W9-BHS-787

The
HUMAN RESOURCES GLOSSARY
Second Edition

The Complete Desk Reference for HR Executives, Managers, and Practitioners

William R. Tracey, Ed.D.
Human Resources Enterprises of Cape Cod, Inc.

S^t_L

St. Lucie Press
Boca Raton   Boston   London   New York   Washington, D.C.

This publication is designed to provide accurate and authoritative information with respect to the subject-matter covered. It should be used with the understanding that it is not the intent of either the author or the publisher to provide legal, accounting, or other professional service. If legal, accounting, or other form of expert advice and assistance is needed, the services of a qualified and competent professional should be engaged.

Library of Congress Cataloging-in-Publication Data

The Human Resources Glossary, second edition: the complete desk reference
    for HR executives, managers, and practitioners / William R. Tracey
       p. cm.
    ISBN 0-57444-160-4
      1. Human resources—terminology.   2. Human resources—teams
    and leadership.   I. Tracey, William R. II. Title.
    RG426.M62 1997
    427.54'7—dc21
                                                                        97-21036
                                                                          CIP

No claim to original U.S. Government works
International Standard Book Number 0-57444-160-4
Library of Congress Card Number 97-21036
Printed in the United States of America 1 2 3 4 5 6 7 8 9 0
Printed on acid-free paper

DEDICATION

for
my mother, Pauline Eva (Burgoyne) O'Neill
my foster mother, Josephine Mary (Burgoyne) Tracey
and
my godmother, Elsie Alice (Burgoyne) Woods

PREFACE

The Human Resources lexicon is growing at a meteoric pace. HR managers and practitioners must understand and be able to use the vocabulary of HR.

This comprehensive glossary of human resources acronyms, abbreviations, and terms and their definitions offers readers the information they need to make sense of the complex, fast-paced world of human resources management, development, and utilization. It contains more than 8,500 entries, including over 1,400 abbreviations and acronyms. Each entry explains the context and application of an acronym, abbreviation, or term, and, in the case of terms rooted in federal law, the applicable legislation is cited.

The book contains brief definitions of the terms that apply to the HR function in business, industry, government, education, and other non-profit organizations. At first glance, many of the words included in the *Glossary* appear to be terms that are common and generally understood. However, some common words have uncommon meanings — their usage is unique to the HR discipline. And, because this volume is intended for global use, some terms that are readily understood by English-speaking Americans would be puzzling, if not incomprehensible, to many for whom English is a second language.

The book also includes the names, addresses, phone and fax numbers, purposes, and other pertinent information, including E-mail and Web site addresses, of professional associations, unions, military and veterans groups, and research organizations and institutes of interest to HR practitioners.

The *HR Glossary* is designed to help readers get maximum results from their HR programs, services, and activities, and assist them to interact and deal effectively with other HR professionals. Every effort has been made to make this book as accurate, complete, and easy to use as possible.

The writer has often had to make arbitrary decisions on the inclusion of terms and their definitions. Inevitably, some users will disagree with the definition given a particular term. In some cases, they may find more complete information on the term in a standard HR text or reference work.

The body of the *Glossary* contains acronyms, abbreviations, and terms arranged alphabetically by subject or topic. Wherever necessary, different terms for the same entity are cross-referenced. Abbreviations and acronyms for organizations and laws and their full titles appear in both forms under the appropriate alphabetical heading.

HOW TO USE THIS BOOK

This book is divided into two parts. The main body of the *Glossary* consists of acronyms and abbreviations with their literal translations heading the entries under each letter of the alphabet. They are followed by the terms with their definitions, including the translations of the acronyms and abbreviations, in alphabetical order. Part two is an index of key terms listed alphabetically under 56 headings, each representing a major area of interest for HR managers and practitioners. Under each heading, key terms are listed, again in alphabetical order.

ACRONYMS AND ABBREVIATIONS

If you want to check on an acronym or abbreviation, go first to the initial entries under the appropriate letter of the alphabet in the main body of the *Glossary*. When you find the correct entry and its meaning, you can then decide whether you need more information. If you do, go directly to the entry for the translated acronym or abbbreviation in the *Glossary*.

PROSPECTING

If you are unfamiliar with a particular area of HR and want to see a sample of what is included, go to the table of contents and scan the major headings in the index of key terms until you find the area of interest. Then go to the appropriate page(s) in the Index of Key Terms and check the listing to find entries that are of potential interest. Go back to the body of the *Glossary* and find the entries and their definitions. Terms *within* a definition that are included in the *Glossary* are set in bold face type.

AIDING RECALL

If you know the term you want but have temporarily forgotten it (we all get a mental block sometimes), follow the steps described in prospecting.

LOOK UP

If you find a word in your reading or hear it in apresentation or conversation and don't know its meaning, go directly to the *Glossary* and look it up. For more detailed information on any term, consult standard HR texts and reference works.

FEEDBACK

If you don't find the word you need in the *Glossary*, if you know of an important word that is not included, or if you think the definition of a word in the *Glossary* misses the mark or is lacking in clarity, please drop the author a note. I'll fix it in the next edition. Send to:

William R. Tracey, Ed.D.

Fifty-four Evergreen Street
South Yarmouth, Massachusetts 02664-5612
508/394-9509 (Voice)
508/760-1103 (Fax)
wtracey@capecod.net (E-mail)

About the Author

William R. Tracey, Ed.D., is president of Human Resources Enterprises of Cape Cod, Inc., an international management, training, and education consulting firm based in South Yarmouth, Massachusetts. He has more than 40 years' experience as a human resources professional, educator, and trainer and holds a doctorate in education from Boston University. Dr. Tracey is also a graduate of the National Cryptologic School, United States Army War College, and the United States Army Management School.

Dr Tracey has been a classroom teacher at the elementary, junior high, and high school levels, supervisor of student teaching, and professor of education at the undergraduate and graduate levels of higher education. His last full-time position in public education was an assignment as Professor of Education and Director of Teacher Training at the Fitchburg (Massachusetts) State College. He has also served in consecutive assignments as Psychologist, Educational Consultant to the Commandant, Director of Instruction, Deputy Commandant for Training and Education, and Director of Training and Doctrine at the U.S. Army Security Agency Training Center and School and the U.S. Army Intelligence School, Fort Devens, Massachusetts.

His consulting career has included assignments with Esso Resources Canada in Alberta and the Northwest Territories, Pertamina, the petroleum exploration and production company in Jakarta, Indonesia, Les Roches, the Swiss Hotel Association's School of Hotel Management in Bluche Crans-Montana located in Switzerland's Valais Canton, and many other assignments in the United States. He has also served three terms as a member of the Commission on Technical and Career Institutions, New England Association of Schools and Colleges, the regional accrediting association.

Dr. Tracey has published 13 books, including the *AMA Human Resources Management and Development Handbook, Designing Training and Development Systems, Critical Skills: The Guide to Top Performance for Human Resources Managers,* and *Training Employees with Disabilities: Strategies to Enhance Learning and Development for an Expanding Part of Your Workforce,* and more than 60 journal articles. His professional affiliations include the American Management Association, American Society for Training and Development, Society of Human Resource Management, Phi Delta Kappa, and the Cape Cod Writer's Center.

CONTENTS

Part I

DEFINITIONS

A

AA　　1. Affirmative action.
2. Alcoholics Anonymous.

AAA　　1. American Arbitration Association. 2. Area Agencies on Aging.

AAAA　　Army Aviation Association of America.

AAACE　　American Association for Adult and Continuing Education.

AADB　　American Association of the Deaf-Blind.

AAFES　　Army Air Force Exchange Service.

AAHE　　The American Association for Higher Education.

AAMR　　American Association on Mental Retardation.

AAOHN　　American Association of Occupational Health Nurses.

AAP　　1. Affirmative action plan.
2. The American Academy of Psychoanalysis.

AAPCC　　Adjusted average per capita cost.

ABA　　1. American Bar Association.
2. Architectural Barriers Act of 1968. 3. The Association for Behavior Analysis.

ABCB　　Architectural Barriers Compliance Board.

ABCD　　Accomplishment-based curriculum development.

ABM　　Applied behavior management.

ABMS　　American Board of Medical Specialties.

ABO　　Accumulated benefits obligations.

ABR　　Accelerated benefit rider.

ACA　　1. American Compensation Association. 2. American Counseling Association. 3. American Chiropractic Association.

ACAA　　Air Carrier Access Act of 1986.

ACBE　　Association for Community-Based Education.

ACC　　Asynchronous computer conferencing.

ACDUTRA　　Active duty for training.

ACE　　1. American Council on Education. 2. Association of Conference Executives.

ACHE　　Association for Continuing Higher Education, Inc.

ACIP　　American Council on International Personnel.

ACL　　Access control list.

ACME　　ACME World Association of Management Consulting Firms.

ACPA　　American Cleft Palate-Craniofacial Association.

ACR　　Adjusted community rate.

ACT　　American College Test.

ACTE　　Association of Corporate Travel Executives.

ACUR　　Ambulatory care utilization review.

ADA　　1. Age Discrimination Act of 1975. 2. Americans with Disabilities Act of 1990. 3. American Dental Association. 4. American Diabetes Association.

ADAA　　Anti-Drug Abuse Act of 1986.

ADARA　　American Deafness and Rehabilitation Association.

ADBs　　Accelerated death benefits.

AD&D　　Accidental death and dismemberment insurance.

ADD　　Attention deficit disorder.

ADEA　　Age Discrimination in Employment Act of 1967.

ADHD　　Attention deficit, hyperactivity disorder.

ADLs Activities of daily living.

ADME Association of Destination Management Executives.

ADR Alternative dispute resolution procedures.

AECT Association for Educational Communications and Technology.

AEDP Adult External Diploma Program.

AEE Association for Experiential Education.

AERA American Educational Research Association.

AESC The Association of Executive Search Consultants.

AFA Air Force Association.

AFB American Foundation for the Blind.

AFDC Aid to Families with Dependent Children.

AFG Al-Anon Family Group Headquarters, Inc.

AFGE American Federation of Government Employees.

AFL–CIO American Federation of Labor–Congress of Industrial Relations.

AFPA Armed Forces Procurement Act of 1947.

AFPI Air Force Procurement Instructions.

AFSA Air Force Sergeants Association.

AFSCME American Federation of State, County, and Municipal Employees.

AFT American Federation of Teachers.

AGBAD Alexander Graham Bell Association for the Deaf.

AGI Adjusted gross income.

AHA 1. American Heart Association. 2. American Hospital Association.

AHD Attention deficit disorder.

AHH Acute health hazard.

AH&MA American Hotel & Motel Association.

AHRSP Association of Human Resource Systems Professionals.

AI Artificial intelligence.

AIA Anti-Injunction Act of 1932.

AIAS Academy of Interactive Arts & Sciences.

AICPA American Institute of Certified Public Accountants.

AIDA Attention, interest, desire, and action.

AIDS Acquired Immune Deficiency Syndrome.

AIMR Association for Investment Management and Research.

AIT Advanced individual training.

AITP Association of Information Technology Professionals.

AJB Americans Job Bank.

AL The American Legion.

ALD Assistive listening device.

ALOS Average length of stay.

AMA 1. American Management Association. 2. American Marketing Association. 3. American Medical Association.

AMD Age-related macular degeneration.

AMI Association for Multi-Media International.

AMOD The Association for the Management of Organization Design.

AMSUS Association of Military Surgeons of the United States.

AMVETS American Veterans.

ANA American Nurses Association.

ANCC American Nurses Credentialing Center.

ANSI American National Standards Institute.

AOCFI The Association of Outplacement Consulting Firms International.

AP American Plan.

APA American Psychological Association.

APEC Asia-Pacific Economic Cooperation.

APEX Advance purchase excursion fare.

APH American Printing House for the Blind, Inc.

API Application programming interface.

AP&QC	American Productivity and Quality Center.
APP	Army Procurement Procedure.
APR	Average payment rate.
APTA	American Physical Therapy Association.
AQL	Acceptable quality level.
AQP	Association for Quality & Participation.
ARC	Aids-Related Complex.
ARCD	Age-related cognitive decline.
ARIA	Arthritis Research Institute of America.
ARL	Action-reflection learning.
ART	Assisted reproductive technology.
ASAE	American Society of Association Executives.
ASAP	As soon as possible.
ASCAP	American Society of Composers Authors & Publishers.
ASCII	American Standard Code for Information Interchange.
ASEAN	Association of South East Asian Nations.
ASEM	American Society for Expert Modeling.
ASHA	American Speech-Language-Hearing Association.
ASHC	American Self-Help Clearinghouse.
ASHHRA	American Society for Healthcare Human Resources Administration.
ASIS	American Society for Industrial Security.
ASL	American Sign Language.
ASPA	American Society of Pension Actuaries.
ASPR	Armed Services Procurement Regulations.
ASQ	American Society for Quality.
ASTA	American Society of Travel Agents.
ASTD	American Society for Training and Development.
ASVAB	Armed Services Vocational Aptitude Battery.
A/T	Assertiveness training.

ATB	1. Automated ticket/boarding pass. 2. America's Talent Bank.
ATEA	American Technical Education Association.
ATM	1. Automated teller machine. 2. Adobe Type Manager. 3. Asynchronous transfer mode.
ATP	Authorization to Participate.
ATS	Applicant tracking system.
AV	Audiovisuals.
AVA	1. American Vocational Association. 2. Activity value analysis.
AVRS	Automated voice response system.
AUSA	Association of the US Army.
AWHP	Association for Worksite Health Promotion.
AWOL	Absent without leave.
AWP	Any-willing-provider.

Abacus   An Asian airline computer reservation system (CRS) consortium formed by Cathay Pacific, China, Malaysian, Philippine, Singapore, and Royal Brunei Airlines.

ability test   In training and development, test instruments used to measure an individual's physical or mental skills or abilities, such as manual dexterity, reasoning, visual acuity, or problem solving. Examples are Revised Beta Examination, 2nd Ed. (Beta-II), Industrial Reading Test, Minnesota Clerical Assessment Battery, Seashore-Bennett Stenographic Proficiency Test, Personnel Tests for Industry (Verbal and Numerical), and Watson-Glaser Critical Thinking Appraisal.

ability to benefit   The likelihood that an individual will complete a program of occupational or remedial training in a successful manner. The ability to benefit may be measured by aptitude, ability, or achievement tests.

ability to pay   In compensation and contract negotiations, the capability of an organization to fulfill a wage and salary increase while remaining profitable and competitive in its industry.

ABLEDATA   An information and referral project operated by Macro International, Inc., the company that operates the National Institute on Disability and Rehabilitation Research. Provides free information from a database listing of more than 20,000 assistive devices for all types of disabilities. *Contact:* ABLEDATA, 8455 Colesville Rd., Ste. 935, Silver Spring, MD 20910-3319 [800/227-0216 or 301/588-9284 (V/TTY); 301/608-8912 (TT) Fax 301/608-8958; E-mail **ABLEDATA@macroint. com**; URL **http://www.abledata.com**].

AboutFace An international information and support organization with about 5,000 members dedicated to providing individual and family support to people who have facial differences. Offers information, practical advice, and the opportunity to network with others who share similar concerns and experiences. *Contact:* AboutFace International, 99 Crowns Lane, Toronto, Ontario M%R 3P4 (800/665-FACE or 416/944-FACE; Fax 416/944-2488; E-mail **aface@io.org**; URL **http://www.io.org/~aface/aface.html**).

absent without leave (AWOL) Unauthorized absence from one's workplace. Usually punished by docking pay.

absolute ratings Rating systems that require the rater to assign a finite value (on a fixed scale) to the trait or performance being rated without reference to any other person. *See also* behaviorally anchored rating scale; checklist; descriptive scale; forced-choice scale; graphic scale; numerical rating.

abstract reasoning In education and training, the ability to perceive problems and issues in symbolic terms and to solve problems and resolve issues in a theoretical rather than in an applied or verifiable manner.

abuse/suppression program An employee benefit, such as a company-sponsored program addressing weight control, smoking cessation, chemical and substance abuse, or gambling addiction control.

academic year As defined by the U.S. Department of Education's Student Financial Assistance Programs, a period of at least 30 weeks of instructional time during which a full-time student is expected to complete at least 24 semester or trimester hours, or at least 36 quarter hours; or, at an institution that measures program length in clock hours, at least 900 clock hours.

Academy of Interactive Arts & Sciences (AIAS) A not-for-profit organization that provides a voice for individuals comprising the worldwide interactive community. Its mission is to promote and advance the common interests of the worldwide interactive community and to recognize outstanding achievement in

interactive content. *Contact:* AIAS, 500 South Buena Vista St., Burbank, CA 95121-7706 (818/623-3730; Fax 818/623-3727; E-mail **academy@interactive.org**; URL **http://www.interactive.org/contact/about.htm**).

accelerated benefit rider (ABR) *See* living benefit rider.

accelerated death benefits (ADBs) Payment of insurance death benefits before death. The amount varies between 100 percent of the face coverage of the policy to a small percentage of the death benefit with a possible monetary cap. When the advance payment is less that the face value, the balance is paid to the beneficiary on the death of the insured.

accelerated learning **1.** Learning designed to be effective and achievable in a short span of time by making the learning environment positive, interesting, supportive, comfortable, nonthreatening, multidimensional, and successful. Also called *speed learning.* **2.** A multi-sensory, brain-congruent, collaborative learning methodology in which the learners are the focal point of the learning experience. It involves both the packaging of the knowledge and skills to be learned and the preparation of the learners so that they can absorb and retain the material faster and more easily.

Accent on Information A nonprofit organization that offers product information for people with physical disabilities through a quarterly publication and a biennial buyers' guide. Accepts phone requests for information. *Contact:* Accent on Information, P.O. Box 700, Gillum Rd. and High Dr., Bloomington, IL 61702 (309/378-2961; Fax 309/378-4420).

accent-reduction training A new benefit offered by a growing number of companies to help employees with heavy foreign accents or strong regional American dialects to improve their pronunciation and enunciation of the English language. Courses typically last as long as 20 weeks.

acceptable quality level (AQL) A method of specifying quality level used by engineers. Largely replaced by **Cpk.**

acceptance In contract law, consenting to an offer under terms agreed to by the offeror. It creates a binding contract.

access In benefits, an individual's ability to obtain needed health care services.

access code An alphanumeric code that allows the user to gain entry to a computer system, program, folder, or file.

access control list (ACL) A means of controlling access to computer files. ACLs can be created on a router or on a server to deny entry to persons who must not be privy to files.

accessible format Materials prepared for people with disabilities in formats other than ordinary print; for example, braille for the blind and extra-large print for the visually impaired.

accessory apartment An alternative way of enabling older persons to remain in their own homes. It involves adding a separate, self-contained apartment unit to the house. Rental of the original dwelling provides the owner with additional financial resources and the security of living apart but not alone.

access-to-care A means of cutting abuse in **medigap insurance**. The measure would require all individuals to have health insurance provided through either their employers or a public plan.

accidental injury An injury caused by an external force or element such as a blow or fall and which requires immediate medical attention. Usually includes animal bites and poisonings.

accidental death and dismemberment (AD&D) In benefits, group insurance that provides coverage for accidental loss of life, limbs, or sight.

accomplishment-based curriculum development (ABCD) A step-by-step system for developing a curriculum from analysis through design, development, delivery, and evaluation phases. It differs from **instructional systems development** in that it looks first at the goals of the organization, then at what exemplary employees produce, and finally at how top performers behave when they produce their results. Attributed to HRD Hall of Famer, Joe Hurless.

accordion management The ability of a company to expand or contract its work force quickly to accommodate changing business conditions.

accountability **1.** Responsibility imposed on a group or individual or assumed by a work team or individual for the effectiveness or success of a program, activity, or project in terms of results achieved; for example, new or improved skills, productivity, cost benefits, or employee motivation. **2.** An implied or explicit requirement to accept responsibility for performance, progress, and accomplishment.

accountability statement *See* job description.

account balance pension (ABP) Benefit plan similar to a defined contribution plan. Benefits are accumulated in an account to which contributions (based on a percentage of pay) are allocated, and fund earnings are credited to the account under a plan formula. Fully vested participants may receive the account balance in a lump sum on termination of employment; on retirement, participants may take the accumulated balance as a lump sum or in the form of an annuity.

accounting A financial control that involves the processes of collecting, recording, classifying, and summarizing transactions, events, and activities that are, at least in part, dollar-oriented, analyzing and interpreting the data, and reporting the results to interested managers or others.

account representative *See* director of sales.

accounts receivable supervisor The hotel functionary responsible for presenting the final bill to the person responsible for a meeting and for explaining charges.

accreditation Certification by a recognized body that an individual, institution, or program has voluntarily undergone a comprehensive study and examination by an objective, impartial, and qualified group of evaluators and that the examination demonstrated that the individual, institution, or program does in fact perform the functions that it claims and that it does so competently. Federal student aid programs require that participating schools and colleges be accredited.

accrued benefit The funds or other form of benefit that a plan participant has accumulated to a particular point in time. For example, for a defined contribution plan, it is the amount of money accumulated in the individual's pension account.

acculturation In multinational operations, the adoption by expatriate managers of the cultural traits, mores, practices, and social patterns of the host country.

accumulated benefits obligations (ABO) The amount needed to finance pension benefits already earned by workers.

achievement competencies Capabilities that portend success in professional, technical, and managerial jobs. They include initiative and concern for order and quality.

achievement-motivation theory A theory that holds that challenging tasks and their successful completion elicit feelings of pleasure; therefore, the solution to motivation is to hire people with a high need to achieve, give them challenging tasks, and provide unambiguous feedback on degree of success.

achievement need A strong need of most **knowledge workers**, characterized by a willingness to take moderate risks to attain the satisfaction that accompanies task completion and positive feedback, particularly with difficult or challenging tasks.

achievement test A test that measures the extent to which a person has acquired certain information or skills as a result of formal or informal training, experience, or self-study. The most common type of test used by HR managers, it measures the knowledge, skills, and abilities of people in specific subject-matter areas. Most often used to determine whether a trainee has achieved the learning objectives of a course or training module or to determine the general effects of previous learning experiences but are also used in screening and selection to test job knowledge. Commercially available standardized achievement tests, such as the Iowa Tests of Basic Skills and the Stanford Achievement Tests, are designed to assess the general effects of previous learning experiences.

acid test A measure of the results of corporate operations that measures immediate solvency or financial soundness. The acid test is calculated by dividing cash plus marketable securities, plus receivables by current liabilities.

$$\text{acid test} = \frac{\text{cash} + \text{marketable securities} + \text{receivables}}{\text{current liabilities}}$$

ACME — World Association of Management Consulting Firms An international association of firms employing more than 55,000 consultants engaged in the practice of consulting to management in over 100 countries worldwide. ACME's mission is to advance the knowledge and quality of the practice of consulting to management, promote better understanding of the profession with the business community, government, academia, and the general public, serve as the voice of the community on major issues, and foster the development of leadership within the consulting community. *Contact:* ACME, 521 Fifth Ave., 35th Floor, New York, NY 10175-3598 (212/697-9693; Fax 212/949-6571; E-mail **info@acmeworld.org**; URL **http://www.acmeworld.org**).

acquired immune deficiency syndrome (AIDS) A viral illness, assumed to be terminal, that attacks the body's immune system leaving it vulnerable to infection. It is the final manifestation of infection with **HIV disease.** The disease cannot be transmitted by casual contact but only by the exchange of body fluids such as through sexual contacts, needles, cuts in the skin, and transfusions of infected blood.

acquisition *See* merger.

acquisitions software A computer program written to perform management tasks associated with the purchase of information systems reference materials.

action learning 1. Usually facilitated by a consultant, it is a systematic and orderly problem-solving process. A group of trainees jointly identify a problem, experiment with a solution, monitor results, and critique the process. Results are used by the learners to redefine the problem and try out alternative solutions. **2.** A middle management training strategy that involves giving trainees released time to work full time on problems in departments other than their own. Trainees meet periodically with a project group to discuss their progress and solutions. **3.** A learning system in which (1) learning is tied to a specific, important, and current project; (2) there is no instructor and trainees learn from and with each other in teams (often cross-functional) as they deal with an issue or problem; (3) emphasis is placed on questioning previous assumptions; and (4) teams continually review their progress and the process itself and question and test their hypotheses.

action or performance learning A learning strategy used by humans (and to some degree by learning machines). It is learning by seeing, hearing, smelling, tasting, feeling, and doing.

action plan Applies to any area of HR following evaluation, such as self-assessment. An action plan is essentially a detailed (sequenced and prioritized) solution for a problem — what is to be done, who is to do it, when it is to be started, when it is to be finished, what resources will be required, and to some degree how it is to be done. In some applications, time and the costs are included in the plan.

action-reflection learning (ARL) A small-group, team approach to learning where the learners learn by doing — by solving actual business problems.

action research **1.** The scientific application of the methods of behavioral science to the solution of practical problems. Involves the processes of diagnosis, data collection and analysis, feedback, and action planning. Attributed to Kurt Lewin. *See also* action plan. **2.** In **organization development**, action research involves identifying and selecting the organizational and interpersonal issues and problems that need to be addressed and finding and applying solutions to those problems in a planned and systematic way.

action skills Skills that are associated with doing or taking action in situations as they are analyzed. They include such specific skills as planning, changing organizational conditions, and behaving effectively in interpersonal situations.

active duty The status of personnel of any component of the Armed Forces assigned to units either indefinitely, for a specified enlistment period, or for some other contractual time commitment.

active duty for training (ACDUTRA) A period of training required of most members of Reserve Component Forces of the military services. A certain number of "drills" is required annually to fulfill a reservist's military commitment — typically one two-hour period per week or four 4-hour periods per month (one weekend) plus 14 days of annual active duty.

active listening In counseling or other person-to-person contacts, concentrating on the other person and the message, not on oneself; giving the other individual total, undivided attention; looking at the person directly but not staring; listening for the central idea, listening for feelings as well as facts, separating facts from opinions, listening ahead, listening between the lines, and responding appropriately.

actives Current workers; preretirement employees.

activities of daily living (ADLs) The basis for determining need for long term care services. Includes continence (control of bowel and bladder functions), dressing, feeding (taking nourishment), toileting, and transferring (getting in and out of a chair or bed).

activity ratio One of the traditional tests of operating performance, activity ratio emphasizes flow rather than financial position. It is calculated by dividing assets into sales individually or in groups, and the result can be expressed as a percentage of sales or a ratio of sales.

activity value analysis (AVA) A cost management strategy that involves quantifying the amount of time and personnel required to accomplish a task and includes that number as a part of the total cost of that activity.

actual charge The amount a physician or supplier actually bills a patient for a particular medical service or supply. The actual charge may differ from customary, prevailing, or reasonable charges (for example, under Medicare).

actual cost projections In project management, a means of determining project costs. The projections are based on prior knowledge of costs involved in a similar project and include various raw material vendor price quotes.

actuarially sound In benefits, pension funds that are adequate, considering the amount accumulated in the fund, current levels of contribution, and assumptions made about interest or return on investment, to meet liabilities accrued and accruing.

actuarial reduction A reduction in the amount of earned pension income payable at age 65 applied when a member of a retirement plan retires prior to age 65 and begins to receive pension benefits. It compensates for the longer period of time that such employees will receive benefits for a longer period of time than those who retire at age 65 or older.

actuating *See* directing.

acupressure An alternative Far Eastern form of medical treatment. Involves light finger, thumb, and hand pressure and massage based on the theory that energy flows along 12 major nerve paths through the body. Illness or stress is believed to cause blockages in energy flow that can be relieved through massage.

acupuncture An alternative form of manipulative medicine developed by the Chinese to relieve pain. Practitioners insert very thin needles into the body and just under the skin at specific locations to treat various kinds of pain and addictions. Practitioners say that it restores or improves the flow of "chi" or "vital life energy" along the 12 major energy pathways, each linked to specific organ systems.

acute care Health care provided for individuals with periodic or short-term illnesses.

acute health hazard (AHH) A substance that has a rapid and adverse effect on the body characterized by severe symptoms.

ADA Guidelines for Tests *See* Enforcement Guidance on Preemployment Disability-Related Inquiries and Medical Examinations Under the Americans with Disabilities Act.

ADARA: Professionals Networking for Excellence in Service Delivery with Individuals Who Are Deaf or Hard of Hearing Promotes and participates in quality human service delivery to deaf and hard of hearing people through agencies and individuals. ADARA is a partnership of national organizations, local affiliates, professional sections and individual members working together to support social services and rehabilitation delivery for deaf and hard of hearing people. *Contact:* ADARA, P.O. Box 251554 Little Rock, AR 72225 [501/868-8850 (voice/TTY); Fax 501/868-8812; E-mail **adarahuie@aol.com**)]

adaptive learning Learning whose purpose is to adapt to what is perceived or known: what is occurring now. For example, a company is using adaptive earning when it employs customer feedback to improve its technical services. Also called *adjustment learning.*

adaptive media For the visually disabled, adaptive media include large-type software and learningware, speech synthesis or talking software, tactile displays, and braille printers.

adaptive test A usually computer-based test in which the choice of test items depends on the testee's responses to earlier items on the same test.

adaptive testing A testing model where an individual testee's cumulative pattern of responses is iteratively assessed and scored. The model is used to determine the effectiveness of training and the remedial treatment needed to improve performance.

additional benefits *See* ancillary benefits.

ad hoc query A question posed to a **database** for information that is not covered in a standard report.

adhocracy An organization that cuts across conventional bureaucratic lines to accomplish a goal or objective. Originally coined by futurist Alvin Toffler.

administrator In estate planning, one who settles an estate for an individual who had either died without a will or whose will-named **executor** could not serve. Performs the same duties as an **executor**.

admission The period from entry into a hospital or other covered medical facility until discharge.

add-on fare A fare calculated from the "home" city to a consolidation point, which is then combined with a negotiated group fare from that point to the final destination.

adjoining In meeting management, two hotel rooms located side by side, with or without a connecting door.

adjunct program In training, supplemental instructions accompanying an instructional system or program designed to guide the trainee to specific modules of the main program or to provide additional information or practice of a skill.

adjusted average per capita cost (AAPCC) In health care, serves as the basis for monthly capitation payments to health maintenance organizations (HMOs) or competitive medical plans (CMPs) under contract to the Health Care Financing Administration. For each county in the United States, for each Medicare member, an HMO or CMP is paid one of 122 monthly capitation amounts, which can vary significantly. The AAPCC represents an actuarial projection of what Medicare expenses would have been for a given category of Medicare beneficiary had the subscriber remained in traditional fee-for-service Medicare.

adjusted community rate (ACR) In health care, a computation that results in a figure indicating the premium an HMO or CMP would charge for providing exactly the same Medicare-covered benefits to a community rated group account, adjusted to allow for the greater intensity and frequency of utilization by Medicare recipients (due to their age) and a normal profit.

adjusted funding ratio The ratio of pension plan assets to the **accumulated benefit obligations,** adjusted to average out companies' differing assumptions about interest rates.

adjusted gross income (AGI) The total of taxable income, less adjustments, that must be reported on U.S. income tax returns.

administrability An essential characteristic of a psychological test. A test is administrable when it can be given to a group with relative ease and with excellent potential for communicating clearly to the test administrator and testees what is to be done and how.

administration The organization function concerned with doing things right. It involves the expert execution of policies established by a higher authority, such as a board of trustees.

administrative support services Office support staff. Traditionally "staff" have been comprised of clerical and secretarial personnel, but now they include word processing and other administrative specialists.

administrator A person responsible for the execution of policies established by higher authority, such as a board of control. Administrators typically direct and control the implementation of policy — they ordinarily don't make it. But when they do, the scope of their authority is limited. Their charter is to do things right. For example, a school administrator doesn't make policy; that is the function of the school board or school committee.

Adobe Type Manager (ATM) In desktop publishing, a utility that can make every size of type look just about as good on the computer screen as it will when printed to a **PostScript** printer. It does this by using the same rasterizing capability that the printer uses. It goes to the printer **font**, gets the outline data to create the characters, and rasterises it to the screen rather than rastering the output to the computer.

adopt-a-country program A means of developing in-house executive expertise to support globalization plans and programs. Participants become expert in a specific country by intensive reading and study of the total culture, language, economy, politics, mores, and traditions and by making frequent visits to the country.

adoption assistance plan Financial assistance provided employees to pay expenses associated with adoption, such as agency, placement, attorney, and other required legal fees, physical exams for prospective parents when required, maternity fees of the natural mother, and temporary foster care charges immediately preceding adoption. May cover adoptions through an agency, private adoptions, or adoptions of children from prior marriages.

adoption benefits See adoption assistance plan.

adoption leave Time off from work granted to the father or mother of a newly adopted child. See also paternity leave.

adoptive program See adoption assistance plan.

adult day care center A center operated by a hospital, nursing home, religious group, or private care organization that provides a variety of health care and social services for people who need assistance for a few hours or all day. Services include grooming and toileting. If licensed by a state and meeting minimum staffing and record keeping requirements, its services may be covered by a long- term care insurer. Not covered by Medicare.

adult education See andragogy; continuing education; human resources development.

Adult External Diploma Program (AEDP) A program that enables workers with sufficient work or life experiences to earn high school credits without taking a written test or attending class. The program uses a pre-screening assessment of basic reading, writing, and math skills and the opportunity to demonstrate 64 general life skills to a trained assessor. Nine states offer the program.

adult foster home See licensed group home.

adult learner Anyone beyond secondary school age, either employed or seeking employment, who is engaged in any type of formal or informal learning activity.

advance booking A computer program that allows an information system or center to book materials in advance for patrons so that the items are available when needed or on a specific date and time.

advanced editing A computer program that allows the staff to add, edit, or delete, in one process, specific data contained in any number of material records.

advanced individual training (AIT) Training provided by the armed forces to entry-level personnel to qualify them for award of a **military occupational specialty**.

advanced manufacturing technology Technologies that have been recently developed or are currently under development for use in product or part design, fabrication, assembly, quality control, or improving the efficiency of production.

advance purchase excursion fare A discounted fare for individuals or groups who meet certain specific requirements, such as tickets purchased three to seven days in advance of travel. Applies primarily to international travel.

adventure education *See* adventure training.

adventure learning *See* adventure training.

adventure training A means of training and developing staff, easing them through corporate change, building teamwork, improving communication, or strengthening leadership to build trust, delegation, and risk-taking. It removes challenges people can control and replaces them with genuinely frightening tasks and obstacles that can be completed or overcome only if participants have faith in themselves and their fellow trainees. Conducted in the wilderness or the woods, rather than in a traditional classroom setting. Participants learn by doing — swinging from ropes, scaling 4-story-high trees, white-river rafting, running obstacle courses, and engaging in group problem solving (physical problems).

adverse action Disciplinary action in the form of formal sanctions to correct or modify unacceptable employee behavior. Includes written reprimand, written warning, suspension, and termination.

adverse impact The negative effects of employment practices. Although not obviously discriminatory, they do in fact affect a protected group differently, significantly, and unfavorably.

adverse medical event Treatment by a health practitioner that is designed to help but instead causes illness, injury, or death, whether from surgical or drug administration mistakes, infections, side effects, misdiagnosis, negligence, or incompetence. Also called *iatrogenic injury.*

adverse selection **1.** Screening and selection policies and procedures established that tend to favor one group over another or affect a protected group differently and unfavorably. **2.** In health care, the problem of attracting members to a plan who tend to be sicker than the general population. **3.** Occurs when an optional insurance plan, such as **COBRA,** is designed in such a way that it will be logically selected by the workers most likely to make the largest claims against the plan.

advisory committee **1.** A method of training needs assessment. A committee representing all levels of management (first-line supervisors, middle managers, and executives), functional specialists (marketing, sales, management information, production, and so on), or organizational levels (supervisors, technicians, staffers, and other workers) is convened to identify, discuss, and set priorities for training. A variant of the method is to convene a panel of outside experts to perform the same function. In both cases the committee provides recommendations; it does not make decisions. **2.** A means of keeping training programs current and consistent with the needs of users. In this sense, an advisory committee consists of a group of six to ten employers of the products of the training system convened periodically to provide advice regarding course content, equipment, and materials. Most often used by vocational-technical schools, institutes, and colleges.

aerobic exercise Any activity that increases heart and respiratory rates, such as aerobics classes, running, some kinds of walking, cycling, swimming, cross-country skiing, jumping rope, dancing, and climbing stairs. An effective means of conditioning the heart, arteries, and respiratory system and burning calories to lose weight.

affect In reference to mental illness, emotional feeling, tone, and mood attached to a thought, including its external manifestations.

affective disorder A mental illness characterized by changes in mood marked by extreme sadness and melancholy (**depression**) or excitement (**mania**).

affective domain **1.** Applied to learning, the learner's feelings, attitudes, values, morals, ethics, human relationships, and self-esteem. **2.** Instructional objectives relating to trainees' interests, attitudes, and values.

affinity card A credit card issued jointly by an airline or hotel and a bank that gives frequent fliers or travelers a mile or so for every dollar charged on the card.

affinity diagram A management and planning tool. Helps group and organize similar items in columns and provides a title or theme for each group of ideas. Used following **brainstorming** or **imagineering** to capture the thread of ideas and make them clear and concise.

affinity plan A Medicare health maintenance organization plan formulated by the HMO industry that would turn the responsibility for providing health care care to Medicare-eligible uniformed services retirees to Medicare HMO firms and allow them to selectively contract with military treatment facilities to provide some health services to uniformed services retirees enrolled in their HMOs. *See also* Medicare subvention.

affirmative action (AA) In equal employment opportunity, the right of employees, regardless of their sex, religion, race, or physical or mental ability, to be treated equally and without discrimination in matters of hiring, pay, and promotion. Also relates to the obligation of employers, as mandated by law, to make positive outreach efforts to assist protected groups to achieve parity in hiring, pay, and promotion to compensate for past discrimination. AA policy has taken two forms: (1) deliberately favoring qualified minorities when hiring or promoting employees and (2) establishing quota systems to regulate the proportion of minority members hired or promoted in accordance with an ideal distribution of employees on the basis of sex, race, creed, or ethnicity. The courts enforce race and sex classifications when necessary to correct past discriminatory practices and patterns. When an employee or labor union is ordered by the court to make concerted efforts to hire minorities who have traditionally been discouraged from seeking employment, the employer is required to to hire or promote additional members of that minority group.

affirmative action plan (AAP) Any company plan designed to correct EEO imbalances or the effects of discriminatory practices on protected groups (women and minorities). It usually involves issuing a corporate policy statement; assigning responsibility to a top official; publicizing the plan; determining the status of minority employment; identifying areas of underutilization; establishing goals, specific objectives, and timetables relating to job assignments, functions, and levels, promotions, and compensation; implementing the plan; and monitoring and evaluating progress.

affordability index A measure of the affordability of home ownership; that is, having sufficient means to purchase property and the ability to bear the expenses of ownership. It is calculated by determining the ratio of average per capita income to median housing prices.

African-Americans Black persons having origins in any of the black African racial groups not of Hispanic origin.

after-acquired evidence A rule established by a federal court decision, *Welch v. Liberty Machine Works* (Eighth Circuit Court of Appeals). The court ruled that after-acquired evidence of employee misrepresentation can be used to defend Title VII liability under the **Civil Rights Act of 1964**, but only if the employer proves that it would not have hired the employee had the misstatements been known. However, in as similar case, *Mardell v. Harleysville Life Insurance*, the Third Circuit Court of Appeals ruled that after-acquired evidence should not be used to defend discrimination charges under any circumstances. The Court emphasized that the defense of federal Civil Rights law superseded employers' rights relating to employee misdeeds and that employee misconduct was relevant only to determine damages should employers be found guilty of discrimination. In 1995, the Supreme Court reviewed a similar case, **McKennon v. Nashville Banner Publishing Co.**, and unanimously held that employees who lose their jobs due to discrimination are entitled to back pay even if the employer later discovers evidence of misconduct that would have justified firing the employee if it had been known at the time. The 9th U.S. Circuit Court of Appeals has subsequently set a standard for employers seeking to prove that they would have discharged an employee for wrongdoing. Rejecting arguments that employers should be required to meet a "clear and convincing" evidence standard, the court ruled that an employer can show that that an employee would have been discharged by producing only a "preponderance of evidence." Note: courts in other federal circuits have yet to rule on this question and are not bound by this decision.

Age Discrimination Act of 1975 (ADA) An act that prohibits discrimination on the basis of age in programs or activities receiving federal financial assistance.

Age Discrimination in Employment Act of 1967 (ADEA) An act designed to promote the employment of older persons based on their ability rather than age and to prohibit arbitrary age discrimination. The Act makes it unlawful to refuse to hire, discharge, or otherwise discriminate against any individual with respect to compensation, terms, conditions, or privileges of employment because of age. As amended in 1978, the Act prohibits the involuntary retirement because of age in the protected age category of 40 to 70 with the exception of (1) *bona fide* **occupational qualifications** necessary to the business and (2) executives entitled to an employer-provided annual retirement income of $27,000 or more. The Act also proscribes job discrimination in terms of hiring, promotions, and layoffs against workers 40 to 70 and applies to employers of 20 or more employees who are engaged in interstate commerce. Effective January 1, 1987, ADEA prohibited mandatory retirement at any age, and the Act continues to prohibit age-based discrimination in all other employment conditions and practices. Formerly the province of the Department of Labor, the **Equal Employment Opportunity Commission** now has jurisdiction. As of 1997, states and local governments may establish mandatory retirement ages and maximum entry-level ages for police, firefighters, prison guards, and other public safety employees. Under the new law, public safety officers may be retired as early as age 55, and the typical entry-level age cutoff for recruits is 30 to 35 years. Job applicants older than 35 can be rejected solely because of their age.

age-based defined contribution plan
A plan that allows employers to make higher contributions to pension plans on behalf of older key employees, independent of compensation, thereby focusing the dollars on those who will need them soonest. The plan is said to offer the best income-replacement features of traditional defined benefit pension plans and provides the simplicity and flexibility of profit sharing plans.

age-based profit sharing
See age-based defined contribution plan.

ageism A new diversity issue for employers — discrimination on the basis of age, with workers 55 and older the fastest-growing segment of the work force.

agency shop In labor-management relations, an arrangement whereby employees who do not belong to the union must pay union dues because it is assumed that the efforts of the collective bargaining unit benefit all workers, not just members of the union.

agents A new kind of software under development that will monitor the outside world, gathering relevant information, screening out unwanted data, tracking appointments, and providing advice and assistance. Also known as *personal assistants.*

age out Describes children of employees covered by an insurance plan who reach a certain age; for example, age 19 for nonstudents and age 23 for students. Also called *emancipation age.*

age-related cognitive decline (ARCD)
A syndrome common among people entering their sixties. It is characterized by a minor increase in forgetfulness, slower recall, and a decrease in retention of inconsequential information. It is not an indicator of the onset of senility or Alzheimer's disease but only a natural part of aging for many people.

age-related macular degeneration (AMD)
A disorder of the macula, a tiny light-sensing spot in the center of the retina, the thin tissue that lines the back of the eye and sends visual signals to the brain. The macula is responsible for central vision, thus the condition makes it difficult to drive, read, sew, watch TV, or do anything that requires "straight ahead" vision.

age wave The dramatic increase in the number of individuals between the ages of 45 and 64 (25 percent or more) that will occur in the decade of the 1990s. Attributed to gerontologist/psychologist Ken Dychtwald (*Age Wave: The Challenges and Opportunities of an Aging America,* with J. Flower, Jeremy P. Thatcher, 1989).

age-weighted defined contribution plan
See age-based defined contribution plan.

aggregative statistics Data recorded for a given period of time, using graphics, that present highly incisive information on ongoing, continuing enterprise operations found useful in guiding the organization. Also called *report statistics.*

agricultural worker law See Migrant and Seasonal Agricultural Worker Protection Act of 1983.

AIDS-related complex (ARC) An early and mild form of the AIDS disease when symptoms begin to appear that may or may not develop into full-blown AIDS. Symptoms include loss of appetite, weight loss, fever, night sweats, skin rashes, diarrhea, fatigue, lack of resistance to infection, or swollen lymph nodes. Positive results on an HIV-antibody test are also necessary for a diagnosis.

AIDS tests Laboratory tests for the presence of HIV antibodies.

Aid to Families with Dependent Children (AFDC) A joint federal and state program for low-income families with children under age five that has no premiums or deductibles.

Air Carrier Access Act of 1986 (ACAA) States that no air carrier may discriminate against any otherwise qualified individual with a disability, by reason of such disability in the provision of air transportation. Designed to prohibit discrimination on the basis of disability and create a framework within which the Department of Transportation can monitor the conduct of the airline industry. Conduct monitored ranges from airline practices in assisting passengers with disabilities to the design of new aircraft.

Air Carrier Accessibility Regulations Written by the department of Transportation to implement the **Air Carrier Access Act of 1986.** Establish rules in three categories; aircraft and airport accessibility, requirements for services, and administrative considerations. New aircraft must be designed to include movable armrests, stowage space for a folding wheelchair, at least one accessible lavatory, and an on-board wheelchair. Existing aircraft are required to conform only if there is a replacement scheduled for cabin interior, seats, or lavatories. Portions of airports or air terminals owned, leased, or operated by one or more airlines must meet the Uniform Federal Accessibility Standards and six additional items (existing facilities must comply by 1995): terminal design, baggage facilities, ticketing system, TDDs, terminal information systems, and gate-aircraft interface. In terms of services, the regulations spell out what what is and is not allowed in such areas as advance notification, seat assignments, stowage and treatment of personal equipment, and accommodations for persons with hearing impairments. The rules also require 48 hours notice to the airline when a group of 10 or more people with disabilities are traveling together and if a passenger wishes to have an on-board wheelchair. Rules

relating to administrative considerations include requirements for comprehensive training programs for air carrier personnel, written programs covering all requirements, and complaint resolution procedures.

Air Carrier Liability Cap Twelve airlines (American, American Eagle, AMR Coombs, Continental, Delta, Hawaiian, Micronesia, Northwest, Tower Air, TWA, United, and USAir) have received approval from the Department of Transportation to raise the $75,000 liability cap, set by the 70-year old Warsaw Convention, for passengers suffering losses. The change is expected to reduce both litigation and legal costs for victims and their families, who may now claim the full amount of damages unless the carrier can prove that it was not negligent.

airfare groups Pricing groups for airfares. They include **business class, business coach, business discount fare, economy class, first class, full coach, leisure discount fare,** and **negotiated meeting fare.**

air fares Various methods used to quote air fares: **add-on, advance purchase excursion, constructed, convention, day-of-the week discount, group/convention, hidden-city, joint, non-refundable, penalty, promotional, round-trip, star numbers; unpublished/preferential,** and **zone fares**.

Air Force Association (AFA) An organization of 200,000 members all of whom have served in the U.S. Armed Forces. Its purpose is to promote public understanding of aerospace issues and national security requirements to ensure support of the national defense and the men and women of the U.S. Air Force. *Contact:* AFA, 1501 Lee Highway, Arlington, VA 22209-1198 (703/247-5800).

Air Force Procurement Instructions (AFPI) In contracting and marketing, procurement procedures promulgated by the US Air Force to supplement the **Armed Forces Procurement Act of 1947**.

Air Force Sergeants Association (AFSA) An association of 167,000 active and retired enlisted personnel of the Air Force, Air National Guard, Air Force Reserve, Army Air Corps, and Army Air forces. Its mission is to serve as the voice of Air Force Enlisted personnel. *Contact:* AFSA, P.O. Box 50, Temple Hills, MD 20748 (301/899-3500).

airline bereavement policies *See* bereavement fare.

Airline Deregulation Act of 1978
Affected the rights of travelers, the ability of meeting planners to negotiate fares, and the viability of the airline industry. The law specifically stated that to maximize reliance on "competitive market forces" and thereby enhance "efficiency, innovation and low prices" in the airline industry, Congress would prohibit states from "enforcing any law relating to airline rates, routes or services of any air carrier."

airside hotel   A hotel located in an air terminal specifically designed for business travelers in transit to ease the transition from one time zone and continent to another. Typically offers guest rooms, cafe, swimming pool, health club, fully equipped business center, secretarial services, and sometimes a nursery.

Air Travel Industry Enforcement Guidelines
Standards governing the content and format of airline advertising, the award of frequent flier premiums, and the payment of compensation to passengers who are bumped or voluntarily yield their seats on overbooked flights. Adopted in 1987 by the National Association of Attorneys General, an organization composed of the chief law enforcement officials of all states. The U.S. Supreme Court reviewed an airline suit (*Morales v. TWA, et al.*) against the Texas Attorney General to bar him from attempting to enforce the guidelines and supported the carriers in their position that the guidelines were preempted by federal law. In effect the Court said that only the federal government, not the states, other airlines, or private citizens, have rights against the airlines for violation of any law, except federal law.

a la carte benefits   *See* flexible benefits/flex benefits program.

Al-Anon   An established community resource for anyone, including Alateen for teenagers, whose life is or has been affected by a problem drinker. The Al-Anon program offers information and help whether the alcoholic is still drinking or not. Although adapted from **Alcoholics Anonymous,** Al-Anon is a separate recovery program that helps the relatives and friends of alcoholics lead happier, more productive lives. It is not allied with any sect, denomination, political entity, organization or institution. There are no dues for membership, and there are groups in most cities and towns across the USA. *Contact:* Al-Anon Family Group Headquarters, Inc., 1600 Corporate Landing Pky, Virginia Beach, VA 23454-5617 (800/344-2666 or 757/563-1600; Fax 757/563-1655; URL **http://www.al-anon.alateen.org**).

Alaskan Natives   Persons who have origins in any of the original peoples of Alaska and who maintain cultural identification through affiliation or community recognition.

Alateen   An integral part of **Al-Anon**, it is a "family group" created to help teenage children affected by the drinking of parents, siblings, or others. Its members follow the same program as member of Al-Anon.

Albemarle Paper Co. v. Moody   A 1975 landmark case relating to testing and discrimination. The U.S. Supreme Court ruled that merely because a psychologist found that tests administered to minorities were valid predictors of on-the-job success that claim was not a sufficient basis for their use.

alcoholic   A person who has become addicted to alcohol, who is powerless over alcohol, and whose life is seriously affected by the addiction.

Alcoholics Anonymous (AA)   A fellowship of men and women who have found a solution to their drinking problem. The only requirement for membership is a desire to stop drinking. There are no dues or fees; AA is supported by voluntary contributions of its members, neither seeking nor accepting outside funding. Members observe personal anonymity at the public level. AA is located in all cities and most towns nationwide. *Contact:* AA, 475 Riverside Dr., New York, N.Y., 10115 (212/870-3400; 212/870-3003; URL **http://www.alcoholics-anonymous.org**).

alcoholism   A disease in which a person becomes physically addicted to alcohol (ethanol). It affects people of all ages and socioeconomic backgrounds. The symptoms of alcoholism are regular or "binge" drinking and the fabrication of intricate strategies to obtain alcohol or conceal the fact that it was consumed. As the disease develops, other symptoms appear, such as absenteeism and tardiness, lapses in memory, frequent accidents or injuries, unusual behavior, unkempt appearance, poor nutrition, failure to function in job or family life, obvious hangovers, blackouts, and cirrhosis of the liver. The causes of alcoholism include psychological problems and excessive tension, and there may be a hereditary element. Self-help and support groups, such as **Alcoholics Anonymous**, have proved to be helpful to people who have an alcohol problem. For some cases, however, intensive treatment, either in a residential facility or outpatient clinic is required to detoxify, reeducate, and provide the needed psychological support.

alcohol testing Final rules were promulgated by the Transportation Department in December 1992 in response to a Congressional mandate passed in 1991 following the Exxon Valdez oil spill in 1989 and several other accidents involving alcohol. The rules became effective in April 1993 and apply to truck drivers, railroad employees, pilots and air traffic controllers, merchant mariners, and others in safety-related jobs. All people starting transportation jobs must be tested for alcohol use before they are hired, and afterward as many as half of them will be subject to random or periodic tests each year. In addition, any worker who is involved in an accident or whose supervisors suspect drinking will be tested. Currently, DOT rules require testing to be done through evidential breath testing devices approved by the National Highway Traffic Safety Administration. These devices could be applied to saliva, breath, or other body fluids. In January 1995, new Department of Transportation rules went into effect. They require employers to conduct random testing just before, during, or immediately after an employee's performance of safety-sensitive duties. Selection for testing is random; however, the number of random tests conducted each year by employers must equal at least 25 percent of all the safety-sensitive employees. The rules also require breath testing using evidential breath testing devices (EBT) that have been approved by the National Highway Traffic Safety Administration. Two breath tests are required to reach a finding with respect to the prohibited alcohol concentration. A reading of less than 0.02 is considered negative, but a reading over that amount requires a second test. A reading of 0.04 or higher disqualifies an employee from continuing in a safety-sensitive position.

Alexander Graham Bell Association for the Deaf (AGBAD) A nonprofit organization comprised of individuals who are hearing impaired, parents, professionals, and other interested persons. Established to empower persons who are hearing impaired to function independently by promoting universal rights and optimal opportunities for such persons, from infancy through adulthood, to learn to use, maintain, and improve all aspects of their verbal communication, including their abilities to speak, speechread, use residual hearing, and process both spoken and written language. *Contact:* AGBAD, 3417 Volta Place, N.W., Washington, DC 20007-2778 [202/337-5220 (voice/TTY) Fax 202/337-8314; E-mail **agbell@aol.com**)].

Alexander technique An alternative form of medical treatment that uses training to improve poor posture to relieve pain.

algorithm 1. In measurement and evaluation, the art of calculating with any class or type of mathematical notation, including rational and irrational numbers. **2.** In multimedia, a series of defined steps that executes an action by input; for example, drawing a pattern of rectangles for an organization chart.

alien employment laws *See* Immigration and Nationality Act of 1952; Immigration Reform and Control Act of 1986.

alimony A monthly payment made by a person to an ex-spouse pending or following a divorce or legal separation.

alliance *See* joint venture; network; strategic alliance.

allopathic medicine Mainstream, regular, or scientific medicine.

allotment system A budgetary control system that allocates funds on a monthly or quarterly basis, rather than allocating the total share of the annual budget to the organizational element at the beginning of a fiscal year. The system insures that obligations and commitments will not exceed the annual budget by imposing controls on the amounts to be expended during a specific period of time.

allowable charge Under the **Civilian Health and Medical Programs of the Uniformed Services (CHAMPUS),** the amount on which CHAMPUS figures beneficiaries' cost share for covered care. The allowable charge is calculated from all bills received during a year from medical care providers.

allowable costs In contracts, costs that are payable or reimbursable to the bidder or contractor. They customarily include direct costs, salary costs, equipment costs, trainee costs, and indirect costs.

allowable expense   In benefits, any item of expense covered by the benefits plan that is necessary, reasonable, and customary. Such items are typically reimbursable.

allowance   **1.** Probate court acceptance and certification that a decease's will is valid. **2.** Court acceptance of the final account of an executor, which is necessary to close an estate.

alpha geek   The most technically knowledgeable and skillful person in an organization or office. From *Wired* magazine's "Jargon Watch."

alteration   As defined by the **Americans with Disabilities Act of 1990,** "a change to a building or facility that affects or could affect the usability of or access to the building or facility or any part thereof."

alternate long-term care facility   A health care facility that provides one or more necessary or medically necessary diagnostic, preventive, therapeutic, maintenance, or personal care services in a setting other than an acute care unit of a hospital, such as a **nursing home** or **hospice**, whether freestanding or part of a life care community. Such facilities provide ongoing care and related services, have a trained and ready-to-respond staff on duty to provide the needed care 24 hours per day, provide three meals per day and accommodate special dietary needs, and are licensed by the appropriate licensing agency.

alternate-form reliability   The correlation between results of the administration of alternate forms of a test, which provides a measure of the degree to which the test measures consistently whatever it measures.

alternation ranking   In job evaluation and performance appraisal, a modified form of relative rating that requires the rater to select alternatively the best employee and then the worst employee from a list of workers until all workers have been appropriately ranked from top to bottom, best to worst.

alternative assessment   Means of evaluating educational attainment by other than traditional, multiple-choice standardized achievement tests. Involves direct examination of student performance on significant tasks that are relevant to life outside of school. Examples include such time-honored means

as oral tests, judging actual performance in athletics, business education, and music, and proficiency testing in language, and competency testing for pilots, dentists, auto mechanics, and other professions and trades. Also called *authentic assessment; direct assessment; performance assessment.*

alternative compensation   Pay system changes, such as skill-based pay, pay for knowledge, group incentives; individual incentives; profit sharing, gain sharing, key contributor programs, job rates, and lump sum payments.

alternative computer input devices   Devices used by people with physical disabilities to enter commands and run software and learningware. Examples are single switch devices, touchscreens, and talking software and learningware.

alternative dispute resolution (ADR) procedures   Procedures designed to settle wrongful discharge claims and avoid costly litigation. The arbitration procedure involves a three-step complaint procedure for any adverse personnel action, other than discharge, and a written complaint step, an automatic appeal to arbitration in termination cases, and a final and binding decision in all cases. Peer review ADR procedures involve use of a peer review board convened for each proceeding in which the employer's challenged personnel decision is reviewed by a board with representation chosen by the employee and management and a facilitator or proctor.

alternative medicine   *See* acupressure; acupuncture; allopathic medicine; Alexander technique; aromatherapy; Ayurvedic medicine; bioenergetics; biofeedback; chiropractic; color healing; crystal healing; guided imagery; holistic medicine/therapy; homeopathy; hypnotherapy; macrobiotics; medicinal herbalism; osteopathic medicine; reflexology; rolfing; shiatsu. Also called *complementary medicine.*

alternative method   In training and development, an instructional approach that may be used as a substitute for the primary or supporting methods when circumstances or resource availability do not permit the use of the optimum method.

alternative therapies   Include such treatments as biofeedback, acupuncture, and homeopathy. Typically lack sufficient documentation on safety and effectiveness against specific diseases and conditions, are not generally taught in U.S. medical schools, and are not usually reimbursed by health coinsurance providers.

alternative work options See compressed workweek; flexiplace; flextime; job sharing/job splitting; phased or partial retirement; V-time programs; work sharing.

alternative work schedule See alternative work site; flextime.

alternative work site A location other than on company premises where employees are permitted to work; for example, at home.

alts Alternative newspapers — weeklys, sometimes free, sometimes countercultural tabloids that feature investigative reporting, arts, and entertainment.

amateur auditor plan A health care cost reduction program that rewards employees for reviewing their own medical bills and reporting overcharges or other discrepancies.

ambulatory care utilization review (ACUR) A new type of utilization review designed to provide employers with the same type of control over outpatient costs and services that they have over employee in-hospital care. Applicable strategies include **preauthorization**, post-treatment/service auditing, and **physician profiling**.

ambulatory surgical facility A facility that provides surgical services not requiring a hospital stay. It may be independently operated or affiliated with a hospital. Part B Medicare helps pay for certain types of surgery performed at approved centers.

amenities In meeting management, complimentary items provided by a facility for its guests. Include toilet articles, writing supplies, bathrobes, fruit baskets, in-room coffee, and emergency items such as razors, toothbrushes, and other toiletries.

The American Academy of Psychoanalysis (AAP) An organization of psychoanalysts and psychiatrists with an interest in the field established to provide a forum for the expression of ideas, concepts, and research in psychoanalysis and dynamic psychiatry in all other respects, and to develop communication among psychoanalysts, psychiatrists, and their colleagues in other disciplines in science and the humanities. Contact: AAP, 47 East 19th St., 6th Fl.,

New York, NY 10003-1323 (212/475-7980; Fax 212/475-8101).

American Action Fund for Blind Children and Adults Provides direct assistance to blind and deaf-blind persons, scholarships and study grants to enable blind students to continue their education, a Hot-Line to the Deaf-Blind (a biweekly news service in Braille), and Twin Vision books with print and Braille text and pictures so that blind parents can read with their sighted children and blind children can read along with their sighted parents. Contact: American Action Fund for Blind Children and Adults, 1800 Johnson St., Ste. 100, Baltimore, MD 21230-4998 (410/659-9315; Fax 410/685-5653).

American Arbitration Association (AAA) A public service, not-for-profit organization dedicated to the resolution of disputes through the use of arbitration, mediation, negotiation, elections, and other dispute settlement techniques. With 38 offices nationwide and cooperative agreements with arbitral institutions in 52 other countries, the Association offers hundreds of education and training programs each year throughout the world. Contact: AAA, 140 West 51st Street, New York, NY 10020-1203 (212/484-4000; Fax 212/765-4874; E-mail: **usadrsrv@arb. com**; URL **http://www.adr.org**).

American Association for Adult and Continuing Education (AAACE) The nation's leading organization dedicated to enhancing lifelong learning and responding to the needs of educators from secondary and postsecondary education, business and labor, military and government, and from community-based organization. AAACE's mission is to promote adult learning and development by providing leadership in unifying individual adult education practitioners; fostering the development and sharing of information, theory, research, and best practices; promoting professional identity and growth; and advocating policy initiatives. Contact: AAACE, 1200 19th St., N.W., Ste 300, Washington, DC (202/429-513; Fax 202/223-4579).

American Association for Higher Education (AAHE) A national organization of more than 8,500 individuals dedicated to improving the quality of American higher education. AAHE's members — faculty, administrators, and students from all sectors, as well as policy makers and leaders from foundations, government, and business — believe that higher education should play a more central role in national life and that our institutions can and must become more effective. *Contact:* AAHE, 1 Dupont Cir. Ste. 360, Washington, DC 20036-1110 (202/293-6440; Fax 202/293-0073; E-mail **mjoyce@ aahe.org**.

American Association of Occupational Health Nurses, Inc. (AAOHN) An association of 13,000 members whose mission is to advance the profession of occupational health nursing by promoting professional excellence through education and research, establishing professional standards of practice and a code of ethics, influencing legislative and regulatory issues that impact health and safety, and fostering internal and external communications to facilitate ASOHN's goals and objectives. *Contact:* AAOHN, 50 Lennox Pointe, Atlanta, GA 30324-3176 (404/262-1162, Ext. 102; Fax 404/262-1165; URL **http://www.aaohn.org**).

American Association of the Deaf-Blind (ASDF) A national consumer advocacy organization for people who have combined hearing and vision impairments. AADB's mission is to assure that a comprehensive, coordinated system of services is accessible to all deaf-blind people, enabling them to achieve their maximum potential through increased independence, productivity, and integration into the community. *Contact:* AADB, 814 Thayer Ave., Room 302, Silver Spring, MD 20910-4500 (800/735-2258 Voice; 301/588-6545 TTY; Fax 301/588-8705).

American Association on Mental Retardation (AAMR) AAMR is an interdisciplinary organization of 9,500 professionals and others in the United States and 55 other countries concerned about mental retardation and related disabilities. AAMR's mission is to advance the knowledge and skills of professionals in the field of mental retardation by exchanging information and ideas. *Contact* AAMR, 444 North Capitol St., N.W., Washington, DC 20001-1512 (E-mail **webmaster@access. digex.net**; URL. **http://www.aamr.org**).

American Bar Association (ABA)
A nonprofit national organization of the legal profession, composed principally of practicing lawyers, judges, court administrators, law teachers, public service attorneys and many non-practicing lawyers who are business executives, and government officials numbering 360,000. ABA's mission is to be the national representative of the legal profession, serving the public and the profession by promoting justice, professional excellence, and respect for the law. Local bar associations are listed in the phone book under municipality or county. *Contact:* ABA, 750 N. Lake Shore Dr., Chicago, IL 60611 (312/ 988-5000; Fax 312/988-6281; E-mail **abasvcctr@ abanet.org**; URL **http://www. abanet.org**).

American Board of Medical Specialties (ABMS) Provides recognition to 23 medical specialty boards, such as the American Board of Family Practice. Each board requires that certified physicians complete a minimum of three years of education in their specialties following medical school and pass a comprehensive examination for qualification. Some boards require physicians to pass additional examinations every few years to demonstrate their continuing competency. ABMS does not maintain records on general practitioners, dentists, podiatrists, chiropractors, psychologists, or optometrists. The board certification status of physicians in covered specialties may be checked by calling 1-800/776-2378.

American Cancer Society A nationwide, community-based voluntary health organization dedicated to eliminating cancer as a major health problem by preventing cancer, saving lives from cancer, and diminishing suffering from cancer through research, education, and service. Provides resources, information, and guidance, programs for women with breast cancer, the Look Good...Feel Better program, cancer support groups, transportation, and limited financial assistance. *Contact:* ACS, 1599 Clifton Rd., NE, Atlanta, GA 30329 (404/320-3333 or check the Yellow Pages for the nearest ACS office; Fax 404/636-2317; URL **http://www.cancer.org**).

American Chiropractic Association (ACA)
A professional organization representing Doctors of Chiropractic. Its mission is to preserve, protect, improve, and promote the chiropractic profession and the services of Doctors of Chiropractic for the benefit of patients they serve. ACA accomplishes its mission by affecting public policy and legislation, by promoting high standards in professional ethics and quality of treatment, and by carrying out a dynamic strategic plan to help ensure the professional growth and

success of Doctors of Chiropractic. *Contact:* ACA, 1701 Clarendon Blvd., Arlington, VA 22209 (800/986-4636; Fax 703/243-2593; E-mail **AMERCHIRO@aol.com**; URL **http://www.amerchiro.org/aca**).

American Cleft Palate-Craniofacial Association (ACPA) Established to encourage the improvement of scientific clinical services to persons with cleft palate and associated deformities. Membership is open to qualified professionals who are involved in the treatment and/or research of cleft lip, cleft palate, and other craniofacial anomalies. Approximately 2,600 members from 40 countries include 30 health care disciplines such as surgeons, dentists, and speech pathologists. *Contact:* American Cleft Palate-Craniofacial Association 1218 Grandview Ave., Pittsburgh, PA 15211-9906 (412/481-1376; Fax 412/481-0847).

American College Test (ACT) A 3-hour achievement test battery sponsored by the American College Testing Program as an alternative to the **Scholastic Aptitude Test**. It tests English, reading, science reasoning, and mathematics knowledge and skills.

American Compensation Association (ACA) A non-profit association of more than 20,000 human resource executives, practitioners, consultants, and academicians engaged in the design, implementation, and management of employee compensation and benefits programs. ACA is committed to excellence in and the advancement of the total compensation profession. It holds periodic meetings to exchange information on compensation trends, conducts salary surveys, and conducts training programs. Sponsors certification program for **Certified Benefits Professional.** *Contact:* ACA, 14040 N. Northsight Blvd., Scottsdale AZ 85260-3601 (602/922-2020; FAX 602/483-8352; E-mail **qllr45a@prodigy.com**; URL **http://www.ahrm.org/aca/aca.htm/**).

American Council of the Blind A consumer organization that acts as a national clearing house for information. Provides referrals, legal assistance, advocacy support, scholarships, and consultative and advisory services to individuals, organizations, and agencies. *Contact:* American Council of the Blind, 1155 15th Ave., N.W., Ste. 720, Washington, DC 20005 (800/424-8666 or 202/467-5081; FAX 202/467-5085; E-mail **NCRABB@ACCESS.DIGBX.NET**; URL **http://www.acb.org**).

American Council on Education (ACE) An independent nonprofit association representing more than 1,800 institutions of higher learning as well as national and regional higher education associations. ACE seeks to advance the interests and goals of higher and adult education in a changing environment by providing leadership and advocacy on important issues, representing the views of the higher and adult education community to policy makers, and offering services to its members. The Council also assists adult learners by reviewing the learning acquired through courses, programs, and training offered by businesses, labor unions, voluntary and professional associations, and the military and recommending credit for the learning, if appropriate **(Program on Non-Collegiate Sponsored Instruction)**, and by administering the international General Educational Development (GED) high school equivalency testing program in cooperation with the states and Canadian provinces. *Contact:* ACE, One Dupont Circle, N.W., Ste. 800, Washington, DC 20036 (202/939-9300; E-mail **web@ace.nche.edu**; URL **http://www.acenet.edu/**).

American Counseling Association (ACA) A private, nonprofit partnership of associations representing professional nearly 60,000 counselors. ACA provides educational programs, publications, and conferences to expand professional knowledge and expertise; promotes recognition of counselors to the public and the media; and represents members' interest before government bodies at the national level. *Contact:* ACA, 5999 Stevenson Ave., Alexandria, VA 22304-3300 (800/347-6647 or 703/823-9800; 703/823-6862 (TDD); Fax 800/473-2329 or 703/823-0252; E-mail **aca@counseling.org**; URL **http://www.counseling.org**).

The American Council on International Personnel, Inc. (ACIP) An organization of more than 250 corporate and institutional members with an interest in the movement of international personnel across national borders. Provides information relating to immigration, publishes a newsletter, holds conferences and seminars, provides job referral services, and sponsors an umbrella

Exchange Visitor Program designed to permit member institutions to bring foreign nationals to the United States for a period of up to 18 months of training. *Contact:* ACIP, 515 Madison Ave., New York, NY 10022 (212/688-2437; Fax 212/593-4697; URL **http://ahrm.org/acip/acip.htm**).

American Deafness and Rehabilitation Association (ADARA) A nonprofit membership organization established to promote development and expansion of services for deaf persons, offers a forum for professionals, students, parents, and lay persons to develop better understanding, encourages research to advance understanding of deaf people and result in improved rehabilitation and related services, encourages recruitment and training of professionals skilled in working with deaf persons, sponsors publications aimed at professionals, and supports the legislative interests of deaf people. *Contact:* ADARA, P.O. Box 55369, Little Rock, AR 72225 (501/868-8850; Fax 501/868-8812; URL **http://www.adara.org**).

American Dental Association (ADA) A professional association of dentists with more than 138,000 members. Its mission is to encourage the improvement of the health of the public and to promote the art and science of dentistry. *Contact:* ADA, 211 East Chicago Ave., Chicago, IL 60611 (312/440-2500; Fax 312/440-7494).

American Diabetes Association A nonprofit organization dedicated to preventing and curing diabetes and improving the lives of all people affected by diabetes through research and education. To fulfill this mission, the American Diabetes Association funds research, publishes scientific findings, and provides information and other services to people with diabetes, their families, health care professionals and the public. *Contact:* American Diabetes Association, 1660 Duke St., Alexandria, VA 22314 (800/ 232-3472 or 202/331-8303; URL **http://www.diabetes. org**).

American Educational Research Association (AERA) A 23,000-member international professional association concerned with improving the educational process by encouraging scholarly inquiry related to education and by promoting the dissemination and practical application of research results. *Contact:* AERA, 1230 17th St., N.W., Washington, DC 20036-3078 (202-223-9485; Fax 202/775-1824; E-mail **aera@gmu.edv**; URL **tikkun. ed.asu.edu/aera/home.html/**).

American Federation of Government Employees (AFGE) The largest federal labor union affiliated with the AFL-CIO. AFGE represents bargaining unit employees from many government departments and agencies, including the Departments of Agriculture, Defense, Education, Health & Human Services, Housing & Urban Development, Justice, State, Veterans Affairs, Office of Personnel Management, Social Security Administration, and others. *Contact:* AFGE, 80 F St., N.W., Washington DC 20001 (202/737-8700; Fax 202/639-6490; E-mail **witiad@afge.org**; URL **http://www.afge.org**).

American Federation of Labor-Congress of Industrial Organizations (AFL-CIO) A voluntary federation of national and international labor unions in the United States established to organize workers in the United States, speak for the labor movement before Congress and other branches of government, coordinate activities such as community services, political education, and voter registration, and represent American labor in world affairs. Since its establishment, the AFL-CIO has expanded to 13.3 million members in more than 100 national unions. Unions affiliated with the AFL-CIO represent bakers, barbers, bottlers, auto workers, actors, accountants, construction workers, steelworkers, machinists, garment workers, engineers, pilots, public employees, janitors, sales clerks, letter carriers, truck drivers, grocery workers, computer operators, and state and federal government employees, among others. *Contact:* AFL-CIO, 815 16th St., N.W., Washington, DC 20006 (202/637-5000; Fax 202/637-5058).

American Federation of State, County, and Municipal Employees (AFSCME) A union within the AFL-CIO representing public employees and health care workers in the United States, Puerto Rico, and Panama. With about 1.3 million members, it is the largest public employee union in the AFL-CIO. Provides collective bargaining and representation for public service workers at every level of government and in the private sector, including clerical employees, social workers, correctional officers, school employees, and health care and hospital workers. *Contact:* AFSCME, 1625 L St., N.W., Washington, DC 20036-5687

(202/429-1000; FAX 202/ 429-1293; E-mail **cot@afscme.org**; URL **http://www.afscme. org**).

American Federation of Teachers (AFT)
A union within the AFL-CIO with 907,000 members. including teachers and school support staff, higher education faculty and staff, health care professionals, and state and municipal employees. Works to improve education, health care, and public services and the working conditions for employees in those areas. *Contact:* AFT, 555 New Jersey Ave., N.W., Washington, DC 20001 (202/879-4400; Fax 202/879-4556; E-mail **dfowler@aft.org**; URL **http://www.aft.org**).

American Foundation for the Blind (AFB)
An organization whose mission is to enable persons who are blind or visually impaired to achieve equality of access and opportunity that will enable freedom of choice in their lives. AFB accomplishes its mission by taking a national leadership role in the development and implementation of public policy and legislation, informational and educational programs, diversified products, and quality services. *Contact:* AFB, 11 Penn Plaza, New York, NY 10001 (212/502-7600 or 212/947-1060; Fax 212/502-7777; E-Mail **newyork@afb-org**).

The American Heart Association (AHA)
A not-for-profit, voluntary health organization funded by private funds. Its mission is to reduce disability and death from cardiovascular diseases and stroke. These include heart attack, stroke, and related disorders. *Contact:* AHA, 5335 Wisconsin Avenue, N.W., Ste. 940, Washington, DC 20015 (202/686-6888; Fax 202/686-6162; E-mail **inquire@amhrt. org**; URL **http://www.amhrt.org**).

American Hospital Association (AHA)
A not-for-profit organization that serves as a national advocate for hospitals, health networks, and their patients. Provides education and information for its members and informs the public about hospitals, health systems, and health care networks. AHA has over 5,600 institutional and 41,000 individual members. *Contact:* AHA. One North Franklin, Chicago, IL 60606 (312/422-3000; URL **http:// www.aoa.dhhs.gove/aoa/dir/41.html**).

American Hotel & Motel Association (AH&MA)   A coalition of state and city lodging associations throughout the United States, Puerto Rico, and the Virgin Islands,

with more than 10,000 members. Provides operations, technical, educational, marketing, and communications services and government affairs representation to the lodging industry. *Contact:* AM&HA, 1201 New York Ave., N.W., Ste. 600, Washington, DC 20005-3931 (202/289-3100; Fax 202/289-3199; E-mail **comments@ahma.com**; URL **http:www.ahma.com**).

American Indians   Persons who have origins in any of the original peoples of North America and who maintain cultural identification through affiliation or community recognition.

American Institute of Certified Public Accountants (AICPA)   A professional society of more than 330,000 accountants certified by the states and territories. The AICPA establishes auditing and reporting standards and prepares and grades national Uniform CPA Examinations for state licensing bodies. *Contact:* AICPA, 1211 Avenue of the Americas, New York, NY 10036 (212/596-6200; Fax 212/596-6213; URL **http://www.aicpa.org**).

The American Legion (AL)   A community-service organization which numbers nearly 3 million members — men and women — in nearly 15,000 American Legion Posts worldwide. The American Legion's national headquarters is in Indianapolis, Indiana, with additional offices in Washington, DC. Membership eligibility in The American Legion is based on honorable service with the U.S. Armed Forces between specific dates. *Contact:* American Legion, 700 N. Pennsylvania St., P.O. Box 1055, Indianapolis;, IN 46206 (317/630-1253; Fax 317/630-1233; URL **http://www.legion.org**).

American Management Association (AMA)   A 75,000-member international education organization, membership-based and not-for-profit. Provides educational forums worldwide where members and their colleagues learn superior, practical business skills and explore best practices of world-class organizations through interaction with each other and expert faculty practitioners. AMA's publishing program provides tools individuals use to extend learning beyond the classroom in a process of life-long professional growth and development through education. *Contact:* AMA, 1601 Broadway, New York NY 10019-7420 (212/586-8100; Fax 212/903-8168; E-mail **cust_serv@ amanet.org**; URL **http://www.amanet.org**).

American Marketing Association (AMA)
An international professional society of 45,000 members in 92 countries and 500 chapters throughout North America. The purpose of AMA is to promote education and assist in personal and professional career development among marketing professionals and to advance the science and ethical practice of the marketing disciplines. Sponsors the **SPIRE awards**. *Contact:* AMA, 250 S. Wacker Dr., Ste. 200, Chicago, IL 60606 (800/AMA-1150 or 312/648-0536; Fax 312/993-7542; E-mail **info@ama.org**; URL **http://www.ama.org**).

American Medical Association (AMA)
A partnership of physicians and their professional associations dedicated to promoting the art and science of medicine and the betterment of public health. Serves physicians and their patient by establishing and promoting ethical, educational, and clinical standards for the medical profession and by advocating for the the integrity of the physician-patient relationship. *Contact:* AMA, 515 N. State St., Chicago, IL 60610 (312/464-5000; E-mail **WebAdmin@ama-assn.org**; URL **http://ama-assn.org/home.amahome.htm**

American National Standards Institute (ANSI) An organization that has overseen standards development in the United States since 1918 and serves as the U.S. member body of the **International Standards Organization** and has accredited the **American Society for Quality Control** as a standards developing organization.

American Nurses Association (ANA)
Nursing's national professional association representing 2.2 million Registered Nurses through its 53 constituent state associations and 13 organizational affiliate members. Advances the nursing profession by fostering high standards of nursing practice, promoting the economic and general welfare of nurses in the workplace, projecting a positive and realistic view of nursing, and by lobbying the Congress and regulatory agencies on health care issues affecting nurses and the public. *Contact:* ANA, 600 Maryland Ave., S.W., Ste. 100 West, Washington, DC 20024-2571 (1-800/284-2378; Fax 202/651-7004; E-mail **WebMaster@ANA. org** or **WebDiva@ANA.org**; URL **http://www.nursingworld.org**).

American Nurses Credentialing Center (ANCC) A subsidiary of the American Nurses Association (ANA). The ANCC's mission is to improve nursing practice and promote high-quality health care services through voluntary credentialing programs and related services. The ANCC certifies nurses in defined functional and clinical areas of nursing, accredits continuing education providers and approval bodies, and recognizes nursing services that meet specified standards. *Contact:* ANCC, 600 Maryland Ave., S.W., Ste. 100 West, Washington, DC 20024-2571 (800/284-2378; Fax 202/651-7004; E-mail **RGROPPER@ANA.ORG**; URL **http://www.nursingworld.org**).

American Physical Therapy Association (APTA) A national professional organization representing more than 70,000 physical therapists, physical therapist assistants, and students. APTA's goal is to foster advancement in physical therapy practice, education, and research. *Contact:* APTA, 1111 North Fairfax Street, Alexandria, Virginia 22314 (703/684-APTA ; Fax 703/684-7343; E-mail **webmaster@apta.org**; URL **http://www.apta.org**)

American Plan (AP) In meeting management, a room rate that includes a bed and three meals.

American Printing House for the Blind, Inc. (APH) Offers braille, computer disk, large type, recorded and regular print books for purchase. Also manufactures the Speaqualizer, a completely hardware-controlled speech access system for IBM personal computers and compatibles. *Contact:* APH, 1839 Frankfort Ave., P.O. Box 6085, Louisville, KY 40206-0085 (502/895-2405; Fax 502/899-2274; E-mail **info@aph.org**; URL **http://www.aph.org**).

American Productivity & Quality Center (AP&QC) An organization of approximately 450 corporate members that provides research, educational, and advisory services to organizations in the public and private sectors to improve productivity and the quality of work life. Sponsors courses, research publications, newsletter, and library. *Contact:* AP&QC, 123 North Post Oak Lane, Houston, TX 77024 (713/685-4637; Fax 713/681-8578; E-mail **apqcinfo@apqc.org**; URL **http://www.apqc.org**).

American Psychological Association (APA) A 142,000 member association dedicated to the advancement of the science and practice of psychology in the public interest. One major division is instructional/

organizational psychology. Publisher of *Applied Psychology* and "Educational & Psychological Test Standards." *Contact:* APA, 750 First St., N.E., Washington, DC 20002-4242 (202/336-5500 or 202/336-6123 TDD; Fax 202/336-6069; E-mail **webmaster@ apa.org**; URL **http://www.apa.org**).

American Self-Help Clearinghouse

An organization established to reduce human suffering and isolation by increasing the awareness, utilization, and development of self-help support groups in dealing with a variety of medical and other stressful life problems. Provides group information services and contacts for any national self-help group, a directory of national and demonstrational model self-help groups, and group/network development assistance. Publishes *The Self-Help Sourcebook. Contact:* American Self-Help Clearinghouse, Northwest Covenant Medical Center, 25 Pocono Rd., Denville, New Jersey, 07834-2995 (201/625-7101; URL **http://www.cmhc.com/selfhelp/**).

American Sign Language (ASL) The language of the culturally deaf, a visual-gestural language that combines the use of space, hand shapes, arms, and movements, fingerspelling, facial expressions, eyes, head, body posture, and body movements. These shapes and movements serve as the words and intonation of the language. It is not English; rather, it is a language in itself, with its own grammar and structure. Sometimes called *Amesian.*

American Society for Expert Modeling (ASEM) A organization of about 96 members established to popularize and support expert modeling and the study of true experts in sales, marketing, and executive leadership. Tools from cybernetics, systems theory, linguistics, and cognitive psychology are used to develop models of top performers and teach those skills to others. *Contact:* ASEM, P.O. Box 2902, Palos Verdes, CA 90274 (213/378-2666).

American Society for Healthcare Human Resources Administration (ASHHRA)

A 3,000+-member organization founded in 1964 and dedicated exclusively to meeting the professional needs of human resource managers in health care. Affiliated with the American Hospital Association (AHA), ASHHRA promotes society development, professional development, professional relationships, and research and monitors public policy. ASHHRA, One N. Franklin, 31st Floor, Chicago, IL 60606 (312/422-3720; Fax 312/422-4579).

American Society for Industrial Security (ASIS) A professional membership organization of management-level security professionals. The association offers an executive referral service for corporations wishing to hire full-time security specialists. *Contact:* ASIS, 1655 North Ft. Myer Dr., Ste. 1200, Arlington, VA 22209-3198; (703/522-5800; Fax 703/243-4954; URL **http://www. asisonline.org**).

American Society for Quality (ASQ) A society of 140,000 individual and 1,100 sustaining members worldwide. ASQ's mission is to facilitate continuous improvement and increased customer satisfaction by identifying, communicating, and promoting the use of quality principles, concepts, and technologies; and thereby be recognized throughout the world as the leading authority on, and champion for, quality. Administers the **Malcolm Baldridge National Quality Award** under contract to the **National Institute of Standards and Technology.** *Contact:* ASQ, 611 E. Wisconsin Ave., P.O. Box 3005, Milwaukee, WI 53201-3005 (800/248-1946; 414/272-8575; Fax 414/272-1734; E-mail **asq@asqc.org**; URL **http:// www.asq.org**).

American Society for Training and Development (ASTD) A 58,000 member nonprofit professional association that provides leadership to individuals, organizations, and society to achieve work-related competence, performance, and fulfillment. ASTD serves practitioners, managers, administrators, educators, and researchers who work in the field of training and human resource development in more than 100 countries. *Contact:* ASTD, 1640 King St., Box 1443, Alexandria, VA 22313-2043 (703/683-8100; Fax 703/683-8103; E-mail **info.center@ astd.noli.com**; URL **http://www.astd.org**).

American Society of Association Executives (ASAE) A 23,500-member organization representing about 10,000 associations established to enhance the competency of association executives, promote the recognition of the role of associations in society, improve the effectiveness of member organizations, and lead in the resolution of public policy issues affecting associations. Offers the **Certified Association Executive** designation. *Contact:* ASAE, 1575 I St., N.W., 12th Floor, Washington, DC 20005-1168 (202/626-2723;

202/626-2003 TDD; Fax 800/622-ASAE or 202/408-9633; E-mail **pr@asae.asaenet.org**; URL **http://www.asanet.org**).

American Society of Composers, Authors & Publishers (ASCAP) A membership organization of 68,000 composers, song writers, lyricists, and music publishers. Established to protect the rights of members by licensing and paying royalties for the public performance of their copyrighted works at meetings, conferences, and exhibits whether held in a hotel, restaurant, conference center, or cruise ship. Fees are based on the number of events or number of attendees. Check your local telephone listings for the nearest office. *Contact:* ASCAP, One Lincoln Plaza, New York, NY 10023 (212/621-6000; E-mail **info@ascap.com**; URL **http://www.ascap. com**). *See also* Broadcast Music Inc.

American Society of Gay & Lesbian Meeting Planners (ASGLMP) *See* International Society of Gay & Lesbian Meeting Professionals.

American Society of Pension Actuaries (ASPA) An organization of 3,100 members established to educate pension actuaries, consultants, administrators, and other benefits professionals and to preserve and enhance the private pension system as part of the development of a cohesive and coherent national retirement income policy. *Contact:* ASPA, 4350 North Fairfax Dr., Ste. 820, Arlington, VA 22203 (703/516-9300; Fax 703/516-9308; E-mail **aspa@pixpc.com**; URL **http://www.aspa.org**).

American Society of Travel Agents (ASTA) An organization of 25,000 members in 136 countries whose mission is to enhance the professionalism and profitability of member agents through effective representation in industry and government affairs, education and training, and by identifying and meeting the needs of the traveling public. *Contact:* ASTA, 1101 King St., Alexandria, VA 22314 (703/739-2782; Fax 703/684-8319; E-mail **astasysop@astanet.com**; URL **http://www. astanet.com**).

American Speech-Language-Hearing Association (ASHA) national professional, scientific, and credentialing organization of 87,000 speech-language pathologists and speech, language, and hearing scientists. Its mission is to ensure that all people with speech, language, and hearing disorders have access to quality services to help them communicate more effectively. ASHA awards the Certificate of Clinical Competence to audiologists and speech-language pathologists who meet strict requirements. *Contact:* ASHA, 10801 Rockville Pike, Rockville, MD 20852 (800/638-8255, voice or TDD; 301/897-5700, voice or TDD; Fax 301/571-0457; E-mail **webmaster@asha. org**; URL **http://www.asha.org**).

American Standard Code for Information Interchange (ASCII) An eight bit code for the interchange of information that can operate at any standard transmission baud (**Baudot**) rate including 300, 1200, 2400, and higher. Provides a means of transmitting information between computers and computer components and a standard for data storage on magnetic tape or disk.

Americans with Disabilities Act of 1990 (ADA) Signed into law by President Bush on July 26, 1990, this Act became effective in 1992. The legislation extends to disabled persons — including persons with hearing and visual impairments, paraplegia and epilepsy, AIDS victims and carriers of the HIV virus, alcoholics, and past users of drug — the same kinds of protections and guarantees that the **Civil Rights Act of 1964** granted African Americans and other minorities. That is, employers may not refuse to hire or promote a person who is qualified to do a job simply because that person is disabled. The bill also requires employers to make reasonable accommodations, without incurring a lot of expense or difficulty, to enable a disabled person to do a job. The bill defines a disabled individual as a person with physical or mental impairment that "substantially limits a major life activity," such as walking, talking, or working. It excludes current users of illegal drugs, homosexuals, bisexuals, transsexuals, transvestites, and people with emotional disorders like kleptomania, gambling compulsions, and pedophelia. It became effective in 1992 for employers with 25 or more workers, and in 1994 for employers with 15 or more workers. The only exceptions are churches and church-run schools. The legislation classifies alcoholism and drug addiction as medical problems and extends new protections to the mentally ill and retarded and to those with learning disabilities. It requires that employers make the workplace accessible to all employees, forces most public service sector businesses to provide wheelchair access, and requires that buses and a percentage of train and subway cars be modified for handicapped access. After 1993, telephone companies were required to establish relay services between special telephones for people with speech or hearing disabilities and people using ordinary telephones. In 1994, the **Equal Employment Opportunity Commission** published guidelines on disability-related inquiries and medical examinations focusing on the hiring process. In general, the guidelines require employers to limit their pre-offer questions to those concerning an applicant's ability to perform job functions. They are also prohibited from making disability-related inquiries at the pre-offer stage. For technical assistance and training for the implementation of the Americans with Disabilities Act of 1990, *see* regional center phone numbers listed under **National Institute for Disability and Rehabilitation**. For ADA technical assistance materials, state and local building codes,and new and proposed regulations, see **http://www.usdoj.gov/crt/ada/adahom1.htm**.

American Technical Education Association (ATEA) A national professional association of 2,000 members dedicated to excellence in postsecondary technical education with emphasis on the concerns of business and industry. Provides professional development opportunities for teachers, administrators, and support personnel in postsecondary education, and networking opportunities for the exchange of ideas among persons in education, business, and industry. *Contact:* ATEA, North Dakota College of Science,800 North Sixth St., Wahpeton, ND 58076-0002 701/671-2240 or 2301; Fax 701/671-2260; E-mail **krump@plains.nodak.edu**; URL **http://members.aol.com/ateainfo**).

American Vocational Association, Inc. (AVA) An organization of 40,000 members whose mission is to provide educational leadership in developing a competitive work force. Specific purposes are to encourage career development, professional involvement, and leadership among members; foster excellence in vocational-technical education, advocate national public policy to benefit vocational-technical education; and market vocational-technical education. *Contact:* AVA, 1410 King St., Alexandria, VA 22314 (703/683-3111; Fax 703/683-7424; URL **http://www.ava.online.org/**).

America On-Line Provides access to the **Internet.**

AmeriCare A proposed joint state and federal program that would replace Medicaid. It would offer a basic health insurance package to people who aren't covered by an employer-provided health care plan.

America's Job Bank (AJB) A job listing service available on the Internet. AJB collects job listings from 1,800 nationwide state employment offices and offers companies the opportunity to enter their job listings directly. URL **http://www.ajb.dni.us/index.html**.

America's Talent Bank (ATB) A nationwide electronic résumé system which allows job seekers to market their qualifications by entering their résumés into this national network, which is then searched by employers for workers who meet their needs. Supported by the Department of Labor, ATB is a product of state employment service agencies. URL **http://www.atb.org.**

AmeriCorps Legislation signed by President Clinton on September 21, 1993 (Public Service Act of 1993) that allows students who complete two years of community service to earn $4,725 per year to apply toward college tuition or student loans. Participants in the program may also earn living allowances of at least $7,400 per year and health care and child day care benefits. The plan funded 20,000 students in 1994, 33,000 in 1995, and 47,000 in 1996 with spending limited to $300, $500, and $700 million respectively in each of the three years.

amicus curiae A legal term that literally means "friend of the court." An *amicus curiae* brief is a petition, declaration, or statement of position on an issue filed by a party not involved in the litigation under consideration by the courts but who may be affected by the outcome. Such briefs usually involve an issue that has far-reaching implications, often involving public policy.

amortization of training expenses
In December 1997, the Internal Revenue Service ruled that certain training expenses incurred in "unusual circumstances" must be amortized over a minimum of five years rather than expensed in the year the costs were incurred. The term "unusual circumstances" was defined as when training costs were incurred "to obtain future benefits significantly beyond those traditionally associated with the

training provided in the ordinary course of a taxpayer's trade or business." Considered by some to be a reasonable ruling because capitalizing training expenses is not a penalty. Considered by others to be a good ruling because it forces companies to treat some types of training as long-term investments rather than tax writeoffs. On the other hand, some fear that the IRS may interpret the "unusual circumstances" clause to penalize companies whose training projects bring long-term profits or those that create new business.

amphetamines A class of legal prescription drugs used in the treatment of colds, hay fever, depression, and obesity. Also commonly used as an "upper", they can be highly addictive and dangerous if abused. Also called *speed; uppers.*

AMVETS National Headquarters (AMVETS) A congressionally chartered nonprofit association of more than 175,000 members who served honorably in the Army, Coast Guard, Navy, Marine Corps, or Air Force after September 15, 1940, or are still serving on active duty in the National Guard or Reserves. Its purpose is to help veterans through a variety of services, promote world peace, and preserve the American way of life. *Contact:* AMVETS National Headquarters, 4647 Forbes Blvd., Lanham, MD 20706-9961 (301/459-6181; Fax 301/459-5578).

amyotropic lateral sclerosis (ALS) A neuromuscular disease characterized by degeneration of a select group of nerve cells and pathways in the brain and spinal cord which leads to progressive wasting and paralysis of the muscles that control movement. There is currently no cure, and it is almost always fatal within a few years. Also called *Lou Gerhig's Disease.*

anagogic or metaphorical learning A learning strategy used by humans (and to some degree by learning machines). It is learning by means of analogy, metaphors, comparison with past experience, or reminders.

analog 1. In data processing, a computer that calculates by using physical analogs (such as the amount of electrical resistance) of the variables of a problem and provides solutions in a graphic representation (such as an oscilloscope pattern). For most data processing applications today, digital computers are used. **2.** In video, the variation of an electrical signal to represent the original

image or sound that is being processed and reproduced. **3.** In multimedia, information and communication technology that uses a continuous scale that is incompatible with digital computers. Data are stored and retrieved as a continuous signal rather than in bits; for example, videocassette and audiocassette recorders and tapes.

analysis exercise Used in assessment centers and other screening and selection strategies. Participants are given information on a situation and asked to recommend appropriate courses of action. Exercises test ability to sift through information, determine critical facts, come to a conclusion, and present a logical argument to support the conclusion.

analysis of variance A statistical means of determining the proportion of explained variance or dispersion between and among "treatment" (experimental) and control groups. In general, the technique helps users to discriminate between causality and mere chance. The complexity of the methodology precludes a cookbook description of its calculation. Computer programs are available to perform the calculations.

analytical decision *See* logical decision.

analytical skills The ability to use logic and inquiry and past experience, research, or experimentation to get the information needed to solve problems, make decisions, innovate, and evaluate. Analytical skills can also be used to clarify objectives, separate the judgment and idea generation phases of creative endeavor, provide cues for association, discover relationships, and examine similarities and differences. They involve observing, listening, diagnosing, analyzing, and assessing situations together with the ability to predict directions that situations are likely to take. They include the ability to reason both deductively and inductively.

analytical survey A research methodology in which data collected in a **polling survey** are subjected to statistical analysis to determine whether there are similarities, differences, or relationships between and among groups.

analytical thinking The ability to differentiate between unimportant and critical details, recognize discrepancies and variances between facts, and draw correct inferences and conclusions from information.

anatomical gift Designation of the use of an organ (heart, liver, lungs, kidneys, cornea, skin, and so on) or donation of the body for medical use following death. May be arranged by completion of special forms, entered in a will, or (in some states) the authorization may be inscribed on the donor's driver's license.

anchoring　The disposition of people to look back to their spiritual foundations to recapture what was soothing and supporting and use it to moor themselves securely in the future. Attributed to Faith Popcorn and Lys Marigold, *Clicking: 16 Trends to Future Fit Your Life, Your Work, and Your Business.*

ancillary benefits　Include such employee benefits as dental care, dependent care, home care, prepaid legal plans, prescription drugs, and vision care. Also called *additional benefits, corollary benefits,* and *fringe benefits.*

ancillary medical benefits　Dental benefits; home care; speech/hearing benefits; prescription drug benefits; vision care.

ancillary probate　Additional probate done in another state where, for example, the decedent owned real estate in his or her name alone.

ancillary services　Medical services such as X-rays and laboratory tests. Also called *support services.*

andragogic learning　*See* andragogy; didactic learning; pedagogic learning.

andragogy　A way of looking at adult learning. It views adults as needing to be self-directing; as having interests and experiences that can provide a sound basis for learning. It also considers their need to know or to do to fulfill their role in society as linked to their readiness to learn; their orientation to learning as life-, work-, and problem-centered rather than subject-centered; and their motivation to learn as directed by internal factors such as self-esteem rather than by external rewards. Attributed to HRD Hall of Famer Malcolm Knowles.

anecdotal records　Individual records that emphasize items and episodes of behavior and performance that are important to the evaluation and development of employees, clients, and trainees. Trainers, supervisors, counselors, and medical and health providers may maintain such records. In addition to being confidential, factual, and objective, such records should include significant items of conduct and performance, not be limited to substandard behavior or performance, and report positive and constructive episodes.

angel　An individual, usually over the age of 40 and affluent, who provides start-up funding (venture capital) for a business undertaking mainly for excitement and challenge.

angina pectoris　Pain or tightness in the chest (sometimes radiating to other parts of the upper body) that occurs when the arteries are partially blocked, resulting in temporary reduction of the blood supply to the heart.

angiogram　A medical diagnostic procedure in which a catheter is threaded through an artery into the heart, a dye is injected, and an X-ray is taken. The procedure shows blockages in the arteries of the heart.

animation　A means of describing (or viewing) and clarifying a visible or invisible process or procedure — a situation in which an element changes or evolves over time — to facilitate comprehension of the relationships between events.

ankylosing spondylitis　A type of arthritis. It affects an estimated 300,000 Americans, usually young men. It is a spinal inflammation that can spread throughout the body.

annual exclusion　The $10,000 per year, per gift allowed by law that an individual can give to another and incur no federal tax liability.

annual leave　The number of hours, days, or weeks of vacation with pay allowed employees by an organization. Based on length of service with the organization, it ranges from one week to six weeks per year, but the most common vacation period is two weeks.

annuitant　A former employee who receives a monthly or annual payment for services rendered upon retirement for which he or she made weekly or monthly contributions while employed.

Annuitants Protection Act of 1994 Technically an amendment to the **Employee Retirement Income Security Act of 1974.** Gives retirees and the Secretary of Labor the right to sue their former employers to obtain relief from ERISA violations involving the purchase of annuities following the termination of a pension plan. The legislation was considered by the Secretary of Labor and many members of congress as a first step toward correcting erroneous interpretations of ERISA, which have had the effect of narrowing the rights and remedies made available to participants and beneficiaries under the law.

annuity **1.** Specified amounts of income paid in a lump sum, yearly, or at other regular intervals. A person receives an annuity for life or for a specific period of time in consideration of services rendered, outstanding performance, or accident or injury. **2.** Contracts purchased from insurers that provide for periodic payments or surrender options.

annuity, joint and survivor *See* contingent annuity.

ANSI X12 A universal health care claims format adopted by the Medicare overseers at the Health Care Financing Administration and officials with The Travelers and Blue Cross and Blue Shield Association. Using **electronic data interchange,** ANSI X12 will eliminate the hundreds of different claims forms now used by major payers.

anti-cutback rule Provides protection against elimination or reduction by plan amendment of certain benefits provided under a qualified plan. Applies to benefits already accrued under the terms of the plan, early retirement benefits, early retirement-type subsidies, and optional forms of benefits. Does not apply to life insurance, accident or health, Social Security supplements, pre- and post-tax employee contributions and direct investments, and plan loans.

anti-discrimination laws *See* Age Discrimination in Employment Act of 1967; Americans with Disabilities Act of 1990; Civil Rights Act of 1964; Civil Rights Act of 1991; Equal Pay Act of 1963; Executive Order 11246; Fair Labor Standards Act of 1938; Pregnancy Discrimination Act of 1978; Older Americans Acts of 1965 and 1978; Older Workers Benefit Protection Act of 1990; Pregnancy Discrimination Act of 1978; Rehabilitation Act of 1973; Vietnam Era Veterans Readjustment and Assistance Act of 1974; Title VII of the Civil rights Act of 1964.

Anti-Drug Abuse Act of 1986 (ADAA) Enacted in October 1986, the Act provided $1.7 billion to be used for law enforcement, treatment for drug abusers, drug research, and school and community education programs.

antigen tests Test for the presence of antibodies in the blood in which the test chemicals react directly with proteins on the coat of the virus to give a definite indication of its presence. Used to detect HIV antibodies.

Anti-Injunction Act of 1932 (AIA) Established and protects the right of employees to participate in union activities by prohibiting **yellow-dog contracts**. It also defines and limits the power of the courts to issue injunctions against certain actions and permits either party to sue if its collective bargaining contract is violated. The law also makes unions immune from antitrust laws (interpreted by the courts to mean when a union acts in its self-interest and not in conjunction with nonlabor groups to achieve its goals). Also known as the Norris-LaGuardia Act.

antitrust and fair trade legislation Legislation directed at prohibition of deliberate commercial injury, such as the acquisition of monopoly power, resulting from unfair, unethical, manipulative, dishonest, or corrupt business practices including conspiracy, coercion, and the elimination of competition. With the exception of Section 5 of the **Federal Trade Commission Act of 1914** and the **Robinson-Patman act of 1936,** which are enforced by the Federal Trade Commission, only the Department of Justice can institute criminal proceedings under the antitrust laws.

antivirus software Utility programs that scan files, boot sectors, and other sections of a compute disk for virus "signatures" or code strings. If the program finds a virus, it notifies the user and removes the virus. Some programs monitor the computer's memory for signs of infection. Others immunize the system by running checks (checksums) on each executable file and, if the checksum changes, the program alerts the user to the potential presence of a virus.

anxiety A persistent feeling of painful uneasiness of mind, apprehension, dread, and impending disaster in response to repressed feelings or internal attitudes. It differs from fear in that it is not referable to specific objects or events. The individual does not know its source.

anxiety attack Sudden, acute, terrifying, panic-like feelings lasting from a few moments to an hour. Victims report rapid heartbeat, palpitation, nausea, dizziness or faintness, diarrhea, and a feeling of suffocation or choking.

any-willing-provider (AWP) *See* any-willing-provider law.

any willing-provider law A state law that is a barrier to managed care. The law permits any provider holding required credentials and willing to conform with the terms and conditions of a network contract to be admitted to that network. Such legislation restricts payers' ability to contract selectively with a limited number of providers to save on premiums.

aphasia A speech defect that results from injury to certain areas of the brain. It is the most disruptive of all communication disabilities. People with aphasia see, hear, and feel, but they cannot integrate this sensory information into logical experience patterns. Aphasia results in inability to use or comprehend words. There are two types of aphasia: expressive and receptive. An individual who can understand what is said but cannot express his or her own thoughts is said to have expressive aphasia. An individual who cannot receive or understand speech has receptive aphasia. Receptive aphasia has its roots in sensory deficiencies, including either or both vision and hearing impairments. Aphasia may be partial, called dysphasia, or total. The most common causes of aphasia are brain tumors, cerebral hemorrhage, and cerebral thrombosis.

Apollo In travel management, a **computer reservation system** (formerly **Covia**). Also provides hardware and software to enhance communications, management reports, quality control and productivity.

apparent authority Established when an individual appears to be authorized to act on an organization's behalf but is not specifically authorized to do so. For example, it occurs when a meeting planner signs a contract with a hotel without authorization from the group represented. If the group, for whatever reason, decides to cancel the meeting, and the contract does not contain a cancellation clause, the hotel may want to recoup damages — for loss of revenue from groups turned away. If the group decides to dispute the claim on the grounds that the planner did not have the authority, the meeting planner has only two options: disagree with his or her employer and risk losing employment or admit that the company is right that he or she knowingly signed a contract without having the authority to do so. In the latter case the hotel may choose to sue both the company and the individual meeting planner.

Apple Internet Connection Kit A software system that allows access to and navigation of the **Internet** simply by pointing and clicking.

applets Small computer applications programs that allow new and powerful interactions between **Web servers** and **Web clients.**

applicant files Files initiated upon receipt of applications for positions and files of persons who were nonselected or who withdrew their applications before a selection was made. Although their useful life is relatively short (usually one or two years), they can be a lucrative source of candidates for vacant positions. Sometimes mistakenly called "active" files.

applicant specifications A staffing document that describes: (1) what an applicant for a specific position *should know* — the technical, professional, and managerial knowledge needed to perform the job; (2) what the applicant should *be able to do* — the technical, professional, and managerial skills required to enter the position; (3) what the applicant *should be* — the educational background, kind and amount of training and experience, and the personal qualities essential for success at the entry level; and (4) what the applicant *can expect* — the nature of the job, compensation offered, job functions, duties, authority, and responsibility, position in the hierarchical structure, and potential for advancement. They are used in recruiting, screening, selecting, training, assigning, developing, and promoting personnel.

applicant tracking system (ATS) A computerized system used to track applicants for positions — from receipt of an application, through the initial interview, to offer and acceptance/rejection — and tabulate evaluations of the organization's recruiting process by the candidates. Some applications provide activity statistics, applicant profiles, custom letters and reports, data sharing, equal employment opportunity applicant flow, electronic posting of job descriptions, invitation schedules, letter history, past employer retrieval, recruiter statistics, résumé scanning, routing status, school and college retrieval, skills retrieval, source statistics, and standard letters.

application A computer program written to perform specific functions, such as inventory control, preparation of spread sheets, and word processing.

application forms Tools for screening applicants for positions. They are also mine fields for the unwary because of the danger of violating equal employment opportunity laws such as **Title VII** of the **Civil Rights Act of 1964, Executive Order 11246, Age Discrimination in Employment Act of 1967,** and **Vocational Rehabilitation Act of 1973.** Areas of potential difficulty include education (dates of attendance and graduation indicate age), military background, arrest record, relatives, physical handicaps, marital and parental status, and housing arrangements.

application programming interface (API) A set of software interfaces that allows unrelated applications to communicate with each other and diverse services.

application software Computer programs that perform tasks for users. Personal productivity software includes spreadsheets, word processing, and databases. Functional or departmental applications include benefits, human resources, information, and payroll.

applied behavior management (ABM) An organizational and individual change process used to assist the organization to involve employees in improving quality, productivity, and profits. It focuses on individual and team performance improvement in areas directly related to the goals and objectives of the organization.

applied billing entry Time spent on specific projects, activities, or clients which can be billed.

applied person-day In calculating HR costs and benefits, an employee's cost per applied person-day is that person's full cost per day divided by his or her applied rate. The calculation should include training costs incurred in preparing for the assignment. Usually for HR professionals with a 70 to 75 percent applied rate, the applied person-day will equal about four times the direct salary cost per day.

applied rate In calculating HR costs and benefits, a worker's applied rate is the number of hours billed to applied projects or clients divided by the total number of hours paid in a given time period. For HR professionals, it is unquestionably the single most important productivity indicator. For them it should remain in the 70 to 75 percent range.

applied research Research directed at discovering new scientific knowledge that has direct application to specific problems and issues or the development of new products, processes, and services that relate to the goals and objectives of the firm.

appraisal See performance appraisal.

appraising Assessing and evaluating objects, processes, products, services, and people.

apprenticeship programs Developed in the Middle Ages by the trade guilds. Although they have declined since the Industrial Revolution, apprenticeship programs remain an important source of skilled workers in the US. The system is used primarily to train laborers, craftsmen, mechanics, and some technicians. A potential craftsman, such as a cabinet maker, is "apprenticed" to a recognized artisan for a period of years during which the apprentice learns the skills by observing and performing the work under the tutelage and guidance of the master craftsman. Currently there are about 1,200 apprenticeable occupations. Each state has a director who, together with field representatives, works with state government, business, industry, organizations, and labor to establish and maintain complete training programs. Apprenticeship program standards are established jointly by the organization, and, where appropriate, labor unions, and the United States Department of Labor.

appropriate penalty A legal doctrine pertaining to cases of unlawful discharge. It asks, "Was the degree of discipline administered by the employer reasonably commensurate with the seriousness of the offense and the employee's record of performance with the organization?"

appropriations bills Annual legislation that provides the funds for the operation of the federal government. There are 13 regular appropriations bills (such as those for defense and agriculture) and an indefinite number of special or supplementary appropriations bills to provide funds for unanticipated expenses.

approved amount See approved charges.

approved charges Medical insurance payments based largely on what the policy (or law in the case of Medicare) defines as "reasonable charges" or the amounts approved by the carrier.

A.P.R.A. Fuel Oil Buyers Group, Inc., et al. A 1996 National Labor Relations Board decision that entitled illegal immigrants fired for union activity to sue for denial of their right to engage in union organizing and collective bargaining activities and ordered their reinstatement with back pay.

aptitude A combination of innate or acquired abilities that indicates a person's ability to develop skill or proficiency in a specific area if appropriate training is provided.

aptitude test A psychological test used in hiring, selecting people for training, and career planning. Similar to tests of general ability but more specialized. Examples of aptitudes are mechanical, space perception, mathematics, art, music, and so on as distinguished from general learning ability. Examples of standardized aptitude tests are Bennett's Test of Mechanical Comprehension, Clerical Abilities Battery, Purdue Mechanical Adaptability Test, SRA Tests of Mechanical Aptitude, Revised Minnesota Paper Form Board Test, and the last four parts of the MacQuarrie Test for Mechanical Ability.

arbitration   A formal form of negotiation used to resolve individual and group disputes including labor-management disagreements. Although it involves a neutral third party, the arbitrator, his or her role is considerably different than that of a mediator. When the parties to a disagreement accept the arbitration process, they also agree to accept the decision of the arbitrator as final and binding. Arbitration is less expensive and time-consuming than **mediation** or litigation. Enforcement is rarely required because both parties agree before the proceedings to accept the decision, and arbitrators are usually better qualified than the courts to rule on specific labor issues.

Archie On the Internet, a computer search system created by McGill University that scans **file transfer protocol** sites around the world for downloadable files.

Architectural and Transportation Barriers Compliance Board (ABCB) A federal entity that provides information and technical assistance regarding accessibility and standards for facilities for people with disabilities. Monitors and enforces compliance with the Architectural Barriers Act of 1968 and investigates complaints about the inaccessibility of buildings. Developed the ADA accessibility guidelines. Created by a 1974 amendment to the **Rehabilitation Act of 1973.** *Contact:* Access Board, 1111 18th St., Ste. 501, Washington, DC 20036 (800/USA-ABLE; 202/272-5434; 202/653-7834 TDD; Fax 202/272-5447; E-mail **info@access-board.gov**; URL **http: www.access-board.gov**).

Architectural Barriers Act of 1968 (ABA) An Act that mandated the design, construction, or modification of public buildings and facilities owned or leased in whole or in part by the federal government (or financed or aided by federal funds) to provide means of access to handicapped individuals. *See also* Americans with Disabilities Act of 1990; Rehabilitation Act of 1973.

architectural privacy The physical privacy (or lack thereof) afforded by office workspace. Believed to have an impact on employees' job satisfaction and productivity.

architecture The set of technical standards that defines the **hardware, system software, application software**, and communication links of a computer system.

Area Agencies on Aging (AAA) Countrywide government-sponsored agencies that serve as focal points for housing and service options for the aging.

area chart A means of displaying data graphically. Employs geometric figures, drawings, or pictures to demonstrate the magnitude of an an effect by the area of the illustration rather than its length or height. Most often used to provide an overview of a trend or the cumulative effects of individual items over time.

Cartoon Viewing by Age Group

area counseling services *See* destination services company.

area differential An allowance paid to employees assigned to a foreign country or certain geographic areas in the United States for hardship factors in the former case and different average pay levels or cost of living in the latter case.

area studies *See* cross-cultural training.

area wage survey A formal or informal survey of the "going rate" for jobs in a particular geographic area used to price benchmark jobs. Surveys may be made by individual firms, professional and technical organizations, and the US government's Bureau of Labor Statistics. BLS conducts area wage surveys annually.

Armed Forces Procurement Act of 1947 (AFPA) In purchasing, contracting, and marketing, a statute covering all Department of

Defense procurement authority. It gives the Department of Defense authorization to publish its **Armed Services Procurement Regulations,** which establish the broad guidelines under which military procurements are made.

Armed Services Vocational Aptitude Battery (ASVAB)   A battery of aptitude tests administered to men and women prior to their enlistment in the Armed Forces. It is used to select military occupational/career fields and to qualify for training in those fields.

Army Air Force Exchange Service (AAFES)   A non-pay benefit for active and retired military personnel and their dependents and some military reservists. Provides substantial savings on products and services, including gasoline stations and automotive services, food services, lawn and garden shops, department stores, flowers, dry cleaning, barber shops and beauty services, tax preparation, video rental, car rental, wedding registry, photo developing, and optical shops. Accepts cash, personal checks, and several major credit cards.

Army Aviation Association of America (AAAA)   An organization of approximately 16,000 members open to all persons who desire to support the advancement of US. Army aviation or its allied pursuits. The purpose of AAAA to advance the status, overall esprit, and the general knowledge and efficiency of persons who are professionally engaged anywhere in the overall field of US Army Aviation. *Contact:* AAAA, 49 Richmondville Ave., Westport, CT 06880-2000 (203/226-8184; Fax 203/222-9863; E-mail **aaaa@quad-a.org**)

Army College Fund   A program of educational benefits. If a service member enlists in one of about 50 Military Occupational Specialties, the Army will contribute up to $14,400 toward the individual's college education, the total amount depending on the number of years served.

Army Procurement Procedure (APP)   In contracting and marketing, procurement procedures promulgated by the U.S. Army to supplement the **Armed Forces Procurement Act of 1947**.

Army Reserve Tuition Assistance Program   A program for which Reservists attending college may apply. If they qualify and complete required military training, reservists may be eligible to receive a part of their tuition for approved college courses.

aromatherapy   A botanical form of alternative medical treatment involving the use of oils from palms in conjunction with facial, massage, or inhalation treatment. Believed to enhance circulation, relieve tension, and improve the skin by stimulating the olfactory nerves.

arrangement item   An objective test item that requires the testee to arrange terms, numbers, symbols, phrases, or sentences in order in accordance with some principle or scheme.

array   In video, a grouping of storage devices, such as a hard disk array.

arrythmia   Irregular heartbeat that occurs when the electrical system of the heart is disturbed. Often caused by a buildup of **cholesterol** plaque inside the coronary arteries, which prevents adequate oxygen from getting to parts of the heart.

arteriography   An X-ray technique used to obtain detailed closeups of affected areas in **arteriosclerosis**. A special dye is injected in the leg or arm and the X-ray reveals the arterial sections which the dyes cannot easily penetrate due to blockage.

arteriosclerosis   "Hardening of the arteries" caused by accumulation of fatty deposits (triglycerides and cholesterol) inside the arteries. The deposits narrow the blood vessels and may lead to spasm of the arteries with partial or complete obstruction.

arthritis   A disease which affects one in seven Americans (36.2 million). It takes several forms: **osteoarthritis, rheumatoid arthritis, gout, fibromyalgia, ankylosing spondylitis, scleroderma, and polymyalgia rheumatica**.

Arthritis Foundation   A not-for-profit organization whose mission if to support research to find the cure for and prevention of arthritis and to improve the quality of life for those affected by arthritis. The Foundation also conducts education programs for health professionals, provides community education and support services for people with arthritis and their families, informs the public about arthritis, and advocates the interests of people affected by arthritis. *Contact:* Arthritis Foundation, 1330 W. Peachtree St., Atlanta, GA 30309 (800/283-7800 or 404/872-7100; E-mail **infocenter@arthritis.org**; URL **http: www.arthritis.org**).

Arthritis Research Institute of America (ARIA)   A research organization devoted to eliminating the pain and suffering of osteoarthritis through research. Sponsors research on related topics. *Contact:* ARIA, 300 S. Duncan Ave., Ste. 240, Clearwater, FL 34615 (813/461-4054; Fax 813/449-9227).

articulation disorders A speech problem manifested in unclear, imprecise voicing of sounds. For example, words involving the "s" sound and its voiced correlative "z" (the most common error); "r" with a "w" substitute; "l" with an "s" substitute; and the "sh" and "zh" sounds. Lallation is a common problem of articulation. In lallation, the *r, l, t, d,* and/or "*s*" sounds are defective.

artificial intelligence (AI) The general term applied to systems and research in the fields of robotics, machine vision, speech recognition, natural languages, and **EXPERT systems** that attempt to emulate or duplicate the various forms of human activity that do not have computational aspects.

artificial reality *See* virtual reality.

Asbestos Regulations Regulations issued by the Occupational Safety and Health Administration that cover employees who are exposed to asbestos at work. 29CFR1910.1001 covers such requirements as air monitoring, ventilation, and engineering controls, use of respiratory protection, protective clothing, and equipment, and clean-up procedures and safe work practices.

ASCII file A computer data file that contains only ASCII characters with no special code for formatting, page layout, and so on. Nearly every computer application program can read and store these files.

Asia-Pacific Economic Cooperation (APEC) A coalition of 18 nations similar to the European Community established to promote economic health and free trade within the area by 2020.

Asians Persons having origins in any of the Far East, Southeast Asia, or the Indian subcontinent countries.

Ask-a-Nurse A toll-free, medical and health hot line operated nationwide. It is staffed by experienced and specially trained registered nurses around the clock, seven days a week. The service provides answers to questions about illnesses, injuries, and general health as well as information on local medical and health resources, including referrals to area physicians, hospitals, and community services. It is not appropriate for emergency calls. Nurses staffing the hot line use a computer data base of clinical protocols approved by physicians as the basis for the advice and assistance they provide. When indicated, nurses also follow up with callers after a few days to check on progress.

assault In law, an apparent offer, attempt, or threat to harm another person without actually carrying out the violent act.

assembly line manufacturing A system of workstations operated by workers who perform only one on two closely related tasks in the manufacturing sequence. The product is moved between workstations on tracks or belts. Designed to simplify and speed up production.

assertiveness training (A/T) Training provided to build assertiveness (not aggressiveness), improve the job performance and satisfaction of managers and supervisors, establish models of managerial behavior, reduce anxieties in handling interpersonal relationships on the job, enhance employees' self-image, and help managers to protect themselves from manipulation or aggression. Strategies are rooted in behavior modification and include personal inventory of participants' skills, attitudes, habits, and values, self-analysis and self-evaluation exercises, group interaction, assertiveness exercises, and feedback on assertive-responsive behavior patterns.

assessment *See* evaluation.

assessment center A structured method of screening and selecting people for assignment or promotion to executive, managerial, or supervisory positions. Over a period of two or three days, and under the direction of a team of evaluators, participants deal with a variety of realistic management problems and situations. They engage in simulations and business games, in-basket exercises, role playing, mock staff meetings, and decision-making exercises; undergo psychological tests and projective techniques, and engage in group discussion and self-evaluation. Evaluators observe, assess, and record participants' behavior and performance, critique group exercises, interview participants, and combine their appraisals in a formal report. Assessment centers can also be used to diagnose training and development needs.

asset appreciation plan *See* book value plan.

assets Items owned by a company, such as cash and bank deposits, marketable securities, accounts receivable, inventories, investments in other companies, land, plant, and equipment, and sometime goodwill or other intangibles, all stated on the basis of purchase prices and not on current or market value.

assignment A process through which a physician or medical supplier agrees to accept an organization's (or Medicare's part B) payment as payment in full except for specific coinsurance and deductible amounts required of the patient. Medicare usually pays 80 percent of the approved amount directly to the physician or supplier after the beneficiary meets the annual part B deductible of $100. The beneficiary pays the other 20 percent.

assignment of benefits In health insurance, authorization by an enrollee or spouse for the insurer to issue payment of benefits directly to the provider.

assistant-to assignment *See* understudy assignment.

assisted housing *See* board and care home; congregate housing; continuing care retirement community; independent living center.

assisted living A housing arrangement in which room and meals, plus help as needed, with bathing, dressing, getting in and out of bed, and protective oversight, are provided.

assisted reproductive technology (ART) Procedures that enable a woman with otherwise untreatable infertility to become pregnant through any artificial conception procedures, such as artificial insemination, in vitro fertilization, and embryo transfer. Neither the procedure on services and supplies related to the procedure are typically covered by health care plans.

assistive device A service or product purchased or rented to help older and disabled persons to function better or more safely at home. May include devices for people with hearing and vision impairments and those who need help in walking or moving around. An example is closed-caption video. Medicare may pay for all or a part of the cost if the device is prescribed by a physician.

assistive listening device (ALD) A device for people with hearing impairments mandated for availability by the **Americans with Disabilities Act of 1990** during all meetings and conventions. Examples of ALDs are infrared and FM systems, both of which can be moved from meeting room to meeting room or permanently installed.

assistive product *See* assistive device.

assistive technology *See* assistive device.

association One of the basic forms of learning in which the learner is helped to make connections between related objects, ideas, or other items or recognize a sequence that must be followed.

The Association for Behavior Analysis (ABA) A 2,500-member international association founded in 1974. It mission is to promote the experimental, theoretical, and applied analysis of behavior and provide a forum for the discussion of issues and the dissemination of information pertinent to the interests of members. ABA, 213 West Hall, Western Michigan University, Kalamazoo, MI 49008-5052 (616/387-8341; Fax 616/387-8354; E-mail **76236.1312@compuserve.com**; URL **http://www.wmich.edu/ABA**).

Association for Community Based Education (ACBE) A national network of organizations, including accredited colleges, that provides educational programs linked to cultures and traditions of their communities. Its mission is to serve the needs of people that conventional public and private educational institutions have not been able to reach through activities that include small business development, health services, job training, adult literacy, and continuing education programs. ACBE, 1806 Vernon St., N.W., Washington, DC 20009 (202/462-6333; E-mail **acbe@aol.com**).

Association for Continuing Higher Education, Inc. (ACHE) A 1,560-member institution-based organization of colleges, universities, and individuals dedicated to the promotion of lifelong learning and excellence in continuing higher education. ACHE encourages professional networks, research, and exchange of information and advocates continuing higher education as a means of enhancing and improving society. *Contact:* ACHE, Trident Technical College, P.O. Box 118067, CE-P, Charleston, SC 29423-8067 (803/722-5546; Fax 803/722-5520).

Association for Educational Communications and Technology (AECT) An international professional association of 5,000 members, the leading organization representing instructional technology professionals. The mission of AECT is to provide leadership in educational communications and technology by linking professionals holding a common interest in the use of educational technology and its application to the learning process. *Contact:* AECT, 1025 Vermont Ave., Street, N.W., Ste. 820, Washington, DC 20005 (202/347-7834; Fax 202/347-7839; E-mail **aect@aect.org**; URL **http://www.aect.org**).

Association for Experiential Education (AEE) A not-for-profit, international, professional organization with approximately 2,500 members in 25 countries. AEE has roots in adventure education, is committed to the development, practice, and evaluation of experiential learning in all settings, and serves as a national resource for experiential education including service learning. Provides materials, training, networking, and information. *Contact:* AEE, 2305 Canyon Blvd. Ste. 100, Boulder, CO 80302 (303/440-8844; Fax 303/440-9581; URL **http://www.princeton.edu/~rourtis/aee.html**).

Association for Investment Management and Research (AIMR) An international, nonprofit organization of over 28,600 investment professionals, including research analysts, investment counselors, portfolio managers, and others in the industry. Offers professional conduct services, continuing education programs, and publications for investment professionals. Sponsors the **Institute for Financial Analysts** which awards the **Chartered Financial Analyst** designation. *Contact:* AIMR, 5 Boar's Head Lane, Charlottesville, VA 22903-0668 (800/247-8132 or 804/980-3668; Fax 804/980-9755; E-mail **info@aimr.org**; URL **http://www.aimr.com**).

Association for Multi-media International, Inc. (AMI) An international association of media professionals who promote, produce, and utilize a wide range of presentation media for communicating, educating, and entertaining. *Contact:* AMI, 10006 N. Dale Mabry Hwy., Ste. 204, Tampa, FL 33618-4424 (813/960-1692; Fax 813/962-7911; URL **http://www.ami.org**).

Association for Quality and Participation (AQP) A 8,000+ member nonprofit professional association dedicated to serving all phases of quality improvement and participation though training, national and regional conferences, publications, and local chapters. AQP's mission is to serve as an advocate and learning resource for individuals, teams, organizations, and communities to design, implement, and sustain quality and

participation processes for high performance. *Contact:* AQP, 801-B West 8th St., Ste. 501, Cincinnati, OH 45203-1607 (800/733-3310 or 513/381-1959; Fax 513/381-0070; E-mail **AQPORG@aol.com**; URL **http://www.nhccd.edu/AQP/index.html**).

The Association for the Management of Organization Design (AMOD) A not-for-profit professional association formed to promote the knowledge and practice of organization design; i.e., the art of fashioning a structure, process, and human talent to organize individuals, groups, and units into an effective total system to achieve the mission of the enterprise. *Contact:* AMOD, P.O. Box 1048, Severna Park, MD 21146-8048 (201-673-2663; Fax 201/765-2325; URL **http:www.greenlake.net/amod**)

Association for Worksite Health Promotion (AWHP) An organization of 2,500 members whose mission is enhance the personal and organizational health and well-being of employees and their families throughout the world. AWHP advocates the value of worksite health promotion, supports health promotion professionals through education, provides resources to those who offer health promotion at the workplace, and serves as a catalyst to advance research and learning. *Contact:* AWHP, 60 Revere Dr., Ste. 500, Northbrook, IL 60062 (847/480-9574; Fax 847-480-9282; URL **http://awhp@awhp.com**).

association management company An organization that manages business, trade, service, and professional associations and provides meeting and conference management services for those organizations. Such organizations provide another career track for meeting management professionals.

association meeting A meeting attended by members of a professional, scientific, or trade association, often including an exposition of products and services by vendors who provide those products and services to the profession or trade.

Association of Conference Executives (ACE) An information center and forum for 600 member organizations involved in organizing, marketing, accommodating, and servicing events. It is the largest U.K. based association in the meetings industry, with the majority of member being buyers. It provides regular training courses for the meetings industry. *Contact:* ACE

International, Riverside House, High St., Huntingdon, Cambridgeshire, GB PE18 6SG (0480-457595).

Association of Corporate Travel Executives (ACTE) A professional association of 1,300 members involved in the business travel industry. ACTE's objectives are to advance educational standards, further professional development, increase activity in corporate, government, and community affairs, and increase communication among members. *Contact:* ACTE, 608 Massachusetts Ave., N.E., Washington, DC 20002 (800/228-3669 or 202/546-5746; Fax 202/546-7140; E-mail **info@acte.org**; URL **http://www.acte.org**).

Association of Destination Management Executives (ADME) A professional association of a relatively new segment of the travel industry, which includes location-specific professionals whose work complements the efforts of meeting planners. Established in August 1995, the association includes representatives from more than 40 of the estimated 4,500 destination management companies in the United States. *Contact:* ADME, 730 17th St, Ste. 710, Denver, CO 80202 (303/825-2406 or 303/825-2022; Fax 303/825-4615).

The Association of Executive Search Consultants (AESC) An organization of professional retained executive search firms. Membership is granted only to firms that have been evaluated by the AESC as having the highest standards of conduct, competence, and professionalism within the executive search community. Firms admitted to membership in the AESC have passed a rigorous admission review by their professional peers. *Contact:* AESC, 500 Fifth Avenue, Ste. 930, New York NY 10110-0900 (212/398-9556; Fax 212/398-9560; URL **http://www.skottedwards.com/aesc.html**).

The Association of Human Resource Systems Professionals, Inc. (HRSP) An organization of approximately 4,500 individual members, representing more than 2,000 organizations located throughout the United States, Canada, and internationally. Established to advance the management of human resources information in support of organizational objectives. Offers accredited continuing education through professional development seminars. Sponsors an annual conference and exposition. *Contact:* HRSP,

14643 Dallas Pkwy, Ste. 525, Dallas, TX 75240 (214/661-3727; Fax 214/386-8180; URL **http://www.ahrm.org/hrsp/hrsp.htm**).

Association of Information Technology Professionals (AITP) An organization of about 12,000 members and more than 5,000 student members representing information systems professionals throughout the United States and Canada. AITP's mission is to promote effective and responsible management of information technology for the benefit of its members, their employers, and society. Formerly the Data Processing Management Association. *Contact:* AITP, 505 Busse Hwy, Park Ridge, IL 60068-3191 (847/825-8124; Fax 847/825-1693; E-mail **70430.35@compuserve.com**.

Association of Military Surgeons of the United States (AMSUS) An association of 13,000 members. Open to past and present enlisted personnel in grades E-5 through E-9, Regular, Reserve, or National Guard commissioned and warrant officers or GS-7 and above civilians in the medical services of the U.S. Air Force, U.S. Army, U.S. Navy, U.S. Coast Guard, U.S. Public Health Service, and Department of Veterans Affairs, officers of military medical services of other nations; and past and present medical consultants to the chiefs of the federal medical services. Its mission is to advance the knowledge of federal health care and increase the effectiveness and efficiency of its membership by mutual association and by the consideration of matters pertaining to constituent services both in peace and in war. *Contact:* AMSUS, 9320 Old Georgetown Rd., Bethesda, MD 20814-1653 (301/897-8800; Fax 301/530-5446; E-mail **stevem@amsus.org**; URL **amsus@amsus.org**).

The Association of Outplacement Consulting Firms International (AOCFI) An association of 120 outplacement firms, with operations in 32 countries, that provide consulting services to assist employers to manage human resource change in the workplace. Services include pre-termination planning and training for corporations and psychological profiling, career assessment, office space and secretarial services, résumé writing, interview techniques, and job search consulting for the outplaced individual. *Contact:* AOCFI, 1200 19th St., N.W., Ste. 300, Washington, DC 20036-2422

(202/857-1185; Fax 202/223-4579; E-mail **daniel_glutzer@sda.com**).

Association of South East Asian Nations (ASEAN) A 25-year old economic and tourism alliance of six East Asian countries: Brunei, Indonesia, Malaysia, the Philippines, Singapore, and Thailand.

Association of the U.S. Army (AUSA) A private, nonprofit educational association of 112,000 individual and 225 industrial members open to all active, reserve, and civilian personnel in the Army and anyone who subscribes to the association bylaws. Its mission is to foster public understanding and support of the Army and the people who serve in it. *Contact:* AUSA, 2425 Wilson Blvd., P.O. Box 1560, Arlington, VA 22210-3385 (703/ 841-4300; Fax 703/525-9039; E-mail **ausa@ aol.com**; URL **http://www.ausa.org**).

association skills In creative problem solving, the ability to do "chain thinking" — gearing the imagination to memory, using sounds rather than words, and causing one thought to lead to another rather than concentrating on a sequential series of steps characteristic of logical thought.

ASTD Member Unit Awards Awards presented annually to members of the **American Society for Training and Development's** Professional Practice and Network organizations who have contributed to the human resource development profession and for service to a specific unit area. Areas included are Career Development, Instructional Technology, International, Management Development, Organization Development, Sales and marketing, Technical and Skills Training, Automotive Industry, Disabilities Awareness, Employee Involvement, Mind/Brain Network, Multicultural Network, Secretarial and Clerical Trainers Network, and Women's Network. Selected by an awards committee from nominees by reviewing documentation and direct contacts with the nominating individual and other person with direct knowledge of the accomplishments of the individual or group. *Contact:* ASTD National Awards Program, Attn: Dawn Temple, 1640 King St., Box 1443, Alexandria, VA 22313-2043 (703/683-8100).

asthma A disease that occurs when the muscles surrounding the bronchial tubes contract, or when the membranes that line the interior of the tubes expand, or when excess mucus is secreted by the mucous glands inside the bronchial walls. These conditions prevent air from passing freely to and from the lungs. Currently affects 13.1 million Americans.

astigmatism Distortion of curvature of the eyeball and its lens, leading to distorted focusing and blurred vision, often accompanied by eyestrain and headaches. Correctable by eye glasses or contact lenses.

asynchronous In multimedia, communicating in other than real time; for example, by E-mail.

asynchronous computer conferencing (ACC) A training delivery option. Uses computers to provide trainee-to-trainee interaction in a high-tech setting, ranging from specially-designed classrooms to individual workstations. An effective means of providing team training. Enables trainees to learn when they need to — or when it is convenient for them. System can incorporate graphics and video.

asynchronous transfer mode (ATM) A high-volume data transmission process.

atherosclerosis Accumulation of deposits of fats and cholesterol (plaques) inside the blood vessels, especially the arteries. May cause hypertension, kidney failure, narrowing of the coronary arteries (angina pectoris), leg cramps, dizziness and headaches, diminished intellectual capacity, and stroke symptoms. A part of the aging process and ultimately the cause of death for many persons.

ATM card A card issued by a bank that allows the user by paying a fee to withdraw cash from an automated teller machine. Some ATMs sell airline tickets, postage stamps, and travelers' checks.

at-risk student A person who will most likely not graduate from high school whether due to a disadvantaged home, poor self-esteem, or an undetected learning disability.

attention deficit disorder (ADD) A learning disability characterized by any eight of the following symptoms: disorganization, distractibility, impulsiveness, overactivity, argumentativeness, low frustration tolerance, mood swings, forgetting, problems with relationships, frequent job changes, underachievement, high intelligence quotient, increased creativity, and compensation for any of the foregoing. The syndrome is believed to be genetic in origin, most likely a neurochemical failure in the system of the brain that controls attention.

attention deficit, hyperactivity disorder (ADHD) A form of **attention deficit disorder**. A neurological syndrome that is characterized by impulsive and excessively chaotic and uncontrolled movement (sometimes playful, oftentimes destructive), distractibility, and hyperactivity or excess energy. Considered by some experts as a motivational disorder. Treatment includes medication (either stimulants, such as dextro-amphetamine sulphate, trade name, Ritalin, or antidepressants, such as desipramine, trade name, Norpramin), behavior management techniques, and psychotherapy.

attention, interest, desire, and action (AIDA) A four-point guide used by specialists when advertising job openings: (1) attract *attention,* (2) develop *interest;* (3) create *desire;* and (4) stimulate *action.*

attestation clause The final paragraph of a will where the witnesses sign.

attitude and opinion survey A device designed to elicit information about employee ideas, feelings, attitudes, concerns, expectations, and preferences on a broad range of managerial issues, from problem identification to in-depth analysis of potential problems identified by other means. The survey can uncover the causes of problems, probe feelings about situations or conditions, and elicit ideas for preventive actions.

attorney-in-fact The agent appointed by the principal or **creator** of a **power of attorney** to act on the principal's behalf.

attribute listing A group ideational technique involving the simple listing of the parts and then the properties, characteristics, basic qualities, distinguishing features, or attributes of the part and the whole object, concept, problem, or idea on a chalkboard for individual attack. Attention then turns to each of the entries, using them as a checklist to force group members to look at all aspects of the item and systematically generate ways to change, modify, or improve it characteristics.

attrition Usually expressed as attrition *rate,* which is the percentage of trainees dropped from training due to failure to maintain normal progress or achieve established standards.

attrition charge A fee assessed by hotels for failure to fill rooms reserved for meetings.

attrition clause In meeting planner contracts with hotels, a clause that states how a decrease in attendance and the number of rooms and meals booked between the signing of the contract and the dates of the event will be handled. Some planning firms have begun including a clause in their group booking contracts that requires hotels to pay full commission on income from penalties assessed to groups that did not use their entire room blocks. Also called *slippage clause.*

at-will-employment *See* employment at will.

audience analysis Scrutinizing and assessing an audience in terms of composition (sex, age, occupation, and so on), objectives, and reasons for attending a presentation or training session for planning and preparation to ensure that objectives, content, structure, methods, materials, language, and examples are appropriate.

audiographics A technology that permits simultaneous transmission of voice communications and graphic images by means of telephone or radio links.

audiographic transmission Using electronic means to convey images such as text, numbers, and graphics (pictures, diagrams, graphs, tables, and so on) from point to point. Devices include computers, word processors, and facsimile machines.

audiologist A hearing care professional who specializes in prevention, identification, and assessment of hearing disorders and provides treatment and rehabilitative services. Practitioners test and diagnose hearing disorders, prescribe and dispense hearing aids and assistive listening devices, instruct people in their use, develop and implement hearing conservation programs, provide aural rehabilitation services such as auditory training, speechreading, and sign language instruction, and conduct research into environmental influences on hearing, new testing methods, and new rehabilitative devices such as cochlear implants.

audio mixing In audio and video production, combining sound from several sources to create the effect desired by the producer.

audiovisuals (AV) Refers to audio visual equipment and materials such as projectuals (slides, filmstrips, and motion pictures); audio and video tapes, cassettes, and discs; photographs, drawings, maps, graphs; and so on.

audiovisual technician The hotel functionary responsible for audiovisual equipment rental and ensuring its trouble-free operation.

audit **1.** A planned and systematic means of assessing the managerial, financial, or other aspect of the status of company planning, operations, and control and the extent to which corporate policies, procedures, and practices are being carried out. It invariably involves interview and observation, review of records and reports, administration, tabulation, and analysis of questionnaires and surveys, and when possible, measurement against standards; identification and analysis of shortfalls, deviations, and violations; determination of causes; identification, selection, and execution of remedial actions, including improvements to systems and procedures; and followup to ensure that corrections have been made. **2.** A complete review and analysis of a human resources information system to ensure that it is meeting user and corporate needs.

auditing **1.** The process of taking an objective and searching look at an organization's plans, objectives, financial position, accounting system and procedures, personnel, facilities, products, programs, services, operations, accomplishments, and deficiencies. **2.** In education and training, the practice of "sitting in" on classes as if the individual were a student but not participating in class discussions or exercises, writing term papers, or taking exams. Auditors are guests or visitors; they receive no grades or credits. Many universities permit senior citizens to audit classes free of charge or for a modest fee when space is available and the instructor gives permission.

authentic assessment
See alternative assessment.

authentic evaluation
See performance assessment.

authoring platform The operating system, such as Windows or System 8, that runs on the computer equipment used to develop informational, educational, or entertainment multimedia programs.

authoring system or software **1.** A program used to develop computer-based training. It typically provides for analysis, management, branching, graphics, and sometimes animation. **2.** In multimedia, the process of programming text, images, audio, and motion picture clips into a sequenced program.

authorization bills Legislation that creates and funds new federal programs, extends authorized programs, or amends programs. Although some authorization bills are effective for only one year, most are multi-year.

authorization cards Cards used by union organizers to sign up the number of employees needed to petition for a union election (30 percent must sign up).

Authorization to Participate (ATP)
An identification card issued to persons enrolled in the **Food Stamps Program** that states how many stamps they are authorized to receive and is valid only for the month issued. The card is brought to an issuing center, usually a bank, store, or post office, where the food stamp coupons are issued. The coupons can be used to buy food at any store that accepts them, but tobacco, pet food, paper goods, alcoholic beverages, and soap cannot be purchased with the stamps.

authorized provider Under the **Civilian Health and Medical Programs of the Uniformed Services (CHAMPUS),** a physician or other individual care provider, or a hospital or supplier, approved by CHAMPUS to provide medical care and supplies.

autism A developmental disability whose manifestations include absence of language or language delays, resistance to affection, and other problem social behaviors. About 70 percent of individuals with autism also have mental retardation. Although the causes of autism are unknown, there is some evidence that it is linked to brain abnormalities. However, following intensive education and training focusing on communication, usually in an institutional setting, autistic behavior can be changed.

autogenetic training or learning Learning that is unprompted and unforced, self-generated and initiated, and spontaneously activated.

autologous transfusion Blood transfused during or following surgery that is obtained in advance from the patient early enough to allow the body to replenish its supply of blood. It is the safest type of transfusion because the blood is totally compatible.

automated data collection. A means of collecting data for work measurement that involves programming computers, whose terminals are used to perform tasks, to record, tabulate, summarize, and report employee performance of those tasks; for example, key strokes per minute, lines of type produced per hour, errors per hour, and so on).

automated teller machine (ATM)
A 24-hour, 7 day per week source of cash to persons having an account and a personal identification number (PIN). Each machine holds from $20,000 to $50,000 in cash in walk-up or drive-up vending machines. There are more than 80,000 in use in the US serving more than 120+ million card holders.

automated ticket/boarding pass (ATB)
In travel management, a card that matches the size of an airline ticket. Usually processed at the boarding gate, it contains an electronic strip encoded with information and is used in place of a ticket/boarding pass.

automated voice response system (AVRS)
A telephone system that enables a caller to obtain information, such as product, corporate or personal account, or tax information 24 hours per day without waiting for a customer service representative. Such systems sometimes require subscribers to enter a confidential personal password identification number, using a touch-tone telephone and a menu of options, and they are "talked through" each step in the process.

automatic enrollment A system for enrolling employees in training programs in which people are automatically and routinely enrolled in appropriate training upon hiring, job change, promotion, and so on.

automation Use of programmable machines, devices, or robots that can perform certain functions. Examples are computer-aided design (CAD), computer-aided manufacturing (CAM), computer-aided process planning (CAPP), automated handling systems (AMH), and automated storage and retrieval systems (AS/RS).

autonomous work groups See work teams.

auto-regression   A statistical technique used to identify a general trend in data rather than individual values.

auxiliary aids and services As defined by the **Americans with Disabilities Act of 1990,** "a wide range of services and devices for ensuring effective communication" (but use of advanced technology is not required), such as **qualified interpreters**, note takers, computer-aided transcription services, written materials, telephone handset amplifiers, assistive listening systems, telephones compatible with hearing aids, closed caption decoders, open and closed captioning, telecommunications devices for deaf persons

(TTY's) videotext displays, or other effective methods of making aurally delivered materials available to individuals with hearing impairments. Auxiliary aids and services also include qualified readers, taped texts, audio recordings, braille materials, large-print materials, or other effective methods of making visually delivered materials available to individuals with visual impairments.

auxiliary personnel
See temporary employees.

availability forecast Used in human resources forecasting. Availability is determined by computer analysis that projects the future capability of the current personnel pool over a specified time frame. The analysis takes into account all anticipated changes in the organization personnel pool due to such factors as projected terminations, hires, and transfers using historical data and statistics to arrive at the projections.

average final compensation A retirement plan provision that bases retirement benefits on a member's earnings in the years immediately preceding retirement. Typically, the average of the five highest earning years in the last ten years or the highest three-year average is used for the calculation.

average length of stay (ALOS)   In health care, the mean number of days of hospitalization required for a specific procedure or the average number of days patients at a given facility remain hospitalized.

average payment rate (APR)   In health care, the amount the Health Care Financing Administration could pay to a HMO or CMP per member per month (PMPM) under a Medicare contract, although not the actual amount because the law requires HMOs and CMPs to compare the **average payment rate** to the group's **adjusted community rate** to determine whether the PMPM is an appropriate amount. See also adjusted average per capita cost.

Aviation Excise Tax of 1997   Reinstates aviation excise taxes, including both the 10 percent ticket tax and the $6.00 international departure tax. The taxes will be levied on all ticket purchases through September 30, 1997 regardless of the travel date.

award An award is a form of reward. It is something bestowed or given, granted for something done. It is not compensation, although it can be either financial or nonmonetary. It is a prize — a bonus, trophy, medal, decoration, citation, honor, premium, gift, present, grant, or testimonial. Awards are given to improve efficiency, encourage, recognize, and reward outstanding achievement or performance, and improve employee motivation and morale. Awards include cash bonuses, savings bonds, jewelry, merchandise, travel, certificates of merit, plaques and trophies, and diplomas.

Award for Professional Excellence   *See* SHRM Award for Professional Excellence.

ayurvedic medicine   An alternative form of medical treatment that originated in India more than 4,000 years ago. It involves use of herbs, diet, and massage therapies by body type.

Azusa   A computer virus that infects floppy disks. It is "caught" by booting from an infected floppy disk. When it has infected 32 disks, it scrambles the serial and parallel ports on the host system so that peripherals no longer work. The virus may also make floppies unusable.

B

BAC   Blood alcohol concentration.

BARS   Behaviorally-anchored rating scale.

BAT   Breath alcohol technician.

BBB   Better Business Bureau.

BBIC   Behavior-based incentive compensation.

BBS   Bulletin board system.

BCNU   Be seeing you (Internet abbreviation).

BEA   Bureau of Economic Analysis.

BEI   Behavioral event interview.

BEO   Banquet event order.

BFOQ   Bona fide occupational qualification.

BHI   Better Hearing Institute.

BI   **1.** Brookings Institution.
     2. Background investigation.

BIA   Braille Institute of America.

BIC   Bank investment contract.

BITC   Basic Instructor Training Course.

BLS   Bureau of Labor Statistics.

BMI   Broadcast Music Inc.

BNA   Bureau of National Affairs.

BPE   Business process engineering.

BPH   Benign prostatic hyperplasia.

bps   Bits per second.

BSEP   Basic Skills Education Program.

BTV   Business television.

BTW   By the way (Internet abbreviation).

BUSG   Burns United Support Groups, Inc.

baby boomers   The "thirty-something" generation of post-World War II adults born between 1945 and 1965, who produced the baby boom of the 1970s and '80s.

baby busters   The **"twenty-something" generation** of young adults born between 1961 and 1972 — the period when the U.S. birth rate fell to one half the rate of the post-World War II peak, resulting in a labor shortage in the 1990s. Also known as *baby busts*.

backbone   The main trunk of a **wide area network**. Smaller **local area networks** feed into the backbone.

back-dating   In travel management, putting a false validation date on a discount ticket that requires advance purchase.

backdoor rationing   A term used by critics to describe a federal rule that would add cost effectiveness to factors considered by the Health Care Financing Administration (HCFA) when deciding whether Medicare will pay for new medical procedures, devices, and drugs. Appropriateness, safety, and effectiveness are the current criteria.

background investigation (BI)   The processes of verifying the accuracy of information provided on application forms and in interviews by job applicants. BIs vary in thoroughness from simple reference checks to verify an applicant's current position and salary, through contact with the applicant's present supervisor by phone or in person, and, in the case of extremely sensitive positions (such as those involving security clearances), complete checks of FBI files, the applicant's home town police records, credit, and interviews with current and former employers, friends, and acquaintances by the Federal Investigative Service.

back office system   In travel management, computer software that is used by travel agency for accounting purposes.

back-to-back ticketing   A faring practice in which two discounted round-trip tickets are booked and the flight coupons are mixed to achieve savings. Considered by some a smart saving strategy; by others, lawbreaking.

back-up   The practice of making a copy of computer or word processor data or documents (usually on external magnetic disks or tapes or on optical disks for off-site storage) to protect them in case the original data are lost or damaged.

bad-boy clauses Punitive contract clauses in executive compensation agreements designed to protect the employer from such practices as recruiting key employees following or at the time of the executive's termination. Such clauses include noncompete agreements, denial of special pension arrangements for recruiting employees, and delaying a portion of bonus award plans until the executive retires.

bad trip Frightening or panic-inducing crises precipitated in some persons by taking a hallucinogen or a narcotic.

bait and switch An illegal sales and pricing strategy — advertising a product at a low price and then only offering higher priced goods to the customer.

balance and reflex performance check A non-medical drug test sometimes used as a substitute for urine tests to determine on-the-job impairment.

balance billing The practice of submitting a bill to the patient for the difference between the original charge for health care services and the amount allowed and paid by Medicare. Part B, Medicare, pays 80 percent of the "allowed" amount. The remainder is paid by supplemental (**medigap**) insurance, **Medicaid**, or the patient. Practitioners can bill the patient for the 20 percent if they have no supplemental insurance. However, it is illegal in some states for practitioners to bill for anything more even if the costs of providing the treatment or service are higher than the amount allowed and received.

Balanced Budget Act of 1997 *Education:* Allows a tax credit of up to $1,500 for the first two years of college or vocational school (Hope Scholarships on tuitions paid beginning January 1, 1998) and up to $1,000 a year, rising to $2,000 in 2002 (for those who owe federal income tax). Credits begin to phase out when adjusted gross income on a joint return exceeds $80,000 ($40,000 on a single return) and drops to zero credit when family income tops $100,000 and individual income exceeds $50,000. The bill also allows a tax credit of up to $1,000 per year for the third and fourth years of college and for graduate study beginning in July 1998. The maximum credit rises to $2,000 after 2002. Employers can provide a worker up to $5,250 per year tax free (beginning December 31, 1996) for undergraduate education; graduate

students must pay taxes on the value of tuition paid by the employers. Education IRAs can be opened beginning January 1, 1998 for children under age 18; families can contribute up to $500 per year per child and pay no taxes on interest as long as the money is spent on education. The full tax break is limited to joint filers with income below $150,000 and single parents with income below $90,000. Interest on student loans is deductible during the first five years of repayment; maximum deduction is $1,000 in 1998 and rises by $500 each year to a maximum of $2,500 in 2001. *Military health care:* Authorizes the Department of Defense (DoD) to test **Medicare subvention** for three years at six sites around the country, starting in January 1998. Participants in the test must: be over age 65 and eligible for Medicare part A benefits (hospitalization); be enrolled in Medicare Part B; agree to enroll in DoD's Tricare Prime managed care plan, and agree not to go elsewhere for care. *Medical Savings Accounts:* The bill allows 300,000 Medicare recipients, to establish medical savings accounts as a trial of that solution.

balance sheet A financial document that presents a tabular statement or summary of the status of a company in terms of its assets, liabilities, and equity. It compares the status of the assets and liabilities of the company at a given point in time, usually at the end of an accounting period, such as a fiscal year. It provides the most accurate picture of a company's financial status.

balance sheet insurance An insurance policy purchased (usually by large companies) to protect a corporation's overseas balance sheet, specifically customer and client payments.

Baldrige Award *See* Malcolm Baldrige National Quality Award.

Balkanized group/society A group of people that has been segregated or divided by race, culture, religion, sexual orientation, or some other attribute.

balloon angioplasty A medical diagnostic procedure in which a deflated balloon is inserted into an artery and inflated to compress fatty deposits to eliminate blockages and head off a heart attack.

banding *See* broadbanding.

bandwidth The range of frequencies within a band. Determines the amount of data that a medium, such as video, can transmit in a given period of time. It is usually measured in **bits-per-second** or **kilobits**. Bandwidth is determined by the types of cable used (copper, coaxial, or fiber optic) and the speed of the switching mechanism that routes the data. Bandwidth is the main obstacle to the widespread use of interactive multimedia communications, due to the large file sizes needed for graphics, audio, and video media.

bank investment contract (BIC)　Issued by banks instead of insurance companies, they are similar to **guaranteed investment contacts**.

bankruptcy　The legally affirmed situation or condition of being unable to meet one's financial obligations.

banquet event order (BEO)　In meeting planning in the United States, detailed instructions for a particular event. Also known as a *function sheet, event order,* or *resume sheet.* Internationally, it is a summary of all the particulars relating to a meeting need.

banquet manager　The hotel functionary who handles meal functions on the day of a meeting event. Responsible for organizing the room setup and supervising the wait staff.

bar code technology　A means of automating a great variety of tasks in almost all industries from checkout stations in supermarkets, inventory control in factories and warehouses, vehicle registration, scanning printed forms in survey organizations, and automating scoring in schools. Bar codes are self-contained messages comprised of bars and spaces printed in a specific pattern on a container, package, envelope, or form. The codes are binary — the black bars and white spaces represent ones and zeros. Uses an **optical mark reader** or **optical scanner** and associated software to provide data input to a computer.

bare bones policy　*See* no frills health plan.

bargaining　*See* collective bargaining; negotiation; unions.

bar manager　The hotel contact with whom meeting planners work out the details of of reception and hospitality suite arrangements, including bar setups, bartenders, liquor brands, and the types and sizes of drinks. More important, the bar manager is the individual responsible for enforcing responsible serving practices that, if violated, could be grounds for legal suits. May also be called *hospitality manager.*

barriers　As defined by the **Americans with Disabilities Act of 1990,** architectural and communication barriers that are structural in nature in existing facilities, where such removal is **readily achievable.** The Act requires the removal of physical barriers caused by the location of temporary or movable structures, such as furniture, equipment, and display racks.

barrister　In the United Kingdom, a **law provider,** one who has the right to plead at the bar in superior courts of law. Equivalent of a licensed lawyer in the U.S.

baseline performance　An organization's actual and current performance level as determined by objective measurement, not subjective judgment.

base pay　*See* base rate.

base rate　The hourly rate or salary paid for a job performed. It does not include payments for overtime, incentives, or other differentials.

Basic Instructor Training Course (BITC)　Training provided by the military services to convert officers, technicians, and other military personnel and civilian employees into instructors. Typically a two- to four-week course.

basic medical coverage　Insurance coverage provided by an organization to its employees whether employer-funded or partially paid by the employees. It typically covers visits to physicians and outpatient clinics for treatment of illnesses and injuries and hospitalization.

basic research　Research directed at the discovery of new scientific knowledge that has no direct application to the current goals and objectives of the organization, although such research may be aimed at areas in which the company has a commercial interest.

Basic Seven　Consist of mathematical, statistical, and graphic tools used to study a problem, display its elements, and communicate the results of its analysis. The tools are **cause-and-effect diagram, check sheet, control chart, histogram, Pareto chart, run chart,** and **scattergram.** Attributed to Kaoru Ishikawa, one of the leaders of Japan's quality movement.

Basic Skills Education Program (BSEP)　A U.S. Army program designed to provide remedial training in the basic skills of reading and arithmetic for newly enlisted personnel with skills deficiencies.

basic skills training　Traditionally seen as encompassing only reading, writing, and computation. Now defined as training provided to upgrade workers' skills, equip them to deal with changes in technology and work processes, and overcome educational deficits.

basic training Initial or entry-level training provided by the U.S. Army and Air Force to introduce enlisted to military life and to develop physical stamina and basic military skills. *See also* boot camp.

batch To batch process computer data according to a fixed frequency of preparation; transactions are collected and held until processing time, often overnight, instead of being processed immediately or on-line, to reduce costs.

batch processing Computerized *monthly* record keeping for employee savings plans that involves two functions: (1) editing participant data to reflect terminations, new hires, and so on, and (2) updating all participant accounts to reflect investment fund earnings and recent employee and company contributions. This type of processing results in delays of four or more weeks in responding to participants' requests for information.

batch program A series of commands initiated by a single user command that is carried out sequentially without the need for further commands.

battery **1.** In law, hitting, beating, or negligent touching of another's person or clothing or anything attached to or held by him or her. **2.** A group of tests that have been validated on the same sample population so that results on the several parts of the battery are comparable.

baud A measure of the speed with which a **modem** transmits data. The higher the baud rate, the faster the information is transmitted and received and the lower the online charges.

Baudot A seven-bit code, only five of which are information bits, used by some text telephones to communicate with each other at a 45.5 baud rate.

Bayesian statistics A system of statistics that provides an advance assessment of the potential value of information to managers in decision making when confronted by alternative paths to a goal or objective.

Be All You Can Be Program Established by the **Higher Education Reauthorization Act of 1992.** It is a program to advertise college opportunities.

bean-counter A term mockingly applied to corporate financial managers or staffers —

accountants, auditors, comptrollers, controllers, and treasurers.

Beck Case A 1988 Supreme Court ruling that established the principle that non-union workers, who are required to pay dues to organized labor under collective bargaining agreements in 29 states that lack right-to-work laws, can be charged only for activities that directly involve the union's collective bargaining activities. However, the Court failed to specify which nonrelated activities were included or how they should be broken out for accounting purposes.

bed and breakfast *See* Continental plan.

Bedeaux plan An incentive plan that provided for productivity bonuses to be shared, with the workers typically receiving 75 percent and the remainder divided between supervisors and the employer. It is not in common use today.

behavior What a person *says* or *does*. It is hearable or observable and reportable. It is not motive, values, personality, or thoughts. Although it is an integral part of performance, it is not the performance itself. 2. The first element of a behavioral objective — the terminal behavior — exactly what trainees must be able to do — things that can be seen and measured. It always begins with a verb, for example, "to operate," "to calculate," and so on.

behavioral event interview (BEI)
A selection interview that provides detailed accounts of how superior and average performers have acted in their most important job successes and failures — and how they felt about the incidents. Interview transcripts are analyzed to assess personal traits, self-concept, motivation, and skills that differentiate between superior and average performers.

behaviorally anchored rating scale (BARS) An expensive, time-consuming, but extremely effective modification of the critical incident approach to rating. Raters are asked to observe and record specific incidents of effective and ineffective performance during a rating period. Those observations are matched against a set of predetermined critical incidents, called a BARS. BARS items are developed as follows: (1) important dimensions of effective performance are identified by workers and supervisors; (2) a second group reviews the incidents to identify effective, average, and ineffective performance; (3) a third group is given the products of the first two groups' efforts and asked to sort the incidents into the dimensions they best represent; (4) a fourth group places a scale value (usually seven or nine points ranging from highly effective to very ineffective) on each incident in each dimension; and (5) the scale is tested by using it with a group of workers, each of whom is rated independently by at least two qualified supervisors.

behavioral health care Prevention and alternative treatments and interventions provided for employees with mental, developmental, and emotional conditions.

behavioral objective A training objective that specifies clearly, precisely, and unambiguously what the trainees must *be able to do*, the *conditions* under which they must be able to perform, and the *standard* or *criterion* of acceptable performance, both at critical points during the development of job skills and at the end of the training program.

behavioral psychology or behaviorism A theory of human behavior that holds that the actions of people are determined solely by stimuli (stimulus-response) and that when behavior is reinforced and rewarded the behavior will be repeated, and when ignored or punished, the behavior will be extinguished. That is, human behavior is the result of its consequences whether immediate or delayed.

behavioral risk management A strategy for managing workplace behavioral problems, such as excessive absenteeism, high accident rate, work slowdowns, stress-related disabilities, complaints and grievances, sabotage, or other forms of dysfunctional employee behavior. The process of behavioral risk management involves the identification of the organization's risks, quantifying and analyzing those risks, and activating new or modified interventions, such as workplace services, benefits, programs, policies, and procedures designed to prevent or remedy behavioral problems. Attributed to Rudy M. Yandrick, *Behavioral Risk Management*. San Francisco, Calif.: Centralink and Jossey-Bass, Inc, Publishers, 1996.

behavioral simulation A controlled exercise used in screening and selecting candidates for positions in which applicants display directly observable behaviors relating to selected dimensions of job performance. Examples are planning, selling, and instructing. There are several types of behavioral simulations: analysis exercises, in-basket exercises, interview simulations, scheduling exercises, and job replica tests.

behavioral technology *See* behaviorism.

behavioral theory of learning The stimulus-response theory of learning.

behavior-based incentive compensation (BBIC) A relatively new and flexible approach to compensation that uses the power of pay as a motivator by sharing the benefits of company growth and return on investment with the employees who made it happen; that is, compensation is tied to the achievement of stated performance criteria. It is considered to be a self-funding plan because the gains in company productivity, service, and profit provide the incentive compensation budget.

behavior-based performance appraisal An approach to employee performance appraisal that focuses exclusively on the individual's behavior — that is, what the person *does* — rather than on what he or she *is like* in terms of personality, traits or characteristics, or skills and abilities.

behavior evaluation An approach to training evaluation that measures the kind and amount of behavioral change that can be attributed to the training provided.

behaviorism *See* behavioral psychology.

behavior management training An approach to managing the observable on-the-job behavior of workers to achieve a planned, measurable, and consistent behavioral outcome, which is translatable into bottom-line payoffs; for example, increased productivity. It makes use of adult learning theory, behavior modeling and modification, performance engineering, goal setting, organization development interventions, and feedback systems.

behavior modeling training Training that focuses on specific situations that the learner must deal with on the job to build skills and confidence in those situations. For example, training may be provided to help managers improve the work environment and the behavior and productivity of their people by demonstrating and practicing the proper methods of interviewing candidates for positions, orienting new employees, conducting performance appraisals, and counseling employees. Strategies include small group discussion, demonstration and performance, simulations and role playing, team training, film, videotape, and multimedia, case studies, exercise and practice of skills, and feedback.

behavior modification Rooted in the psychology of behaviorism. Involves a conscious attempt to change or modify the behavior of people to improve their performance by specifying the desired result, identifying the specific human behaviors that are needed to achieve the result, and immediately reinforcing and rewarding the behavior whenever it appears. Examples of results include training people to be unbiased, to understand diversity, to contribute to the community through community service, to respect and protect the environment, and to be quality producer of goods and services.

bell-shaped curve The normal distribution curve showing the percentage of cases falling within certain portions of the curve of any distribution of scores or ratings. It extends from −3 standard deviations (S.D.) to +3 standard deviations from the midpoint of the distribution. Between −3 and −2 S.D. accounts for 2 percent of the cases; between −2 and −1 S.D., 14 percent; between −1 and 0 S.D. 34 percent; between 0 and +1 S.D. 34 percent; between +1 and +2 S.D. 14 percent; and between +2 and +3 S.D., 2 percent of the cases.

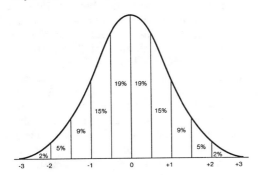

bell staff supervisor The hotel functionary who supervises the bell staff and provides assistance to guests at check-in and check-out times.

benchmarking Determining what competitors and other reputable organizations are doing in such human resources areas as compensation and benefits, customer service, employee assistance programs, orientation, training and development, and so on. Undertaken by on-site visits and document research and then establishing policies, procedures, and standards in those areas.

benchmarks In job evaluation and compensation, a term used to describe jobs that provide an acceptable basis for interorganizational comparisons because they occur in several organizational elements, are reasonably similar in knowledge and skills requirements, and compare reasonably well with respect to accountability and responsibility. Benchmarks are used to anchor a firm's pay scale and slot other jobs based on their relative worth.

benchmark studies Research studies conducted by independent research organizations and think-tanks. They provide a very effective way of obtaining insights into the future.

beneficiary The person for whose benefit a trust is created or designated to receive the proceeds or benefits accruing from an annuity or insurance policy.

benefit limit The lifetime maximum number of days for which a beneficiary will be paid under a **long term care** policy for confinement in a **nursing home** or **alternative long-term care facility**.

benefits manager The corporate manager responsible for evaluating strategies for keeping abreast of developments and government regulations, improving the quality of employee benefits, identifying and correcting access problems, balancing the needs of management and employees, communicating policies and procedures, and managing and containing costs, particularly health care costs.

benefit period A means of measuring a beneficiary's use of hospital and skilled nursing facility services covered by **Medicare**. A benefit period begins the day the insured is hospitalized. It ends after the beneficiary has been discharged from the hospital or other facility that primarily provides skilled nursing or rehabilitation services for 60 consecutive days. If the beneficiary is hospitalized after 60 days, a new benefit period begins, most Part A benefits are renewed, and the beneficiary must pay a new inpatient hospital deductible. Benefit periods are unlimited.

benefits Benefits are economic "goods" granted to employees in addition to base pay. They include financial benefits such as bonuses, merit salary increases, cost-of-living adjustments, stock ownership plans, profit-sharing plans, paid holidays, paid vacations, paid sick leave, paid bereavement leave, group life insurance, group health insurance, group dental insurance, workers' compensation, unemployment insurance, pension plans, survivor benefits, disability benefits, maternity leave, child care and elder care, and tuition assistance and reimbursement, whether paid in whole or in part by the employer. Nonmonetary benefits include flexible work schedules, rest periods and coffee breaks, legal assistance, leaves of absence, medical examinations and treatment, parking facilities, recreation facilities and programs, travel services and opportunities, credit and banking services, discounts on products, training and development, savings plans, and perquisites. Sometimes called **fringe benefits.**

benefits administrator The person responsible for the administration of one or more benefits program. Typically advises employees on eligibility for corporate-supported benefits, amounts of coverage, and claim procedures. Maintains benefit records and prepares forms and other documents needed to implement coverage.

Benefits & Compensation Solutions A monthly journal: $50.00 per year. Address: AMR International, Inc., 10 Valley Drive, Building 9, Greenwich Office Park, Greenwich. CT 06831 (203/661-0101; Fax 203/661-8472; E-mail **AMRSOL1@aol.com**; URL **http://www.BCSolutionsMag.com**).

benefits disclosure Reports required by Department of Labor regulations (summary plan descriptions and Form 5500) covering plan documents, including severance benefits. The **Employee Retirement Income Security Act of 1974** calls for fines of up to $1,000 per day for failure to file properly.

benefits laws *See* employee benefits laws.

benefits manager *See* employee benefits manager.

benefits planning analyst The individual responsible for analyzing and developing policies and benefits plans covering health and accident insurance coverage, retirement and pension plans, income continuance, and holidays and vacations. Determines and maintains status with regard to current benefit trends and legislated requirements and programs.

Benefits Professional of the Year Award *See* Benny Awards.

benign prostatic hyperplasia (BPH) A common medical problem of men, a condition in which the prostate becomes enlarged but is noncancerous. However, the growth of the gland may cause urination problems by constricting the urethra.

Bennett Amendment An amendment to the **Equal Pay Act of 1964**. States that it is not a violation of the Act for an employer

to differentiate (in pay) upon the basis of sex if such differentiation is authorized by the provisions of the Equal Pay Act.

Benny Awards Annual awards presented to the benefits professional of the year and benefits leadership awards. The former is given to the individual who has demonstrated a consistent pattern of creativity and achievement in benefit plan design, administration, communication, and staff management, as well as his or her contributions to the employee benefit profession. The leadership awards are given for excellence in developing and managing programs in three categories: health care, retirement planning, and judges' choice (drawn from full spectrum of benefits programs). Winners are chosen by a panel of *Employee Benefit News'* editorial advisors and staff members from nominations submitted by employers, coworkers, consultants, and benefit suppliers. *Contact: Employee Benefit News,* Awards Dept., 1483 Chain Bridge Road, Ste. 202, McLean Virginia 22101 (703/448-0520).

bequest A gift of personal property under a will. Also called a *legacy.*

bereavement fare In travel management, a special fare for family members of deceased persons. Although policies of airlines differ and are subject to change without notice, all major carriers require immediate family members to prove their relationship to the deceased and furnish the name, address, and phone number of the funeral home for verification. For some airlines, bereavement fares are fully unrestricted and tickets are fully refundable; others require a Saturday night stay and a confirmed return date with charges for changes. And still others have no set policy, leaving decisions up to reservations supervisors on a case-by-case basis. Some airlines require a death or doctor's certificate or an obituary stating the relationship of the deceased to the passenger. Also called *compassionate fare.*

"best practice" group An offspring of the U.S. quality movement. It is a form of **keiretsu** in which a group of companies band together to discuss and exchange information about their management strategies and practices.

BetaSP A professional video format.

beta-test software In travel management, a computer system undergoing tests at a user's site before its release to the public for general use.

Better Business Bureau (BBB) Established to promote ethical business standards and voluntary self-regulation of business practices. Accepts and records consumer complaints of fraud, misrepresentation, poor business practices, or substandard products or services in the area. Has no power to prosecute but will furnish information about any business (or charity organizations) in its area upon request. Offices are located in most U.S. cities. Check you local telephone directory. For an out-of-state BBB, contact Council of Better Business Bureaus, 4200 Wilson Blvd., Ste. 800, Arlington, VA 22203-0100 (703/276-0100; Fax 703/525-8277; E-mail **bbb@bbb.org**; URL **http://www.bbb.org**).

Better Hearing Institute (BHI) A nonprofit, tax-exempt educational organization supported by philanthropic funds. It informs persons with impaired hearing, their friends and relatives, and the general public about hearing loss and available help through medicine, surgery, amplification, and other rehabilitation. *Contact:* BHI, 5021-B Backlick Rd., Annandale, VA 22003 or P. O. Box 1840, Washington, DC 20013 (800/EAR WELL or 703/642-0580; Fax 703/750-9302).

Betts Decision A 1989 Supreme Court Decision (*Public Employees Retirement System of Ohio v. Betts*) that says an employer is not required to meet a cost-justification test for benefits; rather, a worker must show that an employee benefit plan was intended to discriminate. In other words, the high court ruled that employee benefit plans do not violate the Age Discrimination in Employment Act of 1967 if they make age-based distinctions.

Betts legislation *See* Older Workers Benefit Protection Act of 1990.

bicultural A person who behaves or acts according to the cultural orientation, customs, mores, and expectations of his or her own country when that is appropriate and according to those of a host country when that is appropriate.

bidding **1.** In employee selection, a means of recruiting that increases the number of internal transfers and promotions, called job bidding. Lists of all current job openings are posted to give current employees the first option to apply for vacant positions. **2.** In purchasing and contracting, the process of selecting a source of products or services by inviting bids. **3.** In marketing and sales, offering to provide a product or service in response to a **request for proposal**.

bid document In meeting management, a proposal submitted by a destination or property to a potential client group inviting the organization to meet in its venue.

bid manual In meeting management, a written document specifying the requirements of an organization for an event sent to potential destinations or properties. Similar to a request for proposal.

Beit Din A Jewish system of **alternative dispute resolution.** The term literally means House of Judgment. Rather than go to court, the two sides of a dispute agree to allow a rabbinical tribunal (typically three rabbis) who hear the case and decide the outcome. The system has been used by business organizations, such as tour operators and resorts, to settle civil cases.

billing by vendor A means of controlling travel and entertainment costs. Direct billing systems are offered by airlines, hotels, car rental firms, travel agencies, and restaurants.

Bill of Rights *See* Landrum-Griffin Act.

bin In video, a grouping of clips to be incorporated in a program.

biobucks Money earned in the biological technology industry.

bioenergetics An alternative form of medical treatment involving the "exchange of energy" between patient and therapist. *See also* biofeedback.

biofeedback **1.** An alternative form of medical treatment that makes use of machines or electronic feedback devices to train patients to control consciously such involuntary functions as circulation in the hands, jaw tension, blood pressure, heart rate and pulse, digestion, brain waves, and muscle responses. **2.** A stress management technique that makes use of specially designed electrical or electronic equipment to reduce strain, tension, and pressure. Also used in treating chronic pain.

biographical action-research A research methodology that combines studying individual executives and helping them in their professional development. It involves studying people in their current work and collecting data on their early history and present life away from work. Attributed to Robert E. Kaplan and his associates of the **Center for Creative Leadership**.

biometric security systems Virtually foolproof systems that control access to buildings, rooms, and vaults by means of computerized machines that can recognize personal characteristics of people seeking entrance: fingerprints, handprints, blood-vessel arrangement in the eye's retina, and voice patterns. The machines have special sensors that pick up the characteristics, convert them into digital code, and compare them with data stored in the computer. Unless the information matches the characteristics of an authorized person, entrance is denied.

bipolar disorder   A serious mental illness, periodic and recurrent with intervening periods of complete normalcy; a disorder of mood rather than thought, which involves mood swings from depression to mania.. Also called *manic depressive illness* or *manic depressive disorder*. Not to be confused with **schizophrenia**.

bit   The smallest piece of information in a computer file. A bit is a binary digit that is either a *one* or a *zero* — the one turns the circuit on; the zero turns it off.

bitBit   Bit-block transfer. In graphics, a means of moving an entire block of **pixels** as a single unit, such as scrolling a graphics image or sliding a window around a screen.

bitmap font   In topography, a **font** that is displayed by transmitting minuscule electronic bits of information to certain pixels (dots) on the screen and turning those pixels on or off. The on/off information is mapped to a grid of pixels on the computer screen. On Macintosh computers, bitmap fonts are known as screen fonts.

bit-mapped graphics   In desktop publishing, early versions of computer graphics software where every single point in a drawing or illustration had to be defined, which, although more precise than vector graphics, made the process slower and required more computer memory.

bitnick   A person who uses a coin-operated computer terminal in a coffeehouse to log onto cyberspace. From *Wired* magazine's "Jargon Watch" section.

bits per second A measure of bandwidth.

Black Book   A directory of corporate travel product and services providers published annually by ***Business Travel News.*** Categories are hotel chain and management firms, airlines, airline clubs, car rental companies, payment systems providers, consultants and lawyers serving corporate travel, ground transportation providers, industry associations,

affiliates of the **National Business Travel Association** and **Association of Corporate Travel Executives**, technology vendors, tele- and videoconferencing vendors, major travel agencies and consortia, and travel security consultants. *Contact:* Business Travel News, One Penn Plaza, New York, NY 10119-1198 (212/615-2704).

black box approaches   Strategies used by employers to control health care costs by holding providers accountable for the quality of clinical procedures and processes without getting bogged down in detailed evaluation of products and services at the clinical level. Instead, employers hold providers accountable for such broad performance indicators as cost, access, and patient satisfaction, assuming that fear of liability will restrain providers from abuses and shoddy practices.

blanket   In offset printing, a rubber-surfaced fabric that is clamped around a cylinder, to which the image is transferred from the plate, and from which it is transferred to the paper.

bleed   In desktop publishing, describes ink running past the trim or other location where it is not wanted.

blended work force   A combination of full-time, part-time, temporary, and outsourced employees, including independent contractors sued by employers to save money, improve productivity, increase flexibility, and enhance customer service.

blendo   A mixture of different media, such as graphics, text, scanned images, and animation. Also called *meltomedia*. From *Wired* magazine's "Jargon Watch" section.

blind   As defined under Social Security, a person whose vision cannot be corrected to better than 20/200 in the better eye, or if his or her visual field is 20 degrees or less, even with corrective lenses.

blind ad   An advertisement in a newspaper or magazine that does not include the name of the company placing the ad. Readers are asked to mail their response to a post office box number.

blind and vision impaired   People who are totally or partially blind and whose loss of vision places limitations of varying severity on personal, social, or occupational pursuits. Approximately 600,000 Americans are blind.

Gordon M. Bliss Memorial Award
An award presented annually to a national member of the **American Society for Training**

and Development who has excelled in human resource development over a significant period of time. Selected by an awards committee by reviewing documentation and direct contacts with the nominating individual and other persons with direct knowledge of the accomplishments of the nominee. *Contact:* ASTD National Awards Program, Attn: Dawn Temple, 1640 King St., Box 1443, Alexandria, VA 22313-2043 (703/683-8100).

block busting The process of overcoming blocks to creativity.

block diagram A chart or graphic that depicts the route that information, documentation, or materials take from supplier to customer or from one function or department within an organization to others. It is produced by identifying the key steps in the process or system, indicating the offices, departments, teams, or individuals involved, and depicting the steps and hand-offs over time. It helps people see how work moves among individuals and groups of people.

blocked space In meeting management, sleeping rooms, meeting rooms, exhibit space,and other function rooms reserved for use by an organization for a meeting.

blood alcohol concentration (BAC) The percent of alcohol found in a person's blood after drinking. In most states, a persons with a BAC of 0.10 is considered legally drunk.

bloodborne diseases Diseases contracted from exposure to infectious materials borne by human blood or other body fluids; for example, human immunodeficiency virus and hepatitis B (which infects about 8,700 U.S. workers annually and from which approximately 200 die).

Bloodborne Pathogens Standard An OSHA standard (29CFR1910.1030). Requires employers to determine which job classifications or specific tasks and procedures can reasonably be expected to cause worker contact with blood or other potentially infectious materials and to provide appropriate training.

Bloom's taxonomy A classification of instructional objectives that deals with the recall or recognition of knowledge and the development of mental skills and abilities (as contrasted with the **affective domain**, which has to do with a trainee's interests, attitudes, and values and the **psychomotor domain,** which focuses on objectives relating to motor skills).

Attributed to Benjamin Bloom, (*Taxonomy of Educational Objectives: Handbook I, Cognitive Domain,* 1956). *See also* cognitive domain.

blue-collar technical workers Mechanics, repairers, precision production workers, extractive workers (mining, oil and gas, and timber), craft workers, and operator and assembly workers in high-tech industries.

blue-collar workers Wage earners, other than salaried employees. In earlier years, it referred to employees who wore work clothes instead of more formal attire.

blues In desktop publishing, one-color proofs of a document or illustration.

board and care home A plan by which, in exchange for rent, an elderly or disabled individual receives room, meals, utilities, housekeeping and laundry, and daily contact with staff. In addition to a private room, common-user space is also provided.

board certified A designation indicating that a physician has completed a residency program and passed a certifying examination in a particular medical specialty.

boarding care home *See* licensed group home.

body fat measurement Assesses how much of a person's body weight is fat, providing a fairly accurate means of determining how much he or she needs to lose (or gain). Means of measurement include skin-fold calipers, which measure fat under the skin at selected body sites; bioimpedence, which uses a painless electric current; and hydrostatic, in which a person is weighed while under water.

body language Visible signals of an individual's attitude, interest, emotional state, and the like. Includes dress, hair style, and voice cues (tone, volume, and pitch), posture, gestures, facial expressions, and body movements, blushing, contraction of the facial muscles, squirming, blinking, or forced smiles.

body type In typography, type used for extensive composition, usually from 6 to 14 **point**. Also called *text type.*

body work Types of alternative medicine that encompass hundreds of methods of improving the structure and functioning of the body through therapies such as massage, deep-tissue manipulation, movement awareness, and energy balancing.

bold/boldface In typography, type that is heavier and darker than the text type with which it is used.

bona fide occupational qualification (BFOQ)   A legal term used to describe lawfully permissible discriminatory job requirements as an exception to **Title VII** of the **Civil Rights Act of 1964**. Job applicants may be classified based on BFOQ, which permits employers to discriminate in hiring and promotion only if they have a valid reason directly related to performance of the job.

bona fide residence test   As defined by **Section 911, Internal Revenue Code,** a U.S. citizen who has established a permanent home or living quarters in a foreign country while working abroad for an extended or indefinite period of time that includes at least one full tax year, even though the individual intends to return to the U.S. eventually. Brief trips or vacations in the U.S. or other locations do not interrupt this period.

bonanza babies   sPeople born in the five-year period before 1917, who are the recipients of higher Social Security payments than the **notch babies** who receive lower benefits due to legislation passed in 1977 that established a new benefit formula designed to correct and earlier computation, which since 1972 had been paying retirees more than the they should have received.

bond   A legal document under which an individual or corporation (such as an insurance company) agrees to pay, within stated limits, for financial loss caused to another by the principal, default of a third person, or other contingency over which the principal may have no control.

bonding   Occurs when two or more people join and stick together out of respect, regard, and concern for each other.

bonus   After-the fact, discretionary, extra cash compensation (in addition to base salary) paid to employees based on productivity, profits, savings, cost avoidance, or a combination of two or more of these factors, for a period of 12 months or less.

bonus payment   A type of executive incentive plan, whereby bonuses are paid in cash or deferred.

booking code   In travel management, an alphanumeric code used by travel agents to reserve a specific fare. Such codes vary by agent or agency.

booking software   Software that supports and enhances **computer reservation system** information or graphic displays at the point of sale. Such systems enable travel agents to book reservations faster and more accurately.

bookmark   **1.** An icon or position on a computer desktop that allows the user to return to a specific **Web** site by simply clicking the mouse. **2.** A metaphor borrowed from web browsers, it means to make note of an individual for future reference.

book-unit award plans   See book value plan.

book value   The ratio of the total shareholders' equity in an organization divided by the number of outstanding shares.

book value plan   A type of long term executive incentive plan in which the company sells its stock to executives at current book value. They receive dividends on the stock and, as the book value increases, the executive's equity also increases. When the executive leaves the company, he or she must sell back the accumulated shares at the current book value.

Boolean search   A World Wide Web search that allows the inclusion or exclusion of documents containing certain words through the use of such operators as "and," "not," and "or."

boomerangers   Young single men or women who live with their parents.

boom mike   An electronic amplifying device fastened to a long pole, which allows it to be positioned above the head of the speaker and out of camera range. Usually hard-wired.

boot   To activate a computer.

boot camp   The U.S. Navy and Coast Guard's version of basic military training provided to enlistees to introduce them to military life, improve their physical stamina and conditioning, and teach them basic military skills.

bootleg contract   An agreement between union and management designed to circumvent or evade the union's statutory security limitations.

bootleg operation   **1.** An unlawful, or prohibited proceeding or action, such as producing, selling, or distributing products or services illicitly or hiring illegal aliens. **2.** A program, service, funding scheme, or action deliberately and covertly put into effect by an executive, manager, supervisor, other employee or group of workers without prior authorization by the individual or group having jurisdictional authority.

boot up   The process of turning on a computer and initiating its start-up sequence.

The user's first command is initiated by loading a program, application, or set of instructions into the computer. The computer then completes the start-up process.

borderline intelligence A category of persons with mild mental disabilities. As measured by an intelligence test, the condition is represented by an **intelligence quotient (IQ)** of between 70 and 90.

Boss Lift A program designed to inform employers about National Guard and Reserve Training. One-to-three day trips allow employers to witness life in the military services firsthand. Each state is authorized one **National Committee for Employer Support of the Guard and Reserve**-sponsored Boss Lift per year. Participants are transported to the training site by military aircraft. They are reimbursed for meals, incidentals, and travel to and from aircraft pickup points. Most states conduct additional trips using state committee funds. On state-sponsored lifts, participants are responsible for their own expenses, including payment for the use of bachelor officers' quarters.

Boston arm A prosthesis for amputations that is attached surgically. The arm is controlled by the individual's own nerves.

bounty program An internal recruitment and placement method in which current employees are paid a finder's fee for a referral who is hired by the company.

boutique health care Do-it-yourself health care. Includes cosmetic surgery.

Box-Jenkins technique A form of time-series forecast that combines **auto-regression** with the **moving average** approach and then follows a three-step process: (1) identify the forecasting model that best fits the data, (2) fine-tune the model, and (3) make the forecast based on the analysis. Approach is most appropriate when data are not highly irregular.

brachytherapy A treatment for lung cancer that uses a computerized machine (Gammamed 12i) to deliver a high-intensity dose of radiation to cancerous tissue. The radioactive source travels through a catheter (a hollow tube) directly into or near a tumor and eliminates the danger of exposing medical personnel to radiation. The procedure and equipment can also be used to treat breast, esophageal, biliary, and cervical cancer.

Braille Institute of America, Inc. (BIA) A private, nonprofit, privately funded organization established to provide training and services at no charge to people who are legally blind or visually impaired. Services include child development/youth programs, visual aids, career service, adaptive technology, counseling, classes independent living, and braille publishing. Also sponsors a talking book library for blind and physically or reading disabled people. *Contact:* Braille Institute of America, Inc., 741 North Vermont Ave., Los Angeles, CA 90029-3594 (800/BRAILLE or 213/663-1111; Fax 213/666-5881).

brain disease Serious forms of mental illness, such as bipolar disorder (manic depressive illness) major depression; schizophrenia.

brain injuries *See* autism; Down syndrome; perceptually disabled.

brainstorming A free-wheeling group ideational technique designed to produce as many ideas as possible within a short period of time. A group of 7 to 10, under the direction of a leader, generates ideas using four basic rules: no criticism, free-wheeling, quantity, and combination and improvement. Ideas are recorded and subsequently presented to a separate group for evaluation and or use. Attributed to Alex Osborn.

brainwriting A group or individual ideational technique, similar to brainstorming. It encourages people to engage in free association to improve their creative thinking abilities and generate new ideas. Ideas are produced by allowing thoughts to be ungoverned, uncontrolled, and unevaluated.

branching program **1.** A form of **programmed instruction** in which the steps leading to the acquisition of knowledge or skill are determined by the learner's responses to each of the program items. *See also* linear program. **2.** A type of instructional programming that permits trainees to complete training efficiently by skipping whole learning modules (training activities) that represent skills and knowledge already mastered, thereby avoiding duplication or waste of time, and spending more time and effort on modules that represent unknown or unmastered areas of learning.

brand name The most valuable of all intangible company assets. The name given to a product that often transcends its physical properties in the minds of customers. When managed wisely, brand names provide long term revenue.

brand name drug A drug that is sold under a specific **trademark** name. Usually costs more than its generic equivalent. For example, Motrin is the brand name for Ibuprofen.

breach of contract A legal basis for suit when an express oral or written contract is broken.

breakeven analysis A means of determining the point at which revenue derived from sales equals the total cost of producing the product or service. Beyond the breakeven point, an organization begins to show a profit.

breakeven chart A planning and control device that graphically shows the relationship among sales volume, costs, and profits. For the average business, this relationship is the single most important factor in planning for profits.

breakout session In conference and meeting planning, a session convened to accommodate a small group discussion where the "nuts and bolts" of a subject are explored and where learning points are expanded and reinforced. Attendees at a larger **concurrent session, general session,** or **plenary session** are divided into several groups, either in separate rooms or within the main meeting room. Strategies include interactive training, brainstorming, hands-on practice, role playing, team building, and strategy sessions.

breath alcohol technician (BAT) An individual trained and certified to conduct alcohol tests. Required by Department of Transportation rules pertaining to the testing of safety-sensitive transportation workers.

bridge A device that transparently connects dissimilar computer networks.

bridging pay *See* severance pay.

briefing A formal oral presentation to others, such as decision makers, employees, and staff. The purpose may be to inform (familiarize, interpret, clarify, or report on something of importance or concern) or to obtain a verdict or judgment on an issue from an individual or group empowered to make that decision.

brightness In video, the intensity of light, independent of **hue** or saturation. Also called *luminance.*

broadbanding A compensation strategy originally used primarily in the public sector but to an increasing degree now used in private companies mainly for salaried exempt employees, salaried nonexempt employees, and executives, in that order. Broadbanding is used to overcome the constraints of a rigid pay structure (**general schedule**) to meet local market compensation. Most often, large numbers of pay grades are merged into a few broad bands of pay (usually three or four) with larger salary ranges. Another broadbanding approach is called career bands, which employs relatively few bands, involve even wider salary ranges, and emphasizes career development.

Broadcast Music Inc. (BMI) Represents the rights of songwriters, composers, and music publishers. Signed a blanket agreement with the American Society of Association Executives, Meeting Professionals International, the Professional Convention Management Association, and the Religious Conference Management Association which cuts the costs and simplifies paperwork for the use of music at meetings,conventions, and exhibitions. As of 1997, signatory meeting planners will pay BMI annually for a license that covers any use of all copyrighted music represented by BMI, whether taped music at a general session or a band performing at a party. The license fee is based on attendance at all events where music was played during the past year. From 1997 through 2000, the rate for both live and recorded music is 5 cents per attendee (formerly 17 cents for live music and 5 cents for recorded music), and the minimum fee for a license was cut from $175 to $100.

Brock Commission A commission established by the Secretary of Labor in 1990 to study the skills that young people must master to to have workplace know-how.

bronze parachute Severance packages designed for upper-level managers. They are somewhat less lavish than **golden parachutes** received by top executives but more generous than the basic severance plans that cover lower-level employees. In addition, they may be activated by resignation for "good reason" (such as company relocation or change in compensation) as well as by involuntary termination.

The Brookings Institution (BI) A private, independent, nonprofit organization devoted to research, education, and publication in economics, government, foreign policy, and the social sciences. Its principal purpose is to improve the performance of American institutions, the effectiveness of government programs, and the quality of U.S. public policies. Brookings is financed largely by an endowment and by the support of philanthropic foundations, corporations, and individuals.

Contact: Brookings Institution, 1775 Massachusetts Ave., N.W., Washington, DC 20036-2188 (202/797-6000; Fax 202/797-6004; E-mail **brookinfo@brook.edu**; URL **http://www.brook.edu**).

brownout A condition that occurs when voltage drops below the level needed by computers to operate. Brownouts usually result in damaged or lost unsaved data.

browser Software used to explore or surf the **World Wide Web,** using a point-and-click interface, and allowing the display of text and graphics. Most come with **E-mail** software. Examples are **Mosaic, Netscape Navigator, Apple Internet Connection Kit, and Microsoft Internet Explorer.** Some browsers can be downloaded from the Web itself with no charge except for the phone call and any connect charges; others can be purchased for relatively little as part of retail software packages that also include connection software; and others are part of the chief commercial on-line computer services

browsing *See* scanning.

B-school A school that offers the master of business administration (MBA) degree. Originally developed to provide a common language for specialists in accounting and business, the MBA is now considered by many to be an important credential for a career in business, including the human resources area.

The Bubble Generation Japanese term for Generation X.

buddy system An executive, managerial, or supervisory development approach in which a young executive, manager, or supervisor may choose or be assigned a senior executive, manager, or supervisor as a coach and role model.

budget A comprehensive numerical plan for the allocation of resources to achieve corporate goals and objectives. It is a statement of expected results expressed in numerical terms. It determines what resources should be expended by whom and for what (planning) and what resources are being expended where, by whom, and for what (control).

budget chart In meeting management, an estimate of total revenues and expenditures divided into subject categories and used to project cash needed to meet expenses on specific dates. Also called *cash flow chart* and *phased budget.*

budget resolutions Set out annually in general terms by the Congress the amounts of revenues and expenditures the federal government will receive and spend in a particular fiscal year. They are binding only on the Congress. Congressional authorization and appropriation committees have the discretion to change proposals in the budget resolution as long as the spending and reduction targets are met. Actual funding is provided by **appropriations bills** or **reconciliation bills**.

buffet 1. Self-service: a type of meal service where food is presented on a table and guests serve themselves. Popular for receptions, refreshment breaks, and continental breakfasts where time is limited and networking is desired. **2.** Served: A type of meal service where most of the food is displayed on a table and certain items, such as meats, are carved and/or served by chefs or waitpersons.

bug An error or malfunction in computer software that causes it to yield incorrect results.

building block curricula Standard one- or two-week training programs required of employees prior to assignment or promotion to new or more responsible positions. Typically there is a block for first-line supervisors, another for middle mangers, and another for executives.

building-occupant survey
A survey designed to explore employee environmental concerns about the work environment, such as air quality, building noise, lighting, office noise, and thermal comfort. Undertaken to increase worker productivity, demonstrate management's interest in employee well-being, and avoid law suits.

bulletin board system or service (BBS)
In telecommunications and on the **Internet,** a system in which messages are "posted" for subscribers to elicit responses using a **modem.** Files can be sent from the user's computer to the other system (uploaded) or copied from the remote system into the user's system (downloaded).

Donald Bullock Memorial Dissertation Award An award presented annually by the **American Society for Training and Development** in recognition of the outstanding dissertation in human resource development. Candidates must be nominated by their committee chair for a degree granted between July 1 and June 30 of the preceding year. The study must fall within one of the following areas: (1) training and development; (2) work design; (3) organization development/learning; (4) human resource planning; (5) employee assistance; and (6) career development. Selected by an awards committee. *Contact:* ASTD National Awards Program, Attn: Dawn Temple, 1640 King St., Box 1443, Alexandria, VA 22313-2043 (703/683-8100)

bump/bumping   **1.** Displacement of an incumbent employee, such as through layoff or demotion, to make room for an employee with seniority or a **Title VII** litigant — a person who has successfully charged discrimination. Bumping is specifically allowed by the NLRB and the EEOC. **2.** *See* involuntary bumping; voluntary bumping.

bundled case rate   In health care reimbursement, the practice of combining both institutional and professional charges (for example, for cardiac surgery, surgeon, technicians, anesthesiologist, and pre- and postoperative care) into a single payment. Also called *package pricing.*

bundled services   In-house, complete package (investment management, record keeping, and custody) **401(k)** investment services offered employees by companies.

bundled software   Programs sold with a computer as a hardware/software package, typically at a reduced price, to increase attractiveness to buyers.

bundling   The practice of pooling the purchasing of products and services by several organizations as a cost-cutting strategy. Also called *cooperative buying* and *group purchasing.*

burden of proof   In legal actions, the obligation of one of the litigating parties to establish an alleged fact or claim by verifiable evidence or proof.

Bureau of Economic Analysis (BEA) The agency of the Department of Commerce responsible for the preparation and publication of the estimates of gross domestic product and gross national product.

Bureau of Labor Statistics (BLS)   The principal fact-finding agency for the federal government in the broad field of labor economics and statistics. It has a dual role as the statistical arm of the Department of Labor as an independent national statistical agency that collects, processes, analyzes, and disseminates sensitive economic and statistical data to the American public, Congress, other federal agencies, state and local governments, business, and labor. *Contact:* U.S. Department of Labor, 200 Constitution Ave., N.W., Washington, DC 20210 (202/523-6098; URL **http://stats. bls.govblshome.html/**))

burial instructions/checklist   A detailed statement of who should be contacted, what funeral service to employ, whether the remains are to be cremated or buried, the clothing to be worn, the type of ceremony and the name of the church, mosque, synagogue, or chapel, where the services are to be held, where burial is to take place, what newspapers are to be given the information for the obituary, what organizations and government agencies are to be notified, what charities should be suggested for gifts in memory of the decedent, which hymns should be sung, which passages read, and any other instructions that will simplify and make appropriate the final arrangements.

burnout   Physical, mental, or emotional debilitation characterized by exhaustion, frustration, insensitivity to others, detachment, listlessness, loss of concentration, irritability, discouragement, depression, negativism, irritability, low morale, and lack of commitment. It is the result of excessive and prolonged stress generated by such things as pressure of heavy workload, short deadlines, interpersonal problems, or family or financial problems.

Burns United Support Groups, Inc. (BUSG) A national organization established to provide information, assistance, and support to those who have survived being burned and their families and friends. Services include outreach visitation, phone support, and newsletter. *Contact:* Burns United Support Groups, Inc., P.O. Box 36416, Grose Ponte Farms, MI 48236-0416 (313/881-5577; Fax; 313/417-8702; E-mail **156/@concentric.NET**).

burrowing   Describes the practice of getting one's status in the federal bureaucracy changed from political appointee (one who serves at the pleasure of the administration in office) to a *bona fide* career civil service position (one which cannot be terminated for political reasons).

business card   A means of controlling travel and entertainment costs — revolving or nonrevolving corporate cards issued by banks (such as Visa and Mastercard) and offering a standard package or customized reports.

business center In meeting management, the area in a hotel or convention center that contains office equipment, such as copiers, fax machines, computers and printers, modems, and secretarial/clerical services for clients.

business class An unrestricted air fare for travel in a special section of the aircraft and costing less than first class travel.

business-class amenities Include such extra courtesies as 24-hour business center free to guests with fax, copier, and printer, automated check-in and check-out, boardroom and meeting rooms, expanded complimentary breakfast, comfortable and well-lighted work space, cordless phone, free local calls and long-distance access, in-room coffee maker, ironing board, safe exercise room with whirlpool, and two-line speaker phone.

business-class club Offers a 24-hour mini business center, a private lounge, and a separate dining area for use by any hotel guest willing to pay a $40 to $50 per night premium in addition to the regular room rate.

business-class services Includes such items as upgraded bedroom and private lounge with buffet breakfast and late-afternoon hors d'euvres and cocktails. Also called *concierge services.*

business coach An economy class fare with purchase rules that are not too costly to business travelers.

business discount fare An airfare group that affords a small discount to business travelers who book their flights three- to seven days in advance. They rarely carry restrictions or penalties but are limited in number because they depend on seat availability.

business ecosystem An arrangement in which two or more companies work cooperatively to support new products, satisfy clients and customers, and develop new and innovative products, services, and strategies in key market segments.

business espionage The collection and analysis of information about other organizations by illegal or unethical means such as wiretapping, visual, acoustical, and electronic surveillance, "moles" (planted spies), or payment of bribes to employees or former employees of the target organizations.

business ethics Focuses on business practices, institutions, and actions and evaluative judgments about those actions in light of some basic human good or concept of human value.

business-format franchising Occurs when franchisees buy into an entire business concept and program — adopt standardized and prescribed operating procedures, marketing strategy, and management system; e.g., specialized training programs, fitness centers, real estate, and computer outlets.

business intelligence The collection and analysis of information from legitimate and ethical (legal and open) sources about the plans, operations, achievements, problems, products, and processes of other organizations. The information may be obtained from the companies themselves or from secondary sources such as trade and professional associations.

business matchmaking See matchmaker/matchmaking agencies.

business meeting Defined by the Internal Revenue Service as an event (meeting seminar, workshop, or convention) "where the taxpayer (sponsor or attendee) is benefiting or advancing the interest of his trade or business" — and where business is the primary purpose for attendance. In addition, any meeting (lectures, panel discussions, committee meetings, product displays, or similar activities) qualify as a substantial and *bona fide* business discussion. Such meetings, including travel, lodging, food and beverage, entertainment, and recreation, can be deducted by the taxpayer if the items are directly related to the active conduct of business or directly preceding or following a substantial and bona fide business discussion, according to the IRS. However, the costs of business meals and entertainment are subject to a 50 percent deductibility limit.

business necessity Relates to equal employment opportunity. It involves demonstrating that there is an overriding business purpose for any discriminatory practice and that the practice is therefore acceptable. If a practice cannot be defended as a **bona fide occupational qualification**, it is usually justified as a business necessity.

business-process engineering (BPE) See process engineering.

business television (BTV) 1. A form of teleconferencing set up by an organization or group of companies in a specific industry for one-way video used in conjunction with two-way audio for conferences, communication, and training over long distances. The signals are transmitted by telephone lines or satellite. **2.** An information service that includes descriptions of computer software packages with business applications for use with micro- and minicomputers.

Business Travel News: The Newspaper of the Business Travel Industry   A journal published semi-monthly January, February, April, June, July, August and December; three times in March, May, September, October, and November: $95.00 per year (free to qualified subscribers). Address: Miller Freeman Inc., 600 Harrison St., San Francisco, CA 94107 (415-9052200; Fax 415-905-2233; E-mail **crosen@ mfi.com or 74117.126@compuserve.com**; URL **http://www.btnonline.com**).

business unionism   *See* union.

BusinessWeek   A weekly journal (51 issues per year): $49.95 per year. *Contact:* Business Week, 1221 Avenue of The Americas, 39th Fl., New York, New York 10020 (800/635-1200; 212/512-2511; URL **http://www. businessweek.com**).

bust-out   A strategy used by unscrupulous entrepreneurs and businesses that involves this sequence of events: buy a healthy business (preferably one that has been family owned for many years and has a large cash flow), get the purchase financed by the owner and a bank, don't invest anything in the business, use credit to the maximum, fail to pay bills, pocket the cash flow, drain the equity, declare Chapter 7 (liquidation) bankruptcy, and move on to the next business.

Butterfield Ruling   A 1996 ruling of the National Labor Relations Board (*O.E. Butterfield, Inc.*) that reversed a 34-year old precedent (*Pacific Tile & Porcelain Co.*) which presumed that all striker replacements to be permanent employees. The ruling placed the burden of proof on employers to determine if replacements for economic strikers are permanent workers who would be eligible to vote in a union certification election.

buy-back plan   A program designed to cut the costs of absenteeism by buying back unused sick leave time.

buy-back program   In travel management, paying employees cash (usually 50 to 60 percent of the lowest airfare) for earned frequent flier tickets turned in to the company.

buy right   A type of purchasing reform, applied primarily but not exclusively to health care projects, that leans heavily on the use of patient outcome measures as the basis for making buying decisions. Used to select health care providers who can provide the highest quality and most efficient care for the lowest price. Outcome measures include such items as major and minor morbidity and mortality, and patient evaluation of care. The emphasis is on quality, not discounts. The focus of buy right is shifting from managing costs to managing quality — improving the quality of care and eliminating unnecessary variation.

buzz sessions   *See* huddle group.

Byrd Scholarship Program   *See* Robert C. Byrd Honors Scholarship Program.

byte   The smallest unit of access in many computers; typically eight **bits** in length.

by the way (BTW)   Cyberspeak on the Internet.

C

CA	Communications assistant.
CAA	Clayton Antitrust Act of 1914.
CAD	Computer-assisted design.
CAE	**1.** Certified Association Executive. **2.** Computer-assisted engineering.
CAEL	Council for Adult and Experiential Learning.
CAI	Computer-aided (assisted) instruction.
CAJE	Computer-assisted job evaluation.
CAM	**1.** Computer-assisted manufacturing. **2.** Catchment-area management. **3.** Certificate of Advanced Mastery.
CANS	Commission on Achieving Necessary Skills.
CAP	**1.** Closing Agreement Program. **2.** Claims assistance professional.
C&R	Consultation and referral.
CAR	Computer-assisted retrieval.
CARC	Carcinogen.
CASA	Center on Addiction and Substance Abuse.
CASE	Computer-aided software engineering.
CAT	Computerized axial tomography.
CATCAP	Medicare Catastrophic Coverage Act of 1988.
CAT/UB	Center for Assistive Technology/University of Buffalo.
CAV	Constant angular velocity.
CBD	*Commerce Business Daily*.
CBE	Computer-based education.
CBI	Computer-based instruction.

CBL	Computer-based learning.
CBLR	Computer-based learning resources.
CBP	Certified Benefits Professional.
CBR	Computer-based reference.
CBT	Computer-based training.
CBVE	Competency-based vocational-technical education.
CCA/ACR	Canadian Compensation Association/Association Canadiénné de Remuneration.
CCAC	Child Care Action Campaign.
CCD	Charged-coupled device.
CCL	Center for Creative Leadership.
CCLVI	Council of Citizens with Low Vision International.
CCH	Center for Corporate Health.
CCP	**1.** Certified Compensation Professional. **2.** Coordinated Care Program.
CCRC	Continuing care retirement community.
CCR&R	Child care resource and referral programs.
CCTE	Certified Corporate Travel Executive.
CD	**1.** Compact disc. **2.** Career development. **3.** Chemical dependency.
CDC	Centers for Disease Control.
CD-I	Compact disc interactive.
CDMA	Code division multiple access.
CDME	Certified Destination Management Executive.
CDP	Compact disc player.
CDR	Continuing disability review.
CD-R	Compact disc-recordable.
CD-ROM	Compact disc read-only memory.

CD-ROM XA Compact disc, read only-memory extended architecture.

CD-RW Compact disc-rewritable.

CE Conformity Europe.

CEAP Certified Employee Assistance Professional.

CEBS Certified Employee Benefits Specialist.

CEdMA Computer Education Management Association.

CEO Chief executive officer.

CEP Color electronic prepress.

CERCLA Comprehensive Environmental Response, Compensation, and Liability Act of 1980.

CETA Comprehensive Employment and Training Act of 1973.

CEU Continuing Education Unit.

CF Cystic fibrosis.

CFA Chartered Financial Analyst.

CFCs Chlorofluorocarbons.

CFF Cystic Fibrosis Foundation.

CFO Chief financial officer.

CFP Certified Financial Planner.

CFP Board Certified Financial Planner Board of Standards.

CFROI Cash flow return on investment.

CFS Chronic fatigue syndrome.

CG Character generator.

CGA Color graphics adapter.

CGCPOA U.S. Coast Guard Chief Petty Officers Association.

CGI Common gateway interface.

CHAMPUS Civilian Health and Medical Program of the Uniformed Services.

ChFA Chartered Financial Analyst.

CHRIE The Council on Hotel, Restaurant and Institutional Education

CHRP Common hardware reference platform.

CIC 1. Catastrophic illness coverage. 2. Cooperative Information Clearinghouse and Library.

CIM 1. Certificate of Initial Mastery. 2. Computer-integrated manufacturing.

CIO 1. Corporate information officer. 2. Chief information officer.

CIPP Context-Input-Process-Product.

CKO Chief knowledge officer.

CLC Convention Liaison Council.

CLEP College-Level Examination Program.

CLIA Clinical Laboratory Amendments of 1988.

CLMPC Canadian Labour Market and Productivity Centre.

CLO Chief learning officer.

CLV Constant linear velocity.

CM Contact manager.

CMC Certified Management Consultant.

CME Certified Manager of Exhibits.

CMF Career management field.

CMI Computer-managed instruction.

CMIIW Correct me if I'm wrong (Internet speak).

CMMA Communications Media Management Association.

CMO Case management organization.

CMP 1. Certified Meeting Professional. 2. Complete meeting package.

CMS Color management system.

CMT Computer-managed training.

CMYK Cyan, yellow, magenta, and black.

CNCM Computerized numerically controlled machining.

CNO Cost-no-fee contract.

COA 1. Certificate of authority. 2. Commissioned Officers Association of the U.S. Public Health Service. 3. Cost of attendance.

COB Coordination of benefits.

COBOL Common business-oriented language.

COBRA Consolidated Omnibus Budget Reconciliation Act of 1986.

CODA Cash or deferred arrangement.

COHRMA Council on Human Resource Management Associations.

COLA	Cost of living allowance.
COLI	Corporate-owned life insurance.
CON	Certificate of need.
CONAP	Concurrent Admissions Program.
COO	Chief operating officer.
COP	Continuation of pay.
COQ	Cost of quality.
CORF	Comprehensive outpatient rehabilitation facility.
CORPA	Commission on Recognition of Postsecondary Accreditation.
CPA	1. Certified Public Accountant 2. Cleft Palate Foundation.
CPAE	Council of Peers Award for Excellence.
CPAF	Cost-plus-award fee contract.
CPC	Certified Personnel Consultant.
CPDT	Certified Professional Development Trainer.
CPF	Cleft Palate Foundation.
CPFF	Cost-plus-fixed-fee contract.
CPI	Consumer Price Index.
CPIF	Cost-plus-fixed-incentive-fee contract.
CPI-W	Consumer Price Index for Urban Wage Earners and Clerical Workers.
CPM	Critical path method.
CPOA	U.S. Coast Guard Chief Petty Officers Association.
CPR	Cardiopulmonary resuscitation.
CPS	Creative problem solving.
CPT	1. Current Procedural Terminology, 4th Edition. 2. Common procedural terminology.
CPU	Central processing unit.
CRA	Civil Rights Acts of 1964 and 1991.
CRC	Cost-reimbursable contractor.
CRCA	Copyright Remedy Clarification Act of 1991.
CRM	Crew resource management.
CRS	Computer reservation system.
CRT	Cathode ray tube.
CS	1. Cost-sharing contract. 2. Customer service.
CSB	Customer Satisfaction Barometer.
CSE	Child support enforcement.
CSLR	Computer-supported learning resources.
CSP	Certified Speaking Professional.
CSR	Customer service representative.
CSS	Customer service specialist.
CSRA	Civil Service Reform Act of 1978.
CSRS	Civil Service Retirement System.
CSRSEA	Civil Service Retirement Spouse Equity Act of 1984.
CT	1. Computerized tomography. 2. Cycle time.
CTD	Cumulative trauma disorder.
CTI	Corporate Travel Index.
CTO	1. Chief training officer. 2. Chief technology officer.
CTS	1. Certified Temporary Staffing Specialist. 2. Carpal tunnel syndrome.
CTT	Certified Technical Trainer.
CU	Corporate university.
CUA	Common user access.
CUI	Common user interface.
CUPA	College and University Personnel Association.
CV	Curriculum vitae.
CVB	Convention and visitors bureau.
CWA	Communications Workers of America.
CWHSSA	Contract Work Hours and Safety Standards Act of 1962.
CW&WOA	Chief Warrant and Warrant Officers Association, U.S. Coast Guard.
CYA	Cover your anterior.
cabana	In meeting management, a hotel room that is located next to the pool area that may or may not have sleeping facilities.
cabin air	*See* toxic air.

Caesarean section Surgical birth of a fetus. Taking a child from the uterus by cutting through the walls of the abdomen and uterus. Employed when labor is prolonged or normal birth is likely to injure either the child or the mother.

cafeteria A level of food service where food is placed behind a shield and main dishes are served by waitpersons.

cafeteria plan An employee benefit plan that allows employees to select from an array of benefits, within a specified dollar limit, those that most closely match their requirements, and to choose the form in which incentive payments are to be received. Usually a common core of benefits is required, such as minimum levels of disability, health, retirement, and death benefits.

calibration One of the three major components of a **color management system** in desktop publishing. Adjusts measurable deviations from a scanner's, monitor's, printer's, or imagesetter's normal color rendering so that the system consistently conforms to the device's specifications and fits the specified color space.

California Civil Rights Initiative *See* Proposition 209.

The Calix Society Established to help Catholic alcoholics achieve and maintain sobriety through Alcoholics Anonymous. Focuses on total abstinence and spiritual development. Publishes a bimonthly newsletter. *Contact:* Calix Society, c/o Bill Fox, 7601 Wayzata Blvd., Minneapolis, MN 55426 (800/398-0524 or 612/546-0544 mornings only).

call-put-options An investment technique in which a fund invests a small percentage of its assets (say 5 percent), represented by the premium paid, in the purchase of call and put options in respect of specific securities. A call option gives the purchaser of the option the right to buy, and obligates the writer to sell, the underlying security at the exercise price at any time during the option period. A put options gives the purchaser of the option the right to sell, and obligates the writer to buy, the underlying security at the exercise price at any time during the option period.

call-back pay Guaranteed pay for a minimum number of hours when employees are called back to the workplace at a time when they are not scheduled.

call brand In meeting management, a contract provision. A brand of liquor, as distinguished from house brand, selected by the customer by name.

call-girl principle Applies to selling and negotiating: the value of services is greater before they are delivered than after; therefore, it is important to establish the terms of an agreement (the offer) before providing your end of the deal (the consideration). (Attributed to Chester L. Karrass, *Give and Take: The Complete Guide to Negotiating Strategies and Tactics,* Thomas Crowell Publishers.)

calling card A phone card that allows users to dial a special toll-free number for quick long-distance connections, including overseas calls (some one-way, others both ways).

call-in pay Guaranteed pay for minimum number of hours when an employee reports to the workplace and there is no work.

call letter A letter released annually by the Office of Personnel Management (OPM) to every health benefits plan of the Federal Employees Health Benefits Program (FEHBP). The letter sets forth basic guidelines for the plans and thereby determines plan benefits and premium proposals for the following year.

camcorder An item of audiovisual equipment that combines a video camera and recorder in a single unit.

camera-ready In desktop publishing, copy that is ready for photography.

Campus-Based Programs Federal student financial aid programs administered by a school's financial aid administrator. They include the Federal Supplemental Educational Opportunity Grant Program, the Federal Work-Study Program, and the Federal Perkins Loan Program.

Canadian Compensation Association/ Association Canadiénné de Remuneration (CCA/ACR) A not-for-profit professional association of about 1,475 members, in association with the American Compensation Association and the Global Remuneration Organisation, that serves the needs of compensation and benefits practitioners in Canada. Meets the information and training needs of the compensation and management profession and the various publics members serve by proving high-quality education and training programs, information exchanges, and research reports and technical publications. *Contact:* CCA, P.O. Box 294, Kleinburg, Ontario, Canada LOJ 1CO (905/893-1689; FAX 905/893-2392; E-Mail **kleinbrg@netrover.com**; URL **http://www/ahrm.org/aca/cca.htm**).

Canadian Goods and Services Tax
See Goods and Services Tax.

Canadian Labour Market and Productivity Centre (CLMPC) An independent, national organization working with and for the Canadian labor and business communities. With a mission to contribute to economic growth and betterment of society, CLMPC works to improve management-labour relations; promote joint strategies and solutions at the workplace, sectoral, and national levels; and contribute business-labor perspectives to public policy. Services include applied research, organizing conferences, seminars and forums, sectoral labor market analyses, facilitated consultations, and consensus-building activities. *Contact:* CLMPC, 1500-55 Metcalf St., Ottawa, Ontario K1P 6L5 (613/234-0505; Fax 613-234-2482; E-mail **clmpc@magi.com**; URL **http://www.clmpc.ca**).

cancellation clause In contract law, a clause that identifies cut-off dates, advance notice, and monetary penalties, if any, if the activity, event, or other contracted item is canceled.

cancellation fee A fee charged by travel information networks, computer reservation systems, hotels, and car rental companies for canceled bookings. Also known as *kill fee.*

cancer A disease in which cells grow uncontrollably and may spread throughout the body. It takes one of more than 100 forms, the most common of which are bladder, bone, brain, breast, cervical, colon, esophagus, Hodgkin's lymphoma, kidney, larynx, leukemia, lip, liver, lymphomas (non-Hodgkin's), malignant melanoma, mouth, ovary, pancreas, prostate, rectum, skin (basal cell and squamous cell), stomach, testicle, thyroid, and uterus.

cannabis Mood-altering drugs that make time seem to pass more slowly and make sounds, colors, and tastes seem more vivid. Includes marijuana ("pot," "grass"), tetrahydrocannabinol ("THC"), hashish)"hash"), and hashish oil ("hash oil").

canon A model standard of exemplary conduct. Canons express the general concepts and principles, accepted as true, fundamental, and in conformity with good taste, from which more specific rules and regulations are derived.

capital accumulation plan A long-term benefits plan designed to motivate and reward management and encourage employees to save a portion of their income for a time when they will need it to meet capital needs or for supplemental retirement income.

capital expense budget Deals with capital expenditures, which are budget items that represent requests for new, upgraded, rehabilitated, or new or replacement facilities, or equipment for which a predetermined dollar value has been fixed and which has a relatively long life expectancy. Budgets for constructing or improving physical plant and facilities (classrooms, shops, laboratories, libraries, and office space), furniture, furnishing, and equipment fall into this category.

capital gain A profit made on the sale of investments and property, such as stocks, bonds, collectibles, jewelry, and real estate. Capital-gains income is currently taxed at a taxpayer's regular income tax rate, but no higher than 28 percent. However, homeowners who are 55 or older can shelter up to $125,000 profit on the sale of their primary residence from federal income taxes, a once-in-a-lifetime tax exclusion.

capitation **1.** In compensation or reimbursement for services, paying a consultant or provider a set amount of money per member per month. It is calculated by determining the expected volume of referrals, the average cost, and the organization's ability to control utilization, and negotiating strength **2.** A form of **managed care**, viewed by many as a means of controlling health care costs. Instead of a fee for each treatment, health care providers receive a fixed single payment for services per member of their **health maintenance organization** regardless of the type or number of services (ambulatory, in-patient, or home-care) they provide. The plan provides an incentive to providers to curb costs by increasing emphasis on prevention. Capitation programs often include **wellness programs,** such as smoking cessation, blood pressure screening, immunization clinics, prenatal care, diet control, and followup care.

capitation payments   In health care, a system in which the health care provider receives a fixed amount per year, per enrollee for which he or she agrees to provide a predefined health care package.

capping   A method of containing Medicaid costs, adopted by 20 states, described by some as cruel and arbitrary. "Cap states" disqualify anyone with income over a certain amount (even $1 per month over the maximum). The limit applies even if the individual has no savings, no property, and no other assets.

captives   A strategy to reduce the costs of liability insurance coverage (and sometimes workers' compensation). Captives involve the creation of group insurance companies by corporations. They are industry-supported insurance ventures or insurance companies owned by a group of competing firms in an industry. They may also share cost-control ideas, manage claims and reserves, and generate return on investment premiums.

carcinogen (CARC)   Any substance that has been found to cause cancer.

cardiac rehabilitation program   A program operated by a clinic or hospital licensed by the state to treat cardiovascular disease through cardiac rehabilitation treatment or therapy.

cardiac rehabilitation treatment   Cardiovascular services and therapy that involve teaching and monitoring to reduce risk, adjust lifestyle to cardiovascular disease, provide proper exercise, diet, and prescription drugs, and learn self-assessment and self-help skills.

cardiac surgeon   A medical doctor who specializes in surgery of the heart, such as bypasses, valve replacement, and the insertion of pacemakers.

cardiologist   A medical doctor who specializes in the diagnosis and treatment of heart and circulatory disorders ranging from abnormal heart rhythms to congestive heart failure.

cardiopulmonary resuscitation   A life-saving technique frequently taught to supervisory personnel and other workers in first aid, safety training, and employee wellness programs. It involves mouth-to-mouth resuscitation and rhythmic pressure on the chest to restore heartbeat and breathing in heart attack and other life-threatening situations.

card system   The traditional method of containing the costs of providing prescription drugs for employees. It uses a pricing formula that includes the Average Wholesale Price, and adds a nominal dispensing fee to each prescription. The pharmacy files the claim. Many experts believe that card system plans do not save employers any money.

care attendant   *See* personal care attendant.

CareerPath   Contains newspaper ads from six major newspapers in large urban markets (**http://www.careerpath.com**).

career transition program   A downsizing strategy in which salaried employees are offered paid leaves of absence, ranging from six to 15 months, while receiving salaries, health care benefits, and outplacement services, during which time they can search for new jobs.

caretaker   An individual upon whom an elderly person relies for substantial care, including one or more of the necessities essential for physical, intellectual, and emotional well-being, such as food, clothing, shelter, social contact, personal care, and medical care. A caretaker may be a paid live-in companion, a spouse, child, sibling, or other relative if living with the elderly person or providing substantial assistance. A caretaker relationship may also be present when a person is a conservator, guardian, or holder of a power of attorney.

career advising   *See* career counseling.

career anchors   Describes concerns or values that an individual will not abandon. In addition to two primary career supports, technical and functional competence and managerial competence, others include autonomy and independence, creativity, and security. Attributed to Edgar H. Schein (*Career Dynamics: Matching Individual and Organizational Need*, Addison-Wesley, 1978).

career audit   An annual, semi-annual, or quarterly review of career plans and progress. It is a management strategy to help an individual look at the realities of his or her work life. It helps employees examine why they do what they do, how to take responsibility for their own careers, and how to identify the resources they need to manage a career in a changing environment.

career centers   **1.** Offices set up in organizations, usually by outplacement firms, to help employees displaced by downsizing actions find new jobs. The centers provide desks and phones, counselors, and workshops to help employees prepare for job searches or retirement. **2.** Established by the Department of Labor to make the reemployment process easier. The system helps employers by providing computerized labor market information, including job vacancies, worker availability, and salary and wage rates, to improve the process of matching worker skills to job openings. To help people manage their work lives, the centers provide one-stop access in 25 states to a full array of employment-related services, including consumer reports on local education and training, help in filing initial claims for unemployment insurance, information on job training and education, job counseling, and self-help information

career counseling Helping employees learn about their own capabilities, assets, limitations, preferences, and objectives, where they stand in the organization, what opportunities are available to them within and outside the organization, and what they need in the way of training and development to employ their talents and make the most of their opportunities. Then, employees are assisted in developing individual career plans, using information on specific career requirements, career ladders, organizational needs, available development opportunities, and employee interests and needs.

career curves *See* maturity curves.

career development (CD) The process of assessing, aligning, and balancing organizational and individual needs, capabilities, opportunities, and challenges through multiple approaches and methods. It emphasizes the person as an individual who performs, configures, and adapts various work roles. Its major interventions are self-assessment and development processes that affect individual and organizational abilities to generate optimal matches of people jobs.

career ladder A carefully sequenced series of jobs from the lowest to the highest level (in terms of responsibilities, compensation, and challenges) in a career field available in an organization. It marks a clear path for development and promotion. Also called *career path.*

career management field (CMF) A term used by the military services to identify major categories of positions such as intelligence, aviation, electronic maintenance, and the like.

career management profile A means of storing and communicating data about an individual employee; for example, appraisal of performance and potential, training and development needs, and primary and alternate career paths.

career mobility The tendency of people to make several career changes in a lifetime rather than committing to a lifelong career in a given field.

career path The typical hierarchical structure of a career field, it depicts the sequence of positions lowest to highest in that occupation or profession.

career planning The process of establishing short- or long-term career goals and objectives and defining the specific steps required to achieve them (the positions, training, development, and other experiences that will assist in attaining the goals and objectives). It may be done by the employee alone or in concert with a mentor or advisor.

career plateau Reaching a dead end in an organization, with no promotion prospects. It may occur because the individual has reached the top position available in the organization or in the industry or because of age discrimination, downsizing, restructuring, or lack of skills or motivation.

career progression chart *See* progression charts.

career stages Refers to the stages through which people transit during their work-lives. Examples for HRD personnel might be student, apprentice, practitioner, helper, and creator (McLagan, *Training and Development Journal,* July 1987).

Carnegie Corporation of New York Created by Andrew Carnegie in 1911 to promote the advancement and diffusion of knowledge and understanding. The last of Carnegie's great endowments, it is the only one to be established as a grantmaking foundation. Grants must benefit the people of the United States, although up to 7.4 percent of the funds may be used to benefit the people of some countries that are or have been members of the British overseas Commonwealth. *Contact:* Carnegie Corporation of New York, 437 Madison Ave., New York, NY 10022 (212/207-6289;

Fax 212/223-9871; E-mail **gopher.carnegie. org**; URL **http://www.carnegie.org**).

carotid surgery The most common procedure for the relief of carotid blockage or **atherosclerosis** of the main arteries carrying blood to the head. The carotid is exposed by opening it along a short section of the affected area, the plaque is removed, and the incision is stitched shut.

carpal tunnel syndrome (CTS) Said to be the fastest growing occupational injury of the last decade. A neurological disorder or nerve disease, it is caused by repetitive motion injuries that cause tendons and nerves in the hands, wrists, elbows, or shoulders to swell. Unless treated, CTS can cause a person to lose the functions of his or her hand or arm. The tunnel is is a narrow conduit located at the center of the wrist, which encloses tendons and a major nerve.

carrel An individual learning environment typically found in learning centers. One carrel consists of a partitioned area containing a desk and chair, a computer terminal or PC and associated disc drive, cables, telephone, modem, or other devices, and audio, visual, and other materials in document form.

carrier A private insurance organization that contracts with a company or the federal government to handle claims from physicians and suppliers for services covered by the medical benefits package (or Medicare).

carve-outs A means of cutting medical and health care costs, particularly mental health care, substance abuse benefits, chiropractic and physical therapy claims, diagnostic testing services, organ transplants, and drug utilization. Similar to managed care strategies, such as **health maintenance organizations** and **preferred provider organizations** but carve-outs emphasize precertification, utilization review, and case management in specific areas of medical treatment that require more intensive and specialized approaches.

case-based reasoning software
See EXPERT system.

case management A program that has its origins in workers' compensation and long-term disability rehabilitation. Designed to facilitate cost-effective treatment and care and an optimum level of recovery for injured or ill employees. The goal is to identify and coordinate all the resources needed to offer quality options to the patient and maximize

the effectiveness of the health care provided. There are three steps in the process: (1) diagnosis and assessment; (2) planning and coordinating therapy; and (3) monitoring treatment. The process involves the patient, the attending medical professional, the family, and a **case manager.**

case management organizations (CMOs)
Health care management organizations that review medical products and services to help corporations determine their therapeutic value and cost effectiveness.

case manager The key person in a case management program. Usually a registered nurse or physician, the case manager works with the attending health care professional and the employee and his or her family to coordinate medical care. Serves as the patient's advocate with the insurance company, the physician or other medical provider, other care givers, community organizations, and health care agencies.

case method See case study method.

case rate In health care reimbursement arrangements, a flat rate negotiated for a well-defined set of procedures.

case study A research methodology in which systematic investigation is made of a specific situation and the events, circumstances, and consequences associated with it. Data are collected by means of document analysis, interviews, and observations.

case study method A special participative training method that involves in-depth group discussion of real-life situations. It makes use of case reports — factual and accurate word pictures (or visualizations using videocassettes) of a situation that portrays people acting, interacting, and reacting. It requires reading, study, analysis, discussion, and free exchange of ideas as well as decision making and the selling of decisions to others.

cash account pension plan See account balance pension.

cash advance A means of controlling travel and entertainment costs. Funds are issued to employees prior to trips to cover anticipated expenses.

cash arrangement See Section 401(k) plan.

cash balance pension plan A defined benefit plan. Works like a 401(k) in that it is portable. It differs in that the company funds the plan, takes responsibility for investing the funds, and does away with the complex formulas of conventional pension plans. The annuity at retirement is based on earnings of a phantom investment account that must be credited periodically at current market rates. Those calculations give plan participants an estimate of their accrued benefits on a defined contribution equivalent basis. Makes it easier for employees to track the value of their accounts and eliminates the "all or nothing" aspect of most traditional plans whereby full benefits are available only to those who stay with the company for a full career and little or no benefits for those who leave before reaching an eligibility milestone.

cash balance plan   See account balance pension.

cash budget   An analysis of the flow of cash in a company over a short or long time frame. It is a forecast of expected cash intake (receipts) and outlays (disbursements) against which actual cash experience can be measured. It is not an operating statement or an income statement.

cash-deferred [401(k)] plan   A savings plan under which employees are given the options of either deferring part of their income to be invested in a group plan or receiving that same amount in cash on a current basis. Originally, the deferred amount and accumulated interest and dividends could be completely sheltered from current taxation. The deferred amount was considered a reduction in salary and constituted a reduction In the individual's gross taxable income. However, in 1989 Congress tightened its control by including 401(k) contributions in the measurement of taxes due under the **Federal Insurance Contributions Act of 1935** (FICA).

cash flow   The movement of cash derived from operations in and out of a total firm or activity. It is a useful measure of a change in liquidity of assets (convertibility of assets to cash or negotiable instruments) as it is a change in working capital.

cash flow return on investment (CFROI)   A means of assessing the value of a company's assets and measuring the effectiveness of financial management activities. Formerly used almost exclusively for making acquisition bids. Also called *cash flow metrics*. Attributed to Franco Modigliani (Nobel Prize in economics) and Merton H. Miller more than 40 years ago.

cashing out   Refers to working men and women who question the value of a high-powered career and opt for a simpler way of life. Attributed to Faith Popcorn and Lys Marigold, *Clicking: 16 Trends to Future fit Your Life, Your Work and Your Business.*

cash or deferred arrangement (CODA)   See cash deferred [401(k)] plan.

cash plan   A type of profit-sharing plan in which a certain percentage of the profits is distributed in cash at predetermined times to participants in the plan.

casting   Selecting the "talent" — nonprofessional or professional "actors" — for a live dramatization or TV production, whether broadcast, corporate, or educational TV.

casual attire   Typically includes casual slacks, sport shirts, jeans, sweatshirts, T-shirts, sweatpants, and shorts. Evidence of a relaxed employee **dress code**.

casual day   A popular employee benefit of the '90s. One day each week, usually Friday, the organization suspends its normal workplace dress code and allows employees to wear something more comfortable and casual than their usual business clothing. Touted as a morale builder. Also called *dress down day.*

catalog sales   A form of direct marketing used extensively by book publishers, software developers, producers of computer and audiovisual equipment, supplies, programs, and software.

Catalyst   A nonprofit organization with a dual mission: to enable women in business and the professions to achieve their potential and to help employers capitalize on women's talents. Conducts national research, works with corporations and professional firms to provide advice on women's advancement, and sponsors a Speakers Bureau. Catalyst's Corporate Board Placement identifies qualified women for board directorship. *Contact:* Catalyst, 250 Park Avenue South, New York, NY 10003-1459 (212/777-8900; Fax 212/477-4252; E-mail **info@catalystwomen.org**).

cataract   A clouding of the normally clear lens of the eye. The most common type of cataract is related to aging of the eye. Surgery is the only cure for cataract.

catastrophic cap   Under the **Civilian Health and Medical Programs of the Uniformed Services (CHAMPUS),** the upper limit placed on beneficiaries' share of CHAMPUS-covered medical bills in any fiscal year.

Charges beyond the CHAMPUS **allowable charge**, or charges for care not covered by CHAMPUS, are not covered by the cap and must be paid in full by the family members of their military sponsors.

catastrophic illness coverage (CIC)
An optional health insurance plan that provides a higher level of benefits for most services, routine and otherwise, than other plans.

catastrophic protection/coverage
Health care plan provisions that pay full or partial benefits when deductibles and coinsurance of any individual or all covered family members exceed a specified amount in any one calendar year.

catchment-area management (CAM)
The U.S. Navy's method of implementing the Department of Defense **Coordinated Care Program.** It places responsibility for the delivery of health care services at the local command level.

catering director　The hotel functionary who arranges and provides overall supervision of meal and reception functions. In the absence of a convention services department, the catering director may also be responsible for assigning and setting up meeting rooms. May be called a *catering manager, catering sales manager,* or *conference services manager.*

catering manager　*See* catering director.

cathode ray tube (CRT)　**1.** The viewing component of a PC or workstation, located just behind (or serves as) the screen. Similar to the picture tube of a television set, it displays information and graphics. **2.** A basic technology used in large-screen projection. Projectors based on CRTs use phosphor-coated tubes, much like conventional television; however, instead of viewing the image directly off the CRT, it is projected onto a screen.

The Cato Institute　A non-partisan public policy research foundation. The Cato Institute seeks to widen public policy debate to allow consideration of more choices that are consistent with the American principles of limited government, individual liberty, and peace. Toward that goal, the Institute strives to achieve greater involvement of the lay public in questions of policy and the proper role of government. *Contact:* The Cato Institute, 1000 Massachusetts Avenue, N.W., Washington D.C. 20001-5403 (202/842-0200; Fax 202/842-3490; E-mail **Cato@cato.org**; URL **http:www.cato.org**).

causal-comparative study　Research undertaken to establish likely causes for certain changes or effects. For example, to ascertain the characteristics of students who go into marketing, as compared with students who go into other areas of specialization, the investigator might give tests and questionnaires to college juniors and seniors and later compare the data and for students who have gone into marketing with the data from the non-marketing graduates. The researcher would use averages and distributions from the groups for each trait shown in the tests and questionnaires and then compare the groups in terms of averages and spread.

cause-and-effect analysis　A **brainstorming, brainwriting,** and quality circle technique involving the construction of a diagram to aid in recording, organizing, and using the ideas generated during a session.

cause-and-effect diagram　A quality control tool used widely in Japan to study a problem, display its elements, and communicate the results of its analysis. All possible causes of a problem are methodically listed in categories and subcategories as a means of identifying the root problem. Also known as an *Inhikawa diagram.*

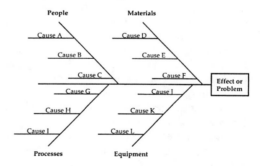

caveat emptor　A legal term that literally means "buyer beware." It indicates an item offered for sale comes with no warranties, so the buyer assumes all risks following the purchase.

C-band satellite　A type of satellite used in business or corporate television, similar to a commercial AM radio system or signal. *See also* Ku-band satellite.

CD-recordable (CD-R)　A compact disc that allows users to write permanently to the disc using their computer. Made possible by a four-layer disc that features a light-sensitive dye layer made of cyanine, ptalocyanine, or azo.

CD-rewritable (CD-RW) A compact disc that allows users to write and rewrite to the disc as many as 1,000 times. Instead of a light-sensitive dye, these discs use a phase-change alloy layer composed of silver, indium, antomony, and tellurium.

Celler-Kefauver Act of 1950 Proscribes stock and asset acquisitions, whether horizontal, vertical, or conglomerate, where the effect may be to substantially reduce competition. It also covers interlocking directorates.

cell manufacturing A manufacturing process used along with or in place of **assembly line manufacturing.** Two or more workers are assigned to each cell or workstation where products are totally built, tested, and shipped. The process requires better trained and higher paid workers and full sets of tools for each cell and is therefore more expensive than an assembly line. However, the approach is more flexible, providing the ability to make changes and manufacture different models each day — plus the advantages of increased employee output (by as much as 20 percent) and product quality (by as much as 25 percent).

Center for Assistive Technology/University of Buffalo (CAT/UB) Provides information, service, research, and education regarding all types of assistive technology for persons of all ages with disabilities. *Contact:* CAT/UB, University of Buffalo, Kimball Tower, 3435 Main St.. Buffalo, NY 14214-3079 (716/829-3217; Fax 716/829-3217; E-mail **jweir@acsu. buffalo.edu**).

The Center for Corporate Health, Inc.
An organization that specializes in health care cost management programs, which educates employees and dependents about leading healthy lifestyles and becoming wise medical care consumers. The "Taking Care" program's communications materials and counseling services in several thousand corporations reach more than 2.5 million employees and dependents nationwide. *Contact:* The Center for Corporate Health, Inc., 10467 White Granite Ave., Ste. 300, Oakton, VA 22124 (703/218-8400; Fax 703/394-7585).

Center for Creative Leadership (CCL)
An international nonprofit educational institution devoted to behavioral science research and leadership education. With branches in Colorado Springs, San Diego, and Brussels in addition to its Greensboro headquarters, and maintaining contact with more than 40 network associates and other partners in the U.S., CCL is one of the largest institutions in the world focusing on leadership. The Center conducts research, produces publications, and provides a broad variety of programs and products to leaders and organizations in the public, corporate, and nonprofit sectors. The Center also serves as a clearinghouse for ideas on leadership and creativity and regularly convenes conferences and colloquia by scholars and practitioners. *Contact:* CCL, One Leadership Place, P.O. Box 27438-6300, Greensboro, NC 27410 (910/545-2805; Fax 910/288-3999; E-mail **info@ leaders.ccl.org**; URL **http://www.ccl.org**).

Centers for Disease Control (CDC)
An independent agency of the Public Health Service, a division of the Department of Health and Human Services. Provides researchers and investigators to search for the causes of epidemics or the outbreak of new diseases and provides educational and prevention programs, particularly in the areas of AIDS, drug and alcohol abuse, accidental injuries, and occupational and health hazards. *See also* Food and Drug Administration.

Center on Addiction and Substance Abuse (CASA) Founded in 1992 to work with experts in medicine, law enforcement, business, law, economics, communications, teaching, social work, and the clergy to determine and combat the impact of substance abuse on the courts, housing, prisons, children, health care, crime, business productivity, and education. *Contact:* CASA, 152 West 57th St., New York, NY 10019 (212/841-5200; Fax 212/956-8020).

centers of excellence Organizations that have developed expertise in disciplines and areas of expertise that are critical to growth, productivity, profitability, and viability. Identified by using industry databases and then applied as a quality control process. For example, in attempting to control health care costs, some organizations have used health care databases to identify providers that have developed expertise in expensive surgical procedures and, in doing so, not only provide excellent care, but also do it.

centralization In organization design, downsizing, or restructuring, consolidating business, industrial, training, or other types of operations and decision making at a central location or headquarters. Centralization consolidates authority in the organization by giving managers of subunits less autonomy in planning and decision making.

centralized billing In travel management, a system of invoicing where the travel supplier sends one bill for all charges incurred by all travelers to the client organization.

centralized network A computing environment in which all processing functions are centrally located and the connected workstations simply input instructions and display responses but do no processing.

central processing unit (CPU) The mechanism that directs and controls a computer's processing capabilities. It consists of a control unit and an arithmetic/logic unit.

central tendency A type of rating error used to describe the situation when raters assign all ratees average ratings. The full range of ratings is not used. *See* error of central tendency.

cerebral palsy A large group of movement and balance disorders that result from brain injury just before, during, or shortly after birth. A person with cerebral palsy usually has an awkward gait, poor balance, and impaired control of movements. Other effects include drooling, facial grimaces, involuntary movements, convulsive seizures, absent or poor speech, visual and hearing impairments, and delayed intellectual development. With advancing age, some muscles become rigid and controlled movements become difficult, if not impossible.

Certificate of Advanced Mastery (CAM) A feature of the proposed **Workforce Development Act of 1996,** the certificate would be awarded after two years of high school vocational training and one year of community college technical training and participants would be eligible to apply for a job at U.S. Job Service Centers.

certificate of authority (COA) License issued by a state to operate a health maintenance organization.

Certificate of Initial Mastery (CIM) A standard of accomplishment set by the **National Alliance for Restructuring Education** that is as high as standards the best-performing countries expect of their students at about age 16. *Contact:* NARE, 700 Eleventh St., N.W., Ste. 750, Washington, DC 20001 (202/783-3668; Fax 202/783-3672; E-mail **nareinfo@mcee.org**; URL **http://www.ecs.org/ecs/2156.htm**).

certificate of need (CON) Requirement that a health care organization get permission from an oversight agency before making plan changes relating to facilities or facility-based services.

certificate of title A document issued by a Land Court that shows the title, property description, and any encumbrances on a parcel of real estate which has been registered or "land courted." The owner must retain physical custody of the certificate and return it whenever there is a transfer of the property.

certification The European term for **registration**, the testing process that determines whether a company has met international standards.

Certified Association Executive (CAE) A designation awarded by the **American Society of Association Executives,** which indicates that the individual has demonstrated high levels of association management knowledge, ethics, leadership, and activity in community affairs. *Contact:* ASAE, 1575 I St., NW, 12th Floor, Washington, DC 20005-1168 (202/626-2798; Fax 202/408-9633; E-mail **pr@asae.asanet.org**; URL **http://www.asaent.org**).

Certified Benefits Professional (CBP) A designation awarded by the **American Compensation Association** following achievement of passing scores on nine examinations: three common core exams, three required benefits exams, and three exams chosen from a list of benefits electives, , each consisting of approximately 100 multiple-choice questions based on the functional area being tested. The ACP also offers a wide range of courses designed to prepare candidates for specific exams. *See also* Certified Compensation Professional. *Contact:* ACA, 14040 N. Northsight Blvd., Scottsdale AZ 85260-3601 (602/922-2020; FAX 602/483-8352; E-mail **qllr45a@prodigy.com**; URL **http://www.ahrm.org/aca.htm**).

Certified Compensation Professional (CCP) A designation awarded by the **American Compensation Association** following successful completion of its certification program, which includes a battery of nine examinations, including three common core, three compensation certification, and three elective exams, each consisting of approximately 100 multiple-choice questions based on the functional area being tested. The ACP also offers a wide range of courses designed to prepare candidates for specific exams. *See also* Certified Benefits Professional. *Contact:* ACA, 14040 N. Northsight Blvd., Scottsdale AZ 85260-3601 (602/922-2020; FAX 602/483-8352; E-mail **qllr45a@prodigy.com**; URL **http://www.ahrm.org/aca.htm**).

Certified Corporate Travel Executive (CCTE) A designation or awarded by the **National Business Travel Association** to individuals who have completed a 4-day series of topical seminars on travel management. A revamped program is now offered by Cornell University. The program requires completion of a two week on-campus session, five regional elective courses, a corporate application project, and a final exam. Total cost is $3,200 plus enrollment fees. After earning certification, graduates must complete at least one elective course per year to keep the CCTE designation. *Contact:* NBTA, 1650 King St., Ste. 401, Alexandria, VA 22314 (703/684-0836 Fax 703/684-0263; E-mail **info@nbta.org**; URL **http://www.nbta.org/nbta**).

Certified Destination Management Executive (CDME) A designation awarded by the **International Association of Convention & Visitors Bureaus** following completion of a two year program consisting of a series of two- and three-day classes taught by University of Calgary and Purdue University professors on such subjects as leadership, destination marketing, international tourism, and strategic planning. Eligibility is limited to CEOs of bureaus, holders of the IACVB Continuing Education Certificate, or professionals who have completed 36 hours of course work, have had senior destination management experience, and have been nominated by their company CEO. IACVB, 2000 L St., NW, Ste. 702, Washington, DC 20036-4990 (202/296-7888; Fax 202/296-7889; E-mail **info@iacvb.org**; URL **http://www.iacvb.org**).

Certified Employee Assistance Professional (CEAP) A designation awarded by the **Employee Assistance Professionals Association** to practitioners who have a minimum of three years of experience (direct employment, internship, or contracted responsibilities), including a total of 3,000 hours, in employee assistance programming, and successful completion of a weighted written examination. The 250-item multiple-choice examination covers work organizations, human resources management, EAP policy and administration EAP direct services, chemical dependency and other addictions, and personal and psychological problems. Recertification is required every three years. *Contact:* EAPA, Inc., 2101 Wilson Blvd., Ste. 500, Arlington, VA 22201-3062 (703) 522-6272; Fax 703/522-4585; URL **http://www.ahrm.org/eapa.htm**.

Certified Employee Benefits Specialist (CEBS) A designation awarded by the **International Foundation of Employee Benefit Plans** following successful completion of 10 courses and examinations covering a comprehensive range of benefit issues. Jointly sponsored by IFEBP and the Wharton School of the University of Pennsylvania. *Contact:* CEBS Department, IFEBP, 18700 W. Bluemound Rd., P.O. Box 69, Brookfield, WI 53008-0069 (414/786-6700; Fax 414/786-8670; E-mail **pr@ifebp.org**; URL **http://www.ifebp.org**).

Certified Financial Planner (CFP) A designation earned by meeting basic and continuing educational, examination, experience, and ethics requirements of the **Certified Financial Planner Board of Standards** *Contact:* CFP Board, 1660 Lincoln St., Ste. 3050, Denver, CO 80264 (303/830-7543; Fax 303/860-7388; URL **http://www.cfp-board.org**).

Certified Financial Planner Board of Standards (CFPBS) Established to benefit and protect the public by setting the qualifications for initial professional certification, to protect the marks CPF® and **Certified Financial Planner®**, to enhance the professionalism of those engaged in the exercise and pursuit of personal financial planning, to develop and administer continuing post-certification requirements and disciplinary procedures for licensees, and to encourage both certification attainment and retention of those persons licensed. *Contact:* CFP Board, 1660 Lincoln St., Ste. 3050, Denver, CO 80264 (303/830-7543; Fax 303/860-7388; URL **http://www.cfp-board.org**).

Certified Management Consultant (CMC) A professional designation granted by the **Institute of Management Consultants** to those who meet membership standards of practice, education, and experience. Certification is based on a point system in which credit is given for documented education, work experience, and professional activity, successful completion of an examination covering professional ethics, and a qualifying interview conducted by certified management consultants. *Contact:* Institute of Management Consultants, 521 Fifth ave., 35th Floor, New York, NY 10175-3598 (212/697-8262; Fax 212/949-6571; E-mail **imcCR@aol.com**; URL **http://www.imcusa.org**).

Certified Manager of Exhibits (CME)
A designation awarded by the **International Exhibitor's Association.** *Contact:* Trade Show Exhibitors Association, 5501 Backlick Rd., Ste. 105, Springfield, VA 22151 (703/941-3725; Fax 703/941-8275; E-mail **tsea@tsea.org**; URL **http://www.tsea.org/maintsea.htm**).

certified medical laboratory A facility certified or licensed by the state or federal government to perform clinical diagnostic tests. If such a facility participates in Medicare, it must accept assignment of claims and cannot bill the beneficiary. Part B pays all charges except in Maryland where beneficiaries can be billed for 20 percent coinsurance for hospital outpatient tests.

Certified Meeting Professional (CMP)
A designation offered by the **Convention Liaison Council** certifying competency in meeting management. Applicants must be currently employed in meeting management, have responsibility and accountability for successful completion of meetings, have a minimum of three years of meeting management experience, and successfully complete the application and examination process. The examination consists of 150 multiple choice questions relating to 25 meeting management functions. Initial certification is valid for five years. Recertification is based on evidence of continued accountability in the field and continued development as a meeting professional. *Contact:* CLC, ASAE Headquarters, 1575 Eye St., Ste. 1190, Washington, DC 20005-1168 (202/626-2709; Fax 202/406-9652).

Certified Personnel Consultant (CPC)
A designation offered by the **National Association of Personnel Services** to individuals who have demonstrated professionalism and commitment to the personnel services industry. *Contact:* NAPS, 3133 Mt. Vernon Ave.,

Alexandria, VA 22305 (703/684-0180; Fax 703/684-0071; E-mail **membership@napsweb.org**; URL **http//www.napsweb.org**).

Certified Professional Development Trainer (CPDT) A designation awarded by The Chauncey Group International (a subsidiary of the **Educational Testing Service** of Princeton, NJ) to classroom trainers. The credential is awarded following evaluation of a classroom trainer's mastery of 14 fundamental instructor competencies identified by the International Board of Standards for Training Performance and Instruction. Evaluation is based on assessment of a 2-minute video of candidates displaying their delivery skills and a 105-question multiple-choice computer-delivered test. Contact: Chauncey (800/258-4914; E-mail **cpdt@chauncey.com**; URL **http://www.chauncey.com**).

Certified Public Accountant (CPA)
An individual qualified by education, successful completion of a comprehensive standardized examination graded by the **American Institute of Certified Public Accountants**, and certified by the state, District of Columbia, or possession as meeting all required professional standards. *Contact:* AICPA, 1211 Avenue of the Americas, New York, NY 10036-8775 (212/525-6200; Fax 212/596-6213; URL **http://www.aicpa.org**).

Certified Speaking Professional (CSP)
A designation awarded by the **National Speakers Association** to individuals who have achieve a proven record of speaking experience including a minimum number of fee presentations, continuing education credits, and consecutive years of professional speaking experience. *Contact:* NSA, 1500 S. Priest Dr., Tempe, AZ 85281 (602/968-2552; Fax 602/968-0911; E-mail **NSAMain@aol.com**; URL **http://www.NSASpeaker.org**)

Certified Technical Trainer (CTT) Program
A certification jointly sponsored by the **Computer Education Management Association** and the **Information Technology Training Association, Inc.** The designation is awarded to technical trainers who have passed tests of 14 competencies identified by the International Board of Standards for Training Performance and Instruction. Evaluation is based on assessment of a 2-minute video of candidates displaying their delivery skills and a 105-question multiple-choice computer-delivered test. Contact: Chauncey

(800/258-4914; E-mail **cpdt@chauncey. com**; URL **http://www.chauncey.com**).

Certified Temporary-Staffing Specialist (CTS) A designation awarded to temporary placement professionals who have passed an examination on employment law, temp operations, and standards of business practice administered by the **National Association of Personnel Services.** *Contact:* NAPS, 3133 Mt. Vernon Ave., Alexandria, VA 22305 (703/684-0180; Fax 703/684-0071; E-mail **membership@napsweb.org**; URL **http//www.napsweb.org**).

C. Everett Koop National Health Awards Awards presented annually by The Health Project, a Washington, DC-based private-public organization, to recognize model work-site health care programs that improve health standards and reduce costs.

chain of custody In law and in charges of use of nonprescription drugs and alcohol, refers to the chain of possession of evidence (such as drug tests involving urine or blood samples) from the time the evidence is obtained until it is finally analyzed or used and reported, and the protection given to that evidence against substitution or tampering during that period of time.

challenge courses In **adventure training**, obstacle courses artificially constructed of cable, ropes, poles or trees, beams, platforms, nets, and hardware. Events involve a series of elements often connected to one another and which can be either elevated or on the ground.

challenged employees *See* handicapped employees.

change agent Persons or groups at any level either inside or outside the organization who, by reason of position, knowledge and skills, or personality, support and influence change. They are invariably skilled problem-sensers, inquirers, and problem-solvers, open-minded and knowledgeable about the organization, and able to obtain the full participation and involvement of others.

change efforts One of the three major stages in learning (the others are **unfreezing** and **refreezing**). This is the point where new behaviors are introduced, in formal learning situations, by a teacher or facilitator. Attributed to Kurt Lewin, pioneer in experiential learning.

change model A form of statistical HR forecasting approach, that assesses the impact of past employment practices and tries to project future human resource availability given certain assumptions about organizational change.

chaos theory A management paradigm. Instead of attempting to impose structure onto an organization from the top, business leaders surrender control and allow employees to function as independent agents, interacting freely with each other to create new business and processes. *See also* complexity theory.

Chapter 7, Federal Bankruptcy Code The most common form of bankruptcy. A proceeding in which most of a business' or individual's assets are taken away by a court officer and divided among creditors according to a set listing of priority payments. Nearly every asset the business or individual holds (except the home, household goods, wages of individuals, and most pension savings) can be taken away and the organization or individual has no say in determining who gets paid and how much. Discharges almost all debts (except taxes due within the past three years, alimony and child support, and most student loans).

Chapter 11, Federal Bankruptcy Code When properly filed in U.S. Bankruptcy Court, Chapter 11 protects a corporation from its creditors. The corporation can continue operations while it tries to reorganize its finances and work out its problems. For individuals with too many assets to qualify for Chapter 13. Not available to stock and commodities brokers, it is the most expensive to file and takes longer to negotiate with creditors resulting in higher attorney's fees. The individual's spendable income is not taken away, nor is personal property. The obligation assumed is simply to make payments as promised under the reorganization plan. Individuals who have heavy debt may work out with creditors a plan to reorganize their debt and devise payment plans so that creditors get at least part of their money.

Chapter 13, Federal Bankruptcy Code A proceeding in which a debt-ridden business or individual having a regular income can ask a court to allow the business or individual to hold onto personal assets and enough money to live on while paying off at least some debt by installments. Some debtors may only have to pay 5 to 20 cents on the dollar spread over three to five years. A trustee is appointed to receive payments monthly and disburse them to creditors. Eligibility is limited to entities that have no more than $100,000 of debts not backed up by some security. Prior to a Supreme Court decision in June 1991, for unsecured debts exceeding $100,000, the only option was to go the Chapter 7 or liquidation route. Now, however, individuals who have heavy debt may work out with creditors a plan, similar to that allowed under Chapter 11, to reorganize their debt and devise payment plans so that creditors get at least part of their money. Creditors have veto power over such a plan and typically insist that they get as much back as they would if the bankruptcy had been filed under Chapter 7. Permits those in financial difficulty to pay off a share of their debt instead of giving up their business.

"Chapter 20," Federal Bankruptcy Code
A euphemism for a scheme that lets a person unload personal debts while preventing a bank from foreclosing on his or her property. The debtor first files under Chapter 7 and, when that has been done, the individual files again under Chapter 13 to renegotiate payments on the debts that are secured.

character generator (CG) In video production, a device used to produce titles and other graphic displays electronically and directly on a video monitor.

characterization One of three main components of a **color management system** in desktop publishing. Provides data profiles that determine the range of color that a scanner, monitor, printer, or image setter is able to capture or reproduce.

chargeback A system for funding training that involves charging back or "billing" the trainee's department for costs incurred by the training department — instructor's fees, training materials, overhead costs, and so on. It can affect positively the way corporations and line managers perceive the value of training and development.

charge card A payment option for travel and entertainment expenses. A means of controlling costs.

charged-coupled device (CCD) In desktop publishing, the most common type of **scanner**, a solid-state electronic device, usually combined in a row to make up the scanning head, that transforms light intensity into electrical voltage. and produces excellent quality images.

charitable organization An organization that is operated exclusively for religious, charitable, scientific, literacy, or educational purposes, if none of its earnings is used for the benefit of any individual, and no substantial part of its activities involve propagandizing or other attempts to influence legislation.

charitable remainder trust *See* charitable trust.

charitable trust An estate planning tool. To provide additional income and improve cash flow during retirement, and avoid the capital gains taxes that would result from selling stocks, bonds, real estate, or other holdings and putting the proceeds into high-yield investments, retirees donate the investment property to a charitable trust, take a tax deduction based on an age-related Internal Revenue Service formula, and receive income for life. The main disadvantage is that the donation is irrevocable — the principal cannot be touched.

charm school A derisive or mocking term applied by cynics to military instructor training courses and civilian train-the-trainer programs.

Chartered Financial Analyst (CFA) A designation conferred by the **Institute for Chartered Financial Analysts** under the auspices of the **Association for Investment Management and Research** upon successful completion of a Study and Examination Program. *Contact:* ICAF, c/o AIMR, P.O. Box 3668, Charlottesville, VA 22903-0668 (804/977-6600; Fax 804/977-1103; E-mail **info@aimr.org**; URL **http://www.aimr.com.aimr.html**).

charter school An independent public school established under state law (19 states as of January 1996) and operated by groups of teachers or nonschool organizations. A part of a campaign to make elementary and secondary education more competitive, innovative, effective, and accountable.

check-in The hour established by hotels for room occupancy, usually later than **check-out** time.

checklist A special form of the questionnaire, a checklist consists of sets of specific statements, questions or items used to collect information about employee feelings, attitudes, or preferences, to gather job and task data, or to rate performance. It is prepared in advance and used to collect objective data and in problem-solving situations to uncover clues for new solutions. The surveyor simply checks the appropriate items as they are observed or reported by the subjects of the survey.

check-off Deduction of union dues or assessments from an employee's pay for transfer to the union.

check-out In meeting management: **1.** The hour posted by hotels by which room occupants must vacate. A penalty of one day's charge may be imposed for failure to vacate on time, although a late check-out may be approved in advance by the hotel management. **2.** The procedure for the departure of hotel guests, including how accounts are to be settled.

check-out trip A trip taken by a buyer to a location which has been selected for a future event. The purpose of the trip is to finalized details with the conference center, hotel, or other host organization.

check-ride *See* employee skills test.

check sheet **1.** An elementary tool of quality control used early in the problem-solving process to compile data from which other quality control tools can be developed. **2.** A means of exercising quality control over a process in which workers are taught to use checklists to insure adherence to standard procedures and to check quality.

chemical dependency (CD) Addiction to prescription or nonprescription drugs, including nicotine and alcohol.

chemotherapy Cytotoxic medication given orally or by intravenous infusion to eradicate a cancer, prevent it from recurring, or control its symptoms. The medication consists of molecules which either destroy cancer cells or slow down their development by interfering with their reproduction and growth. Patients undergoing chemotherapy may experience side effects such as hair loss, fatigue, nausea, and vomiting.

cherry picking The insurance industry's version of **adverse selection**, a form of discrimination. To reduce claims the insurance company writes policies that exclude persons with preexisting conditions and experience-rates the coverage to eliminate high risk individuals, companies, and industries.

chief accountant *See* controller/comptroller.

chief executive officer (CEO) The senior executive responsible for the management of an organization and the individual to whom all other executives report.

chief financial officer (CFO) The executive responsible for overseeing the financial affairs of an organization, including recommending alternative courses of action to the CEO and board of control on important corporate decisions and establishing and managing a system of internal controls (accounting policies, procedures, and reports).

chief knowledge officer (CKO) A new corporate title given to the individual responsible for handling the intellectual assets of a company — its creative, communication, and analytical resources — and coordinating internal learning and skills. Goes beyond traditional training and development in that the objective is to tap the organization's knowledge base to improve processes and develop knowledge-based products and services. May also be responsible for tracking performance using traditional accounting and production yardsticks.

chief learning officer (CLO) The corporate officer responsible for transferring knowledge and strategies, making better use of what individuals, teams, departments, and plants know and can do, and moving knowledge and best practice around the organization. Also called *director of shared learning* or *leader of learning and change.*

chief operating officer (COO) The executive responsible for the day-to-day management of an organization.

chief technology officer (CTO) A corporate officer with responsibility for determining how best to apply new technology, primarily information technology.

chief training officer (CTO) A newly created corporate executive position established to improve the quality of work force training and retraining programs and services. The CTO is the corporate officer responsible for the training function. Equivalent to a finance or marketing executive, the CTO uses business skills to build comprehensive training systems that support corporate goals and objectives.

Chief Warrant and Warrant Officers Association, US Coast Guard (CW&WOA) An organization of 3,300 active duty, reserve, and retired Coast Guard warrant and chief warrant officers. Its mission is to advance the professional abilities of members. *Contact:*

CW&WOA, c/o James Creek Marina, 200 V St., S.W., Washington, DC 20024 (202/554-7753; Fax 202/484-0641; E-mail **cwoauscg@aol.com**).

Child and Dependent-Care Voucher Plan
A system offered to more than 500 employers in 35 states by The Voucher Corp. (TVC) since 1984. TVC contracts with employers to provide the plan on a pretax basis (up to $5,000 in annual benefits) under Sections 125 and 129, **Internal Revenue Code.** TVC provides employers with the master plan document necessary to satisfy federal tax code requirements. The money employees pay for dependent care is deducted from their pay checks, resulting in lower taxes for the employee and lower FICA contributions for employers. Employees are given vouchers instead of cash, which are signed and turned in by providers, who are paid by TVC. *Contact:* TVC, 5836 Corporate Ave., Ste. 150, Cypress, CA 90630 (714/821-4540).

child care A relatively new employee benefit: providing day care facilities and personnel either on-site or near-site to care for the children of employees, or providing full or partial reimbursement for such care.

Child Care Action Campaign (CCAC)
A national, nonprofit coalition of individuals and organizations established to stimulate and support the development of policies and programs that increase the availability of quality, affordable, child care for the benefit of children, their families, and the economic well-being of the nation. CCAC provides information and original research to parents, the general public, and government and corporate policy makers about the needs of families and children. CCAC emphasizes the connection between these needs and the nation's prosperity, and advocates for additional investment in child care by employers, labor, and federal, state, and local governments. *Contact:* CCAC, 330 Seventh Ave., 17th Fl., New York, NY 10001-5010 (212/239-0138; Fax 212/268-6515; E-mail **hn5746@handsnet.org**).

child care facility A building or facility designed or modified to provide child care. Ideally it provides a safe, healthful, and caring environment and fosters creative development and learning in the children it serves.

Child Care Infrastructure Act of 1997
Introduced by Sen. Herbert Kohl, D-Wis. The bill would offer tax credits to private companies and institutions that acquire, build, expand, or repair on- or near-site child care centers or otherwise get involved in increasing the availability of child care through much means as reserving slots in existing centers or contracting with counseling and referral firms for employees.

child care resource and referral program (CCR&R) Services provided to employees through in-house sources or by contract with a community-based resource and referral agency. They may inform employees about the different forms of child care available in the community, identify the ones that have vacancies, provide detailed information about each service, help parents choose the best arrangement for their child, help new child care programs get started, and speak out on child care issues.

child labor law Under federal law, 14- and 15-year olds are allowed to work only three hours per day and a maximum of 18 hours per week when school is in session and only between the hours of 6 a.m. and 7 p.m. They may work longer hours on weekends and during the summer.

children's disability As redefined by the **Personal Responsibility and Work Opportunity Reconciliation Act of 1996** requires that a disabled child under the **Supplemental Security Income** program must meet these requirements: (1) the child has a physical or mental condition that can be medically proven and which results in marked and severe functional limitations: (2) the medically proven physical or mental condition must last or be expected to last at least 12 months or be expected to result in death; and (3) a child may not be considered disabled if he or she is working at a job that is considered to be substantial work. The law also requires a redetermination of disability for a child during the one year period beginning on the individual's 18th birthday.

child support enforcement (CSE)
The responsibility of a variety of public agencies; for example, in Massachusetts, Child Support Enforcement is a division of the Department of Revenue. These agencies track down child support evaders, collect payments by intercepting tax refunds, mailing demand notices, and assessing liens and levies, or by arresting delinquent noncustodial parents. In many cases such agencies

have written agreements with the courts, law enforcement, and other agencies specifying in detail roles and responsibilities in the child support enforcement area.

chip A very thin, square, or rectangular piece of silicon on which the circuit elements of a semiconductor device have been printed or formed.

chiropractic An alternative form of manipulative medical treatment involving "adjustment" of the spine and joints to relieve back pain and other ailments and to improve overall health.

chiropractic care or medicine
Provided by Doctors of Chiropractic. Relies on muscle, skeletal, and nutritional adjustment and manipulation combined with professional counsel to activate the body's own recuperative powers to heal or relieve injuries, disabilities, and pain without drugs or surgery.

chiropractic HMO A **health maintenance organization** that provides managed care and specializes in **chiropractic** treatment.

chi-square test (χ^2) A statistical technique used to screen data to compare observed versus rhetorical frequencies of occurrence of events or phenomena. The test indicates whether the actual differences observed are greater than could be expected by chance alone. Critical values of x^2 are specified for desired probability levels after allowing for a parameter called the number of "degrees of freedom." The calculations are too involved for satisfactory explanation here and are best left to a statistician.

chlorofluorocarbons (CFCs)
Ozone-depleting chemicals used in industrial cleaning operations. Depletion of the ozone layer above the earth allows high amounts of ultraviolet radiation to penetrate the earth's atmosphere, increasing the incidence of skin cancer. About 3 billion pounds of these chemicals are used each year.

choke In desktop publishing, image size reduction.

cholesterol An essential body product for many functions. It is manufactured by many organs such as the liver, the skin, and the intestines and is also found in most foods of animal origin. Plant foods are usually free of the substance. Cholesterol comes from two sources: (1) foods high in cholesterol and saturated fat, and (2) the body itself, which produces cholesterol primarily in the liver. It is indispensable for brain and nervous system growth as well as for the body's manufacture of sex hormones. However, high cholesterol levels increase the risk of of coronary heart disease.

Christa McAuliffe Teacher Program
A program expanded by the **Higher Education Amendments of 1992.** The program is designed to recognize and retain outstanding teachers by providing grants to teachers to cover the expenses of sabbaticals or innovative projects.

chrominance In video, the color, saturation, and he information encoded in a video signal.

chromosome A component of human genes. Each of the 46 human chromosomes contains the **deoxyribonucleic acid** for thousands of individuals genes, the chemical units of heredity.

chronic fatigue syndrome (CFS)
A syndrome of unknown causes and increasing frequency characterized by combinations of such symptoms as emotional distress and/or depression, extreme fatigue, headache, intestinal distress, abdominal pain, low grade fever, sleep disturbances, memory and concentration problems, lymph node swelling, muscle and joint pain, and recurring sore throats. Strikes more women than men, and people who get it are typically in their thirties. Some believe that it is due to a chronic infection with Epstein-Barr virus (EBV), the virus that causes acute infectious mononucleosis (mono). Symptoms may persist for months or years.

chronic illness An illness characterized by repetitive episodes or continuous affliction, usually incurable.

chronic mononucleosis-like syndrome
See chronic fatigue syndrome.

churning 1. In health care, the unethical practice of seeing a patient more often than is medically necessary to increase revenue. Also a performance-based reimbursement system with a heavy emphasis on productivity; for example, rewarding a provider for seeing a large number of patients. 2. In risk management, the illegal and unethical practice of persuading customers to use the built-up cash value of older life insurance policies to finance new and more expensive ones and deceiving them about the cost of the transaction and the extent to which it damages the older policy.

cirrhosis Chronic, permanent scarring of the liver caused most often by alcohol abuse although viral hepatitis and some forms of gallbladder and biliary disease also cause a type of cirrhosis. If the damage continues, progressive liver failure and death may result.

Civilian Health and Medical Program of the Uniformed Services (CHAMPUS) A program that entitles spouses and children of members of the **uniformed services** and retired members to health benefits provided by civilian sources (with some restrictions), such as hospitalization, outpatient care, prescription drugs, treatment of medical and surgical and nervous, mental, and chronic conditions, treatment of contagious diseases, and immunizations when required as a part of medical treatment. Eligibility is limited to (1) dependents (including those between 21 and 23 years of age and enrolled in a full-time course of higher learning or are mentally retarded or physically incapacitated) of service members serving on active duty for more than 30 days or who died while serving on such duty; (2) retired members of the uniformed services entitled to retired, retainer, or equivalent pay or who died in such status. Upon reaching age 65, military retirees lose eligibility for all types of civilian care under CHAMPUS, although they retain eligibility for health care in military facilities.

civilian reduction in force *See* Fiscal 1993 Defense Authorization Act.

civil rights Covers a variety of individual rights created by state and federal constitutions, statutes and regulations, or court decisions in such areas as education, employment, and medical care to identify but a few.

Civil Rights Act of 1866 Established the property rights of all citizens in every State and Territory.

Civil Rights Act of 1870 Established equal rights for all citizens of every State and Territory to make and enforce contracts, sue, give evidence, and enjoy security of person and property.

Civil Rights Act of 1871 Established liability of persons who deprive any rights, privileges, or immunities secured by the Constitution to any citizen or any other persons within the jurisdiction of any State or Territory to an action at law.

Civil Rights Act of 1964 (CRA) Title VII of the Act prohibits discrimination in hiring, firing, promotion, compensation and other terms, privileges, and conditions of employment and facilities based on an employee's race, color, religion, sex, or national origin. Provisions relate to application forms and photographs, help-wanted ads, interviews, physical examinations, formal tests, and assessment centers. The Act applies to state and local governments and all public and private organizations engaged in interstate commerce, including employment agencies and labor unions, which have at least 15 employees. The Act also established the Equal Employment Opportunity Commission (EEOC). The EEOC issued the Uniform Guidelines on Employee Selection. A 1992 amendment (Section 705) created a revolving fund within the (EEOC) which allows it to charge employers and individuals reasonable fees for some of its services to offset the costs of new services, such as developing training programs and producing videos.

Civil Rights Act of 1968 The Act identifies federally protected activities. Among them willful injury, intimidation, or interference by anyone, on account of race, color, religion, or national origin, to dissuade or prevent participation in any benefit, service, privilege, program, facility, or activity provided or administered by the U.S. government, applying for or enjoying employment by any agency of the federal government, and enrolling in any public school or public college. The Act also establishes penalties for violators.

Civil Rights Act of 1990 A bill designed to modify or overturn six recent decisions of the Supreme Court including one in 1989 which adjusted the burden of proof in cases involving disparate impact in employment practices. Passed by both houses of Congress, the bill was vetoed by the President October 22, 1990. The Senate sustained the President's veto October 24, 1990. It voted 66 to 34 to override--one vote short of the number needed to enact the bill over the President's veto.

Civil Rights Act of 1991 Amends the **Civil rights Act of 1964.** It allows employees to receive compensatory and punitive damages when civil rights violations are committed with malice or reckless disregard to an individual's federally protected rights. Requires employers to demonstrate that their allegedly discriminatory practices are job-related and consistent with business necessity. The Act also allows women and employees with disabilities to to sue for compensatory and punitive damages and allows jury trials in discrimination cases. The Act established caps for punitive damages for companies with between 15 and 100 employees at $50,000 and $300,000 for companies with more than 500 employees.

Civil Rights and Women's Equity in Employment Act of 1991 Partially offsets seven Supreme Court decisions that made it more difficult for victims of employment discrimination, including the disabled, to sue and collect damages for job discrimination. In addition to lawsuits for discrimination in promotion and dismissal, the Act permits victims of intentional sexual discrimination, including sexual harassment, to seek compensatory and punitive damages, up to fixed limits (ranging from $50,000 for companies with between 15 and 100 employees and up to $300,000 for organizations with more than 500 employees). Employers are now required to demonstrate that their allegedly discriminatory practices are job-related and consistent with business necessity. The bill (1) allows plaintiffs who litigate intentional discrimination claims under Title VII to have their claims heard by a jury and, if successful, to recover compensatory and punitive damages; (2) requires companies to establish the business necessity of any employment practice deemed to have a disparate impact on members of a protected class; (3) provides that when an employee's race, color, religion, sex, or national origin is a "contributing factor" to an employment decision, that decision is unlawful; (4) ensures that seniority systems developed through collective bargaining agreements, which have the intent of discriminating against a protected class, may be challenged throughout the period that the pact remains in effect; (5) shortens the time during which an employee may challenge any employment practice that follows an earlier consent decree or order which resolved an employment discrimination claim under federal statute; and (6) expands the period for filing discrimination charges with the EEOC from 180 days

to two years. The bill also encourages alternative dispute resolution procedures (such as mediation and arbitration) to avert jury trials. The Act also made it easier to sue for age bias at work by repealing the 2-year statute of limitations for filing job-discrimination lawsuits under the federal Age Discrimination in Employment Act of 1967. Plaintiffs may now go into court at any time following the filing of charges with the Equal Employment Opportunity Commission.

Civil Service Reform Act of 1978 (CSRA) Prescribed certain rights and obligations of employees of the federal government including the right to form, join, or act as a representative for a labor union, or refrain from such activity. It identified specific unfair labor practices, standards of conduct for labor organizations, and grievances, appeals, and review procedures. The Act also outlined the characteristics of a mandated performance appraisal system for federal employees.

Civil Service Retirement Spouse Equity Act of 1984 (CSRSPEA) Requires that any annuitant covered by the Civil Service Retirement System who marries after 1986 to pay a deposit to the Civil Service Retirement Fund if he or she wishes to provide a survivor annuity for a spouse. The deposit equals the difference between the full annuity and the reduced annuity for every month since retirement that the annuitant had not been married, plus a six percent interest charge.

Civil Service Retirement System (CSRS) Until January 1984, CSRS was the only retirement system available to employees of the federal government. At that time the **Federal Employee Retirement System** (FERS) was established to cover all new hires. CSRS, however, still has 1.8 million participating workers, so it will be in effect for many years to come.

claim A request to an insurance carrier or intermediary by a beneficiary or a provider, acting on behalf of a beneficiary, for payment of benefits.

claims assistance professional (CAP) A specialist hired by an individual patient who wishes to challenge a medical or health care claims denial by a commercial insurer and facilitate payment. Some CAPs contract with employers to provide their services for employees. Typically have a background in insurance or have served on the staff of a medical provider.

claims processor A contractor that handles **Civilian Health and Medical Programs of the Uniformed Services (CHAMPUS)** claims for care received within a particular state or country. Also called *fiscal intermediaries.*

claims review In health care, a form of retrospective review that occurs after a case is finished and the patient is discharged. It involves the examination of claims and sometimes review of hospital records for improprieties and errors.

claims substantiation Written benefits statements required by an employer or insurer from a qualified and independent third party stating the date and type and amount of medical service provided by a health care professional or facility and affirming that those services were not reimbursed by another health care plan.

clanning The inclination of people to join up, belong to, or hang out with groups with similar beliefs, interests, or preferences to feel more secure and to validate their own values. Attributed to Faith Popcorn and Lys Marigold, *Clicking: 16 Trends to Future fit Your Life, Your Work and Your Business.*

class action A legal action or lawsuit brought on behalf of a group of people who find themselves similarly aggrieved, injured, or situated.

classroom configuration One of the basic types of room layouts used for small group meetings and conferences. With or without desks or tablet armchairs, the seating arrangement allows all attendees to face the speaker and screens used for audiovisuals.

classroom responder *See* trainee response system.

Clayton Antitrust Act of 1914 (CAA)
A supplement to the **Sherman Antitrust Act of 1890**. The CAA was passed to prevent substantial suppression of competition and the creation of monopolies. It proscribes restraining orders or injunctions by any court in any case between an employer and employees or employees and persons seeking employment involving a dispute over terms or conditions of employment unless necessary to prevent irreparable injury to property. The Act also covers mergers, acquisitions, and interlocking directorates. It states that a corporation is entitled to expand by internal growth, but it may not do so freely through acquisitions and mergers. Section 7 of the Act must be considered before entering into negotiations with respect to the stock or assets of other corporations.

Clean Air Amendments Act of 1990
Enacted to protect human health and the environment by controlling smog, reducing acid rain, protecting the ozone layer, and reducing toxic air pollutants. Implementing regulations have been prepared by the Environmental Protection Agency. Among them is a set of rules that allows utilities and others to buy and sell emission credits Another regulation requires tighter emission controls on new incinerators and chemical plants. Another regulation requires companies with 100 or more employees to reduce the number of automobiles coming to work during the peak hours of 6 to 10 a.m.

Clean Air Amendments Act of 1995
Amends the Clean Air Act to provide an optional provision to reduce work-related vehicle trips and miles traveled in ozone nonattainment areas designated as severe. Allows states to require employers in such areas to implement programs to reduce work-related vehicle trips and miles traveled by employees. and may also require that employers increase average passenger occupancy per vehicle in commuting trips between home and the workplace during peak travel periods. Signed by the President December 23, 1995.

Clean Indoor Air Act of of 1988
Mandates that many public buildings, including post offices, open meetings of governmental bodies, museums, libraries, elevators, supermarkets, all public mass transit, and domestic airline flights (up to 3,000 miles) be smoke-free.

clean sheeting **1.** In general, the practice of scrapping a current policy, program, or system and starting over — establishing a completely new approach from "scratch." **2.** A ploy used by unethical insurance agents to exploit the fears and misconceptions of people who are afraid of medical bills. Here the agent deliberately fails to mention ailments on the application form that the buyer has so that the policy won't be denied by the insurance company. When the insured party files a claim, the company may refuse to pay it on the grounds that the application contained false statements.

Cleft Palate Foundation (CPF) A nonprofit organization dedicated to assisting parents with birth defects of the head and neck and their families. CPF helps patients and their families understand these birth defects through informational brochures and fact sheets. Through CLEFTLINE, a toll-free informational service, CPF refers interested parties to groups of professionals in their area who are skilled in the management of cleft lip, cleft palate, and other craniofacial deformities. CPF is also involved in educating professionals and the public about the problems and treatment of people born with these defects. *Contact:* CPF, 1218 Grandview Ave., Pittsburgh, PA 15211-9906 (800/242-5338 or 412/481-1376; Fax 412/481-0847).

click stream On the **Internet** the path a subscriber follows while locating information.

client-centered counseling
See non-directive counseling.

client/server architecture Describes a new relationship between computers — whether large capacity mainframes, high-powered minicomputers, personal computers, or powerful workstations, permitting front-end and back-end computers to share computing responsibility. One computer operates as the client and the other as the server instead of the earlier relationship where the more powerful computer served as the master and the less powerful as the slave. So, the identities of the client and the server are not fixed — they depend on how the equipment is configured by the manufacturer, vendor, or user. Also known as *cooperative processing*.

client-specific benchmarking
A one-on-one form of benchmarking used to create tailored solutions to improve management for a specific client or organization, evaluating its policies, processes, and procedures against a database.

cliff vesting A form of **vesting** schedule in which full (100 percent) vesting occurs after 10 years of service, with no vesting before completion of 10 years of service.

climate survey A variant of the **attitude and opinion survey**. Attempts to measure employee attitudes toward factors considered important in establishing the climate of an organization: clarity of goals and standards, working relationships, opportunities for personal development, management's credibility, degree of authority and responsibility, and so on. *See also* organization climate survey.

Clinical Laboratory Amendments of 1988 (CLIA) Implemented by the Health Care financing Administration. Effective September 1, 1992, the amendments call for higher fees (as much as 6 percent) when employers send employee and job applicant samples to a laboratory for drug testing unless the laboratory is certified by the National Institute on Drug Abuse.

clinical/major depression A disabling medical illness that costs society billions of dollars for worker absenteeism, diminished productivity, and health care costs. Major depression interferes with working, sleeping eating, and enjoying pleasurable activities. *Also called* unipolar illness.

clinical psychological interview An interview conducted by a therapist (psychologist) that emphasizes psychotherapeutic counseling and uses case-history data and active participation by the counselor in the reeducation of the client.

clinic without walls *See* group practice without walls.

Clintonesque A derogatory term used to describe a style of leadership that is characterized by shifts in position, half measures, temporizing, and questionable strategizing.

Clinton health care reform plan *See* Task Force on National Health Care Reform.

clip A portion of video or audio source material stored on a tape or disc.

clip art In desktop publishing, collections of digitally stored, professional-quality, high resolution art in a large number of subject categories packaged on floppy disks or CD-ROM disks for both Macintosh and IBM-compatible computers.

clock hour A measure of instructor work load and student course load and a means of converting time to credit hours in colleges, universities, and technical schools. One clock hour is a minimum of 50 minutes of instruction, excluding breaks. *See also* credit hour.

close corporation A type of business venture that is limited by law to 30 to 50 stockholders, depending on the state in which the company is incorporated. Close corporations allow business owners to work almost like a partnership without the formalities and record keeping requirements of a general corporation.

closed captions Subtitles of the audio portion (dialog and narration) of a television program or home videocassette printed as large, east-to-read letters on the bottom of the TV screen or monitor. They are similar to subtitles on foreign movies. Closed captioning is a free service of the television industry, but captions remain invisible or "closed" without a decoder. Decoders are easily connected to any TV and are usually compatible with VCRs, cable TV hookups, and satellite receivers. Captions enable deaf and hearing-impaired people to understand all of a program's content and are also used to teach or learn English as a second language. *Contact:* National Captioning Institute, Inc. (NCI), 5203 Leesburg Pike, Falls Church, VA 22041 [1-800/533-WORD (Voice); 800-321-TDDS (TDD); 703/998-2400 (Voice or TDD)].

closed-form questionnaire   A questionnaire that contains a list of items to be checked, a list of alternative responses to be selected, or blanks to be filled in by words or numbers.

closed-loop system   In training, a system that is an organized and orderly whole with clearly definable and interacting components, has a mission or objective, has several interdependent and interacting components, and has some type of feedback mechanism.

closed panel   A managed care plan that contracts with physicians on an exclusive basis for services; that is, the providers are not allowed to see patients of their own.

closed-pay system   A pay system in which the amount of pay employees receive is kept secret. Theoretically, no employee knows what his or her fellow workers are being paid.

closed shop   A union security measure that requires a company to hire only union members. It was outlawed in 1947 but still remains in a few industries.

Closing Agreement Program (CAP) An **Internal Revenue Service** (IRS) enforcement vehicle for qualified pension plans initiated in 1990. The plan allows employers avoid plan disqualification by remedying certain types of violations and paying a fine. The program enables employers to talk to the IRS anonymously and negotiate fines without risk. Also called *John Doe cases.*

Closing the Gap   Publishes an annual resource directory on adaptive equipment and the companies that manufacture and distribute it.

Contact: Closing the Gap, P.O. Box 68, Henderson, MN 56044 (612/248-3294).

clustering   *See* mind-mapping.

coach fare   A full-fare, economy-class published airfare, usually referred to as "Y" class.

coaching   A one-on-one, face-to-face teaching/learning/counseling relationship designed to develop job-related knowledge and skills and improve performance. Involves a continuous flow of instructions, comments, and suggestions from coach to employee — listening, questioning, relating learning to the learner's experiences, and providing guided practice. Also called *tutoring.*

coaxial cable   A type of cable that features a central conductor surrounded by an insulator, a shield, and an outer insulating jacket.

cocaine   An illegal and highly addictive narcotic. Cocaine is a bitter crystalline alkaloid made from coca leaves and is snuffed or snorted. Also called *coke, snow, freebase, rock,* and *crack.*

cochlear implant   A medical device for the profoundly deaf that is surgically implanted in the bone behind the ear with a thin, flexible coil containing electrodes threaded through the cochlea, the snail-shaped portion of the inner ear. The device bypasses parts of the damaged inner ear and stimulates the auditory nerve directly. Although it does not restore hearing, over time, the implant provides sensations of sound, improves compensation skills, such as lip reading, and enhances ability to function fully in the hearing world.

cocooning   The penchant of people to state-at-home to protect themselves from the capricious realities of the outside world. Attributed to Faith Popcorn and Lys Marigold, *Clicking: 16 Trends to Future fit Your Life, Your Work and Your Business.*

codec   From COmpressor and DECompressor. Hardware or software the compresses and decompresses digitized video.

code division multiple access (CDMA) A form of digital wireless technology. Assigns a code to all speech bits addressed to a single wireless phone, transmits a scrambled transmission of the encoded speech, and reassembles the speech in its original format when it is received by its intended recipient.

code gaming   Insurance ripoffs, some bordering on fraud, by unscrupulous physicians and other health care providers to maintain incomes which have been eroded by the increasing costs of operating a medical or related practice, such as malpractice insurance and laws against balance billing. The most common are **upcoding**, **unbundling**, and **exploding**.

codependency Originally applied to spouses, children, and "significant others" of alcohol- and drug-dependent people, "codependency" now is applied to the disorder thought by some to reach all lives touched by substance abuse. It is characterized by loss of contact with one's own feelings, definition of self in terms of the abuser, and attempts to manipulate and control the behavior of the substance abuser. It moves the center of balance of codependent individuals outside of themselves rather than focusing on their own well-being and personal development.

code words Terms that when taken alone do not appear to be discriminatory, but in reality may be inherently racist. For example, referring to a person of a different race as "one of them" or "another one" indicates bias.

codicil An amendment to an existing will executed with the same formalities as the original will.

coefficient of correlation A measure of the extent to which a relationship exists between two sets of measures for the same group of subjects. The most common measure is the product-moment correlation; others used in special situations are rank, biserial, and tetrachoric. Coefficients range from 0.00, indicating a complete absence of relationship, to +1.00 and −1.00 indicating respectively perfect positive or perfect negative relationships.

coercive power Power that exists because certain people are granted or assume the right to apply overt or covert sanctions — to inflict punishment or negative outcomes on others in return for noncompliance with direction or desired behavior.

cognition The capacity for acquiring information or knowledge; the act or faculty of knowing.

cognitive ability test A psychological test used in employee selection or training to measure an individual's mental abilities or ability to learn and reason.

cognitive competencies Capabilities that portend success in professional, technical, or managerial jobs. They include expertise, analytical thinking, and conceptual thinking.

cognitive domain 1. A classification of instructional objectives that deals with the recall or recognition of knowledge and the development of mental skills and abilities. According to **Bloom's taxonomy**, these objectives can be classified into one of six categories: knowledge, comprehension, application, analysis, synthesis, or evaluation. 2. Applied to human learning, the area of learning that is represented by facts, knowledge, and skills, rather than feelings. See also affective domain; psychomotor domain.

cognitive enhancement Use of chemicals, such as food supplements and prescription drugs, to improve mental skills and abilities and memory.

cognitive impairment Deterioration of an individual's intellectual capacity of such severity that it requires continual supervision to protect the person or others. It is typically established by clinical evidence and standardized tests that measure impairment in terms of short or long term memory, orientation to person, place, and time, and deductive or abstract reasoning. Such impairment can results from Alzheimer's disease, other forms of senility, or irreversible dementia.

cognitive modeling Techniques used to teach conceptual skills, thought processes, and language. The approach is rooted in the same learning theory used in behavior modeling. It attempts to make covert mental responses observable.

cognitive psychology A theory that holds that people are self-responsible and that their behavior is entirely dependent on their original thinking, values, and ethics.

cognitive skills See cognitive competencies.

cognitive theory of learning A theory that works on understanding how the mind processes information; that is, how human thought or reasoning occurs. Learning is seen as internal to the individual — the consequence of insight.

cognitivism See cognitive theory of learning.

coinsurance In employee benefits, a cost-sharing requirement. Coinsurance provides that a beneficiary will assume a portion or percentage of the reasonable and customary costs of covered medical or other health care services, usually after paying the deductible. Under Medicare, it is the amount that a beneficiary is responsible for paying — usually 20 percent.

coke The powdered form of cocaine that is snuffed or snorted.

cold leads A ploy used by private insurance companies with official-sounding names. They send out cards to senior citizens, purporting to advise them about changes in their income taxes or their Medicare insurance. The recipients think that the card is from the government or a nonprofit organization. But, when they respond, their names are sold for anywhere from $10 to $25 to a **medigap insurance** company, which then sends salespersons to the respondent.

collaboration The process in which employees at all levels work together, build consensus, and establish alinement and ownership, thereby producing self-esteem, mutual respect, trust, integrity, and positive organization results. Believed by some destined to replace hierarchy as the organizing principle for managing and leading in the twenty-first century.

collaborative appraisal Cooperative appraisal or evaluation of performance involving both the manager and the employee. They jointly establish the standards, choose the performance measures, evaluate progress and accomplishment, identify needed improvements, and establish an action plan.

collaborative community A technique that makes use of group meetings to involve employees in solving organization problems and establishing goals and plans. Attributed to Ronald Lippett and Eva Schindler-Rainman.

collaborative learning Learning that focuses on group or cooperative efforts among instructors (faculty) and trainees (students) to achieve learning objectives. It emphasizes interaction and participation through dialog aimed at idea- and information-sharing.

collaborative marketing See comarketing.

collaborative method "A change process that harnesses the values of collaboration to the power of the workplace culture to produce long-lasting change and breakthrough results for the enterprise." Attributed to Edward M. Marshall, *Transforming the Way We Work: The Power of the Collaborative Workplace,* AMACOM, 1995.

collaborative negotiation Coined by a Harvard Law School study group to describe a new skill needed by HR people to exercise leadership and resolve organization conflicts. In their roles as "negotiators" the Harvard group identified three "hats": arbitrator, advocate, and arbiter.

collaborative relationships 1. Any means of dealing more effectively with the business environment. **2.** Arrangements in which two or more companies share resources and risks to cut the costs of research and development and manufacturing. **3.** Health care organizations that share expensive diagnostic equipment such as cat scanners.

collaboratives See compacts.

collaborative workplace A work environment in which the organization is led and managed by people working in teams but without team bosses, although one team member is typically designated the contact person or spokesman for the team.

collective bargaining Good faith negotiations conducted between a union and an organization to reach an agreement or contract regarding work-related issues and problems such as pay, benefits, hours, working conditions, and the like and the execution of a written contract incorporating agreements reached if requested by either party.

collective bargaining agreement See labor-management contract.

College and University Personnel Association (CUPA) An international network of approximately 6,200 human resource administrators representing over 1,800 colleges and universities. Established to promote the effective management and development of human resources in higher education. *Contact:* CUPA, 1233 20th St., N.W., Suite 503, Washington, DC 20036-1250 (202/429-0311; Fax 202/429-0149; E-mail **arothste@cupa.org** or **gsalguer@nova.umuc.edu**; URL **http://www.cupa.org**).

The College Board A nonprofit membership association of 3.000 schools, colleges, universities, associations, and agencies committed to promoting educational opportunity and improving academic standards. The Board sponsors programs in admissions, assessment, credit-by-examination, financial aid, guidance, and placement to assist in the transition from high school to college. *Contact:* The College Board, 45 Columbus Ave., New York NY 10023-6992 (212/713-8000; Fax 212/713-8277; E-mail **first initial, last**

name@collegeboard.org; URL **http://www. collegeboard.org**).

College-Level Examination Program (CLEP)   Designed to help adults obtain college credits for the knowledge and skills they have acquired through life experience. Sponsored by the College Board, CLEP offers five general examinations that test knowledge in the liberal arts and 30 subject-matter examinations in specific areas such as accounting, economics, foreign language, management, mathematics, and psychology. *Contact:* The College Board, 45 Columbus Ave., New York NY 10023-6917.

colloquy   Similar to a **panel**. Essentially a discussion between two teams, each representing different points of view.

color correction   In desktop publishing, any method of improving color rendition, such as dot-etching, re-etching, and scanning.

color cycling   In computer-generated imaging, a feature of the newer computer paint and animation programs. Provides an easy method of adding special effects to static images and a fast and efficient alternative to animation. For example, color cycling can create the effect of light flashing or glinting across an image.

color electronic prepress (CEP)   Systems that provide acceptable input from desktop equipment and direct input to printing equipment such as metal or paper printing plates (including those mounted on the press) with no film steps in between.

color gamut   In desktop publishing, the range of color a device can produce. A 24-bit color monitor can produce 16 million colors.

color graphics adapter (CGA)   In desktop publishing a low-resolution **bit-mapped** color video standard for IBM-compatible computers having a resolution of 320 by 200 **pixels** and capable of displaying four colors.

color healing   An alternative form of medical treatment in which colored light is shone on the body to alter its "vibrations" or aura.

color management system (CMS)   In desktop publishing and prepress, a means of insuring color consistency throughout a prepress system from the scanner to the computer monitor, to the color printer, and to the final separations. It corrects for differences in in device-specific color so that the image on the monitor matches its source. Composed of three major components: characterization, calibration, and color mapping.

color mapping   One of the three main components of a **color management system** in desktop publishing. Uses the scanner, monitor, printer, or image setter profiles built into the system to compare color spaces and provide an "electronic map" to move a file from the color space of one device into that of another device.

color scanner   An electronic device used to produce color separations from color originals. Color scanners perform one or more of the following functions: analyze the original; input data from the original; compress the tones for contrast, saturation, and brightness; produce the correct color hue; adjust the gray balance of the printing inks; increase the sharpness for better resolution; and store the corrected information in a temporary buffer. Most desktop scanners transfer the data directly to the connected computer, but the information may also be transferred to a page-makeup system, or it may be outputted as halftone positives or negatives.

color separation   The process of preparing a separate electronic or photographic record of the amounts of each process color of cyan, magenta, yellow, or black needed to reproduce an original copy. The record may be a photographic film made through red, green, and blue separation filters or a computer file. A set of four separations, cyan, magenta, yellow, and black, is required to reproduce an original color image. Separations may be made photographically or digitally using electronic scanners and computer programs. The original copy may be a transparency, photographic print, drawing, painting, or printed reproduction.

color space   A way of defining color. Color monitors, which produce colors by firing red, green, and blue phosphors (RGB), use an RGB space. Image setters use the cyan, magenta, yellow, and black (CMYK) color space.

comarketing   Collaboration between companies in such areas as logistics, selling, advertising, promotion, public relations, and distribution. Also called *collaborative marketing* and *alliance venturing*.

combination fee   A fee charged by a lawyer, consultant, contractor, or other nonemployee that incorporates two or more of the following types of fees : **contingency fee, fixed fee, hourly charge, reduced fee, retainer, or reverse contingency.**

combined approach A form of a concepts-based, integrated curriculum. Incorporates aspects of the **holistic approach, infusion approach, interdisciplinary approach, integrative brainwork approach, mind/brain function approach, thematic approach, and topics-within-discipline approach.** Attributed to Betty Jean Eklund Shoemaker, "Education 2000 Integrated Curriculum," *Phi Delta Kappan,* June 1991.

comfort care Hospital care aimed solely at comfort, not therapy, resuscitation, or life extension. Such care would be listed under a "palliative" or "comfort" code on Medicare forms.

command An instruction that causes a computer to do something.

command discipline *See* imposed discipline.

command-driven interface One of the basic types of user interfaces found in microcomputers. Used to get the computer to perform tasks simply by typing in a command — a word or phrase representing the desired action.

Commerce Business Daily (CBD) A publication of the Department of Commerce, the *CBD* is the most comprehensive source of federal solicitation notices (**RFP**s) available. Each CBD contains up to 1,000 procurement notices with entries classified as services or supplies. Another section lists the type and value of recently awarded contracts. *Contact:* Superintendent of Documents, U.S. government Printing Office, Washington, DC 20402-9325 (202/783-3238).

commercial espionage *See* business espionage.

commercial intelligence *See* business intelligence.

commercial paper In investment, short-term, unsecured promissory notes issued to finance short-term credit needs.

commercial rate In meeting management, a special room rate, lower than **rack rate,** for companies that have made prior arrangements with the hotel property.

commissaries *See* Defense Commissary Agency.

The Commissioned Corps of the U.S. Public Health Service Web site provides information on the history and mission of the Service and information about job openings. URL **http://phs.os.dhhs.gov/phs/corps/**

Commissioned Officers Association of the US Public Health Service (COA) An association of 6,900 active duty, retired, inactive reserve, and former commissioned officers of the U.S. Public Health Service. Its mission is to advance the Public Health Service Commissioned Corps by uniting and serving Corps officers and advocating for their interests through leadership and communication. *Contact:* COA, 8201 Corporate Dr., Ste. 560, Landover, MD 20785 (301/731-9080; Fax 301/731-9084; E-mail **mikecoa@aol.com**).

Commission on Achieving Necessary Skills (CANS) A commission established by the Secretary of Labor to study the competencies that children must master to have "**workplace know-how.**" It drew upon educators, state public officials, business people, and labor leaders and reported to the Secretary of Labor in 1991.

Commission on Recognition of Postsecondary Accreditation (CORPA) Created to assure the quality of postsecondary education through the process of voluntary, nongovernmental accreditation. Establishes criteria and provisions for the evaluation and recognition of accrediting agencies. *Contact:* CORPA, One Dupont Circle, N.W., Suite 305, Washington, DC 20036 (202/452-1433; Fax 202/331-9571).

commission-only planner A financial or other type of planner who charges no fees to create plans, but is compensated solely by commissions received from the products sold when the plan is implemented.

Commission on the Future of Worker-Management Relations Established by Secretary of Labor Robert B. Reich and Secretary of Commerce Ronald H. Brown to find ways "to enhance workplace productivity through labor-management cooperation and employee participation" and to consider possible labor law reforms and the use of **alternative dispute resolution procedures** in the workplace.

committee A device used by managers to improve communications, share information and ideas, and provide a means of involving employees in policy making and decision making. Essentially, it is a group of persons appointed or elected to perform a specific function, the nature of which determines the composition of the group, its manner of operation, and its ultimate authority and responsibility. Committees may take the forms of standing (permanent) or *ad hoc* (temporary) committees and perform such functions as policy making (legislative), executive (administrative), judicial (adjudicative), advisory (consultative), or research (investigative).

common business-oriented language (COBOL) A computer programming language used since the 1970s in many mainframe business computers to code programs.

common carrier A company engaged in interstate communications by wire or radio as defined in Section 3(h) of the Communications Act of 1934, as amended.

common gateway interface (CGI) scripts Web server extensions used to control access to compute files.

common hardware reference platform (CHRP) Pronounced "chirp." Boxes that run a variety of operating systems, such as Mac OS, Windows NT, and UNIX (AIX). **common procedural terminology (CPT)** Codes approved by the **American Medical Association** for use in identifying common medical procedures in automated systems for handling insurance claims.

common user access (CUA) A line of applications software that presents a common face to the user regardless of the application.

common user interface (CUI) Provides access to network resources at all work stations using similar or identical screens, commands, and control structures so that users don't have to learn new procedures.

communication The process by which facts, ideas, information, opinions, meanings, emotions, and understanding are exchanged among human beings. It employs speaking and listening, seeing, reading, and writing, and motions, facial expressions, and body language.

Communications Assistance for Law Enforcement Act of 1994 Mandates the installation of undetectable circuits for eavesdropping on wired and wireless voice and data communications from remote surveillance offices located throughout the country. Phone companies are required to install these wiretap circuits or pay $10,000 per day in penalties.

communications assistant (CA) A professional who is specially trained to meet the communications needs of people with hearing and/or speech disabilities including relaying conversation in American Sign Language syntax. Serves as **telecommunications relay systems** operator who relays conversations using a **text telephone** and a regular telephone. The communications assistant transliterates conversation from text to voice and from voice to text.

Communications Media Management Association (CMMA) An organization of about 200 managers of media departments in business and industrial companies. CMMA is dedicated to the professional growth of corporate and education communications managers. Its major objectives are to strengthen the management and technical skills of the membership and maintain an effective network for sharing ideas or seeking answers. Holds two conferences and several regional meetings each year. *Contact:* CMMA, P.O. Box 227, 607 Arbor Ave., Wheaton IL 60189 (630/653-2772; Fax 630/653-2882).

communications server A computer dedicated to providing communications into to a local area network (LAN), and, often, external to the network, including E-mail.

communication training Training provided to improve the skills of employees at all levels of the organization in generating, transmitting, and receiving information. It encompasses training in listening, speaking, writing, and reading.

Communications Workers of America (CWA) A labor union affiliated with the AFL–CIO representing employees in telecommunications, printing and news media, public service, health care, cable television, general manufacturing, electronics, gas and electric utilities, and other fields. CWA has a membership of 600,000 in the United States and Canada in more than 1,200 chartered unions. *Contact:* CWA, 501 3rd St., N.W., Washington, DC 20001-2797 (202/434-1100; Fax 202/434-1279; E-mail **cwa@capcon.net**; URL **http://www.cwa-union.org**).

community mental health centers Specially qualified facilities that provide partial hospitalization for mental health care.

Under certain conditions, Medicare Part B helps pay for care provided these centers.

community property A form of **joint ownership**. The law provides that any property acquired by either spouse by the work, talent, or other productive capacity or effort of either spouse during marriage is owned by both spouses regardless of whose name is on the title. Property acquired by one spouse by gift, devise, bequest, or descent is not included. Arizona, California, Idaho, Louisiana, Nevada, New Mexico, Texas, Washington, and Wisconsin are community property states. State laws differ considerably; however they usually permit one spouse to leave his or her share of community property to whomever he or she chooses. Community property is subject to **probate**.

community rating A health care insurance plan under which an insurance company sets its rates only on the basis of what benefits are offered and the heath claims experience of all those covered in a given community. Therefore subscribers in the "community" (such employers within a state), workers employed by large and small firms and self-employed persons would pay the same premiums. Originally designed to spread the risk of medical costs by charging a single premium regardless of age, gender, income, or medical condition, over the last 20 years it has taken the forms of **cherry picking** and **cream skimming.**

community rating by class A modified form of **community rating** in which premiums are based on age and sex, but not on claims experience.

community relations Actions taken by an organization to build cooperation and mutually helpful relationships and to win public support. It may take the forms of participating in community funding, voter registration, and other types of drives and projects, volunteerism, and cooperative educational ventures.

community standards Values and standards established by custom and accepted by the majority of the members of a region or individual community as right and proper behavior for all people. Examples are concern for wildlife, participation in community political and social affairs, sharing in harvesting activities, and support for youth activities and programs.

compact A partnership or alliance among businesses, educational institutions, and municipal governments to achieve such goals as improved educational opportunity, higher educational standards, reduction in the school dropout rate, increased attendance, and helping high school and college students get summer jobs, part-time jobs while in school, and full-time jobs following graduation.

compact disc (CD) A distortion-free, long-playing digital recording. A means of storing data, the device makes use of small (five-inch) rigid discs, which can store full text, still- and full-motion video, graphics, and audio, and it permits random access. Data can be read into computers for display or manipulation. Storage may be permanent (ROM) or erasable and rewritten once (WORM). Requires special equipment to read and write.

compact disc interactive (CD-I) A interactive multimedia device, a means of combining audio, visual, and computer data on a single medium. A relatively expensive technology for CD-ROM-based consumer multimedia. Consists of a separate device with its own built-in computer. To develop training applications, the device requires tools to provide emulation. A product of Philips Corporation. The three main suppliers of CD-I development tools are Interactive Support Group, Inc. of Chatsworth, California, Script Systems, Inc. of Mohawk, New York, and Optimage, a Phillips/Microware partnership based in Des Moines, Iowa.

compact disc player (CDP) A means of playing back compact discs.

compact disc, read-only memory (CD-ROM) Originally a medium for storing and reproducing music, the technology can be used in training and education, information systems, and a wide range of other areas as a data publication and retrieval medium for use with personal computer systems. Each CD-ROM can store approximately 550 MB of read-only information — more than 150,000 pages of text.

compact disc, read only memory extended architecture (CD-ROM XA) An industry standard for adding audio and video file formats to a CD-ROM disc. Offered by Sony, IBM, Philips, NEC, Chinon, and many other manufacturers.

company creed An organization's **philosophy** of management to which all members of an organization are expected to subscribe. It is usually reduced to written form and consists of a set of simple statements of beliefs and intents.

Company Information A directory of company information that contains mission statements, product descriptions, and annual reports (**http://www.companyname.com** — for example, **http://www.cryslercorp.com**).

comparable factors *See* compensable factors.

comparable worth Applies to job evaluation and the administration of compensation programs. It is a concept and a strategy designed to overcome the male-female salary gap and the pay inequities caused by what have traditionally been female jobs. It promotes the concept of "equal pay for work of equal worth." Male and female jobs, including dissimilar jobs, are compared and matched in terms of difficulty and requirements (skill, effort, and responsibility), and matching salaries are established for the female jobs.

compa-ratio The relationship, expressed as a percent, of actual salaries to the midpoint of the salary range established for a job within the salary grade structure. For example, if an employee in Grade 9 has a salary of $32,000 and the Grade 9 midpoint is $36,000, the employee has a compa-ratio of 88.9 percent ($32,000 divided by $36,000).

comparative ratings An approach to rating that compares people; that is, each person is rated only in comparison with others. Examples are rank order, equal intervals, paired comparisons, and forced distribution rating methods.

compatibility **1.** The ability of a computer to run software and/or use peripheral equipment designed for another computer. **2.** The ability of all parts of a system (computer, printer, software, and so on) to work together.

compbusters Measures taken to eliminate or reduce the incidence of employee accidents, injuries, or other sources of claims for compensation.

compelled self-defamation A legal tort that holds employers liable for giving a false or incorrect reason to an employee for his or her termination, knowing that the employee will have to pass the reason on to a prospective employer.

compensable factors In job evaluation, the basic criteria used to to determine the relative worth of jobs. They consist of the attributes which, in the judgment of management, constitute the basis for establishing relative worth; for example, knowledge, skills, training, experience, accountability, responsibility, working conditions, and so on.

compensation Remuneration for work performed or services rendered in the form of pay and allowances, salaries, wages, stipends, fees and commissions, and bonuses and stock options. For some purposes, such as state taxes, compensation is defined as money paid out over a period of less than 10 years.

compensatory education Educational programs designed to help low-achieving students (the educationally disadvantaged) catch up with their peers and keep up.

compensatory opportunity *See* affirmative action; race-norming.

compensatory time Time off the job and away from the workplace earned by workers by working overtime, on weekends or holidays, or during scheduled vacations. Usually limited to exempt employees; nonexempt workers are paid overtime wages. In 1996, a law changing the minimum wage also specified that employee commute time to and from work in company vehicles would not be compensable.

compensatory training Training provided to remedy worker deficiencies in knowledge and skills. Includes basic skills training, remedial training, and retraining.

competence A social concept involving a comparative judgment about the value or worth of human performance. It is comparative in that it compares typical performance with exemplary performance.

competencies A generic mix of knowledge, skills, and attitudes with broad application. Taught in an integrated way to prepare an individual for many jobs and tasks. Examples are problem solving, troubleshooting, and reasoning.

competency assessment In selection for employment or promotion, evaluation of potential based on appraisal of skills and abilities.

competency-based pay Compensation based on evaluations that focus on individual job skills and behaviors.

competency-based test In selection and training, a test that measures specific skills or competencies, rather than job knowledge.

competency-based training Training that is rooted in the skills and competencies required for acceptable job performance as determined by job and task analysis.

competency-based vocational-technical education (CBVE) Education based on performance objectives that define what the learner must do, under what conditions, and to what standard.

competency evaluation An approach to evaluation that measures the effectiveness of a training or other type of program by comparing the achievement of participants against established competency standards.

competency power Power derived from expertise. It is power and authority based on skills and experience. It is exemplified by leading by example.

competition-based pricing The process of letting competitors establish the prices and then setting your prices low enough to eclipse or keep out the competition to maintain or improve market share. Obviously, price concessions can increase sales. However, irresponsible competitive pricing often results in retaliation by competitors. If carried too far, it can lead to price wars and price attrition.

competitive benchmarking Determining which company or organization, whether a competitor or noncompetitor, provides the best products or services.

competitive intelligence Information collected legally and ethically about how competitors achieve superior performance and productivity. Includes reviewing industry publications, accessing electronic databases, probing internal company experts, and tapping industry observers and commentators, such as academics and consultants, and interrogating customers, clients, dealers, and suppliers. Represents a necessary preliminary step in the **benchmarking** process. *See also* business intelligence; business espionage.

competitive medical plan (CMP) In general, a prepayment health care plan requiring fixed monthly payments and minimal copayments. CMPs with corporate or Medicare contracts offer beneficiaries all services covered by fee-for-service Medicare or other private plans. More specifically, a CMP is

(1) state licensed; (2) provides health care on a prepaid, capitated basis; (3) provides care primarily through physicians who are employees or partners of the entity; (4) assumes full financial risk on a prospective basis with provisions for **stop loss, reinsurance**, and risk sharing with providers; and (5) meets the Public Health Service Act requirement of protection against insolvency.

compiled list A computerized list of of individuals and organizations assembled from existing public and proprietary data sources, such as phone books, trade show attendees, car registrations, association member directories, and product warranty cards.

complaint The original statement made in a civil case detailing the reasons the plaintiff is entitled to the aid or relief of the court.

complementary care Alternative treatments such as **acupressure, biofeedback, guided imagery, hypnotherapy, meditation,** prayer, **reflexology, therapeutic touch,** and **yoga.** Sometimes used with cancer patients as adjuncts to surgery, radiation, and chemotherapy.

completed staff work Products of your people's labor that arrive at your desk ready for your signature — or at least in final draft, ready for review and approval.

complete meeting package (CMP) A pricing method used by conference centers. It is based on per-person, per-day and typically includes room, food, beverage refreshment breaks (except liquor and tax), conference services (meeting room, breakouts, support staff, gratuities, and audiovisual basics), and recreation facilities.

completion item A test item that requires the testee to "fill in the blanks."

complexity theory A spin-off from **chaos theory.** Postulates that, in complex organizations such as businesses, simple agents obeying simple rules can interact to create elaborate and unexpected behavior and positive results.

compliance program Criteria established by the U.S. Sentencing Commission to determine whether a company has an effective program to prevent fraud, theft, or antitrust violations. Its seven elements: (1) the company has policies defining standards and procedures to be used by its agents and employees; (2) a specific high-level person in the organization has been given responsibility for ensuring compliance with policy; (3) the organization has used due care not to delegate significant discretionary authority to persons whom the organization knew, or should have known, had a propensity to engage in illegal activities; (4) the company has effectively communicated it standards and procedures to its agents and employees; (5) the company has taken reasonable steps to achieve compliance with standards, such as monitoring, audits, and reporting systems; (6) the standards have been consistently enforced by means of appropriate disciplinary mechanisms; and (7) when an offense has been detected, the organization has taken reasonable steps to ensure that it could not occur again.

composite review and analysis Evaluation of an organization's operating program as a whole, developed and presented by the head of the organization. It makes use of the vertical reviews and analyses prepared by subordinate managers.

composite score A single score that combines several scores, usually simply by summing them, but sometimes weights are assigned to the separate scores to increase or decrease their importance in the total composite score.

compositing The process of combining multiple layers of video and/or audio into one image.

comprehensive benefit package A health care insurance package in which each participant is covered for as many essential services as the system can afford.

comprehensive budgeting A general term covering all types of budgets used in a company such as the annual budget and supplementary budgets.

comprehensive budget program Characteristic of most for-profit organizations. Consists of two major components: the annual profit plan and the **financial budget**.

Comprehensive Employment and Training Act of 1973 (CETA) Provided for block grants to 475 state and local units of government, which served as prime sponsors. Prime sponsors identified employment and training needs in their geographical areas and planned and operated job training and the services needed to meet those needs. CETA funds were used for classroom instruction in occupational skills and other job-related

training, on-the-job training by public and private employers; recruitment, orientation, counseling, testing, and placement; and support services such as medical and child care services. CETA legislation expired at the end of FY 1982 and was replaced by the Job Training Partnership Act of 1982.

Comprehensive Environmental Response, Compensation, and Liability Act (CERCLA) of 1980 One of five major environmental laws since significantly revised, expanded, and extended. The Act identifies 717 hazardous substances.

comprehensive interview An employment interview in which the interviewer, in addition to asking specific, preplanned questions, is encouraged to probe important points as they arise in the interview.

comprehensive medical coverage Medical insurance plans that cover hospitalization and the fees of medical and surgical practitioners. Often includes prescription drugs.

comprehensiveness One of the characteristics of an acceptable test. A test is comprehensive when it takes liberal and complete samples from whatever is being measured — the objectives of the training program or system.

comprehensive outpatient rehabilitation facility (CORF) A health care facility that provides speech, occupational, and respiratory therapies and counseling and related services. If prescribed by a physician and the facility participates in Medicare, Part B Medicare will pay for services provided.

compressed speech Spoken material recorded at normal speed and played back 3 to 5 or more times faster than the recorded version. It makes use of the known fact that humans can receive and understand aural material much faster than the typical person can articulate it. Used in training to save time.

compressed workweek A scheduling plan that allows employees to rearrange their work hours to help balance work and family responsibilities. For example, the 40-hour work week could be compressed into four 10-hour workdays, or a fortnightly schedule may be used to allow workers one additional day off every two weeks.

compression 1. In wage and salary administration, pay differentials between classes of workers (supervisors and workers, new hires and experienced workers, and job grades, for example) that are too small to be fair and equitable. **2.** Any one of several means of reducing the size of a computer file. Enables the user to fit a large multimedia program on a disc or transmit it over a computer network.

comps Free airline passes; to the airlines, known as non-revenue tickets. They are issued to travel agents, employees of the issuing carrier, employees of other airlines, corporate meeting managers, travel consultants, frequent flier award recipients, and game show or raffle winners. They typically have several restrictions, such as vulnerability to bumping, blackout periods when tickets are not valid, and no advance seat selection or special meal reservations.

comp self-insurance An alternate way of financing coverage for workers' compensation claims. Employers band together in **self-insurance groups** that operate somewhat like risk pools. Objectives include having funding at least match claims payments and building surpluses that can be returned to the employers.

Comp Time Act of 1996 *See* Working Families Flexibility Act of 1996.

CompuServe® An international personal computer network that provides subscribers with instant access, 24 hours a day, 7 days a week, to on-line information, communication, and entertainment products and services for a monthly fee: news, sports, and weather; electronic mail; reference library; shopping; financial information; travel and leisure; entertainment and games; and membership support services. *Contact:* CompuServe®, 5000 Arlington Centre Blvd., P.O. Box 20212, Columbus, OH 43220 (800/848-8199 or 614/457-0802).

computed tomography (CT) A new version of a medical diagnostic imaging technology that makes use of X-rays, a powerful computer, and more sensitive scintillation detectors and provides greater speed, accuracy, diagnostic acuity, and patient comfort than its predecessor, computerized axial tomography (CAT) scanning equipment. Used in scanning the brain for infarcts, hemorrhages, and tumors; the chest for tumors and mediastrinum (spaces between the pleural sacs of the lungs); the abdomen for tumors and other anomalies in the kidneys, pancreas, and liver; and the spine and limbs

for herniated disks, tumors, and other anomalies.

computer A digital device that stores and relays information and images using a series of 1's and 0's. There are several types and many different makes: mainframes, minicomputers, microcomputers, and microprocessors. Also applies to analog devices.

computer-aided (assisted) instruction (CAI) Training that involves the use of computers to conduct, or assist in conducting, instruction. It involves software and learningware that permit the individual learner to proceed at his or her own pace through an instructional sequence or package. Sometimes linked to video or other media, including written documentation. Also called *computer-based training*.

computer-aided software engineering (CASE) Compute programs that capture user requirements and automate the programming process.

computer-assisted design (CAD) A system that uses computers to execute graphic design and engineering analysis functions. In tandem with computer-assisted engineering, engineers and designers can manipulate symbols on a computer monitor, store earlier designs and engineering data, and generate machine instructions directly from the design.

computer-assisted engineering (CAE) A stand-alone manufacturing technology used to create systems applications. The approach can also be used in conjunction with other components.

computer-assisted job evaluation (CAJE) An alternative to the traditional **point-factor method** of job evaluation claimed by some to be capable of producing automatically a job description, a job evaluation, and a quality assurance report on the accuracy of a job analysis. At the very least, the computer-driven system speeds up the job evaluation process, but the ultimate accuracy of the system depends on the appropriateness and quality of the input and the techniques used to establish the standards.

computer-assisted manufacturing (CAM) A system that uses computers to execute manufacturing processes.

computer-assisted retrieval (CAR) A system that links a computer and a microform reader so that data and graphics can be accessed automatically, easily, and quickly. Used in records management.

computer-based coaching Use of a computer as a job aid. The aid is controlled by the workers — that is, they initiate it and decide when they don't need it, based on their performance of job tasks.

computer-based education (CBE) The use of computers in formal education programs at any level of public or private education.

computer-based instruction (CBI)
See computer-based training.

computer-based learning (CBT) Used by some to describe all forms of computer-driven instructional strategies, such as computer-assisted instruction, computer-based education, computer-based training, and computer-managed instruction.

computer-based learning resources (CBLR) Software used to make learning easier, more appropriate, or more enjoyable. The program contains information useful to the learner but does not, in itself, teach; for example, a **database**.

computer-based reference (CBR) Software that delivers text on a computer terminal screen and supports such features as on-line help, on-line manuals, directories, glossaries, indexes, message boards, and connections to or interface with computer-based training.

computer-based training (CBT) The use of computers to deliver instructional packages either at a central training facility or at the workplace through modems. It is used to teach job knowledge or skills. Lessons are presented in the following modes: drill and practice, tutorial, problem solving, instructional games, modeling, problem solving, and simulation. CBT is controlled by others in the sense that others schedule the training, structure the flow, determine alternative sequences, and administer the tests.

computer-based corporate videoconferencing A system that incorporates simultaneous document and data exchange as well as voice and video.

computer conferencing An extension of the electronic mail concept. A system that permits several computer users in different locations and at different times to hold an electronic "conference call" on a particular topic, contributing to a group discussion without the restrictions of time or space. The systems makes use of modems and telephone lines or satellite communications. Also called *computer-enhanced project*

management, expert networking, and *on-line brainstorming.*

Computer Education Management Association (CEdMA) A professional organization made up of individuals who manage training businesses in companies manufacturing computer hardware and software. Provides a forum for managers and directors of computer education organizations. Its goal is to to shape the future of the industry for excellence in education, training and learning in ways that benefit members, customers, partners, and other employees within member organizations. In collaboration with the **Information Technology Association**, created the **Certified Technical Trainer Program**. Contact: CEdMA (512/794-5832 E-mail **board@cedma.org**; URL **http:www.CEdMA.org**)

computer-enhanced project management
See computer conferencing.

computer graphics Sketches, drawings, charts and graphs, and photographs, including 3-dimensional images in black-and-white or color, either generated by a computer or accessed from disks or stacks containing **clip art** or photographs.

computer-integrated manufacturing (CIM) A technology that integrates the process of design and the digital output of design directly down to the loading of instructions onto the assembly line. It combines the storage capacity of CD-ROM with video technology and gives employees immediate access to information right on the work site. The system answers their questions, provides background information, and furnishes video demonstration of processes or procedures on request. Also called *flexible manufacturing system.*

computerized axial tomography (CAT) A medical diagnostic imaging technology (CAT scan) by which a three-dimensional image of a body structure is constructed by computer from a series of plan cross-sectional images made along an axis by radiography.

computerized braces An experimental computerized brace that controls muscle tremors in people with multiple sclerosis and other diseases

computerized numerically controlled machining (CNCM) Stand-alone flexible production machines used with ancillary machines or equipment. Includes systems that permit digital control of machine tools such as cutting and stamping machines, using a series of binary-coded instructions.

computerized reservation system (CRS) In travel management, computer systems, privately owned by airlines, commonly used by travel agents to make inquiries about, reserve, book, and issue travel arrangements.

computerized tomography (CT) A medical diagnostic technology. Employs scanners that use multiple X rays to locate and determine injuries, abnormalities, tumors, and so on.

computer literacy Knowledge of the capabilities of data processing equipment, systems, and software and how to use the services of the data processing department. May or may not involve the ability to use a personal computer.

computer literacy training Training designed to alleviate anxieties about automation, improve manager and user attitudes toward and satisfaction with data processing services, and teach employees how to communicate with computers and computer personnel and how to read and interpret the output of computers. Typically covers the capabilities of company data processing systems, hardware and software components, data communications (teleprocessing and terminals, data base inquiry systems, and on-line and off-line processing), data processing personnel and their functions, data security, and how to use computer services (how to identify input requirements and how to read and use system outputs). Strategies include group discussion, study assignments, computer-assisted instruction, multimedia presentations, demonstration, and hands-on performance and practice.

computer-managed instruction (CMI) The use of a computer with its associated hardware, software, and learningware to manage instructional systems and programs. CMI performs such time-consuming tasks as testing trainees and tracking and recording their progress and accomplishment; developing and implementing training prescriptions tailored to the needs of individual trainees; maintaining inventories and records pertaining to trainees, training space, facilities, equipment, materials, and supplies; and performing other resources allocation, accounting, and reporting functions.

computer-managed training (CMT) See computer-managed instruction.

computerphobia Literally, fear of computers. Often a major hurdle following the installation of computer systems. Employees at all levels sometimes have trouble adapting to the new system and continue to use manual methods of doing things.

computer program A set of instructions, usually written in a special computer language, that a computer uses in processing data.

computer-related training Training provided to employees at all levels of organization to ensure optimum and effective use of data processing facilities and services.

computer reservation system (CRS) A system used to service corporate travel accounts to effect savings, control policy, ensure consistency in the preparation of office reports, and interface with **electronic mailbox/mail**. From an airline's perspective, CRS contributes to profitability by adding booking fee revenues and enhancing market share. Regulations for its use (except by corporations) to prevent anti-competitive practices, are issued by the Department of Transportation.

computer simulation The most widely used and versatile type of simulation. A mathematical model that employs a digital computer to study the behavior of complex systems to represent a real system by incorporating and manipulating large amounts of relevant and realistic detail. Computer simulations are used in such areas as management, engineering, physical sciences, social sciences, and military war gaming.

computer-supported learning resources (CSLR) See computer-based learning resources.

computer synthetic voice translation A technology that converts printed text into artificial speech. Also known as *voice synthesis*.

concentration knowledge and skills One of three types of industry standards to be developed by voluntary partnerships under guidelines issued by the **National Skill Standards Board:** knowledge and skills that relate to a broad area within an economic sector — more specific than **core knowledge and skills** and less specific than **specialty knowledge and skills.** For example, for manufacturing concentration knowledge and skills might be concerned with product assembly.

concept A form or level of learning that involves the acquisition of complex ideas, models, and theories.

concepts-based, integrated curriculum
A generic term used to describe several different approaches to the development and implementation of an interconnected and coherent educational program.

concept search   A World Wide Web search for documents related conceptually to a word, rather than containing the word itself.

conceptual framework   A basic principle of learning. Maintains that the learner must understand where a lesson is leading and provide a structure or pattern for organizing and integrating the knowledge and skills that are the desired learning outcomes.

conceptual skills   Essentially visualizing skills that involve the ability to think incisively and systematically about abstractions, develop and use conceptual models, see the whole picture without being constrained by any of its parts, and tolerate ambiguity. For example, for a manager, they involve the ability to see the organization as a whole, how various functions depend on each other, how they interact, and how changes in one part affect all the others.

concierge   The hotel functionary responsible personal services, such as making arrangements and reservations for transportation (including airline reservations), dining, tours, and theater and sporting events tickets for guests.

concierge level   In meeting management, an entire floor or floors of a hotel reserved for very important persons. Also called *club level* or *tower level*.

concierge benefits   On-site or near-site benefits provided by employers, such as banking, health and medical, ticketing, convenience store, cafeteria take-out, dry cleaning, and hair salon services.

concierge services   Services provided to busy employees by a company for a monthly fee. Examples are shopping for groceries, picking up dry cleaning, running other errands, and planning social events.

conciliation   A formal request "to conciliate" (reconcile) made by the Equal Employment Opportunity Commission when it issues a "cause" finding (reason to believe that discrimination has taken place) following a **fact-finding conference** to investigate a charge of discrimination.

Concurrent Admissions Program (CONAP)
A program for Army or Army Selected Reserve enlistees in cooperation with participating colleges and universities. If the soldier meets the college's admission standards, he or she receives a CONAP Student Agreement, a student file is created, and the soldier is assigned an academic advisor. While on active duty, the soldier may earn credits by enrolling in college courses, the **College Level Examination Program,** taking other national tests, or completing Army Skill Training and for experience in his or her Military Occupational Specialty. The college CONAP advisor helps the soldier transfer the credits to the college and, when he or she leaves the Army or completes initial active duty formal training in the Army Selected Reserve, help in making the transition from soldier to student.

concurrent authoring system   A computer authoring system that has all of the components of a a conventional language plus the ability to interact with an executing application. Attributed to Richard Getler (*CBT Directions,* November 1991, p. 14). He identifies five primary command elements that distinguish it: (1) load and run an application program; (2) write "on top of" the application screen to display prompts and explanations in the form of windows, text, or graphics while the application is on screen; (3) control which keystrokes typed by the user are passed along to the application program; (4) generate keystrokes that are fed to the application as if they were typed at a physical keyboard; and (5) monitor the state of the application by reading the status of the screen.

concurrent engineering   A means of speeding up the design of new products. Involves putting people from different departments together to design the product — such as design and production engineers, quality assurance and reliability specialists, and marketing experts. Also called *integrated product development.*

concurrent receipt   Simultaneous payment of military retirement pay and veterans' disability pay with no decrement to either. Currently, the law requires the reduction of military retired pay by the amount of veterans' disability pay received, but because disability pay is not taxed a net financial gain accrues to the retiree with a disability. Although proponents of a change in the law, who claim that the offset is unfair, the Department of Defense has long opposed any change.

concurrent review   In health care, managing utilization during hospitalization by tracking length of stay, gathering information (utilization management nurses conducting in-person and telephone rounds), and discharge planning and followup.

concurrent session In conference and meeting planning, a session devoted to a particular topic. Typically several concurrent sessions are offered to registrants to enable them to pursue their interests.

concurrent validity In test construction, the practice of comparing the test scores of employees with their current performance as a means of verifying the validity of a test. The approach is questionable because current employees may not be representative of new applicants for positions.

conditioned response In learning theory, classical conditioning, a response that occurs in the presence of a neutral stimulus following repeated pairing of a neutral stimulus with an adequate stimulus without regard to the subject's behavior.

conditions The second element of behavioral objectives. Describe clearly and completely the conditions under which trainees must be able to demonstrate the behavior or performance. Conditions identify what the trainees will be given to use in doing the job (tools, equipment, job aids, references, materials), what they will be denied (tools, equipment, and the like), what assistance they will have (if any), what supervision will be provided, and the physical environment in which they must perform (climate, space, light, and the like). The conditions part of the objective statement invariably begins, "Given:".

conditions of employment Organizational policies and work rules that apply to employees; for example, probationary periods, absences, tardiness, rest periods, vacations, overtime, suspensions, layoffs, dismissals, and such special circumstances as bereavement, pregnancy, childbirth or adoption, and accommodation for religious observances. Such conditions must be clearly defined, codified, and communicated to all concerned.

conductive hearing loss The least common cause of deafness. It affects the outer or middle ear and results when sound waves are not properly conducted to the inner ear. Its causes include ear infections, immobilization of one of the bones in the middle ear, a punctured ear drum, or excessive ear wax.

conduit IRA *See* rollover.

conference **1.** A meeting of members of an association; for example, an annual conference. **2.** A meeting convened for consultation, discussion, or instruction.

The Conference Board A world-wide network of more than 20,000 CEOs and other senior executives in over 50 nations. Its purpose is to improve the global business enterprise system and enhance the contribution of business to society. The Board conducts management and economic research, holds a wide variety of meetings and briefings around the world, and provides forums for business leaders to exchange information and ideas. *Contact:* The Conference Board, 845 Third Avenue, New York, NY 10022 (212/759-0900; E-mail **info@conference-board.org**; URL **http://www.conference-board.org**).

conference center A facility designed and operated to serve the needs of conferees for accessible, dedicated, functional, secure, and attractive meeting, dining, recreation, and sleeping space, which minimizes distractions and provides an effective learning environment. Meeting areas are equipped with podiums, lecterns, flip charts, white boards, audiovisual equipment, including front and rear screen projectors, television, tape recorders, and are wired for personal computers and satellite down links.

conference centers *See* corporate center; executive center; university center.

conference configuration One of the basic types of room layouts used for small group meetings and conferences. Usually includes tables and chairs for two to four (or more) participants arranged in a hollow rectangle or square.

conference method One of the basic instructional methods. Makes use of group discussion techniques to reach an instructional objective. Techniques include questions, answers, and comments from the group leader in combination with answers, comments, and questions from group members.

conference packet In meeting management, a comprehensive collection of conference materials provided all attendees, usually during registration. Includes descriptions of program sessions, information on speakers and participants, agendas, schedules of events and logistical information. Also called *information kit, program book,* or *registration packet.*

conference services manager The hotel functionary responsible for meeting room setups and audiovisual arrangements for small groups.

confidentiality The need of organizations and individuals to protect themselves from others. For example, companies need to protect corporate goals, objectives, financial status, product development, and other information against the forays of competitors. People, too, need to protect the confidentiality of their personal, health, and family status, and their career goals and objectives and job performance.

confidentiality agreement An agreement signed by an employee stipulating that he or she will not disclose company plans, designs, financial position, or other proprietary matters either during employment with the firm or following termination for any reason.

Confined Spaces Standard Rules established by the **Occupational Safety and Health Administration** pertaining to the identification of "confined spaces" and the protection of employees from safety hazards arising from the use of those spaces. Those spaces are defined as areas not intended for employee occupancy, such as storage tanks, boilers, silos, and process vessels, which could have inadequate ventilation, hazardous atmospheres because of toxic fumes, or limited means of entrance or exit. The standards became effective in February 1992.

confirmatory test One of two categories of urine tests for substance abuse. The other is a **screening test**. Confirmatory tests are used when positive screening tests results occur, and they may be the basis for employers denying employment or termination.

confirmed reservation/confirmation In meeting management, an oral or written agreement by which a facility accepts a request for accommodations. To be binding, confirmation must include the intent of the two parties to the agreement, the date, the rate, type of accommodations, and the number to be accommodated. An oral agreement usually includes a requirement for a guest credit card number.

conflict of interest Conditions or situations in which the private financial or other interests of an individual officer, manager, other functionary, or group may profit or stand to benefit in some unacceptable or unfair way from an association, arrangement, or relationship with another group or individual.

conformity assessment An industrial term for laboratory testing that relates to product performance, health, or safety considerations

Conformity Europe (CE Mark) The European Union's standard for product health and safety designed and intended to replace national origins. The term is now only used as CE Mark.

congenital anomaly In health care, a condition existing at or from birth which is a significant deviation from the norm. Typically includes cleft lip, cleft palate, birthmarks, and webbed fingers or toes.

congregate (care) housing Typically sponsored by nonprofit agencies, congregate housing is usually an apartment complex that provides each occupant a full apartment with kitchen, serves meals in a central dining room, provides housekeeping, and sometimes such additional social services as personal and nutrition counseling.

congress In meeting management, the term used outside of the United States to describe a regular meeting of a large organization or group to discuss a subject of issue. A congress may last several days and have several concurrent sessions. National congresses are typically held annually, while international congresses are usually conducted less frequently than annually.

Congressional Accountability Act of 1996 Ended Congress' exemptions from discrimination and workplace laws and from lawsuits by employees. Applies 11 labor laws to Congress, including the Civil Rights Act of 1964, Age Discrimination in Employment Act of 1967, Occupational Safety and Health Act of 1970, Americans with Disabilities Act of 1990, and Family and Medical Leave Act of 1993.

congruity In training, a program in which the strategy or approach used reflects, parallels, complements, and supports the content covered--in other words, mirrors the knowledge and skills taught in the program.

conjoint analysis A marketing tool that involves combining several features of a product or service and presenting them to potential customers or focus groups as a single option or combining alternative levels of each of the desired features. The customers or focus group members then choose among the options.

conjunctive ticket An airline ticket that has multiple parts for multicity trips.

Connecticut v. Teal A 1982 U.S. Supreme Court decision relating to testing and discrimination. The Court ruled that although a large proportion of African-Americans passed a test that had not been validated and were promoted, that fact did not compensate for the possibility that the test discriminated against the African-Americans who failed it. Tests, therefore, must be validated.

connecting In meeting management, two or more hotel rooms with private connecting inside doors that permit access between the rooms without entering the corridor.

connection power A leaders' power derived from his or her associations with important or influential persons in the organization, such as key executives.

consanguinity A blood relationship between people as a result of their common ancestry. The rules of consanguinity in the law define who is closest on the family tree which in turn, for the most part, determines where property will pass upon the death of an individual who has no will.

consciousness-raising training *See* New Age Training.

consent decree An agreement reached between two disputants to resolve a claim of some kind; for example, an employment discrimination claim.

consent form A form used by employers to obtain written consent from employees for specified actions or practices.

consequentialism A theory of ethical reasoning that focuses on the consequences of human actions. All actions are judged in terms of the extent to which they achieve desirable results, and the concepts of right, wrong, and duty are subordinated to the end or purpose of an action. There are two types of consequentialist theory: (1) one that views right action as consequences, weighed against all available actions, that maximize my good; that is, what benefits me the most or hurts me the least; and (2) the more popular type known as utilitarianism, one that maintains that right action must maximize overall good; that is from the standpoint of the entire community.

conservator An person appointed by a probate court temporarily or permanently to make decisions on behalf of an incapacitated individual. Similar to a **guardian**, but authority is limited to managing the ward's property and making financial decisions.

conservatorship A legal means of managing the affairs of an individual who has become incapacitated. A conservator or custodian is appointed by the court and given either wide-ranging power (such as authority to sell property) or specific authority (such as check-cashing) to act for the individual.

consideration A benefit or value gained by the signers of a contract. Without consideration, no contract is valid.

consistency leadership A leadership theory. Holds that there are some constant, unchanging principles and concepts that provide a firm foundation for sound and effective leadership; therefore, consistency in the application of those concepts and principles will provide better results than attempting to adjust leadership behavior to fit the situation or change the situation to make it more compatible with leadership principles.

consolidated medical group A medical practice model in which physicians combine their resources to form a true medical group practice. The members of the group share assets and risks, but they continue to practice medicine in their own offices although they often occupy the same facility.

Consolidated Omnibus Budget Reconciliation Act of 1986 (COBRA) A comprehensive federal law with many provisions covering employee benefit plans. It applies to employers of 20 or more workers; excluded are church plans and government plans. COBRA mandates continuation of group health care insurance plans for up to 36 months, at workers' expense, after they leave the company, their work hours are reduced, or they die, divorce, legally separate, or their dependents **age out.** COBRA has been modified by virtually every comprehensive budget and tax law since its enactment. Effective January 1, 1990, Congress extended COBRA coverage to 29 months (up from 18 months) for disabled employees who receive Social Security benefits. That measure includes a provision requiring companies to offer continuation COBRA coverage to former employees until after their new employer's plan covers preexisting conditions. Other changes relate to new rules on Medicare as a qualifying event; multiemployer plans; controlled groups; self-employed individuals, partners, and outside directors, and other service providers; and partner-only plans. These changes will make it necessary for employers to modify existing COBRA forms and systems and may require reexamination of claims refused under the 1989 rules. Recent court decisions, new regulations and changes to the law: (1) An employer cannot drop COBRA as soon as a former employee is covered by another employer's health plan if the new employer's coverage contains a preexisting condition provision. (2) The spouse and dependents of an employee on COBRA who become entitled to Medicare can elect 36 months of coverage starting on the Medicare entitlement date.

Consolidation Loan   See Federal Family Education Loan Consolidation Loan; Direct Consolidation Loan.

consolidator   Similar to a **travel agent**. Consolidators buy blocks of tickets, mainly for international travel, and sell them at discount.

consortium child care center   A dependent care facility where the costs and responsibilities are shared by several employers, sometimes together with a community agency and/or a union. The consortium may form a not-for-profit corporation to fund a day care center located in downtown areas or in office parks convenient to all businesses contributing to the consortium. *See also* family day care network.

constant angular velocity (CAV)   One of two videodisc formats, methods of placing video frames on an optical disc. With CAV, the frames are set in concentric circles, with each frame having its own 360-degree track on the disc. That provides random access — making it possible for the laser reader to move from one track to the next and from one frame to the next.

constant linear velocity (CLV)   One of two videodisc formats, methods of placing video frames on an optical disc. This format permits placing more than one frame on each 360-degree track of the video disk, which provides longer playing time for the disc but without providing random access to frames.

Constitutional Law   The First (1791, Fifth (1791), Thirteenth (1865), and Fourteenth (1868) Amendments to the Constitution, which include provisions relating to individual rights.

constructed fare   A fare calculated by combining two or more fares in a specific market over either actual or fictional routing to yield a more economical fare than the published one in that market.

construct validity   **1.** In assessment centers and in other instruments and strategies used in selection, promotion, and evaluation, the requirement that the knowledge, skills, or other dimensions of performance to be measured be relevant to job performance. **2.** In tests, the extent to which a test measures some relatively abstract psychological trait. It is used to judge the appropriateness of personality, verbal ability, and mechanical aptitude tests.

consultant   One who offers expert business, professional, and technical advice and assistance to managers and staffers in an organization for a salary (internal) or a fee (external). Consultants guide and assist in solving problems, conducting projects, studies, and surveys, and apply methods and techniques to facilitate change and improvements in management and operations. They may also provide training for employees at all levels.

consultation and referral (C&S)   Services offered to employees to help them balance work/life demands. Include personal assistance to resolve such issues and problems as child, adult, and elder care planning, adoption assistance, school and college planning, school age programs and activities, summer camps and programs, in-home care consultation, sick and backup care planning, and family legal issues. Said to be flexible, personalized, cost-effective, and easy to implement. Formerly called *resource and referral services.*

consultative selling   The process by which a seller identifies the prospective buyer's specific needs and provides specific answers using the solutions of the seller's company. Aligning sales representatives with customer/client interests and concerns and acting as an adviser and consultant in jointly finding the best way to meet customer needs.

consulting pairs   *See* pairing; diversity training.

Consumer Price Index (CPI)   A government (Bureau of Labor Statistics, DOL) calculated and published index reflecting gains or losses in consumer purchasing power. It measures the changes in the price of consumer goods and services by making use of a preselected and fixed list of consumer products and commodities purchased by a hypothetical average family. Used in wage and salary administration and union contract negotiations.

Consumer Price Index for Urban Wage Earners and Clerical Workers (CPI-W)

A government (Bureau of Labor Statistics, DOL) calculated and published index that serves as the basis for computing annual cost-of-living adjustments in federally indexed retirement programs, such as civil service retirement and social security.

contact hours   A measure of instructor workload. The number of hours per week that an instructor is in direct contact with students in a classroom, laboratory, or other learning environment. *See also* credit hour.

contact manager (CM)   Powerful software that provides users with a means of managing their business relationships rather than their daily activities. Combines a database program with word processing capabilities to enable users to write letters and reports and send E-mail and faxes. Particularly useful for a networked business environment because it allows teams to share information and assignments. Examples are *ACT!* 2.0 for Windows and *Goldmine* from Lean Software.

contact signing   Systems of signed English that represent the English language using the hands, facial expressions, body movements, and fingerspelling. They blend the features of ASL and English. They are not a language, per se like ASL; rather, they are a visual depiction of English. The number of signs is infinite, and the rules are variable, depending on the signer's skills, the situation, the topic, and so on. Pidgin sign English, sometimes called contact signing, is used by deaf and hearing people to communicate with each other, so the vast majority of hearing parents, teachers, physicians, psychologists, speech therapists, religious workers, and employers that contact and work with deaf people use Pidgin Sign English.

content   The subject-matter to be learned in a training or education program — the facts, knowledge supports, specific concepts, principles, and elements of skill required for performance.

content standards   In curriculum, standards that establish what should be learned in various subject-matter areas.

content validity   Applies to selection, training, and testing. A selection strategy, training program, or test has content validity if it samples adequately from actual job content; that is, selection mechanisms, training objectives, and test items require performance or simulated performance of real job duties and tasks and the testing procedure requires behaviors and conditions similar to those required on the job.

context evaluation   Assessment of the job environment, including the attitudes of managers and workers toward training and development.

Context-Input-Process-Product (CIPP)

An evaluation model used to measure a program independently and in terms of its own stated goals (rather than comparing it with other programs). Evaluates a program in terms of (1) context (the extent to which goals and philosophy are shared by key program personnel and learners); (2) input (the resources available during program development and implementation and the extent to which they were used effectively); (3) process (the extent to which observed program development and instruction are congruent with program goals and research on instructional effectiveness); and (4) product (the extent to which indicators of program effectiveness and potential for continuation or expansion are present). (Attributed to Stufflebeam & Guba, 1971.)

context leadership   A theory of leadership that advocates shifting (or creating) contexts (how people and organizations see themselves or define their role in the work environment) instead of managing content (information and motivation). Human behavior is seen as a natural manifestation of context (beliefs or assumptions) and not as a function of content.

context-sensitive help   *See* electronic support system.

context variables In training research studies, variables that relate to conditions under which instructors teach, including such elements as trainee characteristics and the learning environment.

continental plan A hotel room rate that includes breakfast, dinner, and a room. Also called *Bermuda rate.*

contingency approach *See* contingency theory of learning.

contingency clause In contract law, a clause that relieves one or both parties of an obligation or pecuniary or other type of liability for the success of a venture due to the nonavailability or poor performance of a third party who is outside of the control of one or both of the parties. to the contract.

contingency fee A fee for services that is paid only under certain preagreed-upon conditions; for example, a fee paid to a lawyer consisting of a certain percentage of the gross amount awarded by the court as the result of a successful law suit. If no cash is awarded to the plaintiff, the lawyer customarily expects payment of out-of-pocket expenses only.

contingency leadership *See* situational leadership.

contingency theory of learning Rests on the assumption that, because people differ from each other in a great variety of ways, different approaches to learning tasks are essential. Two key concepts in the contingency theory are readiness to learn and the teachable moment.

contingency work force *See* contingent work force.

contingent annuity In benefits, an annuity that is payable to the annuitant until his or her death, at which point it becomes payable, in whole or in part, to a named survivor until his or her death.

contingent taker A person or persons named in a will who will inherit property if the first named person predeceases the writer of the will.

contingent worker Part-time, temporary, contract, and various types of free-lance workers. Typically receive low pay, few benefits, and enjoy little or no job security. A cost-saving strategy adopted by more and more organizations. As of 1992, numbered about 30 million workers — one in four in the United States. Also called *disposable worker or independent contractor.*

continuation of pay (COP) Regular compensation (with the usual deductions for taxes, insurance, and so on) paid to employees who have suffered on-the-job injuries. Also applies to compensation paid to employees for a set period of time following layoff or retirement.

continued care Health care benefits provided when a subscriber or employee has a lengthy illness or long recovery period. Typically provided in skilled nursing facilities, chronic disease hospitals, noncustodial nursing homes, home health care, or hospice care.

continuing care retirement community (CCRT) Usually sponsored by non-profit agencies and organizations for retired personnel, CCRTs are apartment complexes and individual housing units that provide health care services and a nursing facility on the premises for an entrance fee and monthly rental. The community makes a commitment to care for patrons, regardless of the status of their health, for as long as they reside in the community. In addition to drop-in assistance and medical care and guaranteed nursing home placement, there is a weekly housekeeping service, linen service, and exercise facilities. for an extra fee, residents can also have dental care, prescription drugs refills, and physical therapy.

continuing disability review (CDR) An evaluation to determine continuing eligibility for Social Security disability benefits required by law. The time between reviews depends on the beneficiary's age and the nature and severity of the medical condition on which the benefits are based, including the chance of medical improvement. Following the review, beneficiaries are placed in one of three medical reexamination categories: (1) medical improvement expected — review scheduled within 6 to 18 months of the most recent medical decision; (2) medical improvement possible — status scheduled for review every 3 years; or (3) medical improvement not expected — status scheduled for review every seven years. A full medical review involves an in depth field office interview, evaluation of the medical evidence of record by a state **Disability Determination**

Services examiner, and a possible consultative medical examination to obtain any additional information needed to assess the possibility of medical improvement of the beneficiary's present condition.

continuing education Programs of education and training offered by private and public educational institutions, professional and technical organizations and associations, and private and public businesses to upgrade the knowledge and skills of adult learners or to enhance and improve their general level of education.

continuing education unit (CEU) A measure of non-degree credit awarded to participants in training programs by professional associations, educational institutions, and some private firms upon completion of courses, seminars, or workshops. One CEU equals 10 hours of participation in an organized educational experience under the sponsorship and direction of a qualified training organization. Sponsored by the nonprofit **International Association for Continuing Education & Training**.

continuing professional education (CPE) Seen by many as a means of preventing obsolescence, remedying deficiencies, preparing for specialization, and maintaining the competency of practitioners in most fields of professional endeavor. Employs a variety of learning strategies. Programs are best developed by a team of planners representing the professionals, employers, clients, professional associations, and credentialing and regulatory agencies.

continuous budgeting A budgeting process that involves a constantly revised time frame achieved by rolling the time interval of the same length; for example, a semiannual budget is revised by dropping the month just ended and adding the next month at the end of the cycle.

continuous learning A process for getting employees to learn the things they need to know as they work. It may take such forms as group meetings of employees and their managers to share ideas and work on real corporate problems and use of inhouse-produced self-guided learning workbooks covering such topics as the corporate mission, culture, and values and the employee's role in the organization.

contract A document which, when it contains the following elements, is legally binding: (1) *offer* — a clear, complete, and unambiguous promise to perform a service or deliver a product; (2) *acceptance* — a clear, unequivocal, and timely expression of consent to the proposed contract or agreement; (3) *consideration* — a legally sufficient price, bargained and paid for an accepted offer; (4) *legal and possible objective* — a purpose to be achieved that is both legal and possible to accomplish; and (5) *competent parties* — legal capacity of both parties to enter into the contract.

contract administration The system by which a labor-management contract or collective bargaining agreement is administered on a day-to-day basis; for example, following the filing of a grievance, whether or not a contract provision has been violated.

contract deliverables A detailed list of of the products that will be delivered by the contractor. It gives the specifications, qualitative and quantitative product data, and any other information that will indicate precisely what the contracting organization will get for the funds expended.

contracting Used in labor negotiations, conflict resolution, purchasing, performance appraisal, coaching and counseling, and training. It is the process of getting two or more parties to arrive at an agreement and a commitment as to what each will do under prescribed conditions to reach a solution or to put a solution into effect.

contracting officer Relevant to marketing and sales in the government sector. Contracting officers are specialists in procurement and the managers of specific government procurements. They have been issued warrants that spell out the limitations of their authority and responsibilities. They manage fact finding, analysis, and planning as well as the actual negotiating process in dealing with bidders.

contract technical workers An alternative staffing option. Contracts with a technical services company to provide highly skilled workers, such as engineers and data processing specialists, to oversee, manage, or conduct long-term, highly complex projects.

contract training Use of outside sources (either on-site or off the premises) to provide training programs for operative, supervisory, or managerial personnel. Sources include colleges and universities, professional societies, management institutes and associations, and management and training companies and consultants.

contract worker Employee who works under contracts as the employee of a technical service firms. Such employees are not independent contractors or contingent workers.

Contract Work Hours and Safety Standards Act of 1962 (CWHSSA) An Act mandating that the wages of every laborer and mechanic employed by any contractor or subcontractor of government (U.S. agency, District of Columbia, or Territory) public works contracts, or for work financed in whole or in part by loans or grants by the federal government be computed on the basis of a standard work week of 40 hours and that a rate not less than one and one-half times the basic rate of pay be paid for all hours worked in excess of the forty hour workweek. The Act further states that no contractor or subcontractor shall require any laborer or mechanic to work in surroundings or under working conditions that are unsanitary, hazardous, or dangerous to health and safety.

contrast effect A type of rating error that is due to the tendency of raters to compare people with each other rather than with some preestablished standard.

contribution analysis A means of identifying noncontributing elements or activities in an organization. It is a way of looking at a department's activities to determine whether they are contributing to the results that some other element of the organization produces as a means of identifying fat to trim.

contributory benefits plan Benefits plan in which employees contribute part or all of the cost of benefits, with the employer covering the remainder of the costs, if any.

control chart Invented in the 1920s by Dr. Walter Shewhart and widely used until the end of World War II, discontinued, and reinstituted in the 1980s. A quality control tool used to monitor a process following the solution to quality control problems by more modern methods such as design of experiments, but experts maintain that they provide minimal return on investment. It is a

moving picture, rather than a snapshot, of the variations in a process. It shows how it is doing now, what its capabilities are, and how those capabilities are affected by changes in the process. Also designed to show how close a process comes on average to meeting desired objectives.

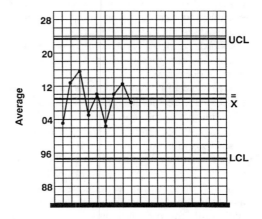

control group In HR research and training evaluation, a group of people who do not participate in the intervention or training program but who are similar to the experimental group in all relevant respects. It is used as the basis for comparing the effects of the experimental intervention or training program. *See also* experimental group.

controlled experiment The most rigorous form of research in which the researcher tests causal hypotheses by manipulating one or more independent variables (hypothesized causes) and measuring one or more dependent variables (hypothesized effects) while controlling all other variables. The technique requires the use of two groups of subjects: the experimental group (the one exposed to the "treatment" being investigated) and the control group (the group not exposed to the "treatment."

controller/comptroller **1.** The staff officer who has overall responsibility for the accounting function in an organization, organizes financial information, identifies problems, insures that all relevant information is properly considered in formulating strategic plans, and serves as the financial disciplinarian for the enterprise by exercising functional authority for financial matters. **2.** For meeting managers, the controller is the person who approves credit for groups and individuals and the itemizes bills relating to a meeting. May also be called the *chief accountant*.

controlling The managerial function concerned with insuring that events, activities, progress, and results match plans. It is the means of keeping plans and performance synchronized and on target. It is accomplished by establishing and applying measurable standards, assessing performance in terms of those standards, and applying corrective measures to remedy observed deviations. It ensures that what is done is what was intended.

control systems Career development processes used to monitor and control the work of individual employees and the organization as a whole; for example, financial reporting systems and performance review.

convenience arrangement An estate planning strategy designed to simplify the process of distributing a deceased person's assets without going through **probate** and with a minimum of difficulty. Essentially, the one persons (the transferor) conveys an asset held in his or her individual name into his or her name and the name of a second individual (the transferee) as joint tenants with the right of survivorship. The transfer results in ready access to funds in the event of death, other catastrophe, or to avoid probate. The transferee is usually a trusted family member, such as an adult child, a brother, or a sister.

convention A general and formal meeting of a professional, trade, social, economic, or legislative group convened to exchange information or obtain agreement on policies and procedures. Usually has a written set of objectives, is of limited duration, and is often accompanied by a trade show featuring suppliers of equipment, materials, and services.

conventionalism An approach to interpreting the U.S. Constitution. The philosophy or belief that says judicial interpretation should reflect accepted community moral principles and judgment.

conventional mortgage A means of financing the purchase of property in which a lump sum is borrowed using the property as security and then repaying the loan by making monthly payments.

conventional staffing Employing full-time, permanent workers at all or selected levels of organization to carry out needed company functions.

convention and visitors bureau (CVB) A nonprofit office established in most large cities that serves as the point-of-contact and source of help to organizations and individuals planning for conventions and meetings. CVBs provide this assistance without charge. They are funded by local appropriations and/or value-added and goods and services taxes. Services include advice on value dates, audiovisual presentations and brochures on local attractions, brochure shells, calendars of events, current local news advisories, facility, rates, and contact information, group familiarization tours, itinerary assistance, local supplier/vendor contacts, media lists, meeting planner guides, multilingual brochures, off-site special event coordination, press and public relations kits, site inspection arrangements, slides and photos, restaurant and attraction guides, spouse activity/event coordination, travel posters, and videos.

convention fare A special fare offered by airlines to attendees at the conferences and exhibitions of professional organizations. Discounts of from 45 to 75 percent off coach and 5 percent off supersaver fares may be offered.

Convention Liaison Council (CLC) An association of 26 organizations representing the convention, meeting, trade show, and exposition industry, and travel and tourism generally. Its purposes are to provide a focal point for the industry to exchange information, recommend solutions to industry problems, develop programs to serve the industry and its publics, and create an awareness of the magnitude of the industry. *Contact:* CLC, ASAE Headquarters, 1575 Eye St., Ste.1190, Washington, DC 20005-1168 (202/626-2709; Fax 202/406-9652).

convention services manager (CSM) In meeting management, a hotel or convention and visitors bureau staffer assigned to assist the organization with all aspects of meeting arrangements. Sometimes called a *conference coordinator*.

convergent thinking *See* vertical thinking.

conversational interview An employment interview that is basically unplanned and open-ended, more of a discussion than an interview. It is considered inefficient and ineffective as a selection device.

conversion insurance Coverage that gives former employees, whose **Consolidated**

Omnibus Budget Reconciliation Act of 1986 (COBRA) health insurance coverage has run out or who can't get health insurance elsewhere, the opportunity to buy coverage. It is more expensive than COBRA coverage, requires higher deductibles and copayments, has low lifetime limits, and doesn't include ancillary coverage (such as treatment for substance abuse). It is most often purchased by people who are between jobs (short-termers) and those who have chronic illnesses or are older but under age 65 and therefore not eligible for Medicare (long-termers).

convertible   In meeting management, a hotel room that contains a couch that opens into a double bed.

convertible security   In investment, a fixed-income security, such as a bond or preferred stock, that may be converted at a stated price within a specified period of time into a specified number of shares of common stock of the same or different issuer.

cookie   A means of tracking activity on the Internet. A cookie is a small file inserted on a user's hard drive when a Web site is visited for the first time. It tells the Web site who the visitor is and what parts of the site the user has visited before. Criticized as an invasion of privacy.

cooperative education Partnerships between businesses, industrial firms, or professional organizations and educational institutions to provide internships or first-hand experience, with college credit and pay, for college or university students engaged in studies relating to the business, industry, or profession. Such programs integrate classroom learning with professional experience in an employment setting related to the student's area of study.

Cooperative Information Clearinghouse and Library (CIC)   Provides a labor relations database and services at no charge. Information is available on about 600 successful labor-management committees, employee stock option (ownership) plans, gainsharing programs, and other cooperative efforts. The database is cross referenced for easy access by industry, union, or program type. The Library contains more than 2,700 books, publication abstracts, articles, and monographs in the area of labor-management relations. *Contact:* CIC, Bureau of Labor-Management Relations and Cooperative Programs, U.S. Department of Labor, Room

N-5402, 200 Constitution Ave., N.W., Washington, DC 20210.

cooperative learning   An interdisciplinary approach to education in which learners are carefully assigned to basic and expert groups on the basis of certain criteria and engage in formalized learning activities. One class session per new unit is reserved for expert groups, where one team member might be responsible for the social science perspective, another for the physical science aspect, one for art, another for literature, and one for media. Each student is held individually accountable for his or her own progress and success. Although all work leading up to the culminating activity, a unit essay, group grades are not given because each student submits his or her own essay. A typical class session consists of basic groups working together on a specific set of questions that direct their attention and get them to think in analytical and critical ways. Questions that encourage the use of high-order, cognitive thinking strategies are addressed to the entire group, which is then asked to discuss the issue briefly and come up with a collective answer. Then a group representative reports on what was discussed.

cooperative processing   *See* client/server architecture.

co-op programs *See* cooperative education.

coordinated care plan   The federal government's term for **managed care**.

Coordinated Care Program (CCP)   A **managed care** program and policy designed to improve the quality, access, and cost-effectiveness of Department of Defense health care. Key features: (1) beneficiary enrollment; (2) changes in beneficiary cost-shares; (3) creation of local networks of military and civilian providers; (4) creation of specialized Military Treatment Facilities; (5) merger of direct care and **Civilian Health and Medical Program of the Uniformed Services** operating and management funds; and (6) local accountability with central oversight. The CCP will attempt to control health care costs by maximizing use of military medical treatment facilities, obtaining better rates for purchased civilian health care, and encouraging better business decisions at the local level. The Defense Authorization Act of 1993 mandated positive incentives for enrolling, including reduced co-payments and deductibles, reduced cost-sharing for primary care services, and expanded benefits, such a preventive services and screening exams.

coordination of benefits (COB) Refers to provisions in a benefits plan designed to prevent double payments when an employee is covered by two health care plans. The primary plan reimburses the individual or the provider first, up to the limits of the plan, and the benefits of the secondary plan are adjusted so that the total amount does not exceed the cost of covered services.

copay See co-payment.

co-payment Refers to patient (employee) out-of-pocket expenses for health care. May be a percentage of the Medicare- or company-approved charge or a flat dollar amount, such as $5 - $10 per office visit.

co-preneurs Married couples who work together as a team in either their own business or in a private corporation. Attributed to *The Organization of the Future,* a newsletter published monthly by Werner & Company of Atlanta, GA.

copyright Protects the creators or owners of visual or written material, including software, videotapes, and videodiscs, from use without permission or infringement under penalty of the law. Copyrights are registered with the Library of Congress.

copyright law Legislation that applies to original works, whether published or recorded. It gives the authors or creators control over how those works can be used and informs the public of how it can legally use the materials. It applies to original works of authorship or creation when they become fixed in a tangible form of expression such as a manuscript, audio or video recording, drawing or painting, or photograph. For a copy of the law, write to U.S. Copyright Office, Library of Congress, Washington, DC 20559. For an application form, write to U.S. Copyright Office, Library of Congress, Register of Copyrights, Washington DC 20559. For 24-hour ordering service call 202/287-9100.

Copyright Remedy Clarification Act of 1991 (CRCA) An Act that seals a loophole in the **Copyright Act of 1976**. That legislation restrained copyright holders from suing state agencies, colleges, and universities for copyright infringements.

core competencies 1. Employee skills and abilities needed to perform the operations that are the heart of a business or industry. **2.** The unique knowledge and skills that distinguish one company from another.

core curriculum Training specifically designed and provided for people at each of several levels in an organization. Typically, there is a central theme, and the only change lies in the scope and complexity of the content and the problems dealt with at each level.

core knowledge and skills One of three types of industry standards to be developed by voluntary partnerships under guidelines issued by the **National Skill Standards Board:** knowledge and skills that are common to and essential for the entire economic sector. For example, for manufacturing core knowledge might include understanding quality control and possessing the skill involved in applying quality control procedures. *See also* concentration knowledge and skills; specialty knowledge and skills.

core process design See reengineering.

core work activities The tasks that must be performed if an organization is to fulfill its mission and achieve its goals and objectives.

core workers Permanent employees who are important to the survival and competitiveness of a business or industry. They are considered to be indispensable.

core work team A group of workers engaged in similar jobs formed into a team based on their jobs, location, and the structure of the organization. **Work team** activities are an integral, essential, and continuing part of the work to be done.

corollary benefits See ancillary benefits.

coronary heart disease The most common type of heart disorder. It occurs when cholesterol and other fatty substances build up and clog the coronary arteries that deliver blood to the heart.

corporate anorexia A business disorder that results from excessive **downsizing**.

corporate attire Typically includes two or three-piece suits, but may also permit sport coats or jackets and ties for men. For women, the attire most often includes suits, dresses, and blouses and skirts.

corporate center A conference center operated by a corporation, typically on company premises. Most often used for management meetings and training programs. Sometimes offers overnight accommodations.

corporate compensation and benefits executive   The officer responsible for all **compensation** and **benefits** programs and services, including their design, implementation, administration, and evaluation.

corporate charge card   A means of controlling travel and entertainment expenses. Company-issued bank cards (American Express, Diners Club, First Banks Visa, MasterCard, Visa Business Card, or other) that are nonrevolving and involve payment of a negotiated fee ranging from $5 to $35. Holders are required to pay off the balance each month with either the company or the employee being billed and held liable for charges. Corporate management receives reports showing spending by employee, vendor, category, and city, and other data to support negotiations.

corporate/chief information officer (CIO)   The executive in charge of an organization's management information system and often the person responsible for contacts with the media.

corporate college   **1.** A training and development organizations, whether actual or virtual, centralized or decentralized, that focuses on one subject, discipline, field of knowledge, or constellation of skills, such as engineering technology or computer repair. **2.** An institution operated by an organization that grants an academic degree, ranging from the associate to the doctoral level. Many corporate colleges of this type are private, nonprofit, and accredited by the **Council on Postsecondary Accreditation** or a regional accrediting association. Degrees are typically job-oriented. *See also* corporate university.

corporate cop   An outside private auditor engaged by a corporations at least annually to audit their financial records as a double check on the adequacy of internal controls and to prevent financial fraud and abuse by insiders. Some members of Congress have proposed legislation to require outside accountants (corporate cops) to inform regulators (Securities Exchange Commission) directly when they discover fraud or other illegalities in their client companies.

corporate culture   The atmosphere or environment surrounding an organization, which influences and shapes the behavior of its people and the quality of interpersonal relationships within it. It is the sum total of the norms of behavior, communication, and management adopted by the organization, and it is strongly influenced by the values and behavior of top management.

corporate gridlock   An organizational condition characterized by a shortage of management positions and a surplus of talented employees, many of whom will, because of the situation, become plateaued and dissatisfied or quit.

corporate identity   The combination of attributes that make a company unique and special. It involves more than a name and logo. It defines what a company is, where it is going, and how it is different from all others.

corporate image   Consists of the sum total of attitudes and opinions toward an organization and its products and services by all of its constituencies: employees, customers, clients, suppliers, consultants, competitors, and the public at large. It includes the company's reputation for competence, responsiveness, concern for clients and customers, and quality of products and services. It is polished by quality products and services, top-notch customer service and satisfaction, fairness and ethical conduct, and general good citizenship. It is tarnished by shoddy products and services, inattention to customers, unethical or unprincipled actions, and lack of community concern.

corporate meeting   **1.** A meeting of corporate officers, managers, supervisors, or other category of employee held to provide information, incentives, motivation, training, or address problems and issues. **2.** The annual meeting of stockholders of a corporation at which officers are elected and other corporate business is transacted.

Corporate Meetings & Incentives: The Senior Executive's Guide to Decision-Making   A monthly journal: $65.00 per year (free to qualified subscribers). Address: CM&I, 420 Lexington Ave., New York, NY 10170-1699 (609/786-6892; E-mail **iscofid@aol.com**; URL **http://www.meetingsnet.com**).

corporate-owned life insurance (COLI)   A means of funding postretirement medical and death benefits limited to executive employees by Congress. Consists of insurance policies on the life of key executives in which the corporation is the beneficiary. The corporation is the owner and beneficiary of the policies and holds all ownership rights, including the right to death benefits and cash value. Employees have no rights to the policies; however, if the insured dies while coverage is in effect, the firm may make an equivalent noninsured payment to the designated survivor(s). In any case, the corporation receives the policy proceeds on a tax-free basis and uses them to fund the benefits or reimburse the corporation for benefits already paid. Beginning in 1992, the Financial Standards Accounting Board required employers to include postretirement benefits on their balance sheets.

corporate renewal *See* restructuring.

corporate sentencing guidelines
See United States Sentencing Commission.

corporate soul A term that describes an organization's reputation and demonstrated concern about earning and retaining the trust and confidence of its internal and external customers and clients. It is revealed by acknowledgement of past mistakes, disclosure of aims, purposes, motives, and aspirations, clarification and acceptance of responsibility and accountability, and definition of pledges for quality, service, or other benefits to constituents, customers, and clients. Attributed to trend watcher Faith Popcorn (*The Popcorn Report*).

corporate strategy A plan whose purpose is to achieve success for the organization in a competitive environment, based on credible estimates of future environmental conditions and the probable actions of others--mainly competitors, customers, employees, suppliers, and government agencies. It consists of policies, objectives, actions, and decisions designed to attain organizational goals.

Corporate Travel Index (CTI) An annual report prepared by *Corporate Travel*. It provides figures that corporate travel decision makers and travelers themselves can use for travel budgeting. It includes per diem costs in 100 cities, most expensive cities by cost category, (lodging, food, car rental, and total per diem cost), luxury lodging rates, and daily travel cost by region.

corporate video Video produced and distributed via satellite communications or telephone lines from a central corporate facility to outlying branches or offices.

corporate university (CU) **1.** In its narrow sense, typical of the 1950s through 1980s, a

corporate-owned campus setting where employees are sent to be trained or developed through formal classroom programs. **2.** In its broader sense, typical of the 1990s, a framework and a process for learning by working on real-life problems and issues on the job rather than in an institutional setting. Designed to link training to the strategic needs of a company and typically involves a process that enables employees, key customers, clients, and suppliers to learn continuously and improve their performance. **3.** A training and development organization, whether actual or virtual, centralized or decentralized, that emphasizes an interdisciplinary organization and approach — one that teaches several different disciplines (such as basic skills, marketing, sales, customer service, technical skills, and clerical skills) and often at several levels (workers, technicians, supervisors, managers, executives, and so on).

Corporate University Review: The Magazine about Organizational Learning and Performance A bimonthly journal published by Enterprise Communications Inc.: $39 per year. Address: Corporate University Review, 1483 Chain Bridge Rd., Ste. 202, McLean, VA 22101-4599 (703/448-0336; Fax 703/448-0270; URL (**http://www.traininggu. ecommunications.com**).

corporation An artificial person, created under the authority of law, from a group of persons, and that has a continuous existence and powers and liabilities separate from its members.

corpus The principal or property that is in a trust.

correcting The process of improving performance, progress toward objectives, and results. It involves taking action to bring variances into line with plans.

corrective discipline
See progressive discipline.

correlation The extent to which two sets of scores or measures are related or the tendency of one score to vary concomitantly with the other. For example, people who score high on intelligence tests often score high in reading ability.

correlation chart A chart used to test for a possible relationship between two process variables, show the strength of any relationship found, and potentially discover and document possible cause and effect.

correlational study A type of descriptive research study that investigates the extent to which variations in one experimental factor or variable correspond with variations in one or more other factors.

correlation analysis A statistical technique, employing manual or computer-assisted mathematical processes, used to determine the statistical relationship between two variables, one independent and the other dependent. For example, the procedure to forecast personnel requirements by correlation analysis would involve determining whether two factors, such as some measure of HR departmental activity and staffing levels, are related.

correlation coefficient *See* coefficient of correlation.

correspondence study Education or training conducted by mail or other means of delivering training packages. It typically involves the completion of reading, writing, problem solving assignments, and tests that are returned by the trainee to the sponsoring organization for review, correction, grading, or other form of feedback. Also called *home study* and *independent study*.

cosmetic surgery A type of service or procedure typically not covered by health care plans. Performed primarily to improve physical appearance and/or treat a mental condition through change in bodily or facial form. Examples are removal of acne scars and breast reduction. Reconstructive breast surgery following a mastectomy is usually covered.

cost analysis An analytical process employed to identify and track the costs of HR activities, programs, and services, including the cost of full- and part-time company personnel, contractors, consultants, and temporary employees, real property, space and facilities, equipment, materials, supplies, and services. It encompasses the processes of collecting, validating, processing, and publishing cost histories, developing cost-estimating models from those data, conducting research to develop new cost analysis methods and techniques, and developing cost estimates during all phases of acquisition and purchasing.

cost-based pricing Involves identifying and assessing all the costs associated with the production, promotion, and delivery of a product or service, adding a factor for profit, and then setting a price based on cost plus profit.

cost-benefit analysis A technique used to compare total resources required with total benefits received from each HR program, system, service, unit, or activity. Also, procedures designed to provide a financial comparison between the full costs (direct, labor, and overhead) of the target system, program, or activity and the savings realized by the intervention and opportunity costs of foregoing other services.

cost center A separate and distinct cost accounting entity that has been identified to provide a means of isolating and tracking costs and to enhance management control by pinpointing accountability for expenditures. More and more HR departments are being identified as cost centers.

cost-containment lump-sum payment A one-time bonus given to employees for performance above a stated level. It does not become a part of the employee's salary.

cost-containment strategies *See* cost-control strategies.

cost contract A Medicare option that allows a subscriber to use medical services outside their plan subject to the usual coinsurance, deductibles, and charges that apply to regular Medicare.

cost control *See* cost management.

cost-control strategies Popular corporate cost-control strategies include flexible benefits, cost shifting/higher deductibles, case management, managed care (HMO/PPO), precertified hospital admissions, second surgical opinions, utilization review, and wellness programs.

cost improvement *See* cost management.

cost of attendance (COA) For federal student aid programs, the total amount it will cost a student to go to school, usually expressed as a yearly amount. It is determined by using a formula established by Congress. The COA covers tuition and fees; on-campus room and board (or a housing and food allowance for off-campus students); and allowances for books, supplies, transportation, loan fees (if applicable), dependent care, costs related to a disability, and miscellaneous expenses; and reasonable costs for eligible study abroad programs. An allowance, determined by the school, is included for reasonable costs connected with a student's employment as part of a cooperative education program. For students attending less than half time, the COA includes only tuition and fees and an allowance for books, supplies, transportation, and dependent-care expenses.

cost management The process of tracking and analyzing expenditures with a view toward eliminating, reducing, or containing the costs associated with all aspects of company planning and operations, or, at the very least, maximizing the value derived from capital and operating expenditures. Methods include statistical analysis, standard hours studies, process charts, line balancing, operations research, short interval scheduling, work sampling, PERT, and machine capacity studies.

cost-no-fee contract (CNO) Used primarily for research studies in which a nonprofit organization or university serves as the contractor. Limits payments to the allowable costs of contract performance.

cost-of-living adjustment (COLA) An across-the-board adjustment to pay or benefits, sometimes contractual, based on changes in the government-published (Bureau of Labor Statistics, Department of Labor) **Consumer Price Index**. It is designed to bring pay into line with increases in the cost of living.

cost of quality (COQ) **1.** An accounting procedure in which the actual costs of poor quality or the expenses incurred as a result of substandard products or services are tracked and measured. **2.** A **total quality management** concept involving the application of techniques to balance the costs of protection and detection activities against the costs of production failure (rejects, reworks, and customer dissatisfaction).

cost per applied person-day A worker's full cost per day divided by his or her **applied rate**.

cost-per-eyeball The cost of a marketer's investment in advertising on the **Internet** based on the total number of people viewing their site.

cost-per-hire A basic element of the employee recruitment budget usually categorized by exempt and nonexempt jobs and often by job category. Sometimes used to measure the effectiveness of the recruitment department and individual recruiters. Cost includes such elements as advertising, applicant travel, and subsistence, recruiter travel and subsistence, employment agency or search fees, and new employee relocation.

cost-per-mile rate of change A **benchmark** used by corporate travel managers to make better comparisons of travel costs than standard industry averages provide. The cost-per-mile rate of change eliminates the factors of specific market conditions and negotiated deals and allows the manager to compare the change in cost per mile to that of the American Express database of 3,000 corporate clients. It is calculated by finding the corporate cost per mile for any month and then applying the following formula. The corporate cost per mile rate of change can then be plotted on a graph and compared with the AmEx database. Attributed to Bonnie Barbareck, director, MIS American Express Travel Related Services ("Leading Travel Indicators," *Corporate Travel*, November 1992, p. 8).

$$\text{Cost per mile rate of change} = \frac{\text{October 1993} - \text{October 1992}}{\text{October 1992}}$$

cost plans One of two types of managed care plans under contract with Medicare. Cost plans do not have lock-in requirements. Persons who enroll in a cost plan can either go to health care providers affiliated with the plan or go outside the plan. If they go outside the plan, the plan usually will not pay, but Medicare will pay its share of charges it approves; however, the subscriber is responsible for Medicare's coinsurance, deductibles, and other charges. The only exceptions recognized by cost plans are for emergency services, which a beneficiary may receive anywhere in the United States and for services urgently needed when the beneficiary is temporarily out of the plan's service area.

cost-plus-award-fee contract (CPAF) An incentive type contract in which contractors are paid based upon the buyer's judgment of how well the contractor is meeting contract requirements. The contract provides no formula for determining final payment of profit to the contractor, but it does provide reimbursement of costs incurred and usually allows a minimum fixed fee to be added for the tasks completed by the contractor.

cost-plus-fixed-fee-contract (CPFF)

The predominant form of cost contracting used when a private organization receives a contract. It pays the contractor for the actual material and labor costs involved in fulfilling a contract, plus a negotiated fixed percentage of the overall cost as profit. It is used when developmental risks are involved, an indeterminable amount of research and analysis are required, or the specifications for the materials and services cannot be totally and accurately defined in advance. Frequently used in contracts calling for job and task analysis, training system development and validation, and other projects involving research.

cost-plus-incentive-fee contract (CPIF)

Contracts that do not have a ceiling price established at the outset. They provide an incentive for completion by the contractor ahead of schedule. May take the forms of either an additional percentage of the value of the contract or a predetermined dollar amount. Used when the risk to the contractor is high but it is advantageous for the contracting organization to complete the project as soon as possible.

cost-reimbursable contractor (CRC)

One of the 200,000 companies, whose federal government contracts include direct reimbursable line items for travel expenses. There are four types of CRCs: (1) commercial companies, which provide products and services to the government; (2) government programs that are managed and operated by commercial companies; (3) government-owned, company-operated facilities; and (4) federally-funded research and development companies. They are required by the government to manage travel with great attention to detail and level of expenditures. Travelers must follow strict spending guidelines to qualify for full reimbursement.

cost-share

Under the **Civilian Health and Medical Programs of the Uniformed Services,** the portion of the **allowable charge** the beneficiary pays on each claim. The cost-share depends on the sponsor's status (active duty or retired). The annual **deductible** for outpatient care, and anything the provider charges above the allowable charge, are paid in addition to the beneficiaries' **cost-share.** The CHAMPUS share is the difference between the allowable charge and the cost-share.

cost-sharing

A strategy to contain health care costs and the costs of other benefits by giving employees more of the responsibility for their own retirement and health care planning and financing. Examples of legislation that has passed responsibility to the individual and the employer include Medicare Benefits Cost-Sharing, FASB Retiree Accounting Rules, Social Security Tax, and the Consolidated Omnibus Budget Reconciliation Act of 1986.

cost-sharing contract (CS)

A contract in which the costs of performance are shared by the contracting organization and the contractor. Usually limited in application to procurement situations where it is evident that the contractor will gain substantial commercial advantage as a consequence of providing the product or performing the service. Uncommon outside of government contracting.

cost-shifting

In benefits, cost reduction strategies designed to transfer more of the costs of providing health care from the organization to employees. It is accomplished by (1) higher deductibles and employee co-payments and contributions, (2) use of the **Consolidated Omnibus Budget Reconciliation Act of 1986** to shift costs to other firms when the employee moves to a new employer; (3) getting employees to opt for managed care programs (HMOs and PPOs) with strong utilization review.

cost-to-complete information

In budgeting, a category of costs often overlooked. It encompasses the costs of completing projects currently underway that may be affected by inflation, higher interest rates, or increased labor costs.

Council for Adult and Experiential Learning (CAEL)

A 600-member nonprofit education association of individuals, colleges and universities, companies, and unions dedicated to serving the needs of adult learners. It provides services and information on adult and experiential learning through workshops, publications, consultations, conferences, and workforce development programs. *Contact:* CAEL, 243 South Wabash Ave., Ste. 800, Chicago, IL 60604 (312/922-5909; Fax 312/922-1769; E-mail **snunes@cael.org**; URL **http://www.cael.com**).

Council of Citizens with Low Vision International (CCLVI)   An international advocacy membership organization for partially sighted people, family members, and professionals. It aims to establish the rights of people with low vision to make full use of their vision through the necessary aids, services, and technology; to educate the public and professionals about the needs and abilities of the partially sighted; to promote research and professional training; and to establish outreach programs to ensure that all partially sighted persons get the services they need. *Contact:* CCLVI, 1400 North Drake Rd., Ste. 218, Kalamazoo MI 49006 (616/381-9566) or CCLVI, c/o 33 Orange St., Woburn, MA 01801-4605.

Council of Peers Award for Excellence (CPAE)   Awarded annually to a maximum of five members of the National **Speakers Association** for demonstrated platform excellence and professionalism. *Contact:* NSA, 1500 S. Priest Dr., Tempe, AZ 85281 (602/968-2552; Fax 602/968-0911; E-mail **NSAMain@aol. com**; URL **http://www.NSASpeaker.org**).

The Council on Hotel, Restaurant and Institutional Education (CHRIE)   The global advocate of hospitality and tourism education. CHRIE's mission is to advance quality education through proactive professional development, research coalitions and networks for all of its members and constituencies. Offers individual, institutional, and corporate memberships. *Contact:* CHRIE, 1200 17th St., N.W., Washington, DC 20036-3097; 202/331-5990; Fax 202/785-2511; E-mail **alliance@access.digix.net**; URL **http://www.access.digex.net/~alliance**).

Council on Human Resource Management Associations (COHRMA)   An organization of 17 human resource management associations, representing more than 200,000 human resource professionals. Meets twice each year to discuss issues of mutual interest, acquaint each other with the goals and operations of their organizations, and examine best practices and new products. *Contact:* SHRM, 606 N. Washington St., Alexandria, VA 22314 (703/548-3440; TDD 703/548-6999; Fax 703/836-0367).

counseling   The process by which two people come together face-to-face and one-on-one to attack a problem so that it can be more clearly defined and the one who has it can be helped to understand, clarify, and find a self-determined solution to it. It is essentially helping people to help themselves.

counteroffer   1. A reply to a **request for proposal** returned to the originator with changes to any items in the original. Unless and until the changes are specifically accepted in writing by all parties, there is no **contract. 2.** A means of retaining valued employees who are considering or have decided to leave their current positions to work for another organization. Involves proffering upgraded compensation and benefits packages to avoid the expenses involved in replacing the individual.

country executive program   A program designed to assist in corporate globalization. Top officers (usually divisional presidents) choose or are assigned a country or area of the world and make themselves responsible for learning its history, politics, culture, and sometimes language through training, individual study, and frequent trips to the country or area. They are often responsible for overseeing visits to the corporate office in the U.S. by natives of the designated country and act as senior business "diplomats."

country-specific training   *See* relocation training.

course developer   A professional training and development specialist. Course developers conduct occupational and job analysis; write performance objectives; sequence learning objectives and activities; identify, select, and organize course content; select and develop learning resources and materials, including audiovisual aids; select or develop evaluative techniques and instruments; prepare programs of instruction, course outlines and schedules, instructor and trainee guides, and lesson plans; develop criteria for the selection of course participants; validate all phases of the training and development program; write course descriptions and announcements; instruct individual or groups in specific training system strategies; and collect, analyze, interpret, process, and report data obtained from the use of internal and external evaluation instruments.

course manager   A professional training and development specialist. Course managers establish objectives for the training and development programs for which they are responsible; develop guidelines for the conduct and operation of programs; determine annual personnel, facilities, and funding requirements for training programs; prepare specifications and **statements of work** for requests for proposals (RFPs) for training; review proposals and participate in the selection of contractors; evaluate the producers and services of contractors and provide feedback to procurement officials; evaluate program results; and prepare reports and statistics on the programs for which they have responsibility.

courseware Software produced for use with computer-based training systems; the programs used for presenting the course content along with the books, film, video, and audio materials that support the training.

covered care Health care services covered by an insurance policy. It typically requires that services be provided by a licensed physician or nurse, a licensed physical, occupational, or speech therapist, other licensed health care provider, home health care agency-furnished home health aide or personal care attendant, or day care services received at an adult day care center.

covered employee A worker protected by (nonexempt from) the provisions of employment laws. For example, under the Omnibus Budget Reconciliation Act of 1989, the term "covered employees" now includes independent contractors, partners, and self-employed individuals covered under a group health plan.

covered period of confinement The number of days that a beneficiary will be paid for inpatient services in a health care facility under an insurance policy, usually beginning with the elimination period.

covered provider A health care professional whose services are covered by Medicare or other health care plan. Includes licensed doctors of medicine (M.D.s), licensed doctors of osteopathy (O.D.s), chiropractors (D.C.s), physician's assistants, nurse practitioners, nurse midwives, nurse anesthetists, dentists (D.M.D.s and D.D.S.s), optometrists (D.O.s), qualified clinical social workers, qualified clinical psychologists (Ph.D.s and Ed.D.s), podiatrists (D.P.M.s), and speech, physical, and occupational therapists.

cover your anterior (CYA) An expression used to describe any action taken by an individual to protect himself or herself from criticism, an adverse action, or other penalty. Actions may take the forms of **memorandum for record**, alibis, or outright deception. Often a less elegant, if not crude, three-letter synonym is substituted for "anterior."

Covia A **computer reservation system** jointly owned by Air Canada, Alitalia, British Airways, KLM Royal Dutch, Swissair, United Airlines, and USAir.

Cpk A universal measure of **process capability**. Used by engineers to specify quality level (parameters) when supplying items to a buyer (in addition to drawings, specification sheets, target costs, and the like). The lower the variation in quality, the higher the Cpk.

crack A highly addictive street drug. Crack is a rock-like, smokable derivative of cocaine. Produces a "high" of less than 30 minutes, so repeated use is typical. Crack may produce bouts of severe depression and paranoia as well as convulsions. Also called *rock, slab,* and *flavor.*

cracker An ill-behaved and highly proficient programmer who uses his or her skills to penetrate the computer systems of others, sometimes by circumventing security systems. Essentially, an electronic burglar who breaks into computers using tools such as Trojan horses, which let the cracker enter networks and private files and hide their tracks when they leave. They often use passwords to presumed secure computers, jeopardizing personnel and corporate information, bank accounts, even national defense systems. *See also* hacker.

cramdown During a bankruptcy proceeding, a court-ordered reduction of a mortgage to the level of a home's current market value to protect a person whose property is worth less than his or her mortgage. The unpaid debt is converted to an unsecured liability.

crank An addictive mind-altering drug. The street name for methamphetamines (speed).

crash **1.** The sudden failure of a computer system due to such causes as power failure, power surge, or an undetected **bug** or virus. **2.** The suicidal depression that drug abusers, especially crack users, experience almost immediately after the burst of euphoria they feel when the drug hits the pleasure centers of the brain.

crawls In video production, the movement of credits (such as producer, directors, and so on) or other graphic material verically on the screen.

cream skimming A corporate competitive tactic. Occurs when an organization challenges the high-profit segment of another company's market or customer base, usually by moving in with an improved second- or third-generation version of a product or service.

creative faring *See* grey fare.

creative imagery The ability to search for, find, identify, and modify, synthesize, or otherwise change the form, size, use, or some other characteristic of an object, concept, or idea to make it truly new.

creative learning A learning environment characterized by exchange and interaction between and among the learners and the facilitator (instructor). It requires original thought and input to the learning process, reexamination of assumptions, critical analysis of processes and trends, and sharing of ideas.

creative problem solving (CPS) The process of addressing problems with these characteristics: the problem is vague; there are few or no criteria of solution; lateral, nonlinear thought, as well as convergent and divergent thinking, are employed; facts are considered but are not central to a solution; a large volume of ideas is sought; judgment of ideas is reserved until later; and the results are sometimes unmeasurable and often involve risk.

creative problem solving training Training designed to unlock creative and innovative talents, help people discover their creative capacities, remove or mitigate obstacles to creative effort, and teach people to use creative thinking techniques and, as a consequence, become more productive, more open to new ideas, and increase their capacity to generate larger numbers of ideas. Strategies include small group discussion, demonstration of problem solving techniques, reading and study assignments, buzz sessions, brainstorming and brainwriting, checklists, morphological analysis, and ideational exercises, both individual and group.

creative staff People representing various disciplines and holding different jobs who develop dramatizations, programs, or shows (writers, artists, drafting specialists, musicians, special effects technicians, set designers, makeup artists, costume designers, and so on).

creative thinking Cognitive activity that results in significant, original, and unique solutions to problems. It is the process of solving problems by adding imagination, invention, inspiration, and a different way of looking at things to logic and competence in finding solutions where only a partial knowledge of the situation is available and some facts are missing.

creative ticketing *See* back-to-back ticketing; gray fare; hidden city fare.

creativity An individual capacity. Bringing something into existence through imaginative skills, using hunches, intuition, and **incubation**. The generation of entirely new, uncommon, original, or unique and potentially useful concepts and ideas.

creator The individual who creates a trust. Also called a *donor, grantor,* or *settlor.*

credentialing Obtaining, reviewing, and verifying documentation of the qualifications of health care providers, such as licenses, certifications, insurance, malpractice history, and so on.

credit hour A measure of instructor work load and student course load and a means of converting time to credit in colleges, universities, and technical schools. One semester hour of credit is generally awarded for each block of 15 clock hours of lecture, 30 clock hours of laboratory, or 45 clock hours of externship/clinical instruction. One quarter-hour of credit is usually awarded for each 10 clock hours of laboratory or 30 clock hours of externship/clinical instruction. *See also* clock hour.

crew resource management (CRM) Training that focuses on communication, team building, work-load management, situation analysis, decision making, and other safety-related subjects. Developed by the airline industry to train cockpit crews, flight attendants, operations agents, dispatchers, and other workers as teams. Now being extended to other industries concerned with teamwork and safety, such as medical and surgical teams, nuclear power plants, and the petrochemical industry.

crisis management   1. Implementing policies and preplanned procedures to deal rationally and effectively with potentially catastrophic events or situations with a view toward reducing negative or damaging effects on the workforce, the community, security, corporate assets, and the company image. *See also* crisis plan; crisis prevention. **2.** Reactive and unwilling or firehouse management where the manager is driven by events.

crisis plan   A formal plan for reacting properly and in a timely manner to a crisis, such as a chemical plant explosion, an oil tanker leak, workplace accident, violence, or other emergency, including the corporate and human aspects of the catastrophe. Its purposes are to prevent crises, reduce uncertainty, and minimize the chances for error, omission, and confusion during and following a crisis. It typically includes a trained emergency response team, a hot-line, mock crises, drills and exercises, and contingency plans for counseling (victims, their families, and fellow employees) and employee assistance, support, accommodations, and emergency funds.

crisis prevention   Policies, plans, and procedures designed to prevent catastrophes, disasters, emergencies, and tragedies.

criterion   1. A standard relating to such things as personnel, space and facilities, equipment, materials and supplies, programs and services, products, productivity, client and customer relations, time, funds, performance, and costs. **2.** A standard by which the value or worth of a test may be judged. **3.** The third and final element of a behavioral object. Describes how well trainees must be able to perform. That is, the criterion establishes the minimum performance requirements for a duty, task, or job element. To do that, the objective statement must prescribe the quality of the work product or service produced (accuracy, completeness, clarity, tolerances, and the like); the quantity of work products produced (the number of work units completed); the time allowed to complete the job, duty, task, or element; or any combination of quality, quantity, and time standards. The criterion invariably begins, "in accordance with the following standard:"

criterion measure   A means of evaluating the adequacy and effectiveness of an instructional system. A test constructed to measure achievement of required knowledge supports and mastery of essential skills at the task or duty level of job performance.

criterion-oriented validity   *See* criterion validity.

criterion-referenced measurement   Measurement of performance by comparing the performance of individuals or groups against a predetermined standard.

criterion-referenced test   A test that is relevant to real-world job requirements; a performance test that focus on the duties and tasks of a job.

criterion validity   Applies to training and testing. There are two types: criterion **concurrent validity** and **criterion predictive validity.** A training program or test has criterion concurrent validity when selection instrument scores or criterion test scores correlate highly with measures of job performance. It has criterion predictive validity when measures of actual on-the-job performance correlate highly with selection instrument scores or criterion test scores during or at the end of training.

critical element   A term used to describe job activities that are most important to managers. The **Civil Service Reform Act of 1978** mandated that federal managers evaluate and rank all of their responsibilities in order of decreasing benefit to the organization.

critical incident   1. In training needs analysis, an analytical tool that involves collecting statements based on direct observation of job incumbents by supervisors or designated observers or recall of job behavior by employees that typify both competent and incompetent performance of a job or task. The technique underscores critical job behaviors for emphasis in training and the supervision of workplace performance. **2.** In performance rating, a descriptive approach in which the rater is asked to observe and record specific incidents of effective and ineffective performance during a rating period. The observations are matched against a predetermined critical incident, often referred to as a behaviorally anchored rating scale. The incidents are discussed with the employee and are used as a basis for developing an improvement plan.

critical-incident survey **1.** A training needs assessment technique. Participants are asked to describe in some detail a specific situation or event that went wrong, identify the cause(s), and determine whether the situation could have been avoided and, if so, how. Responses are analyzed, tallied by problem type, and used in workshops to tailor training to the needs of trainees. **2.** A method of collecting job and task data, it involves asking supervisory personnel to recall, describe in detail, and record job behavior of incumbents that typify both competent and unsatisfactory performance of a job or task. The data are tabulated and analyzed and then used to identify and record critical job behaviors for training.

critical path method (CPM) A method of planning and scheduling projects which usually includes both an "arrow diagram" showing the sequence of related project activities and a computer-based method of determining "slack" times before project activities become critical, cost-time relationships, and total project time. It is a tool that defines the tasks that need to be done to complete a job or project, determines the sequence in which the tasks must be completed, and estimates the time needed to finish the project. The sequence of tasks that takes the longest time to complete is called the "critical path." All scheduling decisions are made on the basis of this critical path.

critical pathway A health care management tool pioneered by a coalition of six Chicago hospitals to reduce costs and improve the quality of care of cardiac cases. The pathway is a planned progression controlled by standard physician orders for diagnostic tests and medication and anticipated activities and treatments for each day of hospitalization, from admission through discharge. The plan will also be used to track variations and, when treatment departs from the path, the reason is recorded. Over time it is anticipated that variations can be linked to outcomes and cost. If successful, the concept may be applied to other types of cases such as mental health/chemical dependency.

critical skills Professional, leadership, managerial, business, technical, people, and personal skills and abilities required for successful performance of the HR managerial job.

critical tasks Job tasks that are crucial and indispensable to the proper performance of a job. Some of the criteria for identifying such tasks are universality, difficulty, cruciality, frequency, achievability, quality, deficiency, and retainability.

critical tracking test A nonmedical drug test that measures fine hand-eye coordination and reaction time. The test is used to detect drug impairment, use of alcohol, sleep deficiency, emotional stress, and illness. Frequently used where safety is a critical factor.

critique In evaluation, fair, unbiased, unvarnished, and accurate feedback on performance, highlighting strengths and weaknesses, provided to employees or trainees by trained, qualified, independent, and objective observers.

croak A street drug. A mixture of crack and regular cocaine smoked like crack.

cross-cultural training Training provided by multinational or multicultural organizations, public and private institutions and agencies, and the military services to increase managerial effectiveness in domestic cross-cultural settings and international operations, negotiations, and decision making, help employees adapt to working, living, and learning environments in cultural settings that differ from their own, establish and maintain friendly, cooperative, and favorable relationships with the people of the host country, and assist HR personnel to adapt training objectives, strategies, methods, and materials to the people of the cultures they are charged to train or develop. Also called *cultural diversity training.*

cross-functional A worker who is required to perform several disparate duties and tasks in an organization that has been so **downsized** that it is grossly understaffed.

cross-functional mapping A basic tool for applying the principles of **total cycle time.** These process maps depict an entire cycle as it moves through the various functional areas of a company. A map is produced as follows: (1) list the functions along the left margin, each function on a separate line; (2) use a box to indicate an activity or task completion; (3) extend each box to cover all functions involved in that activity; (4) use dotted lines to connect sub-processes carried on by different functions simultaneously; (5) trace the flow with input/output arrows between activity boxes. (6) code and label the specific input or output; (7) use a diamond to indicate a yes/no response option; and (8) follow a left-to-right sequence (don't loop back). (Attributed to Philip R. Thomas and Larry J. Gallace with Kenneth R. Martin. *Quality Alone Is Not Enough.* New York: American Management Association, 1992, pp. 71-74.)

cross-functional team A form of participative management involving interdisciplinary teams. Work teams are composed of representatives of different departments or the operating and staff elements of an organization. They are organized to address complex problems in which expertise of several kinds is essential.

cross-impact analysis An integrative technology forecasting technique that uses a small group of experts to address external influences and the interaction of internal and external forces. The process begins with identification of the factors that will most significantly affect the development under consideration. The factors are arranged in a matrix, with the basic development of other factors listed down the left column or Y-axis, and the same arrangement of factors is used to form an equal number of columns across the top or X-axis of the matrix. The experts complete the matrix by placing a notation, such as a "+," "−," or "0" to indicate "increase," "decrease" or "no effect," in each box of the effect of the occurrence of each element on the y-axis on each of the other elements of the matrix on the x-axis (except on itself; that box is left blank). The results are analyzed and presented to the decision maker.

crossover arrangement A plan under which Medicare Part B claim-paying offices automatically transfer information about claims to the patient's supplementary or secondary health benefits insurer. Such arrangements make it unnecessary for medical care providers to submit more than one claim — or for subscribers to submit a claim to their secondary insurers.

cross-promotion The practice of targeting identical customers by two or more companies to improve sales and marketing productivity, using such tactics as putting coupons inside the packages or on the out-side of containers of the partner company, or providing free samples of the partner's product along with a service.

cross-section technique A form of **genetic, developmental, and growth studies** which requires at least a single measurement for each individual within certain groups to calculate an average. Comparisons of the averages (norms or standards) of successive groups indicate trends in the form of changes in the groups as a whole, with which individuals can be compared, although the resulting central trends are not accurate for an individual. For example, leg, arm, and upper body strength measurements for men and women in specific occupations might be taken and the average for each group calculated.

cross-talk **1.** Distracting side conversations between participants at a meeting or training session while the session leader or another participant is speaking to the whole group. **2.** Mixed sounds or unrelated talk heard in radio or telephone transmissions caused by interference from another transmitter.

cross-ticketing A form of booking fraud used by travel agencies to increase their overrides (commissions) from airlines with which they have marketing agreements. The practice involves ticketing all trips, regardless of U.S. origin, on the airline that offers high commissions on sales out of a particular city from that city and sending the tickets overnight to clients.

cross-training A means of developing multi-skilled workers, people who can adapt to changes in job requirements and advancing technology. Cross training is essentially a strategy to make an organization more competitive, increase productivity, promote stability, respond more rapidly to change, avoid layoffs, and compensate for the shrinking pool of qualified workers. It is accomplished by such means as conventional training, on-the-job training, and peer training. Sometimes called *upskilling* or *redeployment.*

cross-validation In test construction, the practice of administering the test to additional groups of subjects and again to recheck the findings of the first validation study; that is, determine whether there is a significant relationship (correlation) between scores (the predictor) and performance (the criterion). Sometimes called *revalidation.*

CRT-based projector The most commonly-used color projector in training and education. It employs three cathode-ray tubes — one each to display red, green, and blue light. Most units require a trained technician to make convergence adjustments every time the unit is moved to ensure sharp images. Newer models make use of digital convergence technology to simplify the adjustment process.

Crystal Awards *See* SITE Crystal Awards.

crystal healing An alternative form of medical treatment. A New Age therapy, adherents maintain that healing energy can be derived from quartz and other mineral crystals.

crystal meth *See* ice.

C-section *See* Caesarean section.

cued speech A form of sign language that uses eight hand shapes and four hand positions in various combinations to display voice sounds rather than words (sounds or phonemes). The system offers the closest parallel to spoken language because it shows what we actually hear (phonetics) rather than words.

cuing **1.** A signal in any form — a word, graphic, phrase, gesture, or facial expression — that initiates a response or action or helps the learner to respond to a stimulus or problem correctly in a learning situation. **2.** A form of feedback that indicates whether an activity or action is proceeding well or poorly as compared with some preestablished standard.

cultural anthropology Used in intercultural training. The study of a given culture so thoroughly that one is able to see the world through their eyes; that is, adopt the native view or perspective.

cultural diversity training *See* cross-cultural training.

culture *See* corporate culture.

cumulative record A record maintained for an individual employee, trainee, or client over a period of years, with successive additions to the record at relatively frequent intervals, as when entering reports of training or counseling. Typically contains all pertinent information concerning the individual, such as personal data, test scores, and subjective impressions, work samples, behavior deviations, and adjustment procedures employed obtained from the individual, supervisors, physicians, and technicians.

cumulative trauma disorder (CTD) Includes three trauma categories, typically computer-associated: hand and wrist, eyestrain, and back discomfort.

currency futures An investment technique whereby a fund purchases and sells currency futures contracts, enabling the fund manager to establish the number of U.S. dollars the fund will receive in a given delivery month for a certain amount of a foreign currency. In that way, if the fund manager anticipates a decline of a foreign currency against the U.S. dollar, the fund can attempt to fix the U.S. dollar value of some or all of the securities held in its **portfolio** that are denominated in that currency. By purchasing foreign currency futures, the fund can establish the number of dollars it will be required to pay for a specified amount of a foreign currency in the delivery month. Thus, if the fund manager intends to buy securities in the future and expects the U.S. dollar to decline against the relevant foreign currency during the period before the future is effected, the fund can attempt to fix the price in U.S. dollars of the securities it intends to acquire.

current assets The total of cash, accounts and notes receivable for the sale of products or services, operating supplies, and prepayments (insurance, interest, taxes, and the like), less reserves for bad debts, advances on merchandise, inventories less any reserves, listed securities not in excess of market, state and municipal bonds, and U.S. government securities.

current debt The total of all liabilities due within one year of the date of the statement, including current payments on notes, mortgages, debentures, or other funded debts. It also includes current reserves, such as reserves for federal and state income taxes and contingency funds. It does not include reserves for depreciation.

***Current Procedural Terminology*, 4th Edition (CPT-4)** Lists five-digit codes that apply to medical services used by providers for billing purposes.

curriculum development The process of designing, developing, validating, and installing training and education programs regardless of target group, content, or length — from kindergarten to graduate degree programs, foreign language to mathematics, plumbing to computer design.

curriculum integration An interdisciplinary approach to teaching and learning in which separate subject areas are linked or fused into a more seamless and thematic curriculum to prepare students for real-world demands.

curriculum vitae A description of an individual's education, training, and experience, written for an academic audience, that focuses on providing evidence of scholarship in the person's field of preparation, interest, and accomplishment.

cursive See script.

CU-SeeMe In multimedia, software that supports desktop **videoconferencing** over a network.

custodial care Care provided primarily to meet personal needs that can be provided by persons without professional medical skills or training but cannot reasonably be expected to restore health. For example, help in walking, getting in and out of bed, bathing, dressing, eating, and taking medication.

customary and reasonable charge See customary charge.

customary charge The amount that physicians or medical suppliers most frequently charge for each separate service and supply furnished. This charge is the usually the maximum amount a health insurance plan will allow for covered expenses.

customary or usual charge See customary charge.

customer-based pricing A pricing process that starts with the market and works back into the company. It sees pricing as a function of what the market will bear for the benefits offered by the product or service. Theoretically, there is no limit on either the upper levels of pricing or profitability other than what the customer is willing to pay. Review and analysis of several factors are key to customer-based pricing: the nature of the market, the number, kind, and quality of competitive offerings, the quality of your products and services, and market share.

customer complaint rate The number of customer complaints about products or services reported to salespersons, dealers, or directly to the producer, through telephone, telex, fax, or correspondence, as compared with the total number of products or services provided over a selected period of time. A measure of productivity.

customer grouping In organization design, one of the basic organizational alternatives in which elements of the organization are grouped by class of customers. For example, in the chemical industry, groups may be formed to serve farmers, the paper industry, and prescription drug manufacturers.

customer partnering A means of improving sales productivity. Involves linking various company levels and functions between a supplier and its customer., including market information, future products, contacts between management levels, accounting, problem solving, quality improvement, training, and so on.

customer rating (appraisal) system Tapping customers or clients for appraisal data on employees such as salespersons, repair specialists, consultants, and the like.

customer relations The kind and quality of a company's relationships with its clients and customers with regard to advertising, financial disclosure, pricing, products, services, quality control, training, and so on.

Customer Satisfaction Barometer (CSB) An index based on an annual survey of customers, both consumers and businesses, of 100 leading companies to measure national quality. Initiated in Sweden, comparable measures are being instituted in Germany, Great Britain, and the United States.

customer service See customer service program.

customer service representative (CSR) A person assigned to the customer service department or office who is responsible for providing support for field representatives by handling orders, credit, and adjustments. Also assists functional support groups (production, distribution, customer financial services, scheduling, and marketing) in performing their functions. Requires a thorough knowledge of company products and applications.

customer service specialist (CSS) A higher level of expertise than that required of the **customer service representative.** Involved in independent problem solving, special projects, hiring and training, and exercising leadership in the customer service function as well as providing technical assistance to functional groups.

customer service program Finding out what customers and clients really want, identifying and analyzing customer service problems, establishing measurable objectives and reward systems, coaching and training customer service representatives and sales personnel, implementing the program, and tracking and measuring results.

customer window model A marketing research technique in which product features and customer requirements are compared on two axes: the first axis ranges from what the customer "gets" to "doesn't get," and the second axis ranges from what the customer "wants" to "doesn't want."

customization/customizing The process of tailoring products (including computer **application software)** or services, marketing, sales, and distribution plans and strategies, packaging, advertising, and pricing, and the like to attract a specific target market.

customized courses See custom training program.

custom training program A training program designed specifically for a particular group of people in a specific organization. Employs problems, situations, and other content unique to the target group.

cut A single transition frame inserted between two video clips.

cut-off date In meeting management, the specific date when a hotel will release a reserved block of sleeping rooms to the general public.

cut score The minimum passing score on an achievement, criterion, or performance test.

cyan One of the subtractive primaries, the hue of which is used for one of the 4-color process inks. It reflects blue and green light and absorbs red light.

cyan, yellow, magenta, and black (CMYK) The four primary colors used in process-color printing.

cyber A prefix that indicates a person, place or thing's residence on the **Internet;** for example, cyberspace, cyberspeak, cyberpunk.

cyber hire Using the **Internet** as a means of advertising for and recruiting prospective employees. Until the Office of Federal Contract Compliance Programs issues guidance for employers who want to be in compliance when they surf for résumés, they would be wise to keep a careful record of the criteria they use to select the résumés of individuals they may want to interview for a position.

cybernetics The comparative study of self-correcting systems characterized by closed-loop devices or servomechanisms.

cyberspace The new "universe" made up of many "planets" which tie together the vast network of modern communications. Includes cable networks, cellular networks, commercial online services, computer bulletin boards, satellite and broadcast television, and telephone networks.

cybrarian A person whose job is online research and information retrieval. Also called a *data surfer* or *super searcher.*

cycles of learning Believed by some to be the ultimate tool in the quest for improved quality. The system requires every manager to monitor performance in every cycle of activity and review feedback to identify clues to do the job better the next time. Similar to **experience curve theory** but relies more on the number of different cycles completed and studied rather than repetition of the same tasks.

cycle time (CT) The average start-to-finish time required to set up, change over, make checks, rework, deliver, and so on. It is a single and automatic measure of quality, cost, delivery, and effectiveness — and a means of integrating those factors. It is calculated by dividing the number of units of work-in-process by the number of units completed with a given time frame. *See also* baseline performance; entitlement performance; first-pass yield; theoretical cycle time; white collar cycle time.

$$\text{Cycle time} = \frac{\text{Number of units of work-in-process}}{\text{Number of units completed}}$$

cyrillic An adjective used to describe something senseless or unintelligible, as in "The

message went cyrillic after retransmission."
It originated as a reference to the difficulty
of the Russian alphabet.

cystic fibrosis (CF)   One of the most common fatal genetic diseases of Caucasians. It
occurs equally in males and females and is
present at birth. The disease causes the exocrine (outward secreting) glands in the body
to fail to function normally. These glands
normally produce thin, slippery secretions,
including sweat, mucus, tears, saliva, and
digestive enzymes. With CF, the mucus-pro-
ducing exocrine glands often generate thick,
sticky secretions that may plug up ducts and
other passageways. These plugs occur most
often in the lungs and intestines and can
interfere with vital body functions, such as
breathing and digestion.

Cystic Fibrosis Foundation (CFF)   A nonprofit organization established to fund
research to find a cure for cystic fibrosis and
to improve the quality of life for the 30,000
children and young adults with the disease.
Funds its own network of 14 research centers in America, finances more than 112 CFF
care centers nationwide, offers general information publications, and supports public
policy and education programs. *Contact:*
Cystic Fibrosis Foundation, 631 Arlington,
Rd., Bethesda, MD 20814, (800/FIGHT CF or
301/ 951-4422; Fax 301/951-6378; E-mail
info@ cff.org; URL **http://www.cff.org**).

D

2DTC	Two-way digital teleconferencing.	**DHMO**	Dental health maintenance organization.
DA	Department of the Army.		
DAA	Deposit administration arrangement.	**DIC**	Dependency and indemnity compensation.
DACUM	Developing a curriculum.	**DI**	Direct imaging.
DAF	Department of the Air Force.	**DIP**	Document image processing.
DAT	Digital audiotape (recorder).	**DIPs**	Deferred income plans.
DB	Database.	**DL**	Distance learning.
DBA	Davis-Bacon Acts of 1931 and 1934.	**DLL**	Dynamic link library.
		DLP	Digital light processing.
DBMS	Database management system.	**DMA**	Direct Marketing Association.
DBO	Docking base option.	**DMC**	Destination management company.
DBP	Defined benefit plan.		
DCAP	Dependent care assistance plan.	**DME**	Durable medical equipment.
DCF	Dependent-care facility.	**DMPA**	Deceptive Mailings Prevention Act of 1990.
DCM	Disability case management.		
DCP	1. Defined contribution plan.	**DN**	Department of the Navy.
	2. Dental capitation plan.	**DNA**	Deoxyribonucleic acid.
	3. Dependent care program.	**DNR**	Do not resuscitate.
	4. Dental care plan.	**DOC**	Department of Commerce.
DCR	Dependent-care reimbursement.	**DOD**	Department of Defense.
DCS	Disk color separation.	**DOE**	1. Department of Education.
DCW	Dependent coverage waiver.		2. Design of experiments.
DDAP	Digital distribution of advertising for publication.	**DOL**	Department of Labor.
		DOMO	Downwardly mobile professional.
DDE	Dynamic data exchange.	**DORS**	Defense Outplacement Referral System.
DDS	Disability Determination Service.		
		DOS	Disk operating system.
DeCA	Defense Commissary Agency.	**DOT**	1. Department of Transportation.
DEERS	Defense Enrollment/Eligibility Reporting System.		2. *Dictionary of Occupational Titles.*
DEFRA	Deficit Reduction Act of 1984.	**DP**	Data processing.
DETC	Distance Education and Training Council.	**dpi**	Dots per inch.
		DPO	Direct public offering.
DFAS	Defense Finance and Accounting Service.	**DPPO**	Dental preferred provider organization.
DFVC	Delinquent Filer Voluntary Compliance.	**DRAS**	Defense Retiree and Annuitant Pay System.
DFWA	Drug-Free Workplace Act of 1988.	**DRE**	Digital rectal exam.

DRGs   Diagnosis-related groups.

DRP   Dividend reinvestment plan.

DSM III-R   *Diagnostic and Statistical Manual of Mental Disorders,* 3rd Edition.

DSS   Decision support systems.

DSVD   Digital simultaneous voice and data.

DTP   Desktop publishing.

DTVC   Desktop videoconferencing.

DUR   Drug utilization review.

DV   Digital video.

DVA   Department of Veterans Affairs.

DVD   Digital virtual disc.

DVH   Domestic violence hotline.

DVI   Digital video interactive technology.

daddy track   The career path taken by male employees who give priority to their families when making career plans. Such workers often demand more job flexibility and invariably place family obligations and considerations ahead of everything including opportunities for promotion. *See also* grandpa track; mommy track.

daily maximum   The largest amount that a health care insurance policy will pay for care (other than for covered equipment purchases) that a beneficiary can receive for any one calendar day of confinement to a health care facility.

daily work log   *See* daily work record.

daily work record   A method of job analysis. Job incumbents are required to fill out daily records of tasks performed over a period of weeks or months. Reports are tabulated and analyzed to identify tasks performed by workers. Results are used to prepare job descriptions, and performance standards, and as a basis for training programs.

data   **1.** A collection of information used or produced by a computer program, including numbers, text, graphics, images, or voice. **2.** A collection of related information in machine-readable form.

database (DB)   A collection of numeric data or textual information that is processed in computer-readable form and stored electronically in a computer's memory for later electronic publishing or distribution. Databases are in full-text, bibliographic, or abstract form. Full-text means just that; bibliographic and abstract mean that a precis, brief summary, or citation is all that is available on-line.

database management system (DBMS)   A software package used to manipulate information. It serves as a repository for stored data, logically unifies all data files, gives multiple users, with different needs and requirements, access to the same data elements, and automatically performs a variety of data integrity checks. Data base management systems eliminate redundancy and superfluous data in the system and reports and thereby reduce costs.

database manager   An individual who is responsible for insuring the technical correctness, cost-effectiveness, consistent usefulness, and security of an organization's computer files.

database producer   Any organization that produces, publishes, or distributes information in machine-readable form.

database record   A collection of related items of information treated as a unit. For example, a bibliographic database would contain complete descriptive information about each document listed: author, title, classification, date of publication, number of pages, the identity of the publisher/sponsoring organization, and an abstract of its contents.

database vendor   An organization that offers for a fee standardized computer access to several databases.

data communications   The technology that enables computers to "talk" to each other (keypunched cards, magnetic tapes, diskettes, mark sense forms, or computer files) and distribute computer output (hardcopy reports, graphics, microfiche, tapes, or diskettes) to those who need the materials in their jobs.

data compression   A technology that makes it possible to store data at lower cost by shrinking numeric, alphabetic, photos, and full-motion video for transport (via satellite or telephone lines) and storage and expanding it back to full size when needed. Enables more efficient transmission or storage of data.

data conversion   Changing data stored in a computer from one form to another or from one application system to another; for example, converting a text file from one word processing system to another.

data element   A single piece of data, such as an employee's last name, date of birth, or salary.

data integrity   Assurance provided by a **database management system** that stored data have not changed except in ways specifically intended by the user.

Data Match A Health Care Financing Administration initiative designed to access information on cases in which Medicare benefits are secondary to those provided by an employer's group plan in an attempt to recover money from employer plans that should have had primary responsibility for claims paid by Medicare. Penalties will be assessed for violations, including failure to supply the requested information on current or past employees' health care coverage.

data mining Using sophisticated technologically advanced tools to find, manipulate, and synchronize data buried deep in corporate databases to support decision decision making. Also called *data drilling, data surfing,* and *data warehouse.*

data processing (DP) The use of digital computers to organize, manipulate, and format data in a business, industry, educational, medical, military, or service organization. *See also* entries beginning with computer.

data processing training   *See* computer literacy training; computer training.

DATA STAR A database vendor. *Contact:* D-S Marketing Inc., 485 Devon Park Dr., Wayne, PA 19087, 800/221-7754 or 215/687-6777.

DATATIMES A database vendor. *Contact:* Datatimes, 14000 Quail Springs Pkwy, Ste. 450, Oklahoma City, OK 73134, 405/751-6400.

Davis-Bacon Acts of 1931 and 1964 (DBA) Require most federal contractors, employers in construction, and those in related areas to pay prevailing wage rates. Amendments provide for employee fringe benefits and mandate records retention requirements. The Acts apply to employers on contracts exceeding $2,000.

Davis v. Michigan A 1989 Supreme Court ruling that states must tax the pensions of state and federal civil service retirees equally. For example, exempting state pensions from income taxes and taxing military or federal retirees or limiting their exemptions would constitute unequal treatment.

day care center   *See* child care facility; child care; elder care.

day care reimbursement account Payments to employees for day care expenses that are nontaxable if certain rules are met:

(1) the annual amount reimbursed must be less than the lower of the employee's or spouse's income; (2) the payment must be for the care of a dependent who is under the age of 13 or who is physically or mentally incapable of self-care; (3) payments cannot be made to a person who is claimed as the employee's dependent on his or her income tax return; (4) when care is provided by a dependent care center or in an individual's home that provides for more than 6 individuals, the center or home must comply with all state and local laws; and (5) the person providing care must sign the reimbursement claim form or provide an invoice or receipt that includes his or her Social Security or care center license number.

daydreaming An individual ideation technique for generating possible solutions to a problem simply by turning the problem, issue, or idea over in your mind rather than addressing it directly. Sometimes called *guided imaging.*

day-of-the-week discount A special discount offered by airlines on days that have historically been low travel days. Includes weekend travel.

day rate A hotel room rate, typically one-half of the regular room rate for a room being used (up to 5 p.m.), by a guest during a given day.

days per thousand   In health care, a standard unit for measuring utilization.

deadbeat dad A term used to describe divorced, non-custodial fathers who have either failed to make court-ordered child support payments or have fallen behind in their payments to their former spouses who have custody of the children.

deadbeat mom A term used to describe divorced, non-custodial mothers who have either failed to make court-ordered child support payments or have fallen behind in their payments to their former spouses who have custody of the children.

dead-tree edition Derogatory cyberspeak for the paper version of a periodical that appears in both paper and electronic (Internet) forms.

deaf and hearing impaired   People who are totally or partially deaf and have sufficient hearing loss to place limitations of varying severity on participation in personal, social, or occupational activities.

dealer training   *See* sales and dealer training.

death care A new employee benefit being offered by some organizations. Such plans offer employees assistance in planning and/or financing funerals for themselves and their dependents.

death benefits Benefits paid to survivors, such as lump-sum preretirement death benefits, preretirement spouse annuities, refunds of employee contributions to pension plans on death before retirement and accumulated interest, insurance (such as individual policy pension trusts or retirement annuities), and death benefits after retirement payable in one of three forms: unreduced, derived by the application of some formula, or optional (elected by the participant).

death spiral Refers to a continuing increase in health insurance premiums, typically in a free-choice setting where losses from underwriting, due to retention of members who cannot change plans because of benefits restrictions or preexisting conditions, mount faster than the premiums can recover.

death tax See estate tax; sponge tax.

deauthorization See deunionization.

debit card A means of controlling travel and entertainment expenses similar to a checking account. Employees charge business expenses to a card, which deducts the amount from an established account (prepaid), thereby eliminating the need for petty cash, cash advances and expense reimbursement payments. Offered by most major bank cards.

debrief The process of questioning a participant in some activity, program, or learning experience to assist that person to analyze his or her performance — or to gather information relating to the feelings and perceptions of the individual about the experience.

debriefing **1.** An exercise following a training session, such as role playing, assessment, or field trip, in which trainees are questioned by the facilitator, evaluator, or other trainees about their experience, what they have learned, and what followup activities they plan to engage in. **2.** One of three crucial elements (and the most important) of all activities used in **adventure training**. The others are **framing** and **implementation**. Debriefing involves reflecting on and discussing the activity to uncover the learning. Also called *processing*. **3.** A discussion with a person or team following return from a trip or mission or completion of an important project, conducted by management, to identify "lessons learned." **3.** An activity conducted following some kind of exercise in which participants discuss and analyze their efforts and performance. Videotapes may be used to help in the analysis.

debt avoidance Includes both legal and illegal, ethical and unethical strategies to evade or escape financial obligations, such as Chapter 11 bankruptcy filing or transferring property to a spouse, a child, or another corporate entity, and liquidation of assets.

debt-loading See bust-out.

debug Eliminating errors from newly developed computer software (programs).

decentralization he practice of placing operations and decision making of business, industrial, training, or other functional elements of organizations near the customers or clients rather than at a centralized headquarters. Like **departmentation**, it divides functions, processes, and personnel into separate groups in an attempt to improve the achievement of the organization's objectives. Decentralization has one additional feature: it disperses authority throughout the organization by giving managers in subunits greater autonomy in planning and decision making.

decentralization of pay The practice of distributing responsibility for compensation to departmental managers instead of holding it at the corporate level.

deceptive advertising Occurs when a company or seller exaggerates the benefits of a product or service. In the case of insurance, the agent or company may exaggerate what the buyer is likely to have to pay for an illness or surgery and overstates the benefits of medigap plans. Endorsements by celebrities on TV have been especially deceptive.

Deceptive Mailings Prevention Act of 1990 (DMPA) An act signed into law November 6, 1990 that prohibits the use of official-looking emblems, titles, seals, or insignia on mailings that are solicitations from non-governmental organizations unless a disclaimer is used on the front of the envelope and on the material contained within it. The disclaimer must alert the recipient that the mailing is not from a government entity but is a solicitation for the purchase of goods or services.

decertification *See* deunionization.

decile Any one of the nine scores or points that divide a distribution into ten equal parts, each containing one-tenth of all the scores or cases. The first decile is the 10th percentile, the fifth is the 50th percentile, and so on.

decision briefing An oral presentation designed to obtain a verdict or judgment on an issue from an individual or group empowered to make that decision. Its purpose is to sell an idea or course of action based on facts and logic

decision-making The central job of all managers — consciously and deliberately choosing what is to be done, who is to do it, when, where, and sometimes, how.

decision-making training Training provided to supervisors and managers to improve their decisions. Typically it focuses on the processes and procedures of problem solving and the nature of risk-taking.

decision matrix A form, table, or format within which a complex of elements takes shape, permitting the selection of the best or most promising option or choice of action.

decision room An arc-shaped room equipped with 10 or more individual computer workstations, a large front-of-the-room viewing screen, and state of the art audiovisual equipment. It is used for brainstorming sessions, group consideration of ideas and problem solutions, and decision making.

decision support systems (DSS) Executive information systems designed to help management make human resources choices.

decision template A model, device, pattern or mold that serves as a gauge or guide to the production of an object or tool. For example, there are templates for choosing a training delivery system.

decision tree A means of arriving at a decision when confronted by alternative routes to the attainment of an objective. It involves answering a series of carefully sequenced questions, usually in terms of "yes" or "no" which leads the decision maker to a high quality decision.

deck A videotape recorder.

dedicated defined contribution plan account A plan for meeting retiree medical liabilities in which benefits are funded by using a portion of profit-sharing accounts to purchase insurance coverage or reimburse annuitants for medical expenses.

dedicated leased lines Lines provided by telephone companies used exclusively to transmit data between sites on a **wide area network.**

deductible The amount of expense a subscriber or beneficiary of a health plan or subscriber must incur before the company plan, Medicare, or other plan (such as the **Civilian Health and Medical Programs of the Uniformed Services**) begins payment for covered services. That is, a deductible is the specific dollar amount the employee or beneficiary must bear before coverage on an insurance policy kicks in. It is a form of cost-sharing.

deductive reasoning The process of reasoning from the general to the specific — of abstracting a general principle from a series of experiences and then applying that principle to other identical or similar situations.

de-employment *See* outplacement.

defamation Aspersions cast on another person. Includes **slander** (oral statements) and **libel** (written statements) that are legally actionable if they are misleading or untrue, result in injury to the person's reputation, and communicated to someone other than the employee. In selection, a potential land mine for anyone who responds to requests for information about present or former employees.

default Failure to carry out any legally binding agreement, commitment, or promise.

defective pricing Illegal pricing tactics, some of which can lead to criminal charges and jail sentences; for example, **bait and switch** and **fraudulent tagging**.

Defense Authorization Act of 1992 Created a mail-order pharmacy benefit for military beneficiaries. Phase-in will occur in at least two multi-state areas by mid-1994. The Act also requires that all DoD managed-care contracts awarded or renewed after January 1, 1993 include a managed-care network of community retail pharmacies for military beneficiaries and Medicare-eligible military retirees affected by the closure of a health care facility as a result of the closure or realignment of a base. Fees, charges, or copayments will be assessed — probably at 20 percent of the cost of the prescription drug.

Defense Commissary Agency (DeCA) Provides a non-pay benefit for active and retired military personnel and their dependents. Offers food at DeCA-operated commissaries, similar to supermarkets, at cost (with a five percent surcharge to cover the cost of commissary maintenance, operating supplies, and new construction) at military installations within the U.S. and abroad.

Defense Enrollment/Eligibility Reporting System (DEERS)   A computerized system used by **uniformed services** health facilities and **Civilian Health and Medical Programs of the Uniformed Services** contractors to confirm an individual's entitlement to services. Retired members receiving retired pay and surviving spouses receiving an annuity are enrolled automatically; enrollment of dependents is the responsibility of sponsors.

Defense Finance and Accounting Service (DFAS)   Operates two centers (Cleveland, OH and Denver, CO) for the administration of the pay accounts of members of the military services. An initiative is underway to convert all Department of Defense military retiree and annuitant pay accounts to a standard pay system and consolidate administration of these accounts to the DFAS.

Defense of Marriage Act of 1996   Legislation, signed by President Clinton September 21, 1996, that defines marriage as a union between a man and a woman, thereby limiting same-sex marriages. The Act prevents gay couples from sharing federal benefits, such as Social Security. Although states have the authority to legalize gay marriages, the federal government would not recognize them. It also allows states the right not to recognize the validity of same-sex marriages performed in another state.

Defense Outplacement Referral System (DORS)   A system that provides mini-résumés of the more than 38,000 military personnel who have registered with the system and have skills that may fit civilian jobs. *Contact:* 800/727-3677.

Defense Retiree and Annuitant Pay System (DRAS)   Administers retiree and annuitant pay accounts for retirees and annuitants of all military services.

defensive bonding   Occurs when a group of employees sticks together out of fear of punishment rather than out of concern for each other.

deferred annuity   An annuity that provides that the money invested in the contract be held by the insurer until some future time (such as the normal retirement age) at which time payments to the beneficiary will begin. In the intervening time, investment earnings are credited to the contract.

deferred arrangements   *See* Section 401(k), Internal Revenue Code.

deferred benefits plan   A retirement plan designed as an incentive for employees to remain with an organization for a full career. It prefunds and guarantees the benefits an employee will receive in retirement. Typically the employer calculates the benefits based on average annual income during the employee's last 3 to 5 years of service. Usually a minimum period of employment is required to vest in the plan.

deferred compensation   **1.** In general, any compensation payments that accrue to an employee at some time in the future (such as pension fund annuities) and are sheltered from taxation until paid. **2.** A form of economic reward for outstanding performance or accomplishments (usually executives). The company invests a specified amount of money each year for a specific period of time in a mutual fund or other investment in the name and ownership of the corporation. Each year, the corporation borrows a certain percentage against the collateral of this investment to buy a cash-value life insurance policy on the life of the insured and owned by the employee. Upon retirement, the executive or his or her beneficiary receives an annual percentage of the net value of the investment at the time of retirement. The executive gets additional current compensation, a substantial life insurance policy against which he or she can borrow, and deferred compensation at retirement.

deferred income plans (DIPs)   **(1)** An executive compensation plan designed to supplement executive earnings by helping overcome limits on the amount of compensation that can be deferred as well as the timing restrictions on distributions imposed by the **Omnibus Budget Reconciliation Act of 1993** and the **General Agreement on Tariffs and Trade** of 1993. **(2)** A type of pension plan in which a portion of a company's profits is credited to each employee's account, placed under the supervision of a trustee, and distributed to the employee or his or her beneficiaries upon retirement or death. There are no guaranteed benefits.

Deficit Reduction Act of 1984 (DEFRA)
Federal legislation that proscribes inclusion of taxable benefits as part of a flexible benefits plans. It also requires employers to give employees' spouses age 65 or older the option of enrolling in group health insurance benefits plans as an alternative to Medicare. New sections (419 and 419A) to the Internal Revenue Code limit the deductibility of contributions to welfare plans and the amount that can be set aside by such plans on a tax-exempt basis. They also require management to explain to employees the technical concepts introduced by the **Employee Retirement Income Security Act of 1974** and its amendments, particularly matters relating to pension plans.

Deficit-Reduction Reconciliation Act of 1989 Established a fee scale for physicians' services under Medicare and limited the amount that physicians could bill patients above what Medicare pays. Medicare generally pays 80 percent of the allowable fee for a particular service, and the patient pays the remaining 20 percent. Physicians who do not accept Medicare's rate as full payment are prohibited by law from charging more than 120 percent (in 1992) and 114 percent (in 1993) of that rate.

defined benefit Keogh plan A plan for self-employed individuals operating in unincorporated businesses. Similar to defined benefit pension plans.

defined benefit pension plan A plan that entitles participants to retirement benefits established in advance. Each year the amount of annual contributions required to provide the defined benefit is determined based on actuarial assumptions such as pre- and post-retirement interest, mortality, turnover, salary scale, and so on. Although retirement benefits are fixed, contributions vary from year to year. The annual benefit at retirement is limited to 100 percent of gross income up to $94,023 (adjusted annually for cost of living). The benefit can be increased or decreased depending on whether retirement benefits begin before or after the individual's Social Security retirement age.

defined benefit plan (DBP) A plan that uses a formula that includes earnings and length of service to calculate the retirement benefits of employees. The employer promises a certain level of benefits at retirement regardless of what happens. The level of entitlement is predefined in terms of any one or a combination of factors, such as level of pay, years of service, and age. The DBP is the type of plan used by most major companies nationwide. For example, a corporate pension plan is a defined benefit.

defined contribution plan (DCP) A retirement plan in which the benefit is not set in advance but depends on plan earnings, length of service, and the amount of of annual contributions. DCPs offer flexibility and control for both the employer and the employee. Retirement benefits are determined by the contributions made by the employee and the employer and their earnings during the period between the contributions and the date of retirement. Benefits are not guaranteed. The employer merely promises to put in a certain amount of money (based on such things as profits, percentage of salary, or an employment-related formula), which the employee may augment in most plans. Contributions are invested on behalf of the named employee, and retirement benefits are whatever accumulated contributions and their investment yield add up to when the employee ceases work. These plans have the advantage of of being portable.

defrag The process of locating data that the disk operating system has scattered over a hard disk and collecting it into contiguous clusters, resulting in accelerating performance of the disk by up to 30 percent or more — and at the same time, extend the life of the disk by reducing wear and tear on the head. It is accomplished by a disk optimizer.

dejobbing The process of dismantling conventional approaches to the division of work in an organization, such as jobs and job descriptions, and using a system in which employees complete tasks on a project-by-project basis. Said to require new forms of organization structure and new hiring, evaluation, and compensation practices but provides greater flexibility, clearer organization focus, a larger pool of talent, and reduced costs. Attributed to William Bridges, *Job Shift: How to Prosper in Workplace Without Jobs*.

delayed retirement credit Under the Social Security system, people who continue to work and do not receive some or all of their monthly checks because of the earnings test are given what is called delayed retirement credit. In effect, it is a bonus for continuing to work beyond age 65. The credit is worth 3.5 percent a year for those who became 65 in 1990 and 1991, rising to eight percent for those becoming age 62 in 2005 or later.

de-layering Restructuring an organization by reducing the number of "layers" or levels of management and supervision.

delay procedure A means of communicating with a deaf person. The nondisabled person stands at least three feet from the individual and waits *at least* five seconds following a question, direction, or request to see whether the individual will give the appropriate response. If the person does not respond within the time allowed, the supervisor or instructor then models or provides the correct response.

delegating A part of the organizing process by which a manager deliberately makes it possible for subordinates to share in the work to be done and the decisions to be made. It is the process of assigning tasks to subordinates, clearly defining what results are expected, giving them a time limit for completion and enough authority to complete the tasks successfully, providing a means for the subordinate to measure and evaluate performance and guidance and assistance as necessary, and exacting responsibility for acceptable performance.

delete tracking A computer utility program that saves basic information about erased files — where the file was stored and how many clusters it occupied — in a small log file. The program may permit the user to view deleted files, estimate undeleted probability, and search and recover data and file fragments.

deleverage/deleveraging The financial strategy of lowering debt to avoid defaults and bankruptcies by shrinking the equity base of a company. Employs such means as repurchasing a company's own stock to lower the overall cost of capital.

Delinquent Filer Voluntary Compliance (DFVC) A Department of Labor program that allows employers to reduce or avoid applicable civil penalties for failing to comply with the reporting provisions of the **Employment Retirement Security Act of 1974** and relief for employers who sponsor certain apprenticeship and training benefits programs or non-qualified, unfunded pension plans for highly compensated executives.

delivery platform The computer operating system, such as Windows or System 8, needed by users to run their multimedia programs.

delivery system **1.** Means of conducting training or learning, from on-the-job training, use of job or work aids, exportable training packages, and correspondence courses, to classroom training, multimedia, interactive video, computer-based training, and self-study. **2.** The specific computer equipment needed to run multimedia programs.

Delphi survey A projective technological forecasting technique involving original individual anonymous input of opinion on a specific issue or subject by a pool of experts, tabulation and feedback of responses or projections to participants, reconsideration of responses by the experts, retabulation of second-round responses with explanatory comments, and retabulation and distribution of projections and comments. The process can be repeated several times until consensus of the experts is achieved.

delusion Fixed, irrational ideas not shared by others and that do not respond to logical or reasoned argument.

deluxe hotel A hotel that features highly personalized attention, services, amenities, and care. In addition to customary services, deluxe hotels greet guests by name, place fruit baskets and fresh flowers in rooms, supply fresh linens, spruce ups, and turn-downs at the guest's convenience, furnish around-the-clock room service, shine guests' shoes each night, and have secretaries and a Concierge on hand to assist in all ways possible.

demand forecast Relates to HR forecasting. A forecast developed from analysis of the projected work load over a specified time frame, usually five years. It may take two forms: a core forecast, which consists of the most certain definition of personnel needs, and a variable forecast, which incorporates less certain variables and permits the inclusion of "what if" scenarios. Actual planning is invariably based on the core forecast, and the variable forecast is held in reserve.

demand management A part of the evolution of the **wellness program** concept, demand management is a means of educating employees so that they can make better health care decisions and, in so doing, reduce costs to employers. Focuses on how, why, when, and were employees access the health care system and tracking what happens when they have sought professional services.

demand pricing A pricing strategy that uses cost and minimum profit as the floor. The actual price is often considerably higher than the floor price due to market demand for the product or service.

de minimus **fringe benefit** A fringe benefit that is so small in value that it would be impractical or unreasonable for an employer to be required to account for them. They do not have to be included in an employee's gross taxable income. Examples are occasional tickets for entertainment or sports events, infrequent parties for employees, meal money when an employee works overtime, and sporadic personal use of company tools and equipment, such as the copy machine.

demo A formal presentation (demonstration) of the capabilities of a computer hardware and/or software package.

demographics Characteristics of a population — race, color, national origin, religion, sex and age distribution, geographical distribution and work force changes in terms of sex, age, marital status, handicapping conditions, and educational and literacy levels.

demonstration method A basic instructional method often used in combination with the lecture (lecture-demonstration) or with performance (demonstration-performance) to teach manipulative operations and procedures, operation and functioning of equipment, team skills, and safety procedures. In demonstration, the instructor actually performs an operation or task, thereby showing the trainees *what* to do and *how* to do it; he or she then uses explanations to point out *why, where,* and *when* it is to be done. The trainees then repeat the operation or task under the guidance of the instructor.

demotion Assigning an employee to a job with lower pay, less challenge, or reduced status and prestige. Although sometimes used as a form of disciplinary action, this is not recommended. Demotion should be reserved for situations in which an employee has been erroneously promoted or is no longer able to perform the duties and functions of the job due to physical, mental, or emotional problems rather than because of unacceptable behavior, conduct, or substandard performance.

dental capitation plan (DCP) A plan that pays dentists a small monthly fee per patient whether service is provided or not.

dental care Typically includes such services as diagnostic and preventive procedures, emergency care for treatment of pain or injury, restorative care, oral and maxillofacial surgery, endodontics, periodontics, prosthodontics, and orthodontics.

dental care plan (DCP) Similar to medical and hospitalization plans, a DCP includes provisions relating to eligibility, cost-sharing, and the determination of benefits. Full reimbursements are limited to minor preventive and restorative procedures. Major restorative (crowns and dentures) and orthodontic (cosmetic) procedures are rarely covered for more than 50 to 75 percent of the cost.

dental health maintenance organization (DHMO) A health maintenance organization organized solely to provide dental benefits.

dental preferred provider organization (DPPO) A dental plan in which an employer contracts with a dentist or group of dentists to provide dental care for its employees. Dentists in the network are paid on a traditional fee-for-service basis but at lower rates, typically giving employees a 10 to 30 percent discount. Although designed to improve monitoring of plan utilization and effect savings, they may not achieve the latter due to increased utilization caused by participating dentists offsetting corporate-negotiated discounts by increasing the number of treatments or office visits.

deontology An approach to ethical decision making. Maintains that duty (rules and principles) should guide actions. There are two forms: (1) Kantian, which focuses on duty and universal rules to determine right actions, where reason, not inclination, should guide the will, and (2) Contractarian or social contract theory, that focuses, not on individual decision making, but on the general social precepts or standards that reasonable persons in ideal situations would accept, approve, and adopt.

deoxyribonucleic acid (DNA) A compound found in the chromosomes of all living things and viruses. It consists of long chain of molecules in two strands wound around each other in a double helix. Two yards of DNA are packed into each one of the 100 trillion cells in the human body, and each strand is more than 37,000 times thinner than a human hair. Every person gets one set of 23 chromosomes for each parent.

departmental walls The invisible walls that separate functional elements of an organization and sometimes result in internal dissension and competition for resources.

departmentation The practice of dividing the functions, processes, and personnel of an organization into separate elements and grouping these subunits in a manner that promises to contribute best to the attainment of the organization's objectives. The most common bases for departmentation are by function, by process, by product, by geographic territory, and by customer or client class.

department cost The benchmarked cost of of a standard procedure or process, the total cost per direct production, research milestone, or other output.

Department of Commerce (DOC) Established to promote American businesses and trade. Its responsibilities include expanding U.S. exports, developing innovative technologies, gathering and disseminating statistical data, measuring economic growth, granting patents, promoting minority entrepreneurship, predicting the weather and monitoring stewardship. An overarching mandate requires DOC agencies to work with the business community to foster economic growth and the creation of new American jobs. DOC is also a source of contracting advice and assistance to firms wanting to do business with the government. *Contact:* DOC, 14th & Constitution Ave., N.W., Room H6411, Washington, DC 20230 (202/377-1472; URL **http://www.doc.gov**).

Department of Defense (DOD) Responsible for providing the military forces needed to deter war and protect the security of the United States. Under the President, the Commander in Chief, the Secretary of Defense exercises the authority, direction, and control over the department, which includes the Joint Chiefs of Staff, National Guard, Army, Navy, Air Force, Marine Corps, and Coast Guard (in time of war). Web home page contains links to the official pages of the Army, Navy, Air force, Marines, and National Guard. (URL **http://www.dtic. mil/defenselink/**).

Department of Defense Interim Rule on Drug-Free Work Force A rule that applies only to Department of Defense contracts involving access to classified information or at such other times as a contracting officer determines it necessary for reasons of national security, health, or safety. The rule states that contractors must have a drug awareness program that includes (1) random testing of employees in "sensitive positions"; (2) an **employee assistance program** that deals with substance abuse; and (3) personnel procedures and practices to deal with drug abusers. The rule became effective October 31, 1988.

Department of Education (DOE) Established to ensure equal access to education and promote educational excellence throughout the Nation. DOE also supplements and complements the efforts of states, the local school systems and other instrumentalities of the states, the private sector, public and private nonprofit educational research institutions, community-based organizations, parents, and students to improve the quality of education. Web site provides education links, describes educational grants and research reports and opportunities, and furnishes guides to the Department. *Contact:* U.S. Department of Education, INet Project Manager, Office of Educational Research and Improvement, National Library of Education, 555 New Jersey Ave. N.W., Room 214b, Washington, D.C. 20208-5725 (202/219-1547; Fax 202/219-1817; E-mail **webmaster@inet.ed.gov**; URL **http://www.ed.gov**).

Department of Labor (DOL) Charged with preparing the American work force for new and better jobs, and ensuring the adequacy of America's workplaces and is responsible for the administration and enforcement of over 180 federal statutes. These legislative mandates and the regulations produced to implement them cover a wide variety of workplace activities for nearly 10 million employers and well over 100 million workers, including protecting workers' wages, health and safety, employment and pension rights; promoting equal employment opportunity; administering job training, unemployment insurance and workers' compensation programs; strengthening free collective bargaining and collecting, analyzing and publishing labor and economic statistics. (URL **http://www.dol.gov**).

Department of Labor 404(c) regulations Among other things, establish rules and standards for the kind of educational effort employers must make to help their employees who have access to multiple portfolio 401(k) and other defined contribution plans understand their investment options. Employers are not permitted to give employees "advice" about investments, but may provide "education" — a distinction that will ultimately be clarified by the courts.

Department of the Air Force (DAF) Mission is to defend the United States through control and exploitation of air and space. The service is organized in eight major commands throughout the world which provide combat aircraft, airlift, refueling, reconnaissance and other support to the Unified Combatant Commands. Web home page provides links to other Air Force Web sites and information for retirees. (URL **http://www.dtic.mil/airforcelink/**).

Department of the Army (DA) Mission is to preserve peace and security, and provide for the defense of the United States, the Territories, Commonwealths, and possessions, and any areas occupied by the United States, support national policies, implement national objectives, overcome any nations responsible for aggressive acts that imperil the peace and security of the United States. Web site provides links to retiree services, useful addresses, and phone numbers. (URL **http://www.army.mil/**).

Department of the Navy (DN) Established to maintain freedom of the seas for the United States and its allies, to be prepared to conduct combat operations at sea in support of the national interests of the United States, and to maintain the ability for power projection ashore. Web site provides links to retiree services, useful addresses, and phone numbers (E-mail **navyonline@ncts. navy.mil**; URL **http://www.navy.mil/**).

Department of Veterans Affairs (DVA) Home page provides an index of services and benefits available to U.S. veterans, a state-by-state listing of veterans' facilities, phone numbers, information on where to get help, special programs for veterans, and links to other veterans' sites. (URL **http:// www.va.gov/**).

dependency and indemnity compensation (DIC) A federal program designed to compensate widows and other dependents of military personnel who die on active duty or of former service members who die from service-connected injuries or diseases. Formerly payments were based on the grade of the service member or veteran. New rates went into effect on January 1, 1993, although surviving spouses of veterans who died before January 1, 1993 will receive the higher of the old and new rates. Under the new rates, all beneficiaries, regardless of the military pay grade of the decedent, receive a flat rate of $750 per month. That rate is increased by $165 for survivors of veterans rated totally disabled for a continuous period of at least eight years immediately preceding death. Additionally, the monthly amount for each child increased $100 in January 1993, $150 per month in October 1993, and $200 per month in October 1994 and thereafter.

dependent care assistance plan (DCAP) Under the Economic Recovery Tax Act of 1981, employers were given the opportunity to offer dependent care assistance in the form of payments or help in finding adequate child care facilities as a fringe benefit to their employees.

dependent care facility (DCF) An employer-sponsored dependent care option.

dependent care program (DCP) Includes child care and elder care. There are four categories of options: financial assistance programs, establishment of child care facilities, workplace information services, and personnel policies.

dependent care reimbursement (DCR) A relatively new employee benefit in which the employer reimburses employees for dependent care expenditures either fully or in part.

dependent coverage waiver (DPW) A health care cost reduction strategy. Employees are allowed to waive dependent coverage.

deposed A legal term. Said of an individual who has given pretrial testimony under oath. *See also* pretrial deposition.

deposit administration arrangement (DAA) A relatively new funding plan vehicle for annuity contracts. Instead of purchasing or insuring pensions for active employees, the assets of these plans are maintained in an accumulation account (an unallocated fund accruing interest). When an employee retires, his or her pension (the amount of which is then known) is purchased from the insurance annuity account and the purchase price is subtracted from the accumulation account. Key features of the plan: (1) greater flexibility than under conventional plans; (2) less extensive guarantees than under fully insured plans such as deferred group annuities or retirement income contracts; (3) purchased benefits for retirees calculated according to the carrier's dividend formula and the experience of all purchased annuities rather than according to the experience of individual deposit administration contracts; and (4) the contract is allocated for retired participants (and possibly terminated but vested participants) and unallocated for actives.

deposition See pretrial deposition.

depression A feeling of sadness or melancholy, which may vary from mild distress to complete despair. In mild cases, the individual is typically quiet, restrained, inhibited, unhappy, and unable to make decisions; in severe cases, the sufferer is often dejected and defeated in attitude and manner. Symptoms include loss of interest in sex and other activities once enjoyed; feelings of sadness or irritability; feelings of unreality, worthlessness, or hopelessness; inability to think, concentrate, remember, or make decisions; headaches; changes in weight or appetite; fatigue or loss of energy; sleep disturbances or changes in sleep patterns, and recurrent thoughts of suicide or death. If an individual experiences at least five of these symptoms, including at at least one of the first two symptoms, for at least two weeks, he or she may be depressed and should consult with a mental health professional. Treatment includes antidepressant medication, psychotherapy, or a combination of medication and psychotherapy.

depressive illnesses The most common of psychiatric disorders, illnesses that often interfere with normal functioning and cause pain and suffering not only to those with the disorder but also those who care about them. However, they are usually less persistently disabling than **schizophrenia**. Depression affects twice as many women as men. The primary disturbance is that of mood.

depth interview See focused interview.

derived objectives Knowledge and skills that contribute to the development of primary job skills — fundamental and integral (or closely related) understandings, concepts, principles and elements of skills that support the attainment of the primary objectives of a training program.

descriptive order A type of instructional sequencing in which the order of presentation is determined by the nature of the material. It is used where the content is highly descriptive or taxonomic; for example, programming and budgeting, data-handling and information systems, and quality control procedures where there are carefully prescribed sequential operations, and descriptions of methodology, equipment, and the like.

descriptive scale A rating scale that uses adjectives or phrases to rate levels of ability, proficiency, or performance. Includes behaviorally-anchored rating scales, essay appraisal, critical incident technique, graphic scales, forced choice scales, and checklists.

descriptive study A study in which data are collected on a situation or area of interest systematically and accurately to determine what the situation really is. Includes opinion and attitude surveys, case studies, anecdotal records, critical incident reports, action research, and performance records. Descriptive studies may report results in either qualitative (verbal descriptions) or quantitative (numerical counts, frequencies, measures of central tendency, or other measurements) terms. However, cause and effect relationships are not established.

design/development cycle One of the two cycles that make up **total cycle time.** It encompasses all activities required to market new products and services — from the time when an opportunity is identified to the time when the product or service is ready for the market.

designer A human resources/human resources development (HR/HRD) competency. A designer is the architect of a HR or HRD system or program.

designer drugs Drugs developed specifically to produce the mind-altering effects of their illegal counterparts. Include analogs of fentanyl ("synthetic heroin," "china white"), analogs of demerol ("synthetic heroin," MPTP [new heroin]"), analogs of amphetamines and methamphetamines ("MDMA," Ecstasy," "XTVC"), and analogs of phencyclidine ("PCPy," "PCE").

design of experiments (DOE) A tool used by workers, usually in tandem with statistical process control and as a part of a participative management strategy, to measure their machine's performance and average and chart the results to improve their productivity. A powerful means of solving quality problems.

de-skilling The practice of dividing low-end manufacturing and service jobs into the smallest and simplest tasks in an attempt to increase efficiency, measurability, and consistency in performance. The reverse of up-skilling.

desktop publishing (DTP) The process of assembling text and graphics using a computer and associated software to produce finished, typeset-looking documents, as contrasted with word processing, which is used to create text. DTP allows the user to experiment with different layouts and designs, mix type sizes and styles, add rules, and insert graphics, line art, and photos. The camera-ready, black-and-white or color masters, including text and graphics, for newsletters, brochures, advertisements, promotional materials, handouts, manuals, and so on are composed by the writer, designer, or editor. Any changes are made by the creator. DPT has three components: a personal computer, with graphics capability, a laser printer, and DPT software.

desktop video An automated presentation created with inexpensive software and a micro-based computer (Macintosh, Amiga, IBM PC, or other and compatibles) and used for either training or promotional purposes. It has two key capabilities: animation and interactivity. The presentation may include images, animation sequences, text, charts, and graphs.

desktop videoconferencing (DTVC) Combines personal computing with audio, video, and communications technologies to provide real-time interaction with other groups of people from a personal computer.

destination management company (DMC) In meeting management, a private full-service professional organization that provides assistance and planning services to corporations and their meeting planners for a fee. Typically operate at overseas locations, including Hawaii, but not exclusively so since many offer their services in U.S. cities. Overseas DMCs make local arrangements before an inspection trip, negotiate with suppliers, greet participants on arrival, find bilingual guides, arrange such things as baggage retrieval, ground transportation, airport transfers, leisure activities, theme parties, and participant and spouse tours at the destination, and provide information on pre-departure agricultural inspections. Domestic DMCs provide baggage and shuttle services, leisure activities, theme events, participant and spousal tours, and other services. Defined by the Association of Destination Management Executives as "a professional management company specializing in the design and delivery of events, activities, tours, staffing, and transportation utilizing local knowledge, expertise, and resources."

destination services Services established to help relocating or transferring employees to adapt to their new surroundings, such as home marketing assistance, school, child day care, and elder care information, and spousal reemployment assistance.

destination services company Often a division of a **home purchase company.** Help employees and their families transferring to a new location to learn as much as possible about the new area before purchasing or leasing a home. They address such concerns as housing and rental costs, utilities, taxes, commuting times and distances, and school quality. Also called *homefinding services* or *area counseling services.*

detection costs In total quality management, costs related to quality assurance measures taken to prevent defects from moving from one stage of a production process to another, such as inspections.

determination evaluation Evaluation strategies designed to assess needs, improve programs, evaluate impacts, and assess processes.

detoxification facility In health care benefits, an institution licensed or certified by the state to provide alcoholism or drug dependency treatment and where such treatment is supervised by a physician or qualified staff member of the treatment facility.

detracking An approach to the restructuring of schools or a means of promoting equal access. Detracking is billed as a promising means of ending inequitable student grouping arrangements and improving educational practice. Essentially it involves terminating such long-standing practices as ability grouping and replacing it with grouping in the basis of interest, themed programs (such as a microsociety school or service academy), or new instructional strategies, such as cooperative learning, interdisciplinary studies, and teaming. Said to require careful planning, overcoming objectors, thorough teacher preparation, and the alinement of organization structures and practices to support the new grouping arrangements.

deunionization The termination of union representation for a particular collective bargaining unit. It is accomplished by a decertification election in which workers vote to disband their union. Also called *deauthorization* or *decertification*.

developing a curriculum (DACUM)
A quick, efficient, and relatively inexpensive approach to curriculum development oriented to current job requirements. Its advocates state that the method cuts the time required for course development to onetenth that of other job analysis methods. It uses a panel of eight to twelve expert-workers and a facilitator to design training. During a two-day session, the panel develops an occupational competency profile for the target job: the duties, tasks, and entry-level tasks, the required supporting skills and knowledge, and the personal traits of successful workers. At a later meeting the panel develops strategies for course development.

development **1.** A planned set of learning experiences designed to improve the skills and job performance of individuals in their current positions in a defined career field or a specific job or to prepare them for advancement to higher-level, more responsible positions in the organization. **2.** In research and development, activities aimed at converting the results of basic and applied research to practical uses, such as marketable products and services.

developmental counseling A form of supervisory counseling in which the employee and the supervisor share ideas and the process of identifying alternatives and selecting the means of remedying a deficiency or solving a problem.

developmental disabilities People whose limitations rest primarily on lowered intellectual capacity attributable to congenital or inherited defects, mental retardation, chromosomal aberrations, disease or injury to the brain, accidents or illnesses in childhood or adulthood, or as the consequence of impaired maturation due to insufficient environmental stimulation from family or cultural sources. *See also* autism; brain injuries; Down syndrome.

developmentalism *See* developmental theory of learning.

developmental theory of learning
Views learners as wanting to be actively involved in their own learning — as oriented toward personal growth. Therefore, learning is facilitated by a supportive training climate where learners choose their own learning experiences.

development costs **1**. All costs incurred during the development of a program or system. **2.** In training, the costs from front-end analysis through the costs of design, development, validation, tracking, evaluation, and redesign.

development program A program designed to encourage and promote improvement and growth in professional, managerial, and technical knowledge, skills, and abilities. Approaches include on-the-job coaching, special assignments, inhouse conferences, clinics, seminars, and workshops, membership on task forces, committees, and research teams, and organization development interventions.

development system The means by which interrelated and interdependent organizational elements are welded into a unified and coherent whole. Includes four subsystem categories: (1) organization development and team building systems, (2) executive, management and supervisory training, (3) employee technical and operational and sales and dealer training, and (4) self-development.

development time The number of hours, days, or weeks required to design, develop, and validate an instructional package or system.

device independence A characteristic of a computer system or program that permits different output devices to image the same file more or less identically.

device independent color Refers to color images that appear the same on different computer output devices, including monitors and various types of printers.

devise A gift of real estate under a will that goes to the devisee as the recipient. *See also* bequest.

devolution In government, reversing the flow of power from the states to the federal government; decentralizing executive and legislative authority; shifting power downward.

diabetes mellitus A disorder of the pancreas that takes one of two forms: Type I, insulin-dependent diabetes mellitus (formerly called juvenile diabetes), a genetic condition in which the pancreas fails to produce insulin thus preventing the body from metabolizing blood sugar, and the more common Type II, non-insulin-dependent diabetes mellitus (formerly called maturity- or adult-onset diabetes), a condition in which the pancreas produces adequate amounts of insulin but the cells are unable to absorb glucose. Although its causes are unknown, researchers believe that individuals can be born with a genetic predisposition towards developing diabetes. Symptoms of Type I usually occur suddenly and include frequent urination, excessive thirst, sudden weight loss, extreme hunger, irritability, weakness and fatigue, and nausea and vomiting. Symptoms of Type II occur gradually and include any of the Type I symptoms, blurred vision, fatigue, recurring hard-to-heal skin, gum, bladder, or vaginal yeast infections, itchy skin, and tingling or numbness in legs, hands, or feet. Treatment for Type I involves daily insulin injections, a balanced diet, limited sugar and fats, and regular exercise. Treatment for Type Two consists of a diet that limits sugar and calories to cause weight loss and a regular exercise program. About 7.8 million Americans have diabetes.

diabetic retinopathy The leading cause of new blindness among adults in the United States. It is a complication of diabetes that is caused by changes in the blood vessels of the eye. When blood vessels in the retina are damaged, they may leak fluid or blood, and grow brush-like branches and scar tissue. This can distort the images that the retina sends to the brain.

diagnosis-related groups (DRGs)
1. Medicare reimbursement levels passed by the Congress in 1983 to control the costs of government health care programs. If a hospital's charges for a particular diagnosis exceed the standard established by the DRGs, reimbursement is reduced to the amount allowed and the provider must absorb the difference. *See also* resource-based relative value scale. **2.** Under the **Civilian Health and Medical Programs of the Uniformed Services,** a new way of paying most civilian hospitals for inpatient services. Under DRGs, CHAMPUS pays most hospitals a fixed rate for inpatient services, regardless of whether or not the hospital bills at a different rate. DRG rates are generally based on national averages of costs for specific services. The DRG system is used in all states except Maryland, and in the District of Columbia and Puerto Rico. Most hospitals are required by law to accept the DRG payment for the impatient care they provide. Beneficiaries are not responsible for the difference between the hospital's billed charges and the DRG payment; they pay only their **cost share**.

***Diagnostic and Statistical Manual of Mental Disorders*, 3rd Edition, revised (DSM III-R)** Provides a coding system for mental and substance abuse disorders.

diagnostic related group reimbursement In health care, a payment system in which a health care provider, such as a hospital, receives a fixed amount per disease category, per admission, regardless of the services actually provided.

diagnostic survey A survey designed and conducted to analyze a specific organizational or employee problem or situation identified by some other means. The survey is conducted to uncover the reasons for it, probe feelings about the situation or problem, and get ideas for its solution.

diagnostic test A test used to identify, locate, assess, and analyze an individual's specific areas of strength and weakness, and where possible, determine their cause. Commonly used to identify knowledge and skills deficiencies.

DIALOG Information Services An on-line **database.** *Contact:* DIALOG, 3460 Hillview Ave., Palo Alto, CA 94304, 800/3-DIALOG or 415/8858-3785.

dial-up connection Allows computers to communicate over a network by means of regular phone lines using a modem.

***Dictionary of Occupational Titles* (DOT)** An authoritative document published by the Department of Labor, available from the Government Printing Office, that lists and defines (in terms of responsibilities, duties, and procedures) more than 20,000 jobs based on analysis of more than 75,000 jobs. In addition the *Dictionary* describes the physical demands of each job, working conditions, and the aptitudes, interests, educational requirements, and vocational preparation required of those seeking employment in each job.

didactic learning A learning strategy used by humans (and to some degree by learning machines). It involves learning facts, principles, or concepts by means of instruction in some form — a teacher, manual, instruction sheet, or multimedia.

didactic teaching Traditional instructor-centered, pedagogic, or instructor-directed learning. It makes use of the presentation and question-and-answer (Socratic) approaches.

diet COLA A permanent reduction in the cost-of-living adjustment for federal and military retirees under the age of 62, resulting in one-half of the full COLA. Proposed in Congress as a spending cut in 1993.

differently abled A term used as a substitute for disabled or handicapped persons.

differing abilities From the phrase, "people with differing abilities," proposed by B. Freer Freeman of Arlington, VA in a contest for a new term to describe people with disabilities. Freeman was awarded the $50,000 first prize by the National Christina Foundation for his entry. The phrase was chosen because it focuses on the abilities of people with disabilities instead of their handicaps.

difficulty *See* item difficulty.

Digispeech A device used to add speech to IBM-compatible software. A special board is installed in the computer and used for speech and sound in the MS-DOS versions of programs. Compatible with **Echo II board** and plug into its speaker jack. Requires IBM PC or compatible, including PS/2 model 25, 30 & 50 (not 50Z). *Contact:* Edmark Corporation, P.O. Box 3903, Bellevue, Washington 98009-3903, (800/426-0856).

digital 1. In data processing, data represented in discrete units, using coded signals (usually a binary code) to express the variables in a problem and provide solutions calculated mathematically. **2.** In video, any device in which an electronic signal is represented by computer-type binary numbers. **3.** Information and communication technology that employs a format compatible with digital computers; information is stored and retrieved as bits.

digital audio tape (DAT) recorder A small (2 1/4" long), expensive recorder that is capable of making distortion-free copies of compact discs and digital broadcasts.

digital distribution of advertising for publication (DDAP) A graphics design system that provides advertising to publications in digital form so that ads can be inserted into the digital flow of data used in publication production thereby making it possible to go directly from computer to plate or computer to press.

digital light processing (DLP) A relatively new American-made projection technology. DLP projectors process light digitally using a microchip, invented by Texas Instruments, that contains thousands of tiny mirrors. *See also* liquid crystal display.

digital photography Using a still video camera/scanner or digital camera that stores images electronically on a magnetic disk rather than on photographic film. Used primarily for certain applications, such as catalogs and newspaper work, due to current quality limitations in terms of image size and resolution. Examples of cameras are the Kodak DCS-2000 and the Sony SEPS-1000.

digital rectal exam (DRE) A medical examination for early identification of prostate problems, including cancer. Recommended annually by the American Cancer Society for men over the age of 40.

digital simultaneous voice and data (DSVD) A standard protocol adopted by major companies in the computer and telecommunications industry, such as Microsoft and Intel, to send both voice and data over a single line either alternately or simultaneously.

digital subtraction angiography An X-ray technique used to obtain detailed closeups of arterial blockage. Special dyes are injected in the arm or leg and the X-ray reveals the arterial sections which the dyes cannot easily penetrate due to blockage.

digital video (DV) **1.** A representation of video images and audio as binary values, 1s and 0s. **2.** A consumer digital video standard. DV provides low-cost, high definition images — 500 lines of horizontal resolution, a signal-to-noise ratio of 54dB, pulse code modulation digital audio, and component recording.

digital video compression A new development in television distribution, which will allow more channels to be delivered to users.

digital-video-disc (DVD) Offers high quality sound and vision, interactive ease, and up to 20 times the storage capacity of a CD-ROM (for dual-layer format, 8,700 megabytes). DVDs differ from compact discs (CDs) in that they use smaller "pits" of data, a more closely spaced track, and special lenses that can focus narrowly on the densely packed pits — thereby achieving great storage capacity. Also called *digital versatile discs.*

digital video interactive (DVI) A hardware and software system, a computer peripheral, a board that is inserted into an existing computer — or incorporated into a new computer equipped with DVI chips. Implements compression of digital audio and video from any source onto a chip set. DVI provides full motion video using a standard CD-ROM disc. Text, images, audio, and motion video can be reduced to digital form (binary code) and stored and manipulated like other data on a computer. That is, once the audio, video, or images are captured, the user can paint, edit, and integrate those components into a multimedia presentation. DVI is preferred by many training and multimedia developers over **videodisc**. Offered by Intel Corporation.

digital virtual disc (DVD) A technological advance that provides high-quality images and audio and can play back CDs and CD-ROMs. A 5-inch DVD disc holds more than 4.7 gigabytes per side — about two hours of video, music, games, and CD-ROM information,either separately or together.

digitize In video, the process of converting an audio or video signal from its analog form into computer-like digital code numbers.

Dilberted The mental and emotional state or condition of an employee after he has been mistreated or disparaged by a intemperate, malicious, or vindictive boss. Borrowed from the comic strip character, Dilbert.

di minimis rule An Internal Revenue Service guideline that exempts business from paying taxes on fringe benefits provided to employees from the 50 percent deduction for meals and entertainment. For example, the subsidized meals provided in a company cafeteria are exempt because the benefit is small when compared with the total compensation of the employee.

dining card A credit card that provides a special discount for subscribers (members) who dine at participating restaurants. With some cards, upon payment of an annual fee, subscribers are allowed to use one or more ordinary credit cards, such as Visa and Mastercard, to pay for meals, beverages, tips, and tax and receive a monthly rebate instead of a discount.

direct assessment *See* alternative assessment.

direct access In travel management, an electronic link between two different **computerized reservation systems** that allows a travel agent to access information and process reservations using both systems.

direct access behavioral health system Offers consumers ease of access and freedom to choose from a select group of health care providers, assuring that subscribers will receive services from qualified providers. The system can be enhanced by structuring provider standards relating to diagnostic examinations, treatment protocols, and centers for emergency access. Such systems are said to benefit payers by improving network management, controlling utilization and cutting administrative costs.

direct billing **1.** In meeting management, the statement of accounts receivable sent to individuals or firms with established credit. **2.** In travel management, a system of invoicing whereby the travel supplier sends the invoice for travel services directly to the traveler who incurred those charges.

direct consolidation loan Under student aid programs, allows the borrower to combine different types and amounts of federal student loans to simplify repayment. The loan pays off the existing loans, and the borrower than repays the consolidation loan over a period of from 10 to 30 years.

direct contracting Describes a provider of integrated health care services involving a delivery system in which contracts are made directly with employers rather than through an insurance company or a managed care organization.

direct contract model A form of **managed care** in which the HMO contracts directly with broad panels of individual physicians (both primary care and specialists) to provide services to their members.

direct costs Expenses associated with specific HR projects, programs, or activities; for example, the costs incurred in conducting a workshop for supervisors. They include out-of pocket expenses (such as air and taxi fares, subsistence, and hotel charges incurred by attending a professional conference) and salary costs (the salaries of instructors or consultants conducting a workshop and the salaries or wages of trainees).

direct deposit An employee benefit. Pay of employees is deposited to their bank accounts electronically — a convenient, reliable, and safe method of depositing pay.

direct drive *See* hard disk.

directed discussion One of three forms of the **conference method**. The objective of directed discussion is to help trainees acquire better understanding of and the ability to apply known facts, principles, concepts, policies, or procedures. The function of the instructor or course leader is to guide the discussion in such a way that the facts, principles, concepts or procedures are clearly articulated and applied.

direct imaging (DI) A printing technology that employs a color electronic prepress system where fully composed pages are prepared and stored in digital form. No film or chemicals are necessary for imaging or developing. The press system interfaces with desktop publishing systems that use IBM and other MS-DOS-based computers, as well as Apple Macintosh computers.

directing The managerial function concerned with establishing and maintaining effective face-to-face relationships with subordinates to get them to do well what the organization has hired them to do, not to avoid reprimand or punishment, but because they want to do it. It encompasses guiding and assisting, motivating and actuating, stimulating and encouraging, communicating, building and maintaining morale, correcting and disciplining, and leading and inspiring.

directive appraisal One-way or one-sided evaluation. The superior observes, evaluates, and provides feedback on performance to subordinates, who are allowed little or no input to the process. The manager establishes the standards, chooses the measures, does the evaluating, reports findings to subordinates at an appraisal interview, makes suggestions for improvement, and records the results.

directive counseling A process in which counselors serve as coaches and teachers. They collect, sift, organize, classify, summarize, and evaluate relevant information to arrive at description of the circumstances surrounding the client's problem. They analyze attitudes, motives, interests, emotional balance, and other factors that may facilitate or inhibit satisfactory adjustment or solution to the client's problem. Counselors may advise, persuade, or explain.

direct labor Labor required to produce or manufacture a product or provide a service.

direct labor budget A budget that displays the estimated costs of the direct labor, expressed in standard labor hours at expected average wage rates, needed to produce the number of products or services to be sold and held in inventory.

direct lending A new system for handling federal student loan programs proposed by President Clinton and endorsed by the Congress in 1993. Instead of allowing banks to provide the loans while the government subsidizes the costs and guarantees the banks against defaults, the banks and state guarantee agencies are eliminated from the system, the federal government raises the money, and colleges and universities make the loans.

Direct Link for the Disabled, Inc. Established to encourage, educate, and empower people with health conditions, disabilities, and rare disorders. Maintains a listing of more than 15,000 organizations and community resource centers nationwide for all types of disabilities. Responds to phone and mail inquiries without charge. *Contact:* Direct Link for the Disabled, P.O. Box 1036, Solvang, CA 93464 (805/688-1603; Fax 805/686-5285; E-mail **linda@directlinkup. com**; URL **http://www.directlinkup.com**).

direct mail A highly effective but relatively expensive marketing technique. It involves identifying the marketing target, obtaining lists of organizations and individuals for solicitation, preparing the marketing media (brochures and response cards), and sending the materials to the target audience by mail.

direct marketing Creating customers and sales by means of mailed brochures and catalogs, **telemarketing,** television shopping channels, and direct factory outlets. No intermediaries (distributors) are involved. The strategy can be justified only if the products or services command sizable gross margins, the number of accounts is manageable, and after-sale service revenue is reasonably attractive.

Direct Marketing Association, Inc. (DMA) A nonprofit organization of more than 3,600 member companies in the United States and 47 other countries that represents the direct marketing industry through educational services, seminars, consumer service programs, research projects, and books and monographs on aspects of direct marketing. DMA's members include direct marketers from nonprofit and public organizations, including catalogers, financial services, book and magazine publishers, book and music clubs, retail stores, and industrial manufacturers. *Contact:* DMA, 1120 Avenue of the Americas, New York, NY 10036-6700 (212/768-7277; Fax 212/719-1946; E-mail **dma@the-dma.org**; URL **http://www.the-dma.org**).

director The person responsible for the staging and performance, including talent delivery and execution, sound, lighting, camera angles, and visual continuity and pacing, of a live dramatization, film, or TV production.

director of food and beverage The hotel functionary who oversees all catering and food operations, as well as the hotel's restaurants. Supervises the the catering director and banquet manager.

director of sales The hotel functionary responsible for booking meetings and the primary contact for corporate meeting managers. May also be called *account representative, marketing manager, sales manager, sales representative.*

directors' and officers' liability insurance Coverage of corporate officers for liability in cases of negligence, malfeasance, misfeasance, or nonfeasance.

directory *See* search engine.

direct public offering (DPO) An offer of the sale of stock made directly to the general public. Regulatory authorities recently recognized that there are fundamental changes occurring in the financial markets and are making adjustments to handle these changes. The withdrawal of restrictive regulations by the Securities and Exchange Commission is making it possible for small and emerging companies to do their own public offering with a decrease in paperwork and costs. *See also* initial public offering; limited offering.

direct reimbursement dental A means of saving time and money and increasing the flexibility of employee dental benefits plans. Employees are reimbursed directly for certain dental and orthodontic procedures within a matter of days on a fixed scale; for example, 100 percent of the first $100, 80 percent of the next $500 up to an annual maximum reimbursement of $750 per covered person.

direct salary costs The prorated salaries of people who conduct or participate in a specific program, usually calculated on a per-day or per-hour basis.

direct transfer A means of moving individual retirement accounts (IRAs) without missing deadlines or incurring taxes or penalties.

disability **1.** As defined by the **Rehabilitation Act of 1973** and the **Americans with Disabilities Act of 1990**: (1) a physical or mental **impairment** that substantially limits one or more of the major life activities of an individual; (2) a record of such an impairment; or (3) being regarded as having such an impairment. It does not include such conditions as transvestism, transsexualism, voyeurism, gender identity disorders not resulting from physical impairments, other sexual behavior disorders, compulsive gambling, kleptomania, pyromania, and psychoactive substance use disorders resulting from current illegal use of drugs. **2.** Under **Social Security**, a person is considered disabled only if he or she is unable to do any kind of work for which suited, and only if inability to work is expected to last for at least a year or to result in death. Therefore, it does not include partial disabilities or short-term disabilities. Benefits continue as long as the individual remains disabled. **3.** In general, disability includes persons who are **physically disabled, mentally impaired, emotionally impaired,** or **learning disabled.**

disability benefits Benefits paid to a disabled employee. A disabled employee is usually defined as one who has a physical or mental condition(s) that prevents the worker from engaging in any substantial gainful work, and the condition is expected to last for a specified period (typically 12 or more months) or result in death. Medical proof is invariably required to support an application for disability benefits. Includes Department of Veterans Affairs disability benefits; state and local government disability benefits; private insurance disability benefits; Supplemental Security Income benefits; Social Security disability benefits; Workers' Compensation.

disability case management (DCM) Case-by-case monitoring of the treatment of employees with disabilities.

disability compensation *See* Veterans' Compensation Rates Amendments of 1993.

Disability Determination Service (DDS) A state agency that makes decisions for the Social Security Administration as to whether an individual claimant qualifies for disability benefits. State DDS evaluation teams, composed of a disability examiner and a physician or psychologist, make the determination using very specific medical and vocational criteria, although many such determinations are made solely on the basis of a treating physician's evidence and recommendations.

disability costs Expenses associated with providing income replacement and medical payments to workers disabled by accident, injury, or illness by such means as workers' compensation insurance and long-term disability policies. Other costs include medical costs paid by health insurance, managerial and supervisory time spent in completing reports and forms, finishing work started, and replacing disabled employees, disability management services, overtime requirements, and lower productivity.

disability management Assigning a single individual responsibility for coordinating and managing disability benefits within an organization. Designed to retain and rehabilitate employees with disabilities and put into place innovative disability management services.

disability manager In the corporate environment, the individual responsible for developing and implementing policies and programs to help persons with disabilities find appropriate jobs and assisting injured, ill, and disabled employees return to work. Positions involving disability management have rapidly grown in number with the enactment of the Americans with Disabilities Act of 1990.

disability plan *See* disability benefits.

disabled person A person who is hearing, vision, or speech impaired, or a person who must use a wheelchair, crutches, cane, or walker due to physical disabilities. A person who has a disability is either unable to do certain things or must do them another way. Sometimes referred to as *handicapped* (objectionable to some) or *challenged* (preferred by some).

disabled and handicapped laws *See* Americans with Disabilities Act of 1990; Architectural Barriers Act of 1968.

disc Optical storage devices or media, such as the laser video disc. *See also* disk.

discharge Termination of an employee for cause. It represents the end of the disciplinary chain. It is reserved for people who cannot or will not subscribe to the rules and who become recalcitrant, insubordinate, or otherwise oblivious to their responsibilities to the organization and their work groups.

discharge planning A process used to limit the number of inpatient hospital stays and assure appropriate care by transferring patients to less expensive health care facilities.

disciplinary layoff A form of disciplinary action involving suspension, usually without pay for a specified number of days or weeks, but almost never for longer than one month.

discipline **1.** Traditionally, discipline has meant complete and total obedience to rules and regulations and to the orders and directives of superiors. Failure to comply resulted in punitive actions. Today, discipline is seen as involving self-control and a sense of personal responsibility for conduct, behavior, and performance. A disciplined organization is one in which members willingly adhere to the rules and principles governing conduct as set forth by the appropriate authorities. Because they accept the rules as right, they are willing to subordinate themselves to the organization. **2.** One of five requirements of the learning organization as described by Peter Senge (*The Fifth Discipline: The Art and*

Practice of the Learning Organization, Doubleday/Currency, 1990). People must master mental models, personal mastery, shared vision, and systems thinking.

disclaimer Refusal or renunciation of property by a beneficiary of an estate or trust. It is usually executed for tax purposes.

disclaimer clause In law, denial or disavowal of authority or responsibility for or renunciation of an event, activity, situation, circumstance, act, interest, right, or property. A complete and unqualified refusal to accept rights to which one is entitled. Recognized by all 50 states. For example, the most effective means of defeating an implied contract claim based upon statements in an employee handbook is to include a clear and emphatic disclaimer in the handbook that it is not a contract and that workers are employed at-will.

disclosure The policy of revealing to the public and or employees situations, conditions, or incidents relating to company policies or operations that cause or have the potential to cause environmental damage or pose health or safety hazards.

disclosure agreement A document that clearly describes the responsibility of the employee to protect company secrets or other items of value to the organization, defines what items are included in that category, and identifies the penalties for violation. It is signed by new employees, witnessed by a corporate official, and filed.

discounting The practices of using disparaging words or nonverbal negative messages when someone proposes an idea or a solution to a problem — or simply failing to affirm the value of an idea or solution. Verbal examples include, "We've tried that before, and it didn't work," or "That is ridiculous." Nonverbal examples are frowns, grimaces, stares, or such structural things as differences in the size of work areas, office furnishings, or benefits for salaried and hourly workers. Attributed to W. Timothy Weaver, Professor of Human Resource Education, Boston University.

discovery learning A system of active learning where the learner's existing knowledge is used to "discover" new information, concepts, and principles through trial and error. It employs critical thinking, problem solving, small group process, and

inquiring. It has been criticized as inefficient, time-consuming, and subject to error.

discretionary bonus *See* bonus; incentive.

discretionary effort Completely voluntary effort by employees to do more than is required by their job descriptions or their supervisors.

discretionary trust A trust with the decision vested in the trustee as to whether and how income and principal should be distributed.

discretionary expense budget *See* expense budget.

discrimination 1. Any policy, procedure, or action that tends to place unfairly an individual or group at a disadvantage in the recruitment, screening, selection, assignment, compensation, testing, training, development, or promotion processes. To prove discrimination, an employee must establish that he or she belongs to a protected group, was rejected although qualified for the job, and the employer filled the position with an individual not in the **protected class**. To rebut a claim of discrimination, employers must refute employees' claims or establish a defense based on one of the following: discharge for gross misconduct, poor performance, or reduction in force. 2. In testing, the ability of a test item to discriminate or distinguish between persons who possess much or little of some trait. 3. In test theory, the correlation of a test item with the total score. 4. In learning, the ability to make useful distinctions between and among a variety of situations and stimuli.

disease management A cost control strategy that is becoming popular among managed care providers, pharmaceutical companies, and other health care professionals. It involves identifying expected outcomes for a certain disease, determining what outcomes a health care plan is actually achieving, and putting policies in place to achieve the desired results.

disenrollment The process of voluntary (the individual simply wants to discontinue membership) or involuntary termination of coverage (when the member changes jobs, or gross offenses, such as fraud and nonpayment of premiums or co-payments).

disfigurement People whose physical appearance is very different from the norm, such a burn victims and those with physical deformities that may be facial or associated with the body, back, head, or limbs. The source may be hereditary, disease, or accident.

disintermediation The practice of buying directly from manufacturers and paying less because it cuts out traditional wholesalers — the middle players.

disk A magnetic storage device, such as a floppy disk, hard disk, or diskette. A means of storing information, instructions, and other forms of computer data. Disks come in three sizes: 3 1/2-inch micro disks (single- and double-sided), 5 1/4-inch (double and quad), and 8-inch single and double. *See also* disc.

disk array Connects two disks through a single controller, which may be hardware or software. A disk array solves the problem of **small-computer standard interface** (SCSI) drive technology: the bottleneck that results from the inability of disks to read or write data as fast as those data can be transmitted across the SCSI interface.

disk-based media A means of storing large amounts of text and graphics.

disk cache Moving portions of a data file from a mechanical disk to a computer's electronic memory, a process that speeds up information retrieval.

disk color separation (DCS) In desktop publishing, a data-file standard defied by QuarkXPress to assist in **color separation**.

disk drive The mechanism that copies information from a disk into the computer's memory and makes it available for use and copies data from the computer's memory to a disk for backup and storage.

diskette *See* disk.

disk operating system (DOS) The operating system of a computer, usually consisting of floppy disks that contain utility functions (for example, copying, deleting information, formatting disks) and disk drives that read those functions.

disk optimizer A utility program that accelerates disk operating system performance by performing a variety of functions, such as surface testing (finding and locking out media defects), low-level format refresher (rewriting tracks), defragging, and extending the life of a hard disk by reducing wear and tear caused by repeated movement of the head.

disparate impact A legal term relating to a form of discrimination in which an employment practice or procedure (such as a psychological test) results in discrimination against a protected class. Such a practice is unlawful unless the employer can demonstrate that the practice is either job-related or a business necessity. Federal agencies have adopted the following formula to determine when disparate impact exists: a selection rate for any racial, ethnic, or gender group which is less than 80 percent of the rate for the highest selection rate. Also referred to as *disparate treatment* and *disparate rejection rates.*

disparate rejection rates *See* disparate impact.

disparate treatment *See* disparate impact.

displacement Describes workers who have lost their jobs as a result of economic change, such as plant closings and layoffs due to shifts in consumer preferences, foreign competition, automation, and robotics.

display bias In travel management, an illegal practice in which the **computer reservation system (CRS)** information screen displays flight information pertaining to its owner before showing the flights of another carrier.

displays *See* exhibits.

disposable worker *See* contingent work force; sheddable worker.

disputed claim A claim for insurance benefits for which the patient or plan enrollee disagrees with the carrier's action. Usually, the individual has the right to appeal and request reconsideration of the claim by the carrier and, if not satisfied, by some higher authority. For example, federal health benefits plan enrollees can appeal to the Office of Personnel Management.

dissatisfiers Factors related to a job's extrinsic content — company policies and procedures, assignments, type of supervision received, working conditions, job security, and pay and benefits — which tend to demotivate people.

dissed A term invented by school-age city kids. It means to be put down, humiliated, or disrespected.

dissolve In video production, slowly fading one image and bringing another image into view in its place.

Distance Education and Training Council (DETC) A nonprofit educational association that servers as a clearinghouse of information about the distance learning/correspondence study field and sponsors the Accrediting

Commission of the Distance Education and Training Council. The mission of DETC is to promote sound educational standards and ethical business practices within the distance study field. Formerly the National Home Study Council. *Contact:* DETC, 1601 18th St., N.W. Washington, DC 20009-2529 (202/ 234-5100; Fax 202/3321386; E-mail **detc@ detc.org**; URL **http://www.detc.org**).

distance learning Learning that is mediated by a person (trainer or instructor) who is not in the same location as the persons who are receiving the training or instruction. It typically involves telecommunication of audio, audiographic, and/or video information using satellite, microwave, cable, telephone lines, or fiber-optic lines.

distance training/education In general, education and training provided for adults at remote locations by such means as satellite-delivered training and interactive video. John R. Verduin, Jr. & Thomas A. Clark (*Distance Education: The Foundations of Effective Practice*) define distance training or education as "any formal approach to learning in which a majority of the instruction occurs while educator and learner are at a distance from one another." They elaborate on the definition by identifying four distinguishing factors: (1) teacher and learner are separated for a majority of the learning process; (2) an educational organization is involved in the process, which includes some type of evaluation of the student's work; (3) some kind of educational media is used to connect the learner and teacher, and to convey course content; and (4) there is some type of two-way communication between the learner and the instructor or educational agency.

Distinguished Contribution to Human Resource Develoment Award An award presented annually to a member of the **American Society for Training and Development** (or an individual nominated by a member) for exceptional contributions over a significant period of time to the field of human resource development. Selected by an awards committee from nominees by reviewing documentation and direct contacts with the nominating individual and other person with direct knowledge of the accomplishments of the nominee. *Contact:* ASTD National Awards Program, Attn: Dawn Temple, 1640 King St.,

Box 1443, Alexandria, VA 22313-2043 (703/683-8100)

distractor In testing, any of the incorrect choices in a test item, such as in a multiple-choice test.

distributed database A computer **database** whose components are stored in more than one location. By linking them over communications channels, such as a **local-area network** or **wide-area network,** the location of the data becomes unimportant to the user.

distributed network A computing environment in which processing capabilities are divided among various workstations throughout the network.

distributed work Describes any type of work done by groups of people who are separated in time and space.

distribution *See* frequency distribution.

divergent thinking An unconventional way of thinking that generates new concepts, ideas, and approaches. It involves tossing, spinning, and rotating a problem in your mind, ruminating and mulling it over in different ways and looking at it from different angles without actually trying to solve it.

diversity In general, diversity refers to the ways in which people in organizations differ, including age, race, native language, gender, ethnic group, religion, personality, cognitive style, physical health, mental health, tenure, organization function, and many others. Recently expanded to include sexual orientation and people with disabilities. In its narrow sense, diversity includes only differences based on race and gender. Some writers define diversity as the great variety of ways, relevant to an organization, in which people people can be grouped, including abilities, age, career aspirations, disabilities, education, family background, geographic origins, interests, marital status, parental status, sex, skills, vocation or profession.

diversity program/strategy A plan and program designed to help employees at all levels of the organization learn new attitudes and adopt new behaviors relating to cultural differences. Includes encouraging diversity in the work force as a priority through hiring practices, creating new internal personnel structures and systems to monitor performance, holding managers accountable for promoting a multicultural work environment, and establishing diversity training and development programs.

diversity training A generic term used to describe any type of training designed to help people understand and value cultural differences in the workplace. Usually provided for managers and supervisors in an attempt to increase productivity and reduce the potential for legal actions resulting from employees' or managements' bigoted attitudes toward people who are different.

divestiture **1.** The process of terminating an investment, arrangement, or affiliation with another organization. **2.** Converting undervalued assets to cash as a part of a capitalization reduction plan.

dividend **1.** In group insurance, return of all or a part of the excess premiums (money not needed to pay claims, meet expenses, establish reserves, and provide a reasonable profit) to the insured. **2.** In investments, money paid to stockholders according to the number of shares held.

***Dividends:* A Magazine for Staples Small Business Customers** Published bimonthly for Staples by Imagination Publishing, 820 West Jackson, Fourth Floor, Chicago, IL 60607 (312/627-1020); $1.95 per copy (free to qualified subscribers). Address: Staples, Inc., 1 Research Drive, Westborough, MA (800/793-3320)

dividend equivalent plan A form of stock equivalent plan in which a number of units of **phantom stock** is granted to an executive, each of which creates rights to a payment equal to to any dividends paid on a share of the company's stock.

dividend reinvestment plan (DRP)
Offered by dividend-paying companies to their shareholders to provide an easy way to nurture the growth of their investments. Such plans give investors the opportunity to purchase additional shares of a company's stock without paying high brokerage fees and without having to make a large outlay of cash. Instead of making a dividend payment and sending a check to the shareholder, the company purchases as many shares of stock as possible with the amount of money due the investor.

divorce benefits A divorced person is entitled to Social Security benefits on the ex-spouse's account if they were married for 10 or more years. Benefits are based on total contributions made by the wage-earner over the entire working career, not just during the marriage. A person married more than once, each time for at least 10 years, may claim benefits against the ex-spouse with the largest Social Security account. If remarried for less than 10 years and no longer married, benefits are claimed against the first spouse. However, as long as a person remains remarried, no benefits can be claimed against the ex-spouse. Benefits of the current spouse of the wage-earner against whom the ex-spouse is making a claim are in no way reduced. Both the current and the ex-spouse both receive full benefits.

DNA fingerprinting A forensic genetic-based identification technology. Said to be a foolproof method of identification by its advocates; however, its use has been disallowed by courts in several states and at several levels.

dock **1.** A penalty for worker tardiness in which the employee loses pay for the lost time. **2.** Sometimes used to describe other penalties for tardiness such as the requirement to make up lost time or be subjected to disciplinary action.

docking base option (DBO) Gives the user the choice of using a laptop computer as a free-standing unit or connecting it to an office printer, other peripherals, or a **local area network**.

docking rules Federal rules governing the reduction of employee pay for time off the job for reasons other than sickness or accident; for example, tardiness or leaving the job before quitting time. Under the law, **salaried workers** cannot collect overtime pay nor have their pay docked for taking a few hours off to do such things as take care of personal business. Under the **Fair Labor Standards Act of 1938**, a salaried employee who is treated like an an hourly worker is eligible for overtime pay and can seek back overtime pay for up to two years. However, under the docking rules, an employer can reduce the pay of a salaried worker if he or she is absent for an entire week, away from the job for an entire day for reasons other than sickness or accident, or is absent for more than a day for reasons of sickness or disability when the employee is covered by a paid-leave policy.

document analysis An individual creative technique that involves analyzing correspondence and reports to cull ideas to improve products and services Examples are travel reports, after-action reports, customer complaints, client requests for assistance, sales reports, consultant reports, and proposals.

documentation **1.** In contracting, the data needed to solicit bids, select a contractor, and monitor contract execution. It includes **statements of work**, a list of **contract deliverables**, proposal evaluation criteria, proposal format, and **quality assurance surveillance plans**. **2.** In training, job and analysis data, results of validation studies, and the like. **3.** In disciplining, all transactions, notices, and forms relating to a disciplinary action, such as records of supervisor-employee discussions, memos, copies of letters of reprimand, warnings, and so on. **4.** The technical information, manuals, user's guides, and accompanying instructions included with computer hardware or software.

document camera In video transmission (including **distance learning**), a desk-mounted, overhead camera and platform, equipped with auto/manual zoom and focus capabilities, used to display text, graphics, transparencies, and small objects in either black and white or color.

document conferencing Software that allows users on different computers to share applications and jointly edit text and graphics files.

document image processing (DIP) A document storage and retrieval system used in such paper-intensive fields as law, medicine, education, communications, and transportation. DIP systems permit better control of work flow in document handling through the integration of microform and computer systems.

document management The technology that permits the creation, revision, distribution, and storage of documents on personal computers.

domain name A means of identifying the computer (**E-mail**) addresses of government offices; educational institutions, companies, networks, organizations, and individuals.

domestic partner Used by organizations, including insurance carriers, to describe a person who lives with an employee or the insured in a relationship, whether gay or straight. Most definitions used by employers include the following: (1) reference to a shared commitment or joint responsibility for each other's common welfare and affirmation that the relationship is permanent; (2) that partners reside together or share a principal residence; and (3) that the partners be financially interdependent or mutually responsible for living expenses for each other.

domestic partner benefits Extends health care coverage to unmarried, same sex, and/or opposite sex partners.

domestic violence hotline (DVH) A hotline telephone number staffed 24 hours per day, every day for victims of domestic violence. The number is 1-800/333-SAFE.

domicile A legal term meaning the place where an individual permanently resides and will return to when "away." An individual's permanent legal home.

domiciliary care See board and care home.

donee The recipient of a gift under a will.

donor The one who gives a gift under a will or who creates a trust.

do not resuscitate (DNR) An order placed on a patient's hospital medical chart directing that attempts will not be made to restore heartbeat or breathing that have stopped naturally.

dot matrix printer An impact printer that forms characters consisting of close patterns of small dots.

dots per inch (dpi) A measure of the **resolution** of computer monitors and laser and dot matrix printers. The standard resolution of computer monitors is 72 dpi; of laser printers, 300 dpi; of image setters, 1270 to 2540 dpi.

double A hotel room with a double bed.

double coverage Describes the situation where spouses with access to and eligibility for work-related health insurance coverage both enroll in the program.

double dipping/dipper **1.** Collecting two (or even three) pensions; for example, military retirement, Social Security, and federal, state, or municipal annuities. **2.** Accepting federal full-time employment following retirement from military service with an annuity. **3.** The practice of counting a spouse's monthly benefits as income for the purpose of determining alimony payments when a lump-sum settlement has been pre-viously granted (disallowed by the courts.).

double/double A hotel room with two double beds.

dower *See* community property.

Dow Jones News Retrieval An on-line **data-base.** *Contact:* Dow Jones News Retrieval, P.O. Box 300, Princeton, NJ 08543-0300, 609/452-1511.

downer *See* sedative.

downgrading **1.** Moving a job or position to a lower level in a general schedule or job evaluation system. **2.** Moving an individual job incumbent to a lower-level job or pay grade.

download Retrieving information or files from a distant or remote computer or the Internet over phone or data lines by means of a computer and a modem.

downloadable font A **font** whose printer font information must be loaded down into the printer before it can be created on the page.

downshifter/downshifting **1.** Describes a career move that involves trading off higher pay and the power of a prestigious job for one that provides a lower salary and status to fulfill personal and family needs and pri-orities. For example, a fast-track middle manager or executive in a large corporation decides to resign and accept a small town secondary school teaching position. **2.** A worker who attempts to slow down work life so that he or she can concentrate on other areas of living. Requires employers to reassess their concepts of what jobs are, how much time it takes to do them, and how to integrate business needs with employees' needs and wants. **3.** Downward movement in the organization accepted by employees to acquire critical competencies and experi-ence that will enable them to change the long-term direction of their careers.

downsizing A management strategy for streamlining an organization, making it more efficient and cost effective by eliminating unnecessary and duplicatory functions and people. It may also have as its objective elimination of noncompetitive or obsolete products, services, and processes or meeting the demands of customers and clients for new products and services. It may stem from an unexpected market downturn, competition, or a hostile takeover.

Down syndrome A chromosome disorder that usually causes delay in physical, intellectual, and language development. Although the exact causes of the chromo-somal rearrangement and primary means of preventing Down syndrome are unknown at this time, it is one of the leading clinical causes of mental retardation in the world — and it is not related to race, nationality, or socioeconomic status. Individuals with Down syndrome vary widely in mental abil-ities, behavior, and physical development, and each has his or her unique personality, capabilities, and talents. The majority of indi-viduals function in the mild to moderate range of mental retardation.

down time Time when equipment is not operational due to a malfunction or other problem.

downwardly mobile professional (DOMO) Typically applied to a person under age 40 who has given up a high-paying job to pursue a more satisfying way of life.

DRAGnet: Disability Resources Activities and Groups Network The local outlet for many national electronic bulletin boards and independent living programs for persons with disabilities in Minnesota. It is available 24 hours a day to people with a personal computer and a modem — and can be used by people with voice synthesizers. The ser-vice is free to users in the 612 area, and plans have been made for satellite expan-sion statewide. The system can be accessed at 612/753-1943.

draw-a-person test A projective technique used to supplement other psychological tests in analyzing and assessing personality. The testee is asked to "draw a person"; then the examiner (a qualified psychometrist or therapist) asks certain questions about the drawing to identify associations the subject makes with the sketch.

draw software In desktop publishing, soft-ware that uses **vector graphics** to create images.

drayage In meeting management, refers to the transfer of equipment, exhibits, and materials from the point of arrival to the exhibit site.

dread disease coverage A life or health insurance policy that covers only specific diseases, such as cancer or AIDS. Banned in some states when some insurers were found to be systematically misleading the public on the benefits of their policies.

dream team A work team composed of an organization's top talent who are brought together to solve a critical problem or develop a plan for the future.

dress code A written company (or other organization) policy on office (or workplace) attire for employees. A relaxed or flexible dress code (**casual attire**) is considered an additional employee benefit by more than half of employees. *See also* corporate attire.

dressing down *See* casual attire.

dressing up *See* corporate attire.

drill and practice A learning strategy that involves practice under supervision of some of the steps in a specific process with critique and feedback. For example, a drill in a golf lesson might focus on hitting balls embedded in a fairway bunker (rather than balls lying cleanly on top of the sand in a bunker near the green).

driver In desktop publishing, software used to control a printer.

driving regulations OSHA has proposed that employees who either drive company vehicles or their own vehicles on company business be subject to new safety regulations including periodic training in driver safety and wearing seat belts. OSHA would also mandate employers to check the driving records of job applicants, monitor driver performance to assure compliance with regulations, and require employees who are guilty of moving violations on the job to attend a defensive driving program.

drop charge A special fee charged by car rental companies on one-way rentals or for returning a car to a different location.

drug abuse Occurs when an individual uses any legal or illegal substance despite the negative effects it may have on his or her physical, psychological, social, or occupational well-being. Initially voluntary, unless treated, it may progress to drug addiction — a compulsion to use the substance to avoid the stress of withdrawal. Although its causes are unknown, it is possible that a tendency toward addiction may be genetically transmitted. There are several classes of drugs: **stimulants, sedatives, opiates, cannabis, hallucinogens, inhalants,** and **designer drugs**. Treatment involves getting the individual off the drugs through a process of detoxification, psychotherapy, after care programs, and support groups

drug formulary In prescription drugs benefits plans, a specific list of drugs by therapeutic grouping that must be prescribed before benefits are received (or are preferred). Formularies are designed by the pharmacy network provider and a multi-disciplinary committee of physicians and pharmacists [Pharmacy and Therapeutics (P&T) Committee]. Each therapeutic group is studied, and drugs are ranked according to clinical effectiveness and cost. The network provider then issues a request for proposals to drug manufacturers. Upon receipt of the proposals, the provider and the P&T designates the drugs within each therapeutic group that will be included in the formulary.

Drug-Free Workplace Act of 1988 (DFWA) Legislation that took effect March 18, 1989. Requires organizations receiving federal contracts of $25,000 or more to meet requirements designed to keep their workplaces free of illegal drugs. It also applies to any organization receiving a grant (including universities) no matter what the amount. To comply, companies must publish and distribute a policy prohibiting the unlawful manufacture, distribution, dispensing, possession, or use of controlled substances in the workplace; notify federal authorities of any convictions of employees for illegal drug activity in the workplace; provide for penalties for employees convicted of drug-related violations on the job; establish an employee-awareness program on the dangers and penalties of workplace drug abuse; and notify employees of the availability of resources for drug rehabilitation and counseling. Violators are penalized by loss of all federal business or grants and face possible disbarment from future opportunities for up to five years.

drug program A health care cost-reduction strategy in which arrangements are made with local pharmacies to waive employee charges if a generic drug is used, and the difference between the generic and name brand is charged if the employee chooses the latter.

drug testing **1.** Testing employees for use of narcotics and alcohol. **2.** Regulations issued by the Department of Health and Human Services in 1988 require employers of certain types of workers to conduct five kinds of drug testing for the presence of marijuana, cocaine, opiates, amphetamines and PCP: random, pre-employment, periodic, reasonable cause, and post accident. Workers include those involved in airline-related functions, railroad operations, interstate truck and bus driving, mass transit, the merchant marines, and natural gas and hazardous liquid pipeline operations. **3.** Rules for drug testing of interstate truck and bus drivers, aviation industry employees, mass transit workers, railroad workers, mariners on commercial vessels, and pipeline industry employees promulgated by the Department of Transportation in November 1989. Rules require pre-employment, periodic, reasonable cause, post-accident, and random testing for marijuana, cocaine, opiates, amphetamines, and phencyclidine (PCP). In February 1994, the Secretary of Transportation announced that, beginning in 1995, alcohol and drug tests are required for safety-sensitive transportation workers, including truck drivers, school bus drivers, mass-transit operators, dispatchers, and maintenance workers, pilots, flight attendants, and aircraft maintenance personnel, railroaders, any other worker with a commercial driver's license, pipeline operators and maintenance personnel, and crew members operating commercial vessels. Alcohol tests, formerly required only after a railroad or maritime accident, must administered on a random basis and at the time of hiring, when a supervisor observes suspicious behavior, and when suspended employees return to work after treatment and rehabilitation. The regulations also eased some provisions by cutting the number of random drug tests from 50 percent of the work force to 25 percent as long as the number of positive tests in an industry remains below 1 percent. Random alcohol tests will also be less stringent. If fewer than 0.5 percent of employees in an industry test positive for two years, required yearly random alcohol tests would drop to 10 percent of safety-sensitive employees. On January 1, 1996, Department of Transportation drug and alcohol testing regulations went into effect for all employers in the United States. The rules apply to anyone working in safety-sensitive jobs (involving driving, being

immediately available to drive, and supervising the loading or unloading of a truck by a driver) within the motor carrier industry.

drug tests *See* balance and reflex performance check; confirmatory test; critical tracking test; enzyme multiplied immunoassay technique; gas chromatography/mass spectrometry; hair analysis; pupillary-reaction test; screening test; urine test.

drug utilization review (DUR) A program for screening prescription drug transactions for potential overdosing or dangerous drug interventions administered by inhouse or contracted utilization review officers, companies, or committees.

dual career ladders *See* dual career tracks.

dual career tracks An approach to employee career development that involves permitting people to move back and forth between managerial and technical or professional jobs over the course of their careers and at the same time allows them to move up in status and compensation. The strategy is adopted to improve retention, motivation, job satisfaction and performance as well as result in the production of creative ideas, practices, and products.

Dual Compensation Act of 1964
Legislation that limited the pensions of military retirees if employed by the federal government.

dual motive case A provision of the **Civil Rights Act of 1991,** in which an employer while making an employment decision, relies on both permissible and impermissible factors. Where formerly the employer could still prevail by proving that the decision would have been the same even if the unlawful factor were absent, the Act makes the burden of proof more difficult. The employee charging discrimination will prevail if it is proven that his or her protected status (race, sex, and so on) was a "motivating factor" in the decision regardless of other factors. In essence, the employer must demonstrate that only lawful factors were used to make the decision.

dual option Describes the offering of both a **health maintenance organization** and a conventional insurance plan by the same carrier.

due process In law, the principle that emphasizes the requirement to protect an individual from arbitrary, capricious, and unfair treatment. Essentially that means that

(1) an employee must be made aware that he or she has committed a rules violation, engaged in unacceptable conduct, or failed to perform satisfactorily; (2) the organization supports the allegation of wrongdoing with credible evidence; (3) the employee is informed of that evidence; and (4) the employee is given an opportunity to question of refute the allegation.

dues check-off   An arrangement negotiated by a **union** whereby the employer deducts dues from the worker's pay and turns the money over to the union.

dummy   In desktop publishing **1.** A preliminary layout showing the position of graphics and text as they will appear in the final document. **2.** A set of blank pages made up in advance to show the size, shape, form, and style of a document.

duplex   In meeting management, a two-story suite with a parlor and bedroom(s) connected by a stairway.

duplication factor   In marketing, the percentage of names on list of organizations or individuals that are also on another list.

durable medical equipment (DME)   Equipment that serves a medical purpose, cannot be useful to people who are not sick or injured, can be used repeatedly, and is prescribed by a physician for use in the home. It typically includes such items as oxygen equipment and wheelchairs and may include seat lift chairs, power-operated vehicles, equipment for care of pressure sores, and transcutaneous electrical nerve stimulators.

durable power of attorney   A legal document prepared by an attorney that gives a named individual the power to act as an agent for the maker or grantor. It can cover general areas of decision making or be limited to specific areas. It is not affected by the disability or incapacity of the maker.

durable power of attorney for health care   A legal (in some states) means of appointing another person to make health care decisions for incapacitated individuals. Because general powers of attorney become null and void when the maker becomes incompetent, some states now permit a power of attorney to be designated as "durable" when stated in the document. An alternative to a living will and often used in conjunction with one.

dustbuster   An E-mail or telephone message sent to someone after a long period of time without any contact — in effect, "shaking the dust off" to see if the connection is still viable.

duty   One of the major subdivisions of the work (job) performed by one individual. A duty has these characteristics: It is one of the incumbent's major functions; it occupies all or a reasonable portion of the incumbent's time; it consists of a cluster of closely related tasks; it occurs with reasonable frequency during the work cycle; it involves work operations that use closely related skills, knowledge, and abilities; and it is performed for some purpose, by some method, according to some standard with respect to speed, accuracy, quality, or quantity. For example, the duties of an electronics equipment repairer include inspecting, adjusting, aligning, trouble-shooting, servicing, and repairing.

duty analysis   A form of occupation analysis that is rarely used. It has been relegated to a back seat in the analysis area where **task analysis** is now primary.

dynamic data exchange (DDE)
See inprocess communications.

dynamic link libraries (DDL)
See inprocess communications.

dynamic random access memory (DRAM)
A type of large memory semiconductor chip used in computers. A DRAM can store up to 1 Megabit (1 million bits of information). It loses memory when the power is cut off.

dynamic revenue estimating   A theory that tax cuts stimulate the economy by means of supply effects and largely pay for themselves.

dynamic scoring   A system for calculating tax reductions based on the assumption that some tax cuts produce economic activity and negate the need for off-setting spending cuts dollar for dollar.

dyslexia   A language disability that takes three forms: visual dyslexia (reversal of letters and numbers, confusing the sequence of letters in words, numbers in series, and events in time, and difficulty in internalizing visual images), auditory dyslexia (problems connecting what is heard with the written words representing those sounds), and a combination of visual and auditory dyslexia. The disability manifests itself in a variety of ways: sometimes confusion of one consonant with another, such as *b's* for *d's*, *p's* for *q's*, or *t's* for *f's*, or as a reversal of syllables, words, or entire sentences. For example, an afflicted person may see a combination of letters as *d-o-g* and another time as *g-o-d*. The language disability typically develops into problems with reading and writing. The causes of dyslexia are unknown; however, researchers have found evidence that the disorder exists in families and may be passed from parent to child. Dyslexia cannot be cured, but it can be alleviated, depending on such things as the severity of the disorder, the age of the individual, the expertise of the therapist, the frequency and duration of learning sessions, and whether training sessions are one-on-one or ingroups. Com-puter games show promise of helping overcome the disorder by elongating hard consonants, spacing them farther apart, making them louder, and providing practice in differentiating among them.

dysthmia A less severe type of depression than **clinical depression** in that it involves long-term, chronic symptoms that are not disabling, but keep the person from functioning at top speed.

dys-stress Tension caused by the pressures of work that are dangerous, cause anxiety and depression, and which unrelieved, can lead to serious physical and emotional illness.

E

EA	Emotions Anonymous.
EAL	Educational Assistance Ltd.
EANGUS	Enlisted Association of the National Guard of the U.S.
EAP	Employee assistance program.
EAPA	Employee Assistance Professionals Association, Inc.
EBB	The Electronic Bulletin Board.
EBI	Employee Benefits Infosource.
EBIT	Earnings before interest and taxes.
EBRI	Employee Benefit Research Institute.
EC	European Community.
ECE	Early childhood education.
ECEDA	Early Childhood Education and Development Act of 1990.
ECF	Extended-care facility.
ECHO	Elderly cottage housing opportunity.
ECI	Economic Cost Index.
ECO	Employee Commute Option.
ECU	European Community (monetary) unit.
ED	1. Electronic document. 2. Emotionally disabled.
EDC	Exhibitor-designated contractor.
EDI	Electronic data interchange.
EDIS	Employee driven idea system.
EDP	Electronic data processing.
EDWAAA	Economic Dislocation and Worker Adjustment Assistance Act of 1988.
EEA	1. Employee educational assistance. 2. European Economic Area.
EEAA	Employee Educational Assistance Act of 1978.
EEO	Equal employment opportunity.
EEOA	Equal Employment Opportunity Act of 1972.

EEOC	Equal Employment Opportunity Commission.
EEPROM	Electronically erasable and reprogrammable memory.
EFA	Epilepsy Foundation of America.
EFC	Expected family contribution.
EFTA	European Free Trade Association.
EFTPS	Electronic Federal Tax Payment System.
EGA	Ethics in Government Act of 1978.
EHA	Emotional Health Anonymous.
EHOP	Employee home ownership plan.
EHS	Extremely hazardous substance.
EI	Employee involvement.
EIA	Environmental Industry Associations.
EIN	Employer identification number.
EIS	Executive information system.
EITC	Earned income tax credit.
ELOS	Estimated length of stay.
EMA	Employment Management Association.
EMF	Electromagnetic field.
EMG	Electromyography.
EMI	European Monetary Institute.
EMIT	Enzyme multiplied immunoassay technique.
EMO	Educational management organization.
EMS	Emergency medical services.
EMT	Emergency medical technician.
EMU	Economic Monetary Union.
ENDA	Employment Non-Discrimination Act of 1996.
E&O	Errors and omissions.
EO	Executive Order.
EOB	Explanation of benefits.
EOI	Evidence of insurability.

EOMB	Explanation of Medicate Benefits.
EOQ	European Organization for Quality.
EP	1. Electronic publishing. 2. Employee participation. 3. European plan.
EPA	1. Environmental Protection Agency. 2. Equal Pay Act of 1963. 3. Epilepsy Foundation of America.
EPCRA	Emergency Planning and Community Right-to-Know Act of 1986.
EPIC	Exemplary Public Interest Contribution.
EPL	Employment practices liability.
EPLI	Employment practices liability insurance.
EPO	Exclusive provider organization.
EPP	1. Employee participation plan. 2. Electronic print production. 3. Employee partnership pay.
EPPA	Employee Polygraph Protection Act of of 1988.
EPSS	Electronic performance support systems.
EPVA	Eastern Paralyzed Veterans Association.
EQ	Emotional quotient.
ERA	Ethics Reform Act of 1989.
ERC	1. Employee Relocation Council. 2. Ethics Resource Center.
ERIC	Educational Resources Information Center.
ERIC/IT	ERIC Clearing House on Information & Technology.
ERIP	Early retirement incentive programs.
ERISA	Employee Income Retirement Security Act of 1974.
ERM	European Exchange Rate Mechanism.
ERTA	Economic Recovery Tax Act of 1981.
ES	Equity sharing.
ESEA	Elementary and Secondary Education Act of 1965.
ESL	English as a second language.

ESOP	1. Employee stock option (ownership) plan. 2. The ESOP Association.
ET	Embedded training.
ETDN	Electronic ticket delivery network.
ETR	External training resource.
ETS	1. Educational Testing Service. 2. Environmental tobacco smoke.
EU	European Union.
EVA	Economic value added.
EVE	Exemplary Voluntary Efforts Award.
EWP	Employee wellness plan.
89	*See* Section 89, Internal Revenue Code.

8-bit color A digital color standard where 8 bits of information are used to describe each color **pixel**, yielding a total of 256 possible simultaneous colors. 8-bit color is standard for color **video graphics array** displays but is inadequate to define the range of colors required for graphic arts reproduction.

The Ear Foundation A nonprofit organization established to lead the effort for better hearing and balance through public and professional education programs, support services, and applied research. *Contact:* The Ear Foundation, 2000 Church St., Box 111, Nashville, TN 37236 (800/545-HEAR or 615/329-7809).

early childhood education (ECE) Education provided to children in the two-to-six age group by public or private agencies, organizations, and businesses. Instead of highly structured, teacher-controlled activities focused on rote learning and memorization, strategies used today emphasize imagination and include one-on-one conversation, interaction, and other approaches. Some programs are funded completely by states, cities or towns, or private organizations; others are partially subsidized by public or private organizations; still others are supported totally by parental tuition payments.

early-out penalty A flat fee ($25 to $50) charged by hotels when guests check out earlier than expected.

early retirement incentive program (ERIP) A strategy designed to encourage retirement of older employees or when budgetary pressures require a significant reduction in personnel within a relatively short period of time. ERIPs have been adopted by many organizations since the passage of the Age Discrimination in Employment Act (as amended in 1987), which prohibits mandatory retirement for most jobs at any age. They have also been used when economic conditions require **downsizing** or **restructuring**. Essentially, such plans establish a period (open window) of from 30 to 90 days during which eligible employees may voluntarily retire with a one-time monetary incentive as well as a full pension — and sometimes additional fringe benefits. Eligibility may be based on age (anyone over age 65 or years of continuous service — for example, the "Rule of 75" whereby any combination of age and years of service total 75 or more). Examples of benefits in addition to an unreduced accrued normal retirement benefit typically include a special "bridge" benefit based on years of service, such as a percentage of final pay amounting to as much as 25 percent for a specified number of years or age, and guaranteed access to coverage of a comprehensive medical plan for the retiree and spouse.

early retirement window　*See* early retirement incentive program.

earned entitlements　Work-related benefits, such as annuities and health insurance, which were paid for in part by deductions from income during the work life of the beneficiary.

earned income tax credit (EITC)　A federal tax credit that provides families earning less than $20,270 per year with credits against their tax liability. The amount of the credit depends on the number of children in the family; some families receive a check from the government if the credit exceeds the tax liability.

earned time off　An employee incentive in which the individual is rewarded for productivity or other contribution to the organization by granting additional time off with pay.

earnings before interest and taxes (EBIT)　A means of valuing a business. EBIT is the market comparison method. It is determined by multiplying earnings before interest and taxes by a multiplier ranging from 4 to 8 and then comparing the resulting value to the selling prices and price earnings of other companies in the industry.

earnings penalty　*See* earnings test.

earnings test　Under the Social Security system, in 1996, beneficiaries who were age 65 through 69 may earn up to $12,500 ($960 per month). Exempt amounts increase annually up to $30,000 in 2002 — $13,500 in 1997, $14,500 in 1998, $15,500 in 1999, 17,000 in 2000, and 25,000 in 2001) without losing any social security benefits. Benefits are withheld at the rate of $1 for each $3 of earnings over that amount. For those under age 65, the limit is $8,280 ($690 per month), and $1 is withheld for every $2 of earnings in excess of that amount. The earnings test does not apply for people over 70.

easel　*See* flip chart.

Eastern Paralyzed Veterans Association (EPVA)　A chapter of the congressionally chartered Paralyzed Veterans of America. EPVA is a nonprofit organization of over 2,000 members residing in New York, New Jersey, Pennsylvania, and Connecticut. EPVA is dedicated to enhancing the lives of veterans with spinal cord injury or disease by ensuring quality health care, promoting research, and advocating for civil rights and independence. *Contact:* EPVA, 75-20 Astoria Blvd., Jackson Heights, NY 11370-1177 (718/803-3782; Fax 718/803-0414; E-mail **info@epva.org**; URL **http://www.epva. org**).

E-based retailing　*See* emotional retailing.

Ebonics　A form of the English language used by many African-Americans. The term combines "ebony" and "phonics." Recognized in some places as a legitimate language, like French or Spanish. Also called *Black English.*

eccentric viewing　Not looking at what you want to see, a technique used by persons to cope with **macular degeneration**, a spot on the retina of the eye which becomes totally insensitive to light. It is done by moving the eyes (not the head) high right or high left of the object to focus the light entering the eye on the retinal tissue beside the macula but not directly on it. The technique moves the blind spot out of the way.

echocardiography　A noninvasive test used by physicians to assess which patients are good candidates for coronary artery bypass surgery. The procedure uses an adrenalin-like drug and an imaging system to predict how well a patient will recover from the surgery.

Echo Headphone　A device that permits trainees to learn privately, filters out ambient noise, and prevents computer sounds from distracting other trainees or workers. A registered trademark of Street Electronics. *Contact:*

Edmark Corporation, P.O. Box 3903, Bellevue, Washington 98009-3903 (800/426-0856).

Echo II Speech Processor Hardware that allows Apple II series software to give oral instructions and provide reinforcement. It is a required component of many **Touch-Window**®-compatible programs and can be used with many other educational programs. The board installs in a slot inside selected Apple computers. It has an external speaker and volume control and a headphone jack for private monitoring. A registered trademark of Street Electronics. *Contact:* Edmark Corporation, P.O. Box 3903, Bellevue, Washington 98009-3903 (800/426-0856).

eclectic counseling An approach to counseling that attempts to make use of the best features of both directive and nondirective methods.

economic analysis A systematic approach to assist HR managers to solve a problem of choice. The full problem is investigated, and objectives and alternatives are searched out and compared in the light of their benefits and costs through the use of appropriate analytical elements.

Economic Cost Index (ECI) By law, the baseline for setting military and federal civilian pay raises. For example, the September 1996 ECI measurement was the guide for setting the 1998 pay raise. The lag between measurement and application is dictated by the 15-month lead time for the budget process. Before 1994, federal civilian raises were supposed to match the ECI. This carried over to military raises, too, because a separate law ties military raises to whatever federal civilian workers get. But in 1994, new legislation started capping Federal civilian raises one-half percentage point below the ECI. The difference was used to fund a "locality pay" additive for Federal civilians that varied by geographic location.

economic benefit A term used by the Internal Revenue Service to identify and determine current tax liability when the employee can receive compensation (backed by a funded plan and instrument, rights that are nonforfeitable, and there is no risk of forfeiture) even though he or she may elect not to do so.

economic conversion A planned shift from military and other defense-related production to civilian consumer products and services to preserve the industrial base and protect jobs.

Economic Dislocation and Worker Adjustment Assistance Act of 1988 (EDWAAA) Amended Title III of the Job Training Partnership Act of 1982 dealing with dislocated workers: terminated, long-term unemployed, and self-employed underemployed blue collar, white collar, mid-level managers, other self-employed people, and displaced homemakers without any economic criteria for assistance. Beginning July 1989, the program was operated at both state and local levels and required states to allocate funds to provide services locally to dislocated workers, such as classroom, occupational skills, and on-the-job training. It also permitted states to provide out-of-area job search and relocation assistance, basic and remedial education, literacy and English as a second language training, entrepreneurial training, and other job-related training. In addition the Act provides readjustment services including testing and assessment and developing individual readjustment plans.

Economic Monetary Union (EMU) An economic monetary union, including a single currency and central bank, for all members of the **European Community**.

Economic Recovery Tax Act of 1981 (ERTA) Authorized the establishment of **incentive stock option plans** and granted deferral of tax liability until the stock is sold. The Act also permitted the establishment of individual retirement accounts (IRAs) for anyone who earned an income regardless of whether the individual was already enrolled in a company pension plan. That provision has since been extensively modified. Another of its provisions gave employers the opportunity to offer dependent care assistance plans (DCAPs) to the employees as a fringe benefit.

economic value added (EVA) A technique for determining whether a company is creating economic value over and above the cost of capital for assets employed. It requires a company to identify its true return (cash flow) for each line of business and for the company as a whole and then determine whether economic value is being added. In some companies, EVA replaces return on assets as a means of measuring performance; in other companies it is used as the basis for linking executive raises and bonuses to stockholder value.

economy One of the characteristics of an acceptable test. A test is economical when a minimum of time, equipment, materials, and personnel is required to administer and score it.

economy class The lowest priced regular air fare.

economy of scale Applicable to some but not all organizations. A concept stating that as an organization gets larger, its operations and other costs per unit decrease. The concept is based on the learning curve and the experience curve.

economy of scope A concept stating that an organization with an extensive and varied product line, broad contacts with potential customers, and wide distribution coverage can achieve substantial savings in operating costs; for example, advertising and promotion and distribution.

ecotourism Most commonly believed to be travel that contributes to conservation. It is more than adventure and nature tourism. It involves positive efforts on the part of the traveler to protect the natural resources of the areas visited.

ecotours Trips, including meetings, incentive travel, and educational tours, taken to show concern for the environment and advance the cause of conservation. Destinations and locales are selected where the area or country is known for its natural qualities of fresh air, wildlife, and pristine surroundings or where significant progress has been made in reducing pollution or achieving environmental improvements.

Ecstasy *See* hallucinogens.

Edison Project An educational undertaking designed to invent, develop, and privately operate for profit 1,000 new American schools and, at the same time, help traditional schools by demonstrating effective practices suitable to their purposes. Critics describe the project as an attempt to create efficient schools driven by technology and the marketplace, schools whose students will achieve high test scores and become highly skilled workers so that the U.S. can challenge the productive capacities of Japan, Germany, and South Korea. Using a core team of seven people led by Benno Schmidt, former president of Yale University, the objectives of the Project will be achieved by a private, for-profit company with a public agenda, according to its cofounder, Christopher Whittle.

The first new schools opened in 1995 on 200 campuses, enrolling 150,000 students between the ages of one an six. In 1998, additional campuses will be opened, and by 2010 enrollment will reach 2,000,000. Ultimately, each campus will contain a day-care center and offer elementary, middle school and high school curriculums. Annual tuition will be the equivalent of the annual cost per student in U.S. public Schools and 20 percent of the funds will be used for scholarships.

editing In video production, the process of adding to, deleting, replacing, extending, shortening, or otherwise changing a videotape from its original form to achieve the coverage, length, quality, and final form desired. The source of the changes may be videotape recorders, audiotape recorders, cameras, character generators, film chains, special effects generators, and so on. Also, any point in a videotape where either or both audio and video content has been changed.

educable A category of persons with mild mental disabilities. Such persons have fair motor development, can learn to communicate, and with supervision and guidance, can perform acceptably in unskilled or semi-skilled occupations.

education Learning programs and experiences that are not directly job-oriented. Education is designed to enrich a person's general knowledge and capabilities over the long term and not to prepare him or her for a profession or an occupation, although it often provides the concepts, principles, and facts upon which job-related skills are based.

educational assistance *See* employee educational assistance. H.R. 127, introduced in 1997 by Reps. Sander Levi D-Mich and Clay Shaw R-Fla, would permanently extend the tax exclusion in the Internal Revenue Code for employer-provided educational assistance for both graduate and undergraduate courses. Also introduced as S. 127 by Sens. William Roth R-Del. and Daniel Moynihan D-N.Y. *See also* the Safe and Affordable School Act of 1997 introduced as a provision of S.1 by Sen. Trent Lott, R-Miss. S. 559 was sent to Congress by President Clinton on April 11 — a bill that contains his education tax incentive proposals, including a permanent extension of the IR Code Section 127 tax exclusion for employer-provided tuition assistance.

Educational Assistance Ltd. (EAL)

An organization that assists corporations to donate excess inventory to colleges, which then provide scholarships to disadvantaged students equal to the value of the equipment or services received. *Contact:* Educational Assistance Ltd., P.O. Box 3021, Glen Ellyn, IL 60138 (630/690-0010; Fax 630/690-0565; E-mail **scholar@eduassist.org**).

educational management organization

(EMO) A private company that operates an individual public elementary or secondary school or an entire school system under contract with the city, town, or school district and assumes responsibility for educating it students. *See also* charter schools.

Educational Research, Development, Dissemination, and Improvement Act of

1994 Established a goal of 1 percent of the total amount of funds spent on education for research. Established the Office of Educational Research and Improvement in the Department of Education to serve as the center and coordinator of efforts.

Educational Resources Information Center

(ERIC) A nation-wide educational database of materials collected by the U.S. Department of Education. ERIC consists of two subfiles (1) Resources in Education (RIE), covering documents, and (2) Current Index to Journals in Education (CIJE), covering approximately 750 journals and serial publications. All records contain abstracts. Sixteen broad subject areas are covered by ERIC: adult, career, and vocational education; counseling and personnel services; elementary and early childhood education; educational management; handicapped and gifted children; information resources; junior colleges; languages and linguistics; rural education and small schools; science, mathematics, and environmental education; social studies; teacher education; tests, measurement, and evaluation; and urban education. Materials, including annotated bibliographies, are disseminated in print, microform, magnetic tape, and CD-ROM. *Contact:* ERIC, Processing and Reference Facility, 833 Rugby Ave., Suite 301, Bethesda, MD 20814 [301/656-9723; URL **http://www.usc.edu/Library/Ref/Ethnic/eric_cd.html** (2k)].

The Educational Society for Resource Management (APICS)

An international organization of 72,000 members that focuses on just-in-time, capacity management, materials requirements, production activity, and master planning. Sponsors an annual conference, seminars and workshops, exhibitions, professional certification, and professional publications. *Contact:* APICS, 500 W. Annandale Rd., Falls Church, VA 22046-4274 (800/444-2742 or 703/237-7202; E-mail **davis@apics-hq.org**; URL **http://www.apics.org**).

educational technology The application of technological advances to employee education, training, and development. Includes computers, **EXPERT systems**, telecommunications, and video.

Educational Testing Service, Inc. (ETS)

A not-for-profit organization that offers products and services for clients in education, government, and business. The purpose of ETS testing is to provide useful and dependable information that will enable individuals and organizations to demonstrate achievements, discover possibilities, and make decisions. *Contact:* ETS, Rosedale Rd., Princeton, NJ 08541-0001 (800/258-4914 or 609/921-9000; 609/734-5410; E-mail **etsinfo@ets.org**; URL **http://www.ets.org**).

Education Amendments of 1992

Reauthorized and significantly changed the **Higher Education Act of 1965.** Signed by the President in July, the law increased the availability of aid for middle-income post-secondary students and families.

Education for All Handicapped Children Act

of 1974 Required the mainstreaming of disabled students into regular classrooms if appropriate and the establishment of individualized educational programs for students with disabilities.

edutainment A combination of educational and entertaining programming used in corporate video. "Edutainment" employs such familiar network formats as magazine shows, newscasts, and game shows to inform, educate, train, and entertain.

EEOC revolving fund A 1992 amendment to the Civil Rights Act of 1964 (Section 705). Created a revolving fund within the **Equal Employment Opportunity Commission** (EEOC), which allows the EEOC to charge employers and individuals reasonable fees for some of its services to offset the costs of new services, such as developing training programs and producing videos.

EEOC waiver policy   States that the right of an individual to file a charge of employment discrimination cannot be waived, that an individual cannot waive the right to testify, assist, or participate in a commission proceeding, and that the no-waiver position is consistent with the commission's strong support of voluntary agreements to resolve employment discrimination disputes.

E-Factor   Environment and economics, empowerment, and efficiency, items that must be incorporated into the way companies due business if they are to prosper in an age of growing environmental awareness. Attributed to Joel Makower, *The E-Factor: the Bottom-Line Approach to Environmentally Responsible business.*

efficiency   A hotel room that contains cooking facilities.

egonomics   Refers to the need of people to make personal statements as a response to the bleak computer era. Attributed to Faith Popcorn and Lys Marigold, *Clicking: 16 Trends to Future Fit Your Life, Your Work, and Your Business.*

eight-ball   One-eighth ounce of cocaine.

E-key system   Electronic key system that employs a plastic card coded with a magnetic strip. Used for hotel/motel room access.

elder abuse   An act or failure to act that results in serious physical or emotional exploitation of an elderly person. Serious physical injury includes any injury, either internal or external, bed sores, malnutrition, dehydration, and inappropriate or harmful administration of drugs and medications. Serious emotional injury includes any extreme emotional condition such as anxiety, fear, depression, and withdrawal. Financial exploitation is an act by another which results in a loss of a substantial amount of money to the elderly person without his or her consent, or when the elder is tricked or forced into giving consent.

elder care   Services provided to the elderly (grandparents, parents, and spouses), including information and consultation, seminars and workshops, on-site peer support groups, and facilities for day care.

elder law   The area of law that deals with estate planning, health care decisions, housing, legal capacity issues, taxation, and government programs, such as Medicaid, which affect people over the age of 65.

elderly cottage housing opportunity (ECHO)   An alternative housing solution for the elderly, ECHO units are small, self-contained, portable, factory-built housing modules that can be placed by means of a crane on a prepared foundation in the yard of a single family house. ECHO units retain the security of closeness to others while retaining privacy.

elective surgery   Any non-emergency surgical procedure that may be scheduled at the convenience of the patient without jeopardizing his or her life or causing serious impairment to bodily functions.

electromagnetic field (EMF)   The area surrounding electrical appliances (such as electric blankets, and motor-driven can-openers, mixers, clocks, and fans), electronic equipment (such as computer video display terminals and television sets), and power lines believed by some to pose health risks, such as cancer. EMF is measured in milligauss.

Electromation Decision   A December 1992 decision of the National Labor Relations Board on the legality of employee action committees or similar team-based work groups established to further the concept of employee participation. The board ruled that employee committees formed at Electomation, Inc., an Indiana electronics firm, were "labor organizations" that violated federal labor laws because of the employer's alleged interference with and domination over the committees. In August 1993, the NLRB issued guidelines to its field offices regarding the ruling. The memorandum stated that an organization is a labor organization if employees participate, and the organization exists, at least in part, for the purpose of "dealing with" employees on mandatory subjects of bargaining, such as grievances, labor disputes, wages, rates of pay, hours, safety concerns, or working conditions. The memorandum deliberately left unresolved the issue of whether any program initiated by the employer exists "for the purpose of achieving quality or efficiency or that were designed to be a communication device to promote generally the interests of quality or efficiency may constitute labor organizations...."

electromyograph (EMG)   An instrument used to convert the electrical activity of skeletal muscles into a visual picture or a sound. It has become one of the principal tools for the diagnosis of neuromuscular disorders, including lower back problems, as well as for biofeedback in subsequent treatment.

electromyography (EMG) A medical diagnostic technology used by neurologists and neurophysiologists to locate and determine the extent of nerve damage. The system uses electrical impulses generated by machine and the human body to develop graphic recordings, which are then measured to produce a diagnosis.

electronically erasable and reprogrammable memory (EEPROM) Semiconductor computer chips that can be erased and reprogrammed. They are smaller, cheaper, and more reliable than disk drives, and they retain their memory in the absence of power.

electronic brainstorming The use of computers to assist in the ideation or creative problem solving process. In elaborate systems, whole rooms are especially designed and furnished for group use. They include work stations with personal computers and specialized software for from 8 to 48 persons and several large wall screens.

electronic bulletin board A comprehensive communication system employing microcomputers, software, modems, and phone lines. Used to transmit electronic mail to specific addresses, post messages to all board users, and send files or other long documents to other users. It also allows distant users to tap into the data base of a central computer to review, send, or obtain information.

The Electronic Bulletin Board (EBB) For on-line security tips for business travelers. *Contact:* Private Sector Liaison Staff, U.S. Department of State Bureau of Diplomatic Security SA-11, Washington, DC 20522-1003. For advisories on conditions affecting travelers abroad, call U.S State Department Citizens Emergency Center 202/647-5225 or U.S. State Department Crisis Center 202/647-0900).

Electronic Communications Privacy Act of 1986 Prohibits interception of **electronic mail** by any extra-organizational third party, including government and law enforcement agencies and individuals, without proper authority, such as a search warrant. Although designed to ensure privacy, absolute security of inter-office, computerized systems is unattainable (unless encrypted by sophisticated codes). They invariably leave an electronic trail, which can be used to recover the messages. Although it is illegal in some states for an employer to listen in on private conversations and telephone calls, there are no clear-cut rules covering electronic mail. In some cases the courts have ruled that, because the company owned the computer system, it had the right to read anything created on it.

electronic data interchange (EDI) Computer-to-computer exchange of business documents between departments, functions, and branches in an organization, with suppliers and contractors, with trading partners, and government offices (for reports, such as first-report-of-injury). EDI technology is affecting internal operations, such as purchasing and financial management, as well as marketing and other external contacts. Among its main advantages are implementation and facilitation of the firm's strategic plan, as well as reductions in time, paperwork, and processing costs.

electronic data processing (EDP) *See* data processing.

electronic delivery system *See* distance learning.

electronic distance learning *See* distance learning.

electronic document (ED) A non-paper document created by computer using specialized software and expertise in document design that automates the document construction process. Electronic publishing software, such as SmarText used with a **Windows**-compatible computer, can create electronic documents using standard word processor and graphics files to build hypertext links, indexes, and tables of contents.

Electronic Federal Tax Payment System (EFTPS) Requires all U.S. companies with 1995 federal employment taxes of $50,000 or more to deposit business taxes electronically as of July 1, 1997 and continue to do so in future years even when their tax liability falls below that level. Failure to file will result in penalties. By 1999, companies with 1997 federal taxes of $20,000 or more must file electronically. A provision mandated by the North American Free Trade Agreement.

Electronic Freedom of Information Act of 1996 Requires federal agencies to provide data electronically, including computer-generated materials, when that form of response is requested.

electronic immigrant A service worker who performs work across an international border by means of a computer and modem — and thereby competes with workers in the more affluent country.

electronic job aid A computer-based system that provides on-line assistance to workers.

electronic mail/mailbox Computer-based message systems, communicating word processors, and communicating facsimile machines connected by modems and telephone lines/radio/satellite links. Anything that can be input to a computer can be transmitted (documents, photos, drawings, and so on). An efficient way to transmit information — reports, memos, other written materials — and an effective way to disseminate information to people dispersed over a large geographical area. Also called **E-mail.**

electronic management A term used to describe the phenomenon of top executives appearing on television screens in cafeterias, orientation sessions, seminars, or team meetings reading carefully scripted speeches instead of appearing in person.

electronic meeting A meeting using a personal computer and presentation peripherals, usually with some kind of outlining software, to help groups of people organize their thoughts, develop ideas, create designs and proposals, present reports, and solve problems.

electronic monitoring Surveillance of employees by such means as monitoring word processing keystrokes, telephone conversations, and E-mail. Employees object to it as an invasion of privacy. Employers maintain that it is a business necessity and can be used as a training and coaching tool for such employees as secretaries, receptionists, customer service representatives, and telemarketers. No laws currently cover telephone monitoring; however, bills have introduced in the Senate and House that would safeguard employee privacy and the right of employees and customers to be notified of monitoring. These bills would require employers to give employees and job candidates written notice of how and when monitoring, including telephone monitoring, would be conducted, what kind of data would be collected, how the data would be used, and how the data would affect performance evaluations. Customers would have to be notified of telephone monitoring.

electronic page-turner Training programs that have simply been transferred from their current format to the computer, failing to take advantage of the potential of the computer for interactivity.

electronic partnering Replacing conventional order-taking, shipping, and invoicing process with **electronic data interchange systems** that hook computers together with modems and telephone lines.

electronic performance aid A job aid that makes use of the computer-based strategies of **artificial intelligence** (AI) and **hypertext systems** instead of paper.

electronic performance support system (EPSS) An integrated computerized system, composed of a database and support functions that provide on-line assistance to workers, in the forms of advice, assistance, data, tools, and images, as the main features of intelligent work stations.

electronic print production (EPP) The process of assembling and formatting information in a computer to serve as output for hard copy (paper). It differs from **desktop publishing** mainly in terms of the quality of the output of the two processes. For EPP, the input device and computer must be able to handle higher-resolution files and deal with multi-image files. They must also be able to transmit layout information to the output device, provide electronic two-way communication between workstations, and handle proofing for offset production.

electronic publishing (EP) Use of such tools as minicomputers or personal computers to write, edit, lay out, and produce sophisticated, professional publications, including text and graphics.

electronic remittance standard Developed by the Department of Health and Human Services to allow health care providers, including hospitals, skilled nursing facilities, home health care agencies, and hospices, to submit Medicare claims electronically and to receive notification of of payment decisions (remittance notices) electronically.

electronic sweatshop   A workplace in which managers use technology to monitor employee performance and productivity; for example, using the same computers on which workers perform such routine tasks as word processing to count worker keystrokes and errors per unit of time.

electronic textbook   A computerized training program that involves the use of graphics, animation, and icons to make learning materials efficient, effective, and visually attractive. Electronic textbooks take full advantage of the capabilities of the computer for meaningful interaction between the learner and the system, such as requiring the trainee to answer questions on the material presented at frequent intervals.

electronic ticket delivery network (ETDN)   A fast and flexible automated ticket delivery service. Certified ETDN networks of printers, located in airports, hotels, and office buildings, print tickets and, using their graphics capabilities, print logos, itineraries, and car or hotel confirmation vouchers. With access to such a network a traveler whose plans change enroute or who must leave his home office on short notice can book a ticket through a designated agency and receive it almost immediately and, in many cases, avoid the fee for ticket changes.

element   The smallest unit of work activity described in occupational or job analysis. Elements are the smallest steps into which it is practicable to subdivide any work operation or task without analyzing separate motions, movements, and mental processes. Elements are also the work units that deal with the details of how the methods, procedures, and techniques involved in a task are carried out. They are very important to developers of training systems. For example, elements performed by an electronics repairer include soldering and unsoldering connections, activating switches, and tightening screws.

element analysis   In job and task analysis, the process of defining the behaviors, conditions, and standards of an element, a component of a task.

Elementary and Secondary Education Act of 1965 (ESEA)   Made Title I, Chapter I, federal funding for compensatory education, a reality. It provided extra instruction in reading, writing, and mathematics for educationally disadvantaged children thereby helping to equalize educational opportunity for needy children. It is the largest single program of federal education aid to elementary and secondary school students and accounts for about 22 percent of the entire Department of Education budget.

Elementary and Secondary Education Reauthorization Act of 1994   A major overhaul of most of the federal government's principal programs of aid for elementary and secondary education. Among other things, the Act requires that children who benefit from federal aid be held to the same high academic standards as all other children and that greater flexibility be allowed in the use of federal funds. The Act also makes inservice training available to all teachers and authorizes several new programs including ones dealing with technology education.

eligible program   Under federal student aid programs, a course of study that requires certain minimum number of hours of instruction and that leads to a degree or certificate at a participating school. There are two exceptions: (1) if the school requires the student to complete certain courses to qualify for admission in to one of its eligible programs, a Direct Loan, an FFEL Program Loan, or a PLUS Loan can be obtained for up to 12 consecutive months while the course work is being completed, provided that the student is enrolled at least half time; (2) if enrolled at least half time in a program to obtain a professional credential or certification required by a state for employment as an elementary or secondary school teacher, a Federal Perkins Loan, Federal Work-Study, and FFEL Stafford Loan, a Direct Loan, or a PLUS Loan can be obtained while the student is enrolled in that program.

eligible small business   In relation to the **Internal Revenue Code** and the **Americans with Disabilities Act of 1990**, a business whose gross receipts do not exceed $1 million or whose work force does not consist of more than 30 full-time workers. Such businesses may qualify for a deduction of up to $15,000 per year for expenses associated with the removal of qualified architectural and transportation barriers and a tax credit of up to 50 percent of eligible access expenditures that exceed $250 but do not exceed $10,250.

elimination period The number of consecutive days an individual must be confined in a **nursing home** or **alternate long term care facility** to qualify for benefits under a long-term care insurance policy. The elimination period initiates a **covered period of confinement.** The elimination period can be anywhere from 30 to 180 days.

ELISA test The most commonly used and the least expensive test to determine whether an individual is infected by HIV. It determines the presence of antibodies, substances produced by the body in response to infection by a foreign agent, and not the AIDS virus itself. However, it cannot be relied upon in the absence of confirmation and retesting.

E-mail *See* electronic mailbox/mail.

E-mail gateway Hardware or software (or a combination of both) that connects at least two dissimilar E-mail systems.

emancipation age *See* age out.

embedded training (ET) Training that is built into the software of computer applications programs — the programs the employee uses on the job — rather than provided in a separate training package. ET is on the same terminal or delivery device as the product it supports. For example, a program that teaches an employee how to use a spreadsheet while using the spreadsheet itself.

emergency child care services (ECCS) A form of direct employer-supported child care service that involves making emergency arrangements, especially when a child is ill, such as helping pay for special sick child infirmaries or family day care homes, or providing health care workers to go to the child's home. Some companies extend the service to situations where usual parental child care arrangements are upset. In such cases, a trained care giver is sent to the employee's home.

emergency medical services (EMS) Medical services provided to victims of accidents and illnesses by physicians, nurses, and emergency medical technicians in hospital emergency rooms, clinics, ambulances, and aircraft.

emergency medical technician (EMT) A person who has received 110 or more hours of medical training to enable him or her to provide emergency medical assistance to victims of life-threatening illnesses or accidents. Typically assigned to ambulance services, EMTs are now being trained to use sophisticated medical equipment, such as automatic heart defibrillators. These devices analyze heart rhythm and deliver a shock to patients suffering from the potentially fatal irregular heart rhythm known as ventricular fibrillation.

Emergency Planning and Community Right-to-Know Act (EPCRA) of 1986 One of five major environmental laws. EPCRA is Title III of the **Superfund Amendments and Reauthorization Act of 1986.** It encompasses four broad areas, three of which require reporting to various local, state, and federal agencies regarding hazardous chemicals used, stored, or transported. The fourth requires the states and localities within the state to set up emergency response plans.

emergency response system A subscription system in which subscribers wear a pendant around their necks (or use a wall-mounted key pad) to summon assistance in an emergency.

emergency treatment Medical services provided in a hospital, trauma center, clinic, physician's office, or other medical facility for an injury or condition that requires immediate care or treatment.

Emerson plan An incentive plan that provided for bonuses to be based on a formula that increases amounts paid at an increasing rate as productivity increases. It is not in common use today.

emoticon Emotion icon. Symbols or icons used on the **Internet** in **E-mail** communications to express feelings or emotions. For example, :-) equals "smiley face," indicating humor or sarcasm; :-(equals "frowny face," indicating sadness or anger.

emotionally disabled (ED) Although out of favor by many who work with people with disabilities, it remains in use. The preferred terms put people first — people with **emotional disabilities**.

emotional disabilities Attention-deficit disorders (short attention spans), psychotic disorders (schizophrenia, paranoia, and manic-depressive psychotic reaction), psychoneurotic disorders (anxiety, hysteria, hypochondria, phobic reaction, and depression), personality disorders (antisocial personality), and substance dependence and abuse, including alcoholism.

Emotional Health Anonymous (EHA)

A group of men and women who are not emotional health professionals but share their experience, strength, and hope with each other so that they may recover from their emotional illness and help others who still suffer to find a new way of life. The only requirement for membership is an honest desire to recover from emotional and mental illness not related to substance abuse. *Contact:* EHA, San Gabriel Valley Intergroup, P.O. Box 2081, San Gabriel, CA 91778 (818/287-6260).

emotionally impaired   Individuals whose limitations rest primarily on psychopathology (abnormal personality functioning) recognizable by easily discernible disturbances of their behavior. These disturbances may be the result of heredity, rearing, traumatic experiences, or stress.

emotional intelligence   Demonstrated by self-awareness and the ability to manage emotions, understand emotions in others, delay self-gratification, repress anti-social impulses, achieve acceptance, and exhibit conciliation skills. Believed by some to be just as important and an even better predictor of success in life and careers than the **intelligence quotient** or scores on the **Scholastic Assessment Test** and other standardized achievement tests. The term was coined by Yale psychologist Peter Salovey and John Mayer of the University of New Hampshire.

emotional quotient (EQ)   *See* emotional intelligence.

emotional retailing   Appealing to customers' emotions, their sense of excitement and fun, their desire for reduced stress, and their concern for moral and family values, rather than logical factors in marketing, promotion, and sales campaigns. Originated by Service Industry Research Systems of R.R. Donnelly & Sons, of Oak Brook, Il.

Emotions Anonymous (EA)   Offers a group approach to the achievement of emotional health patterned after the 12-step program of **Alcoholics Anonymous**. Group meetings are conducted in which participants share their experiences, strength, and hope with each other while practicing the 12 steps to this new way of life, one day at a time. *Contact:* EA, P.O. Box 4245, St. Paul, MN 55104-0245 (612/647-9712; Fax 612/647-1593).

empathy   The ability to see all sides of situation, issue, or dispute and to put one's self in the shoes of others to see the problem or issue from their perspective.

employability doctrine   A new approach used by companies to deal with unstable economic conditions. Instead of offering employment security, they offer workers opportunities to improve their skills — and therefore their employability. Employees are expected to be committed to the goals and objectives of the company while employed, and the company assumes the obligation of offering workers the opportunity to learn new, transferable skills. Employees behave somewhat like independent contractors, assuming responsibility for managing their own benefits, such as training, pension plans, and health care, and developing their own careers.

employee   1. In general, an individual who works for wages or a salary for a company or an individual.   **2.** As defined by the Internal Revenue Service, an employee is a person who works for wages or a salary, works hours set by the company at the company's location, is usually under another's instructions or direction, is paid hourly or other periodic basis, and whose labor and how it is performed are controlled by the employer. Employees receive training, submit reports, are reimbursed for expenses, use tools or materials supplied by the company, and may be fired. *See also* independent contractor.

Employee Assistance Professionals Association, Inc. (EAPA)

A nationwide organization of over 7,000 professional employee assistance practitioners and organizations that assist work organizations and employees and their families with personal and behavioral problems, including health, marital, family, financial, alcohol, drugs, legal, emotional, stress, or other personal concerns which adversely affect employee job performance and productivity. The Association also established policies, procedures, and standards of eligibility for the Certified Employee Assistance Professional credential. *Contact:* EAPA, Inc., 2101 Wilson Blvd., Ste. 500, Arlington, VA 22201-3062 (703) 522-6272; Fax 703/522-4585; URL **http://www.ahrm.org/eapa.htm.**

employee assistance program (EAP)

A program designed to help organizations identify and diagnose a variety of problems and counsel and assist employees in dealing with those problems and issues, such as drug and alcohol abuse, child and spouse abuse, emotional problems, family and social problems, financial problems, career problems, legal concerns, stress management, vocational rehabilitation, stress, and mental and emotional illness.

employee attitude survey *See* organization climate survey.

***Employee Benefit News:* Strategies & Solutions for the Business of Employment.** A journal published 14 times per year: $84.00 (free to qualified subscribers). Address: Enterprise Communications, Inc., 1165 Northchase Pkwy. N.E., Suite 350, Marietta, GA 30067 (770-988-9558; Fax 703-448-0270).

Employee Benefit Research Institute (EBRI) A nonprofit, nonpartisan public policy research organization of some 250 members and 1,500 subscribers. It is committed to the formulation of effective and responsible health, welfare, and retirement policies. *Contact:* EBRI, 2121 K Street, N.W., Ste. 600, Washington, DC 20037-1896 (202/659-0670; Fax 202/775-6312; E-mail **info@ebri. org**; URL **http://www.ebri.org**).

employee benefits *See* benefits.

employee benefits administrator *See* benefits administrator.

Employee Benefits Infosource™ (EBI) A comprehensive on-line database benefits information service offered by the **International Foundation of Employee Benefit Plans**. Designed to help benefits managers, financial officers, employer associations, labor unions, and others gain better and faster access to complex benefits trends and issues, most of which are now the objects of close government scrutiny. *Contact:* IFEBP, 18700 West Bluemond Rd., P.O. Box 69, Brookfield, WI 53008-0069 (414/786-6700, Ext. 8360; Fax 414/786-8780; E-mail **ebinfo@ifebp.org**; URL **http://www.ifebp. org**).

employee benefits laws *See* Consolidated Omnibus Budget Reconciliation Act of 1986; Deficit Reduction Act of 1984; Economic Recovery Tax Act of 1981; Employee Retirement Income Security Act of 1974; Family and Medical Leave Act of 1993; Federal Insurance Contributions Act of 1935; Older Workers Benefit Protection Act of 1990; Omnibus Budget Reconciliation Act of 1990; Pension Protection Act of 1987; Social Security Act of 1935; Tax Equity and Responsibility Act of 1982; Tax Reform Act of 1986; Technical Corrections and Miscellaneous Revenue Act of 1988.

employee benefits manager The individual responsible for designing and administering group health, medical, disability, life, retirement, profit sharing, and thrift plans and for maintaining a competitive corporate benefits posture. Often responsible for selecting and supervising benefits consultants, brokers, trustees, and legal counsel.

employee benefits planning analyst *See* benefits planning analyst.

Employee Commute Option (ECO) A requirement of the **Clean Air Amendments Act of 1990,** which set November 1996 as the date by which employers with 100 or more workers must reduce by 25 percent the number of automobiles coming to work during the peak hours of 6 to 10 am. In 1995, the Environmental Protection Agency announced that it would accept recommendations of the Clean Air Act Advisory Council to relax the requirements, such as allowing states or regions to assume some or all of employers' responsibility to implement trip reduction programs.

employee development *See* development.

employee driven idea system (EDIS) A redefined and redesigned employee suggestion system that focuses on employee involvement and the generation of lots of relatively simple ideas instead of grand suggestions. Management of the implementation of ideas by the person who suggested them is required, and all ideas are equally rewarded with small awards. Attributed to Robin McDermott, Raymond Mikulak, and Michael Beauregard, *Employee Driven Quality.*

employee educational assistance (EEA)
1. *See* Section 127, Internal Revenue Code.
2. An employee benefit that takes the form of a stipend or tuition reimbursement for job-related or non-job-related education or training taken off-the-premises.

Employee Educational Assistance Act of 1978 (EEAA) Codified as **Section 127** of the Internal Revenue Code, the EEAA exempted employees from paying taxes on employer-provided tuition reimbursement benefits for non-job-related college course work (but not those related to sports or hobbies) through the 1983 tax year.

Employee Educational Assistance Reform Act of 1996 In 1996, Congress approved measures to restore the exclusion of taxes on employer-provided tuition reimbursement benefits to cover the period from January 1, 1995 through May 31, 1997. However, tuition for graduate level courses that began after June 30, 1996 will be taxed as income. For undergraduates, up to $5,250 in employer-provided tuition reimbursement remains tax free.

employee education, training, and assistance laws See Economic Dislocation and Worker Adjustment Assistance Act of 1988; Employee Educational Assistance Reform Act of 1986; Job Training Partnership Act of 1982; Lifelong Learning Act of 1976; Manpower Development and Training Act of 1962; Training Technology Transfer Act of 1984; Veterans' Readjustment Benefits Act of 1952; Vietnam Era Veterans' Readjustment and Assistance Act of 1974; Worker Adjustment and Retraining Notification Act of 1988.

employee home ownership plan (EHOP) A benefits plan designed to assist employees to finance the purchase of a home. Employers help their employees find affordable housing and help them finance its purchase. For example, shares of stock contributed by an employer could be used as collateral for borrowing money loaned to employees toward a down payment. The plan would also allow first-time home buyers to use tax-sheltered retirement savings vehicles, such as IRAs and 401(k) plans, toward a down payment on a home. Requires congressional approval.

employee investment plan   See Section 401(k) plan.

employee involvement (EI) The process of engaging workers as individuals and in groups at all levels of organization in making decisions relating to their work. It is characterized by three elements: information, **empowerment,** and rewards. See also Electromation Decision; Gissel bargaining order; employee participation.

employee involvement system   See participative management.

employee leasing See temporary employee. An alternative staffing option. Involves

transferring all or selected employees to the payroll of an employee leasing company or professional employer organization in an formal joint-employment venture. The employee leasing company then leases the workers back to the company and performs most of the functions usually assigned to the HR department, such as compensation and benefits administration and recordkeeping.

employee leasing firm   See professional employer organization.

employee motivation See motivation.

employee opinion survey See organization climate survey.

employee organization plan A health benefits plan sponsored by an organization or association in which members of the plan are primarily federal employees.

employee orientation See orientation.

employee outplacement See outplacement.

employee outreach See outreach program.

employee participation (EP) See participative management.

employee participation plan (EPP) See participative management.

employee participation system See participative management.

employee partnership pay (EPP) A compensation system in which part of a worker's pay is linked to the achievement of various goals or objectives, both financial (profits, earnings, or return calculations) and operational (attendance, cost reductions, output, quality, or safety).

employee performance evaluation See performance appraisal.

Employee Polygraph Protection Act of 1988 (EPPA) Prevents most private employers from requesting or requiring any employee or prospective employee to submit to any lie detector test, requesting or using the results of such tests, or discharging, disciplining or otherwise discriminating against any employee or prospective employee on the basis of the results of such tests. Exempt from the act are Federal government agencies engaged in intelligence or counterintelligence functions (Federal Bureau of Investigation, National Security Agency, Defense Intelligence Agency, and Central Intelligence Agency), organizations that manufacture and distribute controlled substances, and those involved in the protection of nuclear power plants, public transportation, currency, commodities, or proprietary information. Polygraphs may still be administered under severely restricted conditions as a part of an investigation involving suspected wrongdoing. However, employees may refuse to undergo a polygraph test, and they may not be discharged, disciplined, or denied promotions solely on polygraph results.

employee prefunding　A health benefit cost reduction strategy for postretirement health care benefits. The plan requires active employees to contribute to their retiree health plan by making monthly premium payments based on age. Contributions are returned with interest if the employee leaves the company before retirement.

employee privacy　*See* Privacy Act.

employee promotion　*See* promotion.

employee records　*See* records.

employee recruitment　*See* recruitment.

employee relations　*See* employee assistance program; labor-management relations.

Employee Relocation Council (ERC) A professional association of organizations concerned with domestic and international employee transfer. Members include 1,200 representatives of corporations that relocate their employees an well as nearly 11,000 individuals and companies from the relocation industry. ERC was established to provide leadership, services, and assistance to members, enabling them to serve effectively relocated families. *Contact:* ERC, 1720 N St., N.W., Washington, DC 20036 (202/857-0857; Fax 202/467-4012; E-mail **prcomm@ erc.org**; URL **http://www.erc.org/**).

employee retirement　*See* retirement.

Employee Retirement Income Security Act of 1974 (ERISA)　An act that regulates employee benefits such as health care, sickness and accident, disability, and death benefits as well as retirement and capital accumulation plans. It created government-run employee-financed corporations to protect employees against pension fund failures. The Act covers eligibility, funding arrangements, fiduciary responsibilities, and other standards, including financing, vesting, and administration of pension plans in most private businesses and industries. It requires employers to maintain records on employee health and welfare plans and pension plans and descriptions of those plans and report to the DOL, IRS, and **Pension Benefits Guarantee Corporation**. ERISA has been modified by virtually every comprehensive budget and tax law since its enactment.

employee rights　In the context of labor-management relations, employees are protected against unfair labor practices, enterprise interference with employee rights, discrimination in conditions of employment that tend to discourage or encourage membership in a union, and discrimination against an employee for filing a grievance or giving testimony.

employee skills test　A test of important workplace skills administered periodically to help workers maintain important skills and remember little-used but critical procedures. Originated by military aviation and adopted by commercial aviation to maintain the skills of pilots but now used in a variety of occupations. Also called *checkride* or *recertification test.*

employee stock option (ownership) plan (ESOP)　Under such a plan, the benefits of a capital owner are given to employees as an incentive. After they have become vested in the program, employees can redeem their stock when they leave the company through resignation, termination, or retirement. Companies sell bonds, borrow funds from banks, savings and loan institutions, mutual funds, insurance companies, and large institutional investors, or set aside stock. In 1989, Congress repealed the interest exclusion on loans to employee stock ownership plans unless at least 30 percent of company stock is in the hands of employees.

employee support benefits　Include such benefits as employee assistance, health and welfare benefits, wellness and health promotion, and work/family programs.

employee welfare benefit plan A plan that provides benefits to employees due to sickness, hospitalization, surgery, accident, death, disability, or unemployment. Such plans may also provide vacation, day care, elder care, scholarship, prepaid legal services, holiday, severance, and other training benefits.

employee selection　*See* selection.

employee self-service Encouraging employees to use direct access systems, such as kiosks, for information about their benefits instead of going to company benefits offices or outside vendors for assistance.

employee services　Services provided to employees by organizations at reduced or no cost to the employee, such as child care, counseling, recreation, and transportation.

employee task log A means of collecting data for work measurement that involves maintenance by employees of daily or hourly diaries, logs, or check sheets.

employee testing *See* employment tests.

employee termination *See* termination.

employee union *See* union.

employee wellness plan (EWP) *See* wellness program.

employer coalition Originally, an informal arrangement whereby management, labor, insurers, and health care providers collected and shared data on health care utilization. Employer coalitions have now been transformed into coalition purchasing groups called **health care purchasing organizations**.

employer identification number (EIN) The business equivalent of a social security number. Issued by the federal government to companies for use in preparing tax payments, reports, and records. Also required by most banks to open a business account.

employer mandate A legal requirement that employers provide health insurance for their workers. It may include such guidelines as the types of employers that must participate, the classes of employees to be included, and what part of the cost will be borne by the employer.

employer of choice A program and strategy designed to attract top management talent. Involves emphasizing the company's distinctive corporate culture, sterling industry and community reputation, attractive compensation plan, and abundant career development and advancement opportunities.

Employers Council on Flexible Compensation (ECFC) An organization with the mission of representing and promoting flexible compensation through lobbying and publicizing flexible compensation to help create a positive climate for the growth of the concept. *Contact:* ECFC, 927 25th St., N.W., Washington, DC 20005 (202/659-4300).

employer-supported child care services *See* child care resource and referral program; consortium center; dependent care assistance plan; emergency child care services; family day care network; emergency child care services; on-site or near site centers, parent education seminar, child care benefits, voucher program.

employment agencies Public or private organizations that provide placement help to persons seeking jobs. Some are staffed to do applicant screening and counseling; others are strictly in the business of placing clients. In some cases, the individual client pays a fee to the agency; in others the fee is paid by the employer. Such fees are usually a percentage of the applicant's first year's wages or salary, but most will negotiate fees with employers.

employment-at-will A legal doctrine maintaining that it is the right of an employer or employee to terminate the employment relationship at any time and for any — or no — reason. The doctrine has been successfully challenged by employees in the courts in recent years.

employment benefits Benefits granted largely or totally at no cost to the employee.

employment contract A legally binding document that contains the following: (1) duration of the contract (beginning and ending dates) and provision for extension or renewal; (2) compensation, including salary, raises, cost-of-living adjustments, bonuses, profit sharing, and so on; (3) job title and job description; (4) benefits, including pension plan, life and health insurance, sick leave, annual leave, training and development, and so on; (5) provisions for termination/resignation; (6) process for resolving disputes.

employment displacement Involuntary termination of a worker because the job has been eliminated.

employment equity Relates to diversity and equal opportunity in the workplace. Said to occur when members of protected groups, such as African-Americans and people with disabilities, are in the work force in numbers that reflect their status in the community.

Employment Management Association (EMA) A 1,000-member national organization of human resource professionals and providers of employment support services that provides a global forum to exchange ideas and become better informed about staffing and related human resources issues. EMA's goal is to advance staffing as a profession by encouraging member involvement to promote quality and add value to the staffing process through education, innovation, and the identification of technology advances and best practices in the field.

In June 1996, the **Society for Human Resource Management** voted to accept EMA as the newest SHRM Professional Emphasis Group (PEG). effective September 1, 1996. *Contact:* EMA, 4101 Lake Boone Trail, Ste. 201, Raleigh, NC 27607 (919/787-6010; Fax 919/787-5302; E-mail **srexer@ mercury.interpath.net**; URL **http://www. ahrm.org/ema/ema.htm**).

Employment Non-discrimination Act of 1996 (ENDA) A bill that would extend federal employment discrimination protections currently provided based on race, religion, gender, national origin, age and disability to sexual orientation. Thus, ENDA would extend fair employment practices — not special rights — to lesbians, gay men, bisexuals and heterosexuals. ENDA would prohibit employers, employment agencies, and labor unions from using an individual's sexual orientation as the basis for employment decisions, such as hiring, firing, promotion, or compensation. ENDA would exempt employers with fewer than 15 employees and religious organizations,, including educational institutions substantially controlled or supported by religious organizations. ENDA would not apply to uniformed members of the armed forces and would not require an employer to provide benefits for the same-sex partner of an employee ENDA would apply to Congress with the same remedies provided by the Congressional Accountability Act of 1995. The measure failed of passage in the Senate on September 10, 1996.

employment practices liability (EPL) Exposure of an organization to wrongful employment practice claims, such as sexual harassment, discrimination, and wrongful discharge. Some protection against claims is afforded by EPL insurance, particularly if those policies are reviewed and revised to identify and eliminate coverage deficits.

employment practices liability insurance A policy that covers the costs of litigating such employee claims as discrimination, sexual harassment, wrongful discharge, failure to promote, breach of employment contract, misrepresentation, and defamation. Typically does not cover losses from violations of **Employee Retirement Income Security Act (ERISA), Occupational Safety and Health Act (OSHA), Consolidated Omnibus** Budget Reconciliation Act (COBRA), and labor relations, securities, and workers compensation laws.

Employment Termination Act A model law adopted by a national commission after four years of deliberation and recommended for passage by state legislatures. The law would end the **"employment at will"** doctrine that has governed the American workplace since the mid-1980s by prohibiting companies from terminating workers for capricious reasons. It also calls for speedy settlement of disputes using arbitration instead of the time-consuming procedures required to peruse an **Age Discrimination in Employment Act** or other legal basis for complaint. Terminations would be allowed only for "good cause" such as substandard performance, absenteeism, or other non-arbitrary grounds. The proposed law would not apply to union members, part-time or temporary workers, or contract employees.

employment tests Section 106 of the Civil Rights Act of 1991, which became effective November 26, 1991, states, "It shall be an unlawful employment practice for a respondent, in connection with the selection or referral of applicants or candidates for employment or promotion, to adjust the scores of, use different cutoff scores for, or otherwise alter the results of, employment related tests on the basis of race, color, religion, sex, or national origin." In effect, the Act placed the burden of proof on employers to show that there is a business necessity for their tests.

employment torts Grounds for employee lawsuits, the most common of which are invasion of privacy, deceit, intentional interference with contractual relations, and wrongful discharge.

Employment, Training, and Literacy Act of 1997 Reauthorizes the Rehabilitation Act (reauthorized in 1992) through the year 2000. Passed by the House of Representatives May 16, 1997. Awaits Senate action (summer of 1997).

empowered profit sharing A means of enhancing growth in employee morale and productivity and corporate profitability. Involves combining or blending employee **empowerment** and profit or **gain sharing** bonus systems. It uses profit sharing plans, regular and frequent communication on financial results, corporate initiatives, and the solicitation of worker opinions on how the organization can improve its operations to encourage workers to view themselves as partners in the business venture.

empowered training Training on demand and accessed at the time and in the form chosen by the learner.

empowerment Helping people to take charge of their work life. Giving employees responsibility, ownership of their jobs, power over what and how things are done, decision-making authority, and recognition for their ideas and knowledge to improve their performance and productivity. Turning employees loose with the proper training and motivation and encouraging them to get out there and do whatever needs to be done.

emulator An item of hardware or software that performs in such a way that it *seems* to be identical in *function* (as well as compatible with) although it may not look like the type of hardware or software is is designed to imitate; for example, the size of the device or its control panel may be different An emulator often uses specialized software working with a **simulator** to imitate real operations.

EN 29000 The European equivalent of international quality assurance standard ISO 9000.

encounter group *See* sensitivity training.

encrypted English International communication from someone whose command of English is at best marginal although well-intentioned.

encryption A means of securing privacy on networks by employing complex algorithmic codes.

encryption software Scrambles computer data so that unauthorized persons will be unable to read them without a key; includes passwords that unscramble the data.

encumbrance accounting A budget control that requires the obligation of funds in advance of their disbursement. That is, a purchase order must be issued and recorded prior to the purchase of equipment, materials, supplies, or contractual services to reserve funds for the vendor or contractor.

endarterectomy The most common surgical procedure for the relief of carotid blockage or **atherosclerosis**. An incision is made to open a short section of the affected area and the plaque is removed to reveal the healthy arterial wall.

endocrinologist A medical doctor who specializes in the diagnosis and treatment of patients with problems involving the hormone-secreting endocrine glands. These specialized internists consult with other physicians on such medical problems as diabetes, osteoporosis, thyroid disorders, infertility, high cholesterol, and hormone-producing tumors.

endodontics Dental care that encompasses pulpal and root canal therapy.

end-of-course qualification test A test administered to trainees at the conclusion of training. It provides a comprehensive measure of the trainees' ability to perform the full range of job duties and tasks for which training has been provided. It replicates, as realistically as possible, the conditions under which the trainee will be expected to perform when assigned to an operating or managerial position.

endorsement A written "stamp of approval" — praise for a product or service — provided by someone, typically someone well-known if not famous, not connected with the manufacture of the product or delivery of the service. Used as an advertising vehicle.

endoscope An instrument that allows physicians to look inside body cavities thereby displacing conventional surgery for diagnosing many problems in the gastrointestinal tract, urinary system, nasal sinuses, and, most recently, the ear.

eneagram (pronounced "any-a-gram") A personality-typing or self-assessment system that groups people into nine categories by their dominant personality traits. Used in business and industry to get a quick reading on employees or customers and to assist in hiring the right kind of people. Derived from the teaching of Sufi Muslims and introduced to the West by Russian mystic G. I. Gurdjieff.

Enforcement Guidance on Preemployment Disability-Related Inquiries and Medical Examinations under the Americans with Disabilities Act Guidelines issued in 1994 by the **Equal Employment Opportunity Commission** which identify the factors to be considered when determining whether a psychological test is a medical examination (prohibited at the preoffer stage of hiring). In general, the guidelines permit the administration of I.Q., aptitude, personality, and honesty tests during the preoffer stage because they measure an individual's capacity to perform a task successfully. However, tests that by design or implementation assess the existence, nature, or severity of an applicant's mental impairment or general psychological health may be administered only at the postoffer preemployment stage.

engineered expense budgets *See* expense budgets.

engineering control A job injury or illness countermeasure, such as removal of hazards and use of protective clothing, equipment guards, and other devices.

engineering supervisor The hotel functionary responsible for ensuring proper lighting and air conditioning in meeting rooms, providing enough outlets for presentation equipment, and getting draping hung properly.

English as a second language (ESL) Spoken and written English language training provided for persons for whom English is a second language.

enhanced audio compact disc Although marketed as audio compact discs, meant to be played on a compact disc player, these discs contain video that can be viewed on a monitor when the disc is run in a computer compact disc-read only drive.

Enlisted Association of the National Guard of the U.S. (EANGUS) An association of 75,000 enlisted members of the Army and Air National Guard. Its mission is to promote and maintain adequate national security, and foster the status, welfare, and professionalism of enlisted members of the National Guard. *Contact:* EANGUS, 1219 Prince St., Alexandria, VA 22314-2754 (703/519-3846; Fax 703/519-3849; E-mail **natloffc@eangus. org**; URL **http://www.eangus.org**).

enrollment area The geographical area in which an enrollee must live or work to qualify for enrollment in a health maintenance organization or a preferred provider organization.

enrollment fee A one-time charge made by an insurance carrier or health care plan at the time of enrollment to cover the costs of processing the application and establishing records. It is not an annual membership fee.

enterprise computing Integrated, organization-wide computing networks that have these capabilities: (1) meet all computing needs; (2) do distributed computing using dispersed databases; (3) provide communication among all entities; (3) protect the security of

information; (4) adopt and use internal and international standards; and (5) are user friendly.

Enterprise for the Americas Initiative A program announced by President George Bush in June 1990 for closer relationships with Latin American countries. It calls for a new economic and political relationship between the U.S. and its American neighbors involving trade investment and debt initiatives to strengthen the economies of Latin American countries, and ultimately establish a free-trade zone running from Alaska to Tierra del Fuego. Framework agreements have been signed between the U.S. and Bolivia, Chile, Columbia, Ecuador, and Mexico and are in process with most other Latin American countries.

entitlement performance Represents the best that an organization can do, in terms of productivity and quality of products and services, without adding resources. Entitlement performance is not limited by industry standards or incremental **benchmarking**; it is almost always better than either **baseline performance** or the industry benchmark. To perform at this level requires fewer resources than at **baseline performance**.

entitlements 1. Benefits that are totally associated with private or public employment, such as vacations, holidays, overtime, educational assistance, and matching gifts. **2.** Government (federal, state, or municipal) benefits such as Social Security, Medicare, Medicaid, unemployment compensation, and so on that are based on eligibility criteria established by law.

entranet A means of linking companies using World Wide Web electronic technologies.

entrepreneur An individual who establishes, organizes, and manages a business and assumes the risks involved — a "first generation" chief executive. Often a person's response to an innovative idea for a product, service, realization of an opportunity, or dissatisfaction with the values, goals, policies, hierarchy, managerial style, or some other characteristic of a corporation.

entry-level training Training provided to new employees to ensure that they get a good start. It is usually provided for operative employees. It is invariably scheduled for technicians and supervisory personnel upon their initial employment in an HR-related position.

environmental impairment The result of accidents or wanton, irresponsible, or terrorist activities causing air and water pollution. Examples includes oil spills, oil-well fires, and improper disposal of hazardous substances.

Environmental Industry Associations (EIA) An organization represents waste service, engineering, cleanup, and equipment manufacturing firms. Constituent groups are National Solid Waste Management Association, Waste Equipment Technology Association, Hazardous Waste Management Association, and Society for Environmental Management & Technology. *Contact:* Allen Haley, Director, Public and International Affairs, 4301 Connecticut Ave., N.W., Washington, DC 20008 (202/244-4700; Fax 202/966-4818).

environmental laws *See* Clean Air Amendments Acts of 1990 and 1995; Clean Indoor Air Act of of 1988; Comprehensive Environmental Response, Compensation, and Liability Act of 1980; Emergency Planning and Community Right-to-Know Act of 1986; Resource Conservation and Recovery Act of 1976; Superfund Amendments and Reauthorization Act of 1986.

Environmental Protection Agency (EPA) An agency of the federal government that administers and enforces federal environmental regulations such as the **Superfund Amendments and Reauthorization Act of 1986,** the **Emergency Planning and Community Right-to-Know Act of 1986,** and the **Resource Conservation and Recovery Act of 1976.** It has also identified extremely hazardous chemicals and set threshold quantities for each one.

environmental risk A threat to health and life stemming from exposure to hazards in the environment, such as air and water pollution, radon, and new risks such as gradual ocean pollution, global warming, and erosion of the ozone layer.

environmental safety laws *See* Clean Air Amendments Acts of 1990 and 1995; Comprehensive Environmental Response, Compensation, and Liability Act of 1980; Emergency Planning and Community Right-to-Know Act of 1986; Federal Facility Compliance Act of 1992; Resource Conservation and Recovery Act of 1976; Superfund Amendments and Reauthorization Act of 1986.

environmental scanner *See* futurist.

environmental tobacco smoke (ETS) Smoke produced by tobacco users. ETS has recently served as the basis for law suits by employees (passive smokers) for connecting passive smoking to heart and respiratory illnesses. In 1992, the Environmental Protection Agency science review board concluded that ETS should be classified as a major cancer-causing agent.

environmental training A form of technical training, usually conducted by subject matter experts such as chemists and engineers, that focuses on federal and state laws and regulations governing air emissions, water polluting substances, and solid waste disposal. The training is designed to keep employees in compliance with laws and regulations and communities safe from toxic waste and hazardous emissions and conditions. Regulating agencies include the Environmental Protection Agency, Office of Safety and Health Administration, and Department of Transportation.

enzyme multiplied immunoassay technique (EMIT) A drug test used to rule out negative urine samples but is not in and of itself evidence of drug use.

epilepsy A physical condition caused by sudden, brief changes in how the brain works. The person's consciousness, movements, or actions may be altered for a short period of time during a seizure. The cause is unknown in about half of all cases. For the remaining half, epilepsy may be caused by head injury, brain tumors, genetic conditions, lead poisoning, problems in brain development before birth, illnesses like meningitis or encephalitis, or even severe cases of measles. Also called a *seizure disorder.*

Epilepsy Foundation of America (EFA) The national, voluntary health organization dedicated to the prevention and cure of seizure disorders, the alleviation of their effects, the promotion of independence, increased job preparation and employment opportunities, and an optimal quality of life for people who have these disorders. Operates the Training and Placement Service (TAPS) program, an employment initiative funded by the Department of Labor that provides job search assistance, training in job seeking skills, and employer education. *Contact:* EFA, 4351 Garden City Drive, Suite 500, Landover, MD 20785-2267 (800/EFA-1000;

301/459-3700; Fax 301/577-4941; E-mail **postmaster@efa.org**; URL **http://www.efa. org**).

episodes of care In health care management and reporting, time-related intervals that have meaning to the behavior being measured. They may vary both in terms of clinical condition and by the provider type being measured. In obstetrics, caesarean section rate and average length of hospital stay are examples.

EPO In meeting planning, "each pays own" — where charges are divided between the master account and the individual or there is no master account.

equal employment opportunity (EEO) A policy guaranteeing equal opportunity to all prospective and current employees and stating that no employee or applicant will be discriminated against because of race, color, age, sex, national origin, religion, or handicap, that affirmative action will be taken to ensure that equal opportunity is provided to all employees, and that positive actions will be taken to recruit, employ, and promote qualified persons under-represented or under-employed in the work force, with particular attention to African-Americans, Hispanics, Asians and Pacific Islanders, American Indians, Alaskan natives, women, and persons with disabilities. These provisions also apply to screening and selection, assignment and transfer, promotion, compensation and benefits, training and development, discipline, and layoffs and termination.

Equal Employment Opportunity Act of 1972 (EEOA) An amendment to Title VII of the Civil Rights Act of 1964 that made it unlawful to discriminate on the basis of race, color, religion, sex, or national origin in hiring and discharge and in limiting, segregating, or classifying employees or applicants. Administered by the **Equal Employment Opportunity Commission.**

Equal Employment Opportunity Commission (EEOC) A regulatory agency established by amendments to the Civil Rights Act of 1964 to assure compliance with Title VII. The Commission publishes guidelines that define and explain the law, and it serves as the initial forum for claims of illegal employment discrimination. It has guidelines on employee selection, sexual harassment, and age discrimination. Most states and some localities also have equal employment opportunity agencies, some of which have work-sharing agreements with the EEOC in handling discrimination charges. *Contact:* EEOC, 2401 E St., N.W., Washington, DC 202/634-6922 or 1801 L. St., N.W., Washington, DC 20507 (800/USA-EEOC).

equal intervals A form of relative rating that is essentially a variation of the ranking technique. Instead of ranking all items (or people) in order, the rater places them in groupings that seem to be equally spaced. Those who appear to be alike in characteristics, behavior, or performance are then placed in the same grouping.

Equal Opportunity Act of 1996 A bill introduced that would end the use of racial and gender preferences in federal contracting, hiring, and other federally conducted activities. The legislation would prohibit timetables and goals for achieving racial and gender balance in the federal government, equating such approaches with quotas. However, the bill would not bar the government from engaging in "outreach" and recruitment as long as the final selection decision is nondiscriminatory. The bill would also go beyond what the Supreme Court ruled in *Adarand v. Pena* when it said that federal **affirmative action** programs must be narrowly tailored and serve a compelling governmental interest.

Equal Pay Act of 1963 (EPA) An amendment to the Fair Labor Standards Act of 1938 that prohibits sex-based pay differences where the work performed is equal in terms of skills, effort, and responsibility (doctrine of equal pay for equal work). Exceptions include bona fide seniority, merit- or production-based pay systems, or any other job-related factor other than gender. It is applicable to private industry as well as to federal, state, and local governments. To assure compliance, employers need data to analyze pay and job content by sex. Administered by the Fair Labor Standards Board.

equal treatment A legal doctrine pertaining to cases of unlawful discharge. It asks, "Has the employer applied its rules and penalties to all employees evenhandedly and without discrimination?"

equating A statistical procedure used to correct differences in difficulty between different forms of the same test to make the test results comparable. After determining how much the different test forms vary in difficulty, the information is used to adjust the raw scores on different forms of the test to account for those differences.

equipment-specific training   Training that combines instruction in general principles with particular skills; for example, training in electronics principles combined with the skills required to install electronic equipment.

equity   Ownership interest or assets held by stockholders in an organization.

equity adjustment   A permanent salary increase added to an employee's salary because analysis has demonstrated that the person's salary, salary range, or grade increase was too low relative to comparable positions. Merit or cost of living is not a factor.

equity benefits   Benefits that increase in value in connection with one or more of the following: years of service, rate of pay, and age. Examples are pension plans, profit-sharing plans, thrift savings plans, cash-deferred plans, individual retirement accounts, and stock plans.

equity draining   *See* bust-out.

equity model   A form of vertically integrated health care delivery system in which the providers or physicians are the owners.

equity sharing (ES)   A form of employer-assisted housing benefits. Formerly used almost exclusively as loans to get employees to accept assignments in high-cost areas, ES is now more broadly employed. For example, some companies gradually convey full ownership of property to an employee without also transferring potential financial problems by granting employers an annual equity transfer each year that the employee remains with the company. In addition to spreading loans over a longer period of time, insurance policies may also be taken out to help the employee's dependents gain full ownership of the property should the employee die or become disabled.

equity theory   A theory of motivation that holds that when people compare their work/effort, educational level, or experience with those of other employees, their performance will be affected if they perceive inequity in pay, benefits, or prestige.

ergonomic hazard   *See* repetitive strain injury.

ergonomics   The science of making jobs, facilities, equipment, furniture, and furnishing fit people. It deals with the people-machine interface and its impact upon productivity

and health. It includes the design of tools and workstations, placement of furniture, equipment, and materials, the posture and movements required of workers, the size, shape, and height of work surfaces, the pace and repetitiveness of operations, vibrations, noise level, and lighting, and the arrangement of storage areas, as well as the types and arrangement of controls and buttons.

Ergonomic Safety Standards/Rules
Regulations to be issued by the Occupational Safety and Health Administration designed to protect employees from repetitive motion-related illnesses and injuries, such as **carpel tunnel syndrome**. Placed on hold in 1995 when Congress and business groups brought political pressure to bear on the issue claiming that the proposed rules would be both cumbersome and expensive to employers.

ERIC Clearinghouse on Information & Technology (ERIC/IT)   One of 16 clearinghouses in the **Educational Resources Information Center** system. It specializes in library and information science and educational technology. ERIC/IT acquires, selects, catalogs, indexes, and abstracts documents and journal articles in these subject areas for input into the ERIC database. It also offers digests, minibibliographies, monographs, a semi-annual newsletter, an online search simulation package, and other user services. *Contact:* ERIC/IT 4-194 Center for Science and Technology, Syracuse University, Syracuse, NY 13244-4100 (315/443-3640; Fax 315/443-5448; E-mail **eric@ericir.syr.edu**; URL **http://ericir.syr.edu/ithome**).

ERISA bond   A fidelity bond required by federal law that insures tax-qualified pension plans against theft and embezzlement. Must be obtained by all plan trustees and others who handle plan funds.

error of central tendency   A rating error caused by the tendency of some raters to assign all ratees average ratings. The full range of variability is not used.

error of contrast   A rating error attributable to the tendency of some raters to compare people with each other rather than with some preestablished standard.

error of halo   A rating error caused by the tendency of some raters to generalize either positively or negatively from one characteristic of an individual to another characteristic of that same individual.

error of inconsistency A rating error that is caused by variations in the methodology or approach used to evaluation.

error of instability A rating error caused by the passage of time; forgetting.

error of projection A rating error caused by the tendency of some raters to allow their own characteristics or values to influence their ratings.

error of recency A rating error attributable to the tendency of some raters to focus on the work performed most recently (within the last 2 to 3 months) by an employee, rather than taking a broader look at performance.

error of standards A rating error caused by unrealistic or inappropriate rating or rater standards (too high or too low).

error of stereotype A rating error caused by the tendency of some raters to classify or evaluate employees in a certain way because of their membership in a particular group or category, such as religion or national origin.

error of subjectivity Rating errors attributable to the interaction of such factors as lack of rater training and experience, preferences and values, thought processes, personality, and situational influences.

errors and omissions (E&O) A form of insurance, similar to malpractice insurance purchased by physicians.

escalator clause A provision in a collective bargaining agreement for making upward or downward wage adjustments in accordance with changes in the cost of living.

escheat The process by which a person's property passes to the state in cases where there is no will and no lawful heirs.

The ESOP Association An organization of 2,000 members whose mission is to promote employee ownership, especially in the form of ESOPs, as accepted public policy in the United States. *Contact:* The ESOP Association, 1726 M. St., N.W., Ste. 501, Washington, DC 20036 (202/293-2971; Fax 202/293-7568; E-mail **esop@the-esop-emplowner. org**: URL **the-esop-emplowner.org**).

essay appraisal A method of descriptive rating in which the rater simply describes in a narrative style an individual's performance based on observation of behavior and results.

essay test An instrument that calls for written (narrative) responses to questions or problem situations in that testees are asked to discuss, compare, recall, classify, analyze, explain, criticize, organize, apply, describe, evaluate, solve, or the like.

estate planning Preparation of legal and financial documents by the principal to avoid complications and give clear direction to family, friends, health care groups, clergy, and attorneys when the principal dies or becomes incapacitated. Includes wills, trusts, powers of attorney, durable powers of attorney, living wills, health care power of attorney, burial instructions, and anatomical gifts.

estate tax A tax levied on legacies and successions by the federal government and some states (currently five), often patterned after the federal estate tax. The tax is placed on the receipt of property inherited by the beneficiary upon the death of the owner. The federal tax currently applies to estates over $600,000 in value. It also allows a marital deduction for all property transferred to a surviving spouse. The **Internal Revenue Code** of January 1, 1975 also excludes certain retirement benefits from the gross estate. *See also* sponge tax.

esteem needs Human needs for feelings of self-acceptance and self-worth and acceptance, appreciation, and respect of others.

estimated length of stay (ELOS) In health care, an estimate of the number of days of hospitalization required for specific procedures.

estimation In project management, a means of determining project costs in which figures are based on knowledge of the market and the internal and external costs of the project to the firm rather than on past experience with similar projects.

estoppel A legal prohibition against alleging or denying a fact because of one's own actions or words by which the contrary has been demonstrated, implied, or admitted.

est training Aims to transform and expand participants' ability to experience living to the fullest. Founded by Werner Erhard.

Ethernet An access protocol or local area network that operates over coaxial cable or twisted pairs of wires with a data transfer rate of 10 million bits per second. Because of its relatively low cost, it remains a popular method of transmitting data over a local area network.

ethical behavior What should or ought to prevail; unethical behavior is a violation of that standard — making decisions and taking actions under pressure of some sort to do what's expedient or profitable instead of what's good and right.

ethical dilemma Occurs when two or more moral values conflict and one must search for the morally right thing to do. For example, one of your colleagues asks for your help in getting approval for a needed and worthwhile project that clearly involves "creative financing."

ethics A major component of philosophy that is concerned with judgments about "right" and "wrong," "good" and "bad" conduct or behavior of individuals and groups. Ethics involves both the how and the what of behavior and conduct; that is, the means by which actions are carried out are ethically just as important as the ends those acts are intended to achieve.

Ethics in Government Act of 1978 (EGA) Established requirements for public disclosure of the financial interests of high-level government officials, tightened rules restricting post-employment involvement with government agencies by senior officials of those agencies, and created the Office of Government Ethics within the Office of Personnel Management. The Act also prohibited all federal employees from receiving honoraria for lecturing or writing books and articles. This ban was lifted by the U.S. Court of Appeals in 1993 for most executive branch employees, except senior executives for whom honoraria are banned by other existing regulations. It remains in effect for employees of the legislative and judicial branches of government.

ethics laws *See* Ethics in Government Act of 1978; Ethics Reform Acts of 1989; Federal Trade Commission Act of 1914; Foreign Corrupt Practices Act of 1977; Uniform Trade Secrets Acts (states).

Ethics Reform Act of 1989 (ERA) Prohibited all federal employees, except senators and senate staffers, but including military commissioned and warrant officers, from accepting honoraria for speaking and writing even if the outside work was unrelated to their duties or status.

Ethics Resource Center (ERC) A private, nonprofit educational corporation working to strengthen public trust in business, government, and education. Publishes and distributes literature on ethics and produces and distributes video programs to promote higher standards of ethical business conduct. Contact: ERC 1747 Pennsylvania Ave., N.W., Ste. 400, Washington, DC 20006 (202/737-2258; Fax 202/737-2227; E-mail ethics@ethics.org; URL http://www.ethics.org).

ethics training Training provided to executives, managers, and supervisors, and sometimes to customer representatives, marketing, and sales personnel, to promote integrity and ethical practices within and outside the organization, prevent unethical conduct or practices, help personnel overcome pressures to compromise their personal or company standards and values, and avoid violations of community standards and values. Coverage typically includes ethics in interpersonal relationships, rules and proscriptions regarding giving and receiving gifts and gratuities, the pitfalls of coverup and deception, the consequences of tolerating misconduct or violations of policies, rules and regulations, how to confront unethical behavior, proper relationships with clients, customers, dealers, suppliers, contractors, and consultants, responsibilities with respect to facilities, equipment, supplies, products, merchandise, funds, and other company assets, and travel and expense accounts. Primary methods used are case studies, role playing, panels and group interviews, study assignments, and problem solving exercises.

ethnic categories Includes African Americans, American Indians or Alaskan Natives, Asians or Pacific Islanders, Caucasians, and Hispanics.

ethnography In intercultural training, the study of the behavior patterns of specific groups of people or cultures.

ethnological analysis Involves an intense focus on recorded description — what people in a culture do day-to-day — to capture the emic interpretation — the native view of the sights, sounds, symbols, rites, customs, mores, or a culture. Attributed to Polish anthropologist Bronislaw Malinowski in the 1930s.

E-ticketing Electronic ticketing. Similar to reserving a car or hotel accommodations, with passengers receiving only a faxed or mailed confirmation form. In some airports, carriers offer automatic teller machine-like devices into which passengers insert a frequent flier card or credit card, select seats, and receive their boarding passes. Also known as paperless ticketing or ticketless travel.

Euro The currency proposed for use throughout the European Community. It would replace such currencies as the French franc, German deutsche mark, Irish pound, and Italian lira.

euromanagement training Training programs designed to prepare managers and others to accept the challenges, maximize the opportunities, and deal with the problems posed by European operations following the 1992 merger of European markets. Euromanagement training includes language and cross-cultural communications training as well as management development, sales and marketing, technical, and team training.

euromanagers Managers who can operate effectively for global companies in Europe.

European Community (EC) *See* European Union.

European Community (monetary) Unit (ECU) The European Community's common currency, priced at about ECU 1.3 to the U.S. dollar.

European Directive Legislation adopted by the European Union's Council of Ministers for implementation as law in its 15 member states.

European Economic Area (EEA) Established by treaty in January 1994. EEA is made up of the European Union and the European Free Trade Association.

European Exchange Rate Mechanism (ERM) A device designed to keep the value of the currencies of the 15 **European Community** members linked together — in effect, a system of guaranteed exchange rates.

European Free Trade Association (EFTA) An association established in 1960. Currently includes Iceland, Liechtenstein, and Norway.

European Monetary Institute (EMI) The central bank of the **European Union** located in Frankfurt, Germany. It will issue a single currency sometime after 1999.

European Organization for Quality (EOQ) A non-political, non-governmental organization of 31 national European quality organisations, as well as institutions, companies, and individuals all over the world. The mission of EOQ is to facilitate the exchange of information and experience on quality theory and best practice across

Europe to enhance European competitiveness. EOQ pays special attention to the needs of small and medium sized enterprises. *Contact:* EOQ, General Secretariat, P.O. Box 5032, CH-3001, Bern, Switzerland (phone ++41 31 320 61 66; telefax ++41 31 320 68 28).

European plan (EP) A room rate that does not include meals.

European Union (EU) A single European market with more than 375 million consumers and an economy worth $7 trillion a year. Established by the Treaty on European Union (Maastricht Treaty). Its signers were Belgium, Denmark, France, Germany, Great Britain, Greece, Ireland, Italy, Luxembourg, the Netherlands, Portugal, and Spain. Formerly called the **European Community.** As of January 1, 1995, linked 15 nations politically and economically through common foreign policies and a single currency. The union became effective November 1, 1993. In 1994, the Union agreed to admit Austria, Finland, and Sweden as members January 1, 1995. Negotiations were also underway to admit Norway but membership was voted down in that country in November 1994. Operating through its own European Economic Commission and Parliament, the community will lower long-standing barriers to trade and ease the transfer of goods, services, finances and people among its members. Member countries as of this writing are Austria, Belgium, Denmark, France, the Federal Republic of Germany, Finland, Greece, Ireland, Italy, Luxembourg, the Netherlands, Portugal, Spain, Sweden, and the United Kingdom. Waiting in the wings: Bulgaria, Cyprus, the Czech Republic, Estonia, Hungary, Latvia, Lithuania, Poland, Romania, Slovakia, Slovenia, and Turkey. Currently includes a population of 370 million reaching from the Arctic Circle to the Mediterranean Sea and with a combined economy worth about $6.7 trillion. The basic goal is economic and monetary union, including creation of a single currency and a central bank. The Netherlands has proposed that the final state of the economic union, possibly beginning in 1997, be reserved for countries meeting strict conditions on price stability, budget deficits, interest rates, and other measures of economic convergence. In July 1997 Hungary, Poland, the Czech Republic,

Estonia, and Slovenia, former Communist countries, were invited to begin negotiations for membership.

eu-stress Tension in the form of a "high" caused by the pressures of work that is savored because is interesting, stimulating, and challenging. *See also* dys-stress; stress.

evaluation 1. In general, a systematic means of measuring or estimating work in progress and results obtained. *Performance* measures tell managers where their people or their programs and services *are* — that is, the status of programs and services without noting whether good or poor. *Evaluation* tells them how well they *are doing* — whether progress and results are satisfactory or unsatisfactory. In all applications, evaluation involves the establishment of standards, measurement of some sort, identification and analysis of shortfalls, determination of the causes of deviations, identification, selection, and execution of remedial actions, and followup to insure that needed corrections have been made. **2.** In training, the use of tests or other forms of appraisal to measure aptitude, achievement, progress, performance, or potential. **3.** In employee performance appraisal, a measure or estimate of the performance or potential of people.

evaluator A human resources/human resources development competency. A person who assesses the impact of HR interventions on individual or organizational effectiveness.

evidence of insurability (EOI) Used by many insurers as a primary means of combating **adverse selection** by requiring employees and eligible dependents to provide proof of insurability for entry or reentry into a medical benefits plan.

Excellence in Human Resource Development Awards Awards presented annually to national members of the **American Society for Training and Development** and to their employing organizations for exemplary use of training and development, organization development, and career development interventions to improve individual, group, or organizational effectiveness. A maximum of 12 awards is given each year, with up to four individual, team, or organization awards in each of the three categories. *Contact:* ASTD National Awards Program, Attn: Dawn Temple, 1640 King St., Box 1443, Alexandria, VA 22313-2043 (703/683-8100)

Excellence Through Employee Involvement Award Awarded annually by the Employee Involvement Association following an intensive evaluation process that includes site visits, similar to the **Malcolm Baldridge National Quality Award.** *Contact:* EIA, 230 N. Michigan Ave., Ste. 1200, Chicago, IL 60601 (312/616-1100).

excess charge The difference between the Medicare-approved amount for a service or supply and the actual charge, if the actual charge is more than the approved amount.

excess plan A means of providing benefits to executives whose contributions to 401(k) plans are limited. In these "nonqualified plans," higher-paid employees can make voluntary deferrals of the portion of their salary that cannot be legally put into the qualified 401(k) plan. For employees who qualify under these excess plans, deferrals are usually made until retirement, although some companies have allowed employees to defer their salary for a shorter period. Payouts may be a lump sum or a series of payments, with terms spelled out in the initial agreement.

exchanges Provide non-pay benefits for active and retired military personnel and their dependents and some military reservists. Offer substantial savings on products and services, including gasoline stations and automotive services, food services, lawn and garden shops, department stores, flowers, dry cleaning, barber shops and beauty services, tax preparation, video rental, car rental, wedding registry, photo developing, and optical shops. Accept cash, personal checks, and several major credit cards. Include **Army Air Force Exchange Service**, Navy Exchanges, Marine Corps Exchanges, and Coast Guard Exchanges located on military installations in the United States and overseas.

excimer keratorefractive procedure Uses laser and computer technologies to correct nearsightedness and mild astigmatism. The laser, precisely controlled by a computer, reshapes the outer layers of the cornea of the eye to allow the eye to focus properly, thereby eliminating or reducing the need for corrective glasses or contact lenses

excluded costs In contracting, items that cannot be included in bids or submissions for reimbursement as costs. For example, in contracts for training, advertising costs (except for recruitment of personnel or procurement of scarce items), capital expenditures for improvement or acquisition of facilities, entertainment costs (including social activities or cost of alcoholic beverages), interest costs (including costs incurred to borrow funds), costs for attendance at conferences or meetings of professional organizations (unless attendance is necessary in connection with the project, included in the budget, and approved by the contracting officer), and costs for preparation of continuation agreements and other proposal development costs are ordinarily identified as excluded costs.

exclusions Health care services and supplies that insurance plans do not cover. Costs of such items are not counted toward deductibles or catastrophic protection benefits limits.

exclusive provider organization (EPO)
A form of **managed care** similar to preferred provider organizations except that EPOs limit beneficiaries to participating provides for all health care services and usually do not cover services received from other providers. Offers negotiated fee-for-service with bonus pools and incentives for appropriate utilization, a more exclusive network and higher incentives for using network providers than a preferred provider organization. May include the option to go out-of-network for lower reimbursement rate. Provides employer with information on level of utilization and claims experience and greater control of plan design.

executive adventure *See* adventure training.

executive center A for-profit conference center specifically designed to facilitate adult learning. Most often used for management meetings and training programs. Sometimes offers over-night accommodations.

executive chef The hotel functionary responsible for ordering and purchasing food products and kitchen supplies and for supervising all kitchen personnel.

executive development Formal and informal education and training programs, either managerial or functional, designed to improve the performance and potential of selected managers and executives. Most common strategies are formal institutional training, seminars and workshops, coaching, special assignments, and self-study. Specific training topics often include leadership, strategic planning, policy making, decision making, crisis handling, resources allocation, programming and budgeting, financial management, communication, change management, time management, and stress management.

executive housekeeper The hotel functionary responsible for room preparation and cleaning and provides laundry and valet services and extra amenities.

executive information system (EIS)
A computer software program that analyzes the data an executive identifies as critical to his or her business and delivers the analyses to a computer screen as graphics and text. For example, such systems can spot a potential cash flow problem before it happens.

Executive Order (EO) An order issued by the President of the United States directing that something be done or not done. It has the force of law.

Executive Office Accountability Act of 1996 Requires the White House and several agencies to comply with federal employment laws, including the Fair Labor Standards Act, Occupational Safety and Health Act, and Family and Medical Leave Act.

Executive Order 11246 An order that prohibits discrimination in the basis of race, color, creed, sex, or national origin and encourages affirmative action to remedy the underutilization of minorities and women. It applies to federal contractors and subcontractors as well as contractors operating under federally assisted construction contracts.

Executive Order 12564 An order that requires every federal agency to establish a drug testing program for its civilian employees. The program must include testing for cocaine and marijuana and may include testing for opiates, amphetamines, and phencyclidine. Testing for other drugs is not permitted without special permission unless reasonable suspicion, an accident, or an unsafe practice exists. Tests must follow guidelines issued by the Department Health and Human Services. The order became effective on September 15, 1986 when it was signed by President Ronald Reagan.

Executive Order No. 12954 Prohibited federal contractors from hiring workers to replace permanently striking employees. The order allowed the Secretary of Labor to terminate or suspend federal contracts in excess of $100,000 with companies that permanently replace striking workers. However, the order allows contractors to hire temporary employees or subcontract the work during the strike. Signed by President Clinton in March 1995. The U.S. Chamber of Commerce filed a suit against the Department of Labor claiming that the order exceeds presidential authority, and nine trade associations have joined to file an amicus brief with the appellate court in support of the Chamber of Commerce's suit. In the fall of 1995, both the House and the Senate included provisions in the Labor Department's appropriation bills that prohibits funding for enforcement of the executive order. The Executive Order was struck down February 2, 1996 by the U.S. Court of appeals for the District of Columbia Circuit. The Court stated that the Order was an improper and far-reaching attempt to set broad labor policy and concluded that the executive order illegally interfered with private employers' rights to hire permanent replacements. The administration did not carry through with an appeal of the decision.

executive outplacement Generous outplacement services provided to senior executives that go far beyond the customary counseling, résumé preparation, skills assessment, and job search techniques. Some companies set up an office in the executive's home, furnish a dedicated support staff or individual, provide networking opportunities, make travel arrangements, and provide access to compensation and employment law experts.

executive staff meeting A high level face-to-face meeting of the top executives of an organization, such as the president of a corporation and his or her executive president, functional vice presidents, or chief operating officer, and chief financial officer. May be regularly scheduled or called in an emergency.

executive retreat An executive development strategy in which a total top management team moves to an off-premises location for two or more days to examine process issues and engage in team building.

executive search firm A search organization or consultant who works primarily with professional and managerial openings on a retainer basis. Although some work on an hourly or daily fee basis, most compute fees on a percentage of the first year's earnings of the person placed, plus expenses.

executive transformation Learner-centered programs designed to convert *functional* managers and specialists into *general* managers — people who can manage across several organizational functions and make strategic decisions that overcome the inherently insular and conflicting goals of those functions.

executor/executrix In law, the individual (male or female) appointed by a testator (will maker) to execute his or her will.

exemplar learning A learning strategy used by humans (and to some degree by learning machines). It involves learning facts, principles, or concepts by exposure to examples provided by a trainer or the learning environment. The learner generalizes from the examples.

Exemplary Public Interest Contribution (EPIC) Award Awarded annually by the Department of Labor to public interest organizations.

Exemplary Voluntary Efforts (EVE) Award Awarded annually by the Department of Labor to recognize federal contractors that, through "innovative efforts," have increased job opportunities for women, minorities, veterans, and the disabled. Eligibility is limited to federal public interest contractors or federal contractors' organizations covered by Executive Order 11246 who have had a compliance review within the past three years and have had no substantive violations of federal laws or pending enforcement actions.

exempt employee An employee exempt from minimum wage and overtime provisions of the **Fair Labor Standards Act of 1938.** Exempt employees include bona fide executives, managers, supervisors, professionals, administrators, and sales personnel who are salaried and/or commissioned. *See also* nonexempt employee.

exercise program Sometimes a part of employee wellness programs, exercise programs are recreational and promote fitness. They typically center on activities that involve oxygen intake at sustained levels such as calisthenics, aerobic dancing, hiking, and bicycling.

exhaustion A phase in stress response following severe strain over a period of months exhibit   182   expenditure control rules

or years characterized by debilitating physical and emotional illnesses, such as gastrointestinal, cardiovascular, and behavioral disorders, which ultimately result in **burnout**. *See also* stress.

exhibit   A collection of graphic or 3-dimensional aids grouped and displayed to accomplish a specific informational, educational, instructional, or marketing purpose.

exhibitor-designated contractor (EDC)
A person or company hired by trade show exhibitors to set up their booths, circumventing the use of service contractors appointed by the management of the trade show. Trade show managers sometimes charge fees to exhibitors who use EDCs to recoup costs.

exit interview   A structured interview conducted at the time of an employee's termination for cause, resignation, or retirement. In the case of dismissals, exit interviews are used to inform the employee of the termination, the reasons for it, and his or her rights. For resignations and retirement terminations, they are used to inform the employee of his or her rights, benefits, and options and to gather information pertaining to organizational problems.

expanded leave/expanded leave options
Paid or unpaid extended periods of authorized time off from work without loss of employment rights for such reasons as medical attention, family responsibilities, education, and community service.

expanded memory   A type of electronic memory that can be added to all personal computers which use MS-DOS and any Intel processor. Makes compatible programs run faster.

ex parte **proceeding**   A legal term used to describe a hearing conducted by the court with only one of the parties present or even notified. Such proceedings are often scheduled in bitter domestic disputes or where one of the parties, for example, a battered wife, may fear confronting her husband.

expatriate allowance   *See* area differential.

expat/expatriate   An employee who is sent abroad to work for an extended period of time.

expectancy table   A table used to show the relationship between scores on a predictive test and some related result or criterion.

expectancy theory   A theory of motivation that states that challenging tasks and their successful completion elicit feelings of pleasure and are therefore motivating. Explains human behavior as a function of the perceived value of the reward that certain behavior yields and the expectation in the doer that the behavior will actually elicit that reward.

expectational survey   A survey designed and conducted to complement other means of forecasting. For example, expectational surveys may be used to identify significant changes in customer or client expectations and intentions, such as those relating to the purchase of training materials and services.

expected family contribution (EFC)   Under federal student aid programs (except unsubsidized student loans), an amount, determined by a formula established by Congress, that indicates how much of a family's financial resources should be available to help pay for education. Factors considered include taxable and nontaxable income, assets (such as savings and checking accounts), and benefits (such as unemployment and Social Security).

expedited arbitration   A form of **alternative dispute resolution** procedure used by the American Arbitration Association to resolve cases involving small claims under several sets of rules. Hearings are scheduled by phone and are concluded in a day or less.

Expeditionary Learning   A project of seven partners, led by Outward Bound, USA. Applies some of the experience, premises, and language of the Outward Bound enterprise to the operation of entire schools. Schools become communities where students learn to think by taking programmatically related "voyages and adventures" led by adult guides or leaders who work with students organized into multiage groupings of eight to 12 students called watches, which, in turn are clustered into crews of 12 to 18. Schools offer residencies to artists, professionals, scholars, and so on and operate service projects on site, such as theaters, recycling centers, and day care facilities. The academic structure is provided by a world class curriculum, the International Baccalaureate, which is integrated with the rest of the program.

expenditure control rules   Budget control rules established to constrain and manage commitment and disbursement of funds; for example, proscriptions against authorizing expenditures or approving and issuing purchase orders unless sufficient funds are on hand to cover the proposed expenditure or encumbrance.

expense budget There are two types: engineered and discretionary. Engineered expense budgets describe the labor and materials and estimated overhead costs of producing a product or service. Discretionary expense budgets are used when outputs cannot be accurately measured. They set limits on activities to be carried out and the level of effort to be invested in those activities to control costs.

expense reimbursement system In travel management, computer software used to process travel and entertainment expense reports.

experience-based training *See* adventure training.

experience curve One of the underpinnings of **economy of scale**. Postulates that, in addition to gains attributable to the **learning curve** (employee learning and specialization), as an organization increases in size, over time it acquires characteristics that tend to improve efficiency and economy. For example, a firm's reputation may make it able to hire better managers; construction costs for facilities that double available space do not cost twice as much; costs of materials and supplies are lower because they are purchased in greater volume; and so on.

experience curve theory Attributed to the Boston Consulting Group, it postulates that whenever a business' cumulative volume doubles, costs fall by a predictable percentage, producing a downward curve of costs and prices over time.

experience rating A method of establishing the premium for a **fee-for-service plan** (and some health maintenance organizations) which use the amounts actually paid for claims and projected benefits payments for the ensuing year.

experiential learning 1. Training that emphasizes hands-on experiences with the things to be learned rather than hearing or reading about them. 2. *See* adventure training.

experiment A study designed and rigorously managed to rule out as many variables as possible to isolate the cause of a particular

effect (program, intervention, or "treatment"). The treatment is applied only to the experimental group and not to the control group. Statistical tests are used to compare the performance, behavior, or results observed or measured.

experimental drug, device, medical treatment, or procedure A drug, device, medical treatment, or procedure that is investigational; that is, it is being tried out clinically to determine the maximum tolerated dose, its toxicity, its safety, its efficacy, or its efficacy as compared with standard means of treatment or diagnosis.

experimental group A representative group of persons who are exposed to an intervention, training, or "treatment" and whose performance or reaction is compared with that of the control group.

experimental research A research study conducted under carefully controlled conditions — conditions that rule out as many of the potential hypotheses, theories, or explanations of the cause of a particular effect or result. It is characterized by (1) systematic design; (2) use of subjects randomly assigned to treatment (experimental) and control groups to ensure that there is no bias on every variable or factor that could influence the outcomes; (3) specification of how the treatment variables differ between experimental and control groups; (4) total control of the experimental treatment by the researcher, and (5) use of statistical measures to assess the outcomes that clearly represent the variables of interest.

experimental treatments New approaches to the treatment of diseases and conditions under development and investigation at mainstream medical institutions. Include such therapies as bone marrow transplants for breast cancer patients.

expert networking *See* computer conferencing.

expert power Power that derives from followers' judgments that the leader has superior knowledge or ability in the area of endeavor. Its source is specialized skills, knowledge, or information.

EXPERT system A computer program and associated software that simulates the expertise of human experts. EXPERT systems make use of a body of knowledge in a elaborate set of "if-then" rules to narrow the range of possible decision factors, conclusions, or choices. Also called *case-based reasoning software program.*

explanation of benefits (EOB) A statement provided to the insured individual by the insurer (such as Medicare, CHAMPUS, or other insurer) explaining the disposition of a claim. Essentially an EOB summarizes basic benefits information: the name and address of the provider, the date(s) of the service, the service(s) provided, the amount that was invoiced (the charge), the amount approved for payment, an explanation of deductibles and copayments and claims that exceed the **reasonable charge,** and the amount the provider may charge above the approved payment (if any).

Explanation of Medicare Benefits (EOMB) *See* explanation of benefits.

exploding A form of fraud or dishonesty (chicanery) practiced by unscrupulous physicians and other health care practitioners to increase their income. Exemplified by the submission of a bill to the insurer for a series of tests that have all been done on a single sample of blood thereby tripling or quadrupling the dollar value of the claim. .

exponential smoothing A form of time-series forecasting involving comparison of actual and forecast values that includes an adjustable percentage of the error rate of past forecasts.

export Transmission of a data file or computer program to another unrelated program in ready-to-use form.

export license In meeting management, licenses issued by the Department of Commerce to track and control items leaving the country for exposition and other purposes. General export licenses are granted to control high-technology items; validated export licenses are issued on a case-by-case basis for items that are related to armaments (such as radar equipment).

exposition service contractor In meeting management, a supplier of booth equipment, rental furnishings, floor coverings, labor, **drayage,** and signs for trade shows and expositions. Also called *exclusive contractor.*

expository learning Passive learning where trainees are spoon-fed facts and information by a live instructor using lecture or "telling" with or without audiovisuals, expository video, or audio tapes.

ex post facto A legal term that literally means "after the fact." For example, an *ex post facto* law is legislation or regulations that prohibit or outlaw an act after it has been performed. Such laws and regulations are are unconstitutional.

extended care facility (ECF) A health care facility that provides medical care for individuals requiring extended care, including patients who have been discharged from a hospital.

extended family A form of nontraditional household. Involves living with relatives other than parents, spouses, or children, such as siblings, aunts and uncles, cousins, grandparents, or grandchildren.

extended leave programs Leaves of absence granted to employees to meet employee needs (education and personal growth, social service assignments, and extended unpaid personal leave to care for parents or children) and employer needs (rejuvenate the work force, save on temporary worker costs, or downsize the work force).

extended memory A type of electronic memory that can be added to all personal computers that use MS-DOS and a 286 processor or higher to make programs run faster.

extended period of eligibility Under Social Security, a special rule that provides cash benefits and Medicare to disabled persons while they attempt to work. Following a successful **trial work period** if a person is still disabled, for the next 36 months a disabled person is eligible to receive a monthly benefits for any month earnings drop below $500.

extended personal leave Unpaid leave which allows a break of two or more years with return-to-work guarantee for employees. Most often granted to mothers with young children.

extended stay hotel Targets business travelers who reserve rooms for five or more nights. Typically features one room with a full kitchen, work desk with direct-dial phone number, weekly housekeeping, daily light cleaning, and tiered pricing based on length of stay. Some venues may offer grocery-shopping service, in-room fax machine, dry bar, access to a pool, workout room, or other recreation amenity, and even a recording studio and screening room.

external audit An audit conducted by an independent (outside) auditor. It provides a professional judgment on the accuracy and fairness of a company's financial statements using generally accepted auditing standards and procedures. Usually required as a part of the annual report to stockholders.

external consultant **1.** An expert engaged by an organization for a fee to provide advice and assistance to executives, managers, or staffers or to conduct training programs or special studies. **2.** A form of employee assistance program in which professionals, usually psychiatrists or psychologists, are hired to handle employee diagnosis and counseling.

external E-mail An external hook-up that allows communication by computer with others, such as suppliers, contractors, or consultants. Main vendors are Western Union Easylink, CompuServe, Telenet, Dialcom, MCI Mail, AT&T mail, and GE Information Systems.

external evaluation **1.** The application of measures of progress and accomplishment to assess the results achieved by any organizational function outside the organization. **2.** In training and development, assessment of the results within or outside the organization when employees are assigned to or return to the job. Evaluation may focus on changes in job behavior and performance of employees or organization changes attributable to the program or programs offered.

external marketing Has the primary goal of either generating revenue by selling products and services produced inhouse or recovering part or most of the costs of developing programs and services for inhouse use by selling them outside. The potential customers and clients of external marketing, although not necessarily unreceptive to marketing efforts, must be pursued, wooed, and won.

external training resource (ETR) *See* consultant.

externship/clinical instruction A practicum with indirect supervision provided to students. Commonly required of those studying at professional, technical, career, and vocational schools and colleges. Includes, for example, student physicians, teachers, nurses, electricians, and cooks.

extremely hazardous substances (EHS) Any one of 406 hazardous chemicals identified by the Environmental Protection Agency.

extrinsic motivator A behavior reinforcer controlled by the organization, the work group, the boss, a work partner, a spouse, or a friend. Extrinsic motivators include pay, benefits, promotions and incentives, as well as praise, smiles, nods, and pats on the back.

extrinsic reward A reward not controlled by the individual; rather, it is controlled by the organization, the work group, the boss, a work partner, a spouse, or a friend. Extrinsic rewards are not implicit in the achievement; rather, they flow from the action or attainment, such as promotion, improved status, perks, praise, smiles, nods, and pats on the back.

eye care *See* vision care.

E-zine A "paperless" magazine available for readers exclusively on the World Wide Web. Examples are "Hotwired" (**http://www.hotwired.com**), "Mr. Showbiz " (**http://www.mrshowbiz.com**),and "Slate" (**http://www.slate.com**).

F

FAA	Financial aid administrator.
FAP	**1.** Financial assistance program. **2.** Full American plan.
FAQ	Frequently asked questions (Internet abbreviation).
FAR	Federal Acquisition Regulation.
FAS	Financial accounting standard.
FASB	Financial Accounting Standards Board.
FAT	File allocation table.
Fax	Facsimile.
FBP	**1.** Fee-based pricing. **2.** Flexible benefits/flex benefits.
FC	Facilitated communication.
FCP	Family care program.
FCPA	Foreign Corrupt Practices Act of 1977.
FCRA	Fair Credit Reporting Act of 1969.
FDA	Food and Drug Administration.
FECA	Federal Employees' Compensation Act of 1916.
FEEO	Federal Ethics Executive Order of 1965.
FEGLI	Federal Employees Group Life Insurance.
FEHBARS	Federal Employees Health Benefit Acquisition Regulations.
FEHBP	Federal Employees Health Benefits Program.
FERS	Federal Employee Retirement System.
FFEL	Federal Family Education Loan.
FFM	Five-Factor Model.
FFP	Firm-fixed-price contract.
FHA	Federal Highway Administration.
FICA	Federal Insurance Contributions Act of 1935.
FIFO	First-in, first-out.
FLIT	Functional Literacy Program.
FLSA	Fair Labor Standards Act of 1938.
FMCS	Federal Mediation and Conciliation Service.
FMLA	Family and Medical Leave Act of 1993.
FOIA	Freedom of Information Act of 1966.
FPE	Fixed-price contract with economic price-adjustment provisions.
FPI	**1.** Fixed-price-incentive contract. **2.** Future payment index.
FPLET	Fixed-price level-of-effort term contract.
FPP	**1.** Fetal protection policy. **2.** Faculty practice plan.
FPR	Fixed price-redeterminable contract.
FR	**1.** Fixed-rate contract. **2.** *Federal Register.*
FRA	**1.** Federal Rehabilitation Act of 1973. **2.** Fleet Reserve Association.
FSA	**1.** Family Support Act of 1988. **2.** Flexible spending account.
FSC	Foreign sales corporation.
FSEOG	Federal Supplemental Educational Opportunity Grant.
FTA	Free trade agreement.
FTC	Federal Trade Commission.
FTCA	Federal Trade Commission Act of 1914.
FTE	Full-time equivalent.
FTP	File transfer protocol.
FUTA	Federal Unemployment Tax Act.
FWI	Families and Work Institute.

FWIW For what it's worth (Internet abbreviation).

FWS Federal Work-Study.

FYI For your information (Internet abbreviation).

4GL Fourth generation language.

44 *See* Section 44, Internal Revenue Code.

401(a)(4) *See* Section 401(a)(4), Internal Revenue Code.

401(a)(5) *See* Section 401(a)(5), Internal Revenue Code.

401(a)(26) *See* Section 401(a)(26), Internal Revenue Code.

401(a)(17) *See* Section 401(a)(17), Internal Revenue Code.

401(a)(26) *See* Section 401(a)(26), Internal Revenue Code.

401 (h) *See* Section 401(h), Internal Revenue Code.

401 (k) *See* Section 401(k), Internal Revenue Code.

402 *See* Section 402, Internal Revenue Code.

403 (b) *See* Section 403(b), Internal Revenue Code.

410(b) *See* Section 410(b), Internal Revenue Code.

414(r) *See* Section 414(r), Internal Revenue Code.

414(s) *See* Section 414(s), Internal Revenue Code.

415(b) *See* Section 415(b), Internal Revenue Code.

415(c) *See* Section 415(c), Internal Revenue Code.

417 *See* Section 417, Internal Revenue Code.

422(a) *See* Section 422(a), Internal Revenue Code.

457 *See* Section 457, Internal Revenue Code.

501(c)(9) *See* Section 501(c)(9), Internal Revenue Code.

face validity A means of determining the relevance of a test or other instrument (performance rating scale, for example) on "appearances" alone rather than on some more objective means. It is not recognized by the courts as justified.

facilitated communication (FC) The use of special devices through which people with autism, other speech disabilities, cerebral palsy, or deficient motor skills can communicate. The devices include a keyboard input device and a computer screen, and often require help from an aide or instructor who supports the user's arm or hand while the message is being typed by the hunt-and-peck method.

facilitation A strategy for helping a group improve its process for solving problems and making decisions.

facilitator **1.** One who stimulates and helps individuals or groups to develop their own solutions to problems and vision of the organization by nurturing and coordinating the efforts of the person or group rather than imposing solutions or visions from an external position. **2.** An individual who has the role of helping participants in an experiential learning environment, such as group therapy, sensitivity training, encounter group, or professional development group. **3.** The person who is responsible for the *process* in any intervention, such as quality circles or training programs, but without the trappings of formal authority. Responsibility is exercised through persuasion rather than fiat. He or she serves as the teacher, trainer, instructor, moderator, coordinator, counselor, negotiator, ombudsman, marketer, advocate, and record keeper for the group or work team.

facsimile (fax) An electrical means of coding and sending information over telephone lines or radio waves. Similar to a photocopier, facsimiles send and receive exact copies of any type of document (print, handwriting, drawings, or photos) over ordinary phone lines, domestic or international, in from less than 5 seconds to about 6 minutes, depending upon type.

fact finder A neutral person appointed by the President of the United States to study the issues in a labor-management dispute (in circumstances he determines to be a national emergency) and make a public recommendation as to what a reasonable settlement would be.

fact finding An alternative dispute resolution procedure involving investigation of a dispute by a neutral third party who issues a report on the findings, usually recommending a basis for settlement. The report can also assist further negotiations between the parties involved.

fact-finding conference Informal meetings held under the auspices of the **Equal Employment Opportunity Commission** between the employer and the complainant in discrimination cases aimed at defining the issues and determining if there is a basis for negotiation. However, in most cases the EEOC uses the conference as leverage to push for a settlement.

factor analysis Refers to methods of analyzing the interrelationships or intercorrelations among a set of variables, such as test scores. They are designed to identify the root "factors" that account for the interrelationships and determine how much of the variation is attributable to or associated with each of the factors.

factor comparison A quantitative method of job evaluation similar to job ranking. Compensable factors are selected for the jobs to be evaluated. All jobs are then placed in rank order on one of the compensable factors and are assigned a score reflecting their ranking. The process is continued for all compensable factors, one at a time. The scores are totaled for each job resulting in a discrete job ranking or worth/value ranking.

factor income One of the components of the calculation used to convert **gross national product** (GNP) to **gross domestic product** (GDP). Factor income is measured as compensation of employees, corporate profits (dividends, earnings of unincorporated affiliates, and reinvested earnings of incorporated affiliates), and net interest. To convert GNP to GDP one must subtract factor income receipts from foreigners, which represent the goods and services produced abroad using the labor and property supplied by U.S. residents, and add factor income payments to foreigners, which represent the goods and services produced in the U.S. using the labor and property supplied by foreigners.

factor weight In **job evaluation**, a weight assigned to **compensable factors** to indicate relative importance. In a **point-factor** system, the factor weight is predetermined; for example, a firm may value experience twice as much as education and training and assign maximum values of 100 to experience and 50 to education.

faculty practice plan (FPP) A form of group medical practice organized around a teaching program, typically a group of physicians providing services to patients at a teaching hospital.

fade **1.** In video, gradually increasing or decreasing the intensity or volume of the video or audio signal. **2.** In video production, overlapping video signals with the one from the new image increases in intensity while the old image decreases until it is no longer visible.

failure costs In total quality management, refers to internal failures (rejects, reworks, and retesting) and external failures (field repair, return and replacement, warranty costs, product liability, and so on).

Fair Credit Reporting Act of 1969 (FCRA) Regulates privacy and preemployment checks and investigations. The Act protects candidates for employment by covering reports containing information on a person's character, general reputation, or life style regardless of how it is obtained. If the prospective employer intends to use the information, the candidate must be advised in writing that such a report will be requested and also notified of his or her right to request information about the report.

fair employment practices laws *See* Age Discrimination Act of 1975; Age Discrimination in Employment Act of 1967 with amendments; Americans with Disabilities Act of 1990; Civil Rights Act of 1964; Civil Rights and Women's Equity in Employment Act of 1991; Employee Polygraph Protection Act of 1988; Equal Employment Opportunity Act of 1972, Mandatory Retirement Age Law of 1978; Older Americans Act of 1965; Pregnancy Discrimination Act of 1978; Rehabilitation Act of 1973.

Fair Housing Act of 1968 Title VIII of the Civil Rights Act of 1968. Prohibited discrimination in the sale, rental, or financing of housing based on race, color, religion, sex, or national origin.

Fair Housing Amendments Act of 1988 An act that adds to existing protected classes, people with disabilities and families with children, to protect those persons from unfair and discriminatory housing practices. It protects any person who has a physical or mental impairment which substantially limits one or more major life activities, has a record of such impairment, or is regarded as having such an impairment. The law does not extend protections to anyone who is currently an illegal drug abuser. The Act also provides for certain architectural accessibility and adaptable design requirements for new multifamily housing built for first occupancy on or after March 13, 1991. Complaints of discrimination may be filed with the U.S. Department of Housing and Urban Development.

fair investigation A legal requirement that pertains to cases of unlawful discharge. It asks, "Was the employer's investigation of the violation considered and conducted fairly and objectively?"

Fair Labor Standards Act of 1938 (FLSA) The basic federal wage/hour legislation covering companies in interstate or foreign commerce. FLSA established and defined employee categories as exempt (compensation, usually salary, is exempt from the provisions of the Act) and nonexempt (wages are regulated by the act). The Act and its amendments mandated a minimum wage and 40-hour work week for employees of businesses engaged in interstate commerce who are nonexempt. It also established the principle of equal pay for equal work, right to time and one-half for hours worked in excess of the maximum (overtime pay), and prohibited the use of workers under the age of 16 in most jobs and under the age of 18 in hazardous jobs. The Act authorized criminal prosecution for violations. The Wage and Hour Division, Department of Labor, has jurisdiction with respect to private employment, state and local government employment, and federal employees of the Library of Congress, U.S. Postal Service, Postal Rate Commission, and the Tennessee Valley Authority. The Office of Personnel Management is responsible for enforcement with regard to all other federal employees. In recent years, court rulings have created a potential problem that could affect many employers. The courts have ruled that companies activate an unintended aspect of the law when the pay of an exempt employee is docked or accrued leave is debited for partial day absences. Such actions change the status of employees from exempt to nonexempt, making them eligible for overtime for the extra hours worked. Also known as the *wages and hours law.* In 1997, H.R. 1 (filed by Rep Cass Ballenger, R-NC) would allow employees to bank up to 240 hours of compensatory time off annually. With the employer's concurrence, employees could opt to take one and one-half hours of comp time off, with pay, for every hour worked in

excess of 40 during a work week. S. 4 (filed by Sen. John Ashcroft, R-MO) has similar language and, in addition, would allow employers and employees to agree to average weekly hours over a two-week period, with hours worked above 80 to be subject to overtime standards.

fair market value For estate planning and tax purposes, what an unrelated party in a bargaining situation would pay for a particular item or parcel of property.

Fair Pay Act of 1997 Introduced as S. 232 by Sen. Tom Harkin, D-Iowa, the bill would allow payment of different wages under seniority systems, merit system, or systems that measure earning by quantity of quality of production. The bill would direct the Equal Employment Opportunity Commission to issue guidelines specifying criteria for determining whether a job is dominated by employees or a particular sex, race, or national origin.

fair reimbursement law A state law that erects a barrier to managed care (currently on the books of 10 states). The law limits or prohibits differentials in payments to network and non-network **managed care** providers, thereby forcing insurance carriers to limit the amount of network provider discounts.

fair use A part of the **copyright law** that permits people to use a quote, drawing, photograph, or picture of a copyrighted work to study it or use it for teaching, critiquing, news reporting, or scholarly research, without permission and without paying a fee, as long as the source of the material is identified. Frequently used to prove innocence, the principle of fair use has not been fully tested to establish its boundaries. Nonetheless, if only a small amount of the material is used or displayed, or if commercial use is strictly limited, use is likely to allowed without penalty.

Fall Protection Standard A standard promulgated by the Occupational Safety and Health Administration relating to the protection of workers from falls and help them to work safely.

False Claims Act Amendment of 1986 Legislation that permits any citizen who knows of a financial loss to the the federal government from fraudulent activity to go directly to court and sue, in the name of the United States, to recover for the government an amount equal to three times the government's loss, plus a penalty of at least $5,000 for each act of fraud. Successful plaintiffs are entitled to keep up to 30 percent of the proceeds from such suits. The act also gives full legal protection to an employee who files or cooperates with a *qui tam* suit from any form of retaliation on the job, including remedies of job reinstatement and damages doubling the amount of any pay lost due to any retaliatory treatment.

Families and Work Institute (FWI) A nonprofit research and consulting organization with a staff of 22 committed to developing new approaches to balancing the changing needs of American's families and the continuing need for workplace productivity. The Institute's program is unique in that it considers the entire life-cycle of the family from prenatal care through child care to elder care. *Contact:* FWI, 330 Seventh Ave., New York NY 10001 (212/465-2044; Fax 212/465-8637; E-mail **DLOWE35963@gnn.com**; URL **http://www.familiesandwork.org**).

family According to the Conference Board's Work-Family Research and Advisory Panel, there are two definitions: (1) the narrow definition — relationship by marriage, birth, or adoption, and (2) the broad definition — economic dependence (the Internal Revenue Service definition), used for medical, welfare and regulated benefits.

Family and Medical Leave Act of 1993 (FMLA) A bill that requires employers of 50 or more workers to provide up to 12 weeks of unpaid leave per year for childbirth, adoption of a child, or medical circumstances involving an employee or a close member of his or her family. The Act covers employees within a 75-mile radius and applies to nonprofit and government organizations as well as to businesses. Employees retain health benefits while on leave and must be reinstated in the same job or its equivalent upon return to work. Leave is mandated only for employees who have worked for a firm for at least one year and worked at least 1,250 hours, or 25 hours per week, during the period. Companies have the option of applying an employee's paid time off, including vacations and sick pay, toward their leave. Key employees, who constitute the highest-paid 10 percent of the work force, may be excluded. In states that require unpaid family leave, the most liberal law (state or federal) will apply. The law takes effect following the expiration of existing collectively

bargained contracts or a year after the law's enactment, whichever comes first. For most employers FMLA became effective August 5, 1993. In 1997, S. 183 (filed by Sen Christopher Dodd, D-Conn.) would extend FMLA's coverage to employers with 25 or more employees vice the current 50 within a 75 mile radius. A companion bill, S. 280 (introduced by Sen. Patty Murray, D-Wash. would allow working parents to take as many as 24 hours of leave annually to participate in their children's school-related events and family literacy programs. In the House , H.R. 109, introduced by Rep William Clay, D. Mo., combines the Dodd and Murray proposals and also would provide three additional days off annually for employees to attend activities involving routine family needs.

family benefits *See* child care; elder care.

family care program (FCP) An alternative to nursing home care for the elderly and physically disabled established to provide a better quality of life and reduce costs. Care is provided by family members rather than professional health care providers.

family day care network A form of direct employer-supported child care service in which employers contract with local agencies to recruit, train, and assist people to become licensed child care providers in their own homes.

family leave A form of employee benefit in which workers are allowed unpaid leave to care for family members such as newly born or adopted children or seriously ill members of the family. Several states currently mandate unpaid family leave, some of them for new parents only.

Family Sick Leave Act of 1994 Legislation that allows federal employees to use their own sick leave to care for ill family members and to transfer annual leave to other family members who work for the federal government.

Family Support Act of 1988 (FSA)
Focuses on establishing paternity and withholding wages for child support. Includes the **deadbeat dad** provision, effective January 1, 1994. The Act requires employers to withhold court-ordered child support awards from the paychecks of absent parents and send them to a public agency that mails the payments to the recipient. Exceptions are made only when separated or divorced couples agree on alternative arrangements.

family support programs Programs offered by business, industry, community organizations, churches, schools, and youth-serving organizations to help parents balance their work and family responsibilities and compensate for damaging aspects of the social environment Include family leave, job sharing, flexible schedules, part-time work, child care, home-visiting services, parent-child centers, life-skills training, mentoring, and self-help programs.

fam trip One classification of free trips to resort areas taken by corporate meeting planners, users of incentive travel or travel agents, or by travel agents themselves. In a fam trip, the host property owner seeks out the potential client and proffers an invitation, which includes complimentary air and ground transportation, meals and accommodations, and guided tours. The trips are a promotional device to attract meetings and conventions. Fam trip is the shortened form of *familiarization trip*. Attributed to Michael J. Hurwitz, president of the Society of Incentive Travel Executives.

fango A alternative manipulative treatment that involves applying mineral-rich heated mud to the body, which is then wrapped to activate the mud to purge toxins from the skin.

Fannie Mae *See* Federal National Mortgage Association.

Fantasia In travel management, a **computer reservation system** owned by Japan Airlines and Quantas Airlines.

FASB Rule No. 106 A **Financial Accounting Standards Board** rule that was passed in 1991 and became effective December 15, 1992. The Rule requires large companies to pay and account for retirees' health insurance costs up front, and acknowledge the future cost of the promise to pay for their retirees' medical claims. The Rule did not affect small companies until late 1994. Government employees are not affected. The Rule has caused some companies to eliminate health benefits for retirees to avoid listing the liability on their books. Others have cut or plan to cut retiree health benefits to limit their liability, resulting in higher deductibles and retirees paying more for their health insurance.

Fast Company: How Smart Business Works A bimonthly journal: $14.95 per year ($19,95 in Canada). *Contact:* Fast Company, P.O. Box 52760, Boulder, CO 80321-2760 (617/9730350; 800/688-1545; E-mail **loop@fastcompany.com**; **http://www.fastcompany.com**).

fast-trackers Employees who have demonstrated exceptional promotion potential and are being groomed for higher level jobs through coaching, training, and other forms of development. Typically include **knowledge workers**.

fat organization An organization that has more than four layers of management, including the top person and the bottom layer (chairman or president and first-line supervisor).

fax *See* facsimile.

fax board One means of combining the capabilities of personal computers and facsimile machines. It is an electronic component installed directly on the PC by means of an expansion slot. A fax board comes with software that allows the user to initiate fax commands from the computer. A computer printer provides hard copies. A fax board can send only documents created in the attached computer, and it cannot operate while the computer is using memory-intensive programs.

fax machine A machine that scans a document (text or graphics) and converts (digitizes) it to a code that can be sent over telephone lines to another machine, which decodes the signal and converts it back to the original document.

fax security A growing concern among business travelers. In many situations a faxed document containing highly sensitive confidential material can be read by anyone enroute — including the machine operator, hotel desk clerks, and bellmen — and may reach the hands of competitors. Some solutions: (1) have the sender call first and set a definite time for fax transmittal and stand by the fax machine and collect the material as it comes in; (2) use a personal computer to receive documents in the hotel room or office via direct modem-to-modem transfer.

feasibility study A study conducted to determine the need for a new project, product, service, or other type of outcome that requires the commitment of enterprise resources. Such studies have the objective of determining whether the intended results are desirable, whether the plans are complete and effective, whether the design is appropriate and acceptable, whether the hardware and software are efficient and economical, and whether the procedures are foolproof. They typically require comparisons with alternative designs and alternative use of resources. In most organizations today, feasibility studies also include **cost-benefit analysis** to determine whether the expected benefits justify the costs.

featherbedding An unfair labor practice in which the union requires an employer to pay a worker for services not performed.

featherbed rule A union rule that requires an employer to create unneeded jobs, pay workers for duplicate services, guarantee a certain amount of overtime work, or adopt restrictive work rules, such as limiting the amount of work to be done in a day or week.

Federal Acquisition Regulation (FAR) A collection of all the rules and regulations that govern federal procurements, including a detailed section on pricing procedures.

Federal Executive Agency Guidelines Detailed explanations of the procedures to be followed by federal employers in complying with equal opportunity laws issued by the Equal Employment Opportunity Coordinating Council in the 1970s.

Federal Bankruptcy Code *See* Chapter 7, Federal Bankruptcy Code; Chapter 11, Federal Bankruptcy Code; Chapter 13, Federal Bankruptcy Code; Chapter 20, Federal Bankruptcy Code; cramdown.

Federal Direct Loans Low interest loans for students and parents made directly by the federal government with participating schools determining eligibility for a loan and disbursing the funds.

Federal Employees Pay Comparability Act of 1990 Legislation that liberalized the **Dual Compensation Act of 1964.** Enacted November 5, 1990, the act permits the director of the Office of Personnel Management, at the request of the head of a federal executive agency, to waive the application of the dual compensation restriction on a case-by-case basis for employees in positions for which qualified applicants are exceptionally difficult to find and retain.

Federal Employee Retirement System (FERS) Established in January 1984 to eventually replace the **Civil Service Retirement System.** A flexible retirement program that became effective January 1, 1987 and automatically covers all new employees hired after

December 31, 1983, It offers financial security for federal employees and their families and has features that are portable. The components of the system are Social Security benefits, Basic Benefit Plan, and Thrift Savings Plan. Employees pay full Social Security taxes, a small contribution to the Basic Benefit Plan, and a contribution by the employee's government agency of an equal amount, up to 1 percent of the basic pay each period, into the employee's Thrift Saving Plan. In addition, the government matches a portion of those contributions. It now covers more than one million federal workers. Although some employees have elected to join FERS, over 1.3 million workers still participate in the Civil Service Retirement System.

Federal Employees' Compensation Act of 1916 (FECA) Administered by the Department of Labor's Office of Workers' Compensation Program, FECA pays compensation to federal employees who are injured on the job, who develop job-related occupational diseases, or who have an impairment caused by job-related aggravation of a pre-existing condition. FECA also pays claims due to the death of an employee to an employee's widow, widower, child, dependent parent, grandparent, brother, sister, or grandchild if the employee suffers a fatal injury while working or dies as a result of an injury sustained in the performance of duty or as the result of an occupational disease. Benefits include payments for medical services, supplies, and appliances and transportation; continuation of pay for up to 45 days with no charge to sick or annual leave; compensation for temporary total, temporary partial, permanent total, or permanent partial disability; funeral and burial expenses (if death is the result of a work-related injury or disease).

Federal Employees Group Life Insurance (FEGLI) Life insurance provided active and retired (CSRS or FECA) federal employees with premiums withheld from pay or annuity. For most annuitants who retired before December 9, 1980, the face value of their life insurance policies is reduced two percent per month after age 65 until the value is reduced to 25 percent of the original amount. Annuitants who retired after December 9, 1980 have two options: they may elect to have the face value reduced by one percent per month after age 65 until 50 percent of the value is reached or maintain the full policy value at a higher premium.

Federal Employees Group Life Insurance Living Benefits Act of 1994 The bill allows a terminally ill employee or annuitant who has BASIC FEGLI COVERAGE, with a life expectancy of nine months or less, to receive the proceeds of his or her Federal Employees Group Life Insurance (basic life insurance amount less an actuarial deduction). Signed by President Clinton October 25, 1994, and became effective July 25, 1995.

Federal Employees Health Benefit Acquisition Regulations (FEHBARS) Regulations that cover the Office of Personnel Management's purchase of health care benefits programs for federal employees.

Federal Employees Health Benefits Program (FEHBP) A health benefits program offered under several optional plans for active and retired federal employees.

Federal Ethics Executive Order of 1965 (FEEO) Specifically prohibits actions that create the appearance of using public office for private gain and bars government employees from creating the appearance of preferential treatment to any organization or person, or affecting adversely the confidence of the public in the integrity of government.

Federal Facility Compliance Act of 1992 An act that that permits state inspection of federal sites, such as those under the jurisdiction of the Department of Defense and Department of Energy, and authorizes heavy Environmental Protection Agency fines for violation of laws against hazardous waste pollution.

Federal Family Education Loan (FFEL) A low interest loan for students and parents made by private lenders, such as banks, credit unions, and savings and loan associations. Participating schools determine eligibility for the loan and disburse the funds.

Federal Family Education Loan Consolidation Loan Under student loan program, allows the borrower to combine different types and amounts of federal student loans to simplify repayment. The loan pays off existing loans, and the borrower then repays the consolidation loan over a period of from 10 to 30 years.

federal gift tax A tax levied on the total value of property and/or funds transferred or given to an individual. For most gifts, a $10,000 per donee per calendar year gift-tax exclusion is available for money or property of determinable value. If the donee's spouse elects to share in the gift, the annual exclusion can be raised to $20,000 per donee.

Federal Highway Administration (FHA) Responsible for overseeing the implementation of the drug testing rules developed by the U.S. Department of Transportation in 1988. Those rules affect approximately 200,000 employers and 3 million truck and bus drivers. Tests include random, preemployment, periodic (during regular medical exams), post-accident, reasonable cause and followup (for drivers who have tested positive in the past).

Federal Insurance Contributions Act of 1935 (FICA) The Act is the source of Social Security and Medicare withholding requirements (the FICA pay deduction). The Act requires employers to pay the current percentage of the wage base and deduct an identical amount from the employee's pay, and remit the total to the federal government. In 1997, FICA remained at 7.65 % (6.2% Social Security tax and 1.45% Medicare tax). The Act also requires employers to maintain records of all amounts paid to employees for services performed whether payment is in cash or other medium.

federalization In government, increasing the flow of power from the states to the federal government; centralizing executive and legislative authority.

federally qualified health centers Mainly consist of community health centers, Indian health clinics, migrant worker health centers, and health centers for the homeless. They are usually located in inner-city and rural areas and are open to all Medicare beneficiaries for a full range of services.

federally supported clearinghouses on disability Include ERIC Clearinghouse on Disabilities and Gifted Education, 1920 Association Dr., Reston, VA (800/328-0272 or 703/264-9476 voice, 703/264-9449 TTY; Fax 703-620-2421; E-mail **erice@cec.sped.org**); Health Resource Center (on postsecondary education for individuals with disabilities), One Dupont Circle, W.W., Ste. 800, Washington, DC 20036-1193 (800/544-3284, 202/939-9320 voice/TTY,

Fax 202/833-4760; E-mail **heath@ace. nche.edu**); National Clearinghouse for Professions in Special Education, 1920 Association Dr., Reston, VA 22191 (800/641-7824 or 703/264-9476 voice, 703/264-9480 TTY; Fax 703/620-2521; E-mail **ncpse@cec. sped.org**); National Information Center for Children and Youth with Disabilities, P.O. Box 1492, Washington, DC 20036 (800/ 695-0285, 202/884-8200 voice/TTY; Fax 202/884-8441; E-mail **nichcy@ed.org**), and National Rehabilitation Information Center, 8455 Colesville Rd., Ste 935, Silver Spring, MD 20910-3319 (800/641-7824, 703-264-9476 voice, 703/264-9480 TTY; Fax 703/ 620-2521; E-mail **ncpse@cec.sped.org**).

Federal Mediation and Conciliation Service (FMCS)   An independent agency of the federal government whose head reports directly to the President. The FMCS is authorized to institute procedures for a national emergency injunction and stabilize industrial relations for the public welfare. It also provides assistance to labor and management in reaching compromises or settlements when deadlocks or crises occur in negotiations. It maintains lists of arbitrators for the selection of arbitration panels. It has regional offices in various states throughout the United States.

Federal National Mortgage Association (FNMA)   Referred to as Fannie Mae, FNMA is a congressionally chartered private corporation that makes available low-cost housing loans for low-, moderate-, and middle-income Americans. FNMA makes no loans itself but buys mortgages from a national network of 3,000 approved lenders. *Contact:* FNMA, 3900 Wisconsin Ave., N.W., Washington, DC 20016-4667 (E-mail **webmaster@fanniemae.com**; URL **http: www.fanniemae.com**).

Federal Old Age and Survivors' Insurance   *See* Social Security Act of 1935.

Federal Pell Grant   A grant awarded to undergraduate students who have not earned a bachelor's or **professional degree** to provide a foundation of financial aid to which other aid may be added. Eligibility is determined by applying a standard formula which produces an **Expected Family Contribution** (EFC) number. Awards depend on program funding and on the EFC, cost of attendance, whether the student is full-time or part-time, and whether the student attends school for a full academic year or less.

Federal Perkins Loan   A low-interest (5 percent) loan for both graduate and undergraduate students with *exceptional* financial need made through a school's financial aid office. Such loans are made with government funds, paid directly to the student or credited to his or her account, and must be repaid. Depending on the level of need and the funding level of the school, an individual can borrow up to $3,000 for each year of undergraduate study, with a maximum total amount of $15,000; for graduate or professional study, the maximum is $5,000 per year and a combined maximum total of $30,000. If a student is attending school at least half time, monthly repayments begin nine months after graduation, leaving school, or dropping below half-time status. Payment amounts depend on the size of the debt and the length of the repayment period (usually 10 years).

Federal PLUS Loan   A loan made to the parents of dependent students who meet established credit qualifying criteria. Two kinds of loans are available: Direct PLUS Loans and Federal Family Education Loans. Loans are limited to the cost of education minus other financial aid with no annual or aggregate limit. Interest rates are variable. A fee of up to 4 percent of the loan is charged and deducted proportionately each time a loan payment is made. Interest rates are variable and adjusted annually, but they never exceed 9 percent. Repayment begins within 60 days after the final loan disbursement. Maximum term is 10 years; $50 minimum payment per month.

***Federal Register* (FR)**   A publication of government regulations for comment prior to their implementation and the final copies of laws and regulations. *Contact:* Superintendent of Documents, U.S. Government Printing Office, Washington, DC 20402.

Federal Rehabilitation Act of 1973 (FRA)   Legislation that aims to prohibit discrimination against disabled employees. It stipulates that the terms of collective bargaining agreements must be taken into account in protecting the rights of the disabled.

Federal Stafford Loan   A student loan program, open to either undergraduate or graduate students, that is based on financial need as determined by a needs analysis document. Permits loans for undergraduate students of $2,625 (1st year), $3,500 (2nd year), $5,500 (remaining years, and a cumulative total of $23,000. For graduate students, the maximum per year is $8,500 with a cumulative limit of $65,000. Interest rates are variable. Payments of principal and interest are deferred until 6 months after the student ceases to be enrolled on at least a half-time basis. Loans are for a maximum of 10 years; $50 minimum payment per month.

Federal Student Financial Aid Programs
To be eligible, a student must: (1) be a U.S. citizen or eligible noncitizen, (2) be registered with Selective Service (if required); (3) attend a participating college; (4) be working toward a degree or certificate; (5) be making satisfactory academic progress; (6) not owe a refund on a Federal grant or be in default of a Federal education loan; and (7) have financial need (except for Unsubsidized Stafford Loans).

Federal Supplemental Educational Opportunity Grant (FSEOG) A grant offered to undergraduate students who have exceptional financial need, that is, those with the lowest **Expected Family Contributions,** and gives top priority to students who receive Federal Pell Grants. Students may receive between $100 and $4,000 per year, depending upon when they apply, their level of need, and the funding level of the school they're attending. The participating school credits the student's account or pay him or her directly at least once per term (semester, trimester, or quarter). Such grants do not have to be paid back.

Federal Trade Commission (FTC)
An agency of the federal government empowered under Section 5 of the **Federal Trade Commission Act of 1914** to take action against all "unfair methods of competition" and, by amendment in 1938, against all "unfair or deceptive acts or practices." The agency investigates and prosecutes advertising and investment frauds. Although it does not resolve individual complaints, it uses such complaints to develop law-enforcement actions. *Contact:* Correspondence Branch, Federal Trade Commission, Washington, DC 20580.

Federal Trade Commission Act of 1914 (FTCA) An Act designed to prevent unfair competition and deceptive trade practices in interstate commerce. The FTCA proscribes misrepresentation of materials, ingredients, and origin of products and false advertising, trade-restraints, and certain types of sales inducements. It also created the **Federal Trade Commission** as a separate antitrust enforcement agency.

Federal Unemployment Tax Act (FUTA)
Finances unemployment insurance for workers who become unemployed through no fault of their own and who are able, available, and actively seeking work. The tax paid by employers is currently 0.8 percent on the first $7,000 of income per employee. *See also* State Unemployment Insurance.

Federal Work-Study (FWS) A program that provides jobs for undergraduate and graduate students with financial need, allowing them to earn money to help pay educational expenses. Community service work and work related to the student's course of study are encouraged. FWS wage or salary, paid directly at least once per month, must be at least the current federal minimum wage, but it may be higher, depending on the type of work and the skills required. Total amount of the award depends on when the student applies, his or her level of need, and the funding level of the participating school.

FedWorld Information Network An office of the National Technical Information Service established to meet the challenge of accessing comprehensive U.S. Government information online. Includes a database of federal government job openings. *Contact:* NTIS FedWorld (703/487-4850; E-mail **webmaster@fedworl.gov**; URL **http://www. fedworld.gov**).

fee Payment for services rendered, for example, by legal counsel or consultants. Fee arrangements may take any of several different forms: **combination fee, contingency fee, fixed fee, hourly charge, reduced fee, retainer,** or **reverse contingency.**

fee-and-commission planner A financial or other type of planner who charges clients *either* an hourly rate, a set fee per plan, or an agreed-upon percentage of the value of the client's assets or income to establish a base fee for the plan. When the plan is implemented, the planner may receive a commission from some or all of the products purchased.

fee-based pricing (FBP) Paying an organization, such as a travel agency, a fee for its services

feedback Information given to people about their behavior and performance. Used in supervision, performance appraisal, counseling, coaching, and training to reinforce or correct behavior or performance. It may be either positive or negative — the former affirming that something was done correctly (usually accompanied by praise) and the latter pointing out that something has been misapplied and must be corrected (usually accompanied by specific suggestions but sometimes censure, reprimand, or other form of punitive action.).

fee-for-service plan or option A health insurance plan that pays benefits directly to physicians, hospitals, or other health care providers, or that reimburses the patient for covered medical services. It usually gives patients the latitude to seek whatever care they want wherever they want it. Also known as *indemnity plans.* Examples are Blue Cross & Blue Shield and Medicare.

fee maximum The maximum that a professional provider may charge for a product or service.

fee-only planner A financial or other type of planner who charges clients an hourly rate, a set fee per plan, or an agreed-upon percentage of the value of the client's assets or income.

female think The tendency of people to shift from conventional, goal-oriented and hierarchical patterns of thought to more caring, tender, and sharing familial ones. *Attributed to Faith Popcorn and Lys Marigold, Clicking: 16 Trends to Future Fit Your Life, Your Work, and Your Business.*

feng shue A hospitality discipline practiced throughout China. Guest rooms, executive rooms, and ballrooms are structured and furnished in such a way as to keep them in balance with spiritual forces.

fetal protection policy (FPP) A policy that excludes fertile women from jobs involving hazardous levels of exposure to solid, liquid, or gaseous toxic materials, such as lead, to prevent exposure of unborn fetuses to physical harm. Considered by some organizations, such as the American Civil Liberties

Union (ACLU) and the United Auto Workers (UAW), as discriminatory.

fetal risk A matter ruled on by the Supreme Court in March 1991 (*United Auto Workers v. Johnson Controls*, manufacturer of automobile batteries). The case relates to whether an employer may legitimately exclude women of child-bearing age from jobs that might expose them and the fetuses they may carry to dangerous levels of toxic substances, such as lead, glycol ethers, organic mercury (methyl), inorganic mercury, and radiation. The Court ruled that fetal protection is nothing more than an intrusive form of job discrimination. The decision stated, "It is no more appropriate for the courts than it is for individual employers to decide whether a woman's reproductive role is more important to herself and her family than her economic role. Congress has left this choice to the woman as hers to make."

fiber optics A means of sending telephone or video messages over long distances completely interference free. Consist of a bundle of glass fibers that transport light along the length of the fibers at a speed of 100 million bits per second. The sound, data, and images are transformed into waves of light signals by a laser beam. Advanced systems have increased capacity by using such techniques as time-division multiplexing (placing information into the spaces between words and data) and wavelength division multiplexing (using another wavelength to carry more data and increasing the rate at which the signals are sent).

fibromyalgia A type of arthritis that affects an estimated 3.7 million Americans, mostly women, and is often misdiagnosed because many of its symptoms occur with other conditions. Although patients do not show evidence of inflammation, joint, or muscle degeneration, the condition is marked by widespread pain, along with fatigue, insomnia, stiffness, and sometimes psychological distress.

fiduciary A person who is in a position that requires trust, faithfulness, and loyalty, such as executors of wills, trustees of trusts, guardians, and administrators.

Fiduciary Income Tax Return The income tax return that reports income for a trust or estate.

field 1. The location in a **database** designed to accept a particular **data element,** such as a zip code. 2. Every other line of an interlaced video image.

field experiment A research methodology that is a type of **controlled experiment.** Instead of conducting the study under artificial laboratory conditions, the researcher chooses to study the variables in an actual organizational setting. In every other respect the approach is identical to that of the **laboratory experiment.**

field interview A recruitment and screening interview conducted away from company headquarters — literally "in the field." Field interviews are expensive because they require travel, hotel accommodations, subsistence, and usually more than one interviewer.

field test A tryout under typical conditions of a system or program to identify problems before the system is installed as an operating program.

field training 1. In sales, training or coaching conducted by a salesperson's immediate supervisor on the premises of clients and customers in a "live" sales situation. 2. In military training, unit or individual training conducted in the field, away from the classroom or laboratory.

field trip A carefully planned visit or tour to a place away from the training activity to provide first-hand observation of objects, processes, operations, and situations not transportable to, or reproducible in, the training facility. Field trips may be used to orient trainees to the work environment, provide opportunity for first-hand observation of operations, processes, or practices that cannot be readily or safely moved into the classroom or laboratory, stimulate trainee interest and participation in discussion or other types of learning activities, relate theory to practice, or introduce or summarize a topic.

fifty-fifty (50/50) dental plan A cost-cutting dental care plan that pays benefits of $1,000 orthodontic maximum; $1,000 annual maximum, but requires no deductibles.

file In computers, information or data grouped and treated as one unit. A means of organizing stored information for quick and easy retrieval and use.

file allocation table (FAT) Keeps track of where data files are stored on a hard disk

file conversion *See* data conversion.

file server A work station on a computer network that is dedicated to providing file and mass data storage services to other work stations on the network.

file transfer protocol (FTP) Procedures that allow the exchange of files between two computers on the **Internet.** FTP sites are computers dedicated to uploading and downloading files.

filmstrip An older type of audiovisual aid that made use of a sequence of images on a roll of 35mm black and white or color film.

final account An accounting provided by the executor at the conclusion of the settlement of the estate showing the property received, including income, the disbursements, legacies paid to beneficiaries, and a statement that nothing remains in the estate. Acceptance of the final account by the court closes the probate estate and discharges the executor from further liability.

final program In meeting management, a final mailing that contains the definitive conference and social program distributed just prior to the conference or at registration for the event.

Financial Accounting Standard 106
Issued in December 1990 by the **Financial Accounting Standards Board** and become effective in 1993. It requires employers to change from a pay-as-you-go approach to funding medical benefits for present and future retirees to an accrual method of accounting that calls for an estimate of the costs of future benefits. That estimate must then be carried on the corporate balance sheet as a long-term debt payable to employees and, according to estimates, is likely to reduce corporate profits by about 15 percent but *could* impact on profits by as much as 35 to 40 percent. That is, because the standard will make employers account for their costs earlier, it will have the effect of reducing net operating income and earnings per share for many employers.

Financial Accounting Standard 119
Issued by the **Financial Accounting Standards Board** in October 1994, the rule requires new disclosures on the aims, amounts, and positions of derivatives effective in FY 1994 for companies with more than $150 million in total assets and in FY 1995 for all companies.

Financial Accounting Standards Board (FASB) A free-standing body in the private sector, supported by the accounting profession and industry, that establishes "generally accepted" accounting rules and standards for publicly owned organizations and employers. Its standards may be rejected or overruled by the **Securities and Exchange Commission**.

financial advisor A person who, for compensation, provides advice to an individual or corporate client regarding strategies and actions to achieve financial goals and objectives based on an analysis of personal and/or financial condition, resources, and capabilities.

financial aid administrator (FAA) The individual at participating institutions who is responsible for administering student financial aid programs.

financial aid package Under federal student aid programs, the total amount of financial aid a student receives, including federal and nonfederal aid in the forms of grants, loans, and work-study.

financial assessment Measuring or estimating the financial position and strength of an organization by examining long-term, intermediate-term, and short-term indicators and assessing long-, intermediate-, and short-term risk.

financial assistance program (FAP) An employer-sponsored dependent care option. There are four types: flexible spending accounts, flexible benefits (salary reduction plans), voucher programs, and vendor programs.

financial audit An examination of the financial position of an organization, including its balance sheet and its accounting procedures.

financial budget A major component of a comprehensive budget program. A financial budget consists of a budgeted balance sheet showing how the operations plan will affect the company's basic resources and liabilities. It also includes the budget sheet supporting schedules, all in budget format, depicted in cash flow, receivables, inventory, capital expenditures, and depreciation.

financial planning **1.** The development of long-range (five year) financial plans to support the long-range goals and objectives of the enterprise and the HR organization based on study of forecasts, strategic plans, enterprise and HR needs and priorities, anticipated organizational changes, and projected changes in products, services, and processes. **2.** The process of providing advice and assistance to clients for the purpose of achieving the client's financial goals.

financial ratio analysis The interpretation of balance sheets and income statements of an organization in which selected dollar items are compared with another series of dollar items and the resulting figures are related to accepted financial performance standards. Examples of commonly used balance sheet ratios are current assets to current debt, current debt to tangible net worth, total debt to tangible net worth, fixed assets to tangible net worth, net sales to inventory, inventory to net working capital, net sales to tangible net worth, and net profits to tangible net worth. Commonly used income statement ratios are: (1) for gross profit — gross sales, returns and allowances, net sales, cost of goods sold, and gross margin; (2) for operating profit — administrative and general expenses and operating profit; and (3) for final net profit or loss — interest paid, and net profit or loss.

financial reinsurance A type of reinsurance purchased following a loss and after the cost of claims has been determined. It is designed to allow buyers to take tax advantage of incurred losses while removing long-term liability from the corporate balance sheet.

financial reporting The most common method of budget control. Effected by requiring subordinate mangers and supervisors to submit monthly status reports showing encumbered funds and unencumbered balances. It is a very effective means of regulating expenditures.

financial reward A reward given to employees for outstanding performance or contributions to the profitability or image of the organization. Financial rewards include such items as salary raises, promotions, cash bonuses, gift certificates, professional membership dues, fitness club membership dues, and trips to meetings/conventions/exhibits of professional associations for the employee and his or her spouse.

financial risk Long-term risk is estimated by calculating the ratio of long-term debt to total revenue; intermediate risk is determined by calculating either the ratio of restricted revenues (obligated) to total income or the ratio of fixed commitments to total income; short-term risk is determined by calculating the ratio of short-term debt to annual revenue.

financial statement Any report or presentation of financial data in any form or format derived from accounting records of an organization. Primary financial statements include the balance sheet, income statement, statement of retained earnings, and statement of changes in financial position. Secondary financial statements include reports of administrative expenses, cash flow report, accounts-receivable report, and capital expenditure report.

financial strength Financial strength is assessed as follows: long term financial resources are estimated by calculating the ratio of market value of assets to total operating expenses; intermediate financial resources are determined by calculating the ratio of available fund balances to total operating expenses; and short-term financial resources are determined by calculating the ratio of current fund assets to current fund liabilities.

finasteride A generic name for drugs used to treat enlarged prostate glands; for example, the Merck drug Proscar.

firewall protections 1. Safeguards designed to protect from their competitors pricing information of **pharmacy benefit management** firms that offer drug benefit formularies. **2.** Safeguards designed to protect internal computer networks from hackers and other intruders by monitoring incoming and outgoing communications from Internet applications, such as E-mail and file transfer. Firewall products include router packet filtering, authentication, and encryption systems,

firm-fixed-price contract (FFP) The type of contract most commonly used to acquire training programs and services because the items to be purchased can be accurately described and the work effort required to produce the items can be accurately calculated. The vendor guarantees successful performance of the terms of the contract within the proposed time frame and specifies the price of the product or service. The contractor cannot change the specified price or schedule. In return, the buyer agrees to pay the fixed price as specified in the contract without regard to the actual cost of performance of the work required by the contract.

first class An unrestricted air fare providing a special seating section, menu, and free beverages at considerably higher cost than other fares.

first-in-first-out (FIFO) A method of inventory valuation that assumes inventory first purchased (first in) is first used or sold (first out). When materials or products from inventory are used or sold, deductions from the inventory account are made at the cost of the items purchased first, rather than last, thus making the value of the inventory on hand conform more closely to current prices. When procurement prices are changing, FIFO strongly influences stated profits. For example, if prices rise, the value of inventory also rises because the latest purchases remain on the books as the accountant deducts from inventory the lower-priced goods purchased first. The result is higher stated profits. Conversely, if prices drop, the cost of goods sold remains at the higher level and the value of inventory declines. This has the effect of lowering stated profits.

first-pass yield An indicator or effective performance and a measure of quality. First-pass yield is the percentage of tasks completed right *on the first try* (without reworks or corrections). Said by some to be the most important internal measure of quality and competitiveness.

Fiscal 1993 Defense Authorization Act
The Act authorized additional transition assistance for military and civilian personnel affected by the post cold war drawdown. Active duty personnel in nontransferable skills, such as combat arms, are authorized to apply for up to one year of educational leave of absence to obtain civilian job training. Personnel in surplus categories who have 15 but less than 20 years of service are authorized to apply for early retirement. The legislation also contained incentives to encourage service members to leave active duty voluntarily. Selected reservists in surplus categories with 15 but less than 20 years of service are authorized to apply for reserve retirement, with retirement pay commencing at age 60. Selected reservists with at least 20 years of service are authorized to apply for immediate reduced pay retirement for five years or until reaching age 60, whichever comes first. Health care

benefits will not begin until age 60. Reservists involuntarily separated with more than six qualifying years of service are entitled to receive separation pay and transportation benefits, to include two years commissary and exchange privileges. At the discretion of the Service Secretary, they may continue to receive G.I. Bill educational assistance. Civilian personnel are authorized to receive Job Training and Partnership Assistance for 12 months in advance of a base closure or realignment. The Act also authorizes resignation and early retirement incentives of up to $25,000 for civilians in surplus skills categories and for employees at military installations facing closure or realignment. For employees involuntarily separated due to a reduction in force, the Act authorized the Department of Defense to pay for up to 18 months the government contribution for federal health insurance plans.

Fiscal 1997 Defense Authorization Act Among other things, provided the active duty military force a 3 percent pay raise and a 4.6 percent quarters allowance increase, directed the Secretary of Defense to develop a dental plan for retired members and their families, and restored January as the date for retired pay cost-of-living adjustments in all future years.

fishbone chart *See* cause and effect diagram.

fitness In the context of corporate programs, fitness consists of sound physiological components involving cardiovascular, strength, and flexibility fitness, body fat, and nutrition and diet.

fitness for work A document that contains information obtained from employer inquiries into a job applicant's background.

fitness program *See* wellness program.

fitness report The term used by the U.S. Navy and U.S. Marine Corps to describe **officer efficiency reports**.

Five-Factor Model (FFM) A personality assessment model that is based on the **Myers-Briggs Type Indicator** but differs from it in that it is based on experience rather than theory. Used in career development, coaching and counseling, conflict management, customer service, employee selection, job analysis, management and leadership development, team building, and training design. Proponents of FFM claim the following: (1) personality has five dimensions; (2) scores on those dimensions fall along a normal distribution; (3) personality is best described by individual traits rather than types; and (4) the strength of scores indicates preferences. Recently developed Big Five personality inventories include the Hogan Personality Inventory and the NEO Five Factor Inventory. Also called *Big Five paradigm* or *extroversion/introversion*.

Five-Five-Five Plan (5-5-5 Plan) A work proposal featuring a 25-hour work week with five hours of training weekly, phased in over a five-year period. Designed to improve productivity, employee motivation, and job satisfaction. Attributed to futurist Alvin Toffler.

fixed annuity An annuity that guarantees payments of principal and interest with the interest rate changing one or more times annually but guaranteed not to fall below an amount specified in the contract.

fixed assets The sum of the costs (or appraised value) of land and the depreciated book value of buildings, leasehold improvements, equipment, machinery, tools, furnishing and furniture, and fixtures.

fixed budget A budget that is based on fixed costs and therefore does not vary with fluctuations in activity. All costs are assumed to be fixed costs. Also called *static budget*.

fixed costs Costs that are unaffected by the amount of work being done in an organizational element or the total corporation. They accumulate over time and include all costs of operations such as salaries of managers, building maintenance, and so on.

fixed-dollar benefits Health care or other employee benefits plans in which specific dollar limitations are placed on the insurance premiums or claims paid by the company.

fixed fee A set amount paid to a non-employee for completion of a specific service or services regardless of the time or other resources expended by the the contractor.

fixed-price contract with economic price-adjustment provisions (FPE) A contract that allows adjustments to the price when specific and uncontrollable changes (such as labor or materials costs or changes in industry-wide price levels) occur in the cost or price factors set forth in the contract. They have the effect of shifting the risks to the buyer.

fixed-price incentive contract (FPI) A type of contract in which the contractor is paid more profit if performance is completed at a cost below the expected or estimated (target) cost agreed upon in the contract. Similarly, if the costs at completion exceeds the expected or estimated (target) cost, the contractor is paid less profit.

fixed-price level-of-effort term contract (FPLET) A contract that permits firm description of and budgeting for the work to be accomplished by the contractor. Progress in the direction of a goal is what is typically sought rather than completion of the research, such as achievement of a technological breakthrough. Usually limited to research projects of relatively small scope.

fixed-price redeterminable contract (FPR) A type of fixed-price contract that leaves the final negotiation of price until the work has proceeded to the point where costs are clear enough to predict the final costs and the price can be negotiated with confidence.

fixed-rate contract (FR) A contract in which the final amount to be paid to the contractor cannot be determined until performance has been completed. The fixed rate includes direct labor costs, overhead charges, general and administrative or selling expenses, and profit. All of these costs are summed and a rate for reimbursement to the contractor is agreed upon. Close monitoring of performance by the contracting organization is essential to insure that deliverables are acceptable.

flagged rates Rates paid to employees which fall above the **wage curve**. Also called *red circle rates* or *overrates*.

flame/flaming On the Internet, verbal abuse or hate E-mail, usually sent to a user who has violated netiquette.

Flanagan Aptitude Classification Test An **aptitude test** that measures sixteen different areas of knowledge and skill, including basic arithmetic, English grammar and sentence structure, judgment, and problem solving.

flash technology Miniature computer memory chips, some encased in credit-card size packages, that have large storage capacity, random access, immunity from damage by bumps and shaking, the ability to retain information when turned off, and require only one-half the power of conventional chips. They have become the memory for compute notebooks and personal digital assistants, such as Apple's Newton.

flat benefit retirement plan A type of defined benefits pension plan that provides benefits that are unrelated to earnings, such as a certain amount per month or per year of service.

flat effect In mental illness, the absence of or reduction in the amount of emotional tone or outward emotional reaction typically shown in parallel settings or under similar circumstances. Also called *blunted affect*.

flat file database A **database management system** that uses a "flat" file structure,where all data about a particular subject, such as customers or dealers are stored in one or two very large files.

flat/flattened organization An organization structure that has a limited number of hierarchical levels (levels of management and supervision) from top to bottom and hence a wide span of management with many subordinates reporting to one superior.

flat rate The specific room rate for a group that has been agreed on in advance by the hotel or other property and group representative/s.

Fleet Reserve Association (FRA) An organization of 160,000 members open to active duty, drilling reserve, and retired enlisted personnel and commissioned officers with at least one day of prior enlisted service in the Navy, Marine Corps, and Coast Guard. Its mission is to represent its members on military personnel legislative matters, safeguard the compensation, benefits, and entitlements of Sea Services personnel before the Congress, and help with individual career problems through liaison with the Department of Defense, Department of Veterans Affairs, and other government departments and agencies. *Contact:* FRA, 125 N. West St., Alexandria, VA 22314-2754 703/683-1400; Fax 703/549-6610; E-mail **news-fra@fra.org**).

flex *See* flexible benefits/flex benefits program.

flexible benefits/flex benefits programs (FBP) A program that allows employees to adjust their benefits to meet their needs. The employer decides how much money to allocate to benefits, medical for example, and the employee decides how to use those benefits. Such plans often feature less expensive core coverage options with varying deductibles and copayment requirements. Additional benefits may also be offered for purchase by the employee.

flexible budgeting A budgeting process that seeks to identify the factors or activity measures that correlate with increases or decreases in costs with changes in the volume of products or services produced. It helps managers to separate spending from volume variances. Examples of variables are units of output, person-hours, machine hours, number of shifts, and cost-center hours or days. Also called *variable budgeting.*

flexible hours *See* flextime.

flexible leave A plan for personal and parental paid, partially paid, or unpaid leave to allow employees to care for a new baby or for ill dependents.

flexible managed care A combination of a **cafeteria plan** and an **open-ended health maintenance organization** (HMO) plan — adding **managed care** elements to their flexible benefits plans to make the plans more cost-effective.

flexible manufacturing system
See computer-integrated manufacturing.

flexible scheduling A plan to adjust employee schedules as needed to accommodate the business cycles or to increase employee motivation, morale, and job satisfaction.

flexible spending account (FSA) 1. Allows an employee to reserve funds for health care expenses tax-free. A **medical savings account** is one FSA touted as remedy for the health care crisis. A plan that allows employees to use pretax dollars to fund medical expenses not covered by their health plans (and sometimes dependent care). The only cost to the employer is for administrative expenses. Essentially a strategy to reduce health care costs, the plan is offered to employees instead of first dollar coverage of hospitalization and surgery. A specific sum of money is put aside for each employee for prescription drugs, and other outpatient services. The employer decides how much money to put toward benefits and the employee decides how to use that money — and may choose expenses not ordinarily covered by the employer. **2.** An employer-sponsored dependent care option (DCAP) in which the employee chooses from a menu of taxable and nontaxable benefits. Dependent-care options are nontaxable. The dependent must be a child under 15, a dependent, elderly relative, or a mentally or physically handicapped dependent.

flexible staffing A strategy designed to effect substantial savings in salaries and fringe benefits, reduce vulnerability to periodic or seasonal layoffs, and cut turnover. It involves the use of temporary full-time and permanent part-time personnel, consultants, and subcontractors, such as secretarial, accounting, technical, managerial, or executive level employees.

flexible work options Optional schedules and alternative work sites designed to allow employees to balance work and family responsibilities. *See also* compressed work-week, family support options; flexiplace; flextime; homeworker; job sharing/job splitting; phased retirement, V-time programs, and work sharing.

flexiplace An accommodation employers make to help their workers change their lifestyles. Involves the performance of a job in whole or in part away from the company's premises — at home or elsewhere. Also called *flex place* or *telecommuting.*

flex-management Using strategies and tactics that are effective in managing a workforce comprised of females, minorities, older workers, and people with disabilities. Attributed to D. Jamieson and J. O'Mara (*Managing Workforce 2000: Gaining the Diversity Advantage,* Jossey-Bass, 1990).

flex plans Cost reduction strategies designed to transfer more of the costs of providing health care from the organization to employees.

flextime Arrangements made to allow flexibility in start and finish times of the work shift to accommodate employees whose day, hours, or family responsibilities do not match standard work hours. Employees are usually required to be present during "core" time — a set time for all employees. Also called *flexitime.*

flipchart An easel used for illustration during training sessions. The charts hold bond or quadrille paper pads approximately 28" wide by 34" high on a three-legged, folding easel equipped with chart pad clamps and marker storage trays. Colored markers of several different widths are available for writing on dry surfaces.

flip the switch The exact moment when the management information information system department turns off the old MIS and activates the new system. *See also* systems, applications, and products.

floppy disk A removable and transportable computer disk measuring 3.5, 5.25, or 8 inches. Floppy disks provide a computer's secondary memory, a repository for programs and data storage and the information that programs process and produce — documents, applications, and software that a computer can use.

flowchart A graphic representation of an operation used to study, standardize, and improve work processes. It uses symbols (operation, movement, inspection, delay, and storage, for example) to identify common activities that occur in most types of operations. It is also used to as a communications tool to help workers visualize a process in the same way.

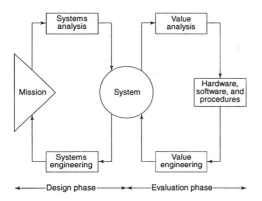

focused interview A research interview with the following requirements: (1) subjects known to have been involved in a particular situation; (2) the investigator has previously analyzed the hypothetically significant elements of the situation and has arrived at a set of hypotheses relating to the meaning and effects of critical aspects of the situation; (3) based on the foregoing analysis, the investigator has developed an interview guide that defines the major area of inquiry and the hypotheses which locate the the pertinent data to be obtained in the interview; (4) the interview is focused on the subject's experiences in the particular situation; and (5) the subject's responses enable the investigator to test the validity of his or her hypotheses and identify unanticipated responses to the situation, thus giving rise to new hypotheses.

focus group An evaluation technique involving in-depth interactive interviews with groups of 8 to 12 people who are in some way associated with the organization, interested in the topic, or use its products or services. Conducted under the guidance of a facilitator, participants share their thoughts, ideas, and opinions.

followup Monitoring results following the completion of any type of HR intervention (for example, training, disciplinary action, job and task analysis, and organization development) to ensure that results conform with plans and that required changes have occurred.

font In desktop publishing, a complete assortment of letters, numbers, punctuation marks, and so on of a given size and design used by the compositor; for example, **12 point Helvetica**.

font caching A technique in which a graphics card stores fonts on board in high speed memory instead of waiting for the computer to send font information every time it displays text.

food and beverage manager The hotel functionary responsible for all food and beverage sales, including dining rooms, coffee shops, lounges, bars, room service, and catering.

Food and Drug Administration (FDA) An independent agency of the Public Health Service, a division of the Department of Health and Human Services. Responsible for testing and controlling drugs, medications, and medical devices and regulating food packaging, labeling, and distribution.

food services Services provided to enhance employee comfort, convenience, and morale, to protect their health, and to reduce travel time and time away from the job. Typical services include beverage and snack vending machines for coffee and lunch breaks on the premises, cafeteria or contract catering service or lunchrooms, and mobile food units or snack bars for large plants or widely dispersed work areas.

Food Stamp Program Designed to help meet the nutritional needs of low-income citizens. Provides low-income households with coupons on a monthly basis which can be redeemed for food at participating stores and eating facilities (such as some soup kitchens and certain restaurants). The program is administered by state departments of public welfare and applications are made to that office (or in the case of households in which one person receives or applies for **Supplemental Security Income** at the Social Security office). Financial eligibility is based on total assets (cash, bank accounts, stocks and bonds, but not the home household and personal goods, life insurance, and certain vehicles), income (less than a gross monthly income standard and a net income standard), and application of a formula. If qualified, applicants receive an **Authorization to Participate** card. In general, a household cannot have more than $2,000 in resources unless it includes a person 60 or older, in which case the limit is $3,000.

food stamps *See* Food Stamp Program.

forced-choice **1.** A rating method that uses two to five descriptions of behavior or performance in each section. Most forced-choice instruments contain 25 to 30 sections. The rater is asked to select the statement that is most characteristic and the one that is least characteristic. **2.** In testing, any multiple-choice test item in which the testee is asked to select one or more of the choices given. However, usage of the term typically focuses on personality measures where testees must choose from among options of equal preference value among the group on which the test was standardized but where one of the options distinguishes between persons high and low on the factor that the choice measures and the others do not.

forced choice scale A type of appraisal that resembles a test. The scale uses two to five descriptions of behavior in each of the 25 to 30 sections of the scale. Both favorable and unfavorable statements are included in each section. Raters are asked to choose the most appropriate statement in each section.

forced distribution A rating method that is essentially a modification of the **graphic scale** to avoid errors of central tendency. Raters are instructed to force their ratings into a normal (bell-shaped) curve — excellent, 10 percent; above average, 20 percent; average, 40 percent; below average, 20 percent; and unsatisfactory, 10 percent.

forced relationships A problem solving technique that involves forcing two or more normally unrelated principles, concepts, ideas, or objects together and squeezing, pressing, or jamming them into forced relationships to develop new solutions.

force-field analysis An approach used in creative problem solving and in planning, organization planning, and implementing training and development interventions. In any situation, there are forces in operation, some driving and some countervailing. When the forces are not in balance, change occurs. Therefore, when change is wanted, the equilibrium of opposing forces must be disturbed, moved to a new balance, and then immobilized in their new state. A diagram of the driving and countervailing forces in a situation is prepared to identify potentially fruitful points of attack. Attributed to Kurt Lewin.

***force majeure* clause** **1.** In law, a termination clause in a contract relieving the parties of their duty to carry out their commitments if performance is made impossible by an unforeseen event beyond the control of either party, i.e., an act of God). **2.** In meeting management, an entertainer's or artist's contract clause that limits liability if the performance must be canceled due to circumstances beyond the artist's control. Does not usually include weather.

forecaster *See* futurist.

forecasting The process of collecting, analyzing, synthesizing, and drawing implications from study of future conditions and events that are most likely to affect practice or operations in a given field over a period of five or more years. It is careful, systematic, deliberate economic, social, and business analysis undertaken to obtain accurate information on future trends and developments in order to prevent costly mistakes in decision making.

forecast A prediction or projection of future conditions or events making use of historical, statistical, and other forms of data, information, systems, assumptions, principles, hypotheses, theories, and laws to arrive at conclusions and identify alternative courses of action to achieve corporate and HR goals and objectives.

Foreign Corrupt Practices Act of 1977 (FCPA) Legislation passed by Congress that (1) prohibits and makes it a criminal offense for any company to offer, directly or indirectly, bribes or payoffs in exchange for foreign contracts; and (2) requires corporations subject to the Securities and Exchange Act of 1934 to have adequate and documented systems of internal accounting control throughout their operations. Penalties for infraction of the FCPA are severe — a corporation can face fines of up to $2 million and an individual can be fined up to $100,000 and be incarcerated for up to five years.

foreign country   As defined by **Section 911, Internal Revenue Code,** any territory under the rule of a government other than the United States, not including American Samoa, the Antarctic Region, Guam, North American Marianas Islands, Puerto Rico, and the Virgin Islands.

foreign earned income   As defined by Section 911, Internal Revenue Code, pay for personal services performed in a foreign country by individuals who maintain a tax home abroad and meet either the residency test or the physical presence test in a foreign country.

foreign housing exclusion   As defined by **Section 911 Internal Revenue Code,** the deductible costs of reasonable housing expenses of employees living abroad that exceed 16 percent of the annual salary of a federal employee at grade GS-14, Step 1. Reasonable housing expenses include furniture rental, nondeductible occupancy taxes, real/personal property insurance, rent or fair market value if provided in kind, repairs, and residential parking fees.

foreign income and housing exclusion   *See* Section 911, Internal Revenue Code.

foreign sales corporation (FSC)   A strategy created by a 1984 act of Congress to help counter the U.S. trade imbalance. An FSC is a foreign corporation established by a U.S. exporter in a U.S. possession (outside of the U.S. Customs Zone) or in one of the more than 20 countries approved by the U.S.. Treasury Department. More than 80 percent operate in the Virgin Islands. An FSC must be a wholly-owned subsidiary of the parent company, have an office and principal bank account in the jurisdiction where it is incorporated, and file pertinent papers with the Internal Revenue Service. When the company makes an export sale, it sends a commission on paper to the FSC. The FSC keeps those invoices on file, and, on its annual corporate income tax returns, the parent company may claim a tax deduction on those commissions. Because commission income is approximately 70 percent tax free, income taxes on export profits are essentially erased.

foreign service premium   A fixed percentage of base pay paid monthly to employees working overseas.

foreign travelers' security   *See* security of travelers.

forgotten widows   Widows of active-duty military service members who died before enactment of the Survivor Benefit Plan (SBP) law in 1972 and widows of reservists who died before enactment of the Reserve Component SBP in 1978, both of whom are currently ineligible for SBP annuities. Their spouses opted for receipt of the total annuity at the time of retirement from military service. Federal civilian forgotten widows were granted annuities 10 years after their SBP was enacted.

Form   A computer virus that simulates key clicks when the keyboard is activated on the 18th or 24th day of the month. The virus may also damage files on the disc. It is "caught" when the computer is booted form an infected floppy disk.

Form 5500 filings   Annual reports to the Internal Revenue Service and the Department of Labor on qualified retirement plans due within seven months of the close of the plan's fiscal year. The reports cover such items as plan operations, level of employee participation, annual expenses, and information on the plan's investment portfolio.

formal logic   The science of deductive reasoning. It is the art of argument exemplified by the syllogism with its major premise, minor premise, and conclusion.

formal plan   A long- or short-term plan based on an organized system involving reflection, study, and research. Formal plans are often the product of a team rather than an individual effort.

formal sanctions   Systems by which individual members of a group or organization are held accountable for their behavior and actions. They include disciplinary actions, such as reprimands, warnings, suspensions, and termination.

format   **1.** The logical arrangement of data inside a file. **2.** The physical arrangement of data on a storage medium such as a floppy disc.

formative evaluation   An approach to the evaluation of training systems that focuses on the system's adequacy in terms of achievement of objectives. It also identifies corrections or changes needed in the system as it is being implemented. *See also* summative evaluation.

formulary A list of drugs that a physician is expected or required to prescribe.

formulary drug A **brand name drug** on a list of prescription drugs specifically approved for special benefit consideration after assessment of their value, efficacy, and utilization by a formulary committee, usually consisting of a group of physicians and pharmacologists. *See also* generic drug.

fortress-hub In travel management, any city where 70 percent or more of the airline seats sold are concentrated in one carrier. Examples are Atlanta, Detroit, Houston, Minneapolis/St. Paul, Philadelphia, Pittsburgh, Raleigh-Durham, and St. Louis. Non-fortress hubs include Boston, Chicago, Dallas, Denver, Los Angeles, New York and Phoenix.

forum 1. In telecommunications, an on-line message base that is limited to a specific topic. 2. In training, discussion groups.

forward averaging A tax accounting technique that enables recipients of lump sum retirement payments to pay taxes on these distributions as if they had been received over a specified period of time, beginning in the year of the distribution.

foster care 1. Arrangements for the personal care and family living of orphaned or abused children in private homes, usually with subsistence pay provided by the state. 2. A social service in which an older person in need of a small amount of daily assistance is placed in a home environment for a small fee paid to the hosting family. In some areas all or a part of the cost is borne by state social service agencies.

foundation model An integrated health care delivery system in which a hospital or other entity creates a not-for-profit foundation, purchases physicians' practices, and places those tangible and intangible assets into the foundation. The foundation governed by a board which cannot be dominated by either the hospital or physicians and includes lay member, manages the the practices.

four-color process In desktop publishing, particularly when describing color press techniques, print that uses the four "primary" process colors: cyan, yellow, magenta, and black.

four fifteen *See* Section 415, Internal Revenue Code.

four-fifths rule A calculation prescribed by the Equal Employment Opportunity Commission to determine whether an employment practice has an **adverse impact** on protected groups. Adverse impact exists where a selection procedure results in hiring a protected group of applicants (African-Americans, for example) at a rate that is less than 80 percent of the rate for white applicants.

four fifty-seven *See* Section 457, Internal Revenue Code.

fourth generation language (4GL) New and advanced computer programming languages that speed up software development.

frame A full screen of video data.

frame buffer In video production, a repository or block of memory that stores one video frame or or still image in system memory for later use.

framegaming A 40-minute group game that encourages participants to express, exchange, capture, and package their suggestions, ideas, or opinions on any subject, problem, or issue. Attributed to Sivasailam Thiagrarajan, editor of *Performance & Instruction* magazine and reported in the September 1988 issue of the *Training and Development Journal.*

frame grabber In video production, the electronic function that freezes one video frame or graphic image so that it can be manipulated.

frame relay A service provided by a long-distance carrier that receives data, packages it, and sends it back over the network via the least costly route.

framing One of three crucial elements of all activities used in **adventure training**. The others are **implementation** and **debriefing.** Framing is the pre-activity of an event in which the scenario is described, goals are established, and rules are announced.

franchise A right conferred contractually by a business to an individual or group to provide a service or sell a specific product in a certain community or geographical area. The franchisee pays an initial fee, furnishes all the capital needed to start the business, assumes full financial and operational responsibility for running the business, pays a continuing royalty (usually a percentage of gross sales), and often buys products from the franchiser. In return, the franchiser allows the franchisee to run the business, assists the franchisee during the start-up period, and provides continuing support in the areas of advertising, purchasing, and operations.

franchising A management system for packaging, selling, and teaching a company-owned idea for marketing a product or service to entrepreneurs. In HR-related areas, franchising is now common in language schools, insurance, day care, fitness clubs, travel agencies, legal services, medical laboratories, printing and photocopying businesses, accountancies, business training, eye care, and career counseling.

fraudulent tagging An illegal sales and pricing strategy — advertising a sale and failing to remark the products with the sales price. *See also* bait and switch; deceptive pricing.

free addressing Describes **telecommuting** employees when they use whatever office space is available on the days they come to work at the company location. *See also* hoteling.

freebase *See* cocaine.

freebies Inducements provided by airlines, hotels, suppliers, and other vendors to agents, travel managers, meeting planners, and travelers. Include cruises, dinners, drinks, gifts, free travel, loans, money, personal services, promotional items, trips to supplier-sponsored trade shows, vacations,

freedom of choice law State legislation that forms a barrier to managed care (currently 11 states have such a law). The law restricts or eliminates an insurer's ability to limit a beneficiary's choice of providers or plans in return for a discount on the premium paid.

Freedom of Information Act of 1966 (FOIA) An act that provides for full and free disclosure to the public information held by administrative agencies of the federal government. Exceptions follow: where disclosure would cause harm to a governmental function, such as national defense or foreign policy, records relating to internal personnel rules and practices of a federal agency, personnel and medical files, properly classified national security information, privileged or confidential information such as trade secrets or confidential business information, audits of financial institutions, and law enforcement investigative materials. Records may be requested by private individuals or entities that are sufficiently particular to be identifiable, and they are not required to show need

or purpose. Doubtful requests for information must be checked with a senior executive, lawyer, privacy officer, freedom-of-information officer, or public information officer.

freelance trainer A temporary trainer who moves from company to company solving trainer shortages either in number or competencies; a viable solution to the staffing problem when training needs expand rapidly.

Freeman Studies Landmark studies of union influence on fringe benefits conducted by Professor R. B. Freeman in 1978 and reported in his article "The Effects of Trade Unionism on Fringe Benefits," NBER Working Paper No. 292, October 1978. Freeman analyzed data pooled from the 1967-72 Bureau of Labor Standards census-style establishment survey, Expenditures of Employee Compensation.

free-text search Describes the process of searching for terms or concepts by computer without relying solely on the words, acronyms, or abbreviations found in a glossary, thesaurus, or dictionary. It often involves use of titles and abstracts of documents.

free-trade agreement (FTA) An agreement between two or more countries to permit economic goods to flow across their borders free of duties.

freeze (frame) In video production or playback, stopping motion in a video image.

frequency distribution A means of shortening a list of test scores to facilitate statistical manipulation. It is the first step determining the range, mean, median, and mode in a collection of scores. Scores are arranged in order of size and the number of times each score occurs is entered to the right of the score.

Test score	Tally	f
86	/	1
84	//	2
80	/	1
78	///	3
74	//// ///	8
70	////	5
69	/	1
67	//	2
65	/	1
60	/	1
Total		25

frequent flier programs Airline-sponsored programs that reward frequent fliers (usually set at 25,000 miles per year of business travel) with "points" for miles flown or the number of round trips — and for dining at participating restaurants. Rewards include travel class upgrades (for example, from coach to business or first-class), free travel, priority seating, priority placement on wait lists for sold-out flights, early boarding, free hotel stays or car rentals, free magazine subscriptions.

free-response questionnaire *See* open form questionnaire.

freestanding ambulatory facility A medical structure that has permanent facilities and equipment for performing outpatient surgical and/or renal dialysis procedures; provides treatment by or under the supervision of physicians or nurses whenever the patient is in the facility, does not provide inpatient accommodations, and is not used as an office or clinic for the private practice of a physician or other professional.

French A high level of meal service in which the waitperson serves from a platter and places the food on each guest's plate.

frequently asked questions (FAQ) A collection of questions (with answers) that new users of the **Internet** ask most often.

friendly takeover A strategy to improve market share, efficiency of scale, or profitability. An agreement between two or more companies to consolidate by swapping shares or purchasing shares of one or more of the merging companies by one organization for a combination of cash and securities under mutually agree-upon terms. Typically, the "buyer" agrees to honor existing stock options and bonus plans of the merged companies.

friendly visitors Volunteers who regularly visit older, ill, and disabled persons who need companionship. They may write letters, read, and run errands. No cost is involved.

fright mail Correspondence that aims to generate fear of a loss of benefits or some other vital asset, such as Social Security, at the hands of unscrupulous or bureaucratic forces. The objective is to raise funds to support a special interest.

fringe benefits Such employee benefits as traditional health, retirement, and savings plans and dental plans, vision care, prescription drugs, life insurance, long-term disability, and accidental death and dismemberment insurance. May also include such items as cab fares and supper money for employees which, by a 1989 ruling of the IRS, are taxable in total for "management" and $100 per trip for other employees.

front-desk manager The hotel functionary responsible for registration and check-in.

front-end analysis A tool or technique used to improve human performance by diagnosing the causes of employee performance deficiencies and determining whether they are due to a lack of skills or knowledge that can be remedied by training or something else. It addresses performance problems by asking these questions: What are the indicators that a problem exists? What are the performance deficiencies revealed by the data? What is the relative value (in dollars) of solving the problem? Attributed to HRD Hall of Famer Joe Harless.

front-office manager The hotel functionary responsible for reservations, room blocks, registration services, early arrivals, late departures, and supervising the reservations manager and desk clerks (and the bell staff if there is no resident manager).

front-office system In travel management, the component of a travel agency's computer system, such as the CRS, that interacts directly with customers.

front-screen A projection system configuration where the projector is positioned in, behind, or above the audience. It is the most common and least expensive system but, in high-ambient-light situations, the image is washed out unless a very strong light source is used.

full American plan (FAP) A pricing method used by hotels and conference centers. Price includes lodging, breakfast, lunch, and dinner.

full coach Completely unrestricted economy class fares.

full costs In cost management and cost-benefits analysis, the sum of direct and indirect costs. It is the most accurate measure of how much it costs to deliver an HR service or product.

full inclusion The practice of having regular teachers or instructors teach both nondisabled trainees or students and disabled or special needs students together, without the assistance of a specially trained teacher or instructor.

full-spectrum learning   An approach to learning that attempts to integrate all the ways that people learn or process information: visually, aurally, tactilely, palpably, olfactorially, gustatorially, and so on.

full-text index   An index on the World Wide Web that contains every word of every document cataloged.

full-time equivalent (FTE)   The equivalent of one full-time employee; for example, two part-time employees are 0.25 FTE each and one employee is 0.50 FTE, for a total of 1.0 FTE.

fully funded pension plan   A pension plan with a funding ratio of 100 percent or more.

functional analysis   In value analysis, the process of identifying and defining the primary and secondary functions of an HR component, program, or service. For example, the primary function of a TV set is to display motion in color — not to entertain or train.

functional authority   Authority typically exercised by staff officers. It is restricted to matters in the functional area assigned to the staffer and is largely advisory, although it is often complemented with the authority provided by knowledge, experience, and expertise and the ability to influence decisions.

functional courses   Training programs provided by the Armed Services that develop knowledge and skills needed in a variety of specialties. For example, leadership training, language training, survival training, communications training, driver training, and instructor training.

functional illiterate   In general, an individual who is unable to read or write well enough to meet the basic demands of everyday life and work. Specifically, anyone who reads and writes below the sixth-grade level, dyslexic adults, recently arrived non-English speaking immigrants, and the high-functioning mentally retarded.

functional language   Communication that permits interaction between two people, one or both of whom have underdeveloped hearing and/or speech abilities. For example, a trainer may communicate with a deaf trainee by pointing with his or her finger, with or without words. The listener will indicate understanding by nodding or pointing to a particular object or graphic. Functional language also means that words that are to be used are words that the individual will need in his or her interactions with others at work or socially.

Functional Literacy Program (FLIT)   A U.S. Army program designed to upgrade trainees' ability to read well enough to locate information, follow directions, complete forms, and master and remember information they need on the job.

functional organization   One of the basic groupings of organizational elements, the nature of the work activities performed and related activities determines the placement of the function. Examples are manufacturing, marketing and sales, finance, management information, and human resources.

functional pricing   Granting a special salary, usually higher, for a special company function or job category in response to market pressure.

functional silos   *See* departmental walls.

functional speech defects   Functional speech defects are caused by psychological factors; they have no physical origins. Also called psychogenic speech disorders.

functional team   A group that has a specific and continuing responsibility for a function within an organization.

function sheet   In meeting management, in the United States, a set of detailed instructions for a particular event. Also known as a *banquet event order* or *resume sheet*. Internationally, it is a summary of all the particulars relating to a meeting need.

function space verification program   A service offered by the **Professional Convention Management Association (PCMA),** serving as an independent third-party auditor, that measures and certifies the "true" size of meeting and function space. PCMA contracts with licensed and bonded civil engineers to measure hotel and conference meeting room space with computer-driven laser equipment. PCMA then processes the measurements with software that provides graphics depicting the layouts of the function rooms in several configurations, taking into account police and fire codes and physical elements such as columns, chandeliers, and beams that may affect visibility.

functional specialists   Employees who have expertise in a particular organizational function, such as training and development, information systems, or finance.

funded debt   Includes mortgages, bonds, debentures, serial notes, or other obligations with a maturity of more than one year from the date of the statement.

funneling A planning and decision making technique practiced by General H. Norman ("Stormin' Norman") Schwarzkopf's Central Command (CENTCOM) management team during strategic meetings to shape operations Desert Shield and Desert Storm in the Persian Gulf. All participants came to daily staff meetings where, having individually explored all possible options and projected outcomes, they were ready to recommend a course of action. Input was then pushed through a narrowing set of criteria to arrive at the best course of action. The commander (CEO) made the final decision.

fusion marketing Involves the use of such strategies as joint or cooperative advertising and innovative bundling or packaging of products and services,

future payment index (FPI) A measure of key financial information created by Dun & Bradstreet Information Services, a division of Dun & Bradstreet Corporation. The FPI measures the degree of risk that businesses will encounter payment problems in the ensuing 6 to 12 months.

futurist A person who specializes in forecasting or predicting the environment of the future. Also called *futurologist, forecaster, environmental scanner,* and *trend spotter.*

futurologist *See* futurist.

future search An employee involvement technique , involving meetings of the people who have a stake in the meeting's outcome — usually a cross-section of the the the whole organization — designed to encourage innovation and empowerment. Attributed to Marvin Weisbord, *Discovering Common Ground: How Future Search Conferences Are Used Worldwide to Achieve Breakthrough Innovation, Empowerment, Shared Vision, and Collaborative Action,* Berrett-Koehler, 1992.

fuzzy search A World Wide Web search that finds matches even when words used in the search are only partially completed or misspelled.

G

G-7	Group of Seven.
G&A	General and administrative.
GAAP	Generally accepted accounting principles.
GATE	Guaranteed Access to Education.
GATT	General Agreement on Tariffs and Trade.
GAW	Guaranteed annual wage.
GBO	Gissel bargaining order.
GBWM	Get back with me (Internet speak).
GC/MS	Gas chromatography/mass spectrometry.
GDP	Gross domestic product.
GDSS	Group decision support system.
GED	General education development.
GHAA	Group Health Association of America.
GIC	1. Guaranteed investment contracts. 2. Graphic item count.
GIF	Graphic Interchange Format.
GIG	General inclusion group.
GIS	Geographical information system.
GLS	Group legal services.
GM	1. Gross margin. 2. General manager.
GMAT	Graduate Management Admissions Test.
GNMA	Government National Mortgage Association.
GNP	Gross national product.
GP	Gross profit.
GPA	Grade point average.
GPHMO	Group practice health maintenance organization.
GPO	Government Pension Offset.
GPWW	Group practice without walls.
GRAT	Grantor retained annuity trust.
GRE	Graduate Record Examination.
GS	General schedule.
GSA	General Services Administration.
GSM	Global system for mobile communications.
GST	Goods and Services Tax/General Services Tax.
GUI	Graphic User interface.
GULP	Group universal life plan.

gag clause **1.** Restrictions included in employment contracts to protect trade secrets and proprietary information **2.** Clauses in contracts between physicians and health maintenance organizations that limit the ability of the health care providers to talk freely with patients about treatment options and HMO payment policies and provide information about the benefits, risks, and costs of various treatments.

gain sharing A type of variable or incentive pay typically used to increase production by linking pay directly to specific improvements in a company's performance. It is used primarily where quantitative levels of production are important measures of business success. Gains are shared with all employees in a unit monthly, quarterly, semiannually, or annually, according to a predetermined formula, calculated on the value or gains of production over labor and other costs. A formula is used to monitor some performance variables such as productivity. Using the formula to measure gains over a targeted baseline, the company shares the resulting benefits with employees. The plan lets employees reap some of the rewards of their efforts based on teamwork and cooperation and by working harder and smarter.

gaishi A foreign company doing business in Japan.

Galileo In travel management, a **computer reservation system** consortium owned by Alitalia, British Airways, KLM Royal Dutch Airlines, Swissair, and others. Shares databases with **Apollo** and **Gemini** in Canada.

Gallaudet University   Funded by the federal government to provide a liberal higher education for deaf persons. Offers more than 80 undergraduate and graduate programs leading to A.A., A.A.S., B.A., B.S., M.S., Ed.D., and Ph.D. degrees and a program of research relating to deafness. Provides information and publishes books and other materials on deafness. *Contact:* Gallaudet University, 800 Florida Ave., N.E., Washington, DC 20002 (202/651-5000; URL **http://www.gallaudet.edu**).

galley proof   In desktop publishing, a proof of text copy that is checked and edited before being made into pages.

games   Contrived activities, involving goals to be achieved and obstacles to be overcome, that are controlled by rules. In training and development, games are contests and matches used in training to develop management skills, improve technical performance, foster cooperation and teamwork, and improve decision making ability. Applications include leadership and human relations training, military war games, research, problem solving, executive testing and selection, marketing, inventory control, and management and supervisory development.

gaming   *See* games.

Gantt chart   Designed for **management by exception**, a device used in project planning, scheduling, and control. Essentially it is a chart with bars representing subprojects, activities, or tasks in a calendar time coordinate, showing dates of start-up and completion and the status of projects between starts and completion, but not relationships or dependencies as in **program evaluation and review technique** and **critical path method**. As time elapses, the bars are filled in to show the time remaining for completion.

Gantt Medal   *See* The Henry Laurence Gantt Medal.

Gantt plan   An incentive plan that provided for large bonuses (30 percent) when productivity standards were first met but then reduced (1.3 percent) for each 1 percent increase in production. It is not in common use today.

gap analysis   A means of measuring and evaluating how well a company is meeting the needs and expectations of its customers and clients. It is done by intensive market research, involving feedback that is charted or graphed and analyzed to identify specific problems and shortfalls in such areas as promotion, product quality, packaging, on-time delivery, pricing, complaint handling, technical service, and professionalism of sales representatives.

garnishee   The act of attaching funds or property sought to be acquired by garnishment (court action).

garnishment   1. An order issued by a court that requires an employer to deduct a stipulated portion of an employee's pay and deliver it to a creditor to settle a debt. 2. The issuance of a notice to a third party to appear in court.

garnishment order   An order issued by a court or other agency having legal jurisdiction that directs an agency (such as Social Security) or employer withhold a certain amount of benefits or pay each month and either send them to the court or agency or other party to forward them to the person or organization entitled to the payment (such as alimony or child support);or pay the stipulated amount directly to the entitled person or organization. States have established maximums, but in no case can federal maximums be exceeded.

gas chromatography/mass spectrometry (GC/MS)   A laboratory test used to confirm the accuracy of the results of drug testing.

gassbuku   A Japanese term that describes an off-site meeting conducted to break down communication barriers between and among workers and managers to promote and facilitate the exchange of ideas.

gastroenterologist   A medical doctor who specializes in the diagnosis and treatment of digestive disorders ranging from intestinal pain and heartburn to ulcers, liver disease, and cancer.

gate array   On a semiconductor computer **chip**, a matrix of transistors that is uncommitted or unassigned, thereby allowing a programmer to customize logic.

gatekeeper   1. An individual (such as a disability case manager) or group (such as a health-care coalition) given responsibility for controlling costs by carefully managing a patient's therapy to minimize unnecessary or duplicate tests and treatment. Usually a family practitioner, internist, pediatrician, or obstetrician-gynecologist. 2. A person who controls the informal organization and communication network in an organization. Gatekeepers are invariably in contact with other gatekeepers in the organization and, when important information is identified, it is quickly passed along.

gatekeeper system A form of **managed care** in which a primary care case management approach is used to control costs.

gateway A device that connects two incompatible networks and translates and transmits information from one to the other.

gay benefits The extension of heterosexual spousal benefits to homosexual couples.

gay rights See Romer v. Evans.

Gemini In travel management, a Canadian **computer reservation system** consortium owned by Air Canada, Alitalia, British Airways, KLM Royal Dutch Airlines, PWA Corp., Swissair, United Airlines, and USAir.

gender gap The difference between men's and women's pay for the same or comparable jobs. Also called *wage gap.*

gene A fragment or sequence of **deoxyribonucleic acid** that holds the chemical formula for making a specific molecule, usually a **protein**.

General Agreement on Tariffs and Trade (GATT) A 44-year-old treaty that governs international trade among nations. On December 15, 1993, representatives of 117 nations approved an accord to lower tariffs and eliminate other trade barriers. The agreement opened foreign markets to U.S. financial institutions and agricultural products, protected patented computer chips, drugs, and other products, scaled back export subsidies on farm products, phased out protective quotas on textiles and apparel in the U.S. and other countries over 10 years, and created a **World Trade Organization.** In 1994, proposed GATT rules slashed tariffs 40 percent, cut subsidies globally, expanded protection of intellectual property, and set rules for investment and trade in services. and extended global trading rules to such areas as agriculture, services, and intellectual property. The **Pension Benefit Guarantee Corporation** provisions of the bill reduced the deductibility of pension plans and raised corporate premiums for pension plan insurance. The U.S. Congress approved the pact during its 1994 lame duck session, and the legislation was signed by President Clinton on December 8, 1994. The accord became effective July 1, 1995.

general and administrative A category of overhead costs (indirect) — the costs of doing business, such as rent, utilities, office equipment, and the like.

General Aptitude Test Battery (GATB) A battery of tests used by about 35 state and 800 local offices of the U.S. Employment Service for prehiring, selection, and making referrals to businesses. The tests measure candidates' verbal, numerical, perceptual, and psychomotor skills.

general corporation The most common type of business structure, a profit-making venture that can have an unlimited number of stockholders/owners. Stockholders' liability is usually limited to the amount of investment in the business. Requires considerable record keeping. Also called a *C corporation.*

General Educational Development (GED) Test A test used to establish high school equivalency. Successful testees are awarded a certificate that qualifies them for admission to many postsecondary institutions and makes them eligible for federal student aid programs.

general inclusion group (GIG) In workplace improvement, GIGs consist of groups of employees such as quality circles, problem solving teams, semiautonomous work groups, employee involvement groups, and so on. Attributed to Stanley M. Herman, management consultant (*Training,* "Lost in the System,"January 1990).

generalist As differentiated from a specialist, a manager who either wears more than one hat or who has the capability to perform more than one enterprise function.

generally accepted accounting principles (GAAP) Broad rules, specific rules, and commonly applied conventions relating to the measurement, classification, and disclosure of financial activities, events, and transactions.

general manager (GM) The hotel functionary responsible for overall policy making, has fiduciary responsibility for the property, manages daily operations of all departments, and serves as the ultimate hotel authority on problems and issues.

General Rule A tax rule that took effect with the repeal of the **Three-Year Rule** for recovery of annuity payments until an employee's total contributions to a federal retirement plan were recovered. Under the **Tax Reform Act of 1986,** all but a small percentage of the annuity is taxed beginning with the first annuity payment.

general schedule (GS) The salary classification system used by the federal government. It ranges from GS-1 to GS-18.

General Services Administration (GSA)
The federal agency responsible for procuring generic or common goods and services for government offices and agencies. A good source of help in locating specific government buyers and completing contracting paperwork. *Contact:* GSA, 17th and D. St., S.W., Washington, DC 20407 (202/501-0800; Fax 202/219-1243; E-mail **public.affairs@gsa.gov** or **webmaster@gsa.gov**; URL **http://gsa.gov**).

general session   In conference and meeting planning, a session at which all registrants are entitled to be present.

Generation X   People born in the late 1950s and '60s who will inherit the world's largest debt and a failing educational system. Sometimes called the **twentysomething generation** or **Xers.** Attributed to Douglas Copeland (*Generation X: Tales for an Accelerated Culture*).

generative learning   Learning that is undertaken to change in accordance with what might occur; to anticipate and react to an expected change. For example, a company is using generative learning when it forecasts and prepares for new client requirements. Also called *predictive learning.*

generic analysis   A means of analyzing an emerging operational system to collect data for the development of a cost-effective and instructionally efficient training system while the operational system is being built. It makes use of a **generic database**. Analysis of current capabilities enables the analyst to develop preliminary task listings and objectives and, following refinement, to identify alternative instructional strategies with associated cost and personnel development factors.

generic database   Data derived from analysis of information available from existing operational systems that perform functions similar to that of an emerging system.

generic drug   A drug that is sold under its chemical name. For example, Ibuprofen is the generic name for Motrin. Generic drugs are required by law to meet the same standards of purity, effectiveness, and strength, and they are usually less expensive than their **brand name drug** counterpart. *See also* formulary drug.

generic skills   A term applied to certain skills believed to be associated with a particular level of management, such as first-line supervision, middle management, and top management.

genetaceuticals   Pharmaceuticals for disorders associated with aging, such as Alzheimer's disease, cystic fibrosis, Lou Gehrig's disease, multiple sclerosis, and osteoporosis.

genetic, developmental, and growth studies   Long-term investigation of the origin, direction, trend, rate, pattern, limit, and decline of growth. Its purpose is to identify causes, interrelationships, and patterns of development among such factors as attitudes, computational ability, experiential background, habits and procedures in problem-solving, interests, learning procedures, length and intensity of instruction, materials of instruction, mental age, methods of instruction, motivation, needs, physiological age, reading ability, social maturity, and socioeconomic status.

genetic testing   Includes several technologies used to detect genetic traits, changes in chromosomes, or changes in **deoxyribonucleic acid** (DNA). Used in the workplace by some companies to screen applicants for predispositions to certain conditions, reduce workers' compensation claims, monitor employees who are frequently exposed to chemicals on the job, and detect and treat conditions in their initial stages to avoid catastrophic medical bills. Such testing raises the issue of employee privacy. In any case, testing should be voluntary and results should be confidential.

genuine assessment
See performance assessment.

geographical grouping
See location grouping.

geographical information system (GIS)
A technology that combines the techniques of automated mapping systems and statistical analysis. GIS provides a means of automatically viewing, analyzing, and correlating data in a new and easily understandable format.

geriatrician   A doctor of medicine who specializes in the diagnosis and treatment of illnesses and ailments associated with aging.

gerontologist   An expert on the aging process and the problems of older persons. Formerly found only on college faculties and the staffs of institutes, growing numbers are appearing on the staffs of corporate training centers where they are assigned the tasks of sensitizing employees to the needs of older customers and clients and tailoring products and services to the requirements of seniors.

Gestalt psychology The school of psychology that sees behavior as a function of perceptions and expectations and emphasizes the tendency of the human mind to organize perceptions into "wholes" by completing patterns from available stimuli. Human behavior is viewed as being composed of the cognitive field of the individual, life space with its opportunities, challenges, and barriers. The theory emphasizes the importance of reorganizing, restructuring, and regrouping and the individual's responsibility for making choices and for his or her own behavior.

gestural systems Visual means of communicating with people who are deaf or hard of hearing. Uses pointing and natural gestures. No equipment or materials are needed, and they are easily learned and readily interpreted by both people with disabilities and nondisabled workers. In recent years, an attempt has been made to create a universal system of gesturing called *Gesticula,* but it has been slow to catch on because most deaf people prefer to communicate in their own country's sign language.

ghost card A means of controlling travel and entertainment expenses. Involves charging air travel expenses to an account number at an agency instead of issuing individual cards to employees. The company pays all expenses in a negotiated time period (from 10 to 60 days after billing. Offered by such card services as Air Travel Card, American Express, Citicorp Diners, enRoute, MasterCard, and Visa.

GI Bill *See* Montgomery GI Bill.

gift splitting Occurs when a spouse joins his or her spouse to use the annual $10,000 per year gift tax exclusion so that $20,000 is available as a gift exclusion amount, even though the property given belongs solely to one spouse.

gigabyte A measure of the storage capacity of a computer. It is equal to 1,000 megabytes.

Gilmer v. Interstate/Johnson Lane Corp.
A 1991 Supreme Court decision that supported the growing use of **alternative dispute resolution procedures** to solve employee conflicts. The Court held that a claim under the Age Discrimination in Employment Act of 1967 is subject to binding arbitration based on an agreement an employee signed with his former employer.

Ginnie Mae *See* Government National Mortgage Association.

Gissel bargaining order (GBO) A **National Labor Relations Board** directive that requires an employer to bargain with a union that has never won an election. Said to be a potential adverse consequence of a finding that an employee participation plan is unlawful.

giveback A benefit, usually one with low monetary value, that the employer requires employees — whether in groups or unions — to surrender to achieve cost savings. Examples are Christmas parties, personalized stationery or notepads, magazine subscriptions, health club memberships, and use of company cars.

glass ceiling The bias barrier that keeps many women from advancing beyond middle management positions into the executive suite.

Glass Ceiling Act of 1991 Short title for Title II of the Civil Rights Act of 1991. The legislation was designed to raise public awareness of the underrepresentation of women and minorities in line functions in the U.S. work force, eliminate barriers to their advancement, and promote work force diversity.

Glass Ceiling Commission A 19-member commission established by the Civil Rights Act of 1991 to conduct a 15-month study of the underrepresentation of women and minorities in the executive, management, and senior decision making positions in business (URL **http://www.ilr.cornell.edu/library/e_archive.GlassCeiling/**)

glaucoma A disease of the optic nerve and a leading causes of blindness in the U.S. Some cases are hereditary and some are due to complications of other eye disorders. Still others cases are due to injuries, certain drugs tumors, inflammation, and abnormal blood vessels. The transparent fluid inside the forward part of the eye does not drain normally, excess pressure builds up within the eye, and the optic nerve is damaged.

global A way of organizing a business across national boundaries in which the company operates on a global scale and attempts to deliver standardized products and services using global human, materiel, and financial resources. Reserved to describe companies that integrate all employees in overseas ventures and establish multicultural teams. *See also* multinational.

global distribution system In travel management, a reservation system that provides uniform and reliable travel booking services throughout the world without regard to country, CRS, or travel agency.

global fee In health care reimbursement, a flat rate that encompasses more than one type of service; for example, a global fee for surgery may include all pre- and postoperative care.

globalization Operating a company without regard to international borders. Instead of exporting goods and services from their "home" countries, firms go where their customers and clients are, and, using foreign nationals, they establish manufacturing and service facilities to serve those customers. That is, they produce, sell, and service their customers from foreign facilities rather than export those products and services from the U.S.

global learning system New courses and other forms of learning systems designed to meet the standards, requirements, and demands of another culture.

Global Paragon Awards Recognize innovation and creativity in meetings sponsored by **Meeting Professionals International**. Entrants are judged in the areas of goals, content, logistics, and results for meetings held between July 1 and June 30 of the preceding year. *Contact:* MPI, Infomart, 1950 Stemmons Freeway, Ste. 5018, Dallas, TX 75207-3109 (214/712-7700).

global pricing In health care, a reimbursement system in which the provider is paid a fixed price for medical products and services for one incidence of illness. Payment includes hospital costs, the primary physician, specialists, surgeon, anesthesiologist, and any other changes incurred by the patient.

global rotational opportunities A means of developing international executives and a strategy for ensuring that employees selected for international assignments do not fail. Typically, participants receive both formal and on-the -job training and spend six months to two years on an assignment so that they can experience a different culture and work environment.

global system for mobile communications (GSM) A digital wireless technology service that carries a subscriber's data in a subscriber identity module or "smartcard," which is inserted into the phone to activate service.

global travel manager Typically a senior-level corporate travel position. The incumbent is responsible for developing and managing worldwide travel operations.

glocal The aspiration of companies to achieve a global posture and presence and, at the same time, satisfy the demands of domestic preferences.

goal A statement of desired long-term outcomes or results — of what an organization wants to accomplish and where it wants to be five or more years down the road. Goals are typically qualitative rather than quantitative. They identify the kind, direction, and degree of change, improvement, or results sought in all programs, services, and activities. Goals provide guidelines for critical organizational programs and activities and ensure that attention and resources are focused on important ends. *See also* objective.

goal congruence That state or condition where there is general agreement among executives, managers, staffers, and employees on the purposes, goals and direction of the organization.

Goals 2000: Educate America Act of 1994 An education plan signed into law by President Clinton March 31, 1994. The Act established a National Skills Standards Board to set educational standards as well as identify broad clusters of occupations for which skill standards are to be developed. The legislation also requires participating states to develop, but not implement, education reform plans that set voluntary standards for U.S. schools and certification for job training programs. It focuses on improved curriculum, student performance, professional development for teachers, increased parental and community involvement, increased flexibility of regulations and greater accountability for schools.

goal-setting theory The motivation theory that suggests that the way to maintain the motivation of all employees is to set difficult but specific and attainable goals and provide feedback on goal accomplishment.

going postal A euphemism for violence in the workplace. It alludes to the rash of violent acts, including murders and assaults, perpetrated by Postal Service employees against their fellow workers

gold-collar workers Scientists, engineers, and other professional workers in short supply who are paid premium salaries to attract and retain them.

golden carrots Incentive programs that involve the use of such inducements to motivation and productivity as company stock, scholarships, all-expense-paid vacations, and "This Is Your Career" home videos.

golden handcuffs A means of retaining key employees, incentives and benefits (such as salary increases or participation in stock option plans) that are tied to continued employment with an organization. Termination of employment for any reason would result in forfeiture of the benefit or incentive.

golden handshake *See* early retirement incentive program.

golden parachute Lucrative severance salary and benefits contractual packages drawn up in advance and activated and awarded to senior executives upon a change in corporate control and at least one of several other triggering circumstances established by Congress in 1984. Examples are the official's subsequent termination without cause by the combined company, reduction in the official's responsibilities, or mandatory relocation. Benefits typically provide for an increase in or acceleration of payments or vesting or other rights of the employee.

golden passport A master of business administration degree from a prestigious graduate school of business, which is often assumed to be the credential for high-level CEO/COO positions, high salaries, and perks.

Gold Awards Annual awards presented to **Convention & Visitors Bureaus** and commercial meeting facilities and services by *Meetings & Conventions* magazine based on the judgments of M&C subscribers. Three classes of awards are made: (1) The Gold Service Award is presented to Convention & Visitors Bureaus that demonstrate professionalism, dedication, and service to corporate, incentive and association meeting planners; (2) the Gold Key is presented to properties that show consistent excellence in serving the meetings industry; and (3) the Gold Platter Award recognizes food and beverage departments that provide outstanding levels of quality, creativity and professionalism. *Contact: M&C,* 500 Plaza Dr., Secaucus, NJ 07094-3626 (201-902-1700; Fax 201-319-1796).

go/no-go standard The point in a training program at which trainees must demonstrate that they have acquired the knowledge and skills needed to progress further in the program or graduate, or receive remedial instruction, or be eliminated.

good cause In union-management relations, a term often used to identify the standard by which employers must justify their disciplinary actions.

Goods and Services/General Services Tax (GST) A form of national sales tax that went into effect in January 1991. It levied a 7 percent tax on all all goods and services bought or sold in Canada (and additional GST of up to 7 percent from individual provinces), The tax affected exhibitors and show managers who have to pay the tax on rental of Canadian exhibit halls and other goods and services. Exhibitors have to pay the tax on space rental, booth rental, and any goods or services. However, exhibitors and meeting organizers may claim a refund on hotel accommodations (for stays of less than one month), meeting rooms, exhibit space, convention show services, audio-visual services, photography services, electrical services, moving services, accounting and legal services, destination management companies, security services, speakers and educational seminars, seminar materials, newsletter services, business equipment, exhibit design and display, and transportation into and out of Canada. Not included for rebates are food and beverages, tobacco, entertainment, car rentals, and other transportation not directly related to the meeting or convention. Planners also have to collect taxes paid on goods and services that they sell at Canadian trade shows before applying for rebates. In 1996 a change in the law required nonresident corporations (and not individual travelers) to file for a refund of eligible taxes paid by all of their employees in Canada and have the refund sent to the company. A reclaim form, "Tax Refund Application for Visitors," is available in most hotels and shops. For more information, call 613/996-7861. For information and rebate forms: in Toronto, 416/954-0473; in Montreal, 514/426-8293; in Ottawa, 613/990-8584.

good faith bargaining In labor-management negotiations, serious and determined attempts on the part of both parties to negotiate and reach reasonable and mutually acceptable terms on issues in question.

good faith effort strategy or system
An approach to achieving results in affirmative action programs that involves changing policies and practices that have tended to contribute to the exclusion or underutilization of members of protected groups (minorities and females), such as advertising vacancies to reach minorities, providing child day care services, and establishing basic skills programs.

Good Samaritan laws   Passed by most states, the laws protect individuals or groups from liability if they provide assistance to people; for example, giving first aid to victims of an accident or donating food to the homeless (soup kitchens, detoxification centers, day care facilities, and so on), although there are certain laws that must be respected, such as keeping hot food hot and cold food cold.

gopher   On the **Internet,** a database of textual information organized by menus. Designed by the University of Minnesota, the computer search system lets Internet users scan for text and data files in large mainframe computers, particularly at college and university sites.

gothic   In topography, usually refers to sans **serif** type designs, but sometimes applied to black letter types.

gout   A form of **arthritis** caused by an accumulation of uric acid in the body, which migrates to the joints where it forms crystals that cause inflammation and pain. It affects about 1 million Americans.

government benefits program   A benefits program supported by the federal government — although some are cooperative programs with state governments and many are administered by state public assistance offices. In addition to Social Security, other benefits programs include **Supplemental Security Income,** unemployment insurance, food stamps, child support enforcement, family and child welfare services, workers' compensation, veterans' benefits, railroad workers' retirement, help for the blind, and other special programs.

government contract laws   *See* Armed Forces Procurement Act of 1947; Contract Work Hours and Safety Standards Act of 1962; Davis-Bacon Acts of 1931 and 1964; Drug-Free Workplace Act of 1988; McNamara-O'Hara Service Contract Act of 1965; Walsh-Healy Public Contracts Act of 1936.

Government National Mortgage Association (GNMA)   An organization that issues government-backed securities (called Ginnie Maes) that typically yield from one to two percentage points more than a 10-year U.S. Treasury Bond yet carry the same "full and faith" credit guarantee by the federal government as to timely repayment of principal and interest. By helping to ensure that mortgage funds are available throughout the country, Ginnie Mae has been instrumental in eliminating regional differences in the availability of mortgage credit for American families and assuring mortgage capital for government housing programs. Ginnie Mae links the capital and Federal housing markets by facilitating secondary market activities for federally insured housing.. *Contact:* GNMA, 451 Seventh St., NW, Washington, DC 20410-9000 (703/918-3907; URL **http://www.ginniemae.gov**).

Government Pension Offset (GPO)   Reduction or elimination of Social Security benefits payments to federal workers or retirees who first became eligible to retire December 1982 or later. Enacted in 1977 and became effective in December 1982, Two-thirds of the amount of government annuity the retiree is eligible for is used to offset whatever Social Security the spouse (wife, husband, widow, or widower) benefit is payable. Several exemptions apply: (1) anyone eligible for a government annuity before December 1982 and meets the 1977 law requirements; (2) anyone who is a federal survivor annuitant; (3) anyone eligible for a government annuity before July 1, 1983 and received one-half support from the male or female spouse; (4) **Federal Employee Retirement System** employees and **Civil Service Retirement System** employees who transferred to FERS; and (5) former CR-SRS employees rehired beginning January 1, 1984 following a separation of one year or more.

graded vesting   A **vesting schedule** in which vesting occurs over a period of 5 to 15 years: 25 percent vesting after 5 years of service, plus 5 percent for each additional year of service up to 10 years and 50 percent vesting after 10 years, plus an additional 10 percent for each year thereafter.

grade point average (GPA) An index of student achievement. It is calculated through the following steps: (1) multiply the grade point value (numerical grade awarded) by the number of credits for each course, (2) take the products of those multiplications and add them up; (3) add up the total number of credits, and (4) divide the sum of the products of the grade point values and credits (see step 2) by the sum of the credits (see step 3). For example: Where the grade point value for an A is 4.0, for a B+ is 3.3, for a C is 2.0, for a C– is 1.7, and for a D is 1.3:

Grade point value	Credits earned
4.0 × 3	= 12.0
3.3 × 3	= 9.9
2.0 × 3	= 6.0
1.7 × 3	= 5.1
1.3 × 3	= 3.9
	36.9

36.9 (total from step 2) divided by 15 (total from step 3 = 2.46 (grade point average)

graduated benefits Health care or other employee benefit plans in which the amount contributed by the employer is determined by the number of years the worker has been employed by the company, so shorter-term workers pay more for their coverage than those who have been with the company for many years.

Graduate Record Examination (GRE) A series of aptitude and achievement tests administered by the **Educational Testing Service** of Princeton, NJ to applicants for admission to graduate schools. Registrants must take three morning tests that measure verbal, quantitative, and analytical aptitude and an afternoon test that assesses achievement in the registrant's major field of undergraduate study. Scores on the tests are reported to the registrant and to the admissions offices of graduate schools selected by the registrant.

grampies Describes the Growing number of people over 60 who are Retired, Active, Monied People In an Excellent State. They are seen as an overlooked source of workers. Attributed to marketing expert Sandra Van der Merve.

grandiose delusion In mental illness, a **delusion** in which the subject believes himself or herself possessed of great wealth, intelligence, importance, power, and the like.

grandparent caregiver A form of nontraditional household. Shared living arrangements in which grandparents care for their grandchildren. Caused by greater distances between family members, higher housing costs, deaths and divorces, less secure retirement, and increased numbers of older Americans.

grandpa track High achieving, seasoned, and valued executives, senior managers, scientists, and engineers who have decided to leave the fast track and pursue a less stressful and more leisurely work pace and life style. They have opted for less job pressure, fewer responsibilities, and more time for family, friends, community, and other interests. Companies have begun to accommodate these employees by implementing human resources policies to prevent them from leaving. Policies include elimination of responsibilities, **flexible work options**, home-based work, **job engineering**, **sabbatical leaves**, unpaid leave with full benefits, and personal leave.

granny dumping The practice of abandoning elderly family members at hospital emergency rooms (or other public places) when their relatives no longer feel that that can (or want to) care for them.

grant A sum of money given to an individual or organization that does not have to be paid back.

granted entitlements Benefits given by Congress on the basis of need or for some other policy purpose, such as Aid to Dependent Children, food stamps, Medicaid, unemployment insurance, and farm subsidies.

grantor The person who creates a **trust** and names a **trustee(s),** and **beneficiaries.** Also called a *settlor, donor,* or *creator.*

grantor-retained annuity trust (GRAT) A means of avoiding estate taxes and gift taxes by putting an investment portfolio into an irrevocable trust. For example, a parent could transfer $200,000 to an irrevocable trust with his or her children as beneficiaries. The trust would provide that a specified percentage of the initial value of the assets, for example 8 or 10 percent, is to be paid out each year to the donor for a definite time. Substantial gift-tax savings would accrue because the gift tax would only be paid on a fraction of what is placed in the trust. At the end of the period the trust terminates, and the remaining assets are distributed to the beneficiaries with no further gift or estate tax. However, if the parent should die before the expiration of the trust, the trust's assets would be included in the estate and taxed.

grapevine An informal communication network or system that operates in most organizations, the grapevine consists of irregular channels by which information, including scuttlebutt and rumors, is passed from one person to another. Its importance lies in what is being transmitted and why rather than in who is on it or how it works.

graphic aids Pictures, drawings, illustrations, photographs, blueprints, templates, chalkboards, bulletin boards, easels, magnetic placards, embossograph placards, maps, charts, diagrams, and flip charts used in training or other forms of communication.

graphical user interface (GUI) Provides users at work stations the ability to interact with software visually; i.e., using a mouse to drag icons representing data from a mainframe window to a work station window. Examples are Apple's Macintosh Interface, Microsoft's Windows 3.x environment for DOS and X Windows for UNIX.

graphic data display See area chart; horizontal bar chart; line chart; pie chart; vertical bar chart.

graphic design The processes of creating and assembling material that is readable, pleasing to the eye, and visually logical for input to and manipulation by a computer and output of the final product is hard copy. It is performed by talented and experienced artisans or practitioners using desktop publishing or software for electronic print production.

Graphic Interchange Format (GIF) The most common format for graphic images on the **Internet**.

graphic item count (GIC) A technique used to analyze individual test items to determine where a multiple-choice test or a subgroup of testees went wrong. GIC is the first step in determining the difficulty of an item. It identifies and tabulates the number of testees selecting each of the alternative answers to every test item.

graphics Drawings, diagrams, photographs, transparencies, graphs, maps, and other materials used as illustrations in documents, books, handouts, projected visuals, videotapes and cassettes, and live presentations and television.

graphics-based training A computer-based interactive training system that employs computerized touch-graphics as the primary training vehicle.

graphic scale A rating scale that combines both numerical scales and adjectives (or descriptive phrases) that describe theoretically equally spaced degrees of performance placed below a horizontal line. The length of the line represents the full range of the ability, performance, or trait to be rated.

graphic scanner An electronic device used in the printing process to make color and tone-corrected color separations and in desk-top publishing to convert drawings and photographs to computer-usable form. There are two types: line art scanners used for black-and-white drawings and lettering and continuous tone scanners that can handle photographs, shaded drawings, and color.

graphics technology Computer hardware and software that allow desktop publishers, designers, and artists to create original art and photographers to retouch or manipulate photos quickly and inexpensively.

graphoanalysis Assessing character traits by analyzing handwriting. It is used much more often in the hiring process in Europe than in the United States.

grass See marijuana.

gray marketing Marketing and sale of a supplier's products by an unauthorized distributor.

Gray Panthers An activist coalition of about 70,000 young and elderly members and supporters founded by Maggie Kuhn in 1970 to eradicate ageism, or discrimination on the basis of age. A primary objective of the group's research, organization, picketing, demonstrating, and lobbying activities has been to cause a revolutionary change in social attitudes toward older people and how private institutions and government agencies deal with older Americans. Campaigns have been aimed at nursing homes, retirement developers, and mass-transit systems, and the organization has worked to ban mandatory retirement, expand job opportunities, and improve housing and medical care for the elderly.

green A person or industry that is environmentally responsible.

green card A permit issued by the U.S. Immigration and Naturalization Service that entitles an alien to permanent residency and employment in the United States. Unless revoked for cause, an alien admitted for "lawful permanent residence" can stay in the United States indefinitely, work anywhere, travel in and out of the country freely, and sponsor qualifying relatives for immigrant visas.

green circle   Used in job plotting charts to highlight an employee who is paid below the minimum of the salary grade set for the job.

green executives   Senior executives in service and consumer-goods companies given responsibility for developing and implementing corporate environmental policies to avoid litigation and Environmental Protection Agency-imposed penalties, improve their image, cash in on the "green" marketing boom, and nurture the earth.

green fund   *See* green tax.

green guest rooms   Environmentally clean hotel rooms that have purer air and water than standard rooms. Special air filters remove smoke, dust, pollen, and other impurities and filters on shower heads and lavatories make tap water pure and drinkable. Some hotels charge extra for these rooms.

green loan   A bank loan offered to help corporate or individual borrowers meet legally binding environmental standards, such as asbestos removal, septic system up-grading, underground fuel tank disposal, lead paint removal, pollution cleanup, and access for people with disabilities.

green mail   The strategy of buying a large amount of stock in a company so that management, suspecting a takeover attempt, will buy it back at a premium price.

green manufacturing   Production of consumer goods that are ecologically friendly or environmentally benign, such as biodegradable packaging and environmentally harmless products.

green marketing   Marketing and selling products that are ecologically safe or environmentally harmless.

Green Seal of Approval   Awarded by a non-profit organization funded by donors that attests that the product has been tested by environmental experts and examines the product life-cycle from raw materials and manufacture to usage, recycling, and disposal. The Seal certifies that the product is ecologically safe.

green rooms   Hotel rooms with water systems that filter out chlorine, iron, sulfur, and other contaminants and air-cleaning systems that remove pollen.

green tax   A tax levy, usually 1 or 2 percent, added to purchases of environmental goods or services to fund measures such as lake and river cleanup, bike paths, biodegradable refuse bags, recycling, and so on.

green training   Training for executives and managers in environmental awareness. It is designed to educate personnel on the things they can do to become environmentally sensitive. In some companies these executives have made wholesale changes in marketing strategies and increased corporate spending to improve the environment.

grey fare   A ticketing practice that exploits fare loopholes, such as **back-to-back ticketing, hidden city fare**, and **meeting fare**. Considered illegal by some airlines and unethical by some companies, but as smart cost reduction strategies by other organizations.

grid training   An approach to team building developed by Blake and Mouton. Based on a "managerial grid" representing several possible leadership styles (depending upon whether the manager is more concerned with people or production), the four-phase program (which may extend over a period of three to five years) aims to develop 9,9 managers — people who are equally concerned about people and production.

grievance   A dispute, claim, complaint, or allegation by an employee or group of employees that a violation, misinterpretation, or misapplication of a provision of the collective bargaining agreement (union contract) has occurred.

grievance procedure   A carefully worded description of the process to be followed by grievants, the union, and management in resolving grievances. The grievance procedure is made a part of the collective bargaining greement or contract and contains the various steps (up to six or more), time limits for each step, and specific rules.

Griggs v. Duke Power   A case tried before the U.S. Supreme Court in 1971, relating to the issue of employment tests, in which the Court stated that **Title VII** of the Civil Rights Act of 1964 focused on the consequences of employment practices and not their intent. Although the Court criticized testing in general, it left companies free to use tests, but it banned tests that have an **adverse impact** on a **protected class** unless they can be demonstrated to be job-performance-related.

gross domestic product (GDP)
An economic indicator that in 1991 replaced (by the Commerce Department) the **gross national product** (GNP) as the primary measure of how well the U.S. economy is doing. The GDP measures all the goods and services produced by labor and property located in the U.S. As long as the labor and property are located in the United States, the suppliers (the workers and, for property, the owners) may be either U.S. residents or the residents of other countries. The change makes the economic indicator compatible with those of most other countries; however, for the U.S. the dollar levels of GDP and GNP differ little. The receipts from foreigners less payments to foreigners of **factor income** have been small mainly due to the fact that the value of the property owned abroad by U.S. residents (U.S. investment abroad) less the value of property owned by foreigners in the U.S. (foreign investment in the U.S.) has been small relative to to the size of the U.S. economy (and the value of labor supplied to and by foreigners is even smaller). In some countries the difference between GDP and GNP is much larger. In December 1995, the Commerce Department's Bureau of Economic analysis made major changes in the way it calculates the GDP to correct flaws in the method of calculation. Instead of using certain "fixed-weight" measures of economic output, the BEA switched to what it calls a "chain-weighted" GDP. For example, instead of measuring the production of a certain item at an index pegged to 1987 prices, the new calculation uses a weighted measure that is closer to current prices. As a consequence, productivity drops and yields a slower growth in GDP than under the old method of calculation.

gross estate   The value of all of a decedent's property, regardless of location, to the extent of his or her equity at the time of death.

grossing up   **1.** Paying the recipient of an incentive award additional money so that he or she can pay the taxes. However, the employee, customer, or independent contractor who

receives the award and the additional money must pay taxes on the total amount received. *See also* incentive travel. **2.** In computing estate taxes of non-residents, the practice of valuing the whole estate of the decedent, regardless of the location of the properties, and then determining the percentage of the property located in each state and applying that percentage to what would have been the estate tax if the decedent had died a domiciliary of the state making the calculation.

grossly retarded   *See* severely retarded.

gross margin (GM)   A measure used in direct costing. Gross margin is the difference between marginal costs (variable or controllable costs) and sales revenue.

$$GM = \text{sales revenue} - \text{marginal costs}$$

gross national product (GNP) An economic indicator, a measure of the performance of a nation's economy or production. GNP is the market value of all the goods and services produced produced by labor and property supplied by U.S. residents whether located in the United States or abroad. To be included, there must be current production as well as a market transaction; therefore, transfer payments (such as receipt of a pension or capital gain) or goods and services produced for one's own use are not included in the GNP. To move from gross national product to **gross domestic product**, one must subtract **factor income** receipts from foreigners, which represent the goods and service produced abroad using the labor and property supplied by U.S. residents, and add factor income payments to foreigners, which represent the goods and services produced in the United States using labor and property supplied by foreigners.

gross profit (GP)   In costing and pricing, it is the difference between total cost (fixed and variable) of goods sold from sales revenue.

$$GP = \text{sales revenue} - (\text{fixed costs} + \text{variable costs})$$

ground operator   *See* destination management company.

group annuity   An annuity that provides benefits to a group of plan participants under a single contract between the employer and the insurer.

group assessment   *See* assessment center.

group auto insurance Employer-sponsored purchase of auto insurance referred to as mass merchandising by the insurance industry. The employer selects the insurance carrier and chooses an insurance agent to handle the enrollment. There are two forms: franchise group and true group programs. In the former, each employee is individually underwritten by the insurance company, pays individual premium rates, and receives an individual policy. With true group programs, participation is based on conditions relating to employment without individual underwriting. The employer selects the benefits, which are provided to all participants, and enters into a contract with the carrier. Participants are issued certificates.

group benefit plan accounting *See* batch processing; transaction-based valuation.

group college benefits Providing employees with a range of services, such as college entrance and financing advice and assistance. Includes on-site workshops, individual consultations with professional advisors, personalized reports on schools that match a student's academic abilities, interests, and needs, and admission essay tips, in addition to financial aid estimates.

group bonus A bonus paid to all members of a work team or task force based on outstanding performance or productivity as a group.

group/convention fare A special air fare offered to large groups of travelers.

group decision support system (GDSS) A system that uses especially designed, interactive computer hardware and software to structure and facilitate ideation, brainstorming, and decision making. Used by human resource professionals to lead successful group or team sessions.

group dynamics **1.** The social processes by which people interact face-to-face in small groups — circles of people who are interacting with regard to a common, explicit goal. **2.** A view of leadership as the property of a group or organization, not of a particular person (the structured or imposed leader) but as a set of functions which, under ideal conditions, become distributed within the group.

group (event charge) card A payment system vehicle designed for corporate meeting planners to help them manage group and meeting expenditures. Such cards enable corporations to track expenses by geographical region, department, meeting planner, or event and track spending by vendor or destination.

group facilitator An HR/HRD competency involving skills in working with groups in either training or problem solving situations.

Group Health Association of America (GHAA) An organization concerned with developing alternatives to the way medical services traditionally have been delivered and financed. GHAA also provides its members with legislative representation, legal counsel, educational programs, research, and publications. *Contact:* GHAA, 1129 20th Street, NW, Ste. 600, Washington, DC 20036 (202/778-3200; E-mail **webmaster@ health.org**; URL **http:www.health.org**).

group health coverage Health care coverage for which a person or covered dependent is eligible because of employment by, membership in, or connection with a particular organization or group that provides payment for hospital, medical, dental, or other health care services or supplies.

group home *See* licensed group home.

group incentives A type of compensation program built around bonuses awarded to small groups or work teams based on their performance. They are typically tied to a company's strategic goals and objectives or productivity measures.

group interview **1.** A method of collecting job data in which a large number of job incumbents is called together to provide information about their jobs. A trained job analyst asks questions designed to elicit job performance data. Following the interview the job analyst combines the data into a single composite job schedule. **2.** An employment interview conducted by a small group of the prospective employee's peers. The format is usually structured and designed to allow the candidate to demonstrate how he or she relates to people. **3.** A training technique involving a 30- to 50-minute dialogue scheduled and conducted between an expert in the field or topic under study and a group of trainees. Interviews are conducted to clarify and analyze problems and issues, to obtain authoritative information, opinion, and impressions on issues, and to set the stage for follow-on learning activities. Interviewees are informed in advance of the kinds of question they are likely to be asked.

group legal care *See* group legal plan.

group legal benefits *See* group legal plan.

group legal plan A type of ancillary benefit illegal in some states but supported by some large unions as a way of ensuring that their members will be able to protect their rights. Such plans provide employees prepaid legal assistance with such problems as wills, divorce, accidents, purchasing a home, and traffic matters, supported in whole or in part by the employer. Sometimes tied in with employee assistance plans.

group legal services (GLS) *See* group legal plan.

group life insurance A type of life insurance policy often provided by organizations to their employees either without cost or at lower premium rates than would be available to individuals. Its main function is to provide death benefits, usually two or three times salary.

group model HMO A type of **health maintenance organization** in which group practices are contracted to provide care to members of the plan. The HMO rents the services of the physicians in a separate group practice and pays the group a per capita rate. The physician group distributes the payment among its members and manages the practices of its physicians.

Group of Seven (G-7) An economic and financial alliance of the seven largest industrial nations: Canada, Germany, Great Britain, Italy, Japan, and the United States. In 1997, Russia was invited to participate but not as a full-fledged member.

group outplacement A cost-cutting approach to the provision of outplacement services to employees, including senior- and middle-level workers, who are losing their jobs because of corporate downsizing. Rather than individual counseling, employees are given assistance in small, goal-oriented groups.

group pension plan A type of pension plan in which employers (and sometimes employees) make set contributions to a pension fund.

group practice **1.** Three or more physicians who deliver patient care, make joint use of facilities, equipment, and support personnel, and divide their income by a prearranged formula. **2.** A training technique in which the instructor leads trainees through a series of questions and answers relating to the current lesson by either calling on volunteers or requiring choral responding (the group calls out answers in unison).

group practice health maintenance organization (GPHMO) An HMO that contracts with teams of multidisciplinary physicians in private practice who agree to provide health care to plan members, often in collaboration with their continuing private practices. GPHMOs deliver a wide range of services at one location and provide inpatient services through affiliated hospitals.

group practice without walls (GPWW) A form of health care delivery system that does not require the participation of a hospital. It is composed of private practice physicians who agree to combine their practices into a single legal entity but who continue to practice medicine in their independent locations. Also known as a *clinic without walls.*

group process Deals with how a task force or work group functions, the roles of the leader, facilitator, members, and resource persons, their actions and interactions, rather than the actual problems, issues, or content addressed.

groupthink The results of a leader's abuse of power and encouragement of group members to defer totally, deluding themselves into believing that the leader is infallible, and becoming blind to opposing points of view or irrefutable evidence contrary to their position. Attributed to Irving L. Janis of Yale University (*Victims of Groupthink*, Boston: Houghton Mifflin, 1972).

group universal life plan (GULP) An extension of group universal life insurance that combines term protection for beneficiaries with an investment element for the policyholder. Such plans are financed by employees' after-tax payroll deduction contributions. Excess contributions may go into an investment fund that earns on a tax-deferred basis, and earnings can be used to pay premiums. Participation is entirely voluntary.

group videoconferencing Systems that can accommodate large groups (as many as 16 users) and up to eight concurrent meetings and allows simultaneous networking of digital networks in a single call. Computer graphics can be displayed on one high-resolution monitor while video can be seen on another monitor. Essentially these systems are miniature video studios controlled by computer.

groupware Computer software that expands the concept of **electronic mailbox/mail** by including group management elements such as communication and interaction, document preparation and tracking, **project management** and record keeping, and scheduling. Permits sharing of databases among computers and team collaboration over time.

grumps Grown-up, mature professionals. They are former, and now aging **yuppies** (young urban professionals), and are now a large marketing target.

guarantee In contracts with hotels or other properties for meetings, the number of meals to be paid for, whether or not they are actually consumed.

Guaranteed Access to Education (GATE) A private pilot student loan program now becoming available. The plan requires no up-front fee and features deferral of interest charges (varying from 8 to 9.75 percent) until after graduation and a 13-year repayment schedule with low monthly obligations the first five years. Participating colleges and universities (named the National Collegiate Trust) pooled loans into a bond issue that was sold to pension funds and other institutional investors.

guarantee agency Under federal student aid programs, a state organization that administers Federal Family Education Loans. Although the federal government sets loan limits and interest rates, these state agencies establish additional limitations within federal guidelines. For further information call the Federal Student Aid Information Center at 800-433-3243

guaranteed annual income Consists of payments made by an employer when a plant must be shut down for equipment repair or replacement and is in addition to unemployment benefits.

guaranteed annual wage (GAW) A compensation plan that guarantees a minimum annual income to employees.

guaranteed investment contract (GIC) A type of defined benefit plan issued by life insurance companies. A funding plan vehicle for annuity contracts. GICs pay a fixed interest rate on a specified deposit for a defined

period of time (typically one to six years) and most are carried under book value. Benefits-responsive GICs permit employees who are eligible for a distribution from their plans to withdraw their investments at book value before the contract reaches maturity without taking any market value adjustment.

guaranteed piecework plan A piece-rate plan in which employees are guaranteed a minimum hourly wage regardless of the number of items they process or produce.

guaranteed room blocks In meeting management and travel management, a group of hotel rooms reserved by a customer who agrees to pay for the rooms even if they are not used. Usually requires established credit with the hotel or cash prepayment.

Guaranteed Student Loan Program Includes Stafford Loans, Supplemental Loans for Students, PLUS loans for parents of dependent students, and consolidation loans. The **Higher Education Reauthorization Act of 1992** expanded eligibility and raised loan limits, particularly to middle income students.

guardian A person or non-profit corporation given authority by a probate court to act on behalf of an individual, called a **ward,** who has been certified by a licensed physician as unable to think, act, or make informed decisions concerning his or her personal health, safety, general welfare, property, or financial interests because of illness or mental incapacity. Has physical control or custody of a minor or incompetent person. Guardians must sign and submit a bond for approval by the court in which he or she accepts the appointment, promises to perform the duties of a guardian, and agrees to make an annual accounting to the court.

guardian ad litem An individual, usually an attorney, appointed by the court to represent the interests of a prospective **ward.** The *guardian ad litem* reviews the facts for the court.

guardianship A legal means of managing the affairs of an individual who has become incapacitated. A guardian, who may or may not be known by the principal, is appointed by the court and given authority to make decisions and act for the incapacitated individual.

guerrilla marketing A means of marketing products and services that is nontraditional, inexpensive, and effective. Targets profits, rather than the generation of sales. Used often by small businesses. Emphasizes a simple marketing plan, followup after sales are made, **fusion marketing**, spying (gathering information on your own company and competitors), and giveaways (freebees). Attributed to Jay Conrad Levinson, author and marketing guru.

guided imaging/imagery **1.** A technique that makes use of the imaginative powers, the "movies of the mind," to review the past, contemplate the present, and speculate about the future to create pictures of possibilities and improbabilities. Sometimes called *visualization* or *visualizing*. **2.** An alternative form of medical treatment in which patients are encouraged to envision their own immune system to help it fight disease.

guided practice An instructional technique in which the instructor engages trainees in using, under close supervision, what they have learned, evaluating performance and providing feedback, and reteaching the skills as needed.

guideline An explanatory statement designed to assist in the interpretation of canons and rules, understand their underlying rationale, and help apply them to real-life situations.

gynecologist A medical doctor who specializes in the diagnosis and treatment of problems originating in the reproductive organs of women. Linked with obstetrics, gynecologists provide counseling on contraception, prenatal care, and routine deliveries.

H

H	Heroin or horse.	**HKNC**	The Helen Keller National Center.
HazWOPER	Hazardous Waste Operations and Emergency Response Standard.	**HLS**	Hue, lightness, saturation.
		HMO	Health maintenance organization.
HBA	Health benefits advisor.		
HBR	*Harvard Business Review.*	**HMOA**	Health Maintenance Organization Acts of 1973 and 1988.
HCE	Highly compensated employee.		
		HOBSO	How Our Business System Operates.
HCEA	Healthcare Convention & Exhibitors Association.		
		HPO	Health care purchasing organization.
HCF	Health care finder.		
HCFA	Health Care Financing Administration.	**HR**	Human resources.
		HRA	Human resources accounting.
HCO	Hearing carry over.	**HRD**	Human resources development.
HCPCS	Health Care Financing Administration Common Procedural Coding System.	**HRE**	Human resources environment.
		HRIC	Human resources information center.
HCS	Hazard Communication Standard of 1988.	**HRIS**	Human resources information system.
HDCD	High definition compatible digital.	**HRM**	Human resources management.
		HRMS	Human resources management system.
HDL	High density lipoproteins.		
HDTV	High definition TV.	**HRP**	Human resources planning.
HEA	Higher Education Act of 1965.	**HRPS**	The Human Resource Planning Society.
HEC	Home equity conversion.	**HRSOPH**	Human resource management practice sophistication.
HEDIS	Health Plan Employer Data and Information Set.		
		HRSP	Association of Human Resource Systems Professionals, Inc.
HF	The Heritage Foundation.		
HFE	Human factors engineering.	**HRU**	Human resources utilization.
HFES	Human Factors and Ergonomics Society.	**HS**	Hazardous substance.
		HSS	*See* U.S. Department of Health and Human Services.
HIPAA	Health Insurance Portability and Accountability Act of 1996.		
		HSWA	Hazardous and Solid Waste Amendments of 1984.
HIPC	Health insurance purchasing cooperative.		
		HTML	HyperText Markup Language.
HIPO	High potential employee.	**HTT**	High-technology training.
HIV	Human immunodeficiency virus.	**HTTP**	HyperText Transport Protocol.

H-1B program *See* Immigration and Naturalization Service H-1B program.

H-2 Form A form required by the Department of Health and Human Services designed to collect health care information with the same filing date as W-2 forms. Employers must report Social Security numbers of employees' spouses and other dependents, names and Social Security numbers of all employees or former employees who elect coverage under the employer's health plan, whether the coverage is single or family, the names, addresses, and identifying numbers of the plans covering the employee or former employee, and the period during the year the coverage was in effect. The first filing of the report was February 28, 1995 for information pertaining to the 1994 calendar year. The form is used by HHS to establish a database to help recover improperly paid Medicare and Medicaid benefits.

habeus corpus A legal term that literally means "to have the body." A writ of *habeus corpus* is a legal document ordering an official, usually a warden, to release a prisoner.

hack Breaking into a computer system without authorization.

hacker **1.** A highly skilled computer programmer; a "good guy." *See also* cracker. **2.** An ill-behaved and highly proficient programmer who uses his or her skills to penetrate the computer systems of others, sometimes by circumventing security systems.

hair analysis A method of screening for drug abuse among employees and prospective employees. The method is based on the theory that chemicals, including illegal drugs, circulating in the bloodstream are incorporated into hair as it grows and remain locked in the hair fibers. Some courts, scientists, and government agencies have warned that current techniques of hair analysis do not stand up as valid drug testing measures.

hai-ten A form of employment adjustment used by the Japanese to reduce labor costs during a recession. It involves reassigning surplus workers to different sections or divisions of the same company. *See also* shukko.

half-time (enrollment) Under federal student aid programs, a measure of the academic enrollment time required to receive Direct or FFEL Program loans. For schools measuring progress by credit hours and academic terms (semesters, trimesters, or quarters), half-time is at least 6 semester hours or quarter hours per term. For schools measuring progress by credit hours but not by academic terms, half-time is at least 12 semester hours or 18 quarter hours per year. For schools measuring progress by clock hours, half-time is at least 12 hours per week.

halftone In desktop publishing, the reproduction of continuous-tone artwork, such as a photograph, by converting the image into dots. In color printing, the process by which three-color dots (cyan, magenta, and yellow) are placed close together so the viewer's eye blends them into a full-color image.

hallucination In mental illness, perceptions or images that occur without any external stimulus.

hallucinogens "Mindblowing" illegal drugs that alter the individual's perceptions of reality, distort the senses or cause to hallucinations. Include phencyclidine ("PCP," "angel dust"), lysergic acid diethylamide ("LSD", "acid"), mescaline and peyote ("mesc," "cactus"), and psilocybin ("shrroms," "magic mushrooms").

halo effect The tendency to base an overall favorable rating or judgment of an individual on one outstanding characteristic despite the presence of negative factors. Here the rater fails to differentiate among discrete traits or abilities and relies on the overall judgment.

Halsey plan An incentive plan that divides the bonus gained from increased productivity between the employer and employees on a set ratio, usually 50-50. It is not in common use today.

hammer clause A clause in a liability insurance policy that requires the insured to settle a claim if recommended by the insurance carrier or be compelled to assume all costs beyond the settlement amount proposed by the insurer.

handicap discrimination laws *See* Americans with Disabilities Act of 1990; Rehabilitation Act of 1973.

handicapped employees Workers in executive, managerial, professional, scientific, technical, marketing, sales, clerical, or other positions who have physical, mental, or emotional disabilities and therefore require workplace accommodations of some sort to enable them to become and remain productive. Also called *challenged employees, disabled employees,* or preferably, *employees with disabilities.*

handling time   A term used in time management to describe time used in getting completed work out of the way of new work or getting materials and components in position for the production of development of new products or services. One form of "handling" time is travel time — getting to and from the place where productive work is done.

handouts   Materials prepared by a presenter or instructor for distribution to attendees or trainees during or following a training session or information briefing. They make take the forms of printed or duplicated text or graphic materials. Also called *leave-behinds.*

handwriting analysis   *See* graphoanalysis.

happiness charts   *See* smile sheets; participant reaction.

harassment   Physical, mental, or emotional hectoring, badgering, intimidation, or torment.

hard-coded   In multimedia production, a predetermined series of statements whose order is not changeable by the user while running a program.

hard data   Information and observations that consist largely of facts, often numerical and measurable, that are objective and independently verifiable.

hard disk   A device that is connected to a computer to increase its data storage capacity. It is made out of metal and can be either built into the computer or externally connected.

hard drive   Provides a computer's secondary memory, a repository for programs and data storage, and the information that programs process and produce.

hardship premium   A monthly payment, typically a percentage of base pay, paid to employees assigned to areas in which unusual or environmental hazards exist.

hardware   The mechanical, magnetic, electronic, and electrical components of a computer system — the actual equipment that you can see and touch — that manipulate information. Examples: video display terminal, keyboard, mouse, printer, hard drive. *See also* software.

hard-wired mike   An electronic amplifying device that has a wire or cord connected between the microphone, the amplifier, and speakers. May be on a stand or hand-held.

harmonizing   A process that would establish international standards of production. In its best sense, harmonizing up, developing countries would adopt the standards of industrialized nations in terms of labor, environmental, and consumer laws and regulations. In its worst sense, harmonizing down, the lax standards found in Africa, Latin American, the old Soviet bloc, and much of Asia would prevail.

Harper v. Virginia   A 1993 Supreme Court decision that made its findings in ***Davis v. Michigan*** retroactive. That is, taxes levied by states on military or federal retired pay and *not* on state retirement annuities *prior to the Davis decision* are illegal, and retirees who paid them may be entitled to refunds.

Harris v. Forklift Systems Inc.
A 1993 Supreme Court Decision that loosened requirements for workers suing employers for sexual harassment. The ruling made it unnecessary for employees to prove psychological damage when defining a hostile work environment in sexual harassment cases. In addition, the Court made it easier for plaintiffs to bring lawsuits against employers convicted of harassment.

***Harvard Business Review* (HBR)**   Published bimonthly by the Harvard Business School Publishing Corporation, Harvard University, 60 Harvard Way, Soldiers Field Rd., Boston, MA 02163: $85,00 per year (professional rate). Contact: HBR, P.O. Box 52621, Boulder, CO 80321-2621 (617/495-6700; URL **http://henry.harvard.edu**).

hash   Hashish, a concentrated form of marijuana.

Hatch Act Reform Amendments of 1993
Amends Title 5, United States Code, to restore to federal civilian employees their right to participate voluntarily, as private citizens, in the political processes of the Nation and to protect such employees from improper political solicitations.

Hawkins-Stafford School Improvement Amendments of 1988   Amendments to Chapter I of the **Elementary and Secondary Education Act of 1965** that mandate accountability for student performance and coordination of the program with the regular school program; provide opportunities for flexibility and creativity in the pursuit of performance improvement; stress higher-order thinking instead of drill and rote learning; and emphasize parental involvement.

Hawthorne effect   Discovered by Elton Mayo in an experiment at the Western Electric Hawthorne Works in Chicago over 50 years ago while trying to isolate factors that would yield greater productivity. He changed the intensity of the lighting in production areas, and productivity rose. He concluded that the change in lighting didn't make the difference. What did was that the experimentation convinced workers that management cared and was trying to improve the work environment. That caused the increase in productivity. He concluded that if you show concern for workers and treat them as human beings with needs and wants, they'll perform better.

Hay Guide-Chart Profile Method   A popular point-factor method of job evaluation.

Haynes plan   An incentive plan that divides productivity bonuses among the employer, supervisors, and workers, usually 40, 10, and 50 percent, respectively. It is not in common use today.

Hay system   A traditional method of job evaluation that focuses on job incumbents' job knowledge and skills, problem solving abilities, and responsibility and accountability as **compensable factors**. Point values are assigned to job characteristics, and benchmarking surveys are often used to calculate minimum salary amounts.

Hazard Communication Standard of 1988 (HCS)   An OSHA requirement aimed at reducing the incidence of chemical-related occupational illnesses and injuries in non-manufacturing workplaces. The regulation requires employers of even one employee in any type of enterprise to establish hazard communication plans and programs to transmit information on the hazards of chemicals to their employees by means of labels on containers, publication and distribution of **materials safety data sheets** (MSDS), and conduct of training programs. Training should cover how the hazard communication program is implemented in the company, how to read and interpret labels and MSDSs, how to get and use hazard information, the hazards of chemicals in the work area, measures employees can take to protect themselves, methods of detecting hazardous chemicals, and specific procedures the employer has put into effect to protect employees. Reference: Chemical Hazard Communication, U.S. Department of Labor, OSHA 3084, Rev. 1988. Also known as the **right-to-know** standard.

Hazardous and Solid Waste Amendments of 1984 (HSWA)   Amendments to the **Resource Conservation and Recovery Act of 1976,** which directed the EPA to establish new requirements to bring small quantity generators of hazardous waste into the hazardous waste regulatory system.

hazardous substance (HS)   Any solid, liquid, or contained gaseous material that could cause injury, death, or damage, or pollute land, air, or water.

hazardous waste   Any solid, liquid, or contained gaseous material that could cause injury or death or damage, or pollute land, air, or water, is no longer used, and is either recycled, discarded, or stored until the quantity is sufficient to treat or dispose of. These wastes are regulated by federal and state public health and environmental laws.

Hazardous Waste and Emergency Response (Standard) (HAZWOPER)   A standard pertaining to hazardous waste promulgated by the Occupational Safety and Health Administration (OSHA 1910.20) that requires that employees be provided training on hazardous waste operations.

hazing   A practice usually associated with college students, particularly fraternities and sororities, but also prevalent in the workplace at all levels and in all types of positions. It is a rite of passage found in corporate offices, hospitals, courts, law offices, banks, factories, construction sites, and service organizations. Its purpose is to test new members of a group and have them prove their mettle, pay their dues, and learn the ropes. It includes practical jokes and assigning intentionally meaningless or humiliating tasks. So long as hazing is mild and does not cause unreasonable emotional or physical pain and suffering it is probably acceptable; but if it creates excessive stress, delay in learning and adjusting to the job, or results in turnover, absenteeism, tardiness, or depression it must be controlled.

headhunters   *See* executive search firm.

head injury Results from traumatic damage to the brain, most commonly due to motor vehicle accidents, falls, assaults and violence, and sports and recreation. Symptoms depend on the extent and location of the injury in the brain. injuries to the left side of the brain may impact language and verbal processing skills, while injury to the right side of the brain may affect visual-spatial problem solving skills. Injury to the frontal lobes may influence general problem solving, abstract thinking, goal setting, attention, concentration, and the ability to perform multiple tasks simultaneously. Injury to the rear of the frontal lobes may impair motor function, and injury to the parietal lobes (upper rear area of the brain) may affect the ability to work with one's hands. Injury to the left side of the temporal lobe (lower middle section of the brain) may affect understanding of spoken words and the ability to speak coherently, and injury to the occipital lobe, (lower rear of the brain) may influence perception and interpretation of visual information. Treatment involves rehabilitative interventions and therapy to develop compensating strategies to overcome cognitive deficits. Also called *traumatic brain injury*.

headquarters hotel In meeting management, the hotel where the administrative and hospitality functions are located when more than one hotel is used for an event.

Head Start Program A federally funded part-day, school-year educational program that serves about 20 percent of eligible disadvantaged preschool children.

health *See* health benefits; occupational health services; wellness program.

Health Insurance Portability and Accountability Act of 1996 (HIPAA) The bill makes it a federal crime for individuals, within three years of applying for Medicaid, to transfer intentionally certain assets for less than fair market value to become eligible for nursing home care paid for by Medicaid. Interim rules governing certification requirements of HIPAA went into effect June 1, 1997 (other HIPAA provisions are generally effective for plan years beginning after June 30, 1997). The rules provide guidance to both employers and employees in the following areas: preexisting condition exclusions, creditable coverage, certificates of creditable coverage, special enrollment rights, and discrimination prohibitions. *Contact:* Pension and Welfare Benefits Administration (800/998-7542 or 202/219-8776; URL **http://www.dol.gov/dol/pwba**).

health and medical disabilities Conditions which often affect not only the work lives of people but also their activities of daily living. For example, alcoholism; epilepsy; heart disease; HIV/AIDS.

health and welfare benefits Ancillary benefits that include dental, employee assistance, legal, long-term disability, long-term nursing care, prescription drugs, short term disability, vision, and wellness programs,.

health benefits The most common of all employee benefits. Consist of medical and hospitalization insurance provided on a group basis to reimburse an employee (and often family members) for all or part of the expenses relating to medical treatment or hospitalization.

health benefits advisor (HBA) A person at a military hospital or clinic who can help **Civilian Health and Medical Programs of the Uniformed Services (CHAMPUS)** users get the medical care they need through the military and CHAMPUS.

health benefits tax cap A proposal by the Association of Private Pension and Welfare Plans, the Health Insurance Association of America, and the Health Policy Committee to the Business Roundtable to limit the tax-free treatment of employer-provided health benefits to the level of the cost of a basic health plan. Some proponents of the plan would make the tax cap a part of a health care reform package and use the revenue derived from it to expand access to the health care system to insured people.

Health Care Amendments Act of 1974 Permits union activities in acute-care hospitals but does not cover nursing homes, psychiatric or rehabilitation hospitals, or other types of health care facilities.

Healthcare Convention & Exhibitors Association (HCEA) An organization of 650 members established to increase the efficiency and effectiveness of health care conventions and exhibits as an educational and marketing medium, promote the value of exhibits and industry as an integral part of these conventions, foster better understanding and cooperation between industry and health care associations, provide information and services useful to industry and health care associations in improving the quality of conventions and exhibit programs, and provide for the professional development of its member representatives. *Contact:* HCEA, 5777 Peachtree-Dunwoody Rd., Ste. 500-G, Atlanta, GA 30342 (404/252-3663; E-mail **hcea@assnhq.com**; URL **http:www.assnhq.com/hcea/index.htm**).

health care cost reduction strategies
Include amateur auditor program, case management, coordination of benefits, dependent coverage waivers, drug program, fifty-fifty dental plan, Medicare carve out, maintenance of benefits, prescription plan, tiered premium system, and wellness program.

Health Care Financing Administration
(HCFA) The agency of the Department of Health and Human Services (HSS) that administers the federal Medicare and Medicaid programs. Enforces federal rules on health care providers' bills by (1) furnishing biweekly lists of overcharges to all health care providers who don't accept assignment and requiring them to make refunds, and (2) informing patients of overcharges by printing the health care provider's maximum fee on the **Explanation of Medicare Benefits** form.

Health Care Financing Administration
Common Procedural Coding System
(HCPCS) Codes used by Medicare that describe services and procedures.

health care finder (HCF) A person at a military hospital or clinic who helps match **Civilian Health and Medical Programs of the Uniformed Services (CHAMPUS)** users with care providers either through the military or the civilian community,

health care power of attorney A legal document that appoints a person(s) who will have the authority to make medical decisions for an incapacitated individual such as ordering or refusing surgery, ordering second opinions, refusing the services of an attending physician, choosing a nursing home, or, if family members disagree on any health matter involving the principal, has the final right of decision.

health care prepayment plan A Medicare option, similar to a **cost contract** but may cover only part of the Medicare benefit package; typically cover Part B expenses (physicians), while enrollees use traditional Medicare for Part A (hospitals and other expenses).

health care proxy A legal document in some states that allows a person to appoint a "health care agent" who may make health care decisions for the principal if the principal lacks the capacity to make or communicate health care decisions. The agent may make a judgment based on all of the circumstances that might prevail, instead of simply considering the circumstances envisioned when the health care proxy was signed.

health care purchasing organization
(HPO) A form of managed health care. HPOs are employer-sponsored purchasing groups organized to buy health care directly from providers (hospitals, physicians, and other professionals) rather than going through health maintenance organizations (HMOs) or preferred provider organizations (PPOs).

health care reimbursement account
An option under a flexible benefits plan. Expenses paid for uninsured medical, vision, hearing, and dental expenses (such as deductibles, copayments/coinsurance, exams, and the like) are reimbursable by the employer on a nontaxable basis provided that rules established by the Internal Revenue Service are met.

Health Care Task Force See Task Force on National Health Care Reform.

health care worker protection rules
See universal precautions.

health insurance Medical and/or hospital insurance coverage provided employees, usually on a group basis, to underwrite or reimburse an employee (and often family members) for all or part of the expenses relating to medical treatment or hospitalization.

Health Insurance Deduction for
Self-Employed Individuals Act of 1995
Amends the Internal Revenue Code to make permanent the deduction for health insurance costs of self-employed individuals. Became effective January 1, 1994. Also Increased the deduction from 25 percent to 30 percent effective beginning after December 31, 1994. Signed by the President. April 11, 1995. *See also* Health Insurance Portability and Accountability Act of 1996.

health insurance indemnity plan
See health benefits.

Health Insurance Portability and Accountability Act of 1996 (HIPAA)
Amends the Internal Revenue Code of 1986 to improve portability and continuity of health insurance coverage in the group and individual markets to combat waste, fraud, and abuse in health insurance and health care delivery, to promote the use of medical savings accounts, to improve access to long-term care services and coverage, and to simplify the administration of health insurance. Signed into law August 21, 1996 and becomes effective July 1, 1997. Provides portability of health insurance, allowing workers to keep their coverage when they change their jobs. The bill also limits to 12 months the period in which a plan could exclude enrollees from coverage because of preexisting conditions. Insurers would also be prohibited from refusing coverage because of an employee's health status. The bill also contains limits on medical malpractice awards; imposes civil and criminal penalties on employers who disclose personally identifiable health information without the consent of the employee; increases the health insurance tax deduction for self-employed persons from 30 percent to 80 percent by the year 2006; makes long-term care insurance and expenses deductible in the same manner as other health costs; allows dying persons, particularly AIDS patients, to draw on their life insurance while they are still living; and sets up a 4-year pilot plan that allows 750,000 Americans to buy experimental tax-deductible Medical Savings Accounts to test whether they can help control health costs without benefiting only the healthy and wealthy. Self-employed persons and employers with 50 or fewer workers would also be eligible to participate in the medical savings account program. The bill also requires employers to revise their COBRA notices and plan documents and change their administrative procedures. *See also* medical savings account.

health insurance purchasing cooperative (HIPC) A state-based agency that arranges insurance for business and individuals under **managed competition** plans. HPICs may also enforce spending ceilings and limit premium increases.

health insurance reform *See* Health Insurance Portability and Accountability Act of 1996.

health maintenance organization (HMO)
In general, an HMO is an organized health care system that is responsible for both the financing and the delivery of a broad range of comprehensive services to an enrolled population. It is a privately established organization qualified by state or federal agencies to offer its services to employees and employers in a specified geographical area. Subscribers who elect to participate in HMOs in preference to employer-sponsored health insurance programs are entitled to a subsidy to their HMO premiums equal to the amount they would otherwise be subsidized under the company plan. Programs provide prepaid routine, round-the-clock medical services at a specific site and usually stress preventive medicine in a clinic. Costs to enrolled employees are limited to a nominal fee (usually $5 to $10 per visit), there are no claim forms to fill out, and the charges of medical care providers to the employer are on a pre-negotiated, fixed annual payment per employee basis. If an HMO-approved health care provider is not used, there is no reimbursement except for life-threatening emergencies when the HMO cannot be contacted prior to a hospital admission.

Health Maintenance Organization Act of 1973 (HMOA) An Act designed to stimulate a nation-wide, prepaid health care system. The HMOA required employers to offer local HMO coverage to employees if the employer is approached by a qualified HMO — a medical organization consisting of several specialists, such as general practitioners, surgeons, psychiatrists, and so on.

Health Maintenance Organization Act of 1988 (HMOA) Legislation mandating a new group-specific rating plan that allows HMOs to set rates based on specific group utilization (similar to the way indemnity insurers set rates); extends the dual choice mandate, which forces employers of 25 or more workers to offer both an indemnity or HMO plan until 1995; and renews the equal contribution for indemnity or HMO plans.

Health Plan Employer Data and Information Set (HEDIS) HEDIS 3.0, released in 1996 by the **National Committee for Quality**

Assurance, is a comprehensive health plan database. It provides a set of performance measures designed to provide meaningful data which can be used to compare plans, make selection easier, and improve overall quality. It includes 60 standardized health plan performance measures.

health-risk appraisal Use of questionnaires and interviews as a part of wellness programs to appraise the health of employees. May also involve a computerized analysis of employee health habits, such as examining how many employees smoke, are overweight, have high cholesterol, and manage stress.

health-risk assessment Use of physical or biomedical screening for specific health conditions as a part of wellness programs.

health-risk factors Items addressed in health-risk appraisals and assessments as part of wellness plans and programs. Include alcohol use, blood pressure, body fat, chemical dependency, cholesterol levels, chronic diseases (such as diabetes), fitness, stress, and tobacco use.

hearing and speech disability cultures and languages Means of communication used by people with speech and hearing disabilities. Include American Sign Language, cued speech, fingerspelling, manual English, speechreading, and speech amplification.

hearing benefits Ancillary benefits. Typically cover audiology testing and may also provide hearing aid and rehabilitation benefits

hearing carry over (HCO) A reduced form of **telecommunications relay services** where a person with a speech disability can listen to the other end user, and in reply, the **communications assistant** reads and speaks the text from his or her display as it is typed on a keyboard by the person with the speech disability. The communications assistant does not type any conversation.

Hear Now A national nonprofit organization whose primary purpose is to provide hearing aids and cochlear implants to low income, hard-of-hearing children and adults. Hear Now also recycles used and broken hearing aids. For more information on recycling or to request an assistance application call 800/648-HEAR. *Contact:* Hear Now, 9745 E. Hampden Ave., Ste 300, Denver, CO 80231-4923 (Fax 303/695-7789; URL **http://www.leisure/an.com/~hearnow/**).

heart disease Takes several forms, such as congestive heart failure, heart block, and cardiac arrhythmia. Affects 21.3 million Americans. Also called *cardiovascular disease*.

hedonism An extremist theory of ethics that holds that whatever gives pleasure is good, and whatever results in pain is bad. Therefore, the pursuit of pleasure, *la dolce vita*, should control human behavior and conduct.

heirs at law Persons designated by the court as the ones to inherit property of a person who dies without a will. Usually referred to as *next-of-kin*.

The Helen Keller National Center (HKNC) The only national program that provides diagnostic evaluation, short-term comprehensive rehabilitation and personal adjustment training, and job preparation and placement for all Americans (youth and adult) who are deaf-blind. *Contact:* HKNC, 111 Middle Neck Rd., Sands Point, NY 11050 [516/944-8900 (voice or TDD); Fax 516/944-7302; E-mail **abigailp@aol.com**].

helping/service competencies Capabilities that portend success in professional, technical, or managerial jobs. They include interpersonal understanding and customer-service orientation.

hemiplegia A form of brain damage and the most common type of neurologic disorder. It paralyzes one half of the body, either the left or the right side of the trunk and its limbs. The most common cause of hemiplegia is a cerebral vascular accident, called a stroke — thrombosis of a cerebral or extracranial artery, hemorrhage in the brain or cerebrospinal space, or embolism.

The Henry Laurence Gantt Medal An award presented annually by the American Society of Mechanical Engineers and the **American Management Association** to an individual from any field of endeavor for distinguished achievement in management as a service to the community. Nominations are solicited for the award in ASME and AMA publications. *Contact:* Patricia Conway, Corporate Secretary, American Management Association, 135 West 50th St., New York NY 10020.

herbal medicine An ancient and alternative form of medical treatment that uses extracts of plant parts to promote natural body functions and speed healing. Although there is evidence that herbs may have health benefits, some have been linked to adverse reactions or more serious side effects.

herbal wrap An alternative manipulative treatment that involves applying warm sheets soaked in a herbal "tea" to the body to encourage the elimination of impurities through perspiration.

The Heritage Foundation (HF) A research/education institute with a staff of 160 whose programs are designed to make the voice of conservatism heard in Washington and throughout the world. HF's policy analysts have expertise in the full range of foreign, defense, domestic, and economic policy issues. *Contact:* Heritage Foundation, 214 Massachusetts Ave., N.E., Washington, DC 20002-4999 (202/546-4400; URL **http://www.heritage.org**).

heroin A morphine derivative, a narcotic diacetyl-morphine, a white, odorless, crystalline substance that is highly addictive. It is dissolved in a base and injected in a vein. Also called *horse, H,* and *junk.*

hickey In offset-lithography, a spot or imperfection in the printing due to dirt in the press, paper particles, and so on.

hidden-city fare An airline fare designed to cut as much as 75 percent off the cost of an normal fare. Essentially it constitutes a loophole in airlines' yield management systems by allowing travel agents to book a ticket at a lower fee, using the traveler's real destination as a stopover. Travelers simply discard the unused portion of the ticket upon arrival at their real destination. Although not illegal, the practice is denounced by the airlines, and it is certainly questionable, if not unethical.

hidden disabilities Disabilities that are not visible to the observer, such as alcoholism, depression, diabetes, drug addiction, epilepsy, head injury, hypertension, and learning disabilities.

hierarchy On the Internet, the broadest area of information covered by a newsgroup.

hierarchy of needs A theory that people constantly seek the satisfaction of needs and that those needs determine human behavior. In ascending order of potency, they are physiological (food, water, shelter, sleep, elimination, and other physical essentials), safety (from the dangers of the environment), belongingness (social interaction), esteem (feelings of self-worth and the appreciation and respect of others), and self-actualization (achievement and self-fulfillment). Attributed to Abraham H. Maslow.

hi-fi High fidelity. Offers top quality sound for prerecorded stereo tapes when coupled with a stereo TV or with multichannel sound hooked up to a stereo system.

high-adventure activities In **adventure training**, such group activities as rock climbing, whitewater river rafting, sailing, mountain climbing, and wilderness travel.

high-deductible medical insurance plan A health care plan with an annual deductible of at least $1,500 and no more than $4,500 for family coverage. Under a 1996 law, employees and self-employed individuals can make tax-deductible contributions of up to 65 percent of their plan's deductible for individuals, and 75 percent of the deductible for family health coverage, to a medical saving account.

high-def *See* high definition TV.

high-definition compatible digital (HDCD) A relatively new form of **compact disc** said to improve realism and natural ambiance when played through an HDCD decoder — although the discs may be played on a conventional CD player.

high-definition TV (HDTV) An advanced television standard, which offers six times the amount of picture information and twice the number of scan lines as conventional TV, so that the picture is clearer and colors are sharper.

high-density lipoproteins (HDL) Cholesterol attached to various fats and proteins (good cholesterol). HDL appears to protect against atherosclerosis by carrying excess cholesterol away from artery walls, so it is associated with a decrease in heart disease.

Higher Education Act of 1965 (HEA) Title IV of the Act provided student aid to help financially needy students attain postsecondary education in colleges, universities, and trade and technical schools. The forms of aid included student loans, grants, work study assistance, and fellowships.

Higher Education Reauthorization Act of 1992 Legislation signed into law July 23, 1992 that boosted college assistance to middle-level families, changed the formula for calculating parental assets, simplified access to student aid, raised the maximum of Pell Grants from $3,100 to $3,700 and income ceilings for students seeking them to $2,400, increased the annual income limits for families of four from $30,000 to $42,000, and extended the life of federal higher education programs and authorized spending of $115 billion over five years.

highly compensated employee/executive (HCE) A term standardized by the Tax Reform Act of 1986 that is used to test for discrimination. At that time, HCEs were considered to be employees who are 5 percent owners, all those earning more than $100,000 from the employer, all those earning more than $66,000 from the employer and in the top paid 20 percent, any officer earning more than $60,000, or one of the highest paid officer of the employer. In August 1996, the Small Business Job Protection Act was signed into law. The Act changed the definition of a HCE. Instead of four criteria, there are now only two: (1) one who was a 5 percent owner of the company during the current or preceding year, or made more than $80,000 in the preceding year. The number of employees considered highly compensated based on compensation over $80,000 can be limited at the employer's discretion to 20 percent of the total number of employees.

high-performance jobs Jobs that rely on worker problem solving, place heavy emphasis on training to upgrade skills, require cooperation between labor and management, and involve the integration of technology into the production process. Proposed as a strategy to help industry and unions survive in a world of intense global competition. Attributed to then Secretary of Labor Robert Reich at the Conference on the Future of the American Workplace held in Chicago in July 1993.

high-performance workplace/work system Organizing work and managing people to make the work environment more effective, improve productivity, product or service quality, and profits, increase market share and customer satisfaction, and make the organization more competitive. Although research has not validated any single set of high performance practices, discussion typically focuses on self-managed teams, quality circles, flat organization structures, new

technologies, innovative compensation arrangements, increased training, total quality management, strategic change management, and continuous improvement.

high-potential employee (HIPO) Employees who have above average talent, skills, and education. Targets for recruitment, retention, training, and development — grooming for leadership positions.

high science Used to describe leading-edge, world-class employees, systems, or equipment.

high season In meeting management, the period when occupancy and room rates are highest for the year.

high-technology training (hi-tech training) Developing and delivering training on leading-edge technologies and evolving processes for technical professionals, scientists, and engineers. It aims to reduce product development time and speed up technology transfer. Examples: the use of computers, telecommunications, interactive video, optical discs, CD-ROMs, WORM discs, laserdiscs, digital video interactive, EXPERT systems, and the like to deliver training.

hiring *See* recruitment, screening, and selection.

hiring bonus A lump-sum bonus paid at the time of employment as an incentive to accept a job offer.

Hispanics Persons of Mexican, Puerto Rican, Dominican, Cuban, Central or South American of either Indian or Hispanic origin, regardless of race.

histogram **1.** A graph that displays the distribution of scores or measures on something being measured or evaluated. Each column represents the number of times a certain measure or score appears. Because the columns are all viewed together, they present a clear picture of the aggregate of the characteristic measured over a specific period of time as well as the trend of those characteristics when the individual columns are converted to a curve. **2.** One of the Basic Seven tools of quality control. A bar chart that shows the distribution of a variance, providing a picture of the way the data are distributed within a range of values and across a broader spectrum of values. A graphic representation of an operation used to study and improve work processes. It uses symbols (operation, movement, inspection, delay, and storage, for example) to identify common activities that occur in most types of operations.

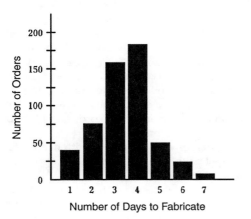

Number of Days to Fabricate

historical study   A type of research in which a retrospective analysis is made of past events and activities. By reviewing organizational documents, data, and the testimony of the people who experienced or observed the events, the research attempts to determine causes and relationships between and among events.

hit   A measure of a Web site's popularity. A hit represents one time that a site has been accessed. Also refers to *leads* or *sales.*

hi-tech   Leading edge technology.

HIV disease   *See* human immunodeficiency virus (HIV).

hold harmless agreement   1. A document signed by service organizations (such as testing companies) stating that they will indemnify the employer from any damage claims in any and all legal actions arising from the use of their services (tests). **2.** In meeting management, a clause in contracts stating that a group, company, or other entity will not be responsible if a claim is filed.

hold harmless clause/disclaimer 1. In contract law, wording that absolves one of the parties of liability for injuries or damages to the personnel or property of the other party to the contract as the result of the misconduct or negligence of its employees or others. **2.** In health care contracts, a clause under which the provider agrees not to sue

or assert any claims against an enrollee for services covered under the contract, even if the health plan becomes insolvent or fails to meet its obligations.

holiday   European term for vacation.

holistic   Treating the whole person or the whole problem rather than one characteristic or one aspect.

holistic approach   May take one of two forms in a concepts-based, integrated curriculum: (1) addresses the needs of the whole child by integrating cognitive, physical, affective, moral, and spiritual dimensions; or (2) offers a curriculum that provides the context in which new knowledge and skills make sense to the learner. Attributed to Betty Jean Eklund Shoemaker, "Education 2000 Integrated Curriculum," *Phi Delta Kappan,* June 1991.

holistic medicine/therapy   An alternative medical treatment that addresses the whole person rather than biomedical therapy of the affected organ. Characterized by its practitioners as an orthomolecular (treatment based on "correct molecules" found naturally in the body, especially vitamins), nutritional, ecologic approach to medicine. It makes use of such tests and procedures as hair analysis for mineral levels, stomach pH tests with a capsule-sized radio transmitter that the patient swallows, six-hour glucose tolerance tests for low blood sugar, chelation therapy (dripping a solution containing an amino acid into the bloodstream for four or more hours), injections of various vitamins and minerals, and week-long diets of vitamin C and liquids. Regarded by some traditional (mainstream) physicians and some state department health agencies as irresponsible, worthless, unethical, or harmful. Has sometimes resulted in charges of professional misconduct and malpractice suits.

hologram   A means of viewing an image in three dimensions. Consists of a thin, flat piece of glass or film, which when used to view the image, allows the viewer to see around different parts of the replication by moving his or her head up and down or side to side.

holographic projection system   Equipment that produces realistic three-dimensional images used in simulations for training purposes.

holographic will A will written entirely in the handwriting of the testator or maker of the will. States vary in their acceptance of such wills.

home adaptation Changes to the home required to accommodate the needs of older and disabled persons. Range from simple change such as installing grab bars or major changes such as widening doorways for wheelchair access to installing first-floor bathrooms. May be tax deductible if required and certified by a physician.

home-based work *See* home worker.

home-delivered meals *See* "meals-on-wheels."

homegrown Computer software that has been developed inhouse.

home office An office set up in an employee's home that substitutes for corporate office space, usually with financial support from the employer.

homeopathic medicine A controversial form of **alternative medicine** that involves the use of carefully selected harmless dilutions of chemicals, plant, mineral, animal extracts, and other natural substances, which are supposed to stimulate healing reactions by working on the body's energy field.

home equity conversion (HEC) Plans that allow individuals to convert the value of their homes into cash without having to move out or repay the loan each month. The plan reduces home equity by making a lump sum payment or gradually reducing the balance due by monthly payments.

home equity loan A loan made by a bank or loan company allowing an individual to borrow against the equity he or she has in his or her home. The borrower must repay the loan with monthly payments. Also called *second mortgage.*

home equity conversion mortgage *See* reverse mortgage.

home finding services *See* destination services company.

home health (care) agency A state-licensed or Medicare-certified public or private organization that specializes in giving skilled nursing services and other therapeutic services, such as physical therapy, in a beneficiary's home.

home health care plan Health services (such as nursing services and rehabilitative therapy) and supplies provided to a covered individual on a part-time, intermittent, or visiting basis in the person's home while he or she is confined due to injury, disease, or pregnancy. Usually a physician must certify that the services and supplies are provided as an alternative to admission to a hospital or skilled nursing facility. Costs range from $25 to $50 per hour. May be covered in part by **Medicare**, **Medicaid**, and **medigap insurance**.

home health care agency An organization that provides nursing care and therapeutic services under a state license or federal certification and maintains records and plans of care for its patients.

home health care plan A written plan for home health care established and approved by a physician.

home leave A periodic leave (usually annually) in the United States (or country of domicile) for employees and their dependents assigned overseas.

home maintenance and repair program A service typically sponsored by nonprofit organizations that includes for a nominal fee home maintenance, home repairs, and help with emergencies such as stopped up sinks and toilets. Does not include major repairs or improvements.

homemaker services Assistance provided to aging, ill, or disable persons by a variety of agencies. Services include assistance with dressing and grooming and help with meal preparation, food shopping, or light housekeeping. Not usually covered by Medicare but may be covered by Medicaid or medigap insurance.

home marketing assistance A relatively new employee benefit instituted to reduce the spiraling costs of relocating employees: purchasing the transferee's home, paying all home sale expenses, covering the cost of finding a home in the destination area, helping the employee sell his or her old home, and transporting the family and household goods to the new location.

home medical equipment Equipment that is prescribed by a physician, is medically necessary, is appropriate for use in the home, fills a medical need, is durable, and is not useful to people who are not sick or injured. Medicare Part B will help pay for equipment that meets those specifications. Examples are oxygen equipment, wheelchairs, artificial limbs, braces, ostomy supplies, and hospital beds.

homeopathy An alternative form of medical therapy in which diseases are treated by administering very small does of natural substances that in larger amounts would cause the same symptoms as the ailment.

homepage On the **World Wide Web,** the opening screen of a site, which can contain text, images (still and motion), and sounds as well as hypertext links that can lead the user to other homepages with a click of the mouse.

home purchase company An organization established to help transferring employees get the equity out of their old homes as fast as possible so they can move to the new location and settle in without worrying about their property. Such companies buy the property.

home sale protection A benefit for relocated and expatriate employees that pays the costs associated with selling a house to take an assignment either overseas or in another geographical area of the United States. If the employee elects not to sell the property, the company may offer home rental protection that provides some property management services and reimburses employees for extraordinary expenses (for example, credit checks) associated with the rental or lease.

home schooling Describes the practice of keeping children at home where they are taught by their parents using self-developed and/or self-guided learning materials.

home sharing A shared household arrangement in which older persons may share their home with others, move into someone else's home, or find a new home that can accommodate several people. Costs are either shared on a pro rata basis or bartered by exchanging services, such as cooking or housework.

home study 1. Employer directed or self-initiated independent study conducted away from the workplace. **2.** Defined by the **Distance Education and Training Council** as an institution that (1) formally enrolls students and maintains student records; (2) retains a qualified faculty; (3) transmits organized instructional materials to students; (3) provides continuous two-way communication on student work and progress; (and (5) offers

courses of instruction that must be studied predominantly at a distance form the institution.

home worker An employee who performs his or her duties at a location away from the plant, shop, or office. A Department of Labor (DOL) rule allows DOL-certified employers to employ home workers, which had formerly been banned because of difficulties in enforcing labor standards. Recently the authorization to employ home workers was extended to the knitted outerwear, gloves and mittens, buttons and buckles, handkerchiefs, embroidery, and nonhazardous jewelry industries.

homogeneous grouping A type of trainee grouping for instruction, characterized by uniformity of the trainee group in achievement, ability, aptitude, background, education, training, or experience. Trainees are assigned to a homogeneous group on the basis of selection instruments or devices that indicate that they are alike in specific attributes, traits, or abilities. Although it cannot be assumed that they are undiversified solely on the selection factor, a narrower range of diversification is established.

honesty test A substitute for polygraph examinations. Honesty tests make use of **pencil-and-paper tests** or **projective techniques** as a part of an applicant screening and selection process to identify persons with tendencies to be dishonest. A study conducted by the U.S. Office of Technology Assessment in 1990 determined that existing research is inconclusive as to whether or not honesty and integrity tests accurately predict dishonest workplace behavior.

honoraria ban *See* Ethics in government Act of 1989.

hook A means of attracting repeat business from current customers or clients or luring new business by using such inducements as free room or travel upgrades, complementary breakfasts, wine hours or cocktails, special amenities and room service, and so on.

Hoover Institution A think tank on War, Revolution and Peace and a center for interdisciplinary and advanced research in the social sciences and public policy on domestic and international affairs. It now has more than 70 resident scholars, and houses one of the world's largest private archives and libraries on economic, political, and social change in the twentieth century, as well as a major scholarly press. *Contact:* Hoover Institution, Stanford University, Stanford, CA 94305-6010 (415/723-0603; E-mail **webmaster@hoover. stanford.edu**; URL **http:/www.Hoover. Stanford.edu**).

Hopwood effect See Hopwood v. Texas.

Hopwood v. Texas A federal appeals court decision involving an admissions plan at the University of Texas Law School, which considered white and minority applicants on separate tracks to increase the number of minority students admitted to the school. The court's ruling found the approach unacceptable and held that the school could no longer use race or ethnicity as factors in admission. That decision has begun ending or modifying **affirmative action** at institutions of higher learning nationwide.

horizontal bar chart A means of displaying data graphically. Most often used to compare and rank items at the same point in time, such as productions of goods or sales.

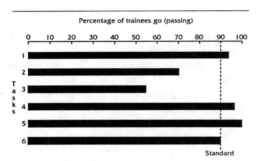

Percentage of trainees go (passing)

horizontal management An organization based on the association of functions that are involved in the same product or process.

horizontal organization A "flattened" organization, one with very few levels, typically involving the use of interdependent cross-functional teams.

horizontal programming One type of satellite-delivered video training. Programs that are applicable across industries, professions, and occupations are packaged by subject. For example, many management, sales, communication, computer literacy, and technical skills programs have wide application.

horse *See* heroin.

hoshin kanri A management planning system initially developed in Japan. It involves analyzing changes in the external environment, setting and linking annual objectives and strategic priorities, creating an integrated

plan of attack, executing the plan, monitoring and controlling progress, and making needed modifications. A key element of the system is the involvement of employees at all levels in developing the methods and procedures for achieving the priorities.

hospice A facility operated by a public or private organization primarily to provide pain relief, symptom management, and supportive services for terminally ill patients and their families. Typically must be certified by Medicare or licensed or accredited by the jurisdiction in which it is located, be supervised by a staff of M.D.s or D.O.s, at least one of whom must be on call at all times, provide 24 hours a day nursing services under the direction of an R.N., and have a full time administrator.

hospice care Programs operated by a licensed or accredited public agency or private organization that engages primarily in providing pain relief, symptom management, and supportive services for terminally ill people and their families. Such programs typically combine acute inpatient, outpatient, and home care for the patient as well as grief or bereavement counseling for his or her family. Typically provide care 24 hours a day, are certified by Medicare (or licensed by the jurisdiction it is in), staffed by at least one physician (M.D., D.O.), one R.N., one iicensed or certified social worker, and have one full-time administrator. Provide skilled nursing services, medical social services, psychological counseling, and dietary counseling.

hospital An institution that is licensed, provides continuous 24-hour per day medical and nursing care, and has facilities for diagnosis and major surgery. The term may also be used to describe a licensed ambulatory surgical center or a facility operated by a hospice or one that provides inpatient care under arrangements made by a hospice.

hospital confinement indemnity coverage An insurance policy that pays a fixed amount for each day that a subscriber is confined to a hospital, up to a specified maximum number of days.

hospital insurance The part of a health benefit plan (such as **Medicare**) that helps to pay for inpatient hospital care, some inpatient care in a skilled nursing facility, home health care, and hospice care.

hospitality   A hotel room used for entertaining, such as cocktail parties.

Hospitality Industry Humanitarian Awards Program   Annual awards presented to corporations or local company units in any hospitality-related business, such as hotels, convention bureaus, national tourist organizations, transportation companies, convention centers, travel companies, and industry buyers and sellers associations and their local chapters by *Successful Meetings* magazine. Eligible programs include efforts in the areas of health, shelter, clothing, nutrition, literacy, environment, and disaster aid. Judges consist of outstanding civic leaders or private-sector individuals who represent leadership positions in the category areas. selected from outside the hospitality industry. *Contact:* Hospitality Industry Humanitarian Awards Program, *Successful Meetings* magazine, 355 Park Avenue South, New York NY 10010-1789.

hospitality manager   *See* bar manager.

hospitality suite   A hotel suite used for entertaining that has an adjoining bedroom(s).

host   A computer to which one or more terminals or other smaller computers are connected or netted. A host can use almost any **Internet** tool, such as WAIS, Mosaic, and Netscape.

host computerized reservation system   In travel management, the primary computerized reservation system (CRS) used by travel agents. It is accessed from a satellite CRS.

Hosteur™   A term coined by the Council on Hotel;, Restaurant, and Institutional Education to capture the essence of the hospitality and tourism career field. The first syllable of the work *Hosteur* related to the basic mission of of hospitality and tourism — hosting and serving the guest; the second syllable, *eur,* is a sound that is recognized internationally.

hostile bid   A strategy for gaining ownership and control of a business by making an overpriced bid for its stock.

hostile environment   In the context of sexual harassment, suggestive comments, leers, sexually explicit photos, graffiti, and so on. *See also* quid pro quo harassment; unwelcome behavior; sexual harassment; reasonable woman standard.

hostile takeover or merger   A strategy for effecting a leveraged purchase of a corporation. It typically involves an over-priced bid for stock.

hostile work environment   *See* sexual harassment.

host site   In distance learning, the site that originates the session or program. the place where the instructor, moderator, or presenter is located.

hotel classifications   In meeting management, categories established to describe amenities, facilities, level of service, and cost of properties. They may vary by country. Typical classifications are deluxe/luxury (five star), first class (four star), standard (three star), and economy or budget.

hotel functional positions   *See* bar manager; catering director; concierge; conference services manager; controller; convention services manager; director of sales; executive chef; executive housekeeper; food and beverage manager; front office manager; general manager; maintenance engineer; recreation manager; resident manager; security chief.

hoteling   In telecommuting, describes employees who call ahead to the company's location or leased space to reserve a particular office on the day they come to work.

hotel rate   Guest room, suite, or meeting room prices, usually excluding applicable taxes, such as continental plan, day rate, European plan, flat rate, full American plan, modified American plan, rack rate, and run-of-the-house rate.

hotel rep firm   Hotel associations of private companies that provide promotion, advertising, marketing, and sales services for small and independent hotels that are not affiliated with a chain or lack the funds to set up their own people in branch offices. Often used by meeting planners to save time and money.

hot work group   A work team composed of high-achieving, productive, and dedicated members which is working on exciting, challenging, and rewarding tasks.

hourly charge   A fee for services based upon an agree-upon hourly rate charged by the contractor for such services. The rate may vary based on the nature of the assignment, its duration, location, and difficulty. Travel time may or may not be included, and minimum time limits may be established by the contract.

hourly part-time worker   A flexible staffing option. Employees hired for part-time work who do not receive any of the fringe benefits given to regular employees.

house count In meeting management, a contract item that refers to the actual number of sleeping rooms occupied during a particular night.

house list In direct marketing, a computerized list of a company's clients or customers, individuals and organizations that have purchased products or services in the past

house organ A company publication prepared and distributed for employees. House organs present company "news" and other information relating to matters of interest or concern to employees and their families.

housing allowance A differential paid to employees to adjust for differences, including both rent and basic utilities, between housing costs overseas and comparable housing in the United States.

housing assistance See Taft-Hartley Amendment of 1990.

How Our Business System Operates (HOBSO) A popular corporate information program of the 1950s. Designed to help employees understand their role in the organization.

HR Canada See Federation of Human Resource Associations of Canada (FHRAC).

HRD Hall of Fame Recognition for exceptional contributions to the human resource development profession over a long period of time. Inductees are selected annually by a board composed of HRD professionals. Sponsored by *Training* magazine. *Contact:* Training, Lakewood Publications, Lakewood Bldg., 50 S. Ninth St., Minneapolis, MN 55402 (612/333-0471)

HR Executive of the Year Award and HR Honor Roll Created by *Human Resource Executive* magazine to honor the top senior-level executives in human resources. A panel of judges evaluates finalists and selects a winner and honor roll members from among nominees, all of whom must be skilled professionals, have a record of innovative solutions to significant HR problems, are active in the HR profession as an integral part of an organization, and have made significant contributions to the HR profession as a whole. *Contact: Human Resources Executive*, Ste. 500, 7747 Dresher Rd., Horsham, PA 19044-0980 (215/784-0910).

HR Magazine on Human Resource Management A monthly journal: $60.00 per year (free to members of SHRM).

Address: Society of Human Resource Management, 606 North Washington Street., Alexandria, VA 22314 (703-548-3440; Fax 703-836-0367).

HR·News A monthly journal: $44.00 per year (free to members). Address: Society for Human Resource Managers,, 606 North Washington Street., Alexandria, VA 22314 (703/548-3440; Fax 703/836-0367).

HR self-audit A means of appraising the quality of the entire HR organization or any of its elements, functions, services, or programs and to institute changes to improve them. Using a specific set of standards, an HR self-audit examines every major aspect of HR management, organization, programs, services, facilities, resources, and outcomes in relation to the organization's goals, using observation, interview, and review of documents. It analyzes purposes and objectives, policies, procedures, and budget, management, staffing, systems, programs, services, and facilities (buildings, space, furnishings, equipment, and materials). It identifies strengths, weaknesses, and problems in organizational structure, services, and programs.

HR Service Excellence Award Presented annually to human resource departments in eight organization-size categories for outstanding and quality service provided to their internal customers. Sponsored by the *Human Resource Executive* and HR Solutions Inc. *Contact:* HR Service Excellence Award, 20 N. Wacker Dr., Ste. 4114, Chicago, IL 60606 (Fax 312/236-3959).

HR strategic plan Management's vision of what the corporation's human needs and requirements will be in the future and what the HR organization must become to meet those needs.

huddle group A training technique used to make possible the exchange of experience and the sharing of ideas in a large group; to identify questions, issues, and problems that members of a large group may wish to have considered; to obtain the contributions of reticent trainees; to gather suggestions from the group for improving learning activities; and to evaluate problem solutions. The group is divided into units of six members, given the problem, and allowed six minutes to discuss it and be ready to report back to the total group.

hue In video, the color of light — red, green, and blue combined in any amount.

hue, lightness, saturation (HLS) In desktop publishing, a model for color definition.

Hughes Act of 1970 Established the National Institute for Alcoholism and Alcohol Abuse (NIAAA) as a separate entity from the National Institute of Mental Health, mandated the establishment of an occupational branch for the NIAAA that granted funds for each state to hire two **occupational program consultants**, charged with developing programs in both the private and public sectors, and mandated the development of programs for the prevention, treatment, and rehabilitation of federal employees with substance abuse problems.

humanitarian awards See Hospitality Industry Humanitarian Awards Program.

human capital Contrasted with financial capital or equipment capital. The assets or wealth of an organization embodied in or represented by the hands, minds, and talents of its employees. Also describes what an organization gains from the loyalty, creativity, effort, accomplishments, and productivity of its employees. Said to contribute more than one-half of an organization's productive capacity. It equates to, and may actually exceed, the productive capacity of machine capital and investment in research and development.

human factors engineering (HFE) Systematic and controlled study and research to adapt the work environment and human tasks to the sensory, perceptual, mental, physical, and esthetic attributes, capacities, and preferences of people. HFE is concerned with workplace layout, equipment controls, instrument design, furniture and furnishings, and environmental conditions (lighting, noise level, and so on).

Human Factors and Ergonomics Society (HFES) An interdisciplinary nonprofit organization of 5,000 members involved in the human factors field. Since its formation in 1957, HFES has promoted the discovery and exchange of human factors knowledge, as well as education and training for students and practitioners. HFES is part of the International Ergonomics Association. Contact: HFES, P.O. Box 1369, Santa Monica, CA 90406 (310/394-1811; Fax 310/394-2410).

human immunodeficiency virus (HIV) The virus that causes acquired immune deficiency syndrome (AIDS and associated conditions, such as Aids-related complex). HIV is present in the earliest stages of infection when there are no symptoms as well as in people with full-blown cases of AIDS. A positive HIV test does not mean that the individual will develop AIDS; however such people can transmit the virus. HIV disease is now considered a chronic, treatable disease. Because people with HIV are living longer, more productive lives, there are likely to be more workers with the disease.

humanistic psychology A theory of human behavior that centers on concern for the rights and resources of the individual and the development of open, caring relationships with others. Humanistic psychology focuses on such matters as creativity, self-realization, and integration of the whole person.

human nature ethics An ethical approach to decision and action. Human nature ethics assumes that all humans have inborn capacities that constitute the ultimate basis for all ethical conduct and behavior. Actions, therefore, are judged in terms of whether they promote or hinder, harmonize or conflict with those human capabilities. So, the criterion for judging the rightness of any action is whether or not the action is compatible with one's inherent human capabilities.

human performance technology See performance technology.

human potential movement See human relations; personal growth training; sensitivity training; T-group.

human relations A term popular in the 1950s and 60s used to describe the integration of behavioral and social sciences principles as they apply people at work. Essentially human relations is the development and implementation of productive and fulfilling group effort. Also referred to as organizational behavior.

Human Resource Award of Excellence An award designed to honor leadership and professional excellence in the practice of human resources management. Presented annually by the American Management Association and Olsten Staffing Services to the human resource practitioner who has demonstrated high levels of originality, innovation, creativity, and inventiveness, implementing or enhancing a program or service, and solving a dramatic challenge. *Contact:* Iris Kapustein, Director, Trade Shows, Awards & Associations, The Olsten Corporation, One Merrick Ave., Westbury, NY 11590 (516/317-1680).

Human Resource Development Quarterly
A journal published quarterly by Jossey-Bass Publishers and sponsored by the **American Society for Training and Development**. Subscription rates are $97.00 per year for institutions, agencies, and libraries; $52.00 per year for individuals if payment is made by personal check. *Contact:* Jossey Bass Publishers, 350 Sansome St., San Francisco, CA 94104-1342 (415/433-1767).

Human Resources Executive   A journal published monthly, except semi-monthly in October, November, and June: $69.95. *Contact:* LRP Publications Company, Suite 500, 747 Dresser Rd., Horsham, PA 19044-0980 (215-784-0910; Fax 215/784-0870; E-mail **jfisher@lrp.com**).

human resource management practice sophistication (HRSOPH)   A measure or index of the effects of overall human resources management practice strategy on company performance. The scale, developed in a Department of Labor study conducted at Columbia University, is a tabulation of management best practices in the areas of attitude assessment, compensation, grievance procedures, information sharing, labor-management participation, performance appraisal, and personnel selection. Attributed to Mark A. Huselid ("Documenting HR's Effect on Company Performance," *HRMagazine,* January 1994, pp. 79-85).

The Human Resource Planning Society (HRPS)   A professional organization of 2,500 individual members and 100 corporate sponsors. HRPS' mission is to increase the impact of human resource planning and management on business and organizational performance. The Society provides access to leading-edge thinking, initiates partnerships and establishes networks, and offers a broad range of learning and growth opportunities. *Contact:* HRSP 41 E. 42nd St., Ste., New York, NY 10017; 212/490-6387; Fax 212/682-6851; URL **http://www.ahrm. org/hrps/hrps.htm**).

Human Resource Professional   A journal published six times per year: $105 per year.

Contact: LRP Publications, Suite 500, 747 Dresher Rd., Horsham, PA 19044-0980 (215-784-0860).

Human Resources (HR)   1. The people that staff and operate an organization — the executives, managers, supervisors, scientists and engineers, technicians, marketing and sales personnel, administrative and clerical personnel, and hourly workers — as contrasted with the financial and material resources of an organization. **2.** The organizational function that deals with the people who manage, produce, market, and sell the products and services of an organization.

human resources accounting (HRA)
A means of measuring employees' costs and value to an organization. A tool to help management make decisions based on facts, figures, and historical data in matters such as hiring, layoffs, transfers, training, and retaining people. Typically performed by the accounting department in conjunction with the HR or personnel department.

human resources development (HRD)
Refers to career development, training and development, and organization development programs offered to employees to develop new or replacement knowledge and skills, improve their performance, potential, and promotability, enhance their general personal growth, and improve group and overall organizational effectiveness.

Human Resources Effectiveness Studies
A joint project of the **Society for Human Resources Management** and the Saratoga Institute that provides figures for checking how well various HR functions are being handled. Conducts annual surveys. *Contact:* SHRM, 606 N. Washington St., Alexandria, VA 22314 (703/548-3440).

human resources engineering   *See* human resources environment.

human resources environment (HRE)
Consists of organization-sponsored activities designed to improve the workplace and work conditions and relationships. Also referred to as *human resources engineering.*

human resources information center (HRIC)   One of the critical components of a human resources information system (HRIS). The HRIC is an administrative element that serves as the interface between the system and its users. The center ensures that required information is being inputted to the system, that required checks, edits, and corrections are being made, and that needed outputs are being accessed, coordinated, and disseminated.

human resources information system (HRIS) A computer-based system for collecting, storing, maintaining, and retrieving data on people, jobs, compensation and benefits, and employment forecasts and conditions to automate HR functions and provide data to managers on demand. Also known as human resources management system, human resources system, and personnel system.

human resources management (HRM) The organization function that focuses on the management and direction of people. HRM deals with the human element in the organization — people as individuals and groups, their recruitment, selection, assignment, motivation, compensation, utilization, services, training, development, promotion, termination, and retirement.

human resources management system (HRMS) An integrated system of human relations, payroll, benefits applications, and the like.

human resources planning (HRP) The process of ensuring that personnel in the numbers and with the skills and experience required by the organization will be available when needed.

human resources utilization (HRU) Refers specifically to the utilization of people within an organization to maximize organizational benefits as well as provide employees with the personal and job satisfaction they need to be productive, effective, and loyal.

human skills The ability to work effectively as a member of a group, the capacity to build cooperative effort within teams, and to deal effectively with interpersonal conflict. Requisites include understanding people and self awareness — understanding one's own motivations, biases, and blind spots.

hurricane writing See mind-mapping.

hybrid organization An organization that balances the use of both horizontal and vertical organization models.

hybrid projector A video and data projection system that combines two or more technologies, such as a combination of an integrated light source with its own lens and a slide projector.

hydrotherapy Most often involves a reclined whirlpool bath with an external water hose used by an attendant to give a person a full body massage. Also includes mineral baths, Scotch showers, Swiss needle showers, and other forms of whirlpool baths.

hypercard See hypertext.

hyperlink A highlighted word or graphic on a **World Wide Web** page that, when clicked on by a mouse, can connect the user to a new location.

hypermedia **1.** A form of **computer-supported learning resource**, tools that integrate performance support for workers. Links different media under learner or worker control. Hypermedia programs are "stacks," and pages (screen images) within a stack are "cards." **2.** On the **Internet,** highlighted text linked to related pages at the same or other Web sites.

hypertalk See hypertext.

hypertension Occurs when an individual's blood pressure is consistently higher than the normal range for his or her age group. It is measured by two numbers: (1) the higher number represents the systolic blood pressure when the heart is working at its maximum and exerts the maximum amount of pressure on the arteries; and (2) the lower number represents the diastolic blood pressure when the minimum amount of pressure is exerted on the arteries. In adults, hypertension is defined as a systolic blood pressure of 140 mm or greater and/or a diastolic blood pressure of 90 mm or greater. Prolonged elevated blood pressure can lead to heart attack, stroke, kidney failure, and atherosclerosis. Although hypertension cannot be cured, it can be treated and controlled with medication, losing weight, restricting alcohol and sodium consumption, regular exercise, quitting smoking, and reducing stress. Affects 27.5 million Americans. Also called *high blood pressure.*

hypertext A type of **computer-supported learning resources.** The term is used generically to refer to interactive media — a means of interacting with a computer in a nonlinear way, a manner that reflects the way people think. Essentially a software program that links graphics and text. Users can use a personal computer to browse rapidly through a document, select a word or phrase, and, with the touch of a button, go directly to linked documents, cross-references, annotations, or footnotes.

HyperText Markup Language (HTML)
The formatting protocol used by World Wide Web sites and interpreted by Web browsers.

hypertext system A computer database (software) that brings several elements together on screen and responds to the non-linear process of human thought. The user can begin with a topic, locate one or more cases of it, and, without having to return to a master menu, branch to associated topics. In essence, users can follow their mental processes directly through the text and save time and reduce frustration.

Hypertext Transport Protocol (HTTP)
The Internet standard coding system that enables users to distribute information and data (links, graphics, and text) across the World Wide Web.

hypnotherapy An alternative form of medical treatment in which therapeutic suggestions are made to relieve pain or speed the healing of patients by placing them in a hypnotic trance state.

hypochondriasis An obsessive preoccupation with a particular illness based on an individual's misinterpretation of bodily sensations. People who suffer from this disorder frequently believe themselves ill when they are not.

hypomania A severe state of **mania** characterized by persistently euphoric or irritable moods, appetite disturbance, decreased need for sleep, increased activity, pressured speech, and loss of judgment and self-control.

hypothesis A shrew inference or guess that is specifically formulated and provisionally adopted to explain observed facts or conditions and to guide in their further investigation in the search for evidence. An educated hunch.

I

IAAVC   International Association of Audio Visual Communicators.

IABC   International Association of Business Communicators.

IACC   International Association of Conference Centers.

IACET   International Association for Continuing Education & Training.

IACMP   International Association of Career Management Professionals.

IACVB   International Association of Convention & Visitor Bureaus.

IAFE   International Association of Fairs and Expositions.

IAPP   International Association of Presentation Professionals.

IADAT   Integrated Applications Digital and Audio Trainer.

IACVB   International Association of Convention & Visitor Bureaus.

IAEDP   International Association of Eating Disorders Professionals.

IAEM   International Association for Exposition Management.

IAF   International Accreditation Forum.

IAFE   International Association of Fairs & Expositions.

IAFP   International Association for Financial Planning.

IAM&AW   International Association of Machinists and Aerospace Workers.

IAPBI   Information Access Project for Blind Individuals.

IAPP   International Association of Presentation Professionals.

IAV   Interactive video system.

IBEW   International Brotherhood of Electrical Workers.

IBT   **1.** Instructor-based training. **2.** Internet-based training.

IC   **1.** Independent contractor. **2.** Information center.

ICCA   International Congress and Convention Association.

ICD-9-CM   *International Classification of Diseases,* 9th revision, clinical modification.

ICFA   Institute for Chartered Financial Analysts.

ICFP   The Institute of Certified Financial Planners.

ICIA   The International Communications Industries Association.

ICM   **1.** Individual case management. **2.** Institute for Crisis Management.

ICPA   Insurance Conference Planners Association.

ICSA   International Customer Service Association.

ICTA   Institute of Certified Travel Agents.

IDEA   Individuals with Disabilities Education Act of 1997.

I-DPO   Internet direct public offering.

IDS   Integrated delivery system.

IDTV   Improved definition television.

IEAP   Integrated Employee Assistance Program.

IEP   Individual education plan.

IFAC   The International Federation of Accountants.

IFEBP   International Foundation of Employee Benefits Plans.

IFHOH International Federation of Hard of Hearing People.

IFTDO International Federation of Training and Development Organizations.

IGLTA International Gay & Lesbian Travel Association.

IHRIM International Association for Human Resource Information Management.

IICS International Interactive Communications Society.

IIE Institute of Industrial Engineers.

III Insurance Information Institute.

IIS Integrated instructional system.

IIRIRA Illegal Immigration Reform and Immigrant Responsibility Act of 1996

IKWUM I know what you mean (Internet speak).

ILEI Index of Leading Economic Indicators.

ILO International Labor Organization.

ILS Integrated learning system.

IM Instructional management.

IMA Interactive Multimedia Association

IMC Institute of Management Consultants.

IME Independent medical examination.

IMHO In my humble opinion.

IMMAC 90 Immigration Act of 1990.

IMO In my opinion (Internet abbreviation).

IMS Interactive Market Systems.

INA Immigration and Nationality Act of 1952.

INFORMS Institute for Operations Research and the Management Sciences

IPA 1. Independent Practice Association. 2. Individual practice association.

IPG Immediate participation guarantee.

IPMA International Personnel Management Association.

IPO 1. Initial public offering. 2. Individual pays own. 3. Independent physician organization.

IQ Intelligence quotient.

IRA Individual retirement account.

IRC 1. Internal Revenue Code. 2. Internet relay chat.

IRCA Immigration Reform and Control Act of 1986.

IRL Institute for Research on Learning.

IRR Individual Ready Reserve.

IRRA Industrial Relations Research Association.

IRS Internal Revenue Service.

IS Information systems.

ISBN International Standard Book Number.

ISCEBS International Society of Certified Employee Benefit Specialists.

ISD Instructional systems development.

ISDN Integrated Services Digital Network.

ISGLMP International Society of Gay and Lesbian Meeting Professionals

ISMP International Society of Meeting Planners.

ISO 1. Incentive stock options. 2. International Standards Organization.

ISO 9000 International Standards Organization 9000 series.

ISP Internet service provider.

ISPI International Society for Performance and Improvement.

ISSN International Standard Serial Number

ISTE International Society for Technology in Education.

IT 1. Instructional technology. 2. Information technology.

ITA Information Technology Agreement.

ITBS International Travel Briefing Service, The.

ITCA International Teleconferencing Association.

ITI   Industrial Technology Institute.
ITS   Intelligent tutoring system.
ITTA   Information Technology Training Association, Inc.
ITVA   International Television Association.
IVD   Interactive videodisc.
IVLA   International Visual Literacy Association.
IVR   Interactive voice response.
IVS   Interactive video system.
IWS   Intelligent work station.

iatrogenic injury   *See* adverse medical event.

IBM National Support Center for Persons with Disabilities   Created to help health care leaders, agency directors, policy makers, employers, educators, public officials, and individuals learn how technology can improve the quality of life for disabled persons in the school, home, and workplace. Responds to requests for information on how computers can help people with vision problems, hearing problems, speech impairments, learning disabilities, mental retardation, or prescribe assistive devices or software. *Contact:* IBM National Support Center for Persons with Disabilities, P.O. Box 2150, Atlanta, GA 30055 (800/426-2133).

IBM's Program to Train Disabled Persons   Helped establish 53 centers nationwide that train people with disabilities for careers in information processing industries. Most centers provide programmer training for individuals with physical disabilities to learn entry-level computer programming skills and to obtain jobs. A second program provides personal computer skills-based training to people with disabilities. *Contact* IBM, 2000 Purchase St., Purchase, NY 10577-2597 (914/697-6595).

ice   An odorless, colorless crystalline, smokable, and highly addictive form of speed (methamphetamine). The drug makes people aggressive and violent. When smoked it provides a high of from 4 to 24 hours. Used over time, the drug can cause permanent mental impairment. Also known as *glass, crank, rock, meth,* and *crystal meth.*

iceberg training   A consequence of corporate downsizing, training budget cuts, and the demand of boards of control to do more with less. Involves training supervisors, technicians, or skilled operative employees to train their employees in the essentials of a particular job (the tip of the iceberg), rather than attempting them to teach them everything they know. Coined by Walter DiMantova, Director of the Center for Corporate Training, Eastern Michigan University, Ypsilanti, Michigan.

icebreaker   An opener, warm-up, energizer, and tension-reducer for training sessions and workshops, such as games, simulations, exercises, and brain-teasers. Icebreakers help the trainer or workshop leader begin sessions with impact, acquaint participants with one another comfortably, and reenergize group members during flat periods.

icon   In computers, a symbol that appears on the screen (CRT) which, when signaled (clicked with a mouse), causes a user's command to the program to be activated.

idea bank   A manual or computerized file of ideas, critical incidents, and events of importance to enterprise planning, management, operations, and control. Used as a source of new initiatives or problem solving approaches.

idea processor   An electronic means of outlining using a personal computer and software that serves as a text editor operating on lines of text instead of individual words. The user enters one idea on each line and then can arrange them hierarchically — the broader concepts broken down sequentially into less comprehensive ones. The user can easily group and regroup ideas until satisfied with the logic of the arrangement.

ideation   Piling up alternative ideas for the solution of problems.

ideational fluency   *See* thinking fluency.

illegal immigrants   *See* A.P.R.A. Fuel Oil Buyers Group Inc., et al; immigration Act of 1990; Immigration Reform and Control Act of 1986.

Illegal Immigration Reform and Immigrant Responsibility Act of 1996 (IIRIRA)   Reduced the number of documents that an employer can accept as proof of identity and eligibility to work in the United States. On a date to be established by the attorney general (but not later than September 30, 1997), employers can no longer accept certificates of naturalization, certificates of citizenship, foreign passports, or birth certificates. Acceptable documents for both identity and employability (List A) are limited to a U.S.

passport, an alien registration card, or other documents designated by the attorney general. Acceptable documents for establishing employment eligibility only (List C) are limited to a U.S. social security card and other documents as determined by the attorney general.

image *See* corporate image; self-image.

image consulting Consulting practice that focuses on public speaking (speech and appearance) training and/or wardrobe/color/style advising.

image database Software that creates a **database** of images, animations, and **digital video** with a single command. It compresses images to save disk space and allows the user to catalog all image formats. The database keeps images organized on a hard drive and enables the user to obtain data on a specific image — what drive and volume the image is on, its name, creator, and the date it was last modified. Some image databases can locate graphics files over a network on servers and on other hard drives.

image doctor *See* spin master.

imagesetter **1.** A high-resolution laser output device that transfers digitized type or images onto photosensitive paper. **2.** Typesetters connected to desktop publishing workstations used to record halftones and line images as well as type.

imagineering Visualizing as an individual or as part of a group how things would be if everything were perfect — no problems, no complications, no obstacles, no errors. The exercise is said to open people's minds to possibilities and opportunities for improvement and, at the same time foster teamwork and collaboration.

imaging *See* creative imagery; guided imaging/imagery; reproductive imagery; speculative imagery; structural imaging/imagery.

imaging software Programs that drive personal computer graphics production such as CAD engineering/architectural drawing, theatrical costume design, digital map-making, 3-dimensional modeling, and photorealism.

immediate annuity An annuity that provides for payments to the beneficiary beginning the year following the purchase of the annuity.

immediate evaluation Evaluation that focuses on ongoing programs and activities. Its objective is to assess the quality of programs and services while they are in operation to provide

supervisors and employees or instructors and trainees the feedback they need to improve their performance. There are three subcategories of immediate evaluation: participant reaction, measurement of behavioral or attitudinal change, and the self-evaluation self-audit.

immediate participation guarantee (IPG) A funding plan vehicle for annuity contracts.

Immigration Act of 1990 (IMMAC 90) Legislation enacted into law on November 29, 1990 that reconstructed the controlling immigration statutes. The Act includes a new classification and quota system for the allocation of immigrant visas (for temporary workers) and affects all persons seeking permanent residency status in the United States. One of the most significant features of the Act is that persons seeking entry on the basis of an offer of employment from a U.S. employer may do so as long as they present unique expertise, training, and experience. It creates a separate category for professionals (such as engineers, scientists, accountants, health practitioners, and teachers) with advanced degrees and gives them priority over lesser-skilled workers. Another feature imposes annual caps on certain occupations for the allocation of nonimmigrant employment-related visas (H-1B employer-sponsored temporary visas). And an employer must now certify to the Department of Labor that the company is offering at least the local prevailing wages and working conditions to H-1B workers and all U.S. workers hold the same job at the employer's facility.

Immigration and Nationality Act of 1952 (INA) An Act that made it unlawful for any person or organization to hire, recruit, or refer for a fee, an alien for employment in the United States, knowing the alien is unauthorized for employment or, after hiring an alien authorized employment, continuing to employ that individual knowing that the alien has become unauthorized with respect to employment. The Act also deals with the admission and employment of special agricultural workers and temporary workers and proscribes discrimination against aliens authorized employment on the basis of national origin or citizenship status.

Immigration and Naturalization Service B-1 status Under the Immigration Reform and Control Act of 1990, a program designed to allow foreign nationals to visit the United States a maximum of one year (with extensions possible) to attend conventions, look for business opportunities, or negotiate agreements.

Immigration and Naturalization Service E-1 status   Available for foreign nationals who are executives, supervisors, or highly skilled workers and who are involved in substantial trade or active investment principally between their home country and the United States; for example, employees of an airline that flies regularly to U.S. cities.

Immigration and Naturalization Service EB-1 status   Designed for aliens with extraordinary ability, outstanding professors and researchers, and multinational executives and managers.

Immigration and Naturalization Service EB-2 status   Designed for professionals with advanced degrees or aliens with exceptional abilities (a somewhat lower level of knowledge and skills than is required for EB-1 status). Requires a sponsoring employer and also permanent labor certification.

Immigration and Naturalization Service EB-3 status   Designed for skilled workers, professionals, and "other workers" who have a parent affiliate or subsidiary abroad and must have worked in a foreign facility for one year in the three years preceding entry into the U.S. Maximum stay in the U.S. is seven years. Applicants must receive labor certification.

Immigration and Naturalization Service H-1B status   Designed to allow nonimmigrant professional workers to enter the United States temporarily to work in specialty occupations which typically require a bachelor's degree or higher. The status is valid only for employment with the sponsoring employer, and the employer must demonstrate his or her status as a professional and may be required to have the alien's credentials evaluated.

Immigration and Naturalization Service TN status   Under the **North American Free Trade Agreement,** allows citizens of Canada and Mexico engaged in professional-level activities to enter the U.S. Must show purpose of entry, professional activity, and educational qualifications, and compliance with applicable state laws, and must state anticipated length of stay and remuneration. Canadians may apply at the border. There is no specific limit on the total number of one-year extensions for Canadians; there is a limit for Mexicans.

Immigration Nursing Relief Act of 1989   Exempts foreign nurses who have legally worked as registered nurses in the United States for at least three years and who began work before September 1, 1989 from the annual national quota. Designed to help U.S. health care facilities to deal with the shortage of registered nurses.

Immigration Reform Act of 1996   Signed into law September 30, 1996. Established three voluntary pilot programs to enhance the ability of employers to confirm new worker eligibility: (1) an enhanced telephone verification system; (2) waiver of certain paperwork requirements if a new employee attests to being a U..S. citizen; or (3) the use of machine-readable documents. Unless reauthorized by Congress, the pilot program expires after four years. The Act also reduced the number of acceptable documents an employee can present for employer verification as follows: For employability and identity, a U.S. passport, a resident alien or alien registration card, or other documents designated by the Attorney General (possibly a visa or foreign passport); for employability only, a social security card or "certain other documents found acceptable by the Attorney General" (such as an employment authorization card; and for identity only, a state driver's license or identification card.

Immigration Reform and Control Act of 1986 (IRCA)   Designed to stem the influx of illegal immigrants, the Act instituted a system of penalties for employers or referral agencies who knowingly recruit, hire, or refer illegal aliens. Employers must file INS form I-9, Employment Eligibility Verification Form, certifying that all newly hired employees are not illegal aliens by ascertaining that they have a U.S. passport, a certificate of U.S. citizenship, a certificate of naturalization, a resident alien card, or a combination of documents (such as social security and birth certificates) showing authorization to work in the United States.

immigration tracking   *See* Immigration Reform and Control Act of 1986.

immunosuppressive drugs   Medication used in immunosuppressive therapy to prevent the rejection of organ transplants.

impact evaluation   An approach to evaluation that focuses on the effects (bottom line results) of programs on individuals or departments, divisions, or corporations. Examples are the extent to which a wellness program reduced absenteeism and accidents or the extent to which an executive succession program, coupled with a cross-cultural training program, provided the executives needed for a global expansion program.

impact wheel   A normative technological forecasting technique that employs a panel of experts to identify important but sometimes obscure impacts and implications of carefully selected changes or developments. A description of the event, change, or development is placed in a circle in the center of a large sheet of paper or on a chalkboard. The panel is asked to identify the direct consequences of the occurrence of the central item, and their responses are placed in smaller circles around the circumference of the initial entry, each connected to the base circle by a single line. Then participants are asked to identify the impacts of each of the first-level consequences, and they are placed in ovals surrounding the first-level entries and connected to them with a single line. The process is continued with additional levels of consequences placed in ovals in a series of concentric circles and connected by single dotted lines to their progenitors until the process loses its usefulness.

impairment   Diminished bodily function resulting from accident or injury that may or may not be disabling depending on the occupation, age, education, work attitude, and so on of the worker. As defined by the **Americans with Disabilities Act of 1990,** "any physiological disorder or condition, cosmetic disfigurement, or anatomical loss affecting one or more of the following body systems: neurological; musculoskeletal; special sense organs (including speech organs that are not respiratory, such as vocal cords, soft palate, and tongue); respiratory, including speech organs; cardiovascular; reproductive; digestive; genitourinary; hemic and lymphatic; skin; and endocrine. It also means any mental or psychological disorder, such as mental retardation, organic brain syndrome, emotional or mental illness, and specific learning disabilities." Impairment does not include homosexuality or bisexuality.

implacement   Helping workers whose jobs have been abolished to identify new career interests and options and develop the skills needed to fulfill them. May involve testing, assessment, career counseling, and retraining. Sometimes undertaken to avoid the costs of recruiting and training new employees.

implementation   **1.** One of the five major steps in getting a computer system up and running. In sequence the steps are design, development, installation, implementation, and operation. It involves modifying or customizing the system to meet specific user needs. **2.** One of three crucial elements of all activities used in **adventure training**. The others are **framing** and **debriefing**. Implementation is the actual conduct of the learning activity.

import   The acceptance of a program or data file by another computer program in a ready-to-use form with all formatting codes intact.

imposed discipline   Discipline that has its roots in the authority of managers. It makes use of deterrents and penalties to secure compliance with organizational rules and policies. Sometimes called *command discipline.*

imposing   *See* imposition process.

imposition process   In desktop publishing, a part of the pre-press process in which the various documents that will be combined to produce a book are placed according to color, section, or content; the press plate is set up using the number of pages per plate, their orientation, the folding style, binding style, margins for spines, press marks; and the imposition sequence that determines the actual page order an signatures sizes (plate styles). Once the plate has been set up, it is combined with other plate styles to form a book style. The last stage of the imposition process is setting the book to film, usually by outputting the plates to an imagesetter.

impression   In printing, the pressure of type, plate, or blanket as it comes in contact with the paper.

Improshare   Translation: *im* proved *pro* ductivity through *shar* ing. A form of gain sharing, it is an employee involvement and productivity scheme that emphasizes performance and reductions in the number of hours invested in the production of goods or services instead of dollars or reduced costs as a measure of results. Management and workers share the same goals and benefit from the same results — productivity and reduced production costs.

improved-definition television (IDTV)
Television sets that feature images that are more accurate, have better definition, and less "noise" than conventional TV sets. The scanning rate of the sets is doubled (from 262 1/2 to 525 lines every 1/60th of a second) so that scanning lines are almost invisible and vertical resolution is improved by 40 percent.

Improving America's Schools Act of 1994
Encourages the integration of vocational training into the school curriculum to produce skilled workers for the labor market.

improvisational ability   The capacity to ad-lib, jury-rig, extemporize. The ability to use familiar objects, concepts, and ideals or their components in new ways or to transform the absurd or incongruous into logical, reasonable, and workable ideas.

inappropriate affect   In mental illness, emotional tone or outward reaction in disharmony or at variance with the idea, object, or thought accompanying it.

inbasket exercise   An instructional method (also used as an assessment center valuative device) involving the use of a representative sample of a month's or even a full year's performance in all aspects of a job. It is used to analyze and evaluate trainees' decision making abilities or to provide practice in decision making. Trainees are given background materials and are then exposed to a structured array of memos, reports, letters, telephone calls, visits, and meetings. In the role of manager, the trainee makes decisions on the incoming "mail." Time limits are established to introduce realism and cause stress. The decision making phase is followed by discussion and critiques of the actions taken and decisions reached. All actions are analyzed, evaluated, and fed back to participants.

in camera   A legal term that literally means "in private." It occurs when a judge determines that it is necessary to conduct a hearing or a part of it "in chambers" because the sensitive nature of the matter in question precludes public exposure.

incentive   A tangible (usually) or intangible reward, financial or otherwise, for performance or achievement that tends to induce, stimulate, or spur individual or group motivation and action. Examples are commissions, bonuses, stock-sharing plans, merchandise, and travel.

incentive bonus   Additional pay awarded as a means of recognizing peak employee performance.

Incentive: Managing and Marketing Through Motivation   A monthly journal: $48.00 per year (free to qualified subscribers). *Contact:* Bill Communications, Inc., 355 Park Avenue South, New York NY 10010 (212/592-6400; Fax 212/592-6459); E-mail **khein@bill.com**; URL **http://www. incentive mag.com**).

incentive pay   Any form of compensation designed to motivate employees to produce specified results or behave in a specific way and to reward them for doing so.

incentive plan   A plan that provides financial rewards to workers whose productivity or contributions to the organization exceed some predetermined standard. Incentives for production workers include piecework plans and group incentive plans; for executives and managers, bonuses, stock options, and the like; for salespersons commissions, bonuses, and special awards.

incentive retirement plan   Incentives offered to encourage early retirement, used as a painless method of reducing personnel during downsizing and restructuring. They involve enhancement of earned retirement benefits and are paid to all eligible employees who volunteer to retire during the period in which the program is offered.

incentives   Bonuses offered to physicians by **health maintenance organizations** for minimizing or reducing health care costs

incentive stock options (ISO)   Authorized by the Economic Recovery Act of 1981, an ISO grants an employee, usually an executive, the right to pay the current market price for shares in the company at a future time. ISOs qualify for favorable tax treatment under Section 422A, Internal Revenue Code.

incentive travel   Considered by the Internal Revenue Service as a business vacation. In the travel industry, it is defined as travel awarded to an employee, customer, or independent contractor as a prize for the attainment of corporate goals or objectives. If the award is given for business reasons, the sponsor may get the full deduction for all expenses incurred in providing the prize. However, the individual who receives the award must pay taxes on the full, fair market value of the incentive travel.

incentive work Used where work output is measurable in units of product, pieces, items, and so on and the rate of pay is stated as dollars paid for each unit or piece produced. Also called *piece rate; piecework.*

incidental graphics The use of a chalkboard, easel, or flip chart to illustrate concepts, or principles by means of drawings, diagrams, symbols, or words during or immediately preceding the presentation of instruction.

incident method A variation of the case method of instruction. With the incident method, only a brief sketch of the climax of a case is presented. It is used to develop judgment, critical thinking, and problem solving ability. Trainees are given a few minutes to study the incident and attempt to determine the information they need to find out what is going on. Trainees then get the facts by asking questions of the instructor in a limited period of time. Questions must be of the type that can be answered yes or no or by a simple factual statement. The group then determines the nature of the problem and the decisions that are needed to solve it.

inclusion A commitment to educate or train people with disabilities (and members of other minority groups), to the maximum extent possible, in the regular school or classroom they would otherwise attend. For people with disabilities, it may involve bringing support services, such as specially trained teachers or instructors, to the person, rather than moving the person to the services. Inclusion is believed to result in increased productivity in the workplace because it allows everyone to participate, not only as employees, trainees, and volunteers, but also as clients and customers.

inclusive rate In meeting management, rates for sleeping rooms, function rooms, banquets, and other activities that include gratuities, service charges, and taxes. May also include breakfast and other meals.

income-based entitlements Federal entitlement programs that pay benefits only to those whose incomes or assets are below established levels, such as **Medicaid**, Aid to Families with Dependent Children, **food stamps**, and **Supplemental Security Income**. Also called *means-tested entitlements.*

income statement One of the key financial documents of an organization, the income statement includes the revenues and expenses applicable to a specific period of time, such as a quarter or year.

income statement method A means of valuing a business. It involves examining the company's current and projected earnings using this formula: value = avg. earnings years 1 and 2 X price-earnings multiple (est. business growth)

in-company counseling A form of employee assistance program (EAP), also called inhouse counseling. Hiring a trained professional counselor or psychologist to conduct all aspects of the EAP from diagnosis through treatment to followup.

in-company diagnosis A form of employee assistance program. The practice of hiring a professional to diagnose the problems of employees and then referring them to appropriate external sources of help. Also called *in-house diagnosis.*

inconsistency One of the primary sources of rating errors. Variations in the methodology or approach used in evaluation cause inconsistency.

in-country support An intercultural intervention in which persons assigned overseas are provided specific contacts and help of all kinds on an as-needed basis for the first three or four months of the foreign assignment.

incremental budgeting A budgeting system that accepts and applies the basic premise that prior funding levels are required for continued operations. It accepts the existing base and permits continuation of the activities, programs, and services of previous years at a minimum of the same level of funding. New or expanded activities, programs, or services, as well as inflation, are evaluated in terms of the costs to be added to the prior budget.

incubation One of the primary steps in the creative problem solving process. Incubation is a period of time in which the individual's attention is deliberately or accidentally shifted or drifted away from the problem to encourage or allow the development of new insights.

incumbent worker training Training designed to update and change worker skills to help them maintain employment and qualify for better jobs.

indemnity Repayment by an insurer for a loss suffered by the insured person or organization.

indemnity insurance Insurance that pays for specific covered services.

indemnity plan **1.** An insurance plan that offers protection against loss or damages, current or future, by providing compensation or remuneration for losses sustained. **2.** In medical and health benefits, typically a benefit provided by an insurance company and which constitutes a plan, such as a major medical plan, that pays an insured's medical expenses or reimburses an employee for "usual and customary" medical expenses in excess of a deductible of $100 a calendar year, 80 percent of the next $5,000, and 100 percent above that amount, and sometimes limited to a semiprivate hospital room.

independent contractor (IC)   An alternative staffing option. Involves contracting with self-employed individuals to perform specialized functions or tasks — typically those that require high-level professional or technical knowledge and skills. Common law rules adopted by the IRS classify workers as *employees* for tax purposes if they: (1) must comply with employer's instructions about the work, (2) receive training from or at the direction of the employer, (3) provide services that are integrated into the business, (4) provide services that must be rendered personally, (5) hire, supervise, and pay assistants for the employer, (6 have a continuing working relationship with the employer, (7) must follow set hours of work, (8) work full-time for an employer, (9) must do their work on the employer's premises, (10) must do their work in a sequence set by the employer, (11) must submit regular reports to the employer, (12) receive payments of regular amount at set intervals, (13) receive payments for business and traveling expenses, (14) rely on the employer to furnish tools and materials, (15) lack a major investment in facilities used to perform the service, (16) cannot make a profit or suffer a loss from the services, (17) work for one employer at a time, (18) do not offer their services to the general public, (19) can be fired by the employer, and (20) may quit work anytime without incurring liability.

Independent Contractor Tax Simplification Act of 1996   Filed in Congress to be effective for services performed by independent contractors. If passed into law, it will be a reworking and refinement of the 20-factor test used to to determine whether a company has the required direction and control over a person, which denotes employee status. Three questions would decide the issue: (1) is there a written agreement between the parties? (2) does it appear that the worker has made some investment, such as the purchase of tools and equipment, incurred significant unreimbursed expenses, or is being compensated primarily on the basis of commissions? (3) does the worker appear to have some independence, such as other customers/clients, his or her own place of business, or flexibility in where or when to work? When the answer to all three of these questions is "yes," the worker is an independent contractor and both parties must continue to report all payments for services in excess of $600 annually to the IRS (Form 1099).

independent living   Arrangements that allow persons with disabilities to live on their own although with some support.

independent living center   A publicly or privately funded agency, usually staffed at least in part by persons with disabilities, established to provide the support services and resources that persons with disabilities often need to live on their own.

independent medical examination (IME) An objective medical examination conducted by an independent practitioner to provide proof of disability in the case of a questionable claim.

independent physician organization (IPO) An alliance formed to help serve employer health needs and reduce costs by establishing a link between physicians and employee-patients. Services include those provided by physicians and selected hospitals, employer health insurance or reinsurance for companies with catastrophic claims, physician-directed utilization review, and claim adjudication.

independent practice   A training technique that involves meaningful and challenging "solo" practice of a skill or task to "set" the learning — for example, homework. It is provided immediately following **guided practice**.

independent practice association (IPA) An HMO that contracts with individual physicians in private practice or associations of independent physicians to provide care to members within a private office setting at a negotiated per capita rate, flat retainer, or negotiated fee-for-service rate to HMO members. Physicians maintain their own offices and often see non-HMO patients on a fee-for-service basis. Other health care services are provided through affiliated hospitals or specialists referred by members' primary care providers.

independent study *See* correspondence study; home study; self-directed learning.

index On the World Wide Web, a searchable catalog of documents created by a **search engine.**

indexing **1.** Automatic adjustment of benefits payments to reflect changes in consumer prices, cost-of-living, or other index of inflation. **2.** A formula for calculating Social Security benefits established to correct a flaw in an old formula that overcompensated for inflation and threw the system out of actuarial balance. Indexing expresses prior year **Federal Insurance Contributions Act of 1935** (FICA) earnings in terms of current dollars.

Index of Leading Economic Indicators (ILEI) The Department of Commerce's primary economic forecasting measure. Used to project economic upturns and recessions by tracking applications for unemployment benefits, buyer traffic, business delivery times, sales activity, stock prices, backlogs of unfilled orders, home building permits issued, and so on.

indirect costs Items of expense that are not associated with specific HR projects, programs, or activities. That is, they are costs that result from common activities that cannot be practically assigned to production as direct costs. Examples are fringe benefits (medical and health insurance, pension payments, and wellness programs) and overhead costs (such as rent, utilities, office equipment, and accounting services.

indirect labor Labor needed to support the production or manufacture of a product or provide a service but is not directly involved in the production or manufacture; for example, training employees in the use of equipment needed in production.

indirect measure A test that measures testees' knowledge, skills, or abilities by means other than actual task performance. For example, obtaining data about testees' ability to repair a carburetor through a paper-and-pencil test that asks them to list the parts of a carburetor, identify the most com-

mon failure points, and describe the steps required to repair the faulty component.

individual account defined benefit plan *See* account balance pension.

individual annuity An annuity purchased individually to meet the needs of specific plan participants.

individual case management (ICM) Monitoring and influencing the treatment of employees with personal, social, or emotional problems.

individual differences In learning, differences among humans in aptitude, ability, habits, ideals, appreciations, interests, learning styles, education, and experience. One of the essential considerations in planning learning experiences.

individual education plan (IEP) A tool to address both academic and personal modifications, specific instructional needs, and measures to determine success and present levels of performance of students with disabilities. It also charts out the daily class schedule, the percentage of time the individual must comply with the regulations within the education plan, and identifies the expectations the school has for the person with the disability.

individual evaluation A form of immediate evaluation that examines changes in the on-the-job behavior of managers, supervisors, workers, clients, customers, dealers, franchisees, or suppliers following training or some other type of intervention. It usually involves questionnaires, rating scales, interviews, tests, or observation.

individual incentive A type of compensation or pay-for-performance plan that ties all or a part of an employee's pay to his or her own performance. It is particularly appropriate where individual output is measurable and quantifiable.

individual interview A method of job analysis in which selected job incumbents are interviewed by a trained job analyst using a standard interview form. Data are collected on duties and tasks performed, the frequency and duration of performance, the sequence of tasks, the importance and difficulty of tasks, amount and kind of supervision received, and the tools and equipment used.

individualized instruction Instructional systems, programs, or modules designed to allow individual trainees to proceed at their own rates through a sequence of learning activities. Activities are designed to provide for individual trainee differences in learning styles, experience, aptitudes, abilities, interests, and needs. The objectives of such systems are to reduce training time, increase learning gain per unit of training time, lower trainee attrition, and reduce instructor requirements and training costs. Also called *self-paced training.*

individualized learning programs Carefully designed learning programs prepared for special needs trainees or students, including those with physical, mental, emotional, and learning disabilities.

individual practice association (IPA) A type of managed care. Similar to a **health maintenance organization,** except that it doesn't operate its own clinics. Rather, it is a loosely organized network of health care providers who treat their patients in their own offices. The providers agree to fees and medical protocols established by the IPA, which pays their bills without having patients submit insurance forms. Physician members can be paid on a fee-for-service basis, a capitated fee, or other means.

Individual Ready Reserve (IRR) The Armed Forces reserve component that is composed of ready reserve members who are fulfilling the remainder of their eight-year military service obligation or are serving in the IRR in a nontraining status voluntarily. They are carried on the rolls of the Reserve Component but are not assigned to units. Although they are not obligated to attend monthly drills or perform annual training, they must keep administrative authorities informed of their addresses and report once each year for a records check, usually at a local recruiting station.

individual retirement account (IRA) A form of defined contribution plan and an inducement to savings and investment. IRAs permit deferral of taxes (and in some cases are tax deductible) on income placed in retirement accounts to be incrementally withdrawn at a later date. To qualify, deferrals are prescribed in terms of annual limits, withdrawal restrictions, and penalties. In 1996, several changes were made to the law. Instead of requiring that individuals begin withdrawing money our of the plan

no later than April 1 of the year following the year he or she reached age 70 and 1/2, even if continuing to work, the new law allows individuals 70 1/2 to delay making distributions until they retire, which allows the funds in the retirement plan to continue to grow on a tax-deferred basis. For someone who is already over the age of 70 1/2 but is still working, the law allows (but does not require) the person to stop making distributions until retirement. Penalty-free IRA withdrawals to pay for medical expenses in excess of 7.5 percent of adjusted gross income, plus penalty-free withdrawals by the unemployed to pay for health insurance will also be allowed in 1997. The new law also allows deductible contributions of up to $2,000 for each spouse, including a homemaker who does not work outside of the home as long as the combined contributions of both spouses at least equal the contributed amount. This change first applies to 1997 (in 1996, the limit of total IRA deductions was $2,250)

Individuals with Disabilities Education Act of 1975 Established education policy for children with disabilities.

Individuals with Disabilities Education Act Amendments of 1991 Extends grant programs for disabled children, including the early intervention program for disabled infants and toddlers. The law also permits funding for preschoolers who reach their third birthday during the program year. The legislation used the phrase "least restrictive environment" to describe the obligation of educators to place children with special needs in regular classrooms whenever appropriate for their educational growth.

Individuals with Disabilities Education Act Amendments of 1996 Contains provisions relating to consolidation of special purposes and programs, discipline, early childhood, eligibility, federal funding, flexibility and waivers, **individual education plan** components and teams, local and state funding formulas, procedural safeguards, and professional development.

Individuals with Disabilities Education Act of 1997 (IDEA) Reauthorized and signed by President Clinton June 4, 1997. Sets educational policy for children with disabilities. Makes teachers from a student's regular classroom a part of his or her Individualized

Education Plan team, writing transition goals for post high school into IEPs when a student is 14 years old, and gives parents who disagree with schools about the education of their child with a disability the option to use mediation to resolve issues. Most provisions took effect with the signing; all others must become effective before July 1, 1998.

induction   Programs designed to introduce new employees to the organization, the work environment, and the job. They typically include introductions to key personnel and co-workers, tours of the office or plant and facilities, and demonstration of selected work tasks.

inductive reasoning   The process of reasoning from the specific to the general — of combining rules or principles to produce new conclusions, rules, or principles. The process of generalizing, going beyond the information at hand to discover new rules, and principles, arguing from particular instances to the general.

industrial democracy   Describes the movement toward employee involvement and empowerment in organizations of all types: project management, task forces, quality circles, self-directed work teams, and so on.

industrial education   Education and training provided at the secondary and postsecondary levels (diplomas, certificates, and associate and baccalaureate degrees) to prepare people for entry-level positions in industry.

industrial engineering   A staff (service) function that is concerned with the design, installation, modification, and improvement of systems composed of people, equipment, and materials. It draws on the physical and social sciences, psychology, mathematics, and, most recently, group dynamics, to analyze and evaluate systems and procedures and recommend changes to make them more effective and efficient.

industrial espionage
See business espionage.

industrial fetal protection policy   See fetal protection policy.

industrial intelligence
See business intelligence.

industrial/organizational (I/O) psychologist
A trained scientist/practitioner who has the dual goals of advancing knowledge and working with practicing managers.

industrial psychology   The application of the science of human behavior to business and industry in the areas of organization planning and development, human resources management, development, and utilization, human engineering, and research.

industrial rehabilitation   Programs and therapies designed to get employees back on the job as soon as possible following accidents or injuries and reduce expenditures for compensation claims.

industrial relations   See labor-management relations.

Industrial Relations Research Association (IRRA)   A 4,000-member organization of academics and practitioners in the areas of labor and industrial relations/human resources. IRRA's mission is to share ideas and keep members abreast of new developments and practices. Contact: IRRA, 4233 Social Science Bldg., 1180 Observatory Dr., University of Wisconsin, Madison, Wisconsin 53706 (608/262-2762; Fax 608/265-4591; E-mail **kbHutchi@facstaff.wisc.edu** or **clcase@facstaff.wisc.edu**; URL **http://www.ilr.cornell.edu/**).

Industrial Technology Institute (ITI)
Offers direct assistance services and applied research to U.S.manufacturers to improve their bottom-line performance and sustain long-term growth. Focuses on applied research, development, and deployment of advanced manufacturing technology, such as **computer-integrated manufacturing, computer-assisted design, computer-assisted manufacturing**, and network management. Contact: ITI, 2901 Hubbard Rd., PO Box 1485, Ann Arbor, MI 48106-1485 (800-292-4484 or 313/769-4000; E-mail **inquiry@iti.org**; URL **http://www.iti.org**).

Industry-Labor Council   A nonprofit organization of nearly 200 corporations that provides information and technical assistance to employers seeking to integrate people with disabilities into the work force. Contact: Industry-Labor Council, National Center for Disability Services, 201 I.U. Willets Rd., Albertson, NY 11507-1599 (516/465-1515; Fax 516/747-2046).

inflation   Increases in prices and wages caused by an increase in the money supply without a corresponding increase in the amount of goods and services available.

influence competencies   Capabilities that portend success in managerial jobs. They include the ability to influence others, organizational sensitivity, and the ability to build relationships.

infobahn *See* information superhighway.

informal organization Groups outside of the formal structure of the organization through which employees satisfy some of their needs (primarily for affection and belonging) and to which they pay considerable personal loyalty. They typically interlock to form a network through which communication moves very quickly.

informal plan A short-term, reactive, intuitive, and unwritten plan, based on past experience and managerial judgment. Informal plans are typically the work of only one person.

informal sanctions Social pressures generated within a group or organization to enforce informal norms of behavior, conduct, and performance.

in forma pauperis A legal term for a pauper or destitute person. It signifies a rule that allows a litigant or party to a lawsuit to obtain a hearing without having to pay normal costs such as filing fees, lawyers' fees, and other charges.

Information Access Project for Blind Individuals (IAPBI) A joint project of the U.S. Department of Justice and the **National Federation of the Blind**. Offers free consultation in meeting the Americans with Disabilities Act's information access requirements. *See also* Job Opportunities for the Blind. *Contact:* IAP, 1800 Johnston St., Baltimore, MD 21230 (410/659-9314; Fax 410/685-5653).

informational database A database that contains abstracts or full text records (such as periodicals, newspapers, and journals) which can be accessed when interfaced with an online catalog or by means of CD-ROM.

information briefing An oral presentation designed to familiarize, interpret, inform, or report on something of interest or concern to the audience, rather than to influence, provoke, indoctrinate, or inspire.

information center (IC) As distinguished from a library, a facility that contains (or has access to) a mainframe computer, outside information systems, and either microcomputers or minicomputers. It is used by professionals, scientists, engineers, educators, technicians, administrators, and clerical

workers for information retrieval and reporting, spreadsheet analysis, word processing, and project management.

information dominance Military jargon used to describe a person who has superior intelligence and the ability to wreak havoc on information networks.

information superhighway **1.** A means of accessing information of all kinds via computer from homes, schools, offices, libraries, or businesses. *See also* I-Way; National Information Infrastructure. **2.** A communication system that has the capacity to interconnect every medium. **3.** The use of Internet.

information refinery A futuristic and somewhat arcane computerized system that screens large volume files and documents for important and relevant information.

information systems (IS) Ways of organizing and distributing computerized data; examples are **human resources information systems** and **management information systems.**

information technology (IT) The full spectrum of information processing, transmission, and storage products, systems, and services. Viewed by some as the key to enhanced organization and individual productivity and performance.

Information Technology Agreement (ITA) A U.S.-crafted agreement signed in December 1996 by the 28 countries that conduct most of the world's info-tech trade. The pact will abolish import duties on computers, software, semiconductors, and telecommunications equipment between July 1, 1997 and January 1, 2000. It will have the effect of reducing prices for personal computers and other equipment needed to access to the **Internet.** Referred to by some as a "global tax cut."

Information Technology Training Association, Inc. (ITTA) An organization of more than 250 commercial, corporate, and associate members representing IT-focused training companies, corporate IT training professionals, and providers of IT. Dedicated to providing vision, leadership, and opportunity for those involved in leaning to enable the effective use of **information technology**. Sponsors instructor development programs, legislative action campaigns, national training partnerships, and business and marketing development efforts. In collaboration with the **Computer Education Management**

Association, created the **Certified Technical Trainer Program**. *Contact:* ITTA, 8400 North Mopac Expressway, Ste. 20, Austin, TX 7875 (512-502-9300; Fax 512-502-9308; E-mail **support@itta.org**; URL **http://www.itta.org**).

information thieves *See* privacy invaders.

information utilities Large computer database and messaging systems to which anyone can subscribe for a fee. Users access the system by means of a **modem** and scan current publications, participate in electronic conferences with special interest groups, and send messages via electronic mail. Examples are America Online, BitNet, **CompuServe**, and **Prodigy**.

Infonuggets Small bits of critical information and segments of training delivered just-in-time, on the job, and on-line by computer networks (corporate intranets with access to Netscape Navigator or Microsoft Internet Explorer) to save time and increase productivity. Also called *granulariation, chunks, and mind snacks.*

informed consent A basic requirement for responsible and principled research. Participants in the study are told that they are involved in a study and are fully informed of the nature of the study, the procedures that will be used, how the results will be used, and alerted to any risks that may be involved.

InfoSeek On the **Internet**, a search tool that specializes in news wires, computer magazines, and company profiles (**http://www.infoseek.com**) *See also* Lycos; Netscape; Yahoo!;

infotainment A combination of information and entertainment in TV commercials or on the **Internet** (home pages) used to create leads or sales

infusion approach A form of concepts-based, integrated curriculum. It integrates and articulates a particular subject, such as computational or writing skills, across the curriculum. Attributed to Betty Jean Eklund Shoemaker, "Education 2000 Integrated Curriculum," *Phi Delta Kappan*, June 1991.

Injury and Illness Record-keeping Requirements Issued by the Occupational Safety and Health Administration early in 1997. Designed to simplify and improve the accuracy of data used by the agency to enforce the law and develop workplace safety standards, the revised rules exempt some businesses that have had low injury and illness rates and employers with fewer than 20 employees in the manufacturing, utilities, wholesale, transportation, and agricultural industries. However, the regulations will be extended to industries that were formerly exempt from the record-keeping requirements, such as auto supply stores, cleaning services, real estate offices, and restaurants.

inhalants **1.** Substances that produce fumes that can be inhaled to produce an immediate high or rush. Used by young people and even some adults. Called "huffing," "bagging," or "sniffing." Many such substances are readily available in stores or in homes; for example, air fresheners, cleaners and solvents, correction fluids, furniture polish, glues, nail polish, and whipped cream in aerosol cans. **2.** Drugs that produce a state of altered consciousness, such as intoxication and dizziness. Include nitros oxide ("laughing gas," "whippets"), amylnitrite ("poppers," "snappers"), butyl nitrite ("rush," "bolt"), chlorohydrocarbons (aerosol sprays), and hydrocarbons (solvents).

inhalation therapy An alternative treatment in which hot vapors, or steam mixed with eucalyptus oil, are inhaled (though equipment or in a steam room) to decongest the respiratory system.

inheritance tax *See* estate tax; sponge tax.

inheritance tax system A death tax system which establishes its tax rate by looking at the relationship of the beneficiary to the decedent.

in-house counseling *See* in-company counseling.

in-house diagnosis *See* in-company diagnosis.

in-house temporary employees An alternative staffing option. Involves placing people on the company payroll for a specific period of time to meet special production or other work requirements.

initial public offering (IPO) A stock offer of the sale of a company's stock to investors. Requires between $50 and $500K to launch and $250K or more annually to satisfy the Securities Exchange Commission's reporting requirements.

initial training *See* entry-level training.

initiative activities In **adventure training**, simple, low-risk, high energy events, such as games, in which the main challenge is one of team work and mental problem solving.

injunction   A court order forbidding an individual or an organization from doing or continuing to do certain things.

injunctive relief   A legal remedy available to individuals or organizations obtained through a court order. For example, an organization may be ordered by the court to provide auxiliary aids or services, modify existing policies, or make facilities accessible to people with disabilities.

injury   In health care benefits and workers' compensation, bodily injury, such as a wound, bone fracture, laceration, or abrasion, sustained accidentally by external means.

inkblot test   *See* Rorschach test.

in-market merger   The marriage of similar organizations, such as banks, in the same market.

in-network   A term applied to flexible benefits plans where employees choose to subscribe to health maintenance organizations (HMOs) or preferred provider organizations (PPOs) each time they use medical services.

innovating or innovation   Deliberate, planned change designed to improve operations, productivity, profitability, products, services, or the quality of work life for employees. It is usually a collaborative activity in which two or more people make a new concept or idea, the product of individual creative effort, practical and usable.

inpatriate   A foreign national employee who has been transferred to the United States for a lengthy work assignment.

inplacement counseling   Counseling provided to current employees to help them move to another job in the organization or adjust to the new job following the transfer.

input evaluation   Assessing the relevance and adequacy of all resources invested in training and development — buildings, facilities, equipment, materials, instructors, support personnel, and so on.

input-output technique   Developed originally as a method of solving dynamic-system design engineering problems. The technique has been adapted for group or individual use in solving problems. The input(s) and output(s) of the system under study are first identified, the specifications or limiting requirements are defined, and

then an attempt is made to find ways to make the input(s) produce the desired output(s) within the specified limitations. In that way, several possible solutions are generated that can then be developed, evaluated, and used.

input technology   Devices used to access and interact with a computer. Includes keyboard, mouse, and pen and voice and handwriting recognition.

inquiring   The process by which facts, ideas, information, opinions, meanings, emotions, and understandings are obtained from others to inform oneself, to solve problems, to make decisions, to innovate, and to evaluate. It makes use of penetrating oral or written questions.

insider   The Securities Exchange Commission (SEC) defines an "insider" as a person in charge of a principal business unit, division, or function or any person who establishes policy in an organization. Whether a person is an insider, therefore, is determined by function, rather than by title.

insider information   Information accessible only to persons working in an organization, such as a member of a board of directors or employees of a brokerage house, which can be used to the individual's own financial advantage or made available to others for the same purpose. Divulging insider information is illegal. For example, **Securities and Exchange Commission** regulations place restrictions on stock purchases and sales by insiders.

Insider Trading and Securities Fraud Enforcement Act of 1988   Specifically addressed trading on insider information in response to the actions of such infamous Wall Street sharks as Ivan Boesky. The Act imposed greater controls on the securities business.

Inside Technology Training   A journal published eight times per year by The Cobb Group, a Division of Ziff-Davis Publishing Company: $69.00 per year (free to qualified subscribers). Address: 9420 Bunsen Pkwy., Louisville, KY 40220 (800/769-2075 or 502/493-3200; Fax 502/491-4200; E-mail **editor@ittrain.com**; URL **http://www.ittrain.com**).

insourcing   Administering benefit plans, such as flexible benefits, internally. Permits valuable control and access to data. Also advantageous when consulting firms and service bureaus cannot support the employer's objectives or does not run on the company's existing computer system. Sophisticated software applications are available commercially for most minicomputer and mainframe computer platforms.

inspection A preventive and control strategy involving planned, scheduled, and sometimes announced visits to administrative, operational, maintenance, training, or other areas of HR operations to evaluate individual or team performance, assess the adequacy of facilities, equipment, and supplies, collect data on potential problems, or follow up on problem remedies.

inspection trip One classification of free trips to resort areas taken by users of incentive travel or travel agents, or by travel agents themselves, to inspect destinations for possible future use. These free trips do not result from a host property owner's invitation; however, the owner does provide complimentary air and and ground transportation, meals and accommodations, and guided tours. No business has yet been booked at the hotel or convention center. Attributed to Michael J. Hurwitz, president of the Society of Incentive Travel Executives.

instability A source of errors in rating due to the passage of time (forgetting).

installation One of the five major steps in getting a computer system up and running. In sequence the steps are design, development, installation, implementation, and operation. Installation involves loading the software onto the computer and running tests to ensure that the program works as designed.

Institute for Chartered Financial Analysts (ICFA) Offers the Chartered Financial Analyst designation. *Contact:* ICAF, c/o AIMR, P.O. Box 3668, Charlottesville, VA 22903-0668 (804/977-6600; Fax 804/977-1103; E-mail **info@aimr.org**; URL **http://www.aimr.com. aimr.html**).

Institute for Crisis Management (ICM) A research-based international consulting network of crisis experts who help corporations, nonprofit organizations, and government agencies prevent business crisis events or minimize the damage when they cannot be avoided. Since 1990, ICM has maintained a database of negative news coverage to analyze business crisis trends and assist those facing crisis situations to anticipate the likely complications and aftershocks. *Contact:* ICM, 1161 East Broadway, Louisville, KY 40204 (502/584-0402; Fax 502/587-6132; E-mail **rbi@crisisexperts.com**; URL **http://www. crisisexperts.com**).

Institute for Operations Research and the Management Sciences (INFORMS) An 11,000 member association dedicated to the development, application, and expansion of a broad field of endeavor encompassing operations research, the management sciences, and related information and decision sciences. *Contact:* INFORMS, 901 Elkridge Landing Rd., Ste. 400, Linthicum, MD 21090-2909 (410/850-0300; Fax 410/684-2963; E-mail **INFORMS@jhuvms.hcF.jhu.edu**; URL **http://www.Informs.org/**).

Institute for Research on Learning (IRL) A multidisciplinary group of education researchers, including physicists and mathematicians, social anthropologists, and cognitive scientists with expertise in artificial intelligence, psychology, and linguistics. IRL's mission is to pursue new kinds of research aimed at understanding the nature of learning in all settings and circumstances, use that understanding to create environments where people can realize their full potential for learning, and bring powerful research results into immediate use. IRL pursues its mission in partnership with schools, workplaces and communities that are seeking to transform themselves into environments for continuous learning. *Contact:* IRL, 66 Willow Place, Menlo Park, CA. 94025 (415614-7900; Fax 415/614-7957; E-mail **webmaster @ WebMaster**; URL **http:// www.irl.org**).

The Institute of Certified Financial Planners (ICFP) A national professional association of 11,000 members founded in 1973. Its mission is to position, assist, and represent the **Certified Financial Planner** professional as the advisor of choice in financial planning matters. The Institute assists human resources professionals to provide top quality, generic financial education to their employees. *Contact:* ICFP, 3801 E. Florida Ave., Ste. 708, Denver, CO 80210-2571 (800/322-4237; Fax 303/759-0749; E-mail **102132.3262@ compuserve.com**).

Institute of Certified Travel Agents (ICTA) A nonprofit organization that provides continuing education for travel professionals. Awards the Certified Travel Counselor designation to those who complete a five-course, 200-hour program and a minimum of 5 years of experience in travel. Currently has 15,000 CTC graduates. *Contact:* ICTA, 148 Linden St., Box 812059, Wellesley, MA 02181-0012 (800/542-4282 or 617/237-0280; Fax 617/237-3860; E-mail **icta-info@icta.com**; URL **http://www.icta.com**).

Institute of Industrial Engineers (IIE)
An international nonprofit association of 24,000 professional industrial engineers dedicated to advancing the technical and managerial excellence of those concerned with improving the productivity of integrated systems of people, materials, information, equipment, and energy. The organization is committed to the dissemination of information and continuing education to improve productivity in the workplace as well as provide products and services to aid in this endeavor. *Contact:* IIE, 25 Technology Park/Atlanta, Norcross, GA 30092 770/4490961; Fax 770/263-8532; E-mail **OS@www.iienet.org**; URL **http://www.iienet.org**).

Institute of Management Consultants, The (IMC) An association of private management consultants throughout the United States and abroad. Its primary purpose is to serve as a voice for those in the field and to establish professional and ethical standards for management consultants. IMC grants the designation of **Certified Management Consultant**. *Contact:* IMC, 521 Fifth Ave., 35th Fl., New York, NY 10175-3598 (212/697-8262; Fax 212-949-6571; E-mail **imcCR@aol.com**; URL **http://www.imcusa.org**).

institutional IRA An **individual retirement account** designed to help employers avoid the 20 percent withholding tax on lump sum distributions and in-service withdrawal plans mandated by the Internal Revenue Service by funneling distributions into the plan instead of distributing the lump sums directly to employees.

institutional partnerships Contractual partnerships established by organizations and area technical schools, colleges, and universities to develop programs, including undergraduate and graduate degree programs, tailored to the needs and requirements of the organization. The institution and the corporation jointly determine enrollment requirements, plan and develop the curriculum, and establish course or degree completion standards and requirements. The school, college, or university provides the instructors (although some courses may be taught by employees of the corporation), and organizes and administers the program. Courses may be conducted either on the premises of the corporation or at the institution — or both.

instructional design *See* instructional systems design.

instructional management (IM) A delivery system for criterion-referenced evaluation. IM also combines a clearly defined curriculum made up of uniquely assessable instructional objectives with computer processing.

instructional management plan A plan used to guide the implementation of an instructional system. The plan includes the learning objectives, a description of the the training setting (facilities, equipment, tools, and materials), instructor and instructor support requirements, the delivery system and instructional strategies, instructor's role, and scheduling, monitoring, and evaluation requirements and strategies.

instructional materials All the materials and audiovisual aids required to implement an instructional system. They include the **program of instruction, lesson plans**, audio only, video only, and audiovisual tapes and cassettes, programmed instruction materials, job aids, computer programs, manuals and texts, handouts, tests, exportable training packages, and so on.

instructional method The basic approach to instruction used. Examples are lecture, conference, demonstration, performance, individual study, programmed instruction, case studies, and simulation.

instructional objective *See* learning objective.

instructional strategy The combination of methods of teaching, mediating devices, and the system of organizing trainees and instructors to accomplish an instructional objective. Selection of strategy is based on the learning objectives, the nature of the subject matter or content, the trainee population, the number, quality, experience, and competencies of the instructional staff, and availability of space, facilities, equipment, materials, time, and costs.

instructional systems design *See* instructional systems development.

instructional systems development (ISD) A rigorous, systematic model for developing instructional systems that was initiated by the Armed Services in the early 1970s. It consists of five phases: analysis, design, development, implementation, and evaluation.

instructional technique A means of instruction that complements a method; for example, questioning, handling trainee responses, and using visual and auditory aids.

instructional technology (IT) **1.** The systems approach to the design, development, and delivery of training and education programs (the process). **2.** Computers, teleconferencing, interactive video, EXPERT systems, audiovisual equipment, and so on used for education and training (hardware and software).

instructional writer An HRD competency. An individual who writes **lesson plans, programs of instruction**, handouts, training manuals, and job aids.

instruction sheet A variation of the job procedures manual, instruction sheets provide written or printed directions to workers on a single sheet of paper. They typically cover a single task and may accompany a piece of equipment to explain how to operate it, or a set of directions written for a temporary employee.

instructor An HRD competency. A teacher or group facilitator.

instructor-based training (IBT) Instruction in the traditional mode where the instructor is the center of activity and attention rather than the learners or trainees. Also referred to as *instructor-centered training.*

instructor camera In distance learning, the camera(s) used to display the instructor (moderator, trainer, or presenter). May include pan, tilt, zoom, preset location, and autotracking capabilities.

instructor-centered training *See* instructor-based training..

instructor development Formal or informal programs designed to improve the performance and potential of employees assigned to instructor positions either full time or part time.

instructor-led training The traditional approach to training involving an instructor, a group of trainees, a classroom or laboratory,

and employing the standard lecture, conference-discussion, demonstration, and performance (practical exercise) methods of instruction and such techniques as questioning and audiovisual aids.

instructor-to-trainee ratio A common instructional standard, often established in the collective bargaining agreement. It is the maximum number of trainees that can be assigned to one instructor expressed as a ratio, such as 1:25.

instructor training Instruction provided to train managers, supervisors, staff personnel, technicians, sales personnel, and operative employees in the principles, methods, and techniques of instruction or to orient, and retrain professional teachers in the procedures and techniques of job training and organizational development. Instructor training typically includes training needs analysis, instructional planning, preparation of instructional materials and lesson plans, methods of presentation (lecture, demonstration, conference, and performance), using role playing, simulation, and case studies, questioning techniques, operating audio-visual equipment, guiding learning activities, counseling techniques, evaluating progress and accomplishment, and practice instruction (with supervision, evaluation, and feedback), usually videotaped.

insurance A contract whereby a carrier undertakes to indemnify or guarantee a person or group security or protection against loss from a specified contingency, event, or peril such as death, dismemberment, injury, illness, disability, damage, vandalism, fire, flood, earthquake, or hurricane/tornado loss or damage, product liability, and directors' and officers' liability, among others.

Insurance Conference Planners Association (ICPA) The insurance industry's meeting planning association. With 400 members representing major insurance companies and related associations in Canada, the United States, Mexico, and abroad, the association was established to promote a high standard of ethical and professional conduct; support a network for exchange of information about conference sites and procedures; disseminate information on meeting management techniques and trends; promote the professional stature, competence, and career growth of members, promote effective communication with airlines, hoteliers, and suppliers, and improve cost efficiency for member companies. *Contact:* Insurance Conference Planners Association, 2801 Woodbine Dr., N. Vancouver, BC, CAN V7R 2R9 (604/988-2054 or 604/988-3933; Fax 604/988-4743).

Insurance Information Institute (III) A nonprofit organization that works to improve public understanding of the property and casualty business. Its computer capabilities provide immediate access to a large data bank of insurance-related information. III also publishes books and newsletters on insurance-related topics. *Contact:* III, 110 William St., New York, NY 10038 800/221-4954 or 212/669-9200; E-mail **Media@ aol.com**; URL **http://www/iii.org/**)

intake interview The initial interview with a client or patient in clinic or other diagnostic and treatment facilities.

intangible personal property Items of personal property which are either not physical in nature, such as bank accounts, certificate of deposit, stocks, and bonds, or which represent something intangible, such as currency

intangible reward A nonmaterial reinforcer. Intangible rewards include social approval in the form of praise, smiles, nods, and pats on the back; assignment to prestigious work groups, committees, and task forces, and special individual assignments; and such forms of recognition as public announcement of achievements and honorary titles.

Integrated Applications Digital and Audio Trainer (IADAT) A communications tool in the form of a sophisticated audio and digital tape recorder produced by Integrated Applications Inc. of Cleveland, Ohio. It is used primarily for developing training and marketing/sales presentations and is limited to IBM DOS and ASCII applications. The unit does not use a camera or half-inch video tape format; it is an interactive recorder that connects directly to a terminal or **personal computer** and continuously records what is on the screen (audio and digital signals) without interfering with the running application. It is said to cut **computer-based training** development time by 50 to 75 percent.

integrated computing
See enterprise computing.

integrated curriculum
See concepts-based, integrated curriculum.

integrated delivery system (IDS) An organized system of health care providers spanning a wide range of health care services. Also called *Integrated Health Care Delivery system.*

integrated employee assistance program (IEAP) An upgraded and restructured form of **employee assistance program**. It retains all of the features and benefits of the traditional variety of EAP, but it is integrated with the organization's overall human resources strategic plan.

integrated human resource management system (IHRIS) A database shared by all corporate human resources functions established to provide a common language and integrate and coordinate all HR services. It includes competency data on all organization jobs and people and is used to manage succession planning, recruitment, selection, compensation, performance appraisal, and training and development.

integrated human resources/payroll system A single computerized database used by both human resources and payroll, thereby eliminating duplicate date entry and processing requirements.

integrated instructional system *See* integrated learning system.

integrated learning An instructional strategy that employs teaching techniques to disseminate information and produce learning on seven levels of human intelligence: linguistic, logical, musical, spatial, kinesthetic, interpersonal, and intrapersonal.

integrated learning system (ILS) A unit of sequenced courseware complemented with management software delivered by networked computers. The courseware addresses a specific content area, and the software provides tracking and reporting capabilities. ILSs are designed to deliver networked-managed instruction. Several manufacturers are now experimenting with CD-ROM technology, and others offer the ability to incorporate different hardware platforms into the same network. Still others give instructors complete control of every aspect of ILS, allowing them to choose exactly which activity is delivered to trainees.

integrated management system A system that integrates all critical aspects of the workplace, such as productivity, outputs or results, corporate climate, meaningful and rewarding jobs, positive discipline, adequate recognition and rewards, creativity and innovation, compensation and benefits, participative policy formulation and decision making, and opportunities for training, development, and advancement for employees.

integrated media A subsystem that represents a complete merging of television and computers and thereby provides greater flexibility and a new environment to facilitate the development of applications software designed to solve interactive training and presentation problems.

Integrated Services Digital Network (ISDN) A system that allows simultaneous digitized communications in almost any form — voice, data, video, and the like — to be sent through a single fiber-optic line. It holds much promise for business communications as well as **distance training or education**.

integrated training Use of a combination of individually-paced, training tools and media, such as interactive video, CBT, and other courseware, to deliver training.

integrated digital videoconferencing Uses video compression algorithms, modems on dial-up lines, access to high bandwidth communications, and a personal computer to deliver image and sound over phone lines.

integrative brainwork approach A form of the concepts-based, integrated curriculum. Employs such information processing strategies as concept attainment, inductive reasoning, advance organizers, concept mapping, and clinical interviews. Attributed to Betty Jean Eklund Shoemaker, "Education 2000 Integrated Curriculum," *Phi Delta Kappan*, June 1991.

integrative disorders Forms of **learning disabilities.** Manifest themselves as difficulties organizing new information and relating it to previously learned information. People with this condition are able to absorb a series of facts but are unable to answer questions using those facts. They are unable to sequence and organize newly learned information and previously learned information into an integrated whole.

integrative techniques A category of technological forecasting techniques used to analyze the impacts of development factors on one another and for presenting decision makers with an integrated picture of projected events. Integrative techniques include cross-impact analysis, scenarios, mathematical models, and the iterative approach.

integrity test **1.** A test used to determine whether tampering has occurred with urine samples taken to identify drug users. The tests may measure pH balance, creatine levels, and gravity levels to detect the presence of bleach or liquid Drano, samples diluted with water or animal urine, or the presence of soap or salt, respectively. **2.** A test administered to applicants for positions to screen out those who are potentially dishonest.

intellectual capital Attributed to Hugh McDonald of I.C.L., the United Kingdom computer manufacturer, it is "the knowledge that exists in an organization that can be used to create differential advantage." (In Thomas A. Stewart, "Brain Power," *Fortune*, June 3, 1991, p. 44.) Thomas R. Horton, former AMA CEO and chairman, maintains that "....intellectual capital is more than that: It is the sum total of the useful knowledge of your employees and your customers....(and is) far more valuable to your business than even your materials and financial resources...." (In *The CEO Paradox: The Privilege and Accountability of Leadership*, New York, AMACOM, 1992, pp. 30-31.)

intellectual property In law, the statutes that protect ideas, trade secrets, inventions, and creative works from being copied or stolen. Protection is provided by copyrights, patents, and trademarks.

Intelligence Authorization for Fiscal Year 1992 Authorizes a $150 million trust fund for foreign language and international studies. The funds are available for undergraduate scholarships to study abroad, graduate fellowships for foreign language and international study, and grants to universities to establish and improve foreign language and international education programs.

intelligence quotient (IQ) A measure of general cognitive ability and sometimes an accurate predictor of worker productivity because it predicts the learning of a job. However, due to several variables including age and experience, it is a much more useful measure for children than for adults.

intelligence test A test that measures learning or problem solving ability, which may be administered in written, oral, or nonverbal form. Intelligence tests are used in screening and selection, promotion, and training and development. Examples are tests of general mental ability (Wonderlic Personnel Test, Adaptability Test, Weschler Adult Intelligence

Scale, and the Thurston Test of Mental Alertness) and tests of specific mental abilities (such as the Differential Aptitude Test and the Armed Forces Standard Aptitude Battery).

intelligent tutoring system (ITS) A system that employs artificial intelligence methods to assist trainees to improve their problem solving skills by monitoring their reasoning, tracking errors to their source, and, based on the diagnosis, providing advice and assistance to strengthen problem solving skills. Not as highly structured as **computer-aided instruction**, which tends to be organized around **decision trees**, ITS allows for more open-ended programs.

intelligent video learning system See computer-based training; interactive video system.

intelligent work station (IWS) A work station that employs an interactive computer-driven job performance support system.

intensive day treatment Outpatient treatment of a mental condition or substance abuse provided at and billed by a facility that meets the definition of a hospital. Treatment consists of individual or group therapy and/or psychological testing.

intent One of four terms in employment law relating to cases of discrimination: **disparate impact**, intent, **business necessity**, and **burden of proof**. In the case of intent, an employer who unwittingly discriminated (by a business practice that seemed to be neutral but produced discriminatory results or effects) would be held accountable be cause the courts look at consequences rather than intent.

intentional survey See expectational survey.

interactive communications In human resources, devices used to give employees the ability to see the results of their choices of benefits. Include special computer software programs, **kiosks**, and **voice response systems**,

interactive learning See computer-based training; creative learning.

Interactive Market Systems (IMS) An on-line **database**. Contact: IMS, 11 W. 42nd St., New York, NY 10036-8088 (212/789-3000).

interactive multimedia **1.** Presentation and training media that make it possible to change images, in terms of sequence and content, at will. Liquid crystal display devices (used in conjunction with overhead projectors), large video monitors, and video/data projectors allow presenters to share computer screen images with large audiences. **2.** The output provided by combining a variety of formerly independent sound and visual media, with a computer in control. That has been made possible by the conversion of analog phonograph records and broadcast TV analog standards to digital formats and standards.

Interactive Multimedia Association (IMA) An organization of over 325 companies whose mission is to promote the development of interactive multimedia applications and reduce barriers to the widespread use of multimedia technology to establish a strong and profitable marketplace for its members. The IMA's key initiatives in compatibility, intellectual property and technology convergence are working to educate, inform and influence in areas that include multimedia standards, patents and federal telecommunications, and information technology policy. Contact: IMA, 48 Maryland Ave., Ste. 202, Annapolis, MD 21401-8011 (410/626-1380; Fax 410/263-0590; E-mail: **info@ima.org**; URL **http://www.ima.org**).

interactive performance accelerator See interactive performance system; performance support system.

interactive performance system On-demand training and learner-controlled training. Computer-driven systems designed to support workers at the job site by providing assistance when needed.

interactive system Computer application programs that process input in real time and make the results immediately available to the user.

interactive training Individualized training provided by means of videotape or videodisc.

interactive videodisc (IVD) A device that allows the user to interact with the video program or lesson stored on the disc. Uses 12-inch discs that can hold thousands of images as animation cells or video frames. Using a computer and videodisc player, the user can stop the video, search for other information or images, and create his or her own route through the material.

interactive video system (IVS) A system that enables random access to the contents of the training or other program by the user through a keyboard, mouse, or finger touch (of the CRT) and responses of the system are determined by the user's input. An example is a flight simulator.

interactive voice response (IVR) *See* voice response system.

interactivity The process of involving learners with the learning materials rather than allowing them to sit and passively listen and observe.

Interactivity: Tools + Techniques for Interactive Media Developers A monthly: journal: $59.95 per year (free to qualified subscribers). *Contact:* Interactivity, 411 Borel Ave., Ste. 100, San Mateo, CA 94402 (415/358-9500; Fax 415-655-4360; E-mail **interactivity@ mfi.com**; URL **http://www.eyemedia.com**).

intercultural training Training provided by intercultural and multicultural organizations, public and private institutions and agencies, and the military services. It is provided to increase managerial effectiveness in international operations, negotiations, and decision making, help employees adapt to working, living, and learning environments in cultural settings different from their own, and establish friendly, cooperative, and favorable relationships with the people of a host country or culture.

interdisciplinary approach A form of the concepts-based, integrated curriculum. It maintains traditional subject-matter boundaries while aligning content and concepts form one discipline with those of another. Attributed to Betty Jean Eklund Shoemaker, "Education 2000 Integrated Curriculum," *Phi Delta Kappan*, June 1991.

interest inventory *See* interest test.

interest test An instrument that reveals an individual's interests and values — the ones that guide and motivate behavior. Interest tests are used in screening and selection for employment and promotion and for training. They do not predict managerial effectiveness. Examples are the Kuder Preference Record, Jackson Vocational Interest Survey, Allport-Vernon Scale of Values, Purdue Job Preference Survey, and Strong Interest Inventory.

interface The connecting of two or more components or entities (people, systems, equipments, and so on) so that they can communicate and interact. For example, the most common computer interface is the keyboard; others are the mouse, touch-sensitive screens, light pens, joy sticks, trackballs, scanners, video cameras, and facsimile machines.

interface charts Used by supervisors in employee orientation and induction programs, they consist of charts showing by name and position the individuals the new employee will interface and interact with on a continuing basis (supervisors, coworkers, staff, committees and workteams, suppliers, consultants, and so on).

interfaced human resources/payroll system Separate computer systems linked to appear to be sharing the same database when they are actually separate. Data fed into one system are transmitted to the other on a scheduled basis.

intergenerational care center A facility that provides both child care and elder care.

intermediarie A private insurance organization that makes coverage and payment decisions on services in hospitals, skilled nursing facilities, home health agencies, and hospices. Some have contracts with the federal government to handle Medicare payments paid through the hospital insurance program.

intermediate evaluation Assessment of trainees' reactions, learning, and performance at the conclusion of training. The evaluation may take either of two forms: individual or organizational. Individual evaluation examines changes in on-the-job behavior of managers, supervisors, workers, clients, or customers, usually following training, development, or other form of intervention. Techniques include questionnaires, rating scales, interviews, tests, or observation. Organizational evaluation examines organizational change in such areas as quality of communications, customer relations, job satisfaction, motivation and morale, and teamwork. Tools include observation, questionnaires, interviews, ratings, and review of records.

intermittent leave Recurring absences authorized by the **Family and Medical Leave Act of 1993** under the rubric of "reasonable accommodations." Typically caused by situations in which an employee's condition prevents putting in a full day's work at the work site but who is capable and often willing to do some work from home. In addition, FMLA allows intermittent leave, with the employer's consent, following the birth or adoption of a child.

internal audit 1. A type of management control. A searching examination of one or more functions of an organization, such as finance or human resources, performed by selected members of the staff of the organization itself rather than an outside agency or auditing firm. It is designed to identify and remedy deficiencies in planning and the conduct of operations. **2.** A financial or HR audit conducted by a team of inhouse auditors. **3.** An audit conducted by an independent, impartial, and autonomous auditor. Internal audits may range from periodic verification of the effectiveness of internal managerial controls to continuing surveillance of all enterprise activities. They may be conducted as a collateral duty by a manager in a very small business or by an audit staff of dozens of professionals in a large business.

internal consultant   A full- or part-time member of the staff of an organization who provides professional or technical advice and assistance in a specified discipline or functional area to executive, managerial, supervisory, staff, technical, and operational employees.

internal criterion test   A test administered at a carefully selected point during the conduct of training. Usually covers a single major task of a job; however, internal criterion tests may also cover clusters of related tasks. Occasionally, even job elements may be of sufficient importance to warrant the development and administration of separate criterion tests.

internal customer evaluation   A relatively new form of performance evaluation in which performance is measured by more than a single boss.

internal evaluation   **1.** Evaluation that focuses on on-going, inhouse HR programs, activities, and services. Its purpose is to assess the quality of the programs and services while they are in operation so that employees, supervisors, managers, and the HR manager get the feedback they need to improve their strategies, methods, and performance. **2.** In training and development, evaluating training and development programs during their conduct. Its purpose is to provide feedback to instructors and trainees and to keep the HR manager informed of progress and accomplishment. The evaluation may take the form of participant reaction, measures of behavioral change during training, or training self-audits.

internal marketing   Promoting HR products and services within the organization to achieve the goals and priorities of the company. The primary goal of internal marketing is to contribute to the achievement of company goals and objectives by providing the programs and services the organization

and its people need to survive and prosper. Customers and clients are "friendlies" who fully expect to be offered (or sold) the products and services of the HR department.

internal motivation   Thoughts or feelings, such as pride or satisfaction, that are evoked in an individual by his or her own behavior or in response to some external stimulus.

internal recruitment   Canvassing the organization to identify employees who can be promoted, transferred, or temporarily assigned to a different position within the organization or one of its subsidiaries.

Internal Revenue Code (IRC)   Specifies the tax treatment of benefits for both employers and employees and the conditions that certain employee benefit plans must meet to receive favorable tax treatment. Of most concern to HR are IRC regulations pertaining to retirement and and capital accumulation plans, group-term life insurance, and health care benefits.

Internal Revenue Service (IRS)   The agency of the federal government responsible for the interpretation of tax law, collection of personal and corporate income taxes, and enforcement of the Internal Revenue Code.

internal temporary pool worker   A flexible staffing option. Hiring former workers or other people and placing them in an "on-call" pool managed by the organization.

international   As distinguished from **global,** describes organizations that may have overseas operations but operate their offshore business separately.

International Accreditation Forum (IAF) An international organization whose purpose is to establish order among accreditation boards worldwide — the bodies that set the rules for **registrars.**

International Association for Continuing Education & Training (IACET)   Formerly the Council on the Continuing Education Unit, IACET is an association of 550 member organizations established to promote and advance quality non-credit adult education and training. It is dedicated to the principle of lifelong learning through research, education and training, and resource dissemination. IACET, 1200 19th St., N.W., Washington, DC 20036-2422 (202/857-1122; Fax 202.223-4579; E-mail **iacet@sba.com**; URL **http://www. interedu.com/iacet/iacet.html**).

International Association for Exposition Management (IAEM)   An organization of 3,600 members established to support the growth and effectiveness of the exposition industry by (1) taking a leadership role in enhancing and advancing exposition management through education, information, and member interaction, and (2) promoting expositions as an effective marketing medium. IAEM represents professionals who conduct and support trade shows. *Contact:* IAEM, 5001 LBJ Freeway, Ste. 350, P.O. Box 802425, Dallas, TX 752380; (972/458-8002; Fax 972/458.8119; E-Mail **julie nelson@iaem@ iaem.org**; URL **http://www.IAEM.org**).

International Association for Financial Planning (IAFP) A non-profit organization of more than 15,000 members in 107 chapters in all 50 states and 22 countries. IAFP provides training, education, information, and other benefits to facilitate the professionalism and success of persons giving personal or corporate advice regarding the achievement of financial objectives, for the ultimate benefit of the consumer. *Contact:* IAFP, 5775 Glenridge Dr., N.E., Ste. B-300, Atlanta, GA 30328 (800/945-4237 or 404/845-0011; Fax 404/845-3660; E-mail **IAFP%2029388@ MCIMAIL.COM**; URL **http://www.AFP.org**).

International Association for Human Resource Information Management (IHRIM) A nonprofit global organization numbering more than 6,000 members. Provides information, products, and services, and sponsors educational events and conferences relating to human resource information management. *Contact:* IHRIM, P.O. Box 801646, Dallas, TX 75380-1646 (214/661-3727; Fax 214/386-8180; E-mail **moreinfo@ ihrim**; URL **http://www.ihrim.org**).

International Association of Audio Visual Communicators (IAAVC) An association of inhouse and independent producers of corporate and organization video, multimedia, and audiovisual presentations involved in the creation of presentations for business, education, entertainment, and government. *Contact:* AVC, 8130 La Mesa Blvd., Ste. 406, La Mesa, CA 91941-6437 (619/461-1600; E-mail **sheemonw@aol.com**; URL **http:// www.cindys.com**).

International Association of Business Communicators (IABC) Association of more than 12,500 communication practitioners in more than 45 countries encompassing the disciplines of employee communication, community relations, corporate relations, shareholder relations, public relations, public affairs, marketing, advertising and audiovisual communication. IABC's purpose is to serve the profession of organizational communication and public relations internationally through its member chapters, districts, and international affiliates. *Contact:* IABC, One Halladie Plz., Ste. 600, San Francisco, CA 94102 (415/433-3400; Fax 415/362-8762; URL **http://www.iabc.com**).

International Association of Career Management Professionals (IACMP) An organization dedicated to building the professionalism of career management practitioners, meeting the associative needs of career management professionals, and achieving recognition for that professionalism. IACMP also aims to unite internationally for mutual and public benefit career management professionals who meet a high degree of competence and integrity, develop and maintain high standards of professional conduct in career management practice, and support the field of career management with information, education and research. *Contact:* IACMP, P.O. Box 1484, Pacifica, CA 94044-6484 (URL **http://www.iacmp.org**).

International Association of Conference Centers (IACC) A global organization comprised of 393 members representing university, corporate, resort, non-residential, and ancillary conference centers. It was founded to foster awareness and understanding of the conference center concept. Conducts an annual conference and provides development workshops for conference center professionals. Membership is limited to conference centers that meet specific criteria for design and services, and to allied businesses. *Contact:* IACC. 243 North Lindberg Blvd., Ste. 315, St. Louis, MO 63141 (800/ 844-2327; 314/993-8575; Fax 314/993-8919; E-mail **info@ iacc.iacconline.com**; URL **http://www. iacconline.com**).

International Association of Convention & Visitor Bureaus (IACVB) An association of 410 not-for-profit member bureaus in 28 countries. These destination marketing organizations act as information clearing houses, convention management consultants, and promotional agencies for the cities they represent. Awards the Certified Destination Management Executives designation. *Contact:* IACVB, 2000 L St., NW, Ste. 702, Washington,

DC 20036-4990 (202/296-7888; Fax 202/296-7889; E-mail **info@iacvb.org**; URL **http://www.iacvb.org/**).

International Association of Eating Disorders Professionals (IAEDP)

An organization of 800 members established to promote a high level of professionalism among practitioners who treat people who suffer from eating disorders. UAEDP establishes ethical and professional standards, offers education and training in the field, certifies those who have met prescribed requirements, promotes professional awareness of eating disorders, and assists in prevention efforts. *Contact:* IAEDP, 123 N.W. 13 St. 206, Boca Raton, Fl 33432 (407/338-6494; Fax 566/338-9913).

International Association of Fairs & Expositions (IAFE)

A voluntary, nonprofit corporation established to organize state, district, and county fairs, state associations of fairs, expositions, associations, corporations, and individuals into one association dedicated to the improvement of the fair industry and related fields. *Contact:* IAFE, 3043 East Cairo St., Springfield, MO, P.O. Box 985, Springfield, Missouri 65801 (800/516-0313 or 417/862-5771; Fax 417/862-0156; E-mail **iafenet@iafenet.org**; URL **http://www.iafenet.org**).

International Association of Machinists and Aerospace Workers (IAM)

A labor union affiliated with the AFL-CIO representing air-transport and automotive mechanics and aerospace and railroad machinists with a membership of 731,780. *Contact:* IAM, 9000 Machinist Place, Upper Marlboro, MD 20772-2687 (301/967-4500; URL **http://www.iamaw.org/**).

International Association of Presentation Professionals (IAPP)

A coalition of corporate and independent producers of presentations in a variety of media, including multimedia, interactive media, slides, overheads, and prints. Its mission is to educate presentation graphics producers in the effective use of software and hardware and to provide a forum for networking. *Contact:* IAPP, 294 Arden Rd., Pittsburgh, PA 15216 (800/688-2748; Fax 412/531-7739; E-mail **74674.325@compuserve.com**; URL **http://www.iapp.org**).

International Brotherhood of Electrical Workers (IBEW)

A labor union representing approximately 800,000 electrical workers. *Contact:* IBEW, 1125 15th St., N.W., Washington, DC 20005 (202/833-7000; Fax; E-mail **gnewton@polarnet.com**; URL **http://www.ibew.org/**).

International Brotherhood of Teamsters, Chauffeurs, Warehousemen and Helpers of America

One of the largest U.S. labor unions whose 1.4 million members are largely employed in trucking and warehousing. Improved wages and working conditions of members and partially stabilized the trucking industry. *Contact:* Teamsters, 25 Louisiana Ave., N.W. Washington, DC 20001 (202/624-6800; Fax E-mail **teamster@teamster.org**; URL **http://www.teamster.org**).

International Brotherhood of Teamsters v. Electromation Inc.

See Electromation Decision.

International Classification of Diseases, 9th revision, Clinical Modification (ICD-9-CM)

A classification of diseases by diagnosis codified into 6-digit numbers. ICVD-10 will use alphanumeric codes.

The International Communications Industries Association (ICIA)

An association of manufacturers, dealers, and installers of presentation equipment. Provides training and services for dealers. technicians, and users of audiovisual/presentation technologies. Publishes the annual *Directory of Video, Computer & Audio-visual Products,* and the *Directory of Multimedia Equipment, Software & Services.* *Contact.* ICIA, 11242 Waples Mill Rd., Ste. 200, Fairfax, VA 22030 (800/659-7469 or 703/273-7200; Fax 703/ 278-8082; E-mail **icia@icia.org**; **http://www.usa.net/icia**).

International Congress and Convention Association (ICCA)

An international association of 460 meeting experts from 65 countries, including all the various groups of suppliers to the international meetings market. Its activities are geared to exchanging market information in various ways, creating business opportunities for its members, and organizing professional training. *Contact:* ICCA, Entrada 121, NL-1096 EB Amsterdam, The Netherlands (+31-20-690 1171; Fax +31-20-699 0781; E-mail **icca@icca.nl**; URL **http://congresscity.com/icca/iccahome.html**).

International Customer Service Association (ICSA)

A 3,000- member association of customer service professionals dedicated to developing the theory and understanding of the total quality service process, advancing the art and science of managing that process, and encouraging professional dialogue in the achievement of customer satisfaction. *Contact:* ICSA,401 N. Michigan Ave., Chicago, IL 60611-4267 (312/644-6610; Fax 312/245-1084; E-mail **ICSA@SBA.com**; URL **http://www.ICSA.com**).

The International Federation of Accountants (IFAC) The world-wide organization for the accountancy profession. The mission of IFAC is the development and enhancement of the profession to enable it to provide services of consistently high quality in the public interest. Developed and issued the "Guideline on Ethics for Professional Accountants," a code designed to serve as a comprehensive standard for all accountants in public practice and in private industry worldwide. Available from the American Institute of Certified Public Accountants. *Contact:* AICPA, 1211 Avenue of the Americas, New York, NY 10036 (800/334-6961 or 212/575-6200). *Contact:* IFAC, 114 West 47th Street, Ste. 2410, New York, NY 10036 (212-302-5952; Fax 212-302-5964; E-mail **judymccrudden@ifac.org**; URL **http://www.ifac.org**).

International Federation of Hard of Hearing People (IFHOH) An international volunteer organization consisting of national organizations of and for hard of hearing and deaf people, consumers, and professional organizations. *Contact:* IFHOH, Radegunder Strasse 10, A-8045 Graz, Austria [++ 43 316 671327 (voice); ++ 43 316 681093 (TDD)].

International Federation of Training and Development Organizations (IFTDO)
A worldwide network of over 150 member organizations with more than one million members in more than 50 countries. IFTDO is committed to identify, develop, and transfer knowledge, skills, and technology to enhance human performance, productivity, personal growth, and sustainable development. The federation is accredited to the U.N. and ILO, helping to ensure that members' voices are heard effectively by international policy makers. *Contact:* IFTDO, P.O. Box 33213. Washington, DC 20033-0213 (202/333-1811; Fax 202/342-6055; E-mail **iftdo@prodigy.com**; URL **http://www.tomco.net/~iftdo**) or OPWZ Austrian Centre for Productivity and Efficiency, Rockhgasse 6, Box 131, A-1014 Vienna, Austria (1/533-86-36/49).

International Foundation for Stutterers, Inc.
An organization established to eliminate stuttering through speech therapy in conjunction with self-help groups. Provides education for the public and professionals about stuttering. *Contact:* International Foundation for Stutters, Inc., P.O. Box 462, Belle Mead, NJ 08502 (609/275-3806).

International Foundation of Employee Benefit Plans (IFEBP) An international organization of 34,000 individuals in the United States and Canada that represents 7,700 corporations, professional advisory firms, trust funds, and public employee funds. Its purpose is to keep members current on industry issues, trends, and developments through its publications, Information Center, online benefits database, and educational programs. The Foundation co-sponsors with the Wharton School, University of Pennsylvania (and in Canada with Dalhousie University) the **Certified Employee Benefits Specialist** designation (CEBS). *Contact:* IFEBP, 18700 W. Bluemound Rd., P.O. Box 69, Brookfield, WI 53008-0069 (414/ 786-6700; Fax 414/786-8670; E-mail **pr@ifebp.org**; URL **http://www.ifebp.org**).

International Gay & Lesbian Travel Association (IGLTA) An international network of about 1,200 travel industry businesses and professionals dedicated to the mission of promoting and enhancing Gay and Lesbian travel throughout the world. *Contact:* IGLTA, 4331 N. Federal Hwy., Ste. 3004, Fort Lauderdale, FL 33308 (800-448-8550; Fax 954/776-3303; E-Mail: **IGLTA@AOL.COM**.

International Interactive Communications Society (IICS) A 3,000-member association of interactive media professionals dedicated to the advancement of interactive arts and technologies. Since 1983, the Society has provided a forum to share ideas, applications, and techniques for the effective use of interactive media. *Contact:* IICS, 10160 S.W. Nimbus Ave., Ste F2, Portland, OR 97223 (503/ 620-3604; Fax 503/620-7857; E-mail **worldhq@iics.org** or **iichq@aol.com**; URL **http://www.iics.org**).

International Labour Organization (ILO)
A specialized, independent agency of the United Nations. Its mandate is to improve working conditions, create employment and promote human rights globally. With a

membership of 173 countries, the ILO represents virtually all nations of the world. The ILO is unique, as it is the only UN agency in which the private sector, represented by labor and business, participates fully and actively with government in decision making. Headquartered in Geneva, Switzerland, ILO recommends international standards for wages, hours of work, vacations, insurance, and other issues affecting employees. *Contact:* ILO, Route des Morillons 4, 1211 Geneva 22 (41-22-799-7126; Fax: 41-22-799-6926; E-mail **webinfo@ilo.org**; URL **http:www.ilo.org**). Washington Branch Office 1828 L Street, NW, Suite 801, Washington, DC 20036 (202/653-7652; 202/653-7687; E-mail **washilo@ilowbo.org**; URL **www.un.org**).

International Organization for Standardization (ISO)   A worldwide federation of national standards bodies from 100 countries. ISO is a non-governmental organization established to promote the development of standardization and related activities in the world to facilitate the international exchange of goods and services and to developing cooperation in the spheres of intellectual, scientific, technological and economic activity. ISO's work results in international agreements which are published as International Standards. *Contact:* ISO, 1, rue de Varembé, Case postale 56, CH-1211 Genève 20, Switzerland (+ 41 22 749 01 11; Telefax: + 41 22 733 34 30; Telex: 41 22 05 iso ch; E-mail **webmaster@isocs.iso.ch**; URL **central@isocs.iso.ch**).

International Personnel Management Association (IPMA)   An organization of human resource professionals, representing the interests of more than 6,000 individual and 1,300 agency members, at the federal, state, and local levels of government. Among the association's purposes and objectives is the promotion of excellence in human resource management through the ongoing development of professional and ethical standards. *Contact:* IPMA, 1617 Duke St., Alexandria, VA 22314 (703/549-7100; Fax 703/684-0948; E-mail **ipma@hr.org**; URL **http://www.ipma-hr.org**).

International Society for Performance Improvement (ISPI)   An association of 10,000 HR managers, training directors, performance technologists, and OD and human factors practitioners throughout the United States, Canada, and more than 30 other countries. ISPI's mission is to increase productivity in the workplace through the application of performance and instructional technologies. Formerly called the National Society for Performance and Instruction. *Contact:* ISPI, 1300 L St., NW, Ste. 1250, Washington, DC 20005 (202/408-7969; Fax 202/408-7972; E-mail **info@ispi.org**; URL **http://www.ispi.org**).

International Society for Technology in Education (ISTE)   A nonprofit professional organization of 12,000 teachers, administrators, coordinators, teacher educators, information resource managers, and educational technology specialists active in learning and contributing to the future of educational technology. Provides information, support, and leadership in the use and integration of computer-based technology in the classroom. *Contact:* ISTE, 1787 Agate St., Eugene, OR 97403-1923 (541/346-4414; Fax 541/346-5890; E-mail **ISTE@oregon.uoregon.edu**; URL **http://isteonline.uoregon.edu**).

International Society of Certified Employee Benefit Specialists (ISCEBS)   A nonprofit educational association of 42 chapters open only to individuals who hold the Certified Employee Benefit Specialist designation — benefits managers, consultants, insurance company representatives, trust officers, administrators, attorneys, investment specialists, government regulators, and others involved in employee benefits. It primary purpose is to provide continuing education opportunities for its members. *Contact:* ISCEBS, 18700 W. Bluemound Rd., P.O. Box 209, Brookfield, WI 53008-0209 (414/786-8771; Fax 414/786-8650; E-mail **iscebs@ifebp.org**; URL **http://www.ifebp.org**).

International Society of Gay & Lesbian Meeting Professionals (ISG&LMP)   'An organization established to provide an arena for communication among gay and lesbian meeting planners and to acknowledge publicly suppliers that are "gay friendly." *Contact:* ASG&LMP, 175 Fifth Ave., Ste. 2172, New York, NY 10010-7703 (212) 982-9324; Fax 212/475-8101; E-mail **ASGLMP@aol.com**).

International Society of Meeting Planners (ISMP)   A worldwide network of professionals involved in all areas of meeting planning, from scheduling to supplying. ISMP was established to improve professionalism and competency in the meeting planning industry as well as create new business opportunities for its members. The Society also offers the professional designations "Registered Meeting Planner" and "Certified Destination Specialist" to qualified applicants. *Contact:* ISMP, 8383 East Evans Road, Scottsdale, AZ 85260-3614 (602/483-0000; Fax 602/998-8022; E-mail **imsp@ iani.org**; URL **http://iani.org/ismp.html**).

International Standard Book Number (ISBN) A number used to identify individual newly published books. Obtained by contacting Books in Print, R.R. Bowker, 121 Chanlon Rd., New Providence, NJ 07974 (908/665-6770).

International Standard Serial Number (ISN) A number used to identify individual issues of periodicals such as magazines and newsletters. Obtained by contacting the Cataloging in Publications Division, National Serial Data Program, Library of Congress, Washington, DC 20540 (202/707-6454; **LCINFO@LOC.GOV** generalLOC info; URL **http://lcweb.loc.gov**). *See also* International Standard Book Number; Library of Congress Book Number.

International Standards Organization 9000 (ISO 9000) A series of standards applicable to products and services, which defines quality assurance systems and the management of the quality mechanism itself. It is based on British Standard 5750 and is used to determine whether companies have their quality systems under control and to certify the attainment of those standards in their operations. EN 29000 is a modification of ISO 9000 adopted by the European Community.

International Standards Organization 14000 The ISO's environmental system standard.

International Teleconferencing Association (ITCA) A non-profit professional association whose 830 members include users, providers, strategists, educators, learners, managers, and employees that use teleconferencing, telecollaborative, and distance education technologies. ITCA's objectives are to foster recognition and research and promote broader application and development, act as the primary resource for information, and provide a forum for the exchange of information among users, providers, and researchers/consultants of teleconferencing. *Contact:* ITCA, 1299 Woodside Dr., Ste. 101, McLean, VA 22102 (703/556-6115; E-mail **dasitca@aol.com**; URL **http://www.itca. org**).

International Television Association (ITVA) An organization of 9,000 members dedicated to serving the needs of the professional video communicator in non-broadcast settings. ITVA provides an open channel of communication connecting video professionals with other practitioners and with companies supplying video equipment, materials, and services. *Contact:* ITVA, 6311 N. O'Connor Rd., Ste. 230, Irving, TX 75039 (972/869-1112; Fax 972/869-2980; E-mail **itvahq@worldnet.att.net**; URL **http://www. itva.org**).

The International Travel Briefing Service (ITBS) Provides on-line security tips for business travelers. *Contact:* ITBS, WSM Publishing Company, Box 466, Merrifield, VA 22116 (301/564-8473).

International Visual Literacy Association (IVLA) An organization of 200 members established to provide a multidisciplinary forum for the exploration, presentation, and discussion of all aspects of visual communication and their applications through visual images, visual literacy, and literacies in general. The association serves as the organizational bond for professionals from many diverse disciplines who are creating and sustaining the study of the nature of visual experiences and literacies and their cognitive and affective bases and who are developing new means for the evaluation of learning through visual methods. *Contact:* IVLA, Inc. c/o Dr. Barbara I Clark, Gonzaga University, E. 502 Boone AD25, Spokane, WA 99258-0001(509/328-4220, X3478; E-mail **bclark@ soe.gonzaga.edu**; URL **http://infoserver.etl.vt.edu/coe/COE-students/Baderku/IVLA.htm**).

Internet A worldwide network of computer networks (more than 32,000 as of January 1996) connecting more than 2 million computers in 135 countries and territories worldwide operated by universities, governments, corporations, individuals, and others. It is neither owned nor controlled by any one entity. The Internet is virtual space in which users send and receive **E-mail,** log in to remote computers, "surf" or browse databases of information, and send and receive files.

internet-based training (IBT) There are two forms: (1) text-based — programs that use simple printed materials And require very little bandwidth (the capacity of a carrier to deliver information); and (2) multimedia — programs that use both sound and video and require relatively large bandwidth.

interval data   Numerical data that can be rank-ordered and have equal distances between all adjacent values.

Internet direct public offering (I-DPO)   An offer to sell a company's stock to the general public. For prices starting at $10,000, a company can sell up to $5 million in stock direct to the on-line general public.

Internet Employment Network   A sizable job bank with free résumé referral. (**http://garnet.insen.com70/1/vendor/napa/jobs/**).

Internet relay chat (IRC)   A communications system that accommodates real-time conversations among multiple users, such as America Online.

Internet server   Allows workstations to connect to the Internet.

Internet service provider (ISP)   An organization that provides access to the Internet. Usually charge by the month and are faster and less expensive than **on-line services**, but they provides few if any extras. To locate an ISP, check The List at **http://the list. iworld.com/**.

intern programs   See cooperative education.

internship   The period prescribed for an intern, in such professions as medicine and teaching, to prepare for entry into the profession.

interpersonal communication   Communication between and among individuals and groups in which information, ideas, and feelings are exchanged mainly by means of face-to-face contacts (spoken words, gestures, and body language).

Interpretative Guidelines on Sexual Harassment   Issued by the Equal Employment Opportunity Commission in March 1980, the guidelines detail employers' responsibilities for maintaining a workplace free of sexual harassment and intimidation.

interpreter/interpretation   A professional linguist who translates the spoken word — oral communication — from one language to another. Used in conferences and training sessions. There are four forms of interpretation: (1) consecutive, in which the speaker pauses after every few sentences to allow the interpreter to render the words in the other language, (2) simultaneous interpretation, requiring the use of headsets, in which the interpreter listens to speech in one language and after a few seconds delay, repeats the content in another language, (3) oral interpretation using two interpreters (because the first interpreter is not a master of the second language, and (4) whisper interpretation, in which each person in a small group of people is assigned an individual interpreter who whispers simultaneous interpretation of what is being said.

interprocess communications   In computer technology, the transfer and sharing of data between two processes running concurrently on the system, through facilities such as dynamic data exchange and dynamic link libraries.

interquartile range   The difference between the third quartile (75th percentile) and the first quartile (25th percentile) in an ordered array of data or **frequency distribution**. It contains the middle 50 percent of the data.

in terroriam clause   States that if anyone contests the will, he or she will receive $1.00 or lose completely any legacy designated for hi or her. Literally means "in terror" of disinheritance. Usually frowned upon by courts.

intervention   A strategy used by managers, facilitators, or practitioners to accomplish some human resources, human resources development, or organization development objective. Examples: creative problem solving exercises, team building, counseling, coaching, training.

interview   A face-to-face meeting with individuals or groups (superiors, peers, subordinates, other employees, customers, suppliers, dealers, and applicants for positions) to give and receive information, identify leads to new or unperceived problems, determine the seriousness of problems spotted by other means, collect information and opinions, and share information. Used in recruitment, screening and selection, assignment, promotion, termination, appraisal, counseling, discipline, attitude and opinion surveys, behavior modeling, evaluation, audits, performance assessment, job and task analysis, market research, needs assessment, productivity improvement, salary review, outplacement, and training and development. Types include nondirective or client-centered, directive, structured, and so on.

inter vivos trust   See revocable living trust.

intestacy rules   Part of state law, they employ the rules of **consanguinity** or closest blood relationship when determining how a person who does not leave a will has his or her property distributed.

intestate A person is said to have died intestate if no will exists at the time of death. Under those circumstances, property of the deceased passes to survivors under the the the state's laws of intestate succession. Although the laws of the various states vary, in most cases the estate will be split between the surviving spouse and children. In some sates, if there are no children, the estate must be shared with the decedent's parents or brothers and sisters.

intestate succession laws Laws that prescribe the persons to whom a deceased individual's property will be distributed if he or she dies without a will.

intra-market merger See in-market merger.

intranet A private corporate network that connects different types of computers in various branches of an organization at widely dispersed locations. Workers at those locations use web browsers to point and click through large databases and communicate with each other. Intranets can be integrated into the **Internet,** allowing users to access data outside the company. Software safeguards, called firewalls, protect the intranet from unauthorized use.

intrapreneur An employee in a managerial position within an organization who is given freedom and autonomy to do what needs to be done and is rewarded for results.

intrinsic motivator A natural outcome of the job and the tasks associated with the work environment, such as feeling of satisfaction and accomplishment following a highly successful decision briefing.

intrinsic reward A reward that is part and parcel of an achievement, whether or not it is recognized and applauded as such by others. Whatever was achieved in and of itself provides the feedback to the doer which says, "You did a good job.!"

intuition training Training designed to teach employees to become more intuitive — to use their instincts, their "sixth sense" or "gut feelings — as a supplement to or substitute for more logical thought processes. Makes use of visualization.

intuitive skill The ability to employ instinctive knowledge or gut feelings, rather than logic, hard facts, or experience, to solve problems, make decisions, innovate, create, and evaluate.

intuitive thinking See lateral thinking.

inventory 1. In testing, a checklist or questionnaire, usually relating to self, designed to elicit non-cognitive (affective) information. Technically not tests, they are most often used to identify personality traits, interests, attitudes, motivation, and the like. 2. The total dollar value of raw materials, materials in process, and finished products on hand in a business, store, warehouse, factory, or processing plant at the time of the statement. 3. A physical count of the number of items of various types of property (goods or stock) on hand in an organization at a given point in time — usually at the end of an accounting period, such as a calendar or fiscal year. 4. A listing of an estate's assets which is filed with probate court for assets in the name of a decedent.

inventory budget A budget that uses the cost of purchases, direct labor, and overhead expenses and budgeted cost of goods sold to determine the budget value of final inventories for raw materials, work in process, and finished products. That budget and the other budgets are then used to determine the budgeted cost of goods sold.

investigation A legal doctrine that pertains to unlawful discharge. Essentially it asks, "Did the employer, before administering the disciplinary action, make an effort to find out whether the employee violated a rule or an order?"

investment techniques See call and put options; currency futures; leverage through borrowing; reverse purchase agreements; short-selling.

The Invisible Industry The meeting planners and hospitality industry.

invitational A graphic or other device used to lure **Internet** subscribers to a marketer's **home page**.

in vitro fertilization (IVF) A medical procedure performed in fertility clinics to make it possible for infertile couples to produce a baby. Involves hormone injections to stimulate the production of eggs, extracting them, fertilizing them with sperm, and inserting them into the woman's uterus. Alternative procedures include assisted hatching; gamete intrafallopian transfer (GIFT); intracytoplasmic sperm injection (ICSI); intrauterine insemination (IUI); zygote intrafallopian transfer (ZIFT).

involuntary bumping In travel management, cancellation of reserved seats of passengers ticketed and already on board an aircraft or ready to board. Caused by overbooking or overselling flights.

involvement *See* employee involvement.

IPO In meeting planning, "individual pays own" — where charges are divided between the master account and the individual or there is no master account.

ipsative scores A means of measuring and reporting differences *within* an individual rather than *between or among* individuals. Used to control constant error in personnel evaluation and rating, such as error of halo or error of standards.

ipso facto A legal term that means "by the fact itself" — that the existence of one fact tends to prove the existence of another fact.

IRA rollover *See* rollover.

irrevocable living trust A legal document prepared by an attorney that allows the maker to transfer ownership of property to a separate entity called a trust, which is managed in accordance with rules established by the maker for the benefit of the beneficiaries named in the trust. An irrevocable trust cannot be changed after it is established; however, it may provide savings on estate taxes and prevent the loss of government benefits to the beneficiary.

Ishikawa diagram *See* cause and effect diagram.

ISO *(isos)* From the Greek word *isos,* which means equal. Often assumed to be an acronym for International Standards Organization.

issue All of a person's future lineage, including children, grandchildren, great-great grandchildren, and so on, descended from a common ancestor.

issue surviving by right of representation A bequest or gift to the closest living family member where the child or children (including grandchildren or great-grandchildren) of a decedent take what their parent would have received if that parent had survived.

Italian boot The Vannina-Rizzoli Limb Orthosis, a prosthesis designed to help individuals with spinal cord injuries stand and/or walk. It facilitates mobility, enhances cardiovascular fitness, and provides increased potential for long-term usage. Light weight and easy to use, the boot is conducive to all-day wearability while promoting standing — without the upper extremity support required by traditional bracing.

italic In typography, type that slants upward to the right, as in *italic.* Used for emphasis.

item analysis The process of analyzing and evaluating individual test items to determine such characteristics as difficulty and discriminating power.

item difficulty A test item characteristic used to determine the worth or appropriateness of individual test items. It is determined by calculating the proportion of a testee group that answers an item correctly. An item with a difficulty of 0.30 or lower is a hard item; one with a difficulty of 0.90 or higher is an easy one.

item distractor An alternative answer to a multiple-choice test item. There are usually three or four distractors per test item, along with the correct or best answer.

item stem The question in a test item that identifies a single, clear, central problem, provides all the information needed for the response, and avoids ambiguity and negative wording.

iterative approach An integrative technique used in forecasting. Several people are selected as forecasters, but their identities are not revealed to each other to prevent cross talk. Questions are sent to all participants in writing simultaneously. As each one replies, the name is checked off on the participant list, the responses are summarized and tabulated, and they are sent out again to all participants for comment. The process is repeated until consensus is achieved.

I-Way A massive network of government, university, and corporate computer data bases which can be accessed either through an on-line service or by a local telephone call.

J

JAIMS	Japan-America Institute of Management Science.
JAN	Job Accommodation Network.
JCAHO	Joint Commission on Accreditation of Healthcare Organizations.
JIT	1. Job instruction training. 2. Just in time.
JOB	Job Opportunities for the Blind.
JPA	Job performance aid.
JPEG	Joint Photographic Experts Group.
JPM	Job performance measure.
JTPA	Job Training Partnership Act of 1982.
JTWROS	Joint tenancy with right of survivorship.
JWV	Jewish War Veterans.

Japan-America Institute of Management Science (JAIMS) A private, graduate-level institute that develops and enhances intercultural communication through management education, training and research. Offers a program for Japanese and American managers who wish to learn how to strengthen economic and political ties and develop an understanding of industrial practices in the two countries. The program includes a 5-month intensive study of Japanese language, culture, and financial management and a 4-month internship in major Japanese firms, institutes, and government agencies. JAIMS, 6660 Hawaii Kai Dr., Honolulu, HI 96825-1108 (800/54-JAIMS or 808/395-2314; Fax 808/396-7111 or 808/396-7112; URL **http://www.jaims.org**). In Japan, JAIMS, 1-17-25 Shinkamata, Ohta-ku, Tokyo 144, Japan [(03)3730-3116; toll-free in Japan: 0120-222-390; Fax (03)3730-4216].

Java Advertised as "a simple, object-oriented, distributed, interpreted, robust, secure, architecture-neutral, portable, high-performance, multi-threaded, dynamic, buzzwork-compliant, general-purpose programming language." A means of creating a standard way to transmit functions, as well as data, over network lines. It could become the language for client/server development. (URL **http://www.javasoft.com/index.html**).

Jerusalem A computer virus having many strains. It reduces free memory and may play "Frere Jacques" at five-minute intervals on Fridays, slow the system, or display a black box one-half hour after a file is infected.

Jewish War Veterans of the U.S.A. (JWV) An organization of approximately 100,000 members open to veterans of wartime service of the Jewish faith. Its mission is service to veterans, Americanism, and to provide a voice on Capitol Hill for veterans' legislation and benefits. *Contact:* Jewish War Veterans of the USA, 1811 R St., N.W., Washington, DC 20009-1659 (202/265-6280; Fax 202/234-5662; E-mail **jwvusa@erols.com**; URL **http://www/penfed.org/jwv/home.htm**).

jitterati The consequence when a member of the "digital generation" drinks too much coffee.

job The duties and tasks that a single worker performs. The basic unit used by personnel to carry out the actions of screening, selecting, classifying, training, assigning, developing, and promoting employees. Examples of a job are electronic equipment repairer and plant superintendent.

Job Accommodation Network (JAN) An international information network and consulting resource to help qualified workers with disabilities to be hired or retained. It enables employers, rehabilitation professionals, and people with disabilities to share information about practical ways, including methods and equipment, of making accommodations for employees and applicants with disabilities. There is no charge for the information; simply a commitment to provide information about accommodations made to JAN for incorporation into the database. *Contact:* JAN, West Virginia University, 918 Chestnut Rodge Rd., Ste., Morgantown, WV 26506-6080 800/526-7234; Canada 800/526-2262; commercial 304/293-7186; Fax 304/293-5407; E-mail **jan@jan.icdi. wvu.edu**; URL **http://janweb.icdi.wvu.edu**).

job aids Materials that provide step-by-step directions for performing specific technical tasks to reduce training time, error rates, and dependence on instructors. They may be in paper (document or manual), computerized, or visual (slides, motion picture, or videocassette) form.

The Job Act *See* Small Business Job Protection Act of 1996.

job analysis The process of collecting, tabulating, grouping, analyzing, interpreting, and reporting data pertaining to the work performed by individuals who fill operative, clerical, technical, staff, supervisory, or managerial positions. Job analysis focuses on the duties, tasks, and elements that make up a job. The results of job analyses are used to identify and organize content for writing and revising **job descriptions** and **applicant specifications**; provide detailed job data that can be used to identify personnel requirements resulting from installation of new equipment, tools, work methods, or processes, and from development of new products and services; project future personnel requirements resulting from restructuring or downsizing; establish accurate and objective information for job evaluation; provide guidance for decisions relating to compensation and benefits, assignment and transfer, on-the-job training and development, and promotion; aid in the development of more effective recruitment, screening, selection, assignment, and classification instruments and procedures; establish measurable job performance standards; identify factors that induce job satisfaction, raise morale, and improve productivity; identify and locate health and safety hazards; and design training and development systems.

job bank A means of compensating for the loss of employees with essential skills. Job banks enroll retired employees for temporary and part-time positions on an "as needed" basis. *See also* U.S. Employment Service.

JobBank USA A national search firm that specializes in employee networking and information services to employers, job candidates, and recruitment firms (URL **http://www.jobbankusa.com**).

job bidding *See* bidding.

job classification A method of job evaluation that involves segregating all jobs in an organization into occupational groups, establishing and defining a series of levels within each group (noting required standards pertaining to knowledge and skills, training and experience, accountability and responsibility, and so on), and finally matching each job to the appropriate level described in the standards. The result is a series of classifications within each occupational group that are not necessarily comparable or equivalent from one group to another.

job codes A means of identifying defined and specific job tasks, typically numeric.

Job Corps A public-private partnership, administered by the U.S. Department of Labor. It is the nation's largest and most comprehensive residential education and job training program for at-risk youth, ages 16 through 24. Since 1964, the program has provided more than 1.7 million disadvantaged young people with the integrated academic, vocational, and social skill training they need to gain independence and get quality, long-term jobs or further education. More than 110 Job Corps campuses exist nationwide, including those in the District of Columbia and Puerto Rico. *Contact:* Job Corps, P.O. Box 193768, San Francisco, CA 04119 (800/733-JOBS or 800/Job-Corps; E-mail **webmaster@jcdc.jobcorps.org**; URL **http://www.jobcorps.org**).

job-cost system In cost accounting, cost reduction, and cost-benefits analysis, a system for assigning production costs to products and services used when production costs are of critical concern. The job-cost system integrates accounting for material and labor costs, use of overhead rates, and cost accounting as a part of the formal ledger. Although time-consuming and costly because of the paperwork involved, it accurately determines factory costs of a product where a variety of products is produced.

job description A document that describes the major duties, functions, and authority assigned to a position and the relationships between the position and other positions in the organization or department, and, when appropriate, the relationship of that job to positions in other departments. It is one of the main products of **job analysis**.

job design The process of developing or redeveloping the dimensions of a job by identifying major functions, duties, and tasks, describing the relationships of the job to other positions in the organization, and documenting them in a written job description.

job dimensions A list of requirements, in terms of knowledge, skills, abilities, education, training, experience, and traits and temperament used in the hiring process. Examples of abilities are analysis, planning, organizing, delegating, and written and oral communication. Examples of traits are judgment, decisiveness, independence, initiative, leadership, tolerance of stress, and energy.

job displacement Job elimination regardless of whether the incumbent is terminated or transferred.

job engineering A performance management technique or intervention in which the job is changed in some way—made more simple, more challenging, more interesting — to promote employee productivity.

job enlargement See job enrichment.

job enrichment Redesigning jobs to motivate people to work to their capacity and level of ability, improve employee morale, job satisfaction, and commitment to the organization, remedy performance shortfalls or problems, develop employee skills and abilities in connection with affirmative action and upward mobility objectives and programs, make accommodations for employees with disabilities, improve the quality of products or services, give job incumbents more prestige and power, increased responsibility, more autonomy, or greater challenge, and preclude employee dissatisfaction, grievances, arbitration, slowdowns, and strikes.

job evaluation A means of comparing jobs to establish their relative level, importance, and value in the organizational scheme of things, including the remuneration that will be allotted, usually resulting in a schedule of position grades or a hierarchy of classifications.

job fair A cost-effective recruitment strategy. Several companies within a geographical area share advertising and site rental costs to stage an employment effort designed to attract candidates for positions as well as identify employment and salary trends and changes in the labor market.

job grade A class or group into which jobs of comparable value are placed for compensation purposes. Typically all jobs at a given grade have the same pay range.

job hangover Loss of enthusiasm that frequently occurs when, after several months or a year in a new job, managers and executives become deeply involved in the day-to-day details of a position and experience a decline in their job satisfaction.

job instruction sheet A set of instructions, usually printed on a single sheet of paper. May accompany a piece of equipment, explaining how to operate it or maintain it. Or the instruction sheet may be a set of directions written for a substitute or temporary employee explaining how to perform a certain task, such as typing a standard company memo.

job instruction training (JIT) A one-on-one training model developed during World War I. JIT included "show," "tell," "do," and "check" steps as well as the additional steps of preparation and introduction. The current version includes these preparation steps: (1) list all steps in the job in the correct sequence, and (2) identify a corresponding key point for each step. The steps show what is to be done, while the key points show how and why it is to be done.

job inventory A shortcut method of job and task analysis useful for identifying the training needs of selected occupations, such as store managers. The inventory lists all of the major activities of the job incumbent, the importance of each activity or task, and the amount of time expended in performing it.

job lock Employees who remain in a job they really want to leave to keep their current health benefits and not chance any break in their eligibility for those benefits. Job lock is evidence of the growing concern about the costs of medical insurance and health care and the increasing numbers of employers who are reducing benefits costs by using cost-sharing strategies.

Job Opportunities for the Blind (JOB)
A joint program of the U.S. Department of Labor and the National Federation of the Blind that provides free workshops, publications, and information about the ADA, reasonable accommodations, and employing blind employees. JOB also provides a free, nationwide service to employers in locating and hiring qualified blind applicants and

assists employees who are blind or become legally blind while on the job. *Contact:* JOB, c/o National Federation of the Blind, 1800 Johnson St., Baltimore, MD 21230 (800/638-7518 or 410/659-9314; E-mail **nfb@access. digex.net**; URL **http://www.nfb.org**).

job paths or job pathing *See* career ladder.

job performance aid (JPA) A document, printed guide, audiotape, videotape, or computer driven program. It is provided to employees for use on the job. Examples are manuals, charts, tables, checklists, and "how to" instructions.

job performance counseling A manager-initiated strategy for improving employee efficiency, effectiveness, and productivity to achieve job adjustment, improve motivation and morale, decrease absenteeism, reduce turnover, foster acceptance of change, release emotional tension, reduce stress, and promote teamwork. It lets employees know where they stand, what they do well, where they are deficient, and how they can improve.

job performance measure (JPM) A test or other evaluative instrument that provides the basis for developing training systems and controlling their quality. JPMs define and describe the job-related outcomes the training should produce.

job performance order A type of instructional sequencing in which the order of presentation of subject-matter is based on the sequence in which a job, duty, or task is actually performed.

job posting Internal or external advertising and recruiting for current position vacancies. Postings include listing the duties, authority, qualifications, supervision received, work schedule, and pay rate.

job pricing The process of determining the appropriate rate of pay or salary for a specific job with due consideration for prevailing industry and regional rates as determined by systematic wage and salary surveys.

job procedures manual A manual written for employees that describes *how* a job procedure should be done, including information on the equipment itself; for example, the sequential steps required to rebuild an automobile carburetor or design, develop, and validate an instructional system.

job profiling A means of defining job requirements based on job definitions and success factors identified by subject-matter experts or supervisory personnel. Also used in employee performance rating.

job ranking The simplest method of job evaluation. All jobs in an organization are ranked by a knowledgeable person or group (usually managers or supervisors) in order of their perceived importance and worth to the organization.

job redesign Restructuring a job by adding, deleting, or changing duties, tasks, or elements to make them more doable or more interesting and challenging.

job reference immunity statutes Laws passed by 26 states designed to shield employers from lawsuits brought by an employee as a result of providing information about the employee to a prospective employer. The typical statute provides qualified immunity to en employer who discloses information about the employee's job performance or work record.

job-related literacy training Training in reading skills provided semi-literate and illiterate employees either in the firm, under contract, or off-the premises.

job relatedness An important legal concept that requires employers to demonstrate that an action, requirement, or program is directly related to the job. Job relatedness is only raised as a consideration when an employer's objection to an employee's refusal to comply with direction is based on protected grounds.

job replica test A behavioral simulation used to test for abilities required by the types of tasks that must be performed in the target job; for example, a driving test for a delivery service position; a typing test for a secretarial position.

job rotation An informal method of training and development, often used in conjunction with coaching. Job rotation is a technique whereby potential managers receive diversified training and experience under close supervision through rotation for specified periods of time in nonsupervisory or managerial jobs, observational assignments, or training or assistant-to positions. It is designed to improve employees in their present jobs and prepare them for future positions. In some cases, managers are rotated through all major departments in an organization for one month each.

job sampling A technique used in employee selection, it involves observing or measuring how an applicant actually performs some of the basic tasks of a job.

job satisfaction The sum of an individual's attitudes and feelings about his or her job — amount and quality of supervision received, working conditions, compensation, job characteristics and challenge, relationships with co-workers, and so on.

job search campaign The use of search organizations, employment agencies, or consultants to identify suitable candidates for key positions or to assist employees who have been terminated to find suitable employment.

Job Service *See* U. S. Employment Service.

job sharing/job splitting An arrangement that allows employees to fulfill their job responsibilities and provide more time for them to care for their dependents by dividing a job and the workday or work week between two part-time employees. For example, one employee may work from 8 a.m. to 12m and the other from 1:00 to 5:00 p.m.; or one employee may work Mondays, Wednesdays, and Fridays and the other Tuesdays and Thursdays. There is a distinction, however, between job sharing and job splitting. Job sharing involves two employees whose duties overlap, think of each other as an extension of themselves, and therefore must communicate. Their shifts may overlap to facilitate such communication, but it is not an essential feature because they may communicate by E-mail or less sophisticated means, such as periodic meetings, phone calls, or notes. Job splitting involves creating two clearly distinct, separate, and independent jobs from one job. No communication between incumbents is needed.

Job Skill Development Act of 1997 Introduced as H.R. 71 by Rep. Joe Knollenberg, R-Mich, the act would amend the FLSA to exempt from the minimum wage and overtime requirements individuals who volunteer their time to enhance their occupational opportunities. Employees would have to initiate the volunteer work, which could consist of no more than 40 hours in a week or 1,040 hours total.

job specifications
See applicant specifications.

job title The specific designation, label, or name given to a job to distinguish it from all other jobs.

JOBTRAK A job bank that, in partnership with 400+ college and university career centers across the country provides the information that students and recent graduates need — over 2,100 new full- and part-time job openings each day. Job seekers visit the JOBTRAK site, search the database and view company profiles. By means of a toll-free phone call, or by using an on-line job listing form, employers may post their job listings at multiple campuses. JOBTRAK service is provided free of charge to colleges. There is a nominal fee to employers to place job listings. *Contact:* JOBTRAK, 990 Westwood Blvd., Suite 260, Los Angeles, CA 90025 (800/999-8725; E-mail **kramberg@ jobtrak.com**; URL **http://www.jobtrak. com**).

Job Training Partnership Act of 1982 (JTPA) The federal government's largest job-skills training program targeted at educationally disadvantaged and displaced youth and adults, especially women, minorities, disabled, disadvantaged, disabled veterans, veterans of the Vietnam era, and veterans recently separated from military service. It funnels federal training funds to the states for local use. The Act replaces CETA, the Comprehensive Employment and Training Act of 1973. The legislation requires states to establish Service Delivery Areas (SDAs), local areas in which JTPA services are developed, implemented, and provided. SDAs provide such services as client assessment, basic education and remediation services, job training, and placement services free of change for all JTPA participants. SDAs broker services — buy them — from community colleges, private proprietary schools, adult basic education programs, and vocational educational training training programs run by local or state agencies. JTPA Title II serves economically disadvantaged individuals. Title III is directed specifically at dislocated workers. The Act also allows employers a 50 percent wage reimbursement of the first six months of employment for disabled individuals who meet established economic guidelines. The program is administered by local private industry councils.

Johari window A model of communication and interpersonal relationships; a graphic means of describing an individual, a group, the psychological climate of an organization, or an entire culture. A square (the window) is divided into four equal parts to represent areas as follows: (I) known to self and known to others, (II) not known to self and known to others, (III) known to self and not known to others, and (IV) not known to self and not known to others. Attributed to Luft and Ingman.

joint The cigarette form of heroin, cocaine, or marijuana.

joint-activities staff Members of the staff paid by both union and management to patrol assembly lines and oversee work teams, cultivate cooperation, and identify opponents of union-management unity and meddlers or obstructionists of union elections. Also called *thought police.*

Joint Commission on Accreditation of Healthcare Organizations (JCAHO)
An independent, not-for profit organization that evaluates and accredits more than 16,000 health care organizations in the United States, including networks and health plans, hospitals, home care agencies, long term care facilities, behavioral health care organizations, laboratories, and ambulatory care centers. Its mission is to improve the quality of health care provided to the public. *Contact:* JCAHO, 1 Renaissance Blvd., Oakbrook Terrace, IL 60181 (630/792-5000; Fax 630/792-5005; E-mail **webmaster@jcaho. org**; URL **http://www.jcaho.org**).

joint fare Special fare pricing established between two carriers for connecting flights or business.

joint labor/management committee
A panel consisting of representatives of employees and management established to study problems, ease conflicts and improve relationships. Such groups typically have clearly defined goals and responsibilities, continuity in their leadership, and meet regularly.

joint life An insurance policy that insures two persons, usually husband and wife. It pays only once on the death of one of the insured. The cost is about 30 percent less than that of buying individual policies on two people.

joint ownership An arrangement whereby an individual shares ownership of property with another. An example is a joint bank account.

Joint Photographic Experts Group (JPEG)
The committee that designed the photographic image-compression standard used on the Internet to compress full-color or gray scale photographic-type digital images.

joint tenancy with right of survivorship (JTWROS) A form of **joint ownership** often used with real property. It can act as a will to avoid probate, but it will not necessarily avoid taxes. It vests the title to the property in the survivor upon the death of the first joint tenant.

joint venture Businesses that have been formally and closely linked to improve market share, engage in mutually supporting activities and endeavors, achieve greater efficiency, and reduce costs. Joint ventures may or may not involve the acquisition of subsidiaries by larger companies. Also called *alliances.*

joint will A legal document, signed by both spouses, which provides that on the death of one of them, all or a specified portion of his or her property will go to the survivor. Upon the death of the second spouse, that person's property, including the remaining part of the first spouse's wealth, will pass to specified relatives, friends, and charitable organizations of each spouse in amounts or proportions agreed to when the will was prepared.

Joshi A computer virus that locks up infected systems on January 5 and displays the message "Type Happy Birthday Joshi!" until the user obeys. The virus causes the system to write to and format 5 1/4-inch disks and 1.2 MB disks as 360K formatted disks, making them unreadable until reformatted. Joshi is "caught" by booting from an infected floppy disk.

Jughead On the **Internet,** a search mechanism that allows users to locate information, files and databases.

junior board A method of developing managers. Junior boards involve the selection of promising employees for management positions, assigning them to committees or task forces where they meet regularly to consider proposals relating to the management of the enterprise. The decisions of these groups are forwarded to the responsible executive who may adopt them, reject them, table them, or refer them back for further consideration.

junior suite A large hotel room with a partition separating the sitting area from the bedroom.

junk *See* heroin.

junket In travel management, a free meeting trip given to lawmakers. Also called *freebies.*

junk fare   A heavily discounted air fare — reduced by as much as 25 percent.

junkfax   Using facsimile machines to deliver unsolicited sales literature to prospective customers and clients, thereby tying up their fax machines and using their fax paper supplies for unwanted and unneeded promotional materials.

jury of experts   A reliable means of collecting and analyzing job data. A group of personnel selected for their experience, expertise, and knowledge of the job are brought together to record the duties and tasks that make up the job. The data are organized and recorded under the direction of a trained job analyst, and in a predetermined and standardized format.

just cause   Legal terminology used in connection with termination or discharge of an employee. To protect itself against litigation, management must insure that it has enforced its rules consistently, that it has made a fair, thorough, and impartial investigation of the facts in the case, that there are credible witnesses to the offense, and the penalty for the offense is fair under the circumstances. Seven tests apply: reasonableness, adequate notice, investigation, fairness, adequacy of proof, equal treatment, and appropriate penalty.

justification evaluation   The form of evaluation most commonly used in the HR field. It involves the collection of evidence to prove the need for initial, continued, or increased funding and other support for programs, services, and activities. Evidence usually takes the form of documentation showing that the programs, services, or activities are effective, save time and money, improve productivity and performance, and so forth.

justified   In desktop publishing, lines of type that are flush at both the left and right edges. In justified type setting, interword spaces are varied to make both margins flush.

Just-in-Time (JIT)   **1.** In management, the practice of waiting until the last possible moment before intervening in a situation, such as in conflict resolution. **2.** In manufacturing, a Japanese approach to inventory reduction. The basic idea is to schedule the arrival of raw materials and parts at the factory at the exact time they are needed and the immediate departure of finished products, instead of maintaining costly stockpiles of materials, parts, and products. **3.** In training, computer-driven performance systems designed to support people in the workplace with help when they need it.

Just-in-Time mentoring   Providing instant linkage between an employee needing help and someone who can give it by providing access to a database and/or by using E-mail to contact an "expert" who has dealt successfully with the same or a similar problem.

Just-in-Time training   Training often (but not always) provided in the workplace that is given when it is needed and is directly related to the work to be done. Typically involves the use of hi-tech training strategies, such as computers, compact disc interactive (CD-I) systems , compact disc-read only memory (CD-ROM), or multimedia, but for some subject-matter, such as leadership and diversity training for managers and executives, personalized, classroom training is often the method of choice.

Just-in-Time work force   *See* contingent work force.

K

k   Kilobyte.

kbps   Kilobits per second.

KISS   Keep it simple stupid. *See* KISS program.

K&R   Kidnap and ransom insurance.

KMAT   Knowledge Management Assessment Tool.

KSAs   Knowledge, skills, and abilities (or attitudes).

kaizen **1.** Attributed to Masaaki Imai, a Japanese term that basically means "improvement" through self-critique in all aspects of an individual's life — personal, social, and work life — getting better to be more productive and competitive. It is a basic principle of achievement motivation. **2.** A Japanese management concept that aims at gradual improvement in the operation and functioning of an organization and achievement of personal and organizational goals by involving everyone from top management to production workers.

Kaleida A cooperative project initiated by Apple and IBM. The objective is to develop the multimedia computer of the future. The company will develop and license multimedia technologies that will operate across platforms.

kanban A Japanese term that describe the "display" or "instruction cards" used to control production and material movement through an inventory (or *kanban*) system. Some kanban cards are request-and-authorization forms that are passed from the assembly line to production areas to indicate that more work pieces are required. They also reduce or eliminate production control person-hours and related paperwork.

kanji Chinese characters adopted by the Japanese for written language more than 1,000 years ago. Characters are used to symbolize various categories of things. Attributed to Professor Noritaki Kano and reported in **Performance in Practice**, Fall, 1996.

Kano model A means of demonstrating the relationship between the presence or absence of a product or service characteristic or feature and the relative satisfaction of customers or clients.

karoshi A Japanese term meaning "death from overwork."

keiretsu A Japanese term meaning "business group"— a group of companies that have forged strategic alliances with other organizations, including competitors, to develop business, increase market share, and dominate their industry. Typically involves the establishment of a network of essentially captive suppliers who provide the raw materials and parts, and meet the component requirements of dominant manufacturers. Adapted and adopted by some U.S. companies.

Keogh Plan A plan that gives a self-employed individual, under strict IRS rules and requirements, the option to establish a qualified tax-deductible pension or profit-sharing plan. Also known as an *H.R. 10 Plan.*

Kerberos An authentication system that employs the government's Data Encryption Standard algorithm. Used to protect computer files from unauthorized entry.

kern/kerning In topography, a term used to describe the practice of selectively adjusting the white space between letters of any size, whether adding or decreasing space. Kerning makes a page of text copy more attractive and, although believed by many to improve readability, studies have shown that it doesn't improve readers' speed or comprehension.

key In video, a special effect achieved by electronically "cutting" or "burning" a hole of any size or shape in the video image and inserting another image or color. The key hole is made by a video camera or a character generator. Keys are used most often for titles.

keyboarding Operating a typewriter, word processor, computer terminal, calculator, keypunch, stenotype machine, or Addressograph.

keyboard system See keypad system.

key contributor program A compensation plan used to recognize and reward individuals or teams whose skills, abilities, performance, or contributions have improved or will significantly improve an organization's products, services, or processes and thereby improve market position, productivity, or profitability.

key cost The cost that is the largest for a company or industry, such as payroll.

key employees Under the **Employee Retirement Income Security Act of 1974** as amended by the **Retirement Equity Act of 1984**, and the **Tax Reform Act of 1986**, key employees are participants in a pension plan who are officers of the employing organization and participants who own a certain percentage interest in the employing organization.

key-man insurance An insurance policy that can be combined with a nonqualified, deferred compensation arrangement when the employer needs both financial protection against the loss of a key employee through death and adequate additional retirement income for the employee in the event that he or she survives a serious accident, injury, or illness and returns to work.

keypad system A 10-digit keypad wired to a computer used make meetings more interactive. Participants respond to questions by pushing the buttons that correspond to their choices. The computer processes the responses and displays them on a matrix on an overhead projector equipped with a **liquid crystal display panel.** Also called *decision support system; keyboard system.*

key points The main teaching points in a lesson plan — the action steps in a procedure, the learning standards, or the most important facts or concepts covered in the lesson.

key result areas Major duties or tasks of a job identified in job evaluation and used in management by objectives and performance appraisal systems to establish objectives and standards.

keyword search A World Wide Web search for documents containing one or more words selected by the user.

kidnap and ransom insurance (K&R) Insurance coverage provided by some companies for their employees who work in areas where there is the possibility of their being taken as hostages by terrorists or maverick governments. Such policies are written on a worldwide basis, and currently there are no restricted areas. Coverage provides for payment of ransom expenses and sometimes includes coverage for lost income. K&R may also provide the services of a protection consultant who can assist a company to avoid difficult situations and respond appropriately to a crisis.

killer app A highly successful application of technology, particularly one that advances or broadens the use of computers and is easy to use. Examples include World Wide Web browsers.

kill fee *See* cancellation fee.

kilobits (kbps) Kilobits per second, a measure of **bandwidth.**

kilobyte (k) A measure of computer storage space. It is equivalent to storage space for about 1,000 characters of text. The actual number is 1024.

kinesics The exploration, research, and study of body movements, facial expressions, and the like as means of communicating.

king A hotel room furnished with a king-size bed.

kiosk A computer-based interactive system installed in corporate cafeterias and work areas to perform a range of functions such as accessing general information about benefits, checking the status of savings plans, making calculations of benefits coverage, and changing the mix of benefits in a flexible benefit program.

KISS program A crude but basically correct creed for marketers, sales personnel, and writers: " keep it simple, stupid."

knowledge Facts, concepts, principles, meanings, understandings, and ideas that support skills and enable people to handle a broad range of assignments. Examples are nomenclature, terminology, symbols, and principles of leadership.

knowledge-based pay *See* pay for skills.

knowledge-based systems   *See* EXPERT systems.

knowledge engineer A job analyst who uses special techniques to codify the knowledge of experts about their specialties for use in expert systems.

Knowledge Management Assessment Tool (KMAT) A diagnostic set of procedures used by the American Productivity Center in collaboration with the Global Best Practices Group, a division of the Arthur Anderson consultancy to analyze the knowledge management practices of 80 companies.

knowledge, skills, and abilities (or attitudes) (KSAs) Common elements in job descriptions and applicant specifications: the knowledge (facts, concepts, principles, and so on), skills (learned and measurable physical and mental behaviors), and abilities (innate or acquired physical or mental capacities), or attitudes (predispositions or sentiments toward others persons, objects, institutions, practices, or ideas) required to perform a job.

knowledge workers People whose work is, for the most part, intellectual: planners, problem solvers, decision makers, managers, scientists, course developers, instructors, technical writers, and so on.

koosh/kooshing A slang expression used to describe rejection for a position.

Kraft joystick A tool to assist trainees to use educational interactive software requiring cursor movement for responses. Compatible with Apple II+, IIe, IIc, IIgs, Franklin, IBM PC and PC jr. *Contact:* Edmark Corporation, P.O. Box 3903, Bellevue, Washington 98009-3903 (800/426-0856).

Krauel v. Iowa Methodist Center A 1996 ruling by the U.S. 8th Circuit Court of Appeals that a self-insured benefits plan violates the **Americans with Disabilities Act of 1990** only if an employer is proven to have reduced or eliminated certain types of coverage to induce workers to quit their jobs or discourage applicants from seeking employment.

KSOP benefits Combined 401(k) and ESOP plans. Viewed by many companies as a cost effective way of funding the matching contributions of a 401k plan despite the complexities, regulatory snares, and additional administrative expenses involved

Ku-band satellite A type of satellite used in business TV, it is similar to police broadcast radio systems. *See also* C-band satellite.

Kuder-Richardson formula A mathematical formula used to estimate the reliability of an objective achievement test in which all items are weighted equally and in which speed of performance is not a consideration. The formula follows:

$$\text{Reliability} = \frac{ns^2 - M(n - M)}{ns^2}$$

where n = number of test items
s = standard deviation
M = mean

kurtosis The shape of a frequency distribution when plotted on a graph. It may be either flat (platykurtic) or humped (leptokurtic). *See also* skewness.

L

LAN	Local area network.
LBO	Leveraged buy-out.
LBR	Living benefits rider.
LCA	**1.** Life cycle analysis. **2.** Labor Condition Application (program).
LCD	Liquid crystal display.
LCI	Learner-controlled instruction.
LCM	Large case management.
LD	Learning disabled.
LDL	Low density lipoproteins.
LEPC	Local emergency planning committee.
LERN	The Learning Resources Network.
L.E.T.	Light at the End of the Tunnel.
LGA	Landrum-Griffin Act of 1959.
LIFO	Last in, first out.
LL	Laubach Literacy.
LLA	Lifelong Learning Act of 1976.
LLC	Limited liability company.
LLL	Life long learning.
LLP	Limited liability partnership.
LMPT	Labor-management participation team.
LMRA	Labor-Management Relations Act of 1947.
LMRDA	Labor-Management Reporting and Disclosure Act of 1959.
LOB	Line-of-balance.
LOC	Library of Congress.
LOL	Laughing out loud (Internet abbreviation).
LOMA	Life Office Management Association.
LON	Local operating network.
LOS	Length of stay.
LP	**1.** Lesson plan. **2.** Law provider.

LPN	Licensed practical nurse.
LSAT	Law School Admissions Test.
LSD	**1.** Lysergic acid diethylamide. **2.** Lump sum distribution.
LTC	Long-term care.
LTCO	Long-term care ombudsman program.
LTD	Long-term disability.
LVA	Literacy Volunteers of America.
L-VIS	Live video insertion system.

labor agreement *See* labor-management contract.

Laboratory Chemical Standard
Regulations issued by the **Occupational Safety and Health Administration** to minimize or eliminate exposure to hazardous chemicals in laboratories. The Standard requires lab operators to train their workers in chemical safety and develop a chemical hygiene plan.

laboratory experiment A **controlled experiment** in which the study is conducted in a "laboratory" (an artificial setting) under conditions selected or created so as to simulate a real setting.

laboratory instruction Application of theory through learner-centered training with an instructor present and supplemented by out-of-class assignments.

laboratory training *See* sensitivity training.

Labor Condition Application (program)
A temporary (H-1B) program designed to protect American jobs and wages from foreign competition. Audited by the Department of labor over a one-year period and concluded that it did not protect American jobs or wages. Some LCA employers were found to be using foreign workers to reduce payroll costs, either by paying less than prevailing wages to their own foreign employees, by illegally treating those employees as independent contractors, or by hiring those workers through job contractors.

labor costs The portion of the total cost of a program, system, or activity that is attributable to instructors, technicians, clerical help, and trainee wages or salaries.

labor demand The highest wage or salary employers are willing to pay for a specific level of employment or number of employees.

labor-hour contract In procurement, a type of fixed-rate contract in which the contractor is reimbursed only for the direct labor applied to fulfill the contract.

labor law posting Federal regulations require four specific **Equal Employment Opportunity** labor law posters as of July 26, 1992. Random inspections will be made by the EEOC and the Occupational Safety and Health Administration to ensure compliance. The posters must cover equal employment opportunity rights under the **Equal Employment Opportunity Act of 1972** and the **Americans with Disabilities Act of 1990**, federal minimum wage rights under the **Fair Labor Standards Act of 1938** and the Amendments of 1990, job safety and health protection under the **Occupational Safety and Health Act of 1970**, and polygraph protection under the **Employee Polygraph Protection Act of 1988**. *See also* state employment postings.

labor-management contract An agreement reached in good faith by negotiators representing a labor union and management and legally binding on both parties. Labor-management contracts contain the following: (1) definition of recognition and representation of the union as the exclusive bargaining agent for employees and the jobs or categories of jobs included and excluded; (2) requirements for union membership and termination of membership; (3) wage rates and methodology for job evaluation, rate changes and adjustments, transfers, upgrading and downgrading, incentive plans, and extent of participation of the union in the foregoing items; (4) management rights; (5) union rights; and (6) union proscriptions. Also known as *collective bargaining agreements*.

labor-management participation team (LMPT) A unit of 8 to 10 hourly workers and supervisors that meets regularly to discuss ways to reduce costs, eliminate waste, raise product quality, and improve health and safety conditions.

labor-management relations Relationships between unions and organizations under the provisions of federal statutes and court decisions covering such things as collective bargaining agreements (labor agreements) wage rates, management and union rights and proscriptions, employee rights, seniority, conduct of negotiations, arbitration, and mediation, grievance procedures, slowdowns and strikes, and adverse actions and discipline.

Labor-Management Relations Act of 1947 (LMRA) An amendment to the **National Labor Relations Act of 1935** (Wagner Act). Proscribed certain union activities and thereby balanced laws that had placed responsibility for unfair labor practices mainly on employers. The Act also prohibited unfair labor practices, enumerated the rights of employees as union members, enumerated the rights of employers, and allowed the President of the United States to temporarily bar national emergency strikes. The law also created the **Federal Mediation and Conciliation Service**. Also known as the *Taft-Hartley Act.*

labor-management relations laws *See* Anti-Injunction Act of 1932; Civil Service Reform Act of 1978; Economic Dislocation and Worker Adjustment Assistance Act of 1988; Employee Polygraph Protection Act of 1988; Labor Management Relations Act of 1947; Labor Management Reporting and Disclosure Act of 1959; National Labor Relations Act of 1935; Whistleblower Protection Act of 1989; Worker Adjustment and Retraining Notification Act of 1988.

Labor-Management Reporting and Disclosure Act of 1959 (LMRDA) Administered by the National Labor Relations Board. Protects the rights of union members to organize, choose their own representatives, and bargain collectively. The Act also increased the power of the Department of Labor (DOL) to investigate internal union financial and political affairs, and it strengthened prohibitions on secondary boycotts and places restrictions on picketing to force recognition by nonunion companies. The law contains a union member's "bill of rights," sets forth ground rules for union elections, regulates the kind of person eligible for service as a union officer, and expands the list of unlawful employer actions. Also known as the *Landrum-Griffin Act.*

labor relations *See* labor-management relations.

labor supply The minimum wage or salary necessary to attract a specific number of employees or level of employment.

labor union *See* union.

lag study A report that informs managers how old health care claims are being processed, how much is being paid out each month (and for earlier months), and compares the payouts to the amount of money that was accrued for expenses each month.

lanai A resort hotel room, usually with a balcony or patio, that overlooks a garden, lake, river, or ocean beach.

Land Court property Land registered with the Land Court as evidenced by a Certificate of Title.

Landgraf v. USI Film Products and Rivers v. Roadway Express Inc. A 1994 Supreme Court ruling that workers who filed discrimination lawsuits before passage of the **Civil Rights Act of 1991** (enacted November 21, 1991) were not eligible for a jury trial, compensatory, or punitive damages allowed by the law.

Landrum-Griffin Act of 1959 (LGA)
See Labor Management Reporting and Disclosure Act of 1959.

laptop computer A small, portable computer that can be operated on batteries, 12-volt DC from a car or boat (with a power converter that converts the DC to 115-volt AC), or from a wall outlet. Some laptops can also be connected to distant systems by means of modems. Weighs less than 12 pounds.

large-case management 1. Management of catastrophic illnesses. *See also* claims review; concurrent review; pattern review; precertification; retrospective review. **2.** Determining the most effective and least expensive way to provide health care services. May involve identifying medically appropriate alternatives to traditional care and the coordination of the revision of plan benefits.

laryngectomy A surgical procedure that involves removal of the larynx, usually due to cancer. Individuals who have undergone the procedure speak through a stoma — an opening in the throat just below the collar line — that enables them, following intensive training, to produce esophageal speech. Vocalization is achieved by forcing air into the stomach and then expelling it through the esophagus. The process produces a husky speech, unvarying in pitch, that is made audible by a hand-held, battery-operated, amplifying artificial voice generator.

laser barcode system A tool in technology-based training and education (similar to the UPC code technology used on items in a

grocery store) that employs a barcode reader to provide an easy-to-use, flexible means of controlling Level II laserdisc systems (laserdisc players with internal manual programming capability plus television or A/V monitor which can also be automatically programmed by means of instructions from a disc), simplifying the integration of written text with laserdisc-generated images and sound.

laserdisc/CD player A combination of a laserdisc and a compact disc (CD) that plays any size disc, from music CDs to movies, with a sharper picture than that provided by an ordinary VCR.

laserdisc technology Videodisc technology that provides three types or levels of interactive systems for training, education, testing, demonstration, desktop publishing, and sales: (1) basic — laserdisc plus television or an audiovisual monitor; (2) intermediate — laserdisc player with internal manual programming capability plus television or audiovisual monitor; and (3) advanced — laserdisc player plus computer plus interactive software plus audiovisual monitor.

laser printer A "light amplification through the simulated emission of radiation" printer used to print high quality text and graphics.

laser videodisc A type of optical disc measuring 8 or 12 inches across and used to store video images in analog format. Laser discs provide better image quality than videotape and are particularly suited to training because they are capable of true still framing and rapid search for individual frames.

last-in, first-out (LIFO) A method of inventory accounting as a means of reducing business taxes and improving cash flow. Users of the system assume that the last items received are the first items sold. During periods of rising costs, the method enables the manager to deduct the most recent, higher cost of merchandise as the cost of sale. That lowers taxable income and tax liability. The system has the disadvantages of requiring additional accounting calculations which lead to increased paperwork and costs, and also make profit margins appear lower, which often creates anxiety among investors and sometimes makes it more difficult to borrow money.

lateral thinking A nonlinear, unconventional, even nonlogical way of looking at problems. It involves thought that challenges assumptions and employs methods other than straight logical thinking. Sometimes called *intuitive thinking*. Attributed to Edward deBono (*Lateral Thinking: Creativity Step by Step,* Harper & Row, 1970).

Laubach Literacy An international nonprofit educational corporation that provides volunteer-based tutoring in English for Americans and nonnative adults, produces materials for tutoring, and trains tutors. *Contact:* Laubach Literacy, 1320 Jamesville Ave., Syracuse, NY 13210 (315/422-9121; 315/422-6369; E-mail **info@laubach.org**; URL **http://www. laubach. org**).

lavaliere mike An electronic amplifying device that can be independently adjusted for sound level and tends to reduce background noises because it is clipped on the speaker's clothing. Also called *tie-tack mike* and *lapel mike.*

law A binding custom, practice, or rule of conduct prescribed by a governing or controlling authority, such as the Congress, state legislature, or the courts,

law provider (LP) A person who provides legal services to clients for a fee or *pro bono.* In the U.S., LPs include licenses lawyers and **paralegal** professionals. In the United Kingdom, LPs include solicitors and barristers; in the Netherlands, advocaats; in Japan, bengoshi. *See also* barrister; solicitor.

layoff 1. Temporary termination of employees due to economic downturn, restructuring or downsizing, assembly line malfunction, equipment outage or replacement, or facility rehabilitation. Employees usually have recall rights to their jobs for a period of time, typically one year. **2.** The final step in a progressive disciplinary system, termination or firing for cause.

LCD-based projector A low-cost alternative to video and data projection. Current units incorporate three convergence-free, solid-state LCD panels (instead of CRTs), an integral 20- to 100-inch zoom lens, a switch for rear projection, industrial video connectors, and connections for standard video sources including computers. They can also be operated by a wireless remote.

LCD panel A liquid crystal display (LCD) projection panel is a form of of projection system that displays computer images. LCD panels are used in tandem with overhead projectors to project the computer image on large screens for viewing by large groups. In effect, they act as electronic transparencies.

leader 1. A person who deals with the human aspects of an organization: the improvement of human performance. Leaders aim to make the most of the human potential in the organization. They may perform all of the functions of managers, but they perform them differently. Leaders influence, motivate, persuade, and empower people to take actions which are in their and the organization's best interests. Leaders use past decisions and intuition as well as reason and logic to guide their decisions. Leaders do the right things right. *See also* administrator; manager. **2.** In desktop publishing, a row of dots, dashes, or hyphens used to guide the reader's eye across the page.

leader-match training Training provided to managers to teach them how to match their leadership style to the situation. The approach assumes that leaders can either exercise some control over the situations they face, or they can adjust their style to the occasion.

leadership The function that deals with the human aspects of organization: the improvement of human performance in the attainment of organizational goals and objectives. It is the process of influencing, motivating, and persuading people to take a desired action which is in their and the organization's best interests. It is doing the right things right, rather than simply doing things right. It is also a relationship between the leader and those led.

leadership development Designed for all levels of management, for supervisors, middle managers, top-level managers, and executives and those preparing for such positions but conducted separately for each group. Focuses on the differences between management and leadership, inventorying leadership abilities, types of leadership, analyzing organizational culture, fostering innovation, learning to use a variety of leadership styles in different situations, and gaining the support and commitment of subordinates.

learner A person who is either passively or actively involved in a learning situation — a situation which either accidentally or purposefully helps people acquire knowledge, skills, habits, attitudes, interests, values, and so on.

learner-controlled instruction (LCI) 1. A form of education or training in which the learner, rather than the instructor, plays the primary role in such activities as planning, objective-setting, selecting the delivery system, instructional methods, and techniques, and evaluating results. **2.** Computer-driven performance systems designed to provide workers with assistance at the job site.

learning Not to be confused with training, learning is the process of acquiring facts, principles, concepts, habits, attitudes, interests, values, appreciations, and skills that result in a change in an individual's behavior or the capacity for such change. It occurs as a result of experience or practice (rather than maturation); it is a relatively permanent change; and it is not directly observable.

learning center A resource facility that offers materials in a variety of formats for individual study: audio and videocassettes, computer-assisted and computer-managed instruction, interactive video, compact laser discs, 8mm and 16mm film, programmed and conventional books and workbooks, periodicals, manuals, organization documents, and a large number of programmed materials in audiovisual forms (sound-filmstrip, 35mm slides, overhead projectuals, and so on).

learning contract A contract made by a person with himself or herself or with an instructor, advisor, or mentor. Contracts are written documents that contain a statement of realistic, attainable learning objectives, definition of the criteria of success in meeting the objectives, delineation of strategies and action plans to attain the objectives, and target dates for the completion of each part of the plan.

learning curve An underpinning of **economy of scale**, it postulates that as workers repeat a task, they are able to do it better and more quickly.

learning disabled (LD) Although out of favor with many, the term remains in use. the preferred term places people first — people with learning disabilities.

learning disabilities Disorders that interfere with an individual's ability to acquire, comprehend, and express information; that is, with the development, interpretation, and/or demonstration of language or nonlanguage abilities, including specific deficits in one or more of the following: academic skills, coordination, expressive language, integration, nonverbal reasoning, oral comprehension, organizational skills, perceptual disorders, social judgment, simple memory deficiencies, or sustaining attention. Learning disabilities is a special cat-

egory of impairment. Learning disorders are considered to be inherent in the individual and are believed to be due to dysfunction of the central nervous system. Learning disabilities do not include learning problems that are due primarily to visual, hearing, or motor disabilities, mental deficits, emotional disturbances, or environmental deprivation.

learning disabled Not to be confused with visually or auditorially impaired persons or mentally retarded individuals, learning disabled persons are individuals who have difficulty receiving and processing information and, as a consequence, have reading, writing, speaking, or computational deficiencies that get in the way of job performance and reduce their trainability.

learning environment The building, facilities, equipment, tools, materials, aids, instructors, facilitators, and other learners that surround a learner and in which he or she is expected to acquire knowledge, skills, attitudes, values, and the like.

learning guides Basic principles relating to learning objectives, trainee participation and response, cues, assistance, and guidance provided trainees, and feedback on performance used to guide the development of instructional systems and their supporting materials.

learning objective An objective that identifies and describes measurable behavior, conditions, and standards needed to acquire enabling or prerequisite skills essential to the achievement of terminal (job-oriented) training objectives. Learning objectives include physical skills, such as gross motor skills, steering and guiding, placing and positioning, operating, and oral communicating and mental skills, such as learning and applying principles and rules, recognizing and classifying characteristics and patterns, identifying signs, symbols, and representations (reading), and recalling information.

The Learning Organization 1. ".....a group of people continually enhancing their capacity to create what they want to create." It involves five disciplines: (1) systems thinking — a discipline for seeing wholes; a framework for seeing interrelationships instead of things; (2) personal mastery — continually clarifying and deepening one's personal vision, focusing energies, developing patience, and seeing reality objectively; (3) mental models — deeply ingrained assumptions, generalization, or pictures or images that influence how we understand the world and how we take action; (4) shared vision — the vision that binds people together around a common identity and a sense of destiny; and (5) team learning — raising the collective IQ of a group above that of anyone in it. Attributed to Peter M. Senge (*Training and Development*, October 1991, p. 42). **2.** An organization that focuses its its attention and resources on the continuous improvement of its operations, products, and services rather than on training *per se.* **3.** An organization that has developed and implemented a continuous and enhanced capacity to learn, adapt, and change.

learning outcome   A basic principle of learning that states that the learner must clearly understand what it is that he or she must be able to do, under what conditions, and to what standard following the learning activity.

learning pattern   The rate and pace at which a learner acquires knowledge and skills. Some start slowly and then learn with increasing speed. Others start rapidly and them slow down. Still others appear to learn at a steady rate. An essential consideration when planning learning experiences.

learning principles   Principles that should guide the planning and conduct of learning activities. They include conceptual framework, learning outcome, primacy or recency, and relevance.

The Learning Resources Network (LERN)   An international nonprofit organization in class programming that serves a range of institutions, organizations, and companies, including colleges, schools, recreation departments, hospitals, associations, trade and technical schools, private businesses, trainers, and companies. These organizations offer a variety of programs, including general interest classes, conferences, contract training, leisure learning, certificate programs, continuing education, recreation, seminars, and staff training. *Contact:* LERN, 1550 Hayes Dr., Manhattan, KS 66502 (913/539-5376;Fax 913/539-7766; E-mail **hq@lern.com**; URL **http://www.lern.com**).

learning skills   The skills and abilities that enable a person to learn — listening, reading, observing, sensing (feeling, smelling, tasting), inquiring, writing, and so on.

learning specialist   *See* course developer.

learning strategy   The approach or game plan an individual uses to acquire knowledge or skills.

learning style   The way that a person processes information and learns. Some are most likely to attend to, retain, and use information that is transmitted orally. Others depend most on visual stimulation — body language and images, whether live or in photographs or video. Still others learn best when they read, reflect on what they have read, and then read again. And still others learn best when they are encouraged to explain a concept or principle to others or demonstrate a skill. An essential consideration when planning learning experiences.

Learning Tomorrow   A national initiative established by the **National Foundation for the Improvement of Education** to stimulate and support the use of technology in restructured schools. It is designed to expand the knowledge and efforts of teachers to effect lasting educational change.

learningware   Computer software programs designed to teach trainees specific knowledge and skills, such as troubleshooting, rather than to perform operations, such as preparing spreadsheets.

leased list   In direct marketing, a computerized list "bought" or rented from its owner for one time use only. Typically contains dummy names and fake addresses to protect them from unauthorized use. Costs average about $100 per thousand names; customized selections add $5 to $15 or more to the base cost.

least-squares method   In statistics (regression analysis), an objective means of fitting a straight or curved line to data plotted on a graph to determine the degree of correlation or significance of the relationship between two variables. (The calculations are too involved to describe here. Consult a good text on statistics — or use a commercially available computer program.)

leave   *See* annual leave; extended personal leave; personal growth leave; sabbatical leave; sick leave; social service leave; voluntary leave.

leave-behinds   *See* handouts.

leave-related benefits   Vacation, sick leave, holiday leave, parental leave, and bereavement leave provided by employers.

leave sharing   An employee benefit that allows workers to serve as both donors and recipients to provide greater financial protection against serious illness or accidents. Employees contribute unused annual and/or sick leave to a coworker whose disability or illness requires long-term medical care or temporary home care. Employees must exhaust all their sick and annual leave to become eligible as recipients, and the amount of leave employees can transfer is determined by employers.

leave stacking The practice of scheduling annual leave in such a way that the leave allowances for two calendar or fiscal years are continuous. For example, if an employer uses the calendar year to measure the 12-month period in which the **Family and Medical Leave Act of 1993** allows an employee to take up to 12 weeks of leave and the employee takes 12 weeks of leave at the end of 1997 and 12 additional weeks beginning January 1, 1998, 24 uninterrupted weeks of leave would be "stacked." The use of the **rolling year** option prevents stacking.

lectern A reading stand or small desk upon which an instructor or speaker places lecture notes.

lecture method One of the basic methods of instruction. A lecture is a semiformal discourse in which the instructor presents a series of events facts, concepts, or principles; explores a problem; or explains relationships. Its basic purpose is to inform. Trainees participate mainly as listeners and questioners. The method is used to orient trainees to course policies, rules, procedures, purposes and objectives, and learning resources; introduce a topic, indicate its importance and job relevance, and present an overview of its scope; give directions on procedures for use in subsequent learning activities; present basic information or data that will provide a common background for subsequent learning activities; set the stage for demonstration, discussion, or performance; illustrate the application of rules, principles, or concepts; or clarify, emphasize, summarize, or review concepts, principles, or facts.

left-brained People whose left brain (the left hemisphere) is dominant. Such people are believed to have more ability to think and function vertically, logically, and traditionally rather than intuitively and creatively.

legal audit A detailed examination and assessment of personnel and employment policies, application forms, handbooks, hiring practices, performance appraisal systems, agreements, contracts, and the like conducted by a qualified lawyer to prevent litigation by identifying and correcting potential problems such as discrimination, performance evaluation, discipline, and discharge practices.

legal plans *See* group legal plan.

legal standards Formal regulatory standards contained in such documents as the Federal Constitution and the Bill of Rights, state constitutions, and the statutes — laws passed by legally constituted authority such as the Congress, state legislatures, and local government, and interpreted and clarified by the Courts.

legitimate power Power that occurs when followers believe that they should comply with the direction of their leader. It derives from group norms about role behavior and what is considered reasonable, acceptable, and correct.

Lehnert v. Ferris Faculty A 1991 Supreme Court decision, which reaffirmed its earlier decision in the **Beck case** by stating that specific union activities, such as political lobbying, ballot campaigns, and public relations programs, could not be included in the fees charged to nonunion employees.

leisure discount fare An airfare group that includes a wide range of restricted and/or penalty fares. Used mainly by travelers whose plans are not subject to change but are sometimes offered to business travelers as the "lowest available fare."

length of stay (LOS) In health care, the number of days of hospitalization.

leptokurtic The shape of the curve of a frequency distribution when plotted on a graph. A leptokurtic curve has a narrow-humped peaked shape.

lesson plan (LP) A document designed to standardize instruction on a given topic. It sets forth the objectives to be attained in a single lesson or group of related lessons, the content (knowledge and skills) to be learned, and the means by which the objectives are to be achieved and the content acquired. It is customarily divided into six parts: identifying information, resources required, introduction, explanation, evaluation, and summary. It serves as a reference for the instructor when preparing for the lesson and as a guide during the presentation of the lesson.

Let's Face It The United States branch of an international mutual help organization dedicated to helping people with facial difference, their loved ones, and the communities in which they live, to understand and to solve the problems of living with this disability. Its goals are to (1) link and educate family, friends, and professionals; (2) educate the public to value the person behind every face; (3) assist facially different people to share their experiences, strengths, and hopes; and (4) educate and provide continuing education to medical, nursing, and allied health professionals. *Contact:* Let's Face It, P.O. Box 29972, Bellingham, WA 98228-1972 (360/676-7325).

letter spacing In desktop publishing, adding space between individual letters within a line of type.

levels of significance Used in determining the extent to which experimental results are valid and important. They are points or values referred to as the *k per cent point* or *points.*

leverage Debt in relation to equity in a company's capital or financial structure; the greater the long-term debt, the greater the financial leverage.

leveraged buy-out (LBO) A business strategy designed to secure control of a company. An LBO may be initiated by an independent investor or the top management of a publicly held company by borrowing heavily to buy or buy back all the common stock shares held by the public. An investor group, often headed by a company's own executives, uses bank loans and high-interest junk bonds to buy a firm and take it private. They are risky ventures because the company becomes debt-ridden. LBOs invariably lose money at first, and they invariably result in severe cost cutting — involving worker layoffs and the selling of divisions or other assets.

leverage ratio One of the traditional tests of operating performance, it is a measure of the extent to which an organization uses the funds of creditors. It is determined by calculating the ratio of debt (creditors') to equity (company's) funds.

leverage through borrowing An investment technique in which a fund borrows for investment purposes. This borrowing is usually unsecured, except to the extent that the fund enters into **reverse repurchase agreements.** Also known as *leveraging.*

LEXIS/NEXIS *See* Meade Data Central NEXIS.

liabilities Sources of assets, such as accounts payable, retained earnings, current portion of long-term debt, accrued expenses and income taxes, stockholders' equity (stock issued), and reserve accounts (such as self-insurance, contingency funds, and funds for lawsuits).

liability coverage Insurance protection against injury and damage claims by third parties purchased by individuals and organizations.

liability claims In air travel, damage claims (for injury or death). Under the Warsaw Convention, $75,000 was set as the limit on such claims unless the victims of an accident or their families could prove the carrier to be guilty of "willful misconduct." In 1996, the Department of Transportation cleared a global airline agreement waiving the ceiling on liability claims for injury or death on international flights from the United States. However, the waiver does not apply to the entire trip. U.S. passengers who wish to sue foreign carriers must do so in the country of the carrier.

liable The condition of being legally responsible for an event or action.

libel Any **defamatory** statement in writing, issued without just cause, that tends to expose another person to public contempt or ridicule. A **plaintiff** established a *prima facie* case of libel by proving that a defamatory statement about him or her was communicated to a third person.

library As distinguished from information centers and learning centers, a collection of books, periodicals, and other documents, mainly in printed form, housed in a centrally located, easily accessible environment that is conducive to study and learning. It is usually staffed by qualified librarians (master's degrees in library science) who serve as chief librarians, catalog and reference librarians, and archivists. Other staff include technicians and microform specialists, clerical assistants, and supply clerks.

Library of Congress (LOC) book number Used to identify newly published books. Usually found on on the back of the title page in the front of the book and in libraries, used to catalog the books either in card files on in computerized systems. Also appears on the spines of shelved books. Obtained by contacting the Cataloging in Publications Division, National Serial Data Program, Library of Congress, Washington, DC 20540 (202/707-6454).

license **1.** A written agreement between the creators or owners of visual or written materials, including software, videotapes, and videodiscs, and a licensee. A license allows the licensee to use or distribute the material (usually a grant of exclusivity) in a defined geographic area or for a specific market for a consideration — payment of a fee. **2.** Court sanctioned permission, such as permission to sell real estate which is part of a decedent's estate.

licensed group home An alternative to **nursing home** care for the elderly and the severely disabled. Licensed by the state, provides a family and less institutionalized atmosphere, typically more personal care and attention due to the limited number of residents — usually 8 to 10, and is 25 to 50 percent less expensive than nursing home care. Also called *residential-care facilities, adult foster home,* and *boarding-care home.*

licensed practical nurse (LPN) A person trained in nursing skills, frequently at the 2-year, associate degree level, and certified and licensed following successful completion of a qualifying examination.

lie detector A machine used to gather information about applicants for positions and to test the veracity of persons suspected of or charged with crimes. Operated and interpreted by a trained individual, the devices record fluctuations in blood pressure and heartbeat when the person answers a series of carefully designed and sequenced questions. A federal law, which took effect in 1988, prohibits most private-sector employers from using polygraphs to screen job applicants or randomly test workers. Exempted from the rules were federal, state and local governments, firms that do sensitive work for agencies such as the Central Intelligence Agency and the Federal Bureau of Investigation, companies that provide security services and those that make or distribute controlled substances. Most states, however, have laws prohibiting the use of lie detectors, including the right of defendants in criminal cases to use the devices to support their alibis. Also called a *polygraph.*

life-care community A housing arrangement in which, in exchange for a one-time entrance fee, plus monthly fees, residents get a guarantee of **assisted living**, personal care, and nursing care as needed.

life cycle A series of stages in the maturation of people, objects, or social organizations/structures; for example, conception,

infancy, puberty, young adulthood, adulthood, late adulthood, and old age. Attributed to Rothwell (*Training & Development Journal,* November 1983).

life-cycle analysis (LCA) A means of identifying a product's environmental impact at every stage from raw material acquisition, through design, manufacturing, and distribution, and use, to disposal.

life-cycle benefits Programs and services, offered by organizations to support employees' needs, that go beyond traditional work and family initiatives. In addition to child-care and elder-care support, typical programs include counseling, educational materials, referral services, support groups for gay and lesbian parents, HIV/AIDS and cancer patients, and workshops on financial planning, weight loss, and so on.

life-cycle cost analysis A means of analyzing the costs of a system, organization, or item of equipment that will be incurred throughout its entire life. The cycle begins with research and development, continues through investment and operations, and extends to disposal of the system, organization, or equipment through redistribution or phasing out.

life-cycle pension plan An actuarial-based pension concept developed by Robert D. Paul, vice chairman of the Martin E. Segal Company. Participants accrue a benefit which, on a lump sum basis, equals 10 percent of final 5-year average pay. The plan is readily communicated to employees because it defines benefits in terms of a *multiple* rather than as a *percentage* of pay. The plan has been acclaimed by some as the **defined benefit plan** of choice for employers seeking to attract and retain fast track employees and meet the needs of the next generation of employees.

life estate An interest in property that provides for income, use, and possession of the property for that "life tenant's life." The interest terminates automatically at death, at which time the property is bequeathed elsewhere in accordance with the directions of the individual who originally created the life estate.

life insurance trust An estate planning option for the affluent. A means of transferring wealth to heirs without paying sizable federal estate taxes (as much as 55 percent). Combines a life insurance policy with an

irrevocable trust. It has the disadvantages of loss of the income and control of the trust's assets, payment of legal fees to draft the trust and accounting fees for professional trustees to manage the trust assets, and payment of possible gift taxes when the trust is funded.

life-long learning (LLL) A concept of learning that holds that learning, and the need for it, never stops. It must be a life-long pursuit.

Life Office Management Association (LOMA) An international association of over 850 life and health insurance and financial services companies established to provide education, research, and information on effective management and operations for the insurance and financial services industry. *Contact:* LOMA, 2300 Windy Ridge Parkway, Suite 600, Atlanta, Georgia 30339 (770/951-1770; Fax 770-984-0441; E-mail **marketing@loma.org**; URL **http://www. loma.org**).

life planning Long-term plans for life, usually associated with retirement planning. Life planning includes plans for all aspects of human living: physical, mental, emotional, social, spiritual, career, family, and decisions relating to work, recreation, leisure, housing, finances, and use of time.

life plans *See* group life insurance.

life skills Interpersonal and communication skills, self-regulation and control, decision making, and problem solving — the skills needed to survive, live with others, and succeed in a complex society.

life stages Describes patterns of cycles through which people go during their lives. Knowing what they are is believed to be useful in personal and career planning. Examples: childhood, adolescence, young adulthood, adulthood, maturity (Erikson, *Childhood and Society,* Norton, 1963); growth exploration, establishment, maintenance, and decline, attributed to Super (*The Psychology of Careers,* Harper & Row, 1957). *See also* career stages.

life support systems Machines that make it possible to sustain or prolong life for severely injured, terminally ill, or incapacitated persons, such as respirators.

lifetime caps Maximum dollar expenditures or total number of days of hospitalization or institutional care available to employees or others under the terms of health benefit plans or insurance policies.

ligature In topography, two or more characters or letters linked together as a single element of type.

Light at the End of the Tunnel (L.E.T.) An integrated set of programs designed to create and foster change and improvement in public schools during an era of low funding and support and increasing criticism and skepticism both inside and outside of education. It was established by Sharon Ryder-Eckert, an organization behavior specialist, in 1988 in a multi-racial urban high school in Little Rock, Ark. The programs are based on cooperative efforts by school administrators and teachers, support by local businesses, positive reinforcement of students, and mentoring and coaching of students by graduates of the program. For more information, Contact Sharon Ryder-Eckert, L.E.T., P.O. Box 14371, Berkeley, CA 94701.

light-valve projector A unit that can produce an image of from 6 to 20 feet wide and can be positioned up to 84 feet away from and project clearly onto a 9 by 12 foot screen. The unit can interface with up to 16 different video and computer formats thereby allowing it to display images from PC, PS/2 and Macintosh computers.

Likert Scales (Profile of Organizational Characteristics) A diagnostic and research tool used in organization-wide surveys. Consists of scales on which respondents are asked to place a mark at the point that describes their experience in the organization and may also be asked to indicate how they would like to see the organization changed. Each scale has 20 points with four areas identified and described. Organization variables measured include leadership processes (five scales), motivation (seven scales), communication (six scales), influence (five scales), decision making (seven scales), goal setting (three scales), control (five scales), and performance and training (three scales). Devised by Rensis Likert.

limited franchising A franchising plan in which the parent company leases only its product line and trade name; for example, car dealerships and gas stations.

limited guardianship *See* conservatorship.

limited liability company (LLC) A business arrangement under some state laws that offers the liability protection afforded by a corporation with the beneficial tax rules that govern partnerships. Owners have the corporate benefits of the LLC to protect their personal assets from business debts as well as the tax advantage of partnerships. LLCs also provide greater flexibility in management and organization of the business and reduce paperwork and record keeping. In many state, LLCs have a life limited to 30 years.

limited liability partnership (LLP)
A business arrangement under some state laws that offers the liability protection afforded by a corporation with the beneficial tax rules that govern partnerships.

limited offering   An alternative means of offering to sell stock in a company to the general public. Rules and regulations of the Securities Exchange Commission allow companies to sell $1 million worth of securities yearly. In addition, 41 states allow companies to sell stock to investors who reside within the same state.

limiting charge   Replaces the term "maximum allowable actual charge" as the basis for Medicare Part B benefit payments for physicians' services. Doctors who don't accept assignment of Medicare benefits are limited in what they can charge their Medicare patients. The maximum amount a physician may charge a Medicare beneficiary for a covered service if the doctor does not accept assignment of the Medicare claim is 15 percent above Medicare's approved amount for a particular service. Limiting charge information appears on the Explanation of Medicare Benefits form sent to beneficiaries after they receive services covered by Part B.

Lincoln incentive system   An incentive plan in which employees work under a **guaranteed piecework plan** and, based on their performance (or merit rating), are given a share of the company's annual profits (less taxes, stockholders' dividends, and reserves for reinvestment).

linear editing   Editing done directly from videotape.

linear program   A form of **programmed instruction** in which the steps leading to the acquisition of knowledge or skill are carefully sequenced.

linear programming   An analytical technique that uses a linear (straight line) programming model to produce an optimal- or minimum-cost solution to a problem. Linear programming can also be used to determine the marginal profitability of adding people, facilities, or equipment to a project to ascertain the sensitivity of a problem solution to cost or

forecasting errors. The technique assumes that all resources converted by operations have costs that are variable and constraints that can be stated as mathematical expressions. Where relationships are not linear, concave, convex, or quadratic programming are applied. Learners proceed through the program by performing all steps in the program in the order presented.

linear regression   The statistical process of fitting a straight line to a set of x, y (two variable) data, using the method of least squares. Although too involved to describe here, the technique is based on the assumption that the relationship between the two variables is linear.

line chart   A quality control tool used to plot data graphically over a period of time, such as a year, quarter, week, or day. Most often used to show changes, cycles, patterns, or trends in continuously variable data over time, such as cash flow or production. Used to display trends, cycles, or patterns. Also called *run chart* or *x/y graph*.

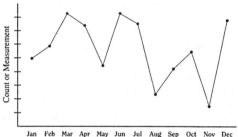

line manager   One who is responsible for supervising or managing and directing one of the levels in the central activity or production aspect of a business or industry rather than a support activity, such as finance or human resources. Line managers have the authority to command, to give orders; they are always someone's boss.

line-of-balance (LOB)   A monitoring tool for projects that use the concept of control by exception. Monitoring focuses on major checkpoints in the overall project schedule and monitors progress as compared with plans. Analysis provides information to the manager on elements of the project that are ahead, behind, and on target.

line of business   **1.** A health care plan, such as a **health maintenance organization**, established as a separate business within another larger organization, usually an insurance company, thereby legally differentiating it from a freestanding company or a company that is set up as a subsidiary. **2.** A unique product type, such as **Medicaid,** within a health care plan.

link   A location on a Web page which when clicked on with a mouse causes a jump to another page with related information or material, conceivably in a completely different Web site in another state or country. Also called a *hyperlink."*

Linking Home and School Through the Workplace   A nonprofit organization that offers courses for parents and others on family reading, mathematics, science, and time management. Cost to train a trainer is $200. *Contact:* Work in America Institute, 700 White Plains Rd., Scarsdale, NY 10583-5008 (914/472-9600).

liquidation   The process of giving up a business; unloading and closing out; terminating by agreement or litigation the precise amount of indebtedness, settling accounts, and distributing the assets of a business.

liquid crystal display (LCD)   **1.** A device made up of rod-shaped molecules, thin polarizing filters, and light to form another type of computer screen. LCDs are used mainly with laptop computers. **2.** LCDs also are the operational part of devices used in conjunction with overhead projectors and large video monitors to share computer screen images with large audiences. Although the resolution and light output of LCD projectors cannot match those of CRTs, their low cost and compact size are an advantage.

liquidity ratio   One of the traditional tests of operating performance, liquidity ratio is a measure of the ability of an organization to meet its cash obligations as they become due and payable. It is calculated by dividing current assets by current liabilities.

listening skills   The ability to listen actively, completely, and non-evaluatingly; the ability to listen for meaning, not just words, speech, or style of delivery; the ability to listen to understand, not to oppose, object, or argue.

listening training   Training provided to improve the listening skills of employees. It is a basic and necessary foundation for all other types of training and development. It involves assessing individual listening habits, abilities, and skills and developing listening skills and techniques.

listservs   On the **Internet,** special interest groups whose participants exchange messages on topics of interest. Automates the creation and maintenance of mailing lists. Similar to a bulletin board, but correspondence is sent directly to subscribers' **E-mail** boxes.

literacy training   Training geared toward adults who can't read or write well enough to fill out a job application or who are only marginally competent in basic skills.

Literacy Volunteers of America (LVA)   A national nonprofit organization that works to promote literacy through a network of community volunteer programs. LVA trains and helps individuals and organizations to tutor adults in basic reading and conversational English and provides training materials and services to literacy tutorial programs. *Contact:* LVA, 635 James ST., Syracuse, NY 13203 (315/472-0001:fax 315/472-0002; E-mail **LVANat@aol.com**; URL **http://archon.edu. Kent.edu/LVA/**).

litigation   A form of negotiation used to resolve individual and group disputes including labor-management disagreements. The issue is decided in a court of law and is invariably a win-lose situation. The judge (or jury) and legal counsel for both sides make use of a large body of procedural law. The decisions of the judge or jury are final unless successfully appealed to a higher court.

live video insertion system (L-VIS)   (Pronounced *Elvis*) An electronic-imaging system used to place logos and ads in the viewer's field of vision on the home TV screen without interfering with the primary scene (such as behind the batter's box in baseball or the goal posts in football). It uses customized computer-generated occlusion technology.

living benefits   Plans that pay up to 30 percent of a life insurance death benefit either in a lump sum or in staggered payments to cover catastrophic or terminal illnesses ranging from cancer and bypass surgery to paying for nursing home stays.

Living Benefits Bill of 1994   *See* Federal Employees Group Life Insurance Living Benefits Act of 1994.

living benefits rider (LBR)   A clause added to insurance policies (usually whole or universal life policies) that provides payouts to the insured, ranging from 10 to 50 percent (average is 25 percent) of the face value of the policy following diagnosis of a grave or terminal medical condition, such as stroke, heart attack, coronary artery disease, kidney failure, or liver disease. Also called *accelerated benefit rider.*

living case method   A modification of the traditional case method pioneered by the Harvard Business School. Instead of using fabricated cases or situations that occurred in the past, participants in executive development seminars work on real strategic or other major unresolved corporate problems.

living life insurance   *See* living benefits.

living trust   A trust that is set up during a person's lifetime. The maker can put property into the trust while still alive, and the property automatically goes to his or her heirs without going through probate court. Such trusts can be revoked by the maker at any time.

living wage   Used in union contract negotiations, a wage rate that will allow employees to maintain their standard of living.

living will   A document that provides the family, physicians, and others concerned with an individual's care with specific directions as to how decisions will be made if the maker becomes unable to participate in decisions regarding medical care and is in an incurable or irreversible mental or physical condition with no reasonable expectation of recovery. The document designates a proxy to act in his or her behalf should the maker be unable to communicate instructions. It is legal in some but not all states. Living wills have limitations. Living wills usually apply to persons who are terminally ill and not to people with such afflictions as Alzheimer's disease, strokes, degenerative disorders, or who are in a coma or persistent vegetative state. Many such wills do not allow medical personnel to withhold food and water.

loading   The part of insurance premiums or pension programs that is added to cover administrative costs, contingency reserves, and profit.

loading up   A ploy used by insurance companies and agents to exploit the fears and misconceptions of people who are afraid of medical bills. Here the agent sells several policies, with similar coverage, to the same buyer. Each policy contains one little benefit that the others don't.

local area network (LAN) 1. Any multi-user electronically linked system for communicating data in the same format, one-way or interactive, in one building or at many sites in the same general area. **2.** In training, a means of facilitating, distributing, or delivering training to individuals and groups.

Local Emergency Planning Committee (LEPC)   A committee established to develop emergency response plans relating to hazardous chemicals.

local operating network (LON)   Applies intuitive control systems to city-wide electric grids to all users, customers, or home owners to enable them to control remotely various utilities, such as lights, electric meters, motion detectors, and television sets.

Local Vocational Rehabilitation Agencies Provide a variety of support services to individuals with disabilities and employers. Check the Yellow Pages under"rehabilitation" or call the National Association of Rehabilitation Facilities (703/648-9300).

location grouping   One of the basic groupings of organizational elements. The location of the work activities performed and related activities determines the placement of the function to facilitate responsiveness to the unique characteristics of a particular region. Used most in marketing and sales organizations.

Lockheed Corp. v. Spink   A Supreme Court decision (1996, U.S. Lexis 3717) which held that the Employee Retirement Income Security Act of 1974 does not prevent employers from conditioning the receipt of early retirement benefits upon plan participants' waiver of employment claims. That is, employers can require participants in early-retirement programs to sign waivers that release any claims they may have against the company.

lockout/tagout rule   An **Occupational Safety and Health Act of 1970** rule that became effective October 31, 1989. The rule covers servicing and maintenance of machines and equipment in which an unexpected start up or release of stored energy could injure employees. Employers must ensure that energy sources for equipment are turned off or disconnected and that the switch is locked or labeled with a warning tag. In addition they must develop an energy control system, ensure that new or repaired equipment can be locked, make use of additional safeguards when tags rather than locks are used, identify and implement specific procedures for the control of hazardous energy and for release of lockout/tagout, obtain standardized locks and tags, conduct annual inspections of energy control procedures, and train employees in specific energy control procedures.

logical order A form of instructional sequencing in which materials are presented either in order of difficulty or in accordance with a logical arrangement of the subject-matter.

longitudinal technique A form of **genetic, developmental, and growth studies** in which a particular group is followed year after year, and repeated measurements of some trait or ability are made. The resulting measurements represent development, growth, or change sequences for that group. For example, hand-eye coordination of a group of surgeons in training and in actual surgical practice could be measured over a period of years.

long-range plan A plan that forecasts what products and services might be offered and where a company's sales and profits might be in 10 or 20 years.

long-term care (LTC) Long-term custodial care provided for the aged and infirm, the chronically ill or functionally disabled, victims of catastrophic illnesses such as stroke and heart attacks, and those with terminal illnesses. Care is provided in either home, medical facility, nursing home, or hospice, for active and retired employees, their spouses or other eligible dependents, or surviving spouses, and sometimes parents-in-law, who are severely and chronically impaired in performing the activities of daily living (such as eating, bathing, dressing, toileting, transportation, or getting around inside homes or or doing other chores).

Long-Term Care Ombudsman Program (LTCO) Created by federal law in 1978 under the federal **Older Americans Act of 1965**. Every state is required to have an ombudsman to serve all residents in nursing homes and adult foster homes throughout the state. A certified ombudsman is trained and authorized to act as an advocate for residents' rights and quality care in nursing homes and residential care in adult foster homes; investigate resident, family, or citizen complaints about long-term-care and services; use his

or her skills in persuasion and mediation to resolve problems when they occur; and monitor the long-term-care system and make appropriate recommendations for its improvement.

long-term disability (LTD) A disabling condition, whether caused by accident or injury, that results in an employee's inability able to perform the duties of his or her occupation and persists longer than six months. Most employer-sponsored long-term disability plans are governed by the Federal Employee Retirement Income Security Act of 1974. The courts have been vigilant in protecting long-term disability claimants under ERISA.

long-term disability insurance Provides employees with an income based on a percentage of their gross base salary in the event of a disability.

long-term incentive (LTI) A type of compensation plan designed to reward executives or other key personnel for corporate or unit performance over a period longer than one year. Examples are performance share plans, performance unit plans, phantom stock plans, restricted stock plans, stock appreciation rights, stock option plans, and stock equivalent plans.

long-term temporary assignments An alternative staffing option. Involves hiring temporary employees to supplement and stabilize the work force over a relative long period of time.

lossless Compressed video that when decompressed has no lost information and suffers no image degradation.

loss of speech Caused by problems of the larynx, the cartilaginous structure at the upper end of the trachea or wind pipe which contains and supports the vocal cords and associated structures. Laryngitis, the most common ailment involving the voice box, is manifested by a change in tone or quality of the voice to a coarse, harsher sound; difficulty in swallowing; and throat pain. Laryngitis is inflammation of the larynx due to inhaling smoke, chemical fumes, gases, or dust; excessive use of alcohol; or diseases such as the common cold, flu, bronchitis, sinusitis, tonsillitis, or pneumonia; overuse or abuse of the voice; polyps in the throat; or cancer. Cancer of the larynx may result in a **laryngectomy,** removal of the voice box.

loss-on-sale assistance   A relatively new fringe benefit to help transferring employees make prudent home purchasing decisions in their new location. Companies reimburse employees for home appraisals and assist those who have lost money on the sale of their home if they have obtained such an appraisal.

loss prevention   *See* safety, protection, and and security services.

lost time   A term used in time management to describe time wasted, squandered, or misspent due to poor planning, procrastination, daydreaming, waiting for equipment, supplies or people, lack of skill or inadequate training, false starts, or time expended between tasks or operations in a job or project.

lottery system   In training research, random selection of participants as members of the experimental or control groups.

low-balling   **1.** A deceptive sales practice in which buyers are offered goods or services at a very low initial cost and then find that costs are significantly higher when they reorder the product or service. For example, unscrupulous insurers offer coverage with very low initial premiums and later increase them dramatically. **2.** In health care, intentionally setting premium rates well below the actual cost of delivering care. It is done to preserve or improve market share or to improve cash flow. Also called *predatory pricing*.

low-density lipoproteins (LDL)   Cholesterol attached to various fats and proteins (bad cholesterol). High levels of LDL result in a buildup of plaque, so it is associated with an increase in heart disease due to atherosclerosis. *See also* cholesterol; high density lipoproteins.

low season   In meeting management, the period when occupancy and room rates are lowest for the year.

low vision   Decreased visual acuity or visual field that is correctable to no better than 20/70, or a field of 30 degrees with best spectacle correction in the better eye. Under these conditions, ordinary eyeglasses, contact lenses, or intraocular implants cannot provide sharp sight.

loyalty program   In marketing, special promotional programs that reward customers and clients for repeat purchases of goods or services.

luminance   In video, the black-and-white information, including brightness, sharpness, and contrast, that is encoded in a video signal.

lumps   *See* lump sum payments or distributions.

lump-sum allowance plan   A means of reimbursing employees for expenses incurred during transfer or relocation. Instead of requiring expense reports and itemized documentation of expenses, transferring employees are granted a lump sum. However, typically employees are required to sign an agreement stating that they will use the money for relocation expenses and will not ask for additional funding. If employees complete the move under the budget allocated, they may keep the balance. This approach offers flexibility, efficiency, controls costs, saves administrative time, avoids unreasonable relocation expense, and gives employees more control over their moves.

lump-sum merit   A form of incentive or variable pay that allows employers to reward performance without committing themselves to an increase in base salaries. Similar to a merit raise, but it is given all at once and only once.

lump-sum distribution (LSD) or payment Payment of the total pension account to employees or their beneficiaries when they retire, change jobs, or become disabled, when a company terminates its retirement plan, or when an employee dies leaving his or her spouse as beneficiary of a retirement plan. Under IRS rules, steps must be taken to defer taxes within 60 days of receipt of the lump sum or the money will be considered money paid to the recipient and may be included in taxable income for the year. Such distributions may also be subject to an additional 10 percent penalty tax if the recipient has not reached age 59 1/2 during the year in which the distribution was made or if the distribution was not made because of death or disability. A 1992 law requires retirement plan sponsors to begin withholding federal income taxes (20 per cent) on certain LSDs in 1993 unless the funds are transferred directly to an **individual retirement account** or other qualified plan. It also simplifies access to the **rollover** option by removing virtually all restrictions on employees' right to roll over amounts received from a qualified retirement plan (previously, partial rollovers were restricted, and an employer's receipt of a partial rollover could threaten the plans qualification status).

lump-sum settlement   A claims settlement arrangement in which the plaintiff receives the total award in a single payment.

lurk/lurking   On the **Internet,** visiting newsgroups without participating in the discussion.

luxury hotel   A hotel that features highly personalized old-world attention, services, and care. In addition to customary services, guests have access to a concierge, laundry, and valet service, round-the-clock room service and laundry and dry-cleaning services, and other amenities.

Lycos   On the **Internet,** a large electronic directory of Web sites that is updated weekly. (URL **http://www.lycos.com**).

Lyme disease   An infectious illness that causes joint pain and inflammation and, if untreated in its early stages, produces complications involving the heart, joints, and nervous system. It is caused by a spirochete form of bacteria that is spread by the bite of a deer tick (also found on birds and rodents). It is treated with antibiotics.

lysergic acid diethylamide (LSD)   A plant-derived hallucinogen that produces vivid alteration of perceptions and kaleidoscopic visual hallucinations, often accompanied by schizophrenic reactions or panic.

M	Mean (average).	**MIC**	1. Multiple incentive contract.
MAC	Maximum allowable charge/cost.		2. Meeting industry council.
MAGI	Modified adjusted gross income.	**MIDI**	Musical instrument digital interface.
MAP	Modified American Plan.	**MIPS**	Millions of instructions per second.
MB	Megabyte.		
MBDA	Minority Business Development Agency.	**MIS**	Management information system.
MBE	Minority business enterprise.	**MITI**	Ministry of International Trade and Industry.
MBGOOTW	Management by getting out of the way.	**MIX**	Member Information Exchange.
MBO	Management by objectives.	**M-JPEG**	Motion Joint Photographic Experts Group.
MBT	Management by trust.		
MBTI	Myers-Briggs Type Indicator.	**MLP**	Midlevel practitioner.
MBWA	Management by walking around.	**MNC**	Multinational company or corporation.
MC	Managed care.	**MOHP**	Multioption health plan.
MCA	The Military Chaplains Association of the USA.	**MOS**	Military occupational specialty.
MCCRA	Medicare Catastrophic Coverage Repeal Act of 1989.	**MOSCA**	McNamara-O'Hara Service Contract Act of 1965.
MCE	1. Medical care evaluation.	**MPC**	Multimedia personal computer.
	2. Management Centre Europe.	**MPEG**	Motion picture experts group.
MCL	Marine Corps League.	**MPI**	Meeting Professionals International.
MCO	1. Managed care organization.		
	2. Medicare carve out.	**MPPAA**	Multiemployer Pension Plan Amendments Act of 1980.
MCROA	Marine Corps Reserve Officers Association.	**MPPP**	Money-purchase pension plan.
MD	1. Muscular dystrophy.	**MR**	Memorandum for record.
	2. Mini disc.	**MRAL**	Mandatory Retirement Age Law of 1978.
MDTA	Manpower Development and Training Act of 1962.	**MRI**	Magnetic resonance imaging.
MEP	Manufacturing Extension Program.	**MRO**	Medical review officer.
		MRR	Motivation/recognition/reward.
MeSH	Medical staff-hospital organization.	**MS**	Muscular sclerosis.
		MSA	1. Medical service agency.
MET	Multiple employer trust.		2. Medical savings account.
MEWA	Multiple employer welfare association.		3. Multisource assessment.
		MSAA	Multiple Sclerosis Society of America.
MHSS	Military Health Service System.		

MSAWA	Migrant and Seasonal Agricultural Worker Act of 1983.
MSD	Musculoskeletal disorder.
MS-DOS	Microsoft disk operating system. *See* Microsoft.
MSDS	Material safety data sheets.
MSGS	Messages (Internet abbreviation).
MSI	Marketing Science Institute.
MSO	Management service organization.
MTF	Military treatment facility.
MUD	Multiuser dungeon.
MVPS	Medical Volume Performance Standard.

Maastricht Treaty The blueprint for the political and economic union of the **European Community (EC).** The Treaty calls for the establishment of a Central European Bank and a common currency by 1999, closer coordination among the EC nations on economic policy, and eventually defense policy. It would also require members to coordinate their positions on political and security matters. On July 23, 1993, the Treaty was ratified by Great Britain, the last of the 12 member nations to do so. During the week of September 14, 1992, Great Britain and Italy declared that they would temporarily abandon the **European Exchange Rate Mechanism** that had maintained somewhat predictable valuations among Europe's currencies. The last of the legal challenges on the constitutionality of the treaty in Great Germany were overcome in 1993, so the treaty became effective November 1, 1993.

machine learning   Computers that can acquire new knowledge and skills as opposed to simply processing and storing information to perform new tasks or organize existing data to perform old tasks faster or better. The objective of research in machine learning is to develop machines with human-like abilities — to accept and react to images, sounds, and distorted or incomplete information. Attributed to Diane E. Kirrane ("Machine Learning," *Training and Development Journal*, Dec. 1990).

macro In computer, facsimile, and telephone operation, a single keystroke that activates a sequence of commands designed by the developer of the macro to perform a specific function or set of functions. For example, with some telephones and fax machines, users can program an 11-digit number into the machine's memory and, by depressing a single key, initiate a call to that number. Computers can also be programmed with macros to save user time in actuating repetitive commands.

macrobiotics   An alternative form of medical treatment in which dietary and health discipline is achieved by balancing "yin" (passive energy) and "yang" (active energy).

macro process   A process that cuts across departmental, divisional, company, or business structures or boundaries.

macular degeneration   An impairment that causes a loss of sharp, central vision due to a spot on the retina of the eye that becomes totally insensitive to light. Although macular degeneration reduces vision in the central part of the retina, it does not affect the eye's side, or peripheral vision. Most people continue to have some useful vision and are able to take care of themselves.

magenta   In desktop publishing, one of the subtractive primary colors, the hue of which is used for one of the 4-color process inks. Magenta reflects blue and red light and absorbs green light.

magnetic board   A porcelain white, beige, or other neutrally-colored board backed with metal. Commercially-available rubber-coated magnets can be used to hang paper, project boards, charts, and letters, numbers, or other symbols for instructional purposes.

magnetic disk   A means of storing data, it can be soft (floppy) or hard (rigid). It stores digital data in the form of text, still images and full motion, and sound, permits random access, and requires electronic equipment to write and read.

magnetic resonance imaging (MRI) A medical diagnostic technology. Employs scanners that provide dynamic, comprehensive views inside the body without the use of ionizing radiation and with no known risk. The system uses radio waves and a strong magnetic field to excite hydrogen nuclei in the body, causing them to emit signals that are converted by computer into two-dimensional images on a video display or film.

mailbox rule   A tenet of contract law that determines when a contract between two parties is accepted. When a signed contract is dispatched by one party to the other, it becomes binding when it is signed by the recipient and placed in the mail.

mailing lists On the **Internet** a means of exchanging information with others with common interests.

mainframe 1. Large capacity, high speed central computer systems (as contrasted with personal computers, minicomputers, and microprocessors) such as the IBM System/36 and System/38, Digital's VAX 9000 System, NEC's ACOS System 3800, and Hitachi's M-800 series. **2.** A computer's central processor.

mainstreaming The practice of keeping special needs trainees, those with mental, developmental, emotional, learning, or physical disabilities, in regular training classes rather than segregating them for separate instruction.

maintenance Scheduled servicing of hardware and software to keep computer systems operating optimally.

maintenance engineer The hotel functionary responsible for the maintenance and repair of all systems, including heating, lighting and electrical service, air conditioning, energy control, and safety facilities equipment, and support. Also called *maintenance manager.*

maintenance fee A fixed percentage of the original cost of computer software paid annually to the supplier for regular maintenance and support.

maintenance manager *See* maintenance engineer.

maintenance of benefits A health care cost reduction plan in which employee benefits are paid by the secondary carrier only up to the amount the employer's plan would pay *less* any amount paid by the primary carrier.

maintenance of membership A union management-agreement in which employees are not required to join the union, but union members employed by the firm must maintain their membership in the union for the duration of the contract.

major depression A serious mental illness that involves depression (loss of interest in normal activities, insomnia, low energy, chronic fatigue, feelings of inadequacy or guilt, social withdrawal, or suicidal tendencies) but not mood swings.

major life activities As defined by the **Americans with Disabilities Act of 1990,** they "include such things as caring for one's self, performing manual tasks, walking, seeing, hearing, speaking, breathing, learning, and working."

major medical coverage Supplementary insurance coverage (in addition to basic coverage) that provides protection against large-scale surgical, hospital, or other medical expenses, treatment, and services, including some health services not covered by Medicare. Typically benefits are paid when a specific (large) deductible has been met. The policies are usually subject to co-insurance provisions, and they may not cover Medicare's deductibles and coinsurance amounts.

make/market cycle One of the two cycles that make up **total cycle time.** It encompasses all customer-related activities--from the time that a potential customer expresses an interest in a product or service to the time when the product or service is paid for.

Malcolm Baldrige National Quality Award An award designed to promote quality achievements of U.S. companies and to publicize successful quality strategies. Awards are made annually to recognize U.S. companies for performance excellence and quality achievement and are given only to organizations that apply for it in writing, are willing to undergo a rigorous on-site evaluation of their operations and share confidential information with examiners and judges, and agree to reveal their quality secrets with other organizations if they win the award. Six awards are made annually, two each in the categories of manufacturing, service, and small business, following a rigorous application and review process including on- and off-site review by teams of private sector judges. Administered by the **American Society for Quality**. Financially supported by the private sector. *Contact:* U.S. Department of Commerce, National Institute of Standards and Technology, Rte. 270 and Quince Orchard Rd., Administration Building, Rm A-537, Gaithersburg, MD 20899-0001 (301/975-2036; Fax 301/948-3716; E-mail **oqp@nist.gov**; URL **http://www.quality. nist.gov/**).

Malcolm Baldrige National Quality Improvement Act of 1987 Legislation passed by the Congress "to provide for the establishment and conduct of a national quality improvement program under which,

(1) awards are given to selected companies and other organizations in the United States that practice effective quality management and as a result make significant improvements in the quality of their goods and services, and (2) information is disseminated about the successful strategies and programs."

malingering The intentional production of false or exaggerated symptoms for a specific purpose, such as avoiding work, fraudulently obtaining money or medication, or seeking attention or sympathy from family or coworkers. The condition affects the body but originates in the mind,

mammography X-ray screening for the detection of breast cancer.

managed account *See* wrap-fee program.

managed care (MC) **1.** A monitoring system for health care benefits plans designed by the employer (not health care providers) to eliminate overutilization by employing a staff of medical and nursing specialists to compare proposed medical care with accepted standards and provide reports to management. It is a means of containing the costs of health care benefits plans, usually involving peer and utilization review, to eliminate over-utilization, unnecessary or inappropriate treatment, and fraud. In the broad sense, it includes everything from hospital review programs and case management to health maintenance organizations and preferred provider organizations. Two types of plans contract with Medicare: **risk plans** and **cost plans**. **2.** In its narrow definition, managed care is the prepaid care provided by **health maintenance organizations** and other groups to contain costs by requiring preadmission approval for hospital stays and closely monitoring other medical services. Typically, subscribers have one primary care physician who acts as a **gatekeeper,** knows the state of the subscriber's present health, refers the subscriber to a specialist within the system when needed, and maintains a record of the recommendations of the specialist in the subscriber's medical record.

managed care organization (MCO) A general term applied to a managed care plan, such a preferred provider organization or a health maintenance organization.

managed chiro Managed chiropractic care, a relatively inexpensive component of employee benefit plans that is becoming increasingly popular. Sometimes involves establishing a network of practitioners, screened by a medical director, integrating chiropractic services with traditional medical services, forging lines of communication between chiropractors and physicians, and instituting quality assurance procedures, such as medical review, peer review inspections, patient surveys, and performance tracking.

managed competition A form of health care plan in which medical consumers, ranging from individuals to small and mid-sized organizations, pool their buying volume and purchase services collectively from competing networks of health care providers, clinics and hospitals, and insurance companies. These consortiums, sometimes called health insurance cooperatives, negotiate for coverage on behalf of individual employers who then choose from a menu of plans, each of which at a minimum offers a basic package of benefits.

managed competition plan A health insurance plan under which health care providers bid for the job of providing care while state governments obtain coverage for the unemployed and part time workers. Employers are allowed to offer their own basic health policies or buy coverage through a nonprofit purchasing organization (**health insurance purchasing cooperatives**) set up by a state government board. In each state, the board negotiates the best rates from HMO-type managed care networks that compete for consumers in a given geographic area. Under some plans, workers pay taxes on part of the money employers now spend to provide health care benefits, that is, anything in excess of the cost of buying the least expensive basic health plan, such as membership in a **health maintenance organization.** Or employers might lose their tax deductions on what they pay. Or both. The idea is to get health care businesses to cut prices to attract customers — to compete to provide customers with more for their money.

managed disability The application of managed care principles and procedures to worker disability and the integration of **short-term disability, long-term disability,** and **workers' compensation.**

managed indemnity A type of **managed care** which requires simple precertification of elective hospital admissions and large case management of catastrophic cases, superimposed on a traditional indemnity insurance plan.

managed pharmacy network A consortium consisting of one or more carefully selected chain pharmacy organizations in a particular region supplemented by independent pharmacies established to provide better geographic access and meaningful discounts below retail pricing for employers. Pricing typically uses the formula of Average Wholesale Price plus a $2.00 dispensing fee. In addition to offering prices that are 15 to 20 percent lower than card systems, managed drug systems take advantage of point-of-sale technology, which allows participating pharmacies to verify coverage before the prescription is dispensed.

management It is the process of doing the right things. It is mostly concerned with planning and control, allocating resources, and solving problems. The role of the HR manager is to make the most of the human potential in the organization. It encompasses five functions: planning, organizing, staffing, directing, and controlling. It makes use of reason and logic; it is objective. It uses both past decisions and intuition to guide the decisions of today.

management audit A searching and open evaluation of an organization with the objective of helping managers to perform their jobs better. It does not appraise individual performance; rather it deals with the functions and interrelationships of activities and the absence of needed activities. The audit may encompass the entire organization, the corporate management audit, or one of its functions, such as human resources. It may be used to reconcile the conflicting interests of different constituencies, retain or restore confidence in the organization's ability to perform its mission effectively, improve performance, profit, efficiency, and growth, and meet the demands and challenges of the highly competitive economic environment. Although an offspring of accounting, it is not just another accounting process. In fact, it is not an accounting function at all since it is not limited to the verification of accounting and financial transactions. Rather, it is broad-scale evaluation.

management by adultery A term coined by Chaparrel Steel to describe its management

philosophy of treating workers like adults instead of children and expecting them to use their brains in their work.

management by exception **1.** A system of management that involves identification of critical deviations from plans, signals the manager that solutions are needed, but withholds the signal when variations are only minor. Its purpose is to simplify and make more efficient the management process itself and allow the manager to focus on important issues and problems. Such systems usually employ numerical measurement, selection criteria to separate important deviations from those of lesser importance, and decision making protocols to assist the manager to take the action required to get performance back on track, adjust expectations and modify objectives, and exploit new opportunities. **2.** The use of control strategies, such as inspections, testing, and client feedback, that identify and bring to the attention of management key problems and shortfalls so that it can concentrate on resolving those deficiencies.

management by getting out of the way (MBGOOTW) Empowering employees by giving them something important to do, giving them the authority to do it, and letting them do it. Attributed to Bob Basso (with Judi Klosek), *This Job Should Be Fun!* Bob Adams, Inc., 80 Summer St., Boston, MA 02127.

management by objectives (MBO)
A relatively uncomplicated means of improving management and productivity in an organization. It is a top-down, sequential, formal, and cooperative means of developing organizational goals and their supporting objectives at each level of organization. It addresses key result areas: profitability, productivity, competitive status, market share, customer service and satisfaction, creativity and innovation, cost management, conservation of resources, management development and performance, employee attitude, training, employee services and career development and performance, and corporate image, public responsibility, and ethics. It includes five steps: identify key result area, establish standards of satisfactory performance, identify objective measures of performance, appraise performance, and mutually determine ways to improve performance.

management by participation *See* participative management.

management by trust (MBT) A system of management that downplays rules, regulations, and disciplinary actions and focuses on establishing and maintaining mutual respect, faith, and trust between managers and their subordinates. It is characterized by management's belief that expectations will be met by subordinates — that people have integrity and the desire and potential to fulfill it.

management by walking around (MBWA) Managing by simply observing; collecting data and impressions by informal visits to work areas. Attributed to Tom Peters and Nancy Austin (*A Passion for Excellence*, 1985).

Management Centre Europe (MCE) The European Headquarters of the American Management Association International. Offers programmes ranging from management training and development through to events that offer top-grade strategic information. MCE's portfolio of products addresses the needs of individuals at all management levels. *Contact:* MCE, Rue de l'Aqueduc 118, B-1050 Brussels (+32 2 543.21.00; Fax +32 2 543.24.00; E-Mail **info@mce.be**; URL **http:www.mce.be**).

management circle A modification of the quality circle process, it involves managers only in an attempt to overcome objections to the implementation of circles as well as to improve the practice of participating managers.

management competencies Capabilities that portend success in professional or managerial jobs. They include assertiveness, ability to use positional power, ability to develop others, and ability to lead teams.

management consultant An individual who provides independent advice and assistance about management processes, issues, and problems to clients who have management responsibilities in public and private organizations.

management consulting A profession in which members provide independent advice and assistance to clients in public and private organizations on management processes, issues, and problems, based on competencies gained through education, training, and experience.

management development Programs designed to meet the needs of an organization for successors to current managers, to help current managers to become more effective, and to provide additional managers to meet the need for expansion of the industry or organization. The programs focus on the management of environmental factors, work force, employee attitudes and values, and technological change. They develop knowledge and skills in leadership and group dynamics, strategic planning and goal setting, organization theory and applications, leadership styles, motivation theory and applications, coaching and team building, and managing change and innovation. Strategies include formal training and education, seminars and workshops, discussion groups and team building, role playing and case studies, simulations, independent study, guided self-analysis and assessment, and coaching.

management-employee collaboration *See* participative management.

management games Used in executive and management development and in **assessment centers**. Exercises, usually computer-driven, require participants to engage in realistic problem solving and decision making, typically as members of two or more simulated companies competing in the marketplace. The objective is to assess participant's planning and organizational abilities, interpersonal skills, decision making skills, and leadership abilities.

management improvement Plans that address opportunities for improving the management, operation, efficiency, profitability of the organization and the HR department. Such plans encompass the full spectrum of programs, activities, and services with the goals of reducing or controlling costs, increasing revenue or return on investment, improving productivity, or enhancing employee job satisfaction, motivation, and morale.

management information system (MIS) A computer-based system designed to generate, organize, store, retrieve, and communicate information for management decisions relating to such things as government regulations, requirements and reports, customer, client, and supplier requirements, union data and requirements, employee, cost, and production data, long and short-range planning and operations data, analyses, impact studies, and model building. An MIS provides on-line, instantaneous, interactive, real-time information access; rapid retrieval and dissemination of information; access to historical data and statistics as well as to current operating information; ability to synthesize and reformat information; and rapid and simple means of inputting, updating, and manipulating information.

management information system report In travel management, a report compiled from data provided by travel suppliers. It shows a company's travel spending and usage patterns.

management meeting A meeting of the officers and principal staff of an organization convened to plan business strategy.

management reinforcement workshop Training provided to improve the reinforcing, feedback, coaching, and modeling skills of managers. It makes use of behavior modeling techniques and role playing.

***Management Review:* The American Management Association Magazine** A monthly publication: $45.00 per year (free to AMA members) Address: American Management Association, P.O. Box 57940, Boulder, CO 80323-7940 (800-262-9699 or 518-891-1500; E-mail **mgmtreview@ amanet.org** or **cust_serv@amanet.org**; URL **http://www.amanet.org**).

management service organization (MSO) An organization that provides services to physicians to support their practices (such as negotiating with managed care organizations) although the physician usually remains an independent private practitioner.

management style Describes a manager's approach to the managerial job: formal, informal, or nonformal; directive or nondirective; person-, task-, or fusion-oriented; positive or negative; democratic, delegative, or free-rein; organizational or personal, laissez-faire, custodial, or coercive, entrepreneurial or bureaucratic; authoritarian, autocratic, manipulative, permissive, participative, or emergent; or charismatic, psychologically distant, or supportive.

manager The officer who provides leadership to the whole organization or one of its major functional elements. Typically serves in supervisory roles, directing and controlling subordinates who perform the work. Responsible for getting a job done through others. Managers are invariably responsible for planning, organizing, directing, and controlling the resources of an organization. They are primarily concerned with planning and control, allocating resources, and solving problems; they make use of reason and logic to resolve issues. Managers do the right things.

managerial grid Developed by Blake and Mouton (*The Managerial Grid,* 1964). Describes several managerial styles (1,1; 5,5; 1,9; 9,1; and 9,9) representing various degrees of emphasis on concern for people and concern for production.

manager-without-portfolio A manager who essentially acts as a contract administrator, monitoring the schedules, costs, and compliance of contractors and outside consultants who are often separated from the manager by hundreds of miles.

managing The process involved in securing planned results with and through the work of other people rather than the work performed by the individual. The task is to establish and maintain an environment that will develop people and facilitate cooperative, effective, and efficient efforts in the attainment of organizational goals. It is accomplished by performing the functions of planning, organizing, staffing, directing, leading, and controlling.

managing diversity Meeting the formidable challenge of embracing people of all racial, ethnic, religious, and cultural backgrounds and tapping their positive and constructive skills and abilities to build a better society and produce a more productive work force.

Managing Diversity A monthly newsletter that provides information, ideas, and tips for people managing a diverse work force: $99.50 per year. Address: Jamestown Area Labor Management Committee, Inc., P.O. Box 819, Fredonia, NY 14702-0819 (716/ 665-3654).

mandated benefits **1.** Benefits that are required by law. **2.** In health care, benefits that are above routine insurance-type benefits, are required by law, and usually apply at the state level, such as defined days of inpatient mental health care or substance abuse treatment.

mandated health care benefits *See* Pension Access and Simplification Act of 1991.

mandatory assignment A state law that establishes a barrier to managed care (eight states currently have such a law). The law prevents insurers from contractually requiring providers to accept the plan's payment as payment in full, except for applicable deductibles and **coinsurance**.

mandatory bargaining item
In labor-management contract negotiations, an item that must be considered and negotiated if it is introduced by either party; for example, pay and benefits.

mandatory drug and alcohol testing
A part of the measure that financed federal transportation programs signed into law in October 1991. The bill mandated random drug and alcohol testing for transportation workers in the airline, trucking, and bus industries, as well as employees of local mass transit systems. Drug and alcohol tests are also required before hire, after an accident, or when an employee is suspected of drug or alcohol abuse. (Earlier laws required drug but not alcohol tests for workers in those industries whose jobs directly affected public safety.)

mandatory outpatient surgery In health care utilization management, requiring that certain procedures be performed on an outpatient basis unless prior approval is obtained from the plan's medical director. *See also* same day surgery.

Mandatory Retirement Age Law of 1978 (MRAL) An Act that prohibits forced retirement of any employee under 70 years of age. Exempt are employees whose jobs have bona fide occupational qualifications, college professors, and business executives.

manding A means of communication between a nondisabled person and an individual with a hearing or speech impairment. It *demands* a verbal or other response from the individual with the disability. The nondisabled may say to the individual, "Tell me what you need." Sometimes called *mand modeling*.

Manhart Decision A 1978 Supreme Court Decision that the use of sex-based mortality tables for determining employee contributions to retirement plans violates **Title VII** of the **Civil Rights Act of 1964** (sex discrimination). *See also* Norris Decision.

mania A mental illness, an **affective disorder**, characterized by periods of abnormal excitement, elation, irritability, increased energy, decreased need for sleep, excessive optimism, and increased activity *See also* depression; hypomania.

manic depressive illness A serious mental illness also called *bipolar disorder*.

manipulative power Power that resides more in the threat of sanctions or pressure rather than on punishment. Followers are maneuvered and used; they are guided into beliefs or actions that they do not fully understand by plausible pretexts.

manpower controls *See* personnel controls.

Manpower Development and Training Act of 1962 (MDTA) Forerunner of the **Comprehensive Employment Training Act of 1973** and the **Job Training Partnership Act of 1982**.

manpower planning *See* HR planning.

manual English A means of communicating with a person who is deaf or hard of hearing. The nondisabled person orally repeats a word as its sign is modeled for the individual. The modeling is accompanied by appropriate gestures, body movements, and facial expressions. Manual English may be used with disabled individuals who have poor articulation, speech intelligibility problems, minimum vocabulary, or inhibiting emotional problems. Sometimes called *total communication*.

manually coded English Systems invented to use signs for coding English. The best known are Seeing Essential English, Signing Exact English, and Linguistics of Visual English. The developers of these visual-gestural codes developed guidelines and principles for inventing new signs or changing existing **American Sign Language** signs to represent English words.

manual system An information and retrieval system that is not automated, such as one based on paper files.

Manufacturing Extension Partnership (MEP) A program of the Department of Commerce's National Institute of Standards and Technology, MEP is a federal-state-private sector partnership that helps small and midsized manufacturers enhance productivity, improve worker skills, and become globally competitive by providing a network of services to assist them in adopting contemporary technologies and business practices. Services are locally-driven through a network of Manufacturing Technology Centers so that they address the specific needs of area manufacturers. Such centers must be affiliated with a U.S.-based not-for-profit institution or organization. Financial support may be provided for a period not to exceed six years. Applicants are required to provide 50 percent or more of the operating costs in years one through three and an increasing percentage in years four through six. *Contact:* MEP, Bldg. 301, Rm. C121, National Institute of Standards and Technology, Gaithersburg, MD 20899-0001 (301/975-4676 or 301-975-5020; Fax 301/963-6556; E-mail **MEPinfo@micf.nist.gov/** URL **http://www. met.nist.gov**).

manufacturing overhead expense budget
A budget based on the production budget that includes expenses of factory and home-office buildings, maintenance and repairs, supervisors' salaries, indirect labor, utilities, supplies, depreciation, insurance, taxes, and wages.

map In video production, making one video image conform to the size, shape, and/or texture of another image.

mapping *See* block diagram; mind mapping.

marginal analysis The process of comparing factors that can be expressed in numbers to evaluate alternative courses of action and arrive at a logical decision.

marijuana An illegal narcotic, cannabis, obtained from the dried leaves and flower heads of the plant *Cannabis sativa.* Smoked in cigarettes. Also called *chronic, grass, hemp, joint, pot, reefers, tasty greens,* and *weed.*

Marine Corps League (MCL) An organization of 45,000 members open to all who have served in the Marine Corps. Its mission is to preserve Marine Corps traditions, promote the interests of the Marine Corps, and aid all Marines and former Marines and their widows and orphans. *Contact:* MCL, P.O. Box 3070, Merrifield, VA 22116-3070 (703/207-9588; Fax 703-297-0047; E-mail **mcl@mcleague.org**).

Marine Corps Reserve Officers Association (MCROA) An organization of 5,500 members open to all Marine officers and officers of other U.S. services who have served with Marines. Its mission is to support and strengthen the Marine Corps and its reserve and reserve officers. *Contact:* MCROA, 110 N. Royal St., Ste. 406, Alexandria, VA 22314-3234 (703/548-7607; Fax 703/519-8779; E-mail **74671.426@compuserve.com**).

marital deduction An estate tax deduction allowed for property in the decedent's taxable estate and passing only to a surviving spouse. The deduction is unlimited on the federal level.

market A group of individuals or organizations that share a common need for products or services, such as educational institutions, hospitals, physicians, the elderly, and so on.

marketer An individual who markets, sells, and contracts to provide HR (or other) services either outside or within the organization.

marketing Long-range promotion of goods or services remote from the point of sale. Marketing is the process of finding out what people need or want and then getting it to them or identifying the people who need what you have and making sure that they know they need it and then getting it to them.

marketing manager *See* director of sales.

marketing plan A written plan, containing as a minimum objectives, potential barriers to success, strategies and tactics to overcome the obstacles, time-phased schedules, measures of progress and accomplishment, and a supporting budget.

market pricing Wage rates and salaries that are pegged to management's best estimate of the going rate in the marketplace for specific jobs.

market reform plan A plan to reduce the costs of health care benefits to individuals by providing tax deductions to moderate income Americans.

market segment A subdivision or subgroup of a market whose members have common secondary needs, values, and concerns, such as elementary education, teaching hospitals, family practice physicians, and so on.

market segmentation The process of matching company or department resources to the appropriate market segment — groups that have a common interest in a particular product or service. Also called *target marketing* and *positioning.*

Marketing Science Institute (MSI) An institute with 60 sponsoring corporations that initiates, supports, and disseminates leading-edge studies by academic scholars addressing research issues specified by member companies. MSI functions as a working partnership and brings together executives from over 55 sponsoring corporations with leading researchers from more than 100 universities worldwide. Provides publications and reports on market research, marketing strategies, market entry, and marketing problems. *Contact:* MSI, 1000 Massachusetts Ave., Cambridge, MA 02138 (617/491-2060; URL **http://cism.bus. utexas.edu/ravi/marketing_science.html**.

marketing strategy The art and science of promoting goods and services with the least cost and the greatest exploitation of corporate strengths and specialized resources, remote from the point of sale. A productive strategy combines efficiency of effort with concentration of force and employs such strengths as proprietary advantage (leading-edge technologies and patented equipment, access to raw materials, and so on), superior knowledge of customer and client needs, and productive alliances with other organizations.

market intelligence Knowledge of current and projected market share and the strengths and weaknesses of self and of strongest competitor(s).

market-oriented plan A mix of middle-class tax deductions and low income tax credits proposed by the Bush administration to offset the cost of private heath insurance.

market penetration The percentage of buyers an organization has compared to the total number of potential businesses in a given area.

market pricing Setting salaries or salary ranges by functional areas or job families on the basis of salary surveys or market pressures with little or no regard for internal ranking or equity. Typically used where there are severe shortages in certain skills areas.

market share A non-financial measure of performance at a specific point in time. Market share can be examined nationally, by region or city, or by market segment or type of customer. It is simply the percentage of business (actual customers) that belongs to your product or service (percent of total sales in terms of the volume of goods sold or net dollar volume of sales) in a product category. To determine market share, you need to know how many customers are out there, what they are buying, how much they spend for the particular product or service, how many are sold by your competitors, and how many your company has sold. You also need to know whether your market share and those of your competitors are increasing or decreasing.

market value plan A type of executive incentive plan that permits executives to purchase company stock, usually with funds borrowed from the company at a low rate of interest. The borrowed funds are either repaid or amortized by means of credits representing compensation for services or bonuses based on performance.

Markov chain A mathematical method used in human resources planning and forecasting. A Markov chain permits the analysis of rates of movement in specific categories of employees on the basis of such variables as salary, age, and sex.

mask **1.** In desktop publishing, in intermediate photographic negative or positive used in color correction during the color separation process. **2.** In offset-lithography, opaque material used to protect open or selected areas of a printing plate during exposure.

mask works A class of **intellectual property** that protects the design of microchips.

massage Involves stroking, kneading, and tapping the skin along muscles and blood pathways. May be light, which is more stimulating, or deep, which is more relaxing and more beneficial to tight, overworked muscles.

mass customization Finding out what customers or clients like and want and building those preferred qualities into all of the products and services a company offers — "efficiently serving customers uniquely." Attributed to B. Joseph Pine II in *Mass Customization: The New Frontier in Business Competition,* Harvard Business School Press, 1993.

massive layoff Defined by the **Worker Adjustment and Retraining Notification Act of 1988** as a reduction in force that is not the result of a plant closing and results in an employment loss at a single site during any 30-day period for at least 33 percent of the employees and at least 50 employees.

massively parallel computer *See* parallel computer.

mass marketing Targeting a very large part of the total market (or several market segments) for the sale of goods and services.

master account In meeting and travel management, the form on which all authorized charges incurred by a group at a hotel, conference center, or other facility for a specific meeting or event are recorded.

master budget *See* profit budget.

master vendor arrangements An alternative staffing option. Involves contracting with a single staffing company to supply all needed temporary employees. Also called *on-site programs* or *vendor-on-premises program.*

mastery test A test that applies an absolute level of performance as the standard to be achieved. That standard separates trainees into two groups: those who are *go* and those who are *no-go* — that is, those who are allowed to continue in the program or graduate and those who are recycled, given remedial training, or dropped from the program.

matching gift A means of discharging corporate responsibility to the community. Involves contributing jointly with employees to charitable, nonprofit, and educational agencies and institutions by matching gifts (usually dollar-for-dollar).

matching item An objective test item that requires the testee to match entries contained in two columns of words, numbers, symbols, phrases, or the like.

matchmakers/matchmaking agency A local or state government agency, private for profit broker, or nonprofit organization that uses marketing and sales techniques to identify pending contracts and, following an intensive canvass of its region, solicits bids and negotiates deals. Instead of attempting to woo new manufacturing plants with expensive incentive packages or opening costly trade offices, matchmakers seek out prospective purchasers of goods and services and pair them with existing businesses in their state or region to improve the local economy.

material safety data sheets (MSDS) Documents required by the Occupational Safety and Health Administration's **Hazard Communication Standard of 1988** and the **Superfund Amendments and Reauthorization Act of 1986.** The data sheets provide detailed information on chemical ingredients: what and where they are, the health hazards they pose, symptoms of exposure, and appropriate protective and emergency treatment measures. Employers must complete MSDS for every type of hazardous chemical in the workplace and keep them accessible to employees in their work areas.

materials developer An HR/HRD competency. An individual who develops and validates learning materials.

maternity and child care A relatively new fringe benefit that includes pre- and post-birth examination with some child care.

mathematical model An integrative technology forecasting technique using simple mathematical models usually manipulated by a computer. Models are developed by constructing a network of events that indicate significant relationships and assigning values to describe those relationships quantitatively. When the model is completed, starting values are assigned to important factors or parameters, and the system is then simulated as the model progresses to determine how the parameters change. Different assumptions or tactics can be tested by changing the input values.

matrix diagram A means of graphically displaying the correlations between two sets of data or categories. The intersection of the two axes of the diagram may use symbols or numbers to indicate the degree or magnitude of the correlation.

Matrix of Training Delivered by Job Classification

	Executives	Middle managers	Supervisors	Technicians	Sales personnel	Admin/Clerical
Customer service	0	0	2	4	16	4
Database	0	0	0	4	4	12
Disability awareness	2	2	6	2	6	2
Diversity training	2	2	2	2	2	2
Finance	4	2	2	2	2	0
Product information	0	0	0	2	8	0

matrix grouping *See* matrix organization.

matrix management A scheme of organization that employs a two-boss or multiple management system and related support mechanisms, a compatible organizational culture, and appropriate behavior patterns. Matrix management attempts to solve the problems associated with the competition of two critical needs in complex organizations: specialization and integration. It promotes the interaction needed to resolve conflicts and find creative solutions to problems, and at the same time improve motivation, coordination, and cooperation. Under a matrix organization, senior managers are in change of an entire function, product, or service, but they are not in full command of the individuals who report to them; that is, they share power with equals.

matrix organization An effective but complex means of achieving integration of planning and effort in an organization. The matrix design is a synthesis of functional and sector departmentation and places employees under two bosses or supervisors: the functional boss who oversees the functional quality of their work and project or program manager who oversees their task assignments, work scheduling, and assignments pertaining directly to the project.

maturity curves **1.** Used as incentives for professionals. Maturity curves predicate annual salary on performance and experience. Individual curves are drawn to reflect different performance levels and provide for annual increases. Typically, curves for higher performance tend to rise to a higher level more rapidly than curves for lower performance. Also called *career curves.* **2.** In engineering and technical jobs, maturity curves are used to determine the appropriate level of a job in an occupational series. Level is determined by the number of years of work experience following attainment of a specific level of formal education where such years represent average or customary achievement for incumbents in a particular job.

maximum allowable charge/cost (MAC) The maximum amount that a vendor may charge for a product or service. Most often relates to pharmaceuticals.

maximum allowable actual charge Until 1991, the basis for Medicare Part B benefit payments to physicians who didn't accept assignment of Medicare benefits. The term has been changed to limiting charge.

maximum payment period The lifetime maximum number of days for which a health care insurance policy will pay for confinement in a health care facility or alternate long term care facility, including any rider benefits.

McCarran-Ferguson Act of 1945 Legislation that provides a limited exemption to the insurance industry from the federal antitrust law. The act provides that the Sherman Act, the Clayton Act, and the Federal Trade Commission Act apply to the business of insurance "to the extent that such business is not regulated by state law." That limited exemption from federal antitrust law does not extend to "any agreement to boycott, coerce or intimidate, or act of boycott, coercion, or intimidation." The act also declares that the business of insurance shall be subject to regulation and taxation by the states. After passage of the act, all states enacted some form of rate regulation to qualify for the exemption. The effect of the antitrust exemption has been eroded in recent years as courts have narrowed the definition of the business of insurance and broadened the definition of boycott, and as an increasing number of states have subjected the industry to state antitrust law.

McCarran-Ferguson Reform Act Legislation, sponsored by Rep Jack Brooks (D-TX) and Sen. Howard Metzenbaum (D-OH) that would amend the McCarran-Ferguson Act by forbidding price-fixing, product tie-ins, geographic division of territories, and monopolization by insurers — a group specifically exempted from such federal antitrust laws, although the original act prohibits coercion, intimidation, and boycotting.

McKinnon v. Nashville Banner Co. A Supreme Court decision that effectively eliminated an employer defense against frivolous lawsuits. **After-acquired evidence** may be used to limit the amount of damages but not to dismiss the case as had previously been the rule.

McNamara-O'Hara Service Contract Act of 1965 (MOSCA) Requires federal contractors who provide services to the federal government at a cost in excess of $2,500 to pay minimum (prevailing) wage rates and provide prevailing fringe benefits, including medical or hospital care, unemployment benefits, life insurance, disability and sickness insurance, accident insurance, vacation and holiday pay, costs of apprenticeship or similar programs and other bona fide fringe benefits.

Mead Data Central NEXIS An on-line **database.** *Contact:* Mead Data Central NEXIS, 9393 Springboro Pike, P.O. Box 933, Dayton, OH 45401-9964, 800/227-4908 or 513/859-1608.

Meals-on-Wheels Hot nutritious meals, including special diets, delivered once or twice daily to the homes of aged or disabled persons by a variety of local agencies at a low, sliding-scale cost.

mean (M)   A measure of central tendency. The mean is the average score in a distribution of scores; it is calculated by summing the scores and dividing by the number of scores in the distribution. *See also* median; mode.

mean difficulty   A measure of the worth or value of a test; an index of the overall difficulty of the test items that make up the measure. The mean difficulty is calculated by finding the average of the percentage scores on the test. The resulting figure gives the analyst an index of average testee achievement in terms of the percentage of items answered correctly.

means-test   Determining eligibility for certain services or benefits, such as health benefits, by looking at income (salary or wages). Income above a certain level makes the individual ineligible for the service or benefit.

measurement   The use of numbers to describe behavior and performance. Observations of the way people behave or perform are assigned numerical values, and these numbers are then used to obtain new information or to describe relationships among the people observed. Measurement is obtained by tests or ratings.

measures of central tendency   Statistical measures useful in evaluating tests. They include the mean, median, and mode.

mechanical   In **offset** printing, a camera-ready pasteup of type, photos, line art, and so on, all on one piece of art board.

med-arb   An **alternative dispute resolution procedure** in which a neutral party is selected to serve as both mediator and arbitrator. Med-arb combines the voluntary strategies of persuasion and discussion, as in mediation, with an arbitrator's authority to issue a final and binding decision.

media   Printed or duplicated materials, graphics, projected still or motion photographic materials, video and sound recordings, and three-dimensional aids and devices.

median   A measure of central tendency. The median is the middle score in a range of scores — that is, one half of the scores are higher and one half are lower than the median score.

mediating device   A specialized piece of equipment, or a system, specifically designed to assist in the presentation of instruction; for example, teaching machines, classroom trainee response systems, computers, and interactive video. Mediating devices are used to supplement other instructional methods, substitute for conventional instructional approaches, relieve instructors from repetitive teaching tasks, provide for automatic test scoring and trainee advancement, record and tabulate trainee responses, control the sequence of instruction and the form of trainee responses, provide immediate correction of errors and the reinforcement of correct responses, and control instructional materials during the development and validation phases of instructional systems development.

mediation   A form of negotiation used to resolve individual and group disputes including labor-management disagreements. Mediation is confidential and private and always involves a neutral third party whose job is to help the individuals or groups to reach a voluntary settlement of the issue. Mediators have no power to make decisions or judgments or to enforce an agreement. Their role is that of facilitators and expediters.

Medicaid   Medical benefits, including hospitalization, payment of health care providers, prescription drugs, and the like, provided for the low income, the poor, and the indigent without charge (no premiums and no deductibles). Medicaid provides benefits only to persons who demonstrate a financial need as determined by federal guidelines and modified by the states. Eligibility is determined by three tests: (1) age 65 or older, blind, or physically or mentally disabled; (2) monthly income not in excess of the maximum allowable amount set by the state; and (3) total assets lower than the established limits. The federal government reimburses states for a substantial portion of Medicaid benefits paid so long as the state's Medicaid program falls within prescribed federal guidelines. In general, coverage is limited to **Aid to Families with Dependent Children** and **Supplemental Security Income**, low income pregnant women, low income children under the age of five, and low income persons in institutions and nursing homes.

medical and health benefits   *See* employee prefunding; fixed-dollar benefits; graduated benefits; hospice care; Medicaid; Medicare; respite care.

medical and health insurance laws See Health Maintenance Organization Act of 1973; Health Maintenance Organization Act of 1978; Medicare Catastrophic Coverage Act of 1988; Medicare Catastrophic Coverage Repeal Act of 1989.

medical assistance company Offers a variety of insurance, medical, and communication products and services for travelers, particularly targeting corporate travelers. Many offer medical records access, crisis assistance (such as emergency evacuation), overseas site inspections, medical consulting, multilingual assistance, and pre-departure kits.

medical care evaluation (MCE) A component of a health care quality assurance program that examines the process of medical care.

medical durable power of attorney See durable power of attorney for health care.

medical herbalism An alternative form of medical treatment in which good health is promoted and illnesses are treated by administering plant-derived potions or medications.

medical insurance The part of Medicare that helps pay for medically necessary physician services, outpatient hospital services, and a number of other medical services and supplies not covered by the hospital insurance part of Medicare, including some home health services.

medical IRA A plan proposed by Republican presidential candidate (1992) Pat Buchanan to provide health care funds by permitting individuals to establish accounts similar to individual retirement accounts that could be used to pay health-care bills.

medical loss ratio In health care management, the ratio between the cost of delivering medical care and the amount of money taken in by the plan.

medically necessary In health care benefits, a requirement for payment of medical and surgical charges. A service or supply is usually considered medically necessary when it is offered by a physician, is effective in treating the condition for which it is prescribed, is part of a course of treatment generally accepted by the American medical community, does not duplicate other services or supplies used to treat the condition, is not experimental, and it is intended to restore health and extend life.

Medical Proxy Act of 1991 See Self-Determination Act of 1991.

Medical Records Confidentiality Act of 1996 Establishes uniform privacy protection for personally identifiable health information whether the information in in paper or electronic form. Also establishes a federal right to review and request corrections to one's medical records and obligates all handlers of patient records to protect their privacy. Imposes civil and criminal penalties on violators.

Medical Records Privacy Act of 1997 A comprehensive federal law, proposed by the Clinton administration, designed to protect the privacy of medical records, allow individuals to ispect their own files, and punish unauthorized disclosure of personal data by hospitals, insurers, health plans, or drug companies. Required by the Health Insurance **Portability and Accountability Act of 1996**, the law would establish minimum federal standards for the use of such information. See also Privacy Act of 1974.

medical resource library A means of empowering employees, promoting **self-care,** reducing stress and anxiety, and emphasizing the importance of prevention. Involves establishing a repository and lending library for books, manuals, pamphlets, videos, audiotapes, and other materials pertaining to such problems as minor ailments, burnout, cardiovascular and cancer prevention, and other health care information that is either unavailable or inaccessible to most employees and their families. The purpose is to enable employees to make informed choices relating to wellness.

medical review officer (MRO) A qualified health care professional, usually a medical doctor, who reviews for medical necessity medical and surgical care provided to employees for an insurance carrier or firm.

medical savings account (MSA) A health care reform measure billed as an effective cost cutter. It works this way: An employer establishes a medical savings account, similar to a savings account, for each employee. The employer then buys employees a health insurance policy with a high deductible (as much as $3,000), resulting in savings of 50 percent or more on premiums. A portion of those savings is deposited annually into each MSA to be used exclusively by employees for their medical expenses, using health care providers of their own choice. Unused funds are rolled over each year and continue to grow. MSAs also follow an employee from job to job, allowing the individual to use its funds to pay for medical bills or insurance premiums between jobs. The system is said to provide incentives for comparison shopping. The **Health Insurance Portability and Accoutability Act of 1996** allows employees and self-employed individuals who have a **high-deductible medical insurance plan** to contribute up to 65 percent of their health plan's deductible (75 percent for families) to a medical saving account.

medical screening Pre-employment medical examinations used primarily to make the best use of employees by placing them in suitable positions. Also used to reduce absenteeism and turnover, avoid **workers' compensation** and other claims against the organization, make needed adjustments to the work area to accommodate the employee, safeguard the health and safety of the employee, other employees, clients, and customers, and identify substance abusers before they are hired.

medical self-care Programs that encourage employees to become better consumers and self-healers to achieve savings on medical plans. Instead or relying on specialized medical care, employees are encouraged to attend seminars and use books, pamphlets, and other materials dealing with preventing and treating common health problems, get more involved in treatment decisions, and work with their physicians to improve the quality and reduce the costs of their health care.

medical service agency (MSA) A coalition of **managed care** organizations designed to overcome the problems of medical service costs and cost-shifting through increased copayments, higher deductibles, balance billing practices, and so on.

medical services Encompass the usual requirements for employee physical examinations, immunizations, and other forms of preventive medicine. May also include consultation or referral for alcoholism or substance abuse, emergency medical or surgical treatment for on-the-job illnesses and injuries, and medical investigation of all accidents and injuries.

medical staff-hospital organization (MeSH)
See physician-hospital organization.

medical supplies Items such as surgical dressings, splints, casts, canes, crutches, and similar medical materials and equipment.

medical underwriting The use of physical examinations and tests of body fluids (urine and blood) by insurers to screen out high risk applicants for life or health insurance (such as those carrying HIV, the AIDS virus).

Medical Volume Performance Standard (MVPS) A benchmark standard established by the Congress in 1989 to recapture excessive fees by capping annually total Medicare physician payments. If total fees exceed the standard in any year, Congress will set a lower cap in subsequent years to recover the excess.

Medicare A federal health insurance program for people 65 or older and certain disabled people under 65 designed to cover medical needs. Medicare is operated by the Health Care Financing Administration of the U.S. Department of Health and Human Services. Unlike **Medicaid**, it is not a financially need-based program; it provides benefits regardless of the financial status of the recipient. It consists of two parts: Part A, hospital insurance, which helps pay for inpatient hospital care, some inpatient care in a skilled nursing facility, and hospice care, and Part B, medical insurance, which helps pay for medically necessary physician's services, outpatient hospital services, home health care, and a number of other medical services and supplies that are not covered by the hospital insurance part of Medicare. Part A is financed by part of the payroll (FICA) tax that also pays for Social Security. Part B is financed by monthly premiums paid by people who choose to enroll. As of January 1, 1997, these Medicare changes took effect: under Part A, Medicare hospital insurance, the deductible for up to 60 days of inpatient care increased to $760; **coinsurance** payments for hospital stays between 61 and 90 days increased to $190 per day; for hospital stays between 91 and 150 days increased to $380; the daily copayment for therapeutic care in a **skilled nursing facility** following a hospital stay for 21 through 100 days increased to $95. The monthly Part B premium, covering physician's fees, and certain services of dental surgeons, optometrists, chiropractors, podiatrists, and chiropodists, outpatient hospital services for diagnosis and treatment, additional medical services including diagnostic X-rays and other tests, and home health services (only if the subscriber does not have Part A coverage), and other items, increased to $43.80 in 1997 with a deductible of $100. Part B generally pays 80 percent of the approved amount for covered services after the subscriber pays an annual $100 deductible. The subscriber is responsible for paying the other 20 percent of deductible charges and for permissible physician charges in excess of the Medicare-approved amount, plus all charges not covered by Medicare. Medicare, in general, does not pay for health care obtained outside the United States. However, there are some limited exceptions for care obtained in Canada and Mexico.

Medicare carve out (MCO)   A health care cost-cutting strategy in which employee benefits are adjusted according to Medicare payout; if Medicare pays more, no additional benefit is paid; if Medicare pays less, a supplement is paid.

Medicare Catastrophic Coverage Act of 1988 (CATCAP)   A law that improved some Medicare benefits but imposed supplemental and graduated premiums on people 65 and older who had income tax liability. Congress repealed the CATCAP surtax November 22, 1989 (retroactive to January 1, 1989). All that remains of the catastrophic coverage is protection against spousal impoverishment (protection of the at-home spouse when the other spouse enters a nursing home and applies for Medicaid), a Medicare buy-in for the impoverished (payment of Medicare Part B premiums), new Medicaid provisions for pregnant mothers and infants, and continuation of the **Pepper Commission** to study health care needs and financing for long-term care and coverage for the uninsured.

Medicare Catastrophic Coverage Repeal Act of 1989 (MCCRA)   An act that preserved one of the features of the CATCAP law — protection against spousal impoverishment. It was enacted December 13, 1989 and provides some financial protection for the at-home or community spouse when the institutionalized spouse is in a nursing home. The law also sets minimums and maximums for the amount of assets a community (non-institutionalized) spouse can retain. Excluded from the computation of assets is the value of the home, personal effects, and household goods.

Medicare continuation   Under Social Security, a special rule that provides continued Medicare coverage to disabled persons for 39 months beyond the **trial work period.** If Medicare coverage stops because of work status, the individual may purchase it for a monthly premium.

Medicare hospice benefits   Available as a benefit under Medicare Hospital Insurance (Part A) to individuals with very limited life expectancy. Beneficiaries who choose hospice care receive non-curative medical and support services for his or her terminal illness. Home care is provided by a Medicare-approved public or private hospice along with necessary inpatient care and a variety of services not otherwise covered by Medicare. Medicare covers nearly all of the costs of the following: physician services, nursing care, medical appliances, medical supplies, outpatient drugs for symptom management and pain relief;, short-term inpatient care, including respite care, home health aide and homemaker services, physical and occupational therapy, speech/language pathology services, medical social services, and dietary and other counseling.

Medicare Hospital Insurance   This is Part A of Medicare. It helps pay for medically necessary inpatient care in a hospital, skilled nursing facility or psychiatric hospital, and for hospice and home health care.

Medicare/Medicaid Databank   The Omnibus Budget Reconciliation Act of 1993 required employers to participate in a Medicare/Medicaid Databank beginning in 1995, but federal compliance guidelines were never issued and funds to administer the program were not appropriated. On September 30, 1996, Congress repealed the legislation and the repeal measure was signed by the President in early October 1996.

Medicare Medical Insurance   This is Part B of Medicare. It helps pay for medically necessary physician's services and many other medical services and supplies.

Medicare risk contract   A contract between a **health maintenance organization** or **competitive medical plan** and the **Health Care Financing Administration** to provide services to Medicare beneficiaries and for which the health plan receives a fixed monthly payment for enrolled Medicare members and in return must provide all services on an at-risk basis.

Medicare SELECT A type of **medigap** supplemental policy that allows senior citizens to buy extra Medicare coverage at a discount by agreeing to use **managed care** and providers from an approved list. When a subscriber receives covered services from a preferred provider, Medicare pays its share of the approved charges and the insurer pays the full supplemental benefits provided for in the policy. Medicare SELECT insurers must also pay supplemental benefits for emergency health care furnished by providers outside the preferred provider network. Medicare SELECT denies payment or pays less that the full benefit if a subscriber goes outside the network for non-emergency services. However, Medicare will still pay its share of approved charges in such situations.

Medicare SELECT Act of 1995 Amends the Omnibus Budget Reconciliation Act of 1990 to permit Medicare SELECT policies to be offered in all States. Signed by the President July 7, 1995.

Medicare-sponsored prepaid health plan A plan that typically offers comprehensive, coordinated medical services through a network of health care providers (physicians, hospitals, and skilled nursing facilities), usually referred to as a **health maintenance organization** or a **competitive medical plan.**

Medicare subvention Legislation that authorizes Medicare to reimburse DoD at a reduced rate for treating additional Medicare eligibles in military hospitals and clinics. However, the authorization is limited to a demonstration test of Medicare reimbursement for three years at six locations beginning January 1, 1998. Participants must be volunteers (and may be limited to 10,000 total enrollees), Medicare-eligible for Part A (hospitalization), enrolled in Part B, agree to enroll in DoD's **TRICARE** Prime mnaged care plan, and agree not to go elsewhere for care. See also **Balanced Budget Act of 1997**.

Medicare supplement insurance plans At the direction of Congress, the National Association of Insurance Commissioners (NAIC), with the help of consumer groups and industry representatives, developed a new set of standards for Medicare supplemental insurance plans. Under these guidelines, beginning July 30, 1992, insurance companies began to offer up to 10 standardized NAIC plans, designated Plans A through J. Companies that sell Medicare supplement insurance must offer Plan A, the most basic plan, and may offer Plans B through J depending on market conditions. In 44 states and the District of Columbia, insurance companies are now allowed to sell only the 10 new standardized medigap policies. In three other states, Delaware, Pennsylvania, and Vermont, insurers now sell 6 of the 10. Three states (Massachusetts, Minnesota, and Wisconsin) have created a standard plan plus standard riders. Among the Plan A benefits: (1) payments for Medicare Part A hospital daily coinsurance charge at the rate of $163 per day (days 61-90) and $326 per day while using the 60 lifetime reserve days (days 91-150); (2) all Medicare eligible charges for hospitalization beyond the 150th day up to a lifetime maximum of an additional 365 days; (3) the first three pints of blood whether required as an outpatient or inpatient; and (4) payment of Medicare Part B medical and outpatient services coinsurance amount after the $100 calendar year Medicare Part B Deductible (20 percent of Medicare "approved charge"). Note that under the law, an insurer cannot make a person wait six months for coverage or preexisting illnesses. Those who have already endured the waiting period in their former medigap policy, insurers are required to cover individuals during the six months after their 65th birthday, regardless of their health. After that, insurers have the option of turning applicants down.

medigap coverage See Medicare supplement insurance plans.

medigap Fraud and Abuse Prevention Act of 1990 See Omnibus Budget Reconciliation Act of 1990.

medigap insurance Private health insurance designed to supplement Medicare (or company insurance) by bridging the gap between the approved rate and the deductible and the provider's charge. Therefore, it typically pays some, but not all, of the medical bills that Medicare (or the company's carrier) doesn't pay. Part B, Medicare, pays 80 percent of the "allowed" amount. The remainder is paid by supplemental (medigap) insurance, Medicaid, or the patient.

meditation An alternative to conventional medicine. Practitioners claim that it is a method of calming the mind controlling emotions by anchoring consciousness in the present moment. Conscious breathing or repetition of a saying or prayer (mantra) is often used to focus attention.

meeting *See* association meeting; corporate meeting; executive staff meeting; management meeting; retreat; sales meeting; strategy/planning meeting; trade show; training meeting; users group meeting.

meeting cost categories Include such items as exposition space, food and beverages, hotel accommodations, meeting space, trade show services, and travel.

meeting facilities Include airport hotels, conference centers, convention centers, cruise ships, midtown hotels, resort hotels, and suburban hotels.

meeting fare A special discounted airfare offered to people attending a convention or meeting. the fare is accessed through a special **star number** in the **computer reservation system.** that can be used on short notice — never more than 7 days in advance and often no advance at all. Meeting fares apply to discounted as well as full-fare tickets and can also be combined with **back-to-back ticketing** to save additional money. Considered by some to be a form of **grey fare**.

meeting industry council (MIC) A coalition of meeting organizations established to bring together key elements of the hospitality industry in order to promote cooperation and collaboration and improve the image of the specific destination. MICs are currently organized in more than 20 destinations in the United States and Canada. Some are dedicated to education and communication, others provide opportunities for networking, and still others focus on a single issue, such as limiting an increase in taxes of one kind or another.

meeting management The processes of planning, organizing, staffing, directing, and controlling corporate domestic and international meetings, conferences, and exhibitions. Involves site selection, transportation, housing, amenities, food and beverage, and entertainment negotiations and arrangements.

Meeting News: **The Newspaper for Meeting, Convention, Incentive Travel & Trade Show Professionals** A journal published monthly in January, February, July, August, and December; three times a month in November; and semimonthly in March, April, May, June,

September, and October: $65.00 per year (free to qualified subscribers). Address: Miller Freeman, Inc., Meeting News, P.O. Box 1189, Skokie, IL 60076-8189 (800/447-0138; fax 708/647-5972; E-mail **jalkon@mfi.com**; URL **http://www.meetingnews.com**).

meeting planner/planning functions Include budgeting, exhibit sales, ground transportation, hotel negotiations, housing, programming, promotion, and site selection.

Meeting Professionals International (MPI) An organization of 14.000 members in 45 countries established to provide opportunities for professional growth and development for those in the meetings industry through educational programs and services, communication, recognition, special interest groups, and networking and to commit to excellence in meetings, continuous international growth, research, a strong chapter network, and high ethical standards. *Contact:* MPI, 455 LBJ Freeway, Suite 1200, Dallas, Texas, 75244-5903 (972-702-3000; Fax: 972-702-3070; E-mail **72662,3077@compuserve.com**; URL **http://www.mpiweb.org**). MPI, European Bureau, Bldg. St. Michel, 15, B-1040 Brussels, Belgium Voice: +32-2-743.15.44; Fax: +32-2-743.15.50).

Meetings & Conventions: The Meeting & Incentive Planner's Resource A journal published thirteen issues per year, $70.00 (free to qualified subscribers). Address: Reed Travel Group, 500 Plaza Drive, Secaucus, NJ 007094-3626 (201-902-1700; Fax 201-319-1796; E-mail **ledelstein@oagmail.oag.com**).

megabyte A measure of the storage capacity of a computer. It is equal to 1,000,000 bytes.

megahertz (Mhz) A measure of the speed at which computers operate. One Mhz equals 1 million cycles per second.

Member Information Exchange (MIX) A network of HR professionals administered by ASTD's Information Center and available only to ASTD members. *Contact:* ASTD, 1630 Duke Street, Alexandria, VA 22313 (703/683-8100).

memorandum for record (MR) A memorandum written for file rather than dispatch. It serves as memory ticklers or documentation of events and decisions that may later be the object of scrutiny — or even litigation.

memory manager A software program that optimizes the extended and expanded memory available in a computer, converting

random access memory to either option as needed.

mental conditions   Mental diseases listed in the International Classification of Diseases as psychoses, neurotic disorders, or personality disorders or other nonpsychotic mental disorders.

mental disabilities   "Slow learners" (IQ range of 75-90), "retarded" (IQ range of 50-75), "severely retarded" or "trainable" (IQ below 50), and "perceptually disabled" (brain injured).

mental health   The condition or presence of emotional well-being. It is observable in behavior that demonstrates awareness of self and a life purpose, a sense of personal autonomy, and an ability to perceive and cope with reality; to interact with others and understand their needs, achieve mutually satisfying relationships, to be active and productive, respond flexibly in the face of stress, and receive pleasure from a variety of sources.

Mental Health Law of 1991   A section of the **Americans with Disabilities Act of 1990** that became effective in July 1992. Once hired, employees with a history of mental illness are entitled to extra support and accommodation from their employers so long as they can perform the essential duties and tasks of their jobs. The rules were extended in 1994 to cover companies with 15 or more employees. The law covers a broad range of mental problems, including mental retardation, learning disabilities, and workers who have overcome substance abuse (recovering victims of drug and alcohol abuse). Other covered illnesses include schizophrenia, manic-depressive disorders, major depression, anxiety disorders, and personality problems. Kleptomania, pyromania, compulsive gambling, and certain types of sexual dysfunctions, such as transvestism, are not covered. In addition, employers cannot reject job applicants because they might add to the organization's medical costs but does not prevent them from limiting benefits for treatment. Accommodations required by the law for the mentally disabled have not been identified but will be clarified as a result of lawsuits. However, special provisions may be as simple and inexpensive as providing more frequent breaks and quieter work areas.

mental health services   Services designed to help employees maintain good mental and emotional health, prevent a breakdown in employee effectiveness, reduce emotional stress, and treat emotional illnesses. They may include individual and group therapy and invariably involve referral to mental health specialists and agencies.

Mental Health Parity Act of 1996
Applies to both self-insured ERISA plans and insured plans, as well as coverage provided federal employees under the Federal Health Benefits Act and collectively bargained plans. Requires that annual and lifetime maximum dollar limits be equal to those for medical benefits when an employer provides mental health coverage (although the act does not require mental health coverage). Therefore, if a group health plan has no dollar limits to plan payments for medical or surgical services, limits are not allowed for mental health services. However, the law specifically excludes substance abuse treatment, including alcohol abuse and chemical dependency, from the requirement for equal maximum benefits. Implementation is effective for group health plans years beginning on or after January 1, 1998. Collectively bargained plans ratified before the law was enacted on September 26, 1996 will be required to comply with the act for plan years beginning after January 1, 1998 or at the end of the collectively bargained agreement, whichever is later.

mental illness   1. Officially defined in May 1993 by the Federal Center for Mental Health Services, Public Health Service, as adults who have or have had in the past year a diagnosable mental, behavioral, or emotional disorder that interferes with one or more major activities of life, like dressing, eating, or working. Provides a national uniform standard to be used by the states in determining eligibility for treatment in state and local clinics that receive federal funds or where patients are treated at no cost or reduced rates. **2.** Generally describes a group of disorders that cause severe disturbances in thinking, feeling and relating and result in diminished capacity for coping with the ordinary demands of life, such as schizophrenia, manic depression obsessive-compulsive disorder, and depression. Mental illness is not the same as **mental retardation**.

People with mental illnesses are usually of normal intelligence. The causes of biologically-based mental illnesses are not understood, although it is believed that the functioning of the brain's neurotransmitters is involved. Heredity may be a factor, and stress may contribute to its onset in vulnerable people. Recreational drugs may also contribute to onset, but are unlikely to be the single cause. Although there are no cures for mental illness, treatment can substantially improve the functioning of persons with those disorders. About 3.3 million Americans are mentally ill.

mentally impaired   Individuals whose limitations rest primarily on lowered intellectual capacity attributed to congenital or inherited defects, mental retardation, chromosomal aberrations (such as Down Syndrome), disease or injury to the brain suffered before, during, or in the immediate period after birth, accidents or illness in childhood or adulthood, or as the consequence of impaired maturation due to insufficient environmental stimulation from family or cultural sources.

mental retardation   People who have diminished intellectual capacity present since birth; that is they are significantly below average in mental functioning and have difficulty in learning and performing daily life functions. About 1.5 million Americans have mental retardation.

mental wellness program   An offshoot of traditional wellness programs, the program attempts to get at the root causes of substandard employee performance, inability of employees to get along with their supervisors and peers, alcohol and drug abuse, or unhealthy life styles. In four- to ten-hour courses, employees are helped to understand themselves and deal with negative self-defeating thoughts. They are also taught how to cope with their irrational fears and their tensions and stresses .

mentor   Senior, experienced, and respected managers or staffers who serve as role models, coaches, counselors, advisors, and advocates for younger or less experienced persons, but who are not directly involved in their charges' personal or work lives.

menu interface   Offers the computer user a choice of commands that are initiated by such means as typing a letter, pressing a cursor key, or pointing and clicking with a mouse.

menu-driven   Software that uses a list of options called a "menu" that is displayed on the screen of the terminal.

merge/purge   In marketing, a software system that combines different input database tapes in varying formats into a common format to eliminate duplications for a promotional or sales mailing.

merger   Consolidating or joining two or more organizations under a single ownership and management They may take the forms of leveraged buyouts (LBOs), friendly acquisitions, or hostile takeovers. Mergers are consummated to improve profitability, market share, or some other financially-related gain or advantage.

merger clause   In contract law, wording stating that the terms contained in a contract represent the total agreement of both parties and that the agreement supersedes any other agreement.

merit budget   A sum of money reserved for annual merit increases on a company, department, or work unit basis. May be expressed in dollars or as a percentage of payroll. Also called *merit pool.*

merit increase   *See* merit pay.

merit pay   Increased compensation paid for outstanding performance of assigned duties and tasks. Focuses on *how well* work is done. The approach assumes, or at least implies, that an objective performance appraisal system is in effect which adequately determines the performance of individual employees. If such a system does not exist, merit pay should not be used. And it should never be linked with economic conditions or increases in the cost of living (COLA).

merit pool   *See* merit budget.

merit rating   A systematic and orderly means of appraising and rating performance; ratings used as a basis for incentive plans such as pay-for-performance.

merit review   Performance review used in a merit rating system.

mesokurtic   Describes the shape of the curve of a frequency distribution when plotted on a graph. A mesokurtic curve is perfectly symmetrical — a model of the normal distribution or bell-shaped curve.

meta-analysis   A statistical study of the results of previous research studies. For example, a study of the validity of tests to see if individual studies consistently produced consistent results.

metacognition   The ability to complete a project or achieve a goal by monitoring one's own thought processes; exercising the "governor" of the mind by thinking about the process of thinking.

metaethics   One of two subdivisions of the discipline of ethics. Focuses on analysis of the meaning of the terms used in ethical or moral argument.

metaphor   A analogy used by a developer to organize the content of a multimedia program. Sometimes adds unnecessary expense to the production without a reasonable return on the investment.

methadone   An addictive synthetic narcotic used to treat addiction to heroin and other opiates. It is taken orally. In some states, methadone clinics are classified by law as centers for the handicapped and are protected against discrimination.

methamphetamine   *See* speed.

method   A basic approach to instruction. Instructional methods include conventional lecture, conference, demonstration, and performance as well as tutorials, programmed instruction, case studies, and simulation, or a combination of the foregoing.

methods analysis   A productivity improvement strategy for new operations and existing processes that involves looking at the job, duty, or task in fine detail, questioning how and why everything is done, and searching for better and more efficient methods.

methods engineering   A systematic means of improving production and product quality by subjecting each phase of an operation or procedure to close scrutiny and analysis to find the most economical, fastest, most efficient, and best method of performing it. Then the procedure is standardized (in terms of equipment, methods and work conditions), operators are trained in the method, and finally the number of standard hours required by a typical operator to do the job is measured.

methods improvement   *See* methods engineering.

Michelangelo   A computer virus that overwrites the first 9MB of an infected hard disk on Michelangelo's birthday, March 6. Lost data are not recoverable. The virus is "caught" by booting from an infected floppy disk.

microcomputer   *See* personal computer.

microdisk   *See* disk.

micromarketing   Targeting highly specialized market segments for clients and customers. Involves catering to a specialized clientele and typically requires the ability to produce a wide variety of goods or services at competitive costs.

microphone   An electronic amplifying device for meetings and conferences.

micro process   A process that remains entirely within a department's or work group's control, direction, or management.

microprocessor   A small electronic chip that contains a complete central processing unit — a computer on a chip — which provides processing capability at the device level and the use of multiple microprocessors in the central processing unit of large computer systems. Microprocessors are often a part of microcomputers.

Microsoft disk operating system (MS-DOS) Originally developed for the IBM personal computer. Most microcomputers, workstations, and mid-range computers can red disks recorded by MS-DOS; however, DOS-based application programs require a specific version of the operating system to run.

Microsoft Internet Explorer   A software system that allows access to and navigation of the **Internet** simply by pointing and clicking.

Microsoft^(R) Windows^{TM}   A graphical computer operating system. It replaces traditional keyboard commands with on-screen symbols and menus that the user can control with a **mouse,** thereby increasing power and ease of use of computers and opens the way for integrating voice, graphics, and video information. In the future, a windows or **MS-DOS** program will work uniformly on virtually any computer so that users can move from workstations to desktops to laptops, yet work in the same way.

microwave   A technology used to transmit telephone messages and television programs point-to-point. Transmissions can also be directed at satellites, which amplify and retransmit the signal to other locations. Uses extremely high frequency radio waves.

midlevel practitioner   Nonphysician health care providers such as physicians' assistants, clinical nurse practitioners, nurse midwifes, and so on.

midlife crisis The end of young adulthood signaled by the approach of the 40th birthday. It is said to be a time of change and adjustment — physiologically, psychologically, socially, financially, maritally, and legally — but more than that, a time for reassessment of what one has accomplished and whether it was fulfilling, what has not been achieved and whether it matters, and what remains useful and doable in the remaining years.

mid-office system In travel management, a computer system that communicates with a front end system, such as a CRS, and processes the information to produce client management information system reports.

mid-range computer See minicomputer.

Migrant and Seasonal Agricultural Worker Act of 1983 (MSAWA) An Act designed to protect migrant and seasonal agricultural workers from unfair labor practices, unhealthful or unsafe living, housing, and working conditions, or discrimination because they have, with just cause, filed a complaint, initiated a proceeding, or testified in any such proceedings relating to the provisions of the Act. It requires employers to obtain a certificate of registration as a farm labor contractor. They are also required to disclose in writing to each worker the place of employment, the wage rates to be paid, the crops and kinds of activities in which the worker may be employed, the period of employment, the transportation, housing, and any other benefit to be provided and their costs, if any, the existence of any strike or other work stoppage, slowdown, or interruption of operations by employees, and any arrangements for commissions or other benefits accruing to the contractor or association resulting from sales to the workers.

migration The movement of data from one computer to another.

The Military Chaplains Association of the USA (MCA) An association of 1,600 active duty, reserve, retired, and former chaplains of the Army, Navy, Air Force, Veterans Administration, and Civil Air Patrol. Its mission is to safeguard and strengthen the forces of faith and morality of our nation; perpetuate and deepen the bonds of understanding and friendship in our military services; preserve our spiritual influence and interest in all members and veterans of the armed forces; uphold the Constitution of the United States; and promote justice, peace, and goodwill. *Contact:* MCA, P.O. Box 42660, Washington, DC 20015-0660 (202/574-2423; Fax 717/642-6792; E-mail **chaplains@charitiesusa.com**).

The Military Coalition (TMC) An alliance of 24 associations representing 5 million current and former uniformed service members plus their families formed to see that America keeps faith with them. TMC works to protect their interests in such areas as compensation, health care, military construction, base closures, and realignment, retirement affairs, taxes and Social Security, and other quality of life issues, such as morale, welfare, and recreation, for active duty and retired, reserve and National Guard veterans, their families, and survivors. *Contact:* The Retired Officer Association, 201 N. Washington St., Alexandria, VA 22314-2539 (800/245-8762 or 703/549-2311; Fax 703/838-8173; E-mail **editor@troaorg**; URL **http://www.troa.org**).

Military Health Service System (MHSS) Provides health care benefits for active and retired military personnel and their families.

military occupational specialty (MOS) An alphanumeric code used to identify specific enlisted occupations in the the U.S. Army and Marine Corps. For example, 11B identifies an Army infantryman; 05H identifies an Army Morse Intercept Operator.

military reduction in force See Fiscal 1993 Defense Authorization Act.

military reservists' rights Under the law, employers are required to hold jobs open for reservists called to active duty for a minimum of four years, extendible if an emergency continues. They must be offered jobs with the same pay, rank, and seniority they would have enjoyed had their employment not been interrupted, but employers are not required to place returning reservists in their old jobs. A 1990 ruling by the Internal Revenue Service mandates that employers offer continuing health insurance coverage to their reservist employees who are called to active duty. Activation of reservists under the ruling are considered a **Consolidated Omnibus Budget Reconciliation Act of 1986** event, and employers are required to furnish notices of COBRA rights to their reservist employees. Such notices explain that under COBRA a reservist employee called to active duty may continue to receive health insurance coverage from the employer, but the employee is required to pay the full premium. Coverage ends when the reservist becomes covered under another group health insurance plan.

military training Training provided officers, noncommissioned officers, and enlisted personnel (and sometimes civilian employees) of the armed forces to prepare them for combat, noncombat, supervisory, managerial, and leadership jobs and positions. The training is provided in military schools and in the units by means of formal and on-the-job approaches by the Army, Navy, Marine Corps, Air Force, and Coast Guard.

military treatment facility (MTF) A hospital or clinic operated by one of the armed services. By October 1995, 95 MTFs throughout the United States will implement a coordinated care plan.

Miller v. Cigma A 1995 U.S. 3rd Circuit Court of Appeals ruling that plaintiffs in cases litigated under the **Age Discrimination in Employment Act of 1967** must prove that their age played a definitive role in the employer's actions, although not necessarily the only factor considered. The decision reversed a ruling of the U.S. Eastern (PA) District Court in favor of Cigma.

millions of instructions per second (MIPS) A measure of the speed the electronic pulses with which a computer communicates with itself — and a means of expressing a computer's price/performance ratio (generally, the higher the MIPS, the higher the price).

mind/brain function approach A form of the concepts-based, integrated curriculum. Employs instructional strategies and classroom organization that engage students in using mind/brain functions. Attributed to Betty Jean Eklund Shoemaker, "Education 2000 Integrated Curriculum," *Phi Delta Kappan,* June 1991.

mindguarding A symptom of **groupthink.** The group discourages the expression of dissenting beliefs to protect itself from threatening ideas and may even suppress documents that go against the direction or decisions of the group.

mind-mapping A simple, useful method for thinking on paper. Mind-mapping employs a non-linear, divergent approach to thought. A mind map is a two-dimensional word sketch that uses a whole sheet of paper to organize ideas into a spider web. Random ideas are recorded on paper, using only key words and phrases, on a subject, problem, or issue, as rapidly as possible without judging their value. These jottings are later subjected to refinement and judgment. The technique is used to solve complex problems, make decisions, plan projects, or take notes. Also known as *hurricane writing, clustering, thought trails,* and *brainstorming on paper.*

minicomputer A computer that is considerably less powerful in processing capabilities, uses less complex software, and has fewer and simpler application programs than the more sophisticated and expensive general purpose computer systems (mainframes).

mini disc (MD) A new piece of stereo equipment developed by Sony. At 2 1/2 inches in size, the MD is small enough to be played on a machine the size of a pack of cigarettes but holds as much audio as a compact disc. Although it does not provide the fidelity of a CD, it out-performs analog tape cassettes. The MD also records as well as plays back, and it will not skip when bumped.

minimalist testing An approach to testing that employs the fewest and simplest test questions to determine whether a learner is "go" or "no-go" on a learning module — that is, whether the trainee advances to the next module, repeats the module, or is provided remedial training of some sort.

minimalist training An approach to training that uses the fewest and simplest training elements or modules and other resources to achieve a given learning outcome. Used to cut training time and costs, the approach is criticized by many as inadequate and inappropriate because it is often carried to extremes and fails to provide enough learner support and a framework for further learning.

mini-max budgeting An approach to budgeting in which two budgets are developed, one for maximum assumed output (high point) and one for minimum assumed output (low point). The difference in cost between the high point and low point budgets divided by the difference in volume will yield the variable rate.

minimum-care package A health-care plan proposed by then presidential candidate Bill Clinton (1992) in which coverage, funded by the federal government, would be offered for those currently without health care insurance.

Minimum Wage Act of 1997 Introduced by Rep. Martin Sabo, D. Minn. as H.R. 687, the bill would increase the minimum wage to $6.50 per hour by the year 2,000 and limit executive compensation to 25 times the salary of the lowest-paid worker.

Minimum Wage Exemption Certificate
A certificate issued by Wage and Hour Division regional offices of the Department of Labor that allows employers to pay between 75 and 50 percent of the minimum wage to disabled workers depending on the severity of the disability. Employers must demonstrate that the subminimum wage reflects the workers low production capacity.

minimum wage law A minimum wage level established by Congress as a part of the Fair Labor Standards Act. Overtime pay at a rate of not less than one and one-half times the regular rates of pay is required for nonexempt workers after 40 hours of work in a workweek. States may have minimums that are higher than those mandated by the federal government. FLSA also provides for the employment of student-learners (vocational education students), full-time students in retail or service establishments, agriculture, or institutions of education, and individuals whose earning or productive capacity is impaired by physical or mental disability, including those related to age or injury, at wage rates below the statutory minimum only under certificates issued by Wage-Hour.

Minimum Wage Act of 1996 In August 1996, the minimum hourly wage was raised to $4.75, effective October 1, 1996; on September 1, 1997, it will be raised another 40 cents to a total of $5.15. The tax portion of the bill provides more generous equipment write-offs for small businesses and allows a new type of simplified pension plan for companies employing 100 or fewer workers.

Ministry of International Trade and Industry (MITI) The powerful Japanese agency responsible, according to many experts, for Japan's economic vigor, dominance, and growth. At the beginning of each decade, MITI produces a position paper that outlines 10-year goals for Japanese industry.

mini-trial An **alternative dispute resolution procedure** involving confidential, non-binding exchange of information with the objective of achieving a prompt and cost-effective settlement of complex litigation. The process seeks to narrow areas of disagreement, reconcile collateral issues, and encourage a fair and equitable settlement.

Minority Business Development Agency (MBDA) A federal agency that can answer questions minority businesses might have about selling products and services to the government. Created to encourage the growth of minority- owned businesses in the United States. MBDA's mission is to (1) coordinate Federal Government plans, programs, and operations which affect minority business enterprise; (2) promote and coordinate the activities of government and private organizations which help minority businesses grow; (3) collect and disseminate information that will help those interested in establishing or expanding a successful minority-owned firm.; and (4) fund organizations to provide management and technical assistance to minority entrepreneurs. *Contact:* MBDA, 14th & Constitution Ave., N.W., Washington, DC 20230 (202-482-4547; Fax 202/501-1689; E-mail **mbda@doc.gov**; URL **http://www.doc.gov/agencies/mbda/index.html**

minority business enterprise (MBE)
A business or nonprofit organization that is at least fifty-one percent (varies by state) owned by, directed by, or in the case of a publicly owned business, at least fifty-one percent of the stock of which is owned by, citizens or permanent resident aliens from minority groups (African-Americans, Hispanics, Asians and Pacific Islanders, and Native Americans).

mission The reasons for the existence of an organization, the purposes it was designed to serve, and the limits of its operations — markets, product line, services, geographic areas, and distribution channels, both current and potential.

mission statement A means of communicating the corporate vision, values, direction, and purposes. It identifies its products. services, customers, markets, and overall strengths. The mission statement includes a snapshot of the company's reason for existing, outlines corporate directives, and describes how the organization should operate. It describes what an organization is, what it does, who it serves, and what makes it unique. The mission statement also forms the basis for strategic and operational plans and a vision that can be shared with the total organization.

mixed model   In health care, a managed care plan that combines two or more types of delivery systems, such as both **closed panel** and **open panel**.

mobile worker   An employee who spends most the time out of the office, on the road, at the customer's site, or in hotels. Typically uses a laptop computer with a modem to connect to information sources and communicate with the home office.

mobility and motion impairments   Disabilities that involve the loss or loss of use of limbs, bones, or muscles and result in inadequacy or incapability of an individual to respond to situations requiring movement of the body, hands, arms, or legs and inability to perform psychomotor skills.

mobility premium   A lump-sum payment made to employees who accept international assignment.

mockup   Similar to a model. Used to simulate environments, machines, systems, and processes in orientation and training programs to provide demonstrations and hands-on experiences.

mode   A measure of central tendency: the score in a distribution of scores that occurs most frequently.

model   A representation of reality. Models are facsimiles or simulations of the components of a system or of an entire system in a defined area of corporate interest and activity. They facilitate understanding, analysis, experimentation, and decision making. Models may be used to develop managerial and leadership skills, improve technical performance, provide practice in decision making, and improve trainees' understanding of management theories. They may take the forms of physical models (typically miniaturized or greatly enlarged representations of reality), analog models (mechanical, electronic, or hydraulic representations of systems or equipment that mirror reality), and mathematical models (composed entirely of mathematical symbols to characterize the dynamic processes found in the real system). The latter must use some computational device, preferably a computer, to trace the implications of the mathematical relationships.

modeling   In marketing, a statistical technique in which the marketer constructs a representative customer or client from a database of customers or clients by identifying similar and dissimilar characteristics.

modem   A modulator/demodulator device that links distant computers by means of telephone lines. A modem converts the computer's digital signals into analog signals, which can be transmitted over the telephone lines. When they reach their destination, the modem demodulates the signals (converts them back to digital).

modified adjusted gross income (MAGI)   The sum of adjusted gross income, tax-exempt interest, the exclusion available to persons living abroad, excluded income from Puerto Rico or other U.S. possession, and the excluded proceeds from U.S. Series EE bonds used for college tuition and fees received during a year. That total must be reported on U.S. Income Tax returns. It is also needed to determine whether Social Security or Railroad Retirement benefits are taxable.

modified American plan (MAP)   In meeting management, a pricing method used by hotels and conference centers. Price includes lodging, breakfast, and dinner.

module   **1.** A format for individually-paced training. A module consists of a self-contained lesson typically including an audio- or videocassette, a workbook, packet of illustrations, samples, or examples (forms, checklists, glossaries, diagrams, and supplemental resources), and a mastery test. Several modules constitute a training program. Used to teach office practices, standard procedures, assembly techniques, operator skills, and the like. **2.** In an **integrated human resources information system**, different applications, each of which work together although performing a specific function. Can often be purchased separately.

mommy track   A term triggered by Felice Schwartz ("Management Women and the New Facts of Life," *Harvard Business Review*, Jan-Feb 1989). She commented on the need for corporate flexibility to accommodate two types of women who need quite different career paths: the Career and Family Woman (women who opt for motherhood regardless of the consequences for career development and progression — the Mommy Track) and the Career Primary Woman (women who are willing to make the most of every opportunity for professional development even if it means sacrifices in their personal lives).

money-purchase pension plan (MPPP)
A type of defined contribution pension plan in which the employer contribution is mandatory and is usually based on a fixed percentage of annual compensation. MPPPs are established and maintained to provide for payment of determinable benefits to employees over a period of years, usually for life, following retirement.

money surrogates   Rewards such as company cars and planes for personal as well as business use, a chauffeured limo, first-class travel accommodations, low or no-cost loans, part-time work with full time pay, early retirement with full pension, payment of professional, technical, or trade association or civic, health, or recreation club dues and memberships, free medical examinations, free dental care, business travel insurance, liberal expense account, in-town apartment, payment of spouses' travel expenses, moving expenses, free financial or legal counseling, home security system, home entertainment expense allowances, savings on vacations, vacation homes, domestic help, free vacation travel, tickets to theater or sporting events, sabbatical leaves, personal liability insurance, child or elder care, and spouse or children tuition payments.

monitor   1. Equipment that consists of a cathode ray tube (CRT) and a plastic or metal casing that displays the computer's information, similar to a television set. Monitors can be either monochromatic or color. **2.** In distance learning, television screens used to display connected sites and provide real-time audio and video communication between the host site and remote sites.

monitoring   1. In training, visiting training classes to observe instruction and learning, validate instructional approaches, rate instructors, and improve learning and instruction. **2.** In technological forecasting, a surveillance technique typically used to take a closer look at changes and development first identified by scanning. It is more focused and disciplined than the scanning technique.

monocultural   Refers to a cultural that is largely undifferentiated in terms of aesthetic, behavioral, religious, linguistic, moral, and/or religious beliefs, customs, and practices.

monoculturalism   A term used to describe the social world that exists and has existed for years. It is a world that separated people into whites, Negroes, and orientals, religions into Protestant, Catholic, and Jewish, people into men and wives, and where gays, lesbians, bisexuals, Muslims, and other racial, ethnic, and religious minorities didn't exist.

mononucleosis   An infectious disease that primarily affects the lymph nodes, particularly those under the jaw, under the arm, and in the groin and an enlarged spleen. It is caused by a type of herpes virus (Epstein-Barr) and results in mild to severe weakness and fatigue. It is treated by bed rest and avoidance of exercise or strenuous activity while the spleen is enlarged.

The Monster Board   A huge index of high-tech and computer job openings (URL **http://www.monster.com/home.html**).

Monte Carlo method   *See* queuing theory/techniques.

Montgomery GI Bill   A federal program of educational benefits for military personnel administered by the Department of Veterans Affairs. The basic monthly benefit is currently $400 for active duty three-to-six year enlistments, $350 for active duty two-year enlistments, and $190 for National Guard and Reserve benefits. Enlistees may elect to contribute $100 per month for 12 months and the government contributes up to $9,600 more. Combined with the **Army College Fund** (up to $14,400), for a four year enlistment, an individual could earn up to $25,200 for college. The 102nd Congress also provided automatic annual cost-of-living increases in Montgomery G.I. Bill benefits effective October 1, 1993. Public Law 104-275, signed October 4, 1996, raised the benefit reimbursement rate for cooperative courses from 80 to 100 percent.

mood disorders   The most common group of serious psychiatric illnesses. Involve periodic disturbances in mood, concentration, sleep, activity, appetite and social behavior. Also called *major affective disorders, major depression,* and *manic depressive illness.*

moonlighting   The practice of holding a second full-time or part-time job in addition to one's normal, full-time occupation. Moonlighting has been prohibited in many organizations because management believes that it detracts from performance of the primary job due to either physical or emotional exhaustion or both.

monthly earnings test Under the Social Security system, during the first year of retirement, beneficiaries are subjected to a monthly earnings test if the yearly limit on income is exceeded in that year. In 1996, beneficiaries who were age 65 through 69 could earn up to $960 per month. Benefits are withheld at the rate of $1 for each $3 of earnings over that amount. For those under age 65, the limit is $690 per month, and $1 is withheld for every $2 of earnings in excess of that amount. Beginning with the month an individual reaches age 70, there is no earning test.

moonrock A street drug made of a combination of crack and heroin.

morale The sum total of attitudes that employees display toward the organization and their feelings and predispositions toward situations which affect and are important to people and call for self-discipline. High morale exists when an employee's (or group's) attitudes are predominantly favorable and low when they are predominantly negative.

morphine An additive drug used to reduce pain. It is a bitter, white, crystalline, narcotic base, the principal alkaloid of opium.

morphing **1.** In multimedia, a short for metamorphosing, a video special effects technique in which one image is seamlessly transformed into another. It is accomplished by means of fast, color Macintosh computers or Windows with lots of memory (minimum of Macintosh Classic II with 5 megabytes of random access memory and 10 megabytes of hard disk storage (better with 8 MB RAM and 30 MB storage). **2.** Doing two or more jobs at the same time.

morphological analysis **1.** In creative problem solving, a system for systematically listing and studying all of the possible combinations of alternatives that might be helpful in solving a problem. It involves stating the problem as broadly as possible and then breaking it into its components for study and analysis. Each of the components or characteristics is treated as an independent variable and is specified or described and inserted into a 2-dimensional grid or a 3-dimensional cube. Each of the intersecting axes of the grid or cube is examined in turn and considered as a possible solution to the problem. The most promising alternatives are selected and tested, modified, evaluated, and developed.

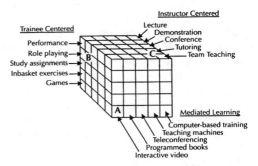

2. In forecasting, a normative technique usually conducted by a group of people using a structured format, typically a grid. Requirements, functions, or characteristics of the issue or problem are listed on one axis and alternative means of meeting them are then entered on the other axis. A current or projected issue, change, or development is examined by determining what the major functions of the development are, ascertaining what methods are being used in present systems to accomplish those functions or deal with the issue, identifying alternative means of accomplishing each function, and considering different ways of combining subordinate solutions or technologies to suggest innovative approaches to accomplish the basic functions or deal with the development.

mortality table A graphic that depicts the rate at which participants in various age groups in a pension plan have died. Used by actuaries to calculate the average life expectancy of men and women of a given age.

Mosaic A popular software system that allows access to and navigation of the **Internet** (World Wide Web) simply by pointing and clicking. Created by the National Center for Supercomputing applications at the University of Illinois.

MOS-producing courses Technical and skills training provided U.S. Army personnel, usually in pay grades E-1, E-2, or E-3, which results in the award of a military occupational specialty. Customarily provided immediately following completion of basic training.

motion picture experts group (MPEG)
A video compression technology that allows personal computer users to play back television-quality video. An MPEG board can deliver full-motion, full-screen video with 16-bit stereo sound.

motivation   A goal-directed stimulus whose components are drives (needs, wants, and desires) and reinforcement (incentives, encouragement, feedback, and rewards). The former reside within the individual and the latter in the work environment. High motivation is manifested by the willingness of people to meet their personal needs, wants, and aspirations by directing their efforts and talents toward attaining organizational goals and objectives.

motivational counseling   A form of counseling initiated by the employee when he or she feels the need for guidance or assistance. Also called *consultative counseling*.

Motivation-Hygiene Theory   The theory postulates that two separate and quite different sets of factors operate in any work situation: satisfiers and dissatisfiers. Satisfiers are related to a jobs's intrinsic content — motivators such as achievement, advancement, and a feeling of challenge and personal growth. Dissatisfiers are related to a job's extrinsic content — hygiene factors such as company policies, type of supervision, working conditions, job security, and pay and benefits. The theory further holds that the absence of satisfiers does not generate job satisfaction. Only when the motivators are activated will people be productive, cooperative, and turn out high quality work. Attributed to Frederick Herzberg.

motivation/recognition/reward (MRR)
Formal programs designed to give employees a feeling of belonging, let them know that they are important, motivate them, improve their morale, enhance their productivity, recognize their achievements, and promote their retention. Primarily involve non-cash awards such as gifts, general merchandise, and jewelry and related items.

mouse   A computer peripheral device used to select computer functions and to enter and delete data. Employs a graphical user interface.

mouse potato   A person who has become addicted to the computer; for example, one who spends and inordinate amount of time daily on the **Internet**.

move-in/move-out   The agreed-upon dates of arrival and occupancy of a set number of hotel rooms (move-in) and departure and vacating those rooms (move-out).

moving average   A "quick and dirty" form of time-series forecasting that involves using a rolling average of past data to predict future trends.

multi-attribute evaluation   A marketing technique used to translate customer's imprecisely stated requirements into objective specifications by listing them in rank order, assigning weights to each in terms of importance, and comparing the customer's rating of each requirement against his or her rating of competition.

multicorporate health care   Consortiums of organizations organized to provide health care to their employees by contracting with health care management firms consisting of physicians, registered nurses and nurse practitioners, therapists, data and information specialists, and support staff. Such cooperative arrangements yield economies of scale.

multicultural   Refers to the variety of cultural backgrounds characteristic of American society — the differences in aesthetic, behavioral, religious, linguistic, moral, and religious beliefs, customs, and practices of different racial and ethnic groups of people.

multiculturalism   A theory that avows the need for social reform. Its goal is to prepare people for a wider and more accepting world — a world where racist, sexist, and homophobic thoughts, as well as speech and action, have been eliminated. Advocates object strenuously to the use of such terms as "freshman" instead of "first year students," "chairman" instead of "chairperson," "Indian" instead of "Native American," " disabled" instead of "different abilities" or "challenged." Adherents are derisively described as "politically correct."

multiculturalist movement
See multiculturalism.

multidisk   A new technology for a single disk drive, an array of eight or nine synchronized devices working in parallel. It allows faster data access, improved reliability, more storage space, and less vulnerability to disk crashes and loss of data.

multidomain job analysis   The process of collecting job information and data relating to job duties and tasks, job knowledge, skills, and abilities, and job performance requirements.

multiemployer benefits plan An employee benefits plan to which more than one employer is required to contribute and which is maintained in accordance with the provisions of one or more collective bargaining agreements. The **Employee Retirement Income Security Act of 1974** defined the original rules for such plans; the **Multiemployer Pension Plan Amendments Act of 1980** increased the number of rules. Also called *multiemployer pension plan*.

Multiemployer Pension Plan Amendments Act of 1980 (MPPAA) Legislation that completely revised Title IV of the **Employee Retirement Income Security Act of 1974** as it applies to multiemployer pension plans. Although too numerous to describe here, the additions included rules relating to administration, reporting, fiduciary responsibility, and enforcement, and for pension plans, to participation, vesting, funding, and termination insurance.

multiemployer welfare plan A plan sponsored by more than one employer that provides nonpension benefits for workers such as life, sick, and accident benefits.

multilateral discounts In travel management, fare reductions of 15 percent or more offered by international air carriers to companies with high-volume and reliable global travel programs. The goal is to achieve a better balance of traffic, retain loyal customers, and improve their global status.

multimedia Combinations of computer hardware, software, and learningware in one easy-to-use package that delivers text, audio, graphics, animation, and video, and eventually including full motion, at one workstation or learning carrel. Includes a variety of systems for bringing information, music, voice, animation, photos, and video images together on a screen. It represents the fusion of television, personal computers, and laser storage systems such as videodiscs and compact discs and permits the user to navigate and interact with the materials. For example, Apple's hardware platform for multimedia is HyperCard.

multimedia personal computer (MPC) A personal computer with a built-in CD-ROM drive and added memory that can produce interactive video.

multinational A way of organizing a business across national boundaries in which the company expands its domestic market to the international market using domestic human, materiel, and financial resources. *See also* global.

multinational company (MNC) *See* transnational company.

multinational pooling A cost containment strategy in which several small insurance policies from each locale where the multinational has a significant presence are combined into a single comprehensive policy. The purpose of pooling is to give global companies financial credibility and some savings on administrative charges. It may also make it easier to deal with the problems of fragmentation caused by distinct rules and regulations governing insurance activities, including the marketing and distribution of private benefits programs, in each country.

multioption health plan (MOHP) *See* cafeteria plan.

multiple-choice item An objective test item that requires testees to select the correct or best answer to a question from among four or more provided alternatives.

multiple employer trust (MET) *See* multiple-employer welfare association.

multiple-employer welfare association (MEWA) A cooperative established to enable members, mainly small employers, to purchase health care coverage at lower costs.

multiple-incentive contract (MIC) A type of contract designed to provide motivation for the contractor to achieve maximum performance. It employs several variables, such as performance, schedule, and costs, to determine the amount of incentive profit to be paid to the contractor.

multiple level password A means of protecting computer from access by unauthorized persons. Employs a series of characters, unique to each user, that must be entered before the computer will perform certain tasks.

multiple regression Too complex for description here, multiple regression is a statistical technique used to assess the impact of several different independent (x) variables on a dependent (y) variable using the method of least squares.

multiple sclerosis (MS) A chronic, episodic, and progressive disease of the nervous system that affects different parts of the brain and therefore produces symptoms in different parts of the body. Its root causes are unknown, but it is a disease of myelin, the coating insulation of the nerves in the brain, spinal cord, and elsewhere in the body, and a disease of the immune system. Approximately 200,000 Americans have multiple sclerosis.

Multiple Sclerosis Association of America (MSAA)   A national self-help organization that offers support group meetings, information and referrals, phone support, conferences, counseling, and a newsletter. *Contact:* MSAA, 706 Haddonfield Rd., Cherry Hill, NJ 08002 (800/833-4MSA; Fax 609/661-9797).

multiple-ticket fare/pricing   A means of saving up to 30 percent over two full-fare round trip tickets, appropriate for travelers with trips to the same destination two weeks in a row. Instead of buying two round trip Saturday-stay fares out of sequence, the traveler books the trip out as a one-way ticket, then a round trip ticket back and forth over the weekend, and a one-way return ticket. Endorsed by the airlines.

multi-point control unit (MCU)   A device that links three or more point-to-point videoconferencing systems.

multipreneur   Simultaneously developing multiple skills and careers to meet the need to be prepared for change, enhance employability, and lock in career success. Attributed to Tom Gorman, *Multipreneuring*, Fireside/Simon & Shuster.

multi-purpose Internet mail extensions (MIME)   A set of Internet functions that extends E-mail capabilities and allows computer files to be attached to E-mail messages.

multi-rater assessment   *See* three hundred sixty degree feedback.

multi-sided icon   Developed and patented by Apple's Advanced Technology group. An icon that produces a new view of an image when clicked on each side.

multi-source assessment (MSA)   A performance feedback system designed to improve the fairness and accuracy of appraisals by increasing the numbers and expanding the levels of assessors. The process can be automated to save the time of respondents and reduce the workload of administrative personnel.

multi-tasking   A system or program that is able to perform two or more tasks simultaneously.

multi-user   A system capable of accommodating users at several terminals.

multi-user dungeon (MUD)   Programmed conceptualizations of rooms, compartments, time zones, and worlds. Used in computer games.

Munchausen syndrome   Describes individuals who lie pathologically about symptoms and illnesses, devoting their time and effort to attempting to get admitted to or remain in the hospital. The condition affects the body but originates in the mind,

Murphy bed   In meeting management, a bed in a hotel room that retracts into the wall.

Murphy's Law   A tongue-in-cheek bromide that says,"If anything can go wrong, it will. If it does go wrong, it's sure to get worse."

muscular dystrophy   A disease that is hereditary, progressive, and produces a pattern of weakness of muscle groups. It takes several different forms; examples include Duchenne, Becker, Emery-Dreifus, facioscapulo humeral, limb-girdle, ocsular, oculopharyngeal, distal, and myotonic dystrophy. The primary cause of the disease is a genetic defect, which results in a gradual weakening and wasting of the muscles that may continue to advance over 20 or 30 years.

musculoskeletal disorder (MSD)   *See* repetitive strain injury.

musical instrument digital interface (MIDI)   A communications prototype for electronic-music equipment developed in 1982 which has since become available for computers. It revolutionized the recording industry by permitting many instruments to be centrally controlled just as if they were one electronic orchestra. MIDI consists of instructions for recreating a musical performance on devices like digital synthesizers by defining notes by parameters, such as pitch, velocity, and modulation. It differs from digital audio, which consists of sounds that are sampled from analog sources at various rates.

mutual learning   An integrated approach to learning and productivity improvement that involves face-to-face sharing of successes and failures, training materials, and business information by representatives, usually senior managers and executives, of several different organizations.

mutual wills   Separate legal documents, one for each spouse, prepared after they have reached agreement as to how their property will be disposed of following their death.

myelography (myelogram)   An invasive medical diagnostic procedure used to identify and locate abnormalities and injuries such as herniated disks (usually in the lumbar area) and tumors. The procedure involves the injection of contrast material into the space surrounding the spinal cord and the use of radiographic equipment to provide pictures for diagnosis.

Myers-Briggs Type Indicator (MBTI)
A highly popular psychological test, refined over a period of 4 years, used primarily but not exclusively in the corporate world by trainers and organization development specialists for personality assessment in team building and communications training. The MBTI divides people into 16 distinguishable personality types. Although highly popular, the test also has its critics who see it as encouraging managers to view personality tests as the easy answer to organization problems. The test is based on the work of Carl Jung and assumes that (1) personality is based on a four-dimensional framework; (2) scores on each dimension fall along a bimodal distribution; and (3) the judger/perceiver dimension is a key determinant of an individual's preferences.

myopia   Nearsightedness. A condition of the eye in which a person can see close objects but is unable to focus on objects farther away, resulting in "blurry" or "fuzzy" vision. It is caused by the shape of the eyeball, which causes light rays from objects to a focus before they reach the retina. The condition can be corrected with special lenses.

myotherapy   A form of physical therapy that uses trigger points to relieve the pain associated with various types of pain syndromes, such as fibromyalgia.

N

NAA 1. National Academy of Arbitrators.

NAAS National Association for Alternative Staffing.

NAB National Alliance of Business.

NABWE National Association of Black Women Entrepreneurs.

NACCRRA National Association of Child Care Resource and Referral Agencies.

NACE National Association of Colleges and Employers.

NAD National Association of the Deaf.

NADPT National Association of Desktop Publishers.

NAEP National Assessment of Educational Progress.

NAEYC National Association for the Education of Young Children.

NAF National Amputation Foundation.

NAFE National Association for Female Executives.

NAFTA North American Free Trade Agreement.

NAHR National Academy of Human Resources.

NAIEC National Association for Industry-Education Cooperation.

NAMI The National Alliance for the Mentally Ill.

NAPEO National Association of Professional Employer Organizations.

NAPFA National Association of Personal Financial Advisors.

NAPS National Association of Personnel Services.

NARE National Alliance for Restructuring Education.

NARFE National Association of Retired Federal Employees.

NARIC National Rehabilitation Information Center.

NAS Non-availability statement.

NASBE National Association of State Boards of Education.

NASE National Association for the Self-Employed.

NATSS National Association of Temporary and Staffing Services.

NAUS/SMW National Association for Uniformed Services/Society of Military Widows.

NAVEX Navy Exchange.

NAVH National Association for Visually Handicapped.

NAWBO National Association of Women Business Owners.

NBEA National Business Education Association.

NBPTS National Board for Professional Teaching Standards.

NBTA National Business Travel Association.

NC Numerical control.

NCADI National Clearinghouse for Alcohol and Drug Information.

NCBMP National Coalition of Black Meeting Planners.

NCD National Council on Disability.

NCI National Cancer Institute.

NCL National Coalition for Literacy.

NCLE	National Clearinghouse for ESL Literacy Education.	**NIL**	National Institute for Literacy.
NCOA	1. National Council on Aging. 2. Noncommissioned Officers Association.	**NIST**	The National Institute of Standards and Technology.
NCPD	National Catholic Office for Persons with Disabilities.	**NLA**	1. Norris-Laguardia Act of 1932. 2. National Literacy Act of 1991.
NCQA	National Committee for Quality Assurance.	**NLP**	Neurolinguistic programming.
		NLRA	National Labor Relations Acts of 1935 and 1937.
NCSA	National Cued Speech Association.	**NLRB**	National Labor Relations Board.
NCSTA	National and Community Service Trust Act of 1993.	**NLT**	No later than (Internet abbreviation).
NCYD	National Center for Youth with Disabilities.	**NLUS**	Navy League of the United States.
NDSS	National Down Syndrome Society.	**NMA**	National Management Association.
NEA	National Education Association.	**NMB**	National Mediation Board.
		NMFA	National Military Family Association.
NERA	Naval Enlisted Reserve Association.	**NMMHMO**	Network and mixed model health maintenance organization.
NESRA	The National Employee Services and Recreation Association.	**NMSS**	National Multiple Sclerosis Society.
NESS	National Easter Seal Society.	**NNF**	The National Neurofibromatosis Foundation, Inc.
NFB	National Federation of the Blind.		
NFIE	National Foundation for the Improvement of Education.	**NOAC**	Next operation as customer.
		NOBC	National Order of Battlefield Commissions.
NFTC	National Foreign Trade Council, Inc.	**NOCA**	National Organization for Competency Assurance.
NGAUS	National Guard Association of the United States.	**NOD**	National Organization on Disability.
NHCE	Non-highly compensated employees.	**NPD**	Navy Procurement Directive.
NHN	National Helpers Network, Inc.	**NQSO**	Nonqualified stock options.
NHP	National Health Program.	**NRA**	1. National Rehabilitation Association. 2. Naval Reserve Association.
NICD	The National Information Center on Deafness.		
NICHY	National Information Center for Children and Youth with Disabilities.	**NRIC**	National Rehabilitation Information Center.
		NRLYD	National Resource Library on Youth with Disabilities.
NIDCD	National Institute on Deafness and Other Communication Disorders.	**NSA**	National Speakers Association.
		NSBA	National School Boards Association.
NIDRR	National Institute on Disability & Rehabilitation Research.	**NSC**	National Safety Council.
NII	National Information Infrastructure.	**NSCIA**	National Spinal Cord Injury Association.

NSEE	National Society for Experiential Education.
NSPA	National Society of Public Accountants.
NTIS	National Technical Information Service.
NTL	National Training Laboratory Institute for Applied Behavioral Science.
NTOs	National Tourist Offices.
NTSC	National Television Standards Committee.
NWA	National Wellness Association.
NWVH	Not working very hard.

nannie An ages-old means of obtaining capable and responsible child care formerly used almost exclusively by wealthy parents. The use of nannies has become an alternative to traditional group child care arrangements. Nannies may be either live-in or non-live-in women, as young as 19 to as old as 70, who provide child care in the home for infants or small children or both. Some may have only a high school education; others may possess college undergraduate and graduate degrees.

nannie placement service A new child care benefit.

nannie tax Social Security taxes paid by employers of household workers (housekeepers and child-care workers) who earn $50 or more in wages in a quarter. To promote wider compliance with the tax law, the House has passed a bill that would raise the threshold for tax payments to $1,250 annually payable either through payroll deductions or one yearly when the employers file their federal income tax returns.

National Academy of Arbitrators (NAA)
A nonprofit honorary association with approximately 670 highly qualified and respected members who may be engaged directly as arbitrators. A non-profit professional and honorary international organization of approximately 670 arbitrators organized to foster high standards of integrity, competence, honor, and character among those engaged in the arbitration of industrial disputes on a professional basis. Members come from the United States, Canada, Australia, and New Zealand, with overseas correspondents in England, Belgium, Netherlands, Israel, Japan, France, Italy, Germany, Mexico, Finland, Wales, Sweden,

and United Kingdom. *Contact:* NAA, Operations Manager, 403 Lowder Bldg., Auburn University, AL 36849 (334/844-2817; Fax 334/844-1498; E-mail **ryan@business. auburn.edu**; URL **http://www.auburn. edu/~hollewh/**).

National Academy of Human Resources (NAHR) Formed in 1992 to recognize distinguished achievement in human resources. Annually selects human resource leaders as Fellows of the National Academy of Human Resources and a limited number of Distinguished Fellows and Honored Organizations. Fellows are individuals whose contributions to the advancement of knowledge human resources, overall contributions to the nation's productivity and global competitiveness, support of the broad principles and objectives of human resources, and overall achievement in human resource practice, management, and theory warrant recognition by their peers. *Contact:* NAHR, P.O. Box 4577, Sante Fe, NM 87502-4577 (505/988-8030).

National Affairs Award An award presented annually by the **American Society for Training and Development** to an individual who has given outstanding public service to the human resource development field while serving in the legislative or executive branches of the United States or state government or in any other national affairs/state policy-making role. Selected by the ASTD National Issues Committee. *Contact:* ASTD National Awards Program, Attn: Dawn Temple, 1640 King St., Box 1443, Alexandria, VA 22313-2043 (703/683-8100)

National Alliance for Restructuring Education (NARE) A partnership of three states, four city school districts, and leading national organizations committed to making the changes necessary to enable all but the most severely disabled students to meet high standards of achievement. The hallmark of its effort is the Certificate of Initial Mastery, a standard of accomplishment that is set as high as standards the best-performing countries expect of their students at about age 16. *Contact:* NARE, 700 Eleventh St., N.W., Ste. 750, Washington, DC 20001 (202/783-3668; Fax 202/783-3672; E-mail **nareinfo@mcee.org**; URL **http://www.ecs. org/ecs/2156.htm**).

The National Alliance for the Mentally Ill (NAMI) An organization of more than 10,000 parents, children, spouses, siblings, and friends of people with serious mental illnesses as well as those people themselves. NAMI is dedicated to the eradication of mental illness and improvement in the quality of life of those whose live are affected by those diseases. It advocates for the mentally ill people by bringing their problems to the attention of local, state, and federal governments. It provides information and resources to make it easier for families to deal with mental illness, and it supports research into causes, treatments, and cures. *Contact:* NAMI, 200 N. Glebe Rd., Ste. 1015, Arlington, VA 22204-3754 (800/950-6264 or 703/524-7600; Fax 703/524-9094; URL **http://www.nami.org**).

National Alliance of Business (NAB)

A business-led, non-profit organization dedicated to building a competitive American work force. In partnership with schools and businesses, the Alliance works in communities to design, implement, evaluate and replicate education and training programs that help students make a successful transition from school to the workplace. The Alliance also researches and chronicles best practices in school-to-work programs and disseminates this information to businesses around the country. *Contact:* NAB, 1201 New York Avenue, NW; Washington, DC 20005 (202/289-2888; Fax 202/289-1303; E-mail **info@nab.com**; URL **http://www.stw.ed. gov/rfi/nab.htm**).

National Amputation Foundation (NAF)

A nonprofit organization with 2,500 members and the largest amputee organization in the United States. Originally established to help veterans who lost a limb in World War I, NAF now serves serves both veterans and civilians of all ages and both sexes by providing legal counsel, vocational guidance, liaison with outside groups, psychological aid, training in the use of prosthetic devices, and publications. *Contact:* National Amputation Foundation, 38-40 Church St., Malverne, NY 11565 (516/887-3600; Fax 516/887-3667).

National and Community Service Trust Act of 1993 (NCSTA)

Amends the National and Community Service Act of 1990 to establish a Corporation for National Service, enhance opportunities for national service, and provide national service educational awards to persons participating in such service. Permits direct government loans to students (up to $100,000 over 5 years) to finance their college education as long as they pay it back with a small percentage of their income over time or with two or three years of national service within the United States. Participants will work for the federal minimum wage in community-designed program and, after two years of full-time service, be eligible for $9,450 in education grants. A new program provides full-time educational awards of $4,725 per year and allow recipients to work before, during, or after postsecondary education. Funds can be used to pay either current education expenses or repay federal student loans.

National Assessment of Educational Progress (NAEP)

A project mandated by Congress in the National Center for Education Statistics, an organization that measures the scholastic achievement of elementary, middle, and high school students to compare and analyze what is occurring in American schools. *Contact:* NAEP, P.O. Box 6710, Princeton, NJ 08541-6710 (800/223-0267; Fax 609/734-1878; E-mail **DRHodes@ets. org**; URL **http:///www.ed.gov/NCES/naep**).

National Association for Alternative Staffing (NAAS)

A nonprofit organization established to educate and assist members in all areas. Also works on the state and national level with governmental agencies, such as the IRS and the Department of Labor, to promote a climate of trust and cooperation. *Contact:* NAAS, 807 Brazos St., Ste. 201, Austin, TX 78701 (512/ 469-9014; E-mail **webmaster@netaci.com**; URL **http: //www.naasnet.org**).

National Association for Female Executives (NAFE)

A 200,000-member association that provides the resources and services — through education, networking, and public advocacy — to empower its members to achieve career success and financial security. Member benefits include the publication *Executive Female,* insurance programs, business start-up guides, financial planning programs, career development events, access to a Web site, and many corporate and travel discounts. It publishes *Executive Female* magazine, conducts conferences, and provides many other member services. *Contact:* NAFE, 30 Irving Place, Floor 5, New York, NY 10003 (212/477-2200; Fax 212/477-8215; URL **http://www.nafe.com**).

National Association for Industry-Education Cooperation (NAIEC)
A voluntary, non-profit organization, NAIEC is the nation's principal advocate for fostering industry-education cooperation/partnerships in furthering human resources/economic development and providing technical assistance on operation and programming related to school improvement. *Contact:* NAIEC, 235 Hendricks Blvd., Buffalo, NY 14226-3304 (716/634-7047; Fax 716/834-7047).

National Association for the Education of Young Children (NAEYC)   A nonprofit membership organization of over 90,000 members, NAEYC acts on behalf of children from birth through age eight by providing professional development opportunities and setting and promoting standards of practice for the early childhood professional. NAEYC also administers a voluntary accreditation system for early childhood programs. *Contact:* NAEYC, 1509 16th Street, NW, Washington, DC 20036 [800/424-2460 or 202/232-8777; Fax 202/328-1846; URL **http://www.social.com/health/nhic/data/hr1900/hr1972.html**).

National Association for the Self-Employed (NASE)   An organization of more than 300,000 entrepreneurs, consultants, and professionals established to support the ability of small businesses to compete and grow. Educates legislators on the needs of small businesses and business people, addresses members' educational, family, and business needs, and publishes *Self-Employed America,* a magazine on small business issues. *Contact:* NASE, National Headquarters, 2121 Precinct Line Road, Hurst, Texas 76054 (800/232-NASE; Fax 817/428-4210; URL **http://www.nselfemployed.ase.org**).

National Association for Uniformed Services/Society of Military Widows (NAUS/SMW)   A military/veterans association of 160,000 members representing all services, ranks, grades, and components — Army, Navy, Marines, Air Force, Coast Guard, Public Health Services, National Oceanic and Atmospheric Administration — officer and enlisted, reserve, National Guard, other veterans, their families, and survivors. Its mission is to represent the interests of the military/veterans community in government by supporting legislation that upholds the security of the United States, sustains the morale of the uniformed services, and

provides fair and equitable consideration of all. *Contact:* NAUS/SMW, 5535 Hempstead Way, Springfield, VA 22151-4094 (800/842-3451 or 703/750-1342; Fax 703/354-4380; E-mail **naus@ix.netcom.com**; URL **http://www.penfed.org/naus/home.htm**).

National Association for Visually Handicapped (NAVH)   An organization of 12,500 members/friends that provides persons with partial vision visual aids, information and referral services, counsel and guidance, and free-by-mail large print library loans and newsletters for adults and children. Works with families, professionals, and paraprofessionals dealing with the partially seeing. *Contact:* NAVH, 22 West 21 St., New York, NY 10010 (212/889-3141;Fax 212/727-2931; E-mail **staff@navh.org**; URL **http://www.navh.org**).

National Association of Black Women Entrepreneurs (NABWE)   A nonprofit organization that provides business and marketing education, financial assistance, and training for women. Sponsors an annual national conference and exposition and four regional conferences. *Contact:* NABWE, Dr. Marilyn French-Hubbard, Executive Director, P.O. Box 1375, Detroit, MI 48231 (313/341-7400).

National Association of Child Care Resource and Referral Agencies (NACCRRA)   A national membership organization of over 400 community child care resource and referral agencies (CCR&RAs) in all 50 states. NACCRRA's mission is to promote the growth and development of high quality resource and referral services and to exercise leadership to build a diverse, high quality child care system with parental choice and equal access for all families. CCR&RAs work closely with community leaders, including employers and unions. NACCRRA and its members offer innovative guidance to policy makers on service delivery and regulatory issues and strategies. Activities include technical assistance; training for referral counselors; information sharing; public education; and coordination of legislation initiatives. *Contact:* NACCRRA, 1319 F St., N.W., Ste. 810, Washington, DC 20004-1106 (202/393-5501; Fax 202/393-1109; E-mail **HN5018@handsnet.org**)

National Association of Colleges and Employers (NACE)   A nonprofit association of human resource professionals and career services counselors in 1,600 member colleges and universities and 1,300 employer organizations involved in career planning and employment of college graduates. Serves as the principal clearinghouse of information of the college-educated work force. NACE provides research and information through annual employer/college surveys, a quarterly survey of starting salary offers to new college graduates, a quarterly journal and biweekly newsletter, and *Job Choices*, a job search and career opportunities guide for students. *Contact:* NACE, 62 Highland Ave., Bethlehem, PA 18017-9085 (610/868-1421; Fax 610/868-0208; E-mail **mimi@ jobweb. org**; URL **http:www.jobweb.org**).

National Association of Desktop Publishers (NADTP) The largest desktop publishing trade association in the U.S. Provides networking, information, and member support services on all aspects of desktop-to-print technologies, from system configuration to illustration, digital photography, typography, design, and layout, imagesetting, scanning, color separation, laser printing, digital proofing, and offset printing. Publishes the *NADTP Journal*, a monthly journal. *Contact:* NADTP, 462 Old Boston St., Topsfield, MA 01983 (800/874-4113 or 508/887-7900; Fax 508/887-6117; URL **http://www.nadtp.com**).

National Association of Personnel Services (NAPS) A trade association of 1,300 member firms that provide private permanent placement and temporary staffing services throughout the United States. The mission of NAPS is to serve, protect, and inform members regarding legislative and regulatory issues affecting personnel services. The Association is dedicated to the professional advancement of the private personnel services industry through continuing education, public information, and leadership. Offers two professional designations: **Certified Personnel Consultant** and **Certified Temporary-Staffing Specialist**. *Contact:* NAPS, 3133 Mt. Vernon Ave., Alexandria, VA 22305 (703/684-0180; Fax 703/684-0071; E-mail **membership@napsweb.org**; URL **http//www.napsweb.org**).

National Association of Personal Financial Advisors (NAPFA) An organization of fee-only financial advisors, academics and students who are not associated with brokers/dealers and who are engaged in activities

directly related to the business of providing comprehensive financial advice. The Association is devoted to promoting consumer and industry awareness of fee-only financial planning through networking, publications, and national and regional conferences. Applicants for full membership must submit a comprehensive financial plan and meet education and experience requirements. *Contact:* NAPFA,355 West Dundee Rd., Buffalo Grove, IL 60089, 847/537-7722; Fax 847/537-7740; E-mail **745354.1052@compuserve. com**; URL **http://www.napfa.org**).

National Association of Professional Employer Organizations (NAPEO) Established to enhance professionalism in the professional employer services industry (companies that provide integrated business services which manage critical human resource responsibilities and employer risks for its clients). Formerly called "leasing" companies. *Contact:* NAPEO, 901 Pitt St., Ste. 350, Alexandria, VA 22314 (703/836-0466; Fax 703/836-0976; E-mail **info@napeo.org**; URL **http:www.podi.com/peo/**).

National Association of Retired Federal Employees (NARFE) A national voluntary association of about 500,000 members in more than 1700 chapters. Membership is open to civilians with at least five years vested service in any agency of the Federal or DC governments including retirees, employees, former employees, and spouses and surviving spouses of persons eligible to join NARFE. Its purpose is to promote and preserve the vested retirement interests and general welfare of its members and secure legislation perfecting the civilian federal retirement law. The association also provides a wide range of member services. *Contact:*: NARFE, 1533 New Hampshire Ave., N.W., Washington, DC 20036-1279 (202/234-0832; Fax 202/797-9698; E-mail **narfehq@ aol.com**; URL **http://www.narfe.org**).

National Association of State Boards of Education (NASBE) A nonprofit, private association of 650 members that represents state and territorial boards of education. Its principal objectives are to strengthen state leadership in education policy making; promote excellence in the education of all students; advocate quality of access to educational opportunity; and assure responsible lay governance of public education.

Contact: NASBE, 1012 Cameron St., Alexandria, VA 22314 (703/684-4000; Fax 703/836-2313; E-mail **boards@nasbt.org**; URL **http://www.NASBE.org**).

National Association of Temporary and Staffing Services (NATSS) Originally established to ensure that competent temporary help services were available to business and industry while simultaneously providing flexible employment opportunities to the work force. NATSS now represents more than 1,400 staffing companies that operate approximately 9,000 offices throughout the United States. NATSS members are active in all types of staffing services, including professional employer services (employee leasing), managed services (often called "outsourcing"), payrolling, placement services, temporary-to-full-time services, long-term staffing, and others. *Contact:* NATSS, 119 South Saint Asaph Street, Alexandria, VA 22314-3119 (703-549-6287; Fax 703-549-4808; E-mail **natss@natss.com**; URL **http://www.natss.com/staffing/**).

National Association of the Deaf (NAD) The nation's largest organization for safeguarding the accessibility and civil rights of 28 million deaf and hard of hearing Americans in education, employment, health care, and telecommunications. Focuses on grassroots advocacy and empowerment, captioned media, deafness-related information and publications, legal assistance, policy development and research, public awareness, and youth leadership development. *Contact:* National Association of the Deaf, 814 Thayer Ave., Silver Spring, MD 20910-4500 [301/587-1788 (voice); 301/587-1789 (TTY; Fax 301/587-1791; E-mail **NADHQ@juno.com**; URL **http://www.nad.org**)].

National Association of Women Business Owners (NAWBO) A nonprofit organization that provides a strong and continuing voice and vision for women business owners within the economic, social, and political communities. Its mission is to strengthen the wealth creating capacity of members, promote economic development, create innovative and effective changes in the business culture, build strategic alliances, coalitions, and affiliations, transform public policy, and influence opinion makers. Local chapters provide managerial training and assistance. *Contact:* NAWBO, 1413 K St., N.W., Ste. 637,

Washington, DC 20005 (301/608-2590; URL **http://www2.nawbo.org/nawbo**).

National Board for Professional Teaching Standards (NBPTS) A board organized to establish high and rigorous standards for what teachers should know and be able to do, certify teachers who meet those standards, and advance related education reforms to improve student learning in American schools. *Contact:* NBPTS, 300 River Place, Ste. 3600, Detroit, MI 48207 (313/259-0830; Fax 313/259-0973; URL **http://www.mnea.org**). For information about National Board Certification, call 800/22-TEACH

National Business Education Association (NBEA) A professional association of about 12,500 members devoted exclusively to serving individuals and groups engaged in instruction, administration, research, and dissemination of information for and about business. NBEA is committed to the advancement of the professional interests and competencies of its members and provides programs and services that enhance members' professional growth and development. *Contact:* NBEA, 1914 Association Drive, Reston, VA 22091-1596 (703/860-8300; Fax 703/620-4483; E-mail **bmurphy@vax2.winona.msus.edu**; URL **http://www.thomson.com/partners/nbea/default.html**).

National Business Travel Association (NBTA) An organization of 1,800 business travel managers, primarily from the Fortune 1000 (direct members), suppliers (allied members), and other travel-related companies and individuals (associate members). NBTA's mission is to enhance the value of travel managers in meeting corporate travel needs and financial goals, provide a forum for members to network, cultivate a positive public image for the industry, educate members about the industry, and promote the safety, security, efficiency, and quality of travel. *Contact:* NBTA, 1650 King St., Ste. 401, Alexandria, VA 22314 (703/684-0836 Fax 703/684-0263; E-mail **info@nbta.org**; URL **http://www.nbta.org/nbta**).

National Cancer Institute (NCI) One of 17 Institutes of the National Institutes of Health. The National Cancer Institute is the Federal Government's principal agency for cancer research and training. Its mission is to eliminate cancer and prevent the devastation that cancer imposes on individuals, families, and society as a whole. *Contact:* NCI, Executive Plaza North, Rm 330, Bethesda, MD 20892 (800/4-CANCER or 301/496-8520; Fax 301/402-0816; E-mail **msears@nih.gov**; URL **http://www.nci.nih.gov/**).

National Catholic Office for Persons with Disabilities (NCPD) A nonprofit organization established to foster the inclusion of people with disabilities in all the celebrations and obligations of the Roman Catholic Church. The organization of 3,700 members works through a network of diocesan directors who oversee access and inclusion at the parish level. *Contact:* NCPD, 401 Michigan Ave., N.E., P.O. Box 29113, Washington, DC 20017 [202/529-2933 (Voice/TDD) Fax 202/529-4678].

National Center for Youth with Disabilities (NCYD) An information and resource center focusing on adolescents with chronic illness and disabilities. Its mission is to raise awareness of the needs of adolescents with chronic illness disabilities, expand the knowledge and involvement of those who provide services to youth, and promote programs and strategies that enhance the ability of adolescents and young adults to grow, develop, work, and participate in community life to their fullest capacity. Provides bibliographic and program services, training materials, publications, and technical assistance. *Contact:* NCYD, University of Minnesota, Box 721, 420 Delaware St. SE, Minneapolis, MN 55455 (612/626-2825; Fax 612/6626-2134; E-mail **ncyd@gold.tc. umn.edu**; URL **http://www.peds.umn. edu/Centers/ncyd**).

National Clearinghouse for Alcohol and Drug Information (NCADI) Established by the Office for Substance Abuse and Prevention as a national resource of up-to-date print and audiovisual materials about alcohol and other drugs. *Contact:* NCADI, P.O. Box 2345, Rockville, MD 20852-2345 (800/729-6686 or 301/468-2600; Fax 301/468-6433; E-mail **info@prevline.health.org**; URL **http://www.health.org**).

National Clearinghouse for ESL Literacy Education (NCLE) An adjunct of **ERIC** clearing house established at the Center for applied Linguistics. Its mission is to provide practitioners and others with timely information on adult ESL literacy education. Collects, evaluates, and abstracts documents in the scope of adult ESL literacy education and native language literacy for the ERIC database. *Contact:* NCLE, U.S. Department of Education, 1118 22nd St., N.W, Washington, DC 20037 (202/429-9292, Ext. 200; Fax 202/659-5641; E-mail **ncle@cal.org**; URL **http://www.cal.org/ncle**).

The National Coalition for Literacy (NCL) A consortium of 11 businesses and associations that seeks to promote the cause of literacy. Fosters collaboration at national, state, and local levels among public and private institutions and serves as an information and communications source for the public and for external organizations. *Contact:* Coalition for Literacy, c/o American Library Association, 50 East Huron St., Chicago IL 60611 (312/280-3217) or NCL Information Center, P.O. Box 81826, Lincoln, NE 68501-1826 (800/228-8813 or 402-464-0602).

National Coalition of Black Meeting Planners (NCBMP) An organization of 925 members established (1) to assist the advancement of Black meeting planners by sharing with them the wealth of information available from their peers, hotel, travel, and convention bureau representatives, consultants, and other suppliers, and (2) to enhance the professional status of Black meeting planners by providing educational opportunities in support of their becoming Certified Meeting Professionals (CMP) *Contact:* NCBMP, 8630 Fenton St., Ste. 126, Silver Spring, MD 20910 (202/628-3952; Fax 301/588-0011; E-mail **103360.152@compuserve.com**).

National Committee for Quality Assurance (NCQA) An independent, not-for-profit organization dedicated to assessing and reporting on the quality of managed care plans, including **health maintenance organizations**. NCQA's mission is to provide information that enables purchasers and consumers of managed health care to distinguish among plans based on quality. Efforts of the Committee are organized around two activities: accreditation and performance measurement. Evaluates and accredits health plans according to 50 nationally recognized standards for quality in six categories: quality management and improvement, physician credentials, members' rights and responsibilities, preventive health services, medical records, and utilization management. *Contact:* NCQA, 2000 L St., N.W., Ste 500, Washington, DC 20036 (202/955-3500 or 800/839-6487; Fax 202/955-3599; URL address, **http://www. ncqa.org**).

National Council on Disability (NCD)

An independent federal agency that makes recommendations to the President and Congress on issues affecting 49 million Americans with disabilities and their families. *Contact:* NCD, 1331 F St., N.W., Ste. 1050, Washington, DC 20004 [202/272-2074 (voice); 202/272-2074 (TT); Fax 202/272-2022; E-mail **mquigley@ncd.gov**; URL **http://www.ncd.gov**].

National Cued Speech Association (NCSA)

Provides information and support services regarding the use of Cued Speech for persons with hearing, speech, and language needs, their families, and professionals. *Contact:* NCSA, Nazareth College of Rochester, 4245 East Ave. Rochester, NY 14617 [800/459-3529 (voice/TTY); Fax 716/586-2452; E-mail **NCSA@naz.edu**].

National Down Syndrome Society (NDSS)

An organization that supports research regarding genetic, behavioral, and learning problems associated with Down syndrome; sponsors scientific symposia and conferences for parents and professionals; advocates on behalf of families and individuals affected by this condition; provides information and referral services through its toll-free number; and develops and disseminates educational materials. *Contact:* National Down Syndrome Society, 666 Broadway, New York, NY 10012-2317 (800/221-4602; 212/460-9930; Fax 212/979-2873; URL **http://www.ndss.org**).

National Easter Seal Society (NESS)

A nationwide network of 135 affiliate societies serving 50 states, the District of Columbia and Puerto Rico. The Societies operate nearly 500 program service sites to meet the needs of more than one million people annually. Established a leadership role in developing quality rehabilitation programs, promoting assistive technology, supporting the enactment of critical legislation and programs, and producing award-winning public education campaigns for people with disabilities, *Contact:* NESS, 230 W. Monroe, Ste. 1800, Chicago, Ill 60606 [312/726-6200; 312.726. 4258 (TDD); Fax 312.726.1494; E-mail **nessinfo@seals.com**; URL **http://www.seals.com**).

National Education Association (NEA)

A union and professional organization of 2.2 million elementary and secondary school teachers and administrators, college and university professors, counselors, and others concerned with education. Seeks support for pubic education, professional excellence and freedom, and economic and professional security for all educators. *Contact:* NEA, 1201 16th St., N.W., Washington, DC 20036 (202/833-4000; URL **http://www.nea.org**).

The National Employee Services and Recreation Association (NESRA)

A nonprofit organization established to represent over 10 million employees. NESRA is dedicated to the principle that employee services, fitness, and recreation programs are essential to sound business management. NESRA promotes programs that serve to improve relations between employees and management, increase overall productivity, boost morale, and reduce absenteeism and turnover. *Contact:* NESRA 2211 York Rd., Ste. 207, Oak Brook, IL 60521-2371 (630/368-1280; Fax 630/368-1286; E-mail **NESRAHQ@aol.com**; URL **http://www.nesra.org**).

National Energy Policy Act of 1992

Legislation, signed by President Bush October 24, 1992, that focuses on conservation and energy sources other than fossil fuel and is designed to reduce U.S. reliance on oil imports. The bill provides tax incentives for renewable energy sources, for some conservation measures, and for independent oil and gas producers. It also calls for new efficiency standards on lights and other equipment, makes it easier for the nuclear power industry to build reactors, and calls for more fleet vehicles by the end of the decade to use fuels other than gasoline.

National Federation of the Blind (NFB)

A consumer group of 50,000 blind Americans whose purpose is to achieve the complete integration of the blind into society by removing legal, economic, and social discrimination, educating the public to new concepts concerning blindness, and ensuring the right of all blind people to exercise to the fullest their individual talents and capacities and work along with their sighted neighbors in the professions, common callings, skilled trades, and regular occupations. With the U.S. Department of Labor, NFB sponsors **Job Opportunities for the Blind**, a nationwide employment service for employers and blind applicants. *Contact:* NFB, 1800 Johnson St., Baltimore, MD 21230 (410/659-9314; Fax 410/685-5653).

National Foreign Trade Council, Inc.

The oldest and largest trade organization in the United States with 550 member companies, including all of the Fortune 500 and 100 other companies beginning to enter the international arena. Focuses on international human resources and serves as a forum for thought leadership. *Contact:* NFTC, Rockefeller Center, 1270 Avenue of the Americas, New York, NY 10020-1702 (212/399-7128; Fax 212/399-7144) or NFTC, 1625 K St., NW, Washington DC 20006-1604 (202/887-0278; Fax 202/452-8160; URL **http://www. ahrm.org/nftc/nftc.htm**).

The National Foundation for the Improvement of Education (NFIE)   A nonprofit foundation, created by the National Education Association, dedicated to improving the quality of education through the empowerment of teachers. It assists teachers to design and implement better learning environments for their students and become leaders in the national education reform movement. *Contact:* NFIE, 1201 16th St., N.W., Washington, DC 20036 (202/822-7840; E-mail **MWu@nea.org**).

National Guard Association of the U.S. (NGAUS)   An association of 58,000 current and former members of of the Army and Air National guard, corporations, and individuals. Its mission is to maintain the freedom and security of the nation by guaranteeing a strong national defense through the provision of a vital and dynamic National Guard, improve the readiness of the National Guard, and provide personnel benefits and entitlements for its members. *Contact:* NGAUS, One Massachusetts Ave., N.W., Washington, DC 20001 (202/789-0031; Fax 202/682-9358).

National Health Awards   *See* C. Everett Koop National Health Awards.

National Health Program (NHP)   A program similar to the Canadian system of national health care introduced by Physicians for a National Health Program. A single insurer would be set up in each state and operate in accordance with national standards enforced locally. All Americans would be covered for medically necessary services including prescription drugs and long-term care. Fees for services would be negotiated by the state insurance company and representatives of health care providers in the state. Physicians would submit claims directly to the state health plan. The plan would be financed by payroll tax contributions which would go into a public health care trust fund. It would replace current

employer and employee premiums for private medical insurance.

National Helpers Network, Inc. (NHN)   A national resource for service-learning in schools and community-based agencies. Works to make service learning a possibility for every young person. Service learning, combining meaningful work with structured reflection, provides adolescents with opportunities to effect change in themselves and their communities. The Network assists schools and agencies to meet the developmental needs of adolescents through program development, staff development, and technical assistance, and information-sharing. *Contact:* NHN, 245 Fifth Ave., Ste. 1705, New York, NY 10016-8728 (800/646-4623 or 212/679-2482; Fax 212/679-7461; E-mail **helpnet@igc.apc.org**).

National Information Center for Children and Youth with Disabilities (NICHY)   Provides sources of information and assistance to parents, educators, care-givers, advocates, and others in helping children and youth with disabilities to become participating members of the community *Contact:* NICHY, P.O. Box 1492, Washington, DC 20013 (800/695-0285 or 202/884-8200: Fax 202/884-8441; E-mail **nichy@aol.org**).

National Information Center on Deafness (NICD)   Serves as a resource center providing information on all aspects of deafness. NICD collects, develops, and disseminates vital, up-to-date information on deafness and hearing loss, and organizations, services, and programs related to people with hearing loss. *Contact:* NICD, Gallaudet University, 800 Florida Ave., N.E., Washington, DC 20002-3695 [202/651-5051 (voice); 202/ 651-5052 (TTY); Fax 202/651-5054; E-mail **nicd@gallux.gallaudet.edu**; URL **http:// www.gallaudet.edu/~nicd**].

National Information Infrastructure (NII)   The federal version of the **Information Superhighway**, composed of telephone, broadcast, cable, and electronics networks, most of which were created by private companies. Offers promise of ultimately providing business, government agencies, hospitals, homes, libraries, and schools access to voice, data, full-motion video, and multimedia.

National Institute for Disability and Rehabilitation Research   A division of the U.S. Department of Education. Has established ten regional centers to provide technical assistance and training for the implementation of the Americans with Disabilities Act of 1990. *Contacts:* in CT, MA, NH, RI, and VT, 207/780-4430; in NJ, NY, and PR, 609/392-4004; in DC, DE, MD, PA, VA, and WV, 703/525-3268; in AL, FL, GA, KY, MS, NC, SC, TN, 404/888-0022; in IL, MI, MN, WI, 312/413-7756 ; in AR, LA, NM, OK, and TX, 713/520-0232; in AK, ID, OR, and WA, 206/438-3168; in IA, KS, NE, and MO, 314/882-3807; in CO, MT, ND, SD, UT, and WY, 719/444-0252; in AZ, CA, HI, NV, and Pacific Basin, 415/465-7884.

National Institute for Literacy (NIL) Established to execute responsibilities listed in the **National Literacy Act of 1991**, which will enable every adult with literacy needs to receive services of the highest quality. The Institute advances the nation's agenda with special emphasis on building public consensus and policy, monitoring programs, sponsoring initiatives, disseminating information on programs and research pertinent to literacy, and building interagency collaboration at the federal and state levels. *Contact:* NIL, 800 Connecticut Ave., N.W., Ste. 200, Washington, DC 20006 (202/632-1500; URL **http://www.nifl.gov/**).

The National Institute of Standards and Technology (NIST) A non-regulatory federal agency within the Commerce Department's Technology Administration. Its primary mission is to promote economic growth by working with industry to develop and apply technology, measurements, and standards. NIST manages the **Malcolm Baldrige National Quality Award** program. *Contact:* NIST, U.S. Department of Commerce Technology Administration, Route 270 and Quince Orchard Rd., Administration Bldg., Rm. A 537, Gaithersburg, MD 20899-0001 (301/975-2036; Fax 301/948-3716; E-mail **oqp@nist.gov**; URL **http://www.quality.nist.gov/**)

National Institute on Deafness and Other Communication Disorders Clearinghouse (NIDCD) An office of the National Institutes of Health, U.S. Department of Health and Human Services, whose mission is to support biomedical and behavioral research and research training in the seven areas of human communication. Established the Clearinghouse as a national resource center for information and resources on the normal and disordered mechanisms of hearing, balance, smell, taste, voice, speech, and

language for health professionals, patients, industry, and the public. *Contact:* NIDCD Clearinghouse, 1 Communication Ave., Bethesda, MD 20892-3456 [800/241-1044 (voice) or 800/241-1055 (TDD/TT); Fax 301/907-8830; E-mail **nidcd@aeric.com**; URL **http://www.nih.gov/nidcd**].

National Institute on Disability & Rehabilitation Research (NIDRR) A part of the **Office of Special Education and Rehabilitative Services,** NIDRR provides leadership and support for comprehensive and coordinated national and international programs of disability and rehabilitation research. *Contact:* NIDRR, OSERS/ED, 330 C St., S.W., Room 3060 Switzer Bldg, Washington, DC 20202-8133 [202/205-8241 or 202/205-8723 (voice/TTY)].

National Labor Relations Act of 1935 (NLRA) An Act increasing government power to ensure employee collective bargaining rights and prohibiting management from engaging in the following unfair labor practices: (1) interfering with, restraining, or coercing employees in the exercise of their right to join or assist in the organization of a union or to refrain from doing so; (2) dominating or interfering with the formation or administration of a labor organization, or contributing financially or otherwise supporting it; (3) discriminating in hiring or tenure of employment or imposing any term or condition of employment to encourage or discourage membership in any labor organization; (4) discharging or otherwise discriminating against employees because they have given testimony under the Act; and (5) refusing to bargain collectively with representatives of its employees. The Act also created the **National Labor Relations Board** to supervise and certify representation elections and prevent unfair labor practices. It also authorized the Board to appoint a representative in court cases involving unions to investigate, prosecute, and judge. Amended by the **Labor Management Relations Act of 1947** (Taft-Hartley), the **Labor-Management Reporting and Disclosure Act of 1959** (Landrum-Griffin), and the Labor Management Cooperation Act of 1978.

National Labor Relations Act of 1947 (NLRA) An act administered by the **National Labor Relations Board** and general counsel. The legislation made it the responsibility of the President, subject to senate confirmation, to appoint a general counsel to a four-year term to serve as investigator and prosecutor in court cases involving unions, thereby protecting the general counsel's autonomy. The Act applies to virtually all industries involved in interstate commerce with a few exceptions.

National Labor Relations Board (NLRB)
A board created by the Wagner Act (**National Labor Relations Act of 1935**) to supervise and certify representation elections and prevent unfair labor practices. The Board is authorized to act only after a petition is filed to request an election or register a charge of unfair labor practice. NLRB representatives monitor the balloting in elections to ensure that only eligible employees vote and count the ballots. The Board issues a certificate recognizing the union as the bargaining agent for the employees when a majority of the eligible employees voted for it. The Board is also authorized to prevent unfair labor practices or order the termination of such practices.

National Labor Relations Board v. Curtis Matheson Scientific Inc. A 1990 Supreme Court decision that upheld an NLRB policy barring companies from assuming that workers hired as replacements during a strike were instinctively opposed to the union. The ruling had the effect of making it more difficult for employers to terminate negotiations on the basis of a lost union majority.

National Labor Relations Board v. Town & Country Electric Inc. A 1995 Supreme Court ruling that individuals paid by labor unions to find employment at nonunion job sites and to organize the work force by **salting** were still considered employees and entitled to protection under the NLRB.

National Leadership Coalition for Health Care Reform (NLCHCR) An alliance of some of the country's biggest unions, U.S. corporations (Chrysler Corporation, Bethlehem Steel, and food, utility, and paper companies), and two former presidents (Gerald R. Ford and Jimmy Carter) that has proposed a plan for a broad restructuring of health care. The plan would require all employers to provide private health insurance to workers or pay a payroll tax of 7 percent, matched by an employee tax of 1.75 percent, to help the government provide the coverage — a so-called "**pay or play**" plan. Workers not covered on the job and the unemployed would receive private insurance policies purchased for them by the states using funds from the 7 percent tax and related taxes. To reduce costs, a government board would set an annual target ceiling for national health spending and set payment rates for all physicians and hospitals.

National Literacy Act of 1991 (NLA)
Legislation designed to enhance the literacy and basic skills of adults and ensure that all all adults acquire the basic skills needed to function effectively and achieve the greatest possible opportunity in their work lives. The Act provides funds for research and quality program delivery at the federal, state, and local levels involving public, community-based, volunteer, business, and industry programs.

National Management Association (NMA)
A 40,000-member association of managers and those who aspire to management positions. NMA sponsors a variety of training programs, team building, and monthly meetings and, through its chapters, works with inhouse HR departments to improve HR programs and services. *Contact:* NMA, 2210 Arbor Blvd., Dayton, OH 45439 (937/294-0421; Fax 937/294-2374; E-mail **NMA1sue@aol.com**; URL **http://www.cris.com/~nmal/INDEX.SHT**).

National Mediation Board (NMB) A mediation board that only deals with the railways and airlines. *See also* American Arbitration Association; National Academy of Arbitrators; Federal Mediation and Conciliation Service.

National Military Family Association (NMFA)
A national organization dedicated to identifying and resolving issues of concern to military families. Its mission is to serve military and other uniformed service families through education, information and advocacy. Membership is open to all uniformed service (active duty, retired, and reserve) families and interested civilians. *Contact::* NMFA, 6000 Stevenson Avenue, Suite 304, Alexandria, VA 22304-3526 (703/823-6632; Fax: 703/751-4857; E-mail: **iamnmfa@aol.com**).

National Multiple Sclerosis Society (NMSS)
An organization that funds research in multiple sclerosis and provides information (brochures, newsletters, and phone contacts), individual, group, and family counseling, and self-help support groups for patients and their families. Provides help in obtaining adaptive equipment and short/long-term

equipment loans. *Contact:* NMSS, 733 Third Ave., New York, NY 10017-3288 (800/FIGHT MS; Fax 212/986-7981; E-mail **info@nmss. org;** URL **http://www.nmss.org**).

The National Neurofibromatosis Foundation, Inc. (NNF) A nonprofit organization with approximately 31,000 associates in all 50 states (23 chapters) and 51 other countries. Its purposes are to (1) sponsor research aimed at finding the cause and cure for both types of neurofibromatosis, NF1 and NF2; (2) promote the development of clinical activities which assure individuals with the disease ready access to the best medical care; (3) develop programs to increase public awareness of neurofibromatosis; and (4) provide support services for patients and their families. *Contact:* National Neurofibromatosis Foundation, Inc., 95 Pine St., 16th Floor,New York, NY 10005 (800/323-7938 or 212/460-8980; E-mail **NNFF@aol.com;** URL **http:// neurofibromatosis.org/**)

National Order of Battlefield Commissions (NOBC) An organization of approximately 1,000 members open to any individual of any service who was commissioned in the armed forces of the United States as a result of combat action. Its mission is to support a strong and responsive national defense by supporting those Americans who follow our flag. *Contact:* NOBC, 4403 Robertson Blvd., Alexandria, VA 22309-3231 (703/780-1753; Fax 703/780-1753).

National Organization for Competency Assurance (NOCA) An organization numbering 120 members. INOCA's mission is to provide a forum for all types of practitioners and organizations interested in learning more about competency assurance and certification. *Contact:* NOCA, 1200 19th St., N.W., Ste. 300, Washington, DC 20036-2422 (202/857-1165; Fax 202/223-4579).

National Organization on Disability (NOD) A private nonprofit organization supported by the contributions of corporations, foundations, and individuals. Its purpose is to increase the acceptance and participation in all aspects of life of all men, women, and children with disabilities. NOD's principal programs are the Community Partnership Program, National Organization Partnership Program, The CEO Council Program, and the Religion and Disability Program. *Contact:* NOD, 910 16th St., N.W., Ste. 600, Washington, DC 20006.

[202/293-5960 (voice); 202/293-5968 (TDD); Fax 202/293-7999; URL **http:// www.nod.org**].

National Patient Self-Determination Act of 1991 Effective December 1, 1991, requires hospitals, nursing facilities, hospices, and other health agencies to furnish information to patients or residents about their right to indicate their wishes regarding the use or refusal of medical care, including life-sustaining equipment and procedures.

National Rehabilitation Association (NRA) Provides referral to more than 400 accessibility surveyors nationwide who can assist employers to meet ADA accessibility guidelines, remove physical and attitudinal barriers, conduct accessibility surveys, and train employers to conduct such surveys. Offers training programs relating to the employment of people with disabilities, and publishes guidelines on accessibility. *Contact:* NRA, 633 S. Washington, St., Alexandria,, VA 22314 (703/836-0850).

National Rehabilitation Information Center (NARIC) A library and information center on disability and rehabilitation serving educators, allied health professionals, administrators, physicians, rehabilitation counselors, information professionals, students, and consumers. NARIC collects and disseminates the results of federally funded research projects. The collection also includes commercially published books, journal articles, and audiovisual materials, totaling 47,000 documents, on all aspects of disability and rehabilitation. *Contact:* NARIC, 8455 Colesville Rd., Ste. 935, Silver Spring, MD 20910-3319 [1-800/346-2742; 301/588-9284; Fax 301/587-1967; URL **http://www.naric. com/naric**).

National Report on Human Resources A newsletter published four times per year by the American Society for Training and Development, free to members. Address: ASTD, 1640 King St., Box 1443, Alexandria, VA 22313-2043 (703/683-8100).

National Resource Library on Youth with Disabilities (NRLYD) A database that provides information related to adolescents, disability, and transition. Contains four files: bibliographic, programs, training/education, and technical assistance. *Contact:* National Resource Library on Youth with Disabilities, National Center for Youth with Disabilities,

University of Minnesota, Box 721, 420 Delaware St., SE, Minneapolis, MN 55455 (612/626-2825, Fax 612/626-2134; E-mail **nycd@gold.tc.umn.edu**; URL **http://www. peds.umn.edu/Centers/ncyd**).

National Safety Council (NSC) A not-for-profit nongovernmental public service organization of 13,400 members devoted to the reduction of preventable deaths, injuries, and illnesses. *Contact:* National Safety Council, 1121 Spring Lake Dr., Itasca, IL 60143 (630/285-1121).

National School Boards Association (NSBA) A federation of all state school boards associations in the United States and the boards of education of Hawaii, the District of Columbia, and the U.S. Virgin Islands. Through this structure, NSBA represents and helps to serve American education through school board leadership. Its mission is to foster excellence and equity in public education through school board leadership. *Contact:* NSBA, 1680 Duke St., Alexandria, VA 22314 (703/838-6722; Fax 703/683-7590; E-mail **info@nsba.org**; URL **http://www.nsba.org/**).

National Science Scholars Program (NSSP) A scholarship program for graduating high school seniors, or individuals obtaining the equivalent of a certificate of graduation, who have demonstrated excellence and achievement in the physical, life, or computer sciences, mathematics, or engineering. Scholarships of up to $5,000 per year or the cost of attendance (whichever is less) for up to five years of study.

National Skills Standards Act of 1994 Establishes a National Skills Standards Board to (1) stimulate the development and adoption of a voluntary national system of skill standards that will result in increased productivity, economic growth, and American economic competitiveness; (2) assist employers to evaluate the skills of prospective employees and to train current employees; (3) enable workers to obtain certification of their skills to protect against dislocation, pursue career advancement, or reenter the work force; and (4) help those offering training and education program to determine appropriate services.

National Skills Standards Board A 20-member board established by the **Goals 2000: Educate America Act of 1994** to identify the work skills needed for certain jobs and develop skill standards for those jobs. Initial standards, reflecting core, concentration, and specialty knowledge and skills, will

be developed for manufacturing, installation, and repair; wholesale and retail sales; and business and administrative services. Members include two neutral, qualified HR professionals, eight business representatives, six at-large members (representing educational institutions, community-based organizations, and state and local governments), the chair of the National Education Standards and Improvement Council, and three Cabinet members (secretaries of Labor, Education, and Commerce).

National Society for Experiential Education (NSEE) A nonprofit association of 1,800 educators and community leaders established to serve as a national resource center for the development and improvement of experiential education programs nationwide. NSEE is committed to fostering the effective use of experience as an integral part of education to empower learners and promote the common good. *Contact:* NSEE, 3509 Haworth Dr., Ste. 207, Raleigh, NC 27609-7229 (919/787-3263; Fax 919/787-3381; E-mail **nsee@datasolv.com**; URL **http://www. tripood.com/nsee/**).

National Society of Public Accountants (NSPA) A nonprofit organization that represents the interests of independent, small business accounting and taxation professionals and provides education, governmental representation, information resources, and accounting, tax, and management assistance to small businesses. NSPA is dedicated to maintaining high standards of proficiency among its members and the accounting profession. *Contact:* NSPA, 1010 N. Fairfax St., Alexandria, VA 22314 (800/966-6679 or 703/549-6400; URL **http://www.nspa. org/**).

National Speakers Association (NSA) An organization of 3,600 members dedicated to advancing the art and value of experts who speak professionally. Its purposes are to define and support standards of excellence in professional speaking, enhance the communication competencies and business skills of professional speakers, promote the value of professional speakers as effective sources of expertise, knowledge, and insight, and expand the marketplace for professional speaking. NSA offers the **Certified Speaking Professional** designation. *Contact:* NSA, 1500 S. Priest Dr., Tempe, AZ 85281 (602/968-2552; Fax

602/968-0911; E-mail **NSAMain@aol.com**; URL **http://www.NSASpeaker.org**)

National Spinal Cord Injury Association (NSCIA) A membership-based, 60+-chapter private nonprofit organization established by the Paralyzed Veterans of America to serve as a national clearing house and primary resource to its members, the general public, and the media regarding spinal cord injury. Provides information and referral on job analysis, job modifications, job accommodations, job restructuring, new technology, adaptive equipment for individuals with spinal cord injuries and information and referral on architectural modifications and building codes. *Contact:* NSCIA, 8300 Colesville, St. 551, Silver Spring, MD 20910 (1-800/962-9629 or 301/588-6959; E-mail **NSCIA2@aol. com**; URL **http://www.spinalcord.org**).

National Technical Information Service (NTIS) A U.S. Department of Commerce service that includes technical reports and other analyses prepared by national and local government agencies and their contractors. The database contains technical reports on training, including training in the Armed Forces. *Contact:* NTIS, U.S. Department of Commerce, 5285 Port Royal Rd., Springfield, VA 22161 (703/487-4600; E-mail **webmaster@fedworld.gov**; URL **http://www.fedworld.gov**).

National Telecommuting Institute, Inc. A nonprofit organization that specializes in filling nonprofessional jobs which can be held by home-based individuals who have disabilities. National Telecommuting Institute uses federal and state vocational rehabilitation funding to recruit, train, and equip individuals with disabilities who need home based work and match them with companies who can employ telecommuters. Common types of work include medical, legal, and business transcripts, customer service work, claims processing, proofreading, and indexing. *Contact:* M.J. Willard, Ed.D., Executive Director, National Telecommuting Institute, Inc., 1505 Commonwealth Ave., Boston, MA 02135 (617/787-4426; Fax 617/787-3806; E-mail **mjwillard@nti.org**).

National Television Standards Committee (NTSC) Established the color television standard used in the U.S. and Japan. This format uses interlacing for broadcasting images; resolution is 525 lines transmitted at 60 half frames per second. It may be compared with PAL (Phase Alternating Line), the system used in much of Europe, which uses 625 lines of resolution.

National Tourism Organization Act of 1996 Signed into law October 11, 1996, the Act established the 48-member National Tourism Organization (NTO), a federally- recognized body that will replace the now-defunct United States Travel and Tourism Administration. NTO will be a private, nonprofit, federally chartered organization with responsibility for developing and implementing a national tourism policy, promoting U.S. tourism abroad, representing U.S. tourism at international trade shows, and conducting tourism market research.

National Tourist Offices (NTOs) Sources of help in planning meetings in a foreign country. Many maintain offices in North America staffed by professionals who understand meeting planners' needs. Most work closely with airlines, hotels, and destination management companies, provide information on rates and social customs, serve as initial contact with hotels, meetings and exhibition facilities, and attractions, interpreters and professional conference organizers, and can arrange site inspections. NTOs provide this assistance without charge. NTOs are funded by value-added and/or goods and services taxes. Other services include advice on value dates, audiovisual presentations and brochures on local attractions, brochure shells, calendar of events, current local news advisories, exchange rates, facility, rate, and contact information, group familiarization tours, itinerary assistance, local supplier/vendor contacts, media lists, meeting planner guides, money transfers, multilingual brochures, off-site special event coordination, press and public relations kits, slides and photos, restaurant and attraction guides, spouse activity/event coordination, travel posters, and videos.

National Wellness Association (NWA) A nonprofit organization (the membership division of the National Wellness Institute) that serves over 3,000 health and wellness promotion professionals. NWA collects and disseminates wellness information to its members and provides the services and networking opportunities necessary to enhance and manage successful wellness programs. *Contact:* NWA, 1045 Clark St., Ste. 210, P.O. Box 827, Stevens Point, WI 54481-0827 (715/342-2969; Fax 715/342-2979; E-mail

nwa@wellnesswi.org; URL **http://www.wellnesswi.org/**).

Native Americans American Indian or Alaskan Native persons having origins in any of the original peoples of North America and maintaining identifiable tribal affiliations through membership and participation or community identification.

natural language processing One area of artificial intelligence: machines that understand and speak (or type) your language or translate one language into another.

natural language report writer A tool, not yet generally available, used to query the **database** and extract reports u ing ordinary English.

natural law An approach to interpreting how the U.S. Constitution applies to individual human rights. The philosophy that individuals have certain basic human rights that are based on universal moral principles or on a "higher law," which is not limited by the letter of the civil law. As proof of the soundness of natural law and the need to protect individuals under civil law, proponents point to the U.S. Declaration of Independence that says, "We hold these truths to be self-evident, that all men are created equal, that they are endowed by their Creator with certain unalienable Rights, that among these are Life, Liberty, and the pursuit of Happiness." In addition, the Declaration of Human Rights, Universal, adopted by the UN General Assembly on December 10, 1948 by which UN members pledged to guarantee not only civil rights such as life, liberty, and freedom from arbitrary arrest, but also so-called social rights, such as the rights to work and to education, on the principle that "all human beings are born free and equal in dignity and rights." *See also* conventionalism; positivism.

Naval Enlisted Reserve Association (NERA) A 16,000 member association of active, inactive, and retired enlisted reservists in the Navy, Marine Corps, and Coast Guard. Its mission is to promote and protect the interests, morale, well-being, readiness, and training of sea service reserve forces. *Contact:* NERA. 6703 Farragut Ave., Falls Church, VA 22042 -2189 (800/776-9020 or 703/534-1329; Fax 703/534-3617; E-mail **nerabob@aol.com**).

Navy Exchange (NAVEX) *See* exchanges.

Naval Reserve Association (NRA) A 25,000 member association of active, inactive, and retired Naval Reserve officers. Its mission is to maintain and strengthen the nation's defense by ensuring a continued strong Navy and Naval Reserve, provide an educational program designed to be informative and professionally helpful to Naval Reservists and potential members entering the Naval Service as commissioned officers, and stimulate and support the Naval sciences and programs. *Contact:* Naval Reserve Association, 1619 King St., Alexandria, VA 22314 (703/548-5800; Fax 703/683-3647; E-mail **deville@navy-reserve.org**; URL **http://www.navy-reserve.org/nra/**).

navigation In multimedia, the indexing and directional tools in a software program designed to help the user find information categories quickly and accurately.

Navy League of the United States (NLUS) A 72,000 member association of civilians, military reservists, and retired military. Its mission is to maintain a strong U.S. maritime posture through support of the Navy, Marine Corps, Coast Guard, and Merchant Marine. Publishes *Sea Power* magazine. *Contact:* NLUS, 2300 Wilson Blvd., Arlington, VA 22201-3308 (703/528-1775; Fax 703/528-2333; E-mail **mail@ww.navyleague.org**; URL **http://www.navyleague.org**).

Navy Procurement Directive (NPD) In contracting and marketing, procurement procedures promulgated by the U.S. Navy to supplement the **Armed Forces Procurement Act of 1947**.

necessary work Work that consists of jobs, duties, or tasks which need to be performed to keep the organization operating but has no value to external customers or clients, such as internal accounting, travel and other types of internal reports.

needs Essentials, necessities, requisites, things that people lack, want, desire, or hope for. They include physiological needs (for food, water, and so on, security needs (for physical and psychological safety) and psychological needs (for acceptance, belonging, and so on).

needs analysis Breaking down a need to identify its causes and its relationships with other needs. It is one of the means of identifying current or projected skills or deficits among employees. It may involve the use of assessment centers, individual interviews, psychological tests, and so on.

needs analyst An HR/HRD competency. An individual who identifies performance deficiencies (either individual or organizational) and identifies the means of overcoming them.

needs assessment **1.** A means of determining the training and development systems and programs needed by the organization, employee groups, or individual employees to make the organization competitive in its industry, improve productivity, build employee morale and job satisfaction, and improve promotion potential and foster career development. Needs assessment identifies gaps in capabilities, abilities, and on-the-job results (performance) and places the identified needs in priority order for resolution. **2.** The process of identifying the capabilities a computer system needs to have to meet the requirements of a human resources department. Used to develop a request for proposal.

needs inventory An instrument that describes the skills and abilities of a specific group or class of workers (for example, clerks, computer programmers, managers) and requires those employees to rate independently the extent to which the skills and abilities apply to themselves or their subordinates. Ratings are tallied by item. The distribution of scores yields a rank order, reflecting the relative importance of specific skills. Decisions on training can then be based on a cut score, for example, all items above a selected score will be included in training.

negative symptoms In mental illness, behaviors that are not found among individuals with **schizophrenia** but are present among normal individuals. Also called *deficit symptoms.*

negligence In law, a tort or civil wrong, a careless violation of the rights of another. It requires proof of a legal duty, breach of that duty, that the breach of duty caused the injury, and actual injury.

negligent hiring **1.** A legal tort recognized by more than 20 states. May be charged when an employer fails to exercise care and caution in hiring and fails to note the consequences of hiring an unsuitable person for the position. Under some conditions, such as contacts with large groups of people and access to private property, this means that

the employer is expected to conduct an inquiry into an applicant's background, short of an independent investigation into an applicant's criminal record. **2.** Employment policies or procedures that omit or neglect to do things that a reasonable person, guided by ordinary considerations as well as the law, would do, or doing something that a reasonable and prudent person would not do. Therefore, employers have the right and the duty to carefully investigate a potential employee's work-related background, and in doing so they are generally protected by the law.

negligent job references Failure to exercise due care in providing information about current or past employees when references are requested by other organizations or agencies.

negligent retention claim Failing to taken corrective, disciplinary, or punitive action when an employee engages in abusive, hostile, threatening, or other unacceptable workplace behavior out of fear of litigation based on a claim under the Americans with Disabilities Act or other employee-rights legislation.

negotiated first class fare A means of attracting corporations that can deliver volume by discounting first class fares from 10 percent to as much as 25 percent. Also used by airlines to increase market share.

negotiated meeting fare An airfare group that usually represents the lowest possible unrestricted fare, amounting to 30 to 50 percent off coach fare — or 5 percent off the lowest available fare.

negotiating skills training Training for executives, managers, corporate negotiators, and members of negotiating teams designed to improve their ability to reach successful agreements and mutually advantageous contracts with clients, collective bargaining units, consultants, customers, financial institutions, and suppliers. Focus is on concepts, principles, procedures, and techniques, preparation and planning, recognizing and dealing with conflict, overcoming barriers and resolving issues, problems, and impasses.

negotiation **1.** in labor-management relations, a process for reaching agreement between or among two or more individuals or groups who have conflicting interests, acting either for themselves or as representatives of organizations. It may take the forms of arbitration or mediation. **2.** In conflict resolution, a form of the confrontation strategy that may make use of indirect persuasion or a type of force agreed upon in advance by both parties (mediation, arbitration, or litigation), which invariably involves a third party. Negotiation is an alternative to argument and, because it is a direct and open process aimed at producing a win-win result, settlements are more likely to be durable than some other means of conflict resolution.

nemawashi A Japanese term that expresses the concept of consensus building.

neonatal care Medical care provided a new-born infant. Intensive neonatal care for low birth weight and other problems can extend to two or three years.

nephropathy Diabetic kidney disease. The disease may be slowed by lowering the blood fat levels (cholesterol).

nepotism Favoritism shown to relatives, usually in the form of patronage, such as in hiring or promotion, based on the relationship rather than on merit.

nerve deafness The most common hearing disability. It is an abnormality of the inner ear, the auditory nerve, or both. The two most common causes of the condition are the aging process and sudden or extended exposure to loud noise, such as noise in the work environment, motorized tools, loud music, and certain hobbies.

net-booking pricing A payment plan offered by travel vendors in which airlines pay only for the number of passengers actually ticketed.

net book value The difference between the assets and liabilities of a company. Often used to set the price in a buy-sell agreement. Also called *net worth*.

NetGuide: The #1 Guide to Everything on the Net A monthly journal: $22.97 per year. Address: CMP Publications, Inc., 600 Community Drive, Manhasset, NY 11030 (516-904-445-4662; Fax 516-562-7406; E-mail **netmail@netguide.cmp.com**; URL **http://www.netguide.com**.

netiquette On the **Internet**, unwritten rules of conduct for users.

netizen A citizen of the **Internet** — someone who uses networked resources.

net profit Net income after depreciation on buildings, equipment, machinery, furniture and furnishings, fixtures, and other fixed assets; after reduction in inventory value to the lower of cost or market; after charge-offs for bad debts; after reserves for federal and state income taxes; and after all other reserves and adjustment; but *before* dividends.

net sales The dollar volume of business over a period of 365 days, net after deductions for returned merchandise, allowances, and discounts from gross sales.

Netscape Navigator A popular software system that allows access to and navigation of the **Internet** simply by pointing and clicking, (URL **http://www.netscape.com**).

netspeak The special vocabulary of the Internet.

network **1.** A group of interconnected computers linked by cable. Networks make information available to several users simultaneously. Enables users separated by geography to communicate with each other. **2.** An informal community of professionals who exchange advice, information, assistance, contacts, and referrals. Some are electronically supported by means of modems and computers. **3.** A diverse but interrelated and closely linked group of businesses with a wide range of ownership structures.

network model HMO A **health maintenance organization** that contracts with two or more independent physician group practice organizations to provide services and pays a fixed monthly fee per patient. The groups manage themselves and determine how fees will be distributed.

network and mixed model health maintenance organization (NMMHMO) A combination of the following types of health maintenance organizations: group practice health maintenance organization, independent practice association, and staff model health maintenance organization. *See also* health maintenance organization.

network-based training A learning system that provides individuals at decentralized locations virtually unlimited interactive learning and information resources through the use of a network of computers.

networked multimedia Storage of still images along with digital audio on a central device that permits simultaneous access by workstations of mixed types on a local area network.

network flow model A method of HR forecasting based on career planning. Concerned with the internal availability of people as shaped or fixed primarily by training and development programs. It forecasts human resources availability by developing projections of individual career paths using a sophisticated career management system. The system uses regularly updated, comprehensive information about position requirements, organization needs, and the gaps between supply and demand for people.

networking The process of acquiring, cultivating, and using a community of professionals to get advice, information, assistance, contacts, and referrals. It is a means of expanding one's learning resources at little or no cost.

net working capital The excess of current assets over current debt as shown on the balance sheet.

network model health maintenance organization A type of **managed care** in which the HMO contracts with more than one group practice to provide physician services to members. These group practices may be broad-based, multispecialty groups or several small groups of of primary care physicians. They may be either closed or open panel plans.

neurocomputer A computer modeled after the human brain. Developed by Ricoh Company, West Caldwlell, NJ, the neurocomputer has processing speeds about 500 times faster than a typical engineering workstation and four times faster than the largest **supercomputer**. The heart of the neurocomputer is a large-scale integrated circuit operating on the principle of pulse density modulation, which is similar to the neural connection used by the human brain. It allows the computer to compare its output to correct solutions and "learn" from its errors. This capability negates the need for slow, preloaded software.

neuroleptic drugs Antipsychotic drugs; the standard drugs currently used to treat the symptoms of schizophrenia.

neurolinguistic programming (NLP)
1. A model for understanding human behavior and a set of communications and learning techniques developed by Gestaultists. It draws from philosophy, cybernetics, psychology, neurology, and linguistics and is rooted in the fundamental belief that people have preferred modes of acquiring and processing information. "Neuro" refers to thought and brain processes; "linguistic" refers to verbal and nonverbal communication, and "programming refers" to behavior, habits, attitudes, and perceptions. Adherents maintain that there is a relationship between what happens within people and their behavior; that is, people's thought processes cause them to behave as they do. **2.** A change process that has its roots in psychotherapy. It is applied to evaluating and facilitating group processes, training, and self-development. NLP involves defining precisely the goal to be reached, the obstacles (lack of information, actions, skills, or beliefs) to be overcome, the purposes those obstacles serve and how they are applied, what works and when and what doesn't, what could work better and when, and determining whether the group functions better as a result of the effort.

neurologist A medical doctor who specializes in the diagnosis and treatment of disorders of the brain and spinal column, such as low back pain, epilepsy, Parkinson's disease, and multiple sclerosis.

New Age Training Training, the avowed purpose of which is to increase the motivation and productivity of employees by encouraging participants to "bare their souls" in rap sessions and other exercises. It may also attempt to get participants "in touch" with spiritual guides, universal masters, higher consciousness, master teachers, and transformational movements. The training may involve motivational talks, relaxation response, brain training, guided visualization, self-hypnosis, transcendental meditation, therapeutic touch, biofeedback, yoga, adventure learning, even walking on fire. It may also make use of blind-trust falls, tree-top team building exercises, and group hugging and cheering. Supporters claim that it builds better people rather than attempting to teach job-specific skills; that it maximizes participants' resources and potential. Critics maintain that it is a possible source of psychological harm and is potentially offensive to employees' values or religious beliefs. Also known as *consciousness-raising training*.

newbie A newcomer to the **Internet** and cyberspace. A patronizing term.

the new breed Young people who are now joining the workforce; typically college-educated professionals.

new hire tax credit *See* Work Opportunity Tax Credit.

newsgroups   On the **Internet,** special interest groups whose participants can read from or post messages to the entire network.

NewsNet   An on-line **database.** *Contact:* NewsNet, 945 Haverford Rd., Bryn Mawr, PA 19010, 800/345-1301 or 215/527-8030.

news puller   On the Web, a service that provides organized, free personalized news based on a user profile defined at the time of registration. Subscribers select categories of interest, such as Computers," "Entertainment," "Finance," "Human Resources," and "Sports," and the service sorts through newspapers, magazines, and Web sites to deliver the news. Works much like basic surfing: the subscriber must go to a Web site and reads its contents. Example: Excite News-Tracker (**http://nt.excite.com**). *See also* news pusher.

news pusher   On the Web, a service that provides organized, free personalized news based on a user profile defined at the time of registration. Subscribers select categories of interest, such as Computers," "Entertainment, " "Finance," "Human Resources," and "Sports, and the service sorts through newspapers, magazines, and Web sites to deliver the news. Specialized software "pushes" information from various sources directly to the subscriber's desktop. Example: Point-Cast (**http://www.pointcast.com**). *See also* news puller.

newsreader   Software used to participate in **usenet** discussion groups. Allows the individual to read or post to the discussion group of choice.

next operation as customer (NOAC)
A concept that employs the following principles as articulated by Keki R. Bhote (*Next Operation as Customer: How to Improve Quality, Cost and Cycle time in Service Operations,* AMACOM, 1991): (1) the internal customer is next in importance to the external customer and needs to be cultivated and satisfied; (2) all work performed, regardless of organizational level can be considered a process that receives input from an internal supplier (the previous operation), and each process has a "User" who adds value to that input and converts it into an output for an internal customer (the next operation); (3) the best measure of the effectiveness of a process is the internal customer's evaluation; (4) there must be consequences, in the form of appropriate rewards and punishment, of performing or failing to perform according to the internal customer's requirements; (5) the thrust of the system is continuous improvement — in terms of quality, cost, and cycle time; and (6) employees must be made true partners with management. Attributed to Dr. Kaoru Ishikawa, the father of the quality movement in Japan.

nexus   A tax concept that is loosely defined as a company's connection, and therefore tax liability, to a place. For example, tax liability is assigned by some states if a company has licensed a trade symbol or made use of some other intangible within their borders. In other states, liability (nexus by agency) is established if someone acted as the company's agent within a state, even though the company had no physical presence or employees in the state. And in still other states, liability (transitory nexus) is determined if a company has sent employees to the state for a number of trade shows or short visits. All types of nexus are being challenged in the courts.

nibbling   In negotiating, asking for small concessions in a contract or other form of agreement.

niche marketing   The process of identifying, analyzing, and selecting strategic marketing segments that have the most potential for payoff.

niches   Things that an organization has discovered it can do better, faster, or cheaper than others.

no balance billing clause   A clause in a health care contract stating that a provider may not bill a member for any payment owed by the plan, regardless of the reason for the nonpayment; however, the provider may bill a member for any amount that the member is required to pay, such as copayment, coinsurance, or for services not covered under the schedule of benefits.

node   **1.** On the **Internet,** a device that stores or relays data. **2.** Any device that is connected to a network.

no frills health plan   A new type of low-cost health policy made available to small businesses (typically fewer than 50 workers) by laws enacted by the state legislatures of Florida, Illinois, Kansas, Kentucky, Maryland, Missouri, North Dakota, Rhode Island, Virginia, and Washington. The new policies cost less because the law exempts insurers from covering several kinds of care mandated by the states in most health plans. Examples are care by a chiropractor or podiatrist, drug abuse treatment, and mental-health costs. The plans are designed to help businesses kept out of the market by high and rising costs of health care insurance premiums. Similar legislation has been introduced in Congress.

No-Int (Stoned 3)   A computer virus that is a variant of **Stoned**. It's undetectable while the virus is resident in memory. It may disrupt utility programs and destroy the boot sector or the partition table.

nominal data   Data that only identify or classify items into groups. *See also* ordinal data.

nominal group conferencing   *See* nominal group technique.

nominal group technique   **1.** In technological forecasting, a projective technique that involves a structured group meeting of five to seven experts conducted by a competent group leader. The members of the group silently consider a question or problem for about 20 minutes and list as many feasible solutions as possible. Following silent listing of the solutions on a chalkboard by participants in turn, each one is discussed and may be modified, combined with others, or divided. Then participants rate or rank each solution independently and privately, the results are tabulated, and presented to the decision maker. **2.** In needs assessment, a structured group meeting designed to develop a list of problems that can be addressed by training. Five to nine participants write down as many problems as they can identify and them in turn, present one idea from the list. the process continues until all lists are exhausted. Structured discussion of each idea follows. The session concludes with individual, independent, private, and silent balloting to select items and establish priorities by rank order.

nominalized experience   A linguistic term that refers to "turning a process into a name or event." Once named, the process can be categorized. The procedure is used in **neurolinguistic programming**.

nomination   A system of enrollment in company training that is based on nominations of employees for specific training by their immediate supervisors. Final selections are

made by a senior manager or a selection board.

non-availability statement (NAS)   Certification from a military hospital stating that it cannot provide the non-emergency inpatient or certain types of outpatient care that a user needs. If **Civilian Health and Medical Programs of the Uniformed Services (CHAMPUS)** users live within certain ZIP codes around a military hospital, they must get a NAS before obtaining non-emergency inpatient (and some outpatient) care at a civilian hospital under CHAMPUS. CHAMPUS does not determine eligibility, nor does it issue NASs; the NAS must be entered electronically in the **defense Enrollment Eligibility Reporting System (DEERS)** computer files by the user's nearest military facility.

Non-Commissioned Officers Association (NCOA)   A 160,000 member association of active, reserve, retired, and veterans of the U.S. armed forces in grades E-1 through E-9. Its mission is to promote and protect the rights and benefits of active duty and veteran NCOs and petty officers in all five branches of the armed forces and provide opportunities for patriotic, fraternal, social, and benevolent activities. *Contact:* NCOA, P.O. Box 33610, San Antonio, TX 78265 (210/653-6161; Fax 210/637-3337; E-mail **ncoaprmark@aol.com**).

noncompete agreement   A contract in which an employee agrees not to compete with an employer during employment or for a specified time following termination of employment. Such agreements may restrict employees from working for direct competitors when they leave. Not controlled by federal law, but in some states laws limit the way in which the agreement can be used by employers. To be valid, such agreements must (1) be supported by valid **consideration;** (2) be made in connection with an **employment agreement;** (3) be reasonable in terms of duration and geographic scope; (4) be necessary to protect a legitimate company interest; and (5) avoid imposing an unreasonable hardship on the employee. Also known as a *restrictive covenant.*

noncompetitive employment contract   *See* noncompete agreement.

noncontributory benefits plan   A plan in which the employer pays the entire cost or full premiums of a funding plan for paying employee benefits.

non-decision The absence or avoidance of decision. Occurs when a manager either ignores an issue or problem or decides to do nothing about it in the hope that the problem will resolve itself, that conditions will change, or that someone else will take action.

non-directive counseling An approach to counseling characterized by actions aimed at establishing and maintaining the conditions necessary for the counselee to achieve insight into his or her problem and thereby achieve control over it. Nondirective counselors do not diagnose, interpret, advise, suggest, reason, persuade, probe, or pass judgment. Rather, they demonstrate warmth and acceptance and concentrate on reflecting and clarifying attitudes.

non-directive interview Used in screening and selection, task analysis, termination, and outplacement. An approach to interviewing characterized by actions designed to establish the conditions necessary for the interviewee to take the lead and discuss subjects of primary concern to him or her.

non-discrimination *See* equal employment opportunity.

non-economic rewards Reward options in the non-economic category that include non-monetary perks. These are special privileges, accommodations, or considerations usually associated with organizational rank and status, although they are sometimes granted on an individual basis and even to lower-ranking persons for specific periods of time. Perks include reserved parking spaces, plush offices, private washrooms, and access to executive dining rooms and airline VIP lounges.

non-exempt employee A worker covered by (not exempted from) the overtime pay provisions of the **Fair Labor Standards Act of 1938**. Nonexempt employees include hourly-paid employees (most occupations related to production, maintenance, and services functions where pay is directly related to the number of hours worked) and some nonexempt salaried workers (clerical, administrative, and paraprofessional job categories).

nonfinancial rewards Typically symbols of achievement or service (quality, length, or retirement) to the organization in such areas as attendance, sales, fund raising, instruction,

production, community service, bravery, cost savings/avoidance, invention, creativity, suggestions, safety, or innovation). The rewards include such things as medals, plaques, badges, trophies, pins, and certificates; corporate "Oscars," "Emmys," or "Nobel Prizes"; office or work area improvements (furniture and furnishings); flexible work schedules; scrolls and VIP certificates, training completion and seminar attendance certificates and diplomas; and certificates of appreciation.

non-highly compensated employee (NHCE) An employee who owns less than 5 percent owners or who is not a family member of owners, who earns less than $75,000 from an employer, or earns less than $50,000 from the employer and is in the bottom 80 percent of employees, or any officer earning less than $45,000.

non-immigrant visa A means of legally bringing into the United States foreign nationals who do not want to reside here permanently. *See also* Immigration and Naturalization Service H-1B status.

nonlinear editing Provides immediate, direct access to any frame of video and audio source material on a disc.

nonlinear regression An arcane form of regression analysis that permits the analyst to construct a model of a non-linear or curvilinear relationship between two variables.

nonparametric methods/statistics A class of statistical techniques that is used when data cannot be quantified readily but can be scaled or ranked in order of relative magnitude and identified as positive or negative in character. Nonparametric methods include techniques that permit easier collection of data from which distributions are unknown because absolute measures are not needed and can be replaced by relative measures such as "better" or "worse." The techniques are particularly useful where small samples are available and the costs of increasing the sample size are prohibitive.

non-participating physician A health care provider who does not accept **Medicare**-approved amounts as full payment for services. Medicare currently pays 80 percent of the approved fee, and the patient is responsible for the remaining 20 percent.

nonprofit/not-for-profit corporation A corporation formed for educational, fraternal, religious, or social purposes.

Members who abide by conditions contained in the corporate bylaws make up such corporations.

Nonprofit World: The National Nonprofit Leadership and Management Journal
A bimonthly journal; $79.00 per year. Address: The Society for Nonprofit Organizations, 6314 Odana Rd., Suite 1, Madison, WI 53719 (608/274-9777; Fax 608/274-9978).

nonqualified pension plan   A plan that does not meet IRS rules and requirements, such as those that provide benefits in excess of those allowed, and therefore do not qualify for favorable tax treatment.

nonqualified stock options (NASO)
A form of stock option plan that does not meet all of the requirements of Section 422A of the **Internal Revenue Code** for incentive options. Nonqualified options usually have a 10-year option term and are usually priced at 100 percent of market value at the time of the grant.

nonrefundable fare   A special fare offered to travelers who are willing to commit themselves to travel plans well in advance of travel.

nonschedule interview   A type of interview conducted without a prepared schedule. The interviewer is thoroughly briefed on what information is required and is then allowed to vary the wording and the sequence of the questions for maximum effectiveness with individual respondents.

nonstandard interview   An interview in which no attempt is made to direct the interviewee's conversation or to obtain the same information from every respondent. The interviewer simply listens carefully and occasionally comments in ways that encourage the interviewee to talk freely about any subject of interest.

nontraditional employment   Applied to women, occupations of fields of work where women constitute less than 25 percent of the individual employed in such occupations. Defined by the Nontraditional Employment for Women Act of 1991, an amendment to the Job Training Partnership Act of 1982.

Nontraditional Employment for Women Act (NEW) of 1991   An amendment to the **Job Training Partnership Act of 1982** administered by the Department of Labor. Awards up to six grants each year to a maximum of $1.5 million to states having the best training programs for both blue collar and skilled workers — programs designed to increase the range of training and job placement for low-income women over the age of 22.

nontraditional household   Sharing living arrangements with other than a spouse and children. Caused by greater distances between family members, higher housing costs, deaths and divorces, less secure retirement, and increased numbers of older Americans. Includes extended family, unrelated roommates and unmarried partners, and grandparent caregiver.

nontraditional risk financing/management
Establishment of **captives** or self-insurance groups.

nontraditional sabbaticals   *See* extended leave programs.

non-value adding work   Work activities that result in rejects, reworks, overproduction, and so on.

nonverbal communications or behavior
Audible or visible behavior used to convey thoughts, feelings, and emotions, such as facial expressions, posture, body movements, gestures, and the like. They may be descriptive (used to illustrate visually), used for emphasis (express a feeling or an idea), or be practical and necessary (reaching for an object), and they may or may not accompany language.

nonverbal test   A test that does not require the use of words in test items or responses, although oral instructions may be included in the description of the task. An example is the Differential Aptitude Tests of Abstract Reasoning.

nootropics   Steroids claimed by some to rejuvenate memory, improve the intellect, revitalize sex drive, and reverse the mental aging process. Some are prescription medicines. Physicians warn that there are risks involved in their use.

normal distribution   *See* bell-shaped curve.

normative ethics   One of two subdivisions of the discipline of ethics, normative ethics focus on the arguments used to attack or defend specific actions or behavior as being good or bad. Normative ethics may be further subdivided into applied and professional ethics.

normative forecasting   A forecasting approach that is based on the premise that future developments will be caused by future needs. If future needs can be projected, the means of meeting the can also be forecast. Also called *goal-oriented forecasting.*

norm-referenced measurement A means of measuring accomplishment and results that compares the achievement of individuals or groups against each other (or groups that have preceded them through the training program).

norms 1. Codes, standards, criteria, or measures and mores, customs, and traditions of conduct or behavior expected under certain conditions and that are commonly acknowledged and accepted by a group as correct, appropriate, right and proper. Conformity brings rewards; deviations result in withholding of rewards, or censure. **2.** In testing, statistical measures and indexes that provide a frame of reference to give meaning to test scores. They are derived from actual performance of individuals of various ages, occupations, or other descriptor in the standardization group for the test. Norms represent average or typical performance on the test in such terms as percentile or stanine.

Norris Decision A 1983 Supreme Court Decision stating that an annuity option in a retirement plan that paid smaller monthly benefits to women than to men discriminated on the basis of sex and was a violation of Title VII of the Civil Rights Act of 1964.

Norris-Laguardia Act of 1932 (NLA)
See Anti-Injunction Act of 1932.

North American Free Trade Agreement (NAFTA) A trading partnership involving the United States, Canada, and Mexico that went into effect January 1, 1994. Over 15 years, the Treaty will eliminate tariffs and other barriers to the flow of goods, services, and investment between the three nations. The agreement creates a trade zone stretching from the Arctic Circle to the Yucatan Peninsula, making it larger in GNP ($6 trillion) and consumer population (378 million) than the European Community. The Agreement, signed by Presidents Bush (United States) and Carlos Salinas de Gortai (Mexico), and Brian Mulroney (Canada) on December 17, 1992, was ratified by the legislatures of the three countries, with the United States being the last. President Clinton signed the legislation December 8, 1993. At a December 1994 Miami summit meeting of the leaders of 34 western hemisphere countries (only Cuba

was excluded), participants agreed to conclude a treaty by the year 2006 to create a free-trade zone (the world's largest) for the Americas (Pan-American Free Agreement). At that meeting, President Clinton and the leaders of Canada and Mexico also agreed to admit Chile to NAFTA. Of interest (and concern) to business owners for security reasons, beginning January 1, 1997, NAFTA requires that federal tax deposit (FTD) transfers of more than $50,000 (IRS Forms 720, 945, 990-C, 990-PF, 990-T, 1042, and CT-1) be made by electronic funds transfer.

no-show 1. In travel industry parlance, an individual who has made a flight reservation, fails to cancel the reservation, and doesn't check in at the appointed time. **2.** In meeting management, a room reservation not used or canceled.

notch babies About 12 million retirees born between 1917 and 1926 receiving Social Security payments that are as much as 20 percent smaller than those paid to people with similar work experiences who were born earlier. The difference in payments, viewed as an injustice by many in the affected age group and more than 230 members of the House, is due to a major overhaul of Social Security passed by the Congress in 1978. Legislation has been filed to increase benefits for notch babies but opponents maintain that there is no discrimination against that group; rather, those born earlier are receiving payments that are higher than they should be.

notebook computer A portable computer that is battery powered, weighs less than six pounds, and is about the size and shape of a looseleaf notebook.

notice A legal doctrine that applies in wrongful discharge cases. In effect it asks, "Did the employer give the employee forewarning of the possible consequences of the employee's disciplinary conduct?"

not working very hard (NWVH)
An approach to career success as a manager attributed to Donald Smith. He refers to the approach as "directed lassitude."

NTL Institute for Applied Behavioral Science A community of members and staff whose purposes are to advance the field of applied behavioral science, eliminate oppression, and foster core our values by: (1) training in the theory and practice of group dynamics, organizational change and societal change;

(2) learning from these experiences; (3) sharing the results of the learning; and (4) engaging in inquiry, knowledge building, and the publication of findings. Its 420+ members — professors, consultants, trainers, psychologists, and OD practitioners — serve as its faculty. *Contact:* NTL Institute, 1240 N. Pitt St., Ste. 100, Alexandria, VA 22314-1403 (800/777-5227 or 703/548-8840; Fax 703/548-3179 E-mail **dedwards@ntl.org;** URL **http://www.ntl.org**).

null hypothesis A statistical statement of the nonexistence of a relationship between two measures; that is that any differences noted amount to nothing — or zero.

number-cruncher A cynical term used to describe people who deal with accounts, budgets, financial matters, and the like, such as accountants and corporate controllers.

numerical control (NC) The process of controlling a machine by feeding it instructions in the form of numbers on punched or magnetic tape, or by setting dials or actuating buttons on a control panel.

numerical rating The simplest form of rating scale. Numerical rating is an absolute method of rating that involves the use of any number of points on a numerical scale, although an odd number is typically chosen so that the middle point represents the average.

nurse case manager A registered nurse employed to avert high case costs and other managed care problems. Provides communication liaison among all involved parties involved and serves as a central source for determining case needs.

nurse practitioner A registered nurse (R.N.) with additional specialized medical training qualified to provide primary medical care in remote or rural areas where no physician is available. Practices under specific written protocols for treatment of specific injuries and illnesses. Supervised (sometimes from a distance) by a doctor of medicine or osteopathy. Payment is authorized by Medicare although at lower rates than it would be for a medical doctor.

nursing home A licensed institution that provides skilled nursing care and related services but does not qualify as a **skilled nursing facility** as defined by Medicare. Usually operated for profit, nursing homes are for people who are seriously ill or need extensive and extended health or personal care. Medicare and private medigap insurance plans reimburse only a small portion of the costs. Medicaid covers the costs for qualified individuals.

nursing home coverage An insurance policy that pays a certain amount per day for services provided in a skilled nursing facility or a smaller amount per day for services in an **alternate long term care facility**. Typically specifies a benefit limit stated in terms of the combined number of days for which the subscriber will be paid. Also usually includes an elimination period, the number of consecutive days of confinement needed to qualify for benefits

nutrition programs Programs sponsored by the federal government a state or local government agencies designed to provide people with information about and access to a more nutritious diet. Include the Special Supplemental Food Program for Women, Infants, and Children (administered by the Department of Agriculture through state health departments), the Nutrition Program for the Elderly (administered by the Department of Health and Human Services through state agencies on aging), and several other food programs administered by the Department of Agriculture (Food Distribution Programs, Child and Adult Care Food Program, School Lunch and Breakfast Programs, and Summer Food Service Program).

nutrition services Inexpensive, nutritious meals served in group setting such as senior centers, churches, synagogues, or senior housing.

nutritional supplements An alternative form of medicine in which vitamin and mineral nutrients are used to supplement a diet that alone may not be supplied in sufficient quantities to maintain overall good health.

Nyetscape A derogatory term used to describe what the speaker believes to be American On-Line's "less than full-feature" **Web** browser.

OAA	Older Americans Acts of 1965, 1978, and 1992.	**OMR**	Optical mark reader.
OASDHI	Old Age, Survivors, Disability, and Health Insurance Program.	**OOH**	*Occupational Outlook Handbook.*
		OOPS	Object-oriented programming system.
OASITF	Old Age and Survivors Insurance Trust Fund.	**OPCs**	Occupational program consultants.
OBE	Outcome-based education.	**OPEIU**	Office & Professional Employ-
OBET	Outdoor-based experiential training.		ees International Union.
		OPG	Oculoplethysmography.
OBRA	Omnibus Budget Reconciliation Acts of 1987, 1989, 1990, and 1993.	**OPHCOO**	Office or Prepaid Health Care Operations and Oversight.
		OPIC	Overseas Private Investment Corporation.
OBT	Outcome-based training.	**OPL**	Other party liability.
OCR	Optical character recognition.	**OPM**	Office of Personnel Management.
OD	Organization development.		
ODDs	Optical disc drive.	**OR**	Operations research.
ODN	Organization Development Network.	**OS/2**	Operating System/2.
		OSAC	Overseas Security Advisory Council.
OEHMO	Open-ended health maintenance organization.	**OSAP**	Office for Substance Abuse Prevention.
OEIC	Optoelectronic integrated circuit.	**OSDBU/MRC**	Office of Small and Disadvantaged Business Utilization Minority Resource Center
OEM	Original equipment manufacturer.		
OEO	Open-ended option.	**OSEP**	Office of Special Education Programs.
OEP	Open-ended plan.		
OER	Officer efficiency report.	**OSERS**	Office of Special Education and Rehabilitative Services.
OET	Outdoor experiential training		
OFCCP	Office of Federal Contract Compliance Programs.	**OSHA**	**1.** Occupational Safety and Health Act of 1970. **2.** Occupational Safety and Health Administration.
O&FM	Organization and functions manual.		
OHS	Occupational health services.		
OHT	Occupational health team.	**OSHA HCS**	OSHA Hazard Communication Standard.
OIC	Oh, I see (Internet speak).		
OJT	On-the-job training.	**OSTD**	Ontario Society for Training and Development.
OLTP	On-line transaction processing.		

OT   Organizational transformation.
OTBH   Out-of-the-box hiring.
OWA   Other weird arrangement.
OWBPA   Older Workers Benefit
                Protection Act of 1990.
125   *See* Section 125, Internal
                Revenue Code.
127   *See* Section 127, Internal
                Revenue Code.
190   *See* Section 190, Internal
                Revenue Code.

objective A specific qualitative or quantitative target. Objectives specify what is to be accomplished by whom and by when. They should be realistic and practicable, meaningful and verifiable, logically related to, derived from, and support goals, cover key result areas, and set forth in writing. They should also cover a specific time frame. Objectives are usually developed annually. In terms of coverage, HR objectives focus on critical HR result areas and encompass all major areas in which resources will be invested, normal or routine work products and innovative improvement projects, and tangible (measurable) and intangible (difficult to measure) products.

objective-line forecast A type of time series forecast. Objective-line forecasts are projections of future activities and operations derived from analysis of historical data and trends and current activities and operations. Also known as *development-line forecast.*

objective test Paper-and-pencil or performance test designed to eliminate the examiners' judgment or bias from the scoring.

objectivity A characteristic of an acceptable test. A test is objective when the judgment or bias of a scorer is eliminated from the scoring; that is, different people scoring the same performance or test paper at different times will arrive at the same score.

object-oriented programming system (OOPS) More powerful than a **module**. Contains not only program code but also data that the code can manipulate. Used by programmers to write applications more efficiently.

objects Computer software modules that can be combined into new, large applications.

O'Brien's Law A law that states, "Murphy was an optimist." *See also* Murphy's Law.

observation A management technique used to identify potential or actual problems and monitor and evaluate processes and worker performance.

observational learning A learning strategy used by humans (and to some degree by learning machines). The learner learns by watching a demonstration or observing a procedure or event.

observational skill In appraisal and evaluation, the ability to collect information about situations and conditions in the environment using a deliberately and carefully worked out plan. It is directed toward fact-finding, is systematic in terms of the timing, length, and number of observations, and is recorded.

observation interview A means of collecting job data. Essentially the same as the interview method except that, in addition to undergoing an in-depth interview by the analyst, the incumbent is observed in the job environment performing all or a substantial part of the job.

obstetrician A medical doctor who specializes in the care of women during pregnancy, labor, birth, and the postnatal period.

occupancy rate In meeting management, the percentage of the total number of sleeping rooms actually occupied in a hotel. The measure has a bearing on the rates charged. *See also* high season; low season; shoulder season.

occupation 1. One's principal calling, business, or employment. 2. A family of jobs common to most areas and industries.

occupational analysis The process of defining the total dimensions and the performance requirements of an occupational field as it is now and is likely to become, describing the job structure and career patterns of that field, and defining the duties, tasks, and elements of each job in terms of behaviors, conditions, and standards. Occupational analyses are used to collect the detailed information needed to identify requirements for new jobs, redesign jobs, project future personnel requirements, and design training and development programs. In addition, occupational analysis defines the boundaries of occupational fields in terms of functions and processes, kinds and numbers of workers, job, task, and skill clusters, and skills hierarchies.

occupational disability Inability to perform one's usual occupation or work for pay due to accident or injury. Usually entitles the person to workers' compensation or similar benefits.

occupational disease A disease that arises out of and in the course of employment and for which a person is entitled to benefits under workers' compensation or similar law.

occupational field The largest meaningful configuration of human work performance. An occupational field consists of all logically related or skills-related jobs. For example, the health services occupational field includes such jobs as physician, registered nurse, licensed practical nurse, and a host of other specialties and subspecialties.

occupational health services (OHS) Replaced the term industrial health activities. The Occupational Safety and Health Administration defines occupational health as "....the theory and practice of the several related professional disciplines of medicine, nursing, and industrial hygiene, whose specialized areas concern exclusively the maintenance, restoration, or improvement of the well-being of the worker." It also involves the prevention of illnesses and disease.

occupational health team (OHT) Consists of practitioners in the following disciplines: occupational medicine (physicians), occupational health nursing (nurses, clinical nurse specialists, and nurse practitioners), and industrial hygiene personnel (industrial hygienists, occupational health engineers, and industrial hygienist chemists).

occupational illness An abnormal condition or disorder caused by exposure to environmental factors associated with employment, including acute and chronic illnesses that may be caused by absorption, inhalation, ingestion, or direct contact with toxic substances or harmful agents.

occupational injury Injury sustained on the job that results in medical treatment other than first aid, loss of consciousness, restriction of work, loss of one or more work days, restriction of motion, or transfer to another job.

occupational orientation An individual's predisposition toward or preference for a certain career field. It is believed by some to be determined by an individual's personality, including needs, wants, motives, and values.

Occupational Outlook Handbook* (OOH)** A companion volume to the ***Dictionary of Occupational Titles. Provides information on jobs, occupations, employment locations, and labor market projections useful in human resources planning.

occupational program consultants (OPCs) Positions mandated by the **Hughes Act of 1970** (two per state). Incumbents are responsible for developing occupational alcoholism programs in both the public and private sectors.

Occupational Safety and Health Act of 1970 (OSHA) Requires employers to provide safe and healthful working conditions, protection against hazards that might cause illness, injury, or death, including hazardous work conditions, methods, materials, and substances. Under OSHA, every employer must be familiar with mandatory OSHA standards and make copies available for employees to review, inform employees about OSHA, inspect workplace conditions to ensure that they conform to safety and health standards, remove or guard hazards, and report and keep records of injuries and occupational illnesses (firms with 11 or more employees). The Act applies to all employers engaged in interstate commerce and is enforced by the Department of Labor. Also known as the *Williams-Steiger Act.*

Occupational Safety and Health Administration (OSHA) A Department of Labor office created by the **Occupational Safety and Health Act of 1970** that oversees the application of the law. (URL http://www.osha.gov).

Occupational Safety and Health Administration Standards Regulations (Standard Section 29 CFR) designed to eliminate or reduce hazards to workers. They include Abrasive Wheel Guarding (1910.215); **Bloodborne Pathogens; Confined Spaces** (1910.146); Employee Exposure/Medical Records Access (1910.20); Flammable and Combustible Liquids (1910.106); Hazard Communication/Construction Industry (1926.59); **Hazard Communication/General Industry** (1910.1200); General Electric Requirements (1910.303); Guardrails (1926.500); **Laboratory Chemical; Lockout/Tagout** (1910.147); Machine Guarding (1910.212); OSHA Notice (1903.2); Power Transmission Equipment (1910.219); Record keeping (1904.2); Respiratory Protection (1910.134); Scaffolding (1926.451); Spray Finishing (1910.107);

Wiring Design/Construction); Wiring Methods/Construction (1926.405); Wiring Methods/General Industry (1910.305).

occupational safety laws *See* Comprehensive Environmental Response, Compensation, and Liability Act of 1980; Emergency Planning and Community Right-to-Know Act of 1986; Hazard Communication Standard of 1988; Occupational Safety and Health Act of 1970; Resource Conservation and Recovery Act of 1976; Superfund Amendments and Reauthorization Act of 1986.

occupational skills *See Dictionary of Occupational Titles.*

occupational therapist *See* registered occupational therapist

oculoplethysmography (OPG) A technique used to locate and determine the degree of carotid arterial blockage by measuring the arterial pulse behind the eye.

off-duty hours Periods during which an employee is completely relieved of duty and is free to use the time for his or her own purposes. In general an employee who is required to wear a beeper while off duty is not working even if on-call unless he or she is subject to additional restrictions that limit activities. In the latter case, the time would be converted to compensable on-call time.

offers in compromise Used by the **Internal Revenue Service** when a taxpayer is unable to pay the full tax, interest, and penalties due and there's doubt that the the full amount can be collected in the future. Such offers settle the taxpayer's obligation at a lower amount.

Office & Professional Employees International Union (OPEIU) An organization representing "white collar" professionals such as accountants, artists, attorneys, bank employees, computer analysts and programmers, copywriters, data entry operators, doctors, engineers, health care certified and licensed employees, hypnotherapists, insurance workers and agents, law enforcement officers and security guards, models, museum curators, nurses, secretaries, Wall Street employees, and many more job classifications. The union represents 140,000 office and professional employees in the United States and Canada. *Contact:* OPEIU, 265 West 14th Street, 6th Fl., New York, NY 10011 (800/346-7348; E-mail **opeiu@opeiu.org**; URL **http:www. opeiu.org/**)

Office for Substance Abuse Prevention (OSAP) A component of the Alcohol, Drug Abuse, and Mental Health Administration of the Public Health Service, U.S. Department of Health and Human Services. Created by the **Anti-Drug Abuse Act of 1986** (and significantly expanded in scope and functions by the Anti-Drug Abuse Act of 1988) to head the government's effort to prevent and intervene in alcohol and drug abuse. Its goal is to promote the concepts of no use of any illegal drugs and no illegal or high-risk use of alcohol or other legal drugs.

Office of Career Opportunities, National Technical Institute for the Deaf Provides special technical education for deaf students from all states. *Contact:* Office of Career Opportunities, National Technical Institute for the Deaf, One Lomb Memboria Dr., Rochester, NY 14623 (716/475-6400).

Office of Federal Contract Compliance Programs (OFCCP) A federal agency charged with responsibility for implementing Executive Orders and enforcing affirmative action regulations for government contractors. OFCC was established as an office of the Department of Labor by **Executive Order 11246**.

Office of National Service (ONS) Coordinates federal service programs, administers the National and Community Service Act of 1990, and provides promotional materials, networking, and recognition. *Contact:* ONS, The White House, Washington, DC 20500 (202/456-6266).

Office of Personnel Management (OPM) The federal agency responsible for promulgating human resource regulations and overseeing civilian personnel matters (workers and retirees) in all agencies and offices of the federal government.

Office of Small and Disadvantaged Business Utilization Minority Resource Center (OSDBU/MRC) An office within the U.S. Agency for International Development. Serves as a clearinghouse for businesses interested in participating in procurements of AID-financed goods and services. *Contact:* Office of Small and Disadvantaged Business Utilization/Minority Resource Center, 320 Twenty-First St., N.W.,Washington, DC 20523 (703/875-1551; Fax 703/875-1862; E-mail **OSDBU@AIDW**: URL **http:// www.info.USAID.GOV**).

Office of Special Education and Rehabilitative Services (OSERS) An office of the Department of education whose mission is to provide leadership to achieve full integration and participation in society of people with disabilities by ensuring equal opportunity and access to and excellence in education, employment, and community living. *Contact:* USDOE, 330 C St., S.W., Room 3132, Washington, DC 20202-2524 [202/205-8241 or 202/205-8723 (voice/TTY)].

Office of Special Education Programs (OSEP) A subdivision of the **Office of Special Education and Rehabilitative Services.** OSEP has major responsibility for programs relating to the free appropriate education of children and youth with disabilities. *Contact:* OSEP/ED, 330 C St., S.W., Room 3086 Switzer Bldg., Washington, DC 20202-2570 [202/205-8241 or 202/205-8723 (voice/TTY)].

Office or Prepaid Health Care Operations and Oversight (OPHCOO) The federal agency, a part of the Health Care Financing Administration, that oversees federal qualification and compliance for health maintenance organizations and eligibility for competitive medical plans.

officer efficiency report (OER) The U.S. Army's annual and special reports on the performance and potential of commissioned and warrant officers.

office skills training Training given to office support staff who provide administrative support services, such as clerical, secretarial, and word processing activities.

off-label drug A drug prescribed by a physician for use for a condition not approved by the Food and Drug Administration (FDA) for that particular condition (although it may be approved by the FDA for a different condition).

off-label prescribing Using a drug to treat a disorder for something other than its approved purpose. For example, prescribing Prozac, a drug approved by the federal Food and Drug Administration to treat depression, to treat obesity.

off-line editing A form of video editing usually done with small format tape to produce an edit decision list, which is used later to automatically assemble the finished program.

offset *See* offset lithography.

offset lithography In printing, the process of using an intermediate blanket cylinder to transfer an image from the image carrier to the substrate.

offset pension formula A formula that results in the subtraction of a portion (limited by IRS regulations) of an individual's Social Security annuity from a defined amount to determine the benefit from the pension plan.

off-the-shelf program A training or other type of program produced for other organizations that are judged to match the needs of an organization *well enough* — although it may not fit either the organization or the industry precisely.

Old Age, Survivors, Disability, and Health Insurance Program (OASDHI) A successor of the **Social Security Act of 1935.** An omnibus social bill passed by the Congress that covers retirement, survivors, and disability insurance (Social Security), hospital and medical insurance for the aged and disabled (Medicare and Medicaid), black-lung benefits for miners, supplemental security income (SSI), unemployment insurance, and public assistance in welfare systems.

Old Age and Survivors' Insurance Trust Fund (OASITF) The largest of several trust funds into which Social Security taxes go. Currently has tens of billions of dollars in it, invested in government guaranteed investments and drawing interest. According to present laws, the funds cannot be used by the government for other purposes. However, "creative bookkeeping" by the administration, and with the help of an acquiescent Congress, has used the mounting Social Security surplus to mask the size of the federal budget deficit.

old boy network People in business and industry who belong to an informal and exclusive "club," are successful, and have considerable power to influence what happens from a financial, production, or other business indicator in their industry (or country). They are typically white, Anglo-Saxon, Protestant males; women and minorities are excluded.

Older Americans Act of 1965 (OAA) An Act to assist older people to secure equal opportunity to the full and free enjoyment of an adequate income in retirement, the best possible physical and mental health, and opportunity for employment without discrimination because of age, among other objectives. Congress has reaffirmed its support for OAA programs 12 times through amendments and reauthorization actions. The most recent reauthorization in 1987 continued a trend to set total funding at about $1 billion. One provision in the 1987 authorization calls for a national assessment of "unsatisfied demand" for supportive services provided at senior centers and other sites.

Older Americans Act of 1978   *See* Long-Term Care Ombudsman Program.

Older Americans Act of 1992 (OAA)
Amends the Older Americans Act of 1965 by including support to family members and other persons providing voluntary care to older persons and needing long-term care services. Provides training and employment counseling to older Americans who have poor employment prospects and economic need. Signed into law by President Bush on September 30, 1992.

Older Workers Benefit Protection Act of 1990 (OWBPA)   An Act signed into law by President Bush on October 16, 1990. It requires that early retirement incentive plans be "consistent with the *relevant* purpose or purposes of this act." It also clarified that the **Age Discrimination in Employment Act of 1967** has authority over employee benefits. In 1997, the 3rd U.S. Circuit Court of Appeals ruled that former employees who waive their rights and accept severance packages may still file suit against their employers for failure to comply with the requirements of the Act. Although ADEA requires employers to provide equal benefits to all workers, it allows reductions in benefits for older workers in cases where added employer costs are incurred as a result of providing those benefits to older workers. The Act of 1990 restores the ADEA to what it was prior to Supreme Court decisions eliminating the requirement for employers to justify lower benefits for older workers by showing increased costs or other economic considerations. Under the law, all waivers and releases of age discrimination must be voluntary. Specifically, all waivers of ADEA rights must (1) be part of an understandable and written agreement between the employer and the employee; (2) refer to rights or claims arising under ADEA; (3) be exclusive of rights or claims that may arise after the date the waiver is signed; (4) be in exchange for consideration in addition to anything of value to which the employee is

already entitled; (5) include a written notice to the employee to consult with an attorney before signing the agreement; (6) allow employees at least 21 days to consider the agreement (or 45 days if part of employment termination); and (7) include a provision that permits the employee to revoke the agreement within seven days.

ombudsman   A person appointed to investigate employee complaints and serve as a mediator between two disputing parties. May also serve as an advocate, counselor, and supporter of the grievant.

Omnibus Budget Reconciliation Act of 1987 (OBRA)   Made significant changes to funding and termination insurance rules applicable to defined benefit pension plans as well changes that affect defined contribution plans. The Act modified rules that limit the holding of employer securities by employee benefit plans and restricts the availability of an estate tax deduction for sales of employer securities to an employee stock option (ownership) plan.

Omnibus Budget Reconciliation Act of 1989 (OBRA)   Modified several of the continuation of health care coverage requirements of the **Consolidated Omnibus Budget Reconciliation Act of 1986**. Part of this bill relates to Medicare as a secondary payer and specifically to periods of coverage for qualified beneficiaries other than the covered employee which "shall not terminate before the close of the 36-month period beginning on the date the covered employee becomes entitled to [Medicare] benefits under title XVIII of the Social Security Act" (36 months after the date of the original qualifying event). The Act also required employers to report certain information to a Medicare Data Bank beginning with calendar year 1994.

Omnibus Budget Reconciliation Act of 1990 (OBRA)   One important provision of this bill established a $22 billion package of tax credits and grant money for poor working families. It was the first federal child care legislation passed since World War II. The Act provided for a three-year, $2.5 billion block grant for states to distribute to parents and day care providers. Recipients of grants could spend them as they wish, but they must meet minimum state health and safety standards, including being immunized to prevent the spread of infectious diseases. That requirement extends to situations where the money is used for child care in private homes. The Act lay the groundwork for a broad federal policy to encourage as well as regulate those who provide child care services. OBRA 1990 also expanded Medicare hospice benefits; provides reimbursement for mammography screening for early detection of breast cancer; mandated states to expand Medicaid coverage to poor children up to the age of 18 by the year 2000; required Medicaid to pay Medicare's Part B premiums, coinsurance, and deductibles for people at the poverty line; gave states more flexibility to provide home- and community-based long-term care services under Medicaid; and required pharmaceutical companies to offer state programs with discounts on prescriptions. To prevent exploitation by unscrupulous insurance agents, the Act prohibited both the sale of duplicative policies to Medicare beneficiaries and the sale of any medigap insurance to low-income older Americans who already receive additional health coverage from the Medicaid program.

Omnibus Budget Reconciliation Act of 1993 (OBRA)   As of January 1, 1994, increased the amount of Social Security subject to tax from the 50 percent base to 85 percent for individuals whose adjusted base income from all sources exceeded $34,000 and for couples with incomes above $44,000. OBRA 93 also reduced the deduction for business meal and entertainment expenses from 80 to 50 percent and made expenses for spouses who travel with an employee no longer deductible. The law eliminated the cap on earnings subject to the Medicare portion of the Social Security Tax; prohibited publicly-held corporations from deducting certain compensation in excess of $1 million per year for the CEO and the four other most highly compensated officers. The law increased income tax rates for high-income individuals from 31 to 36 percent for couples filing jointly with taxable income over $140,000, as well as single filers over $115,000 and heads of households over $127,000, and imposed a 10 percent surtax for individuals with taxable income above $250,000, creating a marginal tax rate of 39.6 percent. The legislation also phased-out

dependency exemption for high-income individuals; and reinstated targeted jobs credit through June 30, 1994. The law also contains changes in employee benefits tax and reporting procedures that become effective in 1994.

Omnibus Transportation Employee Testing Act of 1991   Requires alcohol and drug testing of safety-sensitive employees in the aviation, motor carrier, railroad, and mass transit industries. Rules promulgated by the Department of Transportation cover small employers and large employers, defined as those with 50 or more safety-sensitive employees. Implementation for large employers begins January 1, 1995 and for small employers January 1, 1996.

on-call pay plan   Involves payment of extra compensation to exempt supervisory and technical employees who are required to provide 24-hour services on demand. There are two types of plans: (1) "sandman pay," a pay plan that rewards employees for simply being available to work outside their regular hours — with only the requirement that they must be reachable and able to return to work within a specified period of time; and (2) call-in pay, in which employees are paid extra only when they are called in to perform work, either at the job site or by telephone or computer at home.

on-call time   Off-duty hours during which an employee is required to remain on call either at the work premises or so close to it that he or she cannot effectively use the time for personal purposes. According to the Fair Labor Standards Act, such restrictive on-call time is compensable as working time. An employee who is required to leave word where he or she can be reached is not considered working time, nor is one who wears a beeper while off-duty.

oncologist   A doctor of medicine who specializes in the diagnosis and treatment of cancer, such as **chemotherapy**.

on-demand learning system   A computer-driven learning package available to workers when needed for help on the job or off the job. The systems are designed to support workers at the job site with versatile and productive performance systems. Also called *just-in-time training* and *learner-controlled training*.

one best leadership
See consistency leadership.

one-group technique The simplest of the experimental procedures in which one thing, individual, or group has had introduced, varied, or subtracted some experimental factor or factors, and the resulting changes are reported or measured. For example, a group of trainees might take equivalent forms of a test to determine whether there is any change in their scores on the different forms as a result of the practice effect.

one-on-one training On-the-job, day-to-day learning experiences under the tutelage of a conscientious and experienced coach or supervisor. Strategies include telling or explaining, questioning, showing or demonstrating, drilling or practicing, providing feedback and follow up.

O*Net A comprehensive database, under development by the Department of Labor, that will identify and describe occupations, worker skills, knowledge, abilities and workplace requirements for jobs in all sectors of the economy.

one-ten-one hundred (1/10/100) rule A rule of thumb that holds that for every dollar spent on the prevention of product defects, it costs 10 times as much to inspect products to discover defects and 100 times as much to recall or replace defective products.

on-label prescribing Using a drug to treat a disorder for which it was intended and approved for that use by the federal Food and Drug Administration.

on-line Equipment or a process under the direct control of the **central processing unit** of a computer.

on-line access A means of inputting and accessing information (using a computer and a modem) through the **Internet.** Also called an *Intranet.*

On-Line Career Center A network of networks that offers employment advertising, outplacement services, and communications (URL **http://www.occ.com**).

on-line brainstorming
See computer conferencing.

on-line reference Availability of immediate access to instructions, cues, and other forms of help while using a computer applications program.

on-line services 1. Operations or processing that involve immediate and direct interaction with the database, including inputs and corrections, usually through video terminals connected to the computer. Allow users to enter information into the central computer or display information contained in the computer. Characterized by random transactions, immediate reports, responses to one-time inquiries, and distributed data entry. Examples are America On-line, CompuServe's Executive News Service, Delphi, Desktop Data Inc.'s NewsEdge, Dow Jones Information Services' Dow Vision, Genie, and Meade Data Central's Lexis, and Nexis. **2.** Provide access to the Internet. Tend to be more expensive and slower than **Internet service providers** but are easier to get connected and provide some extras. Examples are America Online, Compuserve, and Prodigy.

on-line transaction processing (OLTP) Data processing that is performed while the user is communicating with the computer. An example: making airline reservations.

on-site or near-site child care center A child care facility for company employees either owned and operated by the employer, constructed by the employer and donated to nonprofit employee-operated groups, or contracted by the employer with a for-profit or not-for-profit organization.

on-site services Services offered employees at their work sites to reduce time off the job, help them meet time constraints, and make them more productive. Services run the gamut from auto repair, shoe repair, beauty salons, barber shops, dry cleaning, and banking services to take-home meals and massage therapy.

One Stop Career Centers Provide comprehensive career planning and employment services through a single state-wide delivery system, accessible to the general public. Currently operating or under development in a majority of states.

Ontario Society for Training and Development (OSTD) Canada's largest training organization representing more than 1,300 training and human resource development practitioners. The Association acts as an advocate for training in Ontario, establishes and maintains professional standards, and serves its members by providing certification, educational programs, annual conferences, and publications. *Contact:* OSTD, 110 Richmond St. East, Ste. 206,, Toronto,

Ontario, Canada M5C 1P1 (416/367-5900; Fax 416/367-5900).

on-the-job training (OJT)   Planned and organized training conducted at the workplace, in the office, shop, laboratory, or in the field, on the production line, on the construction site, or behind the counter by a co-worker or supervisor. It is provided by means of demonstration and example, guided practice, and feedback on performance.

on-time   A measure of organizational, departmental, or work team efficiency determined by calculating the percentage of milestones or planned events achieved on schedule.

opaque projector   A projector that shows an image of solid objects such as pages from a book or a photograph on a screen.

open architecture   A term applied to a system, such as a computer, to which other elements can be added; that is, the system is not fixed but can be altered or modified in some meaningful way.

open-book management   An approach to management that emphasizes empowerment of employees by opening the firm's financial books to them, teaching them the language of finance, and providing them with a continuing flow of financial information. The objectives are to get employees to think and act like business persons and to make them more aware of how their daily decisions impact on the bottom-line.

open-collar worker   A **telecommuter** or other person who works at home and therefore does not have to "dress for success."

Open Competition Act of 1997   S. 606 introduced by Senator Tim Hutchinson, R-AR. would prohibit discrimination in the contract awarding process based on union membership.

open-ended health maintenance organization (OEHMO)   A form of managed care plan designed to contain health care costs by limiting employee choices through the use of such techniques as preauthorization of hospital admission and utilization review. They are "point-of-service" HMOs where there is a primary care physician, and utilization of medical services is tightly managed. OEHMOs are typically difficult to design because of insurance contract limitations and different copayments for regular office visits, prescription drugs, emergency room visits, and appointments with specialists.

open-ended option (OEOs)   See open-ended plan.

open-ended plan (OEPs)   A plan offered by health maintenance organizations that allows members to seek health care from nonparticipating physicians and other health care professionals. In exchange for using these providers, members pay higher premiums, deductibles, and copayments.

open-end questionnaire   See open form questionnaire.

open enrollment   A system where enrollment in company training programs is open to any employee upon application and approval by his or her immediate supervisor. Enrollment forms and schedules are mailed to branches and offices with deadlines for applying.

open enrollment period   **1.** The period when an employee may change health plans. **2.** A period of time during which individuals may sign up for medical or health insurance, for example, people who failed to sign up for Medicare's Medical Insurance (Part B) when they first became eligible, normally age 65, or who dropped Part B for some valid reason.

open form questionnaire   A questionnaire that allows respondents to present a more complete description of a situation by encouraging them to go beyond the numerical or factual data to get into attitudes and feelings, the background of responses, or the reasons for preferences or opinions.

open panel   A managed care health plan that contracts either directly or indirectly with private physicians to deliver health care in their own offices.

open pay system   A pay system in which employees know what other workers in the organization are being paid; for example, the U.S. government general schedule is openly published.

open season   An annual period of about one month's duration during which federal employees, annuitants (including survivors), and those receiving workers' compensation payments who are enrolled in health benefits plans under the **Federal Employee Health Benefits Program** may change plans, options, or type of enrollment (self only or self and family), or any combination of those changes. Federal employees who are not enrolled but are eligible for enrollment may enroll during the open season. Annuitants who are not enrolled may not enroll during the open season.

open shop A nonunionized organization in which workers decide for themselves whether they join the union.

open software technology A computer technology now in development that will facilitate interoperability. The system will enable users to integrate data, such as a spreadsheet, a graphic, and a paragraph of text, each from a different vendor and located on one or more networks, and produce a seamless product.

open window See early retirement incentive program.

operant behavior Emitted responses that occur without known stimuli. They are conditioned by providing a reinforcing stimulus when a desired response is emitted. For example, providing praise or a reward of some kind when a person responds to a conflict situation in a positive way is likely to result in a similar response to other conflict situations.

operant conditioning Calls for strengthening a desired response by reinforcement. Attributed to psychologist B. F. Skinner.

operating budget A budget that deals with individual items of expense, such as salaries and direct labor, supervision, contractual services and utilities, equipment and supplies, travel and tuition, conference and membership fees, and insurance premiums. It also consists of two subdivisions relating to revenues, the budget income statement, and to expenses, the supporting schedules. The supporting schedules include the sales, production, materials, procurement, direct labor, manufacturing overhead, inventory, administrative expense, distribution, and appropriations budgets.

operating system The software that controls a computer's basic functions, including reading and writing data on disks, managing the routing of data, and controlling the interface with the user.

Operating System/2 (OS/2) International business Machine's disk operating system, an alternative to **Microsoft-Disk Operating System** combined with **Windows.**

Operation Able (Ability Based on Long Experience) A nationwide source of help in finding skilled, motivated, and dependable older employees. Local offices assist employers to find full and part-time workers with long experience. Check your local telephone directory.

operational plan A short-term or mid-range plan, usually fit to a quarterly or yearly time frame. Operational plans focus on the human resources needed to support current, scheduled, or projected production or the types of output requirements for the time frame under consideration and the strategies and tactics needed to achieve the desired results.

operational validity The process and result of achieving maximum benefit from a test in terms of such things as administration, testing conditions and facilities, scoring, and use of results. Coined by Byham and Spitzer (*The Law and Personnel Testing,* 1971).

Operation Jobs An employer-friendly approach to solving the problem of illegal immigrant workers launched by the Immigration and Naturalization Service. Over a 30- to 60-day period, INS agents work with employers to remove illegal workers. Companies are then able to fill the vacated positions with unemployed U.S. citizens and legal immigrants without slowing or stopping production. With the help of participating organizations, such as state departments of human services and the Salvation Army (which have client bases of workers with low-level skills) replacements are recruited and hired.

operation process chart See process chart.

operations research (OR) The application of the scientific method to the study of alternative courses of action in decision making. It involves careful definition of the problem and the objective, systematic collection and assessment of facts, orderly development and testing of hypotheses, precise establishment of relationships among the facts, meticulous formulation of predictions based on hypotheses, and painstaking design of measures to evaluate the effectiveness of courses of action.

Operation Transition A massive outplacement program launched by the Department of Defense (DOD) in 1991. The effort was designed to help companies tap the new source of labor that will be created by plans to cut approximately 25 percent of DOD's military and civilian work force over the next

5 to 7 years. Features of the system: on-line access to an automated database of occupations organized by geographic location via a 900 phone number, an electronic bulletin board allowing employers to place free ads for specific jobs; DOD verification of candidate's training and experience at no charge; DOD payment of all moving and storage costs for up to one year for successful candidates for positions; and additional training paid for by DOD for outplaced personnel even if hired by private sector employers.

ophthalmologist A medical doctor who specializes in the diagnosis and treatment of diseases of the eye, such as macular degeneration, glaucoma, and cataracts.

opiates Drugs that give an individual an immediate "rush" of euphoria, follow by several hours of relaxation and reduced anxiety. Include heroin ("smack, "horse"), morphine (pectoral syrup), opium (paregoric, Dover's powder), methadone (dolophine, methadose), and codein.

opinion survey *See* attitude and opinion survey.

Opportunity 2000 Award An award presented annually to organizations by the U.S. Department of Labor to a federal contractor that has instituted "comprehensive work force strategies" to ensure equal employment opportunity and innovative programs and initiatives for "managing diversity and working to break the glass ceiling." Eligibility is limited to federal public interest contractors or federal contractors' organizations covered by Executive Order 11246 who have had a compliance review within the past three years, and have had no substantive violations of federal laws or pending enforcement actions.

opportunity cost **1.** The cost of foregoing other services when an HR/HRD/OD intervention is applied in an organization. *See also* labor costs; personnel costs. **2.** A **benchmark** used by corporate travel managers to make better comparisons of travel costs than standard industry averages provide. It allows companies to measure the cost of their travel policy enforcement in terms of lowest fare opportunities missed by travelers (lost savings due to missed lowest fares). It is calculated by determining the average segment cost for a specific month

and then computing the opportunity cost as follows:

$$\text{Opportunity Cost} = \frac{\text{Average Segment} - \text{Lowest Fare}}{\text{Average Segment}}$$

Opportunity cost can be translated into dollar impact simply by multiplying actual travel expenditures by the opportunity cost percentage as follows: Dollar impact = Travel Costs July 93 × Opportunity Cost July 93, Attributed to Bonnie Barbareck, director, MIS American Express Travel Related Services ("Leading Travel Indicators," *Corporate Travel*, November 1992, p. 8, P.O. Box 1788, Riverton, NJ 08077-9788).

opportunity-to-learn standards In education, standards that establish the conditions and resources needed to give students an equal chance to meet the performance standards.

optical character recognition (OCR) A software program that has data capture and recognition capabilities. The program recognizes and processes documents by converting the characters, including type face kerns and ligatures, foreign language characters, and scientific notation, into computer language.

optical disc *See* compact disc; videodisc.

optical disc drive (ODD) A new addition to the field of computer accessories. ODDs provide storage for 600 MB of existing data or pure storage space on a single 5.25-inch optical disc. They are especially useful for working with subjects that require large contiguous files, such as CAD, video, and multimedia. Three types are currently available: **compact disc, read-only memory; write once, read many;** and erasable. Each drive uses a corresponding type of disc, but they are not interchangeable. ODDs come in two configurations: external units ready to be connected to a computer and internal units designed to be installed inside a computer.

optical mark reader (OMR) A type of scanner that reads barcodes, such as those found on merchandise packages, and makes it possible to automate test grading, survey tabulation, management of library holdings, inventory control, accessing courseware, and many other applications with savings of hundreds of dollars and hours of time.

optical scanner A device which can "read" printed materials. For example, one application has software that can grade tests, assign final course grades, store the data by class, and analyze results. Data can be used for validity and reliability studies.

optical technology   *See* optoelectronic integrated circuit.

optimization model A statistical forecasting model that attempts to provide the forecaster with an ideal or best solution to a given set of needs or constraints to achieve optimal results. Optimization models always begin with predetermined objectives instead of starting with past experience. For example, determining the proper mix of technical and marketing skills in a department or identifying the working conditions most conductive to higher productivity.

optoelectronic integrated circuit (OEIC) A newly developed but not yet commercially available computer chip that transmits data by means of light instead of moving electrons along silicon conduits. OEIC is up to 20 times faster than conventional chips.

optoelectronic technology Systems, mechanisms, and circuitry used to increase the speed of computers. They permit electronic devices to communicate using pulses of laser light as the information conduits. The circuitry translates laser beams into electronic language that computers understand and back again into laser light.

oral and maxillofacial surgery Dental care involving surgery for tooth extractions, fractures of the jaw, reduction of dislocations, manipulation, aspiration, or injection of temporomandibular joints, and other oral surgery, including preoperative and postoperative care.

oral objective test Similar to paper-and-pencil tests except that the testee responds orally instead of in writing. Such tests consist of carefully constructed items in the form of true-false, completion, multiple-choice, or arrangement type questions.

oral reprimand A "Dutch Uncle" talk, given to an employee who has violated a work rule by his or her supervisor. The reprimand is given privately, clearly and tactfully, and specifically and constructively. It focuses on the job behavior, not on personality.

ordinal data Data that can be placed in rank-order.

ordinal measurement A measure that indicates rank order of merit or performance, such as the rankings of employees in terms of productivity or some other measure of performance.

organic speech defects Caused primarily by physical factors, such as accidents, disease, or heredity.

organizational analysis Detailed examination of root causes and effects and how environment, beliefs, systems, structures, processes, roles, policies, rules and regulations, outcomes, and other variables interact and affect each other.

organizational behavior
See human relations.

organizational behavior modification theory A theory of motivation that suggests that people behave in ways that help them avoid unpleasant outcomes (punishment) and attain pleasant ends (rewards). Therefore, the key to motivation is to determine the conditions that trigger desired behavior, establish them, and reinforce by rewards when the behaviors appear.

organizational distance Differences in organizational levels which often create barriers to communication because people at disparate organizational levels (executives, managers, technicians, hourly workers, and so on) have different values, different goals and priorities, dissimilar perspectives and perceptions, and unique ways of thinking.

organizational evaluation The use of instruments and strategies to assess organizational change in such areas as quality of communications, customer relations, job satisfaction, motivation and morale, and teamwork using such tools as observation, questionnaires, interviews, ratings, and records.

organizational survey Periodic and systematic examination and analysis of the organizational structure to ensure that it is consistent with current operating requirements. Such surveys consist of seven steps: planning, data collection, interpretation of data, development of solutions, presenting recommendations, installing and following up recommendations, and evaluating results.

organizational transformation (OT)
A general term covering new or cutting-edge training programs designed to reshape or transform organizations by stimulating motivation, innovation, and excellence through teamwork, empowerment, and participation. OT is viewed as the final stage of a continuum consisting of management-employee development, organization development, and organization transformation. In essence, it is

a long-range program to involve all employees in a major effort to change an organization's culture, values, and management processes and thereby improve productivity, product/service quality, results, and employee satisfaction.

organization and functions manual (O&FM) A document that describes the functions of an organization and all its subordinate elements, defines the relationships between and among elements, and describes the authority and accountability of each unit.

organization characteristics survey *See* organization climate survey.

organization chart A "wiring diagram," a hierarchically-arranged, clear, symmetrical, and unified block diagram, which shows existing activities, functions, levels, and lines of authority in an organization. It includes the title of each element and, by means of connecting lines, shows who is accountable to whom and who is in charge of what activities.

organization climate The corporate atmosphere, felt, rather than observed or defined. It is the product of the collective impact of policies, goals, objectives, priorities, beliefs, values, expectations, managerial techniques, and leadership styles on the motivation and actuation of people to accomplish the mission.

organization climate survey A data collection instrument used to obtain diagnostic information about an organization and used to study its climate and culture. Topics include communication, creativity, pay and benefits, management practices, policies, product and service quality, supervisory practices, the job itself, work conditions, and so on. An organization climate survey gathers employee attitudes, beliefs, feelings, opinions and perceptions, not facts. Also known as *employee attitude survey; employee opinion survey; job satisfaction survey, organization characteristics survey; work climate survey.*

organization culture An organization's basic beliefs and values about itself and its clients, customers, suppliers, and the public at large. It also encompasses an organization's view of its value to society. Culture is embodied in the way things are done in an organization as defined by both written and unwritten policies, procedures, and practices. It is manifested in how the organization defines success and how people are rewarded and punished — the organizational norms that

have become accepted and encouraged (or prescribed) by management.

organization design 1. The skeleton that gives an organization its form and defines the limits of its growth and performance. Organization design encompasses purposes, principles, policies, technical systems, information and decision systems, and people and reward systems. **2.** The process of configuring or reconfiguring the structure of an organization — establishing or changing the arrangement of functions, authority, and relationships between and among various elements of the organization.

organization development (OD) A planned and systematic strategy for changing and improving the management and operation of an enterprise to increase effectiveness, enhance productivity, boost return on investment, improve the quality of work life, and raise the level of employee job satisfaction. In more specific terms, the OD process is aimed at clarifying the mission, goals, and objectives of the organization, align and integrate individual employee, unit, and enterprise goals, make the organization more effective, deal effectively with technical, managerial, and human problems, improve cooperation, collaboration, communication, and teamwork between managers and their subordinates and among units, promote openness and free discussion of differences, issues, and problems, improve decision making processes and promote employee and union acceptance of decisions, build acceptance of and ability to deal with change, improve individual and team performance and interpersonal relationships, and find and articulate consensus and translate it into action.

The Organization Development Institute A non-profit educational organization of 500 members established to promote a better understanding of and disseminate information about organization development to the public and to members. There are three categories of membership: student, regular, and professional consultant. *Contact:* The O.D. Institute, 11234 Walnut Ridge Rd., Chesterland, OH 44026-1299 (216/461-4333; Fax 216/729-9319; E-mail **DoonWCole@aol. com**; URL **http://members.aol.com/odinst**).

organization development intervention A strategy or technique used in the organization development process. Systems interventions include management transition workshops, change management strategies, action planning workshops addressing major issues and problems, benefit-cost analyses for resource allocation, strategic planning, organization planning and design, training and development, job enrichment, enlargement, and redesign, management and HR audits, and group decision making and participative or multiple-management strategies. Organization development interventions include action planning conferences, behavior modeling and modification, communications training, conflict resolution, creative problem solving, goal clarification, intergroup cooperation, leadership training, management by objectives, management improvement conferences, meeting and conference design and management, performance counseling training, process observation, role clarification, small group problem solving, team building, time management, and unit assessment surveys.

Organization Development Network (ODN) A professional association of organization development practitioners and others interested in the field of OD — the management of change in organizations. In addition to its annual national conference, ODN sponsors special-interest conferences on issues of current concern to organizations and publishes the quarterly *OD Practitioner. Contact:* ODN, 76 South Orange Ave., Ste. 101, South Orange, NJ 07079 -1923 (201/763-7337) Fax 201/763-7488; E-mail **mfhoyer@aol. com**; URL **http://www.odnet.org**).

organization diagnosis An important element of the organization development process. Organization diagnosis consists of the collection and analysis of data subsequently used to identify the strengths and weaknesses of the organization and the changes that need to be made to make it more viable and productive.

organization documents All typewritten, photocopied, or printed organization materials, including charts, maps, diagrams, photographs, video- and audiotapes, computer printouts, and so on.

organization history In meeting management, a record of an organization's previous meetings provided to the host property to describe the needs of the group and impact on the property. Typically includes information pertaining to room block, room pick-up, meeting space requirements, and food and beverage revenues generated. *Also called* group history.

organization planning The process of translating an organization's philosophy, vision, goals, and objectives into policies, rules, and practices and taking into full account the firm's culture, structure, environment, competitive position, opportunities, and limitations. It aims at efficiency, effectiveness, and balance among functions that have the greatest impact on achievement of enterprise goals. The resulting plan defines policy, describes structure, philosophy, and goals, identifies communication channels, identifies and describes key positions, authority, responsibility, and accountability.

organization structure The actual configuration of an organization, which identifies reporting chains and authority relationships. It is the hierarchical arrangement of the various functional elements, the authority framework, and the pattern of interrelations of an organization.

organization survey Study of an organization by a team of qualified organization analysts to ensure that the structure of the organization or any of its major components is appropriate and sound. The team completes a six step process involving (1) planning, (2) data collection, (3) data interpretation and evaluation, (4) development of the revised structure, (5) implementation, and (6) monitoring and followup. The team reviews enterprise and employee records, enterprise policies and procedures manuals and other corporate documents, administers and analyzes questionnaires, conducts interviews, occupational, job, and task analyses, analyzes organization charts, organization and functions manuals, work distribution and workflow charts, and direct observation of people at work.

organization taboos Concepts and practices that are fervently held, at least by the upper echelons of the organization, as universal, crystal clear, correct, and accurate portrayals of what cannot or should not be done. Violators are subject to penalties although they may not be overt.

organization vision Top management's articulation of a picture of what the organization should be (in terms of its culture, climate, quality of work life, and performance) and how it should operate in the future.

organized labor *See* union.

organizing The managerial function concerned with identifying the functions and activities that must be conducted, grouping them into logical subdivisions, making clear delegations of authority, clarifying authority relationships both horizontally and vertically within the organization and with other line and staff elements of the company, and assigning each group to a leader with the authority to manage.

organ transplant An important means of maintaining the health and physical capacity of many people who in an earlier time were destined for an early death (such as severe heart disease) or for expensive and lifelong treatments (such as kidney dialysis). Today, many organs can be harvested immediately following the donor's death: heart, liver, lungs, kidneys, corneas, skin, and so on.

orientation A program designed to provide new employees with complete and uniform information about the firm, its organization, mission, functions and policies, compensation, benefits, services, work requirements, standards, rules, safe work habits, and desirable employee-management relations. The objective is to develop confident, loyal, effective, and productive workers and to reduce the likelihood of rule violations, accidents and injuries, discharges, resignations, and grievances. Orientation programs are offered to people following initial hire, transfer, and promotion.

origin The base of reference on a graph — the zero point on both the abscissa (x-axis) and the ordinate (y-axis).

original equipment manufacturer (OEM) The original producer of equipment or components that form a part of a delivered product.

originality The capacity to be inventive and imaginative. The ability to play with concepts, ideas, and relationships, juggle elements into improbable positions, develop wild hypotheses, express the implausible, and think the unthinkable.

orthodontics Dental care involving the supervision, guidance, and correction of developing and mature dentofacial structures.

orthopedic and mobility impairments People who have suffered the loss or normal use of limbs, bones, or muscles due to disease, accident, injury, or deformity (such as cerebral palsy, muscular dystrophy, multiple sclerosis, tuberculosis of the bones or joints, congenital deformities, and amputation). Many must use wheelchairs, crutches or canes, or prostheses (artificial hands or grasping devices, arms, legs, or feet) of one type or another.

orthopedist A medical doctor who specializes in surgery involving the bones, joints, and muscles, ranging from total hip replacement and delicate hand or facial surgery to treating athletes with knee or elbow injuries.

orthotics Devices that can assist individuals with mobility, daily living, and workplace activities. They include such devices as braces, cervical collars, shoe inserts that correct foot alinement, and hand splints to assist individuals with partial or spastic quadriplegia in such tasks as eating, writing, and keyboarding.

The Orton Dyslexia Society An international nonprofit organization of 10,000 members in 45 branches in the United States, one in Canada, and one in Israel. The Society is dedicated to the study and treatment of dyslexia, sharing information with its members through publications, conferences, and a network of volunteers throughout the country. *Contact:* The Orton Dyslexia Society, Chester Bldg./Ste. 382, 8600 LaSalle Rd., Baltimore, MD 21286-2044 (800/222-3123 or 410/296-0232; Fax 410/321-5069; E-mail **info@ods.org**; URL **http: www.ods.org**).

OSHA Under the 1990 OBRA (budget reconciliation package) civil penalties for violation of the federal workplace health and safety standards have been increased by a factor of seven. Maximum penalty for willful violations of standards is now $70,000, (up from $10,000) per violation. Repeat violators are subject to the $70,000 maximum penalty per fine, and for "serious" violations and "other than serious" violations, the fines have increased from $1,000 to $7,000 maximum.

OSHA Hazard Communication Standard (OSHA HCS) *See* Hazard Communication Standard of 1988.

OSHA Process Safety Rule A standard established to prevent catastrophic chemical explosions that became effective May 26, 1993 and was fully implemented in May 1997. Requires petrochemical and chemical companies, natural gas manufacturers, and other industries that transport or mix chemicals to analyze potential hazards at every step of chemical processes, take action to avoid and prevent chemical releases and explosions, adopt detailed management plans, and provide written operating procedures for all safety systems and for each operating phase. The rule also requires employers to train their workers on the specific safety and health hazards, emergency operations, and safe working practices "applicable to the employee's job tasks" and requires contractors to train their workers in chemical processes to ensure the safety of both contract workers and those directly employed by a company and document all training.

osteoarthritis A degenerative condition in which the cartilage in the joints becomes deformed and enlarged, causing pain and preventing normal movement of the joint. The disease is caused by the erosion of cartilage, the spongy tissue at the ends of bones that functions as a shock absorber. Affecting an estimated 15.8 million Americans, it is the most common form of arthritis and occurs in women three times as often as in men.

osteopathic medicine Diagnosis and treatment provided by medical practitioners called osteopaths (D.O.'s). These medical doctors are almost indistinguishable from doctors of medicine (M.D.'s). They prescribe drugs and perform surgery. Some use manipulation as a main modality of treatment.

osteoporosis A crippling disease, caused by loss of minerals, particularly calcium, from the bones mainly as a result of aging. Bones become weak, brittle, and more susceptible to fractures, especially of the hip, spine, arms, and wrist. More common in women, probably due to the lack of the hormone estrogen, although it can also be the result of poor diet, prolonged inactivity, or certain drugs, such as cortisone.

other party liability (OTL) *See* coordination of benefits.

other weird arrangement (OWA) Applies to any novel and unconventional managed care plan.

otolaryngologist A medical doctor who specializes in the diagnosis and treatment of problems of the ear, nose, and throat, ranging from infected tonsils and sinuses to serious ailments like head and neck cancers and deafness.

outcome-based education (OBE) or training (OBT) Assessment of the success of training or education programs based on enrollee performance rather than inputs (number of enrollees, length of training, and so on).

outcomes analysis
See outcomes management.

outcomes management A system for measuring and analyzing the impact of ordinary medical care on the clinical status, function, and well-being of patients. The system relies on epidemiologic principles for making comparisons. "Outcomes" include better quality of life, how soon employees return to work, whether they have pain or resumed their normal activities, whether they feel better, and so on, as well as such traditional clinical measures as lowered blood sugar, blood pressure, and cholesterol level. Attributed to Paul M. Elwood, Jr., M.D., developer of the HMO concept 20 years ago.

outcomes research Studies of the effects of medical and surgical treatment or procedures on such things as whether specific interventions actually save lives and effect cures, how patients feel, their quality of life, presence or absence of pain and its severity, whether they can pursue normal activities, as well as typical clinical measures such as blood pressure, blood sugar level, and cholesterol level.

outdoor experiential training (OET) A method of business-oriented training that combines conventional classroom methods and techniques with hands-on experiences to develop teamwork, often involving the active participation of upper-level managers as well as workers and their supervisors. It uses voluntary physical activities that are challenging but not life-threatening, such as rafting, rock climbing, spelunking, and crossing rope bridges. Activities are usually preceded by classroom briefings on purposes and goals and are invariably concluded with a review and feedback session at which the goals of the activity are repeated and lessons learned are related to the business environment.

outdoor-centered program A training program designed to build teamwork. Participants sleep and eat indoors but many of their activities are conducted outdoors using specially designed facilities such as rope courses (high and low) where activities take place above the ground.

outdoor learning program *See* adventure training; Outward Bound.

outdoor management development *See* adventure training.

outdoor training *See* adventure training.

outlet In meeting planning, a restaurant or lounge in a meeting facility.

outline font On the Macintosh computer, a **font** that has two parts: (1) the **bitmap font** that is seen on the screen and appears in the menu; and (2) the printer font that holds the mathematical outline of the font that tells the **PostScript** printer how to create the letter forms with smooth lines and curves.

out of network A term applied to flexible benefits programs where employees choose to use non-preferred health care providers each time they use medical services.

out-of-pocket direct costs Expenses actually paid in check or cash for a specific project. For example, travel and per diem expenses, training room rentals, learning materials, and coffee for seminar participants.

out-of-pocket payment Expending personal funds for health care not paid for by Medicare or private insurance, such as **deductible** and **coinsurance** payments and other noncovered products and services.

out-of-the-box hiring (OTBH) A staffing strategy dictated by the need for functional competencies rather than industry-specific skills under conditions of changing markets, new technologies, mergers, and intense competition. Involves recruiting workers from other industries having professional competencies that differ from those normally required for a position.

outpatient care Health care provided in a physician's or other health professional's office, in a hospital day-care facility, or in a clinic. Such services as surgery, radiology, pathology, and physical, mental health, and substance abuse therapy are commonly provided. Other services include occupational and speech therapy.

outpatient facility A facility designed to provide one-time or continuing health and medical services to individuals who have not been admitted to hospital inpatient care.

outplacement Comprehensive and integrated services provided to both employees and management in connection with termination of employment. For employees it involves job-finding counseling and assistance to displaced or terminated workers by the organization dismissing the employee. Services may include workshops and training, individual assessment and counseling, access to computerized data banks of job openings, résumé preparation, separate on-site facilities, even private offices, for conducting job searches, secretarial assistance, and financial counseling. For management, it involves providing advice and assistance in planning and administering the termination process: how to terminate humanely and effectively, how to realine human resources planning with corporate strategic planning, how to formulate the severance package, how to conduct the termination interview, how to maintain the morale and productivity of the remaining employees, and how to promote a positive company image to its various constituencies and the general public. Not considered by the IRS (IRS Ruling 92-69) as a part of an employee's income and therefore not taxable unless the terminated employee is given the option of receiving cash or an equivalent amount of outplacement services.

outplacement counseling Counseling provided to terminated employees to help them identify the reasons for the dismissal, accept the finality of the action, identify strengths, skills, and talents that can be stressed in seeking new employment, and provide leads for and assistance in the job search.

output technology Means of retrieving data from a computer. Includes monitors (screens), sound (speech, music, and the like), and printers.

outreach program A means of keeping employees informed of the programs and services available to them, such as the **employee assistance program.** Makes use of group and individual briefings, posters, memos, meetings, kiosks, slide shows, and videocassettes.

outsourcing **1.** The practice of hiring outside consultants, trainers, vendors, or other types of professionals or technicians rather than employing full-time personnel. It is a strategy for freeing management to concentrate on critical functions and activities by transferring routine and repetitive tasks to a third party. and reduce costs. *See also* temporary employee. **2.** Using external consulting firms and service agencies to administer benefit plans, such as flexible benefit plans. Advantageous for small employers and when outside sources can support company objectives and existing company computer systems can manage the program. Main disadvantage is loss of control and access to data. **3.** An alternative staffing option. Involves contracting with a company that has expertise in a certain function to take full responsibility for the performance of that function — rather than just provide personnel to perform it. Often used to provide equipment maintenance, food services, and security.

outsourcing-to-temps A staffing strategy that involves contracting with temp agencies to provide the resources required for entire functions, such as benefits administration — or hiring an agency representative at a company's worksite to manage temporary workers.

outventuring An alternative form of **outsourcing**, in which a department of division of a company scheduled for outsourcing is turned over to the group's own employees, who form an independent business. The new business is owned by some or all of the employees, and their first and primary customer is the corporation they formerly worked for.

Outward Bound Schools operating in 36 countries (plus the military services) that attempt to instill self-confidence and cooperation in participants by placing them in unfamiliar environments (often in a wilderness setting) that develop their abilities to handle challenges. Usually involves physical as well as mental challenges and invariably stresses trust and teamwork.

overhead costs One of the primary categories in the total costs of an HR/HRD/OD program. They consist of support staff salaries, office and classroom rentals, utilities, and the like.

overhead projector A training device that projects an image of anything printed, written, or drawn on a transparent sheet of acetate.

overlap In education, an agreement among colleges and universities to award student financial aid on the basis of need, arrived at through meetings of participating institutions. At those meetings the formula for determining need and the amount to award

students accepted at more than one institution are determined. The practice has been labeled as unlawful collusion and price-fixing by the Department of Justice but a case has not yet been decided by the courts.

overlay In desktop publishing, a proofing technique in which four color-separated contact prints can be viewed separately and overlaid on each other.

overlearning Repeating a fact or practicing a skill until the learning is ingrained or "fixed" — and will be retained even if not used and available for automatic recall when needed, even under extremely stressful conditions.

overpricing In health care, premium rates that are unacceptably high in the marketplace. May be due to avarice, failure to control utilization, excessive overhead; human error, or a panic response to previous low-balling.

overrates *See* flagged rates.

override In travel management, a payment, in addition to standard commissions, made by airlines to travel agencies for preferential treatment when selling space to their customers and clients. The purpose is to increase the airline's market share.

Overseas Private Investment Corporation (OPIC) Provides information on setting up a business overseas. Also offers programs on direct loans, loan guarantees, and political risk insurance. Makes available information packets describing eligibility qualifications and application procedures. *Contact:* OPIC 1615 M. St., N.W., Washington DC 20527 (800/424-OPIC).

Overseas Security Advisory Council (OSAC) Provides liaison between the State Department and the business community. Operates the Overseas Security Electronic Bulletin Board (EBB), which lists the following information by country: State Department travel advisories, security and crime reports, police and diplomatic emergency numbers, profiles of terrorist groups, and so on. Free to U.S. firms with business overseas and accessible via personal computer or telephone modem. *Contact:* DS/DSS/OSAC, 2216 Gallows Rd., Dunn Loring, VA 22027 (703/204-6185).

overtime Work performed in excess of 40 hours in any week for which, under the **Fair Labor Standards Act of 1938,** employees must be paid one-and-one-half times their normal wage rates. Some organizations pay more than one-and-one-half times normal wage rates and some pay for hours worked in excess of 37.5 hours.

overtime by plan Limiting the amount and frequency of overtime assignments in an effort to avoid employee burnout, lowered productivity, and increases in rejects and reworks, Involves communicating the reasons for the overtime, limiting the duration of the overtime program, monitoring employees, checking the quality of products and services, and providing financial and other rewards and recognition for employees' efforts.

P

PA 1. Physician assistant. **2.** Privacy Act of 1974.

PAC Political action committee.

PAPA Participant action plan approach.

PAR Preadmission review.

PASS Plan for Achieving Self-Support.

PAT Preadmission testing.

PATA Pacific Asia Travel Association.

PATC Professional, administrative, technical, and clerical survey.

PAYSOP Payroll-based stock option plan.

PBGC Pension Benefit Guarantee Corporation.

PBM 1. Pharmacy benefit management. **2.** Prescription benefit management.

PBS Public Broadcasting Service.

PBT Performance-based training.

PC Personal computer.

P.C. 1. Politically correct. **2.** Professional corporation.

PCHCARA Pepper Commission Health Care Access Reform Act of 1991.

PCMA Professional Convention Management Association.

PCN Primary care nurse.

PCO Professional conference organizer.

PCP Primary care physician.

PCS Professional conference Specialist.

PD Public domain.

PDA 1. Pregnancy Discrimination Act of 1978. **2.** Personal data assistant. **3.** Personal digital assistant.

PDCA Plan, do, check, act.

PDK Phi Delta Kappa.

PDL Page-description language.

PDP 1. Personal development program. **2.** Prescription drug plan.

PDPO Public Disability Pension Offset.

PDSA Plan-Do-Study-Act.

PE 1. Practical exercise. **2.** Price earnings (ratio).

PEBES Personal Earnings and Benefit Estimate Statement.

PEO Professional employer organization.

PEPP Permanent-equity pension plan.

PERS Personal emergency response system.

PERT Program evaluation and review technique.

PESS Property Essential to Self-Support.

PET Positron emission tomography.

PFC Passenger facility charge.

PFK Pay for knowledge.

PFS 1. Pay for skills. **2.** Personal Financial Specialist.

PGCM Private geriatric care management.

PHO Physician hospital organization.

PHR Professional in Human Resources.

PI Programmed instruction.

PIA Primary insurance amount.

PIC Private industry council.

PIHRA Professionals in Human Resources Association.

PIMS Personal information management system.

PIP Productivity improvement program.

PIT Performance improvement technologist.

PLATO Programmed Logic for Automatic Teaching Operations.

PLC	Permanent Labor Certification (program).	**PR**	Public relations.
PLR	Private letter ruling.	**PRES**	Presentation (Internet abbreviation).
PLS	Please (Internet abbreviation).	**PRK**	Photo-refractive keratectomy.
PLUS	1. Project Literacy U.S. 2. Parent Loans to Undergraduate Students.	**PRO**	Peer review organization.
		Progs	Progressive proofs.
PM	Participative management.	**PROM**	Programmable read-only memory.
PMAA	Personnel Management Association of Aztlan.	**PRWORA**	Personal Responsibility and Work Opportunity Reconciliation Act of 1996.
PMO	Physician ownership model.	**PSA**	1. Personal security account. 2. Prostate specific antigen.
PMP	Participative management process.		
PMPM	Per member per month.	**PSE**	Psychological Stress Evaluator.
PMPY	Per member per year.	**PSI**	1. Professional Secretaries International. 2. Personnel selection inventory.
PMS	1. Premenstrual syndrome. 2. Pantone matching system.		
PMT	Photomultiplier tube.	**PSP**	Performance share plan.
PNHP	Physicians for a National Health Program.	**PSS**	Performance support system.
		PSSMT	Professional Society for Sales & Marketing Training.
PNI	Psychoneuroimmunology.	**PT**	1. Physical training. 2. Performance technology.
PNR	Passenger name record.		
PO	Provider organization.	**PTMPY**	Per thousand members per year.
POA	Power of attorney.	**PTO**	Paid time off.
POD	Payable-on-death (account)	**PTPA**	Portal-to-Portal Act of 1947.
PODN	Professional Organizational Development Network in Higher Education.	**PTS**	Performance to schedule.
		PTSD	Post traumatic stress disorder.
POI	Program of instruction.	**PUP**	Performance unit plan.
PONSI	Program on Non-Collegiate Sponsored Instruction.	**PVA**	Paralyzed Veterans of America.
		PVT	Photovoltaic technology.
POP	Point-of-purchase.	**PWA**	Person with AIDS.
POS	Point-of-service.	**PWD**	People with disabilities.
POTS	Plain old telephone system.	**PWI**	Projects with Industry.
PPA	1. Preferred provider arrangement. 2. Pension Protection Act of 1987.		
PPBS	Planning, programming, budgeting system.		
PPE	Personal protective equipment.		
PPFP	Prepared and perishable food program.		
PPI	Payment performance index.		
PPO	Preferred provider organization.		
PPP	Point-to-point protocol.		
PPS	Prospective payment system.		
PQMI	Process quality management and improvement.		

pacer A device used to speed up the reading process by reducing the amount of time the eyes fix on a group of words. In effect, the device forces the reader's eyes to move across a line of type more rapidly.

Pacer Center, Inc. A coalition of 20 Minnesota disability organizations established to improve and expand opportunities that enhance the quality of life for children and adults with disabilities — physical, mental, learning, and emotional — and their families. Through the Transition and Natural Supports in the Workplace project, funded under a five-year grant from the Departments of Labor and Health and Human

Services, PACER helps businesses hire people with disabilities, develops the support services businesses need to incorporate them into the work force, and identifies the school training needed for them to become successful employees. *Contact:* Pacer Center, 4826 Chicago Ave., South, Minneapolis, MN 55417-1098 [612/827-2966 (voice and TDD) Fax 612/827-3065; E-mail **mnpacer@ edu.gte.net**; URL **http://www.pacer.org**].

Pacific Asia Travel Association (PATA)
An association of approximately 2,200 members whose mission is to contribute to the growth, value, and quality of travel and tourism to and within the Pacific Asia area. PATA member organizations represent all facets of the travel industry. *Contact:*, PATA, One Montgomery St., Ste. 1000, San Francisco, CA 94104 (415/986-4646; Fax 415/986-3458; E-mail **PATAHQ@ix.netcom. com**; URL **http://www.pata.org/patanet**).

Pacific Islanders Persons having origins in any Pacific island; for example, American Samoa, Caroline Islands, and Marshall Islands.

Pacific rim Countries located on the perimeter of the western Pacific Ocean — primarily the economic giants of Japan, South Korea, Taiwan, Hong Kong, Singapore, and the increasingly productive nations of Indonesia, Malaysia, the Philippine Republic, and Thailand.

package A term used to describe any combination of salaries and benefits received by workers as a result of collective bargaining.

packaged program
See off-the shelf program.

page buffer In desktop publishing, a disk incorporated into an image setter that ensures consistent printer output quality. It buffers an entire page image before transmitting it to the recorder. By sending the **raster** lines in one continuous stream, the recorder never has to stop in mid job. Therefore, the film in the image setter is exposed smoothly and consistently.

page-description language (PDL) In desktop publishing, a standard language, such as **PostScript**, that tells the printer's engine how to compose a page. For example, when a printer receives a PostScript file form a computer, it is processed onto a **raster** format that can be recognized by the print engine.

paid family leave Paid time off to attend to family needs.

paid leave bank A program designed to reduce employee absenteeism by allotting

a bank of time for sick leave, vacation, or personal leave. If employees exceed their allotment for a given time period, disciplinary action is taken through a no fault system. Costs are cut by reducing the number of sick days placed in the bank.

paid time off (PTO) **1.** Vacation days (typically 11 days per year the first year of employment, increasing to 24 days after 30 years), sick days (typically 10 days per year with carryover allowed by almost half of American companies), and personal days (provided by only 25 percent of American companies) away from the workplace paid for by the employer. **2.** A flexible benefit plan option in which employees are given the opportunity to buy and sell paid time off. They can buy additional vacation time by trading other benefits for it or sell it for benefits they prefer.

paid time off banking program A system in which a certain number of days of paid time off are allotted to employees to use as they see fit. Established to reduce absenteeism and costs and give employers more flexibility.

paint **1.** In video, altering or enhancing the color, texture, intensity, or any other visual element of an image. **2.** In desktop publishing, software used to create **bit-mapped graphics** images.

paired comparisons A relative rating system that requires the rater to compare the performance of each member of a group with every other member, one at a time. The number of times a person is chosen as the better of the two is tallied; that yields an index of the number of times the person is chosen compared with the number of persons being rated. The total "scores" for individuals identify reverse rank order of the group — the highest scorer is the the best performer and the lowest is the poorest.

pairing Trains employees from diverse backgrounds to mediate disputes, foster cultural sensitivity, and resolve interpersonal problems among workers. Participants, chosen by managers from a group of volunteers to represent a mix of genders, races, ethnic groups, and jobs, learn how to examine all possibilities, overcome communication breakdowns, intolerance, and prejudices, and apply their knowledge of the company's culture to current issues. Following training, consulting pairs who mirror the racial and educational backgrounds and experience may be assigned to employees having difficulties to help them resolve their problems. Created by Pope & Associates, a Cincinnati-based management consulting firm.

Pakistani brain A computer virus that can cause serious damage to computer-stored information.

palmtop A portable computer that is battery powered and about the size and weight of a personal organizer.

panel A training strategy in which 3 to 10 people, under the direction of a moderator, present their views on a particular subject or problem, or present assigned aspects of a broad topic. Panelists are drawn from operating and staff elements or from outside the organization. Trainees themselves sometimes serve as members of panels. Following the presentations by panelists, trainees are encouraged to participate through questions directed to individual panelists. Panels are used to explore unsettled issues and problems, present differing points of view, identify and clarify the advantages and disadvantages of a course of action, and make use of special knowledge, experience, or expertise.

panic disorders Uncontrollable fear responses to ordinary, nonthreatening situations. They can occur in anyone and affect two to five percent of Americans, most often, people in their early twenties. Characterized by sweating, hot or cold flashes, choking or smothering sensations, racing heart, labored breathing, trembling, chest pains, faintness, disorientation, or feeling of dying, losing control, or losing one's mind. May be caused by chemical or hormonal imbalances, drugs or alcohol, stress, or other events.

pantone matching system (PMS) A set of standard color specifications used by desktop publishing designers and printers to ensure precise color matching.

paper-and-pencil objective test A test consisting of carefully constructed questions in the form of true-false, matching, completion, multiple-choice, or arrangement items.

paper-and-pencil test A test that may include objective-, subjective-, essay-, or projective-type test items used to measure achievement, mental ability, specific information, job and trade knowledge, mechanical aptitude and psychomotor skills, cognitive skills, linguistic aptitude, supervisory and managerial abilities, interests, and personality and temperament. Testees respond by writing their answers in long-hand, circling or underlining responses, or marking machine-readable answer sheets.

paperless book A book that is published in electronic form; that is, the text is displayed on "white" pages that replicate ordinary books on the screen of a portable computer, rather than on paper. Instead of scrolling, the user "turns" pages by the touch of a button — and can flip back and forth, underscore passages, or place notes in the margins. Readers can also enlarge the type face, copy passages onto a notebook, and make detailed word, name, or phrase searches.

paradigm shift Looking at an issue or problem from a completely different perspective.

Paragon Awards Annual awards presented by *Corporate Meetings & Incentives* magazine to the hotels, resorts, and conference centers that did the best job of handling meeting and incentive groups during the year. Nominations of hotels are based on the quality of their services to meetings and incentives, while resorts are judged on heir environment, services, and recreational amenities. Conference centers, which must be members of the International Association of Conference Centers (or judged by the editors to be of equivalent purpose and quality), are chosen on the basis of facilities, equipment, and staffing, particularly for small meetings. *Contact: Corporate Meetings & Incentives,* The Graybar Building, #1650, 420 Lexington Ave., New York, NY 10170-1699 (212) 338-9124.

paralegal A law provider; a person who works in a law office but is not a lawyer. May have received formal training at the associate or baccalaureate degree level.

paralinguistic behavior Audible sounds that accompany oral language but are not actual words. Includes inflection, volume, rate, articulated pauses (um, ah, er, and so on), and coughs.

parallel computer A data processor that harnesses tens or hundreds of relatively low-powered computers to work on a single complex problem at superfast speeds, upwards of 9 billion calculations per second. These supercomputers break up problems into thousands of pieces and solve them simultaneously. Examples are the CM-200 developed by Thinking Machines Corporation of Cambridge, MA and the Touchstone Delta computer produced by Intel and installed at the California Institute of Technology.

parallel-group technique   A group method of experimentation in which two or more equivalent groups are used at the same time under conditions that are as carefully controlled as possible and where only a single factor or variable is manipulated or changed. The experimental factor is changed for one group (the experimental group), while the parallel group serves as the control for comparative purposes, undergoing customary, nonexperimental conditions. For example, a researcher may require one group of trainees to take a test under conditions of instructor encouragement, another group under conditions of instructor discouragement, and a third group using the regular directions for administration.

parallel processing computer   *See* supercomputer.

parallel team   A team of employees whose members participate only part time while continuing to perform the duties of their regular jobs.

Paralyzed Veterans of America (PVA) A nonprofit veterans service organization chartered by the U.S. Congress to improve the care, treatment, and rehabilitation of veterans who have a spinal cord injury or disease. PVA funds 58 full-time service offices across the United States. PVA programs include veterans benefits counseling, spinal cord research, advocacy and legislation, barrier-free design, wheelchair sports and recreation, and public education. *Contact:* PVA, 801 Eighteenth St., N.W., P.O. Box 96010, Washington, DC 20006 (800/872-1300 or 202/872-1300; URL **http:www.pva.org**).

paramedic   **1.** A military corpsman or physician who parachutes into inaccessible areas to provide medical attention to persons in need of such services. **2.** Persons who have received 1,000 or more hours of medical training and are authorized to perform technically complex procedures such as administering intravenous medications and surgically inserting airways into the windpipe.

paraphrasing   A technique used in counseling and conflict resolution to verify that a message has been correctly received or to identify where a breakdown has occurred in communication. It is a restatement of what has been heard in different words.

paraplegia   A symptom of spinal cord injury — paralysis affecting the legs and lower parts of the body. Approximately 1.4 million Americans have paralysis of the extremities.

paraprofessional   A person who occupies a position with knowledge and skills requirements that fall somewhere between those of technical and professional jobs; that is, they involve higher-order technical competencies. Examples include drafting specialist, computer software designer, X-ray technologist, and ophthalmic dispenser. Also referred to as *semiprofessional.*

paratransit system   Alternative public transportation or dial-a-ride systems for people with disabilities instituted because most transit systems, including stations and bus stops, are not accessible for those who use wheelchairs or people with hearing, vision developmental , or other disabilities. Most require 24-hour advance notice for reservations.

parental leave   A fringe benefit whereby employees are allowed to use paid sick days or take extended leave without pay after the birth or adoption of a child or to care for a dependent child or parent.

parent education seminar   A form of employer-supported child care benefit in which staff or outside consultants organize forums to inform employees about community resources and provide support on work and family issues.

Parent Loans to Undergraduate Students (PLUS)   Loans available to support tuition and fees for undergraduate students with interest rates at the three-month Treasury-bill rate plus 3.1 percent, adjusted annually, and with a cap of 10 percent. PLUS loans allow participants to borrow the entire cost of education, minus anything received in student aid. Borrowers with no financial need will pay a 6.5 percent up front fee, and those with need will pay anywhere from 5 to 8 percent, depending on the lender.

parent training   Programs offered by nonprofit and proprietary organizations to train corporate trainers or volunteers to teach parents how to help their children in school. Examples are Linking Home and School Through the Workplace; MegaSkills.

Pareto analysis   A method of establishing cost target priorities developed by Alfred

Pareto in the late 19th century. The technique helps separate the important from the unimportant. It is based on a natural phenomenon: that 80 percent of all outcomes results from about 20 percent of a given group of causes. For example, 80 percent of rejected products will be caused by 20 percent of employees; and 80 percent of the profits will come from the sale of 20 percent of the product line. A Pareto analysis is depicted in graphic form, with columns arranged in descending order of importance. Each column represents a different element or problem. Also known as the *80-20 rule.*

Pareto chart   A bar graph ranking in order of importance the causes, sources, types, or reasons for problems and/or opportunities. It serves as a means of exercising quality control and is used extensively in industry. Essentially it employs the principle of management by exception. A Pareto chart displays problems or causes by the magnitude of their effect. Defects or other variables are plotted by type on a **histogram**. A graphic representation of an operation used to study and improve work processes. It uses symbols (operation, movement, inspection, delay, and storage, for example) to identify common activities that occur in most types of operations.

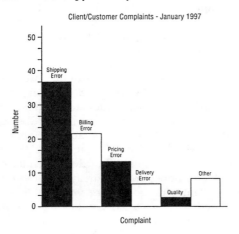

Client/Customer Complaints - January 1997

par GIC   Par guaranteed investment contract issued by insurance companies. Carried at book value and benefit responsive, it is an actively managed investment vehicle that substitutes the credit backing of the insuring company's separate account for the guarantee of the GIC issuer. Interest rates are guaranteed in advance for 6 months to one year,

although par GICs have no maturity date. Funds may be withdrawn by the plan sponsor at any time at their underlying market value.

parking benefits   *See* qualified parking.

Parkinson's disease   A chronic, progressive nervous disease that occurs during middle-age and late years, mainly in men. It is marked by hand or head tremors and weakness of resting muscles and a shuffling gate. It may not be incapacitating for many years. Although not curable, it can be treated by medication. About 1 million Americans have Parkinson's.

Parkinson's Law   States that an individual employee will find work to fill the time available. For that reason it is essential in designing positions to fill the time with useful work. Attributed to C. Northcote Parkinson.

parlor   In meeting management, a living room or sitting room in a hotel that is not used as a bedroom. Also called a *salon.*

par provider   Shorthand term for "participating provider," whether an individual professional or institutional health care provider, who has contracted with a plan to provide services.

partial disability   Inability to perform certain types of work for pay, such as lifting.

partial retirement   *See* phased retirement.

participant action plan approach (PAPA)   An approach to external evaluation of training developed by the U.S. Office of Personnel Management. It determines how participants change their job behavior following training by examining what happened on the job as a result of the training, whether the results were what was intended, and what may have interfered with participants using what they learned in the training program. The program requires that participants develop action plans at the end of training describing the things they want to try out when they get back on the job. Several months following the training, participants are either interviewed or surveyed by questionnaire.

participant camera   In distance learning, the camera(s) used to display participants (trainees or students) at either or both the host and remote sites. Includes pan, tilt, zoom, preset location, and autotracking capabilities.

participant diary or log   A simple means of collecting job data for use in job evaluation and training. Workers are asked to keep a list of the things that they do during the work day and record the amount of time they spend on each activity. The record is supplemented by interviews with the workers and their supervisors by an analyst.

participant reaction The most common, easiest, and most casual and subjective method of evaluating training and development programs. Feelings and opinions of trainees about the training received are collected by means of questionnaires (sometimes by means of interview). Although not entirely lacking in merit, it is neither reliable nor valid. Results do not correlate highly with job performance or the amount and kind of resulting organizational change.

participant in CHAMPUS Health care providers who have agreed to accept the **Civilian Health and Medical Programs of the Uniformed Services** allowable charge (along with the users **cost-share** and **deductible,** if any) as the full fee for the user's care. Those who participate usually file the claim for the user and receive payment from CHAMPUS. Hospitals that participate in Medicare must, by law, also participate in CHAMPUS for inpatient care.

participating physician or supplier A physician or supplier who agrees to accept assignment (the amount that Medicare or other insurance carrier allows) on all claims.

participation The number of employees granted pay increases, submitting suggestions, contributing to a fund drive, involved in volunteer work, and so on, expressed as a percentage of all employees in the group.

participation enhancement strategy See participatory management system.

participative management (PM) A strategy to improve employee motivation, morale, commitment, job satisfaction, and productivity by building mutual trust and respect among workers, supervisors, and managers while eliminating barriers between managers and workers. PM encourages employees at all levels to share in policy formulation and in making decisions in areas that affect them. Mechanisms include work teams and task forces, **Scanlon plan**, committee assignments, quality circles, suggestion systems, and assignment of special projects.

participative management process (PMP) An employee-involvement effort tied to a gain-sharing plan, implemented by Motorola.

participative training A discussion-centered adult learning strategy that emphasizes interaction and exploration of problems and issues and the exchange of experience.

participatory management system A program that recognizes the dignity and potential of employees to become productive members of the management team by playing an active role in the business, maintaining business literacy, and maintaining competence in their own areas of responsibility. The programs employ such devices as work teams, committees and task forces, and quality circles, enhanced by employee surveys and suggestion systems.

partnering **1.** A purchasing trend in which large organizations consolidate their business with one "partner" for multi-year agreements — and often roll the deal over when the contract expires rather than go out again for bids. Partnering is believed to reduce costs and increase quality and profitability because it eliminates stress and the expense of competitive bids, makes internal processes consistent, and focuses attention on fewer suppliers. **2.** See consultative selling.

partnership An association of persons legally joined as partners and co-owners of a business. There are two types: general partnerships where all partners have a say in running the business and any individual partner can obligate the remaining partners; and limited partnerships where the general partner runs the business and limited partners have no say and typically no tax or other form of liability beyond their initial investment.

partnership program A program that lets **Civilian Health and Medical Programs of the Uniformed Services (CHAMPUS)** eligible persons receive inpatient or outpatient treatment from civilian care providers in a military hospital or from uniformed services care providers in civilian health care facilities.

partnerships Advertised as an improved type of work team, characterized by vision, empowerment, focus and discipline, role modeling, and initiative.

part-time employees An alternative staffing option. Involves hiring people to work less than a regular 40-hour work week on a continuing basis. Such employees may be on the company payroll or assigned through a temporary service.

part-time worker An employee hired on the regular payroll to work less than a full 8 hour day, a 40 hour week, or 1,000 hours per year but who has job security and may receive a pro rata share of the benefits received by full-time employees. FICA and other taxes must be withheld.

passenger facility charge (PFC) A user fee or tax (usually $3.00) applied by local airports on passenger boardings for up to two boardings in one direction or four per round trip. The Federal Aviation Administration has ruled that frequent fliers traveling on free tickets must pay the fee while the Congress is trying to pass legislation that would keep free tickets free.

passenger name record (PNR) In travel management, information about a specific reservation that is identified by an alphanumeric code and used to produce **management information system reports**.

pass-through pension insurance Pension insurance coverage provided through an umbrella organization instead of directly to an individual. Currently $100,000 in pass-through pension insurance is permitted for each plan participant. It is a means of protecting the security of retirement funds.

patch Special software designed to fix a bug in a computer system.

patent Legal protection for independent development and marketing of inventions, such as computer algorithms, programs, and interface devices, and equipment, for a period of 17 years. A patent prevents others from making, using, or selling the invention. And, if a device or other patentable object infringes on an existing patent, even if unknowingly, the patent owner may sue for damages. Patents must be registered with the Patent and Trademark Office.

paternity leave Time off from work granted to the father of a newborn.

patient advocate A medical professional, usually a registered nurse with clinical experience and medical/surgical backgrounds, assigned by an employer or an insurance carrier to work with patients and their physicians and coordinate health care from preadmission to discharge.

Patient Self-Determination Act of 1990 Requires that patients be informed of their rights to prepare an advance directive, usually a **living will** or **durable power of attorney** for health care, in which they specify whether they want life-sustaining medical treatments if they become incapacitated. Health care facilities, such a **hospital, hospice, home health agency, nursing home,** and **health maintenance organization,** which receives **Medicare** or **Medicaid** funds, must inform patients and educate them, medical personnel, and the community about the sources and methods of obtaining the appropriate forms.

pattern review In health care, a form of **retrospective review** involving examination of patterns of utilization to determine where corrective action must be taken to reduce costs. For example, several hospitals could be compared on the bases of clinical outcomes, length of patient stay, and charges.

Paul Douglas Teacher Scholarship Program Provides college financial assistance to students in exchange for teaching service, typically two years. Provides up to $5,000 per year, not to exceed $20,000, to students who are in the top 10 percent of their graduating class and who meet other selection criteria established by state agencies.

payable-on-death (POD) (account) A method of avoiding probate. Allows the maker to have full use of the funds until death and to name a beneficiary for whatever remains in his or her bank account following death. There is no limit on the amount that can be passed on to heirs, it costs nothing, and beneficiaries can be changed at any time. Also called a *poor man's trust.*

pay adjustment An effect of inflation, restructuring, other changes in economic conditions, the competitive status of an organization, union demands, or the expectations of workers based on such traditional considerations as experience, seniority, increased responsibility, or simply job tenure. Pay adjustments take the forms of raises and salary cuts. They may also be called *general increases* or *across-the-board adjustments.*

pay-as-you-go strategy A plan for meeting retiree medical liabilities in which benefits are funded as required. The company puts money back into the business instead of into a portfolio of securities.

payback agreement Essentially a contract between a company and relocated employees. Payback agreements state that, if the employee voluntarily leaves the company within a specified period of time (usually one or two years) from the effective date of his or her transfer and receipt of relocation benefits for any reason other than to accept other employment at the same company or one of its subsidiaries, the individual must repay the company, on a prorated basis, all relocation-related expenses, reimbursements, and tax allowances paid on the employee's behalf.

Paycheck Protection Act of 1997
Introduced by Sen Don Nichols, R. Okla. as S.9. the Act would amend the Federal Election Campaign Act of 1971 to protect employees from having their pay involuntarily collected and used for political purposes by a corporation or labor organization. The Act would also prohibit labor unions from collecting dues, initiation fees, special assessments, or other payments from its members or nonmembers if any part of the money is to be used for political purposes.

pay compression Describes the situation where the normal differences in pay between successive job levels or grades gradually erode or actually disappear due to inflation (new hires may receive equal or more pay than workers who have been in the organization for years).

pay-dock proposals A part of the campaign to update the depression-era **Fair Labor Standards Act**. Under these proposals, employers who violate FLSA's pay-docking rules for one employee would no longer be required to convert all of their white collar workers to hourly status.

pay equity Said to occur when equal compensation is paid to workers for work of equivalent value.

pay for knowledge (PFK) See pay for skills.

pay for performance A compensation system in which employees share the risks of business with owners/investors. They earn more when productivity, sales, and profits rise and less when they decline. Such plans typically start with reduced base wages and salaries but bonuses are awarded when production targets, sales, or some other measure of performance is achieved.

pay for skills (PFS) A program designed to keep employee productivity, commitment, job satisfaction, and morale high and turnover down. Although there are several forms of the program, the most common

approach is to define and document the specific skills and knowledge required for each job in the organization and communicate them to employees along with notification that if and when they have mastered the requirements for a particular job, they will be promoted to that position.

pay grades Pay classes, rates, or steps comprised of different jobs of approximately equal difficulty, importance, or value as determined by job evaluation and used for pay purposes.

payment performance index (PPI) A measure of key financial information created by Dun & Bradstreet Information Services, A Division of Dun & Bradstreet Corporation. The PPI measures the change in how fast companies are paying their bills.

payroll-based stock option plan (PAYSOPS) Formerly called TRASOP. Defined contribution plans, established under the Tax Reduction Act of 1975, used to transfer employer stock to employees to provide equity ownership to workers. Describes modifications to tax regulations under the Tax Reduction Act of 1975 and its amendments relating tax credits to distributions that are proportional to payroll.

payrolling An alternative staffing option. Involves identifying specific people to perform needed tasks or functions and referring them to a staffing company, which then employs them and assigns them to work at the company. The staffing firm provides all pre-employment and employment services, such as payroll, records, and workers' compensation coverage, and locates replacements when needed.

payroll method A means of counting employees to determine whether a company is covered by such laws as **Title VII** of the **Civil rights Act of 1964**. The method counts all employees, including hourly and part-time workers, who are on the payroll for each day of a given week regardless of whether they are physically present at work each day. The Court held that the true test of whether an employer has an employment relationship with an individual is to examine the payroll register on the day in question. It should also be noted that both the **Age Discrimination in Employment Act of 1967** and the **Family and Medical Leave Act of 1993** use similar means of determining when an employer is subject to the provisions of those laws. In addition, the **Equal Employment Opportunity Commission** prefers the payroll method, and the U.S. Department of Labor has formally adopted it for determining coverage under FMLA.

payroll tax   *See* Social Security.

pay secrecy   An issue of considerable importance in many organizations. Pay secrecy concerns whether or not employees should know what other workers in their organization are being paid.

pay steps   Specified levels within a pay range on a pay or salary schedule. Employees progress from step to step on the basis of such factors as time in grade, performance, educational level, or the acquisition of new job skills.

pay structure   A tabular or graphic representation of the rate or range of pay that has been approved for each job in an organization, but it does not show the actual wage rates that are paid. It provides the framework for all compensation practices in a company.

PC-based enhancement   One means of combining the capabilities of personal computers and facsimile machines. PC-based enhancement allows the user to transmit computer-generated documents sequentially to multiple addressees. It requires the installation of a special circuit board in the fax machine.

PC fax   A mechanism that translates computer files into a format compatible with a remote fax machine that can then receive and print the document.

peace dividend   An expected (by many) consequence of the end of the Cold War — the reallocation of federal budget expenditures from military-related functions, equipment, and personnel to civilian programs, primarily funding for social programs.

pedagogy   A framework for learning. The practice of teaching (versus facilitating as in **andragogy**). Assumes that adults have many of the characteristics of children — dependent, responsive to authority, and so on. Places emphasis on the transmission of information.

pediatrician   A medical doctor who specializes in the diagnosis and treatment of children's diseases and disorders.

peer appraisal   Performance appraisal performed by an employee's peers — colleagues, team members, or other employees of equivalent rank who have ample opportunities to observe performance. Typically

used as a supplement to either collaborative or reciprocal performance appraisal.

peer coaching   A means of improving employee effectiveness, performance, productivity, cooperation and teamwork, and self-management. Involves developing "partnerships" between and among workers.

peer group learning   A self-improvement vehicle primarily used with executives and managers. Give-and-take periodic meetings of peers from a variety of organizational elements to share ideas, strategies, experiences, philosophies, problems, and issues. Formal presentations by outside speakers may be included, but the basic thrust is informal discussion.

peer review   In health care benefits, examination and study of surgical procedures and other forms of medical treatment by independent medical and health personnel either prior to or following the procedure or treatment to determine its necessity and appropriateness.

peer review organization (PRO)   A group of practicing physicians and other health care professionals under contract to a company (or state or federal government) to monitor and review the quality of the care provided to employees (or Medicare patients). Typically, PROs help decide whether care is reasonable and necessary, is provided in the appropriate setting, and meets the standards of quality accepted by the medical profession.

peer training   Training provided workers by highly skilled or experienced coworkers, usually on-the-job — in the shop, laboratory, office, store, field, or other other operating element.

Pell Grant Program   Expanded by the **Higher Education Reauthorization Act of 1992.** Eliminated the Pell Grant entitlement provision (whereby all students who met eligibility criteria would be guaranteed aid). Increased middle income eligibility to $42,000 and the maximum grant to $3,700 in 1993 and to $4,500 in 1997. Made Aid to Families with Dependent Children (AFDC) recipients automatically eligible.

penalty fare   A fee of 25- to 50-percent of the value of a ticket charged for ticket changes or cancellations.

penalty fee   **1.** In travel management, a charge added to the bills of hotel guests who check out early. **2.** A charge made by restaurants and car rental agencies for no-shows.

pen and notebook system *See* pen-based technology; pen computer.

pen-based technology Devices that use a pen instead of a mouse as a means of inputting data or instructions. Prototype systems operate on notebook computers.

pen-based computer Currently available only in Japan but now being introduced by more than 30 U.S. manufacturers, it is a battery-operated, notebook-size computer that allows users to write on a touch-sensitive screen with a pen-like device instead of using a keyboard or a mouse. The writing is converted into type, which can be combined with electronic sketches or digitized doodles and printed out. Also called *pen tablet, stylus systems* and *smart paper.*

pension A stated allowance or annuity paid regularly to a person upon his or her retirement or to dependents upon his or her death, for past services, meritorious performance, age, loss, or injury. For some purposes, such as state taxes, a pension is defined as money that is paid out over a period of 10 years or more.

Pension Benefit Guarantee Corporation (PBGC) An agency established by the **Employee Retirement Income Security Act of 1974** to guarantee payment of benefits to participants of defined benefit pension plans that meet IRS qualifications. The agency thereby became a trustee for underfunded and terminated single- and multiemployer pension plans and provides financial assistance to those plans. This assistance is funded by premiums paid by participating organizations. Participating organizations are also required to submit annual reports. In June 1990, the Supreme Court ruled that the agency could order an employer to resume its obligations for underfunded pension plans (rather than shifting liabilities to the PBGC) thereby removing a potential liability to the pension agency and causing increases in premiums from the PBGC.

pension equity plan An innovative pension design intended provide an equitable distribution of benefits to diverse employee populations (aging baby boomers and mobile baby busters). Each year, participants are credited with a percentage of pay that will be applied to their final average earnings. The percentage increases with age, typically ranging from 4 percent for employees under 30 to 12 percent for those 60 and over. Additional percentages, typically ranging from 1 percent for participants between 35 and 39 and 3 percent for those 60 and older, are credited to earnings above the Social Security wage base to provide an additional benefit for the portion of pay not eligible for Social Security benefits. The sum of the accumulated percentages is applied to the participant's final average pay to create a lump sum value. That sum can be paid out directly to participants when they retire or leave the company. Departing employees have the option of drawing down the lump sum, converting it into an annuity or rolling it over into an **individual retirement account** or another employer's plan. Attributed to Eric Lofgren, a consultant with the Wyatt Company, who helped develop the plan.

pension equivalent reserve credit plan *See* account balance pension.

pensioner An employee who receives a monthly or annual payment for services rendered upon retirement without having contributed towards the benefit while employed.

pension plan A tax-sheltered savings plan designed to provide sufficient income following retirement so that a reasonable standard of living can be maintained. There are three types: group pension plans, deferred profit-sharing plans, and savings plans.

pension plan retiree medical account An alternative funding vehicle for retiree medical liabilities in which benefits are funded through an existing qualified pension plan.

Pension Portability Act of 1992 (PPA) Included in legislation that extended emergency unemployment insurance benefits and signed into law by President Bush. The law, which went into effect January 1, 1993, enhanced pension portability by (1) permitting direct transfers of lump sum pension payments to an **individual retirement account** (or in some cases into the plan of a new employer); (2) allowing employees to switch any portion of their benefits; and (3) giving employees advance notice of the tax advantages of a direct transfer. One provision of the law requires employers to withhold 20 percent of the withdrawal amount if the employee does not directly transfer the money into an IRA or other plan. The law was designed to encourage workers to save their retirement funds.

Pension Protection Act of 1987 (PPA) Requires companies with underfunded pension plans to pay additional contributions of $6 for every $1,000 of underfunding, up to $34 per employee. The legislation increased premiums that companies pay annually to the **Pension Benefit Guarantee Corporation.** The Act also reduced or eliminated the deduction of contributions by employers for adequately-funded plans.

Pension Protection Act of 1994 A bill designed to overhaul underfunded pension plans. The act changed the formula for calculating cost-of-living adjustments (COLAs) in retirement plan funding and contribution limits under Section 415 of the Internal Revenue Code. COLAs are indexed through the end of the third quarter instead of the fourth quarter and rounded down in $50, $500, and $5,000 increments, depending on which limits are involved.

people knowledge Knowledge of the wants and needs of people, their motivations and biases, and what makes them do what they do. It involves the ability to observe and describe behavior in specific, objective, non-judgmental and non-labeling terms.

people literacy Knowledge about and skill in dealing with people in a workplace setting.

people performance programs Programs designed to get the best performance from all employees (not just the sales force) and customers by involving them in motivational training and offering incentives to link them to corporate goals.

people with disabilities The preferred term for referring to people with physical, mental, developmental, emotional, speech, or learning disorders. It is considered to be more sensitive than such terms as "handicapped" or euphemisms such as "physically challenged."

Pepper Commission A commission established by Congress to study health care plans. In 1990 the 15-member commission endorsed a comprehensive plan for providing health care coverage for uninsured Americans and government-financed long-term care for the elderly and disabled — essentially a blueprint for national health care and long-term care.

per capita In estate planning and settlement, a class gift to only those who survive; for example, a bequest that contains the phrase "to my children who survive me" would not pass on to a grandchild.

perceived disability Refers to a person regarded by his or her employer as having an impairment although the individual does not meet the ADA definition of a person with a disability. Such a person may file a complaint alleging disability discrimination because perceived disability bias is prohibited by the ADA.

percentage score In testing, a score obtained by dividing the number of correct responses by the total number of items on the test.

percentile rank or score A means of indicating the position of a test score in a group of 100 scores. Percentile scores portray relative standing on a test in terms of the percentage of the raw scores equaled or exceeded by any given score. For example, the 95th percentile is the point below which 95 percent of the data falls. Percentiles do not, however, indicate how much better or worse one person's performance is than another's in terms of raw scores. Percentile ranks may be calculated by arranging the raw scores in order of decreasing magnitude and finding for each score the number of scores equaling or lying below it. Each of those numbers is then divided by the total number of scores, and the quotient is multiplied by 100. This formula provides approximate results; if more exact percentile ranks are required, consult any good measurement or statistics reference.

perceptual acuity Said to be a requisite for leaders. It is the ability to analyze and evaluate a situation quickly and then negotiate a practical solution among diverse and opposing groups.

perceptual disorders Difficulty in understanding, comprehending, processing, and interpreting information, concepts, and principles or an inability to make fine discriminations among objects or ideas. Perception and learning are essential concomitants of the thought process. Perception is not sensation; it implies the recognition of an object, an image, or an idea. It takes place only though a lengthy process of repetitive experiencing of the object, image, or thought. Perceptual disabilities often leave a person confused, anxious, and frustrated. A great amount of conscious effort and persistence is required to override distorted visual and auditory information.

perceptually disabled A category of persons with mental disabilities of varying severity. Also called *brain injured.*

per diem reimbursement In health care, a payment system in which a provider receives a fixed amount per patient day, regardless of services provided.

performance **1.** A basic instructional method in which the trainee is required to perform, under controlled conditions, the operation, skills, or movement being taught. The method is used as follow-on instruction to teach manipulative operations or procedures, operation and functioning of equipment, team skills, and safety procedures. There are four types of performance: *independent practice,* in which trainees work individually and at their own pace; *group or controlled practice,* in which trainees work together at a rate set by the instructor step-by-step and by the numbers; *coach and pupil,* in which trainees are paired and members of each pair perform in turn as instructor and trainee; and *team performance,* in which a group of trainees performs an operation or function involving teamwork. **2.** Performance is a term that uses *behavior* as the means and its *consequences* as the end. That is, performance is the act or manner of demonstrating a skill or capacity. It is invariably measurable and involves systematic review and analysis of a specific behavior with the objective of improving that performance. Ideally, it measures how well people do a job or task as compared with a set of performance standards, communicates that information to them, gets agreement on strengths and deficiencies, and results in a plan of action to enhance strengths and shore up weaknesses. Performance can be improved by several means: training, development, coaching, mentoring, networking, peer tutoring, self-development, job rotation, job redesign (re-engineering), and special assignments, such as membership on committees and work teams.

performance accelerator *See* performance support system.

performance achievement plan A long-term, executive incentive plan in which

shares of stock are awarded for the attainment of predetermined financial targets such as return on investment, growth in earnings per share, or profit.

performance analysis Broad-based assessment and study of either organizational or individual performance. Performance analysis is a means of verifying significant performance deficiencies and then determining the most appropriate means of remedying those shortcomings.

performance appraisal Systematic, periodic review and analysis of employees' performance with the objective of improving that performance so that employees can realize their full potential. Ideally, it measures how well people do the job as compared with a set of performance standards, communicates that information to them, gets agreement on strengths and deficiencies, and results in a plan of action to enhance strengths and shore up weaknesses.

performance assessment A test that directly measures skills and abilities — such as presenting testees with appropriate materials and tools and requiring them to produce a product that meets certain specifications. Although not a new concept, performance assessment is currently being promoted as the most reliable means of assessing competency. Some say it is the answer to many social and educational problems. Also called *genuine assessment, authentic evaluation,* and *practical testing.*

performance audit Systematic, comprehensive, and detailed examination and assessment of the systems that comprise the conditions and restraints in which people in an organization work. Performance audits establish baseline data for initiating improvement measures.

performance award plan A form of executive incentive compensation plan in which formulas relating bonus distributions to selected measures of the company's financial performance are used to make payments in cash, stock, or both to executives, usually prorated according to the rank or function of the executive.

performance-based budget *See* program budgeting.

performance-based compensation A form of incentive pay in which increases in compensation are based on the attainment of quarterly or annual targets established before the fact by the manager for individual subordinates or jointly with the subordinate. It is often used in conjunction with management-by-objectives programs.

performance-based licensing In addition to tests of literacy and writing skills and satisfactory completion of an accredited teacher training program, performance-based licensing requirements involve the use of high-quality assessments of teaching performance that would-be teachers would have to pass to obtain a long-term teaching license. (Attributed to Richard J. Murnane, "The Case for Performance-Based Licensing, *Phi Delta Kappan,* October 1991, p. 140.)

performance-based training (PBT) A form of training used to improve substandard performance in a specific area when the skill or knowledge deficiency is clear. Designed for skill mastery in technical areas or where correct procedures mean the difference between life and death. PBT rests on behaviorist theory and instrumental conditioning. Learners practice the correct behavior and then are given feedback and positive reinforcement to shape their responses.

performance benchmarking A form of **benchmarking** used to establish national averages of management practices or purchasing and sales statistics, sorted by industry, geographical locations, or sales volume for peer identification. Usually conducted by means of surveys.

performance budgeting A budgeting system that places primary emphasis on the relationship between input and output. It involves work measurement. Substantive data concerning units of work are developed, such as development hours, equipment hours, instructor platform hours, and output, such as training programs produced or trainees completing a program. Those data are related to the amount of input (resources) required to produce a given estimated output.

performance-centered objective
See behavioral objective.

performance evaluation *See* performance appraisal.

performance feedback *See* feedback.

performance improvement technologists (PITS) Describes the instructional technologists of the 1990s who will need four qualities: (1) ability to think creatively, (2) first-hand

experience with improving performance on the job or in a class, (3) technological know-how, and (4) ability to be a team player. Attributed to Bob Yeager, President of Intercom, Inc. of Woodlands, Texas (*CBT Directions,* March 1991, p. 22).

performance indicator Measurable evidence that a planned result has been achieved. Examples are gains in profit, product quality, productivity, and reductions in interpersonal conflict, training time, costs, and the like.

Performance In Practice A newsletter for forums published four times per year by the American Society for Training and Development, free to members. Address: ASTD, 1640 King St., Box 1443, Alexandria, VA 22313-2043 (703/683-8100).

performance interview A means of selecting candidates for employment used mainly but not exclusively by manufacturing and financial services companies for middle- to senior-level positions. Involves giving the candidate a business problem, asking him or her to define and analyze the problem, develop a response and outline a means of implementing the solution, and presenting the solution to a group of company executives.

performance management **1.** A means of maintaining and improving competent work behavior — employees who do their jobs well — and the relationships between managers and workers. Daily, year-round continuing appraisal, coaching, and feedback that involves helping employees understand the nature and quality of their performance, identify what they need to do to improve, and motivate them to do it. That is, performance management employs strategies designed to foster employee personal responsibility, self-discipline, and individual decision making, rather than traditional punishment, to maintain employee self-esteem and encourage loyalty and commitment. Examples, are **management by objectives; participative management; performance appraisal. 2.** A substitute for performance appraisal said to emphasize teamwork, values, employee career responsibility, and a process that focuses on the needs of customers and clients instead of emphasizing judgment and labeling. The system takes into account the changing values and new definition of the employee-employer relationship.

performance measure A yardstick applied to gauge whether a product or service meets performance standards and the extent to which it deviates from those standards. Performance measures include assessment, inspection, personal observation, audits (quality, product, service, and procedure), questionnaires and interviews, ratings, inventories, and checklists, diagnostic, expectational, attitude, and morale surveys, tests and other evaluative devices, reports and records, and special devices such as Gantt and PERT charts, CPM, and project charts.

performance monitoring Employee surveillance by electronic (telephone or computer), or visual (open or clandestine observation and reports) means or interviews with clients, customers, suppliers. Used to track productivity, accuracy, cordiality, evaluate individuals, establish standards and quotas, identify problems, and provide a basis for training and upgrading programs. Although a wide-spread practice, some forms are renounced and fought by unions.

performance objective *See* behavioral objective.

performance rating Adjectival description or numerical index used to report evaluation of job performance following observation and judgment by a qualified individual either with or without a rating scale.

performance review A less negative term to describe what has traditionally been called performance appraisal. The purpose of performance review is to improve employee performance rather than judge or rate it.

performance share plan (PSP) A stock plan that specifies the attainment of certain predetermined performance objectives before the employee has rights to the stock. The employee pays income taxes on the fair market value of the stock at the time it is issued, but can sell the stock at any time because there are no holding period restrictions.

performance shares A type of incentive plan in which shares in an organization are awarded to top managers based on how well the company does rather than how long the executive survives in his or her position of power.

performance standards 1. In general, criteria used to measure performance in achieving objectives or results. 2. In employee performance appraisal, the yardsticks used to measure efficiency and effectiveness in performing a **job, duty,** or **task**. 3. In job performance measures, criteria that define the amount of time and resources required under normal conditions to complete one unit of job or task output and the characteristics of the product from the standpoint of quality. 4. In education, standards that define the levels of learning that are considered to be satisfactory.

performance support system (PSS) A system that gives users access, via workstations, to the information, guidance, assistance, and other tools they need to learn how to do their jobs and improve their productivity. Sometimes referred to as *interactive performance accelerators.*

performance technology (PT) Systematic approaches to the improvement of human performance on the job; for example, training, organization development, incentives, job redesign, job aids, instructional technology, and ergonomics — interventions that produce results that benefit the organization.

performance test A test that requires the testee to perform a physical or mental skill that is one of the duties, tasks, or elements of a job under conditions similar or identical to those of the work environment. Includes instruments that require the testee to demonstrate some practical application, skill, or operation that is an essential part of a job or task. Sometimes, some kind of apparatus, equipment, or material is involved. The testee's performance is observed and evaluated in accordance with a predetermined standard of performance and/or product of performance.

performance to schedule (PTS) An indicator of quality that is based on measurement of of the ability of an organization to deliver acceptable products to customers on or before a promised date. It is considered to be meaningful and valid only if the customer, rather than the supplier or vendor, sets the delivery schedule.

performance unit plan (PUP) A stock plan that grants units to an executive that can be exchanged for cash payments or their equivalent in stock value at the time of the award if predetermined objectives are achieved.

perinatal care Care provided the mother and infant at about the time of birth.

periodic budgeting Budgets prepared for a specific time period, such as the annual budget, which is usually broken down into semiannual, quarterly, and monthly budgets.

periodontics Dental care involving the treatment of tissues supporting the teeth.

peripherals Components of a computer system: input devices, such as keyboards, the mouse, drawing tools, and scanners, and output devices such as printers and slide makers.

Perkins (Carl D.) Vocational and Applied Technology Education Act Amendments of 1990 and 1991 Replaced the old federal law and established a new course for vocational education. The amendments contain four major changes: (1) shifts the focus of vocational education from its traditional job-skills orientation toward integration of academic/cognitive and vocational skills; (2) places more emphasis on directing federal resources toward school districts in greatest need for reform and improvement in vocational education; (3) restructures the relationship between the states and local school districts aimed at encouraging the districts to provide more leadership in improving vocational education; and (4) distinguishes between secondary and postsecondary levels of vocational education and establishes postsecondary education as a separate program in federal legislation. One of the most significant features of the act is that it identified the need to help states develop the means of measuring the performance of local programs and of setting standards based on that performance. The amendments that went into effect on July 1, 1991 gave states two years to devise performance measures of vocational-technical schools in areas including graduation rates and mastery of basic academic and occupational skills. The law also earmarked $64 million of the total $956 million appropriation to encourage further development of "tech-prep" collaborative programs designed to improve the academic preparation of students and develop partnerships with community and four-year colleges.

perks or perquisites Incentives that involve special privileges and considerations in addition to salary and benefits. They are usually associated with organizational rank and status, although they are sometimes granted on an individual basis. Include athletic/recreation club membership, business class air travel, chauffeur-driven limousines, company car, country club membership, deferred compensation plan, dependent tuition reimbursement, employment contract with takeover protection clause, employment contract without takeover protection clause, ERISA excess plan, executive dining room, executive training programs, financial counseling, first class air travel, free reserved parking, health club membership, legal counseling, low cost/no cost loans, luncheon/supper club membership, outplacement counseling, paid travel for spouses, personal computer for home use, physical fitness program, post-retirement benefit continuation, supplemental executive retirement plan, supplemental life insurance, supplemental long-term disability, supplemental medical insurance, supplemental vacation plan, vacation condominium, and VIP lounge membership.

permanent-equity pension plan (PEPP) A new supplemental pension concept for executive compensation. Stock, rather than cash, is used as the funding vehicle to encourage key employees to develop and keep permanent equity stakes in their company. The plan ties a portion of executive pensions to stock performance. Stock is granted based on a flat percentage of pay or begins as a small percentage of current pay and gradually increases until retirement. Participants are not permitted to sell their stock until retirement or until the desired equity position is reached.

Permanent Labor Certification (PLC) program Designed to protect American jobs and wages by excluding foreigners who seek admission to the United States or status as an immigrant for employment purposes, when qualified and willing U.S. workers are available for the jobs. Audited by the Department of Labor, which found that the program did not serve its intended purposes, although the finding is contradicted by the results of other studies.

per member per month (PMPM) In health care, applies to a revenue or cost for each member per month.

per member per year (PMPY) In health care, applies to a revenue or cost for each member per year.

personal adjustment counseling Counseling provided to employees to help them gain self-understanding, learn how to regulate their own lives, achieve insight into difficult experiences, learn how to use their own resources as well as the resources of the organization and the larger community, and deal with emotional stress.

personal care attendant   Assists the elderly and disabled with such daily tasks as getting out of bed, and bathing, toileting, and dressing thereby enabling people to live in the community rather than in a nursing home or other institution. Supported by Medicaid payments.

personal care home   *See* board and care home.

personal communications services (PCS)   Digital wireless mobile communication technologies that provide a variety of standard features at lower prices and with lower power consumption than cellular services.

personal computer (PC)   Any computer designed for personal, home, or office use. Usually one that can fit in a compact space or on a desk. May be stand-alone or netted with other computers, including minicomputers and mainframes.

Personal Computer Memory Card International Association (PCMCIA)   A standard for credit card-size memory cards used with **personal digital assistants** and personal computers to store information, update software, and support data and fax capabilities.

personal days   A type of employee fringe benefit. Workers are allowed a specific number of paid days off (in addition to paid holidays, annual leave, and sick leave) for any personal reason, such as attending to personal business, attending a school play, keeping a doctor's appointment, or just goofing off. Some employers allow workers to use their personal days on an hourly rather than a full-day basis.

personal development   Training and other activities that encompass such diverse elements as individual and group learning experiences, health and fitness programs, recreational activities, stress management, and assertiveness training.

personal development program (PDP)   A voluntary program designed to help employees achieve personal growth and social and spiritual fulfillment, and help working parents to handle work and family responsibilities and, as a consequence, make them happy and more productive.

Uses such interventions as training in life skills and life planning, workshops on financial planning, dual career, and single parent strategies, sponsoring support groups, and providing third-party mediation services to resolve workplace conflicts.

personal digital assistant (PDA)   A handheld computer device that merges handwriting recognition, personal-organization tools, and state-of-the-art mobile communications in a compact package. Used to store and retrieve information, and may serve as a telephone, fax machine, modem, and electronic date and notebook. Some accept input by means of a keyboard, mouse, stylus, scanner, or printer and also plug into a workstation. Powered by four AAA batteries, the first PDA, the Newton, produced by Apple Computer, weighs less than a pound, measures less than 8 inches in length and 1 inch in thickness, and relies on a pen, rather than a keyboard. The device can recognize handwriting and graphics. Newer models offer controllable back lighting, non-glare screens and can share data with Windows and Macintosh computers.

Personal Earnings and Benefit Estimate Statement (PEBES)   A statement that contains (1) the number of quarters of coverage credits earned; (2) the number of credits needed to be eligible for disability, survivors, and retirement benefits; (3) a year-by-year listing of earnings subject to Social Security Tax; (4) estimates of disability and survivors benefits for the wage earner and his or her family; and (5) estimates of monthly retirement benefits should the individual retire at age 62, 65, or 70. Furnished without charge by the Social Security Administration. In 1995, Special Security began automatically releasing the statement to all people 25 year old or older. Call 800/772-1213 or visit the local Social Security Office.

personal effectiveness competencies   Capabilities that portend success in professional or managerial jobs. They include self-control, resistance to stress, and flexibility.

personal emergency response system (PERS)   A device worn by elderly or disabled persons or installed in their homes, connected by radio to the telephone and in turn to a 24-hour monitoring service. Used to alert emergency medical or law enforcement personnel of an accident or medical emergency involving the individual.

Personal Financial Specialist (PFS) A designation awarded to individuals who are certified public accountants and have passed a six-hour examination given by the **American Institute of Certified Public Accountants**. *Contact:* AICPA, 1211 Avenue of the Americas, New York, NY 10036 (800/862-4272 or 212/596-6200; Fax 212/596-6213; URL **http://www.aicpa.org**).

personal growth leave Paid or unpaid leave granted to employees, sometimes to pursue further education.

personal growth training Training provided on a voluntary basis to workers at all levels to promote self-knowledge and self-acceptance, improve their mental and physical health and well-being, improve their ability to work with others, reduce absenteeism, tardiness, accidents, and injuries; improve productivity; reduce tension and stress; and provide positive personality development. Typically includes medical evaluation prior to enrollment, and may take such forms as physical and recreational activities (such as team and individual sports, aerobic dancing, exercise, orienteering, and wilderness backpacking), introspective exercises, (such as yoga and transcendental meditation), and small-group interactions (such as encounter groups, discussion groups, and workshops).

personal image *See* self-image.

personal information management system (PIMS) A system that manages information with which professionals and researchers work — such as references, notes, and ideas found in reports, research papers, and articles — as well as phone numbers, addresses, appointments, to-do lists, and other personal database items. Traditionally limited to pencil and paper, PIMS now make use of computers, spreadsheets, and databases (some using **Hypertext**) and avoid acquisition, format, and storage problems that limit the individual's ability to work with the data. Examples are *Sidekick* from Starfish Software and *Lotus Organzer*.

personal information manager Software that consolidates details about business contacts derived from business cards, messages, Rolodex files, and other sources and arranges them in a usable form on a computer screen.

personality Enduring personal traits or characteristics that make each individual truly unique — such as assertiveness, self-reliance, dependence, responsibility, dogmatism, defensiveness, openness, warmth, coldness, haughtiness, and the like.

personality and temperament test Usually referred to as personality profiles, inventories, schedules, or scales, personality and temperament tests are used in business and industry to evaluate personality in normal adults and predict human behavior in business for career planning, selection, job placement, promotion, and counseling. They purport to measure some dimension of human personality or temperament, such as whether a person is withdrawn or outgoing, a team player or a loner, mature or immature, emotionally stable or unstable, passive or aggressive, and they are projective in that they disclose a person's needs and values. These tests are usually reserved for the task of selecting individuals for executive or professional positions. They should be administered and interpreted by qualified psychometrists, psychologists, or therapists. Examples are Guilford-Zimmerman Temperament Survey, Gordon Personal Profile-Inventory, Edwards Personal Preference Schedule, California Psychological Inventory, Wonderlic Comprehensive Personality Profile, Taylor-Johnson Temperament Analysis, Thurston Temperament Schedule, Taylor Sales Attitudes Checklist, and Jenkins Activity Survey.

personality test A test used as an employment screening device by an estimated 6,000 U.S. employers. Although their legality or illegality has yet to be proved, several states, including Massachusetts, Minnesota, Rhode Island, and Wisconsin severely restrict or outlaw their use. Their legality is most likely to be challenged in the courts on one or more of the following bases: **disparate impact** or treatment, unlawful inquiry, or invasion of privacy.

personalized benefits Legal, financial planning, educational assistance, and other innovative benefits such as discounts on home and auto insurance (through semi-monthly payroll deductions), massage, exercise and nutrition counseling, and so on.

personal protective equipment (PPE) Equipment designed to safeguard employees from workplace illnesses and injuries, such as surgical gloves, welding gloves, hard hats, goggles, masks, face shields, hot sticks (live electrical wire tools), cold weather outer wear, and metatarsal and safety shoes. Occupational

Safety and Health Administration regulations require employers to determine the appropriate PPE for each hazard, provide and pay for most such equipment, and provide worker training on selecting, inspecting, using, and maintaining the equipment.

Personal Responsibility and Work Opportunity Reconciliation Act of 1996 (PRWORA) Legislation, signed by the President August 22, 1996, that turns welfare over to the states, limits the time anyone can receive benefits to five years, requires one member of every family to find work within two years or the family loses benefits, and requires one half of each state's welfare recipients to be working or in training for a job by the year 2002 or the state will lose some of its federal block grant. The bill also cut food stamp aid to poor families and barred aliens who are not U.S. military veterans from receiving food stamps or Supplemental Security Income benefits until they become U.S. citizens or have worked and paid Social Security taxes for at least 40 quarters. The act allows states to design their own Medicaid programs and contains a requirement for all states to set up new hire directories. Employers have up to 20 days to send information on newly hired employees to the state agencies. The Act also changes the definition of disability for children. A part of the Welfare and Medicaid Reform Act of 1996.

personal security account (PSA) Proposed as a means of setting aside capital well in advance to help workers pay for their retirement instead of the current government Social Security program, which is in financial difficulty. Instead of sending their payroll taxes to the government to be paid out in benefits to current retirees, workers and their employers would deposit all or part of those taxes into private accounts. Proponents of the proposal maintain that workers would benefit since it could raise the declining rate of return people now earn on money paid into the system.

personnel administration The enterprise function that deals with the "people" aspects of operations.

personnel controls Curbs on personnel hiring, utilization, and advancement to manage costs. Control is achieved by establishing realistic performance standards, identifying of deviations from those standards, and correcting deviations.

personnel costs The full costs of people's time including salary or wages and benefits.

personnel director or manager
See human resources manager.

personnel evaluation See performance appraisal.

personnel inventory chart A chart that depicts the status and potential of assigned personnel for advancement to higher-level positions within the HR (or other) organization. The chart assigns each incumbent to one of four categories: immediately promotable, potentially promotable, adequate in present position but not promotable, or release (terminate). Using the chart, a list of positions that will become vacant in the ensuing two-year period period is developed. It identifies vacancies that will occur as a result of promotion and transfer, retirement and resignation, dismissal, and expansion of the organization.

personnel management and administration See human resources management.

Personnel Management Association of Aztlan (PMAA) A 250-member national organization whose purpose is to foster awareness of career opportunities, professionalism, cultural pride, and self-esteem, provide a placement network, share information, expertise, and ideas, and act as a resource for its members, employers, and the community to advance constructive HR policies and practices that have a direct impact on minorities, specifically the Hispanic community. *Contact:* PMAA, Attn: Teresa M. Zaman, Secretary, P.O. Box 31893, Oakland, CA 94604 (415/272-6456).

personnel planning See human resources planning.

personnel records See records.

personnel research See research.

personnel selection inventory (PSI) An instrument designed to measure such qualities as emotional stability, personal values, honesty, and work habits. Used to predict whether or not job applicants are likely to steal on the job. Applicants are categorized as high-, borderline-, or low-risk.

person with AIDS Identified by some as the preferred way to describe an individual who has the AIDS virus — instead of using such phrases as "AIDS victim," which some feel is insensitive or inflammatory.

per stirpes Translated from the Latin as "by right of representation." Used in wills when referring to a gift to children and **issue** and provides that the gift shall go to the closest generational level; however, if anyone predeceases the writer of the will, that person's share will be evenly divided among his or her children.

persuasion or persuasive power Ability to influence, sway, or convince followers of the rightness of a belief or action without using coercion or manipulation.

persuasive behavior The ability to present a product, service, argument, or proposal in terms that others will respond to in a positive way. It is a particularly important skill for salespersons, instructors, and briefers.

per thousand members per year (PTMPY) A common way of reporting health care utilization, such as hospital utilization, which is expressed as days per thousand members per year.

Peter Principle A tongue-in-cheek bromide coined by Laurence J. Peter, psychologist and professor of education (*The Peter Principle*, 1969), which states that in hierarchies a person tends to rise to the level of his or her incompetence.

p-funk A synthetic form of **heroin**.

phantom stock plan The least common of the various forms of long-term incentives, usually limited to the top 2 or 3 percent of exempt employees. Phantom stock plans provide payments in cash or in stock based on hypothetical investments in company stock equal to the gain in fair market value of a designated number of company shares ascribed to each participant in the plan on the date of the grant. Future payments may be based on future appreciation, initial value plus future appreciation, and may provide dividend equivalent payments. Also called *stock appreciation rights plans*.

pharmaco-economist A professional specialist with degrees in both economics and pharmacology who examines the cost-effectiveness and quality of life afforded by new drugs. For example, the pharmaco-economist determines whether one drug more than another can reduce the length of hospital stays or the absences of employees sidelined by illnesses or accidents.

pharmacy benefit management (PBM) Private companies that provide drug benefits packages to organizations advertised as lowering costs and improving health care.

phased retirement A plan for keeping older workers on the payroll for an agreed upon length of time, at least in a part-time capacity, as an effective way to keep long-time employees, strengthen the role of older workers, and help compensate for the growing shortage of workers.

Phi Delta Kappa (PDK) A national honorary professional association for active and retired educators at all levels and graduate students. PDK has both geographical area and campus chapters across the United States and Canada and has more than 139,000 members. It is concerned with educational research, service, and leadership and emphasizes issues, trends and policies in its activities. *Contact*: PDK, 408 N. Union, P.O. Box 789, Bloomington, IN 47402 (812/339-1156; E-mail **headquarters@pdkintl.org**; URL **http://www.pdkintl.org**).

Phi Delta Kappan A journal published monthly, except July and August: $35.00 per year. Address: Phi Delta Kappa International, Inc., 408 N. Union, P.O. Box 789, Bloomington, IN 47402 (812/339-1156).

Phillips 66 *See* huddle group.

philosophy A statement of the fundamental beliefs or values that underlie and govern the actions of an organization and its people and provides guidelines for management planning and decision making. Philosophy deals with principles, truths, and ultimate ends. It typically states the purposes and obligations of the HR department, its responsibilities to the organization, its relationship to the enterprise, its subdivisions, its employees, and other constituencies, the nature and conditions of employee fair treatment, equity, job satisfaction, and development, the roles and relationships of personnel involved in HR, the nature and need of employees at all levels., and the direction in which the HR department should move.

phobias Irrational, involuntary, and inappropriate fear of, or response to, ordinary situations or things. Phobias are usually chronic, and they can lead to other serious disorders, such as depression. Phobias can be successfully treated by a combination of medication, therapy, and support.

The Phoenix Society for Burn Survivors, Inc. An international organization of burn survivors established to assist people who have been burned and their families during and after the hospitalization. Holds national and international conferences, provides books and audiovisual materials, and a quarterly newsletter. *Contact:* The Phoenix Society for Burn Survivors, Inc., 11 Rust Hill Rd., Levittown, PA 19056 (800/888-2786 or 215/946-2876; Fax 215/946-4788).

Photo CD   A product of Kodak, a technology for putting photographic images on compact discs. Photo CD technology includes a proprietary CD player that hooks up to an ordinary television set. Requires a **compact disc, read only memory extended architecture** (CD-ROM XA) drive. To insert photographic images into a computer application, photos are shot with an ordinary 35mm camera, the film is developed, the images are transferred to a compact disc, the disc is placed in a computer's CD-ROM drive, and the images are then selected and inserted directly into the application. Up to 100 images can be accessed on a Photo CD at five levels of resolution: thumbnail (128 lines × 192 pixels), low-resolution (256 × 384), TV and computer display resolution (512 × 768), HDTV resolution (1024 × 1536), and very high resolution (2048 × 3072).

photomultiplier tube (PMT)   In desktop publishing, a type of high-end **scanner** that provides the means of converting light intensity from the scan into electrical voltage. Such scanners are known for high resolution and broad dynamic range.

photo-refractive keratectomy (PRK)   A surgical procedure performed by opthamologists to help correct nearsightedness. It uses an excimer laser to remove a few layers of cells to reshape the cornea of the eye and thereby improve the way light is focused on the retina.

photovoltaic technology (PVT)   The direct conversion of sunlight into electricity. A non-fossil, pollution-free, long-lasting, lightweight, reliable, efficient, and cost-effective power source. Current applications include remote telecommunications, medical care, calculators and portable computers, satellites, and general lighting.

phrase search   A World Wide Web search for documents that contain a word-for-word sentence or phrase selected by the user.

physiatrist   A doctor of medicine (M.D.)who specializes in the nonsurgical management of persons with musculoskeletal and neurological disorders. Also skilled in managing

care for amputees, prescribing prosthetic and orthotic devices, and performing diagnostic evaluations using electromyographic and nerve conduction studies.

physical ability test   A test that is used as a preemployment selection device for positions requiring physical performance. Physical ability tests involve actual performance of the essential functions of a given job. Also called *strength and endurance test.*

physical and mental impairment
As defined by the **Americans with Disabilities Act of 1990,** "physical or mental impairment includes, but is not limited to, such contagious and noncontagious diseases and conditions as orthopedic, visual, speech, and hearing impairments, cerebral palsy, epilepsy, muscular dystrophy, multiple sclerosis, cancer, heart disease, diabetes, mental retardation, emotional illness, specific learning disabilities, HIV disease (whether symptomatic or asymptomatic), tuberculosis, drug addiction, and alcoholism." (It does not include homosexuality or bisexuality).

physical disabilities   Totally or partially deaf, totally or partially blind, speech problems, orthopedically handicapped (loss of normal use of limbs, bones, or muscles due to disease, injury, or deformity, such as cerebral palsy, muscular dystrophy, congenital deformities, and amputation), and health or medical problems (such as AIDS, asthma, epilepsy, diabetes, and heart conditions).

physical examination   In the screening and selection process, a medical examination conducted either by the employer's medical staff or by consulting medical practitioners to determine the applicant's ability to meet the physical requirements of the job; identify medical limitations that must be taken into account in placing the individual or making other accommodations for a disability; establish baseline data and a record for future insurance or compensation claims; or detect communicable diseases that may be unknown to the applicant.

physical fitness program
See exercise program.

physically challenged employees
See handicapped employees.

physically disabled   People whose limitations are attributable primarily to lowered or impaired physical capacity caused by congenital or inherited physical defects, disease or injury suffered before, during, or immediately following birth, accidents or injuries in childhood or adulthood, the result of an inadequate diet, or the consequence of impaired maturation due to inadequate nourishment or insufficient physical activity and stimulation over a prolonged period of time. Includes **blind and vision impaired, deaf and hearing impaired, speech problems, orthopedic and mobility impairments, disfigurement,** and **health and medical problems**.

physical presence test   As defined by **Section 911, Internal Revenue Code,** an employee physically present and working in a foreign country or countries for 330 full days, including vacation days, during 12 consecutive months. The days do not have to be consecutive and the 12 month period can begin on any day of any month. Applies to both U.S. citizens and resident aliens.

physical simulations   Representations of a system that deal with tangible objects — real world objects.

physical therapy   Treatment provided by health care workers to victims of accidents or injury to relieve pain, strengthen muscles, or restore movement. Includes heat treatments, ultrasonography, massage, and electrical-impulse therapies.

physical training (PT)   Training provided by organizations to build and maintain the strength and over-all physical condition of personnel.

physician   In its narrow sense, a medical doctor (M.D. or D.O.); however, in most health care contexts the term includes chiropractors, dentists, podiatrists, optometrists, psychologists, Christian Science Practitioners, licensed independent clinical social workers, and certified nurse midwives. Most have had training in treating physical, mental, or psychiatric disorders.

physician assistant (PA)   A person who has received intensive medical training in patient care. Must be supervised by a licensed physician who employs them. Charges for PAs are allowable under most health care plans although at reduced rates (typically not to exceed 85 percent of a physician's allowable charge).

physician hospital organization (PHO) An organization that at a minimum allows a hospital and its physicians to negotiate with third-party payers. It may also manage the relationship between providers and managed care organizations or provide more services.

physician network   A group of doctors who have banded together to accept the financial risks of covering the health care needs of their patients — a risk traditionally taken by insurers. The objective is to maintain the autonomy of the health care providers and cut costs.

physician ownership model (POM) A form of integrated health care delivery system in which the physician members hold a significant portion of the ownership and equity of the system (more than 51 percent and sometimes all of it).

physician profiling   A means of **utilization review** in which companies track physicians' patterns of practice to reduce the costs of either inpatient or outpatient care.

physician self-referral   *See* self-referrral.

physiological needs   Human needs for food, water, air, shelter, sleep, elimination, and other physical essentials — the things that maintain and sustain life.

physiotherapy   The treatment of bodily weaknesses, defects, or injuries, particularly of the musculo-skeletal system, by physical remedies, especially massage and exercise.

pica   A printer's unit of measurement, used principally in typesetting. One pica equals 12 points or about 1/6 of an inch.

pick list   A computer reference file that shows what can be entered into a specific field of information in human resources **database.** Also called *choice list.*

pictograph   A means of displaying data using pictures of objects typically representing quantities.

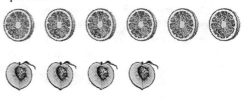

Harvest of Oranges, Peaches, and Avocados, 1996
(in thousands of bushels)

pick-up   Meeting industry jargon for the number of hotel room block reservations filled on a specified date or dates. Most hotels impose monetary penalties for failing to fill reservations, usually on a sliding scale.

In addition, complimentary guest rooms and other meeting-related amenities are determined on the basis of room pick up.

piece rate   In incentive piecework, the rate paid to a worker per piece produced or worked on.

piecework   *See* piece rate; incentive work.

pie chart   A means of displaying data graphically. Most often used to show proportional relationships, such as budget allocations or market share.

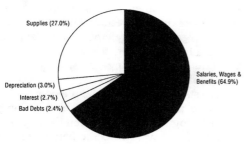

Operating Expenses

pig   In meeting management, a phony meeting fare.

piggybacking   In meeting management, the practice of merging meetings with other organizations or associations to increase and negotiating power and attendance and save time, money, and effort.

pilot   A test vehicle for a program or system designed to make a dry run of a program or system, such as a training system. A systems validation technique. Also known as *piloting.*

pink collar workers   Women who work in low-paying jobs which are in many cases equivalent to higher-paying white collar jobs typically filled by men.

pink slip   An oral or written notice of discharge, firing, layoff, or termination (either for cause, downsizing, or restructuring).

Pinnacle Award Program   Co-sponsored by the **Society for Human Resource Management (SHRM)** and Olsten Staffing Services. The awards recognize original and innovative programs in human resources. All SHRM-affiliated chapters are eligible to compete for eight $1,000 grants from Olsten and national recognition for outstanding achievement. Also known as the *SHRM/Olsten Awards. Contact:* SHRM, 606 N. Washington St., Alexandria, VA 22314 (703/548-3440; TDD 703/548-6999; Fax 703/836-0367; E-mail **shrm@shrm.org**).

Pinnacle Awards   Given annually to outstanding meeting properties (resorts, subur-

ban hotels, downtown hotels, airport hotels, and conference centers) in five geographical regions of the United States and properties in two international categories (Canada and Mexico and all other non-U.S.) that have done an outstanding job of hosting meetings. Facilities are evaluated in terms of overall service, meeting rooms and equipment, recreational facilities, quality of food, exhibit space, accessibility, and social consciousness. Voted by meeting planners and awarded by *Successful Meetings* magazine. *Contact: Successful Meetings,* 633 3rd Ave., New York, NY 10017 (212/986-4800).

pixels   Short for picture elements. Very small square areas that construct the images on a computer screen or bit-mapped images. Pixels are formed by the grid of horizontal and vertical lines that form the screen.

placement   The process of assigning personnel to specific positions following selection and orientation (in the case of new workers) or training, taking into account the needs of the organization as well as the skills, abilities, and, where possible, the needs and interests of the employee. Placement should always be followed by a period of induction.

place of public accommodation

As defined by the **Americans with Disabilities Act of 1990,** "a facility, operated by a private entity, whose operations affect commerce and fall within at least one of 12 specified categories." Includes (1) places of lodging; (2) establishments serving food or drink; (3) places of exhibition or entertainment; (4) places of public gathering; (5) sales or rental establishments; (6) service establishments; (7) stations used for specified public transportation; (8) places of public display or collection; (9) places of recreation; (10) places of education; (11) social service center establishments; and (12) places of exercise or recreation.

plain English laws   Laws passed by several states relating to the clarity, readability, and understandability of legal documents, such as contracts. Although the intent is to structure documents so that their meaning is clear, many such laws only require adherence to superficial measurements such as average number of words per sentence and the average number of syllables per word.

plaintiff   The person who brings a complaint or suit against another in a civil court.

plan   A guide to action; a map managers use to get an organization from where it is to where it wants to be. Plans take the general forms of strategic, operational or tactical, and human resources plans. Examples of plans are goals, objectives, policies, procedures, and budgets.

plan administrator In benefits, the person or organization (often the sponsor) designated by the terms of the instrument as responsible for administering a pension or welfare plan.

plan, do, check, act (PDCA) An elementary tool of quality control. Workers are taught to plan the project or process, do it, check it, and correct it. Also called the *Deming Cycle.*

plan-do-study-act (PDSA) cycle A process improvement methodology that may be used whenever a project or waste or opportunity is identified. Plan by describing the situation, collecting the data, identifying alternatives; do by making the changes; study the effects of the actions taken; if satisfied with the outcomes, act by standardizing the improvements; if not satisfied, plan for further actions. Attributed to Walter Shewart.

Plan for Achieving Self-Support (PASS) A written plan, covering up to three years of activities (extendible for one additional year), that lists the steps a person with disabilities will take to prepare for a job, the amount of money needed, the expenses that will be incurred, the source or sources of the income to be used for the PASS, and a timetable that shows when each phase of the plan will be completed. The plan must be approved by the local Social Security Administration Field Office and is subject to periodic review. A PASS helps persons with disabilities keep income that otherwise disqualifies them from receiving SSI. That income can be earned or unearned as long as it is set aside to help find and keep a job. PASS can be used to help keep Worker's Compensation benefits, insurance benefits, settlement from a lawsuit, and help save money given by the family.

Planners' Choice Awards Annual awards presented to hotels, resorts, conference centers, and convention halls in recognition of delivery of the highest levels of service, accommodations, and meeting facilities by *Meeting News.* Nominations are made by meeting professionals. Awards are given in five categories: urban hotels, convention/commercial hotels, conference centers, resort hotels, and convention centers. *Contact:*

MN, Miller Freeman Inc., 1515 Broadway, New York, NY 10036 (212/944-7363).

planned progression In management and executive development, a predetermined sequence of lateral and vertical job moves for junior or middle managers designed to provide them with exposure to challenges and approaches that will prepare them for broader responsibilities.

planning 1. The keystone of successful management and prerequisite to performance of all other managerial functions. Concerned with assessing the present status of a function or organizational element, articulating a philosophy, predicting the environment of the future, determining goals, anticipating problems, forecasting needs, setting objectives, establishing policies, developing procedures, preparing budgets, establishing special programs, and in general, designing a strategy that will overcome barriers to the achievement of desired results. 2. The first stage in an instructional sequence.

planning, programming, budgeting system (PPBS) A budgeting system that stresses a long-term approach. The system relates three elements: desired outcomes (planning), methods of achieving outcomes (programming), and allocation of funds (budgeting). It attempts to put goals, objectives, strategies, and resources into balance. It combines both operating and capital programs in a consolidated financial plan, and it also provides a framework within which the HR manager can use program analysis techniques effectively. It typically uses a five-year time span so that it takes account of the costs of present programs in future years. Each major program is analyzed, alternative methods of reaching the same goals and objectives are compared, and ways to minimize costs and maximize return on investment are identified.

plant closing As defined by the **Worker Adjustment and Retraining Notification Act of 1988**, the temporary or permanent shutdown of a single site of employment if the shutdown results in an employment loss at the site during any 30-day period of 50 or more full-time employees.

plateaued 1. People who have stopped growing, developing, and improving and simply go through the motions of doing the jobs. 2. Describes employees in dead-end jobs.

plateau program A type of incentive program. Requires individual to reach a certain goal, which leads directly to the award. For example, offering a $100 gift certificate for selling $1,000 worth of product.

plated A type of meal service where each guest is given a plate that has been prepared in the kitchen. Used when time is limited.

platform **1.** A computer — whether a **personal computer, mid-range computer,** or **mainframe.** Includes the **operating system** and **database management software. 2.** In multimedia, the computer used in the production or playback system. **3.** Also used to describe interconnected computer hardware. **4.** The computer **operating system** on which multimedia is authored and delivered.

platform hours An instructor work load measure. The number of hours per day or per week that an instructor is interacting with trainees in an instructional setting. Most collective bargaining agreements establish a maximum number of platform hours per week for instructors.

platform preparation factor A measure of instructor work load. The relationship between the number of hours an instructor can teach a specific block of instruction (determined by the **platform-to-preparation-time ratio**) and the total number of teaching hours available per day.

platform skills The skills involved in presenting a speech or conducting instruction, such as use of voice, speech, and word choice; posture, gestures, and body language; use of notes, audiovisuals, and microphone; style and tone of voice; handling questions, getting audience participation, and controlling a resistant audience.

platform team See cross-functional team.

platform-to-preparation-time ratio The amount of preparation time allowed (or required by contract) per hour of instruction. It varies with such factors as the complexity of the content, availability of reference materials, amount of research required, and number of times the block of instruction is repeated.

Platinum Partners Awards Awards presented annually to merchandise suppliers and incentive travel suppliers by *Incentive* magazine based on motivational appeal, quality and speed of fulfillment or professionalism of service, and degree of customization

or creativity and promotional support. *Contact: Incentive: Managing and Marketing Through Motivation,* 355 Park Avenue South, New York NY 10010 (212/592-6400).

platykurtic Describes the shape of the curve of a frequency distribution when plotted on a graph. It is a broad-humped flattened curve.

play or pay model An approach to health care reform in which employers would be required either to provide health insurance or pay a special payroll tax surcharge to finance a public system that would cover their employees. One plan would require businesses with 25 or more employees to provide coverage or pay a 7 percent payroll tax for uninsured employees, and a federal board would monitor fees and simplify the claims process.

play or pay plan A health care plan that requires employers to provide health care insurance to their employees or pay a payroll tax to help the government provide such coverage.

plenary session In conference and meeting planning, a session at which all voting members of an organization are entitled to be present. The business of an organization, including the election of officers, is transacted at a plenary session.

plug-and-play Refers to a new employee who doesn't need any training.

plus plus Meetings industry jargon for food and beverage events billing — cost per person "plus tax and gratuities."

podium A raised platform or stand (usually small) used by instructors or public speakers. Also called a *dias* or *rostrum.*

point In desktop publishing, the basic increment of typographical measurement. One point is equal to 0.0138 inch; twelve points equal one **pica.**

point-factor method An approach to **job evaluation** in which the desired hierarchical classification of jobs in an organization is achieved by identifying **compensable factors** and assigning to each one scores or points indicating increasing degrees of intensity, scope, difficulty, or value. Each job is then assessed in terms of the appropriate degree for each compensable factor, and separate scores are summed to yield a final point score for that job.

point-of-purchase (POP) In advertising and sales, advertising and sales strategies, devices, and gimmicks used at the location where the goods or services are sold. For example, using window and door signs, non-illuminated signs, mobiles and banners, and floor stands, shelf tags, and danglers (those little pieces of paper or cardboard that hang off the edge of shelves promoting specials).

point-of-sale terminal A replacement for cash registers. Used by retailers to "ring up" sales, collect consumer purchasing data, inventory control, and manage day-to-day operations. Uses **scanners** at checkout stations to input data to a central computer.

point of service (POS) plan A type of managed care. Consists of a formal network of primary care physicians, organized by insurers, who serve as **gatekeepers** to the services of other health care providers (specialists, hospitals, and so on). Members do not have to choose how or where to receive services until they need them, usually with varying costs. For those using physicians on the point of service list of approved providers, a low fee, with no deductible, is charged. For using other providers, the charges are higher in terms of deductibles and coinsurance.

point program A type of incentive program. Rewards employees for performance in point increments. similar to airline frequent-flyer programs which award one point for each mile traveled.

point-to-point protocol (PPP) Allows a computer to connect directly to the **Internet** using a modem and a telephone line.

policy A type of plan that serves as a guide to thinking, discretionary action, and decision making for managers, supervisors, and staff personnel. Policies provide common premises for action. They help insure coordination before decision or action and provide some assurance that recurring problems and issues will be handled with some measure of consistency throughout the organization. They typically cover all critical areas of corporate or departmental operations.

political action committee (PAC) A committee chartered by an organization to administer, disburse, and disclose funds contributed voluntarily and used solely for political purposes, including decisions on which candidate(s) for political office will receive contributions.

political fundamentalism See politically correct.

politically correct Describes people who condemn those who use terms considered to be racist, sexist, homophobic, or discriminatory or practices considered to be multiculturally sensitive. Has resulted in language codes on some university campuses, assaults on freedom of speech and expression, threats to the continued employment of professors, and other forms of intimidation.

political risk insurance Insurance purchased to protect corporate overseas assets against confiscation, expropriation, and nationalization by the host country.

polling survey A type of research study in which a survey is used to investigate current techniques and practices. The results of a polling study are descriptive and are useful for identifying trends, evaluating current practices, or comparing one's practices with those of another organization.

polygraph See lie detector.

polymyalgia rheumatica A type of arthritis that affects an estimated 450,000 Americans, usually older women. It causes muscle pain and neck, shoulder, and hip stiffness.

pooling A flexible benefit plan option in which employees are allowed to draw as needed from an account that combines vacation, holiday, sick, and personal paid time off.

population In a research study, the total group people or things being studied. See also sample.

population comparison A means of determining or proving adverse impact (discrimination) in screening and selection. Population comparison involves comparing the percentage of an organization's minority group employees and the percentage of that minority in the general population in the surrounding community. It is an error-prone method because of the cruciality and difficulty of defining the relevant labor market.

portability **1.** In benefits, a pension plan feature that allows participants to move from one employer to another without changing the source from which benefits, past and future, will be paid. **2.** Guarantees that insurance coverage goes with the individual regardless of change in employment, foreign travel, or change of residence.

portable computer See laptop, notebook computer, palmtop, and transportable computer.

portable pension A pension plan that allows workers who change jobs to have their benefits rolled over into individual retirement accounts, allowing workers to withdraw funds from a **defined contribution plan** as taxable cash, or shifting retirement funds between employers (an uncommon and possibly undesirable practice).

Portal-to-Portal Act of 1947 (PTPA) An Act designed to correct judicial interpretations of the **Fair Labor Standards Act of 1938,** the **Walsh-Healy Public Contracts Act of 1936,** and the **Davis-Bacon Act of 1931** in disregard of long-standing customs and practices between employers and employees. Specifically the Act relieves employers from liability and punishment under the cited laws for failing to pay minimum wages or overtime compensation to employees engaged in walking, riding, or traveling to and from the workplace or area in which the principal activities for which the worker was employed to perform are conducted and for activities that are preliminary to or postliminary to the principal activity or activities. Exceptions include express provisions of a written or nonwritten contract or a custom or practice in effect at the time of such activity between the employee, his or her agent, the collective bargaining unit and the employer.

portfolio An itemized list of investments, commercial paper, and securities owned by a bank, trust, investment firm, or individual investor.

position description *See* job description.

positioning *See* market segmentation.

positive discipline Self-imposed discipline. It comes from within the person and relies on self-motivation, on the willingness, if not the eagerness, of people to do what is consistent with the goals and objectives of the organization and the work group.

positivism An approach to the interpretation of the U.S. Constitution. A philosophy or belief that holds that the only basis for civil law is the will of the sovereign (in the United States, that is the Constitution or the actions of duly elected officials).

positive reinforcement In managing employee behavior, work-team development, instruction, and most other interventions, the process of using feedback (nods, smiles, complimentary comments, praise, pats on the back, rewards, and the like) rather than negative feedback (scowls, withering looks, criticism, condemnation, and punishment) following observation of behavior.

positive-sum game Competition between two individuals or groups where both contestants win, although they may not win equally. For example, labor-management contract negotiations, marketing, and so on.

positive symptoms In mental illness, behaviors that are not found among healthy individuals but are present among individuals with schizophrenia.

positron emission tomogrpahy (PET) A medical diagnostic technology. Employs scanners that use isotopes to track metabolism rates involving a variety of heart, brain, and other organ ailments. The system employs a cyclotron to produce short-lived isotopes that emit particles known as positrons. The isotopes are joined chemically to natural substances like glucose or oxygen and injected into the patient's bloodstream. The scanner then tracks the trace materials as they are metabolized in the body.

post/posting Placing a message on a **bulletin-board system** or entering a message into a network communication system.

post-accident testing Drug and alcohol tests administered to an employee following an industrial accident. Such tests must meet statutory and/or regulatory terms, conditions, and restrictions.

post-claims underwriting The practice of checking an insurance policy-holder's medical and health history only after a claim for benefits is filed.

posters *See* labor law posting; state employment postings.

postnatal care Medical care provided to the mother and infant during the period following birth.

postproduction In TV production, any process that takes place after shooting, such as editing, audio enhancement, and the addition of special effects, graphics, and so on.

PostScript In desktop publishing, a page-description language developed by Adobe Systems. It consists of a specific set of software commands and conventions that forms images on output printers and film recorders when translated through a raster processor.

PostScript font A font that, in addition to screen information, the typeface also contains printer font information that has been defined with the **PostScript** language.

posttest   A test administered following training to determine pass-fail or the amount and kind of behavioral change that has occurred as a result of that training.

post-traumatic stress disorder (PTSD) An emotional illness experienced by victims of assault, rape, natural disasters (such as earthquakes, fires, and floods) and by combat veterans. The triggering event is traumatic to most people and is accompanied by intense fear and a feeling of helplessness. Sufferers relive the traumatic incident, sometimes for years, whether awake or asleep, replaying the event over and over in their minds like a horror movie. Some experience flashbacks, hallucinations, and illusions. Some enter a numbed emotional state in which they become detached and disinterested in what is going on around them. Still others respond with hyperarousal, have difficulty sleeping, are irritable and hostile, and have trouble concentrating. Unless successfully treated (professionally, often with peer group support), sufferers may become victims of substance abuse, broken relationships, and ruined careers.

pot   *See* marijuana.

potential-line forecast   A type of time-series forecast involving projections based on analysis of all opportunities identified in a list of HR (or other) planning issues.

POTS   Plain old telephone system — conventional analog telephone service.

pourover trust   An estate planning strategy designed to prevent individual beneficiaries from finding out how other beneficiaries (such as brothers and sisters) have benefited. The maker sets up individual trusts, each with a separate trustee and instructions. Upon the request of each trustee, funds are provided by a "pourover" trust established by the creator of the trust.

power   The ability to act or influence decisions and action — to effect, persons or groups. It resides in people, not in positions.

power of attorney   A legal document prepared by an attorney that gives a named individual the power to act as the maker's agent. It is revoked by law if the maker becomes incompetent.

power test   A test that measures performance without regard to the speed of response. Test items are typically arranged in order of increasing difficulty, and there is no time limit.

power training   A consequence of downsizing and the demands of boards of control for reductions in training costs. It is training that is carefully designed and focused in short segments on what trainees need to know and be able to do, instead of the lengthy, nice-to-have, and often redundant training programs so commonly offered in the past. Coined by Walter DiMantova, director of the Centers for Corporate Training, Eastern Michigan University, Ypsilanti, Michigan.

practical exercise (PE)   Involves mental or physical hands-on performance of a skill or job task. PE is used primarily as the culminating activity in a series of lessons that may make use of lectures, demonstrations, interactive learning strategies, and the like. Also referred to as *performance method.*

practical testing   *See* performance assessment.

practice   Rehearsal, repetition, and drill provided to "set" or make permanent knowledge or skill.

practitioner   **1.** In general, one who practices a profession. **2.** In health benefits administration, a Christian Science practitioner or nurse.

pragmatism   An ethical theory similar to utilitarianism (*see* consequentialism) but with a slight difference. Pragmatism holds that whatever is right and proper for the greatest number is good, even if it is hard-nosed or painful. Whatever is good only for the individual or the few, or is impractical or ineffective for the many, is bad and should be eschewed.

preadmission review (PAR)   A requirement for certification of medical necessity before an employee can be admitted to a hospital for surgery or other medical treatment. Involves assessment of the appropriateness of in-hospital treatment and the duration of such treatment. PAR typically includes psychiatric and substance abuse as well as other hospital admissions.

preadmission testing (PAT)   In health care, a plan that allows employees planning to be hospitalized, usually for a surgical procedure, to have certain tests, such as X-rays, blood tests, and other pre-surgical tests, performed on an outpatient basis prior to admission.

preauthorization A requirement of health maintenance organizations, preferred provider organizations, and other providers to evaluate the necessity of certain costly medical and surgical procedures before they are performed. Preauthorization is used to determine whether the procedure is necessary, eliminate unnecessary expense, and help patients avoid the costs, pain, and risks associated with such procedures. Examples are angiography, laminectomy, knee arthroscopy, upper gastrointestinal endoscopy, and hemorrhoidectomy.

preaward survey A survey made of a business by the prospective buyer following receipt of bids. The purpose is to look for evidence that the organization is a responsible and responsive firm, with an established quality control system, that can provide the product or service needed and on time. Often used by government agencies.

precert See precertification.

precertification In health care, a means of decreasing utilization by requiring the admitting physician or the subscriber (and often the hospital) to notify the plan before a member is admitted for inpatient care or scheduling an outpatient procedure. Also called *preadmission review* and *precert.*

pre-con meeting In meeting management, a meeting of conference organizers and hotel or property personnel prior to the arrival of meeting participants. The purpose is to review the details of the program and resolve problems and issues with regard to requirements and responsibilities of both parties.

pre-control A simple yet more statistically powerful quality control tool than a **control chart,** it permits monitoring a product or process from the very start rather than waiting for 100 or more readings to calculate control limits. Used primarily in monitoring product, material, or manufacturing processes. Attributed to Frank Satterthwaite.

precursor developments See trailblazer developments.

precycle/precycling Making buying choices that promote and support responsible products and packaging, make recycling simpler and easier, and reduce the amount of trash and garbage you must throw away. Attrib-

uted to Tim Connor, editor of *Recycling World,* the Newsletter of the Environmental Defense Fund. *Contact:* Environmental Defense Fund (EDF), 257 Park Ave. South, New York, NY 10010.

predatory pricing See low-balling.

predeparture training See relocation training.

predictive validity A dependable means of determining the validity of a test. Involves administering the test to applicants before they are hired and then using customary or conventional screening and selection devices (and not the test results) to hire. Following a period of time on the job, such as six months, the performance of the new hires is measured and compared with the test results to determine the accuracy of the tests in predicting successful job performance.

pre-employment testing Drug and alcohol tests administered to by employers to prospective employees to avoid negligent hire claims. It should be noted that to avoid potential liability for claims of defamation, employers should involve an independent medical review officer in the testing process.

pre-existing condition A disease or other type of health problem which predates and frequently results in denial of coverage under a health insurance plan. Some health plans require a waiting period before covering such conditions or will not cover them at all. See Health Care Reform Act of 1996.

preferred provider A provider who furnishes health care services at a discounted fee in exchange for patient volume. Also called *preferred vendor.*

preferred provider arrangement (PPA)
1. See preferred provider organization.
2. Health care plan in which the employer (the payer) makes the arrangement rather than the providers.

preferred provider organization (PPO)
A health care organization comprising medical groups, physicians, and/or hospitals, under contract with corporations or insurance companies to provide medical or other health care products and services that send it patients. In exchange for guaranteeing a certain volume of employee referrals from their firms, employers are granted discount rates from the providers, thereby providing employers a means of monitoring the quality and quantity of health care and better control of costs. PPOs are also seen by employers as

a means of monitoring the quality and quantity of health care. Members may choose from a roster of physicians who provide care according to a set fee schedule. For a higher copayment, members can choose out-of-plan providers.

Pregnancy Discrimination Act of 1978 (PDA)   An amendment to **Title VII** of the **Civil Rights Act of 1964.** Prohibits discrimination in employment practices, including disability, sick leave, and health care benefits, on the bases of pregnancy, childbirth, or related medical conditions. Essentially, the Act requires an employer to treat a woman unable to work because of pregnancy-related conditions exactly the same as any other employee unable to work for other reasons and to provide health care coverage for pregnancy on the same basis as for other medical conditions. It is a violation of PDA to require pregnant women to take leaves of mandatory duration unless a similar requirement is imposed on male employees with disabilities that impair their job performance. However, a mandatory leave policy that affects solely pregnant women may be justified by **business necessity**.

preliminary program   In meeting management, a second mailing to attendees that includes information on program structure, identifies key speakers, and provides details of conference activities and registration forms.

premenstrual syndrome (PMS)   Irritability, depression, tension, pain, headaches, energy loss, or other sensations occurring in some women during the days immediately preceding the onset of menstruation. Can be severe for some women. No treatment is completely effective although some medications have shown some promise.

Pre-Miere Awards   Annual awards presented to creative and prepress production companies by *Pre-* magazine in 20 or more categories, such as annual reports, books, catalogs, brochures and pamphlets, company identification/ stationery, directories, manuals, newsletters, packaging, posters, and print advertisements. *Contact: Pre-,* South Wind Publishing Co., 8340 Mission Road, Ste. 106, Prairie Village, KS 66206 (913/642-6611).

premium   The fee paid by an employee or employer to an insurer for health insurance coverage.

premium pay   Extra pay, in addition to regular wages or salary, for work performed outside or in addition to regularly scheduled work periods, such as Sundays, holidays, nights, and so on.

prenatal care   Consists of medical care, health education, and social support services for both parents to improve the chances that a woman will bear a healthy baby and reduce infant mortality.

pre-need plan   A means of meeting financial obligations associated with one's death and burial. It has two elements: (1) specific instructions regarding the type of burial service desired, and (2) prepayment where money is paid, saved, or invested for services at the time of need. Prepayment can be handled by such means as an individual trust, savings plan, regulated trust agreement, life insurance policy, or annuity contract.

prenuptial agreement   An agreement made before a marriage whereby a couple can provide that, upon termination of the marriage by either death or divorce, each spouse waives certain rights in the property belonging to the other.

prepackaged training   *See* off-the-shelf program.

prepaid health care organization   An organization, such as a health maintenance organization or competitive medical plan, that receives direct payments from the insurance carrier (or Medicare) for the services it provides to subscribers.

prepaid legal plan   A relatively new employee taxable benefit. May include a legal insurance policy, similar to an HMO. Other plans feature unlimited phone advice from and consultation with an attorney by employees and members of their families, will preparation, legal document review, legal representation in the form of letters or phone calls made by an attorney, and referral services for more involved legal counsel. Few plans include representation by an attorney in court cases.

preparation   The second stage in instruction. Involves researching the subject-matter, identifying the specific skills and knowledge to be taught, determining the delivery system, the methods, techniques, and media to be used and the sequence in which they will be used, selecting the means of checking on the effectiveness of the instruction, readying the classroom, shop, or laboratory, and rehearsing and practicing the lesson(s).

prepared and perishable food program (PPFP) Private and public agencies and organizations that collect surplus cooked and fresh food from supermarkets, restaurants, hotels, and caterers and turn it over to community organizations that feed the homeless or others who otherwise might go hungry. Examples are City Harvest in New York City, Daily Bread Food Bank in Miami, and Waste-Not in Scottsdale.

prepayment health plan A health care plan in which a health care provider, such as a health maintenance organization or a competitive medical plan, is paid on a monthly basis for each covered beneficiary. Medicare beneficiaries get all Medicare-covered hospital and medical insurance benefits through such plans.

prerequisites The minimum qualifications a trainee or job applicant must have prior to enrollment in an instructional system or employment/promotion. Prerequisites represent a prediction of the aptitudes, knowledge, skills, experience, and values required for success in the training or in a new position.

pre-retirement counseling Assistance provided to employees prior to their retirement to assist them in making the transition from demanding jobs to a useful and rewarding lifestyle. Typically covers retirement benefits, Social Security, tax planning, budgeting, investment options, wills and trusts, maintenance of physical and emotional health, psychological adjustment, adult education opportunities, volunteer program opportunities, part-time employment, interpersonal relationships, and travel opportunities. Personal consultation, seminars or workshops, small group discussion, pamphlets and fact sheets are the most commonly used delivery systems.

pre-retirement planning
See pre-retirement counseling.

presage variables In training research, variables that relate to the characteristics of instructors and include instructors' formative and educational experiences, and instructors' traits and abilities, competencies, and skills.

presbyopia Aging eyes, a condition that often begins to affect people at about age 40. The lenses of the eye become less flexible, making it more difficult to focus close-up, so that victims have to hold printed material farther and farther from their eyes — and ultimately requires vision correction, usually in the form of bifocals.

prescription drug plan (PDP) A benefits plan in which all or a part (percentage) of the costs of employees' prescription drugs are paid by the insurer. Includes drug card plans, mail-service programs, and integrated plans (a combination of both drug card and mail-service),

prescription benefit management (PBM) Companies that provide prescription drugs to the employees of member organizations. Some PBM companies are independent; others have been acquired by drug manufacturers.

Prescription Drug User Fee Act of 1992 Requires drug companies to pay the Food and Drug Administration (FDA) $100,000 for each drug tested for safety, increasing to $233,000 in five years. FDA will also charge $50,000 to each company annually, rising to $138,000 in five years. It will also charge $6,000 annually for each product already on the market, increasing to $14,000 five years from now. The legislation is designed to cut the time for drug testing in half (down to 6 months for critical drugs and 12 months for all others) and help cover the costs to the government. The Act is also important because it sets a precedent in terms of establishing a way for federal regulatory agencies to raise money to support their programs.

preselection process A voluntary multiple-step process by which current nonmanagement employees are helped to assess their potential and desire for promotion to first-line supervisory positions. Such programs do not focus on actual selection but on self-evaluation of leadership potential. Typically, the program begins with a session where the challenges and realities of first-line supervision are explored. Those who continue with the process are then exposed to strategies, such as coaching, where basic leadership skills are developed. The final step involves evaluation at two or more levels — the coach level, self-evaluation, and an executive-level selection panel.

presentation The third stage in an instructional sequence, it involves the implementation of the instructional plan with the individual trainee or group of trainees.

presentation skills *See* platform skills.

presentation skills training Training provided for employees who must speak to groups and face cameras and microphones. Designed to build skills, confidence, and control in facing an audience or the media. Focuses on planning, organizing, and delivering the presentation, projecting a professional image, maximizing persuasive power, managing anxiety and stress, building and maintaining rapport with listeners, handling questions and objections, and dealing with hostility.

Presentations: Technology and Techniques for Effective Communication Monthly: $24.95 per year (free to qualified subscribers). Address: Lakewood Publications, Presentations Magazine, 50 S. Ninth S., Minneapolis, MN 55402 (612-333-0471; Fax 612-333-6526; E-mail **sheimes@presentations.com**; URL **http://www.presentations.com**).

Presidential ACCESS Scholarship Program Created by the **Higher Education Reauthorization Act of 1992** to reward students who take rigorous academic courses in high school.

President's Committee on Employment of People with Disabilities Offers a toll-free information service about job accommodation methods, devices, and strategies. *Contact:* Rick Douglas, Executive Director, President's Committee on Employment of People with Disabilities, 1331 F St., N.W., Washington, DC 20004-1107 (202/376-6200).

pretermitted child or heir A child or other **issue** intentionally or accidentally omitted from a person's will. The state can provide that such a person is entitled to whatever his or her share would be under the rules of **intestacy.** However, if an individual is deliberately omitted, and the **testator** wishes to avoid the pretermitted heir statute, he or she must state in the will that the omitted person is specifically omitted and was not left out by oversight.

pretest A test administered prior to the initiation of training to determine trainee placement (group or program) and serve as a baseline for measuring the kind and amount of behavioral change attributable to the training.

pre-travel quality control Software systems that access passenger name lists to review for accuracy or other specified checks.

pre-travel reporting Software that accesses reservations prior to ticketing and produces management reports to enhance control.

pre-trial deposition Testimony under oath given by adversaries in a litigation and third-part witnesses elicited by often wide-ranging questions from a lawyer following study of documents and interview of other knowledgeable individuals. The testimony is transcribed and may be used for a variety of purposes at a trial, to gain advantage in other lawsuits, or develop claims against a person or corporation that have not been brought to litigation. Permitted in virtually all federal and state courts.

pretrip One classification of free trips to resort areas taken by users of incentive travel or travel agents, or by travel agents themselves, where business has already been booked and there's a signed contract. The purpose of the trip is to work out the details of the engagement. The host property owner provides complementary air and ground transportation, meals and accommodations, and guided tours. Attributed to Michael Hurwitz, president of the Society of Incentive Travel Executives.

prevailing charge A fee based on the customary charges for covered medical insurance services or items. It is also the maximum charge Medicare can approve for any item or service.

prevailing wage rate The amount typically paid by employers in a labor market or geographical area for similar work.

prevention costs In total quality management, costs associated with the prevention of product or service defects, such as training, problem-solving meetings, quality circles, measurement, preventive maintenance, and so on.

preventive care 1. Health care services designed to prevent illness, such as periodic physical examinations. A new development involves the use of historical data to chart a patient's health over a period of several years so that a health problem is signaled before it becomes acute. Examples are prostate-specific antigen screening (that can detect prostate cancer at a very early stage) and (possibly in the near future) DNA analysis to determine a patient's genetic profile and propensity for disease well in advance of its appearance. Payment is made for preventive health care as contrasted with indemnity plans, which pay for losses incurred following accident or injury. **2.** Well-baby care consisting of physical examinations, infant immunizations, monitoring of growth to detect nutritional problems, treatment of infectious diseases, and checking for injuries or signs of neglect and abuse — and providing guidance and emotional support to the parents.

preventive services   *See* preventive care.

price earnings (PE) (ratio)   The market price of a particular stock divided by that company's earnings per share for the last year or 12-month period. Used as a guide by investors for buying and selling stock.

pricing   The process of establishing a selling price for goods or services. Two methods are commonly used: estimation and actual cost projection.

primacy   A basic principle of learning which holds that people tend to remember best the first and last things they see, hear, or otherwise experience.

***prima facie* case**   A case in which evidence is sufficient to establish or support a presumption of fact. For example, in most states with retaliatory discharge laws, an employee alleging discrimination must establish a *prima facie* case. To win the case, the worker must prove (1) that he or she was seeking the benefits of the workers' comp law, (2) was subjected to discriminatory or retaliatory action while pursuing those rights, and (3) that there was a connection between the pursuit of those rights and and punitive action.

primary care   Care provided by physicians in the specialties of family practice, internal medicine, and pediatrics (and sometimes obstetrics/gynecology).

primary care nurse (PCN)   A registered nurse who assists patients in assessing their medical needs, choosing a health care provider, and deciding among treatment alternatives. Typically expected to be on-call 24 hours per day, seven days per week and have on-line access to physicians.

primary care physician (PCP)   A health care practitioner selected by an insured member of a **health maintenance organization** or a **preferred provider organization** to coordinate health care and make necessary referrals to specialists and hospitals. Usually a family practitioner, pediatrician, internist, or obstetrician/gynecologist.

primary care provider   A health care practitioner, such as a physician, who takes care of all medical needs short of sub-specialty care and surgery. For example, a primary care physician performs physical exams, treats diabetic-related ailments, heart problems, hypertension, and stress-related problems and counsels patients in a variety of areas.

primary health care   *See* basic health care.

primary insurance amount (PIA) The amount to which a social security annuitant is entitled by virtue of his or her average earnings before any deductions, such as a **windfall reduction.** A spouse's social security benefit is usually one-half of the annuitant's PIA; however, if the windfall reduction applies, the spouse's benefit is based on one-half of the reduced PIA until the annuitant's death, at which time the survivor's benefit is based on the unreduced PIA.

primary memory   The **random access memory** component of a computer system, comprised of integrated circuit chips and related components. Primary memory is where the computer's operating system resides and performs its functions, and where programs "do their thing." It is directly addressable by the computer's microprocessor and is almost instantaneously accessible.

primary method   An instructional method that is objectively judged to be the most effective and efficient means of attaining an instructional (learning) objective.

primary objective   One of the core learnings of a training program or a major unit of instruction and an objective of central and dominant importance in an instructional system. It may deal with the development of a manipulative skill, a conceptual skill, or a special ability. It gives meaning, clarity, and unity to all learning activities in the training program.

primary research   Research studies that are conducted directly by the researcher and typically involve such methodologies as field experiments, case studies, and organization surveys.

principal   The individual who appoints a power of attorney or health care proxy.

principles of learning *See* learning principles.

prioritization matrix   A management and planning tool used to help decide what problem of opportunity to work on first, second, third, and so on. It involves listing the items to be evaluated, choosing the criteria against which the importance of items is to be evaluated, the rating scale to be used, and the weight to be given to each rating; rating the items, and tabulating the scores to establish the priorities.

prioritization of resources   A means of determining the level of health care benefits, in terms of which services or therapies should be made available to Americans. Methodologies currently used or in prospect include medical effectiveness of a service (clinical outcomes) and patient characteristics (such as employment potential or income).

print deprived   A person who cannot read due to blindness, vision impairment, or other physical disability, such as Parkinson's disease (unable to hold a book or newspaper steady), or paraplegia (unable to hold a book or turn pages).

Privacy Act of 1974 (PA)   A law designed to protect people against invasions of privacy by federal agencies. Applies to all federal agencies and private firms that keep records for a federal agency under contract. The act permits individuals to decide what records kept by an agency or department are important and to insist that they be used only for the purpose for which the information was collected. The individual also has the right to see the information accompanied by a person of his or her own choice, file information to correct mistakes, amend and add details, dispute records believed to be inaccurate, and make or be provided a copy of all or any portion of a record in a comprehensive form upon request and payment of a reasonable fee that excludes the costs of research or review. The law also requires that records be maintained showing to whom disclosures (other than internal uses) were made and that they be retained for at least five years or the life of the record, whichever is longer. Doubtful requests for information must be referred to legal counsel, the privacy officer, or a senior executive for decision. Reasonable administrative, technical, and physical safeguards must be established to assure protection against inadvertent disclosure and disclosure only to authorized personnel with a need to know.

privacy invaders   Networks or rings of thieves who infiltrate Social Security computer files, stealing confidential personal records and selling the information to whoever will buy it.

privacy laws   *See* Employee Polygraph Protection Act of 1988; Fair Credit Reporting Act of 1969; Freedom of Information Act of 1966; Privacy Act of 1974.

privacy rights laws   State laws making it illegal to fire workers for their private use of legal products (such as cigarettes) or choice of legal activities away from the job. Twenty-three states have passed such legislation and all states, except Alabama, Arkansas, Minnesota, Montana, Ohio, Texas, and Utah, have considered some form of privacy law.

private geriatric care management (PGCM)   A private company that provides counseling services and other forms of assistance for dependent older adults. A PGCM company consists of a team of professionals that makes contacts with physicians and other health care providers, answers questions, provides case workers, plans social activities, arranges for qualified live-in assistance, sees that adult children are made aware of the condition of an aging parent living in another state, and otherwise serves as a surrogate parent.

private industry council (PIC)   A business volunteer board that oversees local job training programs authorized by the **Job Training Partnership Act of 1982** (JTPA). PICs often work with postsecondary institutions to address local education and job training problems. Currently there are approximately 600 PICS that work in partnership with local elected officials to fund and direct training under the JTPA. They must have a majority of private sector employer members, show innovation aimed at streamlining management, and emphasize building a base for private sector ownership and financial support of the system. Most PICs provide job needs surveys.

private inurement   Occurs when a not-for-profit business operates in a way that results in more than incidental financial gain to a private individual, such as a health care provider. Prohibited by the Internal Revenue Service.

private letter ruling (PLR)   A numbered or unnumbered document used by the Internal Revenue Service to announce tax decisions.

privatization **1.** The creation of new private corporate entities (businesses and industries) from what were formerly government-owned and operated enterprises. **2.** Partial privatization has been proposed as a means of shoring up the Social Security system's finances, which will be in serious trouble early in the next decade. If adopted, the proposal would impose government-mandated savings; that is, workers and their employers would be required to funnel all or part of the Social Security taxes currently paid to the government into private accounts — such as personal security accounts.

privileged communication A confidential statement made to a professional, such as a physician, lawyer, priest, rabbi, minister, or spouse, which may not be revealed in a court of law.

probability A statistical term used to describe the possibility or likelihood (the odds) of some event or phenomenon occurring. An absolutely impossible event has a probability of zero. At the other extreme, an absolutely certain event has a probability of one. Events with a likelihood of occurrence between the two extremes are expressed as a decimal fraction between zero and one. For example, an event with a 50-50 chance of happening has a probability of 0.5.

probate process The court-supervised administration of an estate following the death of the owner — the process by which the deceased individual's property is transferred to the persons named in his or her will or to the persons who otherwise inherits the property under the states's laws of intestate succession. It typically includes proving the validity of a will (if there is one), supervising the payment of the taxes and other debts of the estate, and the distribution of the remaining assets to the beneficiaries. May also be known as a *Surrogate's Court* or *Register of Wills*.

probation Policies and procedures relating to the imposition of adverse disciplinary action involving a period of probation during which the behavior and performance of the transgressor will be carefully watched. Such policies invariably address the length (usually no less than 3 and no more than 6 months) and terms of probationary periods, relief from probation, and disposition of records of probation. Probation should be imposed both orally and in writing, and the employee should be told that it is a final warning and will be followed by dismissal unless performance improves to an acceptable level.

probing An effective technique for identifying the origin, nature, or solution of an issue or problem. Probing involves asking detailed and specific questions to uncover hidden feelings, make subtle suggestions, get all the facts, identify the real problem, analyze the problem, and develop alternative solutions.

problem An unplanned and unwanted change or result; a deviation, variance, or aberration; a snag, pitfall, or tangle. A situation that requires resolution and for which there appears to be no obvious answer.

problem-centered order A type of instructional sequencing that employs a series of general problems and then addresses alternative means of solving them. Problems are introduced in increasing order of difficulty.

problem sensing The act of anticipating problems so that they can be headed off.

problem sensitivity The ability to examine potentially troublesome areas to detect deviations from plans either before they surface or early enough in their development to prevent their growth into truly serious and costly issues.

problem solving Directed thinking; the process of channeling thought toward a problem or situation that requires resolution and for which there appears to be no obvious answer. Problem solving thinking is deliberate, sequential, logical, analytical, and evaluative. It uses previously acquired or newly gained knowledge, skills, and experience to take action in an unfamiliar situation.

problem solving skill The ability to resolve a troublesome situation or issue by following a deliberate, logical, reasoned thought process, keeping emotions and personal values in check, and using previously acquired or newly gained knowledge, skills, and experiences.

***pro bono* work** Legal or other types of services provided employees or others without fee or any other charges.

procedural simulations A representation of a system or situation in which the participants have control over what occurs; for example, using a ship docking or a flight **simulator**.

procedure A type of plan that provides specific guides for action. Describes what, when, where, how, and by whom an operation or task is to be performed. It includes all steps necessary for completing the task and is established to ensure maximum efficiency of performance with minimum expenditure of resources. Examples of common procedures: purchase of equipment and materials, operation of equipment, preparation and submission of budgets, fund control, preparation of travel requests, vouchers, and trip reports, recruitment and advertising, and requisitioning supplies.

procedures audit An audit that compares on-going operations and activities, including training, against applicable procedures to determine whether documents, such as standing operating procedures, are current, complete, understood, and used by personnel.

process A transformation or series of changes brought about throughout the life of a system — changes that shape size, function, or some other dimension or attribute of the system.

process action team (PAT) A problem-solving process. A PAT consists of people from different parts of an organization who use statistical problem-solving techniques to attack and solve a specific organizational or business problem. The recommended solutions are delivered to the appropriate executive or other organizational entity for decision with respect to implementation.

process color printing In desktop publishing, four-color printing where all visible colors are reproduced using **cyan, magenta, yellow, and black** inks.

process benchmarking A means of building and sustaining competitive advantage by achieving major improvements in corporate performance. It involves comparing the company's mission and functions, systems and policies, and practices and processes with those of top performing companies inside and outside its own markets to identify areas of competitive superiority and deficiency and then implement actions to maximize the former and minimize the latter. Usually performed in focus groups.

process capability (Cpk) In **total quality management,** a universal measure. The ratio of the specification (what the process is expected to do) to what is actually generated by the process. That is, the capability of the process expressed as the proportion of expectations that will be satisfied by the current process.

process chart *See* flowchart.

process evaluation Assessment that focuses on on-going training programs — use of resources, trainee-instructor interaction, training activities, learning strategies, and so on.

process flowchart *See* flow chart.

process group *See* sensitivity training.

process grouping One of the basic groupings of organizational elements. The stages through which the work or product moves and related activities determine the placement of the function. For example, oil and natural gas companies often group for exploration, production, refining, and distribution.

process improvement *See* quality improvement process.

process innovation *See* reengineering.

process management A concrete, preventive approach to continuous improvement that evolved from total quality, systems theory, and employee involvement. It provides a common language and way of addressing problems, makes work easier and more efficient, and enhances cross-functional teamwork. It involves (1) defining work as a process with inputs, outputs, customers, and suppliers; (2) describing how a process really works; (3) tracking and analyzing the performance of a process; and (4) redesigning a process to improve its performance. Also called *horizontal management.* Adapted from *The Organization of the Future,* November 1991. Werner & Company, 1479 S. Ponce de Leon Ave., N.E., Atlanta, GA 30307.

process observer A member of a work team assigned responsibility for looking at team processes, recording what is seen, reporting findings to the team, and making suggestions to improve team procedures.

process-performance test A test that measures psychomotor skills or a testee's ability to perform a task using a standard sequence of actions while the task is being performed (or evaluation of a videotaped performance) to determine whether the testee followed the prescribed procedures.

process quality management and improvement (PQMI) *See* quality improvement process.

process redesign A low-risk systematic approach to the modification, simplification, and streamlining of existing business processes. May or may not involve technology. May result in incremental or modest improvements but usually leaves work structure intact.

process reengineering A high-risk approach to improvement that involves the creation of new processes and innovative changes to business practices and methods. Typically depends on the use of technology. May result in dramatic improvements but radically changes work structure. (URL **http://www.prosci.com**)

process simulations A representation of a system or situation in which the participants do not have control over what occurs; for example, replicating nuclear fission.

process variables In training research, variables that relate to what instructors and trainees do — their behaviors, separately and interactively, and their impact on each other.

procurement budget Displays the timing, quantities, and estimated costs of each type of raw materials needed to meet production and inventory requirements.

PRODIGY$_{SM}$ Interactive Personal Service An information network that links personal computers across the United States. For a monthly fee, the system creates a file in its customers' computers that provides access to a great variety of sources of information, such as an encyclopedia, stock market reports, and so on.

producer The individual holding overall responsibility for a live dramatization, TV, or motion picture production from concept to post production activities.

producing Developing a creative, cost-effective live dramatization, video program, motion picture, or show from concept through post-production; overseeing or approving the concept, approach, treatment, budget, storyboard, writing, script, casting, set/location selection, shot list, equipment selection, lighting and audio, shooting, visual continuity and pacing, and editing.

product audit An investigation and examination of the production process that involves reinspecting or retesting samples of the product previously tested and accepted. It can be applied to tangible products such as packaged training media and programs and the output of training systems — personnel who have returned to the job following training.

product evaluation 1. A means of assessing employee needs that involves the collection, examination, and evaluation of products produced by managers, supervisors, technicians, or other categories of employees, using a set of quality standards developed for that product, to identify deficiencies that can be corrected by training and development. 2. In training, assessing the competencies, the knowledge and skills, of trainees following training and noting changes in their on-the-job performance.

product grouping One of the basic groupings of organizational elements. The products manufactured or fabricated and related activities determine the placement of the function. For example, a pet supply firm might have groups for pet food, identification and restraining devices (collars and leashes), medication, and flea control.

production company An organization that provides services to meeting planners and managers. They include three types: (1) event production companies that create theme parties or assume responsibility for entertainment; (2) business theater companies that enhance educational and sales meetings by designing sets and providing graphics, custom songs, promotional materials, and live talent; and (3) combination companies that handle both types of functions.

production budget Shows how many units of a product will be produced to meet customer requirements as detailed in the sales budget and the number to be held in inventory.

productive time Used in time management to describe time expended in producing the desired product or service or any element or component of that product or service.

productivity 1. A measure of output or yield. In its simplest form, it is determined by dividing the amount of useful work to be done by the number of people needed to do it. 2. Narrowly defined as efficiency — the ratio of output produced for a given level of input. More broadly defined as effectiveness — the extent to which the output of an activity or program meets a need or solves a problem. In its broadest sense, productivity considers both output production and how well a product, program, or service achieves its objectives and the quality or excellence of those products and services. **3.** Defined by the U.S. Department of Labor as output (products produced) per number of hours worked. In these terms, increased productivity is essential to make American products competitive in global markets and improved standards of living.

productivity improvement program (PIP)
A program that involves employees at all levels and assesses not only how well the organization is doing but also how well it ought to be doing. Applies operational analysis and control to measure the performance of each contributing organizational element to enterprise goals and objectives and employs measures to optimize the utilization of organization resources. PIPs should include analysis of the following factors: (1) *efficiency* in terms of avoiding duplication, minimizing delays and downtime, distributing workload evenly, and applying approved standards; (2) *effectiveness* in terms of making valid assumptions about the relationships between output and desired results, identifying workable alternative approaches, establishing relationships between quality or frequency of outputs and results, selecting proper targets for the application of outputs, and achieving acceptable results; (3) *quality* in terms of clearly defined product and service specifications, readily assessable quality control and feedback mechanisms, procedures, job aids, and training programs, and favorable customer and client reactions and evaluation; and (4) *timeliness* in terms of establishing and applying mechanisms to identify backlogs, the level of timeliness performance, and the importance of timeliness to production service.

productivity tickets A travel industry perk — free tickets given to a meeting's sponsor when a large number of delegates books flights to a meeting or convention on the organization's official airline.

product liability insurance Coverage for potential suits by consumers for faulty products.

product performance test A test that assesses the quality of the products produced by the testee independent of the procedures or behaviors involved in the production. The characteristics of the "products" are compared with those of a standard;

for example, an actual item, a representation, or a template.

product-process performance test
A combination of the product and process performance test where both the product and the process are evaluated.

product specification standards
Standards that describe what customers demand or expect in product or service quality.

product variables In training research, variables that relate to instructional outcomes, including immediate, intermediate, and long-range trainee effects.

professional, administrative, technical, and clerical survey (PATC) One of three types of annual salary surveys conducted by the Bureau of Labor Statistics. The other two are area wage surveys and industry wage surveys.

professional conference (congress) organizer (PCO) An independent meeting professional who specializes in domestic and/or international event management. Engaged by meeting planners to serve as primary liaison between their organizations and the local convention bureau, hotel, and other meeting services and provide logistical and administrative support, including consultation on protocol, customs, and security.

Professional Conference Specialist (PCS)
A designation offered by the Professional Convention Management Association to suppliers following completions of a series of self-study programs. *Contact:* PCMA, 100 Vestavia Office Park, Ste. 220, Birmingham, AL 35216 (205/978-4914; Fax 205/822-3789; E-mail **pcma@internetmci.com**; URL **http://www.pcma.com**).

Professional Convention Management Association (PCMA) An association established to increase the effectiveness of meetings and conventions through education and promotion of the meeting industry to the industry, members, and the general public. Membership includes meeting managers, CEOs, and suppliers in the meetings industry. Of the 3,800 total members, 1,400 are meeting managers, and CEOs responsible for more than 150,000 meetings annually. Offers the Certified Meeting Professional and Professional Conference Specialist Certification Programs. *Contact:* PCMA, 100 Vestavia Office Park, Ste. 220, Birmingham, AL 35216 (205/978-4914; Fax 205/822-3789;

E-mail **pcma@internetmci.com**; URL **http://www.pcma.com**).

professional corporation (P.C.) A corporation formed by a group of individuals who provide services for which a professional license is required; for example, physicians, dentists, lawyers, and architects.

professional degree A college or university degree in such fields as medicine, dentistry, engineering, law, and pharmacy.

professional development **1.** A continuing and deliberate organization-sponsored process aimed at assisting, encouraging, and enabling professionals as individuals to improve their performance and potential — developing their knowledge, skills, abilities, and values. **2.** The process of keeping current in one's occupation or profession, maintaining competence in one's practice, and remaining open to new theories, techniques, and approaches.

professional employer organization (PEO) An outsourcing alternative. A company that assumes the legal and administrative responsibilities for an employer who needs competent performance of payroll, benefits, and other human resource functions and leases employees to perform those functions. PEOs are not involved in the recruitment, training, or management of leased employees.

Professional in Human Resources (PHR) A designation awarded by the Human Resource Certification Institute (HRCI) to HR practitioners, educators, researchers or consultants who have a minimum of four years of exempt-level HR experience, mastered the body of knowledge that constitutes the human resource profession, and are currently working the field. Mastery is demonstrated by successful completion of a written examination covering management practices, selection and placement, training and development, compensation and benefits, employee and labor relations, and health, safety, and security. Recertification is required every three years. *Contact:* HRCI, 606 N. Washington St., Alexandria, VA 22314 (703/548-3440; Fax 703/836-0367; E-mail **hrci@shrm.org**).

professional employer organization (PEO) An out-sourcing option. A firm that leases downsized employees back to the client company to solve staffing problems. The PEO provides benefits comparable with those earned by full-time permanent employees. The client enters into a contract with the PEO and functions as a co-employer. The client directs the employee in the performance of the job but all other functions are handled by the PEO as the employer of record. PEOs are now licensed by 13 states.

professionalization The achievement of social acceptance and approval, as well as high status and pay, by an occupation through the establishment and enforcement of such prerequisites as substantial educational requirements, a definable body of knowledge and skills, a set of key values and code of conduct, licensing or certification by state boards of examination, internship and practice of the specialty, and a system of peer review and regulation.

Professional Organizational Development Network in Higher Education (PODN) An 1,100-member organization of individuals in higher education in the U.S., Canada, and other countries with responsibility on their campuses for instructional, faculty, or organizational development. POD is devoted to improving teaching and learning in higher education. *Contact:* P, David Graf, Manager of Administrative Services, Exhibit Hall South, Iowa State University, Ames, IA 50011 (515/294-3808; Fax 515/294-6024; E-mail **dgraf@iastate.edu**).

Professional Secretaries International (PSI) - The Association for Office Professionals Represents members from different backgrounds and in many fields: secretaries, executive/administrative assistants, information specialists, and office managers. Provides networking opportunities, certification programs, and educational products. PSI's code of ethics sets the standard of professional conduct. *Contact:* PSI, 10502 NW Ambassador Dr., P.O. Box 20404, Kansas City, MO 64195-0404 (816/891-6600; Fax 816/891-9118; E-mail **info@psi.org**; URL **http://www.gvi.net/psi/about.psi.html**).

Professionals in Human Resources Association (PIHRA) A 3,500 member network of Southern California human resources practitioners who wish to stay abreast of current trends, laws, and issues impacting the field. Among other member services, offers a monthly newsletter, professional development seminars, an annual conference, and mentor services. Affiliated with the **Society of Human Resource Managers.** *Contact:* PIHRA, 888 S. Figueroa St., Ste. 1050, Los Angeles, CA 90017 (213/622-7472; Fax 213/622-7450; E-mail **todlipka@ ix.netcom.com**; URL **http://www.pihra.org**).

The Professional Society for Sales & Marketing Training (PSSMT) A professional association of approximately 180 training executives dedicated to helping their own corporations and each other achieve maximum productivity through excellence in training. *Contact:* SMT, 1900 Arch St., Philadelphia, PA 19103-1498 (215/564-3484; Fax 215/564-2175; E-mail **assnhgt@netaxs. com**; URL **http://www.smt.org**).

professional temps A staffing strategy in which companies unwilling or unable to afford the hiring costs and compensation associated with full-time, highly-skilled professionals, such as lawyers, accountants, computer specialists, and top-level managers and executives, employ them as temps. Professional temps are also hired to assist in start-up, restructuring, or closing a business.

proficiency test A test that indicates relative levels of performance or achievement whether in adjectival (poor, fair, good, or excellent) or numerical (raw, standard, percentile, T, or stanine) scores. Although a cut or passing score may be established for them, proficiency tests essentially establish relative ranks or standings on the tasks or information tested.

profile 1. In testing, graphic representation of test results on several tests for either an individual or group using identical or comparable measures such as standard scores and percentile ranks. 2. In marketing, a method of describing the target customer or client group's potential behavioral characteristics.

Profile of Organizational Characteristics *See* Likert Scales.

profit A common corporate financial objective expressed as the excess of income returns or gains over expenditures during a given period of time.

profitability A common corporate objective that focuses on the ability of a company to produce or create new wealth. Exists when there is a probability (or even a possibility) that resources can be used to yield economic values or outputs that are higher or greater than the combined values of the inputs required to produce them.

profit and loss statement A financial statement prepared at the end of an accounting period that provides an indication of the performance of the company's assets during that period. It is a measure of the productivity of the firm's assets.

profit budget A set of projected financial statements and schedules for the ensuing year. A profit budget serves as a profit plan and provides a yardstick for measuring the adequacy of expense budgets. Sometimes called *master budget*.

profit center *See* profit-center management.

profit center management The practice of establishing line or staff departments in an organization as profit centers, making the department or staff element so designated responsible for planning, programming, budgeting, and controlling expenditures in such a way as to produce a "profit" at the end of each fiscal period. The first recognized profit centers were manufacturing and marketing. Later, administration was added. Today, HR is more and more often so designated.

profit plan An annual plan designed to reach the return-on-investment target set by the board of control or top management.

profit-sharing 1. Any procedure under which an employer pays or makes available to all regular employees, subject to reasonable eligibility rules, in addition to prevailing rates of pay, special current or deferred sums based upon the profits of the business. There are three types of profit sharing plans: broad coverage (all or most employees), limited coverage (only certain classes of employees, such as supervisory or salaried employees), and executive profit sharing (limited to a few people at the top of the organization). 2. A type of compensation program used where collective performance or teamwork is needed to produce results. It includes both traditional supplemental retirement plans and cash bonuses paid on the basis of a company's profits.

profit-sharing plan Deferred compensation established and maintained to provide for the participation of employees or their beneficiaries in company profits. Profit sharing plans are defined contribution plans, which are employer-funded and contributions are flexible; that is, the amount of the contribution can be changed annually. Profit-sharing plans do not guarantee a fixed level of benefits; however, to meet qualification requirements they must provide a definite predetermined formula for allocating the contributions and distributing the funds after a fixed number of years, on attainment of a stated age, or occurrence of layoff, illness, disability, retirement, termination of employment, or death. Maximum annual contribution for each employee is 15 percent of gross compensation up to a limit of $30,000; for self-employed persons the maximum is 13.04 percent of net self-employment income.

profit skimming   *See* bust-out.

program budgeting   A budgeting system that deals primarily with broad planning and the costs of functions, activities, programs, and services. Each manager commits to paper specific descriptions of the activities of his or her department for the coming year, expenses for each activity, and a deadline for completion. In HR, program budgeting focuses on the programs carried on and the cost of each program. For example, the training and development budget might be divided into such categories as technical training, safety training, presupervisory training, organization development, and management development.

Program (or Project) Evaluation and Review Technique (PERT)   A manual or computer-based planning, scheduling, and project analysis and control method originally developed by the Navy for the Polaris submarine project. It relates all work on complex projects to time-dependent variables and events (nodes) between activities. It makes use of statistical procedures to predict the amount of time required to complete any element or aspect of a job or project.

program improvement evaluation   Monitoring an ongoing program and remedying deficiencies as they are identified. Also called *formative evaluation.*

programmable read-only memory (PROM)   Semiconductor chips that retain memory in the absence of power.

programmable robot   A device that permits computerized control of mechanical arms or similar devices to do routine or hazardous tasks. Applications include materials handling, tool changing, welding, painting, and assembling.

program manager   *See* course manager.

programmed instruction (PI)   A method of self-instruction in which trainees work through a carefully sequenced and pretested series of steps leading to the acquisition of knowledge or skills representing the instructional objectives. Trainees proceed through the program at their own rates, respond actively (or covertly) to each step in the sequence and receive immediate feedback on the correctness of their responses before proceeding to the next step. The method is used to teach facts, principles, concepts, and problem solving skills; provide practice, remediation, and makeup instruction; maintain previously learned skills; upgrade production, administrative, clerical, or other skills; accelerate capable trainees; provide vertical enrichment (advanced work) or horizontal enrichment (broader contact) in a discipline; or control the variables in an experimental learning situation. Largely replaced by interactive computer and video systems.

programmed learning   *See* programmed instruction.

Programmed Logic for Automatic Teaching Operations (PLATO)   Originally a research project in the field of teaching machines at the Coordinated Science Laboratory of the University of Illinois and supported by the Departments of the Army, Navy, and Air Force in the early 1960s. It is a multiple-student, computer-controlled automatic teaching device. Now the property of a private company, PLATO runs on microcomputer networks and focuses on college-level courseware. The current generation of installations includes color displays and flexible management software.

program of instruction (POI)   A document that spells out the option or combination of options that will be employed in a training system. It is used to communicate to managers, instructors, trainees, and evaluators exactly what is to take place in the training system and when and how. The POI describes all elements of a training or development system. It is essentially a training system blueprint, just as a **lesson plan** is a lesson blueprint. Contents include (1) a title page with complete identifying data, (2) an introductory section defining such items as purpose and objectives, prerequisites for enrollment, length of training in hours, types of instruction, and personnel requirements, (3) job performance requirements with a list of duties, tasks, and elements along with the behavior, conditions, and criteria for each duty and task; (4) learning objectives; (5) performance evaluation strategies; (6) sequence of instruction; (7) space, facilities, and equipment requirements; (8) master list of skills; and (9) a degree of training matrix.

Program on Non-Collegiate Sponsored Instruction (PONSI)   A system for evaluating and certifying corporate training programs for the award of college credit. Teams of impartial faculty evaluators, trained by the **American Council on Education (ACE)** and representing appropriate departments in colleges and universities, are invited by business, industrial, and military organizations and schools to evaluate their courses for equivalent college credit. Colleges are not obligated to accept the credits but more than 1,100 do.

progression chart   A document that depicts planned progression, including alternative routes, from the lowest to the highest positions in specific career fields or in an organization. In some cases, the chart shows progression to positions in other elements of the organization. Progression charts are used as source documents for planning and designing training and development programs, building an in house source of candidates for vacated or newly established positions, and motivating people by identifying specific opportunities for advancement to more challenging and remunerative positions.

progressive discipline   A system involving increasingly severe penalties each time an employee is disciplined for the same violation, a similar offense, or a very serious offense. The sequence from least severe to most severe is as follows: oral reprimand, written reprimand, written warning, suspension without pay (disciplinary layoff), demotion (rarely recommended), and discharge or termination.

progressive payment system   In benefits, a process started in 1983 under which hospitals are paid fixed amounts on the principal diagnosis for each Medicare hospital stay based on payment categories call diagnosis related groups.

progressive proofs   In desktop publishing, proofs made from the separate plates in color process work, showing the sequence

of printing and the result after each additional color has been applied.

progressives   Progressive lenses, a special type of lens that provides clear, continuous vision with no lines, such as those that occur with bifocal lenses.

Project ACTION   Accessible Community Transportation in Our Nation, a cooperative model, initiated in 1988, for accessible public transportation involving national and local disability consumer groups and transit interests managed by the **National Easter Seal Society** and funded by a cooperative agreement with the Urban Mass Transportation Administration. The objective of the project is to improve relations between those groups and develop tools and techniques that can improve transportation services for persons with disabilities. Model projects will (1) identify people with disabilities in the community and their transit needs; (2) develop outreach and marketing strategies; (3) develop training programs for transit providers; (4) develop training programs for persons with disabilities; and (5) apply technology to solve critical barriers to transportation and accessibility.

Project Adventure   A world-wide program that encourages participants to develop confidence by presenting them with increasingly difficult physical challenges, many of which must be met by a team. Used by corporations, community groups, and educational institutions to build team spirit and to help participants develop confidence they need to to achieve goals.

project budgeting   Budgets built around a specific project rather than a time period. Commonly used when appropriating funds for capital expenditures.

project evaluation and review technique (PERT)   *See* program evaluation and review technique.

Project Genome   A monumental medical research now shared by every major industrial nation, the goal of which is to identify every human gene in every cell and and determine how it works. The project will enable medical practitioners to identify both normal and abnormal functions of genes and how they cause disorders and diseases.

projection   In forecasting, an extrapolation into the future using observations and records of past events and data, often coupled with intuition, judgment, and speculation, to arrive at a prediction of the environment to come.

projection system A machine used for video/data projection. There are three configurations: **front-screen, rear-screen**, and **retro**. As distinguished from overhead projectors, these units interface directly with a computer to display text, graphics, animation, and so on. They include CRT-based projectors, rear projection systems, LCD panels and newer hybrid systems that offer versatility in form and function. Many systems can display information from videodiscs, VCRs, camcorders, and other input devices.

projective techniques **1.** Classification of technological forecasting approaches that includes trend extrapolation, trailblazer developments, substitution analysis, Delphi technique, structured interviews, nominal group technique, and modified nominal group technique. **2.** *See* personality and temperament test.

projective test *See* personality and temperament test.

Project LINK: Link to Assistive Products A free information service connecting people with disabilities and others with manufacturers of assistive devices. Catalogs and project information are provided via confidential, targeted mailings. *Contact:* Project LINK, Center for Assistive Technology, State University of New York at Buffalo, 515 Kimball Tower, 3435 Main St., Buffalo, NY 14214-3079 (800/628-2281 or 716/828-3141; Fax 716/829-3217; E-mail **jvrir@acsu.buffalo.edu**).

project management A defined set of activities designed to launch and complete a complex project: defining the job, getting the people, estimating time and costs, breaking the job into tasks, tracking progress and results, setting up change procedures, and establishing acceptance criteria. Project management organizes and manages complex projects on the basis of their technical, schedule, and cost objectives rather than on the basis of existing organizational arrangements, relationships, and procedures.

project management training Designed for project managers responsible for construction, corporate planning, corporate relocation, engineering, new products, research and development, and systems development, and for other executives, managers, and staff officers who may be assigned to project

teams. Focuses on project planning, scheduling, implementation, and control concepts, principles, processes, and procedures and resource allocation, performance measurement, and reporting procedures.

project team An ad hoc or temporary grouping of people to work together in performing a specific job or task or finding a solution to a problem. Often multidisciplinary in that the team is made up of people from different disciplines, such as engineers, marketers, production workers, and trainers.

Projects with Industry (PWI) Federally funded programs aimed at establishing partnerships between business and rehabilitation organizations to facilitate the employment of people with disabilities. *Contact:* PWI, U.S. Department of Education, Rehabilitation Services Administration, 400 Maryland Ave., S.W., Washington, DC 20202 (202/732-1882 for information about nationwide PWI projects or 202/245-2352 to locate the nearest PWI).

promo A promotional product, a give-away premium designed to induce qualified but reluctant buyers to purchase a product or service. Frequently used before, during, or after exhibits and trade shows.

promotion Advancement within an organization involving increased pay, prestige, power and authority, status, or perquisites. Although sometimes used as a reward for productivity and accomplishment, it should be reserved for people who have proved their potential and readiness for assignment to higher-level positions. It may be based on one or more factors: performance, special contributions to the organization, potential, expansion of the company, length of service, and so on.

promotional fare A special limited time lower fare for travel to designated airports (typically for newly scheduled service) to encourage travelers to buy in advance of travel.

promotion progression chart *See* progression chart.

proof A legal doctrine pertaining to cases of unlawful discharge. It asks at the investigation, "Did the 'judge' obtain substantial evidence that the employee was guilty as charged?"

Pro Patria Award Presented annually by each state to an employer who has adopted policies that make it easier for employees to participate in the Army and Air Force

National Guards and the Reserve Components of all services.

property casualty executive
See risk manager.

Property Essential to Self-Support (PESS)
A work incentive for persons with disabilities allowing them to keep property owned (or acquired) that is essential to a job or business in which they earn their living. All tangible goods, such as tools and vehicles are covered completely, as is a home and land on which a business resides or crops are raised for the consumption of the owner. Up to $6,000 of equity in a non-business property needed for self-support is also included in the exclusion.

proposal   **1.** A written or oral message designed to obtain acceptance or to get a favorable decision. **2.** More formally, a response to federal, state, local government, or public or private organizations' requests for proposals (RFPs), bids for the delivery of needed products of services.

Proposition 209   Passed in November 1996 by a majority of California voters. The measure explicitly rejected the idea that women or members of minority groups should get preferential treatment on the basis of race, sex, color, ethnicity, or national origin when applying for jobs, government contracts, or university admission. Implementation has been deferred until the counts rule on its constitutionality. Also known as *California Civil Rights Initiative.*

proprietary information   Business, financial, or technical information that is not generally known or available to competitors that might provide a competitive advantage. Also known as *trade secrets* and *confidential information.*

prospective payment system (PPS)
In health care benefits, a process started in 1983 under which hospitals are paid fixed amounts on the principal diagnosis for each (Medicare) hospital stay based on payment categories called **diagnosis related groups**.

prospective review   In health care, methods for decreasing utilization, such as **precertification, preadmission testing,** and **mandatory outpatient surgery**.

prostate specific antigen (PSA) test
The antigen is a substance formed only by the prostate gland. Higher levels may indicate an enlarged prostate. The test is sometimes used as a screening device, but not a definitive diagnosis, for cancer of the prostate. Recommended annually by the American Cancer Society for men over the age of 50.

Prostatron   A device that uses microwaves to destroy excess prostate tissue in treating enlarged prostate glands. Less expensive than surgery and avoids surgery's worst potential side effects, impotence and incontinence.

prosthetic device   Artificial limbs and eyes, arm, leg, neck, and back braces, orthopedic shoes (as a part of leg braces), corrective lens following cataract surgery, colostomy or ileostomy bags and related supplies, and breast prostheses, including surgical brassieres, after a mastectomy.

prosthetics   The science of developing artificial replacements for limbs lost to amputation.

prosthodontics   Dental care involving the construction, replacement or repair of fixed prostheses, removable partial dentures, complete dentures, and maxillofacial prostheses.

protected characteristics   A legal terms that relates to areas protected by statutes. For example, that an action, program, or requirement conflicts with a person's religious beliefs or discriminates against them or that their privacy has been or will be violated. People can object on some protected ground.

protected class   A legal term used to describe women and minorities (**African-Americans, Native Americans, Alaskan natives, Asians, Pacific Islanders, Hispanics,** people over 40, **disabled persons,** and **Vietnam-era veterans**) who are specifically "protected" from discrimination by the law or court decisions interpreting the law.

protection benefits   Benefits awarded on a contingency basis only, such as accident, illness, injury, disability, or death. Examples are medical and hospitalization insurance, dental and vision care plans, life insurance, sick leave, and safety equipment and clothing.

protein   A key component of all human organs and chemical activities in the body. Made up of amino acids, the function of proteins depends on their shape, which is determined by the 50,000 to 100,000 genes in the cell nucleus.

protocol(s)   **1.** The original copy or draft of a document or record of a transaction. **2.** Rules prescribing etiquette in ceremonies or codes defining deference to rank and position or order of precedence. **3.** In communications, agreed-upon signals used to establish contact, indicate receipt of information, end messages, or correct errors. **4.** Rules and procedures that two computers must follow to exchange data.

prototyping The process of testing a working model of a system or program, or a portion of the model, to ensure that the concept is sound, practicable, and cost-effective. Used by interactive video producers and the TV industry in general, computer software and course developers, architects, engineers, and scientists.

provider An organization, institution, or individual who provides medical services and supplies under an agreement or contract (such as a **health maintenance organization** or **preferred provider organization,** a hospital or nursing home, or an individual physician, nurse, or therapist). Providers include physicians and other health care professionals, hospitals, ambulatory surgical centers, physical and occupational therapists, clinical laboratories, X-ray suppliers, dialysis facilities, and rural health clinics.

provider organization (PO) A direct contracting system of comprehensive medical coverage that allows employers to deal directly with hospitals and physicians. An alternative to other types of managed care organizations, the objective is to lower costs and better or equal quality by creating competition for subscribers at the care delivery level and changing the role of insurers and managed care organizations to that of providing only value-added services. Also known as *physician-hospital networks, physician networks, physician-hospital organizations,* or *provider service organizations.*

Provincial Sales Tax A tax of between 5 and 12 percent levied on restaurant meals and most items sold in shops in the Canadian provinces except for the Northwest Territories, Yukon Territory, and Alberta (which imposes a 5 percent tax on accommodations).

proximity search A World Wide Web search where the user specifies that documents identified must have the words near each other.

Proxy Act of 1991 *See* Self-Determination Act of 1991.

psychiatric interview Similar to psychological counseling, but varying with the personality and philosophical and therapeutic orientation of the counselor and the setting in which the interview occurs.

psychiatric nurse specialist A registered nurse (R.N.), usually with a master's degree in psychiatric nursing, who specializes in treating mental or psychiatric disorders.

psychiatrist A medical doctor (M.D.) who has served a residency in psychiatry and is board certified, licensed to practice medicine and psychiatry in the state in which he or she practices, and a member in good standing of the American Medical Association and the state medical association. Psychiatrists specialize in the diagnosis and treatment of mental disorders and other types of illnesses with accompanying depression or dementia which could lengthen a patient's hospital stay.

psychoanalytic interview A diagnostic or treatment interview used by psychotherapists. The approach rests on the theory that abnormal mental reactions and aberrant behavior are due to repression of desires that the patient consciously rejects but unconsciously accepts.

psychographics 1. Study of the changing patterns of worker values. **2.** In marketing, information relating to the attitudes, values, and behaviors of customers and clients (as contrasted with demographic information).

psychological accommodation A means of integrating disabled workers into the work force. Includes (1) communicating to the staff the individuals' previous accomplishments prior to their arrival; (2) asking disabled workers what they would like to have communicated to coworkers about their disabilities; and (3) demonstrating or modeling the tasks to be performed. Attributed to Harry Levinson, *The Levinson Letter,* December 1, 1992.

psychologically necessary Psychological services that are considered to be "appropriate" and are generally accepted by qualified psychiatrists, psychologists, and other mental health practitioners to be reasonable and adequate for the diagnosis and treatment of the illness, injury or mental disorder.

psychological needs Human needs for belonging and acceptance, attention and affection, self-respect and self-esteem, achievement, independence, freedom, recognition, approval and prestige, and self-realization and self-fulfillment.

psychological order A type of instructional sequencing based on ease of learning. In general, it means that older learnings serve as the basis for new learnings, and that, when possible, the trainee moves from the simple to the complex, from the near to the far, from the familiar to the unknown, and from the concrete to the abstract.

psychological stress evaluator (PSE) A "truth machine" or **lie detector,** an earlier model of the **Verimetrics computer system** co-invented by Charles R. McQuiston, retired Chief of the Technical Committee, U.S. Army Intelligence School, Fort Huachuca, AZ. The machine detects deception by charting (much like a seismograph) stress patterns in the voice. Used by some law enforcement agencies and accepted as permissible evidence by the courts in several states.

psychological test A test instrument used to screen, select, and assign employees, select employees for promotion and for training and development, classify and group trainees, determine the effectiveness and quality of instructional systems, provide a basis for guiding and assisting employees in career development and trainees in improving their performance, diagnose mental and emotional problems and illnesses, and keep management informed about progress and results. Includes tests of mental ability, aptitude, spatial reasoning, psychomotor skills, interests, and personality and temperament.

psychologist A person with extensive education and training in psychology, usually possessing the Ph.D., Psy.D., Ed.D., or master's degree, usually with a concentration in clinical psychology, counseling, psychotherapy, or psychological testing, certified or licensed by the state in which he or she practices, and a member in good standing of the American Psychological Association.

psychology of entitlement "An attitude, a way of looking at life." Those who have it believe that they don't have to earn what they get; rather, they get something because they are owed it — entitled to it. Attributed to Judith M. Bardwick (*Danger in the Comfort Zone,* AMACOM).

psychomotor domain Focuses on instructional objectives relating to motor skills.

psychomotor test A test used as a preemployment selection device, usually for semiskilled, repetitive work that involves manual dexterity, motor ability, and hand-eye coordination. Most psychomotor tests involve

simulation. Examples are the Purdue Pegboard, the Hand-Tool Dexterity Test, and the O'Connor Finger Dexterity Test.

psychoneuroimmunology (PNI) An emerging discipline concerned with the study of the chemical interplay between mind and body — the chemical reactions that occur as the result of thoughts and feelings. It examines the connection between thoughts and emotional events and illness and disease. Involves the manipulation of psychological factors to strengthen the body's immune system and thereby either prevent illnesses or alter the course of a disease. PNI is believed by some to help explain such phenomena as the spontaneous remission of cancer and hysterical blindness and paralysis. Beginning to be used by medical and other practitioners as a means of empowering employees to reduce illnesses and cut corporate health care costs.

psychosis A mental illness or disorder that causes gross distortion or disorganization of a person's mental capacity, emotional response, and ability to recognize reality, communicate, and relate to others to the extent that it interferes with his or her capacity to cope with the ordinary demands of living.

psychosomatic disorder Real physical disorders that can be diagnosed but are exacerbated by stress. The condition affects the body but originates in the mind.

psychotherapy Treatment to correct or ameliorate mental and emotional disorders and illnesses provided by highly trained clinicians: psychiatrists (M.D.'s), psychologists (Ph.D.'s, Ed.D.'s, or M.S.'s) or psychiatric social workers (M.S.W.'s).

Public Broadcasting Service (PBS) A satellite-delivery TV organization that provides narrowcast service, a horizontal type of programming (generic, preproduced video programs). *Contact:* PBS, 1320 Braddock Place, Alexandria, VA 22314-1698 (703/739-5000).

public disability payments Benefits paid under a federal, state, or local government law or plan that pays for disabling conditions that are not job-related. Examples are civil service disability benefits, state temporary disability benefits, and state or local government retirements based on disability.

Public Disability Pension Offset (PDPO) Treats civil service disability retirement as workers' compensation, which offsets Social

Security disability benefits. Enacted in 1981, it affects anyone receiving a disability based on public employment such as federal civil service.

public domain Materials that can be published without obtaining permission or paying a fee. Include literary works, music, films, TV recordings, photographs, and art *no longer covered* by the copyright law. Also include materials created and published by U.S. government agencies.

public domain (PD) software Computer software written, produced, and distributed by someone without charge or fee or who makes payment optional for use of the program. Also called *freeware* and *shareware.*

public relations (PR) The process by which an organization demonstrates the excellence of its products or services by communicating its insights into solutions to problems to its potential customers and clients and the public at large. PR is an important means of attracting and retaining customers, clients, suppliers, and investors, minimizing the impact or dissolving the consequences of conflicts and problems, providing public recognition for employees, obtaining community loyalty and support, and influencing favorable, or blocking unfavorable, legislation.

Public Service Act of 1993
See AmeriCorps.

pull technology One where the user goes to the source to get information; for example, on the Internet, the use of E-mail, surfing the net, or downloading files.

punishment **1.** In operant conditioning, an approach aimed at reducing the frequency of occurrence of undesired behavior. **2.** *See* discipline.

punitive damage award Monetary awards granted by the courts to individuals, groups, or corporations that have been victimized by illegal action, such as fraud or other offense. In March 1991, the U.S. Supreme Court upheld a large award to a person victimized by insurance fraud — and thereby took itself out of the business of granting punitive damage awards except in very extreme situations.

pupillary-reaction test A nonmedical, noninvasive alternative to the **urine test** to detect substance abuse. A trained professional uses a flashlight to determine how the pupils of the subject's eyes react to light.

pure research Research studies designed to add to general knowledge, which may or may not be useful in finding answers to immediate problems or solving current issues.

push technology A system that relies on a user's computer to pull content, via dialing in from servers at specific intervals. That is, its a system where information or services are pushed from somewhere else to the user instead of forcing the user to log on, type a URL, and pull content or services off the Web. Examples are Pointcast (**http://www.pointcast.com**), BackWeb, and Marimba.

put option Worker entitlement to require the employer to repurchase employer stock distributed from an employee stock option (ownership) plan that is not readily tradable on an established securities market under a fair evaluation formula.

Pygmalion effect In managing or training people, when the manager or the trainer expects people to do well, and provides positive feedback, they do. In effect, it is a self-fulfilling prophecy.

QA	Quality assurance.
QASP	Quality assurance surveillance plan.
QC	**1.** Quality control. **2.** Quality circle.
QCD	Quality, cost, delivery.
QCM	Quality of care measurement.
QDRO	Qualified Domestic Relations Order.
QFD	Quality function deployment.
QI	Quality Index.
QIPs	Quality improvement programs.
QM	Quality management.
QMB	Qualified Medicare beneficiary.
QMCSO	Qualified medical child support order.
QRA	Quarterly review and analysis.
QS	Quality Standard.
QSO	Quality strategic objective.
QTY'S	Quantities (Internet abbreviation).
QUALs	Quality-adjusted life years.
QWL	Quality of worklife

quadriplegia A symptom of spinal cord injury — paralysis affecting the level between the neck and chest area involving both the arms and legs.

qualified domestic relations order (QDRO) A court judgment, decree, or order (including property settlement) that relates to child support, alimony payments, retirement plan benefits, or marital property rights to a spouse, former spouse, child, or other dependent made pursuant to a state domestic relations law. Its purpose is to execute and enforce the court judgment. Section 414(p) of the **Internal Revenue Code** requires that employers provide copies of their procedures to employees and potential payees when circumstances regarding the payment of benefits arises. Employers must also follow an unwritten practice by which it places a "hold" on a participant's accounts once it receives confirmation from both parties involved in a divorce that the divorce is final or a QDRO was being sought.

qualified interpreter As defined by the American with Disabilities Act of 1990, "an interpreter who is able to interpret effectively, accurately, and impartially both receptively and expressively, using any necessary specialized vocabulary." The focus is on the ability of the interpreter to facilitate effective communication between a public accommodation and the individual with disabilities.

qualified medical child support order (QMCSO) Similar to a **qualified domestic relation order**, a QMCSO may be ordered by a court to provide health benefits for a child. Employers must determine whether such a court order is a QMCSO. The orders stem from the **Omnibus Budget Reconciliation Act of 1993** that forbids employers from denying health care coverage to children who are not claimed as dependents by a parent in the plan, who do not live with the parent, or live outside the insurer's service area; nor can they exclude children born out of wedlock.

qualified Medicare beneficiary (QMB) A special program for certain elderly and persons with disabilities as a protection against Medicare out-of-pocket expenses. Pays Medicare premiums, deductibles, and coinsurance for those entitled to Medicare Part A. The income of recipients must be at or below the national poverty level, and savings and other assets cannot exceed $4,000 for one person or $6,000 for a couple. Each state administers QMB benefits as a part of its Medicaid program. The monthly income limits for the QMB program in 1996 for all states except Alaska and Hawaii were $665 for an individual and $884 for a couple. In Alaska the monthly income limits were $825 for an individual and $1,099 for a couple; in

426

Hawaii they were $763 for an individual and $1,014 for a couple.

qualified parking As defined by the Internal Revenue Service, "parking for which an employer pays (directly to a parking lot operator or by reimbursement to the employee), or that an employer provides on premises it owns or leases." Employees must pay taxes for parking in employer-provided parking valued at more than $155 per month. Amounts below that are tax free, as is up to $60 per month for employer-provided van pools, mass transit passes, or a combination of both. Employers must determine the taxable amount and include it in the employee's wages.

qualified plan A defined benefit and defined contribution pension or profit-sharing plan that qualifies under statutory requirements and IRS regulations for certain tax advantages, usually accruing to both the employer and the employee. Generally, qualification is dependent upon a determination that the plan does not discriminate in favor of highly compensated employees.

qualified retirement plan Tax-advantaged means of accumulating retirement dollars, the plans come in several forms: traditional defined benefit pension plans, defined contribution plans, and 401(k) plans. The term "qualified" means that the plans are eligible for special tax treatment by both employers and employees under the **Internal Revenue Code** because they meet certain requirements.

qualifying service The number of years of military service required for entitlement to retired pay and associated benefits, such as use of commissary, exchange, and related facilities, and medical care. To qualify at age 60, reservists must have completed at least 20 years of qualifying service, which includes any combination of full time active duty and active participation in a Reserve status. Beginning July 1, 1949, a Reservist must have earned at least 50 points through training or other equivalent duty in the reserve program to be credited with a qualifying year of service.

qualitative methods In judgments of worth or value, use of means other than numbers (for example, estimation or adjectives) to measure achievements, shortfalls, progress, or results. Areas where such judgments may be made include assessment and evaluation, budgeting, forecasting, staffing, research, or

any other area of HR management and development

qualitative research Research studies that rely on the use of non-quantitative information and typically involves such activities as reporting, describing, and interpreting observations.

quality-adjusted life years (Quals)
Pronounced "qual-eez," a measure of the value of medical and surgical treatments in terms of both prolongation of life and quality of life. Quals rank therapies by considering how long a person will live following treatment and multiplying each year of life after treatment by its quality. The value of a year of life is weighted from zero to one, with zero indicating death, and one perfect health with no disability. Thus if a person lives for 10 years with a minor disability measuring 0.8 on the Qual scale, the 10 years of life are reduced to the equivalent of eight non-disabled years. Using the formula, the cost per Qual of various treatments can be compared. Some experts believe that the use of Quals is inevitable because of soaring health care costs and increasing demand for access to it. Opponents argue that Quals are unjust and offensive because they rely on subjective judgment and on healthy people to determine the quality of life of people who are disabled or ill. Attributed to Dr. James Bush of the University of California in San Diego.

quality assurance (QA) 1. Programs designed to ensure that products and services provided to clients and customers meet specifications and are uniformly and consistently of high quality. *See also* quality control. **2.** Plans and programs designed to insure that contract deliverables (products and services) satisfy the requirements of the statement of work.

quality assurance surveillance plan (QASP)
A plan prepared to monitor all contracted services and products based on systematic analysis of the functions contracted. It includes key performance indicators, including realistic rates, times, accuracy levels, and the like; information sources, such as company information systems, random sampling techniques, and customer or user complaints; surveillance tools, such as sampling guides stating what will be checked, the standard of performance, and how the checking will be done; decision guides or tables to establish fault if it occurs; and

checklists to record what has been checked and the results of those checks.

quality audit An inspection conducted periodically to assess the adequacy of a long-established product or procedure to guard against improper practices (due to such things as turnover of personnel, new equipment, rearrangement of work areas, or new facilities) and ensure that the product continues to conform to design criteria and match requirements.

quality circle (QC) A participative management technique. A quality circle consists of a carefully selected homogeneous group of employees who meet regularly for an hour or two each week to consider specific problems and develop recommendations for solutions for presentation to management. Knowledge workers should focus on problems relating to internal departmental and external organizational functions, relationships, and services and performance and quality of worklife programs.

quality control (QC) Plans, programs, policies, and procedures designed and implemented before (materials inspection), during (in-process inspection), or immediately following (post-production inspection) the production of a product or service to ensure that the finished product or service meets specifications and is of uniformly high quality.

quality, cost, delivery (QCD) A Japanese approach to productivity improvement: Keep quality and delivery higher than that of competitors and hold costs down lower than those of rivals.

quality function deployment (QFD)
1. A technique developed by the Japanese in 1972 and used mainly by high-tech and transportation industries. Its purpose is to improve the process of developing and producing products to achieve a competitive advantage in quality, cost, and timing. The QFD discipline uses the framework provided by statistical techniques and quality circles to capture customers' needs and focusing on meeting as many of them as possible. It uses such tools as affinity diagrams, matrix analysis techniques, Ishikawa or fishbone diagrams, fault trees, and Taguchi experimentation, all of which are too complex for description here. In its simplest form, the methodology employs a matrix to display visually customer requirements against different alternatives for satisfying them. Subsequent matrices are used

to relate different aspects of design, test, manufacture, cost, reliability, or technology, thus conserving or deploying the customer's preferences and requirements throughout the process. **2.** In training, a process that involves the development of lists of requirements and then making comparisons and correlations among the lists to identify relationships and bring order to the task and maintain focus on the objectives of the program. Used to understand, evaluate, and make decisions when creating new training programs. For example, to structure a training program that is customer- or client-driven, the development team gathers and prioritizes information pertaining to customer and client needs and then uses that information to design the training.

quality improvement process Any strategy designed to improve the quality of products and services produced by an organization.

quality improvement programs (QUIPs)
Piecemeal programs instituted in the 1970s to pinpoint specific shortcomings and find specific remedies for defects in products and services. Forerunners of **total quality management** efforts.

Quality Index (QI) Similar to the Swedish **Customer Satisfaction Index,** implemented in 1993. The U.S. version reports on the quality of American goods quarterly.

quality inspection *See* quality audit.

quality management (QM) In health care, the equivalent of quality assurance.

quality of care measurement (QCM)
In health benefits, a program to determine what employees are getting from a **utilization review** system — a means of measuring and achieving quality control and cost-containment.

quality of work life (QWL) **1.** A generic term for programs designed to improve worker satisfaction and performance through participative management, quality circles, job enrichment or enlargement, employee involvement, or other job-related human factors strategies. **2.** Labor-management efforts at all levels of organization to enhance the dignity of employees and tap their creative resources to develop a more satisfying and rewarding work environment.

quality review organization A group of practicing physicians and other health care professionals under contract to an organization or the federal government to review the care provided to patients.

Quality Standard-9000 (QS 9000) The first common quality standards to be used by the Big Three automakers — Ford, General Motors, and Chrysler. Based on **ISO 9000,** QS-9000 also contains industry-specific guidelines and special **registration** requirements.

quality strategic objective (QSO) Specific targets for improvement and growth in an organization developed annually by top management. In the area of HR, examples are human resources development, leadership development, on-the-job training, and work team development.

quantitative methods In judgments of worth or value, use of numbers to measure achievements, shortfalls, progress, or results. Areas where such judgments may be made include assessment and evaluation, budgeting, forecasting, staffing, research, or any other area of HR management and development.

quantitative research Research studies that rely on the collection, analysis (usually statistical), interpretation, and reporting of quantitative or numerical data. It typically involves surveys or experiments using controlled groups.

quarter hour *See* credit hour.

quarterly review and analysis (QRA) A control strategy used by managers to evaluate each quarter the efficiency of their organizations in the use of resources (personnel, equipment, facilities, materials, and funds) as related to progress and objectives. Status, trends, deficiencies, progress, and results are reviewed, identified, analyzed, and reported to top management and subordinate activities.

quartile 1. One of the three points (percentiles) in a frequency distribution that defines one of four equal parts. The first quartile (Q1) is the 25th percentile (the value below which 25 percent of the data falls; the second (Q2) is the median or 50th percentile, and the third (Q3) is the 75th. **2.** A range between specific percentiles, for example, the first, between 0 and the 15th percentile, the second between the 25th and the 50th percentile, and so on.

quasi-experimental study A research study undertaken under less than truly experimental conditions, such as without participants who have been randomly selected (nonequivalent groups) or where data are collected under varying conditions or at different times. Although far from ideal, such studies sometimes provide valuable information and insights.

queen In meeting management, a hotel room furnished with a queen-size bed.

query-by-example search A World Wide Web search where the user instructs a search engine to find more documents that are similar to a particular document. Also called *find similar.*

questioning 1. An instructional technique associated with the Socratic method of teaching. **2.** In counseling, a fundamental means of inquiry, of gathering information, of probing. **3.** A means of fact finding and idea generation that can be used in staff meetings and conferences, at information and decision briefings, during interviews, inspections, and casual walk-throughs, by means of questionnaires and surveys, and by **snowflakes** and **taskers**.

questionnaire A written means of collecting information, opinions, and judgments on a variety of problems, issues, situations, and subjects. Used for collecting job and task data and for assessing training and development needs. Closed form questionnaires contain a list of items to be checked, a list of alternative responses to be selected, or blanks to be filled in by words or numbers. Open form questionnaires allow the respondent to present a more complete description of a situation, encouraging the respondent to go beyond the numerical or factual data to get into attitudes and feelings, the background of responses, or the reasons for preferences or opinions.

queuing theory/techniques An approach to waiting-line problems such as equipment waiting to be serviced or the number of waiters needed for each shift in a large restaurant. The objective is to arrive at decisions as to the optimum distribution of service times and the number of people to minimize costs. It uses mathematical models and statistical methods. Monte Carlo methods are a common means of solving queuing theory problems. Their complexity prohibits treatment here; consult any good statistics book.

QuickTime® System software produced by Apple that allows the user to incorporate video footage into a program and play it back on a Macintosh computer.

quid pro quo A legal term that means " something for something" or "what for what" — giving something of value in exchange for something of equal value.

***quid pro quo* harassment** Requiring sexual favors in return for workplace partiality, such as raises, promotion, perks, and so on.

Quimby An acronym for **qualified Medicare beneficiary**.

***qui tam* suit** A suit brought in response to strong private incentives, such as entitlement to keep personally up to 30 percent of the proceeds from successful suits against government cheats and other wrongdoers by whistle blowers. It is an abbreviation for a Latin phrase that means "who brings the action for the king as well as for himself."

quota strategy or system An affirmative action initiative involving steps to achieve balance in an organization by mandating hiring and promotion restrictions that favor protected groups. It also includes the risk of being sued for reverse discrimination.

R

r	Coefficient of correlation.
RA	**1.** Return on assets. **2.** Rehabilitation Act of 1973. **3.** Revenue Act of 1987.
R&A	Review and analysis.
RAM	Random access memory.
RAMDAC	Random access memory digital-to-analog converter.
RBM	Right-brain management.
RBOCs	Regional Bell Operating Companies.
RBRVS	Revenue-based relative value system.
RC	Reserve Components.
RCRA	Resource Conservation and Recovery Act of 1976.
RE	Return on equity.
REA	**1.** The Retired Enlisted Association. **2.** Retirement Equity Act of 1984.
REC'D	Received (Internet abbreviation).
REHABDATA	Rehabilitation data.
RFC	Request for comments (Internet abbreviation).
RFI	Request for information.
RFP	**1.** Request for proposal. **2.** Request for price.
RFQ	Request for quotation.
RGB	Red, green, blue.
RGDS	Regards (Internet abbreviation)
RGIMB	Selected Reserve GI Montgomery Bill of 1985.
RIA	Registered Investment Advisor.
RIAH	Radioimmunoassay of hair.
RICO	Racketeer Influenced Corrupt Organizations Act of 1970.

RIF	Reduction in force.
RISC	Reduced instruction set computing.
RK	Radial keratotomy.
RMI	Repetitive motion injury.
RMP	Registered meeting planner.
ROA	The Reserve Officers Association.
ROE	Return on equity.
ROI	Return on investment
ROM	Read only memory.
ROTFL	Rolling on the floor laughing (an on-line abbreviation).
RP	Retinosis Pigmentosa.
RPA	Retirement Protection Act of 1994.
RQ	Reportable quantity.
RRA	Risk Retention Acts of 1981 and 1986.
RRG	Risk retention group.
RRMIIP	Ready Reserve Mobilization Income Insurance Program.
RRP	Resource referral program.
RSA	Rehabilitation Services Administration.
RSI	Repetitive strain injury.
RT	Repeat trauma.
RTM	Read the manual (Internet abbreviation).
RTFM	Read the (expletive) manual (Internet abbreviation).
RTK	Right-to-know.

rabbi trust A supplemental pension benefit plan in the form of a trust fund that allows executives to avoid being taxed on income earned by the trust until they begin receiving payments at retirement.

race-conscious remedy *See* affirmative action; race-norming.

race-norming The practice of adjusting scores on employment or job-placement tests to compensate for racial differences. For example, the scores of African-Americans and Hispanics on employment tests sometimes have been segregated by racial groups, compared only with their own racial group, and reported not in relation to all those taking the test, but only in relation to others in the individual's racial group. That is, scores are ranked using one of three available scales: one for African-Americans, one for Hispanics, and one for whites and others. As a result, the percentile scores of minorities are increased. The practice was in use for more than 10 years and was commonly applied in about 34 states and by some private employers. The practice was prohibited by the **Civil Rights Act of 1991** because it banned any consideration of race or sex in employment decisions. The ban was implemented on December 15, 1991 by an administration announcement that state employment agencies could no longer increase the scores of minority applicants on one federally sanctioned aptitude test (used for low-level manufacturing or clerical jobs measuring skills like math, reading, and manual dexterity) to raise scores. Other test scores are almost certain to be covered by the same prohibition. However, the Civil Rights Act does allow the use of "lawful affirmative action" programs, so the ban is likely to generate lawsuits as African Americans and Hispanics find themselves dropped from job referral lists.

Racketeer Influenced Corrupt Organizations Act of 1970 (RICO) Legislation passed by the Congress to help the federal government prosecute mobsters but now used for prosecuting cases ranging from white-collar crime, such as securities fraud, to drug trafficking as well.

rack rate The current rate charged and posted for certain types of rooms in a hotel or other property. *See also* day rate; flat rate; run-of-the-house rate.

radial keratotomy (RK) A surgical procedure performed by opthalmologists to help correct nearsightedness. It consists of a series of small spoke-like cuts around the circle of the cornea of the eye, which serve to flatten the cornea and improve the way light is focused on the retina.

radiation theraphy Used in the treatment of cancer. Involves controlled exposure of the cancer to measured amounts of radioactive emissions.

radio generation A generational label applied to people in the "fiftysomething" age group. Said to be conservative, people who want hard facts presented in a logical, slow, and cohesive manner.

radioimmunoassay of hair (RIAH) *See* hair analysis.

radon gas A naturally occurring radioactive gas produced by the decay of radium in the earth's soil. When released into the air out-of-doors, it is relatively harmless, but when trapped indoors, it breaks down into radioactive particles that attach to dust and, at certain levels of concentration, can cause lung cancer. Radon testing, disclosure, and remediation have become a concern of American corporations because of legal issues related to toxic substances. The Environmental Protection Agency and the Surgeon General have recommended that all dwellings be tested for radon and that any home with levels of 4.0 pC/L or higher should be abated or reduced.

ragged In desktop publishing, lines of type that are irregular on either or both ends or margins, such as ragged left or ragged right. In ragged type setting, interword spaced are not varied to **justify** the margins.

raider An individual (or group of investors or professional operators) who attempts to depress stock prices on the stock exchange by concerted selling of stock.

ramspecking Getting hired for a job with the federal government without meeting the usual civil service requirements. Credited to the Ramspeck Act, which gives congressional staffers special access to executive branch positions.

random access memory digital-to-analog converter (RAMDAC) A device in the output section of a graphics card that converts the digital color information in the frame buffer to red, green, and blue analog signals that can be sent to a monitor.

random testing Drug and alcohol tests administered by an employer whether mandated by the government or initiated by a private sector employer. In neither case do such tests violate any constitutional rights of employees. However, since in most states there are laws relating to invasion of privacy, employer-initiated random tests may result in employee litigation.

RAND A private, nonprofit institution that helps improve policies relating to the public interest through research and analysis. RAND researchers, numbering more than 500, operate on a uniquely broad front, assisting public policy makers and private sector leaders in their efforts to strengthen the nation's economy, maintain its security, and improve its quality of life. *Contact:* Rand, 1700 Main St., P.O. Box 2138, Santa Monica, CA 90407-2138 310/393-0411; Fax 310/393-4818; E-mail **gaylord@rand.org**; URL **http://www.rand.org**).

random access memory (RAM)
The main memory of a computer system, made up of integrated circuit chips and related components. It provides temporary storage for the operating system, applications program, and data being processed. Users can alter data on RAM, but RAM information is gone forever when the power is switched off.

random sample or sampling In research and statistical studies, samples of the target group drawn completely by chance and not by some judgmental quota or method that would be certain to introduce some statistical bias to the study.

range A statistical measure of variation. The distance from the highest to the lowest score in a series of scores. It is calculated by subtracting the lowest score from the highest score and adding 1.

$$r = \text{highest score} - \text{lowest score} + 1$$

rank order/ranking method 1. A method or rating where the performance of members of a group or the relative value of objects, processes, or products is determined by arranging them in order from highest to lowest or best to worst. **2.** The simplest approach to job evaluation in which each job is ranked relative to all other jobs based on some criterion such as job difficulty.

rank-order or rank ordered Data that have been arranged from highest to lowest or lowest to highest.

rap session A meeting attended by a manager and a representative group of subordi-

nates (staffers, operative employees, or trainees) *without* their immediate superiors or instructors to provide an opportunity for the representatives to voice their problems and concerns, discuss issues with a top-level decision maker, and offer suggestions to improve the environment.

raster Bit-mapped lines of data on a cathode ray tube or computer screen (where every single point is defined) horizontally scanned, processed, or sequentially outputted, line by line. Creates images on computer and video screens by painting a series of raster lines that change rapidly to produce moving pictures or text.

rasterize In desktop publishing, the capability of a **PostScript** printer to take **font** information, which describes the outline of the characters, covert the outlines into dots, and tell the printer how to print it.

rate buster An individual worker who violates a work team's norms by producing more than his or her fellow workers. Such employees are usually ostracized by the group.

rate guarantees Bargaining chips in negotiations between organizations and insurers.

rating The process of evaluating the attributes or characteristics of objects, processes, or products or the traits or performance of people through observation and judgment. Ratings may be adjectival or numerical.

rating errors *See* error of central tendency; error of contrast; error of halo; error of inconsistency; error of instability; error of projection; error of recency; error of standards; error of stereotype; error of subjectivity.

ratio analysis A simple means of forecasting personnel requirements, it involves determining the ratio between some causal factor, like volume of production, and the number of people to produce it. The resulting ratio can then be used to determine the number of new hires required to support a given increase in production.

ratio chart A variation of the **line chart.** Based on logarithms, the chart is set up so that equal percentage changes show as equal distances. Often conveys more useful information than the more common arithmetic chart, where equal absolute differences show as equal distances.

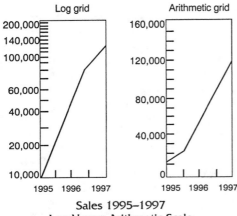

Sales 1995–1997
Log Versus Arithmetic Scale

ratio data   Data that can be rank-ordered with equal distances between adjacent values and have a zero-point with a precise and unambiguous meaning.

rationed care   A controversial cost containment strategy that involves the establishment of a "global budget" for all health care delivered in a region, state, or nation. It limits the availability of specialists and sophisticated medical procedures by establishing a list of services, such as treatment for incurable diseases and infertility therapy, for which state- or federally-sponsored insurance will not provide reimbursement.

rationing   *See* prioritization of resources.

raw score   Any direct or unconverted measure of performance on a test, such as the number of correct responses to test items or the time required for performance.

The REACH Awards for Reengineering Achievement   Honors corporations that have identified key areas for change and the individuals who have successfully implemented new policies and procedures in those areas. In addition to a grand prize for outstanding achievement in financial process reengineering, awards categories include accounts receivable, accounts payable, billing, purchasing, controls and compliance, and information management. Co-sponsored by *CFO* magazine and MasterCard Purchasing Card. *Contact:* The REACH Awards Program, CFO Publishing Corp., 253 Summer St., Boston, MA 02210.

reaction evaluation   An approach to evaluation that focuses on the "reactions" of trainees and their supervisors (and sometimes the instructors and their supervisors) on the effectiveness of training programs.

readily achievable   In the context of the obligation to remove barriers under the **Americans with Disabilities Act of 1990,** "readily achievable" means "easily accomplishable and able to be carried out without much difficulty or expense." It is a lower standard than **undue burden or hardship**.

readiness   In learning, the extent to which the trainee is mentally, psychologically, or physically ready, prepared, or primed for the learning activity. Readiness is an important determinant of the success of a learning activity.

reading rate controller   *See* pacer.

reading training   Training provided by organizations to remedy basic reading skill deficiencies of workers or improve their reading speed and comprehension to improve their readiness for additional training or increase their productivity and their promotion potential. The training may make use of techniques used with young children, such as phonics and flash cards, or sophisticated equipment such as tachistoscopes and reading rate controllers.

read only memory (ROM)   The part of computer memory that contains the information the computer uses throughout the system, including the information it needs to get itself started. It is permanently loaded onto the computer by the manufacturer. It is accessible to users but is not easily altered. ROM is permanent; it doesn't vanish when the power is switched off.

Ready Reserve   *See* Selected Reserve.

Ready Reserve Mobilization Income Insurance Program (RRMIIP)   Enacted as part of the FY 1996 Defense Authorization Act and became effective September 30, 1996. Authorized Reservists to buy income-protection insurance if involuntarily recalled to active duty for more than 30 days in support of war, national emergency, or to augment active forces for an operational mission. Insurance is offered in coverage amounts of $500 to $5,000 per month, in $500 increments. Premium rates were set at $12.20 per month for each $1,000 of monthly coverage. By law, member premiums are supposed to cover the full cost of the program and can be adjusted as necessary to do that. Benefits are payable for up to 12 months in any 18-month period. Current Ready Reservists (except those on full-time active duty) were given 60 days to sign up for the program, starting October 1, 1996. Reserve accessions are automatically covered for $1,000 per month, but must make a specific election to increase, decrease or decline coverage within 60 days of entry. By law, the program can't pay out more than it has collected in premiums. In January 1997, the Defense Department announced that it had to limit initial payouts due to the Bosnian callup. For now, those who signed up for $5,000 a month will be getting $200 a month instead. The Defense Department is preparing a supplemental budget request so the government can follow through in paying the promised benefits.

realism A characteristic of an acceptable test: the extent to which the behaviors, conditions, cues, and standards of a criterion test measure, match, or approximate those of the task. Ideally, test performance is identical to task performance, but that is not always possible because of difficulty, danger, or cost.

rear-end analysis Followup of the results of training on the job to see if the skills learned transfer to the workplace.

rear-screen A projection system configuration that uses a special screen which allows the audience to view an image projected from the other side. Although it is effective in high-ambient-light situations, it has the disadvantage of requiring at least 10 feet of throw distance between the projector and the screen (or the use of expensive mirrors to reduce the space required behind the screen).

reasonable accommodation 1. A legal term relating to measures an employer must take to "accommodate" an employee's objections to an action, requirement, or program on job-relatedness or protected grounds to avoid a lawsuit. 2. A requirement of the **Americans with Disabilities Act of 1990** with respect to hiring or making workplace adjustments for disabled persons: efforts to accommodate the disability of a qualified applicant or employee, such as making existing facilities used by employees accessible to disabled individuals, job restructuring, part time or modified work hours, reassignment to a vacant position, acquisition or modification of equipment or devices, appropriate adjustment or modifications of examinations, training materials, or policies, the provision of qualified readers to interpreters, or other similar accommodations for individuals with disabilities.

reasonable and customary The charge for a health care service or supply that is the usually charge for that service or supply within the geographic area in which the service or supply is provided.

reasonable charge In health care benefits, the amount that is usually charged for the same or similar services or treatment in the same **service area**. However, reasonable charges are usually construed as the amounts approved by insurance carriers, which are typically either the customary charge, the prevailing charge, or the actual charge, whichever is the lowest.

reasonable investigation A legal doctrine that pertains to inquiries relating to a job applicant's fitness for a job, such as preemployment medical examinations, screening for physical disabilities, genetic testing, and so on. It requires that reviews and inquiries be proper, legitimate, and justifiable.

reasonable psychological accommodation See psychological accommodation.

reasonable rule or order A legal doctrine that pertains to determinations of wrongful discharge. In effect, it asks, "Is the employer's rule or order reasonably related to the orderly, efficient, and safe operation of the business and the performance the employer has a right to expect?"

reasonable person (woman) standard A new test that expands the definition of **sexual harassment** in the workplace. Essentially, the standard asks: Would a reasonable *woman* consider the alleged act or action to be sexually harassing or intimidating?

reasonable suspicion testing Drug and alcohol tests administered to an employee because of inappropriate conduct and/ or performance deficiencies, such as excessive or patterned absenteeism or tardiness; carelessness, negligence, or disinterest; poor or declining productivity; erratic or aberrant behavior; or inability to work cooperatively with superiors and/or coworkers.

reassignment Moving employees to positions where either their talents can be used to their own and the organization's advantage or where they can perform the work at the required level. In the former case, reassignment is recognition of the employee's value to the organization. In the latter case, it is a means of salvaging employees whose job performance requirements in their current positions exceed their capabilities.

recall skills The ability to summon, revivify, and review facts, experiences, musings, and reminiscences for use in collecting information, associating events, solving problems, and making decisions. Also called *retention skills.*

recapitalization A strategy for making a company less attractive to predators and takeover artists. Essentially it is restructuring accomplished by repurchasing shares with borrowed capital to shrink the firm's outstanding shares.

recency **1.** A basic principle of learning: principles, concepts, facts, and so on acquired most recently are recalled most easily. **2.** In marketing, describes how recently or organization or individual has bought from your company.

reception operator *See* destination management company.

recertification test *See* employee skills test.

reciprocal review An appraisal system in which the performance of both the manager and the subordinate is evaluated. The subordinate evaluates the manager and the manager evaluates the subordinate based on performance criteria agreed to in advance by both parties. They jointly determine progress and accomplishment, identify shortfalls, and establish action plans.

recognition **1.** Intangible, non-monetary acknowledgement of outstanding performance in the form of praise, accolades, commendations, thank yous, and tributes. May be formal or informal. **2.** In collective bargaining, the process of gaining acknowledgement of a union by management and the **National Labor Relations Board**.

reconciliation The process of designing, debating, negotiating, and deciding on specific legislation to accomplish specific fiscal goals as outlined in Congressional budget resolutions.

reconciliation bills Legislation that enacts (1) increases or decreases in taxes; and (2) changes in entitlement programs, such as Medicare. Because spending is mandatory in entitlement programs, the laws themselves must be changed to increase or decrease funding.

recorder The member of a work team assigned responsibility for keeping a running account of important items discussed during a meeting and recording the decisions or agreements proposed and reached for dissemination to participants and others and for record.

records Information collected, recorded, filed, or included in a data base about individual employees that is essential to the efficient and orderly handling of personnel actions. In the context of the **Freedom of Information Act of 1966** and **Privacy Act of 1974**, records include any item, collection, or grouping of information about an individual in handwritten, typed, printed, microform, computer printout, or audio or video recorded form, which contains the name, identifying number, symbol, photograph, voice print, or fingerprint and associated data, such as education, training, experience, medical history, financial status, or the like.

recovery Describes the truism that in any stable organization of at least several hundred employees, total salaries will decrease by about 1 percent per year in the absence of any merit increases. Recovery is caused by the termination of employees (due to death, transfer, and retirement), promotions, and new hire replacements who are paid less than the former incumbents.

recreation director
See recreation manager.

recreation manager The hotel functionary responsible for arranging and supervising recreational activities and events, such as tennis, golf, water sports, jogging, horseback riding, recreational games and contests, and sometimes supervision of workout and exercise rooms. May also be called *recreation director.*

recreation services Services and facilities provided to attract and retain employees, afford employees opportunities to meet, socialize, and get to know each other, and foster loyalty to the organization. They may include individual and team participatory sports, spectator activities such as sports and theater, attendance at cultural or public events, group tours, arts and crafts, luncheons and dinners, dances, parties, and picnics, and travel.

recruitment The first step in the process of matching job descriptions and applicant specifications with people. The process of surveying all sources of personnel, inside and outside the organization, to locate and attract the best possible candidates for new or vacated positions. The organization actively seeks candidates by advertising both internally and externally in newspapers and professional and technical publications, through search organizations, notices, and personal contacts.

recursive training An approach to training in which the program refers to and reflects itself — that is, it provides a picture within a picture or a story within a story. For example, a seminar on assertiveness in which the instructor is invariably assertive; in an instructor training program, where the instructor displays desirable procedures and practices at all times. The term recursiveness is attributed to Hofstadtr (*Godel, Escher & Bach: An Eternal Golden Braid*, Vintage Books, 1980).

recycle A trainee who repeats instruction because, although his or her performance has been below standard, he or she is judged to have the potential to complete training successfully. Also called *turn-back*.

recycling The practice of requiring a trainee to repeat a module or an entire course of instruction because of inadequate performance.

red circle Used on job charts to highlight employees whose salaries are above the maximum of the salary range set for their jobs.

red circle rates See flagged rates.

redeployment Reassigning workers to openings in other functional areas, departments, or branches rather than laying them off. *See also* cross-training; implacement.

redesign See process redesign.

redlining In insurance and banking, the practice of denying insurance coverage or loans to people who live in ghettos or neighborhoods considered to be at high risk for burglaries, arson, or other criminal activities.

reduced fee A fee arrangement where the contractor and the client agree on a discounted rate but typically sets a minimum amount to be paid by the client over a specified time period.

reengineering See process reengineering.

red, green, blue (RGB) The colors in which computer monitors record color in **pixels**.

reduced instruction set computing (RISC) A new technology that provides the fastest printing available today. It employs a speedy microprocessor that is is more adept at rasterizing (placing an image on the screen of a cathode ray tube) the more graphically-oriented pages that laser printers are being used to produce. Examples are RISC-based PostScript controllers from RIPS and Eicon Technology, high-resolution laser printers from NewGen Systems, and thermal, color PostScript printers from Seiko and CalComp.

reduction in force (RIF) A common consequence of or accompaniment to downsizing — the layoff of employees. That is, voluntary or involuntary termination of employees as a response to competitive pressures, economic downturns, mergers and takeovers, and downsizing and restructuring. Voluntary RIFs usually include financial inducements and other early retirement incentives. Involuntary RIFs are simply layoffs.

re-education Education designed to help teachers and college professors (and to a growing degree, trainers and facilitators in business and industry) to learn the new methods and applications of technology that they need to serve as facilitators of student learning under an **integrated curriculum**. In addition to teaching new skills, the programs convey the benefits of technology and encourage a perception of learning as an ongoing part of professional life.

reengineering A means of achieving gains in productivity. The strategy aims to redesign business and work processes, organizational structures, organizational policies, and resources. Reengineering involves the application of just-in-time inventory controls to all phases of a company's operations and using such techniques as empowerment, restructuring assembly lines and offices, establishing work teams, and training employees in multiple skills. Proponents claim that reengineering should result in faster economic growth, improved international competitiveness, higher real wages for the average worker, and improved living standards. Critics point to the potential displacement of people whose current jobs will be eliminated. Also known as *core process design* and *process innovation*. Attributed to Michael Hammer, a Cambridge, MA consultant.

reentry training   1. Training provided to individuals who, for one reason or another (illness, injury, child rearing, and so on) have been out of the work force for an extended period time and need either initial or refresher training in the skills and knowledge required by the job. **2.** Training provided to returnees from extended overseas assignments to help them adjust to the culture shock when they return to the United States.

reference check/checking   A means of verifying information provided by job candidates on their applications or during interview. Until very recently, most organizations (in excess of 90 percent) made use of this approach by telephone or personal contact with the applicant's current or former employer. Because of the recent flurry of charges of discrimination and violation of privacy, many employers now refuse to provide any information to other firms except the dates the applicant worked in their organizations and the job title held. A total of 18 states (15 since 1995) have enacted laws to limit the civil liability of employers that provide good-faith job references to former or current employees. An additional 16 states have such legislation pending. *See also* background investigation.

referent power   Power that derives from the personality and charisma of the leader, the identification of followers with that person, and the desire of followers to please the leader.

referral agent program   A form of employee assistance program in which a person is selected and given brief and minimum training and information about available community counseling services. The agent's responsibilities are limited to listening to the employee's diagnosis of his or her problem and referring the individual to an appropriate source of help, usually a public agency.

reflexology   An alternative form of manipulative medical treatment in which various parts of the foot, such as the great toe and arches, are manipulated to "clear pathways" and positively affect the remainder of the body.

reframing   In counseling or problem solving, a technique rooted in psychiatry used to help someone see a difficult problem from a new perspective and identify and try a non-standard solution when earlier seemingly logical solutions have not worked.

refreezing   One of the three major stages in learning (the others are **unfreezing** and **change efforts**). Refreezing occurs when the teacher or facilitator attempts to get the learners to embed new skills into their regular behavior or repertoire of skills. Attributed to Kurt Lewin, pioneer in experiential learning.

Regents of the University of California v. Bakke   A 1978 Supreme Court decision declaring that special consideration based on race for admission to graduate school could be acceptable under the Constitution if a school used race as a "plus factor" while reviewing all applicants in one pool. That ruling is analogous to the argument that **affirmative action** to help minority candidates is allowable but that fixed quotas by race would be discriminatory.

Regional Bell Operating Companies (RBOCs)   The regional telephone companies that remained following the breakup of AT&T. In July 1991, the Federal Communications Commission ruled that REBOCs could provide video dial tone services into private homes, at first one or two channels of video over present phone lines and later more channels over fiber optic cables. That privilege could be used to provide interactive multimedia services and/or deliver video programming, the latter allowing them to compete with the TV cable industry.

Registered Investment Advisor (RIA)   A designation granted by the Securities Exchange Commission on submission of a completed registration form and payment of a $150 fee. There are no educational or experience requirements for the designation.

Registered Meeting Planner (RMP)   A professional designation awarded to qualified professional meeting planners by the International Society of Meeting Planners. *Contact:* ISMP, 8383 East Evans Road, Scottsdale, AZ 85260-3614 (602/483-0000; Fax 602/998-8022; E-mail **imsp@iani.org**; URL **http://iani.org/ismp.html**).

registered occupational therapist   A health care professional with special training and expertise in advising people with disabilities in making the kind of adjustments and accommodations needed for daily life and employment, including selecting the right types of wheelchair and adaptive driving equipment, bathing, shopping, cooking, and using special equipment.

registration software   In meeting management, a computer program that stores names, addresses, and other items of information about meeting registrants. Allows the planner to sort and select by any of several data fields and print reports such as rooming and arrival/departure lists.

regression analysis A means of measuring the degree of correlation among variables such as performance ratings and promotions.

regular part time *See* part-time worker.

regular student Under federal student aid programs, an individual who is enrolled in an institution to earn a degree or certificate. In general, to receive federal aid, an individual must be a regular student.

regulation A detailed set of instructions or directives that clarify and implement a law.

Regulatory Fairness Act of 1996
Requires federal agencies that issue regulations to: (1) consider the impact on small businesses, and, where the impact is found to be substantial, to lighten the burden, and (2) issue a booklet explaining new regulations in "plain English" so that they won't require interpretation by legal consultants.

rehabilitation Any program designed to restore a former physical, mental, or emotional capacity.

Rehabilitation Act of 1973 (RA) An act designed to develop and implement comprehensive and coordinated programs of vocational rehabilitation for persons with handicaps to maximize their employability, independence, and integration into the workplace and community by assisting them to obtain employment and secure on-the-job accommodations following hiring. It applied to government contractors and subcontractors, recipients of federal aid, and government employees. The Act prohibited discrimination on the basis of disability in local programs and activities benefiting from federal financial assistance. Enforcement has improved program accessibility for disabled persons to health care, social services, recreation, housing, and transportation and opened educational opportunities to disabled persons at all levels. The Act also proscribes barriers to the employment of the handicapped in the screening and selection processes, particularly during the employment interview. It prohibited employers performing under federal contracts or subcontracts exceeding $25,000 from discriminating against handicapped persons (hearing, vision, speech; cancer, heart

disease, and diabetes; cerebral palsy; epilepsy; mental illness and retardation; muscular dystrophy and multiple sclerosis; and drug addiction and alcoholism). The Act mandated affirmative action to hire handicapped individuals and treat them fairly, including making workplace modifications. The Act also defined a person with a disability as "a person with a physical or mental impairment that substantially limits that person in some major life activity, a person with a record of such a physical or mental impairment, or a person who is regarded as having such an impairment." The amendments of 1974 created the Architectural Barriers Compliance Board, which monitors compliance with the **Architectural Barriers Act of 1968**.

Rehabilitation Act of 1973 The Act established a federal Interagency Committee on Handicapped Employees to establish a focus for federal and other employment of individuals with handicaps, review in cooperation with the Equal Employment Opportunity Commission the adequacy of hiring, placement, and advancement practices with respect to individuals with handicaps, and submit to the EEOC an affirmative action plan for the hiring, placement, and advancement of people with handicaps by departments and agencies of the executive branch of the government. The Act also required the EEOC to develop for referral to State agencies policies and procedures which would facilitate the hiring, placement, and advancement of people who have received rehabilitation services under State vocational rehabilitation programs, veterans' programs, or any other program for individuals with handicaps, including the promotion of job opportunities for such individuals. Title I of the Act encourages State agencies to provide counseling, guidance, referral and placement services; vocational and training services; physical and mental restoration services; an income stipend during the rehabilitation program; interpreter and reader services; transportation to rehabilitation facilities; and assistive aids and devices.

Rehabilitation Act Amendments of 1992
Legislation designed to embed the precepts and values of the **Americans with Disabilities Act of 1990** into the **Rehabilitation Act of 1973** and extend the Act through 1997. The amendments revise the Act to

develop and implement, through research, training, services, and the guarantee of equal opportunity, comprehensive and coordinated programs of vocational rehabilitation and independent living for individuals with disabilities to maximize their employment, independence, and integration into the workplace and the community.

Rehabilitation Data (REHABDATA) A database that contains bibliographic records with abstracts of 30,000+ documents, covering all aspects of disability and rehabilitation, housed in the **National Rehabilitation Information Center** library. *Contact:* NARIC, 8455 Colesville Rd., Ste. 935, Silver Spring, MD 20910-3319 [1-800/346-2742 or 301/588-9284; Fax 301/587-1967; URL **http://www.naric.com/naric**).

Rehabilitation Services Administration (RSA) A subdivision of the **Office of Special Education and Rehabilitation Services,** RSA administers programs to support employment and independence for individuals with disabilities. Annually, the vocational rehabilitation program successfully rehabilitates 200,000 individuals, of which 85 percent enter the competitive labor market or become self-employed. *Contact:* RSA, OSERS/ED 330 C St., S.W. Room 3030, Switzer Bldg., Washington DC. 20202-2531 [202/205-8241 or 202/205-8723 (voice/TTY)].

rehab technology Machines and other devices used by the physically disabled — totally or partially deaf, totally or partially blind, those with speech problems, and orthopedically handicapped (loss of normal use of limbs, bones, or muscles due to disease, spinal chord or injury, or deformity (such as cerebral palsy, muscular dystrophy, tuberculosis of the bones and joints, congenital deformities, and amputation).

reimbursement account An option of most **flexible benefits programs** (plans), in which eligible expenses are reimbursed on a nontaxable basis. Contributions to these accounts come from two sources: employer residual flexible benefits dollars and employee salary deductions. There are two types of reimbursement accounts allowed by the Internal Revenue Service (health care and dependent day care) but only if the following rules are met: (1) annual employee election of the amount of contribution(s); (2) nontransferability of funds; (3) forfeiture of unused funds;

and (4) a contribution limit for day care (determined by the employer) of up to $5,000 per year for married employees who file jointly or are single, and $2,500 for employees who are married but filing separately.

reimbursement contract *See* cost contract.

reimbursement systems *See* capitation payments; diagnostic related group reimbursement; global pricing; per diem reimbursement.

reinforcement A key concept in the behaviorism theory of learning. Reinforcement consists of payback and other forms of positive feedback provided individuals and work groups by supervisors, peers, top management, and the organization following completion of a project, training, or other learning experience.

reinsurance A means of spreading the financial risk incurred by an insurer. Insurance policies are contracted with reinsurers to achieve any or all of the following objectives: (1) increase the capacity of the insurer to do additional business; (2) reduce written premiums to maintain strong premium-to-surplus ratios; (3) provide protection for a portion of the insurer's assets against catastrophic losses; and (4) improve competitive (pricing) status. Reinsurance includes treaty, facultative, and **financial reinsurance**.

reinsurance intermediary A person or company that serves as an reinsurance broker — providing a link between reinsurance companies and their customers. Because of their wide contacts within the insurance industry, intermediaries can provide negotiating expertise, quality assurance, and valuable technical advice with respect to underwriting, accounting, and so on.

reinsurers Insurers that assume for a premium some of the risks of insurance companies to cover a portion of any losses they may incur. The original insurer "cedes" a specific amount of the risk to the reinsurer under a written contract.

regeneration The practice of focusing on employees to keep downsizing from undermining the ability of an organization to be competitive and productive. Includes such strategies as **training, empowerment, upskilling,** tuition-assistance programs, and the establishment of work teams.

registration The testing process used to determine whether a company has met the requirements specified in international standards.

registrars Third party auditors that issue certificates relating to quality system standards such as **ISO 9000, QS-9000,** and **ISO 14000.** Registrars must be accredited to work in a national or regional market.

reject rate A quality control indicator. Identifies the number of products or services rejected as below standard or unacceptable either at the production level or at the supplier or consumer levels as compared with the number produced, shipped, or delivered.

relational database A means of storing and retrieving information. Data are entered into a relational database in "rows and columns," much like a spreadsheet, thereby allowing users to add or remove fields as needed, cross-reference any item of information and relate it to any other.

relationship addict One who has a close and continuing relationship with substance abusers, such as spouse, children, or "significant other" — people who themselves need to "recover." The term is preferred by some therapists as a substitute for **codependency**.

relationship marketing A strategy that encourages and promotes frequent communication between vendors and customers.

relative ratings See comparative ratings.

release agreement Primarily a means of protecting an organization against unlawful discharge suits. However, release agreements are also designed to avoid litigation between an employer and an employee or consultant, a maker and a distributor, or a producer and talent (actors) or other performers. A release agreement is a clearly written legal document executed by either or both parties. In the case of employer-employee releases, they are usually signed by the employee in exchange for some benefit from the employer that the employer is not obligated to give following the employee's discharge, resignation, or layoff. In exchange for the benefit, the employee gives up all claims against the employer in connection with the employment, including termination or resignation. In the case of talent or other "performers," the release permits the public or private performance, broadcast, exhibition, publication, or sale by the producer of the dramatization, comment, speech, article, or other "product."

relevance A basic principle of learning: maintains that people learn best when what they are asked to learn is pertinent and useful or that it will benefit them in some way.

relevance tree A normative forecasting method particularly useful in selecting courses of action that are consistent with organizational objectives and capabilities. That is done by dividing the relevant elements of a decision into consecutively smaller and smaller components. These components are drawn on a sheet of paper with connecting boxes and lines showing relationships (much like an organization chart), establishing criteria for determining the relative importance of each component, assigning numerical values for each component and criterion, and then combining individual ratings to gain new insights about the decision.

reliability A measure of the ability of a psychological test, achievement test, rating scale, or other instrument of appraisal to evaluate consistently whatever is being measured. Expressed as a coefficient of reliability.

reliability coefficient The coefficient of correlation between two forms of a test (alternate form reliability), between halves of a test (split-half reliability), or between scores on two administrations of the same test (test-retest reliability).

religious accommodation In equal employment opportunity, enjoining employers to reasonably accommodate workers in terms of attendance at religious ceremonies, absence due to religious observances and holy days, Saturday or Sunday work, and the like. Work rules that adversely affect certain religious groups are excusable only if religion is a **bona fide occupational qualification** or the employer is unable to reasonably accommodate without undue hardship.

relocating partner The wife, husband, or "**significant other**" of employees being transferred.

relocation allowance A lump-sum payment to domestic transfers or foreign-based employees to cover such things as remodeling living quarters, purchasing furnishings, and obtaining licenses and permits.

relocation assistance Pretransfer and post-transfer assistance provided to domestic or overseas transfers, such as providing information (briefings, information packages, and individual counseling) on such matters as tax and insurance forms required, critical policies and procedures, pay and benefits, and sources of assistance, and getting relocation payments to the individual, helping with the move, and so on.

relocation reluctance   Describes the attitude of employees who, for one reason or another (spouse, children, locations, and so on) are unwilling to move to another city, region, or overseas even for a promotion or salary increase.

relocation training   A form of intercultural training. Designed to prepare a person assigned to work in a foreign country to understand the country, its people, their culture, norms of behavior, customs, and expectations. Also called *country-specific training* or *predeparture training*.

relo policy   Corporate policy relating to **relocation assistance**.

remedial counseling   Counseling given to employees to correct performance problems, careless behavior, or errors of judgment.

remedial training   Repeat training and guided practice provided to remedy or correct deficiencies in trainee performance. It is given *when* it is needed. Remedial training may be provided to groups or to individuals, one-on-one.

remediation   Strategies and interventions designed to overcome deficiencies in the habits, attitudes, knowledge, skills, or performance of employees.

remission   A halt or actual reduction in the progression of an illness resulting in discharge from a hospice care program with no further expense incurred

remodeling   The process of generating leads for a new idea or solution to a problem by changing the existing form of a concept, object, or idea. That may be done by rearranging — doing it backwards, turning it sideways, upside down, moving it from the end to the beginning, front to back, putting it together if it is now separate, separating it if it is joined, and so on. Or the process of substitution can be used — use a different material, a different process, a different sequence, change the players/participants and so on. Or, the processes of addition or multiplication can be used — duplicate the program, make it longer, bigger, more inclusive, add more units, and so on. Or the subtraction process can be used — reduce the length, make it smaller, leave something out, make it less inclusive, cut the number of units, and so on.

remote employee   An employee who (1) works at a site removed from his or her supervisor, or (2) is under contract and works on "secret" projects to which his or her supervisor does not have access.

remote manager   A manager who supervises employees who perform work in places other than the company's location.

remote site   In distance learning, the receiving or destination site(s) where the trainees are located but where the instructor, moderator, or presenter is not present.

remote ticketing system   Non-computer reservation system-issued ticketing machines for remote output of tickets.

rent-a-boss   A temporary executive service. Officials needing a chief operating officer for short periods of time (six to nine months, for example) employ highly qualified and experienced individuals who require no employee benefits and no executive perks.

rent-a-doc   Physicians or other medical practitioners who provide inhouse health care under contract for specific periods of time.

rent-a-judge   An alternative dispute resolution approach in which the parties to the controversy agree to employ a judge, usually a retired jurist, to render an opinion on the dispute. The opinion may be either binding or nonbinding.

rent-a-pro   Any professional who contracts with an organization to provide his or her services for a specified period of time.

repat/repatriate   An employee who returns to the United States following a lengthy assignment abroad.

Repeal of the Mandate for Medicare and Medicaid Coverage Data Bank Act of 1996   Amends the Social Security Act to repeal the mandate for a Medicare and Medicaid Coverage Data Bank (added by the Omnibus Budget Reconciliation Act of 1993). Signed into law by the President October 2, 1996.

repeat trauma (RT)   *See* repetitive strain injury.

repetitive motion injury (RMI)   *See* repetitive strain injury.

repetitive strain injury (RSI)   Injury to the bones, tendons, muscles, or nerves of the back, hands, wrists, fingers, arms, shoulders, neck, back, or lower extremities suffered by data-entry workers, computer programmers, or anyone who spends long hours typing on a computer or word processor keyboard. Also applies to other workers whose jobs require the use of their hands in repetitive motions for long periods of time, such as auto assembly line and other factory workers, meat packers, supermarket checkout clerks, and even musicians — and workers exposed to prolonged static postures, low frequency machine vibrations, and similar conditions. Also known as *cumulative trauma disorder., ergonomic hazard, repeat trauma,* and *repetitive strain injury.*

replacement charts *See* personnel inventory charts.

report Oral or written communication designed to inform or explain problems, situations, or other facts to meet a legitimate organizational, employee, or management need. Examples are trip reports, evaluation reports and critiques, minutes and summaries of meetings, staff studies and decision papers, sales reports, and after-action reports.

reportable quantity (RQ) The quantity of hazardous chemicals released into the environment that exceeds the maximum allowed by the Environmental Protection Agency and must be reported to the **National Response Center**.

report statistics *See* aggregative statistics.

rep payee *See* representative payee.

representative payee A person designated by a federal agency to receive government benefits on behalf of a person determined by the agency to be incapable of managing such benefits as Social Security, Civil Service Retirement, Military Retirement, and Veterans Benefits. Children under the age of 18 and adults who are unable to manage their finances because of severe physical or mental limitations have representative payees. May be a relative, friend or other interested party.

representative sample A sample taken from a group of persons or objects that matches the characteristics of the group from which it was taken; for example, the proportion of cases or subjects of each age, sex, occupation, or socioeconomic level, and so on.

reprimand A form of disciplinary action. An oral or written rebuke.

reproductive imagery The use of memories of past events to search for, find, identify, and modify, synthesize, or otherwise change the form, size, use, of some other characteristic of an object, concept, or idea to make it new.

repurchase agreement In investments, the acquisition of an underlying debt instrument, subject to an obligation of the seller to repurchase, and the buyer to resell, the instrument at a fixed price, usually not more than one week after its purchase. Considered by the **Securities and exchange Commission** as loans by the seller.

repurposing In multimedia, reusing content, such as text, photos, or video, that is readily available "on-the-shelf."

request for information (RFI) A written request sent to potential bidders to learn what products and services they have to offer. The RFI is usually followed up by a **request for proposal** (RFP) to vendors and suppliers who are most likely to be able to deliver the needed product.

request for price (RFP) A federal state, local government, or private corporation request for a price quotation from venders, suppliers, and consultants for products or services identified in the request.

request for proposal (RFP) A federal, state, local government, or private corporation request for detailed bids from vendors and consultants to satisfy some need for a product or service. An RFP is a written document, prepared for distribution to consultants and vendors before selecting products and services to assist them in preparing their bids. It includes functional and technical requirement and specifications, reporting, security, documentation, and training needs, and other criteria to be used in selecting the successful bidder.

request for quotation (RFQ) A formal document distributed to vendors requesting a bid or price quotation for required products or services.

research Meticulously designed and carefully controlled investigative studies in any discipline, function, or area of interest and concern to find solutions to important problems. It accumulates all applicable facts, includes, where appropriate, authoritative opinion and experimentation, discusses all pertinent facets of the problem, accords full consideration to alternative courses of action, incorporates objective analysis of facts, reaches logical conclusions, and presents the results in an understandable form and language.

research skills The skills involved in selecting, developing, and using objective, valid, and reliable data collection, reduction, analysis (including statistical analysis), and reporting methodologies to determine needs, evaluate programs, solve problems, resolve conflicts, compare methods and approaches, develop new approaches, meet reporting requirements (including governmental), and determine the causes of organizational problems.

Reserve Components (RC) Units and individuals either assigned to units or on the rolls of the Armed Forces as individuals who are available for call-up to active duty when ordered by the President.

Reserve Mobilization Insurance The Pentagon decided to ask Congress to suspend the "Ready Reserve Mobilization Income Insurance Program" implemented in October 1996. The suspension would begin October 1, 1997. The benefit grew out of the Persian Gulf War mobilization when a significant number of self-employed Guard and Reserve members were wiped out financially following their activation. Almost all of the reserve soldiers who were called up to support the "third rotation" of troops to Bosnia signed up for the plan, but very few other Reserve members did. Based on earlier (and now questionable) research, DoD estimated that more than 50 percent of reservists would sign up, thus creating an instant deficit in the mobilization insurance fund. As a result, the Pentagon had to ask Congress for $72 million in special supplemental funding. The House Appropriations Subcommittee on National Security voted to approve the $72M request in mid-April 1997, but it still requires endorsement by the full House and Senate. Without enough cash in the fund to pay full benefits, DoD has been limited to paying participants only fractional payments until Congress approves more money.

The Reserve Officers Association (ROA) A 100,000 member independent nonprofit organization of reserve, regular, retired, and former officers of the seven uniformed services Army, Navy, Air Force, Marine Corps, Coast Guard, Public Health Service, and National Oceanic and Atmospheric Administration). Its mission is to ensure an adequate total force of all services including active and reserve components and a force that can be mobilized to meet any contingency. It is operated to benefit uniformed services personnel, and their families and survivors and preserve the earned entitlements and benefits of all members of the uniformed services and their families. *Contact:* ROA, One Constitution Ave., N.E., Washington, DC 20002-5655. (202/479-2200; E-mail **blauer@rog.org**; URL **http://www.troa.org/**)

reservists' benefits Benefits continuance mandated by law when military reservists are called to active duty. They include reemployment following return with the same position of one of equal pay, rank, and seniority, the same treatment they would normally receive under an employer's leave of absence policy, and continuation benefits under **COBRA**. Employers are not obliged to continue salary, contributions to pension or thrift plans, or health insurance coverage.

reshaping *See* downsizing; severance.

residential care facility *See* board and care home.

resident font A **Type I font** whose printer information lives within the **PostScript** laser printer. The printer fonts for several **typefaces** are built into the **read only memory**.

resident manager The hotel functionary responsible for day-to-day management of the property, serving as an assistant general manager. Typically is responsible for front office operations, concierge services, bell captains, security, and housekeeping.

residuary estate The remainder of a person's estate not previously disposed of in the person's will. Such property falls under the residual clause, which usually collects and distributes the majority of the estate and should also provide for contingent beneficiaries should the primary beneficiary predecease the testator.

res ipsa loquitur A legal term that literally means "the thing speaks for itself." It describes a legal theory sometimes used by plaintiffs in jury cases who cannot definitely prove negligence but argue that the defendant's negligence is the only possible explanation for the injury or damage they sustained.

resolution **1.** The disposition of a disagreement through alternative dispute resolution strategies. **2.** The clarity, sharpness, or degree of detail of an image on a computer screen. It is expressed in the number of pixels that run horizontally and the number of lines that run vertically; for example a resolution of 680 dots × 400 lines. The greater the number of **pixels** per square inch, the higher the resolution and the clearer the picture.

resource-based relative value scale (RBRVS) A Medicare cost reduction strategy passed by Congress in 1989 that changes the way health care providers are paid for their services. The results of a Harvard research study, RBRVS forms the basis for new Medicare physician payment legislation that began in 1992 and became fully operational in 1996. It replaces the current "usual, customary, and reasonable" reimbursement system with uniform national set fees based on such variables as the practitioner's time, effort, training and skill, as well as office overhead. Under RBRVS, physicians with family medicine, pediatric, and internist practices receive higher fees than formerly and doctors practicing more invasive medicine (such as heart, thoracic, and orthopedic surgery) receive lower fees than currently. Under the system, such physician services as taking medical histories and counseling patients are valued as highly as surgical procedures.

Resource Conservation and Recovery Act (RCRA) of 1976 Legislation designed to provide "cradle-to-grave" control of hazardous waste. It requires all facilities handling more than 100 kilograms of hazardous waste per month follow Environmental Protection Agency rules for handling waste on site and train all workers to be thoroughly knowledgeable with proper waste handling and emergency procedures. The Act also prohibits employers from placing workers in situations that it "reasonably expects" would be dangerous, such as contact with toxic chemicals. It mandates criminal liability if, in violating provisions of the Act, a party knowingly places others in danger.

resource mother A woman who provides dependable and sympathetic social support to an adolescent mother through the months of pregnancy and beyond. Resource mothers usually live in the same neighborhood, have successfully reared children of their own, and can convey life skills that are most relevant to young mothers.

resource person An expert on the subject at hand invited to work team meetings, discussion groups, or problem solving groups to supply information on request when it seems to be needed or pertinent to the discussion.

resource referral program (RRP) Usually contracted by an employer to assist employees in locating dependent-care services.

respite care Short-term (typically five consecutive days or less) home care or inpatient care in a hospice to a terminally ill patient to give temporary relief to the person who regularly provides or assists with home care

respondeat superior Literally, "let the master respond." An employment doctrine that holds an employer liable for his or her employees' negligent on-the-job actions and does not depend in any way on the plaintiff's ability to prove the employer's negligence.

respondent behavior Behavior elicited by known stimuli. For example, people can be trained to repair an equipment component by repeatedly presenting to them a series of symptoms, demonstrating the correct procedure for fixing them, and providing opportunities for practice.

response list In direct marketing, a computerized list of people and organizations that have responded to a direct mail offer in the past, preferably by actually purchasing something by mail.

response time 1. A quality control indicator. It is the average or mean time that elapses between the identification of the need for a product or service (receipt of the order) and the date of shipment or delivery. 2. In automatic data processing, the interval between the user's input and the computer's reply.

responsive behavior Audible or observable responses to the actions, comments, or questions of others. It takes several forms: direct questions or closed probes (When did it happen?), open-ended questions or comments (Why do you feel that way?), summary or reflective responses (You feel that people are not being very cooperative?) and body language (nods, smiles, shrugs, pats on the back, arm around the shoulder, hugs, and so on).

restatement of tort An advisory standard used by the courts in liability cases. Essentially it states that anyone who, in the course of his or her business, profession, or employment, supplies false information to others to guide them in their business transactions, is subject to liability for monetary loss to them by their reliance on the information provided, if the provider fails to exercise reasonable care in communicating the information. The standard also states that "Communications between employers regarding the previous work history and character of an employee are protected from claims of defamation if the statements are made in 'good faith.' " Therefore, although an employer cannot deliberately submit false information about a former or current employee in response to a request from a prospective employer, he or she is protected from claims of defamation if the statements are made in "good faith."

restraining order A legal remedy available to individuals or organizations obtained through a court order. For example, an organization may be ordered by the court to discontinue an action that may be discriminatory, such as terminating an employee with a disability rather than making a reasonable accommodation.

restricted fares Fare categories used by corporate travelers to save money. They include advance purchase excursion fares, day-of-the week discounts, and group/convention, non-refundable, penalty, promotional, and round-trip fares.

restricted stock plan A form of long-term executive incentive plan that provides the employee with the benefits of stock ownership in the form of dividends; however, restrictions are placed on the disposal of such stock (usually that it revert to the corporation).

restrictive covenant The practice of requiring executives or other highly skilled employees to sign agreements to limit their freedom to work for other organizations, usually for a specified period of time or in a certain geographical area, or with companies that compete directly with the present employer. Other forms relate to nonsolicitation of other employees, prior notice before quitting, or providing the employer with an opportunity to match any offer of employment. *See* noncompete agreement.

restrictive on-call time *See* on-call time.

restrictive policy Prima facie evidence of discrimination in that it demonstrates that an employer (intentionally or unintentionally) has been using a hiring policy or procedure to exclude members of a protected group. For example, a policy against hiring women for assembly line jobs or against hiring women with young children.

restructuring Changing the structure of an organization to make it more efficient and to effect savings.

results evaluation An approach to evaluation that measures the gains or benefits of training (or other intervention) in terms of factors that affect the organization's bottom line — such as profit or productivity.

résumé A document provided by an applicant for a position which identifies his or her career objectives and outlines specialized skills, education, experience, affiliations, and any other information that supports the career objective and will help the decision maker in the screening and selection processes.

résumé scanning system Computer hardware and software that scan and store data from résumés and organize them in an applicant tracking system.

résumé tracking system *See* applicant tracking system.

retailing Selling goods in small quantities directly to the consumer.

retainer 1. A fee paid to a contractor in advance of services as a deposit against future fees. Such payments are applied against fees as incurred on an hourly or projected basis. **2.** A set fee based on an understanding that the contractor will be available to a client and will not accept an assignment from another client if it would conflict with the provision of services to the first client.

retainer agreement A written compact with such professionals as attorneys, actuaries, auditors, and consultants, which describes the services to be provided — what is to be done, by whom and when. Used to avoid funding for the fringe benefits that would be a required to hire a full-time employee. Also called an *engagement letter*.

retaliatory discharge A form of workplace discrimination: discharge designed to punish workers for certain actions. Illegal in most states where, for example, statutes have been enacted to prohibit termination of employees filing for workers' compensation benefits

retarded A category of persons with mental disabilities. As measured by an intelligence test, the condition is represented by an **intelligence quotient (IQ)** between 50 and 75.

retention skills *See* recall skills.

retinal detachment Occurs when the retina of the eye is pulled away from its normal position. The retina does not work when it is detached. It is a very serious problem that almost always causes blindness unless it is treated by laser surgery or cryotherapy (freezing).

retinitis pigmentosa (RP) A condition characterized by degeneration of the retina and choroid (a pigmented vascular layer behind the iris), usually involving development of excess pigment. It is hereditary and begins with night blindness, followed by tunnel vision. Visual loss is progressive, so that by the time most individuals reach young adulthood, they become legally blind.

Retinitis Pigmentosa International
An international nonprofit organization dedicated to the fight against retinitis pigmentosa, incurable hereditary blindness. The organization raises funds for research and helps individuals and their families to accept and deal with the diagnosis of impending blindness. *Contact:* Retinitis Pigmentosa International, P.O. Box 900, Woodland Hills, CA 91365 (800/FIGHT-RP or 818/992-0500; Fax 818/992-3265; E-mail **RPIeyes@aol.com**).

Retired Reserve Members of Reserve Components of the Armed Forces who have completed 20 or more years of active duty or a combination of 20 or more years of active duty and active duty for training. The latter group becomes eligible for retired pay upon reaching the age of 62; those who have completed 20 years of active duty are eligible immediately upon retirement. Under certain conditions and age limitations, members are subject to recall to active duty in an emergency.

retiree skill bank A cost-effective means of attracting skilled and experienced employees and an attractive option for former employees who want to continue to work. A retiree skill bank is a temporary pool of retired employees who are rehired by their former employer on an occasional, temporary, or contractual basis.

retirement *See* preretirement counseling.

retirement benefits Benefits provided to retired employees, usually at age 60 or higher. They may include such things as retirement counseling, relocation allowances, monthly annuity payments, health care insurance, and survivors' benefits.

Retirement Equity Act of 1984 (REA)
An act that liberalized **Employee Retirement Income Security Act of 1974**'s participation, vesting, and service requirements. It extends preretirement surviving spouse protection to all vested employees and requires spousal consent to waive certain benefits. The Act also requires employers to obtain written consent from spouses of retiring workers who choose pension benefits payable only during their lifetimes rather than a joint and survivor plan. A recent General Accounting Office study has recommended that consent forms be written in nontechnical language and include clear explanations of the effects of the consent on the worker's annuity.

retirement planning *See* preretirement counseling.

Retirement Protection Act of 1994 (RPA)
Legislation designed to eliminate the problem of underfunding of pension plans by strengthening funding rules. The Act and subsequent guidelines accelerated contributions to underfunded plans, changed the mandated interest rate for lump-sum calculations from Pension Benefit Guarantee Corporation rates to those based on 30-year U.S. Treasury securities. and eliminated the opportunities that employers now have to avoid funding their plans by enhancing the compliance authority of the **Pension Benefit Guarantee Corporation (PBGC)** and establishing new reporting requirements to provide information to the PBGC on seriously underfunded pension plans. The law also requires employers with pension plans less than 90 percent funded to provide an annual, least-to-read explanation of funding levels of the plan and the limits of PBGC's guarantees. Companies that fail to provide the notice face penalties of up to $1,000 each day they fail to comply.

Retirement Security Act of 1997
Introduced by Sen Tom Daschle D-S.D. as S.14, the Act would expand the number of U.S. workers covered by pensions, with particular provisions aimed at increasing equity for women. A proposed "check off" system would allow employees to authorize their employers to deposit a portion of their paychecks directly into retirement accounts, and businesses would be encouraged to set up new pension plans through such incentives as a $500 tax credit, reduced record

keeping responsibilities, and simplified procedures.

retirement test *See* earnings test.

retouching In computer color prepress, editing the color of an image, pixel by pixel.

retraining **1.** Providing training in a specific job or occupation to enable an employee to perform new processes, procedures, or work with new tools, equipment, and materials. **2.** Providing employees with training in a new job because their old jobs are obsolete and no longer required. For example, retraining assembly workers as accountants.

retreat *See* executive retreat.

retrenchment Layoffs, staff cutbacks, and concomitant benefit reductions effected by public and private organizations during periods of economic decline.

retro A projection system configuration that consists of a screen in front, a projector in back, and some mirrors in between packaged in a roll-away box. They can be used in rooms with high-ambient light, don't require much setup, and can be easily moved.

retrospective review In health care utilization management, a review that occurs after a case is finished and the patient is discharged. Examples are claims review and pattern review.

return on assets (RA) An internal auditing device that indicates how well the assets of an organization are being put to use. It is calculated by dividing net profit by total assets.

$$RA = \frac{net\ profit}{total\ assets}$$

return on equity (ROE) An after-tax measure used by economists to determine the the quality and vitality of a business. It is an estimate of retained earnings for non-borrowed funds invested in a business typically corrected for dividends paid out and for inflation. Or it can also be calculated by dividing net earnings by ending stockholders' equity. Here are the two formulas: return on investment (ROI)

"Real" ROE = return on equity − dividends paid out − inflation rate

or

$$ROE = \frac{net\ earnings}{ending\ stockholders'\ equity}$$

return on investment (ROI) **1.** In finance, the return on invested capital, which is measured as the ratio of reported income to balance sheet book value. ROI has two components: rate of turnover of total assets and rate of earnings per dollar (profit margin) of sales. It serves as a standard measure of performance for each department or element of a business. **2.** In training, ROI is calculated as follows:

$$ROI = \frac{net\ program\ savings\ or\ benefits}{program\ costs}$$

revalidation *See* cross validation.

revamps Conference centers, training facilities, fitness centers, or hotels that have recently been refurbished to bring them up to date and in line with current requirements.

Revenue Act of 1978 Section 530 of the Act provides full "safe harbor" relief from all employment back taxes to businesses if the Internal Revenue service reclassifies workers from independent contractors to employee status. To qualify, the taxpayer must satisfy three requirements: (1) show consistent treatment of workers as independent contractors; (2) apply a reasonable basis for treatment; and (3) file information returns with respect to the workers.

Revenue Act of 1987 (RA) *See* Omnibus Budget Reconciliation Act of 1987.

revenue-based relative value system (RBRVS) *See* resource-based relative value system.

revenue budget The dollar value of projected sales of products or services. These projections establish quotas that must be reached if expense budgets and profit budgets are to be realistic and achievable.

Revenue Reconciliation Act of 1990 Includes provisions for a new tax credit for barrier removal in existing buildings to specifically comply with the **Americans with Disabilities Act of 1990**.

reverse bias or discrimination **1.** In affirmative action plans, particularly with quota systems, charges by the plaintiff that unfair preferences were accorded minorities in hiring, promotion, or layoff situations. **2.** In compensation and benefits, the impact of the Revenue Reconciliation Act of 1993 which took effect in 1994. The Act reduced the compensation limit on qualified retirement plans to $150,000 from $235,840; established a new top marginal income tax rate of 36 percent for high wage earners and placed a surtax on the highest income earners; applies the 1.45 percent Medicare tax to all wages; and limits the amount that can be contributed now in any year to a 401(k) retirement savings program to $9,240. These changes go beyond the near-term reductions in benefit levels by extending them through retirement. Essentially, reverse discrimination means that lower-level employees are allowed to save a greater portion of their current income for retirement compared with highly-paid executives.

reverse contingency fee A fee paid to a contractor that represents the percentage saved the client by the services rendered. For example, an attorney representing a company in a lawsuit receives whatever percentage he or she saves the client, based on the penalties at stake.

reverse discrimination See race bias; reverse bias.

reverse mortgage A federal government sponsored program that enables elderly home owners to meet living expenses or get extra cash by tapping the equity in their property. Mortgages offered by lenders are authorized to make Federal Housing Administration (FHA) insured loans. The loans are available to homeowners 62 years of age and older. The lender disburses money to the borrower in monthly checks or a lump sum or both. The borrower keeps his or her home, and none of the loan has to be repaid until the borrower dies or vacates the property. At that time, the borrower or his or her heirs pays off the debt by selling the property or by using other resources. Also known as a *home equity conversion mortgage.*

reverse redemption Occurs when partners of airlines that sponsor **frequent flier programs,** such as car rental companies, restaurants, telephone companies, florists and the like which offer frequent flier miles, also redeem miles for their services.

reverse repurchase agreement An investment technique involving **leverage through borrowing.** These transaction involve the transfer of an underlying debt instrument to a bank, broker, or dealer in return for cash proceeds based on a percentage of the value of the security. The fund retains the right to receive interest and principal payments on the security. At an agreed upon date, the

fund repurchases the security at principal plus accrued interest.

review A critical analysis of an activity to discover achievements and deficiencies at a given point or for a specified period of time. Review emphasizes critical examination of facts.

review and analysis (R&A) A method of control used by managers to evaluate the efficiency and effectiveness of their organizations in the utilization of resources (personnel, facilities, equipment, materials, and funds) as related to progress and accomplishment. It is concerned primarily with application of the principle of **management by exception.** Typically, the R&A is presented orally to the top manager by subordinate managers and supervisors. The presentation is usually supplemented by visuals. Each subordinate presents the objectives of his or her department, section, or other element, describes accomplishments and shortfalls, analyzes the findings, and makes recommendations to exploit gains and remedy deficiencies.

revocable living trust A legal document that allows the maker to transfer ownership of property to a separate entity called a **trust**, which is managed in accordance with rules established by the maker for the benefit of the beneficiaries named in the trust. The terms of a revocable trust can be changed. Revocable living trusts are used to avoid the **probate process**, probate administration fees and expenses, and legal fees associated with probate.

reward A special tangible (usually) or intangible gain given in return for something done or received to repay an individual or group. It can be recognition for some contribution or service to the organization or the community. Or it can be compensation for exceptional performance of duty, achievements, or service: remuneration, bonus, emolument, stipend, or honorarium. But, a reward is *not* pay, which is regular compensation for doing a job.

reward power Power that derives from the ability of a leader to provide rewards or other positive outcomes in return for compliance of followers with direction of desired behavior.

reward system A system for rewarding employees for their achievement, performance, or creative and innovative products and ideas. Includes awards and recognition such as cash bonuses, merchandise, plaques, trophies, jewelry, and certificates, and letters of appreciation and commendation.

rework Work required only to redo, repair, or remedy products or services not done properly the first time. It does not add value to the product or service.

rework rate A quality control indicator. Identifies the number of products or services that are substandard and must be reworked, fixed, or remedied as compared with the number produced initially.

rheumatoid arthritis An autoimmune disorder that affects approximately 2 million Americans, two-thirds of them women. With this condition, the body's immune system attacks the tissues lining the joints, usually in the hands, arms, and feet, causing inflammation and swelling of the tissues lining the joints as well as fatigue. Its underlying cause is unknown.

rheumatologist A medical doctor (M.D.) who specializes in the diagnosis and treatment of diseases of the muscles, bones, joints, and connective tissues, ranging from arthritis to other types of physical disabilities.

rider An addition or amendment to a legal document, such as a contact or insurance policy. For example, some long term health care insurance providers may offer coverage for **home health care** and **adult day care** benefits in addition to **nursing home** and **alternate long term health care facility** benefits for an additional premium.

rideshare A pollution-control measure mandated by the Clean Air Act Amendments of 1990. Designed to reduce carbon monoxide and ozone-producing automobile emissions by encouraging workers to share rides or work at home. Targets for reductions, calculated by dividing the number of commuters by the number of passenger vehicles in which employees arrive, vary depending on the severity of air pollution in each geographic region. Enticements used by employers include mass transit, car pool, and van pool subsidies; cab fare or preferred parking for car or van-poolers; parking fees for solo drivers; bike racks and shower facilities for employees who commute to work by bike or foot; housing benefits for employees who move closer to the work site or mass transit services; telecommuting; flexible

work hours; compressed work weeks; and **job sharing** and **job splitting**.

rigged deck approach *See* Trojan horse.

right-brained People whose right brain (the right hemisphere) is dominant. Right-brain thinking is more subjective, more feeling and emotion centered. Right-brained people are believed to have the ability to function laterally, intuitively, and creatively.

right brain management (RBM) A concept of managing, developed for the **American Management Association** Executive Effectiveness Course, that focuses on image building, communication, and especially teamwork to get managers to make a habit of "thinking for success." According to Daniel L. Araoz (management consultant and AMA Executive Course Unit Trainer), RBM is a method of enriching one's management style. RBM emphasizes the improvement of managerial effectiveness by maintaining a balance between logical (left-brained) and intuitive or imaginative (right-brained) thinking and right as contrasted with wrong or faulty management.

right of discovery **1.** In litigation, the right to ask for the other side's documentation of its position. **2.** Disclosure ordered by judicial authority of proof on an issue in dispute.

rightsizing A form of downsizing, it is a selective approach to reduce staffing to adapt to change, cut costs, improve quality and productivity, attain a competitive edge, and blunt the impact of labor shortages. In short, it is a strategy for avoiding laying off the wrong people by prioritizing jobs and tasks and targeting unnecessary work rather than focusing on people.

right-to-act Legislation pursued at both federal and state levels that would give workers more authority to refuse to perform duties they believe would put them at risk of serious injury.

right-to-know (RTK) Occupational Safety and Health Administration standards established to protect the health and safety of workers, including those in nonmanufacturing organizations, by keeping them informed of the dangerous substances with which they are working, the hazards and symptoms. Legislation directs that employers inform their employees of hazardous conditions, chemicals, vapors, and the like.

A major provision of the standard requires employee training in chemical safety.

right-to-recovery   A clause included in most insurance policies, it states that the carrier will have the right to recover from the person or organization to whom they made payments in excess of the amount necessary at the time they were made.

"right-to-sue" letter   Issued by the Equal Employment Opportunity Commission to relieve the backlog of employment discrimination cases and allow the Commission to concentrate on high-profile class-action suits while giving individual parties to pursue their charges in federal and state courts. Title VII of the 1964 Civil rights Act gives the EEOC 180 days to resolve a charge, file a suit on behalf of the complainant, or issue a right-to-sue letter. An EEOC rule states that the agency may issue such a letter "at any time prior to the expiration of 180 days" provided that certain circumstances are present. In June 1996, an Indiana federal district court (*Parker v. Noble Roman's Inc.*) ruled that the commission does not have to wait the full 180 days before it issues a right-to-sue letter.

right-to-work   Legislation underscoring the right of employees to work. Twenty-one states now have "right-to-work" membership laws that prohibit mandatory union member-ship.

The Riley Group   A directory of resources and helpful links to other Internet sites relating to employment.

ringi   A Japanese terms that expresses the concept of shared decision making.

risk avoidance   Strategies and tactics designed and implemented to avoid or eliminate financial or other risks. They include such things as policies and work rules, protective devices and clothing, and safety training.

risk contract   A Medicare option in which Medicare pays a set amount to provide for an enrollee's health care. That care includes all Medicare-covered services and, depending on the plan, may include additional services, such as prescription drugs and eyeglasses.

risk management   Corporate insurance management. It is means of coordinating the control of risks to organizational solvency caused by such fortuitous losses as fire damage, liability for injury or death, loss of goods by accidents to the carrier or embezzlement, or theft of trade secrets. Risk management is accomplished by systematic analysis of risks to company assets and profitability and the use of various techniques designed to reduce potential loss from those risks.

risk manager   The buyer and manager of liability and other forms of corporate insurance coverage. Formerly responsible only for insurance, simple loss prevention, and prediction, risk managers are now involved in risk financing, control, and assessment and cost containment in benefits health care. Frequently they have the safety director, claims manager, benefits manager, and risk analyst reporting to them.

risk of loss rule   *See* uniform coverage rule.

risk plans One of two types of managed care plans that contract with Medicare. Risk plans have "lock in" requirements, meaning that a beneficiary is usually locked into receiving all covered care through the plan or through referrals by the plan. In most cases, if the beneficiary receives services that are not authorized by the plan, neither the plan nor Medicare will pay. The only exceptions recognized by such plans are for emergency services, which may be received anywhere in the United States and for urgently needed services when the beneficiary is temporarily out of the plan's service area. Some risk plans offer another exception: for point-of-service care provided outside the plan's network, the plan pays a percentage of the charges, but subscribers are required to pay at least 20 percent of the bill in return for this flexibility.

risk rating   Used by insurance carriers to ensure fairness to all who apply for health insurance coverage, particularly those with lower health risks. Direct risk rating (also called medical underwriting) involves evaluating applicants for insurance to identify those with medical problems whose coverage is reduced or their premiums increased. Insurers may also exclude entire industries or drop specific groups of workers when their claims become large. Indirect risk rating involves the imposition of waiting periods, co-payments, payment ceilings, and the exclusion of certain procedures, tests, or drugs. The practice is condemned by some as systematic discrimination against disadvantaged minorities, older workers, and people with chronic conditions. It is lauded by others who see it as a more equitable system in which risk is assigned to the responsible individual rather than pooled among insureds.

Risk Retention Acts of 1981 and 1986 (RRA) Believed by some experts to have allowed risk retention groups (RRGs) to form and, if licensed in one state, could operate nationally without adhering to the capital and surplus standards of other states.

risk retention group (RRG) A type of alternative market company established to meet the specific needs of companies that have experienced difficulty obtaining liability insurance coverages during the liability insurance crisis of the mid-1980s. Risk retention groups service the needs of such diverse businesses as financial institutions, taxi owners, fitness centers, ski resorts, physicians, and educational institutions.

risk-sharing arrangement A managed care contract that stipulates that both the insured and the insurer share the risks and potential for gain. May involve rate guarantees depending on the size and clout of an employer's preferred provider network, the performance of the managed cared care program, inflation of medical costs, changing technology, and utilization patterns.

risk transfer In purchasing and contracting, clauses or stipulations in a contract or agreement that shift risks from one of the contracting parties to the other; for example, in leasing equipment, the contract may provide that the lessee will bear liability for third-party injury and damage resulting from a defect in the equipment.

road warrior A traveler, such as salespersons, customer service representatives, consultants, and entertainers, who makes frequent and sometimes extended business trips. May make use of high tech devices, such as cellular phones, laptop computers, and portable fax machines to communicate with clients, customers, and the home office.

Robert C. Byrd Honors Scholarship Program Expanded by the Higher Education Reauthorization Act of 1992, it is a program for high school students who have demonstrated outstanding academic achievement and show promise of continued excellence. Eligible students receive $1,500 per year for up to four years of postsecondary education;

however, the amount of the scholarship plus any other aid received cannot exceed the cost of attendance.

Robinson-Patman Act of 1936 An amendment to the **Clayton Act of 1914.** Prohibits discrimination in prices where there may be adverse competitive effects. Section 3 declares illegal certain predatory acts of price discrimination. Most other antitrust laws are enforced by civil, rather than criminal, proceedings.

Robinson v. Shell Oil Company A 1997 Supreme Court Decision which ruled that former employees must be given the same protection against retaliation as current employees and job applicants under Title VII of the Civil Rights Act of 1964. The ruling may have the effect of discouraging employers from providing information or negative references on former employees to avoid law suits under Title VII.

robotics An area of artificial intelligence. Relates to machine vision, movement, and tactile sensing (touching/grasping) devices used in repetitive or dangerous tasks in manufacturing or laboratory work. Robots invariably consist of three elements: a mechanical unit, which performs manipulative functions, a "brain" or controller, which stores instructions and data and directs the movements of the machine, and a power supply, which provides the energy to operate the machine. They are important to HR management because they are likely to replace thousands of workers and are causing a great deal of anxiety among workers and unions.

robot A reprogrammable, multifunctional manipulator designed to move material, parts, tools, or specialized devices through variable programmed motions to perform a variety of tasks.

robust Any system or item of equipment, including training equipment, such as a performance support or multimedia system, that has been designed to withstand extensive use and rough handling, such as in an industrial setting.

rock *See* cocaine.

Roe v. Wade A Supreme Court decision that established a woman's constitutional right to choose an abortion.

rogue executables Potentially destructive Java aplets and ActiveX controls that may be unwittingly downloaded by users from networks assumed to be secure.

role negotiation   A team building approach that centers on the work a group is charged to perform. It typically begins at the upper management level, but it can be launched with any group. Significant changes in work group effectiveness occur when two or more members agree to change their behavior in exchange for some specific change on the part of others

role playing   A laboratory method of instruction that involves the spontaneous dramatization or acting out of a situation by two or more individuals under the direction of an instructor. The dialogue grows out out the situation developed by the trainees assigned to the parts. Each person acts a role as he or she feels it should be played. Other trainees serve as observers and critics. Following the enactment, the group engages in discussion.

rolfing   An alternative manipulative medical treatment that employs deep, and sometimes painful massage, to realign the body.

rolling budget   *See* continuous budgeting.

rolling year   A means of measuring leave taken by an employee under legislation such as the **Family and Medical Leave Act of 1993**. to prevent **leave stacking.** Under FMLA, employers may choose any one of four methods measured backwards from the date of an employee's request for leave: (1) a fixed 12-month period for all employees; (2) 12 months measured from the first date leave is used; (3) a calendar year; or (4) a rolling 12-month period measured backward from the date leave is used, resulting in a constantly changing (rolling) date. So, for each day an employee requests leave, the employer must "look back" 12 months and total the amount of leave the employee has taken to determine how much leave remains available, if any. Once the choice of FMLA leave policy is made, employers must give 60 days' advance notice to employees to change it, and the transition to the new policy must permit employees to retain the full benefit of 12 weeks' leave under whatever method of calculation gives employees the greatest benefit.

rollover   Transfer of funds from one account to another without tax penalty. For example, federal taxes on lump sum distributions can be deferred (or avoided) by placing them in a rollover IRA. Or if an individual is changing jobs, a rollover IRA (also called a *conduit IRA*) can serve as a temporary tax-deferred investment vehicle until the distribution is moved to the qualified plan of a new employer. Once funds are withdrawn from an IRA, the IRS allows only 60 days after receipt to reinvest assets in a new IRA. Assets not reinvested within that period are considered a taxable distribution and, if the individual has not reached age 59 1/2, are not disabled, and do not fall within certain other exemptions, there is also a 10 percent early withdrawal penalty. Only one rollover is allowed per year.

roman   **1.** The Latin alphabet used in English and European languages. **2.** Type that is upright, rather than **italic** or **cursive**.

Romer v. Evans   A U.S. Supreme Court decision of May 20, 1996 that declared illegal state and local laws that deny gays and lesbians legal protection from discrimination. The Court ruled that gays and lesbians are entitled to equal rights, as opposed to special rights that racial minorities and women are given through affirmative action programs. The decision invalidated Colorado state Constitutional Amendment 2 that proscribed legislative, executive, or judicial action at any level of state or local government designed to protect the status of persons based on their "homosexual, lesbian, or bisexual orientation, conduct, practices, or relationships." The ruling is important for three reasons: (1) it may prompt adjustments in workplace attitudes and make the workplace more open to gays and lesbians; (2) it may prod companies to draft sexual orientation, anti-discrimination policies; and (3) it may improve the chances of Congress passing legislation making it illegal to discriminate in the workplace based on sexual orientation. In holding that homosexuality cannot be singled out for disfavorable treatment, the Court contradicts a decision pronounced in 1986 (Bowers v. Hardwick, 478 U. S. 186) which ruled that sodomy is illegal.

room audio   The sound equipment in a classroom or meeting room. It consists of microphones, speakers, and control equipment.

room configurations   Room layouts for meetings and conferences. *See* classroom configuration; conference configuration;

roundtable configuration; theater/auditorium configuration.

rooming list   A list of the names of guests with reservations furnished to the hotel by the corporate meeting manager at least two weeks in advance of arrival.

room rates   *See* continental plan; day rate; European plan; flat rate; full American plan; modified American plan; rack rate; run of the house rate.

room types   *See* adjoining rooms; cabana; concierge level; connecting rooms; convertible room; double; double/double; duplex; efficiency; hospitality room; hospitality suite; junior suite; king; lanai; Murphy bed; parlor; queen; sample; single; studio; suite; twin.

Rorschach Test   Rorschach Personality Assessment, a test used by therapists. Devised in 1921 by Hermann Rorschach, a Swiss psychiatrist, as a means of detecting fundamental personality characteristics, although it does provide some information about the testee's intellect. The testee is shown ten cards on each of which is a complex standard "inkblot" image with two symmetrical halves. Five of the cards are dark gray but with many different shadings; two are dark gray and red; three are multicolored. The testee is asked to state what he or she sees in each of the relatively formless blots, what it looks like, what it makes him or her think of, or what it suggests — and thereby reveals fundamental traits and dominant trends in his or her personality. What the individual perceives and expresses provides the material the psychologist or psychiatrist uses to determine the underlying conflicts against which the testee's symptoms have been constructed as a means of defense.

rotation-group technique   A group technique of experimentation in which groups of subjects (if possible, parallel or equivalent) are exchanged at intervals in terms of the methods or procedures followed. For example, one group of English-as-a-second-language trainees might begin instruction in reading, using the whole word recognition method, while a parallel group would follow the phonetic approach. Then at intervals of one month the two groups would exchange methods. A major limitation of the method lies in the carry-over effect from one instructional method to another, making it difficult to determine whether achievement at the end of a particular month is due to the "whole" method, the phonics method, or a blending of both.

rotator   An employee who works changing shifts; e.g, changing periodically from 7 to 3, to 3 to 11, and 11 to 7 (graveyard shift). Such schedules are believed to disturb circadian rhythms (the body clock), increase stress in employees at work and at home, and result in fatigue, health problems, irritability, reduced job performance, lower productivity, and higher accident rates.

rote learning   A learning strategy used by humans (and to some degree by learning machines). It involves memorizing information without regard to its meaning.

roundtable configuration   One of the basic types of room layouts used for small group meetings and conferences. Includes one or more round tables and chairs for 6 to 8 participants.

round-trip fare   A discounted fare sometimes offered for travel to and return from a singe destination.

router   A device that connects two or more computer networks by the most efficient route. Can handle multiple **protocols** by sending data between dissimilar networks.

routine services/care   Health care services provided periodically to prevent illnesses. Typically include **routine physical examinations**, diagnostic laboratory tests, including pap smears and X-rays, prostate cancer screening, colorectal cancer screening, and mammograms.

routine physical examination   A physical examination, X-ray, laboratory, or other test made on a recurring (annual or semi-annual) basis rather than triggered by symptoms of illness, disease, or injury.

Rowan plan   A type of incentive plan in which worker payments were based on a formula that increased bonus amounts at a decreasing rate as productivity increased. Not in common use today.

Rucker plan   A plan developed by Allen W. Rucker in the 1930s to improve cost management and cost reduction by emphasizing employee involvement through suggestion systems, committees, improved communication, and a bonus plan and the sharing of results with employees.

rug ranking   A colloquial term for compensation policies that determine the pay of secretaries based on the level of the executive or managers they serve, rather than on performance — the higher the rank of the executive or manager (and the more expensive the rug decorating his or her floor), the higher the secretary's salary.

rule   **1.** A uniform and specific statement of a standard of conduct, action, or usage that is mandatory and enforceable. Rules require predetermined and specified courses of action or nonaction in a particular set of circumstances. Rules are prescriptive or proscriptive; they do not permit discretion. Examples are safety rules. **2.** In typography, an element of print in the form of a line.

rule against perpetuities   A common clause in a trust stating that property interest must vest or become current within a period of time defined as the lifetime of all people currently living 0 plus 21 years. Originated in English law to prevent property from being entangled forever in a trust.

Rule No. 106   *See* FASB Rule No. 106.

Rule of Seven   If you want your prospect to take action and buy what you're selling, you must connect with him or her a minimum of seven times within an 18 month period. A rule formulated by Dr. Jeffrey Lant, marketing expert.

Rule of 45   A **vesting schedule** based on age and years of service. Provides 50 percent vesting for an employee with at least 5 years of service when his or her age and years of service add up to 45, plus 10 percent for each year thereafter.

Rule of 72   In investment, a simple formula used to determine how long (in years) it will take for an investment to double in value, assuming that earnings are paid annually and are reinvested in the same account. It is calculated by dividing the number 72 by the stated interest rate.

Rule of 75   In early retirement programs, where the basis for eligibility is established as any combination of age and years of service totaling 75 or more.

rule of thumb   A conventional or customary and non-scientific approach to decision-making or the solution of a problem.

Rule 240   A regulation that is a part of major airlines' Contracts of Carriage. It spells out what the carrier will do for passengers when a flight is delayed, rerouted, or canceled. Although airlines have their own criteria, in most cases they will place customers on competitors' flights to get them to their destination on time

runaround   In desktop publishing, type set to fit around an illustration, a box, or an irregular shape.

run chart   *See* line chart.

running head   In desktop publishing, a book or chapter title that is repeated at the top of every page.

run-of-the-house rate   An agreed upon rate for group accommodations for all available rooms except suites in a hotel or other property.

rural health clinic   A specially qualified outpatient facility located in an area designated as rural, where there is a shortage of health care or rehabilitation practitioners or services. Medicare pays for services provided in these facilities by physicians, nurse practitioners, doctor assistants, nurse midwives, clinical psychologists, and social workers that are a part of the clinic.

Russian (butler)   The highest (and most expensive) level of meal service. Servers present the food on a platter, and guests serve themselves. Usually reserved for banquets and other special occasions.

S

S	Score. *See* test scores.
SAA	**1.** Standards of application architecture. **2.** Sherman Anti-trust Act of 1890.
SAD	Seasonal affective disorder.
SADLs	Significant activities of daily living.
SALT	Society of Applied Learning Technology.
SAP	**1.** Substance abuse professional. **2.** Systems, applications, and products.
SAR	**1.** Stock appreciation rights. **2.** Summary annual report.
SARA	Superfund Amendments and Reauthorization Act of 1986.
SARSEP	Salary reduction simplified employee pension.
SAS	Systems applications software.
SAT	**1.** Scholastic Achievement Test. **2.** Scholastic Assessment Test. **3.** Systems Approach to Training.
SBA	Small Business Administration.
SBIC	Small business investment company.
SBO	Small business organization.
SBP	Survivor benefit plan.
SBS	Sick building syndrome.
SCANS	Secretary's Commission on Achieving Necessary Skills
SCMP	Society of Corporate Meeting Professionals.
SCORE	Service Corps of Retired Executives.
SCSI	Small-computer standard interface.
SD	Standard deviation.
SDA	Service delivery area.
SDI	Selective dissemination of information.
SDWT	Self-directed work team.
SE	**1.** Standard error. **2.** Self-efficacy.
SEC	Securities and Exchange Commission.
SEG	Special effects generator.
SEIU	Service Employees International Union.
SE meas	Standard error of measurement.
SEP	Simplified employee pension.
SEPPA	Single Employer Pension Plan Amendments Act of 1986.
SERCs	State Emergency Response Commissions.
SERP	Supplemental executive retirement plans.
SFA	Student financial aid.
SG&A	Selling, General, and Administrative Expenses.
SGLI	Servicemembers Group Life Insurance.
SHHH	Self Help for Hard of Hearing People, Inc.
SHMO	Social health maintenance organization.
SGMP	Society of Government Meeting Professionals.
SHRM	Society for Human Resource Management.
SHRP	Society of Human Resource Professionals.
SIBP	Self-insured benefits plan.
SIC	*See* U.S. Standard Industrial Classification System.
SIECUS	Sexuality Information & Education Council of the United States.
SIETAR	The Society for Intercultural Education, Training and Research (International).

SIG   Self-insurance group.
SIIA   Self-Insurance Institute of
             America, Inc.
SIM   Single Internal Market.
SIMPLE   Savings Incentive Match Plan for
             Employees.
SITE   Society of Incentive & Travel
             Executives.
SKA   Skills, knowledge, and
             attitudes.
SLA   Special Libraries Association.
SLIP   Serial Line Internet Protocol.
SLMA   Student Loan Marketing
             Association.
SLMB   Specified low-income Medicare
             beneficiary.
SLOB   Separate line of business.
SLS   Supplemental Loans for
             Students.
SMA   Self-managed account.
S.M.D.I. Society for Muscular Dystrophy
             Information, International.
SME   1. Society of Manufacturing
             Engineers. 2. Subject-matter
             expert.
SMERF   Social, military, educational,
             religious, and fraternal.
SMHMO   Staff model health maintenance
             organization.
SMOCTA   Service Members Occupational
             Conversion and Training Act of
             1993.
SMPTE   Society of Motion Picture and
             Television Engineers.
SMWIA   Sheet Metal Workers' Interna-
             tional Association.
SMWT   Self-managed work team.
SNF   Skilled nursing facility.
SNO   The Society for Nonprofit
             Organizations.
SOP   Standing operating procedure.
SOW   Statement of work.
SPBA   Society of Professional Benefit
             Administrators.
SPC   Statistical process control.
SPD   Summary plan description.
SPHR   Senior Professional in Human
             Resources.

SPIMM   Self-paced interactive
             multimedia.
SQG   Small quantity generator.
SQL   Structured query language.
SRMC   Society of Risk Management
             Consultants.
S-R theory Stimulus-response theory.
SSA   Social Security Act of 1935.
SSCRA   Soldiers and Sailors Civil Relief
             Act of 1991.
SSI   Supplemental Security Income.
SSO   Second surgical opinion.
STAG   Society of Travel Agents in
             Government.
STC   1. Short-time compensation.
             2. Society for Technical
             Communication.
STD   1. Sexually transmitted disease.
             2. Short-term disability.
STEPS   Severance trust executive plans.
STP   Satellite ticket printer.
STS   Sociotechnical system.
SUB   Supplemental unemployment
             benefits.
SUI   State Unemployment Insurance.
SV   Still video.
SVD   Simultaneous voice and data.
SW   Software.
SWAP   Short wavelength autoperimetry.
SYSOP   System operator.
16   Section 16, Securities Exchange
             Act of 1991.

sabbatical 1. In business and industry, a fringe benefit offered to employees by some companies to combat job burnout, promote personal growth, teach, pursue advanced training, or perform public service. Employees on sabbatical receive full pay and benefits for from 6 to 12 weeks and with a frequency range from once every four years to once in a career. 2. In education, a leave of absence sometimes granted to members of college and university faculties every seventh year for rest, travel, or research for either a semester at full pay or a full academic year at half pay.

sabbatical leave   An incentive plan commonly used by colleges and universities (and by a growing number of corporations) to foster staff longevity, commitment, and development and prevent **burnout**. Typically awarded after six years of continuous and superior service, employees are encouraged to pursue new, but job-related, courses of study or other developmental activities, such as teaching or work in a nonprofit organization. Awardees are paid salary and benefits for up to a full year and typically return to the same jobs at the end of the leave.

Sabre In travel management, A **computer reservation system** owned by American Airlines. Also provides assistance on site and by phone in linking systems, including electronic mail systems and local area networks.

Safe fax See fax security.

Safe Harbor Regulations Regulations issued by the Department of Labor on September 3, 1987 to interpret the requirements of Section 404(c) of the **Employee Retirement Income Security Act of 1974.** In brief, the regulations offer employers relief from fiduciary responsibility for investment performance if they offer participants in individual account plans a range of investment options, an opportunity to invest the assets in his or her account in a "safe" investment, and control over assets.

safe harbor relief See Revenue Act of 1978.

Safety and Health Improvement and Regulatory Reform Act of 1995
Legislation that would radically change the **Occupational Safety and Health Administration.** Its main provisions: (1) reserves at last 50 percent of OSHA funds for consultation, training, education, and compliance assistance programs; (2) expands small business programs; (3) makes the Voluntary Protection Program a central part of OSHA's mission and program; (4) creates a Voluntary Compliance Program, which allows certified individuals to conduct advisory safety and health review for employers; (4) protects and encourages employee participation committees or plans that address safety and health issues; (5) encourages the adoption of voluntary substance abuse programs; (6) strengthens antidiscrimination provisions; (7) encourages employers to conduct internal safety and health audits without OSHA penalties; (8) amends the **Occupational Safety and Health Act of 1970** to include regulatory impact, risk assessment, and cost benefit reform; and (9) requires risk assessment and cost-benefit analysis to be industry-specific.

safety needs Human needs for safety from the dangers of the environment.

safety, protection, and security services
Programs designed to protect employees from the devastating effects of accidents, injuries, and personal attacks and the organization from the loss of productive time, payments for treatment and time away from the job, increased insurance premiums, loss due to theft, pilferage, industrial espionage, sabotage, or unauthorized disclosure, and the expenses that result from litigation. Protective strategies include visitor identification and control, area entry and exit control, material and document control, vehicle control, conduct of inspections and inventories, use of alarm systems and security devices, guard surveillance, safes, vaults, key control, training, and so on.

safety training Training provided to employees, clients, and customers to promote their concern for safe and healthful working conditions, reduce accidents, injuries, and illnesses by detecting, analyzing, and correcting unsafe or unhealthful conditions, ensure compliance with federal, state, industry, insurance, and enterprise rules, regulations, requirements, and practices, reduce the threat of litigation, and train people in safety procedures, practices, and the use of safety equipment. Strategies, processes, and techniques include formal training involving demonstrations and the use of multimedia, safety meetings and conferences, safety publications, bulletins, and posters, safety contests, signs, and slogans, example of supervisors, immediate correction of errors, and the elimination of hazards.

salaried planner A financial or other type of planner who receives compensation from his or her company, rather than from the specific products or services they sell.

salaried workers In general, defined by the law as executives and administrative and professional employees, people who receive predetermined annual pay that isn't affected by the quantity or quality of the work performed.

salary-based deductible Health care coverage that ties the deductible to salary — to ability to pay. That is, the deductible increases for those who can afford to pay and decreases for those who cannot.

salary compression A consequence of inflation. Symptoms are higher salaries for new hires than for current workers, and hourly pay increases for workers that have matched or overtaken supervisory compensation levels.

salary continuation plan *See* supplemental executive retirement plan.

salary grade A level of compensation, usually a **salary range** and not an individual amount, established for a group of similar jobs.

salary range A band of salaries, from minimum to maximum, set for a specific job.

salary reduction plan *See* 401K plan.

salary reduction simplified employee pension (SARSEP) A retirement plan in which employees were allowed to contribute to their retirement through an IRA. The **Small Business Job Protection Act of 1996** terminated that option. This means that a tax exempt employer will not be able to establish an employee deferral-only plan without following the full **Section 401(k)** approach.

salary survey *See* area wage survey; professional, administrative, technical, and clerical survey.

sales and dealer training Training provided to the sales force, franchisees, and dealers to teach them what they need to know about the products and services they market and sell, how to demonstrate the effectiveness of their products and services, how to conduct their business, and help them develop the attitudes, skills, and habits they need to influence prospects and customers to make decisions to buy.

sales budget Displays projected sales by month, product line, and geographic areas.

sales manager The hotel functionary who books meetings, blocks sleeping rooms, reserves meeting space, and negotiates rates.

sales meeting A meeting of marketing and sales personnel convened to develop sales forecasts, marketing and sales strategies, and motivate and urge personnel to renewed effort.

sales representative *See* director of sales.

Sallie Mae *See* Student Loan Marketing Association.

salting A tactic of labor unions in which non-union workplaces are infiltrated in order to organize them. Protected by federal labor law.

"same actor" inference A postulate or ground rule adopted in the 1st, 4th, 6th, and 7th U.S. Circuit Courts of Appeals as a defense to a claim of age discrimination. The inference recognizes that it would be illogical for an employer to hire a person who is a member of a **protected class** and later fire the employee because of membership in that class.

same day surgery In health care utilization management, requiring a member who is to be hospitalized on an elective basis to undergo routine preoperative tests as an outpatient and admission on the day the surgery is to be performed.

sample **1.** In meeting management, a hotel room used solely for display of merchandise. It may or may not have sleeping facilities. **2.** In a research study, a relatively small number of cases drawn from the **population**.

sandbagging Where compensation of executive compensation is directly tied to business plans, the unethical practice of establishing a plan that is easily achieved in order to win a large raise or bonus.

sandwiched employee An employee sandwiched between two generations. **1.** The post-World War II generation of employees who are having children late in their lives just at the time they're being called on to take care of their aging parents. **2.** Adults who have reared their own children, now gone and on their own, who suddenly find themselves responsible for the care of a dependent parent or other relative.

sandwiched generation *See* sandwiched employee.

sanity track People who have opted for a normal, 40-hour work week, instead of six 10-hour days, to allow them to balance their personal and professional lives. Coined by Harvard Business School Professor Lawrence Schlesinger.

satellite ticket printer Computer reservation system-issued ticketing machines for remote output of tickets, usually at corporate offices.

satisfiers Factors related to a job's intrinsic content, such as achievement, advancement, and a feeling of challenge and personal growth.

satellite In **telecommuting,** a small office designed to accommodate only a few employees and is usually located near their homes.

satellite communications A means of linking remote sites with corporate mainframe computers and conferencing facilities, called

very small aperature terminal systems, that provide up to 56-**Kbps** interactive service.

satellite ticket printer (STP) In travel management, a device that prints travel documents, such as tickets and itineraries, on ticket stock. Found in airports, offices, and some hotel lobbies.

satisfactory academic progress Under federal student aid programs, to be eligible for aid, an individual must meet the school's written standard of acceptable progress toward a degree or certificate.

Saturn Project A General Motors labor-management experimental program involving total redesign of G.E.'s traditional manufacturing plant, changes in management style and focus, downsizing, a team-based management system, redesigned jobs and tasks, and automation.

sauna A therapy of Finnish origin that uses dry heat in a wood-lined room to sweat out impurities in the body. A steam room is similar but uses wet heat.

savings and thrift plan A type of **defined contribution plan** in which an employee's contributions to a pension plan are matched in whole or in part by the employer.

Savings Incentive Match Plan for Employees (SIMPLE) A part of the Minimum Wage Bill that became effective January 1, 1997. Allows businesses with 100 or fewer employees to establish a retirement plan option funded by employer contributions and allows for employee elective salary reduction contributions of up to $6,000 annually on a pre tax basis and thereby reduce their taxable income. Savings grow tax-deferred up to withdrawal. Employers must either match up to 3 percent of participating employees' compensation or make non-elective contributions of 2 percent of each employee's compensation on behalf of eligible employees. Such contributions are tax-deductible for employers.

savings plan A type of pension plan in which employees set aside a fixed percentage of their weekly wages or salary for their retirement; the company usually matches from 50 to 100 percent of the employee's contribution.

scalable font A **font** that can be enlarged or reduced to any size, whether that size has been installed in the system or not. It will print smooth at the selected size even if it looks ragged on the screen.

scalar principle A principle of organization. States that there must be a hierarchical structure in every organization which clearly depicts superior-subordinate, authority-accountability, and direction-reporting relationships.

scaled scores A procedure used to to convert the actual raw scores (number correct) on different forms of a test to a uniform scale following **equating.** This procedure ensures that all testees are required to demonstrate the same level of ability to achieve a passing score on the test regardless of whether or not they took an easier or more difficult form of the test.

scam trip One classification of free trips to resort areas taken by bogus users of incentive travel or unethical travel agents who steal free vacations by pretending that they are potential clients. Attributed to Michael J. Hurwitz, president of the Society of Incentive Travel Executives.

Scanlon Plan A team approach to management initiated in the late 1940s similar to quality circles. It gives employees a financial share in the productivity gains of an organization. Shares depend on cost reductions achieved. Proposals for cost-cutting are screened by committees prior to their implementation.

scanner A peripheral mechanism that automatically transfers information, from text to graphics, into the computer without need for keyboarding. It is essentially a tiny camera that converts optical information into digital electronic data that can be interpreted and manipulated by a computer. The scanner software converts the digital image into a form that various applications programs can use. Scanners are most often used to capture illustrations for insertion into other documents. They may produce black-and-white output (even from color originals) or full color.

scanning 1. In self-development, the process of skimming research reports, books, professional and technical magazines, newspapers, advertisements, catalogs, brochures, and the like (including materials that are only vaguely related or totally foreign to the reader's areas of interest and competence) to gain insight into what others are doing and thinking. **2.** In forecasting, a surveillance technique that involves observation of changes and developments in an area of interest to identify early-on potentially important impacts on the organization.

scatter diagram A quality control tool. The product of plotting a series of numbers representing measures or readings on two variables on the x- and y-axes of a graph. The objective is to discover relationships or correlation (positive or negative), if any, (but not cause-and-effect) between the two variables.

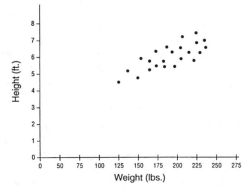

Weight (lbs.)

scattergram A tool used to compare salaries and determine the internal equity and effectiveness of a compensation program. Shows maximum, minimum, and actual salaries and indicates higher and lower than maximum and minimum by using red and green circles.

scenario 1. An integrative forecasting technique involving the development of "stories" or "scripts" about future real world conditions. Scenarios add depth and breadth to decisions about future plans and operations because they can present the interactions of several factors and developments in an integrated way. **2.** An outline or synopsis of a dramatization or the plot of a video program prepared prior to production showing the development of the production scene by scene.

schedule A plan for allocating people, time, space, facilities, equipment, and materials to various activities and projects, monitoring the progress of those activities and projects, and insuring the smooth operation of the organization or program. Examples are work schedules, production schedules, annual schedules of courses, classes, and programs, and weekly training schedules.

schedule interview An interview in which every respondent is asked for precisely the same information. The interviewer reads the

questions from a prepared schedule to insure consistency in the wording and sequence of questions.

schizophrenia A serious mental disease that interferes with the brain's ability to think clearly and logically — a disorder of thought processes — that can include confused or illogical thinking, delusions, extreme withdrawal, hallucinations, or dulled or inappropriate feelings. Frequently results in withdrawal of the individual's interest in other people.

Scholastic Aptitude Test (SAT) A two and one-half hour multiple choice examination designed by the Educational Testing Service of Princeton, New Jersey to measure reasoning skills, mathematics and verbal, and readiness for college entrance. The maximum score on each of the two parts of the test is 800. Until recently, most colleges required applicants to submit SAT scores. Criticism of the test has centered on the charge that the tests contain built-in cultural and class biases and therefore discriminate against minorities.

Scholastic Assessment Test (SAT) Replaced the **Scholastic Aptitude Test** in March 1994. Scores on the verbal and mathematics portions of the SAT range from 200 to 800, with 500 representing the average score, although test norms are now based on a reference group of 1 million students who graduated from high school in 1990 rather than the original grading scale of 1941 which was based on the results of 10,000 testees. These tests result in scores that are as many as 100 points higher than earlier scores because of adjustments made in the scoring system made to reflect more accurately the larger, more diverse student population of today.

school delivery standards A term included in the the House of Representatives' bill on restructuring the public schools that makes it incumbent on the education community to heed. School delivery standards, as defined by the House, are those necessary to ensure "that each student in a school has a fair opportunity to achieve the knowledge and skills set out in the national content standards and work force readiness standards." Evidence of "fair opportunity" includes: (1) that the school has formally adopted a curriculum that is in line with national standards; (2) that the curriculum is being taught in classrooms; (3) that teachers understand the curriculum and are able to teach it; (4) that teachers have access to curricular materials necessary for the mastery of the standards; (5) that the school has instructional methods and policies in place to promote mastery by all students; (6) that administrators are well prepared; (7) that schools have the libraries and laboratories necessary for learning; and (8) that the foregoing indicators will be consistent with state policies.

school holiday care A form of family and work program, a fringe benefit. The company provides care for school-age children when schools are not is session (including summer vacation).

school matching A service offered to employees as a benefit by a growing number of companies. The service helps employees find schools that match the needs of their children. Initially offered to families who were relocating and wanted to buy homes in an area with good schools, the service is now offered to all employees to enhance recruitment, retention, and morale.

School to Work Opportunities Act of 1994 Legislation designed to improve the transition from school to jobs for the approximately 75 percent of high school students who do not go on to college. The bill (1) establishes a national system of community partnerships among the education, business, and government sectors to provide apprenticeship training for high school juniors and seniors; (2) provides federal seed money to develop combined academic programs and supervised work experiences to give students "career majors"; (3) requires each school-to-work program to contain work-based learning in the form of job training and paid work experience to develop job skills; and (4) incorporates a program of study based on academic and job skills standards identified under the **Goals 2000: Educate America Act of 1994.** The program is jointly administered by the U.S. Departments of Labor and Education.

scientific management Emphasizes the need to evaluate each job scientifically to determine the best method of performing it. Attributed to Frederick Taylor.

scientist and engineer development Programs conducted to restore, refresh, and update the professional and technical vitality of scientists and engineers, improve their productivity, retrain personnel whose skills and knowledge have become obsolescent or unneeded in the organization, extend their productive life, and promote and support learning and growth. Delivery systems include formal and informal communication networks among professionals within and outside the organization, attendance at programs and conferences sponsored by professional societies, enterprise-sponsored seminars, symposia, workshops; lectures, and tutorials, laboratory observation and experimentation, industrial, government and university exchange programs, and sabbatical leaves for study and research.

scleroderma An arthritis-related condition, characterized by thickening of the skin. It may also affect joints, blood vessels, and internal organs. Affects more than 50,000 Americans.

score Impressing or indenting a mark on paper with a string or rule to make folding easier.

S corporation A special tax designation applied for by corporations that are already in existence. The status eliminates federal corporate income taxes and avoids double taxation. S corporations must be domestic, permit only one class of stock, and require that stockholders be U.S. citizens. S corporations can have up to 75 stockholders (formerly only 35), and they can now include individuals, estates, one-person trusts, and tax exempt entities.

Scotch hose An alternative medical treatment that involves the use of high-pressure hoses that alternate hot and cold water. Used to improve circulation.

screen In desktop publishing, the dot pattern in a separation, usually expressed as the number of lines per inch.

screening The first step in the process of reviewing applicants for positions. It involves review of application forms and résumés, telephone checks to verify information supplied by the candidate, the administration, scoring, and analysis of psychological tests [aptitude, job knowledge, achievement, and (sometimes) personality and temperament tests], analysis of self-reports, interviews, visits and observation, medical exams, and assessment centers.

screening test One of two types of urine drug detection tests. A screening test is less expensive, less time consuming, and less accurate than a **confirmatory test**, which is conducted when positive results occur.

screen linking   A tool featured by some human resources and other software that automatically presents in correct sequence all of the screens needed to complete a particular task. When one screen is completed, the next one appears.

script   **1.** A carefully developed, painstakingly worded, written and tested monologue or dialogue used by the "talent" or actors in a live or recorded dramatization or in making telemarketing calls. **2.** In desktop publishing, type designed to resemble handwriting or writing with a brush. Also called *cursive.*

scuzzy   A disk that uses the **small computer interface**, an industry standard way for peripheral devices to communicate with small computers.

sealed bid   An organization's bid for a contract that is sealed and opened along with all other bids at a set time and place to preserve the element of competition.

search   In database management, examining a data file to locate records that meet a specific set of criteria.

search engine   An electronic directory on the **World Wide Web** that searches for documents, pages, or sites indexed by subject, key words, or concepts. Examples are AltaVista, Lycos, WebCrawler, and Yahoo!.

searches   See Web searches.

search firm   An organization or consultant who has employers as clients. Working on a retainer, hourly, daily, or fixed-fee basis, the firm searches for qualified candidates for key professional, scientist, engineer, and managerial openings and sometimes recommends appropriate compensation packages. Also called *headhunters.*

search key   One or more characters of information which are to be compared with file keys to locate matches.

seasonal affective disorder (SAD)
A phenomenon associated with the impact of the amount of daylight on the mental state of workers. In winter, when light is less intense and of shorter duration, workers often feel depressed, irritable, and unable to concentrate.

Seattle foot   A flexible, life-like prosthesis for amputees that allows considerable freedom of movement — including such activities as basketball, baseball, and golf.

secondary memory   Computer devices, such as floppy disks, hard drives, and the circuitry that controls them. Secondary memory is used for data storage, providing a repository for the information that programs process and produce.

secondary method *See* alternative method.

secondary payer rules   Federal government rules that give private insurers primary coverage responsibility for certain beneficiaries, resulting in substantial savings to Medicare.

secondary research   Research studies conducted by individuals or organizations that make use of materials and research findings found in journal articles and other published documents.

second-party registration   Occurs when a corporation or company audits its own suppliers for conformance to international quality standards.

second surgical opinion (SSO)   An opinion provided by an independent physician, a requirement of many company medical and health benefits plans, such as health maintenance organizations, designed to prevent unnecessary surgery or other therapy or reduce or contain costs.

second-to-die life insurance   A policy that provides coverage for both spouses under one policy, with the death benefit paid at the time of the death of the second of the two insured. Thus, the insurance payments enable the survivor to avoid the forced sale of assets to pay estate taxes, administrative expenses, probate charges, and executor fees.

Secretary's Commission on Achieving Necessary Skills (SCANS)   A 31-member commission formed by the Secretary of Labor in 1990 to identify the skills needed by employees in a high-performance workplace. The report of the commission, "Learning a Living: A Blueprint for High Performance," published in 1992, called for a partnership of employers, schools, parents, and government to make education more relevant to the needs of the future work force. Five critical skills were identified: (1) ability to use resources (time, money, materials, space, and staff); (2) interpersonal skills to work with people with diverse backgrounds (in team building, teaching, customer relations, leadership, and negotiations); (3) acquiring and evaluating data; (4) understanding social, organizational, and technological systems;

and (5) selecting and maintaining technological tools. The Commission emphasized (The SCANS Know-How) that workers must also be proficient in basic competencies: reading, writing, mathematics, speaking, listening, and thinking skills for decision making, problem solving, and reasoning. In addition, the Commission identified personal qualities, such as responsibility, self-esteem, sociability, and integrity as necessary attributes.

secret benefit Enacted by the Congress in 1988, known as the **Qualified Medicare Beneficiary Program**. It provides protection against Medicare out-of-pocket expenses for low-income elderly and disabled persons. In many instances, the government has failed to make the rules known to eligibles, resulting in needless Medicare premium deductions from Social Security checks.

Section 16, Securities Exchange Act of 1991
Effected changes in the Act of 1934. Made it mandatory for corporate insiders to file reports of a stock purchase or sell in a timely manner as follows: Form 3, to designate an individual who becomes an insider and must comply with insider report requirements; Form 4, to be filed within 10 days after the end of the month, to report all non-exempt transactions that have liability attached to them; and Form 5, to be filed within 45 days of the close of a fiscal year, to report stock splits, deferred transactions, and gifts. Effective May 1, 1991.

Section 44, Internal Revenue Code
Allows an eligible small business (with annual gross receipts under $1 million) to elect a nonrefundable tax credit equal to 50 percent of the amount of eligible disability access expenditures for any tax year between $259 and $10,250; consequently the maximum amount of the credit for any taxable year is $5,000. An "eligible small business" is defined as any person or corporation that (1) had gross receipts (reduced by returns and allowances) for the preceding taxable year that did not exceed $1 million or (2) had no more than 30 full-time employees, and (3) elects the application of the disabled access credit for the tax year. An employee is considered full time if employed at least 30 hours per week for 20 or more calendar weeks in the tax year. Eligible access expenditures include amounts paid or incurred: (1) to remove architectural, communication, physical, or transportation barriers; (2) to

provide qualified interpreters or other means of making aurally delivered materials available to individuals with hearing impairments; (3) to provide qualified readers, taped texts, and other methods of making visually delivered materials available to individuals with visual impairments; (4) to acquire or modify equipment or devices for individuals with disabilities; or (5) to provide other similar services, modifications, materials, or equipment.

Section 89, Internal Revenue Code
A provision of the **Tax Reform Act of 1986,** which made benefits received by employees taxable unless employer-provided benefit plans met certain nondiscrimination requirements set out by the IRS as Section 89, Internal Revenue Code. The intent of the Act was to avoid giving tax-favored status to benefit plans that benefit only highly paid employees. The Act was repealed in 1989. As a consequence, nondiscrimination and qualification rules were completely repealed, the pre-Tax Reform Act nondiscrimination rules for group term life insurance plans, self-insured medical plans, and cafeteria plans were restored, nondiscrimination rules for dependent care assistance plans, with certain changes, was retained, and relief from the separate-line-of-business rules that apply to qualified pension and profit sharing plans was provided. Specifically, employers will have to comply with several restored parts of the Internal Revenue Code subject to nondiscrimination rules. They include Section 79 group term life policies, Section 105(h) self-insured medical reimbursement plans, Section 129 dependent care assistance programs, Section 125 cafeteria plans, and Section 505(b) benefits provided through **voluntary employees' beneficiary association** trusts.

Section 125, Internal Revenue Code
A section of the Internal Revenue Code covering flexible spending accounts (FSAs) or "cafeteria style" benefits plans, in which employees can choose from several different benefits to make up largely individualized benefits packages. Two types of flexible spending accounts may be established: health care FSAs or dependent care FSAs. FSAs begin when an employee authorizes contributions to one or both types of accounts. Contributions to these accounts are tax-exempt for all federal and most state and local taxes.

Section 127, Internal Revenue Code

An on again, off again rule. Since its enactment by Congress, Section 127 (Employee Educational Assistance) has expired and been reauthorized several times. It made employer-provided tuition reimbursement for tuition, books, or fees for non-job-related undergraduate and graduate courses a tax-free benefit. EEA allows workers to deduct employer-paid tuition reimbursements from their gross income. In 1996, Congress approved measures to restore the exclusion to cover the period from January 1, 1995 through May 31, 1997. However, tuition for graduate level courses that began after June 30, 1996 will be taxed as income. For undergraduates, up to $5,250 in employer-provided tuition reimbursement remains tax free.

Section 162(k), Internal Revenue Code

Specifies health insurance continuation requirements.

Section 162(m), Internal Revenue Code

Imposes a $1 million deduction limit on compensation received by the chief executive officer and the next four highest-paid officers of publicly-held corporations. The rule exempts compensation, including amounts received from stock options that qualifies as being "performance based."

Section 190, Internal Revenue Code

Allows an annual tax deduction of up to $15,000 by any taxpayer who removes barriers to people with disabilities in a place where a business or trade is conducted, including places of public accommodation and transportation systems. The deduction applies only to the removal of barriers at existing places of business or trade. Areas covered include controls, doors and stairways, elevators, entrances, floors, grading, hazards, identification, parking lots, public telephones, ramps, toilet rooms, walks, warning signals, and water fountains. An additional provision covers removal of other substantial barriers to the access or use of a facility or public transportation vehicle or a barrier to one or more classes of people (such as blind or deaf persons or individuals using wheelchairs). To qualify for the deduction, the modification must conform with design standards issued by the **U.S. Architectural and Transportation Barriers Compliance Board** and the **Uniform Federal Accessibility Standard.**

Section 401 (a)(4), Internal Revenue Code

Regulations governing retirement plan discrimination released in September 1991. Originally scheduled to be effective January 1, 1992, implementation of the rules was postponed to the start of the plan year beginning on or after January 1, 1994.

Section 401(a)(5)

Regulation governing retirement plans (permitted disparity) that became effective at the start of the retirement plan year beginning on or after January 1, 1994.

Section 401(a)(17), Internal Revenue Code

Regulation setting a $200,000 annual limit on compensation that became effective on the start of the plan year beginning on or after January 1, 1994.

Section 401(a)(26), Internal Revenue Code

See Section 414(r); separate line of business regulation.

Section 401(h), Internal Revenue Code

A tax-exempt method of pre-funding for retiree medical benefits by which employers are permitted to make tax-deductible contributions (as well as interest on earnings), to retirement medical accounts. In 1989, Congress repealed a 1989 IRS ruling liberalizing the use of trusts under Section 401(h).

Section 401(k), Internal Revenue Code

Deals with employee investment plans as modified by the **Tax Reform Act of 1986, Small Business Job Protection Act of 1996,** and IRS rulings. A type of **defined contribution plan** providing retirement or salary deferral benefits, also known as cash or deferred arrangements. Beginning after December 31, 1996, any tax-exempt employer can adopt a 401(k) plan; however, state and local governments remain prohibited from maintaining such plans. Plans can be funded entirely by the employee, entirely by the employer, or jointly by both. Combined employer and employee contributions are limited to 20 percent of gross annual compensation to a maximum of $160,000, including annual employee contributions of up to $9,500 (1997) (adjusted yearly for cost of living) on a pretax basis. Employer contributions are deductible from current income, and both employer and employee contributions grow tax-deferred. Employers have the discretion to allow only employee deferrals, or to make employer matching contributions at any rate, or to make a contribution to every plan participant without regard to employee elective deferrals. Employer contributions can be subject to a vesting schedule so that employees are entitled to keep the total contribution after not more than seven years of work. All plans must be written, and annual reports must be filed. Where there are more than 100 plan participants, the law requires audits of the plan.

Section 402, Internal Revenue Code

Included in the **Unemployment Compensation Amendments Act of 1992** as a means of funding emergency unemployment benefits. Allows any portion of a distribution from a qualified pension or annuity plan or tax-sheltered annuity, other than a minimum required distribution or a distribution of equal payments over the remaining lifetime or more than 10 years to be rolled over tax-free into an **individual retirement account** or other qualified plan or annuity. Requires qualified plans to permit participants to elect to have any distribution eligible for rollover transferred directly to an eligible transferee plan designated by the participant. However, withholding is to be imposed at a rate of 20 percent on any distribution that is eligible to be rolled over but is not transferred directly to an eligible plan.

Section 403(b), Internal Revenue Code

A pension and annuity plan similar to a 401(k) plan except that it applies to not-for-profit and public organizations such as educational institutions, churches, hospitals, and others officially classified as "charitable" under Sections 501(c) (3) of the Internal Revenue Code. Elective deferrals can be made of sums up to $9,500 annually. The Small Business Job Protection Act of 1996 allows 403(b) plan participants to make more than one elective deferral each calendar year, effective retroactively to January 1, 1996. The main difference between 401(k) and 403(b) plans: the former were established as a supplement to other pension sources, while 403(b) plans were intended to be a primary provider of retirement income. Contributions are deducted from base pay in a 401(k) plan, while salary is reduced by a pre-agreed amount under a 403(b) plan.

Section 404A, Internal Revenue Code

The Code prescribes stringent rules for recognizing contributions to U.S. pension plans as tax deductible expenses. Plans must meet qualification standards and contributions must be invested in pension trust funds. Section 404A was passed by the Congress to legitimize deductions for foreign pension contributions, which formerly would not qualify under U.S. rules. In general, the Section makes tax deductible contributions eligible for U.S. recognition without application of the full U.S. qualification standards if a foreign pension plan has tax-deferred status in the foreign country. In May 1993, the IRS issued proposed regulations under Section 404A that could impact harshly on the tax treatment of foreign contributions by imposing higher taxes with retroactivity. Involvement of both the Benefits and Tax Departments of multinational corporations in determining tax deductibility appears to be imperative.

Section 404(C), Internal Revenue Code

An **Employee Retirement Income Security Act** regulation that governs qualified business retirement programs. The regulation states that if participants in a plan are allowed to make their own investment decision by "self-directing" their individual account balances, the employers are not generally liable for those investment decisions. On October 13, 1992, the Department of Labor issued new regulations for compliance with Section 404(C) which became effective for most qualified plans on January 1, 1994. In general, to comply, sponsors must provide employees with a broad range of investment choices, detailed information on investment options offered, and the opportunity to change investment funds frequently.

Section 410(b), Internal Revenue Code

Regulation covering nondiscrimination coverage ("coverage rules") that became effective at the start of the retirement plan year beginning on or after January 1, 1994. The rules require that "qualified" retirement plans must cover enough employees to meet either the "ratio percentage test," the "average benefits test," or qualify under the "separate line of business" (SLOB) exception.

Section 414(r), Internal Revenue Code

Regulation governing retirement plans (separate lines of business) that became effective at the start of the retirement plan year beginning on or after January 1, 1994. *See also* separate line of business pension regulation.

Section 414(s), Internal Revenue Code

Regulation governing retirement plans (definition of compensation) that became effective at the start of the retirement plan year beginning on or after January 1, 1994.

Section 415(b), Internal Revenue Code
A section of the Internal Revenue Code that limits the amounts paid from defined benefit plans. In the case of single benefit plans, the limit is the lesser of 100 percent of the high 3-year average pay or in 1997 $125,000 per year at the Social Security Normal Retirement Age. For individuals participating in one or more defined benefit plans and one or more defined contribution plans, there are combined plan limitations. There are also separate limits for workers participating in defined contribution plans.

Section 415(c), Internal Revenue Code
Limits the annual contribution to an individual's defined contribution account. In 1997, the maximum was $30,000.

Section 417, Internal Revenue Code
Promulgates rules for making qualified joint and survivor preretirement survivor annuity elections, including notification and consent requirements and the periods during which elections may be made and revoked.

Section 419A(f)(6)   Deals with executive compensation plans, such as severance trust executive plans and deferred income plans.

Section 422A, Internal Revenue Code
Provides favorable tax treatment for **incentive stock options,** provided that the following major requirements are met: (1) option term does not exceed 10 years; (2) option price is 100 percent of fair market value at the time of the grant; (3) specific requirements of the plan have been approved by shareholders; and (4) vesting is limited to $100,000 aggregate fair market value during any calendar year.

Section 457, Internal Revenue Code
A section of the Internal Revenue Code modified by the **Tax Reform Act of 1986**. It extended the section to cover deferred compensation plans for nongovernmental tax-exempt organizations to treat nongovernmental, tax exempt employees the same as state and local government workers for deferring income.

Section 501 (c)(9), Internal Revenue Code
The section of the Internal Revenue Code that exempts from tax entities (such as trust funds) funds that provide life, sickness, accident, or similar benefits for employees. Often used as a pre-funding method of financing

long-term disability benefits and life insurance coverage for retirees. A trust fund is created in which the employer can deposit regularly an amount actuarially calculated to be necessary to fund the claims that can be expected to arise from the benefits provided to covered employees. To be tax exempt, membership must be voluntary (not a condition of employment), the fund must be operated only to provide life, sickness, accident, or similar benefits, benefits for highly compensated employees cannot be disproportionately greater than those for other employees, and funds cannot revert to the employer upon termination of a plan.

Section 704(a) of Title VII   A section of the Civil Rights Act of 1964 that protects employer retaliation against employees and job applicants "who have made a charge, testified, assisted or participated in any investigation, proceeding or hearing." In a unanimous ruling in 1997, the Supreme Court extended the provision of the act to former employees.

Section 911, Internal Revenue Code
Allows employees of U.S. businesses working in a foreign country to exclude up to $70,000 of foreign earned income from taxable income each year provided that the employee's tax home is in a foreign country and the employee meets either the bona fide residence test or the physical presence test.

Section 6672, Internal Revenue Code
Establishes guidelines on withholding income, Social Security, and Medicare taxes, in processing tax payments, and in filing tax reports. The regulation states that if income, Social Security, and Medicare taxes are not withheld or are not truthfully accounted for and paid to the IRS, a penalty of 100 percent will be imposed on all persons who are determined by the IRS to be responsible for collecting, accounting for, and paying these taxes, and who acted willfully in not doing so.

secular humanism   A philosophical position that holds that there are no absolutes or final truths beyond debate.

secular trust   Similar to the popular **rabbi trust**. A relatively new executive perk which provides taxable supplementary pension benefits for corporate executives.

Securities and Exchange Commission (SEC)
An agency of the federal government charged with enforcement of the Securities Act and promulgating rules and regulations

on financial issues, such as insider trading and disclosures on executive compensation.

security chief The hotel functionary responsible for maintaining the security of hotel and guest property and guests themselves, for planning and installing special security equipment, and for supervising security guards.

security information *See* security of travelers.

security needs Human needs for physical, psychological, and financial safety and security.

security of travelers For on-line security tips for business travelers. *Contact:* Private Sector Liaison Staff, U.S. Department of State Bureau of Diplomatic Security SA-11, Washington, DC 20522-1003. For advisories on conditions affecting travelers abroad, call U.S State Department Citizens Emergency Center (202/647-5225) or U.S. State Department Crisis Center (202/647-0900).

security-related tests *See* drug testing; honesty test; lie detector; psychological stress evaluator.

sedative Legal prescription drugs which can be dangerous when abused. Also called a *downer.*

Selected Reserve A Reserve Component of the Armed Forces made up of reservists assigned to units or pre-trained members of any of the Armed Services. Selected reservists are required to attend monthly drills and perform annual active duty for training.

Selected Reserve Montgomery GI Bill of 1985 (RMGIB) A federally funded educational benefit for military reservists. Participants must agree to serve in the Selected Reserve for six years, complete Initial Active Duty for Training, have a high school diploma or equivalent prior to eligibility start date, and can use benefits only while drilling satisfactorily (except if separated for a disability not the result of willful misconduct or, if involuntary separated for Reserve Transition Benefits). If combined with another DVA benefit program, the total number of months of entitlement cannot exceed 48 months. Maximum benefit of RMGIB (full time) is 36 months.

selection The process of matching people and jobs. The decision-making process in hiring, it typically involves multiple interviews and interviewer ratings, and it may make use of performance tests and assessment centers. Ideally, it is a deliberate, integrated, standard-

ized, comprehensive, efficient, and cost effective system, which is preceded by the formulation of job descriptions and applicant specifications, design and distribution of application forms and interviewer evaluation forms, construction or selection of appropriate tests or other evaluation instruments, preparation of advertisements, administration and interpretation of tests, conduct of employment interviews, use of group selection procedures such as assessment centers, making of reference checks, arranging for medical screening examinations, and evaluation of candidates before the hiring decision is made.

selective dissemination of information (SDI) An information service that automatically conducts a search of user-specified databases whenever the files are updated, and the results of the search are stored in the user's mailbox on that system.

self-actualization needs Attributed to Abraham Maslow. Human needs for achievement and self-realization or self-fulfillment — attainment of the highest level of functioning that the person is capable of — being all that one can be.

self-assessment *See* self-audit.

self-audit **1.** In career planning, self-exploration and evaluation to identify strengths and limitations. **2.** In performance appraisal, evaluation of self carried out by the ratee. **3.** In intermediate evaluation, a technique used to appraise the quality of the entire organization or any one of its elements, functions, services, or programs and to institute changes to improve the organization, function, or service.

self-care Using various strategies to provide workers with information on health self-management. Encouraging employees to manage health care problems, such as allergies, backaches, colds, cuts and bruises, headaches, and rashes, at home and without the help of a health care professional. Includes these options: (1) handbooks that contain quality health care information to care for oneself and thereby reduce the number of acute visits or phone calls to health care providers; (2) use of community group presentations of health-related messages; (3) establishment of a health resource library; and (4) setting up a health hotline.

self-critical analysis *See* self-evaluation privilege.

self-defense training A new benefit that companies are offering to their workers, particularly, but not exclusively, for women employees. Typically contracted with outside self-defense schools, given on company premises, often on company time, and supported in whole or in part by company funding.

self-designed pay plan A form of executive incentive plan that allows participants to choose the form in which their incentive payments are to be made. Sometimes called a *cafeteria plan*.

Self-Determination Act of 1991 Effective December 1, 1991, a federal law that requires hospitals and other health care facilities to inform patients of their state health care proxy law — laws designed to safeguard a person's autonomy. Such laws typically allow individuals to appoint an "agent" to make medical decisions for them, including decisions about use of life-sustaining procedures and equipment when the individual is not able to make such decisions.

self-development A means of planning and carrying out strategic career and life planning. Self-development takes into account an individual's strengths, aspirations, challenges, and opportunities and seeks to identify and remedy deficiencies and shortfalls and integrate strengths and aspirations into an optimal career and life plan. It includes all dimensions of self — personally, socially, and professionally, intellectually, physically, mentally, emotionally, experientially, and spiritually. It makes use of such means as correspondence and home-study courses, technical school, college, and university study, membership in trade, technical, and professional associations, membership in civic and community groups, service clubs, and personal improvement groups, and professional reading.

self-directed learning Self-motivated and self-managed planning and execution of a process of learning, changing, and improving. It may be undertaken with the assistance of an advisor, mentor, or trainer, but it always involves learner control over the learning goals, strategy, methods and materials, and evaluation.

self-directed work team (SDWT) *See* self-managed work team.

self-discipline A standard of personal behavior, job performance, work habits, courtesy, consideration of others, appearance, and ethical conduct that enables people singly or in groups to perform their mission, functions, and duties efficiently and effectively.

self-efficacy (SE) One of the requirements for facilitating performance. Refers to people's judgments about their capabilities to use their skills to do specific things or their beliefs about their ability to influence events that affect their lives. Attributed to HRD Hall of Famer, Robert F. Mager ("No Self-Efficacy, No Performance," *Training*, April 1992, pp. 32-36.) According to Mager, the other three elements needed to perform a job successfully are skill, opportunity to perform, and a supportive environment. He notes that SE has five main effects on behavior: (1) choice of behavior, (2) motivation, (3) perseverance, (4) facilitative (positive) thought patterns ("I can do this"), and (5) vulnerability to stress and depression.

Self Employed Professional: Technology · Management · Lifestyle A bimonthly journal: $29.97 per year (free to qualified subscribers). Address: Business Media Group, Self Employed Professional, 462 Boston St., Topsfield, MA 01983-1232 (800/874-4113 or 508-887-6855; Fax 508/887-6117; E-mail **sepedit@aol.com**).

self-evaluation *See* self-audit.

self-evaluation privilege Protection for employers under the law of some states designed to promote an organization's self-criticism of it policies and procedures. Investigations or self-evaluations, even if not conducted under the direction of the employer's attorney or in anticipation of litigation, may be protected from disclosure of the criticism, opinions, deliberations, and evaluative aspects of such a report.

self-funded indemnity plan A combination of a **self-funded plan of benefits** and an **indemnity plan** of benefits.

self-funded plan of benefits A plan in which employers provide an indemnity type plan to their employees on a self-funded basis (not through an insurance company) and purchase stop loss coverage from a reinsurer to reimburse the self-funded plan when claims exceed a set amount (usually $20,000) for any one individual. Typically such a plan also has an aggregate stop loss, which establishes that if claims exceed a set amount, such as $200,000, on all employees and dependents, the reinsurance carrier would also reimburse the self-funded plan for the excess aggregate amount.

self-funding *See* self-insurance.

Self Help for Hard of Hearing People, Inc. (SHHH) A nonprofit, non-sectarian volunteer international organization of hard of hearing people, their relatives, and friends, with local chapters in major cities. It is devoted to the welfare and interests of of those who cannot hear well but are committed to participating in the hearing world. Publishes the bimonthly *SHHH Journal. Contact:* SHHH, 7910 Woodmont Ave., Suite 1200, Bethesda MD 20814 [301/657-2248; 301/657-2249 (TTY); Fax 301/913-9413; URL **http://webcom/~houtx/shhh.html**).

self-image The way in which an individual sees himself or herself — how he or she feels about himself or herself. Self-image centers on the amount of self-esteem an individual possesses. In the workplace it is influenced by actual job performance, how the person views his or her performance, and how the individual perceives that others view his or her job performance.

self-insurance **1.** In risk management, risk retention with a funded or unfunded reserve. **2.** In benefits administration, an arrangement in which an employer pays claims for such benefits as medical care and short-term disability as they are incurred.

Self-Insurance Institute of America, Inc. (SIIA) An organization of 1,000 members established to promote and protect the concept of self-insurance. *Contact:* SIIA, 17300 Redhill Ave, #100., Irvine, CA 92614 (714/261-2553; Fax 714/261-2594).

self-insured benefits plan (SIBC) A benefits plan administered and supported in its entirety by the organization rather than by other insurance carriers.

self-inventory A list of an individual's knowledge, skills, and other attributes developed by the person and used in self-assessment to identify goals, objectives, capabilities, deficiencies, constraints, and resources.

self-knowledge Knowledge of who one is, what one would like to be and isn't, and how others react to one's persona. Also knowledge of one's strengths and limitations, talents and shortcomings, capabilities and faults.

self-managed account (SMA) Allowing employees to choose from among such investments as mutual funds, fixed-income securities, and stocks listed on domestic exchanges when creating their investment portfolios with the intention of making them satisfied with their 401(k) plan.

self-managed work team (SMWT) A work team that has been given complete autonomy in a specific area of work.

self-paced interactive multimedia (SPIMM) An indicator or measure of the appropriateness and effectiveness of computer-based training programs using a checklist that addresses three factors: (1) self-pacing (difficulty level and rate of instruction); (2) interactivity (ability of the program to reply to user's questions and provide feedback); and (3) multimedia (quality of audio and video). Attributed to Charles MacNelly, General Dynamics Corp., Fort Worth,TX (*Training*, February 1993).

self-paced training *See* individualized instruction; self-directed learning.

self-rating An approach to performance evaluation in which employees rate themselves, typically using a rating scale and in conjunction with supervisors' ratings.

self-reflective learning A learning process directed at personal change. It is a means of encouraging learners to think about their experiences, analyze their attitudes, assumptions, and beliefs, and gain insights that will allow them to change their behavior. Self-reflective learning is often used to help individuals learn about their jobs and their roles on a work team or task force.

self-referral The health-care industry's term describing the practice of referring patients to clinics, clinical laboratories, or other medical facilities in which the referring physician is an investor; for example, for magnetic resonance imaging (MRI). In 1989, Congress passed legislation designed to restrict self-referral. Starting January 1, 1992, the government prohibited physicians from referring Medicare and Medicaid patients to clinical laboratories in which the doctors have a financial interest.

self-regulated work group *See* self-managed work team.

self-reimbursement A means of controlling travel and entertainment costs. Employees submit their expense reports to the company and write their own reimbursement checks on one handwritten form or by electronic means.

self-report A personal history or inventory of biographical information that has been systematically designed and statistically validated in much the same way as a psychological test. The information is provided by respondents in a prescribed format.

self-study *See* self-audit.

self-insurance group (SIG) An alternative means of obtaining insurance coverage for workers' compensation claims in which employers band together to finance exposure to insurance risk and, at the same time, earn investment income on the funds.

selling, general, and administrative expenses (SG&A) Include such items as executive salaries, promotional expenses, legal fees, supplies, and the like. A new focal point for reengineering financial and administrative components and benchmarking because those items account for expenditures of upwards of 15 percent of the revenue of large public companies.

semester hour *See* credit hour.

semiautonomous work group *See* work team.

semi-bundled services Investment services offered employees by organizations that permit workers to choose a combination of inhouse and outside sources, including those offered by independent outside sources.

semiconductor chips The building blocks of computers and other electronic devices.

seminar A meeting or conference at which a group of people study and discuss a subject or topic under the leadership of a facilitator.

seminar method A variation of the conference method in which the purpose is to find an answer to a question or a solution to a problem. The instructor or leader does not have the answer or solution; in fact, there often is no known best or correct solution. The leader or instructor simply presents the problem and encourages full and free discussion aimed at identifying the real problem, determining and evaluating alternative solutions, arriving at a conclusion, and making recommendations to support or arrive at a decision.

seminar selling Selling products or services to customers in groups, rather than one at a time. For example, several organizations sell management training materials or audio-visual equipment and materials to groups of human resources development managers and trainers at seminars with heavy educational content. Instead of hard-sell sales pitches, they focus on developing concepts and applications. The intent is to generate interest in the products and services among those who influence corporate purchases.

semiprofessional *See* paraprofessional.

senior center A center established for older people at usually no or low fee. Offers a variety of social, educational, and recreational services.

Senior Professional In Human Resources (SPHR) A designation awarded by the Human Resource Certification Institute (HRCI) to HR practitioners, educators, researchers or consultants who have a minimum of eight years of exempt-level HR experience and who have mastered the body of knowledge that constitutes the human resource profession and are currently working in the field. Mastery is demonstrated by successful completion of a written examination covering management practices, selection and placement, training and development, compensation and benefits, employee and labor relations, and health, safety, and security. Recertification is required every three years. *Contact:* HRCI, 606 N. Washington St., Alexandria, VA 22314 (703/548-3440 or 703/548-6999).

seniority Priority given to employees due to length of service with a company or superiority in rank or status and to which certain rights, such as promotion or retention, accrue.

sensitivity analysis A marketing technique used to assess the customer's preferences for an increase or decrease in the cost of a product or service by varying each stated requirement or specification slightly upward and downward.

sensitivity training A deliberate effort to apply behavioral science to problems of motivation, communication, problem solving, and teamwork. It is small-group interaction under stress in an unstructured group composed of volunteer learners and a trained and skilled leader. To attain the objective of behavioral change, a permissive and supportive environment is established. Participants, guided by a trainer, are encouraged to act their own roles, receive feedback, examine their concepts of self, experiment with and practice new patterns of behavior, and learn how to maintain changed behavior back on the job. Content of the training varies with the nature of the individuals and groups participating. Also called *T-group.*

sentry strategy   A computer utility technique used to restore damaged or recover deleted files by storing deleted files in a hidden sub-directory. Its main disadvantage is that it uses a great amount of space on the hard disk.

separate line of business (SLOB) pension regulations   A final set of IRS regulations published September 3, 1993 covering requirements of "qualified" retirement plans. Originally a part of the massive IRS rule-making effort for ERISA changes mandated by the **Tax Reform Act of 1986,** the new rules are promulgated by Internal Revenue Code Section 410(b) and become effective for plan years beginning on or after January 1, 1994. The regulations describe when employers can subject different benefit plans covering distinctly separate operating divisions to percentage, ratio, and average benefit tests under code section 410(b) *individually* rather than merging or lumping all plans together. Also known as *coverage rules.*

sequester/sequestration   A legal terms that means "to take possession of" or "withhold" property or funds until some demand is satisfied. For example, **cost-of-living adjustments** for certain groups, such as federal and military retirees' annuities, have been withheld by the Congress in an attempt to balance the budget.

serial line Internet protocol (SLIP)   Allows a computer to connect directly to the **Internet** using a modem and a telephone line. Also known as a *Dialup-IP (point-to-point protocol).*

serif   In desktop publishing, the short, cross-line at the end of main strokes of many letters in some type faces.

serious health condition   Regulations covering the **Family and Medical Leave Act of 1993** provided a new definition that removed the requirement of incapacitation for more than three consecutive business days for conditions such as asthma, diabetes, epilepsy, and any incapacity due to pregnancy. It also qualified substance abuse as a serious health condition.

server   A system that stores computer files and runs applications for networks of personal computers, called clients. Gives workstations access to shared resources, such as printers and sets of files.

server-push/client-pull technology   On the World Wide Web, animation techniques that allow designers, with a single request, to create graphics that move and change. The difference between the two approaches lies in the way the information is delivered. Server-push maintains an open connection between the browser and the server. With client-pull, the connection is closed after each request.

service animal   As defined by the **Americans with Disabilities Act of 1990,** "any guide dog, signal dog, or other animal individually trained to provide assistance to an individual with a disability." For example, animals that guide individuals with impaired vision, alerting individuals with impaired hearing to intruders or sounds, providing minimal protection or rescue work, pulling a wheelchair, or fetching dropped items. The term is used in the context of the requirement that public accommodations modify policies, practices, and procedures to accommodate the use of service animals.

service area   The geographical area defined in a managed care plan within which the plan will provide health care services to its members.

service-based operations cycle time   *See* white collar cycle time.

service benchmarks   A means of quantifying the service a company receives from its suppliers or service providers, such as travel agencies. Standards are derived from assessing the company's current arrangements as well as making comparisons with other corporate/agency relationships to pinpoint problems and improve service.

service bureau   A form of integrated health care delivery system in which a hospital, managed care plan, or other organization provides services to a physician's practice at a fair market price.

service charge   In meeting management, charges for the services of waitpersons, other food and beverage function personnel, housepersons, electricians, and other technicians (such as audiovisual specialists).

service contract   In purchasing and contracting, an agreement with a vendor to provide services either on preventive basis (regular and periodic servicing) or per call basis (service when the equipment fails).

Service Contract Act of 1965   Requires payment of prevailing wage rates and fringe benefits on contracts in excess of $2,500 to provide services to the federal government. And, where a collective-bargaining agreement covers such service employees, compensation must in accordance with the rates for employees provided for in the agreement, including prospective wage increases.

Service Corps of Retired Executives (SCORE) A 12,400-member volunteer program, sponsored by the U.S. Small Business Administration (SBA). The program matches volunteers with small businesses that need expert advice. Men and women business executives share their management and technical expertise with present and prospective owners/managers of small businesses. They offer free, confidential counseling in accounting, human resources management, marketing, real estate, financing, inventory control, plant management, computer systems, and business and product analysis and low cost training programs. To locate the nearest SCORE office, call 800-8-ASK-SBA or 202/205-7064; Fax 800/634-0245; TDD 202/205-7333; E-mail **feedback@www.sbaonline.sba.gov**; URL **http://www.sba.gov/SCORE/**).

Service Delivery Area (SDA)   A local area in which **Job Training Partnership Act of 1982** (JTPA) services are developed, implemented, and provided. SDAs provide such services as client assessment, basic education and remediation services, job training, and placement services free of charge for all JTPA participants.

Service Employees International Union (SEIU) An international union of 1 million service workers. SEIU is dedicated to leadership in fighting for good jobs, fair wages, rights, and respect for American working families. *Contact:* SEIU, 1313 L St., N.W., Washington, DC 20005 (202/898-3200; E-mail **webmaster@seiu.org**; URL **http://www.seiu.org/altman.html**).

Service Members Occupational Conversion and Training Act of 1993 (SMOCTA) Legislation administered jointly by the departments of Defense (DOD), Labor (DOL), and Veterans Affairs (DVA) that offers employers monetary incentives to hire and train eligible veterans. DOL is authorized by the Act to reimburse employers up to $10,000 of a trainee's wages during the training period and $12,000 if the veteran has a service-connected disability. To be eligible, veterans must have served on active duty for more than 90 days and been discharged after August 1, 1990. The veteran must also meet one of the following criteria: (1) be unemployed for at least eight of the last 15 weeks before applying; (2) as determined by DOD, have a **military occupational specialty** not easily transferable to the civilian workplace, or (3) have at least a 30 percent disability rating from DVA. To be eligible, employers must provide training programs of between six and 18 months in duration and be approved by DVA. Training for seasonal or or temporary jobs, jobs based on commissions, positions with the federal government, or jobs outside the United States are ineligible.

Servicemembers's Group Life Insurance (SGLI) Low cost, group live insurance provided to members of all branches of the military service, active duty, Ready Reserve, and Retired Reserve. Maximum coverage was increased from $100,000 to $200,000 as of December 1, 1992. Eligible personnel may purchase the additional $100,000 in increments of $10,000 to reach the maximum amount. Premiums are $8.00 per month for $100,000.

service plan   A type of **managed care,** which has contractual relationships with providers to address maximum fees, prohibit balance billing, and use the same utilization management techniques as **managed indemnity.** Examples are Blue Cross and Blue Shield plans.

service provider   An on-line service, university network, or corporate server that allows users to connect with the Internet and the World Wide Web.

service worker   Any person who provides a "service" to others — from housekeepers and butlers to nurses and physicians.

servo-systems   In organization development, training, marketing, and the like, closed-loop processes that provide for organizational and individual feedback and responsiveness.

settlor   The person who creates a **trust**. Also called the *donor, creator,* or *grantor.*

settling-in support   *See* in-country support.

severance/severance pay A standard benefit for employees who are terminated due to economic downturn, **downsizing**, **rightsizing**, **restructuring**, **redeployment**, reshaping, or job elimination (and sometimes even for substandard performance). Usually uses years of service as the basis for calculating the amount of the benefit and typically pays one week's pay per year of service. For executives and other key personnel, is often based on an employment agreement or contract. Often awarded to an employee in addition to base pay to lighten the economic and psychological impact of discharge and prevent litigation. Sometimes used as an incentive for voluntary `employee resignation during downsizing and restructuring actions. Payments may range from three or four day's pay to as much as a year's salary.

severance program A program designed to ease the problems associated with unexpected termination of employees. It may include the award of salary and bonuses, continuation of benefits for a specified period of time, and outplacement, career, and psychological counseling.

severance trust executive plans (STEPs) According to an IRS ruling, benefits paid to executives in the event of job terminations "resulting from unanticipated events that are supported by a genuine business purpose" as long as they do not exceed two times final pay over a period of not more than two years. A strategy for overcoming the restrictions imposed by the **Omnibus Budget Reconciliation Act of 1993** and the **General Agreement on Tariffs and Trade** of 1993.

severely retarded A category of persons with mental disabilities. As measured by an intelligence test, the condition is represented by an **intelligence quotient (IQ)** below 50. Such persons are incapable of self-maintenance and need complete care and supervision, although they may have some motor and speech capabilities.

sex discrimination Discrimination, mainly but not exclusively against women, in such areas as denial of employment, quality of employment, differences in wages, pregnancy, and opportunities for advancement.

Sexuality Information & Education Council of the United States (SIECUS) An organization of 2,500 members established to advocate the right of individuals to make responsible sexual choices. SIECUS develops, collects, and disseminates information and promotes comprehensive education about sexuality. It maintains a library available to the public. *Contact:* SIECUS, 130 W. 42nd St., Ste. 350, New York, NY 10036 (212/819-9770; E-mail **siecus@ siecus.org**; URL **http://www.siecus.org**).

sexual harassment **1.** Defined by the Equal Employment Opportunity Commission as "unwelcome sexual advances, requests for sexual favors, and other verbal (such as telling sexual jokes) or physical conduct (pinching, putting arms around a person, or touching) of a sexual nature. . . when such submission to or rejection of this conduct explicitly or implicitly affects an individual's employment, unreasonably interferes with an individual's work performance or creates an intimidating, hostile, or offensive work environment." **2.** A form of discrimination resulting from different treatment of the sexes, such as unwanted overt or subtle sexual overtures leading to differential job-related outcomes. Unlawful sex discrimination may take either of two forms: (1) *Quid pro quo* harassment occurs when a supervisor conditions the granting of an economic benefit, such as promotion, upon the receipt of sexual favors from a subordinate or punishes the subordinate for refusing to submit to his or her request (termination, loss of salary increases, or demotion) and (2) *hostile work environment* harassment occurs where supervisors and/or co-workers create an atmosphere so infused with unwelcome sexually oriented conduct that an individual's reasonable comfort or ability to perform his or her job job is affected. Examples of the latter include intimidation, hostility, physical contact, suggestive comments, off-color jokes, and pressure for dates. On November 9, 1993, the U.S. Supreme Court provided greater leeway to file a sexual harassment claim, made it easier to win a sexual harassment suit, and allowed more leverage for people convicted of harassment to seek legal redress. The Court ruled that a plaintiff need not prove psychological harm and rejected a standard adopted by several lower federal courts that required plaintiffs to show that sexual harassment resulted in "severe psychological injury." Using the broad rule of workplace equality, the Court stated that the law was violated when, for any one of several reasons," the (workplace) environment would reasonably be perceived, and is perceived, as hostile or abusive" and that "no single factor is required." The decision means that employers must consider all relevant facts when examining sexual harassment cases to determine (1) the severity and frequency of the conduct of the accused; (2) whether the conduct placed the plaintiff in a physically threatening or humiliating situation; and (3) whether the conduct interfered with the employee's work performance or access to promotion, or caused psychological harm.

sexually transmitted disease (STD) A disease spread by sexual contact; for example, genital herpes, gonorrhea, HIV/AIDS, human papillomavirus or chalmydia, syphilis.

shadow stock plan
See phantom stock plan.

sham union A nonunion organization which purports to represent workers but is completely controlled by management. Prohibited by Section 8(a)(2) of the **National Labor Relations Act of 1935** as an unfair labor practice.

shareware Software produced and distributed free of charge, similar to public domain software, but that should be paid for if kept or used by the recipient.

sheddable worker One that is a part of a force of contingent workers hired to supplement a core group of full-time employees that operate the business from day to day — workers that can be laid off when not needed.

Schengen Agreement Aimed at providing visa- and passport-free travel throughout Europe. Became effective March 1, 1995 in France, Germany, Holland, Luxembourg, Portugal, and Spain. Austria, Denmark, Finland, Greece, Italy, and Sweden at likely to participate in the near future. Ireland and the United Kingdom have elected not to participate.

sedatives Drugs that serve to reduce anxiety, and after causing a brief period of euphoria, produce calmness, tranquility, and sleep. Examples include barbiturates ("downers," "barbs"), methaqualone ("Quaaludes," "ludes"), and tranquilizers (Valium, Xana).

shadow pricing Setting health care premium rates at a level just below the rates charged by competitors whether or not

those rates can be justified. The practice is unethical and may be illegal.

shareware *See* public domain software.

Sheet Metal Workers' International Association (SMWIA) An international labor union with membership in the AFL-CIO and the Canadian Labour Congress with approximately 134,000 members. SMWIA provides policy direction and program support on behalf of its membership in maintaining the union's jurisdiction over various types of sheet metal and related work in the United States and Canada. SMWIA members work in the building and construction trades, in production manufacturing, and in the railroad and shipyard industries. *Contact:* SMWIA, 1750 New York Avenue, N. W., Washington, DC 20006 (202/783-5880; Fax 202/662-0891; E-mail **webmaster@onweb.com**; URL **http:www.smwia.org**).

shell A template for a **CD-ROM** training programs produced by instructional design firms for sale or lease to organizations. The discs combine high-resolution, digital video and audio with interactive text and graphics. The template allows a user to customize, update, and revise digital files on the disc by changing or inserting text, graphics, and video.

Sherman Antitrust Act of 1890 (SAA)
An Act that makes any contract, conglomerate, cartel, partnership, syndicate, association, conspiracy, collusion, or plot in restraint of commerce or trade and all monopolies or attempts to corner and control trade illegal and subject to criminal sanctions. It also grants victims the right to recover damages. The law was last amended October 8, 1982.

Shiatsu massage A Japanese alternative manipulative medical treatment that employs therapeutic acupressure massage using pressure points.

shoppers Total market coverage publications distributed to households in most cities and towns. They may contain only advertising or they may be a weekly newspaper published on a market's heaviest shopping day.

shop steward A union representative to whom members of the union may go with complaints and who serves as an on-site contact for management on union matters.

short-selling An investment technique involving transactions in which a fund sells a security it does not own in anticipation of a decline in the market value of that security. The fund borrows the security to deliver it to the buyer. The fund is then obligated to replace the security borrowed by purchasing it at the market price at the time of replacement. The price at that time may be more or less than the price at which the security was sold by the fund. Until the security is replaced, the fund must pay to the lender amounts equal to any dividends or interest that accrue during the term of the loan, and it may also have to pay a premium, which would increase the cost of the security sold. The proceeds of the short sale are retained by the broker, to the extent necessary to meet margin requirements, until the short position is closed out. *See also* call and put options; currency futures; leverage; leverage through borrowing; reverse purchase agreement.

short-term disability (STD) A disabling condition, whether caused by accident or injury, that persists no longer than 6 months. However, in many traditional STD programs, the employee controls the duration of the disability. Generally, short-term disability benefits are offset by workers' compensation benefits.

short-term disability insurance *See* workers' compensation.

short-term income protection State-administered and, with a few exceptions, entirely employer-financed programs designed to protect workers during periods of joblessness.

short-term trust An estate planning strategy in which an individual transfers income-producing properties to a trust for the benefit of a person or an institution that receives all the income for the duration of the trust, which is selected by the grantor and must be longer than 10 years. At the end of the duration, the trust terminates and the remaining principal goes a predetermined beneficiary or beneficiaries. (The principal cannot revert to the grantor or his or her spouse unless the reversion applies in the case of a lineal descendant.) Also called a or *give-and-keep* trust.

short-time compensation (STC) The use of partial payments from unemployment insurance systems for workers whose salaries have been reduced to support continued employment rather than waiting until workers have been laid off. The practice has been facilitated

by legislation in Arizona, Arkansas, California, Florida, Kansas, Louisiana, Maryland, Massachusetts, Missouri, New York, Oregon, Texas, Vermont, and Washington.

short wavelength autoperimetry (SWAP) A field-of-vision test for the diagnosis of glaucoma three to four years earlier than with older diagnostic tests.

shoulder season In meeting management, the period between **high season** and **low season** when hotel occupancy and room rates are most negotiable.

shovelware A collection of materials from existing (and often old) manuals, training films, and computer-based training files place on CD-ROM, sometimes enhanced with sound and visual effects.

shrinkwrap licensing A notice on a software box, visible through its plastic covering, that spells out the terms of the "contract" and informs the buyer that opening the package constitutes acceptance of the license agreement as a binding contract. Used to protect the authors of the software from copyright infringement (unauthorized copying) and ensure them of profits from sales of the product.

shrooms Psychedelic mushrooms containing psilocybin, an illegal drug.

SHRM Award for Professional Excellence Awarded annually to three outstanding HR professionals in recognition of their consistently high performance and whose creative approaches have benefited both their employers and their business and professional communities. *Contact:* SHRM, 606 N. Washington St., Alexandria, VA 22314 (703/548-3440).

shukko A form of employment adjustment used by the Japanese to reduce labor costs during a recession. It involves sending surplus workers to subsidiaries or affiliated companies in the second layer of the Japanese economy. *See also* hai-ten.

sick building syndrome (SBS) Buildings in which there has been a high incidence of serious illnesses among occupants, such as cancer and pulmonary diseases, or less critical ailments, such as headaches, nausea, and dizzy spells.

sick leave Compensation paid to employees when they are absent from work because of illness or injury. Most sick leave policies grant full pay for a specified number of sick days accumulated at a specified rate per month of service.

the sidestep Lateral movement within an organization by an employee, rather than upward progress, accepted as a means of remaining employed or embraced to broaden one's knowledge and developing new skills and competencies.

Signet Awards Sponsored by the **Society of Incentive Travel Executives**, a worldwide program of awards that recognizes the top employers who motivate their employees with incentive travel. Eligibility is limited to companies that have used incentive travel as a means of achieving business objectives for five years or more. There are two categories of awards: companies with up to 500. employees and up to $200 million in sales and companies with more than 500 employees and $200 million in sales. *Contact:* SITE, 21 W. 38th St., New York NY 10018 (212/575-0910). *See also* SITE Crystal Awards.

significant activities of daily living (SADLs) In the health care field, to qualify for benefits under a long term care insurance policy, the insured must be totally dependent on human assistance in performing a specific number (usually three) of the following significant activities of daily living: bathing, eating, dressing, toileting, transferring from bed to chair, and maintaining continence.

significant figures Used by researchers and statisticians to indicate and report the accuracy of the original measurements used in a study; thus the figure $46,221,000 could be reported as $46M. The reported figures must not indicate a degree of accuracy higher than that which exists, nor should they fail to indicate a high degree of accuracy when such measurements have been obtained.

significant other Describes a spouse, sweetheart, lover, partner, parent, child, grandparent, daughter/son-in-law, friend, or companion, an individual who has an important impact on one's welfare, happiness, or emotional security. Attributed to Harry Stack Sullivan, noted psychiatrist.

silent sabotage Includes a wide range of organization problems that occur when values perceptions become skewed. Examples are workers who come in late and leave early; managers who equate achievement with making money; personnel who place greater emphasis on making money than serving customers. Attributed to William M.

Morin, "Silent Sabotage: Mending the Crisis in Corporate Values," *Management Review,* July 1995, pp.10-14.

SIMPLE Individual Retirement Accounts (SIMPLE IRAs) *See* Savings Incentive Match Plan for Employees.

simple memory deficiencies A form of learning disability which results in such problems as inability to join ideas one to another in imagining, conceiving, and other processes, and the formation of new ideas from these processes; disorders in the "stream of thought" — a coherent sequence of related ideas passing from an initial idea to a goal idea; or frequent lapses in ability to reproduce or recall facts and ideas.

simplified employee pension (SEP) A group of individual retirement accounts (IRAs) established by employees but funded by the employer. Allowed by the Revenue Act of 1978. Replaced by Savings Incentive Match Plans (SIMPLE).

simulation **1.** A technique that involves the use of a manual or computerized model of a large, complex, nonlinear problem. The approach simulates or imitates operations and responses to problems and situations to test the ability of a person, system, or procedure to overcome obstacles and meet variations. Simulations are also used to predict results or provide answers to "what if?" type questions. **2.** Sophisticated computer networks that integrate voice-recognition software, artificial intelligence, robotics, and holographic projections to produce **virtual reality**. **3.** A special participative instructional method that may take any one of three forms: physical simulations, procedural simulations, or process simulations.

simulator A machine, device, item or equipment or system that replicates or imitates the real system. It assumes the appearance, characteristics, or capabilities of the real device, equipment or system. A simulator looks exactly like and works exactly like the real thing. It may be used in tandem with a live instructor (controlled simulation) or it may be a stand-alone device. Primarily used in training. For example, flight simulators are used to train military and commercial pilots.

simultaneous voice and data (SVD) A transmission capability used in products for the office and home.

single A hotel room with a double bed for one-person occupancy.

Single Employer Pension Plan Amendments Act of 1986 (SEPPA) Included in the **Consolidated Omnibus Reconciliation Act of 1986.** Revised funding requirements for pension plans. Requires employers who maintain defined benefit or money purchase defined contribution plans to give due notice to employees after adopting an amendment to the plans not less than 15 days prior to the effective date before implementing amendments which significantly reduce benefits.

Single European Act of 1987 Reinforced economic unification among **European Community** countries (now totaling 15) by detailing 279 European Community proposals for the elimination of trade barriers by 1992.

Single Internal Market (SIM) A **European Community** information service established by the U.S. Department of Commerce to provide background data, copies of proposed and approved laws, and help with problems. *Contact:* SIM, 1992 Information Service, Office of European Community Affairs, U.S. Department of Commerce, Room 3036, 14th St. and Constitution Ave., NW, Washington, DC 29230 (202/377-5276).

single-payer plan An advanced form of universal health-care plan, similar to Canada's health-care system, in which the federal government would eliminate Medicare, Medicaid, and employer-funded insurance, replace private insurers, underwrite the coverage, and negotiate physicians' fees. The term single payer refers to the the *system of payment* and not the *delivery system* of health care.

sip and puff machine Computerized equipment that persons without the use of their arms or legs can use to perform many actions, such as steering wheelchairs, switching on the TV and changing channels, telephoning, and using computers.

SITE Crystal Awards Awards presented annually by the **Society of Incentive Travel Executives** for innovative incentive travel programs. Include awards for Creative Use of Incentive Travel to Solve a Marketing Problem, Promotion & Communication, Best Incentive Travel for Non-Sales Program, Trip Delivery (four nights or less), Trip Delivery (five nights or more), Outstanding Event, and Achievement Award for Excellence. *Contact:* SITE, 21 W. 38th St., New York NY 10018 (212/575-0910).

site inspection A visit to a potential meeting site by a meeting planner, usually incognito and at their own expense to ensure that the property is seen as it would be seen by participants during a meeting.

sit-in Organized, usually passive, occupation of an office, shop, or other facility to protest discrimination or express some other grievance.

situational HR Reacting to changes in the business environment with ineffective practices, such as eliminating training and development during a business down-turn. *See also* virtual HR.

situationalism The ethical theory that holds that nothing is absolute, demonstrably correct, right, or good. The goodness of an action depends on the circumstances and the conditions surrounding it. Therefore, the situation itself, and not moral or ethical concepts, rules, or principles, is the determinant of the rightness or goodness of the action or behavior.

situational leadership The theory that there is no one best way to lead, but that there are likely to be preferred or more promising ways of leading under certain conditions or circumstances. Therefore, the best approach to leadership at any particular moment depends on the people being led, the task to be accomplished, and the circumstances surrounding the two variables.

skewness A measure of the positive or negative departures of frequency distributions from normality (the normal or bell-shaped curve). The degree of skewness varies between the limits of −3 and +3. A normal distribution will have a value of 0. Skewness is measured by the following formula:

$$\text{skewness} = \frac{3\left(\text{mean} - \text{median}\right)}{\text{standard deviation}}$$

skill Learned mental or motor behavior that requires some degree of facility in the performance of all or part of a complex act. Examples are writing, calculating, problem solving, counseling, and interviewing.

skill-based compensation *See* skill-based pay.

skill-based pay A nontraditional form of compensation; pay for what employees can do regardless of their positions, length of service with the organization, or whether the skills are used. Typically based on the number of specific skills mastered by the worker under the assumption that those skills may support the organization's future needs. It works this way. Using the job description as a guide, skills are identified and monetary values are assigned to all components of the base job (minimum to midpoint of the salary range). New employees start at the minimum for that job, and salaries are adjusted only when employee either gain new skills or lose existing ones. That is, employee compensation levels are based on individual initiative and mastery of job skills. Recent versions of the plan focus on payment for the acquisition of core or strategic skills — competencies that are essential to the success of the organization.

skilled nursing facility (SNF)   A specially qualified institution or facility that has the staff and equipment to provide 24-hour per day skilled nursing care or rehabilitation services and other related health services by or under the supervision of a registered nurse (RN) and a physician.

skill gap   Basic skill deficiencies — in reading, writing, mathematics, and oral communication.

skills   "How to" procedures or techniques that apply to a specific situation. Typically taught to prepare an individual to perform a job or task. Examples are interviewing, keyboarding, and soldering.

skills and technical training   Training provided to compensate for deficiencies in the knowledge and skills of entry-level workers, remedy employee performance deficiencies due to inadequate skill or knowledge, or upgrade or retrain employees as required by the introduction of new systems, equipment, tools, processes, procedures, techniques, or products. Such training makes extensive use of demonstration and performance, equipment, tools, models, mockups, and multimedia, task lists, and job aids. It focuses on correct procedures, practice of cognitive and manipulative skills, the development of safe work habits, and the use of protective clothing and safety devices.

Skills, knowledge, and attitudes (SKA)   Categories of educational or training objectives. Conform with Bloom's Taxonomy of Educational Objectives: psychomotor (skills), cognitive (knowledge), and affective (attitudes).

skills test   A test specifically designed to yield data pertaining to the training and development needs of employees. In addition to identifying skills inadequacies, including such higher-level skills as decision making, skills tests can also reveal deficiencies in job knowledge.

skip-a-generation trust   An estate planning strategy designed to avoid payment of estate taxes on transfers of property along generational lines. Such a trust leaves a life interest to the grantor's children, with either a further life interest or a distribution to the grandchildren, great-grandchildren, and so on. In 1976, Congress imposed a skip-generation tax which was repealed by a new law that was retroactive to 1976. The complexities of that law make it advisable that anyone contemplating a skip-generation arrangement seek competent professional counsel.

skunk works   Refers to a creative, innovative, fast-paced, and somewhat unconventional undertaking operating at the periphery of the organization. A term borrowed from the L'il Abner comic strip, it was applied to business by the Lockheed California Company where it is called Skunk Works, a registered service mark. The term was also used by Tom Peters and Nancy Austin (Foreword to *A Passion for Excellence*, New York, Random House, 1984).

slander   A false oral statement or report maliciously issued that tends to expose another person to public contempt or ridicule. A **plaintiff** established a ***prima facie*** case of slander by proving that a defamatory statement about him or her was communicated to a third person.

sleep deprivation   An emerging workplace problem common to shift workers, chronic fatigue, which impacts adversely on productivity, benefit costs, and industrial accidents and is linked to work-and family conflicts. Remedies include **compressed workweek** and encouraging naps during the day.

sleep room   A hotel room designed to help long-haul travelers to recover from jet lag so that they can be more productive following arrival at their destination or when returning to their office from abroad. Rooms are equipped with soundproofed windows, white noise and nature-sound machines, insulated carpet, door seals, and extra-heavy drapes. Rooms also stock a variety of blankets and pillows, relaxation audiotapes, and provide continuous music of the guest's choice. Instead of alcohol and caffeine-laden drinks, minibars are stocked with milk, herbal tea, fruit juice, cheese and crackers, and cookies.

slippage clause *See* attrition clause.

slotting allowance *See* slotting fee.

slotting fee   A fee charged by large store chains, mainly grocery stores but not limited to them, as a kind of one-time "price of admission" for new products. Theoretically, and sometimes in reality, a manufacturer who pays enough in slotting fees can get enough shelf space to squeeze out competing products.

slow learner   A category of persons with mental disabilities. As measured by an intelligence test, the condition is represented by an **intelligence quotient (IQ)** between 75 and 90.

slow screw   A form of computer sabotage, it is a computer virus that destroys a file bit by bit over time.

Small Business Administration (SBA)
An independent agency of the federal government established to aid, counsel, and protect the interests of small and disadvantaged businesses, ensure that small business concerns receive a fair portion of Government purchases, contracts, and subcontracts, as well as of the sales of Government property; make loans to small business concerns, State and local development companies, and the victims of floods or other catastrophes, or of certain types of economic injury; and license, regulate, and make loans to small business investment companies. The U.S. Business Advisor, an on-line service, provides businesses with access to a full range of plain language regulatory guidance and compliance assistance, as well as to government forms, business development software and topic-specific information. *Contact:* SBA, 409 Third Street, SW, Washington, DC 20416 (800-U-ASK-SBA or 202-205-6600; TDD 704/344-6640; Fax 202/205-7064; URL **http://www.sba.gov**

small business investment company (SBIC)
Organizations that provide loans and equity investments to small companies. Such investments are backed by the U.S. government, but they are administered by private companies who evaluate the merits of business

plans just as any banker or venture capitalist might do.

Small Business Jobs Protection Act of 1996   Signed into law August 29, 1996. Contains these important changes: (1) simplified pension distribution rules and nondiscrimination provisions that make it easier for employers to establish and administer retirement plans, including 401(k) plans; (2) retroactively extended Section 127, the tax exclusion for employer-provided educational assistance; (3) simplified the definition of "highly compensated employees"; (4) raised the expensing limit on business equipment the year it is put in service to $18,000 (in 1997 and, by 2003 to $25,000); and (5) created a new type of retirement plan called a Savings Incentive Match Plan for Employees.

small business organization (SBO)
A business or nonprofit organization that is independently owned and operated, not dominant in its field of endeavor, and employs a small number of workers (typically 100 or fewer).

small computer standard interface (SCSI)
A receptacle (called a "port") usually located on the back of a personal computer, used to connect high speed disks, modems, and other devices to the system.

small quantity generator (SQG)   Storers or users of hazardous chemicals who generate between 220 pounds (100 kilograms) and 2200 pounds (1000 kilograms) (approximately 240 gallons) per month of hazardous waste or more than 2.2 pounds (1 kilogram) approximately 1 quart) of acutely hazardous waste per month and therefore must be in compliance with all requirements of the Resource Conservation and Recovery Act of 1976.

smart bars   Pubs and lounges that dispense what are described as "cognitive enhancing" amino acid cocktails instead of beer and hard liquor.

smart building   An office building where offices are prefurnished with computer and telephone equipment and where temperature, lighting, and "talking" elevators are all computerized.

smart card   A plastic card, resembling a credit or debit card, that uses embedded microprocessor chips instead of a magnetic strip to store data. Transactions are conducted by passing the card through a terminal, like a swipe card, or transmitting the funds over the Internet.

smart computer *See* neurocomputer.

smart drugs *See* cognitive enhancement; nootropics.

smart meeting room A meeting room equipped to handle computer and communication needs, such as abundant power outlets built into movable tables, videoconferencing equipment and conference telephones, Internet access via ISDN lines, digital light processing projectors, lighting and temperature controls (adjustable by attendees), and a support staff specially trained for high-tech troubleshooting.

smart paper *See* pen computer.

smile sheet A trainee reaction form. A common approach to the evaluation of training in which trainees are asked for their opinions about the value of the course, seminar, or workshop, the instructor, and the training setting.

smile training A cynical term recently applied to customer-service training that focuses on developing people who can act friendly toward customers by teaching nonverbal behaviors that convey friendliness.

smiley On the **Internet 1.** Key strokes that convey emotion by means of "faces." **2.** A synonym for positive feelings; for example, "Give me a smiley."

Smokers' Rights bill A bill under consideration in a few states that would prohibit employers from discriminating against workers who smoke off the job. Smokers who believe that they have been discriminated against could take their employer to court for damages, including attorney's fees and court costs. Compromise bills would allow employers to differentiate between smokers and nonsmokers in cases where they can show a rational basis related to the job.

smoking gun approach *See* Trojan horse.

SMPTE "Simp-tee" — an acronym for the **Society of Motion Picture and Television Engineers** and also for the standards it established for film, video, and audio devices. Simp-tee is represented by a series of digital bits, but the values of 0 and 1 are portrayed on analog tape as two distinct frequencies.

snail mail Used by **Internet** sophisticates to describe the U.S. Postal Service.

sneaker net Jokingly considered the simplest form of **local area network.** One user copies a file onto a floppy disk and then "runs" it over to another person who needs the data.

sniffer 1. Software that can read all the data that passes information into or out of a computer. It can be programmed to "search" for keywords, such as proxies or mergers, suggesting financial transactions. **2.** A synonym for a spy.

sniffing The use of **inhalants** to get an immediate high. The practice often turns out to be a life-threatening experience.

snow *See* cocaine.

snowflake A short (usually one page or less) memo sent to subordinate managers and staffers to get facts, opinions, or ideas on a single subject quickly, briefly, and in writing. Sometimes called a *tasker.*

social engineeering A technique used by unscrupulous operatives to obtain a computer user's password and identification to gain access to computer files. The operative uses cajolery to get the information.

social health maintenance organization (SHMO) A rare form of **health maintenance organization** that provides social as well as medical care for its members,

social, military, educational, religious, and fraternal (SMERF) In the meeting/conference industry, SMERFs are low budget groups, as contrasted with corporate business, which are pursued by conference centers during "off seasons" to provide income.

social needs Human needs for acceptance, belongingness, appreciation, and respect of others. Also known as *affiliation needs.* Attributed to Abraham Maslow.

social- or economic-based entitlements Federal entitlement programs, such as veterans' compensation, deposit insurance, student loans, farm price supports, foster care and adoption services, and rehabilitation services, that provide benefits based on criteria corresponding to their intent.

Social Security Act of 1935 (SSA) Legislation that created and implemented a worker-employer-government insurance program covering retirement, survivors, disability, and **Medicare** benefits. In 1997 individuals pay 7.65% on earnings up to $65,400 through withholding. That amount is matched dollar for dollar by the employer and sent to the Social Security Administration. The amount attributable to Social Security tax for 1997 is 6.2% on the first $65,400 of earned income and the Medicare tax is 1.45% on any amount of earned income. The maximum Social Security tax liability for 1997 is $3,887.40; there is no maximum limit for Medicare. Retirement benefits begin at age 65 (full benefits) or 62 (reduced benefits). The amount people can earn annually in 1997 (earnings test) without losing Social Security benefits is $13,500 (increasing annually up to $30,000 in 2002 — $14,500 in 1998, $15,500 in 1999, $17,000 in 2000, and $25,000 in 2001), and $1 in benefits is withheld for every $3 of earnings in excess of that amount. For individuals under the age of 65, the annual exempt amount in 1996 was $8,280. For every $2.00 earned over that amount, $1.00 is deducted from benefits. The earnings test does not apply for people over 70. Beginning in 2003, the age for full retirement will be raised to 65 years and two months; by 2027, the age will be 67. Other benefits include **Supplemental Security Income**, unemployment insurance, food stamps, child support enforcement, family and child welfare services, workers' compensation, veterans' benefits, help for the blind, and several other special programs. Some are cooperative programs with state governments; many are administered by state public-assistance offices. (800/772-1213; TTY 800/325-0778)

Social Security Act Amendment of 1995 Amended title XVIII of the Social Security Act to permit Medicare Select policies to be offered in all states. Became law July 7, 1995.

Social Security Administration   For help with problems or customer service complaints, contact the nearest Social Security Office (Yellow Pages) or write to Social Security Administration, Office of Public Inquiries, Rm. 4100 Annex Bldg., 6401 Security Blvd., Baltimore, MD 21235 (800/772-1213).

Social Security disability benefits Eligibility is based on prior work under Social Security, inability to do any kind of work for which suited, and the disability is expected to last at least a year or result in death. Disability benefits can be received at any age. Certain family members may also qualify including: (1) unmarried children (including stepchildren or grandchildren) under the age of 18 or under 19 if still in high school full time; (2) unmarried children 18 or older if their have a disability that started before age 22; (3) a spouse who is 62 or older (or any age if caring for a child who is under 16 or is disabled and also receiving benefits); or (4) a disabled widow or widower 50 or older if the disability occurred before the death of the individual covered by Social Security or within seven years after his or her death. (800/772-1213; TTY 800/325-0778)

Social Security family benefits   Children eligible for Social Security benefits receive up to one-half of a parent's full benefit; however, there is a limit to the amount of money that can be paid to a family.

social security notch   *See* notch babies.

Social Security retirement benefits   As of 1997, full retirement benefits qualification is age 65; for early retirement, age 62, but the benefit amount is permanently reduced based on the number of months the individual will receive benefits before reaching full retirement age (a reduction of about 20 percent at age 62; 13.33 percent at age 63, and about 6.66 percent at age 64. People who decide to continue working beyond full retirement age can increase their benefit when they start receiving them or reach age 70. For example, an individual born in 1943 or later who delays receipt of benefits will add 8 percent per year to his or her benefit. Full retirement age will be increased in gradual steps until it reaches age 67 in 2003.

Social Security spousal benefits   Individuals eligible for spousal benefits who begins taking the benefit at age 65 will receive 50 percent of the amount the covered spouse receives. If the eligible spouse elects to receive a spousal benefit at age 62, the benefit is 37.5 percent of the amount the spouse receives. For qualified spouses, the spousal benefit is paid *in addition* to the earned Social Security benefits (800/772-1213; TTY 800/325-0778).

Social Security survivor benefits   Individuals eligible for survivor benefits include widows, widowers, divorced widows, divorced widowers, children, and dependent parents of individuals who have worked, paid Social Security taxes, and earned enough credits. The number of credits needed depends on age and when the death occurs. Benefits can also be paid to children and a spouse who is caring for the children if the decedent has credit for one and one half years of work in the three years just preceding death. Full benefits are paid at age 65 or older (or reduced benefits as early as age 60 for widows or widowers and, if disabled, at ages 50 to 60). Benefits can be paid to unmarried children under age 18 (or up to age 19 if attending elementary or secondary school full time), at any age if disabled before age 22 and remains disabled, and under certain circumstances to stepchildren or grandchildren. Survivors benefits can also be paid to dependent parents at age 62 or older.

social security windfall reduction
Not to be confused with the **government pension offset.** It is a formula that reduces a government annuitant's *own* (not a spouse's) social security benefit. Anyone who first became eligible for a non-social security covered government annuity after 1985 is subject to a reduction of as much as 50 percent unless he or she has 30 years of substantial earnings under social security. Federal workers hired after December 31, 1983 are exempt from the windfall reduction.

social service leave   A leave of absence granted to an employee, often with full pay, to serve for an extended period of time (frequently a whole year) with some social service agency.

social system   A formal or informal set of relationships among people who must work (or play) together, perform tasks, and interact.

social worker A person with a degree in social work, usually a master's degree (M.S.S.W.) who has specialized training in counseling.

Society for Applied Learning Technology (SALT) A 1,000 member society oriented toward professionals whose work requires knowledge and communication in the field of instructional technology. The Society provides a means of enhancing knowledge and job performance through its publications and professional meetings. *Contact:* SALT, 50 Culpepper Street, Warrenton, VA 20186 (800-457-6812 or 540/347-0055; Fax 540/349-3169; E-mail **info@SALT.org**; URL **http://www.SALT.org**).

Society for Human Resource Management (SHRM) Formerly named the American Society for Personnel Administration (ASPA). With a worldwide membership of 85,000 professional and student members, SHRM is the world's largest professional membership organization dedicated exclusively to excellence in human resource management. Provides its membership with education and information services, conferences and seminars, government and media representation, and publications. *Contact:* SHRM, 1800 Duke St., Alexandria, VA 22314 (703/548-3440; TDD 703/548-6999; Fax 703/836-0367; E-mail **shrm@shrm.org**; URL **http://www.shrm. org**).

The Society for Intercultural Education, Training and Research (International) (SIETAR) An interdisciplinary professional and service organization of 2,100 members whose purpose is to implement and promote cooperative interactions and effective communication among peoples of diverse cultures, races, and ethnic groups. *Contact:* David Santini, 808 17th St., N.W., Ste. 200, Washington, DC 20006-3953 (202/466-7883; Fax 202/223-9569; E-mail **75250. 1275@compuserve. com**; URL **http://www.public.asu.edu/ ~shogun/sietar/welcome/index.html**).

Society for Muscular Dystrophy Information, International (S.M.D.I.) Established to share and encourage the exchange of nontechnical, neuromuscular disorder and disability-related information. Provides referrals to support groups, publishes a networking newsletter, and operates a publications exchange. *Contact:* S.M.D.I., International, P.O. Box 479, Bridgewater, Nova Scotia, Canada B4V 2X6 (902/685-3962 or 902/682-8086; Fax 902/682-3142; E-mail **smdi@atcon.com**).

The Society for Nonprofit Organizations (SNO) A nonprofit membership organization of about 6,000 members. SNO' mission is to draw together all elements of the nonprofit world, to encourage open communications and sharing, to identify the common ground that can unify, and to foster a sense of community in the sector by encouraging networking, alliances, collaborations, and sharing, providing wide-ranging education, training, and support services, and conducting research to identify emerging trends, issues, and opportunities for nonprofit organizations. *Contact:* SNO, 6314 Odana Road, Suite 1, Madison, WI 53719-1141 (800/424-7367; 608/274-9777; Fax 608/274-9978; E-mail **snpo@danenet.wicip.org**; URL **http://www. uwex.edu/danenet/snpo**).

Society for Technical Communication (STC) A worldwide association of 20,000 members in 141 chapters, dedicated to meeting the needs of professional technical communicators. Members include writers and editors of scientific and technical material and computer documentation, managers, educators and students, graphic artists, audiovisual specialists, and consultants. *Contact:* STC, 901 N. Stuart St., Ste. 904, Arlington, VA 22203-1854 (703/522-4114; Fax 703/522-2075; E-mail **stc@stc-va.org**; URL **http://www.stc-va.org**).

Society of Corporate Meeting Professionals (SCMP) A membership group consisting of convention services managers, including those who have sales responsibilities. *Contact:* SCMP, 1819 Peachtree St., N.E., Ste. 620, Atlanta, GA 30309 (404/355-9932; Fax 404/351-3348; E-mail **asshq@mindspring.com**).

Society of Government Meeting Professionals (SGMP) A nonprofit professional organization of 2,600 members who are involved in planning government meetings — either on a full or part-time basis — and those individuals who supply services to government planners. Its objective is to improve the quality and promote the cost-effectiveness of government meetings. *Contact:* SGMP, 219 E. Main, Mechanicsburg, PA 17005 (717/795-7467; Fax 717/795-7473).

Society for Human Resource Management (SHRM) (Update) 85,000 professional and student members. Contact: SHRM, 1800 Duke St., Alexandria, VA 22314 (800/283-77476 or 703/548-3440; TDD 703/548-6999; Fax 703/836-0367; E-mail **shrm@shrm.org**; URL **http://www.shrm.org**).

Society of Human Resource Professionals (SHRP) A 700-member chapter of the The **Society for Human Resource Management**. It offers a monthly newsletter, workshop programs, and a job referral service. *Contact:* SHRP, 8 South Michigan Ave., #1000, Chicago, IL 60603 (312/368-0188; Fax 312/580-0165 E-mail **SHRP@gss.net**).

Society of Incentive & Travel Executives (SITE) A world-wide nonprofit organization of 2,200 business professionals representing 80 countries dedicated to increasing corporate recognition and use of incentives, including travel, as motivators and rewards. Members include airlines, consultants, corporate executives, cruise lines, destination management companies, hotels and resorts, incentive travel houses, trade publications, official tourist organizations, travel agencies, and other supporting organizations. *Contact:* SITE, 21 W. 38th St., 10th Fl., New York NY 10018-5584 (212/575-0910; Fax 212/575-0910; E-mail **site/@ix.netcom.com**; URL **http://www.info-now.com/site/**).

Society of Manufacturing Engineers (SME) A professional organization that focuses on the advancement of manufacturing technology, including robotics and computer integrated manufacturing. Dedicated to serving its 70,000 members (in 70 countries) and the manufacturing community through the advancement of professionals, knowledge, and learning. Sponsors seminars, conferences, exhibitions, technical publications. *Contact:* SME, 1 SME Drive/P.O. Box 930, Dearborn, MI 48121 (313/271-1500; URL **http://www.sme.org**).

Society of Motion Picture and Television Engineers (SMPTE) An organization of over 9,000 members worldwide established to gather and disseminate information, provide seminars and workshops, and organize conferences and forums on all aspects of motion picture and professional TV arts and sciences. SMPTE also established the standards by which film, video, and audio devices could synchronize elements using the reference of hours:minutes:seconds:frames. *Contact:* SMPTE, 595 Hartsdale Ave, White Plains, NY 10607-1824 (914/761-1100; Fax 914/761-3115; E-mail **smpte@smpte.org**; URL **http://www.smpte.org/**)

Society of Professional Benefit Administrators (SPBA) A national association of 400 third party administration (TPA) member firms that provide outside employee benefits administration to client employee benefit plans. SPBA's member firms administer employee benefit plans representing every size and format of employment and every type of business. Its goal is to have TPAs provide the best possible services to their clients. *Contact:* SPBA, Two Wisconsin Cir., Ste 670, Bethesda, MD 20815-7003 (301/718-7722; Fax 301/718-9440).

Society of Travel Agents in Government (STAG) A 500-member non-profit educational forum consisting of travel agents, air/lodging/car rental suppliers, and federal and other government travel managers and contractors throughout the U.S. Established to enhance the competence of travel agencies engaged in providing travel services to governmental bodies through education and to promote professional standards. *Contact:* STAG, 6935 Wisconsin Ave., N.W., Washington, DC 20815 (301/654-8595; Fax 301/654-6663; E-mail **govtvlmkt@aol.com**).

sociotechnical systems (STS) Systems that bring technology and people together based on the belief that every organization is simultaneously a social and a technical system and that ignoring either system is an invitation to disaster. Such concepts and strategies as organization design, labor-management cooperation, participatory management, and employee involvement, and such **organization development** interventions as team building, job redesign and enlargement, have their roots in sociotechnical theory. The objective of such systems is to achieve high performance (technology, equipment, materials, space, and facilities) and people working productively and in harmony.

sociotechnical work design A means of raising both the quality of work life and productivity, it gives the workers who actually perform a job an opportunity to assist engineers and other specialists to design the jobs. In that way, the human factors carry equal or greater weight than technical considerations in job design and redesign.

SOCKS A free computer product that allows a user to modify a client program, such as a **file transfer protocol,** and run a generic SOCKified server.

soft data Information and observations that consist largely of individual personal perceptions, recollections, and impressions that are subjective and not independently verifiable.

soft skills Interpersonal skills such as speaking, listening, interviewing, counseling, negotiating, and conflict resolution.

software Any information in a form that a computer can use. Software includes the instructions or programs that direct the hardware. Software may be installed in the computer by the manufacturer or loaded into memory by the user by means of a disk and a disk drive. Examples are applications programs such as spread sheets and word processing programs.

sokaiya A Japanese term used to describe extortionists who threaten to disrupt corporate meetings unless they are paid to "maintain order."

solar electric technology *See* photovoltaic technology.

Soldiers' and Sailors' Civil Relief Act of 1991 Amended the Soldiers' and Sailors' Civil Relief Act of 1940 to clarify veterans' reemployment rights and improve veterans' rights to reinstatement of health insurance. Temporarily limited the financial obligations of military personnel while on active duty, as well as creditors' remedies against such personnel in certain circumstances. Among its vital protections for members of the Armed Forces called to active duty in the Persian Gulf War, the Act increased from $150 to $1,200 the monthly rent threshold protection against eviction, provided for the reinstatement of employer-provided health insurance immediately upon return to civilian life, delayed until July 1, 1991 any civil actions against members, and clarified existing reemployment rights for reservists called to active duty for periods of 90 days or longer.

sole proprietorship An arrangement under the law that gives an owner the exclusive right to transact business. It also has the advantage of allowing the proprietor to hire part-time or full-time workers on a project basis without have to incur the long-term expense of company benefits.

solicitor In the United Kingdom, a **law provider,** one who is qualified to advise clients, plead cases in lower courts, and prepare cases for barristers to plead in higher courts.

somatization disorder Vague physical complaints that last for several years but cannot be diagnosed. The condition affects the body but originates in the mind,

soundboard *See* sound card.

sound byte A short (usually 30-seconds in duration) bit of comment or conversation on television or radio. Believed by many to be misleading because it often lacks context.

sound card Hardware that fits into a slot in a computer's central processing unit that allows the computer to play sounds.

source tax **1.** A tax placed on income earned in the years an individual lived and worked in a state. **2.** A state income tax on retirement income or other disbursements of qualified pension plans to nonresidents. Assessed on former residents who have relocated. Currently California, Idaho, and Oregon have source taxes. Colorado, Florida, Louisiana, Nevada,

Texas, and Washington now have laws protecting residents against source taxes.

space verification program
See function space verification program.

spam/spamming On the **Internet,** the unwelcome practice of broadcasting an advertisement to several newsgroups or mailing lists. Also called *garbage* or *junk postings.*

span of authority *See* span of management

span of control *See* span of management.

span of management A principle of management that states that there is a limit to the number of persons one individual can supervise. In early management theory, the ideal span of management was narrowly defined as five to eight subordinates. Today, span of management is seen to hinge on several factors: the nature of the process being performed, the complexity of the task, the ability of the workers, and the physical proximity of workers to each other.

speak out program A means of communicating with employees and providing answers to their questions and responses to their concerns. May employ a mail-in system, telephone hot-line, meetings, and employee surveys.

Spearman-Brown formula A method for calculating the coefficient of reliability of a test which indicates how consistently the test measures whatever it purports to measure. The test is scored in two parts as well as in total; that is, separate scores are calculated for the total test, for odd-numbered test items, and for even-numbered test items. The formula is as follows:

$$r_n = \left(\frac{1 - s_a^2 + s_b^2}{s_t^2} \right) \left(\text{Spearman-Brown formula} \right)$$

where s_a = standard deviation of the first half of the test (odd-numbered items)
   s_b = standard deviation of the second half of the test (even-numbered items)
   s_t = standard deviation of the total test

special assignment A strategy for building the data bases of employees by bringing them into contact with new and different people, situations, problems, and ideas. They include assignment to investigations, studies, audits, quality circle membership, and assignment to work teams and task forces, temporary positions, and travel.

special cash award A form of variable pay. Cash awards are given to nonexecutive employees who have done something noteworthy and special for the company — such as developing a new procedure or a means of cutting costs.

special-effects generator (SEG) In TV production and transmission, an electronic device usually installed in the video switcher and used to produce wipes, split screens, inserts, keys, and the like.

specialization An organizational principle that states that as organizations grow, work must be divided, otherwise jobs will become so complex and require so many different skills that they cannot be performed by one person. Therefore, clear areas of specialization must be defined at all levels of organization and work divided accordingly.

Special K An animal tranquilizer snorted by teenagers to get high. The drug is dangerous in that it causes delusions, irrational behavior, and impairment of motor functions. It may also cause cardiac and respiratory problems. Also called *cat.*

Special Libraries Association (SLA) A network of 15,000 professional librarians whose areas of specialization include the arts, business, education, engineering, environmental and resource management, law, medicine, information technology, news, social science, and telecommunications. The Association provides support and services for special librarians, including employment assistance, continuing education, scholarship aid, research, publications, conferences, consultation, and networking. *Contact:* SLA, 1700 Eighteenth St., N.W., Washington, DC 20009-2508 (202/234-4700; Fax 202/265-9317; URL **http://www.sla.org**).

special performance targets A form of variable pay in which employees are given specific performance goals, such as the number of pages of technical material produced per day, and are rewarded for meeting or exceeding the target.

special practitioner Specially qualified medical professionals who are not physicians but are approved by insurance carriers and Medicare to provide services to beneficiaries. Examples are certified nurse anesthetist, certified nurse midwife, physician assistant, and clinical psychologist.

special training Training programs provided for special groups of workers, such as **fast-trackers** and employees with disabilities.

specialty benefits Additions to employee benefits packages such as mortgage assistance, vehicle leasing, and company credit card programs.

specialty knowledge and skills One of three types of industry standards to be developed by voluntary partnerships under guidelines issued by the **National Skill Standards Board:** knowledge and skills that are the most detailed and specific jobs and functions within an economic sector or firm — much more specific than **core knowledge and skills** and **concentration knowledge and skills**. For example, for manufacturing specialty knowledge and skills might be those required of a computer repairer.

special work team A work team formed to address specific problems or issues. Special work teams engage in cooperative efforts to identify, analyze, and solve job-related or other problems, make recommendations, integrate organization and individual needs and goals, or improve communication and understanding. They are often interdepartmental or departmental. Examples are executive search teams, task forces, quality circles, employee participation groups, and committees.

specified disease coverage An insurance policy that provides benefits only if the subscriber becomes ill because of a particular disease, such as cancer. Benefits are usually limited to a certain dollar amount. Not available in some states.

specified low-income Medicare beneficiary (SLMB) A program for persons entitled to Medicare Part A whose incomes are slightly higher than the national poverty level. The program pays only Medicare Part B premiums. Monthly income limits for the program in 1996 for all states except Alaska and Hawaii were $794 for an individual and $1.057 for a couple. In Alaska, the monthly limits were $986 for an individual and $1,314 for a couple; in Hawaii the limits were $912 for an individual and $1,213 for a couple.

specimen integrity The condition of a blood or urine sample. In drug testing, the need to insure that samples used in drug testing are authentic and accurate in accordance with government (Federal Drug Administration) guidelines regarding measurement precision, storage and transport, and time requirements.

speech benefits An ancillary benefit. Typically cover speech rehabilitation treatment, ranging from ten covered visits per year up to unlimited visits.

speech and language disorders Individuals who have difficulty making themselves understood, due primarily to neurological or mechanical disabilities involving the voice. An individual is considered to have a speech impairment or disability when (1) speech is so deviant that listeners pay more attention to how the person speaks than to what is said; (2) speech is difficult or impossible to understand; or (3) the speaker reacts to his or her own utterance in such a way as to affect the communication adversely. There are two basic causes of speech impairments, functional and organic. Functional (or psychogenic) speech defects are caused by psychological factors; they have no physical origins. Organic speech defects are caused primarily by physical factors, such as accidents, disease, or heredity.

speech/hearing benefits See hearing benefits; speech benefits.

speech-language pathologist A professional who helps people develop their communication abilities as well as treat speech, language, and voice disorders. Services include prevention, identification, evaluation, treatment, and rehabilitation of communication disorders including stroke victims and those who have language delays, stutter, or have other voice and articulation problems. They also work with people who are nonspeaking and use augmentative communication aids ranging from sign language to computers.

speech problems People who have speech difficulties or impediments to oral communication such as stuttering, aphasia, cleft palate, laryngectomy, lisping, and lallation.

speech recognition See voice and speech recognition.

speech synthesizer Converts various types of text signals, such as keyboard, scanner, and switch input, into speech for use by people who are blind. Most synthesizers provide inflection, tonal quality, and variable pitch, and many can be customized by the user for special acronyms, words, and trade terms.

speed An addictive street drug, methamphetamine, taken as pills or injected.

speedball See moonrock.

speed learning *See* speed reading.

speed reading A means of rapid reading. Overcomes such habits as word-for-word reading, excessive fixations, vocalizing, inaccurate return sweeps, loss of concentration, and so on. It emphasizes thinking, increasing eye span, accurate return sweeps, skimming, comprehension, and the like to increase speed and comprehension. May make use of reading rate controller equipment and tachistoscopes.

speedwriting A technique for organizing thoughts, packaging them for impact, and getting them on paper quickly.

spend down Reducing one's assets and income to reach the low levels that will enable an individual to qualify for Medicaid.

spent time A term used in time management to describe time consumed or used before, during, or after completion of a job, task, or project. Although work is done during spent time, it is unproductive. Examples are searching for equipment, tools, materials, or people, setting up and resetting equipment, machines, or automated equipment, or redoing or correcting defective products or poor quality services.

spendthrift trust An estate planning strategy designed to protect a beneficiary against his or her own carelessness, voluntary extravagance, or financial misfortune. The trust is established with income-producing assets, and the trustee is given discretion as to when, under what conditions, and in what amounts the beneficiary will receive the income from the trust.

spider On the world Wide Web, software that scans documents and adds them to an index by following links.

spike A sudden burst of electrical power lasting less than a second. Spikes may damage computer hardware as well as unsaved data. Protection against spikes is provided by surge suppressors — devices that plug into regular electrical outlets and which have several receptacles into which the computer and its peripherals are plugged.

spinal cord injury A lesion of the cord that results in paralysis of certain parts of the body and corresponding loss of sensation and ability to move. There are two primary symptoms: **paraplegia** and **quadriplegia**. Other symptoms may include impairment of bladder, bowel, and sexual function, reduction in pulmonary function, impairment of the circulatory system, muscle spasms, and chronic pain.

spin master Applied to a new breed of public relations personnel, people who are skilled at crafting and spinning the "right" corporate image — a company that is stable, healthy, socially conscious, politically correct. Sometimes called *image doctor.*

SPIRE awards Gold, silver, and bronze awards given annually by the **American Marketing Association** for outstanding promotional campaigns, judged on creativity, planning, presentation, and success. *Contact:* AMA, 250 S. Wacker Dr., Ste. 200, Chicago, IL 60606 (312/648-0536).

split city fare A method of cutting fares by splitting a trip into two legs. For example, a direct, full-fare ticket between two cities some distance apart is often more expensive than the sum of the lowest fare from the departure city to an intermediate destination and from the intermediate destination to the final destination.

split-dollar insurance An insurance arrangement involving an agreement between the employer and the employee (usually an executive) to share or split the cost of insurance premiums, the benefits of the plan, or both.

split-half reliability *See* Spearman-Brown formula.

spondyloarthropathies A collection of disorders that tend to affect the spine. They include Reiter's syndrome, psoriatic arthritis, intestinal arthropathy, reactive arthropathy, and ankylosing spondylitis (the most common type) in which the spinal bones fuse. Their causes are unknown.

sponge tax A means of recovering or reducing the state tax paid on estates by applying credit for taxes paid to the state against the federal estate tax. That is, the state takes a share of the tax the estate pays to the federal government when the tax exceeds the current federal exemption of $600,000 instead of adding a state estate tax. (Actually, the estate tax paid to the state is credited toward the federal estate tax — effectively canceling out the state tax). The $600,000 federal exemption can be used for both gift of assets while living and when leaving an estate to U.S. citizen beneficiaries. An unlimited amount of gift or estate assets can go to a U.S. citizen spouse without incurring federal tax liability. The limit for non-citizen spouses is currently $100,000.

spooling Use of an intermediate computer storage device, such as a disk, to overcome the bottleneck created by the production of output reports at a rate faster than they can be printed. The device accumulates reports in a file for later printing, allows the operator to control when and in what order they will be printed, and permits the operator to use the computer while the reports are being printed.

spot report A brief, hand-written, formatted report of the observations of managers, supervisors, staff personnel, technicians, other employees, customer service representatives, suppliers, or sales personnel to sound the alert about problems and events that could blossom into severe problems.

spousal impoverishment Individuals who become penniless as a consequence of poor financial planning or massive medical or long-term health care costs due to catastrophic illness (and may therefore become eligible for Medicaid). Some protection against spousal impoverishment was provided by **Medicare Catastrophic Coverage Repeal Act of 1989**.

Spousal Impoverishment Law of 1989 The law requires each state to build in protections for at-home spouses and established certain maximums and minimums of income and assets to be set aside for the at-home spouse to keep. Before 1989, all assets owned by a patient in a nursing home had to go to pay for care. Because the majority of institutionalized spouses were husbands, and because typically the couple's assets were held in the husband's name, the wife was rapidly forced into poverty.

spreadsheet A computer program used to analyze numbers in row-and-column accounting format. Formulas can be entered to calculate totals, percents, and other data summaries. Recalculations can be readily made by changing inputs.

spread spectrum See code division multiple access.

springing power of attorney A legal document permitted in some states. Prepared by an attorney, it gives a named individual the power to act as the maker's agent. Unlike a general power of attorney, it "springs" into effect when the maker becomes incompetent.

squatters In travel management, hotel guests who check in a day early and refuse to check out and remain an extra day or days, bumping those with reservations for those days. Used by travelers and convention attendees whose first choice hotel is booked solid. Some states have "inkeeper's rights" laws which give hoteliers the right to evict guests who fail to vacate a room on their confirmed and intended checkout date.

staffing The managerial function concerned with the acquisition (recruitment, screening, and selection), orientation and induction, training, assignment, compensation, development, promotion, reassignment, and retirement or termination of personnel). It employs personnel inventories, projections of position vacancies, and promotion progression charts, carefully designed applicant specifications, job descriptions, recruitment and advertising strategies, and screening and selection procedures. The staffing function involves the use of top quality orientation and induction, performance appraisal, training and development, compensation, promotion, reassignment, and termination systems and programs.

staffing options See contract technical workers; conventional staffing; employee leasing; independent contractors; in-house temporary employees; long-term temporary assignments; master vendor arrangements; outsourcing; part-time employees; payrolling; temp-to-lease programs; temp-to-perm programs; traditional temporary help.

staff leasing Used originally by small businesses and professional practices to minimize the cost of providing benefits to lower-skilled employees, leased staff are now employed to save time and costs, provide professional skills unavailable within the company, and reduce turnover. Staff leasing differs from **temporary employees** in that leased staff are hired by the employing company, stay on the job for an indefinite period of time, and enjoy portable benefits, while temporary employees are recruited by the temp agency, remain on the job for a limited period of time, and lack comprehensive benefits.

staff model A form of **integrated health care delivery system** in which physicians are employed by the system and integrated either through practice purchase or being hired directly. Often the system is a larger and more comprehensive organization than a hospital.

staff model health maintenance organization (SMHMO) An HMO that owns and operates health care centers staffed by physicians employed directly by the HMO. Centers may provide laboratory, x-ray, drug and alcohol treatment programs, prescription drugs, and other medical services. Affiliated hospitals provide inpatient services to members. Also called *closed panel HMOs.*

staff officer or staff manager A head of an organizational element who is not in the direct chain of command — the line of authority leading from the CEO to the lowest hourly worker. Staff officers are responsible for advising and assisting line and other staff elements. They serve as the heads of staff or support elements and have only functional (a defined area) authority over line and other staff officers, although they almost always have line authority within their own organizations. Examples are the controller; manager, training and development.

Stafford Loans The basic, government-subsidized student loan available to everyone. If the individual's college application shows financial need, the government pays the interest on the loan while the student is in school, and repayments don't start until the student leaves school. Maximum loans for freshmen total $2,625 annually; for sophomores, $3,500; for juniors and seniors, $5,500, and for graduate and professional students, $8,500. The interest rate is pegged at the three-month Treasury-bill rate plus 3.1 percent, adjusted annually. These loans are capped at 9 percent for everyone, regardless of income. If rates exceed that amount, the government will pay the difference.

stand-alone software A computer program that does not automatically share data with another program.

standard An objective criterion against which methods, performance, products, services, and results can be measured and evaluated. Standards describe the conditions that exist when a job or function is being done in an acceptable way or the characteristics of a product or service when it meets requirements, conforms to design criteria, or falls within established tolerances.

standard deviation (S.D.) A statistical measure of variation, it is derived by mathematical formula from either a frequency distribution or grouped data. It shows how the scores on a test (or numbers in another type of distribution) distribute themselves around the mean score (or number).

$$\text{Standard deviation } (s) = \sqrt{\frac{\Sigma\, fd^2}{N}}$$

where Σ = sum of
    f = frequencies
    d = deviations from the mean
    N = number of scores

A simplified formula for calculating the standard deviation, accurate for most purposes, is:

$$\text{Standard deviation} = \frac{\text{sum of the high sixth} - \text{sum of the low sixth}}{\text{half the number of testees}}$$

standard error (SE) A statistical estimate of the possible size or scope of error present in an individual test score or a group measure such as a mean or coefficient of correlation.

standard error of measurement (SE meas) A statistical measure of the reliability of a psychological or achievement test expressed in the score units of the test. It indicates the upward or downward distance between the theoretical "true" mean of a test and the actual scores. An individual's true score is considered to lie within a band of scores on the total score continuum; the width of the band depends on the size of the standard error of measurement.

$$\sigma\, \text{meas} = \sigma_1\sqrt{1 - r_{11}}$$

where σ meas = standard error of
               measurement
    σ_1 = standard deviation of the test
    r_{11} = reliability coefficient of the test

standard hour plan Similar to a piecework incentive plan, the standard hour plan rewards workers by granting a percent premium above the base rate that equals the percent by which their performance exceeds the prescribed standard.

standard infection control rules
See universal precautions.

standard interview
See standardized interview.

standardizability A characteristic of an acceptable test. A test is standard when a systematic sample of performance has been obtained under prescribed conditions and scored according to definite rules. Factors in standardization include equipment, tools, and working aids, materials, arrangement, difficulty of problems, and the testing environment; all conditions must be identical for all testees.

standardization Developing and establishing uniform specifications for systems, equipment, machines, tools, materials, procedures, practices, or any type of product or service.

standardized interview An interview that deals with exactly the same subject matter, using identical questions (and usually in the same sequence), and whose answers are comparable and classifiable. Differences in responses should reflect actual differences between interviewees and not to the questions they were asked or the meaning they attached to the questions.

standardized test A test designed to provide an objective and systematic sample of individual performance when administered under carefully prescribed conditions and interpreted according to specified normative information. Also called *standard test*.

standard report A template for a recurring report, usually delivered with the software that is retained as a permanent part of a human resources information system so that it can be reproduced as needed.

standards 1. Benchmarks, criteria, or yardsticks. 2. Criteria agreed upon by computer hardware and software venders that make it possible for them to work together.

standard score A derived score that takes into account the mean performance of a given group on a test and also the relative performance of all people taking that test. If a test is neither too easy nor too difficult for the group tested, scores will be distributed normally: that is, their arrangement will be similar to the normal probability curve. Standard scores are calculated by dividing the deviations of testees' raw scores from the mean by the standard deviation of the group. Also called a *z score*. The formula follows (see also T-score):

$$\text{standard score (z)} = \frac{\text{raw score} - \text{mean}}{\text{standard deviation}}$$

standards of applications architecture (SAA) A set of common (industry-wide) standards by which all computer systems will be transportable and can interface. It will allow users to operate different makes of computers with similar sets of commands.

standards of care Standards that describe circumstances under which certain medical or surgical procedures should and should not be performed. They are developed and refined by expert physicians based on review of published research and personal experience.

standards of performance
See performance standards.

standard test *See* standardized test.

standing operating procedures (SOP) Sometimes mistakenly called "standard" operating procedures. SOPs are painstakingly written, carefully communicated, and thoroughly monitored procedures for performing recurring functions, duties, or tasks.

standing work team A group of employees assigned to either identical or similar jobs and formed into teams based on their location, their jobs, and the structure of the organization. Work team activity is a regular and ongoing part of getting the work of the organization done.

stanine score A form of standard score (standard nine) that divides the score distribution into nine groups. The mean of a set of stanines is 5, and its standard deviation is approximately 2. Each stanine represents a band of scores on the base line of the normal probability curve of one-half of a standard deviation. The entire range of scores is divided into nine such bands. The middle stanine is the band including one-fourth of a standard deviation on each side of the mean. This is numbered the fifth stanine. On either side are four stanines; each is one-half a standard deviation. Those below the middle are numbered one to four and those above, six to nine. The formula is as follows:

$$\text{Stanine} = 5 + 2\left(\frac{\text{Raw score} - \text{mean}}{\text{Standard deviation}}\right)$$

star measurement In productivity improvement, measuring the quality of key processes and results in five areas: products and services; use of resources (people, funds, materials, equipment, facilities, technology, and market position); work processes and environment; employee, management, and labor relations; and customer, client, supplier, and public relations.

star numbers Confidential passwords or booking codes used to identify private discount airfares, such as convention fares, which offer discounts of from 5 to 45 percent. These fares have often been advertised in convention brochures or released by corporations, travel agents, and individual travelers to the detriment of the airlines concerned.

Star Schools Program Created by Congress in 1990 to establish high technology learning centers throughout the country to provide educational programs and materials to low-income students. Technologies employed include Web sites, interactive video and computer systems, and teleconferencing.

State Emergency Response Commissions (SERCs) Commissions or agencies established or designated under the federal law to enforce the provisions of the Superfund Amendments and Reauthorization Act of 1986.

state employment postings Mandatory employment postings required by all 50 states, although requirements differ from state to state. Most states require fair employment law, minimum wage, state occupational safety and health, and workers' compensation posters.

Statement No. 95, FASB Issued by the Financial Accounting Standards Board in November 1987, Statement No. 95 requires public companies to replace the standard Statement of Changes in Financial Position (SCFP) with a Statement of Cash Flows in financial reports.

statement of account In meeting management, a document that lists income and expenses following an event.

statement of non-availability
See non-availability statement.

Statement of Support A pledge make by employers never to deny employment based on Reserve or National Guard Service and to grant leaves of absence for military training of their employees.

statement of work (SOW) A complete, detailed, and realistic statement or specification of an organization's needs and requirements upon which prospective suppliers base their bids to provide products or services. SOWs are developed following systematic analysis of the functions to be contracted or procured using organizational, job, task, and performance analysis procedures. The SOW contains the following:

(1) definitions of all special terms and phrases; (2) description of the facilities to be used and maintained by the contractor; (3) facilities to be constructed by the organization and by the contractor during or prior to contract performance; (4) a list of equipment, supplies, records, and publications that will be provided to the contractor; (5) provisions for accountability of facilities, equipment, supplies, and the like; (6) obligations of the contractor at the end of contract performance; (7) a list of all property that the contractor must furnish; (8) a description of the specific tasks to be performed by the contractor; (9) definition of applicable professional and technical specifications; (10) quality assurance provisions that detail how each task will be received and accepted; (11) a delivery schedule; (12) criteria for measuring the effectiveness of contract performance; (13) a list of all records that must be maintained by the contractor; and (14) a list of all reports the contractor must provide.

State Taxation of Pension Income Act of 1995 Prohibits states from taxing the retirement income of nonresidents. Important to human resources managers because without the legislation employers would have been required to recreate the retirement account history of of former employees, including rollovers and other services in different states. The law mandates that anything that "looks like a pension" can be taxed only by the state in which the retiree is a resident.

State Unemployment Insurance (SUI) Supports workers who become unemployed through no fault of their own and who are able, available, and actively seeking work. Paid for by employers based on a company's unemployment experience rating. Varies from 0.01 to 13 percent of an employer's taxable wages, depending on state regulations

static budgeting *See* fixed budget.

static scoring Assumption that a tax cut produces an equivalent drop in revenues; for example, a 10 percent reduction in tax rates inevitably results in a 10 percent drop in revenue.

statistical analysis An approach to determining or measuring the differences or relationships between variables, treatments, processes, or persons that are mathematically- or numerically-, rather than judgmentally-based.

statistical map   A graphic device for depicting numerical information on a geographic basis. The way the map is shaded, hatched, or colored, for example, can be used to show the magnitude of the phenomena being analyzed or studied.

Language

□ German

▨ French

▧ Italian

▦ Romansch

Switzerland

statistical model   Used in HR forecasting to develop a clearer picture of forces and their impacts on human resources availability. There are two types: the **change model** and the **optimization model**.

statistical process-control (SPC)
1. A strategy for avoiding massive unplanned manufacturing stoppages and controlling the quality of products delivered to customers by programming small breaks into the production system and checking quality at each step in production against standards set in advance. Those standards establish mathematical limits of acceptable performance for each step to eliminate as much variation as possible. Instead of focusing on the final product as most quality control (CQ) systems do, SPC focuses on the process, the true source of QC problems. At prescribed intervals, workers measure a representative sample of their output. The measurements are averaged, the difference between the high and low measurements is determined, and the numbers are recorded and compared with preestablished standards. If the figures fall within tolerances the customers will accept, work is resumed. If not, the problem is fixed. **2.** Techniques and tools manufacturers use to measure their output, which are now being applied to the measurement of training effectiveness and as a means of teaching workers to become more productive. Although used primarily in controlling

product work but recently applied to services and white-collar work.

statute of frauds   A law that requires certain contracts to be in writing in recognition of the fact that the written word is more durable, reliable, and legally enforceable than the spoken word. For example, an individual's promise to pay the debt of another, to indemnify or hold harmless another party, to sell real property, and any contract in consideration of marriage require a written contract. Under this statute, oral contracts are not enforceable unless some kind of written document exists, which is signed by the person against whom the terms of the contract would be enforced. The purpose is to avoid memory lapses, preclude legal disputes, prevent parties from claiming that there was a contract where none existed, clearly identify the terms and conditions of a contract where one does exist, and improve business relationships. The statute of fraud is the law in all 50 states and all Common Law countries.

statutory benefits   Benefits mandated by federal and state laws. They include social security (FICA), workers' compensation, and unemployment compensation. Sometimes partly supported by employee contributions.

steering   In risk management, the ethically questionable practice of influencing a patient to deal with a particular insurance carrier or viatical settlement firm when an agreement exists between the health care provider and the insurance carrier or firm stipulating that the provider will receive a certain percentage of the face value of all life insurance policies the carrier or firm buys.

stepped-up basis   The new tax cost basis an appreciated asset receives when it is listed on a decedent's estate tax return. The capital gains received on such an asset escape income taxes.

stereotyping   The practice of assigning traits or abilities to people based on assumptions made that people with certain characteristics or representing certain races, nationalities, religions, regions, and so on have certain traits, abilities, disabilities, and the like.

still-frame storage unit   A digital device used to store individual video frames, which can then be instantly retrieved by entering its coded address. The device eliminates the need for slides and camera cards in TV production.

still video (SV)   A method of imaging that provides a useful and convenient alternative to "silver" photography. Using still video cameras, which resemble standard 35mm cameras in size, shape, and function, single video frames (still images) are stored on a mini magnetic disk, similar to a computer floppy disk but only 2 inches in diameter. A single disk can hold up to 50 images. Some systems are capable of recording a few seconds of audio with each picture. The images can then be played back over a conventional TV set. Some cameras also have a built-in playback mode. Hard copies can be printed out using a video printer. Its greatest advantage is that still video can be tied in with other electronic media. Images can be transmitted to computers and modified using graphics software; they can be combined with motion video, or transmitted from one location to another just like regular video.

stimulants   Drugs that create a feeling of euphoria or a "high." Repeated use often make the user feel anxious, hyperactive, and irritable. Include cocaine ("coke" "snow"), crack-cocaine ("freebase rocks," "rock"), amphetamines ("speed," "uppers"), and methamphetamines ("crank," "crystal meth").

Stimulus-Response Theory (S-R Theory)
The stimulus-response theory of association or the conditioning process of learning. The theory states that connections are made between stimuli.

St. Mary's Honor Center v. Hicks   A 1993 Supreme Court decision that prevents an employee from winning a job-discrimination suit if he or she makes false statements in court, whether knowingly or unknowingly, about the reason a worker was treated less favorably than other employees. The plaintiff must prove bias based on race, gender, religion, or national origin.

stock appreciation rights plan (SAR)
An executive compensation plan that allows for the payment of undetermined amounts tied to the dividend record of the company or to the gain in the company's stock price over a specified period of time without the actual purchase of stock by the participant. Employees are credited with a number of stock units without ownership rights in the stock itself.

stock equivalent plan   A form of long-term incentive plan. Includes book value plans, phantom stock plans, and dividend equivalent plans.

stock grant   A plan in which employees, usually executives, are given stock in the company as an incentive to improve the organization's bottom line performance. *See also* stock options.

stock incentives   *See* stock grant; stock options.

stock options   Financial incentives to improve effort and productivity, usually directed toward managerial, scientific, and technical employees. Employees are given the right to purchase a specified amount of stock at a certain price for a stated period of time when they have qualified for such reward. Options prices are usually considerably lower than the prevailing market prices, and the difference between the option and the market price is the value of the option at any given time. Include **incentive stock options**, **nonqualified stock options**, and **stock appreciation rights**.

Stoned   A computer virus that displays the message "Your PC is stoned!" on every eighth system boot up. The virus may overwrite the computer's hard disk **file allocation table** and make it difficult to retrieve files from infected floppy disks. The virus is "caught" from an infected floppy.

stop loss   **1.** A provision in health or disability insurance policies that places a ceiling on the amount the employee has to pay (the deductible) as his or her share of a claim. **2.** A provision that limits aggregate losses in self-funded health or disability plans to a specific agreed-upon annual amount. The carrier pays the employer (policyholder) for claims in excess of the agreed-upon amount.

stop words   On the World Wide Web, conjunctions, prepositions, articles, and other words, such as "and," "to," and "a," that appear in documents but alone have little or no meaning.

storing   A learning strategy used by humans (and to some degree by learning machines). It involves storing information in memory that is frequently needed to avoid the need for repeating the problem-solving process. Also called *caching*.

storyboard   In television or audiovisual production, a document that contains statements of the video, company, and audience objectives and sketches showing the information to be covered, style of photography or video shots, action flow, and transitions. It is used to help management and other staff officers visualize what the final product will look like.

straight piecework plan   A type of incentive plan in which workers are paid on the basis of the number of units produced or worked on and where there is no guaranteed minimum wage.

strategic alliances   Business ventures that involve contractual and cooperative efforts toward the achievement of common goals. Alliances may last from only a few months to ten or more years.

strategic future conference
See future search.

strategic leadership team   A group of people who provide overall direction and guidance to a company, department, or unit.

strategic plan   A means of matching the resources of an organization with the internal and external conditions within which it must operate to attain its mission and achieve its goals and objectives. It is a tool to plan for the future and to develop more creative and innovative solutions to organizational problems. The strategic plan examines the effects of potential changes in government policies, demographic and social changes, economic trends, and technological advances, among others. The plan also contains corporate goals and objectives, organization structure, financial data, and break even analysis.

strategic planning   The process of identifying the probable or most likely issues, opportunities, threats, and options that an organization will face over the next five or more years. It involves a look into the future as a means of avoiding disasters and crises.

strategic quality management (SQM)
See total quality management.

strategic staffing   The growing practice of employing only a small core group of permanent employees and making frequent use of temporary employees for highly specialized positions.

strategic thinking   The ability to think in terms of the total business, analyze external factors and their influence on the organization, and see problems and solutions in a new light.

strategy   A compatible combination of goals, objectives, policies, and programs that will enable a manager to accomplish optimum

results under a given set of conditions or circumstances.

strategy/planning meeting   A high-level, face-to-face meeting of key individuals devoted to the formulation of strategic, long-range, tactical, or operational plans or the development of a stratagem to deal with a problem, issue, or crisis.

street name   Listing of stocks, bonds, or other securities in the name of a broker without issuing certificates in the name of the real owner. Useful in the settlement of estates, street names make it unnecessary to change the names on certificates from the decedent's name, to the estate, and then to the beneficiary.

strength and endurance test   *See* physical ability test.

stress   The negative effects of unfavorable job or home conditions on people. The condition adversely affects the physical, mental, and emotional health or productivity of people. Examples are role conflicts, lack of peer or superior support, responsibility for others, pressures of time, work overload, and marital and family problems.

stress interview   An employment interview in which the interviewer deliberately subjects the candidate to tension and pressure to determine how he or she reacts. The practice is not recommended because interviewees are already under considerable stress.

stress management training   Training conducted to eliminate or reduce the consequences of excessive stress to individual employees, their families, and the organization in terms of adverse effects on physical and mental health, damage to personal and family life, increased absenteeism and tardiness, strained interpersonal relationships, complaints and grievances, substandard performance, and lower productivity on the job. Strategies and techniques used include medical referral, psychotherapy, exercises and fitness programs, counseling and self-awareness training, diet consultation and nutritional assays, relaxation tapes and exercises, breathing techniques, meditation, self-hypnosis, and autosuggestion, autogenetic training, massage, biofeedback, seminars and discussion groups, and spouse or couples workshops.

strike   A work stoppage, walkout, or sit-in of employees as a group (usually members of a union or collective bargaining unit) in an attempt to force an employer to grant wage or salary increases or improved benefits.

striped-collar workers   A blend of blue- and white-collar workers. Possess a higher level of technical knowledge and skills than **blue-collar workers** but do not have college degrees as **white-collar workers** typically do.

stroke   Occurs when the brain's blood supply is reduced due to the narrowing of arteries by the long-term buildup of plaque, a process called **atherosclerosis.** May lead to long-term speech loss, memory loss, partial paralysis, and sometimes death. Also called a *cerebrovascular accident.*

structural imagery   The ability to convert mentally a two-dimensional image into three dimensions.

structured experiences   Training activities that involve participants in learning by doing, have specific objectives, involve step-by-step directions, and make use of prepared materials. They are particularly appropriate for management development in such areas as leadership, negotiating, strategic planning, conflict resolution, role clarification, team building, and internal consulting.

structured interview   **1.** In relation to forecasting, a projection technique that makes use of a panel of experts in a series of face-to-face interviews employing a pre-structured standardized interview format, using identical questions and procedures in the same sequence with each interviewee. The results of each interview are recorded and constitute a data base for the next interview. When all of the experts have been interviewed, feedback is furnished to participants by phone or in written form. **2.** In relation to interviewing, *see also* behavioral event interview; comprehensive interview; conversational interview; group interview; nondirective interview; nonschedule interview; nonstandard interview; standardized interview; stress interview; structured interview.

structured query language (SQL)   Computer software used to acquire fast and accurate responses from a relational database.

structured settlement   An alternative to an insurance lump sum settlement. A financial arrangement that allows the defendant in a lawsuit to pay off today's claims with tomorrow's dollars — clearing the books of every-

thing from $3,000 personal injury claims through million-dollar malpractice claims to multimillion-dollar class action suits — by stretching out payments over a period of five, 10, or 20 years, or a lifetime. Typically, the defendant buys an annuity from a life insurance company (or the annuity is self-funded by a corporation or institution) that makes payments to the injured party over several years. The defendant also gets a fast settlement and reduced settlement costs. The plaintiff receives tax- and worry-free guaranteed income tailored to his or her needs over the payment period.

Student Aid Bill of 1992   Made it easier for students from middle-income families to pay for college with government grants and loans. It extended the life of federal higher education programs and authorizes spending of $115 billion over five years. The bill dropped equity in home or farm and college savings accounts from the calculation of assets used to determine student aid eligibility. Raised student income ceilings for students seeking Pell grants of up to $2,400 per year. Students from families of four with an annual income of up to $42,000 (formerly $30,000) a year qualify for the grants. The bill also required all lenders of federal guaranteed student loans to offer borrowers either graduated on income-sensitive repayment options. And the bill established a new unsubsidized loan program for students and families who now do not qualify because their incomes are too high. In addition, the bill established a direct loan pilot program at 200 to 250 schools that eliminated banks and other intermediaries, such as the **Student Loan Marketing Association.**

Student Loan Marketing Association (SLMA) (SallieMae)   One of the nation's largest financial services companies and the leading source of funds, account servicing, and other operational support services for federally insured student and parent loans. Currently funds approximately 40 percent of all insured student loans. Purchases loans from lenders to replenish their funds so they can make more student loans. Sallie Mae is headquartered in Washington, D.C. and maintains education loan servicing centers around the country. One of the nation's largest financial services companies and the leading source of funds, account servicing, and other operational support services for federally insured student and parent loans. Currently funds approximately 40 percent of all insured student loans. Purchases loans from lenders to replenish their funds so they can make more student loans. Sallie Mae is headquartered in Washington, D.C. and maintains education loan servicing centers around the country. *Contact:* **http://investors.salliemae.com/.**

Student Loan Reform Act of 1993
Amended Part D of title IV to make funds available to eligible students (and their parents) attending participating institutions of higher education by means of direct loans made by the participating institutions, consortia, or alternative organizations that had agreements with the Secretary of Education to originate loans.

Student Loan Repayment Program
For each year of service in the Reserve, 15 per cent of the reservist's student loans (Guaranteed Student Loan, National Direct Student Loan, or Federally Insured Student Loan), or $500, whichever is greater, will be repaid, up to a total of $10,000, or up to $20,000 for selected military occupational specialties.

studio   In meeting management, a one-room hotel parlor with one or two couches that can be converted to beds.

study assignment A traditional method of instruction in which the instructor assigns readings in books, periodicals, manuals, or handouts; requires the completion of a project or research paper; or prescribes problems and exercises for the practice of a skill.

stuttering Usually described as excessive repetition or a break in speech rhythm. More accurately, stuttering is a deviation in the fluency of speech. There are three possible causes: (1) physical or constitutional, (2) emotional problems, or (3) learned behavior or response. It is most likely to be the result of environmental or hereditary factors or their interaction. However, no theory about the origin of stuttering has been proved. People who stutter are just as intelligent and well-adjusted as nonstutterers. There are no quick cures. Qualified speech therapists, however, can help people at any age make significant progress in overcoming the disorder.

Stuttering Foundation of America
Formerly the Speech Foundation of America, a non-profit organization established to work toward the prevention and improved treatment of those who stutter. Publishes books and brochures and provides information packets for adults who stutter, parents of children who stutter, Speech-language pathologists, the American Academy of Pediatrics, and the American Academy of Family Physicians. *Contact:* Stuttering Foundation of America, P.O. Box 11749, Memphis, TN 38111-0749 (800/992-9392; Fax 901/452-3931; E-mail **stuttersfa@aol.com**).

stylus system *See* pen computer.

subacute care Comprehensive health care provided immediately following, or instead of, acute hospitalization. Typically involves conditions that do not require complex diagnostic procedures or hi-tech monitoring.

sub-chapter S corporation   A business arrangement under the law, common among smaller firms, that permits the organization to have as many as 35 shareholders and eliminate dual taxation on income and corporation revenues. Under Internal Revenue Service rules, profits and losses are included on a personal return, an alternative that is unavailable to larger C corporations.

subjective disability Illnesses with symptoms that cannot be medically documented; that is, self-reported conditions that can be described but not verified by medical exams. Examples are chronic fatigue, chronic pain, depression, and sick building syndrome.

subject-matter expert (SME) A person with considerable training and experience in an occupation, profession, or discipline used by training or course developers as a resource person to help identify the knowledge and skills required for job performance.

subnotebook A new type of laptop or portable computer being produced by Dell Computer (320SLi) and Gateway (2000 Handbook). Weighing 2 to 4 pounds and measuring about 6 by 10 inches, they are smaller and lighter than other notebooks, yet have a keyboard large enough for touch typing.

subordinate appraisal system   A system that uses appraisal by subordinates to improve managerial performance. It may involve the use of opinion surveys and questionnaires.

subrogation   The contractual right of an entity (such as a health care plan) to recover payments made to a member for services after that member has received such payment for damages in a legal action.

subsidized housing A relatively new benefit in which employers help employees buy their own homes, from providing loans to offset purchasing costs to forming coalitions with local organizations to work with developers and contractors to build houses.

subsidized loan Under federal student aid programs, a loan awarded on the basis of financial need. For qualified students, the federal government pays interest on the loan until the individuals begin repayment and during authorized periods of deferment thereafter.

subsidized payment A means of controlling travel and entertainment costs. Employees pay for all business-related travel expenses either in cash or by personal credit cards and get reimbursed after payment.

substance abuse Misuse of or dependence upon chemicals or other substances such as alcohol, narcotics, or hallucinogens. Usually requires treatment in the form of therapy and support.

substance abuse laws *See* Anti-Drug Abuse Act of 1986; Drug-Free Workplace Act of 1988; Transportation Act of 1989.

substance abuse professional (SAP)
A person who is eligible to provide substance abuse counseling and/or treatment. Includes medical doctors and osteopathic physicians, psychologists, licensed or certified social workers, and alcohol and drug counselors certified by the National Association of Drug and Alcohol Abuse Counselors. Beginning in 1996, all employers with safety-sensitive employees are required to follow federal Department of Transportation regulations mandating that the services of SAPs be made available to employees who test positive for alcohol and/or drug abuse.

substitution analysis A projective technique used in forecasting that seeks to project the rate of substitution that has either started or not yet begun by examining the nature of the substitution, and, based on regression analysis of a set of similar substitutions, develops a specific mathematical substitution formula. The objective is to identify substitutes that can perform a required function more effectively or less expensively. Examples: teleconferencing instead of travel; facsimile instead of overnight mail.

substitution of benefits or employee stock option (ownership) plan (ESOP) benefits
A plan for meeting retiree medical liabilities in which benefits are funded by reducing the benefits of the retiree medical plan and compensating employees with other increased benefits such as pensions or ESOPs.

subtractive color theory The principle underpinning the printing of cyan, magenta, and yellow inks on paper to absorb portions of the red, green, and blue light illuminating a surface to prevent it from reflecting back to the viewer's eye (different combinations of cyan, magenta, and yellow create the appearance of the visible spectrum on the paper).

Successful Meetings: **The Authority on Meetings and Incentive Travel Management** A monthly journal: $48.00 per year (free to qualified subscribers). Address: Bill Communications, 355 Park Avenue South, New York, NY 10010 (212-592-6403; Fax 212-592-6600; E-mail **72262.427@compuserve. com**; URL **http://www.successmtgs.com**).

succession planning Specific plans developed to insure that the needs of an organization for senior managers and executives will be met. The plans identify current and projected personnel resource requirements, current and projected fill, and the sources and means to fill future vacancies with top quality people. Succession planning involves identifying and analyzing key positions, assessing potential candidates against job and personal requirements, creating individual development plans, and selecting the people to prepare for assignment to the key positions.

successor trustee In a trust instrument, the person appointed to take over the duties of the original trustee when that person is unable to serve.

suggestion system A formal or semi-formal means of getting to management the ideas of employees for changes to policies, procedures, and practices, facilities, equipment and materials, products and services, and working conditions. Systems offer employees a ready way to voice their complaints about policies, procedures, and practices, and equipment, materials, products, and working conditions, including hazards to health and safety. Suggestion systems provide an effective means of collecting employee ideas for more effective use of human, material, and financial resources and expand the body of technical, professional and human knowledge to increase enterprise growth, productivity, and profitability.

suggestology An instructional method that uses the power of suggestion and allusion as a means of encouraging, facilitating, or accelerating learning. "This is easy," or "You can do it." Attributed to Ostrander, Schroeder, and Ostander (*Superlearning*, 1979).

suitcasing A traditional method of delivering classroom training to groups workers at remote locations. All materials required to conduct the training are packaged and either sent or hand-carried to the training location where they are used by a "traveling" trainer.

suite In meeting management, a hotel parlor connected to one or more bedrooms.

summary annual report (SAR) A summary of key financial information taken from annual **Form 5500 filings** about a company's retirement plan as required by federal law. Copies of the SAR must be distributed to all plan participants.

summary jury trial An alternative dispute resolution approach in which the parties to the controversy agree to employ a mock, six-member jury, empaneled by a court, to render a non-binding verdict on the dispute. The purpose of the procedure is to demonstrate to the parties how a jury might decide the case.

summary plan description (SPD) A written description of a the key features and benefits of a company's benefit plan. An important part of a plan to communicate benefits information to employees, required by the **Employee Retirement Income Security Act of 1974**. SPDs should be specific, simple, complete, written in plain English, and meet these requirements: (1) be filed with the Department of Labor; (2) be distributed to employees; (3) be updated when significant changes are made to the plan or the law changes; (4) be republished and distributed to employees and the Department of Labor whenever changes are made and every five years at a minimum.

summative evaluation An approach to the evaluation of training systems that focuses on the effectiveness of the program in terms of the results obtained as compared with the resources expended.

summer day camp A form of employer-supported child care service in which summer day camps are organized by community agencies or unions and are partially subsidized by the company.

Summit Award Presented annually by the **Association of Human Resource Systems Professionals, Inc.** to individuals in recognition of their professional excellence within the human resource information system industry. *Contact:* HRSP, P.O. Box 801646, Dallas TX 75380-1646 (214/661-3727).

supercomputer An ultrasophisticated high-powered number-crunching computer with the capability of solving problems (typically scientific) that defy solution by ordinary means. One genre makes use of parallel computing architectures in which tens or hundreds of smaller processors are harnessed together; others consist of one ultra fast computer.

super crip Term used by disabled persons to describe their physically challenged peers who are "overachievers" or have triumphed over their disabilities and become exceptionally competitive, remarkably independent, and highly competent.

Superfund Amendments and Reauthorization Act of 1986 (SARA 1910:120) An act relating to health and physical hazards of chemicals in the workplace and hazardous waste operations. It significantly revised, expanded, and extended the provisions of the **Comprehensive Environmental Response, Compensation, and Liability Act of 1980**, commonly known as the Superfund Law.

Superfund Law *See* Comprehensive Environmental Response, Compensation, and Liability Act of 1980.

Super VHS A recent development in VHS, it offers picture resolution that is twice as good as the standard VHS picture. Super VHS is to video recorders what high definition TV is to television.

supervisory counseling *See* job performance counseling.

supervisory development Training and development provided to selected employees with the potential for promotion to supervisory positions or to incumbent supervisors to remedy performance deficiencies.

supplemental executive retirement plan (SERP) A tailored financial arrangement that functions as a retirement plan for key employees where there is no qualified retirement plan. SERPs help retain key executives, make compensation packages more competitive, help with necessary or desirable early retirement, protect benefits in a merger situation, and restore benefits stripped from higher-paid executives by recent changes in tax laws. Sometimes called a *salary continuation plan*.

supplemental health insurance *See* medigap insurance.

Supplemental Loans for Students (SLS)
Government subsidized loans for certain undergraduate and all graduate students. If the individual's college application shows financial need, the government pays the interest on the loan while the student is in school, and repayments don't start until the student leaves school. The interest rate is the three-month Treasury-bill rate plus 3.1 percent, adjusted annually, and with a cap of 11 percent. Maximum loans for freshmen sophomores, juniors, and seniors is $4,000 annually and $10,000 for graduate and professional students.

supplemental pay benefits Benefits paid for time not worked. They include unemployment insurance, vacation and holiday pay, sick pay, bereavement pay, severance pay, and **supplemental unemployment benefits**.

supplemental protection plan Benefits designed to afford additional protection to workers while they are employed and after retirement. Examples are death, disability, and medical insurance policies that provide higher amounts of coverage than the group plan in effect and, mainly for executives, equity-based plans funded by the company that provide post-retirement income and equity.

Supplemental Security Income (SSI)
A joint federal and state program for low income persons that has no premiums and deductibles. It pays monthly checks to people who are 65 or older, who are blind, or who have a disability and who have little or no property or income. A single person may be able to receive SSI with assets worth up to $2,000; a couple may be eligible with assets of up to $3,000. In neither case is the home lived in and the land it's on counted. Personal property, household goods, life insurance policies, and a car usually do not count. Disabled and blind children are also eligible for monthly checks. People who receive SSI usually eligible for the **Food Stamp Program** and **Medicaid** as well. Basic SSI payments are the same nationwide; however, many states add money to the basic check.

supplemental unemployment benefits (SUB)
Supplements to state unemployment insurance payments funded and paid by employers to unemployed workers. They are typically paid during periods of layoff, reduced work weeks, and relocation.

supplementary benefits Benefits provided by employers, often partly supported by employee contributions, such as health care, life insurance, disability insurance, and pensions.

supply side economics An economic theory that holds that an increase in the money supply provided by lowering taxes will increase productivity and, in turn, profits.

support Services provided by a hardware or software vender after the sale, such as installation, implementation, problem solving, and modifying software.

supported employment Arrangements made by social service and rehabilitation agencies to buy or deliver coaches or tutors to help clients with severe disabilities to learn a job.

support group A group of employees established to provide attention to the needs or special interests of certain categories of employees, such as recovering alcoholics and substance abusers, single working parents, divorced or separated employees, women in non-traditional jobs, disabled persons, and gays and lesbians.

supporting method An approach to instruction that is objectively determined to be an essential complement to a primary method; that is, it must be used in conjunction with the primary method to ensure attainment of the instructional goal.

surcharge In pricing, a charge passed along to the customer resulting from higher business costs at certain locations.

surf/surfing Scanning or browsing through the information superhighway or **Internet** to locate and access needed data or information of interest.

surge A sudden flow of electrical power that can last several seconds and can damage hardware as well as unsaved data. Protection against surges is provided by surge suppressors or protectors — devices that plug into regular electrical outlets and which have several receptacles into which the computer and its peripherals are plugged.

surgical procedure A procedure performed by a licensed physician (M.D. or D.O.) or other licensed medical practitioner, which involves cutting, suturing, treatment of a fracture, reduction of a dislocation, electrocauterization, radiotherapy, diagnostic and therapeutic endoscopic procedure, injection treatment (hemorrhoids and varicose veins), or laser beam operation.

surveillance techniques Passive or observational techniques used in forecasting. They require a large data base, computer support, and a responsive management system.

survey A means of collecting data for use in identifying and diagnosing problems, determining the expectations of people, measuring employee attitudes and morale, and determining status in specific areas of concern to management. Either or both the questionnaire and the personal or group interview may be used to collect the required information.

survivor benefit plan (SBP) An option offered to retired military personnel by which a surviving spouse receives a percentage of the deceased retiree's annuity, currently 55 percent until the survivor is 62, after which the annuity is reduced to 35 percent for life. The premium for SBP is the lower of the current formula (2.5 percent of the first $349 of retired pay and 10 percent for the rest) or a flat premium of 6.5 percent of retired pay, but the premium is dropped if the retiree's spouse dies before the retiree.

survivor insurance An insurance policy that insures two persons, usually husband and wife, but does not pay benefits until both insured persons die. It is usually less costly than insuring the life of one person. Typically used to pay estate taxes and other obligations at the death of the second person insured.

survivors benefits **1.** Lump sum or monthly payments made by an organization to the surviving spouse or children of an employee or annuitant. **2.** In addition to private corporations, survivors benefits are also paid by federal and state governments (Social Security and Armed Forces annuitants, for example). Invariably, maximum payments are established and age limits set for the surviving spouse and dependent children. Under Social Security, survivors benefits are paid to survivors) of workers who have enough credits (depending on age, from 6 up to 40 credits based on 1 credit for each $540 in earnings with a maximum of 4 credits in any single year) for work in jobs or self-employment covered by Social Security and, under a special rule, benefits can be paid to children and spouses even if the individual doesn't have

the number of credits needed. Widows or widowers receive full benefits at 65 or older or reduced benefits as early as age 60. A disabled widow or widower can receive benefits at 50 - 60. Widows or widowers at any age receive benefits if they take care of the decedent's child under 16 or disabled who receives benefits. Unmarried children under 18 (or 19 if attending elementary or secondary school full time) or at any age if disabled before 22 and remains disabled receive benefits. Dependent parents at age 62 or older are eligible for benefits. Under certain circumstances, benefits can be paid to grandchildren. Former wives or husbands (divorced) can receive benefits under the same circumstances as a widow or widower if the marriage lasted 10 years or more. The 10-year rule doesn't apply if the former spouse is caring for a child of the decedent under age 16 or disabled who receives benefits. In general, surviving spouses cannot get benefits if they remarry. However, remarriage after age 60 (50 if disabled) will not prevent benefit payments.

suspense A deadline or target date for completion of an action, project, or task; a "not later than" target date.

Sutton's Law A maxim that says, "Go where the money is!" Applied to health care management, it means, "Pay attention to where the money is spent." Attributed to Depression-era bank robber Willy Sutton who, when asked why he robbed banks, replied, "That's where the money is."

swash letters In topography, type characters that use fancy flourishes instead of a terminal or serif.

sweetheart contract A contract that is let to favored bidders — and sometimes provides exceptionally favorable terms that result in higher profits. In many cases they are illegal because they involve collusion or fraud.

sweetheart deal Preferential treatment afforded to individuals or groups in such areas as contracts, perquisites, compensation (raises and bonuses) and benefits (retirement).

switcher In television production, a device used to control two or more video signals to create special patterns such as wipes, dissolves, and keys.

symbiosis Two employees or others working closely where each person, as well as the organization, benefits in some fashion from the association or relationship.

symposium   A meeting or conference at which a particular subject or topic is freely and openly discussed and opinions are gathered.

synectics   A group problem solving technique that makes use of analogy and metaphor. New ideas are developed by joining two apparently irrelevant and incompatible elements. Exercises are used to break rigid mind sets and generate idea fluency.

synergy   The combined effects of any project, process, or activity in which more can be accomplished by the cooperation and collaboration of two or more people than by their separate efforts.

synthesis   Putting the elements of of ideas, problems, or concepts together.

synthetic GIC   Synthetic guaranteed investment account. Carried at book value and benefit responsive. Issued by banks or financial intermediaries, rather than by insurance companies, a synthetic GIC uses a passive investment approach that substitutes the credit backing of the underlying bonds for the guarantee of the GIC issuer. Synthetic GICs have a maturity date that coincides with the maturity of the underlying securities, but that date may be uncertain when backed by mortgages.

synthetic skills   The opposite of analytical skills, but invariably used after analytical skills. They involve a logical process of combining or merging several facts, concepts, or ideas to create new or improved concepts and ideas.

system life cycle   All phases of a computer system's life, from design, development, installation, implementation, and operation to eventual replacement.

System One   In travel management, a **computer reservation system** owned by Continental Airlines and Electronic Data Systems. Also offers documentation of its systems, consulting on-site and by phone, and certification in its laboratories.

system operator (SYSOP)   The gatekeeper, referee, or "fixer" for a multiuser computer system or bulletin board.

system software   The internal programming of a computer.

sysadmin   Computer vernacular for the systems administrator — the person in charge of the corporate management information system.

systems analysis   The process of breaking a whole system into its component parts and relating those parts to each other and to the whole. The objective is to enable the manager to acquire a better understanding of the behavior and operation of the whole system by studying the behavior and interactions of its parts.

systems, applications, and products (SAP)   An integrated, money-saving, time-saving, enterprise-wide information system, replacement software that replaces conventional individual production, inventory, sales, purchasing, accounting, and other system components with modules that mesh and communicate seamlessly with each other.

systems applications software (SAS)   The computer software that produces a needed product: word processing documents, spreadsheets, budgets, and the like.

Systems Approach to Training (SAT)   The U.S. Army's streamlined approach to the **instructional systems development (ISD)** process. The approach simplifies and abbreviates the ISD process and focuses on evaluation (control) throughout the five-step process.

systems engineering   A systematic search for ways and means of satisfying the functional requirements of a system, it relates mission and system. Systems engineering also translates concepts into procedures that produce the desired system output.

Systems I organization   An organization managed by people who have little trust or confidence in their subordinates, so planning and decision making remain centralized. Attributed to Rensis Likert.

Systems IV organization   An organization managed by people who have complete trust and confidence in their subordinates and share planning and decision making with them. Attributed to Rensis Likert.

systems quality control   Periodic checks on the operation of an on-going system (such as a training system) to insure that it continues to operate as intended and that the quality of the output remains within design tolerances or standards.

systems validation   A means of determining the effectiveness of the various elements of a system (such as a training system) and its suitability to serve the intended purpose prior to its final acceptance and installation as an operational system.

T

TA	1. Task analysis. 2. Transactional Analysis. 3. Transportation Act of 1989. 4. Teaching assistant.	**THA**	Taft-Hartley Act of 1947.
TAB	Training Advisory Board.	**THR**	Target heart rate.
TAMP	Travel Agents in Meeting Planning.	**THX**	Thanks (Internet abbreviation).
TAMRA	Technical Corrections and Miscellaneous Revenue Act of 1988.	**TI**	Toastmasters International.
		TIA	1. Transient ischemic attack. 2. Travel Industry Association of America. 3. Thanks in advance (Internet speak).
TAW	Train America's Workforce.	**TIC**	Technical information center.
TBC	Time-based corrector.	**TIFF**	Tagged image file format.
TBL	Technology-based learning.	**TL**	Team learning.
TBOR2	Taxpayer Bill of Rights 2.	**TLO**	Terminal learning objective.
TBP	Target benefit plan.	**TM**	Transcendental meditation.
TCM	Total compensation management.	**TMA**	Training Media Association.
		TMC	1. Total market coverage. 2. The Military Coalition.
TCP/IP	Transmission control protocol/Internet protocol.	**TMIS**	Travel management information system.
T&D	Training and development.	**TMJ**	Temporal mandibular joint syndrome.
TDA	Tax-deferred annuity.		
TDCA	Television Decoder Circuitry Act of 1990.	**TMRW**	Tomorrow (Internet abbreviation).
TDD/TTY	Telecommunications device for the deaf/teletypewriter	**TNA**	Training needs analysis.
		TNSTAAFL	There's no such thing as a free lunch (Internet abbreviation).
TDMA	Time division multiple access.		
TDU	Total defects per unit.	**TODR**	Transfer-on-death registration.
TDUR	Therapeutic drug utilization review.	**TPA**	Third-party administrator.
		TPL/S	Third-party liability/subrogation.
T&E	Travel and entertainment.	**TPQ**	Threshold planning quantity.
TEA	Technology in Education Act of 1993.	**TPS**	Tiered premium system.
		TPT	Total person training.
TEAM	Teamwork for Employees and Management Act of 1996.	**TQC**	Total quality control.
		TQI	Total quality improvement.
TEI	Total employee involvement.	**TQM**	Total quality management.
TEFRA	Tax Equity and Fiscal Responsibility Act of 1982.	**TQO**	Total quality organization.
		TRA	Tax Reform Act of 1986.
TELNET	An Internet protocol.	**TRASOP**	Tax Reduction Act (1975) stock ownership plan.
TF	Technology forecasting.		

TREA	The Retired Enlisted Association.
TROA	The Retired Officers Association.
TRS	**1.** Telecommunications relay services. **2.** Time recorder system.
TS	Technology sucks (Internet speak).
TSA	Tax-sheltered annuity.
TSEA	Trade Show Exhibitors Association.
TSP	Thrift Savings Plan.
TT	**1.** Text telephone. **2.** Team teaching.
TTTA	Training Technology Transfer Act of 1984.
TULIP	Transurethral ultrasound-guided laser-induced prostatectomy.
TURP	Transurethral resection prostatectomy.
TVCR	Tabletop videocassette recorder.

24-bit color The highest digital color standard currently available where 24 bits of information are used to describe each color **pixel**, yielding more than 16 million colors.

360-degree feedback A means of increasing employee participation, demonstrating company commitment to the work force, and identifying areas for both organizational and individual improvement. Involves multi-rater assessment or group appraisal by collecting behavioral observations from several organizational levels, and external contacts (managers, supervisors, team members, peers, clients, and suppliers) including employee self-assessment. Also called *multirater feedback* and *360-degree assessment.*

T1 line A dedicated data/video transmission linkage that is capable of moving the large quantities of data required by multimedia over a network.

T&E expense management system Software that automates the entry, tabulation, and processing of post-travel T&E expense data to traveler reimbursement and posting to the general ledger.

table **1.** A graphic display of data in tabular form — containing headings and columns. **2.** In human resources information systems, a means of storing detailed data common to a class of employees (such as supervisors) or a set of procedures, referenced by a simple code. For example, a benefits plan table carries all characteristics of the different plans in effect, each with its own code. A benefits change, such as a new premium rate, can be made to the table instead of changing the records of all affected employees.

tabletop videocassette recorder (TVCR) A compact, portable delivery system that combines a standard VHS videocassette player and an 11- or 13-inch television monitor in a single unit.

tachistoscope A device used to present visual stimuli (letters, words, phrases, figures, or colors) for one-fifth of a second or less. Used to increase reading speed.

tactical plans *See* operational plans.

Taft-Hartley Act *See* Labor-Management Relations Act of 1947.

Taft-Hartley Amendment of 1990 Legislation that allows unions to negotiate for housing assistance for their members. In addition to earlier anti-corruption provisions prohibiting management from making direct payments to unions except for certain purposes such as employee education, health care, and retirement, the amendment adds housing to the list of exemptions.

tagged image file format (TIFF) In desktop publishing, a standard graphics file format for both bit-mapped images and a common format used by scanners.

tailored training Training that is customized for a particular group of people in a specific organization so that it is relevant to the trainees, real jobs, the organization, and the industry.

take-home pay An employee's earnings after taxes, Social Security deduction, and other voluntary and involuntary deductions (such as life, medical and health insurance, union dues, contributions to charitable organizations, and garnishments).

takeover *See* merger.

talent The professional or nonprofessional "actors" in a live dramatization, film, or TV production.

tall organization An organization with a narrow **span of management** and many levels of authority where only a few subordinates report to one superior.

tangible net worth The sum of all outstanding preferred and common stock, surplus, and undivided profits, less any intangible items included in the assets, such as good will, trademarks, patents, and copyrights, leaseholds, mailing lists, treasury stock, organization expenses, and underwriting discounts and expenses.

tangible personal property   Items of a physical nature; for example, cars, furniture, jewelry, paintings, and antiques.

tangible reinforcer   *See* tangible reward.

tangible reward   A reward that is concrete and touchable, such as savings bonds, trophies and plaques, certificates, and merchandise.

target benefit plan (TBP)   A hybrid type of **defined contribution plan** in which contributions are determined as though the plan were a **defined benefit plan**; however, the amount of benefit received at retirement depends on the value of the assets in the worker's account, just as it does in a defined contribution plan.

targeted jobs tax credit   An employer tax credit of 40 percent of the first $6,000 earned by a qualified disabled worker. To qualify for the credit, the disabled worker must be certified for the program by a State Employment Service, a Private Industry Council, or a State Vocational Rehabilitation Program prior to beginning work.

target heart rate (THR)   The safest number of heartbeats per minute that a person's heart should pump during aerobic activity. To improve cardiovascular fitness, the American College of Sports Medicine and the American Heart Association advise that during workouts people should keep their heart rates within a safe range; that is, somewhere between low and high heart rates. THR is determined as follows: (1) calculate the maximum heart rate by subtracting your age from 220; (2) calculate the high THR by multiplying the maximum heart rate by 0.80; (3) calculate the low THR by multiplying the maximum heart rate by 0.60. Heart rate may be checked by taking the pulse immediately following exercise. Count the pulses for 10 seconds and then multiply by 6. The resulting number should be somewhere between the low and the high THRs. The formulas for calculating maximum, high, and low heart rates are as follows:

$$\text{Maximum heart rate} = 220 - \text{age}$$

$$\text{High THR} = \text{maximum heart rate} \times 0.80$$

$$\text{Low THR} = \text{maximum heart rate} \times 0.60$$

target marketing   *See* market segmentation.

target plan   *See* target benefit plan.

task   A level in the structure of work. One of the work operations that is a logical and essential step in the performance of a duty. That is, every duty is made up of one or more tasks, and a task has the same relationship to a duty as a duty has to a job. A task is a work unit that defines and describes the methods, procedure, and techniques by which a duty is carried out. Each task has these characteristics: It is performed in a relatively short period of time (seconds, minutes, or hours but rarely days or longer); its occurs with reasonable frequency in the work cycle; it is an independent and finite part of a duty; it is performed by one person (not shared or divided with another worker); it involves closely related skills, knowledge, and abilities; and it is performed in accordance with some standard. For example, an electronic equipment repairer's servicing duty might include cleaning, lubricating, replacing tubes, and filling reservoirs with hydraulic fluid.

task analysis (TA)   The lowest practicable level of analysis; the process of defining the behaviors, conditions, and standards of a task and identifying the elements that distinguish that task from other tasks.

tasker   *See* snowflake.

tax cost basis   When the cost of an item is subtracted from the the proceeds of the sale of the property, the result is the taxable gain. The cost of something sold is seen as a return of capital and is not taxed.

tax-deferred annuity (TDA)
See tax-sheltered annuity.

Tax Equity and Fiscal Responsibility Act of 1982 (TEFRA)   Legislation that made Medicare the secondary insurer and employer-provided plans under contract with **health maintenance organizations** the primary insurance source for active employees aged 65 to 69. The law has since been amended to include working spouses younger than age 65 and active employees older than 69. Regulations implementing the act became effective February 1, 1985. TEFRA simplified risk contracting requirements, brought them more in line with the way HMOs operate, and introduced the practice of returning saving to Medicare beneficiaries rather than to the government.

tax extender A term used by some to describe legislative proposals giving tax-favored status to employee benefits such as group legal and education assistance plans.

tax home As defined by **Section 911, Internal Revenue Code,** the general area of an individual's place of business, employment, or post of duty, where he or she is permanently or indefinitely engaged as an employee. A tax home is not necessarily a person's residence or family home. If an employee's regular abode is in the U.S., it cannot be in a foreign country. The location of the home is determined, in part, by whether the overseas assignment is temporary or indefinite. A foreign assignment that is expected to last or actually lasts two years or longer is considered indefinite. Circumstances determine whether an overseas assignment that lasts less than one year is temporary or indefinite. If the overseas assignment lasts for more than one year but less than two years, it is considered an indefinite assignment unless the employee plans to return to the same home in the U.S. after the assignment and the U.S. home is the individual's regular abode.

tax law: incentive programs Sales and nonsales incentives are not tax deductible. Length of service and safety programs are partially tax deductible — up to $400 per employee; however, the employee will be taxed on any sum exceeding the first $400. If the rules of the length of service or safety program are in writing and kept on file by the employer, up to $1,600 per person is deductible, but the average payout per employee must not exceed $400.

TaxLink A system of reporting that became effective with the signing of the **North American Free Trade Agreement** in 1994. The Internal Revenue Code was amended to require employers to pay their taxes electronically. Taxes affected include payroll, excise, corporate, unemployment, and railroad retirement. The program will be phased in over a six-year period that began January 1, 1995 based on certain thresholds of tax liability.

Taxpayer Bill of Rights 2 (TBOR2) A sequel to the TBOR of 1988. Provides added protection against alleged Internal Revenue Service abuses — such as intimidating taxpayers, placing liens on homes and businesses, and confiscating property — by appointing a taxpayer advocate, speeding up agency responses to disputes and refunds, giving IRS agents more leeway to accept **offers in compromise**, providing relief to innocent spouses (who signed joint returns containing understatement of tax liabilities), and allowing higher damages (up to $1 million) for "reckless" and intentional disregard of the law pertaining to collection methods.

Tax Reduction Act (1975) stock ownership plan (TRASOP) *See* payroll-based stock option plan.

Tax Reform Act of 1986 (TRA) Established nondiscrimination standards for employee compensation and benefits, limited certain salary deferral plans, and set new standards for pretax benefit plans, loans, and pensions. The Act greatly reduced the usefulness of IRAs by restricting the tax deductibility of contributions, based on adjusted gross income for active participants in company pension plans. New IRS regulations, effective January 1, 1991, provided guidance on the retirement plan nondiscrimination rules added or changed by the Act. Among other things the regulations were designed to simplify the previously proposed minimum participation requirements under Section 401(a)(26) and provide new tests to insure that benefit plans do not discriminate in favor of highly compensated workers. The Act also clarified a travel issue: A corporation cannot deduct a cruise meeting as a business expense unless the ship is a U.S.-registered ship whose every stop is in U.S. ports, and such deductions are limited to $2,000 per year.

tax-sheltered annuity (TSA) Provides retirement income for workers of certain tax-exempt organizations. Amounts saved can accumulate tax-free and sometimes provide other tax advantages; however, amounts paid to annuitants at retirement are treated as ordinary income and so taxed. The **Tax Reform Act of 1986** modified the amount that may be contributed to TSAs. Also referred to as *tax-deferred annuity*.

teachable moment That relatively brief and often unpredictable period when a learner is eager for advice, assistance, or training.

teacher certification A credential that has historically been used to verify that an individual is qualified to teach in the public schools of a state.

Teacher Corps Programs Created by the Higher Education Reauthorization Act of 1992 to provide college aid to prospective teachers in return for their commitments to teach in under-served areas.

teaching assistant (TA) A graduate student assigned to a university professor (or professors) to help with their course loads by providing assistance to students, grading papers, and so on.

team See cross-functional team; functional team; parallel team; project team; strategic leadership team; work team.

team-based pay A compensation plan that uses work team performance measures to determine the amount of pay awarded or compensating members of a work team in such as way as to encourage collaboration and productivity.

team building A strategy for helping a work group improve its unity of purpose and functioning by learning to identify, analyze, and solve its own problems. The basic strategy is group discussion centering on encouraging team members to listen attentively and express their ideas and feelings openly, insisting on frankness in expressing disagreement, resolving disagreement by consensus, maintaining focus on the tasks to be accomplished, and periodically examining how well the group is doing and how its members are contributing. Content typically includes long- and short-term planning, allocation and redistribution of resources, communication and coordination, motivation and morale, conflict resolution, training and development of subordinates, decision making, and designing and implementing controls.

team concept A view of on-the-job working relationships that emphasizes collaboration, cooperation, and teamwork rather than individualism, self-reliance, and competition.

team hiring Using organization teams to perform significant parts of the hiring process. Companies that use the approach typically train team members in the law, company policy, how to ask questions and how to listen, what to look for in a candidate, and how to rate or rank candidates.

team incentive A reward earned and shared by a small group, rather than an individual, for meeting or exceeding special performance targets.

team learning (TL) 1. A form of organization in which a group of trainees, under one instructor, is subdivided into smaller groups or teams for instruction and performance. Under the supervision and guidance of the instructor the teams engage in learning activities of a variety of types aimed at the development of verbal or manipulative skills. It is a means of handling individual differences, teaching team skills, providing guided practice in developing verbal or manipulative skills, and developing problem solving ability. **2.** An **organization development** strategy that provides a means of designing and delivering management training that focuses on work team problem solving.

team pay See team-based pay.

team selling A team approach to sales designed to overcome the problems associated with the complexity and global nature of corporate business today. Teams may be cross-functional groups of people from various departments of the company such as research and development, engineering, customer service, maintenance, and training, a coordinated group of sales persons that forms an international team, or a team assembled from several divisions of the company representing different product lines.

Teamsters Union See International Brotherhood of Teamsters, Chauffeurs, Warehousemen and Helpers of America.

team teaching (TT) A form of training that uses a team of two to eight instructors. One member is designated as the team leader and the others, who represent a range of subject-matter and teaching competencies, jointly plan, conduct, and evaluate all learning activities for a relatively large group (up to 30) of trainees. The system is used to handle large and diversified groups of trainees with greater efficiency, maximize the use of available instructor knowledge and skills, provide a means of dealing more effectively with individual trainee differences, and individualize instruction to the maximum.

team training See team learning.

Team Work: Your Personal Guide to Working Successfully with People A newsletter published by Dartnell, 4660 Ravenswood Ave., Chicago, IL 60640-4595 (800/621-5463)

Teamwork for Employers and Managers Act of 1996 (TEAM) Legislation that would have amended the **National Labor Relations Board** ruling in the **Electromation decision** to permit employers to establish and maintain **employee involvement** programs, including joint labor-management committees, without fear of litigation to discuss matters of mutual interest, including issues of quality, productivity, safety, and efficiency. Although passed by both the House and Senate, the bill was vetoed by President Clinton on July 30, 1996. Reintroduced in 1997 by Rep. Harris Farwell R-Ala. as HR. 634 and in the Senate as S. 295, by Sen. Jim Jeffords, R-Vt. **Teamwork for Employers and Managers Act of 1997** would amend the NLRA to allow an employer to establish assist, and participate in programs that address "matters of mutual interest" to employers and employees, provided that the workers participate in the program "to at least the same extent practicable" as their managers.

techies Technical experts; usually used in connection with the use of technical experts as a training resource.

Technical Corrections and Miscellaneous Revenue Act of 1988 (TAMRA) The Act requires employers to report the total amount of dependent care assistance provided for each employee.

technical education and training personnel A category of technical workers that includes professors, teachers, and trainers who prepare technical work force for their jobs.

technical information center (TIC) *See* information center.

technical professionals A category of technical workers that includes scientists, engineers, architects, and health professionals (physicians, dentists, podiatrists, and so on), computer systems analysts, and computer scientists.

technical skills Occupationally related, concrete, and functional skills — the kinds of skills that operating employees and managers have in common, although the specific skills the two groups possess vary both in kind and complexity. For example, a computer operator may be skilled in the use of Lotus 1,2,3; a training manager should be skilled in the selection and use of instructional methods.

technical support employees A category of technical workers that includes managers of technical workers and marketing and sales personnel who work in industries and institutions where technical products or services are produced or provided. They require some technical education and training.

technical systems analysis Examination of the key variables that impinge on, interact with, or interfere with the accomplishment of the core work or objectives of the organization and detail the specific steps required to convert inputs into outputs.. The analysis includes statistical quality control and **sociotechnical systems** redesign.

technical training Training that focuses on the application of mathematical and scientific principles to the creation of products, services, or processes. It is provided for workers who use technology in their jobs. Most technical training in industry is geared to upgrading and updating skills in jobs that require certification or licensing; for example, in health care.

technical trend extrapolation A projective technological forecasting technique that begins by identifying the characteristics of a technology that are key to its performance (such as accuracy, maintainability, cost, and so on) and plots them against time in an attempt to discern a regular development pattern, which can then be extended into the future to make the forecast.

technical workers Employees whose work requires technical knowledge and skills. The category includes technical professionals, technical support personnel, technologists, technicians, blue-collar technical workers in manufacturing, transportation, and utilities industries, and technical education and training personnel.

technical writer An HR/HRD competency. Technical writers convert highly technical materials into readable and usable form. They produce technical manuals, instruction sheets, job aids, and the like.

technician An individual highly trained and skilled in the methods and procedures associated with any technical occupation, profession, or trade. A specialist or expert in a technical field.

technobabble Language that sounds scientific; the technification of ordinary language. It makes use of euphemisms and sometimes attempts to obfuscate ideas or replace accuracy in descriptive language to make things appear to be more positive or more believable. Examples are "sleep deficit" for "overtired," "human interface" for "human interaction" or "human relations," and "lethality system" for "weapon" or "weapons system."

techno hobo A free-lance technology expert of some sort who is often on the road pursuing his or her business calling.

technographer An individual trained and experienced in acting as a cofacilitator of a meeting by selectively recording information and displaying the evolving record for all participants to see, edit, and reorganize on the spot. *See also* facilitator; technography.

technography A computer-enhanced approach for organizing, managing, presenting, and distributing the information generated in meetings. It involves interactive recording and employs two components: equipment and a person who can manipulate software while listening for and organizing pertinent information.

technoliteracy Knowledge of the capabilities of technology-based equipment, such as computers, compact disks, interactive/multimedia, and computer-assisted design and manufacturing systems.

technologist *See* technician.

technology Industrial science; systematic knowledge in the industrial arts and sciences.

technology assimilation A goal of many organizations: ensuring that technology is being used to best advantage for both the organization and its employees.

technology-based learning (TBL) A general term that describes computer-driven applications of educational/training technology. Encompasses **computer-based training** (CBT), **computer-based learning resources** (CBLR), and **computer-managed instruction** (CMI).

technology forecasting (TF) Techniques used to predict, preferably in a quantifiable, logical, and credible way, the nature, direction, rate, and effects of changes in technology. *See also* integrative techniques; normative forecasting; projective techniques; surveillance techniques.

technology integration A growing challenge for human resources personnel posed by the power of the personal computer, the variety of products being marketed, and the trend toward centralizing HR responsibilities. Involves the integration of combinations of hardware, software, and personal computer components to support HR projects and services.

Technology Preparation *See* Tech Prep.

Technology-Related Assistance for Individuals with Disabilities Act of 1988 An Act that established grants to states to set up programs to encourage the use of assistive technology for people with disabilities and national programs, including studies to investigate the financing of technology, the development of an information and referral network (Title I), and a public education campaign to enable workers with disabilities to live more independently, perform a greater variety of jobs, or return to work more quickly (Title II). The Act encourages employers and employees in states that have such technology programs to obtain help from the local organization to develop technological accommodations for employees.

Technology Training A journal published eight times per year by The Cobb Group, a Division of Ziff-Davis Publishing Company: $69.00 per year (free to qualified subscribers). Address: 9420 Bunsen Pkwy., Louisville, KY 40220 (800/769-2075 or 502/493-3200; Fax 502/491-4200; E-mail **editor@ittrain.com**; URL **http://www.ittrain.com**).

technophobia Fear of complex machines, such as computers, faxes, photocopiers, and videocassette recorders. Technophobes are intimidated by complicated devices.

technotraining High-tech means of conducting training such as computer-based instruction, interactive video, and teleconferencing.

Tech Prep Technology Preparation, a federally funded program established to prepare students attending vocational-technical secondary schools for the jobs of the future as skilled technicians having two or more years of college training in such fields as manufacturing, communication, health care, and electronics. Tech Prep integrates the curriculums of the last two years of secondary school and two subsequent years at a post-secondary institution, resulting in award of an associate degree. Students take some college-level courses while attending high school under a cooperative arrangement between a postsecondary institution and a vocational high school.

telecomputer A utility that combines the telephone, television, and computer into a single unit used to access information and convert it into meaningful knowledge. The term is attributed to George Gilder.

telecommunications Transmission of audio, video, or both audio and video information, documents, data, and visuals by means of telephone land lines, radio waves, or satellite communication links.

telecommunications device for the deaf/teletypewriter (TDD/TTY) *See* telecommunications relay services.

telecommunications relay services (TRS)
Telephone transmission services that enable individuals with hearing or speech disabilities to communicate by wire or radio with hearing persons in a manner that is functionally equivalent to the ability of an individual who does not have a hearing or speech disability to communicate using voice communication services by wire or radio. Hot line telephone numbers are staffed 24 hours per day, every day for those who are deaf, hard of hearing, or speech impaired and cannot communicate by means of a standard telephone to call anyone, anywhere in the United States or Canada with no limits on the length or number of calls. Specially trained communications assistants (operators) connect users with hearing or speaking persons. The system requires the installation of special telephone equipment. Most states have 800 numbers. There are no extra fees or charges for the service. For toll calls, TRS users pay rates no greater than the rates paid for equivalent telephone services with respect to such factors as the duration of the call, the time of day, and the distance from the point of origin to the point of termination. In most areas, discounted rates are given to those eligible for direct-dial, station-to-station calls outside the local calling area but within the geographic area. To qualify, a physician, otolaryngologist, licensed speech-language pathologist, audiologist, or representative of an authorized agency must sign a form indicating the service is needed for communication over the phone line. Formerly called *telecommunications device for the deaf/teletypewriter (TDD/TTY)*.

telecommuting/telecommuters Participants in part-time or full-time work-at-home programs, with or without computers and modems tied into the corporate home office.

telecenter/telecommuting center A modification of work-at-home programs. Instead of traveling to their normal offices, workers drive to a center established within their area containing workstations, phone lines, modems, fax machines, and copiers. The arrangement cuts commute time and eliminates the interruptions they might encounter at home. Also called *telework center*.

teleconferencing Satellite or phone line TV point-to-point communication links established between two or more groups at two or more locations to provide instant interchange of aural and visual information or for training. Teleconferencing may take any of four modes: (1) video conferencing, which uses TV images plus sound at all locations; (2) computer conferencing, where computers at several sites are netted; (3) audio-graphic conferencing, where audio via telephone and visual images via FAX are the means of communication; and (4) audio conferencing, voice communication by means of telephone, radio, or satellite.

telecourses Whole secondary- or college-level courses dealing with a single subject available on videotape (or cassettes) supplemented by ancillary materials.

telephonic health care services A call-in service offered by many managed-care organizations to help employees make better-informed health care decisions and help employers avoid unnecessary expenses. Typically use registered nurse-answered, round-the-clock 800 numbers and rely on information technology, such as hundreds of physician-approved protocols that serve as a basis for decisions with respect to a variety of illnesses and injuries.

TELNET An **Internet protocol**/application program that allows a user to log in to another computer remotely to retrieve data if they have the Internet address where the information is stored.

telephone monitoring Listening in on telephone conversations in the workplace. Considered an invasion of privacy by many employees and necessary to meet business needs by some employers.

telemarketing Contacting potential customers and clients by phone, either within the company or outside, to identify unmet needs for HR products and services. It may also be used to qualify sales leads, sell new products or services to old and new customers, clients, or prospects, renew service contracts, complement standard marketing efforts, and obtain data from prospects for market research on company products and services.

Telemarketing and Consumer Fraud and Abuse Prevention Act of 1994 Legislation that gave the Federal Trade Commission broad authority to regulate **telemarketing** by adopting a rule that prohibited deceptive and abusive telemarketing acts. The final rule, which became effective in January 1996, includes a requirement for marketers to disclose the following information: (1) cost of the product; (2) restrictions or conditions on the purchase of the product; (3) refund policy; (4) the odds of winning a prize, or if odds cannot be calculated in advance, the factors used in calculating the odds, that no purchase is necessary to win, and how to participate in the promotion without making a purchase or a payment; and (5) all costs that must be incurred or conditions that must be fulfilled to redeem a prize. The rule does not apply to America Online, Prodigy, the Internet, E-mail, and other types of communication, which the FTC will decide how to regulate at some time in the future.

telemarketing rule *See* Telemarketing and Consumer Fraud and Abuse Prevention Act of 1994.

telemedicine Use of telecommunications technology to diagnose illnesses and injuries and provide patient care over long distances. Uses one- or two-way video over ordinary telephone lines or fiber optics (or telephone communication tied in with satellites) with digital signal compression to examine patients, discuss symptoms, and send the results of such diagnostic tools as echocardiograms, CAT scans, and fetal monitoring from one physician to another.

telephone checks A screening device used to verify information supplied by candidates for employment either in application forms or in interview.

telephone reassurance or support A service offered by volunteers who call aged or disabled persons daily to check that all is well with the individual called. *See also* homemaker services; friendly visitors.

telephone service A means of transmitting low-resolution multimedia over copper wires. Represents the lowest level on the **bandwidth** spectrum.

telephonic health care services A call-in service offered by many managed-care organizations to help employees make better-informed health care decisions and help employers avoid unnecessary expenses. Typically use registered nurse-answered, round-the-clock 800 numbers and rely on information technology, such as hundreds of physician-approved protocols that serve

as a basis for decisions with respect to a variety of illnesses and injuries.

TelePrompTer An electronic device that displays a speaker's script, running at a speed that matches the individual's delivery. Modern devices include a transparent screen that is not visible to the audience.

teleradiology A telecommunications technology that allows health care providers to exchange medical and dental images for consultation and medical review purposes. It uses an all-digital, fiber-optic telephone network to transmit diagnostic quality angiogram, **computerized tomography**, **magnetic imaging**, **positron emission tomography**, sonogram, thermogram, and X-ray readings and images in seconds.

telerecruiting A nontraditional, low cost, and increasingly popular means of expediting the hiring process. Potential candidates are screened and interviewed for open positions by in-house or contract recruiters. It is controversial because it targets people who are currently employed.

telescoping Describes the phenomenon of women developing alcoholism more rapidly than men. Although women tend to start drinking at a later age than men, they appear for alcoholism treatment at about the same age.

teletraining *See* teleconferencing.

Television Decoder Circuitry Act of 1990 (TDCA) An amendment to the Communications Act of 1934, the Act required, as of July 1, 1993, that all television sets with screens of 13 inches or more have built-in decoder circuitry capable of displaying closed captions, making it unnecessary for the deaf and hearing impaired to use portable decoders and achieve compliance with the auxiliary aids and services requirements of the Americans with Disabilities act of 1990.

teleworking A work environment change, usually voluntary, in which employees no longer have offices with desks and report in person daily. Instead, each worker is given a personal computer, modem, answering machine, and fax so that they can work at home or at another specified location. Hours and days of work and any type of flexibility allowed should be clearly defined.

temp A person who temporarily fills vacated positions. Includes "hired gun" financial officers and controllers, executives, professional personnel directors and corporate counsels, and "high-rent" managers, as well as accountants, clerks, and secretaries.

temping Using contingent or temporary workers to provide labor flexibility, acquire needed expertise, control employee head count following downsizing, fill in for absent employees, screen candidates for future employment, and control benefits costs.

temporal mandibular joint disease/ syndrome (TMJ) Pain or discomfort, limitation of motion of the jaw, or cracking in the jaw due to inflammation or degenerative changes in the jaw joint most often resulting from aging, arthritis, injury, or muscle tension caused by repeated jaw-clenching or tooth-grinding.

temporary agency hire A flexible staffing option. Hiring professionals or other workers for specified time periods or projects. They remain the employees of the agency and not of the company that contracts for their services.

temporary employees Corporate executives, managers, technicians, physicians, nurses, pharmacists, accountants, or office workers hired on a temporary basis to meet seasonal or emergency requirements, which cannot be met through organizational resources. Provide a means of remaining globally competitive and avoiding the ups and downs of market cycles and the growing burdens of employment rules, antidiscrimination laws, health care costs, and pension plans. Also called *contingent workers, contractors, disposable workers, extra workers, fill-ins, free-lancers, just-in-time employees, part-timers, per-diem workers, leased employees, peripherals, short-timers, supplementals,* and *temporary staffers.*

temporary trainer *See* free-lance trainer.

temp-to-hire A staffing strategy in which temps interested in full-time positions are recruited and assigned for a trial period during which time the company evaluates the temp's skills and the temps evaluate the workplace. The temps are paid by the temp agency during the trial period, and the company avoids the cost of poor hiring decisions and saves money in unemployment benefits and workers' compensation.

temp-to-lease programs An alternative staffing option. Involves contracting with two staffing firms, usually a temporary service and a professional employee organization (PEO). The temporary service performs all of the screening, selection, and assignment function for what become long-term temporaries at the client company. After a specified period of satisfactory employment, the temporary employee is moved to leased employee status and transferred to the PEO's payroll.

temp-to-perm programs An alternative staffing option. Involves hiring employees on a temporary basis, typically through a temporary worker company, with the understanding that if they perform well for a specific period they will be offered regular (permanent) employment.

tenancy by the entirety A form of joint ownership, recognized by about 24 states, where property is owned by and cannot be sold without the consent of both spouses. Upon the death of the first spouse, the entire interest in the property passes to the surviving spouse. Property held in a tenancy by the entirety is not affected by the terms of a will and is not subject to probate.

tenancy in common A form of joint ownership in which the tenants in common own a share in the property (for example, a one-third or one-half interest) and are free to do whatever they wish with their share — sell it while they are alive or leave it to someone in their will. Property held as a tenant in common is subject to probate.

teraflops computer The next generation of supercomputers. They can perform one trillion operations per second.

terazosin A generic drug for the treatment of enlarged prostate glands; for example, Abbott Laboratories' Hytrin.

terminal A peripheral device linked to a **mainframe** or **minicomputer** that includes a keyboard, monitor, and a video generator. It has little or no processing power.

terminal emulation Occurs when a personal computer or workstation communicates with a mainframe, performs no processing, and simply displays signals from the host computer. When the communication is disconnected, the equipment resumes its full processing power.

terminal learning objective (TLO) In the design phase of instructional systems development, objectives written for each job performance measure. TLOs include the behavior or action, the conditions of performance, and the criterion or standard to be attained by the learner.

termination Separation from the organization for reason of transfer, resignation, retirement, layoff, or dismissal for cause (incompetence, violation of polices or rules, insubordination, and so on).

termination-at-will The traditional rule that where there is no contract, the employment relationship can be terminated "at will" (for any reason or no reason) by either the employer or the employee. That rule has been superseded due to litigation.

termination clause In contract law, wording that allows either party to the contract to cancel for reasons of acts of God, war, civil disorder, disaster, government regulation, strikes, bankruptcy of either party, and so on. Also called *force majeure clause.*

termination counseling See outplacement.

term life insurance A life insurance policy that remains in effect only as long as premium payments are made. Such policies have no surrender value.

test A means of observing and describing how people perform in a specific, controlled situation. Tests are instruments used to measure such things as general mental ability (intelligence or scholastic aptitude), specific mental abilities (deductive, inductive, and spatial reasoning), specific information, job knowledge, trade knowledge, mechanical aptitude and psychomotor skills, cognitive skills, linguistic aptitude, supervisory and managerial abilities, interests, and personality and temperament.

testamentary capacity The legal ability to write a valid will, which includes awareness of one's possessions (rational), knowledge of who would be eligible as heirs to inherit property, and the ability to devise and comprehend a plan for the distribution of that property.

testamentary trust A trust established during the lifetime of the maker that can be used to protect an estate at the time of the maker's death. It comes into existence after the death of the maker. It is created by drawing up a **will** which must go through the **probate system.**

testator A person who has made a will.

tester An individual dispatched by civil rights and community rights groups to masquerade as a job or housing applicant and potential real estate purchaser to uncover discriminatory practices. The practice was endorsed by the **Equal Employment Opportunity Commission** but is now being litigated on the basis that testers apply for jobs they don't plan to accept. In December 1990, the Equal Employment Opportunity Commission began accepting complaints from testers in the area of job discrimination.

testimonial A form of endorsement in which the endorser *speaks* the words of praise for a product or service. It is provided by someone, typically someone well-known if not famous, not connected with the manufacture of the product or delivery of the service. Used as an advertising vehicle.

testing The quality assurance phase of software development. Includes a search for bugs and running sample data to assess software speed and performance.

test items The individual questions that comprise an achievement, aptitude, or other type of test. The most common types of test items are true-false, multiple choice, matching, arrangement, and essay.

test-retest reliability coefficient A reliability coefficient obtained by administering the same test a second time or different forms of the same test (after a short interval) and correlating the resulting sets of scores.

test scores Test results of all kinds. Scores are reported as adjectival, raw numerical, rank order, percentage, percentile, standard, and stanine scores, frequency distributions, graphic scales, and descriptive statements of performance.

test security **1.** The right of a testee to privacy of information relating to test results and the right to informed consent about the use of those results. **2.** The right of a testee to expect that no one taking the test has access to the test or information about its contents that would give him or her unfair advantage over other test takers.

tests of significance
See levels of significance.

text telephone (TT) Replaces the term **telecommunications device for the deaf** (TDD). Machines, usually electronic devices, that have a keyboard and a readout display. Coded signals are sent and received by text telephones through telephone lines.

T-group See sensitivity training.

thalassotherapy An ancient Greek treatment that uses sea water, seaweed, algae, and sea air to reduce stress and rejuvenate and cleanse the skin.

theater/auditorium configuration A basic type of room layout for meetings or conferences. Used for medium- to large-size groups, with seating that allows all participants to face the speaker and audiovisual screen. No tables are provided. The configuration usually includes a podium or stage.

***T.H.E. Journal:* Technological Horizons in Education** A journal published monthly, except July: $29.00 per year (free to qualified subscribers). Address: 150 El Camino Real, Suite 112, Tustin, CA 92680-3670 (714/730-4011; Fax 714/730-3739; URL **http://www.thejournal.com**).

thematic approach A form of the concepts-based, integrated curriculum. Subordinates subject matter to a core topic, causing boundaries between disciplines to become indistinct. Attributed to Betty Jean Eklund Shoemaker, ("Education 2000 Integrated Curriculum," *Phi Delta Kappan*, June 1991).

The Military Coalition (TMC) An alliance of 24 associations representing 5 million current and former uniformed service members plus their families formed to see that America keeps faith with them. TMC works to protect their interests in such areas as compensation, health care, military construction, base closures and realignment, retirement affairs, taxes and Social Security, and other quality of life issues, such as morale, welfare, and recreation, for active duty and retired, reserve and National Guard veterans, their families, and survivors.

theoretical cycle time The time required for a single unit to undergo every essential step in the production process without encountering any delays or bobbles. It includes *only* value-adding actions.

Theory X The traditional assumptions and beliefs about people: They dislike work, wish to avoid responsibility, lack ambition, like to be told what to do, and show little concern or loyalty toward their organizations. As a result Theory X managers use firm direction and control over their people — close surveillance, coercion, and threats or punishment. Attributed to Douglas McGregor.

Theory Y Sees workers as people who find work as natural and either a source of satisfaction or a source of punishment (depending upon conditions), who seek responsibility, who become committed to objectives through the satisfaction of their esteem and self-actualization needs, and who have the capacity to demonstrate imagination, ingenuity, and creativity in solving organizational problems. Theory Y managers, therefore, delegate authority, enlarge jobs, and permit greater participation of workers in policy and decision making in the areas that affect them. Attributed to Douglas McGregor.

Theory Z Emphasizes the importance of job security and opportunities to gain recognition, rewards and advancement in motivating people, the criticality of employee participation in planning, problem solving, decision making, and quality control, and the importance or significance of adapting managerial strategies and tactics to the national culture and life styles of employees. Attributed to William Ouchi.

therapeutic drug utilization review (TDUR) Programs designed to reduce costs by identifying inappropriate or overly costly prescribing patterns of therapy regimens within an employee prescription drug plan. Studies typically target high-dollar-volume therapeutic categories, such as anti-ulcer, anti-arthritis, and cardiovascular medications.

therapeutic listening Listening that focuses on tuning in to an employee or counselee, concentrating actively, and reacting positively by words, facial expressions, and gestures. Its objective is to elicit comments and content through the use of encouragement and blocking or breaking techniques.

therapeutic touch An alternative treatment involving the "laying on of hands."

therapist A medical, psychological, physical, or other health-related and highly trained practitioner who provides treatment for physical, mental, or emotional disorders, injuries, and illnesses. Examples are psychologists, physical therapists, and psychiatrists.

The Retired Enlisted Association (TREA) An association of 80,000 enlisted retirees from all branches of the Armed Forces, their surviving spouses, and active duty members with more than 15 years of service. Its mission is to represent retired enlisted personnel before Congress and other appropriate federal agencies. *Contact:* TREA, 909 N. Washington St., Ste. 300, Alexandria, VA 22314 (703/ 684-1981; Fax 703/548-4876; E-mail **mzabko@aol.com**).

The Retired Officers Association (TROA)
An independent, nonprofit association of 396,000 past, present, active and reserve, commissioned, or warrant officers of the Army, Navy, Air Force, Marine Corps, Coast Guard, National Oceanic and Atmospheric Administration, and Public Health Service. Its mission is to support a strong national defense and represent members' and their dependents' and survivors' interests in a wide range of compensation, benefits, and retirement issues. Sponsors educational assistance program, survivor assistance, and retiree employment services. *Contact:* TROA, 201 N. Washington St., Alexandria, VA 22314-2539 (800/245-8762 or 703/549-2311; Fax 703/838-8173; E-mail **troa@troa. org**; URL **http://www.troa.org/**).

thermotherapy   A nonsurgical outpatient procedure that uses microwaves to destroy excess prostate tissue — a treatment for enlarged prostate. It costs less than surgery and lacks surgery's worst side effects, including impotence and incontinence.

thesaurus   On the World Wide Web, a list of synonyms a **search engine** can use to locate matches for particular words if the words themselves do not appear in documents.

thinking flexibility   The ability to keep an open mind and produce many ideas related to each other. It requires receptivity and openness to suggestions.

thinking fluency   The ability to generate an abundance of ideas, quickly and seemingly effortlessly and to move easily from one idea to another. Also called *ideational fluency*.

think tank   An organization that employs futurists whose primary occupation is to forecast trends and developments in terms of such things as demographics, politics, social change, technology, and so on; for example, Brookings Institution; Hoover Institution; Hudson Institute; Rand Corporation.

third-party administrator (TPA)   A company that handles Medicare and other health care insurance claims and utilization review for the federal government or corporations. TPAs may offer precertification, a second opinion program, and catastrophic case management. Essentially the job of TPAs is to settle claims problems. They also provide a means of reducing costs by providing outside experts to monitor, evaluate, and control health care services.

third-party liability/subrogation (TPL/S)
A process that enables an employer to recoup funds from settlement proceeds recovered by insured employees. Subrogation is the legal right to sue a negligent third party. The process requires automation to identify, investigate,track, litigate, and recover money from negligent third parties and is typically managed by legal counsel or outsourced.

third-party registration   Occurs when a corporation or company hires an independent organization to audit its suppliers for conformance to international quality standards.

third-party sexual harassment   Harassment of an employee by a customer or client, a violation of Title VII of the Civil Rights Act of 1964, for which employers can be held liable even they don't know the offender personally.

"thirtysomething" generation
See baby boomers.

Thomas Lawson Syndrome   Describes the ruinous tendency of organizations to stick to old beliefs and values and obsolete technologies. The Thomas Lawson was a sailing ship that became obsolete when steam-powered vessels appeared.

thought disorder   In mental illness, a symptom of **schizophrenia**, in which clear, goal-directed thinking becomes increasingly difficult as shown in redundant, repetitious, fuzzy, or muddled speech.

thought police   *See* joint-activities staff.

thought trails   *See* mind-mapping.

three hundred sixty degree feedback
A form of **performance evaluation** that involves direct and constructive verbal (oral and instrumented) feedback from an individual's superiors, peers, and subordinates.

three-year rule   A three-year recovery rule that allowed a federal retiree tax free annuity payments until an amount equal to his or her total contributions to the federal retirement system had been recovered. The rule was repealed by the Tax Reform Act of 1986.

threshold planning quantity (TPQ)
The maximum quantity of any of the 406 hazardous chemicals listed by the Environmental Protection Agency to be used or stored. If larger quantities are used or stored, the organization is required by law to notify the **State Emergency Response Commission**, its **Local Emergency Planning Committee**, and the local fire department.

thrift savings plan (TSP) **1.** A form of equity benefit, a thrift savings plan serves as an adjunct or supplement to noncontributory pension plans. Employees are given the option of saving through payroll deductions a designated percentage of their regular pay in one or more available investment opportunities, usually matched dollar for dollar by the employer. **2.** A retirement savings plan for both **Federal Employees' Retirement System (FERS)** and **Civil Service Retirement System (CSRS)** employees. Participants pay no taxes on TSP contributions or earnings until they withdraw their savings after they leave federal service. Participants covered by FERS may contribute up to 10 percent of their basic pay each pay period (up to the IRS limit). The first 3 percent contributed each pay period is matched dollar for dollar with agency contributions to the account, and the next two percent is matched 50 cents on the dollar. The Agency automatically contributes an amount equal to one percent of basic pay each pay period whether an FERS employee contributes or not. Participants covered by CSRS may contribute up to five percent of their basic pay each pay period (up to the IRS limit), but they do not receive any Agency contributions. There are three investment options: Government Securities Investment (G) Fund, Common Stock Index Investment (C) Fund, and Fixed Income Index Investment (F) Fund.

thrombosis A clot or coagulation of a blood vessel. When it occurs in a coronary artery and completely blocks the flow of blood, the result is a heart attack. When blood and the oxygen it carries are cut off, damage to the heart muscle or death can result.

tic Involuntary but apparently purposeless movements of interconnected muscles. Tics frequently involve the muscles of the eyelids with blinking or squinting, repetitious frowning, grimacing, snorting, grunting, swallowing, head twisting or shaking, or explosive verbalizations. They often first occur in childhood and may disappear or continue through adulthood. To some degree they can be controlled by medication.

ticketing abroad In travel management, the practice of issuing tickets for international travel originating in the United States from a foreign location to get a lower fare. The ticket is then mailed to the traveler.

ticket transfer In travel management, the practice of transferring a nonrefundable ticket or part of a back-to-back ticket issued in one traveler's name to another traveler for use.

tiered benefits plan A cost savings device that expands employees' eligibility for benefits over a specified period of time rather than granting full benefits immediately upon employment.

tiered marketing The practice of marketing products and services by targeting potential customers separately in two or more groupings or channels, using different approaches for each group. For example, using a direct sales for one group (top-of-the-line products), resellers for another group (upper-range products), dealers for a third (mid-range products), and retailers for a fourth (lower-range products).

tiered premium system (TPS) A health care cost-cutting strategy in which premiums for coverage are established at different rates for employee only, employee and spouse, and employee, spouse, and children.

time analysis A time study method that involves the employee directly. The individual records on a prepared form all of his or her activities and the time spent on them for a week or longer. Originally used to establish a standard time for items produced, such as rate-per-hour, time analysis is now used as the basis for analyzing how time is spent rather than establishing a work measurement standard.

time code Typically consists of four two-digit numbers, representing hours, minutes, and seconds. Used to number video frames.

time division multiple access (TDMA) A form of wireless technology that sends bursts or packages of digitalized information through "timeslots." The packets are reassembled into a voice or data signal by the receiver.

time and materials contract In procurement, a type of fixed-rate contract in which, in addition to the fixed rate agreed upon in the contract, there is a provision for the delivery of materials required by the performance of the specified work at cost.

time and motion study The oldest of the accepted work measurement techniques. An approach that involves the study of the motions and time required for task performance of workers using observation, stop watches, or video recordings.

time-based corrector (TBC)　In video production, a device that allows synchronization and editing of video materials produced by two different sources at different speeds. Used to correct technical errors in helical scan VTR formats and permits the tape to be broadcast or dubbed up to larger tape formats.

time grouping　One of the basic means of grouping organizational elements where the number of shifts required to perform the work is the determining factor. This alternative is common in manufacturing and service organizations.

time management　The art and science of using time prudently and well to achieve personal, professional, career, and organizational goals and objectives. It is the practical and effective system of taking time to save time so that you can get more of the things done that have to be done and have time left over to do some of the things you want to do. It involves a systematic approach to the management of programs, projects, activities, priorities, and schedules.

time management software　Personal computer programs that can maintain daily diaries and office schedules, track appointments, provide memory "ticklers" for correspondence, monitor referrals to leads, check sales calls against "closings," estimate staffing requirements for projects, schedule meetings, track the scheduling of facilities, equipment or projects, monitor resource use, and print reports.

time management training　Offered for employees at all levels to improve their use of and control over time on and off the job. Focuses on a systematic approach to the control of time, identifying and analyzing time problems, avoiding procrastination, eliminating time wasters, making the most of delegation, and developing and implementing action plans.

time off from work options　Include adoption leave, paid family leave, paid time off, paternity leave, personal days, sabbatical leave, use of sick days for sick dependents, vacation buying/selling, and vacation carryover.

time-on-tasks　The most critical element of interactive systems or courseware design. The amount of time the system or courseware can hold the trainee on a task — the determining factor in achieving mastery. The amount of time required varies with the type of knowledge or skill being presented and the objectives of the training session.

time recorder system (TRS)　A computerized time clock that can record time and attendance data as they occur and accumulate the data. May be interfaced with a payroll system.

time series forecast　A method of forecasting that makes use of past data to predict future performance, taking into account seasonal factors and trends. It may take any of four different forms: momentum-line, objective or development-line, and potential-line forecasts or model building.

time-sharing　A system that includes a central computer that permits multiple users with terminals at several remote locations to access and interact with large-scale data processing resources at a central location simultaneously.

time study　*See* time and motion study.

tinnitus　An ear disorder in which the individual hears sounds, such as buzzing, roaring, banging, hissing, or ringing, that do not really exist. May be caused by ear infection, a foreign body in the ear, tumor, or otosclerlosis.

tin parachute　A novel type of severance plan designed to protect employees when company ownership changes. A variant of the **golden parachute**, which guarantees hefty payments to key executives in the event of takeovers or mergers, tin parachutes assure lower-level employees of similar benefits. For example, some plans entitle all employees to cash payments of up to two and one-half times their annual compensation, including bonuses and incentive pay, if company ownership changes as a consequence of a hostile takeover. Because of the number of employees they apply to, the plans serve as a deterrent to raiders by making takeovers prohibitively expensive.

tint　In desktop publishing, an even tone area of a solid color.

Title I/Chapter I　*See* Elementary and Secondary Education Act of 1965.

Title VII of the Civil Rights Act of 1964　In 1997, the U.S Supreme Court adopted the Equal employment Opportunity Commission's method of counting employees to determine whether an employer is covered by Title VII. The payroll method, which counts all employees including hourly and part-time workers who are on the payroll for each day of a given week regardless of whether they are physically present at work each day, is also used to determine coverage under the **Age Discrimination in Employment Act of 1967** by the EEOC and the **Family and Medical Leave Act of 1993** by the Labor Department.

Toastmasters International (TI) A 180,000-member international organization dedicated to the improvement of the oral expression of thoughts, ideas, and opinions and leadership potential through an educational program that emphasizes learning by doing. *Contact:* TI, 23182 Arroyo Vista, Rancho Santa Margarita, CA 92688-0000 (800/9WE-SPEAK or 714/858-8225; fax 714/858-1270; E-mail **tminfo@toastmasters.org**; URL **http://www.ni.net.toastmasters.org**).

Token Ring Technology adapted by International Business Machine Corporation to move great quantities of data through a local area network.

Top 25 An annual list of the travel executives (travel buyers, suppliers, consultants, public policy makers, or association leaders) who have most influenced the industry. Selected by the editors of *Business Travel News* from individuals nominated by subscribers and the editors. *Contact:* BTN, One Penn Plaza, New York NY 10119-1198 (212/615-2212; Fax 212/279-3945; E-mail **crosen@mfi.com**; URL **www.btnonline.com**).

top-hat account *See* nonqualified 401(k) wraparound plan.

top-heavy plan A pension plan in which the accrued benefits or the account balances of **key employees** exceed 60 percent of the accrued benefits or account balances of all participants. In addition, if an employer maintains more than one plan, the 60 percent rule may be applied to some or all of the employers' plans in the aggregate. To be tax qualified, a top-heavy plan must comply with special vesting rules: 10 percent vesting for each employee who has completed at least 3 years of service, *or* 20 percent vesting for each employee who has 2 years of service and 20 percent for each year thereafter until the employee is 10 percent vested after 6 years of service.

topics-within-discipline approach A form of the concepts-based, integrated curriculum. Combines several segments of the same discipline within the instructional setting. For example, integrated language arts and integrated mathematics programs. Attributed to Betty Jean Eklund Shoemaker ("Education 2000 Integrated Curriculum," *Phi Delta Kappan*, June 1991).

Torch Awards Awards presented annually to national members (maximum of four) of the **American Society for Training and Development** whose leadership in ASTD over a significant period of time has made a difference in helping the society accomplish its goals and fulfill its vision. Selected by an awards committee from nominees by reviewing documentation and direct contacts with the nominating individual and other person with direct knowledge of the accomplishments of the nominee. *Contact:* ASTD National Awards Program, Attn: Dawn Temple, 1640 King St., Box 1443, Alexandria, VA 22313-2043 (703/683-8100).

tort In law, a wrong or wrongful act committed against an individual or group or their property without a breech of contract (independent of a binding agreement).

tort reform A proposal to restrict jury power and discretion in awarding punitive monetary damages to individuals victimized by fraud or other forms of wrongdoing initiated in response to the enormous sums awarded to plaintiffs in recent years. In a 1991 7 to 1 ruling (*Cleopatra Haslip v. Pacific Mutual Life Insurance*), the Supreme Court refused to limit such awards and left such decisions in the hands of state legislatures to adopt or reject such reforms, thereby disappointing broad segments of the American business community.

total compensation management (TCM) Management of both cash compensation (direct pay) and all benefits provided by an organization to attract and retain employees. Includes retirement benefits, deferred compensation, tuition reimbursement, training and development, memberships, discounts, and stock.

total cycle time The time required to complete the two interdependent cycles involved in the production of any product or service: **make/market cycle** and the **design/development cycle**. Improvement in performance and quality is achieved by simplifying both cycles of activity within an enterprise, eliminating non-value adding steps, and reducing the number of tasks or actions in each process.

total debt The sum of current debt and any outstanding funded debts (debts with a maturity of more than one year from the date of the statement).

total defects per unit (TDU) A measure of product quality.

total employee involvement (TEI) A form of participative management, the objective of which is to involve all employees in a program of continuous improvement — in terms of self, procedures, products, and services.

total fertility rate (TFR) A measurement used by demographers to document by country increases and decreases in the number of births per woman during child-bearing years.

totalization agreement An agreement between the United States and another country to allow foreign national employees transferred to the United States for five years or less to avoid paying U.S. Social Security taxes as long as they continue to pay into their home country's welfare or retirement system.

totally disabled A person who has a disability to the extent that he or she is unable to perform the usual and customary activities of a person in good health and of comparable age; that is, the individual is unable to perform the duties of any occupation. However, federal and state courts have rejected excessively stringent interpretations of "total disability" definitions. Courts have held that long-term disability plans must consider all relevant circumstances, including the claimant's age, educational background, training, and availability of suitable employment in the claimant's geographical area.

total market coverage (TMC)
See shoppers.

total person training (TPT)
See personal growth training.

total quality control
See total quality management.

total quality improvement (TQI)
An approach to the improvement of the quality of products and services that requires massive changes in an organization. In addition to the traditional objectives of controlling, assuring, and guaranteeing quality, TQI aims to make certain that the needs of customers and clients are identified early in the process of designing products and services and revamping the organization to insure that it responds to those needs.

total quality management (TQM) An all-out and integrated approach to organizational improvement and the upgrading of production and service quality. TQM involves sweeping changes in company culture and its way of doing business. It focuses on quality as a central concern to meet customer needs and uses measurement tools, techniques, and training to analyze and solve quality problems. TQM employs such strategies as employee development, cross-training, and empowerment, team building, consolidation of jobs, redirection of union-management relations, and enlistment of the assistance of suppliers. The term was coined by the Naval Air Systems Command in 1985, although its origins can be traced as far back as World War II.

total quality organization An organization that focuses its efforts on continuous improvement strategies in all areas of operation and does it successfully.

TouchWindow® A device that attaches to any standard computer monitor with self-adhesive Velcro strips and plugs into a port on the computer. Users simply touch the screen to interact with the software. Available for Amiga, Apple II series, IBM and compatibles, and Macintosh/GS-OS. A registered trademark of Edmark Corporation. *Contact:* Edmark Corporation, P.O. Box 3903, Bellevue, Washington 98009-3903 (800/426-0856).

Town and Country Electric v. NLRB
A November 1995 Supreme Court decision that reversed a federal appeals court ruling and protects the jobs of union organizers. Confirms a National Labor Relations Board ruling that a worker can be a company "employee" and at the same time be a paid union organizer in that company. The decision makes clear that there is no inconsistency in loyalty to the collective bargaining process and allegiance to the company for which an employee works. The Court's decision gives license to a new union organizing tactic known as **salting.**

toxic air Air in aircraft cabins that contains chemicals, cleaning agents, carbon dioxide, pesticides, and germs from passengers caused by recycling cabin air as a means of reducing the cost of fuel. Toxic air results in headaches and discomfort and possibly the spread of other diseases and health risks, such as colds.

Trace Research and Development Center
Offers literature on adaptive technology and a public information program on computer access for people with disabilities, including a database of organizations and products. There is no fee for mail or phone inquiries. *Contact:* Trace, University of Wisconsin, Madison, Rm. S-151, Waisman Center, 1500 Highland Ave., Madison, WI 53705 (608/ 262-6966).

tracking   **1.** Grouping students by ability to accommodate differences in career goals, talents, skills, abilities, and interests. For years it has been the standard practice in a majority of U.S. schools although its unacceptability, on grounds of unfairness and unproductiveness, has been growing for several years. 2. Used in technological forecasting. The most focused, disciplined, and intensive form of surveillance. It is reserved for following changes and development of crucial importance to the organization.

trade down   In travel management, encouraging or requiring travelers to use limited-service accommodations or economy hotels, which provide such amenities as complimentary breakfasts but lack room service and lavish lobbies, restaurants, and meeting rooms.

trade loading pricing   The traditional approach to pricing in which manufacturers stockpile supplies and produce products around-the-clock to increase output for short term promotion; freight companies charge higher prices to accommodate peak-and-valley distribution cycles; manufacturers advertise incentives and deals to encourage dealer loading; dealers rent additional warehousing space to store products and pass on the added costs to the consumer. Products sit in warehouses waiting for demand to catch up with supply.

trademark   A name, symbol, design, word, or phrase that distinguishes a product from the products of other companies. It cannot be granted if it is being used by some other company in the same industry. A trademark cannot be granted for general words, nor can it be registered before it is used. It can be lost if it is not used. Trademarks must be registered with the Patent and Trademark Office.

trade name   The name of a business or company, such International Business Machines, Chrysler Corporation, or Apple Computers, Inc.

trade secret   Any device, process, or compilation of information used in a business that gives the owner an advantage over competitors who don't know about it. To have legal status, a trade secret (1) must not be public knowledge or generally known in an industry; (2) must not have been described in detail in a trade journal or other journal available to the public; and (3) must have been guarded or protected from disclosure to unauthorized persons.

trade show   A meeting and exposition, usually scheduled during national and regional conferences of professional and trade associations, at which manufacturers and producers of consumer products and vendors of services display their wares. Rather than a sales focus, trade shows are marketing ventures.

Trade Show Exhibitors Association (TSEA)
A 1,600+ member organization representing the interests of firms that use exhibits as a marketing or promotional medium, as well as suppliers to the exposition industry. Its goals are (1) to foster programs that elevate the exhibit manager's professionalism and improve the industry's overall effectiveness; (2) to encourage effective communications among all sectors of the exhibit industry; (3) to educate about the cost-effectiveness and marketing value of trade shows; and (4) to encourage cooperation with international partners in the trade show industry. Also sponsors the **Certified Manager of Exhibits** program. *Contact:* Trade Show Exhibitors Association, 5501 Backlick Rd., Ste. 105, Springfield, VA 22151 (703/941-3725; Fax 703/941-8275; E-mail **tsea@tsea.org**; URL **http://www.tsea.org/maintsea.htm**).

traditional licensing   The issuance of a license to teach a particular subject or group of grades based on satisfactory completion of a state-approved teacher training program offered by a four-year college or university and, in most states, achievement of a score above a prespecified level on one or more multiple-choice tests, most commonly parts of the National Teachers Examination.

traditional temporary help   An alternative staffing option. Involves assigning workers recruited, screened, and hired by a temporary help firm to work at a client's site for a specified period of time, usually to compensate for temporary skill shortages, cover employee absences, meet unusual production requirements, or perform special assignments.

traditional valuation *See* batch processing.

trailblazer developments A projective technique used in forecasting, it involves the identification of technological developments in one area or discipline as harbingers of developments in another area or discipline. Also called *precursor developments*.

trailing spouse Describes the wife or husband of an employee being transferred. In addition to having a negative connotation, the term is inaccurate because many who move with transferred employees are not spouses because they are not legally married. An acceptable replacement term is "relocating partner."

training advisory board (TAB) A group representing departments and staff elements of an organization established to keep the training manager abreast of corporate issues that relate to or impact on training and development. Typically meets quarterly.

transactional human resources Refers to such HR functions and activities as compensation, benefits, recruitment and selection, and training.

transfer-on-death registration (TODR) A means of avoiding probate in some states. Allows the maker to register ownership of securities in a beneficiary form, which can be changed until his or her death.

trial work period Under Social Security, a special work incentive rule that allows disabled persons to earn as much as they can for a 9-month period (not necessarily consecutive) without affecting benefits. The 9 months of work must fall within a 5-year period before the trial work period can end. A trial work month is any month in which the individual earns more than $200. After the trial work period ends, the work is evaluated to determine if it is substantial. If earnings do not average more than $500 per month, benefits will usually continue. If earnings average more than $500 per month, benefits continue for a 3-month grade period before they are discontinued.

trainability The degree to which a worker can take advantage of additional training and education, either formal or on-the-job. Sometimes referred to as the *trainability index.*

trainable A category of mental disability. As measured by an intelligence test, it is represented by an **intelligence quotient (IQ)** below 50. Such persons have poor motor development and minimal speech. They sometimes may be able to contribute to their own support under supervision and function at a minimum useful level in a controlled environment.

Train America's Workforce (TAW) A campaign initiated and sponsored by the American Society for Training and Development. Its purpose is to encourage and promote the additional training American workers (executives and managers, technicians, customer service workers, and other employees) will need over the next decade to keep up with the changes demanded by their jobs. TAW will cover all 50 states. For further information call the TAW hotline 703/683-9599.

trainee response system A mechanical, electrical, or electronic means of establishing two-way communication between an instructional program or an instructor and trainees. Systems of this type are designed to be used by instructors in conjunction with media such as projectuals, motion pictures, TV, and audio recordings, and live lectures and demonstrations to check on the understanding and reactions of trainees. Periodically throughout the presentation, all trainees are simultaneously asked to respond to questions by depressing keys or switches. Responses may be recorded on punched cards or paper rolls, displayed by indicator lights or meters that indicate the percentage of correct responses, thereby providing immediate feedback to the instructor and the trainees.

trainer liability A very real present day legal risk for trainers. Many situations have the potential for lawsuits against trainers or coaches and for the injured party to seek damages: (1) where the trainer (supervisor, coach, or instructor) had a duty to exercise a standard of care that represented the minimum required to protect the trainee (or worker) from unreasonable risk; (2) that the trainer failed to act according to that standard; (3) that there is a causal connection between the (in)action of the trainer and the resulting injury; and (4) that there was actual damage or injury. Examples are injuries in the classroom, shop, or laboratory (negligence), injuries to the trainee or a third party caused by poor or incorrect instruction (malpractice/negligence), or improper supervision of trainees (negligence).

trainer malpractice   Grounds for a lawsuit against an instructor who despite being unqualified to provide training does so.

trainer   **1.** An instructor or facilitator in business and industry. **2.** Equipment or system used to train individuals and groups, such as flight trainers and simulators.

trainer training   *See* instructor training.

TRAINET   A computerized database of 100,000 public seminars that is accessible over personal computer terminals. Produced for ASTD members only by Timeplace, Inc., Waltham, MA. *Contact:* ASTD, 1630 Duke Street, Alexandria, VA 22313 (703/683-8100).

training   Formal or informal, group or individual, instructor-facilitated or media-delivered short-term learning experiences designed to impart or improve the skills, knowledge, and job performance of employees, franchisees, dealers, or clients. Its immediate goal is to develop new job skills or improve competency in the performance of current skills — to create the ability to do something new or do it better. It takes place *before* it is needed.

training aid   A graphic, photographic, projection, three-dimensional, or other form of audio and visual equipment, device, software, or material used in training.

Training & Development   A monthly journal: $85.00 per year (free to members of ASTD). Address: American Society for Training and Development, 1640 King Street, Alexandria, VA 22314 (703-683-8100; Fax 703.683-9203; E-mail **mbox@astd.org**; URL **http://www.astd.org**).

training and development   All of the planned learning experiences provided individual employees to bring about changes in on-the-job behavior and performance that will promote the attainment of the goals and objectives of the organization and at the same time develop the potential, enhance the career advancement, and improve the job satisfaction of individual employees.

training and development self-audit
A technique used to appraise objectively the quality of specific aspects of training and development with the objective of upgrading and improving all facets of training management and operations, including philosophy and goals, plans, policies, and procedures, organization and relationships, building and facilities, management and supervision, staff, curriculum development and operation, and instructional support services. Self-audits may be performed annually, biennially, or triennially. They determine where the training activity is, where it is heading, and where revisions are needed to meet both organizational and departmental objectives.

training and development self-study
See training and development self-audit.

training conference   A variation of the conference method in which the objective becomes one of pooling the knowledge and past experience of trainees to arrive at improved or more clearly stated principles, concepts, policies, or procedures. The issues discussed in a training conference are less likely to have pat answers than the issues talked about in a directed discussion. The task of the leader is to elicit contributions from the group, based on past experiences, that have a bearing on the topic. Balanced participation is the goal.

training development
See curriculum development.

training director   *See* training manager.

training document   Printed, duplicated, or graphic materials used in developing, validating, conducting, and evaluating training programs. Includes questionnaires and surveys, lesson plans, programs of instruction, training management master plans, trainee handouts and advance sheets, and tests and examinations.

training manager   The officer responsible for planning, developing, conducting, and controlling corporate training and development programs and activities in any type of organization. Also known as *human resources development manager; training director.*

training materials   Documents (lesson plans, programs of instruction, tests, and handouts) in printed, duplicated, or graphic form, and training supplies used in the conduct of training programs.

Training Media Association (TMA)   A nonprofit association whose mission is to use the collective efforts of its 95 members to protect their intellectual property through copyright education and enforcement programs and to foster growth in the industry. *Contact:* TMA, 198 Thomas Johnson Dr., Ste. 206, Frederick, MD 21701 (301/662-4268; Fax 301/695-7627; E-mail **RHGTMA@aol.com**; URL **http://www.trainingmedia.org**).

training meeting A meeting of employees at any level and in any profession or occupation convened *to* provide training in specific knowledge or skills.

training needs analysis (TNA) The first step in the training process. Designed to identify performance gaps that can be remedied by training. It consists of surveillance, investigation, and data analysis.

training objective The desired outcome of a lesson, training session, seminar, workshop, course, or other means of training and developing people. Training objectives include such learning outcomes as knowledge, skills, habits, attitudes, ideals, appreciations, and interests.

training on demand A system of scheduling company training (courses, seminars, and workshops) whenever required or requested by organizations or departments.

training program design *See* instructional systems design.

training program management *See* human resources management.

training research Carefully designed studies conducted to try out alternative solutions to training and development problems under controlled conditions. The objective is to provide data that will assist in decision making, offer alternative solutions and new approaches to training problems, insure adequate planning, programming, and budgeting for and management during the execution of research efforts, and prevent duplication of research efforts and eliminate studies that have low payoff potential.

training systems development
See instructional systems development.

Training Technology Transfer Act of 1984 (TTTA) Established the Office of Training Technology Transfer to facilitate the transfer of training technology from the agencies of the federal government, including the Department of Defense, to the private sector and state and local governments with special attention to the requirements of small business.

Training: The Human Side of Business
A monthly journal: $78.00 per year. Address: Lakewood Publications, Lakewood Building, 50 S. Ninth St., Minneapolis, MN 55402 (612-333-0471; Fax 612-333-6526; E-mail **TrainMag@aol.com**; URL **http://www. lakewoodpub.com**).

training via the Internet A growing means of reaching trainees separated by time, distance, location, and schedules. Used primarily to deliver computer-based training and other distance learning strategies that do not require a great deal of video support. Due to bandwidth and modem speed limitations, video and complex graphics are time-consuming to download. E-mail can be used to provide interaction between and among inhouse subject matter experts and trainers and trainees.

training wage *See* minimum wage law.

transaction-based valuation A form of daily valuation specifically designed for group benefit plans. The system can value any account on the date a transaction is effected thereby giving participants more investment choices, the ability to move funds between investments quickly, faster access to withdrawals and loans, and up-to-date account information. Essentially it's a calculation of the value of an individual's account as of any given day, based on the amount of money in the account and the actual performance of the funds in which the account has been invested.

transactional analysis (TA) Training conducted to improve the interpersonal skills and productivity of personnel by developing their self-understanding, self-acceptance, and self-confidence, helping them gain insight into the motivation, life scripts, and games played by others, assisting them to analyze the causes of interpersonal problems and facilitate supportive, cooperative, and productive relationships with subordinates, opening and improving face-to-face communications, and learning to develop meaningful, productive, and game-free relationships with others.

transaction-based pricing A payment plan offered by travel vendors in which airlines pay for every transaction pushed through the computer reservation system.

transcendental meditation (TM)
An approach to tension reduction, relaxation, and reflection bordering on the idealistic, supernatural, or metaphysical. It employs a philosophy based on the doctrine that reality can only be discovered by emphasizing the intuitive and spiritual above the empirical.

transfer 1. In education, the transfer of learning, which is the ability to transfer knowledge or skills learned in one discipline or context to another field of endeavor or situation. For example, the ability to solve algebraic equations to the ability to solve problems in physics. **2.** In corporate training, the ability, inclination, and habit of applying knowledge and skills learned in a training program to the performance of the job. **3.** In job assignment, the practice of moving an employee from one job, location, or work shift to another.

transfer of training   *See* transfer.

transformational leadership   Leadership that is focused on change, innovation, and entrepreneurship. It is systematic, purposeful, and organized, and it looks for changes and movement of resources from "lesser to greater productivity."

transient ischemic attack (TIA)   A form of **stroke** that occurs when the brain's blood flow is reduced only for a short period of time. Its short-term symptoms include brief numbness of the limbs, weakness, and impaired speech or vision.

transitional employment   Providing alternative work for a limited time that will be useful to the organization and, at the same time, serve as rehabilitative assignments for employees who have been absent due to illness or injury. Rather than paying disability benefits, the organization brings workers back to the workplace as soon as medical providers approve of the return and places them in temporary modified-duty, light-duty, or restructured jobs until they are sufficiently recovered to return to their original positions.

transition assistance   *See* Fiscal 1993 Defense Authorization Act.

transition-assistance office   One of 62 offices established by the U.S. Army at major military installations worldwide in 1992 to ease the transition of Army families to civilian life following downsizing and base closures. The offices offer workshops on how to assemble a portfolio, résumé, and cover letter, list prospective employers in an extensive database, counsel on entitlements and how to obtain them, and assist in job searches up to 180 days before separation. *Contact:* Army Career and Alumni Program, PERSCOM, ATTN; TAPC-PDC, 2461 Eisenhower Ave., Alexandria, VA 22331-0479 (800/445-2049).

transition planning   A legally mandated, dynamic process, involving students with disabilities, their parents, educators, and community agencies, for developing a set of coordinated plans and activities to promote school to postschool activities.

transition services   A coordinated set of activities for a (disabled) student, designed within an outcomes-oriented process, that promotes movement from school to postschool activities, including secondary education, vocational training, integrated employment (including **supported employment**), continuing and adult education, adult services, **independent living**, or community participation.

translator   A professional linguist who works with the written word and translates letters, reports, brochures, proposals, graphics, and training materials from one language to another. Additions or deletions are not permitted.

transitions   Occur when organizations move from one stage to another during the corporate life cycle. Corporations grow, develop, and age just like people.

transmission control protocol/Internet protocol (TCP/IP)   Protocols used on the Internet to connect dissimilar computers and offer services such as Telenet.

transnational   A way of organizing a business across national boundaries in which the company operates on a worldwide scale with local responsiveness and global human, materiel, and financial resources.

transnational company   A company that does business in countries other than the one in which it is headquartered. Formerly referred to as *multinational company*.

transplants   Manufacturing facilities owned and operated by foreign corporations in the United States or U.S.-owned and operated plants overseas.

transportable computer   A portable computer that weighs less than 20 pounds, has a handle, but is used on a desk while plugged into an electrical outlet.

Transportation Act of 1989 (TA)   A bill that includes mandatory drug and alcohol testing of transportation workers. Specifically, the bill calls for random, preemployment, post-accident, and for-cause testing of employees in safety-sensitive positions in the airline, rail, bus, and trucking industries.

transportation benefit   Payment to a health care plan beneficiary for transportation costs to travel to an approved medical facility for treatment. Usually includes reasonable and temporary expenses for the recipient and one other individual (or, in the case of a minor, two other individuals).

transurethral ultrasound-guided laser-induced prostatectomy (TULIP) An investigative technology for treating non-cancerous enlargement of the prostate gland. It uses a miniature ultrasound device to guide the delivery of laser energy to the site of prostate obstruction inside the urethra.

transurethral resection prostatectomy (TURP) The standard treatment for non-cancerous enlargement of the prostate. With this procedure, an instrument called a resectoscope is passed through the penis and the urethra and into the bladder, where the urologist uses an electrical loop under direct visual control to shave away the prostate from within to improve urine flow.

trapping In desktop publishing (color prepress), adjusting overlapping color areas to account for misregistration on the press. Typically, light colors are spread (enlarged) or choked (reduced) into darker colors. Trapping may be done by desktop designers or publishers themselves by working within the applications program or using a commercially available dedicated trapping program.

travel agent A individual or agency that provides full travel services, dealing with all aspects of travel for all types of transportation, car rentals, and hotel reservations.

travel and entertainment card A means of controlling travel and entertainment costs. Issued by the company, travelers use these limited-use travel cards only to pay for air, hotel, car rental, or other specified T&E costs. Some bank and other card companies offer this option.

travel and transportation services Services established to improve the efficiency and economy of company operations and make jobs involving travel more convenient, less burdensome, and safer for employees. Such services may include provision of free or low-cost parking facilities, assistance in establishing and maintaining car pools, arrangements for convenient public transportation to and from the workplace, provision of special public, private, or company-owned or leased conveyances for disabled employees, provisions for emergency transportation,

arrangements for short-distance travel for necessary business activities, and long-distance travel services within the continental United States and overseas.

travel coordinator An entry-level travel position responsible for booking reservations, communicating with travelers, and administering various aspects of travel services. Reports to the **travel manager**.

Travel Industry Association of America (TIA) An organization of approximately 2,000 travel-related businesses, associations, and local, regional, and state travel promotion agencies. Represents the common interests and concerns of all components of the U.S. travel industry. Promotes travel, protects the industry from governmental initiatives that would impede travel, and seeks to enlarge an understanding of tourism as an industry. Provides forums and marketing programs and publishes a monthly newsletter. *Contact:* Travel Industry Association of America, 1100 New York Ave., NW,, Suite 450, Washington, DC 20005-3934 (202/408-8422; Fax 202/408-1255; E-mail **scook@tia.org**).

travel management Performance of the functions of planning, organizing, staffing, directing, and controlling policies, procedures, and budgets relating to corporate travel and transportation arrangements including air and ground transportation, lodging, meals and entertainment, expense reports and reconciliation, enforcement, automation, selecting a travel agency, negotiating rates, ticketing, itineraries and booking, and delivery.

travel management consultant An outside specialist contracted to work on corporate travel projects, typically reporting to the senior-level executive who is responsible for travel.

travel management information system Computer software used to automate various travel management-related functions. Includes software to (1) enhance the reservation process at the point-of-sale and enable travel agents to book reservations in a computer reservation system (booking software); (2) access passenger name records to check for accuracy and alternatives (pre-travel quality control); (3) access reservations prior to ticketing and produce management reports (pre-travel reporting); (4) generate reports following ticket issue (travel management reporting); (5) agency accounting and preparation of post-ticketing management reports to clients (office accounting system); and (6) facilitate entry, compilation, and processing of post-travel travel and entertainment expense data through to the reimbursement of travelers.

travel manager A mid-level corporate travel position. Responsible for negotiating with vendors, communicating with travelers, and monitoring policies, travel operations, and costs.

travel management reporting Software that produces reports after tickets have been issued. Typically a part of an accounting system.

travelers' security *See* security of travelers.

treatment A written description of what the viewer or user of a video or multimedia program will see, hear, and experience in the program. Usually includes preliminary sketches of graphics and sample sections of text.

Treaty of Asuncion An agreement signed on March 26, 1991 by Argentina, Brazil, Paraguay, and Uruguay, a bloc of 190 million people, which calls for the establishment of a free-trade zone by the end of 1994.

Treaty of Rome of 1958 The origin of the **European Community** and the **European Union.** It abolished tariffs and quotas among its six nation (at that time) members (France, West Germany, Italy, Luxembourg, The Netherlands, and Belgium).

Treaty on European Union *See* European Monetary Institute; European Union; Maastricht Treaty;

trend analysis A means of forecasting personnel needs, it involves studying an organization's employment patterns over the last five years or more with attention focused on such things as the number employed at the end of each year or some other point in the year, the number of workers in each group and subgroup, and so on to identify trends that might be expected to continue.

trend extrapolation A projective technique used in forecasting that involves plotting the values of key parameters or characteristics of change in any area against time to detect patterns of development. When such patterns are established, they can be logically extended for a period of time into the future.

trend guarantee *See* rate guarantee; risk sharing.

trend spotter *See* futurist.

TRICARE A reform of the **Military Health Care System** required by the Defense Autho-

rization Act of 1994. TRICARE is a triple-option health care program for all military services that combines military and civilian health care providers and resources. Involves a phase in of a **managed care** approach, which relies on arrangements with pools of military and civilian health care professionals who provide services to local beneficiaries. Under the plan, active duty members continue to receive care through the services' military facilities while their families and retired military families will be treated through TRICARE. *TRICARE Prime*, an HMO-type plan and the least costly option, requires an annual enrollment fee and copayments. Enrollees receive health care through **military treatment facilities** (MTFs) or a supporting network of civilian providers. With *TRICARE Extra* , military members pay no enrollment fee, but a yearly deductible is charged and heath care is delivered through a network of civilian providers who accept payments from the **Civilian Health and Medical Program of the Uniformed Services** (CHAMPUS) and provide services at negotiated, discount rates. Beneficiaries also pay copayments, but they are lower than those paid by standard CHAMPUS users. *TRICARE Standard*, the most expensive option, is a fee-for-service plan, which includes deductibles and co-payments, as does standard CHAMPUS. The program was implemented in many U.S. locations in 1995 and will be implemented throughout the country by 1997. (URL **http://www.nmclanna.nadn. navy.mil.trica.htm**).

tricky ticketing Unethical means of offsetting reduced travel budgets, such as back-dating, back-to-back ticketing, cross-ticketing, hidden-city fare, ticketing abroad, and ticket transfer.

triggering condition or event The physical or mental circumstance or status that activates insurance coverage. For example, the inability of a person covered by long term care insurance to perform two or more of the activities of daily living.

trip chainer A person who combines trips to or from work with such errands as delivering kids to school or day care and picking them up, grocery shopping, or picking up laundry.

triple option Offering a health maintenance organization, a preferred provider organization, and a conventional insurance plan by s single insurer.

triple option point-of-service health care plan   A managed care model. Gives enrollees three options at the point where they need health care: (1) go through their primary care physician (least expensive); (2) go directly to another network; or (3) go outside of the network (highest deductibles and copayments).

trip-planning software   Programs that display travel options to assist decision makers at corporate sites.

Trojan horse   1. In connection with computers, a potentially destructive computer program disguised as something friendly, such as a game. It is designed by malicious employees or other saboteurs to quietly change files or erase data from an existing program while you play the game. **2.** In forecasting, an approach that consists of finding out what has happened or is about to happen in a given area before anyone else knows about it, or using information before anyone else decides to use it. It involves rapid use of insider information, whether the insider is the forecaster, or someone who will tell the forecaster what he or she needs to know in time to do something with the information. Also known as the *smoking gun approach* or *rigged deck approach.*

true-false item   A test item that requires the testee to indicate whether a statement is true or false.

true score   A hypothetical and unreachable value. A score that is entirely free of error. Theoretically it is the average score from an infinite number of measurements from the same or equivalent tests with all other variables, such as the identity of testees, held constant. The standard deviation of the infinite number of samplings is the **standard error of measurement**.

TrueType font   A font that is **scalable,** but is not a **PostScript font** or a **Type I** font. TrueType uses a different outline and scaling technology, but it can be used with PostScript printers. Unlike PostScript, it has both screen and printing information built into a single unit.

true 24-hour coverage   A single policy of coverage for both health care benefits and workers' compensation purchased by an employer; that is, the policy must include management of disability benefits as well as health benefits.

trust   A legal arrangement in written form that allows the maker to transfer ownership of property to the trust. It is then managed by a trustee for the beneficiaries named in the trust. A trust can ensure that one's wealth or its income will be protected against inexperience, diminished abilities in advanced years, or the impact of unpredictable events.

trustee   The person named in a trust document who is responsible for managing the trust or has legal title to the trust property.

truth machine   *See* lie detector; psychological stress evaluator.

T-score   A variation of the **standard score**. Because standardized scores are often fractional and those below the mean are negative, it is often helpful to set up a distribution of standard scores with a mean sufficiently greater than zero to avoid minuses and a standard deviation sufficiently greater than 1.0 to make decimals unnecessary. The result is a T-score. A T-score is calculated by converting the mean of the distribution to 50 and the standard deviation to 10. The formula is as follows:

$$\text{T-score} = \frac{10 \times z\text{-score}}{\text{Standard deviation}} + 50$$

$$\text{T-score} = \frac{10\left(\text{Raw score} - \text{mean}\right)}{\text{Standard deviation}} + 50$$

tuition-aid program   A formal corporate program and plan that provides financial assistance to employees who take credit or noncredit courses from accredited schools and colleges on their own time. In some cases financial backing is provided only for training and education programs that are directly related to the employee's current job. In other organizations, tuition aid is granted for high school equivalency courses (GED), general postsecondary education programs and cultural courses, and advanced degree programs for employees — and sometimes for the employee's spouse and/or children.

turkey trot   The practice of transferring a marginal, incompetent, or problem employee from one department or job to another in the hope that a new environment and a new boss will give the person a fresh start. Used most often to describe in a disparaging way the transfer of incompetent, failing, or marginal teachers to a new school and principal.

turnaround document A report generated by the human resources information system (HRIS) that is returned to the source of the information for confirmation and return to the the the HRIS.

turnaround time In meeting management, the amount of time required to disassemble and remove equipment for a function from a room and then reset the room for another function.

turn-back *See* recycle.

turnkey program A packaged program developed by an outside vendor contractor, or consultant, often tailor made for the purchasing organization, ready for installation without modification and immediate operation by the buyer. Examples are wellness programs and awards and recognition programs,

turnover Usually expressed as rate of turnover. Describes the change in the composition of the work force due to termination (disciplinary, resignation, transfer, or retirement). Its importance lies in its impact on employee morale, recruitment, and hiring and training costs.

tutoring A form of one-on-one instruction. The instructor works with an individual trainee — explaining, demonstrating, questioning, coaching, and guiding practice. Used primarily to teach complex skills and operations, those that present danger to the trainee or hazard to expensive equipment, or for remedial instruction.

twenty-four hour coverage
See true 24-hour coverage.

"twentysomething" generation
See baby busters.

twin In meeting management, a hotel room furnished with two single or double beds.

twisting A ploy used by unscrupulous insurance agents, particularly with the elderly. The agent persuades the buyer to cancel his or her present policy for a "better" one. A few months later, the ploy is repeated. Then it happens again. The agent earns more for new policies than the small commission paid for renewals. That is the incentive. Constant replacement may leave the customer uninsured because of the waiting period on pre-existing conditions.

two-tier pay structure A compensation plan that brings new hires into the work force of an organization at a lower rate of pay (as much as 50 percent lower) than was given to employees hired earlier for similar jobs.

two-way digital teleconferencing (2DTC)
A high-tech training delivery method. Requires telecasting equipment at the trainer's and the trainees' site. Employs compressed video technology, which produces a slightly jerky screen image. Permits more interaction than video teleconferencing

two-way interactive video In distance learning, the ability to see and hear presenters, moderators, participants, and trainees simultaneously and continuously from comparably equipped rooms at the host site and remote locations.

type-A (personality) A behavior pattern characteristic of people who are aggressive, intense, competitive, hard-driving, impatient, and emotionally expressive, hostile, and often angry workaholics.

type-B (personality) A behavior pattern characteristic of people who are laid-back, calm, considerate, empathic, restrained, patient, kind, trusting, slow to anger, and good listeners.

typeface In topography, within a **type family**, one of the different forms of type available, such as Bookman Regular, Bookman Italic, and Bookman Bold. The term **font** has come to means the same as typeface.

type family In typography, a collection of all the sizes and styles of a type design with the same characteristics. Examples of type families are Bookman, Chicago, Helvetica, and Times. Usual components are **roman**, **italic**, and **bold**.

Type I font Formerly an Adobe proprietary **font**, a Type I font is a **PostScript font** that is now open to everyone.

types of research *See* analytical survey; applied research; basic research; case study; controlled experiment; experimental research; field experiment; historical study; laboratory experiment; polling survey; primary research; pure research; qualitative research; quantitative research; quasi-experimental study; secondary research.

Typhoid Mary *See* virus.

U

UAFA	United Armed Forces Association.
UAW	United Auto Workers.
UBIT	Unrelated Business Income Tax.
UCC	Uniform commercial code.
UCEA	University Continuing Education Association.
UCPA	United Cerebral Palsy Associations.
UCR	Usual, customary, and reasonable.
UFCW	United Food and Commercial Workers Union.
UFTS	Uniformed Services Treatment Facility.
UHWM	Uniform Hazardous Waste Manifest.
UI	The Urban Institute.
ULPs	Unfair labor practices.
UM	Utilization management.
UMWA	United Mine Workers of America.
UNCCISG	United Nations Convention on Contracts for the International Sale of Goods.
UPC	Universal Product Code.
UR	Utilization review.
URAC	Utilization Review Accreditation Commission.
URL	Universal resource locator.
URO	Utilization review officer.
USAWOA	U.S. Army Warrant Officers Association.
USCPOA	U.S. Coast Guard Chief Petty Officers Association.
USDLA	United States Distance Learning Association.
USDOC	U.S. Department of Commerce.
USERRA	Uniformed Services Employment and Reemployment Rights Act of 1994

USES	U.S. Employment Service.
USFSPA	Uniformed Services Former Spouse's Protection Act of 1983.
USSC	U.S. Sentencing Commission.
USTDC	U.S. Travel Data Center.
UTMA	Uniform Transfer to Minors Act of 1994.
UTSA	Uniform Trade Secrets Acts.
U.S. VIP	Uniformed Services Voluntary Insurance Program.
USWA	United Steelworkers of America.

ubiquitous computing Computers that will be an invisible part of the infrastructure and keep the user connected to the world. Attributed to John Seely Brown, Director of Xerox Corp's Palo Alto Research Center in California (*Computer World*, August 17, 1992),

ultimate evaluation Examination and assessment of the changes in the results achieved by organizations, departments, managers, supervisors, or employees when they have experienced or been subjected to some organization development or training and development intervention. Measures used focus on such outcomes as increased productivity, improved quality of products or services, and reduced operating costs. Examples are decreases or reductions in absenteeism, accident rates, customer complaints, grievances, labor disputes, machine damage and downtime, operating costs, rejects and reworks, and turnover and increases or improvements in attendance, customer satisfaction, new processes, new products, product quality and quantity, profit and return on investment, and sales.

Ultimedia A new family of IBM **multimedia** platforms that embodies powerful features, most notably a digital signal processor chip that provides 16-bit audio capabilities and can handle image compression. The first platform with the Ultimedia label was the PS/2, Model M57 SLC multimedia computer.

ultrasound A diagnostic technique that uses sound waves to create images of certain parts of the body. Similar to an X-ray but without the dangers of radiation exposure (although the safety of the technique is being questioned). High frequency sound waves are directed toward a body organ or cavity, and the sound is reflected back from the selected organ or tissue to form the image.

unapplied billing entry Time spent on activities that cannot be directly associated with a specific project or client and therefore cannot be billed. Examples are administration (handling correspondence, attending meetings, and so on), staff work (research, preparing reports, and the like), professional development (attending courses and reading professional books and journals), and holiday, sick, and vacation time.

unbundle Similar to **unbundling** — when computer manufacturers charge separately for software or services that had previously been included in the total price of the computer system.

unbundled services Options offered employees that permit workers to choose whatever investment alternatives they would like, including those offered by independent outside sources such as those offered by national full-service 401(k) vendors.

unbundling A form of **code gaming** practiced by unscrupulous physicians and other health care providers to increase their income. It is exemplified by the submission of a bill to the insurer for several separate surgical or other procedures, all of which where performed at the same time and customarily considered a single procedure.

understanding A form or level of learning in which the learner is able to acquire, comprehend, and interpret concepts, principles, ideas, and theories.

understudy assignment A method of providing management training and development that involves assignment of the trainee to a competent senior manager or executive who tailors the training and coaching to the needs of the individual by providing experiences and feedback that will enhance skills development.

underutilization In affirmative action, when determining the status of minority group employment in a company by geographic area, department, and job, the finding that members of protected groups are not adequately represented or that there is a concentration of nonminority workers. Analysis of data provides a basis for remedies in the form of affirmative action programs.

understanding, urgency, direction, and discipline (U2D2) A prescription for credible, effective, and successful leadership: (1) working to to ensure that everyone n the organization understands why change is necessary; (2) injecting a sense of urgency into the organization; (3) ensuring that people in the organization share a vision, a common philosophy, purpose, and a set of values and ideals; and (4) being consistent in the execution of discipline — keeping one's word, rejecting lip-service and expediency. Attributed to Oren Harari, "'U2D2: The R_x for Leadership Blues," *Management Review*, August 1995, pp. 34-36.

underwriting **1.** Bearing the risk for something as insurance companies do for the payment of premiums. **2.** Analysis of an entity to determine whether it should be offered insurance and/or the rates that should be charged for such coverage.

undue burden or hardship Under the **Americans With Disabilities Act of 1990**, the term means an action requiring significant difficulty of expense to a business to make "reasonable accommodation" to the disability of a qualified applicant or employee. Factors included for consideration in determining if a reasonable accommodation actually constitutes an "undue hardship" include the nature and cost of the accommodation, the financial resources of the employer, and the impact of the accommodation on the financial resources of the employer. "Undue burden is a higher standard than "readily achievable."

unemployment compensation A form of statutory benefit. State laws or regulations provide that employees who are involuntarily unemployed may receive compensation in stated amounts and for a stipulated period of time unless they are able to secure gainful employment. Programs are funded by payroll taxes levied entirely upon employers (except in Alabama, Alaska, New Jersey, and Pennsylvania, where employees are required to make small contributions) although they are sometimes supplemented by federal funds (usually during periods of severe and general high unemployment), and administered by the states.

Unemployment Compensation Amendments Act of 1992 Extended emergency unemployment benefits programs for long-term jobless workers who had exhausted their regular 26 weeks of benefits. Included a provision designed to pay for the increased unemployment benefits involving a change in qualified plan distribution and rollover rules. The law requires that all qualified retirement plans permit rollover of any taxable portion of a distribution from another qualified plan or tax-sheltered annuity, unless it is a minimum required distribution or part of a series of long-term payments. Qualified plans making distributions must permit their distributions to be rolled over into an **individual retirement account** or another plan specified by the plan participant. If the plan participant does not specify a rollover into another plan or IRA, the employer plan making the distribution must withhold 20 percent of the distribution in addition to any penalties for early withdrawal that apply. Signed by President Bush July 3, 1992 and became effective December 31, 1992.

unemployment insurance *See* unemployment compensation.

unfair labor practices (ULPs) 1. As defined by the **Wagner Act of 1935**, such employer practices as (1) interfering with, restraining, or coercing employees in exercising their legally sanctioned right of self-organization; (2) dominating or interfering with either the formation or administration of labor unions, including bribery of employees, company spy systems, moving a business to avoid unionization, and blacklisting union sympathizers; (3) discriminating in any way against employees for their legal union activities; (4) discharging or discriminating against employees because they have filed unfair practice charges against the company; and (5) refusing to bargain collectively with their employees' representatives. **2.** As defined by the **Labor-Management Relations Act of 1947** (Taft-Harley), by unions, practices such as (1) restraining or coercing employees from exercising their guaranteed bargaining rights; (2) causing an employer to discriminate in any way against an employee in order to encourage or discourage membership in a union; (3) refusing to bargain "in good faith" with the employer about wages, hours, and other employment conditions (and certain types of strikes and boycotts); and (4) engaging in "featherbedding" (requiring an employer to pay for services not performed).

unfairly discriminatory Any policy or action that results in unequal probabilities of selection for training, hiring, or other favorable outcome for persons (members of a minority group or women) who have equal probabilities of success (with nonminorities) in the job or training program.

unfreezing One of the three major stages in learning (the others are **change efforts** and **refreezing**). Unfreezing occurs when barriers to the acquisition of new or replacement knowledge, habits, or attitudes are reduced or eliminated. Attributed to Kurt Lewin, pioneer in experiential learning.

unified credit A tax credit for federal estate taxes. The credit now amounts to $600,000 for the equivalent of the value of the taxable property.

Uniform Commercial Code (UCC) Prescribes standards and procedures for commercial operations and transactions within the United States. Included is treatment of the problems of "offer" and "acceptance," binding contract formation, and the problems of discrepancies between the Seller's standard form documents (sales order and order acknowledgements) and the Buyer's standard forms (purchase orders and order confirmations).

uniform coverage rule An Internal Revenue Service rule. States that plan participants who elect health care flexible spending accounts (FSAs) must be afforded uniform coverage throughout the coverage period, just as with other medical plans. Employers may not withhold FSA claims reimbursements until the FSA balance of employee pretax contributions justifies the reimbursement. Instead, employers must make reimbursements for qualified FSA claims at all times during a year on the basis of the total amount of annual contributions made by the employee during enrollment.

uniform durable power of attorney An enabling law passed by a state to allow an individual to appoint another as an agent to manage his or her property and finances. Such a power of attorney remains in effect even if the creator or principal is incompetent.

uniformed services The Army, Navy, Marine Corps, Air Force, Coast Guard, Commissioned

Corps of the Public Health Service, and the Commissioned Corps of the National Oceanic & Atmospheric Administration.

Uniformed Services Employment and Reemployment Rights Act of 1994

(USERRA)   Replaced the Veterans Reemployment Rights Act of 1940. Effective October 13, 1996, required all public and private employers to: (1) grant a leave of absence for members of the National Guard and Reserve to perform military service whether voluntary or involuntary; 2) reinstate seniority, pay, and benefits at the level service members would have attained if they had not left for military service; (3) allow service members to purchase continued health care coverage for up to 18 months at a cost not to exceed 102 percent of the plan cost for individual or family coverage; (4) reinstate insurance coverage immediately for returning veterans; (5) restore all life and disability insurance benefits as if the employee had remained on the job; and (6) credit returning veterans with all benefits accruals under a defined benefit plan and all employer contributions to a defined contribution plan as if the veteran had not left employment (for plans involving employer matching funds, the returning vet must be permitted to — and may be required to — make up the contributions paid during military service in order to receive the employer's contribution). Applies to employees returning from military service after December 12, 1994. The Act also entitled employers to (1) advance notice of upcoming military duty; (2) proof of an employee's military duty; and (3) timely return of the employee upon completion of military duty.

Uniformed Services Former Spouses Protection Act of 1983 (USFSPA)

Authorizes state courts to treat military retired pay as *either* the property of the retiree *or* the property of the retiree and his or her spouse in accordance with the law of the jurisdiction of such courts. Amended several times since its enactment, the Act entitles an unremarried former spouse of a military member to certain military-related benefits and privileges. For example, the Act permits a court to award a portion of military retired pay to a former spouse as his or her property (in addition to any other court-awarded spousal and/or child support and/or division of other marital property). Although a court can award more than 50 percent of a retired service member's pay to the ex-spouse as property, the government is only authorized to send up to 50 percent of "disposable" retired pay directly to the ex-spouse as property.

Uniformed Services Retirees and Dependents Health Care Availability Act of 1997

Introduced by Rep. William (Mac) Thornberry (R-Texas (H.R. 1456. The bill would restore health care equity to uniformed services personnel and their dependents, includes a Federal Employees Health Benefits Program option for Medicare-eligible uniformed services beneficiaries and Medicare subvention, and have DoD pay late enrollment penalties for uniformed services beneficiaries who did not enroll in Medicare, Part B, and would increase **TRICARE** and **CHAMPUS** benefits to the highest level of benefits provided under the **FEHBP**.

Uniformed Services Treatment Facility

(USTF)   One of nine U.S. Public Health Service hospitals and clinics transferred to non-governmental organizations in 1981. Nine, located in Maine, Massachusetts, New York, Maryland, Ohio, Texas, and Washington, are operated by civilian health organizations under contract to DOD, offering comprehensive medical care to military retirees and eligible family members, including Medicare-eligible beneficiaries.

Uniformed Services Voluntary Insurance Program (U.S. VIP)

A voluntary health insurance program available for purchase by ex-members of the uniformed services and their dependents and paid for entirely by policy holders. The plan provides up to one year of coverage and is designed to cover the insured until they are enrolled in a permanent program or become eligible for group health insurance.

Uniform Federal Accessibility Standard

(UFAS)   Provides design specifications to provide accessibility to buildings and facilities for the disabled. The **Americans with Disabilities Act of 1990** requires compliance with USFAS.

Uniform Guidelines on Employee Selection Procedures

Approved in 1978 by the **Equal Employment Opportunity Commission**, Civil Service Commission, Department of Labor, and Department of Justice, and published by the Equal Employment Opportunity Commission to help employers comply with regulations on nondiscrimination. Contain "highly recommended" procedures for such things as employee selection, record keeping, preemployment inquiries, and affirmative action programs.

Uniform Hazardous Waste Manifest (UHWM)   A multi-copy shipping and tracking document required by the **Resource Conservation and Recovery Act of 1976** as essential to cradle-to-grave management of hazardous waste. The hazardous waste generator, the hauler, and the designated facility must each sign this document and keep a copy and a copy must be returned by the recipient to the generator to acknowledge receipt of the shipment.

uniform resource locator (URL)   See universal resource locator.

Uniform Trade Secrets Acts (UTSA)   Acts adopted by 19 states that protect business secrets that have "independent value" to people outside the company, are generally unknown to outsiders and are unlikely to be discovered by lawful means, and the owner has instituted measures to try to maintain secrecy.

Uniform Transfer to Minors Act of 1994 (UTMA)   Replaced the Uniform Gifts to Minors Act. Allows stocks, bonds, insurance contracts, and real estate to be held by a custodian for the benefit of a minor and provides an alternative to a court-appointed guardian or trust to hold property for the benefit of a minor until he or she reaches the age of 21.

union   A formal organization of employees, recognized by management and certified by the **National Labor Relations Board** and authorized by the Board to act on behalf of it members on such matters as working conditions, wages, benefits, and job security.

union busting   Strategies and tactics used by management in an attempt to abolish or dissolve a union. See labor-management contract.

unionization   The establishment of collective bargaining between an employer and the work force as a unit.

The Union of Needle Trades, Industrial and Textile Workers (UNITE)   Formed by the merger of the International Ladies' Garment Workers' Union and the Amalgamated Clothing and Textile Workers Union in July 1995. Members work in basic apparel and textile, auto parts and auto supply, millinery, shoe, laundry, glove and tanning, bag and packaging, retail, and related industries. Dedicated to advancing workers' rights, leading in organizing new workers, pioneer in labor-management relations to better the lives of working people, and build international alliances with workers around the world. UNITE represents workers in Canada, the United States, and Puerto Rico. *Contact:* UNITE, 1710 Broadway, New York, NY 10019-5299 (212/265-7000; Fax 212/265-3415; E-mail **JMORT@uniteunion.org** ; URL **http://www.uniteunion.org**).

union relations   See labor-management relations.

union shop   An accommodation or arrangement with a union where the firm can only hire union employees. If the company hires nonunion employees, they must join the union after a prescribed period of time and pay dues; it they don't, they can be fired.

United Armed Forces Association (UAFA)   An organization of approximately 20,000 members open to E-1 through O-10 active duty, retired, Reserve, National Guard, and veterans of all five uniformed military services. UAFA's mission is to provide benefits, consumer discounts, and information and to provide legislative representation before Congress on all matters affecting members. *Contact:* UAFA, P.O. Box 2603, Waco, TX 76702-2603 (Fax 804/750-7789; E-mail **uafa@iamerica.net**; URL **http://www.uafa.org**).

United Auto Workers (UAW)   (International Union, United Automobile, Aerospace, and Agricultural Implement Workers of America). Members are employed as skilled and unskilled workers, clerical, technical, and professional employees in both the public and private sectors, including automobile, farm equipment, aerospace, aviation, metal, parts, academic, and health care industries.*Contact:* UAW, 8000 E. Jefferson Ave., Detroit, MI 48214 (313/926-5000; Fax 313/926-5009; E-mail **FAQ@uaw.org**; URL **http://www.uaw.org**).

United Cerebral Palsy Associations (UCPA)   A nationwide network of 155 state and local affiliated agencies that provide direct services to people with cerebral palsy, act as advocates for people with disabilities, are involved in public and professional information and education, and support research on cerebral palsy and the neurosciences. UCPA's mission is to advance the independence, productivity, and full citizenship of people with cerebral palsy and other disabilities, through commitment to the principles of independence, inclusion, and self-determination. *Contact:* UCPA,1660 L St., N.W., Suite 700, Washington, DC 20036-5602 [800/USA-5-UCP or 202/776-0406; 202/973-7197 (TTY); Fax 202/776-0414; E-mail **ucpanatl@ucpa. org**; URL **http://www.ucpa.org**).

United Food and Commercial Workers (UFCW)   A labor union representing 1.4 million food and food service workers throughout the United States and Canada. Members work in dozens of industries for employers large and small, in multinationals, regional companies, and local firms. *Contact:* UFCW, 1775 K. St., N.W., Washington, DC 20006-1598 (202/223-3111; E-mail **webmaster@ ufcw.org**; URL **http://www.ufcw.org/**).

United Mine Workers of America (UMWA)   An independent labor union composed of 240,000 members, representing coal miners and other workers throughout the United States and Canada, with jurisdiction over both anthracite and bituminous coal mining. *Contact:* UMWA, 900 15th St., N.W., Washington, DC 20005 (202/842-7200; URL **http://www.access.digex.net/~miner/ index.html**).

United Nations Convention on Contracts for the International Sale of Goods (UNCCISG)   A law affecting international commercial operations and transactions that became effective in the U.S. and several other countries in 1988. As of March 1992, the number of countries that have adopted and completed the ratification process increased to a total of 30. Commercial documentation used in international sales drafted prior to 1988 is now inadequate. The Convention applies to contracts for the sale of goods between commercial buyers and sellers located in different countries. Consumer goods purchased for the personal use of the buyer are excluded, as are transactions involving investment securities, negotiable instruments, ships and aircraft, and purely local transactions between businesses in the same country. The Convention is significantly different from the Universal Commercial Code.

United States Copyright Act of 1976   The fourth major revision of the United States Copyright Act of 1790. *See* copyright law.

United States Distance Learning Association (USDLA)   A non-profit association formed to promote the development and application of distance learning for education and training. Constituents served include K through 12 education, higher education, continuing education, corporate training, and military and government training. The USDLA carries out an international role through liaison with other national and international organizations and its annual International Distance Learning Conference. The association has also become the leading source of information and recommendations for government agencies, Congress, industry and those entering upon the development of distance learning programs. *Contact:* USDLA, P.O. Box 5106, San Ramon, CA 94583 (510/820-5845; E-mail **shelley@usdla.org**; URL **http://usdla.org/**).

United States Tourism Organization Act of 1996   Established a public-private national tourism office, the U.S. National Tourism Organization, with responsibility for promoting all aspects of travel to the United States, from vacation travel to the meeting industry.

United Steelworkers of America (USWA)   Represents over 700,000 working men and women throughout the United States and Canada in the steel, aluminum, and other metal refining industries. Affiliated with the AFL-CIO. *Contact:* USWA, 5 Gateway Ctr., Pittsburgh, PA 15222 (412/562-2400; URL **http://www.uswa.org**).

unity analysis   The process by which the cost or value of worker competency is determined. The difference between a marginal and average or an average and superior performer is estimated to be between 40 and 70 percent of the average annual salary for a job. That points to the need for effective training to ensure optimum worker performance.

unity of command   An organizational principle stating that no subordinate should report to more than one superior.

universal and variable life insurance   Policies that allow policyholders to invest portions of their premiums in mutual funds or other investment vehicles.

universal coverage   Providing health insurance for everyone in the population regardless of health, employment, income, or other factor.

universal health care plan   A plan by which the federal government would draw up a catalog of minimum health care benefits for all Americans. Private companies would continue to offer coverage to workers under employer-funded plans and develop policies to cover the costs of experimental or high-risk procedures.

universal precautions Mandatory regulations issued by the Department of Labor's Occupational Safety and Health Administration in December 1991 that became effective in March 1992. Designed to protect workers, primarily but not exclusively health care providers, from health risks associated with their work. The regulations cover all health care facilities, including hospitals, clinics, hospices, nursing homes, and doctors' and dentists' offices. They also cover other occupations in which workers may be exposed to contaminated substances, such as funeral homes, emergency teams, law enforcement units, correctional facilities, linen services, and medical equipment repair companies. Employers are required to provide, at their own expense, voluntary inoculations for their employees to prevent hepatitis B. The regulations also require employers to institute engineering controls, such as puncture-resistant containers for used needles, and protective equipment, such as impermeable gowns, gloves, and face masks, and the enforcement of work practices to reduce infections, such as handwashing. The standard also requires appropriate labeling and training to alert workers to the risks posed by bloodborne organisms. Facilities that use concentrated viruses are required to post warning signs. Employers are required to keep records of incidents of exposure, postexposure followup, hepatitis B vaccinations, and employee training.

Universal Product Code (UPC) A rectangle of bold black lines with numbers underneath found on most packaged retail products. The codes, when electronically scanned and inputted to a computer, identify the product by name, type, size, and price on the register receipt and also provide a means of updating the inventory.

Universal Product Code (UPC) Bar Code
Used by publishers to identify books and periodicals. Printed on the back of most books and on the front or back of many magazines. Available from *UPC Barcode* CPDA (212/818-0234), Publication Identification Processing, 436 E. 87th St., New York, NY 10128-6502 (212/996-6000 Fax 212/410-7477), or (do it

yourself software) Bear Rock Software Co., 6069 Enterprise Drive, Placerville, CA 95667 (916/672-0244; Fax 916/622-4775).

universal resource locator (URL)
An address for a "Website" — a specific site that identifies both the location and type of resources on the World Wide Web.

university center A conference center located on the campus of a college or university. Most often used for management meetings and continuing education programs. May offer overnight accommodations and recreational facilities.

University Continuing Education Association (UCEA) Consists of more than 400 accredited, degree-granting higher education institutions and non-profit organizations with a substantial involvement in continuing higher education and about 2,000 professionals. Founded in 1915, the Association promotes expanded opportunities and high quality in continuing higher education. *Contact:* UCEA, One Dupont Cir., Ste. 615, Washington, DC 20036 (202/659-3130; Fax 202/785-0374; E-mail **postmaster@nucea. edu**; URL **http://www.nucea.edu**).

Unix A multitasking, multiprogramming environment originally developed by AT&T and commonly used as the basis of multiuser **computer-based training** systems and human resource applications. It enables CBT developers (as well as developers of other applications) to take the software used to drive real displays, introduce identifiers and locations of targets, and have the software do the computations. It makes it possible to invoke any function of the system. It allows the CBT author to build instruction directly into an application as well as call up and run portions of an application. Two of its versions are IBM's Aix and Microsoft's Xenis.

unlimited access Means that a worker eligible for health care benefits may not be limited in using the plan because of high deductibles, copayments, or other restrictions.

unnecessary work Jobs, duties, or tasks that are not needed for the operation of the organization, such as internal reports that no one needs or reads, and work that does not add value to a product or service.

unpublished/preferential fare A specially priced fare offered to a customer which has been customized to meet the specific travel requirements of the buyer.

Unrelated Business Income Tax (UBIT)
A policy that allows the government to tax non-profit institutional or association revenues unrelated to the organization's tax-exempt status and purpose; for example, publications advertising income and royalties. UBIT statutes, first enacted in 1950, outline the types of income that are exempt from federal income tax. One standard is the "relatedness test," which says that activities "substantially unrelated" to an association's purpose are tax-exempt. For example, it an association receives funding from a corporation to finance a banquet, seminar, or coffee break, that income is exempt from taxation. The **Internal Revenue Service,** however, could require meeting planners to pay income tax on what they consider to be advertising; for example, display of corporate names and logos on souvenirs and trophies.

unrelated roommates and unmarried partners A form of nontraditional household. Shared living arrangements whether all men, all women, or a combination, regardless of age.

unsafe acts Such causes of accidents and injuries as distractions (horseplay or startling), failing to secure equipment or tools, failing to wear safe clothing or use protective equipment, lifting improperly, making safety devices inoperable (removing or disconnecting them), operating or working at unsafe speed (either too fast or too slowly), throwing objects or materials, using unsafe equipment or tools, using equipment or tools unsafely, using unsafe procedures in arranging, loading, placing, combining, or mixing, and taking unsafe positions under suspended loads.

unsafe conditions Such hazards as defective equipment and tools, hazardous arrangement or congestion of machines or equipment, hazardous procedures in using equipment and tools, improperly guarded equipment and tools, improper illumination, inadequate ventilation or impure air sources, overloading, and unsafe storage.

unsolicited proposal A proposal to provide products or services initiated by a marketer and sent to a potential customer or client.

Unsubsidized Federal Stafford Loan (Dependent Students) A loan program open to dependent undergraduate students who do not qualify in whole or in part for the **Federal Stafford Loan.** Interest rates are vari-

able but do not exceed 8.25 percent. For loans disbursed on or After July 1, 1995, the interest rate during in-school, grade, and deferment are 0.6 percent lower than the rate during repayment. Borrowers can receive both subsidized and unsubsidized Federal Stafford Loans totaling up to their applicable Federal Stafford limits of $2,625 (1st year), $3,500 (2nd year), $5,500 remaining years, and a cumulative limit of $23,000. Payments of the principal are deferred until 6 months after the student ceases to be enrolled on at least a half-time basis, but the student is responsible for interest that accrues. Maximum term is 10 years with a $50 minimum payment per month.

Unsubsidized Federal Stafford Loan (Independent Students) Loans available to independent undergraduate or graduate students who are eligible for Federal Stafford Loans. Interest rates are variable but do not exceed 8.25 percent. For loans disbursed on or After July 1, 1995, the interest rate during in-school, grade, and deferment are 0.6 percent lower than the rate during repayment. Independent undergraduate students may borrow up to these maximums, less any subsidized Stafford amounts: $6,625 (1st year), $7,500 (2nd year), $10,500 (remaining years), cumulative $46,000. For independent graduate students the maximum loan is $18,500 per year with a cumulative total of $138,500. Payments of the principal are deferred until 6 months after the student ceases to be enrolled on at least a half-time basis, but the student is responsible for interest that accrues. Maximum term is 10 years with a $50 minimum payment per month.

unsubsidized loan Under federal student aid programs, a loan that is not awarded on the basis of financial need. The borrower is charged interest from the time the loan is disbursed until it is paid in full. However, the borrower may chose to pay the interest or allow it to accumulate. It interest is allowed to accumulate, it will be capitalized — that is, the interest will be added to the principal amount of the loan and increase the amount the borrower has to repay.

unwelcome behavior Unwanted, undesirable, unacceptable, or objectionable conduct by workplace superiors, peers, or subordinates, such as touching or other types of sexual advances. See also hostile environment; *quid pro quo* harassment.

upcharges/upcharging Room rates that are generally $15-$20 higher for business-class rooms which include such amenities as spacious desks, special lighting, and business technology (fax and photocopy machine services and rental of desk- or lap-top computers).

upcoding A form of **code gaming** practiced by unscrupulous physicians and other health care practitioners to increase their income. Exemplified by the submission of an insurance claim form for removal of a tiny (three-millimeter) squamous skin lesion as a relatively large (two-centimeter) basal cell carcinoma.

upgrade An improved version (new edition) of existing computer software or hardware.

upload Sending information to another computer(s) by means of a **modem**.

uppers *See* amphetamines.

upskilling *See* cross-training; incumbent worker training.

upstream research In marketing, conducting studies on prices and materials for products still in the vision, dream, or early development stages.

uptraining Training designed to improve employees' performance of current skills and teach new skills. Sometimes called *redeployment*. Includes cross-training.

upward mobility **1.** Readiness of employees to assume more responsible or more demanding positions. Refers primarily to the preparation and promotion of minorities into more demanding and remunerative jobs, including managerial positions. **2.** Programs designed to identify specific jobs as targets for underdeveloped employees, advertise projected vacancies in those jobs, identify and advertise bridge positions leading to the target jobs, identify specific qualifications for each job, restrict competition for bridge and upward mobility jobs to underemployed, underdeveloped, and underutilized employees and applicants, prepare individual development plans for selected individuals, and identify and implement specific training and development activities for each upward mobility position.

The Urban Institute (UI) A private, non-profit policy research and educational organization with a staff of 200 established to investigate the social and economic problems confronting the nation and the government policies and programs designed to alleviate such problems. The Institute's objectives are to sharpen thinking about society's problems and efforts to solve them, improve government decisions and their implementation, and increase citizens' awareness about important public choices. *Contact:* The Urban Institute, 2100 M. St., N.W., Washington, DC 20024 (202/833-7200; E-mail **webmaster@urban. org**; URL **http://www.urban.org/**).

urine test The most common technique used to detect drug use. There are two types: **screening test** and **confirmatory test**. Both can result in false positives.

urologist A medical doctor that specializes in the diagnosis and treatment of disorders of the urinary tract in men and women, such as severe bladder infections, kidney cancer, and reproductive disorders in men, mainly prostate cancer.

usability testing Testing the features of any system, including training systems, using such techniques as paper and pencil studies, prototyping, behavioral benchmarking, and field observations. In computer-based training (CBT), for example, testing such features as screen design, navigation, and on-line help.

U.S. Army Warrant Officers Association (USAWOA) An association of 5,000 active duty, National Guard, reserve, and retired Army warrant officers. Its mission is to recommend improvements in the Army and promote technical and professional information among warrant officers. *Contact:* USAWOA, 462 Herndon Pkwy, Ste. 207, Herndon Pkwy., VA 22070-5235 (703/742-7727; Fax 703/742-7728; E-mail **usawa@erols.com**).

U.S. Bipartisan Commission on Comprehensive Health Care *See* Pepper Commission.

U.S. Coast Guard Chief Petty Officers Association (CGCPOA) An association of 10,000 active, retired, and reserve Coast Guard chief petty officers (E7, E8, and E9). Its mission is to promote and protect the rights and benefits of members and all Armed Forces personnel *Contact:* CPOA, 5520-G Hempstead Way, Springfield, VA 22151-4009 (703/941-0395; Fax 703/941-0397; E-mail **CGCPOA@aol.com**).

U.S. Department of Commerce (USDOC) Through its 343 district offices, USDOC employs international trade specialists who provide guidance to businesses on getting started in exporting. *Contact:* USDOC, International Trade Administration, 14th and

Constitution Ave., N.W., Washington, DC 20230 (202/377-5261).

U.S. Department of Health and Human Services (HHS) The government's principal agency for protecting the health of all Americans and providing essential human services. The department includes more than 300 programs covering a wide range of activities; for example, medical and social science research, assuring food and drug safety, Medicare and Medicaid Financial assistance for low-income families (AFDC), substance abuse treatment and prevention, and services for older Americans. *Contact:* HSS, Hubert H. Humphrey Building, 200 Independence Avenue SW, Washington, D.C., 20201 (301/443-3400; Fax 301/443-0041; URL **http://www.os.dhhs.gov/**).

use it or lose it rule An Internal Revenue Service rule that prohibits income deferrals (of benefits) throughout the implementation of cafeteria plans. For example, unused flexible spending account credits from the current year plan may not be saved or deferred into a later plan year. If no other option is selected, they are paid to the employee as fully taxable income. Similarly, elective vacation purchases must be used in the year purchased or they are forfeited.

US Employment Service (USES) An agency of the Department of Labor. Operates the Job Bank. Jobs listed by employers are matched by computer with people who are seeking jobs. There is no charge for the service to either employers or job seekers, but it is used primarily by the unemployed because they are required to register with U.S. Employment Service to collect unemployment compensation. USES has offices in most cities and in all states.

usenet newsgroups On the **Internet,** upwards of 7,000 topic-oriented message bases and discussion groups that can be read and addressed or posted to.

use of sick days for sick dependents A policy that allows employees to use their sick days to care for a spouse or other dependent who is ill.

user fee 1. A charge, usually nominal, for services otherwise provided for free. **2.** A fee proposed for outpatient care or for prescription drugs when provided by a **Military Treatment Facility.** Specifically prohibited by the Congress in 1988 and 1990, but imposed on prescription drugs in Veterans Administration medical facilities only in the Omnibus Budget Reconciliation Act of 1990.

user-friendly Describes the human-machine interface: hardware or software that is relatively simple to use.

userid A compression of "user identification," the unique signature of an **Internet** user that usually precedes the @ (at) sign in an E-mail address.

U.S. Sentencing Commission (USSC) An independent agency within the federal judiciary. USSC provides guidelines for sentencing corporations and other organizations convicted of federal criminal offenses such as fraud, theft, or antitrust violations. The guidelines offer corporations four mitigating factors to reduce fines: (1) the offense was voluntarily reported or an effective program was maintained to prevent and detect violations; (2) no individual in a policy-setting position had knowledge of the offense; (3) the company cooperated fully with the government's investigation; and (4) the company accepted responsibility and took steps to remedy the harm caused.

users group meeting A meeting of consumers of products and services that band together to exchange information, discuss problems and issues, and network; for example, users of desktop publishing equipment, computer software, and computer hardware.

U.S. Coast Guard (USCG) The primary federal agency with maritime authority for the United States. It is an organization of people, ships, aircraft, boats, and shore stations and responds to tasks in four main mission areas: Maritime Law Enforcement, Maritime Safety, Marine Environmental Protection, and National Security. When directed by the president, operates as a Service in the U.S. Navy. Web site contains facts, images, and the history of the Coast Guard. (URL **http://www. dot.gov/dotinfo/uscg/**)

U.S. Coast Guard Chief Petty Officers Association (USCPOA) An organization of approximately 10,00 members open to active, retired, and reserve Coast Guard chief petty officers. Its mission is to promote the welfare of chief petty officers, to promote and protect the rights and benefits of all Armed Forces personnel, and to aid in Coast Guard recruiting. *Contact:* USCPOA, 5520-G Hempstead Way, Springfield, VA 22151-4009.

U.S. Government security In investments, a security issued or guaranteed by the U.S. Government or its agencies or instrumentalities. Includes U.S. Treasury securities that differ only in their interest rates, maturities, and times of issuance. Treasury Bills have initial maturities of one year of less; Treasury Notes have initial maturities of one to ten years; and Treasury Bonds generally have initial maturities of more than ten years.

Usher's syndrome An inherited disorder present at birth or early in life. It involves hearing loss and a progressive loss of vision caused by retinitis pigmentosa. There is no treatment for the visual effects of the disease. Cochlear implants may provide some benefit for those with severe hearing loss.

U.S. Marine Corps (USMC) The Marine Corps is organized, trained, and equipped primarily to: (1) provide Fleet Marine Forces of combined arms, together with supporting air components, for service with the United States Fleet; (2) provide detachments and organizations for service on armed vessels of the Navy, and security detachments for the protection of naval property at naval stations and bases; and (3) provide Marine forces for airborne operations, in coordination with the Army, the Navy, and the Air Force. Web site provides access to fact files and publications and contains information on the history and traditions of the Corps. (URL **http://www.usmc.mil/**).

U.S. Standard Industrial Classification System (SIC) A formal system established in the 1950s to standardize industrial production in a variety of areas, including measurements, statistics, and reports, and track industrial output.

USTF Managed Care Plan An alternative to health care in a **military treatment facility (MTF),** the plan is offered by **Uniformed Services Treatment Facilities (USTF)** to beneficiaries eligible under the **Defense Enrollment/Eligibility Reporting System**, reside in the ZIP code specific service area of a USTF, and be enrolled in the plan. Enrollees exchange their **Civilian Health and Medical Programs of the Uniformed Services** and MTF benefits for the benefits of the USTF Managed Care Plan. The USTF is responsible for meeting all of the enrolled beneficiaries' medically-necessary health care needs.

U.S. Travel Data Center (USTDC) The research and consulting affiliate of the **Travel Industry Association of America,** the recognized source for domestic and international travel and tourism research. Members of the Center receive annual and quarterly publications that examine U.S. domestic travel trends and the economic impact of the travel industry. The Center also performs proprietary marketing and economic research for corporations, associations, state and county governments, and convention and visitors bureaus. *Contact:* U.S. Travel Data Center, 1100 New York Ave., N.W., Ste. 450, Washington DC 20005 (202/408-8422).

usual, customary, and reasonable (UCR) In it acronym form, used by insurance companies in connection with setting base fees. UCR means that payment will be made for charges the subscriber is legally responsible to pay based on the normal, fair, and established charge for a covered service or treatment (the same or similar) in the same service area.

utility programs *See* utilities.

utilities Software programs provided by the manufacturer, independent vendors, or developed inhouse that increase the efficiency of computer systems and salvage deleted files and damaged directories. Examples are programs for sorting, cueing, merging, moving data, undeleting/unformatting, disk optimizing, backup preparation, memory managing, and virus protection.

utilization management (UM) Management of health care programs to control costs. Involves data analysis of claims, identification of specific utilization problems, evaluation of benefits to ensure that employees have incentives to use alternative less costly treatment settings, and, based on findings, revise benefits packages.

utilization review (UR) 1. A common part of employees' health benefits packages. Involves a focused review of the use of the benefits over time. UR seeks to identify specific problems relating to variations in practice among specific categories, such as providers, facilities, or geographic areas, and the severity of illnesses, through sophisticated data analysis. Following review and analysis of the problems, **utilization management** programs are used to address the problems, the program is implemented, results are audited and measured, and information is fed back to the provider. **2.** A process used for deciding whether to approve treatment or referrals recommended by health care providers. Typically required in managed care plans and some traditional plans.

utilization review officer (URO) A medical practitioner given responsibility for precertifying the need for various medical procedures, admission to a hospital, verification that continued stay is essential, and discharge planning, including tentative arrangements for continued care at home or in an extended care facility.

Utilization Review Accreditation Commission (URAC) A voluntary non-profit organization that evaluates external utilization review agencies, such as free-standing companies, utilization management departments of insurance companies, and utilization departments of managed care plans. Created as a subsidiary of the American Managed Care and Review Association, which recently merged with the **Group Health Association of America**. Some states require certification by URAC for authorization to operate a utilization management organization. *Contact:* GHAA, 1129 20th Street, NW, Ste. 600, Washington, DC 20036 (202/778-3200).

V

VA Value analysis.

VAT Value added tax.

VC Virtual classroom.

VCO Voice carry over.

VCR 1. Videocassette recorder.
2. Voluntary compliance resolution.

VDT Video display terminal.

VE Value engineering.

VEAP Veterans' Education Assistance Program.

VEBA Voluntary Employees' Beneficiary Association.

VESA Video Electronic Standards Association.

VEVRA Vietnam Era Veterans Readjustment and Assistance Act of 1974.

VFW Veterans of Foreign Wars.

VGA Video graphics array.

VNA Visiting Nurse Association.

VNR Video news release.

VOD Video-on-demand.

VR Virtual reality.

VRA Veterans Readjustment Act of 1952.

VRAM Video random access memory.

VRBA Veterans' Readjustment Benefits Act of 1966.

VRML Virtual reality modeling language.

VRR Veterans' reemployment rights.

VRS Voice response system.

VSAT Very small aperture terminal.

VSI Voluntary separation incentive.

VTC Video teleconferencing.

VTR Video tape recorder.

VTT Video teletraining.

V/TTY Voice/teletypewriter.

VVA Vietnam Veterans of America, Inc.

vacation *See* annual leave.

vacation buying/selling A time off from work option. Employees are permitted to buy vacation hours or days from other employees who wish to sell them.

vacation carryover A leave policy that allows employees to keep unused vacation time in one year for use in the next year.

validity An essential characteristic of tests, ratings, and other psychological measures. Indicates the extent to which the instrument measures what it was supposed to measure and that scores or ratings provided by the instrument predict or correlate significantly with important aspects of job performance.

validity generalization A concept that holds that inconsistencies in traditional test validation studies are caused by statistical errors that can be eliminated by **meta-analysis**. When that is true, validity is judged to be "generalized."

value added 1. The value added to a product by the resources invested in the materials which comprise it — mainly the value that labor added. Sometimes calculated as net sales minus inventory charge (increase) less material and supplies used equals production value (value added). 2. In meeting management, services or items that are not regularly offered in the contracted cost but are negotiated between the meeting planner and the supplier.

value added tax (VAT) A tax levied on the increase in the value of a product or commodity attributed to the labor involved in producing, marketing, selling, and delivering it to customers or clients. An increment of value is added at each stage of the production process, and the tax is ultimately borne by the consumer. Also called a *consumption tax*.

value added tax (VAT) rebate services Firms that obtain VAT refunds for companies that qualify for a VAT refund (mainly for-profit companies) from Canada and European countries which impose such taxes. Most charge fees ranging from 15 to 40 percent of the refund.

value-adding work Activities and processes, from production to delivery, that transfer raw materials, parts, and data into products and services that can be delivered to customers. Work that increases the value of a product or service to a potential customer or client.

value analysis (VA) A process that involves the evaluation of basic systems functions and alternative design approaches to determine which design contributes the most to overall systems value in terms of effectiveness and costs.

value analysis and engineering A productivity improvement strategy that examines the value added to a product or service by the materials specified for its production. It focuses on the function of the product or service and seeks to eliminate costs that do not contribute to that function.

value creating work Innovative strategies and activities that enhance productivity and elevate quality. It is work that streamlines processes and improves products and services.

value engineering (VE) A systematic effort to analyze the function of HR systems, equipment, facilities, procedures, methods, and supplies to achieve the necessary functions at the lowest overall cost, consistent with requirements for performance, reliability, quality, and maintainability. In other words, value engineering is a logical, organized method of studying hardware, software, and procedures and design, construction, procurement, installation, and maintenance of systems to ensure that the required systems functions are achieved at the lowest possible cost. Value engineering relates the system to hardware, software, and procedures.

value pricing A new pricing strategy. Manufacturer keeps supplies at an as-needed level, saving warehousing costs, and runs normal production shifts; freight companies distribute on a normal schedule, saving on shipping costs; products are sold at one value price, with income from incentives passed on to the consumer; dealer profits by selling rather than buying the product; need for warehousing is eliminated by implementing a just-in-time supply schedule, saving money

for both dealers and consumers; products reach the consumer earlier at lower prices.

value research A subset or branch of value engineering. In marketing it seeks to determine the client's strongest preferences or dislikes and satisfactions or dissatisfactions, as well as features of the product or service on which the customer is neutral.

values The set of objects, activities, principles, or concepts that an individual or group considers important — things that they will sacrifice for and work diligently to get or support. In addition to compensation, achievement, progress, and development, **knowledge workers** value recognition by their peers, opportunities to provide professional assistance and leadership to groups of people, and acceptance and membership in closed and highly select groups.

values code *See* ethics.

values education Programs designed to instill certain principles considered to be fundamental to the continuation of a free society. Proponents believe that the nation cannot survive unless the values upon which it was grounded are fully comprehended and practiced by each succeeding generation. The program is typically infused into elementary, middle school, and high school curriculums. In earlier years, values education focused on inculcating and modeling such values as promptness, neatness and cleanliness, working hard, and respecting the property of others. Today the thrust is as much if not more often on helping students clarify their own values and acquire moral reasoning and value analysis skills.

values statement A corporate document that states precisely what is important to the organization or business. Such statements have been used as the primary means of changing the culture of an organization.

value sustaining work Activities essential to sustain the production process — administrative, record keeping accounting, payroll, and training.

VA Medicare Subvention Legislation
On April 17, 1997 House Veterans Affairs Committee Chairman Bob Stump (R-AZ) and 24 other Committee members introduced a Medicare subvention bill for the VA (H.R. 1362). The bill would establish a demonstration project to allow Medicare to reimburse the VA for treating Medicare-eligible veterans

in VA hospitals. The Secretary of Veterans Affairs would be able to designate up to three sites for the test, effective January 1, 1998. Initially, it would only test Medicare reimbursement on a treatment-by-treatment basis, but the bill would direct VA and Medicare to send Congress a report by March 1, 1999 on the feasibility of extending the test to VA's enrollment-based managed care plans. Only veterans who have both Medicare Part A and Part B would be eligible to participate in the test.

vaporware   Software that does not exist except in the minds of the producers, yet is announced or discussed.

variable annuity   An annuity or pension in which the amount paid to retirees varies according to the investment yield of the funds set aside to provide it.

variable budgeting   See flexible budgeting.

variable compensation   Any kind of pay given strictly on the basis of employee or organizational performance and contributions to the achievement of organizational goals; a reward for outstanding performance. Options include special cash awards, special performance targets, lump sum merit, profit-sharing, team incentives, and gain sharing.

variable pay   See variable compensation.

variance   A measure of the dispersion in a set of data that is equal to the the average of the squared deviations of each item from the mean.

variance analysis   In budgeting, the process of isolating and identifying deviations from expected results and resolving significant variances into their components to determine causes. These findings are presented to the decision maker for appropriate remedial action.

variance forecast   In human resources forecasting, a measure of the an organization's ability to to meet future personnel needs, and it drives the recruitment process. The variance forecast makes use of both the demand forecast and the availability forecast to calculate and graphically display the variance between the two.

Varity Corp. v. Howe   A 1996 ruling of the U.S. Supreme Court on the issue of whether workers have the right to sue on their own behalf under the **Employee Retirement Income Security Act of 1974.** The Court ruled that workers who have been denied benefits in violation of ERISA can seek individual remedies and ready access to the federal courts.

VAT reclaim/refund   The practice of recovering value added taxes (VATs) on consumer goods and services paid to foreign governments, particularly in Europe, and especially by organizations whose employees are frequent international business travelers. By filing the appropriate forms, U.S. corporations can recover VATs on such items as hotels, meals, car rentals, gasoline, taxis, conferences, phone calls, and other business expenses (ranging from 3 to 18 percent) because European governments consider businesses as intermediaries, rather than end-users, which are the target of the VAT. Under terms of a 1966 agreement, U.S. firms are eligible for refunds of the 15 percent VAT taxes paid in Germany.

VDT disease   A hazard or occupational illness attributable to the use of video display terminals in the workplace: hand and wrist muscle strain, neck and back problems, other musculoskeletal disorders, hypertension, eyestrain and vision problems, and potentially dangerous levels of radiation as a consequence of long-term exposure.

vector graphics   In desktop publishing, a type of software that uses a line between two points. Most illustration software uses vector graphics instead of the slower (but more precise) bit-mapped drawings used in earlier computer graphics software. Vectors can be processed as a series of points and connections making it easier and faster for a computer to store and manipulate.

vendor program   In benefits, an employer-sponsored dependent care option in which an employer subsidizes dependent care slots in group day care centers or family day care homes.

venture capital   An equity financing option for growing businesses and the early stage of financing used by many high-risk companies. It involves commitment of funds by venture capital firms following assessment of several factors: the background and skills of the management team, marketability of products and services, size and projected growth of the market, and anticipated return on investment.

ventures   In planning and marketing, separate business units established by a corporation to develop and bring new technologies and products to market as a means of dealing with the growing competitiveness of the business environment.

venturing Establishing partnerships with other companies to share costs and risks.

Verimetrics analyzer A **lie detector** invented by Charles R. McQuiston, retired Chief of the Technical Committee, U.S. Army Intelligence School, Fort Huachuca, AZ. The system is billed as a more accurate machine than its predecessor, the **Psychological Stress Evaluator**. It is said to detect lies by measuring and graphically tracing changes in stress levels in the subject's voice and has been adopted by law enforcement departments in California, Florida, and Louisiana.

Veronica A software program that helps **Internet** users find the information they seek by entering keywords to locate the site where the information is stored. An alternative to **Archie**.

vertical bar chart A means of displaying data graphically. Most often used to compare similar data in different time periods, such as monthly sales or production, or to measure performance against a standard.

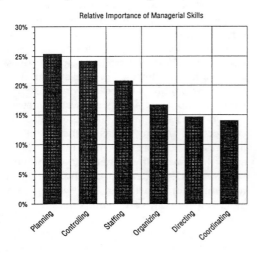

Relative Importance of Managerial Skills

vertical disintegration Describes corporations that shed layer after layer of full-time workers until their operations are performed largely by contract employees.

vertical management The traditional line and staff organization structure, composed of the primary functions of engineering, manufacturing, marketing and sales, finance, and quality assurance, each with its own manager, reporting to the COO or general manager.

vertical organization The traditional line and staff structure, often with multiple levels of authority and responsibility.

vertical programming One type of satellite-delivered video training program — usually programs aimed at a specific audience; for example, software designers or professional nurses.

vertical review and analysis A review of the performance of elements of an organization by function. For example, review and analysis in turn of the marketing, sales, and production departments an organization.

vertical thinking The conventional approach to thought. Vertical thinking uses techniques to eliminate uncertainty and error, simplify complexity, and improve decision making. It involves breaking a problem into smaller and smaller pieces to get it to manageable size and perspective. It focuses on an answer; for example, it is the process involved in calculating your tax liability. Also called *convergent thinking*.

very small aperture terminal (VSAT) A system of **satellite communications** that links remote sites with corporate computer mainframes and conferencing facilities.

vestibule training Induction training provided to new hires outside the work site to acquaint them with the equipment, tools, and procedures used on the job. Most frequently used when the job involves costly equipment and materials, involves hazardous work, or where inexperienced workers would slow production. Sometimes makes use of simulators, as in flight training.

vested or vesting **1.** An employee is said to be vested when he or she acquires a legal right to accrued benefits at retirement. A vested benefit is a nonforfeitable immediate or deferred benefit which an employee has gained. **2.** A benefit plan provision that entitles employees to all or a portion of accrued benefits in company pension plans even if they are placed on long-term or permanent layoff prior to retirement. The **Employee Retirement Income Security Act of 1974** specifies the standards for vesting of employee contributions and were made more restrictive by the **Tax Reform Act of 1986. 3.** That point in time when an executive can exercise stock option or **stock appreciation rights** or some other executive compensation plan can no longer be forfeited.

vesting schedules *See* cliff vesting; graded vesting; rule of 45.

Veterans' Benefits Improvement Act of 1994 Authorizes compensation to Persian Gulf Veterans suffering from disabilities resulting from undiagnosed illnesses possibly incurred during service in the Persian Gulf. Authorizes the Secretary of Veterans Affairs to compensate Gulf War veterans who suffer chronic disabilities that become apparent during or within a specified time after their service in the Gulf region. Signed by the president November 2, 1994.

Veterans' Compensation Rates Amendments of 1993 Legislation that amended Title 38, United States Code, to provide cost-of-living adjustment in the rates of disability compensation for veterans with service-connected disabilities and the rates of dependency and indemnity compensation for survivors of such veterans.

Veterans' Education Assistance Program (VEAP) Now authorizes active duty participants, who entered service between January 1, 1977 and June 30, 1985, to switch to the **Montgomery G.I. Bill** program, which offers higher benefits. Signed into law October 4, 1996.

Veterans Employment Opportunities Act of 1997 Passed by the House April 9, 1997 (H.R. 240). The bill improves a veteran's ability to seek administrative and legal redress for violations of federal employment preference laws. This would mark the first opportunity to pursue legal remedies through the courts. The bill would also broaden application of veterans preference to certain positions at the White House, Congress, and the Judiciary. Senators Chuck Hagel (R-NE) and Max W. Cleland (D-GA) introduced a companion bill, S. 1021, on July 16, 1997.

veterans' employment and training laws *See* Job Training Partnership Act of 1982; Veterans' Readjustment Benefits Act of 1966; Vietnam Era Veterans' Readjustment and Assistance Act of 1974.

Veterans' Group Life Insurance (VGLI) Low-cost group life insurance available to veterans of all military services following separation from active duty. Effective December 1, 1992, veterans may increase their coverage to a maximum of $200,000 but they cannot obtain more coverage under VGLI than the total of their coverage in force

under **Servicemens' Group Life Insurance.** Veterans are also guaranteed VGLI coverage on a five-year term-renewable basis.

Veterans Health Care Reform Act of 1996 Requires the VA to establish an annual patient enrollment system. Mandates that, by October 1, 1998, all veterans not enrolled will no longer be able to use the VA health care system. Veterans requiring care for a service-connected condition, or who are 50% or more service-connected disabled, are exempt from the enrollment requirement.

Veterans' Medicare Reimbursement Model Project Act of 1996 The bill would establish a model demonstration project at a limited number of sites under which the Department of Veterans Affairs would be reimbursed by the Department of Health and Human Services for health care provided to certain Medicare-eligible veterans. The purpose of the bill is to expand the choice of health care for older veterans; bring new resources, utilization, and operational experience to the VA health care system; and produce savings for the Medicare Trust Fund. Approved by President Clinton August 8, 1996, at which time he directed the Secretary of Veterans Affairs to submit the enabling legislation to Congress.

Veterans of Foreign Wars (VFW) An organization of approximately 2.1 million members, open to all grades and ranks of past and present members of the U.S. Armed Forces discharged under honorable conditions and awarded a Department of Defense-authorized campaign or foreign service medal. Its missions are fraternal, patriotic, historical, and educational. *Contact:* VFW, 200 Maryland Ave., N.E., Washington DC 20002 (202/543-2239; Fax 202/543-6719; URL http://www.vfw.org).

Veterans' Readjustment Benefits Act of 1966 (VRBA) [As amended by the Vietnam Era Veterans Readjustment Assistance Act of 1974 (P.L. 93-508) and by P.L. 100-212 of 1988.] An Act designed to meet the special employment and training needs of disabled veterans and Vietnam-era veterans and increase their opportunities to obtain employment, job training, counseling, and job placement services. The Act established an Assistant Secretary of Labor for Veterans' Employment and Training within the Department of Labor to promulgate and administer policies and programs to provide employment and training services and programs.

veterans' reemployment rights   Federal statutes designed to encourage noncareer service in the military by reducing the employment disadvantages that result from such service. The original VRR law was passed in 1940 and has been amended many times since.

Veterans' Reemployment Rights Acts of 1993 and 1994   Guarantees that employees who enlist or called to active military duty have a right to return to a job of similar seniority, pay, and status upon release to civilian life. The Act also defined compensation for purposes of defined contribution plans as salary or wages paid to the worker just prior to his or her entry into military service and determined that the length of time a returning veteran has to make retroactive savings plan contributions should be any reasonable period agreed to by both the employer and the employee.

Veterans Reemployment Act of 1994   Specifically protects the pension benefits of employees called to active duty in the Armed Services. Applies to any pension plan protected under the **Employee Retirement Income Security Act of 1974**, including both 401(k) and traditional pension plans.

viatical settlement   A form of **living benefit** by which companies (not insurance carriers), backed by private investors and pension and corporate funds, purchase life insurance policies for between 15 and 95 percent of their face value in exchange for being named the beneficiary. The shorter the individual's life expectancy, the higher the percentage paid. The industry has come into being since 1989, largely precipitated by the AIDS epidemic. People with huge medical bills and short life expectancies sell their policies to get immediate cash; companies purchase the policies to get a quick return on investment. Considered unconscionable, even ghoulish, by some, but realistic and defensible by others. Also called *death futures.*

vicarious liability   The liability of a trainer or others responsible for training if injuries occur as a result of an employee's application of the skills taught in a training program.

Vichy shower   An alternative treatment in which hot and cold sea water is sprayed on the body by means of low-pressure hoses. Said to cleanse and heal the body.

video board   Computer hardware that enables it to play back video. *See* video card.

video capture card   Equipment and associated software that allow the user to run videotape signals into a computer, convert them to digital video, play them back on a monitor, and save them as digital video files.

video card   A device that fits into a bay or slot in the central processing unit of a computer and enables the computer to play digital video files.

video cassette recorder (VCR)   A device that allows the user to play back videotapes on a television screen and to record programs that are being received by a television set for playback at a later time.

video compression   In multimedia, the process of reducing the number of digital bits required to store information or images to save memory; in some cases no information is lost by the process; in others, some is lost but enough information is retained to represent the original image.

video conferencing   Point-to-point communication between two or more groups at two or more locations using satellite communications or phone lines.

video decompression   In multimedia, the process of restoring previously compressed information or images into the format from which it was compressed. With some processes some information may be lost; with others, no information is lost.

video disc   A means of storing data, it makes use of large (12 inches in diameter) rigid discs using analog, rather than digital, technology. Such discs can store full text, graphics, still and full motion video, and audio. They hold about 30 minutes of linear play video on each side and can accommodate 54,000 still pictures with limited audio per frame. Files can be accessed randomly, and images can be accessed by computer for display. Storage is permanent (ROM). Requires special equipment to read. Digital videodiscs may replace videocassettes and compact disc-read only memory as a universal storage medium.

video display terminal (VDT)   The viewing screen of a computer on which the files and the data inputted by peripheral devices or outputted by the computer can be seen and manipulated.

Video Electronic Standards Association (VESA)   An organization that creates, establishes, disseminates, and supports industry-wide video graphics standards for the benefit of producers and consumers. Contact: VESA, 2150 North First Street, Suite 440, San Jose, CA. 95131-2029 (408/435-0333; Fax 408/435-8225; E-mail **ftp.vesa.org**; URL **http://www.vesa.org**).

video, full-motion Broadcast quality video — full screen video that is played back at 30 frames per second.

video graphics array (VGA) A color graphics standard introduced by IBM. VGA has a resolution of 640 by 480 pixels, providing an 8-bit color bit-marked display.

video information system (VIS) A set of specifications for interactive compact disc players that are simply connected to a television set and are operated by a remote control device. VIS is an open system based on Windows 3.1 that will be licensed to both hardware and software vendors.

video news release (VNR) Satellite technology used by corporations, associations, and government agencies to transmit to the public audio, visual, and textual information across the country or anywhere in the world. Video clips average 90 seconds and are accompanied by background visuals. Prior to transmission in the U.S., more than 750 TV stations are sent a VNR alert by fax.

video-on-demand (VOD) High performance, real-time transmission, storage, and retrieval imaging systems. May be interactive.

videophone A device that uses fiber optics, digital signal compression, and telephone lines and satellite communications to transmit detailed still or motion pictures over very great distances. Used in telemedicine projects.

video random access memory (VRAM) A special kind of high-speed memory used in frame buffers.

video stream In multimedia, a sequence of video images played back by means of computer command.

video tape recorder (VTR) A recording and playback tape deck.

video teleconferencing (VTC) A form of distance training or education that links classrooms at two or more locations with live, full-motion video using telephone or satellite communications. Enables instructors to be televised live to multiple training locations. Interaction between and among instructors and trainees can be achieved by means of open telephone, fax, and computer lines.

video teletraining (VTT) A delivery system used by the military services to provide training at remote sites using satellite communications. VTT differs from conventional TV training in that it is two-way communication using large screen TV, video cameras and audio systems at both the sending and receiving sites thereby allowing instructors and trainees to see each other and conduct discussions in real time.

Video Toaster A customized Commodore Amiga personal computer that serves as a desktop video production facility. It manipulates video signals directly instead of having to convert them, and, by means of a video digitizer, brings any image a camera can see into a computer, and integrates the output of as many as seven other devices to create video effects formerly produced only by expensive, large-scale production facilities. It has an on-screen icon display accessible by the click of a mouse for 132 preprogrammed special effects.

Vietnam Era Veterans Readjustment and Assistance Act of 1974 (VEVRA) Legislation passed by Congress to promote the hiring of "qualified disabled veterans" and "veterans of the Vietnam era." The Act proscribes discrimination against those veterans and requires affirmative action to hire and promote them. Qualified disabled veterans are those who receive disability compensation for a 30 percent or greater disability or who were discharged or released from active duty for an injury received or aggravated in the line of duty. Veterans of the Vietnam era are individuals who were on active duty more than 180 days between August 5, 1964 and May 5, 1975, were not dishonorably discharged or were on active duty between those dates and were released for a service-connected disability. The Act requires employers to take affirmative action to employ and advance qualified disabled and Vietnam era veterans. It applies only to federal contractors and subcontractors with contracts of $10,000 or more. Larger contractors (with contracts worth $50,000 or more and 50 or more employees) must also prepare affirmative action programs. The Office of Federal Contract Compliance is empowered to bring actions in federal court to enforce this legislation.

Vietnam Veterans of America, Inc. (VVA) Established to help, encourage, and promote the improvement of the condition of the Vietnam veteran, advance the physical and cultural improvement, growth, and development, self-respect, self-confidence, and usefulness of those veterans and others, eliminate discrimination suffered by Vietnam veterans, and develop channels of communication which will assist Vietnam veterans to maximize self-realization and enrichment of their lives and enhance life-fulfillment. Contact: VVA, 1224 M Street, N.W., Washington, D.C. 20005-5183 (800/VVA-1316 or 202/628-2700; Fax 202/628-5880; E-mail **71154.702@compuserve.com**; URL **http://www.org**).

virtual classroom (VC) The name is copyrighted by the Computerized Conferencing and Communications Center, New Jersey Institute of Technology, Newark, NJ.) A teaching-learning environment contained within a computer-mediated communication system; that is, it is a set of group communication "work" spaces and facilities fabricated in software rather than steel, bricks, and lumber. Its purpose is to facilitate "distance" or remote learning and to improve the quality of education and training.

virtual HR **1.** Human resource services that are available to employees instantaneously any time and at any place. *See also* situational HR. **2.** Use of technology to provide "self-service" human resources programs, such as benefits enrollment, data base updating, and employee performance evaluation. Examples of virtual HR are interactive, multimedia computer programs, information kiosks, and voice-response telephone systems. Relieves HR managers of routine or repetitive tasks and, at the same time, empowers workers to take charge of their own careers.

virtual office The "workplace" (such as hotel rooms, cars, and clients' offices) of sales people, field engineers, customer service representatives, auditors, and other employees who work off the company premises when and where it is convenient and remain connected by computer links and telephone modems. Said to replace real estate with technology.

virtual organization An organization, built on flexibility and employee empowerment and valuing diversity, speed, teamwork, communication, and a highly skilled work force. Such organizations are based on networks or

teams, which are focused on a single problem. They can be internal or external to the firm and can be extended to include customers, clients, suppliers, and even competitors in strategic alliances. Also called virtual teams. Attributed to Joseph R. Cleveland, president of Lockheed Martin of Orlando, Florida.

virtual reality (VR) Systems that create computer-generated, three-dimensional, multisensory, real-time, interactive artificial environments through the use of graphics and animation technology. Using sensing and interface devices (such as stereoscopic headgear or eye phones) and software (such as data suits, and tracking equipment), the systems create three-dimensional, directly interactive environments that immerse users into worlds that appear real and allow them to interact with those worlds. Used in training, manufacturing, and entertainment.

virtual reality modeling language (VRML) Codifies into a standardized formal such complex tasks as simulating artificial environments, inputting control data, outputting visual, aural, or feedback data, storing and manipulation of 3-D worlds, and communicating virtual reality data to others. Essentially VRML is a means of describing objects in 3D space.

virtual team A network of employees in different locations who can be interconnected by fax, phone, E-mail, videoconferencng, or an intranet and who focus on accomplishing a goal, objective, or project as a team.

virtual workplace A term used by some companies to indicate a broader interpretation of the virtual office. Employees may work in hotels, at the client's site, or elsewhere.

virus A hostile short code segment of a computer program that attaches itself to the beginning or end of a code piece and gives commands to modify or destroy data. Computers get "sick" when they pick up a virus that is hitchhiking on foreign floppy disks or program files downloaded from bulletin boards. Viruses can attack any executable computer file, overlay file, allocation table, partition table, or boot sector. Some viruses instruct the system to do a variety of abnormal activities such as drawing a picture on the screen, printing a message, erasing files, or performing other destructive acts. Some are intelligent enough to look for an unused piece of code within a program. For that reason they are difficult to detect.

vision **1.** A leader's sense (that is, his or her intuitive feeling), that an idea is good, believable, and worthwhile to attempt to carry out, and that leader's ability to instill in others that it was, in fact, their idea in the first place. **2.** A view, shared by all constituencies of an organization, of the purposes, values, and principles toward which the organization is moving and around which it can shape its culture.

vision care An ancillary benefit that typically provides one eye examination per year, plus eyeglass frames and lenses as needed.

vision care plan A form of protection benefit, a plan by which reimbursements are provided to covered employees for limited optometric examinations and lens prescriptions.

visioning Developing a "vision statement" for an organization. Prophesying the future — what the world of work and business will become, what the organization will become, who it should be ready to serve, and how it might best serve them.

visioning meeting An employee involvement technique. A group of employees is convened to develop a vision statement for an organization.

vision statement A description of the future (typically ten years ahead) as a planner would like to see it. It includes key components of the external and internal environments, the position of the organization in its industry, and the role and status of the HR department in that context.

Vision World Wide, Inc. Publishes materials that that are encouraging and motivating to people who are vision impaired and their families, informative to health care professionals, senior centers, radio reading services, and libraries, and enlightening to the general public. Also provides information and referral services through a nationwide toll-free help line. Contact: Vision World Wide, Inc., 5707 Brockton Dr., #302, Indianapolis, IN 46220-5481 (800/431-1739 or 317/254-1332; Fax 317/251-6588; E-mail **visionww@netdirect.net**; URL **http://www. netdirect.net/vision-enhancement/**).

Visiting Nurse Association (VNA) An agency licensed by a town, city, county, or state which provides part-time, intermittent skilled nursing services in a person's place of residence.

visualization See guided imaging/imagery.

visualizing See guided imaging/imagery.

visual literacy **1.** A group of vision competencies a human being can develop by seeing and at the same time having and integrating other sensory experiences. **2.** The learned ability to interpret the communication of visual symbols (images), and to create messages using visual symbols. **3.** The ability to translate visual images into verbal language and vice versa. **4.** The ability to search for and evaluate visual information in visual media. (As defined by the International Visual Literacy Association).

vocational education Occupational education and training provided at the secondary and postsecondary (vocational, technical, career institutions) levels in trades and semi- or paraprofessions.

Vocational Rehabilitation On-the-Job Training Program An incentive to hire disabled workers in the form of a wage reimbursement awarded to the employer for a limited period of time. To qualify, the disabled worker employed must be an Office of Vocational Rehabilitation client and the job must be full-time and permanent.

Vocational Rehabilitation Services Workers who are ineligible for Social Security disability benefits may be considered for vocational rehabilitation services by state Vocational Rehabilitation Agencies. Those agencies provide counseling, training, and many other services that disabled persons may need to help them get back to work.

voice and speech recognition Use of digitized sound, recorded and integrated into a program. In addition to identifying a speaker's speech patterns, systems can "guess" what a speaker means and make corrections as feedback is received.

voice response system Uses touch-tone telephones as computer terminals for requesting or entering data. Users are prompted to press keys by a computer-generated voice.

voir dire A legal term that means literally "to speak the truth" — it refers to the jury selection process.

voluntary reduced hours An arrangement that allows employees to reduce their work hours for a specified period with a corresponding reduction in income. Also called V-time.

voice activated Computer software designed to recognize and perform commands spoken by the user.

voice carry over (VCO) A reduced form of telecommunications relay services where the person with a hearing disability can speak directly to the other end user. The communications assistant types the response back to the person with the hearing disability where it appears on a readout display. The communications assistant does not voice any conversations.

voice mail Automated telephone or other form of electronic answering system.

voice-over In video and audio production, a voice speaking over music or other sound background; narration added to the original soundtrack during the post-production phase.

voice recognition Software that enables users to enter text and numbers into a computer without using a keyboard, mouse, or pen.

voice recognition unit A device that can be programmed to recognize and respond to oral commands. For example, a computer user might say, "Print the letter," and the device transmits the command to the computer, which responds by printing out the document.

voice response system (VRS) A means of streamlining and speeding up benefits administration and making it more responsive to employees' requests for information and assistance. VRSs are customized communications tools that give employees access to information stored in a computer by calling a toll-free number at any time of the day or night. A recorded message provides them with step-by-step directions and a list of options. Specific information is retrieved when the employee presses certain numbers on a touch-tone phone and enters his or her access code.

voice synthesis See computer synthetic voice translation.

voice/teletypewriter (V/TTY) A telecommunications device for the deaf/teletypewriter Relay Center that provides assistance to the deaf, hard of hearing, and communication disabled persons using the devices to make local and long distance calls through the center.

voids In travel management, the practice of voiding or back-dating a ticket without imposing a penalty on the purchaser.

voluntary bargaining item In union contract negotiations, an item over which bargaining is neither required (mandatory) nor prohibited (unlawful), and neither party can be compelled to negotiate.

voluntary benefits Insurance plans paid for by employees, such as group term life insurance and disability and cancer assistance policies.

voluntary bumping In travel management, a result of overbooking. Ticketed passengers with reserved seats, either on board an aircraft or ready to board, are offered a reward, such as a free flight or cash, to give up their seats.

Voluntary Compliance Resolution (VCR) An experimental Internal Revenue Service (IRS) tax amnesty program aimed at inducing voluntary compliance with pension plan rules. The VCR plan allows eligible qualified pension plan sponsors to voluntarily disclose the defects in their operational plans, pay a fixed compliance fee, agree to make full correction, and, when necessary, implement procedures to keep the plan in compliance. The program applies to plans that have received a favorable determination letter from the IRS that considered the Tax Equity and Responsibility Act of 1982, the Tax Reform Act of 1984, and the Retirement Equity Act of 1984. Originally set to expire at the end of 1993, the VCR has been extended to December 31, 1994. It has also modified eligibility criteria to include corrections for aggregated plans with certain errors, clarified treatment of defective benefit plans that are not eligible for retroactive correction under the Section 401(b) remedial amendment period, and lowered compliance fees to $350 for certain violations. The program is an extension of the IRS Closing Agreement Program.

voluntary employees' beneficiary association (VEBA) Defined in Section 501(c) of the Internal Revenue Code as a separate organization "providing for the payment of life, sickness, accident, or other benefits to the members.....or their dependents or designated beneficiaries." Companies may establish VEBAs for employees, subject to specific IRS rules and regulations, to which the VEBA makes tax-deductible contributions. The VEBA invests the funds for payment of benefits to employees on a tax-exempt basis; however, with the repeal of Section 89 of the Internal

Revenue Code (IRC), VEBA trusts will lose their tax-favored status unless the plans are nondiscriminatory under Section 505(b) of the IRC.

voluntary reduced work time A program that allows workers to make time and income/benefits tradeoffs (reduced pay and benefits for a reduced work week) by pre-arrangement for specified periods of time and with a defined process for returning to full-time work.

voluntary leave Leave without pay voluntarily taken by workers for a specified period of time to help an organization reduce costs.

voluntary separation incentive (VSI) An incentive bonus offered to military personnel who volunteer to leave the service during the downsizing of the armed services (1992-3). For Army personnel, it consists of 2-1/2 percent of basic pay per year of service, which applies to those who have served from six to 20 years.

Volunteer Protection Act of 1996 Legislation introduced in Congress that would protect volunteers working on behalf of nonprofit and government organizations from personal financial liability in the event of a lawsuit. The bill would encourage prompt adoption of state laws to exempt unpaid volunteers from tort liability, except in cases of willful misconduct. The law would protect both officers and "direct service" volunteers. Since the bill was first introduced in 1985, more than 30 states have enacted their own volunteer protection laws; however, they vary widely in score and coverage and therefore cause confusion. or fail to shield volunteers completely from liability.

volunteerism   Promotion of volunteer employee service by means of company-sponsored or paid leave for up to one year with full salary and benefits for community service or non-profit organization assignments.

Volunteer Protection Act of 1997 Legislation that protects a volunteer from liability for harm caused while properly engaged in volunteer work unless the harm was caused by willful or criminal misconduct; conscious, flagrant indifference; or resulted from a crime of violence, international terrorism, a sexual offense, or a violation of civil rights law. Passed by both the House and Senate May 21, 1997 and sent to President Clinton for signature.

voucher program An employer-sponsored and -financed dependent care option in which the employee submits monthly vouchers for dependent care expenses to the provider and the employer covers all or a part of the cost of the services.

voucher system A training plan that would replace some 50 federal job training programs with stipends of up to $2,600 per year for two years to eligible people. Recipients would be free to spend the money on education or classroom or on-the-job training.

V-time programs   A type of alternative work schedule in which work time and compensation are voluntarily reduced. These programs allow employees to make time/income tradeoffs by enrolling in a program rather than negotiating with their immediate supervisors.

vu-graph See overhead projector.

W

WA	Wagner Act of 1935.
WAG	Wild-ass guess.
WAIS	Wide area information servers.
WAN	Wide-area network.
WARNA	Worker Adjustment and Retraining Notification Act of 1988.
WATS	Wide Area Telecommunications Service.
WAW	Waiter-actor-webmaster.
WBE	Women-owned business enterprise.
WBT	Web-based training.
WCA	Wellness Councils of America.
WCRI	Workers' Compensation Research Institute.
WELCOA	Wellness Councils of America.
WEP	Windfall Elimination Provision.
WFD	World Federation of the Deaf.
WFS	World Future Society.
WHA	Work Hours Act of 1962.
WHPCA	Walsh-Healy Public Contracts Act of 1936.
WID	World Institute on Disability
WIRs	Work injury reports.
WOOPIE	Well-off older person.
WORM	Write once, read many.
WPA	Whistleblower Protection Act of 1989.
WRI	World Resources Institute.
WRT	With respect to (Internet speak).
WSA	Williams-Steiger Act of 1970.
WSJ	*The Wall Street Journal.*
WTO	World Trade Organization.
WWW	World Wide Web.
WYSIWYG	What you see is what you get.

W-2 Form The form employers give to workers at the end of each calendar year which shows total earnings reported to the government and sums withheld for various purposes, such as federal state, local, and FICA taxes.

W-4 Form The form employers issue to workers for completion at the time of hiring to estimate and report probable tax liabilities for withholding considering such factors as number of dependents and outside income.

wage and salary administration The procedures and processes used to plan and administer compensation programs for employees at all levels of organization. They include job analysis and evaluation, job pricing, and pay structures for executives, exempt employees, and nonexempt hourly paid and salaried workers.

wage and salary survey An employee survey designed to provide information to help the HR manager deal with important compensation policy matters, including making salaries and wages attractive and competitive. Such surveys are also essential preliminaries to the conduct of other management actions such as union negotiations.

wage curve Used to assign pay rates to pay grades (jobs of approximately equal difficulty that have been grouped together). Depicts graphically the pay rates currently being paid for jobs in each pay grade relative to the points or rankings awarded to each job or grade during job evaluation.

wage gap The difference between men's and women's pay for the same or comparable jobs. Also called *gender gap.*

wage garnishment A legal procedure through which the earnings of an individual are required to be withheld by an employer for the payment of a debt. Most garnishments are made by court order.

wages and hours laws See Equal Pay Act of 1963; Fair Labor Standards Act (FLSA) of 1938; Portal-to-Portal Act of 1947.

wage structure Graphically depicts the range of pay rates (such as dollars and cents per hour) to be paid each pay grade in a series of jobs. Derived from the **wage curve,**

but additional information, such as market wages, compensation policies, and required rate changes are taken into account to produce the final wage structure — the wages to be paid by the company categorized by pay grades and indicating rate changes.

Wagner Act of 1935 (WA)   *See* National Labor-Management Relations Act of 1935; unfair labor practices.

waiter-actor-webmasters (WAW) Describes shady graphics designers and **Web** consultants who try to exploit the current Web boom.

waiting line problems   *See* queuing theory.

waitlist   A list of names of individual air travelers present in the terminal without reservations (in the order received) awaiting cancellations of flight reservations. Some airlines give priority to those on the waitlist for emergency reasons or to members of their clubs and other VIPs.

waiver   **1.** A document signed by employees or candidates for positions by which they give up or relinquish certain specified rights, such as the release of personal information. **2.** A document signed by candidates for positions prior to making their application stating that they take preemployment tests (such as honesty tests) voluntarily and waive all claims against the company for the administration of the tests.

walk   In meeting management, a guest with a confirmed reservation who is sent to another property because of overbooking.

"walking" clause   A clause in a contract with a hotel that describes the requirements for obtaining a guaranteed reservation and the hotel's obligations if a reservation is not honored due to overbooking.

walking the talk   Congruence between what a person says and how he or she actually behaves. Doing something instead of merely talking about it. Taking action expeditiously after committing to do something.

walk-out   *See* strike.

wallpaper   An Internet term for the often-distracting background pattern behind the text on a "page."

The Wall Street Journal (WSJ)   *Contact:* (800/975-8609; E-mail **inquiries@interactive.wsj.com**; URL **http://www.wsj.com**).

Walsh-Healy Public Contracts Act of 1936 (WHPCA)   An act that established basic labor standards for such items as minimum (prevailing) wage rates, overtime, health and safety requirements, and fringe benefits. The Act also establishes liability for breaches of contract for the manufacture or furnishing of materials, supplies, articles, and equipment. It applies to organizations working on federal government contracts of $10,000 or more. Amendments require payment of minimum wage rates an overtime pay on contracts to provide goods to the federal government.

Walters v. Metropolitan Educational Enterprises, Inc.   A 1997 Supreme Court decision on how employees must be counted to determine which federal laws, such as the Americans with Disabilities Act, apply to a business. The court ruled that anyone who has an "employment relationship with a business (a person who is on the company payroll, including a temporary or part-time employee) is to be included, regardless of whether that person is actually at work on a particular day."

want list   A person's wish list — consisting of things they want, but which are not necessarily the things that they need.

ward   A legal term that describes an incapacitated person who is under the **guardianship** of a court-appointed temporary or permanent **guardian** who has the authority to make personal, financial, and medical decision on behalf of the ward.

warehousing   Placing physically or mentally disabled persons in long-term care facilities, such as mental institutions, with the assumption that their disabilities are irremediable and that they require permanent custodial care.

warning   A form of disciplinary action; usually the first formal stage of progressive discipline. It is invariable written: a letter describing the offense, reminding the employee of a previous written reprimand, and informing the employee that a repeat of the offense will result in more stringent disciplinary action.

warrant   In investments, an instrument issued by a corporation that gives the holder the right to subscribe to a specified amount of the corporation's capital stock at a set price for a specified period of time.

Washington Alert   A data base vendor; for example, Dow Jones News/Retrieval.

watchdog utilities   Computer software programs that help recover data from damaged or accidentally formatted files by making a copy of the file allocation tables.

Watson v. Fort Worth Bank & Trust
A 1988 decision of the U.S. Supreme Court relating to tests and discrimination. The Court ruled that subjective employment practices, such as ratings and performance evaluations, are subject to the same standards as are objective criteria, such as tests, used in making hiring decisions.

Web-based HR applications
Human resources functions performed by or with the help of the World Wide Web. Examples include benefit information/enrollment, corporate communication, job posting/application, thrift/savings/401(k)/profit sharing, research, and training and development.

Web-based training (WBT) Distance training conducted via the Internet to reduce training costs and increase accessibility for workers.

Web client A computer terminal that simply displays documents.

WebCrawler A free service provided by most commercial services as well as specific locations that allows the subscriber or user to search the **Internet.**

webmaster/webmistress In organizations, the individual responsible for **World Wide Web** site design, administration, and maintenance, currently filled by professionals of widely varying experiences. Some come from information systems backgrounds and others are former communications managers. Typically have a high profile in the organization, reporting directly to the chairman or CEO or the chief information officer.

Web searches Boolean search, concept search, fuzzy search, keyword search, phrase search, precision search, proximity search, query-by-example search.

Web server A computer terminal that responds to requests from users by sending a **hypertext** document.

Website An address on the **Internet** which brings a user to the opening screen of a specific site. A website may contain many home pages. *See also* universal resource locator.

webwrap licensing A notice on a Web page, readable on the user's computer monitor, that spells out the terms of the "contract" and informs the individual that downloading the package (accomplished by a click of the mouse) constitutes acceptance of the license agreement as a binding contract. Used to protect the authors of the software from copyright infringement (unauthorized copying) and ensure them of profits from sales of the product.

webzine A paperless magazine available on the World Wide Web. Originally noncommercial, communal, and free, online publications are beginning to carry advertising and bill subscribers. *Also called* E(lectronic)zine.

weed *See* marijuana.

Weingarten Rule (or Rights) Interprets the **National Labor Relations Act of 1935** in relation to unfair labor practices and the questioning of employees by employers. States that an employer violates the NLRA by requiring an employee to take part in an investigatory interview without union representation if the employee requests representation. However, an employer may refuse to bargain with any union representative permitted to attend an interview. An employee is not entitled to representation at a meeting with management where management has already decided in advance of the meeting to terminate the employee and the sole purpose of the meeting is to inform the employee of that fact.

welfare plan A benefits plan that provides for medical, surgical, or hospital care for sickness, accident, disability, death, or unemployment. Under provisions of the **Employee Retirement Income Security Act of 1974** such plans may also offer such benefits as vacation or scholarship plans.

welfare reform *See* Personal Responsibility and Work Opportunity Act of 1996.

well child care A health care benefit that pays all or part of the reasonable and customary charges for such services as doctor office visits, including the costs associated with routine physical examinations, laboratory tests, and routine childhood immunizations recommended by the American Academy of Pediatrics. Typically includes the first routine newborn examination and routine inpatient or outpatient screening.

Wellness Councils of America (WELCOA)
A national nonprofit organization of 2,000 corporate members in 27 Councils established to promote healthier lifestyles for all Americans, especially through health promotion activities

at the work site. WELCOA acts as a national clearinghouse for information on workplace health promotion and has set national criteria to measure achievement in this area. Develops products and services for any company anywhere. *Contact:* WELCOA, Community Health Plaza, Ste. 311, 7101 Newport Ave., Omaha, Nebraska 68152 (402/572-3590; Fax 402/572-3594; URL **http://www.social.com/ health/nhic/data/hr2300/hr2346.html**).

wellness program   A means of heading off employee illnesses and accidents, as well as medical claims, by installing corporate fitness centers, supporting wholly or partially fitness programs off site, and sponsoring health screenings and wellness education. Wellness programs typically include (1) developing awareness of the need for wellness; (2) assessment and monitoring of the overall health of employees (occupationally, physically, nutritionally, intellectually, emotionally, spiritually and ethically, and socially and environmentally); (3) skills training and the provision of supportive environments; (4) maintenance of minimal levels of performance by reducing risks through systematic exercise and life-style modification (annual physicals, smoking cessation programs, weight reduction, blood pressure control, drug and alcohol assistance, fitness centers, comprehensive health risk assessment, stress management, exercise programs, back care, and other educational programs); and (5) **demand management** training.

well-off older person (WOOPIE)   Applied to people who have retired with an ample annuity, supplemented by Social Security.

Western blot test   A reliable but complicated and expensive test for the HIV antibody used to confirm the results of ELISHA or other tests.

what-if?   A common term for software functions that allow users to test hypotheses.

what you see is what you get (WYSIWYG) In personal computer vernacular, refers to the capabilities of such aids to the user as graphical software.

whipsawing   A term used by labor to describe the practice of forcing plant-against-plant competition or bidding for jobs. The threat of closings, whether specifically made or only implied, is used as a lever to gain approval of cost-saving measures unless unions make concessions with

respect to such items as compensation, benefits, scheduling, or work rules.

whistleblower   An employee who reports unsafe, dishonest, unethical, or questionable employer practices.

Whistleblower Protection Act of 1989 (WPA)   An Act designed to protect the rights of federal employees who make disclosures of illegality, corruption, fraud, waste, abuse, and unnecessary government expenditures, prevent reprisals, and help eliminate wrongdoing within the government. The Act established the Office of Special Counsel to receive and investigate allegations of prohibited personnel practices, bring petitions for corrective actions, file complaints or make recommendations for disciplinary action, and where appropriate forward to the Attorney General or an agency head disclosures of violations of any law, rule, or regulation, gross mismanagement, waste of funds, abuse of authority, or substantial and specific danger to public health or safety. In 1997, the Labor Department expanded the whistleblower protection responsibilities of the Occupational Safety and Health Administration by requiring the agency to prevent retaliation against employees alleging violations of the Superfund Hazardous Waste Cleanup Act, Clean Air Act, Safe Drinking Water Act, Resource Conservation and Recovery Act, Clean Water Act, Toxic Substances Control Act, and Energy Reorganization Act.

whiteboard   Document conferencing that accommodates multiple users and allows them simultaneously to view and annotate those documents with pens, highlighters, and drawing tools. Advanced programs handle multipage documents and provide tools for delivering them as presentations.

white collar cycle time   A measure of quality. It is calculated by dividing the number of actions-in-process (partially completed tasks) by their completion rate. Examples of actions in process: number of positions being filled; number of courses being developed; number of reports to be completed, and so on.

$$\text{Cycle time} = \frac{\text{Number of actions in process}}{\text{Completion rate}}$$

white-collar workers   Salaried employees, e.g., managers, supervisors, technicians, salespersons, and clerical workers, whose work doesn't usually include manual labor and therefore dress somewhat more formally than blue collar workers.

Whittle New American School   A project launched by Christopher Whittle to build a new American school to replace what he describes as outdated and inadequate. The venture is called the **Edison Project.** It is described by critics as an threatening step toward privatization of public schools.

wholistic   *See* holistic.

wholesaling   Selling goods in large quantities to jobbers or retailers rather than directly to consumers.

wide area information servers (WAIS)
A text search system that lets **Internet** users conduct topical or keyword searches of large text files.

wide-area network (WAN)   A group of computers interconnected over long distances using telephone lines or satellite links. There are basically two types: **distributed networks** and **centralized networks.** Attributed to James H. Russell, Jr. (*T.H.E. Journal,* November 1991, p. 62).

Wide Area Telecommunications Service (WATS)   An efficient and cost effective long-distance telephone service for incoming or outgoing telephone calls or both.

widow   In topography, the end of a paragraph or a column of printed material that is undesirably short, such as a single short word or the end of a hyphenated word, such as "ing."

wild-ass guess (WAG)   A crude term used by engineers to describe conclusions reached by intuition or instinct rather than deduced from factual evidence.

wild duck   Attributed to IBM founder Thomas Watson. Describes a creative and innovative professional, often an engineer or technician, who lives and works by different rules than other employees. Wild ducks are not motivated by traditional pay or other incentives, nor do they respond well to conventional management approaches and techniques. They require special handling.

wilderness training   As distinguished from outdoor-centered programs, participants live outdoors and engage in relatively strenuous physical activities such as mountain climbing, white river rafting, and sailing.

will   A legal document that determines who will receive the property of the maker upon his or her death. It also specifies how and when the beneficiary is to receive the property. Wills can often save taxes on estates.

willful misconduct   Deliberate, conscious, and premeditated violation of company rules or regulations. Willful misconduct requires the imposition of sanctions or disciplinary action.

Williams-Steiger Act of 1970 (WSA)   *See* Occupational Safety and Health Act of 1970 (OSHA).

Windfall Elimination Provision (WEP)
A reduction of as much as 50 percent in Social Security benefit payments to federal workers or retirees. Enacted in 1983, it affects federal employees first eligible to retire after 1985 if they are also eligible for an annuity based in whole or in part on work not covered by Social Security. Exemptions include (1) anyone who has 30 years of substantial earnings under Social Security; (2) anyone who is a federal survivor annuitant; (3) anyone whose pension is based solely on noncovered employment before 1957; (4) anyone whose only pension from noncovered employment is based on Railroad Retirement covered work; (5) any federal worker first hired after December 31, 1983 or a federal worker performing service January 1, 1984 who became mandatorily covered under Social Security January 1, 1984; and (6) anyone employed December 31, 1983 by a nonprofit organization that became mandatorily covered under Social Security on that date. *See* windfall reduction.

windfall reduction   A provision of the Social Security law that subjects those who are eligible for government pensions, based in whole or in part on non-covered social security employment, to a reduction in their Social Security benefit payments. The formula affects annuitants who reached age 62 or become disabled after 1985 and who first become eligible to retire after 1985. The reduction could reduce benefits by up to 50 percent. To become eligible for a Social Security disability benefit, an individual must have worked in a job covered by Social Security for five years out of the 10 years before he or she became disabled. Exempt from WEP are all employees first hired January 1, 1984 and after, or a federal worker performing service on January `1, 1984 who became mandatorily covered under Social Security on January 1, 1984 Also exempt is anyone, whether retiring from the **Civil Service Retirement System** or **Federal Employee Retirement System** if he or she has had 30 years of substantial earnings in Social Security covered employment. The Social Security minimum benefit was eliminated in January 1982; benefits are now based on average earnings. Also known as the *windfall elimination provision*.

windows Refers to Microsoft® Windows™, a graphical computer user interface that makes use of pull-down menus and intuitive commands, and **"what you see is what you get"** displays. It permits users to do more with personal computing than can be done with character-based software and do it more quickly and more easily. Used in most leading disk operating systems.

wipe In video production, changing the video image from one scene to another by sweeping away the old one either side to side, top to bottom, bottom to top, or diagonally.

wireless data communications Wireless **local area networks** that will offer greater convenience and mobility to millions of users by the year 2,000 or sooner. Systems will connect users by radio frequency (frequency modulation), giving them data and voice communications anywhere, anytime.

wireless mike A hand-held electronic amplifying device that has no cords or wires. It is essentially a miniature transmitter that sends radio waves to a receiver, which sends the signal to an amplifier and then to speakers. Allows the speaker to move about freely but is subject to radio frequency (RF) interference from electrical wiring or other electrical devices in or near the room.

wireless technology Devices that enable people to communicate (voice and data) over the electromagnetic spectrum. Includes cellular telephones, pagers, microphones, and package delivery tracking systems.

wish-list See want-list.

withdrawal **1.** In drug culture, deprivation of recreational drugs, resulting in depression, sweating, and delirium tremens. **2.** In mental illness, retreat from society and relationships with others. Typically indicated by aloofness, apathy, lack of interest in socializing, and difficulty in communicating with others.

within group score conversion *See* race-norming.

Wizard Award An award given by the **Professional Convention Management Association** that recognizes innovation in the meeting industry. *Contact:* PCMA, 100 Vestavia Office Park, Ste. 220, Birmingham, AL 35216 (205/823-7262).

Women for Sobriety Established to help women alcoholics achieve sobriety. Addresses the need to overcome depression and guilt. Provides group meetings, conferences, information and referrals, newsletter, and phone support. *Contact:* Women for Sobriety, P.O. Box 618, Quakertown, PA 18951-0618 (800/333-1606; Fax 215/536-8026; E-mail **WFSoBRIETY@aol.com**; URL **http://www.mediapulse.com/WFS/**).

women-owned business enterprise (WBE) A business enterprise or nonprofit organization that is at least fifty-one percent owned by, directed by, or in the case of a publicly owned business, at least fifty-one percent of the stock of which is owned by citizens or permanent resident aliens who are women, and such ownership is real, substantial, and continuing.

Women's Pension Protection Act of 1997 S. 320, introduced by Sen. Carol Moseley-Braun (D-IL) and H.R. 766, introduced by Rep. Barbara Kennelly (D-CT). The bills would improve the security, equity, and accessibility of pension programs for women. Include a provision that would pay survivor benefits to spouses and former spouses of men who died prior to receiving a Civil Service Retirement System deferred annuity. Another bill, S.14, introduced by Sen. Tom Daschle, (D-SD), includes a wider range of proposals that would improve pension access, security, and portability in the private sector as well as pay survivor benefits in Civil Service Retirement System deferred annuities.

womyn Coined by feminists and now listed as an alternative spelling of "women" in the Random House *Webster's College Dictionary*.

wonk A theorist and expert in any line of work who invariably exhibits singular dedication and intensity toward his or her occupation.

"woo woo" factor Tongue-in-cheek description, attributed to Philip Jones, former editor of *Training* magazine, of training activities that are pseudo job-related and highly subjective, where goals are personal and individualistic, and that people accept as being cost effective on "faith" alone.

word processing Systems designed to produce company publications, correspondence, advertising copy, contracts, training and development materials, instruction sheets for dealers and distributors, technical manuals, installation, and assembly, operating, maintenance, and repair instructions quickly, accurately, and relatively inexpensively.

work Jobs, duties, or tasks performed by people, machines, computers, energy, chemical processes, water, air, and so on to meet an objective or produce a product or service, which is measured by the time taken, its cost, and the quality of the output.

workaholic Most commonly describes people who work too hard. In its complementary sense, workaholics are productive workers who put in long hours. It its worst sense, they are people who compulsively rework, rewrite, and redo tasks. Research psychologists have described workaholism as an addiction, a behavioral dysfunction, that causes people to work themselves to death.

work and family programs Work accommodations and benefits programs designed to help equalize benefits, serve as recruiting and retention incentives, and build good will among employees. Examples are adoption assistance program, dependent care assistance plan, employee home ownership plan, family care program, flexible leave, **flexiplace**, home leave, home marketing assistance, home sales protection, **job sharing/job splitting**, maternity and child care, and parental leave.

work-at-home A form of work and family program in which employees are allowed to work at home one or more days each week (although they may maintain a desk or office at the company site) so that they can care for their children or others.

work-based learning Job-related training — training in which the learners get practical, hands-on practice on the job, as well as classroom training; for example, youth apprenticeships. The term was coined by the Office of Work-Based Learning of the U.S. Department of labor. Sometimes called *structured work-based learning*.

work climate survey *See* organization climate survey.

work count chart The last step in the work simplification process. Its objective is to collect information which can be used to balance employee workloads by determining how much work is being done at each work station. The count is made by using the stroke or operation tally method (counting the strokes or operations), recording items using a meter, or recording the numbers of the first and last documents handled if they are numbered serially.

work distribution chart A device used to improve work flow, allocate time to work processes, distribute work evenly, and reduce employee boredom or fatigue. The chart is developed by determining what tasks are being performed in a work area, who by name is doing them, and how much time is spent on each one. The chart is analyzed by a knowledgeable supervisor to improve task assignment and performance.

Worker Adjustment and Retraining Notification Act of 1988 (WARNA) An Act requiring that as of February 4, 1989, workers in companies with 100 or more full-time employees receive a minimum of 60 days' written advance notice in the event of a **massive layoff** (50 or more people) or **plant closing**. The law allows employers to provide less than 60 days' notice when they are seeking new customers, trying to raise capital, or when the closures or layoffs are due to unforeseen conditions or natural disasters.

worker gang A new corporate security problem that consists of workers who band together and conspire to steal from their companies. They use the company's facilities and time to conduct their outside drug, money laundering, and mail fraud businesses.

workers' comp EAP A new form of **employee assistance program** designed to help employers and injured employees address the emotional and psychological aspects of workplace injuries to speed up claims procedures, keep employees satisfied, and avoid lawsuits. It involves one-on-one counseling by trained counselors who act as liaisons between workers who file workers' compensation claims and claims adjustors, determine what, if any, emotional needs exist; and provide treatment and followup.

workers' compensation Statutes passed by all states designed to protect workers from the hazards and consequences of accidents, injuries, illnesses, and death to themselves and their families as a result of their employment. Benefits are paid to workers suffering job related physical, mental, or emotional accidents, injuries, disabilities, or disfigurement or who aggravate preexisting physical or mental conditions at work. In addition to death benefits, they typically include weekly payments, based on earnings and size of family, medical and hospital bills, scheduled loss (amputation, loss of use or loss of a bodily function), payments for scarring, rehabilitation, retraining, settlements, travel expenses, and attorney fees paid to the employee or his or her surviving spouse or children. Businesses must either have adequate funds to pay claims or carry appropriate workers' compensation insurance coverage. The laws also provide some protection to employers against excessive liability.

workers' compensation payments
Benefits paid to workers because of job-related injuries or illnesses. Such payments may be made by federal or state workers' compensation agencies, employers, or insurance companies on behalf of employers.

Workers' Compensation Research Institute (WCRI)   An independent, not-for-profit research organization with a staff of 30 that provides high-quality objective information about public policy issues involving workers' compensation systems. Those who benefit from the Institute's work include public officials, insurers, employers, injured workers, organized labor, and others affected by workers' compensation systems across the United States and around the world. *Contact:* WCRI, 101 Main St., Cambridge, MA 02142 (617/ 494-1240; Fax 617/494-5240).

work ethic   An attribute whose strength is considered by many managers to be more important than intelligence, education, or enthusiasm when hiring employees. It is exemplified by industriousness, commitment to quality, conscientious attendance, practical knowledge, helpfulness to co-workers, high levels of motivation, subordination of self, coolness in crisis, company loyalty, willingness to take responsibility, effectiveness in team situations, and attention to customer/client needs.

work-family audit   A step-by-step procedure for exploring dependent care and related issues within a company. It involves two stages: preplanning, where the company addresses key aspects of the company, the labor force, and the community to determine the need for and feasibility of initiating work-family programs, and the audit itself that involves five steps: (1) identifying work-family options; (2) establishing objectives; (3) developing an implementation plan; (4) specifying outcomes and benefits of each program; and (5) measuring outcomes and costs. Developed by Raymond C. Collins, President of Collins Management Consulting Inc. and Renee Magid, President of Initiatives: The Center for the Advancement of Work and Family Life (reported in"Work and Family Issues," Chapter 15 in Mary F. Cook, Editor, *The AMA Handbook for Employee Recruitment and Retention*, AMACOM, 1992).

work-family benefits   Ancillary benefits that include alcohol and substance abuse counseling, child care, education benefits, elder care, family leave, family/marital problems counseling, flexible work hours, mortgage assistance, part-time work options, psychological/emotional stress counseling, sabbaticals, savings plans for child care, and work at home programs.

work-family programs   *See* child care; elder care; family leave; flexible scheduling; job sharing/job splitting; work-at-home.

workflow automation   **1.** The practice of moving documents, materials, and parts among workgroup members in an organization to improve efficiency and productivity. **2.** In human resources, the practice of moving documents to improve information flow and services between HR and its customers and to create, strengthen, and maintain the links between customers and HR systems. It employs such technologies as résumé tracking, interactive voice response systems, kiosks, and most recently, the Internet. **3.** One of the last steps in reengineering undertaken to achieve optimum efficiency in delivering information, ensuring completion of transactions, tracking the effectiveness of processes, and providing positive returns to the organization. It involves examining specific events, processes, and ways of managing a given activity and then integrating new technologies developed specifically to support and improve workflow.

workflow software   Uses computers to connect human resources systems and payroll, time, attendance, accidents and injuries, and other related functions and records. Designed to reduce redundant data entry and provide immediate access to employee information.

Workforce 2000 Revisited   A sequel to the Hudson Institute's *Workforce 2000*, published in 1987, which became a definitive document on the changing workplace. Considers the impact of globalization, technology, and demographics on workers and businesses and calls for a new educational model to prepare both young and older people for work.

Workforce Development Act of 1995 (WDA) Passed overwhelmingly by the Senate in October 1995, S.143 would shift responsibility for job training programs to the states by creating a single block grant to states totaling $8.1 billion in fiscal 1998 — a 15 percent reduction from current spending levels. Proposed legislation that would repeal virtually all federal job training, adult, and vocational education programs and turning funds over to the states to find ways to train workers and help them find jobs. The Job Training Partnership Act of 1982 and the Perkins Vocational and Applied Technology Education Act Amendments of 1990 and 1991 would be terminated. States would be required to spend 25 percent on work force employment activities, such as job-search programs for out-of-school youths. Another 25 percent would be allocated to state agencies to support work force initiatives in vocational education and school-to-work programs. The remaining 50 percent would be placed in "flex accounts" for governors to spend as they see fit on work force training programs or other programs aimed toward youth.

work force development boards Commissions established by states to steer work programs for "at risk" youth. Members typically represent business and industry.

Workforce: The Magazine for Leaders in Human Resources   A journal published monthly by ACC Communications Inc.: $59 per year. Address, ACC Communications Inc., 245 Fisher Ave., B-2, Costa Mesa, CA 92626 (800/444-6485 or 714/751-1883; Fax 714/751-4106; E-mail **mailroom@workforcemag. com**; URL **http://www.workforceonline. com**).

work force planning   *See* human resources planning.

work hardening   Four- to six-week programs provided for injured workers following physical or occupational therapy to give them the self-confidence and stamina need to resume an active role in the work force. Frequently simulates the work that got employees injured in the first place to get them back on the job.

Work Hours Act of 1962 (WHA) Mandates that wages be computed on the basis of an 8-hour day, 40-hour week, with payment of overtime for all hours in excess of the basic day and week to certain classes of laborers.

work incentives   Special Social Security rules that provide cash benefits and Medicare for disabled workers while they attempt to work.

work incentives rules   Designed to provide support for disabled **Social Security** and **Supplemental Security Income** (SSI) beneficiaries who want employment. Although there are different rules for Social Security and SSI, both programs provide cash benefits and continue **Medicare** or **Medicaid** while the disabled person attempts to work on a regular basis, help with the work expenses resulting from the disability, help with vocational rehabilitation, and training for a new type of work.

Working Families Flexibility Act of 1996 Would amend the **Fair Standards Act of 1938** to allow employers to provide and employees to receive compensatory time off at time and one half in lieu of overtime pay and requires employers to give employees 30 days notice before cashing out employees' compensatory time banks or discontinuing the policy. Also would limit the employees' ability to cash out if the compensatory time bank has accumulated over 80 hours. Employees desiring time off could choose when to take the time, as long as reasonable notice was given and the absence would not disrupt business operations. State and local government employees have enjoyed the option since 1985. Passed by the House, July 30, 1996 by a 225 to 195 vote. The bill is under consideration by the 105th Congress. Also called the *Comp Time Act.*

work injury reports (WIRs)   Used by the Bureau of Statistics, U.S. Department of Labor to identify and describe in WIR surveys the occupational injury and illness situation in the United States. The surveys are based on employee questionnaires, workers' compensation reports, and filed claims and show the number of injured workers in various categories and the percentage who reported that they did not receive safety training for the tasks they were assigned.

work life initiatives Policies and strategies designed to make workers feel part of a supportive, caring organization. Designed to win their support and loyalty and increase product and service quality and productivity. Include such services as emergency dependent, dependent care referral, income tax preparation, legal information, on-site child care, on-site fitness centers, personal or family counseling, subsidized tutoring for children, and summer day camp for children.

work measurement A method of determining the amount of output produced by a specific amount of input during a set period of time. It involves these steps: definition of the basic units of measurement (for example, words per minute); development of data collection instruments and procedures; collection, tabulation, and analysis of work data; definition of work standards; and implementation, followup, and (when necessary) revision of the new standards.

work methods analysis The process of analyzing procedures, operations, and systems, establishing standards of performance, and controlling performance to reduce labor costs. It involves systematic study of each job in an organizational element or process to eliminate unnecessary operations, standardize equipment, tools, procedures, and working conditions, and measure the time required to perform each operation.

Work Opportunity Credit Pre-screening Notice and Certification Request, IRS Form 8850 Required by the IRS to be submitted by the employer (signed by both the employer and the employee) to qualify for the **Work Opportunity Tax Credit.** The form must be submitted to the state employment service agency within three weeks after the employee starts work.

Work Opportunity Tax Credit The Internal Revenue Service allows employers a credit of up to $2,100 for each targeted low-income new hire, generally 35 percent of the first $6,000 in wages. The credit applies to employees who started work after September 30, 1996 and before October 1,

1997. The targeted groups include qualified recipients of Aid to Families with Dependent Children or its successor under welfare reform, veterans, felons, high-risk youth, vocational rehabilitation referrals, summer youth, and food stamp recipients.

work orientation factors Approaches or orientations to work that people prefer and under which they are most motivated to work best — that is, the conditions under which a job is most effectively and efficiently performed. Attributed to Stephen L. Cohen, "The Future and HRD," Chapter 4 in William R. Tracey, *Human Resources Management & Development Handbook,* AMACOM, 1993.

work participation method *See* work performance.

work performance A time-consuming and expensive (yet effective) method of collecting job data, it involves performance of job tasks by the job analyst. Simple operations may be performed without prior instruction; more complex job activities require training and supervision until learned.

workplace basic skills training
See literacy training.

workplace chaplain A member of the clergy (minister, priest, rabbi, or other) employed by an organization and made available to employees on a voluntary basis to provide spiritual guidance and counseling. The objective is to show compassion and concern, improve communication between employees and management, reduce stress, and meet other special needs of employees for assistance.

workplace diversity Having a work force that at all levels is representative of the general population in terms of ethnic, racial, religious, and cultural backgrounds and genders and lifestyles.

workplace information services
An employer-sponsored dependent care option. May include parent seminars and resource referral programs.

workplace know-how Five competencies identified by the Secretary of Labor's **Commission on Achieving Necessary Skills**. In 1991 it reported that children must master the following: (1) resources — allocating time, money, materials, space, and staff; (2) interpersonal skills — working on teams, teaching others, serving customers, leading, negotiating, and working well with people from culturally diverse backgrounds; (3) information — how to acquire and process data, including file management and computer literacy; (4) systems — understanding social, organizational and technological systems, monitoring and correcting performance and designing or improving systems; and (5) technology — selecting equipment and tools, applying technology to specific tasks and maintaining and trouble shooting technologies. In addition, the commission stated that young people also need a foundation that stresses thinking skills: being able to make decisions, solve problems, and reason.

Workplace Safety and Health Program Standard   A standard under development by the Occupational Safety and Health Administration that is scheduled for implementation during fiscal 1997. The standard will require employers to institute comprehensive safety and health programs in the workplace.

workplace search   The practice of conducting probes and surveys to locate contraband, stolen property, or illegal nonprescription drugs.

workplace surveillance   The practice of observing or eavesdropping on workers by human or technical means (such as video cameras and telephone taps and recordings) to prevent or detect criminal activity or violations of company policies and rules.

work practice control   Any one of several job injury countermeasures, such as information, education, training, and supervision.

work process chart   A work simplification technique that documents the flow of a single unit (form, document, equipment part, component of a system) through an operation, series of operations, or series of work stations, and enables analysis of the process and subsequent improvement of efficiency. Symbols are used to create a chart showing stages in the work process: operation, transportation, inspection, and storage or delay.

work-related entitlements   Federal entitlement programs that base eligibility for benefits on a work history, usually in combination with an age requirement, such as Social Security, Medicare, civil service retirement, military retirement, and unemployment compensation.

work rules   Workplace requirements and proscriptions established, communicated, interpreted, and enforced to guide the actions of employees, supervisors, and collective bargaining units, maintain discipline, prevent injuries and accidents, and maintain productivity. They deal with such items as absence and tardiness, rest periods and coffee breaks, safety procedures, and protective equipment and clothing.

work sample test   An assessment test that requires the testee (job candidate) to perform one or more of the tasks of a job. Commonly used to select cashiers, computer operators, secretaries, stenographers, and so on.

work sampling   A method of measuring work that requires a trained analyst. The job is broken down into tasks, random observations are made of individual performing the job or tasks using mathematical formulas to establish the proper sample size, and the preparation of a report describing how job incumbents spent their time and the number of work units produced during a specified period of time. Analysts also report the amount of time used to produce each unit of work output.

works council   Councils established for the information and consultation of employees. Required by the **European Union** of any company in Europe, including American companies, with more than 1,000 employees and more than 150 employees in each of at least two countries, effective September 22, 1996.

work sharing   An alternative to layoffs during recessions or restructuring in which all or part of a company's work force temporarily reduces hours and salary. In some states, employees can collect unemployment insurance to offset part of the wages lost.

workshop   A meeting or conference at which a group of people, under the leadership of an **instructor** or **facilitator**, intensively studies, discusses, and *applies* principles, procedures, and processes.

workshop method   A program designed to involve participants directly in the learning process. It makes use of such methods and techniques as panels, discussion, group interviews, group problem solving, and role playing.

work simplification   A systematic attempt to improve the way work is performed. Its goal is to make work simpler and easier to do. It uses work distribution, work flow, and work process charts to determine exactly how a duty or task is performed; reviews, analyzes, questions, and challenges every step in the work process; develops and tests alternative methods; implements the best and most workable methods; modifies the new method as needed; and repeats the process after an appropriate period of time.

workstation A stand-alone position for one person consisting of a personal computer and associated peripherals or keyboard entry to a computer along with a desk and chair, and storage space (and sometimes a communications interface with other positions or stations).

work stoppage Cessation of work by employees in sympathy with a cause or to express a grievance.

work-study Federal programs that allow students to work and earn money while attending postsecondary education programs.

work team **1.** Employees who work permanently and exclusively as members of a team. **2.** A form of participatory management designed to place management and decision making authority at lower levels in the organization. Teams are trained and then given autonomy in specific areas of work or for carrying out specific functions. Three of the most common types are: (1) problem-solving teams, consisting of five to twelve volunteers who meet weekly to discuss ways of improving the work environment; (2) special teams, consisting of two to twelve members, established to serve a variety of purposes, such as designing and introducing new technology or meeting with customers, clients, and suppliers; and (3) self-managed teams, consisting of five to fifteen workers who learn all production tasks, rotate from job to job, order materials, and schedule work.

work team development Provided for leaders and members of committees, project teams, quality circles, self-directed work teams, and task forces to improve their performance. Focuses on the selection and development of members, how to structure and manage the team, how to resolve conflict, and how to increase collaboration and productivity.

work to the rule A tactic used by members of collective bargaining units to underscore their dissatisfaction with management policies or practices. Instead of going on strike, the workers refuse to engage in any work-related activities that are not specifically identified in the labor contract as their responsibility. For example, unionized teachers are expressing their frustration and anger over low salaries, layoffs, imposed pay cuts, and larger class sizes by refusing to write letters of recommendation for student applicants for college admission and scholarships, after-school tutoring, evening parent interviews, and club sponsorship.

World Federation of the Deaf (WFD) Advocates for the rights of deaf people around the world. Promotes the exchange of research findings, ideas, and reports about deafness. Encourages national federations of deaf people to establish aid programs for deaf people in developing countries. *Contact:* WFD, International Disability Centre, 13D, Chemin Du Levant, F. 01210 Ferney-Voltaire, France.

World Institute on Disability (WID) A public policy center that uses research, public education, training, and model program development to create a more accessible and supportive society. *Contact:* WID, 510 16th St., Oakland, CA 94612 (510/763-4100; Fax 510/763-4109; E-mail **wid@wid.org**).

World Resources Institute (WRI) An independent center for policy research and technical assistance on global environmental and development issues. Dedicated to helping governments and private organizations of all types cope with environmental, resource, and development challenges of global significance. Through policy research and technical assistance, WRI helps address the question: How can societies meet human needs and nurture economic growth without destroying the natural resources and environmental integrity that make prosperity possible? *Contact:* WRI, 1709 New York Ave., N.W., Washington, DC 20006 (202/638-6300; Fax 202/638-0036; E-mail: **philip@wri.org**; URL **http://www.wri.org/wri/**).

Worldspan In travel management, a **computer reservation system** jointly owned by Abacus, Delta, Northwest, and TWA. Also offers phone consultation, technical specifications, compatibility certification, and marketing.

World Trade Organization (WTO) Created by the **General Agreement on Tariffs and Trade** on December 15, 1993, the WTO, if approved by the legislatures of the countries involved, will be a permanent institution that will enforce trade rules covering more than 10,000 products and nearly all business services in 117 nations. The decisions of the WTO will be binding unless unanimously reversed by it members.

World Wide Web (WWW) A spider-web-like network of **Internet** information sources, and the glitzy part of the **Internet** with pictures, sound, and text. It involves a **hypermedia** information storage system that employs software and a **graphical user interface** to assist the user in browsing or navigating through the **Internet** simply by pointing and clicking.

world/world class standards In education, standards that are based on the content presented to and expectations held for students in countries that have demonstrated superior academic performance on international assessments.

worm A malicious computer program designed to propagate itself as the user unknowingly performs routine functions, such as copying files. It can continue to propagate across a computer network or over a modem.

wrap *See* wrap-fee program.

wraparound plan **1.** A deferred compensation plan designed to augment existing 401(k) investments to enable highly compensated employees to save for their retirement. **2.** Insurance or health care plan coverage, often used for Medicare, for copayments and deductibles that are not covered under a member's basic plan.

wrap-fee program A program that allows an investor to define and cap the expense of investment advice and brokerage execution costs by paying a fee (usually a percentage of the dollars invested) for such services. Originally consisting of a simple flat fee in lieu of a commission, or a fee covering both money management services and brokerage execution fees, wrap-fee programs now offer such services as evaluation of investment objectives, assistance in allocating assets among various types of investments,

custodial services, securities transactions, and portfolio management.

write once, read many (WORM) Compact disks that are erasable and can be rewritten only once but read many times.

write protection A method of protecting a disk so that its information cannot be altered. Users can read the contents of a protected disk, but they cannot add or delete any information unless the disk is "unlocked."

writing training Training provided employees at any level to improve their writing ability through content, exercises, and activities designed to develop skills for creating specific pieces of writing, such as correspondence, decision papers, reports, job descriptions, policy statements, proposals, and performance evaluations.

written reprimand A short memo or letter addressed to the employee that clearly and succinctly describes the offense or unacceptable behavior, underscoring the fact that the incident represents repeat behavior. It reminds the employee of previous discussions about the behavior and states that additional incidents will result in more stringent action. Usually a copy of the memo or letter is placed in the individual's personnel file.

wrongful discharge Unfair or unjust termination. A corollary to the legal doctrine of "employment at will." In a decision by the Supreme Court in June 1988, employees covered by a collective bargaining agreement who have bargained for grievance and arbitration of discharges that violate their contracts have the additional remedy of going to court to sue for compensatory and punitive damages. There are three basic grounds for such a suit: breach of contract, violation of public policy, and breach of an implied covenant of good faith and fair dealing.

wuppies Wired upwardly mobile professionals. Aficionados of electronic devices, microchips and cybergadgets, and the World Wide Web.

X

x-axis The abscissa on a two-dimensional Cartesian coordinate system (a graph) for locating points in a plane; the horizontal line which intersects the origin and the ordinate (the vertical line which intersects the abscissa and the origin). It is one of the elements of reference by which a point, as on a curve, is referred to a system of fixed rectilinear co-ordinate axes.

Xers A label for a generation, a demographic generalization applied to the generation following the **baby boomers**, the twenty-something generation brought up on video and accustomed to technology, that came of age in the late 1980s and early 1990s. Said to be pragmatic, highly competitive, self- and fulfillment-oriented. Attributed to Douglas Copeland in the novel *Generation X: Tales for an Accelerated Society.*

Y

YIU   Yes, I understand (Internet speak).

YR   Your (Internet abbreviation).

YSA   Youth Service America.

yahoo!   On the **Internet,** a **search engine** that enables the user to type in a key word to find **homepages** of sites that include the same word. (URL **http://www.yahoo.com**)

y-axis   The ordinate on a two-dimensional Cartesian coordinate system (a graph) for locating points in a plane; the vertical line which intersects the origin and the abscissa (the horizontal line which intersects the ordinate and the origin). It is one of the elements of reference by which a point, as on a curve, is referred to a system of fixed rectilinear co-ordinate axes.

yellow-dog contract   An agreement not to joint a union forced on employees before they were hired by employers. The practice was prevalent in the early days of unions (prior to the 1930s), but it is now illegal. *See also* Labor-Management Relations Act of 1935.

yield management   A marketing and sales technique, often computerized, that combines human behavior forecasting using historical data and just-in-time product pricing (moving the product out of inventory at just the right moment). The yield manager makes sales projections while changing the pricing. Used by airlines to continually adjust the number of seats to be sold at a given fare and hotels to quote prices for blocks of rooms two years in advance.

yiffies   Translates to "young, individualistic, freedom-minded and few" persons. Applies to persons under 26, who decide for themselves where they're going, are not totally dedicated to their jobs, and are in the post 1964 generation of people more interested in job satisfaction, a laid-back life style, and having fun than they are in money.

yoga   An alternative treatment involving mental and physical exercises designed to develop mental, physical, and spiritual health by withdrawing the senses from all external objects.

Youth Service America (YSA)   An alliance of of 171 National Service Affiliates committed to community and national service. YSA's mission is to build healthy towns and cities, and foster citizenship, knowledge, and personal development through a powerful network of service opportunities for young Americans. Provides technical assistance, materials, policy development and national newsletter. *Contact:* YSA, 1101 15th St., N.W., Suite 200, Washington, DC 20004 (202/296-2992; URL **http://www. servenet.org/ysanet2/index.html**).

yuppie flu   *See* chronic fatigue syndrome.

yuppies   Young, upwardly mobile urban professionals.

Z

ZBB   Zero-base budgeting.

zero-base budgeting (ZBB)   A budgeting system in which management carefully examines the basis for allocating resources during the period when budgets are being formulated and programs and services are being planned. Rather than using the previous year's funding levels as a base, ZBB uses zero funding as the starting point. So, prior funding levels are essentially ignored, and all activities and programs compete on an equal footing for funding.

zero-based staffing   A staffing strategy commonly used after extensive downsizing and restructuring. Involves eliminating, reevaluating, and redesigning positions within the organization structure and requiring employees to reapply for configured positions.

zero defects   A program designed to achieve the objective of "zero defects" in products and services delivered to customers and clients.

zero-sum game   Competition between two individuals or groups where only one of the contestants is the winner — and the victor wins at the expense of the loser. For example, labor-management contract negotiations, marketing, and so on.

zine   A Web journal — no paper, no printing, no postage, no delay, and no waiting. For example, *Word* (**http://www.word.com/index.html**), *Salon* (**http://www.salon1999.com/**), *Slate* (**http://www.slate.com**), and *Feed* (**http://www.feedmag.com**).

Z-list   Four tables of hazardous substances identified in the OSHA Hazard Communication Standard. The list is available from the Superintendent of Documents, U.S. government Printing Office, Washington, DC 20402-9325.

Zoe Baird problem   Failure to pay Social Security taxes (7.65 percent paid by the employer and a matching amount withheld from the wages) on a domestic employee's wages every three months when those wages exceed $50 per quarter. Baird is the corporate lawyer whose nomination for the position of Attorney General in the Clinton cabinet was withdrawn after disclosure that she had failed to pay Social Security taxes for her maid and chauffeur who were illegal aliens.

zone fare   A marketing initiative; a method of fare calculation used to simplify fare structures and budgeting for the customer — and a good buy for companies with 100 or more persons traveling to a meeting when their departure points are scattered geographically. Rates are quoted based on geographic zones within a region (usually 4 to 5 zones).

Z-score   *See* standard score; T-score.

Part II

INDEX OF KEY TERMS

Note to the Reader: This section contains sample lists of key items arranged by HR area. They are included to assist the user in recalling or locating terms in a given area of interest. The list does *not* contain *all* of the terms included in the Glossary. The HR areas and the pages in this part on which they begin follow.

1 Associations

ABLEDATA
AboutFace
Accent on Information
ACME World Association of Management
 Consulting Firms
ADARA
Al-Anon
Alateen
Alcoholics Anonymous
Alexander Graham Bell Association for the
 Deaf
The American Academy of Psychoanalysis
American Action Fund for Blind Children and
 Adults
American Arbitration Association
American Association for Adult and
 Continuing Education
American Association for Higher Education
American Association of Occupational Health
 Nurses
American Association of the Deaf-Blind
American Association on Mental Retardation
American Bar Association
American Cancer Society
American Chiropractic Association
American Cleft Palate-Craniofacial Association
American Compensation Association
American Council of the Blind
American Council on Education
The American Council on International
 Personnel
American Counseling Association
American Deafness and Rehabilitation
 Association
American Dental Association
American Diabetes Association
American Educational Research Association
American Federation of Government
 Employees
American Federation of Labor-Congress of
 Industrial Organizations
American Federation of State, County and
 Municipal Employees, AFL-CIO
American Federation of Teachers
American Foundation for the Blind
American Heart Association
American Hotel & Motel Association
American Hospital Association
American Institute of Certified Public
 Accountants
American Management Association
American Marketing Association

American Medical Association
American National Standards Institute
American Nurses Association
American Nurses Credentialing Center
American Physical Therapy Association
American Printing House for the Blind, Inc.
American Productivity & Quality Center
American Psychological Association
American Self-Help Clearinghouse
American Society for Expert Modeling
American Society for Healthcare Human
 Resources Administration
American Society for Industrial Security
American Society for Quality
American Society for Training and
 Development
American Society of Association Executives
American Society of Composers, Authors &
 Publishers
American Society of Pension Actuaries
American Society of Travel Agents
American Speech-Language-Hearing
 Association
American Technical Education Association
American Vocational Association, Inc.
Arthritis Foundation
The Association for Behavior Analysis
Association for Community Based Education
Association for Continuing Higher Education
Association for Educational Communications
 and Technology
Association for Experiential Education
Association for Investment, Management,
 and Research
Association for Multi-Media International, Inc.
Association for Quality and Participation
Association for the Management of
 Organization Design
Association for Worksite Health Promotion
Association of Conference Executives
Association of Corporate Travel Executives
Association of Destination Management
 Executives
Association of Executive Search Consultants
The Association of Human Resource Systems
 Professionals, Inc.
Association of Information Technology
 Professionals
Association of Management Consulting Firms
The Association of Outplacement Consulting
 Firms International
Better Hearing Institute
Burns United Support Groups, Inc.
The Calix Society

Canadian Compensation Association
Canadian Labour Market and Productivity
  Centre
Carnegie Corporation of New York
Catalyst
Center for Assistive Technology
Center for Corporate Health, Inc.
Center for Creative Leadership
Certified Financial Planner Board of Standards
Child Care Action Campaign
Cleft Palate Foundation
The College Board
College and University Personnel Association
Commission on Recognition of Post-
  secondary Accreditation
Communications Media Management
  Association
Computer Education Management
  Association
Computer Education Management
  Association
The Conference Board
Convention Liaison Council
Council for Adult and Experiential Learning
Council of Citizens with Low Vision
  International
The Council on Hotel, Restaurant and
  Institutional Education
Cystic Fibrosis Foundation
Direct Link for the Disabled
Direct Marketing Association, Inc.
Distance Education and Training Council
DRAGnet: Disability Resources Activities and
  Groups Network
The Ear Foundation
Eastern Paralyzed Veterans Association
Educational Assistance Ltd.
Educational Testing Service
Emotional Health Anonymous
Emotions Anonymous
Employee Assistance Professionals
  Association
Employee Benefits Infosource
Employee Relocation Council
Employment Management Association
Environmental Industry Associations
Epilepsy Foundation of America
The ESOP Association
Ethics Resource Center
European Organization for Quality
FedWorld Information Network
Group Health Association of America
Healthcare Convention & Exhibitors
  Association

Hear Now
The Helen Keller National Center
Human Resource Planning Society
Information Access Project for Blind
  Individuals
Information Technology Training Association,
  Inc.
Information Technology Training Association,
  Inc.
Institute for Chartered Financial Analysts
Institute of Certified Financial Planners
Institute of Certified Travel Agents
Institute of Industrial Engineers
Institute of Management Consultants
Insurance Conference Planners
  Association
Interactive Multimedia Association
International Association for Continuing
  Education & Training
International Association for Exposition
  Management
International Association for Financial
  Planning
International Association for Human Resource
  Information Management
International Association of Audio Visual
  Communicators
International Association of Business
  Communicators
International Association of Career
  Management Professionals
International Association of Conference
  Centers
International Association of Convention &
  Visitors Bureaus
International Association of Eating Disorders
  Professionals
International Association of Fairs &
  Expositions
International Association of Presentation
  Professionals
International Communications Industries
  Association
International Congress & Convention
  Association
International Customer Service Association
International Federation of Accountants
International Federation of Hard of Hearing
  People
International Federation of Training and
  Development Organisations
International Foundation for Stutterers, Inc.
International Foundation of Employee Benefits
  Plans

International Gay & Lesbian Travel
 Association
International Interactive Communications
 Society
International Personnel Management
 Association
International Society of Gay and Lesbian
 Meeting Professionals
International Society for Performance
 Improvement
International Society for Technology in
 Education
International Society of Certified Employee
 Benefit Specialists
International Society of Gay & Lesbian
 Meeting Professionals
International Society of Meeting Planners
International Standards Organization
International Teleconferencing Association
International Television Association
International Travel Briefing Service
International Visual Literacy Association
Job Accommodation Network
Job Opportunities for the Blind
Joint Commission on Accreditation of
 Healthcare Organizations
Laubach Literacy
The Learning Resources Network
Let's Face It
Life Office Management Association
Literacy Volunteers of America
Management Centre Europe
Meeting Professionals International
Multiple Sclerosis Association of America
National Academy of Arbitrators
National Academy of Human Resources
National Alliance for Business
National Alliance for Restructuring Education
National Alliance for the Mentally Ill
National Amputation Foundation
National Association for Alternative Staffing
National Association for Female Executives
National Association for Industry Education
 Cooperation
National Association for the Education of
 Young Children
National Association for the Self-Employed
National Association for Visually Handicapped
National Association of Black Women
 Entrepreneurs
National Association of Child Care Resource
 and Referral Agencies
National Association of Colleges and
 Employers

National Association of Desktop Publishers
National Association of Personal Financial
 Advisors
National Association of Personnel Services
National Association of Professional Employer
 Organizations
National Association of Retired Federal
 Employees
National Association of State Boards of
 Education
National Association of Temporary and
 Staffing Services
National Association of the Deaf
National Association of Women Business
 Owners
National Board for Professional Teaching
 Standards
National Business Education Association
National Business Travel Association
National Cancer Institute
National Catholic Office for Persons with
 Disabilities
National Center for Youth with
 Disabilities
National Clearing House for Alcohol and Drug
 Information
National Clearinghouse for ESL Literacy
 Education
The National Coalition for Literacy
National Coalition of Black Meeting Planners
National Committee for Quality Assurance
National Council on Disability
National Cued Speech Association
National Down Syndrome Society
National Easter Seal Society
National Education Association
The National Employee Services and
 Recreation Association
National Federation of the Blind
National Foreign Trade Council
National Foundation for the Improvement of
 Education
National Helpers Network
National Information Center for Children and
 Youth with Disabilities
National Information Center on Deafness
National Institute for Literacy
The National Institute of Standards and
 Technology
The National Institute on Deafness and Other
 Communications Disorders Clearinghouse
The National Management Association
National Multiple Sclerosis Society
National Neurofibromatosis Foundation, Inc.

National Organization for Competency Assurance
National Organization on Disability
National Rehabilitation Association
National Resource Library on Youth with Disabilities
National Safety Council
National School Boards Association
National Society for Experiential Education
National Society of Public Accountants
National Speakers Association
National Spinal Cord Injury Association
National Telecommuting Institute, Inc.
National Wellness Association
Office of Special Education and Rehabilitative Services
Office of Special Education Programs
Ontario Society for Training and Development
Organization Development Institute
Organization Development Network
Orton Dyslexia Society
Pacer Center
Paralyzed Veterans of America
Personnel Management Association of Aztlan
Phi Delta Kappa
The Phoenix Society for Burn Survivors, Inc.
Professional Convention Management Association
Professional Organizational Development Network in Higher Education
Professional Secretaries International
Professionals in Human Resources Association
Professional Society for Sales & Marketing Training
Project LINK
Rehabilitation Services Administration
Retinitis Pigmentosa International
Self Help for Hard of Hearing People
Self-Insurance Institute of America
Service Corps of Retired Executives
Sexuality Information & Education Council of the United States
Society for Applied Learning Technology
Society for Human Resource Management
Society for Intercultural Education, Training, and Research (International)
Society for Muscular Dystrophy Information, International
Society for Nonprofit Organizations
Society for Technical Communication
Society of Corporate Meeting Professionals
Society of Government Meeting Professionals
Society of Human Resource Professionals
Society of Incentive and Travel Executives

Society of Manufacturing Engineers
Society of Motion Picture and Television Engineers
Society of Professional Benefit Administrators
Society of Travel Agents in Government
Special Libraries Association
Stuttering Foundation of America
Toastmasters International
Trade Show Exhibitors Association
Training Media Association
Travel Industry Association of America
United Cerebral Palsy Associations
United States Distance Learning Association
University Continuing Education Association
U.S. Travel Data Center
Utilization Review Accreditation Commission
Video Electronics Standards Association
Vision World Wide, Inc.
Visiting Nurse Association
Wellness Councils of America
Women for Sobriety
World Federation of the Deaf
Youth Service America

2   Benefits

accidental death and dismemberment
accrued benefit
accumulated benefit obligations
actuarial reduction
adjusted funding ratio
alternative work options
adult day care
age-based defined contribution plan
age out
Aid to Families with Dependent Children
ancillary benefits
annual leave
annuity
authorization to participate
average final compensation
backdoor rationing
Benny Awards
bonanza babies
buy-back plan
cafeteria plans
call letter
capital accumulation plan
career centers
cash balance pension plan
cash deferred (401 [k]) plan
Certified Benefits Professional

network model HMO
noncontributory benefit plan
nonqualified pension plan
notch babies
nutrition programs
outsourcing
outplacement
paid leave bank
paid time off
parental leave
parking benefits
pension equity plan
pension plan
pension plan retiree medical account
performance share plan
permanent equity pension plan
personal days
personal growth leave
point-of-service plan
pooling
portability
portable pension
preferred provider organization
prepaid legal plan
primary insurance amount
prospective payment system
protection benefits
psychology of entitlement
public disability pension offset
qualified parking
qualified plan
rabbi trust
rationed care
reimbursement account
Reserve Mobilization Insurance
reservists' benefits
retirement benefits
rider
rolling year
Rule of 45
Rule of 75
sabbatical leave
savings and thrift plan
savings incentive match plan for employees
school holiday care
school matching
secret benefit
Section 162(k)
self-managed account
sick leave
SIIMPLE Individual Retirement Accounts
social-or economic-based entitlements
Social Security disability benefits
Social Security family benefits

Social Security retirement benefits
Social Security spousal benefits
Social Security survivors benefits
social service leave
specialty benefits
spousal career assistance
State Unemployment Insurance
statutory benefits
substitution of pension or ESOP benefits
summary annual report
summary plan description
supplementary benefits
Supplementary Security Income
survivors benefits
tax extender
third party liability/subrogation
thrift savings plan
tiered benefits plan
top-hat account
top-heavy plans
total compensation management
trial work period
triple option point-of-service health care
    plan
tuition aid program
uniform coverage rule
universal coverage
unlimited access
use it or lose it rule
variable annuity
vesting or vested
vesting schedules
viatical settlement
voluntary employees' beneficiary
    association
voluntary leave
V-time programs
welfare plan
Windfall Elimination Provision
windfall reduction
work and family programs
work/family benefits
workers' comp EAP`
work incentives
workplace chaplain
work-related entitlements
work sharing

3   Budgeting

capital expense budget
cash budget
comprehensive budgeting

continuous budgeting
cost-to-complete information
direct labor budget
expense budget
financial budget
fixed budget
flexible budgeting
incremental budgeting
inventory budget
lump-sum allowance plan
manufacturing overhead expense budget
mini-max budgeting
operating budget
performance budgeting
periodic budgeting
planning, programming, budgeting system
procurement budget
production budget
profit budget
program budgeting
project budgeting
revenue budget
sales budget
zero-base budgeting

4 Child Care and Elder Care

accessory apartment
adult day care center
Area Agencies on Aging
board and care home
continuing care retirement community
early childhood education
elderly cottage housing opportunity
family support programs
foster care
friendly visitors
gerontologist
granny dumping
Gray Panthers
home adaptation
home health care
home maintenance and repair
 programs
homemaker services
home sharing
licensed group home
life skills
meals-on-wheels
MegaSkills
nannie
Parents: Homework Helpers Not
 Hinderers
parent training

personal care attendant
prenatal care
preventive care
resource mother
senior center
telephone reassurance or support
work and family programs

5 Communication

alts
dead tree edition
decision briefing
facsimile
global system for mobile communication
grapevine
groupware
house organs
informal organization
information briefing
Information Superhighway
Integrated Services Digital Network
internet
interpersonal communication
interpreter
interview
keypad system
kinesics
kiosk
National Information Infrastructure
networking
nibbling
nonverbal communication or behavior
organizational distance
paralinguistic behavior
personal communications services
protocol(s)
rap session
service provider
surfing
teleradiology
translator
universal resource locator
voice mail
voice response system
web site
whiteboard

6 Compensation

ability to pay
area differential
area wage survey

reverse contingency fee
rug ranking
salary continuation plan
salary grade
salary range
sandbagging
sandman pay
scattergram
Section 911, Internal Revenue Code
sequester/sequestration
severance pay
severance trust executive plans
short-time compensation
skill-based pay
source tax
stock appreciation rights
stock equivalent plan
stock option plan
supplemental pay benefits
survivor benefit plan
tax home
team-based pay
tin parachute
total compensation management
training wage
two-tier pay structure
unemployment compensation
variable pay
wage and salary survey
wage curve
wage gap
wage structure
wages and hours laws
workers' compensation
Workers' Compensation Research
  Institute
Zoe Baird problem

7   Computer-Related Terms

access control list
acquisitions softward
ad hoc query
advance booking
advance editing
agents
alternative computer input device
America Online
American Standard Code for Information
  Interchange
analog
antivirus programs
applets

applicant tracking system
application
application programming interface
application software
architecture
artificial intelligence
audit
authoring system
Azusa
backbone
back up
bandwidth
barcode
batch
batch processing
baud
bit
bookmark
Boolean search
boot up
bridge
browser
bug
bulletin board service
bulletin board system
bundled software
byte
CD-recordable
CD-rewritable
centralized network
central processing unit
chip
click stream
client/server architecture
coaxial cable
command
command-driven interface
common business-oriented language
common gateway interface
common user access
common user interface
communications server
Compact Disk-Read Only Memory
compatibility
CompuServe
computer
computer-aided instruction
computer-aided software engineering
computer-assisted instruction
computer-assisted design
computer-assisted engineering
computer-assisted manufacturing
computer-assisted retrieval
computer-based coaching

fuzzy search
gate array
gateway
gigabyte
Gopher
graphical user interface
graphic design
Graphic Interchange Format
groupware
hack
hacker
hard disk
hard drive
hardware
homegrown
homepage
host
hypermedia
hypertext
hypertext system
icon
idea bank
idea processor
imaging software
implementation
import
index
informational database
information dominance
information refinery
information utilities
InfoSeek
infotainment
installation
integrated human resource management
    system
integrated human resources' payroll
    system
integrated services digital network
integrated software
intelligent workstation
interactive communications
interactive system
interface
Internet
Internet relay chat
Internet service provider
interprocess communications
intranet
invitational
Java
Jerusalem
jitterati
job codes

Joint Photographic Experts Group
Joshi
Kaleida
Kerberos
keyword search
killer app
kilobyte
laptop
laser printer
learningware
link
local area network
lurk/lurking
Lycos
machine learning
macro
magnetic disk
mainframe
maintenance
maintenance fee
manual system
mathematical model
megabyte
memory management-driven
menu interface
Michelangelo
microcomputer
microdisk
microprocessor
Microsoft Disk Operating System
Microsoft® Windows™
mid-range computer
migration
millions of instructions per second
minicomputer
modem
module
monitor
morphing
Mosaic
mouse
multidisk
multimedia
multimedia personal computer
multiple level password
multipurpose Internet mail extensions
multisided icon
multi-tasking
multi-user
multiuser dungeon
natural language processing
natural language report writer
navigation
needs assessment

netiquette
Netscape
network
network file system
neurocomputer
newbie
newspuller
news pusher
node
No-Int(Stoned 3)
notebook computer
Nyetscape
object-oriented programming system
objects
on-demand learning system
on-line
on-line reference
on-line transaction processing
open software technology
operating system
Operating System/2
optical character recognition
optical disc drive
optical mark reader
optoelectronic integrated circuit
optoelectronic technology
Pakistani brain
palmtop
parallel computer
PC-based enhancement
peripherals
personal digital assistant
phrase search
pick list
platform
point-to-point protocol
portable computer
post/posting
primary memory
production report
programmable read-only memory
protocol
prototyping
proximity search
public domain software
pull technology
push technology
query-by-example search
QuickTime
random access memory
read only memory
reduced instruction set computing
relational database
response time

résumé scanning system
robotics
rogue executables
router
scanner
screen linking
scuzzi
search
search key
secondary memory
semiconductor chips
sentry strategy
serial line Internet protocol
server
shareware
simulator
slow screw
smart computer
snail mail
sneaker net
social engineering
SOCKS
software
sound card
spam/spamming
spider
spreadsheet
stand-alone software
standards
standards of application architecture
standard report
Stoned
stop words
structured query language
subnotebook
supercomputer
support
surf/surfing
system life cycle
system operator
systems, applications, and products
systems applications software
system software
table
technography
technology integration
Telnet
teraflops computer
terminal
terminal emulation
testing
thesaurus
time recorder system
time sharing

Token Ring
TouchWindow®
transmission control protocol/Internet
  protocol
transportable computer
Trojan horse
turnaround document

Ultimedia
unbundle
universal resource locator
Unix
upgrade
upload
user friendly
utilities
VDT disease
Veronica
video graphics array
virtual classroom
virtual reality
virtual reality modeling language
virus
voice activated
voice response system
waiter-actor-Webmaster
wallpaper
watchdog utilities
Web client
WebCrawler
Webmaster
Web searches
Web server
Web site
webzine
what-if?
what you see is what you get
wide area information servers
wide-area network
windows
workstation
World Wide Web
write once, read many
write protection

8   Cost Management

activity value analysis
actual cost projections
applied billing entry
applied rate
black box approaches
capping
captives
card system

carve-outs
centers of excellence
check-out trip
collaborative relationship
compbusters
composite review and analysis
comp self-insurance
computer reservation system
Corporate Travel Index
cost analysis
cost-benefit analysis
cost centers
cost containment strategies
cost-control strategies
cost of quality
cost per applied person-day
cost-sharing
cost shifting
debit card
dependent coverage waiver
detection costs
development costs
direct costs
direct labor
direct salary costs
drug program
employer coalition
failure costs
fifty-fifty dental plan
flexible staffing
flex plans
full costs
general and administrative expenses
genetic testing
group outplacement
health care cost reduction strategies
Health Plan Employer Data and Information
  Set
human resource accounting
indirect costs
indirect labor
industrial rehabilitation
insurance
job-cost system
life-cycle cost analysis
maintenance of benefits
medical self-care
Medicare carve out
multinational pooling
opportunity costs
overhead costs
out-of-pocket direct costs
Pareto analysis
personnel controls
personnel costs

physician profiling
preferred provider organization
prevention costs
product liability insurance
quality of care measurement
queuing theory/techniques
risk retention group
self-insurance group
therapeutic drug utilization review
tiered premium system
trade down
unapplied billing entry
unity analysis
utilization management

9 Creativity and Innovation

affinity diagram
attribute listing
block busting
brainstorming
brainwriting
creative imagery
creative problem solving
creative problem-solving training
creative thinking
daydreaming
electronic brainstorming
forced relationships
force-field analysis
guided imaging/imagery
huddle group
hurricane writing
idea bank
idea processor
ideation
imagineering
imaging
imaging software
incubation
lateral thinking
mind-mapping
morphological analysis
prioritization matrix
reproductive imagery

10 Desktop Publishing

8-bit color
24-bit color
Adobe Type Manager
bitmap font
bit-mapped graphic

blanket
bleed
blues
body type
bold/bold face
calibration
camera-ready
characterization
charge-coupled device
choke
clip art
CMYK
color correction
color cycling
color electronic prepress
color gamut
color graphics adapter
color management system
color mapping
color scanner
color separation
color space
cyan
desktop color separation
digital photography
direct imaging
disk array
downloadable font
draw software
dummy
font
four-color process
galley proof
gothic
halftone
headline
hickey
image database
image setter
imposition process
impression
International Standard Book Number
International Standard Serial Number
italic
justified
kern
kern/kerning
leader
letterspacing
Library of Congress Book Number
ligature
magenta
mask
mechanical
offset

11   Disability

speech-language pathologist
speech problems
speech synthesizer
spinal cord injury
spondyloarthropathies
stuttering
subjective disability
super crip
supported employment
Technology-Related Assistance for Individuals
    with Disabilities Act of 1988
telecommunications for the
    deaf/teletypewriter
telecommunications relay services
text telephone
TouchWindow®
trainable
transition services
translator
undue burden or hardship
Uniform Federal Accessibility Standard
Usher's syndrome
Vocational Rehabilitation On-the-Job Training
    Program
voice carry over
voice/teletypewriter
work incentive rules

12   Education

academic year
accreditation
alternative assessment
America 2000
American College Test
Army College Fund
Army Reserve Tuition Assistance
    Program
at-risk student
Be All You Can Be Program
B-school
Byrd Scholarship Program
Campus-Based Programs
charter school
Christa McAuliffe Teacher Program
clock hour
combined approach
compensatory education
competency-based vocational-technical
    education
computer-based education
concepts-based, integrated curriculum
Concurrent Admissions Program
Consolidated Loan

content standards
continuing education
continuing education units
continuing professional education
cooperative education
cooperative learning
correspondence study
cost of attendance
credit hour
curriculum development
curriculum integration
Direct Consolidation Loan
distance training or education
diversity programs
early childhood education
Edison Project
educational management organization
educational technology
edutainment
Elementary and Secondary Education Act of
    1965
eligible program
Expeditionary Learning
employee education, training, and assistance
    laws
expected family contribution
externship/clinical instruction
Federal Direct Loans
Federal Family Education Loan
Federal Student Financial Aid Programs
Federal Pell Grant
Federal Perkins Loan
Federal Supplemental Educational
    Opportunity Grant
Federal Work-Study
financial aid administrator
financial aid package
General Education Development
Goals 2000: Educate America Act of
    1993
grade point average
grant
guarantee agency
Guaranteed Access to Education Stafford
    Loans
Guaranteed Student Loan Program
half time
Hawkins-Stafford School Improvement
    Amendments of 1988
Higher Education Reauthorization Act
    of 1992
home schooling
Individuals with Disabilities Education Act
    Amendments of 1991
industrial education

13   Employee Development

scientist and engineer development
self-audit
self-development
self-knowledge
seminar method
special assignment
time management training
understudy assignment
uptraining
workshop method

14 Employee Discipline

adverse action
appropriate penalty
compelled self-defamation
conditions of employment
demotion
discharge
disciplinary layoff
dock
downgrading
due process
employment-at-will
equal treatment
fair employment practices laws
fair investigation
good cause
formal sanctions
imposed discipline
informal sanctions
just cause
layoff
notice
oral reprimand
pink slip
positive discipline
probation
progressive discipline
punishment
reasonable rule or order
release agreement
self-discipline
warning
willful misconduct
written reprimand
wrongful discharge

15 Employee Participation

committee
cross-functional team

Electromation Decision
employee driven idea system
employee involvement
industrial democracy
labor-management relations laws
participatory management system
quality circles
quality of worklife
participative management process
Scanlon Plan
sham union
suggestion systems
total employee involvement

16 Employee Services

behavioral risk management
career audit
career counseling
career development
career planning
client-centered counseling
clinical psychological interview
coaching
developmental counseling
directive counseling
disabled and handicapped laws
eclectic counseling
employee assistance program
employee educational assistance
employee home ownership plan
environmental safety laws
group outplacement
implacement
in-company counseling
inplacement counseling
job performance counseling
just-in-time mentoring
medical services
mental health services
motivational counseling
networking
nondirective counseling
occupational health services
occupational safety laws
Operation Transition
outplacement
outplacement counseling
personal adjustment counseling
preretirement counseling
preventive care
private geriatric care management
psychiatric interview

17 Equal Employment Opportunity

18 Ethics

conflict of interest
consequentialism
deontology
ethical behavior
ethical dilemma
ethics laws
Ethics Reform Act of 1989
Ethics Reform Act of 1991
ethics training
fair employment practices laws
hedonism
human nature ethics
industrial espionage
metaethics
normative ethics
pragmatism
privacy laws
situationalism

19   Finance and Accounting

acid test
activity ratio
actuarially sound
affordability index
allotment system
allowable costs
amortization of training expenses
angel
assets
audit
auditing
balance sheet
bean counter
book value
break-even analysis
call and put options
capital gain
cash flow
cash flow return on investment
Certified Financial Analyst
Certified Financial Planner
Chapter 7, Federal Bankruptcy Code
Chapter 11, Federal Bankruptcy Code
Chapter 13, Federal Bankruptcy Code
"Chapter 20," Federal Bankruptcy Code
chargeback
charitable trust
commercial paper
conflict of interest
contribution analysis
controller/comptroller
convertible security

corporate cop
currency futures
current assets
current debt
debt avoidance
deleverage/deleveraging
direct public offering
divestiture
dividend
dynamic scoring
earnings before interest and taxes
Economic Cost Index
economic value added
encumbrance accounting
equity
European Exchange Rate Mechanism
expenditure control rules
external audit
factor income
Fannie Mae
FASB Rule No. 106
Federal National Mortgage Association
Financial Accounting Standards Board
Financial Accounting Standards Board Rules
financial advisor
financial assessment
financial planning
financial ratio analysis
financial reinsurance
financial reporting
financial risk
financial statement
financial strength
fixed assets
fixed costs
flexible spending account
funded debt
future payment index
generally accepted accounting principles
Ginnie Mae
government contract laws
Government National Mortgage Association
grantor retained annuity trust
green loan
green mail
gross domestic product
gross national product
gross profit
home equity conversion
home equity loan
human resources accounting
income statement
income statement method
index of leading economic indicators

initial public offering
insider
insurance
internal audit
Internal Revenue Code
Internet direct public offering
investment techniques
leverage ratio
leverage through borrowing
liabilities
life insurance trust
liquidation
liquidity ratio
marginal analysis
net book value
net profit
net sales
nexus
net working capital
nontraditional risk financing management
Overseas Private Investment Corporation
par guaranteed investment contract
payment performance index
portfolio
price earnings (PE) (ratio)
product liability insurance
profit
profit and loss statement
profit center
profit plan
raiders
recapitalization
reinsurance
repurchase agreement
return on assets
return on equity
return on investment
reverse repurchase agreement
risk avoidance
rollover
Rule of 72
Securities and Exchange Commission
semi-bundled services
short-selling
spreadsheet
Statement No. 95, FASB
static scoring
tangible net worth
total debt
U.S. Government security
venture capital
Voluntary Compliance Resolution
warrant
wrap-fee program

20   Forecasting

availability forecast
benchmark studies
Box-Jenkins technique
change model
exponential smoothing
futurist
impact wheel
iterative approach
Markov chain
mathematical model
monitoring
morphological analysis
moving average
network flow model
nominal group technique
normative forecasting
objective-line forecast
optimization model
potential-line forecast
projection
projective techniques
ratio analysis
relevance tree
scanning
scenario
statistical model
structured interview
substitution analysis
surveillance techniques
technology forecasting
time series forecast
tracking
trailblazer developments
trend analysis
trend extrapolation
variance forecast

21   Health Care

acupressure
adjusted average per capita cost
adjusted community rate
affinity plan
allopathic medicine
allowable charge
alternate long term care facility
alternative medicine
alternative therapies
ambulatory surgical facilities
American Managed Care and Review
   Association

AmeriCare
anxiety
anxiety attack
approved charges
assignment of benefits
assisted reproductive technology
authorized provider
auxiliary services
average payment rate
balance billing
basic medical coverage
benefit limit
biofeedback
board certified
bundled case rate
bundled services
capitation
capitation payments
cardiac rehabilitation program
cardiac rehabilitation treatment
cardiac surgeon
cardiologist
carve-outs
case management
catastrophic cap
catastrophic protection/coverage
catchment-area management
certificate of authority
certificate of need
certified medical laboratory
C. Everett Koop National Health Awards
chemotherapy
chiropractic HMO
churning
Civilian Health and Medical Program of the
   Uniformed Services
claims processor
claims review
cognitive impairment
coinsurance
comfort care
community mental health centers
complementary care
comprehensive medical coverage
comprehensive outpatient rehabilitation
   facility
concurrent review
continued care
Coordinated Care Plan
Coordinated Care Program
coordination of benefits
copayment
cosmetic surgery
cost contract

cost plans
cost-share
covered period of confinement
covered provider
credentialing
custodial care
daily maximum
days per thousand
death spiral
deductible
Defense Enrollment/Eligibility Reporting
   System
demand management
dental care
dental care plan
dental preferred provider organization
dependent coverage waiver
detoxification facility
diabetes
diagnostic related group reimbursement
direct contracting
direct reimbursement dental
disability case management
disability costs
Disability Determination Service
discharge planning
disease management
disputed claim
domestic partner benefits
drug formulary
dual option
durable medical equipment
elimination period
employee benefits laws
employee prefunding
endocrinologist
episodes of care
equity model
evidence of insurability
exclusive provider organizations
experimental treatments
explanation of benefits
experience rating
extended care facility
faculty practice plan
Federal Employees Health Benefits Program
federally qualified health centers
fee-for-service plan
fee maximum
fire wall protections
fixed-dollar benefits
flat rate
flexible managed care
flexible spending account

formulary
freestanding ambulatory facility
gag clause
gastroenterologist
gatekeeper
geriatrician
global fee
global pricing
Group Health Association of America
group model HMO
group practice
group practice health maintenance
    organization
guided imagery
gynecologist
health benefits
health care prepayment plan
health care purchasing organization
health care reimbursable account
Health Care Task Force
health insurance purchasing cooperative
health maintenance organization
hold-harmless clause
holistic medicine
home health care agency
home health care
home medical equipment
homeopathic medicine
hospice
hospice care
hospital confinement indemnity coverage
hypnotherapy
incentives
immunosuppressive drugs
indemnity insurance
independent physician organization
independent practice association
individual case management
individual practice association
integrated delivery system
lag study
large case management
lifetime caps
limiting charge
line of business
long term care
Long-Term Ombudsman Program
low-balling
magnetic resonance imaging
major medical coverage
managed care
managed chiro
managed competition
managed pharmacy network

mandated benefits
mandatory outpatient surgery
market reform plan
maternity and child care
maximum payment period
Medicaid
medical and health insurance laws
medical insurance
medical loss ratio
Medical Records Confidentiality Act of 1996
medical review officer
medical savings account
medical service agency
Medicare
Medicare risk contract
Medicare SELECT
Medicare subvention
medigap insurance
meditation
mental health
midlevel practitioner
military treatment facility
mixed model
myelography
National Committee on Quality Assurance
network model HMO
neurologist
no balance billing clause
non-availability statement
non-participating physician
nurse case manager
nurse practitioner
nursing home coverage
obstetrician
Office of Prepaid Health Care Operations and
    Oversight
off-label drug
off-label prescribing
Old Age, Survivors, Disability and Health
    Insurance Program
oncologist
on-label prescribing
open-ended health maintenance organization
open-ended plan
open panel
open season
ophthamologist
orthopedist
oral and maxillofacial surgery
osteoarthritis
osteopathic medicine
otolaryngologist
outcomes management
out-of-pocket payment

overpricing
par provider
participant in CHAMPUS
patient advocate
pattern review
pay-as-you-go strategy
pediatrician
pension plan retiree medical account
per diem reimbursement
pharmacy benefit management
photo-refractive keratectomy
physiatrist
play or pay model
play or pay plan
point of service plan
positron emission tomography
post-claims underwriting
preadmission review
preadmission testing
precertification
predatory pricing
preexisting condition
preferred provider arrangement
preferred provider organization
premium
preventive care
primary care nurse
private inurement
prospective payment system
prospective review
provider organization
qualified Medicare beneficiary
Quimby
radial keratotomy
radiation theraphy
reflexology
remission
resource-based relative value system
retainer
retrospective review
rheumatoid arthritis
rheumatologist
rider
risk contract
risk plans
routine services/care
rural health clinics
salary-based deductible
same day surgery
self-care
self-funded plan of benefits
service area
shadow pricing
shoe-box effect

significant activities of daily living
single payer plan
skilled nursing facility
special practitioners
specified disease coverage
specified low-income Medicare beneficiary
staff model
stop loss
subacute care
subrogation
Sutton's Law
Tax Equity and Fiscal Responsibility Act of
  1982
telemedicine
therapeutic touch
transportation benefit
triggering condition or event
triple option
triple option point-of-service health care plan
Uniformed Services Treatment Facility
underwriting
universal coverage
upcoding
urologist
user fee
utilization review
Utilization Review Accreditation Commission
well child care
wraparound plan
yoga

22 Health, Fitness, and Wellness

acquired immune deficiency syndrome
aerobic exercise
AIDS-related complex
AIDS tests
amateur auditor plan
ambulatory care utilization review
angina pectoris
ankylosing spondylitis
arrythmia
arthritis
asthma
atherosclerosis
behavioral health care
biofeedback
boutique health care
burnout
call letter
cancer
cardiac rehabilitation program
cardiac rehabilitation treatment

23 Instructional Strategies and Techniques

demonstration method
didactic learning/teaching
directed discussion
discovery learning
distance learning
document camera
drill and practice
experiential learning
expository learning
field trips
framing
games
graphic aids
group interview
guided practice
handouts
high adventure activities
homestudy
homogeneous groups
host site
implementation
in-basket exercises
independent study
individualized instruction
initiative activities
instructional management plan
instructional method
instructional objective
instructional strategy
instructional technique
instructor camera
instructor-led training
interactive multimedia
interactive performance system
interactive video system
job aids
job instruction training
job procedures manual
laboratory training
learning center
lecture method
mediating device
method
mockup
model
monitor
multimedia
one-on-one training
on-the-job training
panels
participant camera
peer group learning
performance
performance support system

physical simulations
preparation
presentation
procedural simulations
process simulations
programmed instruction
questioning
recycle
remote site
role playing
room audio
seminar method
sensitivity training
shell
simulation
structured experiences
study assignments
suggestology
supporting method
team learning
team teaching
teleconferencing
telecourses
two-way interactive video
trainee response system
training conference
tutoring

24   Instructional Systems Development

accomplishment-based curriculum
   development
behavior
branching program
conditions
course developer
criterion
critical incident
decision matrix
decision template
decision tree
delivery system
descriptive order
duty analysis
element
element analysis
field test
front-end analysis
generic analysis
high-technology training
holistic approach
infusion approach
instructional systems development

Integrated Applications Digital and Audio
 Trainer
integrative brainwork approach
interdisciplinary approach
job performance order
learning environment
learning guides
learning objective
learning skills
learning strategy
learningware
lesson plan
logical order
mind/brain function approach
module
multimedia
needs assessment
needs inventories
nominal group technique
objective
pilot
problem-centered order
producer
program of instruction
prototyping
psychological order
rule of thumb
script
storyboard
systems approach to training
systems validation
thematic approach
topics-within-discipline approach
training needs analysis
training objective
training program design
training systems development

25   Job Analysis and Job Evaluation

accountability
benchmarks
comparable factors
comparable worth
compensable factors
computer-assisted job evaluation
critical element
critical incident survey
critical tasks
documentation
duty
factor comparison
factor weight

group interview
Hay plan
individual interview
job
job analysis
job classification
job description
job design
job dimensions
job enrichment
job evaluation
job inventory
job paths
job ranking
job redesign
job title
jury of experts
key result areas
knowledge, skills, and abilities
multi-domain job analysis
occupational analysis
occupational field
participant diary or log
task
task analysis
work participation method
work performance

26   Jobs and Functions

actives
administrative support services
administrator
alpha geek
audiologist
authorized provider
bean-counter
benefit manager
benefits administrator
benefits planning analyst
bitnick
blue collar workers
blue collar technical workers
The Bubble Generation
Certified Association Executive
Certified Benefits Professional
Certified Compensation Professional
Certified Corporate Travel Executive
Certified Destination Management Executive
Certified Employee Assistance Professional
Certified Employee Benefit Specialist
Certified Financial Planner
Certified Management Consultant

Certified Manager of Exhibits
Certified Meeting Professional
Certified Personnel Consultant
Certified Professional Development Trainer
Certified Public Accountant
Certified Speaking Professional
Certified Technical Trainer
Certified Temporary Staffing Specialist
change agent
Chartered Financial Analyst
chief executive officer
chief financial officer
chief knowledge officer
chief learning officer
chief operating officer
chief technology officer
chief training officer
claims assistance professional
claims processor
commission-only planner
contingent work force
controller
convention and visitors bureau
co-preneurs
core competencies
core workers
corporate compensation and benefits
   executive
course developer
course manager
creative staff
cross-functional
curriculum development
customer relations
customer service representative
customer service specialist
cybrarian
daddy track
data base manager
data processing
decision making
dejobbing
designer
directing
director
disability manager
displacement
disposable workers
distributed work
downwardly mobile professional
downshifter/downshifting
electronic immigrant
electronic partnering
electronic sweatshop

employee
employee benefits manager
ergonomics
exempt employee
expats/expatriates
facilitator
fee-only planner
fee-and-commission planner
financial advisor
financial planner
free addressing
free-lance trainer
functional specialists
futurist
gatekeeper
generalist
global rotational opportunities
gold collar workers
grampies
grandpa track
green executive
group facilitator
health benefits advisor
health care finder
high-performance jobs
high potential employee
home worker
hoteling
image consulting
independent contractors
industrial engineering
industrial/organizational (I/O) psychologist
internal consultant
job lock
job sharing
joint-activities staff
knowledge workers
leader
licensed practical nurse
manager
manager-without-portfolio
managing
management consultant
management consulting
marketer
materials developer
meeting management
mentor
mobile worker
mommy track
moonlighting
mouse potato
needs analyst
nonexempt employee

27 Labor-Management and Industrial Relations

28   Laws and Legal Terms

29   Leadership

30   Learning and Behavior

behavioral psychology
behaviorism
change efforts
cognition
cognitive domain
cognitive enhancement
cognitive modeling
cognitive psychology
computer-based learning
concept
conceptual framework
conceptual skills
conditioned response
contingency theory of learning
creative learning
cuing
deductive reasoning
developmental theory of learning
didactic learning
discovery learning
discrimination
dyslexia
emotional intelligence
expository learning
feedback
full-spectrum learning
functional illiterate
Gestalt psychology
holistic
humanistic psychology
individual differences
inductive reasoning
industrial psychology
integrated learning
integrated learning system
intelligence quotient
interactivity
learning disability
learning environment
learning outcome
learning pattern
learning principles
learning skills
learning strategy
learning style
learningware
lifelong learning
mainstreaming
needs
neurolinguistic programming
nominalized experience
nootropics
observational learning
operant behavior
operant conditioning

overlearning
physiological needs
primacy
practice
psychological needs
readiness
recency
refreezing
reinforcement
relevance
respondent behavior
responsive behavior
right-brained
rote learning
security needs
self-efficacy
self-reflective learning
skills, knowledge, and attitudes
social needs
storing or caching
strategic thinking
teachable moment
understanding
unfreezing
vertical thinking

31   Management

accordion management
actual cost projections
administrator
behavioral risk management
benchmarking
chaos theory
collaboration
collaborative method
collaborative workplace
complexity theory
correcting
country executive program
crisis management
critical path method
cross-functional team
decision making
delegating
devolution
Dilberted
directing
discretionary effort
empowerment
entrepreneur
euromanagers
federalization
flex management

flip the switch
franchising
friendly takeover
functional authority
functional team
generalist
generic skills
globalization
goal congruence
group decision support system
hai-ten
high performance workplace/work system
hoshin kanri
human capital
human resources
human resources environment
human resources management
human resources planning
human resources utilization
instructional management
integrated management system
internal audit
just in time
keiretsu
long-range plan
management audit
management by adultery
management by exception
management by objectives
management by trust
management by walking around
management improvement
management meeting
management style
manager
managerial grid
managing diversity
matrix management
Office of Personnel Management
operational plans
organizing
outsourcing
overtime by plan
performance management
policy
process capability
project management
project team
property casualty executive
reengineering
regeneration
scientific management
shukko
span of management
strategic alliances

strategic leadership team
strategic plan
temping
Theory X
Theory Y
Theory Z
training advisory board
work-based HR applications

32 Marketing, Pricing, and Sales

affinity
Air Force Procurement Instructions
antitrust and fair trade legislation
Army Procurement Procedure
ASCII
bait and switch
benchmarking
blind ad
brand names
business ecosystem
business espionage
business format franchising
business intelligence
call-girl principle
catalog sales
client-specific benchmarking
cojoint analysis
comarketing
competition-based pricing
competitive benchmarking
competitive intelligence
compiled list
complete meeting package
consultative selling
cost-based pricing
cream skimming
cross-promotion
customer-based pricing
customer partnering
customer relations
Customer Satisfaction Barometer
customer service program
customer window model
customization
deceptive advertising
defective pricing
demand pricing
direct mail
direct marketing.
disintermediation
duplication factor
economy of scale
economy of scope

electronic data interchange
ethics laws
European Community
external marketing
Federal Acquisition Regulation
Federal Trade Commission
fee-based pricing
foreign sales corporation
franchising
fraudulent tagging
free trade agreement
fusion marketing
gap analysis
General Services Administration
global
globalization
glocal
Goods and Services/General Services Tax
government contract laws
gray marketing
green marketing
Green Seal of Approval
Group of Seven
guerrilla marketing
hook
house list
internal marketing
joint ventures
Kano model
key cost
leased list
leverage
life cycle analysis
limited franchising
limited offering
lowballing
loyalty program
Maastricht Treaty
marketing plan
Marketing Science Institute
marketing strategy
market intelligence
market penetration
market pricing
market segmentation
market share
mass customization
mass marketing
merge/purge
micromarketing
modeling
multi-attribute evaluation
Navy Procurement Directive
niche marketing
North American Free Trade Agreement

O'Brien's Law
performance benchmarking
point-of-purchase
pricing
privatization
process benchmarking
profile
promo
proposal
proprietary information
psychographics
quality function deployment
recency
request for proposal
relationship marketing
response list
retailing
Rule of Seven
sales meeting
seminar selling
sensitivity analysis
slotting fee
Small Business Administration
spin master
team selling
telemarketing
telemarketing rule
testimonial
tiered marketing
total quality improvement
trade loading pricing
trademark
trade name
trade secret
trade show
United Nations Convention on Contracts for
    the International Sale of Goods
Universal Product Code
upstream research
value pricing
value research
ventures
venturing
video news release
wholesaling
yield management

33   Measurement and Evaluation

appraising
behavior evaluation
Myers-Briggs Type Indicator
competency evaluation
construct validity

content validity
context evaluation
context-input-process-product
correlation
criterion measure
criterion-referenced measurement
criterion validity
critical incident survey
critique
cross validation
determination evaluation
external evaluation
factor analysis
Five-Factor Model
focus group
follow-up
forced-choice
forced distribution
formative evaluation
go/no-go standards
graphic scale
immediate evaluation
impact evaluation
individual evaluation
input evaluation
inspection
intermediate evaluation
internal audit
internal evaluation
interval data
job evaluation
job performance measures
justification evaluation
management audit
measurement
monitoring
nominal data
norm-referenced measurement
null hypothesis
observation
ordinal data
participant reaction
performance measure
procedures audit
process evaluation
product evaluation
product-process evaluation
program improvement evaluation
qualitative methods
rank order/ranking method
rank order/rank ordered
ratio data
reaction evaluation
reliability
results evaluation

smile sheet
standards
summative evaluation
training and development self-audit
ultimate evaluation
utilization review
validity

34 Medical Terms

acupressure
acupuncture
acute care
adverse medical event
affect
affective disorder
age-related cognitive decline
age-related macular degeneration
Alexander technique
alternative medicine therapy
anatomical gifts
angina pectoris
angiogram
aromatherapy
arteriography
arteriosclerosis
atherosclerosis
assistive devices
astigmatism
audiologist
autologous transfusion
Ayurvedic medicine
balloon angioplasty
benign prostatic hyperplasia
bioenergetics
biofeedback
bipolar disorder
brachytherapy
brain diseases
brand name drug
Caesarean section
cardiopulminary resuscitation
chiropractic
carotid surgery
cholesterol
chronic fatigue syndrome
cirrhosis
cochlear implant
cognitive enhancement
color healing
computed tomography
computerized axial tomography
critical pathway
delusion

depression
digital subtraction angiography
digital rectal exam
DNA fingerprinting
do not resuscitate
Down syndrome
drug formulary
echocardiography
electromyograph
emergency medical services
emergency medical technician
emergency response system
emotional disabilities
endarterectomy
endodonics
endoscope
epilepsy
excimer keratorefractive procedure
finasteride
flat affect
formulary drug
generic drug
genetaceuticals
genetic testing
grandiose delusion
guided imagery
hallucination
high density lipoproteins
holistic medicine/therapy
homeopathy
hydrotherapy
hypnotherapy
hypochondriasis
inappropriate affect
independent medical examination
Italian boot
life support systems
limiting charge
low density lipoproteins
Lyme disease
macrobiotics
macular degeneration
managed chiro
manic depressive illness
major depression
malingering
mania
massage
medical herbalism
medical underwriting
medically necessary
mononucleosis
mood disorders
Munchausen syndrome

myopic
myotherapy
negative symptoms
neonatal care
nephropathy
neuroleptic drugs
nootropics
oculoplethysmography
off-label drug
oral and maxillofacial surgery
organ transplant
orthodontics
osteoporosis
outcomes research
panic disorder
paramedic
paraplegia
Parkinson's disease
perinatal care
physical therapy
positive symptoms
postnatal care
premenstrual syndrome
prenatal care
presbyopia
prostate specific antigen
prosthodontics
psychologically necessary
psychoneuroimmunology
psychosomatic disorder
psychosis
quadriplegia
quality-adjusted life years
reflexology
repetitive strain injury
rolfing
sauna
schizophrenia
Seattle foot
self-referral
Shiatu massage
short wavelength autoperimetry
sip-and-puff machine
sleep deprivation
somatization disorder
spinal cord injury
stroke
telemedicine
teleradiology
temporal mandibular joint disease/syndrome
thermotherapy
thought disorder
tinnitus
transient ischemic attack

transurethral resection prostatectomy
transurethral ultrasound-guided laser-induced
  prostatectomy
ultrasound
withdrawal

35 Meeting Management

adjoining
amenities
American plan
association management company
association meeting
attrition charge
banquet event order
bar manager
bid document
bid manual
blocked space
breakout session
budget chart
buffet
business center
business class amenities
business meeting
cabana
cafeteria
call brand
catering director
check-in
check-out
classroom configuration
commercial rate
concierge
concierge level
concurrent session
conference
conference center
conference configuration
conference packet
conference services manager
connecting
confirmed reservation
congress
continental plan
controller
convention
convention and visitors bureau
convention services manager
convertible
corporate center
corporate meeting
cut-off date

day rate
destination management company
direct billing
director of sales
double
double/double
drayage
duplex
early-out penalty
efficiency
European plan
executive center
executive chef
executive housekeeper
executive staff meeting
exhibitor-designated contractor
export license
exposition service contractor
fam trip
feng shue
final program
flat rate
food and beverage manager
force majeure clause
French
front office manager
full American plan
function sheet
gassbuku
general manager
general session
Gold Awards
Goods and Services Tax
green rooms
group (event charge) card
guarantee
guaranteed room blocks
high season
hold harmless
house count
hospitality
Hospitality Industry Humanitarian Awards
  Program
hospitality suite
hotel classifications
hotel functional positions
hotel rep firm
inclusive rate
The Invisible Industry
junior suite
keypad system
king
lanai
low season

management meeting
maintenance engineer
master account
meeting cost categories
meeting facilities
meeting industry council
meeting planner/planning functions
modified American plan
move-in/move-out
Murphy bed
no-show
organization history
outlet
parlor
pick up
piggybacking
Pinnacle Awards
plated
plenary session
plus-plus
pre-con meeting
preliminary program
professional conference (congress)
   organizer
Provincial Sales Tax
queen
rack rate
recreation manager
registration software
resident manager
retreat
room block
room configurations
room rates
room types
roundtable configuration
run-of-the-house rate
Russian
sales meeting
sample
security chief
seminar
service charge
shoulder season
single
site inspection
smart meeting room
sokaiya
statement of account
strategy/planning meeting
studio
symposium
TelePrompTer
theater/auditorium configuration

trade show
training meeting
turnaround time
twin
university center
Unrelated Business Income Tax
users group meeting
value added
value added tax rebate services
walk
"walking" clause
workshop

36   Military and Veterans Organzations

Air Force Association
Air Force Sergeants Association
The American Legion
AMVETS National Headquarters
Army Aviation Association of America, Inc.
Association of Military Surgeons of the United
   States
Association of the United States Army
Chief Warrant and Warrant Officers
   Association, U.S. Coast Guard
Commissioned Officers Association of the
   U.S. Public Health Service
Eastern Paralyzed Veterans Association
Enlisted Association of the National Guard of
   the U.S.
Fleet Reserve Association
Jewish War Veterans of the USA
Marine Corps League
Marine Corps Reserve Officers
   Association
The Military Chaplains Association of
   the USA
National Association for Uniformed
   Services/Society of Military Widows
National Guard Association of the U.S.
National Military Family Association
National Order of Battlefield
   Commissions
Naval Enlisted Reserve Association
Naval Reserve Association
Non Commissioned Officers Association of
   the USA
Navy League of the United States
The Reserve Officers Association
The Retired Enlisted Association
The Retired Officers Association
United Armed Forces Association
U.S. Army Warrant Officers Association

U.S. Coast Guard Chief Petty Officers
  Association
Veterans of Foreign Wars of the United States
  of America
Vietnam Veterans of America

37 Motivation, Incentives, and Awards

achievement-motivation theory
achievement need
ASTD Member Unit Awards
award
Bedeaux plan
Council of Peers Award for Excellence
Gordon M. Bliss Memorial Award
book value plan
Donald Bullock Memorial Dissertation
  Award
capital accumulation plan
cash-deferred (401[k]) plan
cash plan
compressed work week
comps
deferred benefits plan
deferred compensation
dissatisfiers
Distinguished Contribution to Human
  Resource Development Award
employee stock option (ownership) plan
employer of choice
empowerment
Excellence in Human Resource Development
  Awards
Exemplary Public Interest Contribution
  Award
Exemplary Voluntary Efforts Award
expectancy theory
extrinsic motivator
extrinsic reward
fam trip
financial reward
flextime
golden carrots
golden handcuffs
golden parachute
Hawthorne effect
Haynes plan
Henry Laurence Gantt Medal
hierarchy of needs
home office
hoteling
HRD Hall of Fame
HR Executive of the Year

HR Honor Roll
HR Service Excellence Award
incentive pay
incentive plan
incentive retirement plan
incentive stock option
incentive work
intangible reward
internal motivation
intrinsic motivator
intrinsic reward
job satisfaction
job sharing/job splitting
key contributor program
Lincoln incentive system
long-term incentive
lump-sum merit
Malcolm Baldridge National Quality
  Award
market value plan
maturity curves
money surrogates
motivation
motivation/recognition/reward
National Academy of Human
  Resources
National Affairs Award
noneconomic rewards
Opportunity 2000 Award
people performance programs
performance achievement plan
performance award plans
performance shares
phased retirement
Pinnacle Awards
profit sharing
Pro Patria Award
recognition
reinforcement
restricted stock plan
reward system
Rowan plan
sabbatical
sabbatical leave
satisfiers
scam trip
secular trust
SHRM Award for Professional Excellence
special cash award
stock grants
stock options
Summit Award
supplemental executive retirement plan
tangible reward

team incentive
telecommuting
telework center
Top 25
Torch Awards
voluntary reduced hours
work-at-home option
work orientation factors

38 Organization Design

adhocracy
blended workforce
centralization
close corporation
committee
compact
contract technical workers
conventional staffing
core work activities
corporate anorexia
customer grouping
decentralization
departmentation
downsizing
economy of scale
employee leasing
experience curve
flat organization
friendly takeover
functional organization
general corporation
hostile takeover or merger
hybrid organization
in-house temporary employees
job displacement
job engineering
job redesign
leveraged buy-out
limited liability company
location grouping
long-term temporary assignments
master vendor arrangements
matrix organization
merger
mission statement
multinational
nonprofit/not-for profit organization
organizational analysis
organizational evaluation
organizational survey
organization and functions manual
organization chart

organization diagnosis
organization documents
organization planning
organization structure
outsourcing-to-temps
part-time employees
payrolling
process grouping
product grouping
professional corporation
professional employer organization
professional temps
reduction in force
restructuring
rightsizing
scalar principle
S corporation
small business investment company
staffing options
tall organization
temp-to-hire
temp-to lease programs
temp-to-perm programs
traditional temporary help
transitions
transnational
vertical organization
virtual organization
virtual team
visioning
zero-based staffing

39 Organization Development

management by objectives
management reinforcement workshop
organizational analysis
organizational evaluation
organizational survey
organizational transformation
organization climate
organization culture
organization design
organization development
organization development
   interventions
organization diagnosis
organization vision
performance analysis
performance audit
performance indicator
team building
time management

40   Performance Appraisal

360-degree feedback
absolute ratings
alternative ranking
assessment center
behavior
behaviorally-anchored rating scale
behavior-based performance
   appraisal
central tendency
Civil Service Reform Act of 1978
collaborative appraisal
comparative ratings
competence
competency assessment
contrast effect
critical element
critical incident
customer rating (appraisal) system
descriptive scale
directive appraisal
equal intervals
error of contrast
error of halo
error of inconsistency
error of instability
error of projection
error of recency
error of standards
error of stereotype
error of subjectivity
essay appraisal
face validity
fair employment practices laws
feedback
fitness report
forced choice scale
forced distribution
graphic scale
ipsative scores
key result areas
merit rating
merit review
multisource assessment
observational skills
officer efficiency report
ordinal measurements
paired comparisons
peer appraisal
performance analysis
performance management
performance measure
performance monitoring

performance review
performance ratings
performance standards
privacy laws
rank order/ranking method
reciprocal review
self-rating
stereotyping
three hundred sixty degree
   feedback

41   Problem Solving

abstract reasoning
action research
action skills
analytical skills
analytical thinking
association skills
attribute listing
Basic Seven
block busting
brainstorming
brainwriting
cause-and-effect analysis
cause-and-effect diagram
checklist
checksheet
climate survey
closed-form questionnaire
control chart
creative imagery
creative problem-solving training
decision tree
deductive reasoning
diagnostic survey
document analysis
economic analysis
electronic brainstorming
funnelling
histogram
inductive reasoning
input-output technique
inquiring
intelligent tutoring system
intuitive skill
lateral thinking
linear programming
marginal analysis
morphological analysis
Pareto chart
problem sensitivity
problem solving

problem-solving skills
reframing
run chart
scattergram
synthetic skills
thinking fluency

42 Productivity, Standards, and Quality Control

acceptable quality level
advanced manufacturing technology
assembly line manufacturing
baseline performance
"best practice" group
block diagram
cause and effect diagram
cell manufacturing
certification
concentration knowledge and skills
conformity assessment
conformity Europe
check sheet
computer-integrated manufacturing
control chart
core knowledge and skills
correlation chart
cost of quality measurement
cross-functional mapping
cross-training
customer complaint rate
Customer Satisfaction Barometer
cycles of learning
cycle time
design/development cycle
EN 29000
design of experiments
detection costs
empowerment
entitlement performance
experience curve theory
failure costs
first-pass yield
fishbone chart
Five-Five-Five Plan
flow chart
handling time
histogram
Improshare
International Accreditation Forum
International Organization for
    Standardization
ISO 9000

ISO 14000
keiretsu
labor-management relations
    laws
learning organization
make/market cycle
methods analysis
methods engineering
mutual learning
necessary work
next operation as customer
non-value adding work
on-time
operations research
Pareto chart
peer coaching
performance to schedule
plan, do, check, act
pre-control
prevention costs
process benchmarking
process capability
process management
product evaluation
productivity
productivity improvement program
product specification standards
QS-9000
quality control
quality function deployment
quality improvement process
quality improvement programs
Quality Index
queuing theory/techniques
reengineering
Registrars
registration
reject rate
rework
rework rate
run chart
schedule
specialty knowledge and skills
star measurement
statistical process control
theoretical cycle time
total cycle time
unnecessary work
value adding work
value analysis and engineering
value creating work
value sustaining work
white collar cycle time
workflow automation

work simplification
zero defects

43   Professional Journals

Benefits & Compensation Solutions
Business Travel News
BusinessWeek
Corporate Meetings & Incentives
Corporate University Review
Dividends
Employee Benefit News
Fast Company: How Smart Business Works
Harvard Business Review
HRMagazine on Human Resource
   Management
HR.News
Human Resource Development Quarterly
Human Resource Executive
Human Resource Professional
Incentive
Inside Technology Training
Interactivity
Managing Diversity
Management Review
Meeting News
Meetings & Conventions
National Report on Human Resources
NetGuide
Nonprofit World
Performance In Practice
Phi Delta Kappan
Presentations
Self Employed Professional
Successful Meetings
Team Work
Technology Training
T.H.E. Journal
Training
Training & Development
The Wall Street Journal
Workforce: The Magazine for Leaders in
   Human Resources

44   Purchasing and Contracting

acceptance
Air Force Procurement Instructions
Armed Forces Procurement Act of 1947
Army Procurement Procedure
Commerce Business Daily
contract

contract administration
contract deliverables
contracting
cost contract
cost-no-fee contract
cost-plus-award-fee contract
cost-plus-fixed-fee contract
cost-plus-incentive-fee contract
cost-sharing contract
Department of Commerce
disclaimer clause
documentation
ethics laws
excluded costs
firm-fixed-price contract
fixed-price contract with price-adjustment
   provisions
fixed-price-incentive contract
fixed-price level-of-effort term contract
fixed-price-redeterminable contract
fixed-rate contract
government contract laws
guaranteed investment contract
labor-hour contract
multiple-incentive contract
Navy Procurement Directive
Office of Federal Contract Compliance
   Programs
pre-award survey
precycle/precycling
proposal
quality assurance surveillance plan
quality audit
quality control
request for information
request for proposal
risk sharing arrangement
risk transfer
service contract
statement of work
sweetheart contract
time and materials contract
turnkey program
United Nations Convention on Contracts for
   the International Sale of Goods

45   Recruiting, Hiring, and Promoting

achievement competencies
agricultural worker law
alien employment laws
America's Job Bank
America's Talent Bank

46   Research Organizations and Institutes

The Cato Institute
Center for Corporate Health
Centers for Disease Control
Educational Resources Information Center
The Electonic Bulletin Board, Inc.
Employee Benefit Research Institute
ERIC Clearinghouse on Information &
    Technology
Ethics Resource Center
Families and Work Institute
Federally Supported Clearinghouses on
    Disability
FedWorld Information Network
Food and Drug Administration
The Heritage Foundation
Hoover Institution
Human Factors and Ergonomics Society
Industrial Relations Research Association
Industrial Technology Institute
Industry Labor Council
Institute for Crisis Management
Institute for Operations Research and the
    Management Sciences
Institute for Research on Learning
Institute of Industrial Engineers
Insurance Information Institute
Japan-American Institute of Management
    Science
Marketing Science Institute
National Assessment of Educational Progress
National Institute on Disability and
    Rehabilitation Research
National Institute on Deafness and Other
    Communication Disorders
National Rehabilitation Information Center
National Technical Information Service
RAND
The Urban Institute
Workers' Compensation Research Institute
World Institute on Disability
World Resources Institute

47   Research, Statistics, and Information Systems

aggregative statistics
analysis of variance
analytical survey
applied research
area chart
auto-regression
bar chart
basic research

Basic Seven
Bayesian statistics
bell-shaped curve
case study
causal-comparative study
cause-and-effect diagram
checklist
checksheet
chi-square test
CompuServe(R)
context variables
control groups
control chart
controlled experiment
correlational study
cross-section technique
database
database management system
DATA STAR
DATATIMES
descriptive study
DIALOG Information Services
Dow Jones News/Retrieval
Educational Resources Information Center
expectancy table
experimental group
experimental research
feasibility study
field experiment
generic data base
genetic, developmental, and growth studies
hard data
histogram
historical study
horizontal bar chart
human factors engineering
human resource information system
human resources information centers
Human Resource Information Network
human resources information system
hypothesis
information refinery
informed consent
Interactive Market Services
interquartile range
kurtosis
laboratory experiment
least squares method
leptokurtic
levels of significance
library
linear regression
line chart
longitudinal technique

48 Safety and Security

49 Service and Information Agencies and Organizations

American Board of Medical Specialties
Ask-a-Nurse
Canadian Labour Market and Productivity Centre
Center on Addiction and Substance Abuse
Council of Citizens with Low Vision International
Defense Outplacement Referral System
Educational Assistance Ltd.
Educational Resources Information Center
Educational Testing Service, Inc.
The Electronic Bulletin Board
Epilepsy Foundation of America
ERIC Clearing House on Information Resources
Institute for International Research
Insurance Information Institute
International Travel Briefing Service
Job Accommodation Network
Linking Home and School Through the Workplace
National Center for Youth with Disabilities
National Down Syndrome Society
National Foundation for the Improvement of Education
National Information Center on Deafness
National Organization on Disability
National Rehabilitation Information Center
National Spinal Cord Injury Association
Overseas Private Investment Corporation
Overseas Security Advisory Council
Service Corps of Retired Executives
Sexuality Information & Education Council of the United States
U.S. Department of Commerce
Youth Service America

50 Substance Abuse

abuse/suppression program
alcohol testing
amphetamine
bad trip
balance and reflex performance check
Center on Addiction and Substance Abuse
Clinical Laboratory Amendments of 1988
codependency
confirmatory test
crack
crank

critical tracking test
crash
Department of Defense Interim Rule on Drug-Free Work Place
Drug Free Workplace Act of 1988
drug testing
drug tests
enzyme multiplied immunoassay technique
Executive Order 12564
Federal Highway Administration
hair analysis test
hallucinogen
hash
heroin
Hughes Act of 1970
ice
joint
lysergic acid diethylamide
mandatory drug and alcohol testing
marijuana
methadone
methamphetamine
moonrock
morphine
occupational program consultants
Office for Substance Abuse Prevention
p-funk
pupillary-reaction test
relationship addict
screening test
specimen integrity
speed
speedball
substance abuse laws
support group
urine test
withdrawal

51 Teams and Team Building

action learning
action-reflection learning
autonomous work group
collaborative community
concurrent engineering
dream team
facilitator
future search
group dynamics
group facilitator
group incentives
groupthink
groupware

hot work group
human relations
mindguarding
neurolinguistic programming
parallel team
partnerships
peer coaching
process action team
project team
recorder
role negotiation
role playing
self-directed work team
self-managed work team
self-regulated work group
semiautonomous work group
sham union
special work teams
standing work team
synectics
synergy
team building
team concept
team hiring
visioning meeting
work team
work team development

52   Technology

array
artificial intelligence
asynchronous
asynchronous transfer mode
audiographics
authoring platform
authoring system or program
automated voice response system
automation
bandwidth
bar code technology
BetaSP
bin
bits per second
blendo
brightness
bulletin board service
business television
camcorder
C-band satellite
character generator
chrominance
client/server architecture

clip
codec
code division multiple access
compact disc
compact disc interactive
compact disc, read-only memory
compact disc, read only memory extended
  architecture
compositing
compressed speech
compression
computer
computer-assisted design
computer-assisted engineering
computer-assisted manufacturing
computer-assisted retrieval
computer-based coaching
computer-based corporate videoconferencing
computer-based learning resources
computer-integrated manufacturing
computerized numerically controlled
  machining
computer simulation
computer synthetic voice translation
constant angular velocity
constant linear velocity
corporate video
cut
cybernetics
deck
delivery platform
delivery system
desktop publishing
desktop video
desktop videoconferencing
Digispeech
digital audiotape
digital light processing
digital photography
digital simultaneous voice and data
digital video disc
digital video interactive technology
digital virtual disc
digitize
direct imaging
disk-based media
disk drive
disk operating system
distance learning
document camera
educational technology
edutainment
electronic data interchange
electronic job aid

electronic mailbox/mail
electronic management
electronic meeting
electronic performance aid
electronic performance support system
emulator
enhanced audio compact disc
EXPERT system
fax machine
fiber-optic cable
fiber optics
field
flaming
frame
frame grabber
freeze (frame)
global system for mobile communication
graphical user interface
graphic scanner
group videoconferencing
hardware
high definition compatible digital
high definition TV
hologram
host site
hue
Industrial Technology Institute
information highway
information systems
information technology
instructor camera
interactive videodisc
interactive voice response
Integrated Applications Digital and Audio
   Trainer
integrated digital videoconferencing
Integrated Services Digital Network
interactive videodisc
interactive video system
Internet
Internet service provider
I-way
keypad system
kilobits
Ku-band satellite
laser barcode system
laserdisc
LCD-based projector
LCD panel
linear edition
liquid crystal display
live video insertion system
local area network
lossless

luminance
lurk/lurking
map
metaphor
microwave
minidisc
modem
monitor
motion picture experts group
multidisk
multipoint control unit
multimedia
musical instrument digital interface
netiquette
networked multimedia
nonlinear editing
numerical control
on-line access
optical mark reader
optoelectronic technology
overhead projection
pacer
paint
paperless book
participant camera
PC-based enhancement
pen-based technology
personal emergency response systems
personal information management system
Photo CD
photovoltaic technology
programmable robot
point-of-sale terminal
projection systems
repurposing
robotics
room audio
satellite communications
scanner
shovelware
simulator
smart building
sociotechnical systems
software
soundcard
spam/spamming
special-effects generator
still frame storage unit
still video
supercomputer
Super VHS
surfing
tabletop videocassette recorder
technology-based learning

telecommunications device for the
  deaf/teletypewriter
teleconferencing
telemedicine
Telenet
telephone service
time-based corrector
time code
time division multiple access
treatment
two-way interactive video
ubiquitous computing
usenet newsgroups
vaporware
Verimetrics Analyzer
Veronica
very small aperature terminal
video board
videocapture card
video card
video cassette recorder
videocompression
videodisc
video, full motion
video news release
videophone
videostream
video teleconferencing
virtual reality
voice recognition
voice and speech recognition
voice recognition unit
voice response system
wide area information servers
wipe
wireless data communications
wireless technology
workflow automation
workflow software
write once, read many
World Wide Web

53   Tests and Testing

ability test
achievement test
adaptive test
adaptive testing
administrability
Albemarle Paper Co. v. Moody
alternate-form reliability
aptitude test
arrangement items

battery
checkride
cognitive ability test
competency-based test
completion items
composite score
comprehensiveness
concurrent validity
Connecticut v. Teal
construct validity
content validity
correlation
correlational study
correlation analysis
criterion measure
criterion-referenced test
criterion validity
cross validation
cut score
diagnostic test
distractor
draw-a-person test
employee skills testing
end-of-course qualification test
eneagram
equating
essay test
face validity
fair employment practices laws
field test
Flanagan Aptitude Classification Test
frequency distribution
General Aptitude Battery
graphic item count
Griggs v. Duke Power Co.
histogram
honesty test
indirect measure
intelligence test
interest test
internal criterion test
inventory
item analysis
item difficulty
item stem
job performance measures
job replica test
Knowledge Management Assessment Tool
mastery test
matching items
mean difficulty
minimalist testing
mode
multiple-choice items

55 Travel Management

56 Work Measurement